HISPANIC LITERATURE

CRITICISM

SUPPLEMENT

Guide to Gale Literary Criticism Series

For criticism on	Consult these Gale series
Authors now living or who died after December 31, 1959	*CONTEMPORARY LITERARY CRITICISM (CLC)*
Authors who died between 1900 and 1959	*TWENTIETH-CENTURY LITERARY CRITICISM (TCLC)*
Authors who died between 1800 and 1899	*NINETEENTH-CENTURY LITERATURE CRITICISM (NCLC)*
Authors who died between 1400 and 1799	*LITERATURE CRITICISM FROM 1400 TO 1800 (LC)* *SHAKESPEAREAN CRITICISM (SC)*
Authors who died before 1400	*CLASSICAL AND MEDIEVAL LITERATURE CRITICISM (CMLC)*
Authors of books for children and young adults	*CHILDREN'S LITERATURE REVIEW (CLR)*
Dramatists	*DRAMA CRITICISM (DC)*
Poets	*POETRY CRITICISM (PC)*
Short story writers	*SHORT STORY CRITICISM (SSC)*
Black writers of the past two hundred years	*BLACK LITERATURE CRITICISM (BLC)* *BLACK LITERATURE CRITICISM SUPPLEMENT (BLCS)*
Hispanic writers of the late nineteenth and twentieth centuries	*HISPANIC LITERATURE CRITICISM (HLC)* *HISPANIC LITERATURE CRITICISM SUPPLEMENT (HLCS)*
Native North American writers and orators of the eighteenth, nineteenth, and twentieth centuries	*NATIVE NORTH AMERICAN LITERATURE (NNAL)*
Major authors from the Renaissance to the present	*WORLD LITERATURE CRITICISM, 1500 TO THE PRESENT (WLC)*

HISPANIC LITERATURE
CRITICISM

SUPPLEMENT
VOLUME 2

Guimarães Rosa – Viramontes

Indexes

Susan Salas, Editor

GALE GROUP

Detroit
San Francisco
London
Boston
Woodbridge, CT

Library of Congress Catalog Card Number 99-067761
ISBN 0-7876-3755-6
Vol 2 ISBN 0-7876-3757-2

Printed in the United States of America

10   9   8   7   6   5   4   3   2   1

Contents of Volume 2

João Guimarães Rosa
1908-1967

Brazilian short story writer and novelist.

INTRODUCTION

João Guimarães Rosa is one of Brazil's most acclaimed writers, a master of both the short story and novel. His preoccupation with language, usually a hallmark of poetry, was redirected into prose, writing so demanding he was compared to James Joyce for his virtuoso manipulation of syntax, borrowings and intermixings of Portuguese with other languages, multiplied levels of meaning through metaphor and puns, and his juxtapositions of demotic and erudite expressions. Conjoined with the linguistic dimension were Guimarães Rosa's experiments in form. He produced a substantial body of fiction, including his masterpiece *Grande Sertão: Veredas* (1963; *The Devil to Pay in the Backlands*).

João Guimarães Rosa was born in Cordisburgo, Minas Gerais, on June 27, 1908 in rural Brazil. He was the eldest of six children, and his father a successful businessman. João was a good student, skillful in languages and sciences. In medical school, Guimarães Rosa wrote his first short stories, and when he graduated in 1930, he became a rural physician for two years and then a medic during the Revolution of 1932. During this time he learned more languages and published a few short stories and poems. In 1934, Guimarães Rosa passed a civil service exam and that same year joined the Ministry of Foreign Affairs. During this time he also devoted himself to writing in his spare time. In 1937, his only volume of poetry, *Magma,* won the Brazilian Academy of Letters prize. In 1938, Guimarães Rosa served as a diplomat in Germany and later that year won second prize for a thousand-page manuscript of short stories in the Humberto de Campos fiction contest. When Brazil joined the war against Hitler in 1942, Guimarães Rosa was interned in Germany for four months and then released to return to Brazil. During World War II, he served as Secretary of the Brazilian Embassy in Bogotá until 1944. In Colombia, he worked on his prize-winning manuscript of short stories, publishing *Sagarana* in 1946. The successful collection won a prize from the Society Felipe d'Oliveira. During this period, Guimarães Rosa served as Director of the Ministry of State's Documentation Service and then became Secretary of the Brazilian delegation to the Paris Peace Conference. More government posts would follow through the late sixties, the last being head of the Frontier Demarcation Service (1962-67). After *Sagarana,* Guimarães Rosa's next publications occurred within four months of each other: a collection of novellas, *Corpo de Baile* (Corps de Ballet), and then the six-hundred page *Grande Sertão: Veredas,* both works published in 1956.

Guimarães Rosa's next publication, *Primeiras Estórias* (*The Third Bank of the River and other Stories*) occurred in 1962. The following year he was elected to Brazilian Academy of Arts and Letters. In 1967, Guimarães Rosa represented Brazil at the First Latin American Congress of Writers and upon his return to Brazil, he published the collection of short stories, *Tutaméia.* On November 19, 1967, three days after his acceptance speech to The Brazilian Academy of Letters, Guimarães Rosa died in his study of a heart attack. In his speech he had said, "People do not die," he said, "they become enchanted." His two major posthumous works were *Estas Estórias* (1969; *These Stories*) and *Ave Palavra* (1970; *Hail, Word or Bird, Word*), a volume of previously uncollected or unpublished *crônicas,* poems, and short stories. Four films have been made of Guimarães Rosa's works: *The Devil to Pay in the Backlands* (1965), "A hora e vez de Augusto Matraga" (1966; "Augusto Matraga's Hour and Turn"), *Sagarana, a Duel* (1973), and *Noites do Sertão* (1984; Backland's Nights).

Sagarana is a collection of nine stories set against the backdrop of the Brazilian backlands and contains a variety of protagonists including a donkey, two friends dying of malaria, a duo of vengeful males in a love triangle, and a witch doctor. The work is a dynamic and sympathetic portrayal of the diversions, tensions, and problems common in Brazil in the early twentieth century. Guimarães Rosa's next collection, *Corpo de Baile,* is comprised of seven, partially autobiographical novelettes of differing lengths in which several characters reappear periodically as a unifyng thread within the stories. A six-hundred page monologue, *Grande Sertão: Veredas* is Guimarães Rosa's most ambitious work and has been compared to Joyce's *Ulysses* (1922). Considered an epic because of its theme of honor and deception, its journeys and trials, and, predominantly, its concern with the battle between good and evil, it is the first-person narration of Riobaldo, a retired ex-bandit chieftain, to his auditor. The book was also praised for its colorful descriptions of the Brazilian provinces of Minas Gerais and Bahia. *Primeiras Estórias* is a collection centered around the idea of epiphanies in the lives of children and other relatively powerless members of society. The title story is told by a young male narrator whose father leaves his family on the canoe he has built and drifts endlessly, ghostlike, just out of reach on a nearby river, never to return to land or to his family. After many years, the son reaches the conclusion he must replace his father on the canoe, but suffers a failure of nerve. Full of guilt, the son consoles himself that once he dies, he will have his corpse set adrift on a canoe to eventually merge with the river. *Tutaméia*, subtitled "Third Tales," is the last of the author's work to be published while he was alive. Its forty tiny "anecdotes of abstraction" are, at various points, punctuated with longer essays (called "prefaces") which treat such issues as the nature of imagination and originality, the concept of the genre of *estória* (tale), the rationale of neologisms in both everyday and erudite language, and the author's own perspective on inspiration and the essence of life. Guimarães Rosa's two major posthumous works are *Estas Estórias* and *Ave Palavra*. The first is similar to the style of *Sagarana* and the second is collection of fifty-four brief entries called a "miscellany" by its author. Included here are poems, short stories, lyrical essays, poetic reportings, maxims, travel notes, and fragments of a diary, most of them published in journals and periodicals from 1947-67. Subjects range from vignettes of zoos in Italy, France, Germany, and Brazil, to memoir-like pieces set in both urban and rural contexts. These pieces leave readers with a one-world point of view reflecting the well-traveled author.

Guimarães Rosa is usually placed in the third generation of the modernist movement in Brazil, a generation preoccupied with means more than message. Guimarães Rosa took the medium further than most of his contemporaries, believing that it could not be neglected for message. Guimarães Rosa "attacked" the clichés of language on several fronts: words, expressions, syntax. He also hammered at clichéd form, often bending the straight narrative line into forms that curved and branched poetically. In attacking formal and linguistic clichés, the author hoped his writing could be revolutionary, less in the way of its message, more in the way of medium, redefining his use of his chosen genre. Few writers are able to effect such a revolution in form and language while at the same time constructing a narrative. Critics have commented on the importance of good translation of Guimarães Rosa's works for this reason.It is this thatmakes Guimarães Rosa one of the greatest prose writers of twentieth-century Brazil, and his *Grande Sertão: Veredas*, one of the most respected novels in Latin American fiction.

PRINCIPAL WORKS

Magma (poetry) 1934
Sagarana (short stories) 1946
Corpo de Baile (short stories) 1956
Grande Sertão: Veredas [*The Devil to Pay in the Backlands*] (novel) 1956
Primeiras Estórias [*The Third Bank of the River and Other Stories*] (short stories) 1962
Tutaméia: Terceiras Estórias (short stories) 1967
Estas Estórias (short stories) 1969
Ave, Palavra (short stories) 1970
Correspondência com o Tradutor Italiano (letters) 1972
A Volta do (short stories) 1973
Sagarana Emotiva: Cartas de J. Guimarães Rosa (letters) 1975
Contos (short stories) 1978
Jardins e Riachinhos (short stories) 1983
Rosiana (short stories) 1983

CRITICISM

Mary L. Daniel (essay date 1971)

SOURCE: "Joao Guimarães Rosa," in *Studies in Short Fiction,* Vol. 8, No. 1, Winter, 1971, pp. 209-16.

[*In the following essay, Daniel provides an overview of Guimarães Rosa's major works.*]

The isolated backlands of the interior Brazilian state of Minas Gerais—its cowboys, outlaws, and primitive dirt farmers—these are the raw material of Brazil's most original short story writer of the twentieth century. Strange to say, this creator of stories so congenitally rooted in the *sertão* is no mere picturesque "regionalist" but an erudite master of language and a bold stylistic-linguistic innovator. He is João Guimarães Rosa (1908-1967), whose debut on the Brazilian literary scene at the age of thirty-eight shattered the status quo of comfortable literary regionalism, shocked the critics, puzzled the public, and opened an exciting new era in Portuguese-language fiction.

Guimarães Rosa is primarily a *teller of stories,* carrying on in literary fashion the oral tradition of time immemorial, a tradition replete with talking animals, extrasensory communication between beasts and humans, and a pervasive teluric mystique. In no work are these features more evident than in his first published collection of stories—*Sagarana* (1946), a set of nine tales of the *sertão* that introduce into Brazilian literature on a decisive scale numerous elements of backland vocabulary and syntax hitherto unknown outside of Minas Gerais. Similar in character and style to *Sagarana* is *Corpo de Baile*, a collection of seven short novels published in 1956, the same year as Guimarães Rosa's best-known work—the monumental novel of the Brazilian hinterland, *Grande Sertão: Veredas*.

Whereas the stories of *Sagarana* are mutually independent one of another, certain interrelationships exist among several of the *Corpo de Baile* novellas, principally with regard to a number of their characters, whose careers may be followed in rather sketchy fashion throughout the sequence. After its second edition, this work was subdivided into three smaller volumes, published under the titles *Manuelzão e Miguilim*; *No Urubuquàquá, no Pinhém*; and *Noites do Sertão*. It is in this *Corpo de Baile* collection that the reader becomes keenly aware of Rosa's extraordinary talent for re-creating the world of childhood as interpreted by a child's mind in terms comprehensible to adults. Guimarães Rosa's psychological insight is profound and on occasion uncanny, and his sensitive probing of the age-old problems of the human personality as these are experienced by the simple inhabitants of the *sertão* is one of the most universal and authentic aspects of his total work.

Grande Sertão: Veredas, with its 600 pages of epic prose uninterrupted by chapter divisions, clearly falls outside consideration as short fiction; its style and character, however, are identical to that of the author's more numerous shorter works. The impact of this, Guimarães Rosa's only full-length novel, is evident in the fact that it was the first of his works translated into English [*The Devil to Pay in the Backlands*, James L. Taylor and Harriet de Onís, tr. (Knopf, 1963)] and other European languages. The overwhelming presence of *Grande Sertão: Veredas* has perhaps drawn attention from some of the author's shorter works, though in the last few years there have been successive editions and foreign translations of *Sagarana* and of *Primeiras Estórias*, a short volume of twenty-one brief stories published in 1962. *Sagarana* appeared in English translation under its original title in 1966 [Harriet de Onís, tr. (Knopf)] and *Primeiras Estórias* has been translated by Barbara Shelby under the title *The Third Bank of the River* (Knopf, 1968).

In *Primeiras Estórias* and *Tutaméia*—a similar volume of extremely brief *estórias* (forty in all) published in 1967 just three months before the author's premature death—one will note increasing variety of subject matter, with the strictly rural tales alternating with subjective, quasi-essayistic vignettes of a philosophical or psychological nature. This feature is most evident in Rosa's last work published in his lifetime *Tutaméia*, (subtitled *Terceiras Estórias*), which may serve as his own analysis and evaluation of his literary creation as though by some metaphysical foresight he had been made aware of his impending death and had felt moved to leave his readers some sort of personal confession. *Tutaméia*, in addition to its forty minuscule stories, contains four "prefaces," spaced at intervals throughout the book and comprising intimate essays in which Guimarães Rosa discusses elements of his literary creation: the essence of *estórias* as an imaginative genre that should be understood intuitively; the creation of neologisms (as much a trademark of his style as of that of James Joyce) to renew language and fill existing conceptual gaps; the nature of the creative process as experienced by the author himself, with the strong inference of subliminal and metaphysical influences operative in his own career. *Tutaméia* answers certain questions latent in the minds of many readers of Guimarães Rosa, and probably raises just as many others, which is as the author would want it—that the reader should project himself into the work and perceive it experimentally.

To date one posthumous volume of Rosean compositions has appeared—*Estas Estórias*, published late in 1969. Partially sketched out as to its table of contents by Guimarães Rosa himself before his death, the book contains nine short novels dating in composition from 1947 to 1967, most of them from the early 1960's. Several of these tales had appeared individually in magazines, but at least four others had never been officially "polished" for publication by the author. So in a sense *Estas Estórias* is at once a tentative and final work, including in footnote form occasional variant readings indicated in the typewritten originals of several of the tales. The volumes is eclectic as to content, admitting even a sea story (unique in Rosean prose) and an Andean episode in addition to the more typical Brazilian backland sequences, and reveals both the simpler and more complex aspects of the author's style.

Within the totality of Guimarães Rosa's short fiction, be it *estórias* or novellas, appear a goodly number of characters created not merely for transitory appearance on the printed page but for mind-sticking survival within the reader's consciousness. Such are Augusto Matraga, the questing soul of *Sagarana*; Miguilim, the myopic eight-year-old, and adult protagonists Manuelzão and Soropita of *Corpo de Baile*; the anonymous narrator of **"A terceira margem do rio"** (**"The Third Bank of the River"**) in the *Primeiras Estorias* collection; **"Rebimba o Bom"** of *Tutaméia*, who never appears but whose spiritual presence is decisive in the careers of others; and the "jaguar-man" of *Estas Estórias*. And who can forget the **"Burrinho pedrês"** ("dappled donkey") of *Sagarana*, representing the animal kingdom in this gallery of personalities? Guimarães Rosa's characters are remembered for what they *are* existentially rather than for whatever role they may play in the selection in which they appear: a curious phenomenon, this essentially introspective orientation throughout the author's extensive collection of "Wild West" stories. These are authentic types from one of Brazil's most isolated areas, accessible only recently to vehicular traffic; their human drama is conditioned by their circumstances and their careers determined by their environment. They are not idealized, nor do they serve as grist for a "social document" mill. Since their life is the only one they know, comparisons are beside the point; empathetic presentation, rather than interpretation, is Guimarães Rosa's approach, for he is after all one of them and speaks as an insider.

If we are to compare João Guimarães Rosa with other contemporary Brazilian fiction writers, it is fairly obvious that the most distinctive feature of his prose is his use of the Portuguese language in new and sometimes startling ways. These innovations generally fall into three broad categories: vocabulary, grammar-syntax, and rhetorical technique. His diction is the confluence of many sources, ranging from the archaic (kept alive in the speech of the *sertão*) to the purely creative, and presents a constant juxtaposition and interaction of erudite and colloquial elements. The result is a language generally Brazilian, strongly regional, and at the same time international because of its admixture of foreign words in Brazilianized form: a curious and heterogeneous literary language, readily identifiable as "Rosean" by the reader in the same manner as the uniquely "Joycean" style in English prose.

Guimarães Rosa's incessant search for "just the right word" and his passion for conciseness and simultaneity of expression (prime elements in his preferred genre) have led to the creation of numerous lexical neologisms of both functional and poetic quality. This task of language renewal is not carried out willy-nilly but rather adheres to the primitive traditions and historical development of the Portuguese language; the most common neologistic technique that Guimarães Rosa uses is the partial alteration of well-known words to create new perspectives for familiar concepts. Guimarães Rosa's linguistic philospohy is one of "deconditioning" and "reconditioning" of his readers; to use a current phrase, he would like to "blow the minds" of his public to open up new awarenesses, both sensorial and intuitive. Underlying all this is his basic yearning for universal communication; he longs to possess a linguistic vehicle having the completeness and flexibility that no single existing language in itself possesses. He would wish, if possible, to recreate the language of pre-Babel—primitive, virile, and beautiful.

It is in the area of grammar and sentence structure that Guimarães Rosa's prose differs most markedly from traditional norms. He takes constant liberties, inverting normal word order, using one grammatical category in place of another or substituting phrases or single words for complete clauses, dropping prepositions and subordinating conjunctions, omitting articles and on other occasions doubling the same. His punctuation is capricious, reveling in use of the comma and in general corresponding directly to vocal inflection and breath groupings rather than to the grammatical logic of written prose. The Rosean style is strongly substantive, concrete, and the frequent substantivation of non-nominal elements contributes to this. Guimarães Rosa uses coupling of derivative pairs for intensive effect or implied simultaneity, and he delights in creating adjectival, substantive, and verbal clusters as points of maximum focus within passages of on-flowing prose. The overall effect of such techniques, together with actual word shortening by way of apocopation of final syllables (Guimarães Rosa favors a strongly consonantal language), is the presentation of a sometimes telegraphic, frequently agitated, always dynamic onrush of prose. Dialogue, fairly frequent in the author's rural works but less common in *Primeiras Estórias* and *Tutaméia*, occurs in abrupt fashion with a minimum of "bridging," true to the style of oral narrative. We find, then, an essentially linear, paratactic prose formed of concise, co-ordinated word groupings of great verbal economy. The effect on the reader-listener of such a literary torrent may be either exhilarating or overwhelming, but will in any case challenge his response. No one can read Guimarães Rosa passively, for a moment's inattention risks the loss of a key word or phrase as the storyteller spins his narrative.

One cannot overemphasize the *oral* basis of Guimarães Rosa's stories and short novels, even of his full-length novel; his works are better heard than read, and are best read aloud. Numerous poetic and rhetorical devices may be discovered by the ear in Rosean prose, though these may easily slip by unperceived by the eye. Among such are full-scale or assonant rhyme, rhythm (on occasion sustained through entire paragraphs), alliteration, onomatopoeia, repetition and echo, rhetorical questions, oratorical structuring of paragraphs, and an overall appeal to the inherent musicality of the spoken word. Perhaps what Guimarães Rosa writes is not strictly prose at all, but a kind of confluence of prose and verse which might bear any name the reader chooses to bestow, such as *prosoema,* though such pigeonholing would violate the

free spirit of his work and its delightful evasion of analysis. It is barbarously primitive one moment, delicately poetic and consciously thetorical the next, a sometimes bewildering interaction of contrasts and paradoxes that constitutes by its internal tension and dynamic appeal the underlying structure of the author's verbal workmanship.

Throughout his work, Guimarães Rosa shows an almost mystical esteem for words as inviolable entities of sound and personality as well as conceptual symbols. He revels in the use of words as does a composer with the infinite varieties of musical sound at his disposal, and writes with a refreshing though sometimes bewildering lack of rigidity. The spontaneity of Guimarães Rosa's creation is somewhat deceptive, however, for no one can be said to labor more studiously over literary production than he, as those who have seen his works in manuscript form can testify. There are at work within his creative consciousness two strong forces—the "feeling" and the "thinking." The former is fundamental to the conception of his artistic and human inspiration, the thematic and ambiental aspects of his work; the latter is essential to the process of transferring the latent story from its inception to its final form on the printed page. That these forces should be complementary and evidently coexistent throughout his work, with the resultant tension and sometime paradox of character such interplay may bring forth, is a distinctive feature of Rosean prose. It is a prose that is outwardly complicated and difficult while inwardly roughhewn and simple, accessible most directly by intuition. This is not to imply that what we have is a hermetic, Joycean style, though many Brazilian readers have been put off by this very notion, given the fact that Guimarães Rosa is obviously something "different" within the field of typical socio-regionally oriented Brazilian prose fiction. Our author's primary preoccupation never ceases to be the matter of interpersonal communication, and he is essentially a man of the people whose multifaceted vision of life finds its most natural and expedient means of expression in the angular, dynamic torrent of words with which he speaks.

A key to understanding Guimarães Rosa's works is an awareness of the constant intersectioning of multiple levels of reality that they involve. Just as the author has avoided the confining narrowness of regionalism, the common plateau of standard usage, and the subjective exclusivenes of esoteric poetic language by integrating elements of all three in his style, so the subject matter of his *estórias* incorporates and intersects the multiple perspectives of human consciousness, from the crudest elements of marginal physical existence in the *sertão* to the most intimate ontological probing of the human soul in its solitude. The result is a polyvalent work with a strong sense of unity within diversity: Life is one, though its manifestations be multiple and diverse. By being true to many perspectives simultaneously, Guimarães Rosa has denied none of them; his preoccupations and his style reflect both the primitive and the cultured mind, and his language is in effect a stylization of regional speech resulting from a process of selectivity and modification with an ear to continual beautification and perfection of the original.

All of this points to an underlying Neoplatonic tendency in Guimarães Rosa's concept of reality and his re-creation of that reality through his literature. The ascensional process that recognizes the simultaneous existence of various levels of awareness but strives inevitably toward attainment of the highest, fullest, and best is basic to the author's interpretation of his own works. He envisions in them a three-stage existence, present in their language as well as their thematic content:

1) the underlying charm (enchantment),

2) the level-lying common meaning,

3) the "overlying" idea (metaphysic).

He intends that his poetic prose should find resonance within the many areas of human awareness, from sense perception through logical intelligence to the realm of the spirit. In a sense this tripartite vision finds a parallel in the development through which Guimarães Rosa's work has passed. In *Sagarana* the "underlying charm" of auditory appeal as revealed in rhythm, rhyme, and neologistic creation is a predominant feature; it is also the author's least complex work. In *Corpo de Baile* and the novel *Grande Sertão: Veredas*, there comes to the fore the "level-lying common meaning" of syntactic concentration and fuller plot and character development, while in most of the stories of *Primeiras Estórias* and *Tutaméia* the metaphysical element or "overlying idea" is a distinguishing and pervasive factor, presenting the intangible conflicts and ecstasies of the human spirit in its ascensional pathway of *becoming*. *Estas Estórias*, the posthumous collection, offers a composite of all these elements in varying degrees.

What unique contribution has Guimarães Rosa made to Brazilian language and literature? He has brought *renewal, flexibility,* and *universality*. By revitalizing familiar morphological patterns, he has drawn attention to the inherent potential of the *wood,* and through his original and dynamic syntax and sensitive use of poetic and rhetorical techniques he has created a prose of aesthetic beauty and expressive power. In his concern for both the content and form of his works, he has made the latter a colleague rather than a slave of the former. Insofar as contemporary Brazilian literature is coming to form an increasingly important and well-known part of the wider field of Latin American and international letters, Guimarães Rosa's most vital role as a writer of fiction may be that of an "international regionalist" who has succeeded in universalizing an area (the Brazilian *sertão*) and a way of life whose interest had hitherto been generally limited to local color and sociological research and who has stylized a vigorous manner of expression lifted from its *mineiro* origins through aesthetic re-creation to the pages of literature.

Relatively little scholarly bibliography exists to date, particularly in English, on João Guimarães Rosa. Readers conversant with the Portuguese language, or with a good enough knowledge of Spanish to read Portuguese by analogy with the help of a bilingual dictionary, will find a more detailed stylistic analysis of the author's works in my book *João Guimarães Rosa: Travessia Literária* (Rio de Janeiro: José Olympio Editôra, 1968). A memorial volume of speeches, photographs, reminiscences, and interpretative sketches on Guimarães Rosa by contemporary Brazilian writers was published under the title *Em memória de João Guimarães Rosa* a few months after his death (Rio: José Olympio Editôra, 1968) and is noteworthy for its complete bibliographical listing of all Rosean works and scholarship on them in all languages, current to mid1968. An impressionistic interpretation of the author's personality and work, together with ample biographical data in English, may be found in an interesting interview-based volume—*Into the Mainstream (Conversations with Latin-American Writers)*—by Luis Harss and Barbara Dohman (New York: Harper and Row, 1967, chapter IV). One hopes that Guimarães Rosa will receive increased attention from foreign readers and critics in the near future, for the works of this robust, refreshing, and profound writer in the vanguard of contemporary Latin-American fiction have clearly become a landmark and must be reckoned with.

Alfred J. Mac Adam (essay date 1977)

SOURCE: "João Guimarães Rosa: Honneur des Hommes," in *Modern Latin American Narratives,* The University of Chicago Press, 1977, pp. 69-77.

[*In the following essay, Mac Adam discusses significant themes in Guimarães Rosa's* Grande Sertão: Veredas.]

Language as a sign of life, and linguistic play as a sign of fecundity are the hallmark of João Guimarães Rosa's *Grande Sertão: Veredas* (1956), one of the very few texts we shall consider which may be construed as optimistic. Language in *Grande Sertão* is a bridge between nature, the *sertão* (backlands), and culture and is used by men, who also constitute a bridge between the two worlds, both to name their artifacts and to imitate the sounds of the natural world. The narrator of the text, Riobaldo, continues the bridge metaphor by living on the edge of the backlands, a citizen both of nature and of culture. The effect of his bridge identity on his discourse is that of deformation, a condition in which we see the narrator mutilating and recreating the language he inherits from his society. There is no sense here that the turbulent, rural language of the narrator belongs to the past, in the way the *porteño* slang of *Rayuela,* or the Cuban Spanish of Cabrera Infante do when they intentionally evoke the language of a particular era, the 1950s in both of these cases. Language in Guimarães Rosa is the "honneur des hommes" of which Valéry speaks, not raw material to be sifted and purified, but natural energy which demonstrates man's dynamic status. Language here constantly reminds the reader that nothing in man is fixed, that while individuals and cultures have a personality and a continuity, they are nevertheless bound up in the ebb and flow of a universe in flux.

Grande Sertão argues against one of man's own inventions, which the text takes to be man's worst enemy, linear time. When the flux of undifferentiated time or time taken as a series of recurrent cycles is transformed by man into linear history, he loses contact with a part of himself, the part belonging to nature. The great opposition in the text, Riobaldo's perpetual speculation about the existence of God and the Devil, is actually an erroneous representation of the difference between the world of culture and the world of nature. Riobaldo wonders if there is a Devil, although he never doubts the existence of God. For him the problem is one of morality, but for the reader the opposition is a false problem, since morality is not the text's principal subject. Instead of representing good and evil, God would seem to symbolize the universe as eternal, an essence, while the Devil stands for the world of phenomena (or language), the visible world of chaos and flux. While *Grande Sertão* might at first seem to recreate Pico della Mirandola's platonism, a system which shows how man participates in the lower world of flesh and how he may purge himself of base matter to become an angel, it is in fact an inversion of that system.

There are no hierarchies in *Grande Sertão*, because the text enacts the doctrines of Heraclitus in autobiographical form. Heraclitus's stress on the individual's need to comprehend the principles that govern both himself and his universe are represented metaphorically in Riobaldo's discourse by language itself, by the act of narrating. It is not what Riobaldo says but what he means that concerns the reader, not what he intends but what his discourse says through him. Riobaldo, virtually the "other" in Lacan's formula *"the unconscious is the discourse of the other,"*[1] is his own message. He is the *logos,* the reason or order of things representing itself for us, and he is, like all men in Heraclitus's sense, what he seeks. The dichotomy he senses, the split between God and the Devil, is really not a dichotomy but a basic principle of universal harmony, the harmony of opposites, of flux itself, which he expresses without comprehension. He reminds us several times, "The important thing is this: you listen to me, listen to me more than just listening to what I say; and listen disarmed" (p. 86/91),[2] or, "I don't know how to tell things in a straightforward way. I learned how to a little with my buddy Quelemém, but he sort of wants to know everything differently. He doesn't want the event itself, but the beyond-thing, the other thing" (p. 152/166).

These last two remarks would seem to be a restatement of Heraclitian fragment 50: "Listening not to me but to the Logos it is wise to agree that all things are one."[3] As usual, the utterance is paradoxical; we have no choice but to listen to the speaker, while at the same time we are required to interpret his words, to look beyond them. Riobaldo's advice also recalls fragment 93: "The lord whose oracle is in Delphi neither speaks out nor conceals, but gives a sign" (p. 211). *Grande Sertão* is a vast ideogram composed of language, containing an autobiography, yet standing as a huge metaphor about man's eternal condition. It demands elucidation because the articulation of its parts is confusing; but whatever values are

assigned to those elements, one basic lesson is reiterated throughout: man is part of a cosmos in flux; he is not limited by history or circumstance, and his principal business in life should be to find the *logos,* the order of the universe, within himself. The microcosm is a metaphor for the macrocosm.

The *mise en scène* of this idea is strange and yet oddly familiar, especially for North American readers. Just as Melville used the first-person narrator and the world of whaling to deal with ethical and theological problems, Guimarães uses a first-person format and the *sertão* as his stage. Both the sailing ship and the *sertão* have the benefit of being *loci* divorced from historical contingency. They are isolated worlds within a macrocosm, and while their ultimate significance can only be seen in terms of the macrocosm, they use metaphors to express their ideas. Both *Moby Dick* and *Grande Sertão* utilize a setting derived from the world of romance; their characters too are heroic, just as the actions they describe are titanic in scale. *Grande Sertão* even resorts to such epic conventions as catalogs of warriors' names and councils of heroes in which decisions are made on the basis of what bards will sing about those present. All of this makes the vehicle of expression correspond to the high seriousness of the ideas at stake. Familiar problems are thrown into relief by being made strange and alien. Neither text is ironic and each attempts to make a statement about the human condition. Perhaps this is why the divorce from the "real world" of the novel and from the grotesque world of satire is necessary.

Of course, Riobaldo's tale is quite different from Ishmael's account of the Pequod's voyage. Whereas Ishmael's tale is about matters he witnesses and in which he participates marginally, Riobaldo's story is an autobiography. He makes the usual distinctions between the "I" narrator and the "I" actor usually formulated by picaresque narrators, but it is not his intention to confess his sins. Riobaldo is himself a truth which must be revealed, and it is for this reason the silent "o senhor" who listens, and in whose position we readers find ourselves, is so significant. This listener does not seem to be present in order to give absolution to the speaker, but rather to record his story. There are few references made to what it is the listener does as Riobaldo speaks, but one passage makes it clear: "Crossing of my life. Guarravacã—you look, you write" (p. 220/241). Riobaldo is not speaking figuratively here, and it would seem that we are to imagine the "learned" listener as a stenographer. It is tempting to identify him with Guimarães himself, recording the lessons gleaned from his sojourn in the backlands as a young doctor, but this association is of no special significance. The burden of interpretation lies with the reader, who must be diligent if he is to keep up simultaneously with the language and with the story Riobaldo tells.

Riobaldo's addresses to his public, beginning with his first words, tend to be soothing and adulatory, but his discourse is oddly ritualized: "A visit, here at home in my house, with me, lasts three days" (p. 22/19). Our visit in Riobaldo's house (the book itself) may last much longer than three days, but this magic number informs us that we are embarking on a rite of passage, from a kind of death (belief in linear history) to a resurrection, a realization that the world is in perpetual flux and that time moves in no single direction, an idea found also in the Cuban writer Alejo Carpentier's *El siglo de las luces*. Later Riobaldo puts us on our guard, "I tell things for myself; I tell things for you. When you don't understand me, wait for me" (p. 112/122), and again, "I tell you what I know and you don't know; but mainly I want to tell what I don't know that I know, and that maybe you know" (p. 175/192). The oracle is certainly speaking, urging us to keep up with him, not trying either to scare us away or to challenge us. Riobaldo is holding up a mirror to his audience throughout his discourse, but it is up to the reader to discern his own image.

The actual sequence of events in Riobaldo's life history reflects the message it propounds. Unlike Machado's Brás Cubas, Riobaldo does not worry about whether he should begin his autobiography at the end or the beginning: Guimarães resolves the problem of unity in the first person narrative, not by using a dead narrator, but by declaring constant change to be the only perspective. Riobaldo begins therefore nowhere, neither *in medias res* nor at one of the extremes. We have come to him, in some mysterious way, and in a similarly ambiguous fashion he will tell us what he has to say. He moves backwards and forwards through his past (and to this extent, his having a past, he is like traditional narrators), remembering in both directions, letting his story meander from one topic to another, imitating the Heraclitian rivers that run through the narrative.

The paradoxical mixture of metonymy and metaphor at the root of all narrative is almost bewildering here. In the first paragraph Riobaldo mentions, in this order, these subjects: the shots, heard by the listener, which were only target practice; the people who wanted to borrow Riobaldo's guns to shoot a deformed calf they assumed was the Devil; what a real gun fight is like; where the *sertão* might be in relation to where Riobaldo and his listener are (which concludes that the *sertão* is ubiquitous). At first there seems to be a kind of regression, but this sequence (shots, practice, visit, birth of calf) is dissolved when the obsessive theme of the *sertão* appears. Nevertheless, because of the presence of such topics as the Devil, violence, and the *sertão*, it is possible to see the first paragraph as the matrix from which the entire text is derived. The tumult of subjects, the haphazard movement from idea to idea, and the emphasis on the *sertão* as a world of perpetual war also recalls Heraclitian fragment 53, concerning the harmonious discord of nature: "War is the father of all and king of all, and some he shows as gods, others as men; some he makes slaves, others free" (p. 195).

The action of **Grande Sertão** is a series of wars between rival groups of outlaws (*jagunços*). The association of these groups with ideologies is tenuous at best (although one chief, Zé Bebelo, wants to liquidate the *jagunços*) and, for Riobaldo's own development, irrelevant. He is

involved, but it is his own inner struggle which most concerns him (and us), an inner struggle like that of Jason in the *Argonautica,* not like Isabel Archer's in *Portrait of a Lady*. The culminating battle in the text, motivated by revenge, takes place with Riobaldo offstage. It is in a sense merely another element in his self-revelation and not a culmination. The idea of culmination or ending is avoided in **Grande Sertão**, and the most significant events occur when they are least expected. Again, this is because life is unpredictable, and despite the moral implications of Riobaldo's concern about belonging either to God or to the Devil, the universe at war is neither good nor evil. In fact, Riobaldo's moral dilemma—he does not know whether or not he sells his soul to the Devil—is subsumed into the greater statement made by the text concerning the world as flux.

The *sertão* is the place where opposites coexist, and Riobaldo's life is progressively revealed to be a metaphor for the *sertão*, just as it is a metaphor for him. But existing in close conjunction with Riobaldo are other characters, the mute *jagunços*, their chiefs, and Diadorim, the most important figure in Riobaldo's life. Guimarães tantalizes the reader with the antinomian idea that a woman, Diadorim, could disguise herself as a *jagunço*, fight, and not be recognized. Here again we see Guimarães using romance fixtures to make his text strange and alien. The subject of Diadorim's masquerade is never raised and, despite some similarities, she is not the amazon or warrior maiden of Ariosto or Calderón. She is a symbol of unsuccessful harmony, a violation of a natural state of affairs. She is a renunciation of the individual's search for his own image, because she has fixed her identity by attempting to define herself as what she is not.

Diadorim's role in Riobaldo's life is that of a catalyst. When she first appears, she is the mysterious "boy" ("o menino," of pp. 80-86/84-91) who involves Riobaldo in a curious rite of passage. Riobaldo is made to cross the São Francisco River in a canoe, a frightening experience. On the other bank he sees the "boy," who urged him to make the crossing, stab a man who suggests that she and Riobaldo are homosexuals. Riobaldo and Diadorim then recross the river. Either something or nothing has happened, but Riobaldo makes no real explanations, simply noting, "I didn't feel anything. Only a transformation I could sense. Lots of important things have no name" (p. 86/91). Riobaldo learns he can be brave, the first step in learning he is not limited in any way. Later he assumes he has reached his limits, but only because he cannot see that he has passed them: "I cross through things—and in the middle of the crossing I don't see!" (p. 30/27). Passage or crossing (the last word of the text is the single word *travessia* accompanied by the symbol for infinity) is reality in **Grande Sertão**: it is an error to invent, as Diadorim does, impassable boundaries.

The relationship between Riobaldo and Diadorim is deceiving. While they seem to constitute an opposition (one darkness, one light) they are in fact mirror twins. Riobaldo and Diadorim are versions of human life itself, one with self-imposed limits, one without; and this is reflected in their biographies. Riobaldo is a bastard who flees when he learns that his godfather and patron, Selorico Mendes, is his father (p. 95/102), as if to deny any but an autochthonous origin. Diadorim, like Camilla, never knew her mother and identified so strongly with her father, Joca Ramiro, that avenging his death became her only reason for living. Diadorim's lust for revenge is like the wrath of Achilles: it shapes the drama of the text, but it does not constitute its total significance.

Riobaldo's ambivalent attitude toward Diadorim is the result of his loving her sexually and hating himself for what he thinks is unnatural. The actual source of disharmony is Diadorim's fixity, her all-consuming passion for revenge, which blinds her to her responsibilities to herself. Her ancestor worship is no virtue in the *sertão*. But of course there is some ambiguity in this. Human life in the text leads inexorably to death; there is no deviation from that pattern. However, human perception of time and the transformation of that interpretation into history is another matter. Diadorim's attempt to "correct" the past is a failure, although this failure must be understood in the exemplary context of what the entire book seems to be saying. That is, within the text's statement about human fulfillment in the universe of flux there is a negative sign, Diadorim, whose fixity and denial of self represent death-in-life.

Augusto de Campos's ingenious deciphering[4] of Diadorim's name, his pointing out that the letter *d* is a sign both of God ("Deus") and the Devil, is aimed at demonstrating Diadorim's fundamental ambiguity. It would seem however that more than being ambiguous, Diadorim is a negation, negation of sex, negation of self (ancestor worship), and negation of life. We must recall in passing that God is, in the Heraclitian sense, the *logos* or order of the universe; the Devil is His manifestation in the world of phenomena. Riobaldo tells this to the reader without knowing it himself; but he is, after all, a narrator, not an interpreter.

Why it should be Diadorim who initiates Riobaldo into the world of change and violence is a difficult problem. In her role as the boy, Diadorim reveals to Riobaldo the infinite possibilities latent within him, and later it is Diadorim who introduces Riobaldo to the life of the *jagunços*, teaching him how to maintain his individuality and self-respect. Diadorim's function is like that of Virgil in the *Divine Comedy*; she reveals paths she herself cannot take. She must be discarded if Riobaldo is to discover his true mode of being, but this is not easily done because memory, the vast pool out of which Riobaldo draws his narrative, lets nothing die.

The relationship between the individual and his past, between the individual and his progenitors, is ambiguous in *Grande Sertão*. Clearly, Diadorim exaggerates her fealty to her father, and the text seems to say that the dead, locked in the immobility of death, can have no claim on the living, no claim except memory. What an individual should do, either symbolically or literally, is what the character Medeiro Vaz does when he becomes an outlaw:

he got rid of everything; he divested himself of what he owned in land and cattle; he shed everything as if he wanted to return to what he was when he was born. He had no dependents, no heirs. At the end, with his own hands he set fire to the ranch house, the ranch house which had belonged to his father, his grandfather, his great-grandfather, and waited until it was ashes. Today that place is all overgrown. Finally he went to where his mother was buried, a little cemetary at the edge of the pasture; then he knocked down the fence, pushed over the stones. Soon he felt better; nobody could find, to stir up with dishonor, the place where his family's bones could be found.

(pp. 36-37/35)

This is more than a romantic gesture, more than an existentialist belittling of objects and relationships in order to exalt the individual. Medeiro Vaz embraces the *logos* and is reborn.

Guimarães restores the myth of a world where people may retain their dignity in the face of the unknown, a world not necessarily of heroes and *jagunços* but of ordinary individuals who are told their lives are determined by economic and political forces beyond their control. This is not to say that **Grande Sertão** is a reactionary text; to the contrary, it demonstrates that the Medusa of depair is not a genuine threat to those who realize that history, like all fictions, is what they make of it, not what it makes of them. In this sense, Guimarães and Cortázar coincide: they both want to change the reader's life. Cortázar informs us that we are threatened by routines which rob us of identity; and Guimarães, echoing Heraclitus, simply points out the folly of believing in the reality of anything which is essentially a metaphor.

In "Tlön, Uqbar, Orbis Tertius," Borges describes a situation in which a fiction, a world made of words, becomes reality; and this is exactly the kind of fiction, one which stifles life instead of nurturing it, against which Guimarães fights. To take a version of reality as reality is to abdicate part of one's individuality. It is impossible not to bear the yoke of any order, any fiction; but absolute faith in anything but one's power to change fictions is an error. In *Cien años de soledad*, García Márquez sets out to demythologize a national history so that everyone may return to a *tabula rasa* and find better fictions. The difference between *Cien años* and **Grande Sertão** is between a text which is an image of an inexhaustible universe and one which is aimed at proving the unreality of a particular world. One twists its plot, as it twists language itself, into the figure eight of infinity; the other draws the line of linear history back on itself in a circle in order to end it.

NOTES

[1] "Seminar on 'The Purloined Letter,'" p. 45.

[2] *Grande Sertão: Veredas,* 6th ed. (Rio de Janeiro: José Olympio Editôra, 1968); trans. by James L. Taylor and Harriet de Onís, *The Devil to Pay in the Backlands* (New York: Alfred A. Knopf, 1971).

[3] G. S. Kirk and J. E. Raven, "Heraclitus of Ephesus," in *The Pre-Socratic Philosophers* (Cambridge: Cambridge University Press, 1963), p. 188. All Heraclitian quotations are taken from this edition.

[4] Augusto de Campos, "Um lance de 'Dês' do *Grande Sertão*," in Pedro Xisto, Augusto de Campos, and Haroldo de Campos, *Guimarães Rosa em três dimensões* (São Paulo: Conselho Estadual de Cultura, Comissão Estadual de Literatura, 1970), pp. 55-58.

Stephanie Merrim   (essay date 1983)

SOURCE: "Sagarana: A Story System," in *Hispania,* Vol. 66, No. 4, December, 1983, pp. 502-10.

[In the following essay, Merrim explores the themes of "Song and Artifice" in Sagarana.*]*

João Guimarães Rosa's first published work, *Sagarana* (1946),[1] as its translator into English aptly noted, comprises a "cycle of stories"[2] so densely interwoven as to form a discernible system whose components we can identify and whose design we can chart in a manner reminiscent of folktale analysis. Because, as we shall see, *Sagarana* is so obviously conceived as a system, a formal analysis should not betray but rather illuminate the ambitious thematic concerns of the text, for each of the nine stories of *Sagarana* plays out a drama involving a battle between two fields of motifs[3] whose themes, taken together, attempt to embrace man's whole being. The full and sensual presence of nature, a macrocosm, provides the backdrop for each of these dramas. To capture the totality of man and nature without exceeding the bounds of empirical reality is a goal descriptive of the epic:

> Great epic writing gives form to the extensive totality of life. . . . For the epic, the world at any given moment is an ultimate principle, it is empirical at its deepest, most decisive, all-determining transcendental base . . . it can never, while remaining epic, transcend the breadth and depth, the rounded, sensual, richly ordered nature of life.[4]

It is no accident, then, that as the first feature of our system the epic theme of voyage and return, of confronting one's destiny, unites the stories of *Sagarana* and appears in some form in each.

The next, and defining, feature of the system are the two basic forces underlying *Sagarana*'s stories and which we shall term Song and Artifice: all that is ultimate, be it concrete or abstract, falls to song and all that is relative, to artifice. Song, in the first place, is nature's song: its lyricism, dynamism, and multivalent diversity. Nature, in our text, is *the* absolute identified with God, the fullest presence, a force of such richness and enormity that it is beyond the reaches of man's conceptualization. A totality, nature contains all possible movement, shape and color. Nature is God's handiwork and man God's creature; no mortal imagination could conceive anything not already present in nature, as in the moon, "onde cabiam todos os devaneios e em que podia beber qualquer imag-

inação" (p. 218). Yet nature, far from being a utopia, is a non-human force: it is both beauty and violence, beyond comprehension or control. In the end, the inscrutable powers of nature prescribe man's death or fate.

Guimarães Rosa populates this vastness with a wealth of natural subjects, a seemingly endless procession of flora and fauna which surge from the narrative with the vitality of a newly born language. The descriptions of nature or "natural orchestration" of the stories are songs in themselves, language realigned with nature by recapturing the origins of the word—poetry, according to one critic: "A poesia volta . . . aos seus começos que terão sido os própios começos de linguagem, o homem descobrindo e abordando a natureza . . . e marcando com o signo verbal a sua posse."[5] For Guimarães Rosa, poetry is the "canto e plumagem" (p. 238) of the word, its music and exotic trappings, such as that of these names listed sheerly for their own sake in **"Minha Gente"**:

> Meu esp ito fumaceou, por ares de minha só posse—e fui, por inglas de Inglaterra, e marcas de Dinamarcas, e landas de Holanda e Irlanda. Subi à visão de deusas, lentas apsaras de sabor de pétalas, lindas tôdas: Dária, da Circássia; Ragna e Aase; e Gúdrun, a de olhos côr dos fiordes; e Vívian, violeta; e Erika, sílfide loira; e Varvára, a de belos feros olhos verdes; a a princesa Vladislava; císnea e junoniana; e a princesinha Berengária, que vinha, sutil, ao meu encontro, no alternar esvoaçante dos tornozelos preciosos. . . .

> (pp. 201-02)

Nature and the poetry of natural orchestration are free motifs, the song background of each story. In each specific plot, however, song commands a system of motifs, a set of allies which are in harmony with the primal forces. One set are magic forms of language, and the other, magical characters. First, obviously, there is song itself— the inlaid poetry, usually *cantigas*—which exercises an orphic influence over man and beast. Other verbal creations may also have a magical effect when they indicate an alliance with nature. Religion, in *Sagarana*, represents a covenant with nature's creator: thus religious language, prayer, brings man into contact with God. Witchcraft, the charm (verbal or otherwise) is equally as potent as non-pagan religion, being the magic which arises from nature. And, as does poetry, man's words when shaped into literature, such as Lalino's stories in **"A Volta do Marido Pródigo"** which enchant others and even himself, can have magic effects.

Lalino himself has special traits: "Um mulato dêsses pode valer ouros. . . . Não sei se é de Deus mesmo, mas uns assim têm qualquer um apadrinhamento. . . . É uma raça de criaturas diferentes, que os outros não podem entender" (p. 98). Certain types of people who live close to nature, such as children, simple people, blacks, are song characters, as are animals, the children of God (such as oxen: "Que santos de grandes que não fazem mal a ninguém; criação certa de Deus," (p. 307). Song characters, unencumbered by formal learning, follow nature's course. Living by instinct, they *know* intuitively; without thinking they are privy to life's secrets. A special place in this scheme is reserved for women, who are always and inevitably magical, on a different plane from men. The love they weave and inspire, as does Lalino's wife, "Enfeitou-se melhor, e, silenciosa, com quieta vigilância, desenrolava, dedo a dedo, palmo a palmo, o grande jôgo, a teia sorrateira que às mulheres ninguém precisava de ensinar" (p. 82), is also of song.

If nature's forces are primal, those of man, in general, are but secondary, hence the category of artificer, maker of things not natural: "O homem é um bicho esmochado, que não devia haver" (p. 292), think the oxen in **"Conversa de Bois."** Although he is a potential ally of nature, man is alienated *a priori* from intuition and thus reduced to an impoverished relative of nature, ruled by it and impotent before it. In this respect, Guimarães Rosa seems to adhere firmly to the biblical tradition that, exiled from Eden for the discovery of wisdom, man's form of knowledge can only approximate the state of intuition lost. And by the same fall removed from the eternity of nature, man lives in time—days of rushed and confused movement, reminiscent of Bergson's external time.

In our system of motifs, man is above all the artificer who crafts devices, and who can change the world: "—Eu acho que nós, bois—Dansador diz, com baba—assim como os cachorros, as pedras, as árvores, somos pessoas sôltas, com beiradas, comêço a fim. O homem, não: o homem pode se ajuntar com as coisas, se encostar nelas, crescer, mudar de forma e de jeito" (p. 310). Again, though, man's magic is secondary, compensatory. Be it from arrogance, naïveté or desperation, man strives in vain to impose his schemes on nature and bring it under his domination. Nature is beyond comprehension; man tries to parcel it out into small units of meaning within a scheme he himself invents. He builds fences, houses and yokes to scale down nature's enormity to a tangible space, and to tame its creatures. And most importantly in *Sagarana*, he invents complicated schemes, strategies and plots—artifices—futile attempts to outwit his fate and determine his own destiny.

Destiny, a capital letter word for Guimarães Rosa, cannot be manipulated; it can only be fulfilled by man aligning himself with nature. As does Jorge Luis Borges, Guimarães Rosa conceives of destiny as the divine plan formulated by God for each man, and of the attaining of one's destiny as the sum of one's entire life. In his "Poema conjetural" Borges describes the fatal moment in battle where his ancestor, Francisco de Laprida, achieved his destiny and saw his whole life encapsulated into that one instant:

> Al fin he descubierto
> le recóndita clave de mis años,
> la letra que faltaba, la perfecta
> forma que supo Dios desde el principio.
> En el espejo de esta noche alcanzo
> mi insospechado rostro eterno. El círculo
> se va a cerrar. . . . [6]

All the arbitrary twists of fate and masks one has worn reach their definition, molded into the "insospechado rostro eterno." In fulfilling one's fate, one day stands as the condensation of a whole life, as Borges says: "Yo he sospechado alguna vez que cualquier vida humana, por intrincada y populosa que sea, consta en realidad de un momento: el momento en que sabe para siempre quien es."[7] The many are resolved into one in this moment, or as Guimarães Rosa puts it, "a estória de um burrinho, como a história de um homem grande, é bem dada no resumo de um só dia de sua vida" (p. 4), a moment which can only be one of intuition. Man must therefore give over his artifices to song to attain it. The heart (song), as this *cantiga* from **"São Marcos"** tells us, and not the mind (artifice) wins out:

> Chegando na encruzilhada
> eu tive de resolver:
> para a esquerda fui, contigo.
> Coração soube escolher!
>
> (p. 240)

The stories of *Sagarana* are characterized by what we might call an "epiphany" structure, for each story details its protagonist's realization of his destiny. Like Augusto Matraga, each character has his "hora e vez." In formal terms, the epiphany is defined as the resolution of artifice and song in which the tension between the two is dissolved, resulting in harmony. Harmony or equilibrium are the key words here, for the initial impulse of every story is the disruption of equilibrium through a transgression of nature, in other words, the violation or negation of a natural element. In the end, the equilibrium which has been upset must be restored. Harmony is reinstated, destiny is realized, we emphasize, by artifice ceding to song, or in other words, man merging with nature in some way. The focus of the stories is on this coming together of artifice and song; as to whether they remain fused, there is only an implied "happily ever after."

The "happily ever after" ending is a property of all the five stories to which we now turn,[8] and particularly of the first, **"Minha Gente."** One need reshape the terms only slightly to distinguish in **"Minha Gente"** (and in the others) traces of the mythos of spring, comedy: "What normally happens, is that a young man wants a young woman, that his desire is resisted by some opposition, usually paternal, and that near the end of the play some twist in the plot enables the hero to have his will."[9] Overcoming the obstacles in his path, there is often a kind of conversion in the character that, on a large scale, represents the progress toward a new society or "a kind of moral norm"[10] which leaves the audience with a happy sense of "this should be" ending.

In the lighthearted love story, **"Minha Gente,"** the obstacles to the protagonist's happiness, his own plots to win the wrong woman (his cousin, Maria Irma), comes from within, as does the conversion, for the return home to his own kin is also the return to nature. At the same time, the hero's problem, if not conversion, resounds in every corner of the story. **"Minha Gente"** takes on the shape of an object lesson in the opposition of artifice and song, with each major character falling to one or the other side.

A markedly ironic treatment is accorded the artificers. Santana, who accompanies the protagonist on his journey home, is the first artificer we meet. Withdrawn into a world of abstractions and moves (much like the pursuing schemers in the previous story, **"Duelo"**), blinded to what surrounds him, Santana converts life into a chess game:

> Santana se encaramujou: está ausente dêste mundo, no departamento astral dos problematistas. E êste deve ser um dos motivos da segurança com que êle enfrenta qualquer roda ou ambiente: haja algum senão, sejam os outros hostis ou estúpidos, ou estúpidos e hostis a um tempo, e Santa se encosta em qualquer parte, poste ou árvore, e problemiza, problemiza sem parar.
>
> (p. 179)

Upon returning home, the hero also finds his Uncle Emílio, once bland and easygoing, transformed into a plotter, a consummate and wily politician. Emílio's maneuvers to engineer his election resemble nothing more than a chess game whose board is the entire district. This artificer's fate is not enviable: although he wins the election, he is ruined financially. The unhappy end of another artificer, Bento Porfirio, is presented in a substory. Killed while plotting the seduction of his adulterous sweetheart, Bento leaves this comment on man's impotence over his fate: "Aı, que mundo triste é êste, que a gente está nêle só p'ra mor de errar! . . . E, quando a gente quer concertar, ainda erra mais . . ." (p. 193). Thus, Emílio and Bento's tragedies suggest the ruin to which scheming leads.

To the characters on the side of nature corresponds the Buddha's song:

> Aprende do rolar dos rios,
> dos regatos monteses, da queda das cascatas:
> tagarelante, ondeia o seu caudal—
> só o oceano é silencio.
>
> (p. 201)

From nature José Malvino and the *moleque* Nicanor learn the facts which they perform when challenged by the skeptical protagonist. José, the guide, reconstructs whole events by reading the signs of nature, while Nicanor charms wild animals. Maria Irma has also learned from nature a love-in-spired sorcery, to lead her cousin to his fated love Amanda. Yet, unwittingly, she works another kind of witchcraft, enchanting the protagonist and inciting him to poetic reveries of exotic images and names. Part of the enchantment is an awakening to nature, whose vibrant richness dwarfs man's paltry games.

The comic hero in recognizing his folly moves from illusion to reality: "Illusion is whatever is fixed or definable, and reality is best understood as its negation: whatever reality is, it's not that."[11] This is an apt representation of what happens to our nameless protagonist. In the attempt to make Maria Irma jealous and win her, he plays

out his own chess game of moves and ploys, until receiving a letter from Santana. A continuation of their chess game, the red rook is placed in checkmate, surrounded by black pieces. The youth catches the message in a minute: his games are futile because destiny is stacked against him. Repentant, he thinks:

> Por aí, tive cansaço e vergonha de tudo o que antes eu dissera e fizera, e foram notáveis os meus pensamentos. O pio do zabelê é escandido e gemido. A estrada do amor, a gente já está mesmo nela, desde que não pergunte por direção nem destino. E a casa do amor— em cuja porta não se chama e não se espera—fica um pouco mais adiante.
>
> (p. 221)

Having abandoned illusion, and artifice, he meets his destiny, in the form of Amanda, upon arriving home.

"São Marcos" carries the theme of sorcery beyond the human sixth sense of love to the level of real witchcraft. The story picks up the motif of exotic names, which played a minor rôle in **"Minha Gente,"** and in a self-styled "sub-estória" develops it into a commentary on the poetic value of certain kinds of words. João, the protagonist, wanders through the woods, and finding an old *cantiga* carved in a tree, responds with a list of Egyptian kings which form a poem through their melodious inner rhyme:

> E cra para mim um poema êsse rol de reis leoninos, agora despojados de vontade sanhuda e só representados na poesia. Não pelos cilindros de ouro e pedras, postos sôbre as reais comas riçadas, nem pelas alargadas barbas, entremeadas de fios de ouro. Só, só por causa dos nomes.
>
> (p. 238)

Divorced from their original referents (the Egyptian kings), these words are poetry by sheer virtue of their sounds and shapes. Words with "canto e plumagem" (p. 238) exercise a fascination over the people of the *sertão* as well; the narrator/protagonist describes how the *sertanejos* deem the mysterious sounds of the Latin whose meaning they cannot understand a necessary part of the Mass. For João, however, it is fitting that the poetic words are written on a tree, since nature itself inspires their coining:

> Porque, diante de um gravatá, selva moldada em jarro jônico, dizer-se apenas *drimirim* ou *amormeuzinho* é justo; e, ao descobrir, no meio da mata, um angelim que atira para cima cinqüenta metros de tronco e fronde, quem não terá ímpeto de criar um vocativo absurdo e bradá-lo—Ó colossalidade!—na direção da altura?
>
> (p. 238)

Be it neologism or not, devoid of any supposed meaning the word is a living entity with powers of its own.

The purpose of the above subplot is to establish language as magical and nature-inspired. Departing from this belief, the larger plot of **"São Marcos"** concerns a transgression of song language and of nature itself through language. An educated outsider like the hero of **"Minha Gente,"** João is given to superstition (which, standing more on the side of man than God, equals artifice) but utterly scorns deeper magic, sorcery. On his way to the woods he mocks the renowned João Mangolo, ironically hitting on the truth that every black is a "feiticeiro." João's second transgression of nature is to take lightly the sacred prayer of St. Mark by reciting it gratuitously. "Pára," cries his friend Aurísio, "Isso é reza brava, e o senhor não sabe com o que é que está bulindo" (p. 232). And as a caution, Aurísio retaliates with a series of anecdotes—part of the lore of the town—recounting the ominous consequences of defying sorcery.

Passing through the woods and narrating its beauties for the reader, João commits a third, and most subtle, transgression, that of anthropomorphizing nature. Each grove, each clearing or pool, suggests an atmosphere or image to him: the Rendas da Yara evoke medieval thoughts, his erotic "Venusberg" demands sin, another clearing is purely Egyptian. The personification of nature goads him into a false sense of security, of believing he has control over nature. It turns out, nevertheless, to be another illusion: the places in the woods, "tão estáveis e não-humanos," are of an alien order beyond man's reach which João betrays with his anthropomorphic comparisons.

Suddenly the adventure of sight becomes an unsuccessful adventure of the mind as João stumbles about, blinded by João Mangolo's spell. Nature, before so human and orderly, becomes threatening and incomprehensible to João, who is unable to orient himself. His prayers ineffectual, he abandons himself to nature's rhythm: "Ir. Sem tomar direção, sem saber do caminho. Pé por pé, pé por si. Deixarei que o caminho me escolha" (p. 251). Cancelling one transgression is not enough: all at once he remembers the prayer of St. Mark and blares it out. The restoration of the prayer to its just and sacred function resolves the transgression, and the fury of the prayer leads the blinded man to Mangolo's house where the curse is removed after the two Joãos, doubles in their anger, battle it out.

As we proceed to examine the five stories, it becomes more and more apparent that the tales of *Sagarana* form a chain, an interlinking system of partial units. No single story fully defines any one motif (such as witchcraft, poetry, love, etc.): the next or a later story will pick it up again, building on it or rerouting it in another direction. **"Corpo Fechado,"** for example, relegates the educated outsider, the protagonist and first person narrator of the two preceding stories, to a secondary position, converting him into the witness and interlocutor of the protagonist. The defending of one's honor, which motivated the chase in **"Duelo"** and Lalino's return, leads Manuel Fulô, the hero of **"Corpo Fechado,"** to take recourse to a spell, echoing the theme of sorcery from **"Minha Gente"** and **"São Marcos."**

Perhaps of greater importance to **"Corpo Fechado"** is the act of passing on a town's legends from **"São Marcos,"** in that the subject and organization of this next tale

reveal it to be part of the lore of a town's badmen. Composed of anecdotes like Aurísio's, **"Corpo Fechado"** starts out with accounts told to the outsider or "doutor," of the town's former badmen, Desidério Cabaça, Miligido, José Boi, and the present bully, Targino. Before the newest badman, Manuel Fulô, can assume his position, however, the "doutor's" story is subject to several false starts. When Manuel comes to announce his engagement to Maria das Dores, the narrator states, "e aí foi que a história começou" (p. 266). But at the moment in which Targino informs Manuel of his intention to steal Maria, we are told: "E foi então que de fato a história começou" (p. 279). Then again as Manuel locks himself in with the magician, it is repeated: "Mas, de fato, cartas dadas, a história começa mesmo é aqui" (p. 283).

What is meant by these postponed beginnings?[12] For one thing, they are a comment on the writing of history. It is a truism that any event has many angles, many beginnings and ends. Despite claims to objectivity, the historian must always make a choice, either in the selecting of his data or the perspective from which to approach his material, thus, artifice-like, betraying the real flow of time and experience. In any case, our historian-narrator is aware of the problem and, for this reason, envisions several beginnings to what will be Mané's legend. An analogous explanation of the same phenomenon is that though the whole of it is the tale of badman Manuel Fulô, the single story is comprised of many: the first start begins a love story, the second that of the making of a badman, and the third the story of a charm to make Manuel bulletproof. The importance of these plays between the one story and the many will soon become apparent.

Almost paradoxically, the last and shortest story is both the essence and the whole of **"Corpo Fechado."** The "real" story which the others narrow down to concerns the avenging of Targino's transgression of his opponent's love by means of a charm to make Manuel invulnerable. Manuel is a centaur, half artificer and half song creature. On the one hand, he is a crafty fellow whose wiles outsmart even the tricky gypsies who trained him. On the other, Manuel is descended from the Indians, people of nature, and his alter ego is an animal, his mule. The credibility of the charm is therefore diluted, wavering between artifice and song: is it a trick to fool himself and gain courage, or is he really bulletproof? No matter; to have faith in the charm is to ally oneself with magic and it enables Manuel to rise to his fate in the showdown which earns him the title of badman.

The Chinese boxes of story-within-story found in **"Corpo Fechado"** assumes two further shapes in **"Conversa de Bois."** A frame story, **"Conversa de Bois"** presents itself as a yarn told aloud, with some liberties, by a nameless narrator to his friend Manuel Timborna (notice how even the names carry over from one tale to the next). Even more striking is the splitting of this story into two distinct, yet interwoven substories: the essential difference between men and beast as developed in the oxen's musings, and the rectification by the oxen of their cart driver's violation of nature.

Men, say the oxen, are pest-like creatures peripheral to the immensity of nature. Brought under man's domination and living close to him, unlike their brothers in pasture, the carter's oxen bemoan the forced alienation from their natural state:

> Não podemos mais deixar de pensar como o homem. . . .
> Estamos todos pensando como o homem pensa.
>
> (p. 295)

> Mas é melhor não pensar como o homem [. . . .]
> Começamos a olhar o mêdo . . . o mêdo grande . . . e
> a pressa. . . . É ruim ser boi-de-carro. . . . É ruim
> viver perto dos homens. . . . As coises ruins são de
> homem: tristeza, fome, calor—tudo, pensado, é pior.
>
> (p. 294).

That the forced assimilation of animal to humanity, underlining the distinction between artifice and song creatures, involves an infringement of nature's plan, is illustrated by the story of the ox Rodapião, whose man-like schemes led to his death: "Chegou e quis espiar tudo, farejar e conhecer. . . . Era tão esperto e tão estúrdio, que ninguém não podia com êle. . . . Só falava artes compridas, idéia de homem, coisas que boi nunca conversou [. . .] êle tinha ficado quase como um homem, meio maluco" (pp. 302-03).

The carter, Argenor Soronho, has committed a sin against two of nature's creatures, the oxen and the child Tiãozinho. Soronho has enslaved and beaten the saintly oxen; they, in turn (and this is also the crux of **"O Burrinho Pedrês"**), rail against confinement and coexistence with man. By courting Tiãozinho's mother while the boy's father lies dying, mistreating the boy, and showing disrespect for the now dead father whom they cart to his grave, Soronho inspires a thirst for a revenge that the child is unable to effect by himself.

In the final and stunning portion of narrative, the oxen and boy become one through their thoughts and avenge the outrage. Tiãozinho's dream-thoughts bridge the final gap between himself and the oxen" "O bezerro-de-homem sabe mais, às vêzes. . . . Éle vive muito perto de nós, e ainda é bezerro. . . . Tem horas em que êle fica ainda mais perto de nós. . . . Quando está meio dormindo, pensa quase como nós bois" (p. 318). The two strands of narrative become one as oxen and boy, negating their separate beings, merge into the single shining power of vastness: "Não há nenhum boi Capitão. . . . Mas todos os bois. . . . Não há bezerro-de-homem! . . . Todos . . . Tudo. . . . Tudo é enorme . . ." (p. 319). During the exalted interval of primal alliance and destiny, the oxen rebel, killing Agenor Soronho.

At one point in **"Duelo,"** the narrator remarks, "é verídica a narrativa" (p. 145), while in **"A Hora e Vez de Augusto Matraga,"** we find the comment, "esta aqui é estória inventada, e não é um caso acontecido, não senhor" (p. 343). We can suggest two reasons why the last and best-known story of **Sagarana** is called "invented" by its own author. First off, the concluding story of the

work is in a sense more contrived than the others. Just as the first and last stories of Joyce's *Dubliners* contain the seeds of the rest, so does **"Augusto Matraga"** bear almost all the major motifs of *Sagarana*. We shall point them out in analyzing the story. Secondly, **"Augusto Matraga"** elevates the themes of the epic journey and destiny to a clearly allegorical level, providing a spiritual framework within which to regard the body of the text.

The allegory here developed is that of an existential Christ, reborn within this world to fulfill his humanity and fate on earth. A cattle brand composed of a triangle inscribed in a circle is described in the story: three points in a continuum, it depicts Augusto Matraga's death, rebirth and transformation within one lifetime as well as the avenging of his sins through a three-stage religious conversion. Trinity-like, the all-as-one and one-as-all movement is again reflected in the first lines of the story, which encapsulate the process of the negation of being, "Matraga não é Matraga, não é nada," and the three phases of transformation: "Matraga é Estêves, Augusto Estêves, filho do Coronel Afonsão Estêves, das Pindaíbas e do Saco-de-Embira. Ou Nhô Augusto—o homem . . ." (p. 324).

Soronho Argenor's arrogance and cruelty are reincarnated in Augusto Matraga, who sins against love (the backwoodsman's love for Sariema, whom Matraga buys in auction; conjugal love, for he abuses his wife) and life, since he is a killer. When informed that his wife has left him, Matraga departs in a fury, zealous for revenge (**"Volto,"** **"Duelo,"** **"Corpo Fechado"**). However, his henchman, including the backwoodsman he wronged, get to him first. Dragging Matraga along the purgative "caminho de pragas e judição" (p. 335) the men beat him—they believe—to death, the symbolic murder of his old self.

During the battle Matraga's body "parecia querer partir-se em dois" (p. 335). Half of him dies while the other half is freed for spiritual and physical rebirth, a task assumed by the devoted black couple (**"Sarapalha"**). Weakened, Matraga is reduced to the essentials of life (**"O Burrinho Pedrês,"** **"Volta"**) and, as if in the womb, to a state of innocence. He emerges from his stupor with a renewed faith in God. The priest shrives him of his past sins, sowing a faith in just reward and destiny in their own time—Matraga's charm (**"São Marcos"**), and a motto for *Sagarana*: "Cada um tem a sua hora e a sua vez: você há de ter a sua" (p. 339).

In the second stage of self-redemption, Matraga denies his humanity and manhood, appointing himself to the ascetic route of self-denial and faith of the saints: "porque para êle, féria feita, a vida já se acabara, e só esperava era a salvação da sua alma e a misericórdia de Deus Nosso Senhor. Nunca mais seria gente!" (p. 340). Matraga and the blacks travel to another town where he is viewed as "meio dôido e meio santo" (p. 341), a Christ figure. Nonetheless, it is a different, non-ascetic, kind of saint that he is meant to be: angered by the news that a man has been killed and his daughter led to ruin because of him, Matraga feels his mortal cravings reawaken, he abandons asceticism and opens his eyes and ears to nature.

The final and most prolonged phase of self-realization is Matraga's reintegration into humanity. Though at first fearing it a sin to enjoy life, he gradually discovers in nature "os sinais da mão de Deus" and his sights shift from heaven and salvation to something of a *carpe diem:* "Nem pensou mais em morte, nem em ir para o céu" (p. 356). Therefore, when Joãozinho Bem-Bem and his badmen (**"Corpo"**) arrive in town, Matraga delights in their presence—though he refuses to join their band. Having now come full circle, Augusto is fit to tackle his fate. Two omens, a dream and a bird's song, impulse the journey he takes mounted on a mule, "um animalzinho assim meio sagrado, muito misturado às passagens da vida de Jesus" (p. 360) (**"O Burrinho Pedrês"**). Like the narrator of **"Minha Gente,"** Matraga abandons himself to nature, letting the donkey take him to Joãozinho Bem-Bem. And now it is Augusto who averts the other man's sin against nature (the murder of an innocent man), reversing the original transgression and restoring equilibrium.

Heralded as a saviour by the townspeople, and nicknamed "o Homem do Jumento," Matraga actually discards sainthood to regain his humanity in dying: there are no gods and no devils on earth, just brave men, the moral seems to be, for the saintly Matraga and his "parente" Joãozinho Bem-Bem become doubles in their courage (the two Joãos in **"São Marcos"**), finishing each other off. Christ proved his mortality and humanity with his death. In like manner, Matraga, already reincarnated, ceases to be "o Homem do Jumento" and reclaims his original name and being, Nhô Augusto Estêves of Pindaíbas, in his final moments.

Augusto Matraga's three names being resolved into one, the triangle within the circle—both of these recall the Trinity, whose dual movement of the three-as-one and one-as-three bears further-reaching consequences for *Sagarana* and, indeed, for the rest of Guimarães Rosa's later works. Let us term the former, the many as one, *telescopic* and the latter, where the one proves to be many, *microscopic,* and proceed to consider their implications.

From a microscopic perspective, every component divides into many, things-within-things, with each resulting element partial, interdependent on the text. In much the same way does each story of *Sagarana* contain many elements and form a partial unit of the whole system which is the complete field of motifs, the text. Each story develops a certain nucleus of the overall field of motifs of *Sagarana*, motifs which carry over throughout the work, appearing separately and in varying combinations. In the course of the text each motif, such as love, poetic language, honor, the charm, etc., finds fuller and fuller expression, often encountering explicit definition in a particular story. And the whole field of motifs, as stated previously, converge in the "invented" story, **"A Hora a Vez de Augusto Matraga."** By the same token, each story is comprised of smaller parcels—*cantigas,* anecdotes, substories—which do not stand alone, but complement particular aspects of the whole story. In fact, a subplot of one story, such as the motif of names in **"São Marcos,"** may only make full sense in the context of the following narration.

From a telescopic perspective, on the other hand, everything is contracted into one point which stands on its own as a kind of microcosm, subsuming all else; in the case of a literary work, they would stand as microcosms of the text. Within this framework, those same anecdotes, *cantigas* and substories which but worked into the larger scheme of the story before, acquire special meaning. Though these elements are indeed partial, they can and should also be considered as a progressive stripping-down of the story, a reduction into its most essential elements which contain the whole of it.

To illustrate further the play between expansion and contraction, microscopic and telescopic, let us examine the generic possibilities of our work. *Sagarana* is potentially a text of many genres of subgenres. It has been classified, variously, as a collection of stories by most of its critics, as a "cycle of stories," by its English translator, and it has also been suggested that "each story should be read as a chapter of a novel."[13] While the first two represent a telescopic point of view, the last, we shall see, reflects a microscopic attitude.

The isomorphic traits of the stories, which telescope all the tales into one paradigm, have been mentioned several times. Briefly, they are a transgression of nature, the reappearing drama of achieving one's destiny, and the ultimate fusing of artifice and song. In this manner, each of the collected stories contains the seeds of the others. On the other hand, *Sagarana* is also a cumulative system or cycle of stories, not by virtue of having the same characters reappear in each story, but for its formal characteristics, being a fabric of progressively developing, growing motifs. The motifs as presented in each *individual* story thus qualify as what has been called "double-edged" discourse,[14] since they evoke the other meanings the themes had assumed in previous tales. Gathering meanings and resonance as the system evolves, by the end of the cycle each motif is not only double, but multiple-edged.

To perceive *Sagarana* as a novel, or consistent development, involves some special consideration, for we must first try to understand what a novel is. Lukács sees the inner meaning of the novel as a biographical form which gives expression to a person's journey toward the full recognition of self: "The inner form of the novel has been understood as the process of the problematic individual's journeying toward himself, the road from dull captivity within a merely present reality—a reality that is heterogeneous in itself and meaningless to the individual—towards clear self-recognition."[15] If we accept this definition, then *Sagarana*, with its epiphany structure, is certainly faithful to the inner sensibility of the novel. But what of the formal shape, the consistency of development and characters? The key is to be found in *Sagarana* itself. An unknown voice, in **"São Marcos,"** calls out: "Güenta o relance, Izé!," to which the narrator/protagonist replies: "Estremeci e me voltei, porque, nesta estória, eu também me chamarei José" (p. 228). With this clue, Guimarães Rosa subtly indicates that all the narrators (postulated by the work) are one person who merely assumes different masks or narrative personae. Reinventing himself with each tale, he tells the same story—perhaps his own—both from different narrative points of view (first person, third person) and from different perspectives. Put another way, *Sagarana* is a novel which refracts a cohesive theme (the meeting of one's destiny) into its many possible phases and perspectives. Taking recourse to a more formal view of the novel, that of B. Eichenbaum,[16] we find that in comparison with the short story's single focus, a novel has many centers within a unified evolution. From this standpoint it is clear that *Sagarana* can be seen as a novel with multiple centers, illustrating the shifting facets of a theme.

Despite its many generic possibilities, this *Sagarana* nonetheless appears as straightforward as a folktale when compared to Guimarães Rosa's later works, such as his convoluted *Grande Sertão: Veredas*—a *sertão* text into which few clear critical paths have been carved. Yet perhaps Guimarães Rosa left a trail of his own, in *Sagarana*, for each of *Grande Sertão: Vereda's* two central leitmotifs and the themes they synthesize represent the development of features from *Sagarana:* (1) *Travessia* (crossing): the conflict between artifice and song (an analytic vs. an intuitive outlook on life), so neatly resolved in *Sagarana*, gives rise to the confounding ambiguity of *Grande Sertão: Veredas* as its protagonist, Riobaldo, crosses from one state to the other, finally remaining in the first, from which perspective his tale is told; (2) "O diabo na rua no meio da redemoinho": from this standpoint of analysis, the microscopic point of view which refracts the world into chaotic multiplicity (the "redemoinho") comes to define Riobaldo's attitude and ultimately reveals itself as a full-blown philosophical perspectivism. To conclude, then, in this and other aspects—enough for several articles—the astute reader will discern in *Sagarana* not only a story system, but the system that *Grande Sertão: Veredas* effectively explodes and expands.

NOTES

[1] João Guimarães Rosa, *Sagarana*, 17th ed. (Rio de Janeiro: José Olympio, 1956). All quotations will be taken from this edition and page numbers will appear in the text.

[2] Harriet de Onis entitled her translation *Sagarana: A Cycle of Stories* (New York: Knopf, 1966).

[3] I refer here to Boris Tomashevsky's concept of the motif as the smallest, indecomposable unit of a text. Further explanation of this concept can be found in Tomashevsky's "Thématique," in *Théorie de la littérature*, ed. Tzvetan Todorov (Paris: Seuil, 1965), pp. 267-303.

[4] Georgy Lukács, *The Theory of the Novel*, trans. Anne Bostock (Cambridge, Mass.: MIT Press, 1971), p. 46.

[5] Pedro Xisto, "A Busca da Poesia," in Pedro Xisto, Augusto de Campos, and Haroldo de Campos, *Guimarães Rosa em Três Dimensões* (São Paulo: Conselho Estadal de Cultura, 1970), p. 26.

[6] Jorge Luis Borges, *Obra poética*, p. 148.

[7] Jorge Luis Borges, "Nota sobre Carriego," in *Otras inquisiciones* (Buenos Aires: Sur, 1952), p. 42.

[8] I have chosen to focus on five stories instead of all of them for matters of space; I have chosen these five in particular for the presence of "São Marcos" and its discussion of poetic language, and for the presence of "Augusto Matraga," which includes the whole field of motifs.

[9] Northrop Frye, *Anatomy of Criticism* (Princeton: Princeton University Press, 1957), p. 163.

[10] Frye, p. 169.

[11] Frye, pp. 169-70.

[12] These several beginnings become several endings in the perspectivism of the concluding lines of Riobaldo's narrative in GS: V:

"Aqui a estória se acabou.

Aqui a estória acabada.

Aqui a estória acaba." (p. 454)

[13] Franklin de Oliveira, Introduction to the translation of Sagarana, p. ix.

[14] The term is Mikhail Bakhtin's from Chapter V of *Problems of Dostoevsky's Poetics*, trans. R. W. Rotsel (Michigan: Ardis, 1973), and refers to discourse with a double focus which, like parody, contains the word of another source.

[15] Lukács, p. 80.

[16] Boris Eichenbaum, "O. Henry and the Theory of the Short Story," in *Readings in Russian Poetics*, eds. Ladislav Matejka and Krystyna Pomorska (Cambridge, Mass.: MIT Press, 1971), pp. 227-72.

Mary L. Daniel (essay date 1986)

SOURCE: "Redemptive Analogy in the Fiction of João Guimarães Rosa," in *Romance Notes*, Vol. 27, No. 2, Winter, 1986, pp. 127-34.

[*In the following essay, Daniel discusses the theme of grace in Guimarães Rosa's works.*]

João Guimarães Rosa (1908-1967) is a Brazilian fiction writer recognized internationally as the giant of his generation and of XX century Brazilian letters. A native of the interior state of Minas Gerais, he was fluent in nearly ten languages, practiced medicine for several years, and for the last three decades of his life served as a member of the Brazilian diplomatic corps in several foreign posts. Though his first volume of short stories was composed in the mid-1930s, the enforced hiatus of the war years delayed its publication until 1946. Guimarães Rosa thus appears as a writer whose literary debut occurred fairly late in life, though in fact his creativity predates his publication by at least a decade.

Guimarães Rosa has been likened to Melville because of his sensitive treatment of the inner/outer world, and has been called the "James Joyce of the Portuguese language" because of his linguistic innovations: neologisms, widespread lexical borrowing from ancient and modern languages, syntactic inversions and a unique "telegraphic syntax," and the consistent utilization of an orally-based style of storytelling possessing medieval and archetypical qualities. Guimarães Rosa is also frequently referred to as a "universal regionalist" or "surregionalist" because the thematic content and physical context of his narratives involves almost exclusively the remote backlands of Brazil—the savanna country where cowboys, outlaws, and cattle roam in a frontier environment which is a law unto itself—while at the same time a metaphysical dimension overarches nearly every work and high dramas of conscience and theological inquiry pervade Rosean prose. Of his gigantic novel *Grande Sertão: Veredas,* a 600-page first person monologue free of chapter divisions published in 1956, the author himself said: ". . . *Grande Sertão: Veredas*—que, por bizarra que V. ache a afirmativa, é menos literatura pura do que um sumário de idéias e crenças do autor, com buritis e capim devidamente semi-camuflados."[1]

This author, who has inspired awe, puzzlement, desperation and excitement among readers and critics alike, has given us a helpful hint as to the multi-dimensionality of his fiction in a letter to one of his English-language translators:

> Nos meus livros . . . tem importância, pelo menos igual ao do sentido da estória, se é que não muito mais: a poética ou poeticidade da forma, tanto a "sensação" mágica, visual, das palavras, quanto a eficácia sonora delas . . .—transmitindo ao subconsciente vibrações emotivas subtis. Tudo em 3 planos (como os ensinos das antigas religiões orientais):
>
> 1-The underlying charm (enchantment).
> 2-The level-lying common meaning.
> 3-The "overlying" idea (metaphysic)[2]

There is throughout the works of Gimarães Rosa a basic concept of *esoteric* (versos *exoteric*) religious belief, experience, and practice. The author has reiterated in personal correspondence that he considers spiritual themes the most important of all. Critic Suzi Sperber, basing her analysis on Rosa's private library, observes his devotional readings in the works of Bernanos and Romano Guardini, his extensive and exhaustive study of both the Old and New Testaments of the Bible (particulary the Gospels), and his knowledge of the Hindu *Upanishads,* Tao, Plotinus, Theosophy, Christian Science, and diverse esoteric texts. In a letter to his Italian translator four years before his death, Guimarães Rosa summed up his personal perspective in the following terms:

> Sou profundamente, essencialmente religioso, ainda que fora do rótulo estrito e das fileiras de qualquer confissão ou seita: antes, talvez, como Riobaldo de *Grande Sertão: Veredas*, pertença eu a todas . . . Daí todas as minhas

constantes preocupações religiosas, metafisicas, embeberem os meus livros. Talvez meio-existencialista-cristão (alguns me classificam assim), meio neo-platõnico (. . .) e sempre impregnado de hinduísmo . . . Quero ficar com o Tao, com os Vedas e Upanixades, com os Evangelistas e São Paulo, com Platão, com Plotino, com Bergston, com Berdiaeff — com Cristo, principalmente.[3]

Suzi Sperber calls Gimarães Rosa's personal religion "um cristianismo *sui-generis.* Un cristianismo de fé e oração, um cristianismo em que o Espírito Santo teria algo de milagroso, de mediador com a transcendência—inerente à sua natureza intrínseca—mas não forçosa e indissolu-velmente ligado ao Pai e ao Filho."[4]

Transcendence and intuition play major roles in Guimarães Rosa's life awareness and consideration of his own fictional works. He speaks of these qualities frequently in the confessional "prefaces" intercalated in the last work published during his lifetime—*Tutaméia*—among which the following is typical: "Sei que o autor, ademais de cauto, tem, para o mais-que-natural, finas úteis antenas."[5] Running through his fiction is a deep vein of what may be called, besides "metaphysical," frankly *theological,* though never doctrinarian, concerns. In her investigation and cataloguing of the books in Rosa's private library, Suzi Sperber notes a number of telling marginal comments and underlinings of passages the author found especially appealing or relevant. One such passage, the key to our present topic, is the following from Romano Guardini's book *Le Seigneur,* which Rosa had underlined: "L'homme devient exactement ce qu'il est de par le décret eternel de la grâce et de par sa propre volonté la plus profonde."[6]

Divine grace and human free will, according to Rosa's reasoning, collaborate to liberate humankind from the bondage of blind destiny or karmic cyclicity. Grace is the providential intervention of divine benevolence in human life wherever created beings will facilitate its reception. It is proper for us to include all created beings here, for in the primitive Brazilian backland ambience of Guimarães Rosa's short stories, novel, and novelettes, there is an organic interdependence among men, women, cattle, horses, children, birds, and other living things. A kind of Franciscan oneness prevades the Rosean universe, so animals as well as people may be the agents of grace or of cosmic justice to right wrongs and restore equilibrium in relationships. Let us consider now in the fiction of Guimarães Rosa typical examples of such *redemptive analogy*—stories or traditions understood and/or interpreted as suggestive of the redemption of humankind through divine intervention.

Sagarana (1946), the author's first published volume of short stories, bears a title meaning "primitive saga" or "almost a saga." Of its nine tales, at least four contain elements which may be interpreted as aspects of redemptive analogy or even as outright parables. In **"O Burrinho pedrês"** and **"Conversa de Bois,"** the agents are quadrupeds and a child, and the linking factor among them is innocence. The little dust-brown donkey is named Sete-de-Ouros, and he is pressed into action for a cattle drive simply because there aren't enough horses for all the cowhands to ride. No one wants to ride the donkey, of course, for he is far too lowly. Yet, as in the Biblical citation, "the stone which the builders rejected has become the head of the corner." Sete-de-Ouros comes into focus as a life-preserver when flood waters swell the stream the cattle drive attempts to ford: The horses and their riders are lost in the swirling current, but Sete-de-Ouros faithfully crosses the treacherous channel, bearing on his back the drunk cowhand Badu (whose life had been threatened by a malicious partner) and with the peace-making cowboy Francolim hanging on to his tail. Badu, as "low man on the totem pole" among the herders, had been assigned the lowly donkey, but in being brought low, with no potential for rescuing himself, he has been saved.

The story **"Conversa de Bois"** exemplifies the dictum that "a little child shall lead them," though in this case the child, named Tiãozinho, is paired with the yokes of oxen he is leading as the oxcart bearing his deceased father to burial creaks along the rutted dirt road. The cruel Agenor, owner of the team and rig and brutalizer of the child's family, sits atop the cart, nodding off to sleep as the journey progresses. A kind of sonambulant, subliminal communication is established among the oxen, who also have suffered abuse at the hands of their owner, Agenor, and between them and the child who walks ahead of them. Suddenly they lurch, the oxcart jerks forward, and the sleeping Agenor falls off and is killed. After the trauma, the oppressive atmosphere lifts and we read:

> O caminho melhorou. Tiãozinho — nunca houve melhor menino candieiro - vai em corridinha, maneiro, porque os bois, com a fresca, aceleram. E talvez dois defuntos dêem mais para a viagem, pois até o carro está contente — *renhein* (. . .) *nhein* — e abre a goela do chumaço, numa toada triunfal.[7]

In yet another story of the *Sagarana* collection— **Duelo"**— cosmic justice is wrought and equilibrum restored in the case of a pair of men hunting each other down; the agent is a simple and innocent young man named Timpim Vinte-e-Um, who enters the story as a kind of third party unaware of the cat-and-mouse game that is in progress. An even more eloquent example of human agent of divine providence and justice is the last story of the collection, a Christological parable entitled **"A hora e vez de Augusta Matraga."** Combining elements of the Good Samaritan, the Prodigal Son, and the Calvary defeat of death through death, Gimarães Rosa offers in this narrative the career of one Augusto Matraga, brawler and bully, who descends to the depths of well-merited physical punishment, is rescued and restored by a pair of poor and virtuous country folk, experiences repentance and conversion, undergoes a period of ascetic self-castigation (a kind of Lenten interlude) and subsequent liberation of spirit, feels the call of destiny in his new life, lets a donkey choose his route in search of "the right place at the right time," resists the temptation to backslide into his previous pattern of violence,

and eventually protects the life of the population of an entire village by killing, without malice and somewhat reluctantly, an old bandit friend who vindictively threatens the innocent villagers. But in saving them, he dies himself. The townspeople gather to express their gratitude as he breathes his last:

> E o velho choroso exclamava:—Traz meus filhos, para agradecerem a ele, para beijarem os pés dele! (. . .) Não deixem este santo morrer assim . . . Então, Augusto Matraga fechou um pouco os olhos, com sorriso intenso nos lábios lambuzados de sangue, e de seu rosto subia um sério contentamento.
>
> Daí, mais, olhou . . . e disse, agora sussurrado, sumido:
> —Põe a bênção na minha filha (. . .) seja lá onde for que ela esteja (. . .) E, Dionóra (. . .) Fala com a Dionóra que está tudo em ordem. Depois, morreu.[8]

And so the words of reconciliation with family members and other estranged persons have been spoken to complete what is the fullest model of redemptive analogy among many in the fiction of Guimarães Rosa.

In one of the novelettes of the *Corpo de Baile* collection (1956) and several of the short stories included in *Primeiras Estórias* (1962), we find messianic figures of both sexes, though predominantly male, who intervene graciously and usually unexpectedly in the lives of others to bring restoration, protection, or new life. These interveners may have much in common with those they aid or be of a more transcendent, liminal nature. Among the first are the traveling doctor of **"Campo Geral"** (*Corpo de Baile*) who opens new worlds to a nearsighted seven-year-old in a primitive, debauched backland environment by sharing his thick glasses with the youngster and taking him to an urban clinic to be fitted with his own glasses at the doctor's expense. The doctor, himself extremely myopic, is able to diagnose the child's problem at a glance and graciously offers the cure which had previously been totally outside the realm of possibility. He partakes simultaneously of two worlds, that of his own professional expertise and that of the child's limitation, and so can raise the young boy to a new and higher level of living. Equally benevolent and intervening from a position of strength, albeit in a somewhat more veiled manner, to aid and infuse new life and courage into vulnerable men and women, are Meu Amigo (**"Fatalidade"**) and Tio Man'Antônio (**"Nada e a nossa condição"**) of the *Primeiras Estórias* collection. Meu Amigo draws the attention of readers acquainted with the New Testament by his direct quotations from St. Paul's Epistle to the Romans on the interaction of *faith* and *grace,* laconically interspersed within his own direct action to save another. Of a more other-worldly nature than the above-mentioned mediators of grace are Nhinhinha (**"A menina de lá**) and the **"Moço muito branco"** of the *Primeiras Estórias* tales of the same name. Both seem to partake of the tentative presence more recently exemplified in popular culture by E. T.: They are children or adolescents who dwell for a brief time among a somewhat incomprehending humanity and minister a heavenly awareness (the gleaming young man through his glance and touch, since he is mute), only to depart abruptly as though by foreordained timetable, leaving behind an aura of tenderness and wonder.

A few months before his death, Guimarães Rosa published a volume of very short narratives and fictionalized essays entitled **Tutaméia**, which he himself referred to as *anecdotes of abstraction,* reflecting spiritual allegories and metaphysical sensibilities. Among the protagonists created in this volume is **"Rebimba, o Bom,"** a man who never appears physically but whose presence, via the references of those who have known him or heard of him, serves to inspire and direct the life of the story's narrator in undying hope and constructive action. The fundamental optimism and confidence of the author himself are patent in the four theoretical essays, called "prefaces," included in **Tutaméia**, in one of which he affirms: "O mal está apenas guardando lugar para o bem. O mundo supura é só a olhos impuros. Deus está fazendo coisas fabulosas."[9]

The contraposition of good and evil constitutes the essential theme and fictional framework of Guimarães Rosa's monumental novel, **Grande Sertão: Veredas**. Its central figure, a retired and respectable ex-bandit named Riobaldo, is searching his past in a rambling monologue, seeking to determine once and for all to his own satisfaction whether or not he once made a pact with the Devil to successfully defeat a malevolent rival bandit named Hermógenes. The novel is a gold mine of theological and metaphysical questions, which though absorbing in themselves are not germane to our present consideration. What *is* germane is the role of a young bandit named Diadorim (also called *Reinaldo* by some of the outlaws), closest companion of Riobaldo and guiding light and inspiration of his career. This figure is the agent of grace in the redemptive analogy portrayed throughout the novel, bringing equilibrium, calm and courage to Riobaldo when he falters or loses his sense of orientation and stability. In the final showdown battle of Riobaldo's career, his forces face those of Hermógenes, who is known to have a pact with the Devil. Riobaldo, supposedly the sharpshooter of the band, faints just as he is in an ideal position to kill Hermógenes; he regains consciousness only after the enemy has been defeated, and then discovers what has happened: Diadorim has engaged Hermógenes in hand-to-hand combat and killed him. But in a parallel to the case of Augusto Matraga, Diadorim also has died at the hands of Hermógenes. Though Riobaldo had been tempted by the potential power deriving from a pact with the Devil, Diadorim was free of such temptation to collusion with evil and had chosen to do combat voluntarily to save the life of a friend and to vindicate the name and honor of the band's founder—Diadorim's father, Joca Ramiro. In the novel's most moving scene, Riobaldo, overcome with remorse and grief, helps prepare the body of Diadorim for burial; as his friend's bloody clothes are removed, Riobaldo discovers for the first time that Diadorim is a woman. After her burial he seeks to discover why she would have so carefully disguised her true identity by dressing as an adolescent male to integrate into the crude existence in which the battles of mankind are fought and become unnecessarily vulnerable to violence in order to serve as sacrificial lamb to restore order out of chaos and inspire Riobaldo himself (a kind of *Everyman*) to lay down his weapons and seek a life of peace. After some searching, Riobaldo is able to ascertain the complete and original name of his friend: It is *Deodorina,* whose etymology may be understood as "adorer of God." Diadorim has mediated grace in the life of Riobaldo and has marked his conscience permanently for the better.

The worldview expressed in the fiction of Guimarães Rosa, while taking into account the essential sinfulness of humankind and the brutality of life in its natural state, never ceases to be cognizant of the availability of divine grace to ameliorate and transform the most desperate of situations. Guimarães Rosa's "holy sinners," liminal creatures, and providential quadrupeds join forces in this creation of an authentic regionalism which grapples with deep spiritual and ontological concerns.

NOTES

[1] Suzi Frankl Sperber, *Caos e Cosmos* (São Paulo, 1976), p. 89.

[2] Mary L. Daniel, *João Guimarães Rosa: Travessia Literária* (Rio de Janeiro, 1969), p. 172.

[3] Sperber, pp. 144-145.

[4] Sperber, p. 40.

[5] João Guimarães Rosa, *Tutaméia: Terceiras Estórias* (Rio de Janeiro, 1967), p. 159.

[6] Sperber, p. 92.

[7] João Guimarães Rosa, *Sagarana* (6th ed.—Rio, 1964), p. 318.

[8] Rosa, *Sagarana,* pp. 364-5.

[9] Rosa, *Tutaméia,* p. 165.

FURTHER READING

Avelar, Idelber, "The Logic of Paradox in Guimarães Rosa's *Tutaméia,*" in The *Latin American Literary Review,* Vol. 22, No. 43, January-June, 1994, pp. 67-80.

Analyzes the use of paradox in *Tutaméia.*

Valente, Luiz Fernando, "Fiction and the Reader: The Prefaces of *Tutaméia,*" in *Hispanic Review,* Vol. 56, No. 3, Summer, 1988, pp. 349-62.

Considers that the prefaces of *Tutaméia* "emphasize . . . the mutually enriching partnership between the writer and the reader."

Valente, Luiz Fernando, "Affective Response in *Granda Sertão: Veredas*" in *Luso-Brazilian Review*, Vol. 23, No. 1, Summer, 1986, pp. 77-88.

Examines the relationship between the reader and the text of *Grande Sertão* and analyzes the theme of history versus fiction within the narrative.

Additional coverage of Guimarães Rosa's life and career is contained in the following sources published by the Gale Group: *Contemporary Literary Criticism,* **Vol. 23;** *Contemporary Authors,* **Vols. 89-92, 175; and** *Dictionary of Literary Biography,* **Vol. 113.**

Manuel Gutiérrez Nájera
1859-1895

Mexican essayist, poet, journalist, and short story writer.

INTRODUCTION

Manuel Gutiérrez Nájera earned distinction as one of a formidable generation of modernist writers, including Nicaraguan Rubén Darío and Venezuelan Manuel Díaz Rodríguez. By the time he died at age thirty-five, he had had three careers: journalist, poet, and short story writer. It was he who helped transform the turn-of-the-century short story into a literary landmark, endowing the genre with a pathos embedded in a syntactical economy previously found only in lyric verse, a style which still predominates the Latin-American short story today. In poetry, Gutiérrez Nájera is known for the changes he brought to the mood of the poetic image, accomplishing a mix of stilted expression with borrowings from French romantic and symbolist poetic styles. He also followed the modernist tenets of restraint, objectivity, and precision, and, employig a Romantic sense of musicality, refined expression, and exquisite sensibility, his verse acts as a kind of bridge between the Romantic and the modern eras. Gutiérrez Nájera also contributed to literature in the area of the *crónica*, or journalistic prose—an area in which he did much of his work. Because of his influence, this type of prose became a popular style among the writers of the next generation.

Manuel Gutiérrez Nájera was born December 22, 1859, to a middle-class family in Mexico. His father also was a journalist, editor, poet, and dramatist whose work was performed at Mexico City's National Theater in 1862. Gutiérrez Nájera was educated at home, first by his mother, a devout Catholic, and later by tutors of mathematics, physics, Latin, and French. Early on his mother encouraged him to become an ecclesiastic, so Gutiérrez Nájera read the works of the great Spanish Christian mystics, San Juan de la Cruz, Santa Teresa de Jesús, Fray Luis de Leon, and Fray Luis de Granada. Prolific and precocious, he continued publishing after his first article appeared, at thirteen in the journal, *La Iberia*. Gutiérrez Nájera was initiated into journalism when he was sixteen. His entire life was spent working for the daily press as an editor or writer. In this capacity he used a plethora of pseudonyms: M. Can Can, Junius Puck, Recamier, El Cura de Jalatlaco, Perico el de los Palotes, Omega, XX, and the most famous, El Duque Job. These pseudonyms allowed him to recycle older texts in new contexts, enabling him to make more money with less work. In addition to his career in newspapers, he founded, with his friend Carlos Diaz Dufóo, *Revista Azul,* a publication that became the focal point for Modernist literature in Spanish America. In 1888, he was appointed deputy to the national congress from Texcoco, a position providing enough income to allow him to marry. From that time on, his wife, two daughters, his newspaper, *La Partido Liberal,* and his journal, *Revista Azul,* became the bulk of his life. Though he longed to travel, Gutiérrez Nájera never left Mexico, and rarely traveled outside Mexico City. In 1895, the Associated Press of Mexico named him its president but an illness prevented him from assuming the post. Following surgery in Mexico City, he died at the height of his career on February 3, 1895.

"By dint of scribbling so much I'm beginning to hate the ink I use," Gutiérrez Nájera once wrote. His ink spilled into three areas: poetry, short fiction, and *crónicas* (chronicles). Derived from the French word *chronique,* the *crónica* is a prose genre Gutiérrez Nájera is said to have invented. the *crónica*, and which was a central form used by modernist Spanish-American writers. Gutiérrez Nájera's prose fused traditional imagery with chromatic metaphors, fleeting impressions, French and English words, and exotic names and places from Europe—especially Paris. His *crónicas,* entitled *Crónicas color de rosa* (Rose Colored Chronicles), *Crónicas color de lluvia* (Rain Colored Chronicles), *Crónicas color de oro* (Golden Chronicles), *Crónicas de mil colors* (Myriad Colored Chronicles) reflect the imaginative correlations and synaesthesia that would later become conventions of this genre. The *crónicas* address art, literature, cultural problems, national identity, theatrical performances, and political and social questions in a simple style showcasing unique syntax or colloquial expression. Anger is often tempered with humor and with an attempt at geniality. In Gutiérrez Nájera's short fiction such as, "La mañana de San Juan" ("The Morning of St. John's Day"), "La novela del tranvía" ("The Novel in the Streetcar"), and "Los amores del cometa" ("The Loves of the Comet"), melancholy dominates. These stories of the luckless and unfulfilled are the writer's response to those trapped in a set of circumstances where joy is juxtaposed to misery, as life is to death. In "La balada del año nuevo" ("The Ballad of the New Year") where the death of Bebé inside is laid against a celebration outside. In many of his stories, narrators dream of an ideal world, a "happy land [where] there is no legislative chamber, no government, no municipality . . . No pedestrian is robbed of his watch, because there are no watches . . . and the river waters are as blue as the eyes of the angels and the tiny leaves of the forget-me-nots." Such sentimental qualities and juxtapositions also appear in Gutiérrez Nájera's poetry, a Romantic sense of reality as set to modernist stylistic and metric experiments to reveal one of modernism's most prevalent artistic moods: anguish. So prevalent are pain and suffering, and so profound the existential anguish in Gutiérrez Nájera's verse that they are frequently countered with dream, remembrance, abandon, and passion.

Gutiérrez Nájera might best be characterized as a "bridge writer" who spanned the gap between Romantic and modernist writers. His Romantic outpouring is moderated by his concern for refinement and sophistication in expression. While much of Gutiérrez Nájera's work might now be considered sentimental or escapist because of his occasional forays into fantastic worlds that acknowledge the need for their own existence, realms where "Neither children nor birds have invented gunpowder."

PRINCIPAL WORKS

Cuentos frágiles (short stories) 1883
Plato del dia (collected works) 1895
Poesías (poetry) 1896
Obras de Manuel Gutiérrez Nájera 1: Prosa (short stories) 1898
Obras de Manuel Gutiérrez Nájera 2: Prosa (short stories) 1903
Amor y lágrimas (poetry) 1912
Hojas sueltas: Artículos diversos (articles) 1912
Cuentos de Manuel Gutiérrez Nájera. Cultura (short stories) 1916
Sus mejores poesías (poetry) 1916
Poesías escogidas (poetry) 1918
Cuaresmas del Duque Job (short stories) 1922
Cuentos, crónicas y ensayos (short stories) 1940
Cuentos color de humo (short stories) 1942
Manuel Gutiérrez Nájera. Poesías inéditas recogidas de periódicos de México (collected works) 1942
Obras inéditas de Gutiérrez Nájera: Crónicas de Puck (short stories) 1943
Cuaresmas del Duque Job y otros artículos (collected works) 1946
Poesías completas (poetry) 1953
Cuentos completos y otras narraciones (short stories) 1958
Obras 1: Crítica literaria (criticism) 1959
Escritos inéditos de sabor satírico: "Plato del día." (satire) 1972
Obras 3: Crónicas y artículos sobre teatro (1876–1880) (articles) 1974

CRITICISM

Harley D. Oberhelman (essay date 1974)

SOURCE: Review of *Escritos inéditos de sabor satirico "Plato del dia,"* in *Hispania,* December, 1974, p. 1020.

[*In the following essay, Oberhelman praises the arrangement of the "Plato del dia" anthology.*]

This handsome volume collects the two hundred and sixty-four short articles published by Manuel Gutiérrez Nájera in *El Universal* between April 8, 1893, and January 10,

1895, under the general title, **Plato del día**, but it does a great deal more. Prof. and Mrs. Carter provide the reader with a well-written "Estudio preliminar" whose purpose is to "dar idea general del contenido, forma y tono de los doscientos sesenta y cuatro **Platos** que integran la serie." At the end of the volume seven pages of "Notas" elucidate references to proper names in the **Platos**. There are two indices: the "Indice de materias" reproduces the original newspaper titles plus a parenthetical subtitle invented by the compilers to give additional clarification of the contents, and the "Indice alfabético" provides a key to proper names and titles which appear in the **Platos**. There is a bibliography which includes the best known studies of Gutiérrez Nájera as well as general studies of the literary, cultural, and political scene in late nineteenth-century Mexico.

The tremendous value of this volume lies in the fact that it collects all of the **Platos** for the first time: only two had previously been published. Of almost equal value is the **"Estudio preliminar"** which gives a general overview of the principal themes, ranging from satirical comments on the contemporary scene to considerations of such diverse topics as crime, literature, journalism, the theatre, public health, politics, the Church, suicide, justice, and prostitution. There is a brief study of Gutiérrez Nájera's use of humor and pseudonyms (all of the **Platos** except one were signed with the pseudonym "Recamier"), and the preliminary study concludes with a general analysis of the structure and style of the **Platos**, using carefully selected examples of the genre to support the conclusions. Finally, an effort is made to relate the **Platos** to the total production of **"El Duque Job."**

The arrangement of the **Platos** themselves is chronological with the purpose of preserving thematic unity. Each is numbered, and the original date of publication (when available) is given. Footnotes are keyed to the numbers assigned to the **Platos**, and while they total well over one hundred, in no case do they cover all possible questions of interpretation which might arise—a fact readily admitted by the compilers in the "Advertencia."

This excellent and meticulous work must be viewed in the historical perspective of previous *estudios najerianos*. One naturally thinks of the late E. K. Mapes whose pioneering investigation and early publication of source material provided the way for later studies produced by his student, collaborator, and friend, Boyd G. Carter. It is most fitting that this latest volume be dedicated to Mapes and to his wife, Laura Hinkhouse Mapes, whose devotion, assistance, and collaboration aided the late mentor in much the same way that the present investigator is assisted by Mary Eileen Carter.

Harley D. Oberhelman (essay date 1981)

SOURCE: "The Literary Generation of the *Revista Azul*," in *In Honor of Boyd G. Carter: A Collection of Essays,* edited by Catherine Vera and George R. McMurray, 1981, pp. 67-75.

[*Here, Oberhelman discusses the influence of Gutiérrez Nájera's literary journal* Revista Azul *on Mexican literature.*]

Manuel Gutiérrez Nájera was the leader of a brilliant group of Mexican literary artists who contributed to his journal and who commonly have been called the generation of the *Revista Azul* by later critics. While the bonds which held this group together were never tight, the emergence of this association was unique and significant in Mexican literature. Never before had a Mexican literary journal been the focal point for a group of writers. The *Revista Azul* consolidated the new generations of the *Revista Moderna* and *Savia Moderna*. The only journal of earlier Mexican literature comparable to the *Revista Azul* was Altamirano's *El Renacimiento* (1869, 1894) which published articles by leading literary figures of widely divergent viewpoints, but Altamirano's publication was a forum where various attitudes could be expressed and not a unifying, consolidating force as was the *Revista Azul*.

The Mexican modernists of the *Revista Azul* generation were by all measures the most significant group of contributors to Gutiérrez Nájera's journal. In the organization and publication of the first issues of the periodical about twenty of the leading literary and political figures of late nineteenth-century Mexico participated. Many of these figures were themselves romantics or neo-classics who became associated with the movement but who never really adapted their style to its new esthetic principles. Other supporters of the new movement were journalists and political figures.

While Justo Sierra had been the *maestro* of this new generation, it was Gutiérrez Nájera to whom the younger poets turned directly for leadership and critical analysis of their earliest works. From time to time they would hold afternoon meetings where they would read their latest efforts, and "El Duque Job" would lead the discussion that followed. In the "Azul pálido" section of volume five, number eleven, there is a description of such a meeting where José Peón y Contreras read his latest poetry and a long discussion followed. "Y pronto, cuando las estrellitas de luz eléctrica tiemblen alli abajo, en el esqueleto de la ciudad, las manos se tenderán, la banda se disolverá, y luego pasarán dias y dias, sin volver á encontrarnos, ignorados unos de otros, como viajeros que han perdido la vereda de la casa."[1] / Thus one can see that this generation was individualistic, united only in a mutual love for "el verso azul." Many days would pass between meetings, but on some afternoon later "volveremos á reunirnos—quizás no estemos ya todos—y de nuevo el Maestro estará alli con su prosa musical é irónica, su frase vigorosa, mientras los martillos formarán un coro épico á la vigorosa página del arte" (*RA*, **V**, 176).

The young writers of this emerging generation whose contributions to the *Revista Azul* were most numerous included Carlos Diaz Dufóo, Luis G. Urbina, Jesús Valenzuela, José Juan Tablada, Jesús Urueta, Angel de Campo, and later Amado Nervo. The first two authors were, of course, closely associated with Gutiérrez Nájera in the enterprise and were largely responsible for the editorial policy of the publication, especially after the death of "El Duque Job." Another of Mexico's great modernists, Salvador Diaz Mirón, is the author of seven compositions published in the *Revista Azul*, all of which are reprints of lesser-known works. There is no evidence that he was directly associated with the magazine in any way. Diaz Mirón was especially hostile to such literary journals. Ormond makes the following comment regarding this matter: "Diaz Mirón would be far better known had he not conceived a violent prejudice against appearing in columns of periodicals. This decision was taken in reprisal for the early pirating of his verse."[2] This observation is substantiated in the *Revista Azul* by a number of references to pirated editions of his works which appeared in the United States. Other Mexican modernists of note who contributed fewer compositions than those noted above include Francisco M. de Olaguibel, Bernardo Couto Castillo, Francisco A. de Icaza, and Balbino Dávalos. The latter was important to the *Revista Azul* principally for his translations of works by the French Parnassians.

From the mere standpoint of numbers Carlos Diaz Dufóo contributed far more articles to the *Revista Azul* than any other writer, even more than Gutiérrez Nájera. His signed compositions total nearly a hundred, but he was also the author of a vast number of unsigned editorial sketches in the "Azul pálido" sections and of numerous articles which he signed with the pseudonym "Monaguillo." It is indeed remarkable that such a prolific contributor to Mexico's leading modernist journal of the day should not be considered by most critics as even a member of the modernists' ranks. He frequently is mentioned as the co-founder of the *Revista Azul*, but his greatest claim to fame is as an economist and contributor to the editorial pages of some of Mexico City's leading newspapers. His artistic prose and literary criticism have been neglected for years, very possibly due to the fact that he wrote most of these compositions during the last decade of the nineteenth century when Gutiérrez Nájera was at the height of his popularity. Diaz Dufóo lived until 1941, but during his later life his journalistic prose was far less artistic than that which appeared in the *Revista Azul*.

Prose sketches, *crónicas,* critical articles, essays, and short stories by Diaz Dufóo can be found in profusion throughout all five volumes of the *Revista*. He obviously seeks to emulate the style of Gutiérrez Nájera in a number of his *crónicas* in order to keep the same mood and tone which pervaded the *Revista Azul* in its first year of publication. It must be admitted, however, that his style quite frequently suffers in comparison with that of his master whose innate *gracia* was inimitable. In *crónicas* such as *Fin de año* the tendency to philosophize at the end of the year, a characteristic of several of Gutiérrez Nájera's compositions, can be observed. "¿Por qué al concluir el año recordamos á nuestros muertos—á nuestros muertecitos, como decia Manuel Gutiérrez Nájera, ¡ay! arrebatado en la túnica de ese pérfido anciano que ya comienza su agonia?" (*RA*, **IV**, 130). Imitations of the style of **"El Duque**

Job" are not limited to a similarity of themes, for in such prose fragments as *Nocturno* it is possible to see the influence of such works as "La serenata de Schubert." The opening sentences serve as an excellent example of an attempt to emulate the slow, even rhythm and the mood of serenity seen in the poem of Gutiérrez Nájera: "La sombra se ha ido arrastrando, poco á poco, absorbiendo luz, devorando reflejos, lentamente, perezosamente, en asecho de los colores, haciendo flotar sus átomos oscuros, inundándolo todo en su oleada negra. Hasta mi llegan los acordes lejanos de una vaga melodia de Chopin. El piano solloza sus lágrimas musicales que caen en el silencio de la noche como gotas de lluvia sobre una bandeja de plata (*RA*, III, 248). Identical in theme and in style is *La serenata*. Diaz Dufóo follows the traditional devices employed by the modernists in such compositions: an opening passage describing the scene, the gradual introduction of the musical passage with a description of the music's effect on the listener, and a conclusion in which the last note fades away into the distance.

In compositions such as the ones just discussed Carlos Diaz Dufóo seems to be experimenting with the esthetic principles recently introduced by the young modernists. However, such a style certainly is not typical of the majority of his journalistic articles where he deals with contemporary problems of society: the excesses of positivism, the theories of naturalism, and the unconventional characteristics of certain Bohemian artists and writers. A severe criticism of the *mal du siècle* attitude can be found in *Un problema fin de siglo,* and in *Los tristes* he challenges the men of the nineteenth century who, educated in the principles of Christianity, have substituted for belief in God a belief in liberty, science, and democracy. His theories are sometimes supplemented with a narrative to illustrate a point as in *Una duda* where the problem of the impact of evil on humanity is illustrated by an account of a shipwreck. At times these narratives become almost surrealistic as the author probes beyond common truisms for the causes of world phenomena. Carlos Diaz Dufóo is always conscious of contemporary problems and currents of thought. The compositions of his that can be termed modernistic are relatively few, and his position in the *Revista Azul* is more that of the journalist who is constantly analyzing and evaluating the problems of his generation.

Luis G. Urbina was the third member of the group closely associated with the *Revista Azul*. As *secretario de redacción* Urbina exercised considerable influence in the determination of the journal's contents, but of his own compositions there are included only sixteen prose articles and four poems. These are his earliest writings, for Urbina was only twenty-five when the periodical began publication. According to Max Henriquez Ureña, at this period in his life Urbina was still a romantic,[3] and Arturo Torres-Rioseco adds that "Luis Urbina (1868) ha tenido el valor de permanecer siempre romántico."[4] It is no wonder, therefore, that Urbina is mentioned most often as the continuer of the romantic-modernistic style of Gutiérrez Nájera. It was **"El Duque Job"** himself who wrote an extensive criticism of Urbina's poetry for the

June 16, 1895 issue of the *Revista Azul*. The entire issue is devoted to a study of Urbina and contains other critical articles on his work by Justo Sierra, Angel de Campo, and Diaz Dufóo. The following lines by Gutiérrez Nájera, reprinted in this issue from *La Revista Ilustrada* of New York, clearly indicate the type of poetry that young Urbina was writing: "Urbina es muy joven. Dice que ya conoce el dolor; pero no es cierto; á la que conoce es á la primera novia del poeta: á la Melancolia. Tienen sus versos la tristeza apacible de la madrugada. Los envuelve, por decirlo asi, una obscuridad azul. . . . Porque la poesia de Urbina se inclina á la tristeza, como sien hermosa y soñolienta que busca el hombro de la buena amiga. Hay poetas asi, que nacen enamorados de lo pálido y Urbino es uno de ellos (*RA*, III, 99). The statement on the same page that "Urbina es rico en verso y pobre en prosa" cannot be verified in the *Revista Azul* where only four of his poems appear, and all except "En un álbum" are reprinted from other sources.

Urbina's prose in the *Revista* consists of a series of *crónicas,* literary criticisms, and reviews of important musical events. His *crónicas* show a definite stylistic and thematic similarity to those of Gutiérrez Nájera, but he often loses himself in verbosity and highly complicated imagery. Urbina lacks the precision and clarity seen in Gutiérrez Nájera.

Throughout much of his prose there is a certain romantic nostalgia reminiscent of "El Duque Job." In *Almas solas y casas vacias* the author revisits a solitary plaza, the scene of many of his romantic escapades as a youth. Stimulated by strains of familiar music, the past is suddenly reconstructed. "¡Toca tu wals, memoria, pero no tan aprisa! ¡Quiero contemplar esos deslumbrantes minutos de gloria que llevan palmas; ese instante de dicha que cruza sonando besos, ese rato de meditación que pasa cantando estrofas, esas noches azules de citas, esa puesta de sol de los juramentos!" (*RA*, I, 47). Such a passage is much more effective than his earlier verbose descriptions. He has taken more care to select "le mot juste" in his images; they are less complex and more comprehensible to the reader. Gutiérrez Nájera often wrote similar nostalgic passages in which a happier past was recalled in a not-so-happy present, and it is in such *crónicas* that the close parallels between the two contemporaries can readily be observed.

While Manuel Gutiérrez Nájera, Carlos Diaz Dufóo, and Luis G. Urbina are the Mexican modernists whose literary personalities are best defined in the pages of the *Revista Azul*, there are three other poets represented who were to become the leaders of the *Revista Moderna* generation. These poets were Amado Nervo, Jesús E. Valenzuela, and José Juan Tablada; the former two were founders of the *Revista Moderna,* and Tablada was one of its outstanding contributors. Both Nervo and Tablada were in their early twenties when the *Revista Azul* first appeared, but Valenzuela was some fifteen years older. Nervo had just arrived in Mexico City from Mazatlán where he had begun a career as a journalist. He had just started to write poetry, and many of his first efforts were reprinted by the editors of the *Revista Azul.* His reputation as a poet was steadily growing, and in 1896 a poem of his recited on the first anniversary of the death of Gutiérrez Nájera increased his popularity tremendously. This was the famous "In memoriam" with the familiar opening lines:

> Era un ritmo: el que vibra en el espacio
> Como queja inmortal y se levanta
> Y llega del Señor hasta el palacio
> ¡Un ritmo! y en el cielo de topacio
> Se perdió: como todo lo que canta!
>
> (*RA*, **IV**, 237)

Even in this early work the mystical, religious tendency of Nervo's poetry is clearly seen. Likewise, in contrast with Gutiérrez Nájera and Urbina, his preoccupation with the central idea of the passage is paramount. Any attempt to stimulate the visual senses is subordinate to the ideas expressed in the lines. A somewhat different mood dominates the conclusion to **"Ojos negros,"** a poem written especially for the *Revista Azul*.

> ¡Oh noche! ven á mi llena de encanto;
> Mientras con vuelo misterioso avanzas,
> Nada más para ti será mi canto,
> Y en los brumos repliegues de tu manto,
> Su cáliz abrirán mis esperanzas. . . . . .
>
> (*RA*, **II**, 302)

Whether the theme is religious or not, there is a kind of mysterious mysticism already obvious here that was to dominate much of his later poetry. Also it should be pointed out that Nervo relies heavily on nouns and verbs in the creation of his images whereas most of the other modernists of this period were using a plethora of adjectives. An excellent example of this extensive use of adjectives for purposes of ornateness can be seen in the lines of José Juan Tablada, a poet whose work reflects a deep skepticism and contains frequent outbursts of irony and sarcasm. A connoisseur of Japanese art and culture, Tablada often chose exotic settings for backgrounds to his verse and prose. Max Henríquez Ureña sees a Parnassian influence in his poetry, and parallels with Baudelaire can be found both in his literary art and his personal life.[5] The French Parnassian style is apparent in **"Abanico Luis XV"** where images of plastic beauty occur in almost every stanza. Of all of Tablada's poems in the *Revista Azul*, "Venecia" is one which best reveals the above characteristics. The first two stanzas set the mood for the entire work.

> ¡Oh, la ciudad de las palomas blancas,
> De las góndolas negras!
> ¡Ciudad de las ruidosas mascaradas,
> Oh soñadora y lánguida Venecia!
>
> ¡Poetica imagen de mi triste vida!
> ¡El lóbrego canal de mi existencia
> Cual cortejo de góndolas sombrias
> Surcan también mis fúnebres tristezas!
>
> (*RA*, **II**, 327)

Sadness, even an occasional tone of bitterness, permeates the constant flow of plastic, colorful images. The use of contrasting colors and moods creates a feeling of duality which is always left unresolved. At times Tablada allows the ugly and the morose to dominate his work to such a degree that he assumes a Baudelairian style as in the following prose passage: "El árbol siniestro, el árbol fetiche, donde el vampiro venerado se resguarda, un país de canibalismo y de fanatismo, de sol caliginoso y ardiente, una horda de zoulohs que aúlla y se entrega al rito hierático y brutal . . ." (*RA*, **III**, 318).

Both Nervo and Tablada contributed only nine poems each to the *Revista Azul*. While Nervo already showed indications of the direction his poetry was to take in later years, Tablada had not yet developed his interest in Japanese culture. Jesús E. Valenzuela, on the other hand, was considerably older than both Nervo and Tablada, yet he never was able to develop his poetic skill to as high a degree of mastery. His greatest claim to literary fame is the *Revista Moderna* which he founded with Amado Nervo and financed until his death in 1911. Throughout the pages of the *Revista Azul* Valenzuela demonstrates that he is a man of considerable culture, one well-read in the works of classical literature, yet when he attempts to mingle the ancient with modern esthetic principles, the resulting lines often seem forced and somewhat artificial. His unlimited generosity in supporting the *Revista Moderna* won him high esteem in Mexico, but later critics have assigned him only a secondary literary role in the movement he so eagerly supported.

Also closely connected to the *Revista Azul* generation and later an affiliate of the *Revista Moderna* writers was Jesús Urueta, one of the great Mexican orators of his day. While he is not generally considered among the leaders of modernism in Mexico, he did contribute ten prose articles to the *Revista Azul*. Many of them reflect his interest in current literary theories and in sociological problems of the late nineteenth century. His article on Taine is an attempt to apply to José Zorrilla and Guillermo Prieto the theory that an author reveals himself in his works, which are the products of heredity, environment, and historical time. Certain *crónicas* explore in detail the theories of naturalism, but it is in a series of extremely short prose sketches that one sees certain modernist tendencies. *Del caballete* is a group of five word paintings of which an excellent example is *Indolente*: "La tarde. El remanso oculto por un cortinaje de espesas frondas. Bulle el agua en remolinos de cristal agitando las arenas de oro, y oscila en el fondo un pedazo de cielo azul, desgarrado por el tejido de las ramas" (*RA*, **I**, 6). It should be noted that the first two sentences, both of which lack verbs, set the stage for the rest of the sketch. In the third sentence movement begins, and a series of words suggesting brilliant color is added. In *Viñetas* a similar opening is used effectively in a description of downtown Mexico City: "La calle de Plateros. Domingo. Medio dia. Grupos, carruajes. . . En una esquina, el poeta; pantalón claro, levita negra con un clavel rojo en el ojal, narigudo, algo más que narigudo; un *porfirista* apagado en el rincón de la boca: bigote de eléctricas púas . . ." (*RA*, **I**, 109). The detail and precision of this sketch reveal a great power of observation. While there is nothing in *Viñetas* that could not have been written by a confirmed realist, one must conclude that it was his ability to choose "le mot juste" and his ability to write polished, colorful prose that won for him a small niche in the *Revista Azul*.

Diaz Dufóo, Urbina, Valenzuela, Nervo, Tablada, Urueta— these were the principal followers of Gutiérrez Nájera who were associated in varying degrees with the *Revista Azul*. But there were many other contributors from within Mexico whose works generally are not considered strictly modernistic but who found nevertheless a place in Gutiérrez Nájera's publication for many of their compositions. It is beyond the scope of the present work to study in detail the contributions of these literary figures, but for the sake of a total picture of the journal it is necessary to comment on the outstanding contribution of Angel de Campo, considered a leading *costumbrista* by most literary critics, yet a writer closely associated with the modernists of the *Revista Azul* generation.

A product of his environment, "Micrós," as Angel de Campo signed all seventy-eight of his prose articles in the *Revista Azul*, was able to sketch vividly and accurately the everyday activities of the middle and lower classes of society for the readers of the daily press. While he is often critical, he tempers his judgment with feelings of deep tenderness and pity for the sufferings of the humble and unfortunate. At times he is even humorous, but above all he is an admirable literary artist who is able to reproduce with keen understanding the panoramas unfolding before his eyes. No doubt it was the color and the brilliance of his style which won the admiration of the Mexican modernists.

"Micrós" contribution to the *Revista Azul* was extensive. His seventy-eight prose articles and three poems almost equal the number of entries by Gutiérrez Nájera. Although his poetry is negligible, his influence as a prose writer can be seen throughout all five volumes. While he is best known for his copious articles on everyday themes, he also wrote for the *Revista Azul* several short stories and articles of literary criticism.

In many of his prose articles and sketches "Micrós" describes in a realistic style the many activities he observes about him. Such a realistic sketch is *En un dia de fiesta* where he relates a quarrel between a man and a woman as they walk down the highway. Careful attention is given to details of the rustic setting with special emphasis on the description of the various sounds connected with the harvesting of grain. Only the beginning of the quarrel is recorded directly, for as the couple moves along the highway, their gestures alone are described, and the rest of the dialogue is a matter of supposition. In other *crónicas* such as *Misa de siete* Angel de Campo writes with a more elaborate descriptive technique closely paralleling some of the *crónicas* of Gutiérrez Nájera and Urbina. Here he paints a comprehensive picture of a church and the surrounding neighborhood shortly before seven o'clock mass. The ringing of the church bell opens the scene, and the sound of the bell mixes pleasantly with the whistling of the wind. There is a minute description of the church and of the people moving in the street in front of the facade. There are bricklayers, street sweepers, an old lady going to mass, and a "pobre ciego con cortinas verdes en los ojos" (*RA*, V, 139). In the conclusion the author listens to the conversations of these various people and notes how sad most of them are in contrast to the gaiety expressed by the bell "que canta á la diafanidad azul de la mañana" (*RA*, V, 140).

There were many other literary figures who, like Angel de Campo, have never been considered among the principal adherents to modernism but who for various reasons were welcomed as contributors to the *Revista Azul*. Two of these contributors, Juan de Dios Peza and José M. Bustillos, were direct followers of Altamirano. Many of the poets generally considered romantics, including Guillermo Prieto, Laura Méndez de Cuenca, José I. Novelo, Adalbento A. Esteva, Antonio Zaraguza, José Peón Peón del Valle, and Luis Gonzaga Ortiz, had several of their poems published within the pages of Gutiérrez Nájera's *Revista*. This is not surprising in consideration of the fact that the roots of modernism in Mexico go directly back to romanticism via many of the works of **"El Duque Job"** and Urbina. Poets whom most critics consider neo-classics likewise contributed a number of compositions, many of which displayed a Parnassian perfection of form. The poetry of Manuel José Othón is an excellent example of this quality. Other poets whose lines show a definite classic influence include José M. Roa Bárcena, Joaquin Arcadio Pagaza, Enrique Fernández Granados ("Fernangrana"), and Juan B. Delgado.

It should be pointed out that there is still another group of poets sometimes considered as minor modernists or as poets related to the movement of modernism who were beginning to write during the period between 1894 and 1896. None of these figures wrote extensively for the *Revista Azul,* and some never succeeded in rising above the depths of literary obscurity. Maria Enriqueta Camarillo de Pereyra, better known simply as Maria Enriqueta, hardly belongs to any literary school. Related to the modernists somewhat more closely were the poets Francisco M. de Olaguibel, Francisco A. de Icaza, Manuel Puga y Acal, and Manuel Larrañaga Portugal.

However, in spite of the fact that none of these secondary literary figures radically altered the general composition of the *Revista Azul* with their poems and articles, without them the journal would have lacked variety, something vitally important in a weekly publication. By including prose and poetry from so many heterogeneous sources the editors were able to give their publication a more cosmopolitan spirit and free it from the narrow bonds of being the *portavoz* of a single literary movement. The *Revista Azul*, in addition to being the leading modernist publication of its day, was also truly representative of Mexican literature at the end of the nineteenth century. The great variety of authors included in its pages is aptly characterized by Genaro Estrada in the following terms: ". . . aunque no fué un periódico de rigurosa selección de los escritos, si lo fué de escritores selectos."

NOTES

[1] RA V, 176. Subsequent references to the *Revista Azul* will be cited parenthetically within the text.

[2] Irving Osmond, "Mexico's New Poets," *The Bookman*, XLIX (March 1919), 104.

[3] Henriquez Ureña, *Breve historia del modernismo*, p. 470.

[4] Torres-Rioseco, *Bibliografia de la poesia mexicana*, p. xxiv.

[5] Henriquez Ureña, "Las influencias francesas en la poesia hispano-americana," *Revista Iberoamericana*, II (1940), 411.

[6] Genaro Estrada, *Poetas nuevos de México* (México: Ediciones Porrúa, 1916), p. ix.

José María Heredia
1803-1839

Cuban poet, dramatist, essayist, and historian.

INTRODUCTION

Widely recognized as Cuba's premier lyricist, Heredia was one of the earliest proponents of the Romantic movement in Latin America, and his verse represents the beginnings of a transition from colonial literature to an indigenous literary identity. Heredia spent most of his career exiled from Cuba for espousing pro-independence ideals. He led a sad life, at times overwhelmed by nostalgia for his distant native country, as reflected in his poetry and his ideological and literary themes. Best known for the poem "En el teocalli de Cholula" (1820; "In the Aztec Temple of Cholula") and the ode "Al Niágara" (1824; "To Niagara"), Heredia embodied the Romantic spirit in both his life and his verse, despite his frequent emulation of neoclassical form and meter. A wandering patriot inspired by the new ideals of equality and fraternity, Heredia was considered "the first Hispanic American Romantic."

Born in Santiago de Cuba on December 31, 1803, Heredia was the son of a Dominican immigrant who worked for the Spanish judiciary in Cuba, Florida, Venezuela, and Mexico. For this reason, constant change and instability marked Heredia's childhood. When his father died in Mexico in 1820, Heredia assumed responsibility for his family. Although he had begun taking university courses in law, he returned to Cuba, completing his studies at the University of Havana in 1821. After practicing law for a short while, Spanish officials accused him of plotting an insurrection against the imperial government and banished him from Cuba in 1823. Heredia fled to Boston, and then to New York, where he taught Spanish for a short time. For eighteen months he endured loneliness and poverty in a Brooklyn boarding house where he began writing verse, most notably "Al Niágara," after the famous waterfall. In 1825, he published the poetry collection *Poesías*. That year, the imperial court of Cuba sentenced him to death in absentia; at the invitation of the president of a newly independent Mexico, Heredia moved to Toluca, the capital of Mexico province, where he launched a campaign for Cuban independence. In Mexico, Heredia held various governmental positions, serving as a judge on the superior court, minister of the Audiencia (court of common pleas), and president of the Mexican Institute; he also continued his writing. In addition, Heredia worked as a journalist, editing the periodical *La Gaceta Especial de la República*, and contributed stories and essays to various newspapers. Heredia gradually became disillusioned with Mexican politics. Taking advantage of an amnesty issued in 1836, he requested approval from the imperial government of Cuba to return to his homeland. Under strict watch, Heredia visited there from November 1836 to March 1837 but was saddened by the state of co-lonial affairs. He returned to Toluca, where he died of tuberculosis on May 7, 1839.

Heredia is said to have lived the life of an existential romantic, a life of great suffering which he poured into his poems. . . . His work is considered lyrical and sentimental, tragic and epic, civil, patriotic, religious, Europeanized, and frequently Americanist. His early verse reflects the influence of Romantic European poets, such as the autobiographical poem "En mi cumpleaños" ("On My Birthday"), written when he was nineteen, in which he complains of misfortune in love. His mature poems, however, often contemplate nature and human existence, through a predominantly melancholic outlook. Heredia's most celebrated poem, "En el teocalli de Cholula," which some scholars consider an example of early Latin American romanticism, describes the sunset at the Mexican city of Cholula, site of a famous ancient temple. Infused with melancholy and subjective reflections, the narrator meditates on the civilization and culture of indigenous people. In his nature poems "Al Niágara" and "En una tempestad" ("In a Storm"), the landscape in presented in spiritual terms, contrasting the grandeur of natural phenomenon with the temporal insignificance of humanity as the narrator searches for spiritual support and affirmative identity. A neoclassical ode composed of *octaves reales* (eight lines of eleven syllables), "Al Niágara" conveys the desolation of a suffering soul, emphasizing themes of displacement and loss while reflecting the anguish of marginalization. In other poems, pronounced themes of exile as a condition of being abound, detailed by an evasive sense of the present to express feelings of loss. Besides his poetry, Heredia wrote drama, history, and an aesthetic treatise *Ensayo sobre la novela* (1832; Essay on the Novel), which posits and rejects the historical novel genre on the basis of apposition between historical truthfulness and fictional invention. He also composed the literary essay collection *Poetas ingleses contemporáneos* (1832) and numerous translations and theatrical adaptations. His *Ultimos versos* (1839; *Last Verses*), published in the year he died, are decidedly religious in theme and tone.

Heredia received a great deal of critical acclaim from his contemporaries and exerted broad influence on Latin American literary life during the first half of the nineteenth century. Considered an important critic in the nineteenth century and one of the pre-eminent classic poets of Latin America, Heredia's writings are among the earliest examples of Cuban exile literature. He is widely recognized as the first Romantic to write in Spanish. As one scholar has stated, "Heredia. . . .is the incarnation of the first image of the romantic hero in the New World, unfortunate, without a homeland, rebellious and liberal, trapped in an irremediable destiny."

PRINCIPAL WORKS

Poesías (poetry) 1825
Los últimos romanos (drama) 1829
Ensayo sobre la novela (essays) 1832
Lecciones de historia universal (history) 1832
Poetas ingleses contemporáneos (anthology) 1832
Ultimos versos [*Last Verses*] (poetry) 1839
Obras poéticas (poetry) 1875
Prédicas de libertad (speeches) 1936
Antología herediana (poetry) 1939
Poesías, discursos y cartas de José María Heredia
  (letters) 1939
Poesías completas 1940–1951 (poetry) 1951
Trabajos desconocidos y olvidados (poetry) 1972

CRITICISM

Lee Fontanella (essay date 1972)

SOURCE "J. M. Heredia: A Case for Critical Inclusivism," in *Revista Hispanica Moderna, Vol. XXXVII, No. 3,1972-1973, pp. 162-79.*

[*In the following essay, Fontanella explores Professor Luis Monguió's argument that scholars have mistakenly labeled Heredia as a Romantic poet.*]

Professor Luis Monguió, in his review of the book by Manuel Pedro González (*José María Heredia. . .*), seems to say that the Romantic poet is not properly represented when a single aspect of his style is favored by the critic for the purpose of derogating other aspects of the writer's style.[1] It is methodologically wrong, Professor Monguió says, to rest the claim that Heredia was a Romantic upon the detection of a *tónica romántica* in the poetry that Heredia wrote during 1820-1825 (see González, pp. 17, 59-65); and it is wrong to qualify the Cuban-born Heredia as Romantic for this limited number of years. The reviewer adds that the interpretation of Heredia that is based almost exclusively upon the poet's link with the Spanish Escuela Salmantina of poetry is likewise mistaken, and as an example of this erroneous critical approach, outstanding at the end of the nineteenth century, he cites that of Chacón y Calvo.[2] The review ends with the following wise observation: "La obra del Sr. González pone de realce los aspectos románticos de la obra herediana. Otros críticos prefieren colocar el énfasis en sus aspectos neo-clásicos. Ni el uno ni los otros [la critica desde Andrés Bello hasta José María Chacón y Calvo] tienen toda la razón; ni al uno ni a los otros falta toda la razón." In other words, Heredia's works encompass a range of expressive possibilities that oblige the critic to regard the poet's literature retrospectively and prospectively at the same time. I would extend Professor Monguió's closing remark: Not only in the example of the individual poet,

but also in the example of the single poem, it is critically erroneous to reduce stylistic or tonal possibilities to one. A look at **"Poesía"** and the internationally famous **"Niágara"** (June 15, 1824) will serve to explain the idea.[3]

Professor Monguió observes that González avoids dealing critically with **"Poesía"**; in contrast, Professor Monguió attaches special importance to this poem. Professor Monguió s interest in **"Poesía"** derives from the quizzical note that Heredia added to the New York publication of this poem. With this note, the poet wondered if this attempt (**"Poesía"**) to express the poetic spirit might not be extravagant ("¿Se tendrá por extravagancia esta tentativa de expresar el espíritu poético?"). Monguió discovers a significant ambivalence in this seemingly rhetorical query, and he arrives at the conclusion that this ambivalence is what detains Heredia on the threshold (unibral) of Romanticism. It is possible to relate Heredia to an ism, if we first recognize that different expressive styles are operative within the limits of the ism and that these styles of course apply to Heredia's works. The ambivalence that Professor Monguió finds in Heredia's quizzical note is characteristic of Hispanic Romanticism. A unifaceted Hispanic Romantic style is a questionable concept; the evolution toward a relatively fixed style (which the word umbral seems to indicate) is a critical concept that effaces the concept of dynamic stylistics, which is indeed Professor Monguió's point of critical departure.

Professor Monguió stops to inquire what it might have been that caused Heredia to vacillate and to discern extravagance in his attempt to express the poetic spirit. He concludes that Heredia might have detected an air of Platonism in **"Poesia."**[1] Perhaps we can clarify this conclusion with a view toward genre. **"Poesía,"** instead of teaching how to go about the poetic art, is concerned with poetry as essence, that is, poetry prior to the poet's art. Mostly, the poem is concerned with *poesía* as metaphysic, rather than with *poesía* as artifact. As such, the poem represents a departure from its forerunner, the *ars poetica*. The very title of Heredia's poem indicates that here, artistic procedure (ars) is not the principal question. Also, the odic address in the direction of Poesía, rather than to a public, reduces the likelihood of discursive quality in this poem; consequently, one assumes a reduction in discursive purpose and, with this, a tendency away from didacticism. This tendency is characteristic of the *ars poetica* after the vogue of the *ars poetica* even when the *ars poetica* is so entitled but does not conform strictly to the neoclassical type.[6] Nevertheless, the final moment of **"Poesía"** represents a consummation of its subject, metaphysical *poesía*, and in this sense, the poem may be said to approximate its forerunner. Seen from one point of view, metaphysical *poesía* is transformed into artifact; it becomes *poema*. So, the *ars poetica*, wherein poetic expression should stand for the doctrinal truths that it proffers, is ultimately a paradox: It represents—as soon as it fulfills its explanatory purpose while it is the example of what is explained—a departure from the rationalism in which it is esthetically rooted. The *ars poetica* has as its end to be a symbolical consummation. Where the focus is the poem as idea, the rationalist esthetic is rendered unproblematic, since the matching of sign to idea is no longer the focus of poetry.

The **"Poesía"** poet, throughout much of the poem, veers from a rationalist esthetic, although rationalist esthetic, although rationalist esthetics did persist in the theory of the Romantic period as an ideal of adequate expression. For example, evident throughout **"Poesía"** are the formal patterns for art, and model artists superior to the individual poet, which are corollaries of the rationalist esthetic, as if in spite of the rationalist esthetic, in Heredia's poem *poesia* is usually a universal, rather than an empirical fact. But in the course of the poem the subject changes meaning: while poesía has been metaphysical, it is finally conceived as *poema*. With this, the poem embraces more than one esthetic fashion, and it reflects more than a single ideology.

Metaphysical *poesía*, which is the breath of God *(espíritu divino)* here, is interpretable as the Word that is literally breathed into man and nature from a source superior to both. *Poesía* is the breath *(aliento)* that vivifies and sets everything aflame, as does the desert wind *(soplo abrasador de los desiertos)*. So, it is also *sublime inspiración*. One could cite many occasions on which *inspiración* is mentioned or metaphorized in **"Poesía."** This idea, or the periphrasis thereof, pervades the poem:

> Hay un genio, un espíritu de vida
> Que llena el Universo: él es quien vierte
> En las bellas escenas de Natura
> Su gloria y majestad: él quien envuelve
> Con su radioso manto a la hermosura,
> Y *da a sus ojos elocuente idioma,*
> Y *música a su voz,* él quien la presta
> El hechizo funesto, irresistible,
> Que embriaga. y enloquece a los mortales
> En su sonrisa y su mirar: *él sopla*
> Del mármol yerto *las dormidas formas,*
> Y *las anima,* si el cincel las hiere. [my underscoring]

These references to *inspiración,* although they are figures of poetic speech, do have a theological relationship which ought not to be overlooked.[7] Divine revelation is the means by which the poet is inspired: "la celeste llama / . . . los misterios de un horror profundo / A los hombres atónitos revela." If blessed, the poet, like Pindar, Herrera, Quitana, Homer, Tasso, Milton (foremost), and nature itself, will be the passive receptor, then minister of the poesia that derives from the divine source:

> Pero a mi alma fogosa es muy más grato
> Dejarme arrebatar por tu torrente,
> Y ornada en rayos la soberbia frente,
> Escuchar tus oniculos divinos,
> Y repetirlos; como en otro tiempo
> De Apolo a la feliz sacerdotisa
> Grecia muda escuchaba,
> Y ella de sacro horror se estremecía,

> Y el fatídico acento repetía
> Del Dios abrasador que la agitaba.

The poet whose voice is heard in this poem is still distant from the poet creator of "poem." The conception of *poesía* as metaphysic prior to its being *poema* may be understood as problematic for him who would be creator *(poeta)*. In the hiatus between reception and transformation of metaphysical *poesía* into *poema* exists that moment which makes impossible the ideal identification between inner life and poem, for which the subjectivist poet strives. While *poesía* is for the poet a thing apart, while it is inspirational and genius in itself, the poet must forego the inborn faculty, genius. (In **"Poesía,"** *genio* derives from a *fuente de luz* [*sacra fuente*]; it is in apposition to *espíritu de vida,* which is tantamount to *alma del universo* and *sublime inspiración.*) The "Poesía" poet is not born into language, which notion gained favor with Romanticism and was developed by subsequent linguistic theorists; instead, the Word, God's *Poesía* (cf. language), is inspired, breathed into the poet.[8] Nevertheless, **"Poesía"** leads toward a poetic solution for the dichotomy between *inspiración* and language. Poem subsumes poetry, one might say, as the poem runs its course.

As God's breath becomes poem, God's receptive minister becomes creator poet. With the final word, the poetic self is identified with poem: "Al ver como su lienzo se animaba, / El Correggio exclamaba: / '¡Yo también soy pintor!—¡Yo soy poeta!'"[9] What occurs at the close of **"Poesía"** is miraculous. By virtue of the parallel between the segments of the final line, there is a parallel between the artists Correggio and the poet: as Correggio regarded his canvas, so our poet regards his completed poem. In the association of the poetic self with the Correggio example, the poet resolves the dichotomy between passive poet and poet creator *(poeta)*, thereby between metaphysical *poesía* and artifact, or *poema*. So, while the final verses of **"Poesía"** indicate that the result of metaphysical *poesía* is artifact, they also point to a reevaluation of the poetic self. At this moment, the poet is another milestone in a tradition of accomplishment: he has achieved what the models Pindar, Herrera, Quintana, Homer, Tasso and Milton had achieved before him. The poet's final words permit a metaphorical interpretation, too: this poem is a poem of poems, poetic works up to, and including, this final three-word declaration.[10]

The foregoing speculations with regard to the final moment of **"Poesía"** bring to mind Professor Monguió's suggestion that ambivalence may explain the note that Heredia added to **"Poesía."** The assertive exclamation that the final words of the poem constitute another manifestation of the tone of surprise that Heredia proffered in that added note upon achieving another concept of the self. Granted the entire course of **"Poesía"** it is the recognition on the part of the poetic self of his status as *poeta* that is as extraordinary for the poet as is the subject of his poetic achievement, or as is his expressive mode. In poems of Heredia that are usually thought to be more Romantic than **"Poesía"** appear indications of both the new poetic stance that the final moment **"Poesía"** may signify and that poetic stance which the final moment of **"Poesía"** may mean to negate. In other words, the afore-mentioned "ambivalence" is ideological while it is esthetic. Since we are dealing here with one poet, who is subject to a variety of ideologies, works, words and symbols at once, not only is ambivalence a necessary consideration, but so is ambivalence in more than just the esthetic realm.

A view of **"Poesía"** indicates that the correspondence between ideology and esthetic formality is inconstant; or else, that despite an odic strain a poetic voice may be distinct from that of the poet in reality. Heredia's **"Niágara"** serves to validate further this observation. Although the lyric ode is arelaltively subjective mode, The poet's voice is a fictitious voice. On the one hand, the sum of the poet's expression is an artistic working of the poet's own experience. On the other hand, a part of this experience is a general verbal experience, which must be taken into account, in order to gain a proper perspective on the verbal art of the poem. Although the poet's expression may seem to have a largely empirical basis, as it does in the case of **"Niágara,"** a prior verbal experience may be primary, and for this reason, the poet's expression in any given instance may not always be entirely his own.[11]

There is a coincidence of diction between the **"Niágara"** text and a version of Chateaubriand's *Atala* that Heredia must have seen prior to his composition of **"Niágara."** Heredia wrote from Brooklyn (May 8, 1824) to his mother and sister and advised his sister to read the description of Niagara Falls in Chateaubriand's *Atala*; on June 15, he composed a version of **"Niágara"** in the album in which visitors to the Falls signed their names and wrote down their impressions of the view.[12] We have, in addition to these biographical facts, the opinion of Marcelino Menéndez y Pelayo, who affirms a certain resemblance between the *Atala* text and a descriptive portion of Heredia's ode.[13] The admission of Menéndez y Pelayo is well founded, as the following examples from **"Niágara"** and *Atala* serve to show:

El abismo horrendo	Celle [masse du fieuve] qui tombe
Devora los torrentes despeñados:	au levant descend dans une combre effrayante on diroit une
Crúzanse en 61 mil iris, y asordados	colonne d'eau du déluge. Mille arcs-en-ciel se coursent et se
Vuelven los bosques el fragor tremendo. Al golpe	crousent sur l'abyme. Frappant le roc ébranlé, l'eau
violentísimo en las peñas	rejaillit en tourbillons d'ecume,
Rómpese el agua, y salta, y una nube	qui s'élèvent au-dessus des forêts, commes les fumées d'un vaste
De revueltos vapores	embrâsement.[14]
Cubre el abismo, en remolinos, sube,	
Gira en torno, y al cielo	
Cual pirámide inmensa levanta,	
y por sobre los bosques que le cercan	
Al solitario cazador espanta.	

The memorable passage from the *Atala* epilogue probably influenced in Heredia's imaginings during the act

of poetic composition. Heredia's own words in this descriptive portion of the ode reflect the verbal experience that *Atala* must have meant for Heredia. In turn, Heredia's famous letter, dated Manchester, June 17, 1824, is a prosed expression of the subject of the verses that Heredia composed two days before he composed the ode.[15] The historical coincidence of these two compositions naturally leads to a certain coincidence in imagery and diction, outstanding upon comparison of the two. [16]

Literary language cannot always be attributed to the assimilation of rhetoric; the influence of psychological motive in the choice of literary language may be operative. Furthermore, the psychological motive may help to explain the choice of a particular verbal context as basis for the **"Niágara"** ode. Heredia's identification of his own circumstance with a particular thematic situation could have led him to associate his own composition with the suggestive precedent. This is what occurs, in some degree, in Heredia's letter dated Tarpaulin-Cove, November 31, 1826; from off the coast of Falmouth, Mass., Heredia writes: "Paréme estremecido, y creía que me hallaba con Milton en la inmensa soledad donde se alza el trono de la muerte."[17] And surely, this is what Heredia intimates when in his letter of June 17 (see note 15) he writes:

> Después de haber errado en los bosques eriales de. Goat-Island, me senté al borde de la Catarata inglesa, y mirando fijamente la caída de las aguas y la subida de los vapores me abandoné libremente a mis meditaciones. Yo no sé qué analogía tiene aquel espectáculo solitario y agreste con mis sentimientos. Me parecía ver en aquel torrente la imagen de mis pasiones y de las borrascas de mi vida. Así, así coma los rápidos del Niágara hierve mi corazón en pos de la perfección ideal que en vano busco sabre la tierra. Si mis ideas, como empiezo a temerlo, no son más que quimeras brillantes, hijas del acaloramiento de mi alma buena y sensible, ¿por qué no acabo de despertar de mi sueño? ¡Oh! ¿Cuándo aca-bará la novela de mi vida, para que empiece su realidad?

> Allí escribí apresuradamente los versos que te incluyo y que sólo expresan débilmente una parte de mis sensaciones. [my underscoring]

For the expatriot Heredia, the Niagara site that is described in the epilogue to *Atala* could have signified, conceivably, a place of exile.[18] Earlier in *Atala* (end part II), it is Chactas who foretells the exile motif of the epilogue. In the epilogue, with the granddaughter of René (the narrator's guide to the Falls) and her spouse, the motif is extended. And in the closing words of the narrator, who is the literary analogue to Heredia himself the motif is enhanced to fullest extent: ". . . car j'erre, ainsi que vous, á la merci des hommes; et moins heureux dans mon exil, . . ." As the diction in the description of the Falls indicates, the poet's identification of his own circumstance with the situation depicted in the epilogue might have spurred him to compose within the context of descriptive words that appears in *Atala* along with the exile motif.

Although the poet's expression in any given instance may not always be entirely his own, his expression is not that of any other poet, ultimately. In the aforementioned verses that describe the Falls, language is worked poetically to the effect that by these verses **"Niágara"** becomes the representation of its subject.[19] Suffice it to mention, as an example, verses to which we shall attend later: the repetition of phrase and vocalic elision at the end of the third stanza ("Y otras mil, y otras mil ya las alcanzan, / Y entre espuma y fragor desaparecen"), and the intention to effect in verse the "waves innumerable / [that] meet there and madden. . ." (the 1827 translation; see note 21). just as Heredia must have composed within the context of other authors' descriptive terms, so did poetizers of Niagara who succeeded Heredia. Who can deny a similarity between the above lines by Heredia and these by Carlos Fernández Shaw?:

> Y las aguas sin fin se precipitan,
> se empujan, se atropellan,
> se entrechocan rugiendo, se quebrantan,
> y al caer, ya se estrellan,
> y ya sobre las rocas se levantan,
> y formando mil círculos de espuma,
> y envueltas en tremendo remolino,
> y entre el fragor y la creciente bruma,
> siguen, siguen, y siguen su carnino . . . [20]

Here, there is a similarity not only in diction (see, also, my text corresponding to note 14); there are similarities in poetic mechanics and apparent intention behind the mechanics. Fernández Shaw, like Heredia, uses repetition of phrase and vocalic elision, in order that his verses represent the subject.

Thus, the difficult distance between poem and meaning is narrowed. Through representational versification, the poem grows symbolic of its subject; whereby the poet establishes an analogy between his art and the divine Creator's natural art, the Falls. And this is in keeping with the idea of the eternal quality that, for the poet, characterizes the Falls: ". . . ¡Duren mis versos / Cual tu gloria inmortal! . . ." As Heredia's poem—inspired, in part, by the Falls—would be in the image of the natural poetry that is Niagara—inspired, literally, by God (". . . el Señor. . . /. . . / Dió su voz a tus aguas despefiadas")—so would be Heredia in the image of the Creator.

If the bold aspiration to godhood distinguishes the poet of the Romantic era from the classicist, what seems just as significant with respect to the poet's Romanticism is the intervention of nature as the linguistic vehicle through which that aspiration is achieved. It is not the objective of so many Romantic odes that have as their subject lofty nature to be the vehicle by which the poet attempts to elevate himself (as if he were the lofty natural object itself) to a supra-human, more godly level? Is not William Cullen Bryant's "To a Cloud" (1924) such an example?: "Beautiful cloud! I would I were with thee / . . . / To. . . look / On Earth as on an open book."[21] But these odes to natural objects are paradoxical, insofar as the end of the sensationalist experience depicted herein is a departure from the material realm and its consequences. (In William Cullen Bryant's "To a Cloud," the poet would ". . .linger, till the sunset . . .," "O'er Greece, long fettered and oppressed.") Despite this paradox, the Venezuelan Rafáel María Baralt called these depictions of sensationalist experience truthful, in comparison to poems that were rooted in that "poesía de convención, de estudio retórico, de formas mentirosas"; he referred specifically to **"Niágara,"** it appears:

> Hasta. entonces en Francia y, generalmente hablando, en la Europa literaría no se contemplaba ni se describía la naturaleza sino al modo como la contemplaron y describieron Teócrito y Virgilio. Mr. Chateaubriand transplantó (permítaseme la expresión) la naturaleza virgen, portentosa, variada y colosal del Nuevo Mundo al antiguo, y abrió por este medio a la poesía moderna los anchos caminos y las vastísimas regiones homéricas. Inspirado, como Ossian, con la contemplación profunda y el sentimiento fntimo de la creación en sus formas mis pintorescas y sublimes, cantó como él el mundo real, y lo cantó por haber visto, por haber sentido, por haber padecido. Antes de Mr. de Chateaubriand la poesía descriptiva había sido una poesía de convención, de estudio retórico, de formas mentirosas; con él y por él fue la poesía. de la sensación, y por consiguiente la de la verdad.
>
> De aquí, señores, sus caracteres de exactitud y de majestad; de aquí sus efectos sorprendentes, análogos a los que nos producen la vista del Niágara, del lago Ontario, del Chimborazo, del Amazonas, de los Andes.[22]

In **"Poesía,"** where the work of artists inspired by God serves as model for the poet, and where *inspiración* is still what makes possible the poetic act, nature, as imagistic vehicle for the poet or as a model for art, is foregone. The image of nature is not instrumental in **"Poesía"** with respect to the development of either poetic self or poem; that is, the poet neither requires nature as means of transcendence, nor is versification executed in order that the poem be a representation of nature. Representational versification of the words that describe the natural phenomenon Niagara is, perhaps, an indication of a genuinely empirical stance on the part of the poet. These observations seem all the more significant when, in comparison, we recall that in the course of **"Poesía"** natural phenomena do manifest *poesía*: ". . . él [espíritu] es quien vierte / En las bellas escenas de Natura / Su gloria y majestad"; ". . . o [este espíritu] con sus gritos / Anima las borrascas...." In **"Poesía,"** the poet delineates a universal hierarchy, wherein the metaphysical bypasses nature, for all practical purposes, and inspires man. Here, nature is not the immediate source of the poet's inspiration. There occurs no "sympathy" between the poetic self and nature; nor is there reason for such to occur, since *poesía* is *espíritu divino*, which requires no natural intervention prior to reaching man. Thus, nature in **"Poesía"** remains abstract **"Natura,"** quite separate from sensationalist man. Nevertheless, it is in the realm of nature that the poetic self has taken cognizance of *poesía* as a fact: De el etéreo cielo / Baja, y se manifiesta a los mortales / En la nocturna lluvia y en el trueno. / Allí le he visto yo: . . ." This manifestation of *poesía,* in spite of the fact that it is depicted as tumultuous and atmospheric, has constituted a past experience of the poet; the experience lacks the actuality that one associates with the representation of sensationalist experience.

The universe of the **"Niágara"** poet is not essentially unlike that of the **"Poesía"** poet, although the experience of the two poets depicted in each poem differs. The configuration of the universe remains essentially the same, but the poet, rather than casually observing the Word in **"Natura,"** experiences the Word through nature. This is possible, since the Falls, like both mortal man and the natural world mentioned in **"Poesía,"** is recipient of the eloquent voice of a divine being. The poet addresses the Falls: "Abrió el Señor su mano omnipotente, Cubrió tu faz de nubes agitadas, / Dió su voz a tus aguas despeñadas. . . ." So, the "Dios de la verdad" in **"Niágara"** retains his aspect of Word, or *poesía*; and *verdad,* in **"Niágara,"** is tantamount to *poesía* in the poem **"Poesía."** In general, the different experience of the Word calls for a shift in rhetoric. The accentuation of nature's role with respect to the poet, which we find if we pass from **"Poesía"** to **"Niágara,"** is, naturally, marked by an accentuation of sensationalist precept and rhetoric. However, this does not diminish the need to consider poetic rhetoric to which one might ascribe a Platonic basis. For example, the opening verses of **"Niágara"** are in contradiction to the sensationalist accent in the poem: "Dadme mi lira, dádmela, que siento / En mi alma estremecida y agitada / Arder la. inspiración." While these verses are representative of classical rhetoric, they are also reminiscent of the norm of diction in **"Poesía."**[23] Although the example seems atypical of the norm of rhetoric in "Nid"gara," we cannot deny the existence of these verses of adopted poetic diction in the poem. Obviously, a shift in rhetorical priorities does not necessarily signify a radical alteration in Heredia. Furthermore, there are imagistic and lexical coincidences in the descriptions of nature in **"Poesía"** ("De las aguas con furia despeñadas / El tremendo fragor") and **"Niágara,"** such that a part of **"Niágara"** appears to be an elaboration of **"Poesía."**

While lexical and imagistic coincidences do not mean that the poetic self is the same from poem to poem, they do support the impression that there is no radical alteration in Heredia from poem to poem. The **"Niágara"** poet's inquiry into the workings that lie behind natural phenomena, or the fact that he approaches God empirically, does not mean the total displacement of an ideology by a revolutionary contradiction of that ideology. Behind all of the poetic efforts that may point to a sensationalist philosophical background, there is the "¡Dios, Dios de la verdad!," which the poet finally accepts as a solution to his inquiry into the origin of the Falls ("¡Dó. . .? ¿Quién. . .? ¿Qué poderosa mano. . .?"). [24]

The ambivalence means, of course, that **"Niágara"** approximates **"Poesía,"** while it differs from it. Both poems have models of human invention but **"Niágara"** has models of divine (Niagara), as well as human (*Atala*)

invention. Correspondingly, we also find in **"Niágara"** the poet's analogy between himself and God the Creator and the space between poetic art and the divine Creator's natural art. Obviously, the analogies between the poet and God and between poetic art and God's natural art are distinct from the analogy with human models and their art, which is what we find in **"Poesía."** The poetic selves represented in **"Poesía"** and **"Niágara"** are similar insofar as they both are enhanced in the course of the poems. In both it is the poetic self that is hypostatized, ultimately, whatever the subject apostrophized at the start. Each in its own way, the poems affirm the liberation of the poetic self through art. In each, the poetic self achieves, by virtue of his poem, a superior status, but the range of this superiority differs from poem to poem.

The transcendence that the poetic self achieves in **"Niágara,"** finally, is not only represented in climactic occurrence; it is also represented in poetic process, in the interreference between the words *frente* and *faz.* Initially, the poetic voice informs that his own brow (*frente*) has not shone with radiance for some time, and he awaits the divine gift that he can achieve only through contemplation of the aspect (*faz*) of the Falls. The poet's contemplation of Niagara, which is the natural art of the Creator and, as such, His reflection, is the means through which a *profunda impresión* occurs in the poet. The **"Niágara"** ode, which is the consequence of this *impresión*, is thereby the translation of divine art such as this is in a state of nature. (We have already mentioned versification as a means by which the poet's own work represents Niagara such as Niagara is in its natural state.) So, through his own poetic art, the poet establishes an analogy between God and self. The withered brow (*mi faz marchita*) and the subsequent wrinkled brow ("Y la profunda pena . . .Ruga mi frente,. . .") are destined, in the course of the poem and by virtue of the poem, to acquire the radiance which the poet would recover from the start. *Mi frente*, lacking radiance initially, is displaced in the image of the final line of the poem by the radiant brow (*radiósa frente*) that the poet lifts into the clouds on a climactic voyage toward godhood. By virtue of this image, poet approaches *Criador* physiognomically. So, the poet approximated godhood both figuratively (*radiosa frente*) and literally, upon his climactic ascent toward God.

Only by knowing something about Heredia's alternatives of expression, can we appreciate Heredia as a stylist, or as representative of a given ism. Heredia revised many of his poems for the 1832 publication of his poetry, so his poems lend themselves for a consideration of stylistics.[25] Revision of **"Niágara"** begins with the opening word; we have no longer "dadme (mi lira)" repeated. We seem to have, now, a more reflective poem, retuned, as it were, for the betterment of art: "Templad mi lira, dádmela,. . ." In effect, this initial change is representative of the very idea of revision, and it accentuates the concept of poetry as artifact. In the newer version, there is only one extensive revision, the seventh stanza, where Heredia briefly expressed opposition to unorthodox philosophical doctrine:

¡Dios, Dios de la verdad! En otros climas
  Oí mentidos filósofos, que osaban
  Escrutar tus misterios, ultrajarte,
  Y de impiedad al lamentable abismo
  A los míseros hombres arrastraban.
  Por eso siempre te buscó mi mente
  En la sublime soledad: ahora
  Entera se abre a ti; tu mano siente
  En esta inmensidad que me circunda,
  Y tu profunda voz baja a mi seno
  De este raudal en el eterno trueno. [my
underscoring]

Heredia extended ". . .En otros climas / Oí mentidos filósofos,. . ." with the following verses:

  ¡Omnipotente Dios! En otros climas
  Vi monstruos execrables,
  Blasfemando tu nombre sacrosanto,
  Sembrar error y fanatismo impío,
  Los campos inundar en sangre y llanto,
  De hermanos atizar la infanda guerra,
  Y desolar frenéticos la tierra.
  Vílos, y el pecho se inflamó a su vista
  En grave indignación. Por otra parte
  Vi mentidos filósofos,. . .

In other words, Heredia chose to elaborate his condemnation of lying philosophers of other climes by associating
them with execrable blasphemers and civil disorder.[26] So
the orthodox philosophical note in **"Niágara"** is inseparable from the exile motif, just as it is in the epilogue by
Chateaubriand, best known for his *Géne du Christianisme*
(1802). While in the former version the epithet "Dios de
la verdad" reinforces by contrast the qualifier *mentidos,*
the replacement of "Dios de la verdad" by "omnipotente
Dios" in the newer version renders a new aspect to God;
with the change there is added a literal reinforcement (*omnipotente*) of God's position in the universal hierarchy.
On the other hand, the displacement of the former epithet
could be ascribed to mechanics of quantitative versification. In large part, the changes that Heredia made seem not
to have been for the purpose of new literal significance,
rather for imagery and versification. The critic should
naturally be concerned with the comparison between the
results in each case; even changes of this proportion can
have significance with respect to style and meaning. For
example, where "tu profunda voz baja a mi seno" becomes
"tu profunda voz hiere mi seno," Heredia recaptured imagery cultivated in Spain's sixteenth-century lyric.[27] Also,
the mere removal of the comma from "Y otras mil, y otras
mil. . ." makes for a verse that better depicts the maddened
confusion of waves represented in this instance. That is,
the removal of a comma where one is expected amounts to
an elimination of the semiological logic that detracts from
the depiction of confusion in the earlier version; depriving
the verse of the sign that is indicative of sequential logic
imparts to the verse itself the confusion that the verse is
meant to depict. In a much broader sense, the removal of
the sign that is indicative of logic may indicate opposition
to neoclassical style and a tendency toward a more Romantic style.

The critic, in his involvement with style, touches upon
the broader phenomena. that tend to inform stylistic selection, as E. H. Gombrich explains: "Style is any distinctive, and therefore recognizable, way in which an act
is performed or an artifact made or ought to be performed and made . . . . only against the background of
alternative choices can the distinctive way also be seen
as expressive. . . . If the term 'style' is thus used descrip-
tively for alternative ways of doing things, the term 'fashion' can be reserved for the fluctuating preferences which
carry social prestige." [28] One reason why critics still floun-
der in treating of Romantic style is the failure to apply a
critical procedure that takes into account alternatives and
preferences that may appear, init-ially, external to the
writer's final option. While Heredia's work spans a gamut of expressive possibilities, it reflects more than a single guiding fashion. Manuel Pedro González (*op. cit.*, pp.
43-44) does recognize that Here-dia's poetry, like that
of the peninsular Escuela Salmantina, "es una encrucijada
en la que convergen múltiples y hasta contradictorias
corrientes líricas: reminiscencias latinas, influjos clásicos españoles, una fuerte dosis de ascendencia bucólica.
y el venero naturista rousseauniana." But he is bent on
condemning the earlier traditions in favor of the newer
Romanticism: "Todo [lo anterior] adobado y regido por
el prosaísmo a que la inflexibilidad de la poética vigente
condenaba a las musas. De ahí el amasijo lírico, incoloro
e insípido, sin vigor ni carácter, que es la poesía de estos
simuladores de todos los modelos que no se atrevieron a
ser ellos mismos. No hay inconveniente en reconocerles
el título de prerromáticos [sic], con el cual lo finico que
se quiere significar es que no fueron clásicos ni tuvieron
la sinceridad y el arranque lírico necesario para llegar a
ser románticos." González is vindictively persistent in
his attack:

> Es ardua tarea, sin embargo, cribar las esencias román-
> ticas que vitalizan la poesía herediana entre 1820 y 1825
> de la afectación sentimental, y del atuendo bucólico
> salamantino que pervirtieron su gusto y entorpecieron su
> evolución literaria. Por otra parte, el calco de los aderezos
> retóricos de Cienfuegos y Meléndez, tan evidente en la
> producción del cubano por estos aflos—y tan próximos
> ya al estilo romántico—dificulta aún más la tarea de
> desligar en el numen herediano lo romántico genuino de
> lo seudo romántico que los modelos españoles le impu-
> sieron, lo que en él era ya inconsciente conjunción de
> insurgencia e impulso romántico legítimo de la mendaz
> postura rousseauniana heredada de los prerrománticos
> (*op. cit.*, p. 68).

If ultimately our interest is art, there is no inherent positive value in the Romanticism of Heredia; on the other
hand, there is value in the dynamics of artistic choice, if
ultimately our interest is art. Literary elements that hark
back to tradition, or literary elements that foretell trends,
make literature none the better or worse intrinsically.
Literature gains nothing for its Romantic characteristics,
just as it loses nothing for any—let us say—pre-Romantic traits that it may exhibit. Any negative stigma attached
to the term "pre-Romantic" or any positive value attributed to "Romantic" (and viceversa) is unjustifiable when
the topic is art.

The study of **"Poesía"** and **"Niágara"** confirms that it is right to discourage the critical application of rhetorical criteria for the delimitation of isms. This is, in fact, what Professor Russell Sebold does for Peninsular Romanticism; thus, he disputes the "pre-Romanticism," or "pseudo-Romanticism," of the Salamantine poets,

> The "Romantic traits" which critics usually mention can be considered authentically Romantic only in those works in which they are found as functions of a Romantic cosmology, and the fact that we have discovered in certain Spanish poems written between 1768 and 1773 a relationship between man and the universe that is exactly the same as that found in the so-called Romantic works of the nineteenth century, and established the philosophical basis for this relationship in the thought, of the Enlightenment means that we are justified in considering these poems Romantic and in dating the emergence of Romantic poetry in Spain in the early 1770's.[29]

Romanticism, here, is a *Weltanschauung* always definable by a "thread of sensationalism," the result of the assimilation of the new materialism derived from Locke's and Condillac's sensationalist epistemology. According to Professor Sebold, it is in the poetic works of Salamantine poets such as Melédez Valdés and Cadalso that one finds the initial signs of Romanticism, hat is, of a "total shift in the European *forma mentis*" (p. 117). For example, Cadalso's elegy, "A la muerte de Filis" (1773) represents a fusion of "*natura naturans* with *natura naturata*" (p. 135) whereby the universe becomes a projection of the self, in proportion as man is acted upon by nature. The "fusion of *natura naturans* with *natura naturata*" is a prior stage in the evolution toward an "egocentric pantheism."[30] In disputing the pre-Romanticism of the Salamantine poets, Professor Sebold reduces Romanticism to an essential; whereby the following concepts are possible: "authentically Romantic"; "a relationship. . .that is exactly the same as that found in the so-called Romantic works of the nineteenth century,. . ."; a total shift in the European *forma mentis*; total fusion of "*natura naturans* with *natura naturata*." The ideology that one finds expressed in the poets that succeeded the era called "pre-Romantic" is an ideology that "remained the same as in the earlier works that are usually called pre-Romantic" (p. 136).

On the one hand, it is possible to argue, from a philosophical standpoint, that the above claims concerning a "Romantic cosmology" are too holistic to constitute a sound point of departure. When Romanticism is reduced to an essential, it seems none the less easy to name it. Professor Sebold also notes that Spanish writers were giving names to Romantic grief years before writers in France and Germany were so doing.[31] The case in point is, specifically, Meléndez Valdés, in 1794: the phrase *fastidio universal*, in "Elegía II: A Jovino, el melancólico." In apparent contradiction, Manuel Pedro González (*op. cit.*, p. 43) says: "El tratamiento de la naturaleza en Meléndez es de filiación rousseauniana—como en sus amigos y colegas—pero es convencional y falso, según el historiador inglés [E. Allison Peers] . . . En ninguno de Dos poetas finiseculares de orientación' rousseauniana

que el señor[a] Allison Peers nos ofrece] penetró el espiritu romántico legítimo y aun su emulación de Rousseau es superficial—convencional—y con frecuencia apócrifa." (Incidentally, González [p. 65] mentions that he finds no use of the terms *romántico* and *romanticismo* in the prose and poetry of Heredia until 1839, the year of the poet's death.) The poetic assignation of a name to a sensibility is not proof of that sensibility as psychic fact in the poet. The answer to the question "What's in a name?" is "A degree of truth, but not exclusive truth."

Also, one might be tempted to contest the "thread of sensationalism" tenet. If the "thread of sensationalism" tenet, tried and tested, is borne out over a long history of Romanticism, one must also grant that another indication of its pervasiveness over time is the negative responses to sensationalist doctrine in the course of time. The critical treatment of Romantic literature must take into account not only the interrelationship between stylistic trends, but, simultaneously, ideological dynamics, too. Even in narrow perspectives, such as the single poem, it is necessary to observe fluctuations among the ideologies that serve as basis for that dialogue. (Cf. note 29: ". . . justified in considering these poems Romantic. . . .") Professor Sebold, despite his intention to discourage the critical application of rhetorical criteria for the delimitation of isms, claims that whereas the Romantic *Weltanschauung* remained essentially the same, it was the expression of the *Weltanschauung* that varied over time: "It is significant that all the major literary styles of the nineteenth century (Romanticism, Realism, Naturalism) are merely variations on the same concept of man as a sentient material being in dialogue with a material universe" (p. 138). My argument, then, is with regard to critical procedure, rather than with philosophical essentialism or the definition of the essence. Since ideology does bear relationship to expressive choice, it is difficult to imagine the essential constancy of the one in the light of the variability of the other."

NOTES

[1] The review of *José María Heredia, primogénito del romanticismo hispano: Ensayo de rectificación histórica* (México: Colegio de México, 1955) appeared in *Hispanic Review*, XXV, No. 2 (April 1957), pp. 148-150.

[2] See, especially, chapter U1 ("Las influencias de la Escuela Salmantina del siglo XVIII") of José María Chacón y Calvo, *Estudios heredianos* (La Habana: Ed. Trópico, 1939).

[3] I quote from the critical edition *Poesias completas*, I-II, prepared under the directorship of Emilio Roig de Leuchsenring (Municipio de La Habana: Colección Histórica Cubana y Americana, 3, 1940-1941). "Poesía" and "Niágara" appeared in the first volume of Heredia's verses: *Poesias de losi Maria Heredia* (New York: Behr and Kahl; Gray and Bunce, Printers, 1825). The former poem was probably written between 1819 and 1824, prior to "Niágara," judging by the table of contents, with dates for some of the poems, that Francisco González del Valle reprints in his *Cronología herediana, 1803-1839* (La Habana: Secretaría de Educación, 1938), pp. 165-166.

[4] Manuel Pedro González also expresses the umbral concept, in other terms, and he deals with style as a circumscribed entity: "La edad, el temperamento, el ambiente histórico y politico que respiraba [Heredia], los ideales patriáticos que alentaba, la pasión de la libertad y la justicia, que lo consumía; todo ello, estimulado por el reactivo de sus lecturas en lenguas extranieras, hace de él una figura romántica y el primer poeta hispano que si no se incorporó nunca del todo a la nueva sensibilidad, supo sentirla y expresarla antes que nadie en español. De esto creo que es prueba irrecusable el poema titulado "Proyecto," escrito en 1824— acaso el más incontrovertiblemente romántico de cuantos escribió" (*op. cit.,* pp. 112-113).

[5] Professor Monguió mentions "Poesía" once again, in another article, elaborating somewhat upon Heredia's place within a history of poetry: "El concepto de poesía en algunos poetas hispanoamericanos representativos," in *Revista Hispánica Moderna,* XXIII, No. 2 (April 1957), pp. 112-113, especially.

[6] See William Leonard Schwartz, "Some Twentieth Century *Arts Poétiques,*" in *PMLA,* XLVII No. 2 (June 1932), p. 593.

[7] 1 am grateful to Professors Yolanda Sold and Robin L. McAllister for their helpful editing of this text and for their suggestions. Professor Sold would de-emphasize the theological implications of *inspiración.* Professor McAllister also calls my attention to the fact that *inspiración,* here, is probably less theological than esthetic, and in conformity with Plato and Longinus. If so, and if we were to limit the idea of *inspiración* to csthetics, it is obvious that those esthetics would have to be considered in the light of an extranational and extracontemporaneous background.

[8] The origin of language, one facet of the polemic with Lockean sensationalism, was still a topic in the later half of the nineteenth century. Juan Valera rejected Grimm's conclusion that man would invent his own language, if the need for one existed (see "Discurso leído por el Ilmo. Sr. D. . ., en el acto de su recepción el día 16 de marzo de 1862," in *Discursos leídos en las recepciones públicas que ha celebrado desde 1847 la Real Academia Española,* III [Madrid: Imp. Nacional, 1865], p. 236). In the same year, Pascasio Lorrio, as spokesman for Madrid's Sociedad de Lengua Universal, scoffed at Rousseau for having denied that language was human convention (see the "Discours sur l'inégalité parmi les hommes" of Rousseau), and he asserted instead: "animado el hombre, no tuvo que hacer de su parte sino poner en ejercicio y uso el deseo que Dios le inspiró para traducir en signos externos lo que en su alma sentía" C'La palabra. Idioma primitivo," in *Boletín de la Sociedad de Lengua Universal,* 1, No. 8 [1862], pp. 243-249). Ten years later, the periodical *El Liceo de Granada* printed two installments by José de España Lledó: "Origen del lenguaje," in IV, No. 4 (April 15, 1872); "Relaciones de la palabra con el pensamiento," in IV, No. 6 (May 15, 1872). When España Lledó distinguished among, and evaluated, the linguistic theories of several tradicionalistas (for example, De Bonald, the principal representative of *tradicionalismo,* and an enemy of Condillac), he rejected both the opinion of Grimm, as had Valera, and the extremes of traditionalist dogma, with respect to the origin and function of language.

[9] The edition (Roig de Leuchsenring) that we follow rightly indicates by quotation marks that the last three words are uttered by the poet himself. The Mexico (Rafael y Vilá, 1852) edition (*Poesías del ciudad-ano José M. Heredia, Ministro de la Audiencia del Estado de México*) lends the same impression, since "¡Yo también soy pintor!" appears in italics, whereas "¡Yo soy poëta!" does not; no quotation marks are used. Two other editions that I have seen are alike, except in their orthography, but they are somewhat equivocal, for neither uses quotation marks. In them, the final lines read: "¡Yo también soi pintor!—¡Yo soi poeta! " (*Obras*

poéticas de José María Heredia, I ("Poesías") [Nueva York: N. Ponce de León, 1875], p. 196); "¡Yo también soy pintor!—¡Yo soy poeta!" (*Poesías líricas de José María Heredia,* ed. Elías Zerolo (Paris: Gamier Hermanos, 1893), p. 174). The *Encyclopaedia Britannica* (VII, IIth ed., p. 195) leads one to believe that the attribution to Correggio must end with the word *pintor,* in Heredia's poem, thus confirming the punctuation of the Roig de Leuchsenring edition of the *Poesías:* "The famous story that [Correggio] was gratified by seeing a picture of Raphael's, and closed an intense scrutiny of it by exclaiming 'Anch'io son pittore,'. . . cannot be traced to any certain source. It has nevertheless a great internal air of probability; . . ."

[10] Perhaps a remark by Juan Valera sheds light on the final image in "Poesía"; "....todo poeta romántico debía hablamos de sí mismo. . . . Un pagano no hablaba de sí mismo sino cuando, después de haber hecho grandes hechos, tenía razón para creerse un prodigio de ingenio, de valor o de doctrina; y aun asi, hablaba poco" ("Del romanticismo en España y de Espronceda (1854)," in *Obras completas,* II, ed. Luis Araujo Costa, 2nd ed. [Madrid: Aguilar, 1949], p. 10). Would Valera have seen in the final words of this poem a pagan classicist whose great feat led him to believe of himself that he was a prodigy?

[11] Cf. Manuel Pedro González (*op. cit.,* p. 27), who presumes, with Alberto Zum Felde (*Proceso intelectual del Uruguay y crítica de su literatura*), that individual temperament is a fixed thing, and that authors and ideas influence the individual in a significant way, only when they respond to individual temperament.

[12] See González del Valle, *op. cit.,* p. 147. Although the original text of "Niágara" has not been discovered, it is known that Tomás Gener came across the text on July 5, when he went to sign the guest album; Gener then sent a copy, with brief critical commentary, to his wife in Matanzas (*ibid.,* p. 154).

[13] *Ibid.,* pp. 147-148. Because of the tremendous success of *Atala,* there were numerous editions that Heredia might have seen prior to May 8, 1824. In the Spanish language alone, there were a dozen editions issued between 1801—the first French edition of *Atala* is April 2, 1801—and 1824; of course, there were also editions in English and French. For an idea of the magnitude of this bibliographic problem, see Pedro Grases, *La primera versión castellana de "Atala"* (Caracas: "Cromotip" offprint, 1955). It is not at all surprising, then, that other poets versified the prose of *Atala.* Professor Enrique Anderson-Imbert points out that José Joaquín Olmedo did so in the poem "Canción indiana" (*Historia de la literatura hispanoamericana,* 1, 3rd ed. [Mexico; Buenos Aires: Fondo de Cultura Económica, 1961], p. 191). In this regard, one might consider another poem by Heredia, "Atala." Incidentally, the three-act *Atala,* by José Fernández Madrid, was reviewed under Heredia's directorship, in *La Miscelánea:* Periódico Critico y Literario, 2nd Ser., 1, No. 6 (November 1831) (see José María Heredia, Revisiones literarias, ed. José María Chacón y Calvo [Havana: Publicaciones del Ministerio de Educación (Grandes Periodistas Cubanos, 6), 1947], p. 269).

[14] I cite the definitive edition of 1805, in the critical edition by Armand Weil: Chateaubriand, *Atala* (Paris: José Corti, 1950). pp. 126-127. I shall take up shortly the matter of the definitive text (1832) of Heredia's "Niágara"; above, I cite the 1825 edition of the poem, which was more proximate, of course, to the *Atala* experience.

[15] The letter is reprinted by Chacón y Calvo, ed., Revisiones [*op. cit.*], pp. 48-60.

[16] Adolfo de Castro, aiming to exemplify the literary phenomenon of poetic prose, claims the superiority of the letter over the ode "D. Manuel

José Quintana. D. José María de Heredia [sic]. Sus poesías en prosa," La España Moderna. Revista Ibero Americana, I, No. 8 [August 1889]. pp. 61-81).

[17] Reprinted by Chacón y Calvo, ed., Revisiones (*op. cit.*), p. 131.

[18] Heredia was denounced as a conspirator, first by Antonio Betancourt and Aranguren brothers, Pablo and Juan Guillermo, in Matanzas. The denunciation rested upon Heredia's former membership in a branch (Caballeros Racionales) of the order Soles y Rayos de Bolívar. In a letter to his mother (New York, May 25, 1824), Heredia claimed that he had broken with the Caballeros Racionales nearly a year prior to the accusations leveled against him. In early November, Heredia hid for a week in the residence of José Arango y Castillo called Los Molinos de la Marquesa, before fleeing for the United States (see González del Valle, *op. cit.*, pp. 135-139). The "Himno del desterrado: Canción escrita a la vista de las costas septentrionales de Cuba el 7 de septiembre de 1825," which Heredia apparently wrote while aboard the schooner that carried him from New York (August 22) to Alvarado, Mexico (September 15), lends an impression of the poet's impression of himself around that time: "...errante y proscripto me miro."

[19] This must be what Max Henríquez Ureña e'Literatura cubana," in Archipiélago [Santiago de Cuba, November 30, 1928], p. 116) means to say when he speaks of a "reflection of the poet's agitation": "Frente al Niágara, bástale reflejar su propia agitación interior para traducir la terrible majestad de la catarata." The critic of literature should remember that this agitation is linguistically figurative, rather than just imagined.

[20] "Al salto de Niágara," in *Poesías completas*, ed. Melchor Fernindez Almagro (Madrid: Gredos, 1966), 305. Adolfo de Castro (op. cit., p. 76) mentions that he heard this ode recited before the Ateneo de Cádiz. There is a thematic similarity between the odes of Heredia and Fernández Shaw, too. Fernández Shaw's *desventuras largas* turn to spiritual *alegría* before the Falls. Likewise, Heredia had undergone spiritual enlightenment before the Falls; he had found temporary solace for "las borrascas de [su] vida" (letter of June 17, *op. cit.*). Still another commentator on the Falls, Ramón. de la Sagra (*Cinco meses en los Estados Unidos de la América del Norte*) learned how minimal were social man's preoccupations and intrigues, beside the immense grandeur of the Falls (see two letters (July 31; Aug. 1, 1835], written on the site, published in *Semanario Pintoresco Español*, III, No. 109 (Apr. 29, 18381, 548-550).

2

[1] Apart from the literary contexts which I have already cited, and which might have framed Heredia's thought, Manuel Pedro González (*op. cit.*, pp. 92, 99) remarks *tantas analogías* between the work of William Cullen Bryant and Heredia. González argues that Heredia, whose knowledge of the English language must have been superior to what Heredia would have had his correspondents believe (P. 111), must have read Bryant during his visit to the United States (pp. 93, 97). On the other hand, any personal acquaintance between Heredia and Bryant is more questionable. On the subject of "The Alleged Acquaintance of William Cullen Bryant and José Maria Heredia," see José de Oafs (*Hispanic Review*, XXV, no. 3 [July 1957], pp. 217-220), who, judging by a particular letter written by Bryant denies the fact of a personal acquaintance between the two poets. This opinion is unwittingly contradicted, it appears, by Charles H. Brown (*William Cullen Bryant* [New York: Charles Scribner's Sons, 1971], pp. 139, 155), who also claims that "Niágara," in The United States Review and Literary Gazette, is Bryant's translation. It remains uncertain whether or not William Cullen Bryant was the translator of "Niágara" into English; Bryant was a contributor to the Gazette, were the first English translation first appeared (1, No. 4 [January 1827]. pp. 283-286). Quotations from Bryant are from *William Cullen Bryant: Representative Selections* ed. Tremaine McDowell (New York, Cincinnati, Chicago, Boston, Atlanta: American Book Co., 1935).

[22] "Chateaubriand y sus obras," in *El Siglo Pintoresco*, III (1847), p. 123; the text of Baralt's speech before the Ateneo de Madrid. Manuel Pedro González (*op. cit.*, pp. 35-36, 69), also recognizes functional nature as an aspect of Heredia's Romanticism and he cites Rousseau Chateaubriand, Ossian (James Macpherson). Lamartine. and Byron as tributarv writers in the mode of nature poetry.

[23] See, for example, the opening verses of the "Oda III" of *La lira de Medellin,* by José Iglesias de la Casa (1748-1791): "Dame, dame, muchacho, / Dame la lira, ¡ea!" (in *Poetas líricos del sigto XVIII*, I (BAE, LXI], ed. Leopoldo Augusto de Cueto [Madrid: Atlas, 1952], p. 442).

[24] In a discussion of Heredia's religiousness (". . . suma religiosidad, pero sin sectarismo"), Alfonso E. Páez fixes upon the very lines of the letter of June 17, which correspond in diction and sentiment to these inquiries that appear in "Niágara" (*Recordando a Heredia Estudio crítico* [Havana: Cultural, 1939], pp. 187-188). The letter is reprinted in Madrid's *Semanario Pintoresco Español,* 4th Ser., V, No. 47 (Nov. 1850), 370-371.

[25] *Poesias del ciudadano José María Heredia, Ministro de la Audiencia de México.* Segunda edición corregida y aumentada, I-II (Toluca: Imp. del Estado (Juan Matute]), 1832. Again, I quote from the Roig de Leuchsenring edition. Manuel Pedro Gonvález (*op. cit.*, pp. 121-122) accepts the hypothesis that there were other versions of "Niágara," prior to the 1825 publication.

[26] Manuel Pedro González (*ibid.*, p. 125) attributes the alteration of these verses to the poet's experience in México, following his return from the United States. As a consequence of this experience, González claims, Heredia "se aburguesa ripidamente, se torna didáctico, conservador, legalista, moralizante. El poeta civil—según la definición de Piñeyro—se acentuaná cada día más" (p. 141); ". . . Heredia se hace cada día mis conservador, mis apegado al orden, a la tradición, a la legalidad, por injusta que sea,. . ." (p. 143).

[27] It is not only to Manuel Pedro González's butt of attack, Cienfuegos and the Escuela Salmantina, that one should look in order to appreciate to fuller extent Alez himself (*ibid.*, p. 24) the stylistic possibilities that Heredia had available. González informs that Heredia was "un adolescente dotado de extraordinaria precocidad, acostumbrado a leer y traducir de corrido a los grandes clásicos latinos desde los ocho años." Nevertheless, the critic's flagwaving in favor of Romanticism leads him too often to state unjustifiable claims that the reader must overlook as mere affirmations of personal taste. For example, in dealing with the question of the 1832 version of "Niágara," he says: "Todo en [la penúltima estrofa] lo ha trasegado casi literalmente de Cienfuegos. Como siempre le ocurre, lo que a Cienfuegos le tomé aquí afea y demerita este hermoso canto. Es la estrofa más endeble y afectada del poema. En todas las otras referencias personales que la oda contiene, Heredia se revela narcista, egotista, ufano de su genio, es decir, romántico. En ésta, en cambio, se muestra sentimentaloide y cursi. Los préstamos de Cienfuegos jamis enriquecieron la heredad podtica del cubano. Lejos de añadirle mirito redundaron siempre en detrimento, de su musa" (*ibid., p. 123*). Here, Gon7Alez appears to echo Alberto Lista. A critical Lista, from whom Domingo del Monte had solicited an evaluation of Heredia's poems, corresponded with Del Monte on Jan. 1, 1828 (letter reprinted in the Mexico edition [*op. cit.*] by Rafael y Vilá, 1852). While Lista urged a second, more polished edition of Heredia's verses, he also used his commentary as vehicle for condemning Cienfuegos.

[28] "Style," in *International Encyclopedia of the Social Sciences*, XV, ed. David Sills (New York: Crowell, Collier, & Macmillan, 1968), p. 353.

[29] "Enlightenment Philosophy and the Emergence of Spanish Romanticism," chapter V of *The lbero-American Enlightenment* (Urbana: Univer-

sity of Minois Press, 1971), p. 135. Angel I. Augier ("Reencuentro y afirmación del poeta Heredia," in the Roig de Leuchsenring edition of Heredia, *op. cit.*, pp. 53-77) denies pre-Romanticism in the particular case of Heredia. He writes about the *romanticismo sustantivo* of in Heredia, of course, moments of the *aspecto negativo* of the truer, social demo- cratic Heredia; his basis for rejecting the *calificacidn ambigua* (*pre- romántico*) is the social revolutionary Romanticism that Heredia might be said to have espoused. Augier finds Romanticism, but the latter is not characteristic of Heredia. For Augier, Heredia was a *pura estamnpa romántica* and had not degenerated, essentially, into Romanticism's morbid psychological varieties of the *mat du siécle* sort.

[30] This term, from Professor Américo Castro, upon whose thesis Profesior Sebold bases his own (see Professor Castro's introduction to *Les Grands Romántiques Espagnols* (Paris: La Renaissance du Livre, n.d. (1922)], p. 13). Manuel Pedro González differs from Professor Sebold in his view of the Salamantine poets (and in his critical procedure, often), but not with respect to this criterion for Romanticism: "Mas si la originalidad de Heredia es poco robusta, en cambio poseía una fina sensibilidad, un rico temperamento poético, una imaginación exaltada y plástica y, sobre todo, una profunda sinceridad, and de otros rasgos idiosincrásicos, y de un modo de *proyectar su ego en el drama de la naturaleza* que lo apartan del falaz bucolismo de sus modelos salarnantinos y lo aproximan al perfecto 'mood' romántico antes que nadie en lengua castellana" (*op. cit.*, pp. 67-68; my underscoring).

[31] "Sobre el nombre español del dolor romántico," in *Insula*, XXIII, No. 264 (November 1968). Professor Sebold also notes that Meléndez Valdés wrote to Jovellanos and mentioned that through Locke, he (Meléndez), had acquired the ability to think (*discurrir*) ("Enlightenment. . .," p. 116). Such extraliterary claims are probably better approximations to the truth in this matter, since they are not so subject to the factor of rhetorical tradition as are literary utterances that purposefully involve style.

[37] My caveat contrasts with the argument of Francisco González del Valle (cited by Enrique Gay-Calbó, "Heredia: Apuntes para un estudio sobre su vida y su obra," in the Roig de Leuchsenring edition [*op. cit.*], 1, 41): "En Heredia el hombre es uno y el poeta es otro." Rafael Esténger bases a book upon just the opposite point of view: ". . .la fatalidad de Heredia es siempre que la realidad y la poesía se confunden, el mundo real y el ilusorio se entrelazan. . ." (*Heredia: La incomprensión de si mismo* [Havana: Ed. Trópico (Biograffas Cubanas, 7), 1938], 55). My caveat is an extension, into today's criticism, of esthetics that were upheld in Heredia's time. It is, also, a logical extension of the classical esthetic of harmonious matching of expression to idea, while it admits a more mod- ern, individualist principle. Heredia's contemporary, Esteban Echeverría, in imitation of French and German Romantics, claimed:

> "El estilo es la fisonomía del pensamiento, a cuyos contornos y rasgos dan realce y colorido el lenguaje: los periodos y las imágenes; así es que las obras del ingenio reflejan siempre formas de estilo originales y caracteísticas. Los escritores mediocres no tienen estilo propio porque carecen de fondo; y ora imitan el de este o aquel autor que consideran clásico, ora hacen pepitoria de estilos, pero sus obras correctas y castizas a veces, ni salen del linaje común, ni hieren, ni arrebatan.
>
> Cada pensamiento, pues, cada asunto, requiere expresión conforme y de aqui nace la diversidad de estilos, cuya clasificacióa menuda podrá verse en los retóricos" ("Estilo, lenguaje, ritmo, método expositivo," in *Clasicismo y roman- ticismo: Los consuelos,* ed. Eros Nicola Siri (Buenos Aires: Sophos, 1944], 58-59; first published posthumously, by Juan María Gutiérrez, in *Revista del Rio de la Plata*, V [1873]).

Ted E. McVay, Jr. (essay date 1994)

SOURCE: "The Sublime Aesthetic in the Poetry of José Maria Heredia," in *Dieciocho,* Vol. 17, No. 1, 1994, pp. 33-41.

[In the following essay, McVay explores Heredia's works as sublime aesthetic forms inspired by the European Romantic movement.]

Much of what has been written about José María Heredia has revolved around a controversy over whether to clas- sify his poetry as belonging to the neoclassical or ro- mantic periods. As stylistic elements of both movements are present in his poetry, he is often treated as a transi- tional figure or as a precursor of the later period. Al- though the word "sublime" has been used in describing Heredia's nature poetry in support of the romantic argu- ment (Lazo xxxi), the sublime as an aesthetic concept, as it was developed in eighteenth-century Europe and as it is manifested in Heredia's works, has not yet been exam- ined. In this article, I will begin that examination by briefly describing the development of the concept into a pre- romantic aesthetic theory, and by demonstrating Heredia's familiarity with it through an analysis of the ode, **"En una tempestad."**

The earliest major work dealing with the sublime is the treatise, *On the Sublime*, written in the first century B.C. and long attributed to Longinus, in which the author's principal interest is the high rhetorical style.[1] He does, however, distinguish the sublime in rhetoric — passages which elevate our souls and fill us "with a proud exalta- tion and a sense of vaunting joy" (Longinus 107) — from those things in nature which have the same effect. Fol- lowing Boileau's translation of and commentary on the work in 1674, interest in the sublime increased dramat- ically, especially in England, and the focus of inquiry gravitated more toward the causes in nature of the sub- lime response. Until late in the eighteenth century, the- orists generally held that objects themselves embodied sublimity, and they proposed vastness, terror, and great power as qualities productive of the phenomenon. Later writers considered sublimity to lie within the subjective imagination of the person who experienced it; such is the position of Kant in his *Critique of Aesthetic Judgment*. The list of those who wrote on the sublime in England includes the essayist Joseph Addison, the poet Mark Akenside (whom Heredia includes in a list of English poets he has read), a physician, John Baillie, the philos- opher Edmund Burke, and Hugh Blair, a professor of Rhetoric and Belles Lettres at the University of Edin- burgh. While the treatises of these theorists often differ fundamentally, I will summarize only those of Burke and Blair. Burke's work is important not only because of its relation to the poem I have chosen to analyze here, but also for its value to Heredia's aesthetics. Blair's *Lec- tures* serve as a synthesis and summary of other theories, and are especially relevant to Heredia's patriotic poems.

Burke published his work, *A Philosophical Enquiry into the Origin of our Ideas of the Sublime and Beautiful,* in

1757. It was translated into Spanish and published at Alcalá in 1807 (Montiel 218), but Heredia's knowledge of English renders that fact irrelevant to our study. Burke differs from other theorists by insisting that the sublime is founded on terror:

> Whatever is fitted in any sort to excite the ideas of pain, and danger, that is to say, whatever is in any sort terrible, or is conversant about terrible objects, or operates in a manner analogous to terror, is a source of the *sublime;* that is, it is productive of the strongest emotion which the mind is capable of feeling.
>
> (39)

In order for this feeling to arise, there must be a distance of the subject from actual danger:

> If the pain and terror are so modified as not to be actually noxious; if the pain is not carried to violence, and the terror is not conversant about the present destruction of the person, . . . they are capable of producing delight; not pleasure, but a sort of delightful horror, a sort of tranquillity tinged with terror.
>
> (136)

The highest degree of sublimity for Burke is astonishment—"that state of the soul in which all its motions are suspended," the mind being "so entirely filled with its object, that it cannot entertain any other, nor by consequence reason on that object which employs it"; lesser effects are admiration, reverence and respect (57). Positing terror as the underlying source of all sublime experience, Burke lists the following as its immediate causes: obscurity, great power, privation, vastness, infinity, difficulty, magnificence, light, color, loudness and suddenness of sounds, and fierce animals and their cries. Obscurity evokes the sublime because we are afraid of what we cannot discern, and power, because we may suffer violence from forces stronger than our own. God is, of course, the highest power. Privation ("*vacuity, darkness, solitude* and *silence*" [146]), vastness (length, height and depth), and infinity (temporal vastness) are also causes of the sublime. He defines "difficulty" as the effort required to perform great tasks and "magnificence" as great numbers of things. Sound and loudness, as of waterfalls, storm winds, thunder and artillery, evoke the sublime as well. While this catalogue of sublime objects is similar to those of other theorists, its foundation upon the terrible is peculiar to Burke.

Hugh Blair delivered lectures in the 1760s at Edinburgh and published them in 1783 as *Lectures on Rhetoric and Belles Lettres* (Monk 120). Blair's work was influential at the time in the cultures which influenced Heredia's poetry: those of North America (Jacobs 20), Spain and Latin America (Montiel 223). He had also published in 1763 his *Critical Dissertation on the Poems of Ossian* which was often printed together with editions of the Ossianic poems (Montiel 219). Heredia, who later translated Ossian into Spanish, was probably familiar with that aspect of the Scotsman's work as well.

For Blair, the quality of sublimity or grandeur (he used the terms synonymously) lay in external objects.

> This quality produces a sort of internal elevation and expansion; it raises the mind much above its ordinary state, and fills it with a degree of wonder and astonishment which it cannot well express. The emotion is certainly delightful; but it is altogether of the serious kind; a degree of awfulness and solemnity.

Whereas John Baillie grounded his theory in the idea of vastness as the cause of the sublime and Burke based his theory on terror, Blair lists several causes. That which is vast—boundless prospects, limitless plains, the heavens, the ocean—"produces the impression of sublimity" (32). In the case of the heavens, the effect is augmented by great height and in the case of the ocean by the continual motion and great force of its immeasurable quantity of water. Blair sees a hierarchy of sublimity: height and/or depth produce a higher elevation of mind than expanse alone. Things immaterial also cause sublime responses: loud sounds such as thunder, cannon fire, the roaring of winds, the shouts of multitudes and the sound of vast waterfalls; and great power and strength as manifested in earthquakes, volcanoes, conflagrations, storms, floods, and lightning. Darkness, solitude and silence, which Burke would group as examples of privation, serve to heighten the effect, but not to cause it for Blair: examples are hoary mountains, solitary lakes, aged forests, and night scenes. For Blair, the whole catalogue points to a supreme power which underlies them:

> No ideas . . . are so sublime as those taken from the Supreme Being; the most unknown, but the greatest of all objects; the infinity of whose nature, and the eternity of whose duration, joined with the omnipotence of his power, though they surpass our conceptions, yet exalt them to the highest.
>
> (34-35)

The ultimate underlying source of the sublime for Blair, then, is mighty force or power.

While Heredia undoubtedly owes his concept of the sublime to English theorists, in his poetry he makes it his own. The fact that he was self-consciously employing the idea is made evident by its occurrence in at least seventy-eight of the one hundred eleven poems that comprise his *Poesías completas*, beginning with **"A Elpino,"** written in 1819 when he was only fifteen years old:

> la vista
> de sus ondas fierísimas, hirviendo
> bajo huracán feroz, en mi alma vierte
> sublime inspiración y fuerza y vida.
>
> (10-13)[2]

In his ode **"Niágara,"** which is perhaps his highest expression of the sublime in nature, we have his own testimony that he was aware of the sublime experience as a concept, that he had become acquainted with the idea separate from the experience:

. . . siempre
lo común y mezquino desdeñando,
ansié por lo terrífico y sublime.
Al despeñarse el huracán furiso,
al retumbar sobre mi frente el rayo,
palpitando gocé: vi al Océano,
azotado por austro proceloso,
combatir mi bajel, y ante mis plantas
vórtice hirviente abrir, y amé el peligro.
Mas del mar la fiereza en mi alma no produjo
la profunda impresión que tu grandeza.

(14-25)

Heredia also employs the sublime skillfully in his patriotic poetry to express his political ideology, using the idea of the sublimity of high moral conduct, as described and disseminated by Blair, along with Burke's terror-based concept. However, the most striking occurrences of the sublime in Heredia lie in his nature poems where the sublime experience itself is the subject of the work. The poem I have chosen to analyze is a case in point.

"En una tempestad," written in 1822 when the poet was eighteen, could have been composed with an open text of Burke's *Enquiry* in one hand, a pen in the other, and the hurricane howling fiercely around him.[3] The idea of terror is established by the words *pavor* (10), *terrible* (10), *aterrador* (27) and *horror profundo* (44), and by the images of the trembling sun, the hiding birds, and the earth which "contempla con pavor su faz terrible" (10). The use of obscurity, one of the immediate causes of the sublime cited by Burke, increases through the length of the poem beginning with the veiling of the sun's face in haze and clouds, growing with the spreading of the storm's terrifying and majestic mantle, and culminating in "oscuridad universal" (34). All becomes dark, confused, finally disappearing totally, leaving the poet in utter privation, completely cut off from the world: "Al fin, mundo fatal, nos separamos; / el huracán y yo solos estamos?" (50-51). Privation, as I indicated earlier, is an immediate cause of the sublime listed by Burke. Yet another is a sense of vastness, created here by the use of the words *espacio inmenso* (6), *tremendo* (7) and *gigante* (28), and by the images of a personified storm whose outstretched arms embrace all the poet can see, a darkness that covers the entire world, and lightning whose brilliance inundates the heavens. The eerie light of the sun and the drab color of the personified storm's apparel are other elements cited by Burke. Another cause, great power, is indicated here by the words *irresistible* (7), *furor* (16), and *majestuoso* (27). Power is portrayed by the image of the storm racing through immense space ("vedle rodar por el espacio inmenso" [6]), by the image of the overturning of God's chariot, which causes lightning bolts to be hurled to the earth.

En las nubes retumba despeñado
el carro del Señor, y de sus ruedas
brota el rayo veloz, se precipita,
hiere y aterra al suelo . . .

(37-40)

and by the image of the storm turning an ocean in the sky: "La tormenta umbría / en los aires revuelve un océano / que todo lo sepulta . . ." (47-49). In his discussion of power, Burke mentions the image of the bull: "The idea of a bull," he writes, "is . . . great, and it has frequently a place in sublime descriptions, and elevating comparisons" (65). Heredia uses the bull in precisely that way:

¿Al toro no miráis? El suelo escarban,
de insoportable ardor sus pies heridos:
la frente poderosa levantando,
y en la hinchada nariz fuego aspirando,
llama la tempestad con sus bramidos.

(11-15)

The sounds of the bull and the storm bellowing, the echo from the distant hills, the thunder, and the low rumble of the rain, all are great sounds which echo the voice of God. And just as the storm caused the sublimely powerful bull to seem insignificant, now God becomes the higher end to whom the sublime storm points.

The poet's reaction to what he experiences is the astonishment described by Burke:

that state of the soul, in whch all its motions are suspended, with some degree of horror. In this case the mind is so entirely filled with its object, that it cannot entertain any other . . .

(57)

The poet, after calling the tempest sublime, describes his reaction: "¡Sublime tempestad! ¡Cómo en tu seno, / de tu solemne inspiración henchido, / al mundo vil y miserable olvido . . ." (52-54). Burke also says that terror, when not directly threatening to the life of the person is "capable of producing delight; not pleasure, but a sort of delightful horror, a sort of tranquillity tinged with terror" (136). The poet describes himself "de delicia lleno (55). He is elevated—"alzo la frente" (55) —, and his mind is raised to the highest point possible as he addresses the storm directly:

Yo en ti me elevo
al trono del Señor; oigo en las nubes
el eco de su voz; siento a la tierra
escucharle y temblar. Ferviente lloro
desciende por mis pálidas mejillas,
y su alta majestad trémulo adoro.

(57-62)

Burke's comment: "If we rejoice, we rejoice with trembling; and even whilst we are receiving benefits, we cannot but shudder at a power which can confer benefits of such mighty importance" (68).

The use of so many of the standard catalogued sublime objects and the understanding of terror as the basis for the sublime experience point directly to Burke's *Enquiry* as an important source of Heredia's aesthetics manifested in this poem.[4] Other important poems which treat the sublime experience using terror as its basis include

"**Al Popocatépetl,**" "**En el Teocalli de Cholula,**" "**Niá-gara,**" and "**Al cometa de 1825,**" although the last one mentioned relies on a terror which exists only in the imagination. In his later natural sublime poems, the influence 1968.

Even if we are never able to determine the historical facts of Heredia's contact with them, our having an acquaintance with eighteenth-century English theories of the sublime is imperative in approaching his poetry. Knowing the concepts which obviously informed his aesthetic ideas and provided him with the language he used to express his experience of reality opens his work to greater understanding and appreciation.[5]

NOTES

[1] Samuel Holt Monk provides an informative overview in *The Sublime: A Study of Critical Theories in XVIII-Century England,* Ann Arbor: U of Michigan P, 1960.

[2] All quotations of Heredia's poetry will be taken from the Porrúa edition, ed. Raimundo Lazo, México: Porrúa, 1974. Citation numbers refer to lines.

[3] The complete poem in Lazo's edition omits the third line, which I have inserted from the Ortiz edition (66):

> Huracán, huracán, venir te siento,
> y en tu soplo abrasado
> [respiro entusiasmado]
> del señor de los aires el aliento.
> En las alas del viento suspendido   5
> vedle rodar por el espacio inmenso,
> silencioso, tremendo, irresistible
> en su curso veloz. La tierra en calma
> siniestra, misteriosa,
> contempla con pavor su faz terrible.   10
> ¿Al oiro no miráis? El suelo escarban,
> de insoportable ardor sus pies heridos:
> la frente poderosa levantando,
> y en la hinchada nariz fuego aspirando,
> llama la tempestad con sus bramidos.   15
> ¡Qué nubes! ¡Qué furor! El sol temblando
> vela en triste vapor su faz gloriosa,
> y su disco nublado sólo vierte
> luz fúnebre y sombría,
> que no es noche ni día . . .   20
> ¡Pavoroso color, velo de muerte!
> Los pajarillos tiemblan y se esconden
> al acercarse el huracán bramando,
> y en los lejanos montes retumbando
> le oyen los bosques, y a su voz responden. 25
> Llega ya . . . ¿No le veis? ¡Cuál desenvuelve
> su manto aterrador y majestuoso . . . !
> ¡Gigante de los aires, te saludo . . . !
> En fiera confusión el viento agita
> las orlas de su parda vestidura . . .   30
> ¡Ved . . . ! ¡En el horizonte
> los brazos rapidísimos enarca,
> y con ellos abarca
> cuanto alcanzo a mirar de monte a monte!
> ¡Oscuridad universal . . . ! ¡Su soplo   35

> levanta en torbellinos
> el polvo de los campos agitado . . . !
> En las nubes retumba despeñado
> el carro del Señor, y de sus ruedas
> brota el rayo veloz, se precipita,   40
> hiere y aterra al suelo,
> y su lívida luz inunda el cielo.
> ¿Qué rumor? ¿Es la lluvia . . . ? Desatada
> cae a torrentes, oscurece el mundo,
> y todo es confusión, horror profundo,   45
> cielos, nubes, colinas, caro bosque,
> ¿dó estáis . . . ? Os busco en vano
> desaparecisteis . . . La tormenta umbría
> en los aires revuelve un océano
> que todo lo sepulta . . .   50
> Al fin, mundo fatal, nos separamos;
> el huracán y yo solos estamos.
> ¡Sublime tempestad! ¡Cómo en tu seno,
> de tu solemne inspiración henchido,
> al mundo vil y miserable olvido,   55
> y alzo la frente, de delicia lleno!
> ¿Dó está el alma cobarde
> que teme tu rugir . . . ? Yo en ti me elevo
> al trono del Señor; oigo en las nubes
> el eco de su voz; siento a la tierra   60
> escucharle temblar. Ferviente lloro
> desciende por mis pálidas mejillas,
> y su alta majestad trémulo adoro.

[4] The first published edition of the poem, "**Versos escritos en una tempestad**" (1825), differs somewhat from the version cited here. Several of the changes made to the poem for its 1832 appearance seem to highlight the emphasis on the sublime. For example, in the earlier poem, the bull's "frente" is described as "armada" instead of "poderosa" (13), and line 21 is changed from "y al mundo tiñe de color de muerte" to "¡Pavoroso color, velo de muerte!" In the earlier version, the birds of line 22 "callan" instead of "tiemblan," and the hurricane "viene volando" instead of "bramando." Other changes seem to be stylistic in nature. At any rate, the 1825 version indicates that at least by then (if not in September, 1822, the date given in the original volume [86]), Heredia was greatly under the influence of the sublime aesthetic.

[5] An earlier version of this article was presented at the 37th Mountain Interstate Foreign Language Conference, October, 1987, in Richmond, Virginia.

WORKS CITED

Addison, Joseph. *The Spectator.* Nos. 411-421. 1712. *The Works of the Right Honourable Joseph Addison.* Ed. Richard Hurd. London: T. Cadell and W. Davies, 1811. Vol. 4, 336-377.

Baillie, John. *An Essay on the Sublime.* 1747. Los Angeles: The Augustan Reprint Soc., 1953.

Blair, Hugh. *Lectures on Rhetoric and Belles Lettres.* Philadelphia: James Kay, Jun. & Brother, 1844.

Burke, Edmund. *A Philosophical Enquiry into the Origin of our Ideas of the Sublime and Beautiful.* Ed. James T. Boulton. Notre Dame: U of Notre Dame P, 1968.

Heredia y Heredia, José María. *Poesías.* New York: Behr and Kahl, 1925.

————. *Poesías completas.* Ed. Raimundo Lazo. Mexico: Porrúa, 1974.

————. *Poesías discursosy cartas de José María Heredia.* 2 vols. *Colección de libros cubanos,* vol. XLI. Fernando Ortiz, dir. Habana: Cultural, 1939, Tomo I.

Jacobs, Robert D. *Poe: Journalist and Critic.* Baton Rouge: Louisiana State UP, 1969.

Lazo, Raimundo. "Estudio preliminar." *Poesías completas* de José María Heredia. Mexico: Porrúa, 1974. VII-L.

[Longinus.] *On the Sublime. Classical Literary Criticism.* Trans. T.S. Dorsch. New York: Penguin, 1984. 97-158.

Monk, Samuel H. *The Sublime: A Study of Critical Theories in XVIII-Century England.* Ann Arbor: U of Michigan P, 1960.

Montiel, Isidoro. *Ossián en España.* Barcelona: Editorial Planeta, 1974.

Juana de Ibarbourou
1895-1979

(Born Juanita Fernandez Morales) Uruguayan poet, playwright, novelist, and children's fiction writer.

INTRODUCTION

Juana de Ibarbourou was an extremely popular twentieth-century Uruguayan poet, known throughout the Spanish-speaking world. She is regarded as one of the most important writers to come from the smallest country in South America, and her influence has also loomed large on other women poets from Uruguay. Ibarbourou's reputation primarily rested on her early poetry, including *Las lenguas de diamante* (1919; *Tongues of Diamonds*). The poems were simple in language yet rhythmic and sensual, focusing on aspects of nature and love. Her expressly feminine perspective, sometimes bordering on narcissism, often drew comparisons to Sappho.

Ibarbourou was born Juanita Fernandez Morales on March 8, 1985 in the small village of Melo, Cerro Largo, Uruguay. She led an idyllic childhood on a farm, interacting daily with nature—a theme that would often turn up in her later poetry. Her father, a Spaniard, recited poetry from his native land to his daughter; from her nanny, Ibarbourou learned many fables. Ibarbourou was educated in local schools, including a state-run *escuela mixta*, with children of both sexes. A teacher encouraged Ibarbourou's early writing efforts. While still a student, Ibarbourou began publishing poems in local newspapers and magazines, some under the pseudonyms "Sid" and "Jeannette d'Ibar." In June 1914, Ibarbourou married an army officer, Captain Lucas Ibarbourou. After living in a number of army garrisons in Uruguay and giving birth to her only child, Julio Cesar in 1917, the family settled in Montevideo in 1918, where Ibarbourou spent most of her life, writing poetry. Her literary career began when she submitted seven of her poems to the literary editor of the local newspaper, *La Razón*. Struck by the power of her work, he praised them in print, which led to the publication of her first book in 1919.

Ibarbourou's directness and force of vision in her first three volumes of poetry, from 1919's *Las lenguas de diamante* through 1922's *Raiz salvaje* (*Savage Root*), garnered her immediate acclaim and life-long attention. She became known throughout South America and the Spanish-speaking world for her happy, exuberant erotic-tinged poems. In August 1929, the Uruguayan government dubbed her Juana de America for her contributions to literature at a ceremony at the Legislative Palace of Montevideo. More than 10,000 people attended the ceremony and she was give a ring to commemorate the moment—one of many honors she received throughout her lifetime.

Las lenguas de diamante, set the thematic stage for the rest of her early poetry as well as her career. The 65 poems concentrated on two topics: nature and love. Using an uncomplicated vocabulary and sensuous rhythm, Ibarbourou boldly celebrated youth and its power. Her direct point of view and openness about love was uncommon for women at the time. Many of these poems concern a lover, and the bold and youthful ecstasy Ibarbourou feels toward him. She also celebrates the beauty of the female body. In poems like "El furete lazo" ("The Strong Tie"), Ibarbourou expresses the fury of her passion in an overtly erotic way. For Ibarbourou, love is an essence of life just as the poet is an important part of the natural world. Death is only thought of in terms of reincarnation, as a flower or flame, or something in nature. Nature played a bigger role in Ibarbourou's next collection, *El cantaro fresco*. The poems are simple and sensual, contemplating the beauty of everyday life and the things found within it, such as the joy of the sun. Ibarbourou also suffers with nature, empathizing with trees cut down to make furniture. While death comes into play in this book, the poems do not reflect any fear of it. *El cantaro fresco* is more a personal reflection, tinged with a sense of nostalgia for the poet's passing youth. *Raiz salvaje* continues with that poems are more about nature than love, though nature is still a place of and for love. In *Raiz salvaje*, Ibarbourou relates nearly everything to elements of nature, such as flowers, trees, and forests. Some critics believe the best poems in the collection are her recollections of water images. In Ibarbourou's next collection of poetry, *La rosa de los vientos*, the poems were neither as simple nor as joyous, and her stance became darker and more intricate, the effect of the deaths of many members of her family. While Ibarbourou's images became more rich and elaborate, the poems were seen as less forceful and beautiful. She did not publish poetry again until 1950. During this time, she published religious prose, stories of her childhood and a collection of radio dramas and lullabies for children. In *Estampas de la Biblia* (1934), Ibarbourou discusses figures in the Bible as universal types and analyzes them in physical and spiritual terms, recreating the Bible in her own way.

In 1947, Ibarbourou became a member of the National Academy of Literature and in 1950 she served as president of the Uruguayan Society of Authors. That year, Ibarbourou published her last important collection of poetry, *Perdida* (*Lost*). The images were rich and the poems complex, but the book, like others of Ibarbourou's in this time period, was received with a mixed reaction. Ibarbourou published two more major collections of poetry in the 1950s. Presenting poems of loss and the passage of time, some critics believe this to be her finest collection, culminating the life of a robust and sensual woman with pain and lament. *Perdida* won the first National Prize of Literature to be awarded in Uruguay in 1959. She continued to write prose and poetry in seclusion until the end of her life. Upon her death on July 14, 1979, in Montevideo, her remains were brought to the same Legislative Palace where she was proclaimed Juana de America 50 years earlier so her many admirers could pay their final respects.

Many critics and contemporaries agree that Ibarbourou's first three collections of poetry are her most important and influential, and thus, her most well-known. Ibarbourou's early work is not seen as fitting in any specific school, save a hint of modernism: her poems are simple and freely formed, except for a handful of sonnets. These poems followed her own original tone and train of thought. Ibarbourou used her feminine point of view to describe nature and life around her in a sensual, spontaneous manner. Her critics found these early poems to be fresh and full of the exuberance of youth and the love of life.

PRINCIPAL WORKS

Las lenguas de diamante   (poetry)   1919
El cantaro fresco   (poetry)   1920
Raiz salvaje   (poetry)   1922
Ejemplario   (poetry)   1925
La rosa de los vientos   (poetry)   1930
Estampas de la Biblia   (prose)   1934
Loores de Nuestra Senora   (prose)   1934
San Francisco de Asis   (poetry)   1935
Los mas bellos versos   (poetry)   1936
Antologia poetica   (poetry)   1940
Poemas   (poetry)   1942
Chico Carlo, cuentos   (short stories)   1944
Los suenos de Natacha, cinco obras de teatro para ninos   (drama)   1945
Perdida   (poetry)   1950
Azor   (poetry)   1953
Obras completas   (poetry)   1953
Romances del destino   (poetry)   1955
Oro y tormenta   (poetry)   1956
Tiempo   (poetry)   1962
Angor Dei   (poetry)   1963
El dulce milagro   (poetry)   1964
Elegia   (poetry)   1967
La pasajera, diario de una islena: Elegia, Losada   (memoirs)   1967
Juan Soldado   1971

CRITICISM

Sidonia Carmen Rosenbaum   (essay date 1945)

SOURCE: "Juana de Ibarbourou," in *Modern Women Poets of Spanish America,* Cocce Press, 1945, pp. 229-56.

[*In the following essay, Rosenbaum offers a thorough review of Ibabourou's life, her most famous writings, and her enormous literary influence.*]

The last of the great poetesses of [the modern] period is Juana de Ibarbourou of Uruguay, who was known simply as Juanita Fernández until her marriage to the army officer with the Basque name which, according to Unamuno, means "head of the valley."[1] She was born in 1895, in Melo:

> . . . *Ciudad de coloniales casas*
> En medio de la pánica llanura
> *Y cerca del Brasil . . .* [2]

She passed her childhood, and the ardent years of dream-filled adolescence, in those rustic—almost wild—surroundings. They in turn communicated to her all their fragrance and élan, and planted deep that "savage root" that long, weary years of civilized life have not been able to eradicate.

Her culture, never profound, has undoubtedly been nurtured in the last few years when her position in the world of letters has permitted—and, perhaps, required—her to enlarge her literary vision. Her first books revealed a freshness, a spontaneity, a charming lack of profundity[3] which only a mind untaught can produce. Her superficiality of thought has always made the sensorial appeal which her verses evoke stronger.

She has inspired many paeans of praise, in prose and verse.[4] And her name, exalted to fetichistic heights by warm admirers, reached the pinnacle of glory when on the tenth of August, 1929, in the Palacio Legislativo of Montevideo, it was consecrated in the annals of literature as *Juana de América.* No greater honor has ever been bestowed on any other poet of the Continent!

Juana de Ibarbourou has published three books of verse, and three of prose—equally poetic. Numerous selections of her works have appeared; for her popularity, even over a long period of non-publication, has never waned.

Vicente A. Salaverri, who is credited with having occasioned her literary début by publishing seven sonnets of hers in the pages of *La Razón,* tells of her arrival at the editorial office of the then-popular Montevidean review with two notebooks of verses which she timidly handed over for him to read. He opened them with distrust, he admits, but closed them with enthusiasm and admiration; for the poems—some of them lamentably incorrect in form—evinced "an extraordinary temperament." "She was an Hebraic poetess," he writes, "of a contagious pantheism and a fragrant sensuality."[5]

Her poems were read with interest; and shortly after (1919) **Las lenguas de diamante**, her first book, was published, bearing a gracious prologue by the Argentine writer Manuel Gálvez. *El cántaro fresco*—in prose—appeared a year later (1920), and was followed by **Raíz salvaje** (1922), which definitely enshrined the poetess in the high literary niche she occupies to this day.

During the eight years that intervened between *Raíz salvaje* and her most recent book of poems published more than a decade ago: *La rosa de los vientos* (1930), several selections of her works appeared—in Barcelona, in Madrid, in Chile; and numerous translations in English, in French, in Italian . . . the most extensive being Miomandre's notable rendering of most of the poems of her third book under the title of *La touffe sauvage*. She has written for outstanding magazines and newspapers, contributing not only poems but also children's tales and berceuses. In recent years her interest in pedagogy has prompted her to compile two textbooks: *Ejemplario* and *Páginas de literatura contemporánea*.

Always deeply devout—in spite of the pantheistic and pagan qualities of her work—she has of late sought inspiration in religion and the Bible, publishing three notable works—two books in prose: *Loores de Nuestra Señora* (1934) and *Estampas de la Biblia* (1934), and a poem: *San Francisco de Asís* (1935).

But the modality of Juana de Ibarbourou which is best known, and which won her an undisputed place in Spanish American letters, is that of her first books—the most typical, the most *Ibarbourian*. In them she sings only of the elemental things, and, therefore, the eternal ones: of love, of life, of death—but above all, and enveloping everything in a vibrant, translucent veil, of *nature*.

Her first book—*Las lenguas de diamante*—sings of love unbounded, and of youth; and although some poems, especially those she includes in the section "Anforas negras," speak of pain and bitterness and even of death, they are, as Unamuno said, "more imagined than felt." The elegiac note in this, her book of joy, of springtime and of youth, made him feel as if she, possessing a lyre of exceptional quality and tonal range, had wanted to pluck all its chords—even though some might have been borrowed. Leave sadness until it comes, he cautioned.

Although preeminently one of love, this book reveals all the facets of personality and moods, and all the themes that are to reappear in later books. Basically, then, this book *is* Juana de Ibarbourou. For there is little in *Raíz salvaje* or even in *La rosa de los vientos* that is not already here, except that certain concepts change, certain ardent thoughts are tempered, certain illusions, as well as certain fears, are dispelled—as they are in life. But what she gains in depth, in "philosophic" concept, in form and expression, she loses in ardor, in freshness, and in spontaneity. She is now a better versifier, a more polished stylist, a follower of "the new trends" in poetry, with a superabundance of symbolism, of imagery. But there is nothing *distinctive* about all this. And were it not that the old Juana—she who threatened to be "a scandal" as the unwilling passenger in Charon's grim ferry ("Caronte: yo seré un escándalo en tu barca")—is still present, never quite hidden behind the thick wall of modernity, these new verses of hers would be merely another of the many examples of good poetry which is now being produced in all Spanish America, but, as we said, not distinctive as those first books of hers were.

Received somewhat as Delmira Agustini's books had been a decade earlier—although with less sensationalism—some praised the "chaste daring" of her verses; some censured their excessive and uncalled-for frankness. Yet all recognized a new note in feminine poetry: a rustic note that was to be widely imitated by countless women who thought it prudent to clothe their erotic verses, offtimes uninspired, in the revealing yet chaste garments of nature.

Love—in all its forms—is here: passionate, healthy, ardent, happy love; sometimes a little sad, yet not quite tragic. Never before had anyone in the ardent tropics—and a woman at that—sung so unperturbedly of the "chaste impudicity" of love. Never before had a woman offered herself in a manner that was really a command to take her—take her *now* and not tomorrow. Yet never was the surrender so beautifully, so unaffectedly expressed. And she offered herself, not as Delmira did—with the somber grimace of one who sounds the pith of love, and feels its poignancy—but with a naturalness that belied the urgency of her plea: "Descíñeme, amante; descíñeme, amante." For here was a woman ruled not by morals, or conventions, which she dared to overlook—nor even by those yielding, but sheltering barriers that the "timidity" of the sex imposes—but by a primitive urge to be taken simply as one plucks a fruit, picks a flower, or drinks in the refreshing water of a stream:

> Crecí
> Para ti.
> Tálame . . .
>
> Florí
> Para ti.
> Córtame . . .
>
> Fluí
> Para ti.
> Bébeme . .
>
> (L,[6] 29)

This primitive love, this constant ardor which youth inspires, and which she records in pages that breathe the purifying air of nature—and exude its fragrance—is what made her unique, and, in her manner, unsurpassed in Spanish American letters.

The mood this first book of hers translates is characterized by an exuberance, a superabundance of life, which is marked by a constant need of light, of movement, and a consequent dread of darkness and immobility—synthesized in death. And she who is young only feels happy in the presence of the freshness, the fragrance, the verdancy of nature; and dejected in the ocher aridity which suggests lifelessness, decomposition and death. She, therefore, feels an ardent cult for water, which in the form of rivers, or of rain, keeps things alive and verdant.

Characteristic of the "primitive" manner she popularized—and unsurpassed in later books—are poems like "Salvaje", "*Fugitiva*", "*Panteísmo*"; poems that have been imitated countless times yet never rivaled by poetesses who erroneously attempt to reproduce, without her talent, their most salient features.

The poems of *Las lenguas de diamante*, although written down much later, probably took form when Juana de Ibarbourou was still living that wild, joyous life of which she sings. *El cántaro fresco*, published but one year later, shows her as a woman far more mature who only comes upon the life that was in the nostalgic paths of remembrance. The change is abrupt: from adolescence to womanhood; from carefree childhood to motherhood. And the fact that these pages are written in prose seems to indicate a sobering effect upon her intoxicating moods of love, of life and of narcissism.

She suddenly becomes serious, proper and domestic. And the disturbing thoughts of love, and those of daring and sweet surrender, are no longer here. For she is now the mother of a son, the manager of a home, and the rustic paradise is no more. But in her heart she lives the life that was—going back to the "happier days" with undue facility (*Selva*, *La mariposa*, *Los grillos*, *El trigo*, *Los parrales*, *El haz de hierba*, *Las chicharras*). Her thoughts are more solemn now, and less self-centered. But the same fears persist: the dread of immobility, of darkness, and of death. The fear of growing old is now more acute than in her youthful plea to the lover to take her now, and not tomorrow, "ere youth and freshness fade." And she feels the same joys in sunshine, in color, and in movement; the same avidity for life; the same irrepressible attachment for nature, grown, if anything, more tender. The simple joys are glorified; the simple pleasures exalted. And a certain sweet melancholy pervades.

In *Raíz salvaje*, which has been rightfully called a commentary in verse of *El cántaro fresco*, she again is "la hembra primitiva"—although seldom with the lightness of heart that characterized the first love songs. And, strangely enough, in poetic garb she again resorts to her characteristic frankness in matters erotic. Yet many of these poems, like the compositions in prose of *El cántaro fresco*, are written from the point of view of one who, chained to a life of what must seem "repression and immobility," recalls with hungry avidity the vibrant joys of the past.

These are more tranquil verses as a whole—more polished in form, more terse in concept. They evince a successful effort to eliminate most non-essentials. And there is a greater variety of verse structure; for she succeeded in freeing herself from the bondage of the sonnet, which in her case never attained the limpidity and perfection sometimes arrived at by more expert stylists, and which proved somewhat tyrannical and monotonous in her first book of poems.

This book is ruled by the thought expressed in the title, *Raíz salvaje*, and by the rebellious mood of the monostanzaic, untitled poem with which it opens:

> *¡Si estoy harta de esta vida civilizada!*
> *¡Si tengo ansias sin nombre de ser libre y feliz!*
> *¡Si aunque florezca en rosas nadie podrá*
> *cambiarme*
>   *La salvaje raíz!*

For she is deeply aware of the inextricable savage root that lies within her; a root which a civilized covering may hide from other eyes—but never from her own consciousness. She never feels a part of the present "sheltered" life; for her roots, planted in the lusty soil of the wild and open country, bind her irrevocably to its "nourishing breast." That is why she always finds moral sustenance and strength in nature—and spiritual regeneration. And she looks to its wise teachings for her own spiritual guidance:

> *Río elástico y largo:*
> *Enséñale a mi alma*
> *A formarse un remanso*
>   (**R**, 50)

> *Vieja selva que miras cómo nos marchitamos*
> *Sin encontrar la clave para reverdecer:*
> *Dime si siendo humildes, dime si siendo puros*
> *Lo graremos tu fuerte y gallarda vejez*
>   (**R**, 52)

As in *El cántaro fresco*, the past is repeatedly evoked—nowhere more touchingly than in "**El vendedor de naranjas**", where the sight of an Indian boy selling oranges, and the sweet, fragrant spheres in his basket, bring back memories that make the meaning of the word "nostalgia" trenchantly clear:

> *Si a otro pago muy lejos del tuyo*
> *Indiecito, algún día te llevan,*
> *Y no eres feliz, y suspiras*
> *Por volver a tu vieja querencia,*
>
> *Y una tarde en un soplo de viento*
> *El sabor a tus montes te asalta,*
> *Ya sabrás, indiecito asombrado,*
> *Lo que es la palabra "nostalgia"!*
>   (**R**, 100)

Yet there is no mention of the past in poems like "**Como la primavera**",[7] "**La sed**",[8] "**La tarde**",[9] which breathe an air of actuality that proves her verily to be, as she claimed, "la misma muchacha salvaje".

Her fondness for nature, if anything, is intensified; the water,[10] the trees,[11] always so much a part of her, become still closer. And there is now in her verse a pictoric quality, a terse colorfulness, that was lacking in her first book of poems.

Love is now more serene, probably because she has matured. The restlessness which haunted her in her uncontrollable ardor ("esta inquietud constante" . . .) has evolved into a more placid regard for the lover. But the feeling is deeper. The love scenes are more tranquil, too, for all words have been spoken. He knows now what she is for him (**"Lo que soy para ti"**, L, 15). And so there is no need for her to repeat those ardent phrases of surrender. The general agitation and the fervor that attend love in its first stages are absent from **"Como la primavera"** y **"La sed"**, for instance, where tenderness and a deep understanding unite to make the bond still stronger.

There is a gentle air of melancholy—more genuine now, and more restrained; for life has taught her many things. There is nothing in *Las lenguas de diamante*, with all its talk of suffering and pain, comparable to the depth and authenticity of:

> *Yo estoy triste y sola tirada en la sombra*
> > **(R**, 40)

> *Ahórrame, mi Dios, la cruel angustia*
> *De sentarme boy también, sola, a la mesa*
> > **(R**, 88)

> *—¡Quién pudiera ser niño y sentarse en la calle*
> *Sin angustias ni trabas, a jugar con el lodo!*
> > **(R**, 15)

Calm, sleep—and even death!—are held blessed; for they have the power to dull anguish, to relax strained, tired nerves and "to refresh":

> *Y es tan serena la noche*
> *Y es tan intensa la calma,*
> *Qua se adormece mi angustia*
> *Y se evaporan las lágrimas*
> > **(R**, 42)

> *. . . ¡delicia del sueño que afloja*
> *La loca y eterna tensión de mis nervios!*
> > **(R**, 73)

> *He visto la muerte de cerca, de cerca,*
> *Era tal como una mariposa negra.*

> *¡Y yo necesito sentir la frescura*
> *Que dan sus dos alas de gamuza negra!*
> > **(R**, 37)

This growing feeling for the need of "un minuto de desprendimiento" becomes characteristic in her most recent phase of poetic evolution.

From the pages of *La rosa de los vientos* a far more conscious artist greets us; one who has felt the need—or was it the advisability?—to discard the old familiar garb and don the new; to be "à la page", as some one said. Reading this book one often has the impression that the poetess wished to astound by her modernity; that she wanted all to know that she could achieve the latest stylistic pirouettes with as much dexterity, fluency and ease as any one. The result is almost a labyrinth of images, picturesque and ingenious for the most part, through which one has to wind to arrive at the actually limpid—and often surprisingly elementary—thought expressed. For any obscurity in these

last poems of hers is only in form, never in essence. These poems differ from the earlier ones mainly in her apparent change of attitude in respect to life. But rather than a change we consider it an evolution. Basically she is the same, although, naturally, somewhat "toned down" and "awakened" by maturity. Yet we have seen that already in *El cántaro fresco* there had been a considerable change; that the restless "muchacha salvaje" of *Las lenguas de diamante* had been superseded by a quiet, serious, taciturn woman; and that all the joy those pages held was that which translated the moods and evoked the scenes of the past.

The changes apparent then were mainly those of perspective. For while her first book related events of the past in the light of the past, *El cántaro fresco* and *Raíz salvaje* speak of the present, and of the past, but view-ed—especially in the former book—in the light of the present. Her more recent book of poems deals wholly with the present—a far from joyful one, we gather, and too distant now from the happy past to find solace in its remembrance. But that "raíz salvaje" is still there, still deeply rooted within. And in her images (invariably inspired by nature), in old thoughts that are sometimes visible behind their modern garb, in characteristic gestures and moods, one discerns but little fundamental change.

If she sang before because life was good, and love and youth lighted her spirit, she now finds need to express those other things life holds: bitterness, hopelessness, pain—those haunting things which shut out laughter and light from her soul. If there was any doubt before as to her sincerity in respect to these bleaker moods, there is none now; for the time that Unamuno presaged[12] came, and she who once, perhaps, only imagined she knew sorrow and pain—and almost revelled in it—now truly appears to know of days "bitter like a newly-formed fruit."

Her joy is no longer the spontaneous, irrepressible spark of yore, but a conscious torch she carries in an effort to keep herself from falling into the fathomless depths of despair. Her repeated allusions to happiness,[13] to hope;[14] her constant desire to be jubilant and gay,[15] strike a pathetic and frustrated note. And there is bravery in her wish to dance upon her bleeding heart (. . ."yo bailaré sobre mi corazón herido"); strength and purpose in her desire to go and conquer destiny ("Ir a conquistar el destino"); and a will to preserve whatever happiness is meted out to her, which is almost a challenge:

> *Pero mi alegría queda intacta y la veré*
> *   multiplicada*
> *En los caireles fulgurantes del sueño.*

> *. . . la llevo como un clavel del aire*

> *Ahora es mía y la levanto en alto,*

> *Alegría de un día que yo he de salvar*
> *Del maleficio de las horas brujas*
> > (33-34)

Before, she could find balm in nature and in memories of an idyllic past; but now she has to resort to more toxic, and less curative measures. For she finds her "artificial paradise" in dreams—dreams of realized hopes, of painless days, and the tantalizing ones of travel.

She did not always have this vice of dreaming that made an endless night—brilliant and jubilant with stars—of Delmira Agustini's life. Yet at times she feels that she must seek a dream to compensate her for the vacuity and drabness of a day—the craziest dream she can find; one that might have a puppet player's cap, or a tattooed, fantastic face:

> Yo quiero un sueño que me compense de este día
> Claro, vacío, monótono . . .
>
> Elegiría el sueño más loco
> El que tuviese un gorro de titiritero
> O la cara tatuada y fantástica

(p. 80)

This desire to dream—which she attributes to having, as a child, drunk of the waters of the Tacuari river, and which formerly had taken the form of youthful reverie—becomes more of a necessity as the realities of life become sharper. And her soul clamors for the minute of release, of detachment, when the spirit sets out alone on the soft road of dreams:

> Toda mi alma clama por el minuto de
>   desprendimiento
> Cuando el espíritu se echa a andar solo
> Por los caminos blandos del sueño . . .

(10)

—a road that leads to the "país de los caminos iluminados / por el mirasol giratorio de los sueños", where the world, and even life, cease to exist.

She who once felt that "savage love" for light; who had such dread of darkness and the night that brought it on, now becomes ill from the violent perfume which the tunic of light brings. And she feels the need of night which shuts her eyes, fatigued by the sight of faces; the night that dulls the sharpness of words and brings to the ears an echo of throats without hate. She is wearied by the "heroic pain" of nightly fashioning for herself a pair of wings; for the day, indefatigable grinder of shears, steel daggers and iron swords, rudely cuts them off and leaves her again bereft of her only means of escape.

Still, in spite of the fascination night now holds for her, she knows that it is "arbitrary and toxic," and that "only the day can save us"; for "from the small death of every night things are born pure," and, with the dawn, everything acquires an air of birth. If she once needed night "to duplicate hope," she now wants to turn her back to it and to the afternoon, its harbinger, and nevermore to dream. Yet she has faith and hope in the future. For the Potter Who fashions the clay jars of the coming days makes each one different and unique. And if yesterday's had

borders of harsh stone and the opaque concavity of an empty cistern, others will come nestled in honeycombs, or in the softness of a live petal. She now awaits one, clear and pure, which will have the golden hue of untouched honey (**RV**, 44).

But stronger than her bent for dreaming, far more persistent, and having the same heritage: the Tacuari river,[16] is her desire to travel. She who knows that every dawn will bring only "a sterile peace of inert hands upon the knees," is beset by an immense longing to go and lay her head upon the knees of the Unknown.[17] For in her drab horizon she has discovered a new hue: "the color of the desire to go through unknown places to far-off cities."

Only in imagination and in dreams can she satisfy this "ansiedad constante", this "afán de partida"[18] that fill her. It is not surprising, therefore, that so many of these later poems should be inspired by themes and motives of the sea. In these imaginary voyages on the nocturnal oceans of dreams, through the unnavigated seas of the abstract, she goes in search of "the little red fish of happiness." And knowing that the shores of day are still far-distant, she laughs as she flings her cast-off sadness into the port of Rejoicing.

Except for some poems which appear from time to time—similar in mood and form to those of **La rosa de los vientos**—one can say that Juana de Ibarbourou has entered upon a new literary phase. With the publication in 1934 of **Loores de Nuestra Señora** and **Estampas de la Biblia**, and of the poem **San Francisco de Asís**, a year later, she lays aside her former manner of auto-description and self-revelation to sing, in limpid prose, the praises of the Virgin; to depict, in chiselled portraits, the dramatic figures of the Old Testament; and to relate, with lyric fervor, the vibrant episode of Saint Francis and the Leper.

The **Loores** are poetic commentaries—or amplifications—of the various "praises" of the Litany: Mater amabilis, Rosa sine spina, Turris eburnea, Porta coeli, Stella matutina . . . These are pages filled with all the beauty, the love, the tenderness, the veneration and the fervor which the Virgin—Consolatrix afflictorum—inspires in her. And she offers them as she would a floral tribute—simple and pure and fragrant—to the "sweet and divine protector" who has guided her through the night of "confusion" to the clear day of faith; to serenity, fortitude, beatitude and hope. From the diaphanous depths of her spirit flow these fervent "loores": Mater boni consilii, Turris davidica, Domus aurea, Spes ultima.

The **Estampas** are succinct but inspired "self-portraits" of some of the outstanding and moving Biblical figures: Adam, Cain, Noah, Abraham, Jacob, Moses, David, Solomon, Daniel, Sarah, Rebecca, Ruth, Judith, Esther. Each identifies himself clearly and simply, sketching in words and images of distinct Biblical flavor, a highly dramatic, warm portrait; for rather than static pictures these are live, vibrantly human descriptions that reveal the inner workings of mind and soul of these men and women—

some austere, some gentle, some pathetic—who have served as inspiration to countless comments in prose and verse. By no means inferior in poetic concept and interpretative value, these **Estampas de la Biblia** add some creditable pages to the ever-growing literature that finds an inexhaustible source of material in "the book that has no peer".

In these books her expression is always clear and direct, with an elegant simplicity that bears slight comparison with the somewhat rococo leanings of **La rosa de los vientos,** and that seems closer to the fragrant, nostalgic pages of **El cántaro fresco.** And as she herself was seeking spiritual anchorage in the tempestuous seas of uncertainty, so did her pen essay distinct modes of expression until, like her spirit, it found a limpid, tranquil lake to reflect its steady and clear image. Whatever road she takes in the future, she will always carry with her the sacred dust of these paths she followed to arrive at "la montaña de la serenidad definitiva".

As one reads the poetry of Juana de Ibarbourou one sees how everything that concerns her most: *love,* life, death, herself . . . is seen and interpreted as part of nature; for nature is the mirror that reflects her thoughts, her emotions, her moods, her manner of expression. It is difficult, therefore, to isolate her themes and attempt to define them singly; for not only are they all interrelated as regards nature, but there is a deep inner unity of thought and concept—not necessarily premeditated—that makes each an indispensable part of the other. The thought of love, for instance, immediately evokes the desire for life, the fear of death, the pleasure she finds in offering to the lover her sun-browned, elastic, fragrant body; the thought of life summons up appetizing feasts of love, as she proffers her tempting beauty with a joy marred only by the haunting thought that youth, alas!, is not everlasting, and that death will one day extinguish the starry gaze in her eyes, will pale the bloom of her cheek, will reduce arms that embrace and lips that burn to lifeless ashes; the thought of death steals short-lived joy from what might otherwise have been cloudless hours of love, it awakens the desire for endless life as part of nature, for ever-verdant beauty; the thought of herself, fragrant with nards, and proud of her youth, her beauty, her desirability, calls up visions of the lover waiting to pluck the flowers and the fruits of love, while life still lends them fragrance and flavor—before death wilts and robs them of their power to lure . . .

Set against a background of nature, each one of these themes is presented simply—one might almost say *naively*—without great depth of thought, without philosophical implications, but with a freshness and spontaneity which only poetry of this type can possess. For her ideas upon life, upon death, upon love, are not transcendental, but the direct, basic ones of a person who does not seek to comprehend what there is, or may be, beyond that which meets the eye. She bases her ideas of love upon her feelings and desires; those of life upon what she sees of nature; those of death upon what she knows of life. She does not attempt to pry or indagate into the unknown—or to deduce the why and the wherefore of things; for she is as simple and elemental and direct in her thoughts and in her emotions, as the flowers, the fruits, the trees and the other creatures of nature that fill her verses and with which more than once she identifies and compares herself.

Her love of nature, in every form, is intense—all embracing. She feels a sort of kinship with it; for, as she says, she is convinced that in a past life she herself had roots and sprang flowers, and felt, hanging from her branches, terse fruits, heavy with sweet juice:

> Estoy convencida de que en una vida ancestral, hace ya miles de años, yo tuve raíces y gajos, dí flores, sentí pendientes de mis ramas, que eran como brazos jugosos y verdes, frutas tersas, pesadas de zumo dulce . . .
>
> (**CF**, 21).

Perhaps that is why her body still retains that "odor of springtime," and her mouth is fresh and fragrant like a newly-cut rose . . .

She loves the forests, the fields, the meadows, the long green roads ("las selvas, los campos, los prados, los largos caminos verdes" . . .), but in her heart she harbors a true predilection for water:

> *¡Cuánto me gusta el agua!*
> *¡Cuánto me gusta el agua!*
> *Hacia ella se inclina*
> *Como un junco mi alma*
>
> (**R**, 18)

She feels for it a sisterly affection ("yo siento por el agua un cariño de hermana"); and so she wonders if in another "ancestral life" she may not have been a cistern, a fountain or a river:

> *Acaso, en otra vida*
> *Ancestral, yo habré sido*
> *Antes de ser de carne,*
> *Cisterna, fuente o río . . .*
>
> (**R**, 18)

She loves the water not only for the physical joy she finds in its refreshing sweetness, but also because to her it typifies goodness, tenderness, sincerity, purity, charity . . . and "tastes of truth". And so she calls it "la buena criatura", or "Sor caridad". For when one is tormented by a burning thirst, this "kindly creature" offers her breast that one may drink; when one is suffering from a gaping wound, her clear current forms a refreshing and soothing bandage; when one feels tired, or feverish, or depressed, there is nothing that comforts more. And so when she feels as if a hidden hand were hurling pebbles of sorrow at her soul, she goes to the well and instantly finds her panacea. The mere touch of the humid clay pitcher against her cheek, or a little rain water in the hollow of her hand, brings comfort and fills the moment with gladness.

Besides being a physical and spiritual balm, water—rain—brings about that fragrant freshness which the earth exudes; it decks the fields in verdant softness; it weighs down the tree branches with sweet loads of turgid fruit; it adorns and scents the world with its crown of sweet-smelling flowers. Life, verdure, color, aromas—what Juana de Ibarbourou loves most—are the result of the vivifying power contained in those drops whose sound charms her ears and whose touch sets her body tingling.

But she is also familiar with the reverse side of the picture; for under the implacable rays of the sun, in the aridness of the dry season, she has walked the long ocher roads which traverse parched fields—devoid of plants or verdure. And she sees the elm trees as sentinels—looking over the "yellow anxiety" of the fields; awaiting "the dreamed-of message of rain," as they watch the clouds and question the winds, that they may announce its approach, jubilantly, to the alert ears of the suffering roots. And she pictures, too, the millions of little green mouths open to receive its generous life-giving stream after a long drought, while the birds huddle close under the protecting umbrellas of the leaves.

That is why water holds so sacred a meaning for her; water in all forms—whether it be the far-off, powerful water of the sea, or the rain, or the more familiar one of rivers, lakes, ponds, wells or faucets; whether turbulent, running or still—water, which to her is a live creature that "talks, dreams, sings, kisses and comforts".

A mere listing of all the plants she mentions, of all the trees, the flowers, the fruits, the animals and insects that appear in her poems, would only serve to confirm, once more, that there is nothing in nature that escapes the notice, or fails to arouse the interest, of this poetess who always sees herself—in life as well as in death—as an integral part of it.

Her thoughts and sympathies are with the water, the trees, the plants and all the other components of nature with which she feels such a deep and significant kinship. She can understand their gestures—for her so meaningful—and interpret their mute language:

> Es un montón de álamos rumorosos y agudos
> Aferrados en medio de la árida llanura,
> Las raíces pequeñas de los pastos resecos
> Les claman el mensaje soñado de la lluvia.
>
> Y ellos miran las nubes, e interrogan al viento,
> Y hacen ¡no!, con la verde cabeza de sus copas,
> —¡Aún el agua demora!—sus piran las gramíneas
>   Que bajo el sol se enroscan
>   (R, 47)
>
> Yo entiendo lo que dicen las gotas cantarinas.
> La lluvia, en mi ventana, tiene voces divinas
>   (L, 123)

She can sense the supreme sanctity of the water which administers kindness like a Sister of Charity; the friendly benignity of the sun that warms the fragrant earth on which she loves to lie; the staunch nobility of the elms that "like a row of good boys" hold steadfast watch over all; the never-ending sadness of the cypress that has become a citizen of all the cemeteries of the earth; the bitter suffering of the fig tree that writhes in the pain of its ugliness. And she walks among them all like a friend, finding solace and freshness, food, fragrance and rest in the water, the fruits, the plants and flowers, the trees, and in the sun-warmed carpet of the earth.

Often she is alone with nature ("He huroneado en la selva milenaria de cedros . . . y he corrido por todos los pedrosos caminos" . . . L, 91; "Siento un acre placer en tenderme en la tierra", L, 149; "He bebido del chorro cándido de la fuente . . . Elástica de gozo cual un gamo he corrido/por todos los ceñudos senderos de la tierra," R, 57). But she finds the greatest joy in sharing these things she delights in with the lover:

> Bajo la luna llena, que es una oblea de cobre,
> Vagamos taciturnos en un éxtasis vago . . .
>   (L, 7)
>
> Me vestiré de blanco, me aromaré de rosas,
> E iremos por las rutas que huelen a tomillo . . .
>   (L, 119)
>
> Iremos por los campos de la mano,
> A través de los bosques y los trigos . . .
>   (L, 139)
>
> ¡Qué alocado retorno hacia la aldea,
> Ceñidos por los hilos de la lluvia . . .
>   (L, 152)
>
> Tómame de la mano. Vámonos a la lluvia
> Descalzos y lijeros de ro pa, sin paraguas . . .
>   (R, 97)

Like Adam and Eve they seem to be alone in the world ("Somos grandes y solos sobre el haz de los campos"); and any other people they encounter—shepherds, laborers—are always unidentified and have far less individuality than the trees, the flowers, the wind, the water, and even the odors that greet her at every step.

All the flora of her region find entrance in her poetry—not in a disinterested or detached manner, nor as casual "color," but as a complement to herself, as an emotional expansion, as a friend, as an accomplice. For the many plants that scent the roads, like the trees, like the flowers, are silent but sympathetic witnesses of her joys and sorrows, mute spectators at her trysts, artful adjuncts to her charms.

She does not tire of speaking of the "dulce *laurel* hospitalario", the *hiedra*, the fragrant *tomillo*, the *gramíneas, camalotes* . . . nor of the trees: the "*pinos* olorosos y negros", the "*ceibos* frondosos", the "*álamos* rumorosos y agudos"; of "la *higuera* . . . aspera y fea", the "*ciruelos* redondos", "*limoneros* rectos", "*naranjos* de brotes lustrosos", and all those others under whose rustling branches she so often found comfort and rest—and love.

Many flowers—alive with color, and of penetrating aroma—appear in the course of her poems: poppies, pansies, daisies, sunflowers, azaleas, jasmines. But those she mentions most frequently, and which lend her beauty (when pinned to her breast, or in her dark hair) and that tantalizing fragrance which so charms the lover, are roses, lilies, violets, dahlias and nards.

As one reads the poetry of Juana de Ibarbourou one sees how everything that concerns her most: *love,* life, death, herself . . . is seen and interpreted as part of nature; for nature is the mirror that reflects her thoughts, her emotions, her moods, her manner of expression. [Ibarbourou's] ideas upon life, upon death, upon love, are not transcendental, but the direct, basic ones of a person who does not seek to comprehend what there is, or may be, beyond that which meets the eye. She bases her ideas of love upon her feelings and desires; those of life upon what she sees of nature; those of death upon what she knows of life. She does not attempt to pry or indagate into the unknown—or to deduce the why and the wherefore of things; for she is as simple and elemental and direct in her thoughts and in her emotions, as the flowers, the fruits, the trees and the other creatures of nature that fill her verses and with which more than once she identifies and compares herself.

Flowers give an indefinable, alluring fragrance to her body as a whole—and to her hair—but fruits make her lips luscious and tempting. And as she goes in avid search of blackberries or strawberries, which make her lips fragrant and vivid, she knows that eating them is a prelude to the kiss:

> *¡Canastito repleto de fresas!*
>
> *Y después que las hemos comido,*
> *Lentamente besarme en los labios*
> *Que ellas ponen fragantes y vivos*
>
> (**R**, 79)

—the kiss that other lips, "dulces como de *fresa*", and that give her a "sensación de agua viva y *moras* negras", will let fall upon her own like a ripe fruit.

She sinks her healthy teeth into "el fruto dulce y sano/ de las rústicas vides y los higos/que coronan las tunas"; into "the compact meat" of juice-filled peaches, plums, pears, grapes, apples, oranges and all the other fruits she gathers in her rich orchard. But she relishes the rustic blackberries and strawberries the most; and quinces, because of their pungent odor. She uses the "membrillos redondos y pintones" to perfume her closets, and her clothes absorb that "olor frutal" which gives her body its "constant flavor of spring".

As prolific as the plant life, as varied and as typical, are the small animals and birds, and especially the insects whose movements so intrigue this "intuitive and rustic entomologist." Butterflies, glowworms, moths, ants, beetles, crickets; lizards, moles, frogs, toads, sparrows, magpies, parrots . . . all appear as part of that exuberant and animated landscape which serves as background to her own tempestuous moods.

Passionately fond of the sun, the warmth, the bustle and the joy of life upon earth ("el sol, el calor, el ruido y la alegría de la vida sobre la tierra") she cannot think of ever forgoing them. Yet knowing that She who puts out the lamps of life ("la apagadora de las lámparas") cares nothing for her "solicitous anxiety of life, of clarity, of sky" . . . she implores the lover that if she die, he bury her not deep, but near the earth's surface where she can still be lulled by the wild chirping of the birds or the joyous chatter of the fountain; where the sun can warm her bones, and her eyes, stretched into growing shoots, can come up to behold once more "the savage lamp of the red sunsets". For she foresees the struggle of her flesh to come up again—the need to feel, in its particles, the freshness of the wind. Therefore she asks that he strew seeds on her grave so that they may take root in her "diminished bones." On the ladder of the live shoots she will come up to see him through the purple lilies!

Death, then, may effect changes in her flesh, but her desire to feel the warmth of the sun, or the fresh caress of the breeze; to hear the "divine" chatter of the birds and of the fountains, and to see the lover, will never be dulled. This belief in the continuance of one's likes and desires after death—of the same joys she experiences in life—and in the perpetuation of one's being in some form or another, is nowhere better expressed than in her oft-quoted "**Vida garfio**":

> *Amante: no me lleves, si muero, al camposanto.*
> *A flor de tierra abre mi fosa, junto al riente*
> *Alboroto divino de alguna pajarera,*
> *O junto a la encantada charla de alguna fuente.*
>
> *A flor de tierra, amante. Casi sobre la tierra*
> *Donde el sol me caliente los huesos, y mis ojos*
> *Alargados en tallos, suban a ver de nuevo*
> *La lámpara salvaje de los ocasos rojos.*
>
> *A flor de tierra, amante. Que el tránsito así sea*
> *   Más breve. Yo presiento*
> *La lucha de mi carne por volver hacia arriba,*
> *Por sentir en sus átomos la frescura del viento.*

Yo sé que acaso nunca allá abajo mis manos
  Podrán estarse quietas.
Que siempre como topos arañarán la tierra
En medio de las sombras estrujadas y prietas.

Arrójame semillas. Yo quiero que se enraícen
En la greda amarilla de mis huesos menguados.
¡Por la parda escalera de las raíces vivas
Yo subiré a mirarte en los lirios morados!

(**L**, 47-48)

The certainty of immortality with the same essential characteristics and feelings she has now, serves as a balm for the dire thought of leaving life's inexhaustible feast. And the horror of death ("yo le tengo horror a la muerte", **R**, 45) is mitigated by the comforting thought that her body, when put into the earth, may furnish the fertilizer to nurture some huge tree which will increase her present stature a hundredfold (**R**, 45). And as she feels her muscles, her hair, her shoulders, she is again filled with the joy that she is now touching that which someday may become the branches of a tree, the tender straws that line a cozy nest, the earth that fills a furrow that is warm—like woman's flesh (**R**, 45).

Her life in the flesh will terminate at death; but her spirit will live on to reap the joys and blessings that nature, in its insatiable bounty, will continue to bestow. And so, in the lovely purple lilies, in the gracefully-turned vase, in the happy atoms that go dancing along enchanting paths, in the vivid, yet small flame that will comfort the lover in his long hours of desolation, and in so many other ways, she will continue to live on—for death does not annihilate; it merely *transforms* . . .

But these spiritual joys are for later. Now there is in her a constant avidity to take a palpable part "in the feast". And so she drinks in joy and love and life with the furor, the fervor and the fruition of one who knows that

The Bird of Time has but a little way
To flutter—and the Bird is on the wing . . .

of one who knows that someday she will be forever still and silent—"in perpetual repose"—under the black earth, while life above her continues to buzz like a drunken bee:

Ha de llegar un día en que he de estarme quieta,
  ¡Ay, por siempre, por siempre!
Con las manos cruzadas y apagados los ojos,
Con los oídos sordos y con la boca muda,
Y los pies andariegos en reposo perpetuo
  Bajo la tierra negra

Mientras encima mío se oirá zumbar la vida
  Como una abeja ebria

(**L**, 92)

of one who knows that her mouth, her hands, her hair, will some day all have turned to the proverbial ashes and dust:

No codicies mi boca. Mi boca es de ceniza
Y es un hueco sonido de campana mi risa.

No me oprimas las manos. Son de polvo mis
  manos,
Y al estrecharlas tocas comidas de gusanos.

No trences mis cabellos. Mis cabellos son tierra
Con la que han de nutrirse las plantas
  de la sierra.

(**"Laceria"**, **L**, 103)

And she who is so alive wonders if the dead are content to sleep on without interruption; or if tired of their unending rest they have a longing for movement, for noise, for *verticality*:

¡Oh, muertos para quienes el silencio es enorme
Y no se acaba nunca! ¿Será bueno dormir
Como ellos, sin nada que les aje el reposo?
¿Se está bien allá abajo o desearán salir

Un día a correr campos, a buscar a los hombres,
El movimiento, el grito, la verticalidad,
Cansados del descanso sin tregua, llenos de ansia
Por la inquietud ardiente, viva, de la ciudad?

(**"Cementerio campesino"**, **L**, 177-178)

Yet there are times—rare times—when tired of this eternal wishing, hoping, dreaming that is life, she is beset by a wild longing to rest; by an unbounded desire to stretch out in the dust and be only dust:

¡Oh, este eterno anhelar!
¡Oh, esta eterna inquietud!
¡Como a veces te sueño,
Sueño del ataúd!

Hasta el cuerpo me duele
De soñar y soñar.
Muerte, anúlame. Hoy tengo
Un ansia de reposar . . .

Esta noche la tierra
Es un imán tenaz.
¡Oh, tenderme en el polvo!
¡Oh, ser polvo y no más!

¡Oh, ser polvo, ser tierra,
Disgregarse, volver
A la nada, que ignora
La fatiga de ser.

(**"Cansancio"**, **L**, 159-160)

And there are others when, tortured by the thought of old age—when youth and beauty are no more—she thinks of the clemency of death. The slow approach of an old woman evokes these mournful thoughts, as she wonders if she, too, so fresh and young, will some day have those deep ridges on her cheeks; if the terse, rich ivory of her dark body will break into those same sinuous pleats. What will happen to her constant desire to walk through woods and meadows and to "the sonorous bell of her happiness?" Will they be transformed into this same sadness—into this quiet anguish? Will she be able *to live* without the pride of being *strong* and *young* and *desired?* Oh, Lord— she cries—why can't the legend of the Fountain of Youth be true? (**CF**, 128-129).

Knowing, then, that time is at a premium, she urges the lover to take her *now* "while it is still early"; while her flesh is still fragrant and soft with the dahlias and the nards of youth; for later his desire may have no echo of response—like an offering placed upon a silent tomb:

> Tómame ahora que aún es temprano
> Y que llevo dalias nuevas en la mano.
>
> Tómame ahora que aún es sombría
> Esta taciturna cabellera mía.
>
> Ahora, que tengo la carne olorosa,
> Y los ojos limpios y la piel de rosa.
> . . . . .
>
> Después . . . ¡ah yo sé
> Que ya nada de eso más tarde tendré!
>
> Que entonces inútil será tu deseo
> Como ofrenda puesta sobre un mausoleo.
>
> ¡Tómame ahora que aún es temprano
> Y que tengo rica de nardos la mano!
>
> ("**La hora**", **L**, 17-18)

And so she loses no time in enjoying to the full the sweetness which each fleeting moment brings. And she gives herself to the lover joyfully and without reserve— offering her lithe, brown body "like a gift of love."

The naturalness with which she speaks of this love, and the constant analogies with nature—which lend it an idyllic note—obviate any feeling of crudeness or lust that one might sense in poetry of a more "sophisticated" type. Her reiterated claim to purity and chastity ("soy casta como Diana"), expressed in paradoxical terms ("puro impudor", "casta impudicia"), is abetted by critics who laud her "castísima desnudez espiritual" (Unamuno), her "desnuda virginidad" (Torres Bodet), her "casto impudor" (Ballesteros de Martos). And so she can with all frankness speak of

> . . . la suprema delicia
> De la más casta impudicia
> Dormir desnuda en tus brazos
>
> (**R**, 25)

for she knows that her love—like her soul—is always tendered with "the *pure impurity* of a fruit, a star or a flower."

Seldom is their passion brought within the orbits of a room, for her dislike—one might almost say *distrust*— of anything "civilized," and her almost religious cult for nature make her always seek "unfettered love in rustic

peace."[19] This results in so close an identification of love with nature that many of the sensations she experiences in one or the other are at times so fused—or even *confused*—that she can, with all naturalness, say: "he mordido manzanas y he besado tus labios" . . . implying that the sensation derived from biting apples was comparable, similar, or perhaps *identical* to that occasioned by kissing the lover on the lips! This thought is borne out by frequent allusions to a kiss falling upon her lips as would a fruit, and producing a like sensation:

> Donde una tarde alguien puso en mi boca
> Como un fruto extraordinario
> El primer beso amoroso
>
> (**R**, 27)
>
> Sensación de agua viva y moras negras
> Me dió tu boca, amante
> . . . . .
>
> Y me cayó tu beso entre los labios
> Como un fruto maduro de la selva . . .
>
> (**R**, 43)

The body and the kiss, like water, infuse a freshness that allays the burning thirst of love. And so when the lover is parched by desire, she, the good Samaritan, offers the live fount of her body:

> La sed era en su boca como un largo rubí,
> Y yo el cántaro vivo de mi cuerpo le dí
>
> (**L**, 90)

while for her thirst there is no greater comfort than the refreshing sweetness of his kiss:

> Tu beso fué en mis labios
> De un dulzor refrescante.
> . . . . .
>
> Y me cayó tu beso entre los labios
> Como . . .
> . . . un lavado guijarro del arroyo
>
> (**R**, 43)

All nature seems to breathe love, and the lover's presence is felt in the strong, yet tender embrace of the wind, in the fragrant warmth of the green-carpeted earth, in the caressing waters of the river; his lips in the turgid sweetness of the rustic fruits; his fire in the burning copper of the sun that bends all vegetation to its will.

This woman whose breast, as she says, harbors a live coal instead of a heart ("un ascua viva encendida en lugar de corazón"), at times loves with ardor, with passion, with a certain savageness that knows no moral bonds or restrictions. And like Delmira Agustini who felt that the lover's soul and hers were tied in an unyielding knot which Destiny and the Fates could not undo, Juana de Ibarbourou also says:

> Mi alma frente a tu alma se ha hecho un nudo
> Apretado y sombrío.

. . . . .

Y es un abrazo inacabable y largo
Que ni la muerte romperá.

. . . . .

Mi raíz se ha trenzado a tus raíces
Y cuando quieras desatar el nudo,
Sentirás que te duele en carne viva
Y que en mi herida brota sangre tuya!

                                    (**"Fusión"**, **L**, 87-88)

It is then that the kiss, which most often is wholesome and refreshing, becomes an insatiable, flame-devouring fire; a harrowing life-sipping thirst—a kiss that bites flesh and mouth and soul, opening a wound through which she feels life fleeing.

But most often she is in a far gentler and less tempestuous mood, and is filled with the need of being all things for the lover; of giving him all—her youth, her dreams, herself:

> *Y te dí el olor,*
> *De todas mis dalias y nardos en flor.*
>
> *Y te dí el tesoro,*
> *De las hondas minas de mis sueños de oro.*
>
> *Y te dí la miel,*
> *Del panal moreno que finge mi piel.*
> *Y todo te dí!*

                                    (**L**, 23)

for rather than possessive, she wants to be subservient to him.

One of the most touching poems in this tenor is "Enredadera", where she says that for the rich privilege of being always at his side she will be merely a fragrance or a shadow. She will be silence itself, if he wants silence, and when he returns from the street—weary, bitter, thirsty—her body will be there for him, like the clear water of the river. Her arm will be a pillow of fresh clover; her hands, refreshing to his burning brow. There is a sort of *tameness* in her then, and a certain humility which is ingratiating, as she chooses the meeker attitudes that a woman so often likes to assume in love. This feeling of humbleness—of complete surrender—is akin to that of weakness, of "smallness", that she feels next to "him" who is aptly the strong one, the protector, in whose company she feels no fear: "Contigo en el nido no sé lo que es miedo".

Her poetry is marvelously alive and fresh and fragrant. It is redolent of sweet-smelling grass and newly-hoed earth; of thyme and moss and wind-swept wheat; of violets and marguerites, dahlias and nards; of fruits, of sunshine, and of spring. For Juana de Ibarbourou has a keen, almost primitive, sense of smell and is constantly referring to the many and varied odors that greet her—"like a friendly dog"—as she walks through the woods or fields, or even at home as the delightful aroma of fruits and flowers permeates her rooms.

All these rustic odors are transmitted to her brown, lithe body and to her dark hair which she loves to spread "like a black wing" on the lover's knees:

> *Mi cuerpo está impregnado del aroma ardoroso*
> *De los pastos maduros. Mi cabello sombroso*
> *Esparce, al destrenzarlo, olor a sol y a heno,*
> *A salvia, a yerbabuena y a flores de centeno.*

. . . . .

> *Y huelo a hierba clara nacida en la mañana!*

                                    (**L**, 130)

> *Tiene aún mi epidermis morena,*
> *No sé qué fragrancias de trigo emparvado*

                                    (**R**, 29)

And that is why she tells him that he can kiss a thousand women but not one will give him that "impression of rustic love," that "impression of rivulet and forest" that she does.

Accustomed to the boundless freedom of fields, meadows, open roads, woods; to the joys of unlimited wind and rain and sunshine; to the pungent, invigorating or delicate fragrance of fruits, plants and flowers; to the caressing song of birds, crickets, brooks, of her native Melo, in the city she somehow feels like "a wild plant in a conservatory". But, as she says, all the sweet memories of the past are in her soul, and in her blood; and so, in spite of the years that have gone by, she does not forget . . . Nor can she, for there is always something—a word plethoric with reminiscence (*selva, pinos* . . .); the fresh and healthful smell of pasture grass, or the balsamic one of amber-colored oranges; the crickets' or cicadas' song at siesta-time or in the summer eve; a butterfly in flight; a passing cart filled with golden sheaves of wheat—that summons up "remembrance of things past".[20]

There are times when she seems to find quiet contentment and serenity in the steady rhythm of her present life. But she is too restless of spirit—too anguished at the sign of immobility in any form—to be long satisfied with "sterile peace". And so she begins to envy "the traveling destiny of the winds". A violent desire for change, a constant urge to rid herself of the strangling hold of monotony—most often externalized in a longing for travel—takes possession of her.

This wanderlust, also rooted, undoubtedly, in her dread of immobility, comes into evidence in the earlier books. But it is not until *La rosa de los vientos* that one feels its merciless and relentless grip. For it is no longer a caprice then—as it may have been some time before—but a spiritual necessity to set out in search of new stimuli to enliven her youth, aged prematurely in the stifling air of sameness; a pressing urge to find the road that may lead to a new life, to a new land of hope where she can discard the garb of sorrow that now hangs heavy upon her and don anew the long-sought, radiant one of joy.

The ships—small, live worlds—had long sent her mute invitations from afar. But the Atlantic, a friendly hand that opens to receive all travelers and sailors, for her is a clenched fist, and has no roads. This ocean, she well knows, will never balance on its undulating back the boat that would take her from this small land of hers to those others—wondrous ones!—of which her "motionless youth" and her melancholy dream. She looks at it, then, as she would a fruit into which she will never bite, or as a fertile field that she will never reap (**"Atlántico", RV**, 93-94).

Sitting alone on the shore—among the shadows—she devours with avid eyes the divine feast denied to her. And the realization that she "bites an impossible desire" rends from her that "cutting cry" with which she hopes to sever the cable that binds her to one land—*to only one land!*—of which she knows even the dust that dances on the wind; but her vain cry falls limp upon the sea, like a wounded gull (**"El grito", RV**, 72-73).

But if she dwells on the miracles of travel to a soul crushed by routine, she also writes, at much greater length, of the simple joys of seeing familiar scenes, familar plants, flowers, insects . . . ; of homely duties and motherly cares; of her garden, her trees, her well, her native river.

In a poem which sounds truer depths than those in which she sang of other horizons, other shores, she speaks of the familiar aromas that greet her as she follows near-by roads, and of burying her face among the flowers "de olor cordial y antiguo". And, suddenly, as she says, "all the lies of the sea become clear." For in common with other Americans who, like her, have not a sailor's soul, she loves the land:

> La montaña, la pampa, la colina y la selva,
> La antiplanicie brava y los llanos verdeantes
> Donde pasta la vaca y galopa el bisonte . . .
>
> (**R**, 67)

Returning home she feels the deep joys of "reconquest." All her poems are a paean to this brilliant, fragrant land of hers:

> ¡Qué brillantes y qué bien huelen
> Mis tierras de América . . .
>
> (**RV**, 86)

And she herself, in her exuberance, in her sensuousness, in her zest for life, in her fire, in her fondness for light, is an ardent fragment of that huge, colorful tropical expanse—"todo el trópico de oro, de escarlata, de añil"—which knows the burning fire of midday, the long and restless twilights, the vivid dawns, and that odor of forests which gallops on the wind to kindle dreams and desire . . . (**RV**, 102).

The reminiscences of other authors one may discern in the works of Juana de Ibarbourou—in her concepts, in her themes, in her images even—are due, undoubtedly, more to analogy than to direct influence. For her literary antecedents, as has been pointed out, may have been Omar Kháyyám, Ronsard, Anacreon—of whom she had probably never heard when she wrote those poems that bear their stamp. It is true one can find similarities—too obvious to be accidental or casual—between certain lines of hers and others of Delmira Agustini's.[21] But it is also true that there is much in common between the general tone and concept of her poems and some of Anna de Noailles, of whom, it is claimed, she never heard until striking resemblances in their work were noted. They have many things in common: their love of life, their dread of death and of old age, their passion for nature, their sensuousness and narcissism, their constant concern for love. But the Comtesse, as Zum Felde says, is as typical of the Old World with its culture, its finesse, it mundanity, its sophistication and refinement, as Juana is of the New, with its freshness, its naiveté, its spontaneity, its artlessness.

Physically both petite and alluring (the Comtesse more *femme du monde;* Juana more ingenuous), they differ greatly in personality and background. One had education and wealth and travel, and the company of outstanding men of letters; the other was a simple country girl—unread, practically untaught—who felt lost even in Montevideo. Yet, in spite of all this, their themes, their thoughts, and even their modes of expression are often surprisingly alike.[22]

Anna de Noailles' horizon—even the physical one—is far vaster than Juana de Ibarbourou's. She is constantly evoking the many countries, cities, landscapes—of Europe, of the Orient—that she has seen. Her desire for travel, therefore, although repeatedly sounded, lacks the poignancy and eagerness that one discerns, for instance, in *La rosa de los vientos*, for it is merely a longing to revisit familiar places, and not a spiritual need as in Juana.

The author of *Les éblouissements* makes innumerable and repeated allusions to writers—past and present—with whom she is familiar; and her poems abound in literary and mythological references—all indicative of a wide and heterogeneous culture, but which, at times, seem superfluous and cumbersome. Juana de Ibarbourou does not do this—for obvious reasons—and one cannot help thinking that for the type of poetry she writes this lack of learning is almost an asset.

The Comtesse de Noailles has a wider range of themes and interests, and yet, perhaps because she wrote so much more, she seems far more repetitious even than Juana de Ibarbourou whose insistence on the use of certain thoughts, words and expressions has often been criticized. The author of **Raíz salvaje** seems, therefore, by comparison, to give us the same themes simplified—reduced to the essentials—and not unduly ornate as they sometimes appear in the more effusive verse of the French poetess.

Because we know the Comtesse to be a woman of the world her "primitiveness" seems, at times, almost an affectation. She is, in all ways, far more experienced than Juana. In love, her desire and her pleasure are keener and wiser—based on a recollection of repeated voluptuous and sensual joys—and her surrender lacks the "purity," one might say, of that of the poetess of Melo, who never had cause, as did Anna de Noailles, to evoke her innocence with nostalgia . . .

Juana likewise differs from the other major poetesses of Spanish America, for her poems do not disclose those erotic yearnings, dissatisfactions and contradictions one so readily and commonly discerns in their piteous cries. She needs love for a happy, normal, healthy existence; and she is fortunate in having found it. But to her it is never that unbounded passion which to Delmira Agustini was "greater than life, greater than dreams"; nor that fruitless chastity that crucified María Eugenia Vaz Ferreira; nor that fever of possession that burned within Gabriela Mistral; nor that torturing emptiness that hounded Alfonsina Storni . . . And her reactions to the lover are always natural, sound; for he is *the end,* the goal, of her yearning, and not merely *the means* of getting to the pith of that inexplicable something which is love.

In all ways simple—without phobias, without complexes—she does not feel frustrated or misunderstood. Nor does she ask of the lover any but those things most easily granted and mutually desired. And she is willing to give as much as she demands, if not more. In this, as in many other ways: in her coquetry, in her "weakness," in the preponderance of the sensory, the instinctive, rather than the rational, mental attitudes, she is the most truly feminine of the major poetesses of Spanish America; for it is said that in those qualities lies the true essence of femininity.

NOTES

[1] From a letter written to J. de I. after having read *Las lenguas de diamante,* her first book. It is dated: Salamanca, 18-9-19.

[2] Emilio Oribe: "El grito" from *El castillo interior,* Montevideo, 1917.

[3] Vargas Vila, the Colombian novelist, recalling his recent visit to Montevideo, said of her: "Es sumamente ignorante, pero quizás allá resida el encanto de sus versos" (R. Maya, "Entrevista con Vargas Vila", in *Nosotros,* Buenos Aires, 1924, XLVII, p. 225). Very different was the impression she was to create some years later on another writer from Colombia, for Nieto Caballero says of her: "Estudia. Se ocupa en labores tan serias como la de investigar la razón de la influencia de grandes estadistas. Su comprensión es muy vasta" . . . (*Repertorio Americano,* San José, Costa Rica, Nov. 17, 1928).

[4] Notable among the poems are those written by Luisa Luisi, Alfonsina Storni, Emilio Frugoni and Fernán Silva Valdés.

[5] In *Nosotros,* Buenos Aires, 1919, XXXI.

[6] The following abbreviations will be used when quoting from the books of Juana de Ibarbourou: L: (*Las*) *Lenguas de diamante,* Buenos Aires, 1926; CF: *El cántaro fresco,* Montevideo, 1920; R: *Raíz salvaje,* Montevideo, 1924; RV: *La rosa de los vientos,* Montevideo, 1930.

[7]
Como un ala negra tendí mis cabellos Sobre tus rodillas.
Cerrando los ojos su olor aspiraste Diciéndome luego:

—¿Duermes sobre piedras cubiertas de musgos?
Con ramas de sauces te atas las trenzas?
Tu almohada es de trébol? (R, 11)

[8]
Tu beso fué en mis labios
De un dulzor refrescante.
Sensación de agua viva y moras negras
Me dió tu boca, amante.
Cansada me acosté sobre los pastos
Con tu brazo tendido, por apoyo (R, 43)

[9]
He bebido del chorro cándido de la fuente.
Traigo los labios frescos y la cara mojada . . . (R, 57)

[10]"Noche de lluvia", "Melancolía", "La laguna", "El baño", "La sed", "El remanso", "El pozo", "El estanque", "La copa", "El agua corriente", "Millonarios".

[11] "Los pinos", "Los árboles en la llanura", "El bosque", "Camino de álamos", "La higuera", "El nido".

[12] ". . . debe usted dejar las tristezas hasta que ellas vengan—que, desgraciadamente, teniendo como usted tiene un alma sensible y hasta ardiente, le vendrán . . ."

[13]
En la piragua roja del mediodía
He arribado a las islas de la Alegría sin causa (21)

Iremos por mares nunca navegados
A pescar los rojos pececitos de la alegría (35)

(Pudo tenerme cuando yo era un gajo de alegría
Curvado hacia su hombro grave) (41)

Llevo este don de felicidad
Como una lámpara encendida resguardada en las manos (49)

[14]
Mi alma sesga sobre los cauces sombríos
La garúa luminosa de la esperanza (18)

El navío de la esperanza
Ha olvidado los caminos claros de mi puerto (53)

Toda la tarde alisé un madero de esperanza
Para que fuera la proa
De un avión o una nave de triunfo (60)

[15]
"Canción del deseo de júbilo" (35)

Hervor del deseo de cantar alegre (37)

Avidez de tomar parte alborozada en la fiesta
De las cintas de colores y las cuentas fulgurantes (38)

[16]
Los que han probado sus aguas
Se han hecho soñadores y vagabundos (106)

[17] Ir,

> *Y apoyar la cabeza en las rodillas de lo desconocido* (48)

[18] The following poems best reflect this "longing for departure": "Día de felicidad sin causa", "Timonel de mi sueño", "Hora de espera", "Canción del deseo de júbilo", "Ir a conquistar el destino", "Días sin fe", "El grito", "Las olas", "El Atlántico".

[19] "Vida aldeana" evokes an idyllic picture of love which she likens to "a verse of Virgil lived before the luminous stars". (L, 139-140).

[20] "Selva: he aquí una palabra húmeda, verde, fresca, rumorosa, profunda . . . ¡qué palabra para mí tan llena de reminiscencias! Huele a eucaliptus, a álamos, a sauces, a grama; suena a viento, a agua que corre, a pájaros que cantan y pían, a roce de insectos y croar de sapitos verdes; evoca redondeles de sol sobre la tierra, frutas silvestres de una dulzura áspera, caravanas de hormigas rojas cargadas de hojitas tiernas, penumbra verdosa y fresca, soledad. ¡Oh, Dios mío, evoca mis quince años y toda mi alegría sana, inconsciente y salvaje!" (CF, 11-12)

> *Yo digo ¡pinos! y siento*
> *Que se me aclara el alma.*
> *Yo digo ¡pinos! y en mis oídos*
> *Rumorea la selva.*
> *Yo digo ¡pinos! y por mis labios pasa*
> *La frescura de las fuentes salvajes.*
>
> . . . . .
>
> *Yo digo ¡pinos! y me veo morena,*
> *Quinceabrileña,*
> *Bajo uno que era amplio como una casa . . .* (R, 27)

Ha pasado ante mí un hombre inclinado bajo un gran haz de pasto maduro . . . Por un instante un olor fresco y saludable se esparció en el camino y flotó en torno mío, llenándome de recuerdos . . . (CF, 75)

Mi hijo ha cazado un grillo y viene a traérmelo porque alguien le ha dicho que, guardándolo bajo una copa de cristal, recibiremos una alegría. ¿Una alegría? Entonces, pequeño mago chillón y negro, llévame con mi niño a aquel sendero que yo cruzaba todas las tardecitas cuando volvía de la escuela a mi casa. Muchos grillos cantaban entre los pastos del ribazo y yo hacía el camino abstraída y encantada, con una inconsciente y honda poesía en mi corazón. (CF, 23)

Una mariposita pequeña y amarilla ha venido a revoltear en torno de la luz . . .

—¿De dónde vienes, pequeñita? ¿Has estado acaso en aquel bosque rumoroso que yo recorría encantada y sin miedo cuando era niña? ¿Bebiste tal vez una minúscula gota de agua en aquella laguna toda bordada de juncos y de mimbres, que hay cerca del bosque de que te hablo? (CF, 15)

> *Me ha quedado clavada en los ojos,*
> *La visión de ese carro de trigo,*
> *Que cruzó rechinante y pesado,*
> *Sembrando de espigas el recto camino.*
> *¡No pretendas, ahora, que ría!*
> *¡Tú no sabes en que hondos recuerdos*
> *Estoy abstraída!* (R, 29)

[21] Juana reiterates Delmira's desire for a "raza nueva" in almost identical words:

> *Espera, no te duermas. Esta noche*
> *Somos acaso, la raíz suprema*
> *De donde debe germinar mañana*
> *El tronco bello de una raza nueva* (R, 14)

Many of her images and expressions re-echo Delmira's:

> *Y en el triángulo estéril que es hoy mi corazón*
> *Sólo ha brotado el* hongo *de la* desolación (L, 170)

> *O caza las arañas del tedio, o traga amargos*
> Hongos de soledad (Agustini, I, 55)

> . . . *¿No sientes*
> *Como me* nutro de *tu misma* sombra? (L, 87)

> . . . *algún alma . . . fué mía*
> *Se* nutrió de *mi* sombra (Agustini, II, 34)

> Silencio *en nuestros labios una* rosa *ha florido* (L, 7)

> *Y el* silencio *es una* rosa
> *Sobre su pico de fuego* (Agustini, I, 83)

[22] As we have given a rather full analysis of Juana de Ibarbourou's themes we do not deem it necessary to repeat here some of the thoughts or lines that will, inevitably, recall these of Anna de Noailles:

> *Je vais aller goûter et prendre dans mes mains*
> *Les bois, les sources d'eaux, la haie et ses épines*
> Le coeur innombrable, p. 68

> *Baiser l'air, goûter l'eau glissante, avoir le coeur*
> *Simple et chaud comme un fruit qui donne son odeur*
> Ibid., p. 81.

> *Je suis pleine d'élan, d'amour, de bonne odeur*
> Les éblouissements, p. 268.

> *Je sais tous les secrets des plantes et des eaux*
> L'ombre des jours, p. 68.

> *Etre dans la nature ainsi qu'un arbre humain*
> Le coeur innombrable, p. 73.

> *Et j'ai tenu l'odeur des saisons dans mes mains*
> Ibid., p. 7.

> *Mais l'odeur de l'été reste dans tes cheveux*
> Ibid., p. 76.

> . . . *ivre d'air, d'azur, de vent, de sel* . . .
> Les éblouissements, p. 103.

> *Lvre d'espoir, ivre d'amour, ivre d'été* . . .
> Ibid., p. 394.

> . . . *ivre d'odeur, de soleil et d'azur*
> Ibid., p. 398.

(Juana de Ibarbourou had said: "Estoy ebria de tarde, de viento y primavera", (R, 57).

Je demeure joyeuse, ardente et désirable
Le coeur innombrable, p. 107.

Que je vous aime, douce Vie
Les éblouissements, p. 159.

Mourante, je dirai qu'il faut jouir et vivre
Ibid., p. 5.

Déjà la vie ardente incline vers le soir,
Respire ta jeunesse,
Le temps est court qui va de la vigne au pressoir,
De l'aube au jour qui baisse.
Le coeur innombrable, p. 185.

Pourtant tu t'en iras un jour de moi, Jeunesse.
Tu t'en iras, tenant l'Amour entre tes bras.
L'ombre des jours, p. 3.

Tu dis que c'est l'heure de vivre,
Que le moment de vivre est court . . .
Les éblouissements, p. 14.

(The "tempus fugit" theme strikes a more personal—and dolorous—note in the poetesses who set so much store by their youth and desirability. They follow, to the letter, Robert Herrick's advice "To the virgins": "Gather ye rosebuds while ye may" . . .

Vivez si m'en croyez; n'attendez à demain:
Cueillez dès aujourd'hui les roses de la vie.)
Ne plus jamais vous voir, ô lumière des cieux!
Hélas! je n'étais pas faite pour être morte . . .
Les éblouissements, p. 52.

On songe au temps qui fuit, aux plus jeunes années
Ibid., p. 3.

Avoir quinze ans, rêver dans l'herbe haute et chaude
Où le soleil s'ébat . . .
Ibid., p. 15.

J'étais contente alors . . .
 . . . . .

Je me disais . . .
Ce sera tout un jour à courir dans le thym,
Près du merisier rose et près de la cigale,
Tout un jour à goûter la feuille et le pétale . . .
Ibid., p. 374.

Je me souviens des soirs en mai sur ma terrasse,
L'odeur d'un oranger engourdissait l'espace . . .
Ibid., p. 4.

WORKS CITED

Benvenuto, O. M. B. De. "La poesía femenina." In *Circunstanciales*, Montevideo, 1941, pp. 35-43.

Bula Piriz, R. "Sobre poetisas uruguayas." *Hiper*, [1943], no. 92, pp. 2-12; no. 93, pp. 8-16. [Agustini, Ibarbourou, Vaz Ferreira and Esther de Cáceres.]

Castillo Ledon, A. G. C. De. "Poetisas modernas de México." *BUPan*, 1940, LXXIV, 645-656.

Console, A. *Dos conferencias literarias: Poetas a los veinte años. Nuestras poetisas de boy.* Buenos Aires, Gráfs. Ferrari, 1935.

Cuenca, H. "Apunte sobre poesía femenina venezolana." *UniversalCar*, March 3, 1940.

Delgado, J. B. & V. Salado Alvarez. *Nuevas orientaciones de la poesía femenina.* México, Imp. Victoria, 1924.

Dumbar Temple, e. "Curso de la literatura femenina a través del período colonial en el Perú." *TresL*, 1939, no. 1, pp. 25-56.

Franulic, L. "Panorama de la literatura femenina actual." *Hoy*, 1937, VII, no. 316, pp. 63-66.

Goldberg, I. "Literary ladies of the South." *AmM*, 1926, VII, 448-452. [María Enriqueta, J. de Ibarbourou, G. Mistral, A. Storni].

Gonzalez Y Contreras, G. "Interpretación de la poesía femenina." *RNC*, 1941, II, no. 25, pp. 84-104.

Gonzalez-Ruano, C. *Literatura americana. Ensayos de madrigal y de crítica. I: Poetisas modernas.* Madrid, Imp. Artística, 1924.

Guiteras, J. P. "Poetisas cubanas." RCub, 1877, II, 481-502.

Ibarra De Anda, F. *Las mexicanas en el periodismo.* 2a ed. México, Edit. Juventa, 1937.

Jimenez, N. "Libros femeninos de memorias." In *Biografía y crítica*, Quito Ecuador, 1933, pp. 129-132.

Labarca, E. "Poetisas uruguayas." *A*, 1924, I, no. 1, pp. 60-62. [Adela Castell, María Eugenia Vaz Ferreira, Delmira Agustini, Juana de Ibarbourou, Luisa Luisi].

Labarca, E. "Mujeres de letras argentinas." *A*, 1924, I, no. 3, pp. 248-250. [Alfonsina Storni, Margarita Abella Caprile, Susana Calandrelli, Emilia Bertolé].

Latcham, R. A. "Aspectos de la literatura femenina en Chile." *RCChile*, 1923, XLV, 783-792.

Lee, M. "Puerto Rican women writers: The record of one hundred years." *BAbr*, 1934, XIII, 7-10.

Llach, L. "Tres escritoras mexicanas." *LyP*, 1934, pp. 165-174. [Laura Méndez de Cuenca, Isabel Prieto de Landázuri, Dolores Correa Zapata].

Mandolini, H. "Genio y lirismo femeninos." *Nos*, 1932, LXXVII, 326-340.

Medina, J. T. *La literatura femenina en Chile. Notas bibliográficas y en parte críticas.* Santiago de Chile, Imp. Universitaria, 1923.

Miranda S., Estela. *Algunas poetisas de Chile y Uruguay: Su sentido de la vida y su interpretación del paisaje.* Prólogo de N. Pinilla. Santiago de Chile, Nascimento, 1937. [G. Mistral, María Isabel Peralta, M. Monvel, Ma. E. Vaz Ferreira, D. Agustini, J. de Ibarbourou].

"La mujer dominicana en la literatura." *AmerH*, 1939, IV. no. 2, pp. 42-44.

Nano Lottero, r. *Tre poetesse dell'Uruguay*. Introduzione di Emilio de Matteis. Genova, Casa Editrice Nazionale, [1930?]. [M. E. Vaz Ferreira, D. Agustini, L. Luisi].

Nuñez Y Dominguez, J. De J. "La producción literaria femenina hispan-oamericana." *RRaza*, 1928, XIV, nos 151-152, pp. 28-30.

Oliva, A. "La sensibilidad infantil en nuestras poetisas." *Cal*, August 11, 1940.

Ossorio Y Bernard, M. *Apuntes para un diccionario de escritoras americanas del siglo XIX*. Madrid, La España Moderna, 1891-1892.

This bibliography is limited to the general works dealing with feminine Spanish American poetry, and to the modernist poetesses studied. There are excellent bibliographies on the poetesses of the past such as Sor Juana Inés de la Cruz and Gertrudis Gómez de Avellaneda. Likewise excluded are the studies on the history of woman in Spanish America, and feminine world literature, as well as other works consulted as general reference.

Myriam Yvonne Johnson (essay date 1982)

SOURCE: "Four Women in Search of Freedom," in *Revista / Review Interamericana*, Vol. XII, No. 1, Spring 1982, pp. 87-99.

[*In the following essay, Jehenson claims that careful inspection of Ibarbourou's poetry reveals the great emotional price she paid for conforming to conventional female roles.*]

Juana de Ibarbourou's life is almost wholly conventional. Unlike plain Alfonsina Storni, Ibarbourou was a beautiful woman. Unlike Delmira Agustini, she was happily married and the mother of a child she adored. At twenty four she publishes *Lenguas de diamante* (1919) which brings her immediate recognition. At thirty four she was crowned "Juana de América" in Montevideo; and is designated "Woman of the Americas for 1953" by the Union of American Women in New York. What was this woman like, then, whom women chose as their model, and who was lauded by the men and women of Latin America?

Ibarbourou's poetry pulsates with hedonistic joy and with a disdain of death. Like Titian's uninhibited and pagan Danaë, the Danaë of Ibarbourou's *Matinal* is wholly natural.[17] Juana de Ibarbourou's vision, unlike Delmira Agustini's Dionysian and anguished search for the transcendent, has a calm, Apollonian quality which is satisfied with living and with loving in the present (*Visión pagana*). Her poetry images that Golden Age which paganism has always seemed to offer with its uninhibited love of the body and of the body's natural functions.[18]

There are indications, however, that the *carpe diem* philosophy that seems to permeate her poetry is not consistent. The very thin line that has always separated the

Dionysian from the Apollonian is apparent in her poetry. In *La hora* a desperate awareness of time passing permeates her so called hedonism:

> Tómame ahora que aún es temprano
> Y que llevo dalias nuevas en la mano.
>
> Tómame ahora que aún es sombría
> Esta taciturna cabellera mía.
>
> Ahora, que tengo la carne olorosa,
> y los ojos limpios y la piel de rosa.
>
> Ahora, que calza mi planta ligera
> La sandalia viva de la primavera.
>
> Ahora, que en mis labios repica la risa
> Como una campana sacudida a prisa.
>
> Después . . . ah, yo sé
> Que ya nada de eso más tarde tendré!

Later she will admit that it is in solitude, when she knows no one is watching, that she removes her false smile and the simulated brilliance of either pride or joy from her eyes. There are reflections of the ambiguity already felt in *La hora*, however, even in her happiest verses. In *Hastío*, for example, she longs for a double example life, for the sexually active life of a Mary Magdalen which, filled with its "cien mil amores," is devoid of the monotony of her own life:

> Magdalena: yo a veces envidio lo que fuiste.
>
> Me aburre esta existencia tan monótona y triste.
> Hoy daría mi alma por los mil esplendores
> Y el vértigo de abismo de tus cien mil amores. . . .
>
> El inmenso bostezo de mi paz cambiaría
> Por el barro dorado de tus noches de orgía,
> Para luego ofrendarlo en un gran vaso lleno
> De ungüento de nardos, al rubio Nazareno.
>
> ¡Hoy daría mi alma por los mil esplendores
> Y el vértigo de abismo de tus cien mil amores!

In *Inquietud* she claims that regardless of how hard she tries, her beloved's kisses do not really soothe the nameless anxiety she experiences. In *Silencio* she laments having to live a life so slow and tiresome, and she describes it to some extent in her poem *El ruego*. Here she waits for her husband to come home to the dinner table she has so carefully prepared for him. She prays that he will not eat downtown once more with his friends while she awaits in tears. As she checks the strawberries yet once more, she prays, "Ahórrame, mi dios, la cruel angustia de sentarme hoy también, sola, a la mesa." At times she echoes Storni's most devastating poem *La que comprende*, although Ibarbourou seems devoid of Storni's bitterness. She wants to leave, to walk and walk but cannot because of the restrictions of being a woman and she laments: "Qué pena honda me da ser mujer." She reiterates the same dissatisfaction later on in her poetic-prose series in *Andar*. In her later book *Raiz Salvaje*, she will admit that she is tired of her well-ordered and civilized life, that she longs to be free and happy (Introduction). Yet in the once "happy" days of the well known *Despecho*, Ibarbourou had already recorded the ambiguity of her feelings:

> Ah, que estoy cansada! Me he
> reído tanto
> Tanto, que a mis ojos ha asomado
> el llanto
> Tanto, que este rictus que
> contrae mi boca
> Es un rastro extraño de mi
> risa loca . . .
>
> Mentira! No tengo ni dudas
> ni celos, ni inquietud, ni
> angustias, ni penas, ni
> anhelos. Si brilla en
> mis ojos la humedad del llanto
> Es por el èsfuerzo de reírme tanto . . .

The woman who emerges from her last book, *Perdida*, written after her mother and her husband have died, experiences the loneliness traditional in the "feminine" condition to which she has subscribed all her life. In *La hermanita* she longs for another child since she is alone now that her only child is grown. With nostalgia, she remembers in *La enredadera*, the almost symbiotic relationship she once enjoyed with her husband; and in *Mi voz, tu voz* that they both spoke with one voice. She lives now for her son (*Ensueño: Diario de una joven madre*), and with the memories of what she once had (*El cántaro fresco*).

As she gazes with envy in *Lunita* at the seventh child of her friend, the reader cannot help but feel pity for the successful "Juana de América" as she describes what for her would be a blissful future for the little girl, that she be blond, blue-eyed, and that she marry a prince. In a paradoxical way, it is with the "happy" and successful poet Ibarbourou who dreams of Prince Charmings as boons for little girls, and not with her tragic precursors, Storni and Agustini, that the reader experiences genuine discomfort. It is a suspicion that Ibarbourou has paid a price for the tranquility and contentment that have accompanied her internalization of conventional roles.

NOTES

[17] For her complete works, see *Juana de Ibarbourou: Obras Completas,* introd. Ventura García Calderón (Madrid: Aguilar, 1960).

[18] Erwin Panofsky and Fritz Saxl, "Classical Mythology in Medieval Art," *Metropolitan Museum Studies,* 4 (1932-33), 275-278.

FURTHER READING

Davies, Catherine. "Expression and Silence in the Poetry of Juana de Ibabourou and Idea Vilariño." In *Women Writers in Twentieth-Century Spain and Spanish America,* pp. 157-75, Lewiston: The Edwin Mellen Press, 1993.

> Compares Ibarbourou's writing style with that of fellow Uruguayan Idea Vilariño.

Dorn, Georgette M. "Four Twentieth-Century Latin American Women Authors." *SECOLAS ANNALS: Organization of the Southeastern Conference on Latin American Studies,* Vol. X, (March, 1979): 125-33.

> Offers a condensed explication of Juana de Ibarbourou's poetry and her contribution to Latin American literature.

Additional coverage of Ibarbourou's life and career is contained in the following sources published by the Gale Group: *Hispanic Writers*.

Sor Juana Inés de la Cruz
1651-1695

(Baptized Juana Inés de Asbaje y Ramirez) Mexican feminist, poet, playwright, scholar, and autobiographer.

INTRODUCTION

Embraced by her contemporaries as "la décima musa de México," or "the tenth muse of Mexico," Sor Juana Inés de la Cruz was a Hieronymite nun whose eloquent lyrical poetry has earmed her the reputation as the finest poet of seventeenth-century colonial Spanish America. An erudite scholar and early feminist, she wrote many *canciones,* sonnets, ballads, and *villancicos* (carol sequences) as well as *loas* (dramatic prologues), *autos sacramentales* (allegorical verse plays), and secular *comedias.* In addition, two of her prose works survive, including the famous *Respuesta a Sor Filotea de la Cruz* [1691; *Reply to Sister Philotea*], which is widely considered a defining document of feminist literature. In her writings, Sor Juana cultivated the themes and techniques of *conceptismo* and *culteranismo,* the typical baroque literary styles of contemporary Spain. Her works evince the breadth of her varied interests, which range from philosophy, theology, history, and science to music, art, and literature, and her themes generally concern the status of women and colonial culture. Although she published just two poetry collections in her lifetime, numerous editions appeared during the late seventeenth- and early eighteenth-centuries, a testament to her popularity throughout the Hispanic world. Since then, Sor Juana has been admired as an avatar of literary elegance and feminist sensibility.

Juana Inés de Asbaje y Ramirez was born in San Miguel, in the Nepantla of Mexico in 1651. Mostly self-educated. and an intellectual prodigy, she learned to read at the age of three. At the age of eight she wrote a *loa* honoring the Eucharistic sacrament. Her family moved to Mexico City when she was nine, where she mastered Latin in twenty lessons. By the time she was a teenager, she attended the viceroy's wife at the court of New Spain, dazzling the assembly with her beauty, wit, intellect, and knowledge. At court, she wrote all sorts of poetry celebrating social, ecclesiastical, and political events. In 1667, for unclear reasons, she withdrew from court life and entered the Order of the Discalced Carmelites. She grew ill as she adapted to the nuns' austere lifestyle and left after three months. Some biographers have ascribed her retreat to a soured love affair or an aversion to the vapidity of court. However, as she later revealed in her *Respuesta,* a cloistered life allowed her enough time to continue her intellectual pursuits, so she joined the convent of San Jerónimo in 1669. As a nun, Sor Juana studied the range of humane arts and sciences, collected scientific equipment and musical instruments, amassed a personal library comprising about 4000 books, and corresponded with many of the leading poets and scholars of her day as she continued to write plays and poems. She dedicated many works to the viceroy's family members and friends, one of whom arranged the publication of *Inundación castálida* (1689), her first poetry collection. As her repute spread, some authorities of the Catholic church disapproved of her secular studies, and they sought to curtail them. In 1690, the bishop of Puebla published Sor Juana's *Carta atenagórica,* which responds to the text of a sermon delivered in 1650, along with a letter reprimanding her. Since the letter was signed "Sor Filotea," Sor Juana addressed her own letter appropriately, the text of which is known as the *Respuesta.* Upon the publication of *Segundo volumen de las obras de Sóror Juana Inés de la Cruz* (1692). Juana relinquished her studies, sold her possessions (directing the proceeds to relieve the poor), and turned almost wholly to religious contemplation. During an epidemic in Mexico City, she became infected while caring for others and died on April 17, 1695.

Sor Juana's writings were first published in Spain, including a third volume of collected verse, *Fama y obras pósthumas de Fénix de México y Dézima Musa* (1700; *Fame and Posthumous Works of the Mexican Phoenix and Tenth Muse*). Encompassing a variety of forms and meters, her poetry exemplifies typical baroque prosody, featuring conceits and neologisms, Latinate syntax and vocabulary, and a highly ornate, artificial style. Sor Juana's lyric poetry represents her best known and most significant work, including, for instance, a verse portrait of the Countess of Paredes, the patron of *Inundación castálida*; a sonnet on a painting of herself that she saw as a vain effort at immortality; a number of "carpe diem" sonnets centering on the image of a rose; poems about hope and the vanity of human desires; several ballads expressing feminist ideals; the *villancicos* to Ste. Catherine of Alexandria; and verses on fidelity in love, always presented as a feminine quality, most notably in five sonnets paying tribute to mythological heroines who died for honor's sake. Perhaps her most famous and popular poem is "Hombres necios que acussés" ("Foolish Men Who Accuse [Women]), a witty commentary about men who unfairly blame women for iniquities instigated by those very men. *El Sueño* (1951; *The Dream*), a long poem containing 975 verses, probes the nature of human thought. As the world falls asleep and the poet dreams, her soul escapes her body and sees fantastic things; it tries to intuit all being but cannot, and returns with the awareness that true learning comes only through patience and perseverance. *El Sueño* condenses contemporary scholastic and scientific thought, covering the ancient philosophers, the Church Fathers, Florentine hermetic wisdom, and the ideas of Kircher and Descartes. The poem also features poetic commonplaces of the Renaissance, recast in Spanish baroque forms. The autobiographical *Respuesta a Sor Filotea* carefully argues a defense of her secular interests and pleads for equal educational opportunities for women. In a gentle display of her sense of humor, she promises to read more sacred literature, then proceeds to pack her letter with arguments, allusions, and quotations that show her knowledge of the Bible, the Church Fathers, the medieval Scholastics, and the religious writers of her own era. Recalling her childhood eagerness to learn to read and write, her adolescent rejection of marriage and her choice of the convent as a place to study, the *Respuesta* describes Sor Juana's intellectual vocation and cites many famous women from the Bible and from classical antiquity. Sor Juana's theatrical works consist of several *loas,* which relate Aztec mythology through female allegorical figures; two *comedias,* including *Amor es más labertino* (1689; Love is More a Labyrinth) and *Los empeños de una case* (1689; Trials of a Noble House), a parody of Calderónian "cape and sword" dramatic form; and three *autos sacramentales*: the biblical *El cetro de José* (Joseph's Scepter), the hagiographic *El mátir del Sacramento San Hermenegildo* (The Martyr of the Sacrament of St. Hermenegildo], and *Divino Narciso* [The Divine Fop], which combines the classical myth of Narcissus with the Aztec ritual sacrifice of the Corn God.

Interest in Sor Juana's life and works has revived considerably since the early twentieth century, and today she is acknowledged as the most significant lyric poet of colonial Spanish America. Although many critics have found the majority of her verse thematically trivial and stylistically derivative, her love poems have intrigued most scholars, who generally consider them her finest work. However, readers have puzzled over the tone and intent of these lyrics, for nearly all have detected the ambiguity informing them. Hence, critics have debated whether the love poetry belongs to the tradition of eroticism or mysticism, or both. This debate extends to the scholarship regarding Sor Juana's life, which has attracted as much criticism as her art— and has provoked similar contention. While many biographers have characterized her as a sincere, deeply religious woman and possibly a mystic, others have described her as a cautious cunning hypocrite, perhaps even an agnostic or atheist: in the 1940s a series of books appeared that questioned her fidelity to Catholicism, regardless of her *auto sacramentales*. These studies led to the so-called "black legend of Sor Juana," which more recent biographers, while not entirely dismissing it, suggest that it reflects the cultural conditions of the society in which Sor Juana lived and wrote. Indeed, a growing number of critics have emphasized her contributions to the struggle for women's liberation, particularly her *Respuesta.*

PRINCIPAL WORKS

Neptuno alegórico (poetry) 1680
Inundación castálida (poetry) 1689
Amor es más labertino [*Love is More a Labyrinth*] (drama) 1689

Los empeños de una case [*Trials of a Noble House*] (drama) 1689
Poemas (poetry) 1690
El mátir del Sacramento San Hermenegildo (drama) 1690
El cetro de José (drama) 1690
Auto sacramental del divino Narciso (drama) 1690
Respuesta a Sor Filotea de la Cruz [*A Woman of Genius: The Intellectual Autobiography of Sor Juana Ines de la Cruz; Carta athenagórica*] (autobiography) 1691
Fama y obras pósthumas de Fénix de México y Dézima Musa [*Fame and Posthumous Works of the Mexican Phoenix and Tenth Muse*] (poetry) 1700
Obras poéticas (poetry) 1715
El sueño [*The Dream*] (poetry) 1951
Obras completas. 4 vols. (poetry, essays, and drama) 1951-1957

CRITICISM

Kessel Schwartz (essay date 1975)

SOURCE: "'Primero Sueño'—A Reinterpretation," in *Kentucky Romance Quarterly,* Vol. XXII, No. 4, 1975, pp. 473-90.

[*In this essay, Schwartz examines "Primero Sueño" as a deeply symbolic poem that reveals Cruz's subconscious desires.*]

"Primero Sueño" was composed at a time when Sor Juana was undergoing a physical and spiritual crisis of the first magnitude. One can, of course, only guess at her psychological state and its reinforcement of the latent symbolism of her unconscious, but the poem seems to have offered her the opportunity to sublimate various thinly disguised impulses. Apparently unintentional symbols, when subjected to analysis, appear to be well-motivated, and her selection of relevant imagery reinforces the belief that in her case the unconscious influences were so overwhelming that her creative process was simply a transmutation, into an artistically and socially acceptable form, of her neurotic fantasies. Psychoanalytic investigations into origins may overlook some significant aspects of experience; one cannot prove that the principles of psychoanalysis have absolute validity, especially as they apply to the analysis of dream mechanisms and the metamorphosis of latent into manifest content. Yet through this approach the reader may understand the unconscious and hidden motivations of which Sor Juana herself was not aware, which, when analyzed, clarify certain distortions dwelling in the dark corners of the human mind and provide flashes of recognition of symbols that one knows or almost knows as his own.

Ludwig Pfandl, in his exploration of Sor Juana's psychoneurotic states, stresses the narcissistic fantasies and father fixation in **"Primero Sueño."**[1] Although one may agree with the clear evidence of the poetess's neurotic character in this poem, a completely different interpretation of her symbology seems indicated. Superficially the recall of the process of falling asleep, her lyrical masterpiece concerns the freedom of the soul in this state to seek universal knowledge, its ensuing failure and return. Intrinsically, allowing for the Gongoristic flights and the learned classic allusions, the poem, a combination of hypnagogic imagery and dream, appears to relate intimately to both the "Isakower phenomenon" and the "Dream Screen."

The "Isakower phenomenon" is associated with well-known hypnagogic manifestations of a visual, auditory, and tactile nature which occur when one is falling asleep or (more infrequently) awaking. It usually involves mouth sensations, feelings of giddiness, bodilessness, and floating or sinking. Often the drowser feels small in the presence of something large or heavy, described as a kind of balloon, and may hear indistinct, indecipherable murmurs. The visual impression is that of something shadowy, indefinite or jagged, and of vast size, occasionally accompanied by fire. Most striking of all is "the blurring of the distinction between quite different regions of the body . . . and between what is internal and what is external, the body and the outside world. We note too the amorphous character of the impressions conveyed by the sense organs."[2] In short, says Isakower, the dark masses which approach the person falling asleep, accompanied by the latter's inability to ascertain the division between body and mass, are reproductions of a little baby's sensations on falling asleep at the breast.

According to Isakower, sleep, even in adults, repeats an orally determined infantile situation, consciously or unconsciously associated with the idea of being a satiated nursling. Bertram D. Lewin, complementing this concept, postulates the idea of the dream screen as "the surface on to which a dream appears to be projected. It is the blank background, present in the dream, though not necessarily seen, and the visually perceived action in ordinary manifest dream content takes place on it or before it."[3] The representation of the mother's breast during this nursing situation (the dream screen) may be through a variety of solid or convex shapes or fluid objects, which, although not screens, serve as their equivalents since they are derived from the same nursing experience. The dream screen, an hallucinatory rather than real fulfillment of a wish to sleep, tells the dreamer that he is asleep and that there is a breast for him to sleep at. In other words the dream screen has the metapsychological structure of a dream, forming the background or projection drop for the dream picture.[4]

In the very first stanzas of **"Primero Sueño"** Sor Juana seems to reflect the dream's sleep-guarding function, and through her visual hallucinations, several repressed wishes:

> Piramidal, funesta, de la tierra
> nacida sombra, al Cielo encaminaba
> de vanos obeliscos punta altiva,
> escalar pretendiendo las Estrellas;
> si bien sus luces bellas . . .
> la tenebrosa guerra
> que con negros vapores le intimaba

> la pavorosa sombra fugitiva
> burlaban tan distantes,
> que su atezado ceño
> al superior convexo aún no llegaba
> del orbe de la Diosa . . .
> quedando sólo dueño
> del aire que empañaba
> con el aliento denso que exhalaba . . . [5]

In these lines we learn that the earth's dark shadow advances like some vain obelisk wishing to reach the unattainable light of the stars, which resist its treacherous attack and black emanations. The black tip, unable to reach the superior curve of the moon, attains only the concave surface of its sphere, creating a thick vapor or fog in the atmosphere. This threatening shadow, resembling closely the manifest element of a dream that frightens the child, is a true disturber. It involves a repressed impulse which "breaks through as a displacement or projection,"[6] and as an awakener is also often associated with the father's penis,[7] a phallic symbolism to which Pfandl alludes at some length in his own analysis of this poem.[8] The father intrudes into the timeless relationship or immortality at the breast. The moon, a standard mother symbol of regeneration, through its plane or segment of curved surface seems homologous to the dream screen as an idea of curved space reflecting early life experiences.

In immediately following lines the nocturnal birds utter dull, scarcely heard noises, an incomprehensible susurration:

> sumisas sólo voces consentía . . .
> tan obscuras, tan graves,
> que aun el silencio no se interrumpía.
>
> (p. 335)

Reemphasized later on as "solos la no canora componían capilla pavorosa . . . / y pausas más que voces, esperando . . ." and "sacrílego rüido, violador del silencio sosegado" (pp. 336-37), the sound is definitely associated with the process of falling asleep:

> Este, pues, triste son intercadente
> de la asombrada turba temerosa
> menos a la atención solicitaba
> que al sueño persuadía . . .
> su obtusa consonancia espaciosa
> al sosiego inducía
> y al reposo los miembros convidaba.
>
> (p. 337)

The murmurs recall the "Isakower phenomenon." Reinforcing a psychoanalytic interpretation, the poem's following passages appear to refer to repressed wishes, allayed and gratified by the revival of early situations of bliss in order to supplant disturbing genital instinctual wishes directed toward an incestuous object.

In these passages we meet Nictimene, in mythology turned into an owl for her incestuous relationship with her father. In the poem she hides in shadows and drinks olive oil from holy lamps. In other mythological references the daughters of Minias, turned by Bacchus into wingless bats, produce a kind of cloud within a cloud, "segunda forman niebla, / ser vistas aun temiendo en la tiniebla" (p. 336); Actaeon, seeing the moon goddess in her naked beauty as she bathed, was changed into a stag and torn to pieces by his own hounds, "El de sus mismos perros acosado . . . / tímido ya venado" (p. 338). These associations fuse with a series of breast images. The sea is a blue cradle in which the sun sleeps; the fish lie on dark cavernous breasts; destructive and fearful wild animals repose in concave rocky mountain caverns as if on hidden maternal breasts:

> El mar . . . ni aun la instable mecía
> cerúlea cuna donde el sol dormía . . .
> y los dormidos, siempre mudos, peces,
> en los lechos lamosos
> de sus obscuros senos cavernosos . . .
> senos escondidos . . .
> cóncavos de peñascos mal formados.
>
> (p. 337)

Sor Juana's shadow, myths, and breast references reveal her unconscious complexes and the archemotives behind the primitive triangle of mother, father, child. Sleep, stemming from oral satisfaction, is supposedly dreamless; but later, the child has more contact with the world and a longer waking life filled with more complex wishes which penetrate his world. The wish to sleep at mother's breast is opposed then by other wishes, the unconscious and disturbers which at times with some distortion, generate the manifest content of later dreams. Occasionally, the ego's censorship, surprised, allows deeply dreaded erotic, incestuous, and aggressive wishes passages into consciousness, sometimes with their full emotional charge.[9]

Again combining her dream with hypnagogic fancy, Sor Juana returns to the Isakower phenomena:

> De Júpiter el ave generosa . . .
> por no darse entera al descanso, . . .
> a un solo pie librada fía el peso
> y en otro guarda el cálculo pequeño
> —despertador reloj del leve sueño—,
> porque, si necesario fue admitido,
> no puede dilatarse continuado,
> antes interrumpido
> del regio sea pastoral cuidado . . .
> El sueño todo, en fin, lo poseía;
> todo, en fin, el silencio lo ocupaba . . .
> así, pues, de profundo
> sueño dulce los miembros ocupados,
> quedaron los sentidos
> del que ejercicio tienen ordinario . . .
> si privados no, al menos suspendidos,
> y cediendo al retrato del contrario
> de la vida, que—lentamente armado—
> cobarde embiste y vence perezoso
> con armas soñolientas . . .
>
> (pp. 338-39)

The eagle, with a rock in his claws, guards the king's sleep. Were the censor (eagle) to fail or drop the rock,

one would awaken. On falling asleep, the ego withdraws its interest and its cathexes from the external world in a gradual process. The world does not vanish suddenly, but various ego functions disintegrate and differentiations diminish. Part of the perceptual apparatus observes the body ego as its boundaries become blurred and fused with the external world, and perceptions become localized as sensations in a particular body region.[10]

Sor Juana next presents us with the powerful image of death, which in the poem changes the body into a corpse with a soul (alive when compared with real death). She reveals a neurotic wish for death, basically the desire for oral satisfaction and the ensuing sleep, of which death fears are the anxious equivalents,[11] transmutations of the original pleasure of falling asleep:

> y con siempre igual vara
> (como, en efecto, imagen poderosa
> de la muerte) Morfeo
> el sayal mide igual con el brocado.
>   El alma, pues, suspensa
> del exterior gobierno . . .
> solamente dispensa
> remota, si del todo separada
> no, a los de muerte temporal opresos
> lánguidos miembros, sosegados huesos,
> los gajes del calor vegetativo,
> el cuerpo siendo, en sosegada calma,
> un cadáver con alma,
> muerto a la vida y a la muerte vivo,
> de lo segundo dando tardas señas
> el del reloj humano . . .
>
> (p. 340)

Paradoxically, sleep which brings pleasure also involves the anxiety of being eaten and dying.[12] The young baby, feeling threatened by the aggression of its own id, projects that hostility onto the breast which it then fears as destructive, dreading being devoured and its own death.[13]

In the opening statement of the poem the poetess revealed her apprehension of being smothered and of being in the dark. The sudden separation from the outer world involves a fear of losing contact with waking life and of being engulfed in the breast or the intramaternal world of sleep (recall the host of maternal sleep symbols). It repeats childhood fears of going to sleep or of being put to sleep, the fantasy of being alive and not dead, which means being awake. The child fears bad dreams, that he will be hungry and unsatisfied. In the moment of relaxation that intervenes between the infant's satiation at the breast and the subsequent falling asleep, memory traces lend content to the wish to be eaten and help explain the reference to death and sleep as one, "cadáver con alma."[14]

The soul (ego), freed from the exterior guidance of the body, now affords vegetative heat to its weakened members; the heart, "este, pues, miembro rey y centro vivo/ de espíritus vitales" (p. 340), aided by the lungs, brings lifesaving breath to the entire body. Yet the tongue is dull and useless: "la lengua . . . torpe, enmudecía" (p. 341). The digestive apparatus changes food into energy for the parts of the body and provides *quilo* (a white, innocent liquid) to satisfy the system's voracious appetite:

> Y aquella del calor más competente
> científica oficina,
> próvida de los miembros despensera,
> que avara nunca y siempre diligente,
> ni a la parte prefiere más vecina
> ni olvida a la remota,
> y en ajustado natural cuadrante
> las cuantidades nota
> que a cada cual tocarla considera,
> del que alambicó quilo el incesante
> calor, en el manjar que . . .
> entre él y el húmedo interpuso
> su inocente substancia,
> pagando por entero
> la que, ya piedad sea, o ya arrogancia,
> al contrario voraz, necia, lo expuso . . .
>
> (p. 341)

The stomach then channels the refined vapors to the brain which interprets the sensory impressions, first using its imagination and reasoning facilities and then its memory to allow free play to fantasy and the creation of diverse imagery:

> ésta, pues . . .
> templada hoguera del calor humano,
> al cerebro envïaba
> húmedos, mas tan claros los vapores
> de los atemperados cuatro humores,
> que con ellos no sólo no empeñaba
> los simulacros que la estimativa
> dió a la imaginativa
> y aquésta, por custodia más segura,
> en forma ya más pura
> entregó a la memoria que, oficiosa,
> grabó tenaz y guarda cuidadosa,
> sino que daban a la fantasía
> lugar de que formase
> imágenes diversas.
>
> (pp. 341-42)

Associations of food and sleep are common phenomena in psychiatric literature. The patient, like an unsatisfied baby, wishes to eat so that he may sleep. Simmel sees in sleep, which he terms "nirvana," a turning "inward of the interest directed previously to objects and primarily to food. This interest . . . follows the food down the digestive tract, which supplies a kind of topographical indication, like a road map, of the locus of libidinal and aggressive internal action. The organism attacks the food internally as it had externally."[15]

In the next section of the poem Sor Juana writes that just as one can see all the boats which plow the sea in the magic mirror of the lighthouse at Pharos so fantasy views and copies the images of all things, including the spiritual beings who belong to the heavens. It reports the invisible and immaterial for the soul (ego) in mental, luminous colors but without light. Insofar as it is possible to conceive of the invisible, the ego reflects it in a kind of blank dream:

> así ella, sosegada, iba copiando
> las imágenes todas de las cosas,
> y el pincel invisible iba formando
> de mentales, sin luz, siempre vistosas
> colores, las figuras
> no sólo ya de todas las criaturas
> sublunares, mas aun también de aquéllas
> que intelectuales claras son Estrellas,
> y en el modo posible
> que concebirse puede lo invisible,
> en sí, mañosa, las representaba
> y al alma las mostraba.
>
> (p. 342)

Restored to its immaterial being and liberated from bodily ties, it reaches, as it travels the spiritual infinite spheres, for the divine being in whose image it was created:

> La cual, en tanto, toda convertida
> a su inmaterial ser y esencia bella,
> aquella contemplaba;
> participada de alto Ser, centella
> que con similitud en sí gozaba;
> y juzgándose casi dividida
> de aquella que impedida
> siempre la tiene, corporal cadena,
> que grosera embaraza y torpe impide
> el vuelo intelectual con que ya mide
> la cuantidad inmensa de la Esfera . . .
>
> (p. 342)

Isakower, postulating two parts of the ego, has demonstrated that a kind of estrangement occurs between them. One, wider awake, remains on a higher level of differentiation. The other, observed by the first part, regresses in order to enjoy the hallucinatory possession of a previously lost object. At the point of sleep the body ego reverts to an infantile phase of development, a primitive attitude from the ontogenetic standpoint. However, the attitude is always one of intensified self-observation at a certain distance from the experience.[16]

In **"Primero sueño"** the ego has the sensation of being on top of a mountain beside which Atlas seems a dwarf and Olympus scarcely a hill. The clouds which crown its proudest peak are, from the ego's vantage point, only a mist, a kind of girdle clinging around the mountain's wide thighs, to be ruptured by the wind or dissipated by the heat of the sun which drinks it up:

> puesta, a su parecer, en la eminente
> cumbre de un monte a quien el mismo Atlante . . .
> y Olimpo . . .
> aun falda suya ser no merecía:
> pues las nubes—que opaca son corona
> de la más elevada corpulencia,
> del volcán más soberbio que en la tierra
> gigante erguido intima al cielo guerra—,

apenas densa zona
de su altiva eminencia,
o a su vasta cintura
cíngulo tosco son, que—mal ceñido—
o el viento lo desata sacudido,
o vecino el calor del Sol lo apura.

(p. 343)

It must be remembered that in semi-waking states everything looks as though it were at an enormous distance,
which helps create a feeling in one that he is a giant. The
gigantic size represents the reproduction of the relative
proportions of things during childhood. Objects seem large
to a tiny observer. The extraordinary magnitude of the
hallucinated mass, therefore, denotes that a breast is being portrayed in respect to size as it was directly experienced by the baby. The mass, sometimes associated with
a feeling of dizziness and deep emotional stirring, is often
accompanied by an awareness of a vaporish white cloud
which may produce awe or grandeur.[17]

This idea is further reinforced by the following lines. Two
pyramids, solid masses, stretch upward so that their tips
disappear and become invisible to the sharpest eye: "Las
Pirámides dos . . . a la vista . . . entre los vientos se
desparecía . . ." (pp. 343-44). Attempting to reach the heights
of the celestial spheres, the ego's vision, frightened, falls
shattered at the base, which is bathed in shadowless light:
"hasta que fatigada del espanto / no descendía, sino des-
peñada / se hallaba al pie de la espaciosa basa" (p. 344). In
the same way that tongues of fire reach toward Heaven like
pyramidal points, so the human spirit, aspiring to find God,
the core of all essence, goes straight toward the center of
the circle which contains the entire eternal being:

las Pirámides fueron materiales
tipos solos, señales exteriores
de las que, dimensiones interiores,
especies son del alma intencionales:
que como sube en piramidal punta
al Cielo la ambiciosa llama ardiente,
así la humana mente . . .
a la Causa Primera siempre aspira
—céntrico punto donde recta tira
la línea, si ya no circunferencia,
que contiene, infinita, toda esencia.

(p. 345)

The two real pyramids, compared to the spiritual one, are
insignificant, as the ego tries to penetrate an area completely strange to it:

Estos, pues, Montes dos artificiales . . .
y aun aquella blasfema altiva torre . . .
si fueran comparados
a la mental pirámide elevada
donde—sin saber cómo—colocada
el Alma se miró, tan atrasados
se hallaran, que cualquiera
gradüara su cima por Esfera:
pues su ambicioso anhelo,
haciendo cumbre de su propio vuelo,

en la más eminente
la encumbró parte de su propia mente,
de sí tan remontada, que creía
que a otra nueva región de sí salía.

(pp. 345-46)

Pyramids, in mass and shape, would be almost perfect
representations of breasts; their relationships to the intruding tower and the search for the point of the circumference which contains all essence seem pertinent. In
psychoanalysis the common fear of falling from a height
usually portrays falling asleep and "clinging to a rock or
cliff . . . represents the mother . . ."[18]

Joyful, although somewhat restrained, the soul (ego) views
the totality of infinite space and creation, but frightened
by its incomprehensibility, "cúmulo incomprehensible,"
seeks escape in the shadow from the overblinding sun of
knowledge:

retrocedió cobarde . . .
no menos de la inmensa muchedumbre
de tanta maquinosa pesadumbre
(de diversas especies conglobado
esférico compuesto),
que de las cualidades
de cada cual, cedió: tan asombrado,
que . . .
por mirarlo todo, nada vía . . .
con la sobra de luz queda más ciego . . .
y a la tiniebla misma, que antes era
tenebroso a la vista impedimento . . .
sirviendo ya—piadosa medianera—
la sombra de instrumento
para que recobrados
por grados se habiliten . . .

(pp. 346-48)

The ego, in attempting to borrow some means of control
for its own fantasies, musters its defenses in an elaboration and transformation of wishes involved in the oral
triad (to eat, be eaten, and to sleep).

Like a ship driven onto a sandy beach, the ego seeks to
recover and engage in renewed effort to achieve the sweet
fruit of its desire, but the phenomena are so disconcerting
that the ego suffers the same catastrophe which previously had overtaken it:

permitiéndole apenas
de un concepto confuso
el informe embrión que, mal formado,
inordinado caos retrataba . . .
ciñendo con violencia lo difuso
de objeto tanto, a tan pequeño vaso . . .
mal le hizo de su grado
en la mental orilla
dar fondo, destrozado . . .
besando arena a arena
de la playa en bajel, astilla a astilla,
donde—ya recobrado . . .
juzgó conveniente

a singular assunto reducirse,
o separadamente
una por una discurrir las cosas . . .
advertido . . .
de no poder con un intüitivo
conocer acto todo lo crïado . . .

(pp. 349-50)

It therefore appeals for help to the thought processes to attempt to make some order out of the chaos overwhelming it and to understand the individual parts of the totality. In her search for omniscience Sor Juana's own perception and knowledge cannot provide her with a valid way to investigate the repressions which are responsible for her failure. She therefore shifts to an all-powerful, knowing Supreme Being:

sigue . . . y el prolijo, si blando,
continuo curso de la disciplina,
robustos le va alientos infundiendo,
con que más animoso
al palio glorïoso
del empeño arduo, altiva aspira,
los altos escalones ascendiendo . . .
hasta que insensiblemente
la honrosa cumbre mira
término dulce de su afán pesado
(de amarga siembra, fruto al gusto grato,
que aun a largas fatigas fué barato),
y con planta valiente
la cima huella de su altiva frente.

(p. 350)

The ego wishes to possess the "honroso cumbre" of the "altos escalones, término dulce de su afán" (the breast). The feeling of smallness and the merging with a larger unit, associated with going to sleep, and a corresponding anxiety, as expressed here, represent an orally based fear of being devoured and are related to agoraphobia and sensations of falling away from a height.[19] The thirst implicit in the references to the sandy desert waste, an image repeated later in the poem, may be the original gritty mouth feeling translated into a distinct visual form and projected onto the symbol of the breast. The invisible and formless elements, perceived in a direct immanent fashion, in the breast situation "may be brought into juncture with God, the invisible, so that He may be perceived in this same way, directly."[20] The mystic in his union with God enjoys an ineffable experience, outside of time, neither localizable or nameable, much as a dreamer of a "blank dream joins the invisible or formless but directly apprehended breast."[21]

Freud discussed the primary processes as the language of dream and delusion, "a process in which many thoughts may be condensed into one sign, in which emotions become mobile, metaphorical expression retains literal meaning, and the dangerous or the immoral is disguised in 'symbols'. In the structure of dreams not only the instinctual impulses and the repressed wishes of the id driving towards the primary process could be studied, but also the attempt of the ego to reorganize this chaos in semantics. This attempt Freud calls 'the secondary elaboration' of the dream."[22]

The continual associations are with breast imagery. The earth goddess offers terrestrial sweet food, the liquid of its maternal breast:

Thetis—el primero
que a sus fértiles pechos maternales,
. . . dulces apoyó manantïales
de humor terrestre, que a su nutrimento
natural es dulcísimo alimento . . .

(p. 351)

The ego, attempting to separate the essential from the secondary, thinks of mortal man whose mouth will eventually be closed with dust, "que, cuanto más altiva al Cielo toca, / sella el polvo la boca" (p. 352), but it is unable to fathom God's creation. Indeed, the mind balks at understanding any number of things such as a stream which appears and disappears or a flower, an exquisite mixture of red and white:

quien de la fuente no alcanzó risueña
el ignorado modo
con que el curso dirige cristalino
deteniendo en ambages su camino
—los horrorosos senos
de Plutón, las cavernas pavorosas
del abismo tremendo . .
quién de la breve flor aun no sabía . . .
mixtos, por qué, colores
—confundiendo la grana en los albores . . .
que—roto del capillo el blanco sello—
de dulce herida de la Cipria Diosa
los despojos ostenta jactanciosa,
si ya el que la colora,
candor al alba, púrpura al aurora
no le usurpó y, mezclado,
purpúreo es ampo, rosicler nevado . . .
preceptor quizá vano . . .
de industria femenil . . .

(pp. 353-54)

The structure of the universe is too overwhelming without the loving support of the Creator with whom it is impossible to identify, so the ego feels overcome by the oppressive weight of a very heavy globe:

¿cómo en tan espantosa
máquina inmensa discurrir pudiera,
cuyo terrible incomportable peso
—si ya en su centro mismo no estribara—
de Atlante a las espaldas agobiara . . .
y el que fué de la Esfera
bastante contrapeso,
pesada menos, menos ponderosa
su máquina juzgara, que la empresa
de investigar a la Naturaleza?

(p. 354)

As we have seen, Sor Juana is exhilarated by a feeling of liberation and union which, for the short time it lasts, seems clear. But it is a nonverbal or preverbal bliss, a primitive, narcissistic trust in sensory experiences which cannot be communicated, even by analogy. The common double phenomenon of good and bad sleep revealed here involves the sensation of immortality, heaven, or blank state following nursing, along with frustration and a feared death, unfulfilled anxieties, and guilt. Typically, one may fall from the heights to the foot of a cliff or rock where there will be a pool or yawning chasm or canyon to swallow the dreamer.[23] The "horrorosos senos de Plutón" and the mysterious caverns of the gigantic abyss to which Sor Juana alludes, even though she relates them to the myth of Persephone, are associations which are too apt to be accidental. As we have previously mentioned, the breast may be a shelter or a place of terror. The reference to the rose and the aureole and the association to feminine beauty seems to relate to the nipple more than to the whitish expanse of the breast. Since two sets of experience may combine (from the original nursing situation and elsewhere), this may be a later impression.

The ego searches for a solution, its will wrecked on sandy shoals, "entre escollos zozobraba" (p. 356). The stupor begins to vanish and the bonds of the dream to relax, "las cadenas del sueño desataban" (p. 356). The arms and legs begin to stir, although the mind is still fogged by sleep. The apparitions of sleep become diluted like vapor or light fog, smoke dispersed by the wind:

> los miembros extenuados . . .
> ni del todo despiertos ni dormidos,
> muestras de apetecer el movimiento . . .
> ya daban, extendiendo
> los nervios, poco a poco, entumecidos . . .
> a cobrar empezaron los sentidos . . .
> Y del cerebro, ya desocupado,
> las fantasmas huyeron,
> y—como de vapor leve formadas—
> en fácil humo, en viento convertidas . . .
>
> (pp. 356-57)

It seems as if a magic lantern were projecting on to a white wall unreal images painted with quivering reflections, helped by the obscurity as well as by light, so that the fleeting shadow represents an imagined body of three dimensions where in reality there scarcely exists a surface. Sor Juana's imagery clarifies a complex and confused corner of experience as it transmits verbally the precise picture of the dream screen:

> Así linterna mágica, pintadas
> representa fingidas
> en la blanca pared varias figuras,
> de la sombra no menos ayudadas
> que de la luz: que en trémulos reflejos
> los competentes lejos
> guardando de la docta perspectiva,
> en sus ciertas mensuras
> de varias experiencias aprobadas,
> la sombra fugitiva,
> que en el mismo esplendor se desvanece,
> cuerpo finge formado,
> de todas dimensiones adornado,
> cuando aun ser superficie no merece.
>
> (p. 357)

In the "Isakower phenomenon," large masses (breasts) approach beginning sleepers, grow, and finally merge with them. The dream screen, on the contrary, curves over into a convex surface and disappears, ending the process which begins with going to sleep. In this poem the shadow is the screen on which the dream is really projected, the flattened breast. Intruding preconscious or unconscious wishes that threaten to wake the sleeper from visual content and project the sleeper's ego onto the screen. Representations of the body or of its parts in the visual content of the dream mean that the body or that part is awake. It is an intruder and disturber of sleep, opposite to the tendency of the dream screen, pure fulfillment and the wish to sleep.[24]

Meanwhile, the half light of dawn approaches, confronting the night with the young soldiers of her radiant army, "contra la noche armada" (p. 358). Night deploys her own troops, her shadowy cape pierced here and there by luminous rays, and tries to gather her black squadrons to effect an orderly retreat:

> cuando—como tirana al fin, cobarde . . .
> intentó de sus fuerzas, oponiendo
> de su funesta capa los reparos,
> breves en ella de los tajos claros
> heridas recibiendo . . .
> a recoger los negros escuadrones
> para poder en orden retirarse . . .
>
> (p. 358)

But the light assaults the darkness which, stumbling over its own fear, cedes and retreats, surrounded by shadows, as the sunlight takes over and the sleeper awakens:

> cuando de más vecina
> plenitud de reflejos fue asaltada,
> que la punta rayó más encumbrada
> de los del Mundo erguidos torreones.
>   Llegó, en efecto, el Sol cerrando el giro
> que esculpió de oro sobre azul zafiro . . .
> líneas, digo, de luz clara . . .
> pautando al Cielo la cerúlea plana;
> y a la que antes funesta fué tirana
> de su imperio, atropadas embestían:
> que sin concierto huyendo presurosa
> —en sus mismos horrores tropezando—
> su sombra iba pisando,
> y llegar al Ocaso pretendía
> con el (sin orden ya) desbaratado
> ejército de sombras, acosado
> de la luz que el alcance le seguía . . .
> restituyendo
> entera a los sentidos exteriores
> su operación, quedano a la luz más cierta
> el Mundo iluminado, y yo despierta.
>
> (pp. 358-59)

The body, through with food, wants to sleep more but is awakened. The wish to sleep was the reason for the dream which serves as sleep's guardian. The fight between the sun and the night, involving the rolling away into the distance, and the striped blue paper sky, is a typical dream screen ending, which occurs just before awakening. Waking up itself involves flight from the object upon which the anxiety was displaced, just as the shadows, trapped in their own horror, flee the waking sun. In a reversal which provides a symmetrical ending to the poem, the light, in all its phallic symbolism, is now the disturber and awakener instead of the phallic shadow.

Some may choose to regard **"Primero Sueño"** as an anecdotal base on which to project a poetic experience rather than the record of a dream. Yet the latter interpretation also allows the reader to achieve an archetypal response. As with all difficult poetry the reader must seek the truth behind Sor Juana's feelings and slight suggestions in his own way, but it seems fairly clear that Sor Juana elucidates unconscious motives, activated by sleep, to achieve gratification through dream content. It seems obvious, also, that the poem reflects anxieties and emotional experience which she herself feels but cannot logically explain. In any event, in the ever-fascinating search for the real Sor Juana Inés de la Cruz, this admittedly limited interpretation of that anguished nun's unconscious motivations and their ontogenetic origins expressed in **"Primero Sueño"** may help the reader understand what she was trying to convey. Most of her poem seems deeply rooted in her unconscious depths, and she seems to have written it consciously to evade but subconsciously to clarify her creative and destructive impulses.

NOTES

[1] Ludwig Pfandl, *Sor Juana Inés de la Cruz: La décima musa de México* (Mexico, 1963), pp. 205-230.

[2] Otto Isakower, "A Contribution to the Patho-Psychology of Phenomena Associated with Falling Asleep," *International Journal of Psycho-Analysis*, XIX (1938), p. 333.

[3] Bertram D. Lewin, "Sleep, the Mouth, and the Dream Screen," *The Psychoanalytic Quarterly*, XV (1946), p. 420.

[4] Bertram D. Lewin "Reconsiderations of the Dream Screen," *The Psychoanalytic Quarterly*, XXII (1953), pp. 174-99.

[5] "Primero Sueño," in Sor Juana Inés de la Cruz, *Obras completas* (Mexico, 1951), p. 335. Further citations are to this edition.

[6] Bertram D. Lewin, "Phobic Symptoms and Dream Interpretation," *The Psychoanalytic Quarterly*, XXI (1952), p. 302.

[7] Ibid., p. 308.

[8] Pfandl, p. 340.

[9] See Bertram D. Lewin, *The Psychoanalysis of Elation* (New York, 1950), pp. 83-98.

[10] Isakower, p. 340.

[11] Lewin, "Sleep, the Mouth, and the Dream Screen," p. 431.

[12] Lewin, *The Psychoanalysis of Elation*, p. 112.

[13] Melanie Klein, *Contributions to Psychoanalysis, 1921-1945* (London, 1948). See also, Melanie Klein, "The Early Development of Conscience in the Child," in *Psycho-Analysis Today*, ed. by Sandor Lorand (New York, 1944), pp. 64-74.

[14] Lewin, "Phobic Symptoms," pp. 304-05.

[15] Lewin, *The Psychoanalysis of Elation*, pp. 126-27.

[16] Isakower, pp. 331-345.

[17] Lewin, "Reconsiderations," pp. 178-181.

[18] Lewin, *The Psychoanalysis of Elation*, p. 111.

[19] Lewin, "Phobic Symptoms," p. 313

[20] Lewin, "Reconsiderations," p. 191.

[21] Ibid.

[22] Ernst Kris, "Approaches to Art," in *Psychoanalysis Today*, ed. by Sandor Lorand (New York, 1944), p. 364.

[23] Lewin, *The Psychoanalysis of Elation*, p. 111.

[24] Lewin, "Sleep," pp. 427-33.

Octavio Paz   (essay date 1976)

SOURCE: "Sor Juana Inés de la Cruz," in *The Siren and the Seashell and Other Essays on Poets and Poetry*, translated by Lysander Kemp and Margaret Sayers Peden, University of Texas Press, 1976, pp. 3-15.

[*In the following essay, Paz favorably reviews Cruz's major works and provides an in-depth analysis of* Respuesta a Sor Filotea de la Cruz.]

In 1690, Manuel Fernández de Santa Cruz, bishop of Puebla, published Sor Juana Inés's criticism of the Jesuit Antonio de Vieyra's famous sermon, "Christ's Proofs of Love for Man." This **Carta atenagórica** [Letter worthy of Athena] is Sor Juana's only theological composition, or at least the only one that has survived.

Taken up at a friend's behest and written "with more repugnance than any other feeling, as much because it treats sacred things, for which I have reverent terror, as because it seems to wish to impugn, for which I have a natural aversion," the *Carta* had immediate repercussions. It was most unusual that a Mexican nun should dare to criticize, with as much rigor as intellectual boldness, the celebrated confessor of Christina of Sweden. But, if her criticism of Vieyra produced astonishment, her singular opinion on divine favors must have perturbed even those who admired her. Sor Juana maintained that the greatest beneficences of God are negative: "To reward is beneficence, to punish is beneficence, and to suspend beneficence is the greatest beneficence and not to perform good acts the greatest goodness." In a nun who loved poetry and science and was more preoccupied with learning than with her own salvation, this idea ran the risk of being judged as something more than theological subtlety: if the greatest divine favor were indifference, did this not too greatly enlarge the sphere of free will?

The bishop of Puebla, the nun's publisher and friend, did not conceal his disagreement. Under the pseudonym of Sor Filotea de la Cruz, he declared, in the missive that preceded the *Carta atenagórica*: "Although your discretion calls them blessings [the negative beneficences], I hold them to be punishments." Indeed, for the Christian there is no life outside of grace, and even liberty is a reflection of that grace. Moreover, the prelate did not content himself with demonstrating his lack of conformity with Sor Juana's theology but manifested a still more decided and cutting reprobation of her intellectual and literary affinities: "I do not intend that you change your nature by renouncing books, but that you better it by reading that of Jesus Christ . . . it is a pity that so great an understanding lower itself in such a way by unworthy notice of the Earth that it have not desire to penetrate what transpires in Heaven; and, since it be already lowered to the ground, that it not descend further, to consider what transpires in Hell." The bishop's letter brought Sor Juana face to face with the problem of her vocation and, more fundamentally, with her entire life. The theological discussion passed to a second plane.

Respuesta a Sor Filotea de la Cruz [*Reply to Sister Filotea de la Cruz*] was the last thing Sor Juana wrote. A critical autobiography, a defense of her right to learn, and a confession of the limits of all human learning, this text announced her final submission. Two years later she sold her books and abandoned herself to the powers of silence. Ripe for death, she did not escape the epidemic of 1695.[1]

I fear that it may not be possible to understand what her work and her life tell us unless first we understand the meaning of this renunciation of the word. To hear what the cessation of her voice says to us is more than a baroque formula for comprehension. For, if silence is "a negative thing," not speaking is not: the characteristic function of silence is not at all the same thing as having nothing to say. Silence is inexpressible, the sonorous expression of nothingness; not speaking is significant: even in regard to "those things one cannot say, it is needful to say at least that they cannot be said, so that it may be understood that not speaking is not ignorance of what to say, but rather is being unable to express the many things that are to be said." What is it that the last years of Sor Juana keep silent from us? And does what they keep silent belong to the realm of silence, that is, of the inexpressible, or to that of not speaking, which speaks through allusions and signs?

Sor Juana's crisis coincided with the upheaval and the public calamities that darkened the end of the seventeenth century in Mexico. It does not seem reasonable to believe that the first was an effect of the second. This kind of linear explanation necessitates another. The chain of cause and effect is endless. Furthermore, one cannot use history to explain culture as if it were a matter of different orders: one the world of facts, the other that of works. Facts are inseparable from works. Man moves in a world of works. Culture is history. And one may add that what is peculiar to history is culture and that there is no history except that of culture: the history of men's works and the history of men in their works. Thus, Sor Juana's silence and the tumultuous events of 1692 are closely related facts and are unintelligible except within the history of colonial culture. Both are consequences of a historical crisis little studied until now.

Denying this world and affirming another were acts that could not have the same significance for Sor Juana that they had for the great spirits of the Counter Reformation or the evangelists of New Spain. For Saints Theresa and Ignatius, renunciation of this world did not signify resignation or silence, but a change of destiny: history, and human action with it, opened to the other world and thus acquired new fecundity . . . . The truly personal portion of Sor Juana's work does not touch upon either action or contemplation, but upon knowledge— a knowledge that questions this world but does not judge it. This new kind of knowledge was impossible within the tenets of her historical universe. For more than twenty years Sor Juana adhered to her purpose. And she did not yield until all doors were definitely closed. Within herself the conflict was radical: knowledge is dream. When history awakened her from her dream, at the end of her life, she ceased to speak . . . .

In the temporal sphere New Spain had been founded as the harmonious and hierarchical coexistence of many races and nations under the shadow of the Austrian monarchy; in the spiritual sphere, upon the universality of the Christian revelation. The superiority of the Spanish monarchy to the Aztec state was somewhat similar to that of the new religion: both constituted an open order capable of including all men and all races. The temporal order was just, moreover, because it was based upon the Christian revelation, upon the divine and rational word. Renouncing the rational word—keeping silent—and burning the Court of Justice, a symbol of the state, were acts of similar significance. In these acts New Spain expressed itself as negation. But this negation was not made against an external power: through these acts the colony negated itself and renounced its own existence, but no affirmation was born out of this negation. The poet fell silent, the intellectual abdicated, the people rebelled. The crisis led to silence. All doors were closed and colonial history was revealed as an adventure without an exit.

The meaning of the colonial crisis may be misunderstood if one yields to the temptation of considering it as a prophecy of independence. This would be true if independence were solely the extreme consequence of the dissolution of the Spanish Empire. But it was something more and also something substantially different: it was a revolution, that is, the exchange of the colonial order for another. Or say it was a complete beginning again of America's history. In spite of what many think, the colonial world did not give birth to an independent Mexico: there was a rupture and, following that, an order founded on principles and institutions radically different from the old ones.[2] That is why the nineteenth century has seemed remote from its colonial past. No one recognized himself as being in the tradition of New Spain because, in fact, the liberals who brought about independence were of a different tradition. For more than a century, Mexico has lived without a past.

If the crisis that closed the period of the Austrian monarchy did not prophesy independence, then what was its meaning? Compared to the plurality of nations and tongues that comprised the pre-Hispanic world, New Spain presented a unitarian structure: all peoples and all men had a place in that universal order. In Sor Juana's *villancicos* ("Christmas carols") a heterogeneous multitude confesses a single faith and a single loyalty, in Nahuatl, Latin, and Spanish. Colonial Catholicism was as universal as the monarchy, and all the old gods and ancient mythologies, scarcely disguised, could be accommodated in its heavens. Abandoned by their divinities, the Indians, through baptism, renewed their ties with the divine and once again found their place in this world and in the other. The uprooting effect of the Conquest was resolved into the discovery of an ultraterrestrial home. But Catholicism arrived in Mexico as a religion already formed and on the defensive. Few have pointed out that the apogee of the Catholic religion in America coincided with its European twilight: sunset there was dawn among us. The new religion was a centuries-old religion with a subtle and complex philosophy that left no door open to the ardors of investigation or the doubts of speculation. This difference in historical rhythm—the root of the crisis—is also perceivable in other orbits, from the economic to the literary. In all orders the situation was similar: there was nothing to invent, nothing to add, nothing to propose. Scarcely born, New Spain was an opulent flower condemned to a premature and static maturity. Sor Juana embodies this maturity. Her poetry is an excellent showcase of sixteenth- and seventeenth-century styles. Assuredly, at times—as in her imitation of Jacinto Polo de Medina—she is superior to her model, but she discovered no new worlds. The same is true of her theater, and the greatest praise one can offer of *El divino Narciso* [*The divine Narcisus*] is that it is not unworthy of the Calderonian sacramental plays.

(Only in **"Primero sueño"** [*First dream*], for reasons that will be examined later, does she surpass her masters.) In short, Sor Juana never transcended the style of her epoch. It was not possible for her to break those forms that imprisoned her so subtly and within which she moved with such elegance: to destroy them would have been to repudiate her own being. The conflict was insoluble because her only escape would have demanded the destruction of the very foundations of the colonial world.

As it was not possible to deny the principles on which that society rested without repudiating oneself, it was also impossible to propose others. Neither the tradition nor the history of New Spain could propose alternative solutions. It is true that two centuries later other principles were adopted, but one must remember that they came from outside, from France and the United States, and would form a different society. At the end of the seventeenth century the colonial world lost any possibility of renewing itself: the same principles that had engendered it were now choking it.

Denying this world and affirming another were acts that could not have the same significance for Sor Juana that they had for the great spirits of the Counter Reformation or the evangelists of New Spain. For Saints Theresa and Ignatius, renunciation of this world did not signify resignation or silence, but a change of destiny: history, and human action with it, opened to the other world and thus acquired new fecundity. The mystic life did not consist so much of quitting this world as of introducing personal life into sacred history. Militant Catholicism, evangelical or reformist, impregnated history with meaning, and the negation of the world was translated finally into an affirmation of historical action. In contrast, the truly personal portion of Sor Juana's work does not touch upon either action or contemplation, but upon knowledge—a knowledge that questions this world but does not judge it. This new kind of knowledge was impossible within the tenets of her historical universe. For more than twenty years Sor Juana adhered to her purpose. And she did not yield until all doors were definitely closed. Within herself the conflict was radical: knowledge is dream. When history awakened her from her dream, at the end of her life, she ceased to speak. Her awakening closed the golden dream of the viceroyship. If we do not understand her silence, we cannot comprehend what **"Primero sueño"** and *Respuesta a Sor Filotea de la Cruz* really mean: knowledge is impossible, and all utterance flows into silence. In understanding her silence one

> *deciphers glories*
> *amid characters of devastation.*

Ambiguous glories. Everything in her—vocation, soul, body—was ambivalent. While she was still a child her family sent her to live in Mexico City with relatives. At sixteen she was lady-in-waiting to the Marquesa de Mancera, vicereine of New Spain. Through the biography by Father P. Diego Calleja we are able to hear the echoes of the celebrations and competitions in which the young prodigy Juana shone. Beautiful and alone, she was not without suitors. But she chose not to be the "white wall upon which all would throw mud." She took the habit, because, "considering my totally negative attitude toward matrimony, it seemed the most fitting and most decent thing I could choose." We know now that she was an illegitimate child. Had she been legitimate, would she have chosen married life? This possibility is dubious. When Sor Juana speaks of her intellectual vocation she seems sincere: neither the absence of wordly love nor the urgency of divine love led her to the cloister. The convent was an expedient, a reasonable solution, offering refuge and solitude. The cell was an asylum, not a hermit's cave. Laboratory, library, salon, there she received visitors and conversed with them; poems were read, discussions held, and good music heard. She participated from the convent in both intellectual and courtly life. She was constantly writing poetry. She wrote plays, Christmas carols, prologues, treatises on music, and reflections on morality. Between the viceregal palace and the convent flowed a constant exchange of rhymes and civilities, compliments, satirical poems, and petitions. Indulged child, the tenth Muse.

"The tender phrases of the Mexican language" appear in her *villancicos* along with black Congolese and the unpolished speech of the Basque. With complete awareness, and even a certain coquetry, Sor Juana employs all those rare spices:

> *What magic infusions*
> *known to the Indian herbsmen*
> *of my country spread their enchantment*
> *among my writings?*

We would be in error if we confused the baroque aesthetic—which opened doors to the exoticism of the New World—with a preoccupation with nationalism. Actually one might say precisely the opposite. This predilection for languages and native dialects—in imitation of Luis de Góngora—does not so much reveal a hypothetical divination of future nationalism as a lively consciousness of the universality of the empire: Indians, Creoles, mulattoes, and Spaniards form one whole. Her preoccupation with pre-Columbian religions—apparent in the prologue to *El divino Narciso*—has similar meaning. The functions of the church were no different from those of the empire: to conciliate antagonisms and to embrace all differences in one superior truth.

Love is one of the constant themes in her poetry. Scholars say that she loved and was loved. She herself tells us this in various lyrics and sonnets—although in **Respuesta a Sor Filotea de la Cruz** she warns us that everything she wrote, except for **Primero sueno**, was commissioned. It is of little importance whether these were her loves or another's, whether they were experienced or imagined: by the grace of her poetry she made them her own. Her eroticism is intellectual; by that I do not mean that it is lacking in either profundity or authenticity. Like all great lovers, Sor Juana delights in the dialectic of passion; also, for she is sensual, in its rhetoric, which is not the same as the rhetorical passions of some female poets. The men

and women in her poems are images, shadows "fashioned by fantasy." Her Platonism is not exempt from ardor. She feels her body is like a sexless flame:

> *And I know that my body—*
> *never inclining to one or the other—*
> *is neuter, or abstract, everything*
> *the soul alone safekeeps.*

The question is a burning one. Thus she leaves it "so that others may air it," since one should not attempt subtleties about things that are best ignored. No less ambiguous is her attitude toward the two sexes. The men of her sonnets and lyrics are fleeting shadows exemplifying absence and disdain. However, her portraits of women are splendid, especially those of the vicereines who protected her, the Marquesa de Mancera and the Condesa de Paredes. Sor Juana's poem that "paints the beautiful proportions of the Lady Paredes" is one of the memorable works of Gongoristic poetry. This passion should not scandalize:

> *To be a woman and to be absent*
> *is no impediment to loving you,*
> *for souls, as you know,*
> *ignore distance and gender.*

The same rationale appears in almost all her amorous poetry—and also in the poems that treat the friendship she professes for Phyllis or Lysis: "Pure love, without desire for indecencies, can feel what profanest love feels." It would be excessive to speak of homosexuality; it is not excessive to observe that she herself does not hide the ambiguity of her feelings. In one of her most profound sonnets she repeats:

> *Though you may thwart the tight bond*
> *that enclasped your fantastic form,*
> *it is little use to evade arms and breast*
> *if my fantasy builds you a prison.*

Her loves, real or imagined, were without doubt chaste. She loved the body with her soul, but who can trace the boundaries between one and the other? For us, body and soul are one, or almost so: our idea of the body is colored by the spirit, and vice versa. Sor Juana lived in a world based on dualism, and for her the problem was easier to resolve, as much in the sphere of ideas as in that of conduct. When the Marquesa de Mancera died, she asked:

> *Beauteous compound, in Laura divided,*
> *immortal soul, glorious spirit,*
> *why leave a body so beautiful,*
> *and why bid farewell to such a soul?*

Sor Juana moved among shadows: those of untouchable bodies and fleeting souls. For her, only divine love was both concrete and ideal. But Sor Juana is not a mystic poet, and in her religious poems divinity is an abstraction. God is Idea and Concept, and even where she visibly follows the mystics she resists mixing the earthly and the heavenly. Divine love is rational love.

These were not her great love. From the time of her childhood she was inclined toward learning. As an adolescent she conceived the project of dressing as a man and attending the university. Resigned to being self-taught, she complained: "How hard it is to study those soulless marks on the page, lacking the living voice of the master." And she added that all these labors "were suffered for the love of learning; oh, had it only been for the love of God—which were proper—how worthwhile it would have been!" This lament is a confession: the knowledge she seeks is not in sacred books. If theology is the "queen of the sciences," she lingers on her outer skirts: physics and logic, rhetoric and law. But her curiosity is not that of the specialist; she aspires to the integration of individual truths and insists upon the unity of learning. Variety does not harm general understanding; rather, it exacts it; all sciences are related: "It is the chain the ancients imagined issuing from the mouth of Jupiter, from which all things were suspended, linked one with another."

Her interest in science is impressive. In the lines of **"Primero sueño"** she describes, with a pedantry that makes us smile, the alimentary functions, the phenomenon of sleep and fantasy, the curative value of certain poisons, the Egyptian pyramids, and the magic lantern that

> *reproduces, feigned*
> *on the white wall, various figures,*
> *helped no less by the shadows*
> *than by light in tremulous reflections . . .*

Everything blends together: theology, science, baroque rhetoric, and true astonishment before the universe. Her attitude is rare in the Hispanic tradition. For the great Spaniards learning resolved into either heroic action or negation of the world (positive negation, to state it differently). For Sor Juana the world is a problem. For her, everything stimulates questions; her whole being is one excited question. The universe is a vast labyrinth within which the soul can find no unraveling thread, "shifting sands making it impossible for those attempting to follow a course." Nothing is further removed from this rational puzzle than the image of the world left us by the Spanish classics. There, science and action are blended. To learn is to act, and all action, like all learning, is related to the world beyond. Within this tradition disinterested learning is blasphemy or madness.

The church did not judge Sor Juana mad or blasphemous, but it did lament her deviation. In ***Respuesta a Sor Filotea de la Cruz*** she tells us that "they mortified and tormented me by saying, These studies are not in conformance with saintly ignorance, she will be lost, she will faint away at such heights in her own perspicacity and acuity." Double solitude: that of the conscience and that of being a woman. A superior—"very saintly and very candid, who believed that study was a matter for the Inquisition"— ordered her not to study. Her confessor tightened the ring and for two years denied her spiritual assistance. It was difficult to resist so much opposing pressure, as before it had been difficult not to be disoriented by the

adulation of the court. Sor Juana persisted. Using the texts of the church fathers as support, she defended her right—and that of all women—to knowledge. And not only to learning, but also to teaching: "What is unseemly in an elderly woman's having as her charge the education of young ladies?"

Versatile, attracted by a thousand things at once, she defended herself by studying, and, studying, she retreated. If her superiors took away her books, she still had her mind, that consumed more matter in a quarter of an hour than books in four years. Not even in sleep was she liberated "from this continuous movement of my imagination; rather it is wont to work more freely, less encumbered, in my sleep . . . arguing and making verses that would fill a very large catalogue." This is one of her most beautiful confessions and one that gives us the key to her major poem: dreaming is a longer and more lucid wakefulness. Dreaming is knowing. In addition to diurnal learning arises another, necessarily rebellious form of learning, beyond the law and subject to a punishment that stimulates the spirit more than it terrorizes it. I need not emphasize here how the concept that governs **"Primero sueño"** coincides with some of modern poetry's preoccupations.

We owe the best and clearest description of the subject matter of **"Primero sueño"** to Father Calleja's biography: "It being nighttime, I slept. I dreamed that once and for all I desired to understand all the things that comprise the universe: I could not, not even as they are divided into categories, not even an individual one. The dawn came and, disillusioned, I awoke." Sor Juana declared that she wrote the poem as a deliberate imitation of *Soledades* [Solitudes]. But **"Primero sueño"** is a poem about nocturnal astonishment, while Góngora's poem is about daytime. There is nothing behind the images of the Cordovan poet because his world is pure image, a splendor of appearances. Sor Juana's universe—barren of color, abounding in shadows, abysses, and sudden clearings—is a labyrinth of symbols, a rational delirium. **"Primero sueño"** is a poem about knowledge. This distinguishes it from Gongoristic poetry and, more finally, from all baroque poetry. This very quality binds it, unexpectedly, to German Romantic poetry and through that to the poetry of our own time.

In some passages the baroque verse resists the unusual exercise of transcribing concepts and abstract formulas into images. The language becomes abrupt and pedantic. In other lines, the best and most intense, expression becomes dizzying in its lucidity. Sor Juana creates an abstract and hallucinatory landscape formed of cones, obelisks, pyramids, geometric precipices, and aggressive peaks. Her world partakes of mechanics and of myth. The sphere and the triangle rule its empty sky. Poetry of science, but also of nocturnal terror. The poem begins when night reigns over the world. Everything sleeps, overcome by dreams. The king and the thief sleep, the lovers and the solitary. The body lies delivered unto itself. Diminished life of the body, disproportionate life of the spirit, freed from its corporeal weight. Nourishment, transformed into heat, engenders sensations that fantasy converts into images. On the heights of her mental pyramid—formed by all the powers of the spirit, memory and imagination, judgment and fantasy—the soul contemplates the phantasms of the world and, especially, those figures of the mind, "the clear intellectual stars" of her interior sky. In them the soul re-creates itself in itself. Later, the soul dissociates itself from this contemplation and spreads its gaze over all creation; the world's diversity dazzles it and finally blinds it. An intellectual eagle, the soul hurls itself from the precipice "into the neutrality of a sea of astonishment." The fall does not annihilate it. Incapable of flight, it climbs. Painfully, step by step, it ascends the pyramid. Since method must repair the "defect of being unable to know all of creation in an intuitive act," it divides the world into categories, grades of knowledge. **"Primero sueño"** describes the progress of thought, a spiral that ascends from the inanimate toward man and his symbol, the triangle, a figure in which animal and divine converge. Man is the site of creation's rendezvous, life's highest point of tension, always between two abysses: "lofty lowliness . . . at the mercy of amorous union." But method does not remedy the limitations of the spirit. Understanding cannot discern the ties that unite the inanimate to the animate, vegetable to animal, animal to man. Nor is it even feasible to penetrate the most simple phenomenon: the individual is as irreducible as the species. Darkly it realizes that the immense variety of creation is resolved in one law but that that law is ineffable. The soul vacillates. Perhaps it would be better to retreat. Examples of other defeats rise up as a warning to the imprudent. The warning becomes a challenge; the spirit becomes inflamed as it sees that others did not hesitate to "make their names eternal in their ruin." The poem is peopled with Promethean images; the act of knowing, not knowledge itself, is the battle prize. The fallen soul affirms itself and, making cajolery of its terror, hastens to elect new courses. In that instant the fasting body reclaims its own dominion. The sun bursts forth. Images dissolve. Knowledge is a dream. But the sun's victory is partial and cyclical. It triumphs in half the world; in the other half it is vanquished. Rebellious night, "recovered by reason of its fall," erects its empire in the territories the sun forsakes. There, other souls dream Sor Juana's dream. The universe the poem reveals to us is ambivalent: wakefulness is dream; the night's defeat, its victory. The dream of knowledge also means: knowledge is dream. Each affirmation carries within it its own negation.

Sor Juana's night is not the carnal night of lovers. Neither is it the night of the mystics. It is an intellectual night, lofty and fixed like an immense eye, a night firmly constructed above the void, rigorous geometry, taciturn obelisk, all of it fixed tension directed toward the heavens. This vertical impulse is the only thing that recalls other nights of Spanish mysticism. But the mystics seem to be attracted to heaven by lines of celestial forces, as one sees in certain of El Greco's paintings. In **"Primero sueño"** the heavens are closed; the heights are hostile to flight. Silence confronting man: the desire for knowledge is illicit and the soul that dreams of knowledge is

rebellious. Nocturnal solitude of the consciousness. Drought, vertigo, palpitation. But, nevertheless, all is not adversity. In his solitude and his fall from the heights man affirms himself in himself: to know is to dream, but that dream is everything we know of ourselves, and in that dream resides our greatness. It is a game of mirrors in which the soul loses each time it wins and wins each time it loses, and the poem's emotion springs from the awareness of this ambiguity. Sor Juana's cyclical and vertiginous night suddenly reveals its fixed center: **"Primero sueño"** is a poem not of knowledge but of the *act of knowing*. And thus Sor Juana transmutes her historical and personal ill fortunes, makes victory of her defeat, song of her silence. Once again poetry is nourished by history and biography. Once again it transcends them.

NOTES

[1] Among the few things found in her cell was an unfinished poem "in recognition of the inimitable writers of Europe who made their works greater by their praise."

[2] It is true that many colonial traits were prolonged until 1587—even to our own time—but as inertia, obstacles, and obstinate survival, like facts that have lost their historical meaning.

Janis L. Pallister   (essay date 1979)

SOURCE: "A Note on Sor Juana de la Cruz," in *Women and Literature,* Vol. 7, No. 2., Spring 1979, pp. 42-46.

[*In this essay, Pallister analyzes Cruz's poetic style and favorably reviews "Primero Sueño" and the* Rendondillas.]

Sor Juana Iñez de la Cruz (1651-95),[1] reputedly the illegitimate daughter of a *Mexicana* and a Spaniard, was an extremely learned woman, highly educated, and endowed with extraordinary literary gifts. Early in life, as Juana de Asbaje, she was a lady-in-waiting to the viceroy's wife. But since she lost no love on men, and since she was alienated from the men of her period (who lost no love on erudite women), some believe Sor Juana entered the convent to avoid the opposite sex and the need to marry. Yet, others say she escaped to the convent to console herself over the death of a lover. In either case, her chosen life as a nun afforded her the opportunity to develop her poetic abilities and to branch out into many realms of study, especially philosophy and theology.

Sor Juana's poetic style is highly formal, as would be expected from a poet of her period. She practiced the traditional *romance* and *redondilla,* and she wrote many sonnets, both devotional and secular. In both the devotional poetry and the secular verse we encounter a considerable amount of allegory. The poems of religious inspiration, although not really mystical, are reminiscent of Santa Teresa de Avila and of Christobalina Fernandez de Alarcón; the secular ones (in the Renaissance tradition and sometimes suggesting Góngora) reveal a rather heavy use of classical mythology. But despite these characteristics, which always tend to give us a sense of the old-fashioned, Sor Juana's work is characterized not only by elegance, but also by power, freshness and especially by modernity of attitude. In such a sonnet as the one addressed to a linnet ("**A un jilguero**") she reveals her profound lyricism and great tenderness:

> Sweet linnet, sad small bird,
> Who scarcely saw how beautiful the dawn
> when at the first note of your melody
> You met with death and therefore lost your cadence
> . . . . .
> Oh fortune ever sought-for, ever feared
> Who would have thought that your own life
> Would, by not stifling song, be death's accomplice?

This same sad and tormented sense of loss is expressed in many of the sonnets, but unfortunately we can scarcely quote them all here.[2] But let us at least say that the idea of death's omnipotence and omnipresence, and of the transitoriness of human life has perhaps never been more poignantly stated than by Sor Juana, who, reflecting upon "praises dedicated to a portrait of her by truth," concludes her refutations to these praises by saying:

> es cadáver, es polvo, es sombra, es nada.
> (it's a cadaver, dust, a shadow; it is nothing).

Sor Juana's "**Primero Sueño,**" considered by Elias Rivers to be "the most ambitious philosophical poem written during the Golden Age of Spanish letters,"[3] for all its complexity and density, abounds in energy and force. Many passages of this poem—which depicts the struggle between darkness and light and contemplates the limitations of the human mind in its struggle to grasp reality—announce the methods of symbolism and surrealism. The description of the nocturnal birds and bats is overwhelmingly beautiful in its rich Mediterranean orientation and in its awesome, majestic sweep:

> With slowest flight and chant, heard
> scarcely by the ear and even less by soul
> shameful Nictimene[4] peeks
> through the chinks of the sacred doors
> or the most propitious skylights, which
> open up a breach large enough for her aims,
> and she, most sacrilegious, reaches the gleaming
> sacred lamps of a perennial flame,
> which she puts out and even desecrates
> devouring from the clear liquor
> all the fatty matter which Minerva's tree
> (weighed down by fruit, by presses)
> oozed in its anguish and gave forth by force.[5]

And yet, within the context of the battle of the sexes, Sor Juana perhaps had more to say to her male contemporaries than she did about many other things. Despite her great talents as a lyric and philosophical poet, she is nevertheless best known for the *Redondillas*[6] in which she roundly scolds men for corrupting women and then spurning

them for not being pure. The practice, she says in essence, is enough to justify a woman's rebellion. Indeed, one can do no better than to offer here a sampling of these lines, in a translation which hopefully captures the original's realism, satire and irony, and thus shows yet another, indeed the most engaging, aspect of Sor Juana's personality and style:

> Stupid and simple-minded are you men who
> irrationally discredit every woman
> not seeing that you are yourselves the reason
> for all the things you tend to blame and boo.
>
> If with unequalled and with eager zest
> you harvest nothing but disdain from them
> why then, when you yourselves to ill provoke
>   them,
> is their good work your ever constant quest?
>
> Fiercely do you combat their each resistance
> and yet with the most solemn gravity
> you say that it was due uniquely to their levity
> rather than to your own great diligence.
>
> Your wild opinion and your fierce leers
> are of your own imagination merely figments;
> your valor's like the child's when he invents
> the bogeymen whom he then deeply fears.
>
> You'd find with simple-minded obstinacy
> that the ideal woman whom you seek
> is now-pursued-Alissa of the rosy cheek;
> but, having caught her, then you're after Nancy.
>
> What whim of man can be more curious
> than when he with a very dirty hand
> smudges the mirror in complete abandon
> and then declares the image spurious?
>
> You treat with the same attitude
> a woman's favors and a woman's scorn:
> for if she treats you badly you're forlorn;
> but should she yield you scold her and are rude.
>
> No woman wins a place in your regard
> since she who takes the very greatest care
> if she refuses you is thankless and unfair;
> but entertaining you is stained and marred.
>
> You are so simple-minded and so stupid
> that with no trace of constancy whatever
> one woman is as "cruel" branded forever,
> another as too easy mark for Cupid.
>
> Pray how indeed shall she herself be tempered,
> she who aspires to your little world of love,
> if she who spurns offends the heavens above,
> and she who was too easy has but angered?
> Between the anger and the bitter pain
> brought on by you at your most treacherous whim
> happy is she who has no Jack or Jim;
> So go ahead then, if you dare complain.

The pains of love brought on by all your rantings
which, having caused a woman to turn evil,
nevertheless expect to find in her no devil
simply invite her liberty to sprout wings.

Which one of them do you think more to blame
in any passion which has gone astray:
she who gave in, who could not hold at bay
the fallen man, or he who begged her without
    shame?

Or which one do you think is more to blame
(leaving aside whatever harm is done):
she who for money sins to give you fun,
or *you* who, giving money, sin the same.

But why should you feel guilt at what you've
    wrought
or be astonished that you feel such shame?
Accept them faulted as, because of you, they came,
or model them to suit what'er you sought.

Cease all of this your wild soliciting
and then it seems to me you might with reason
attack and criticize a bitch in season
should she your service try eliciting.

I am quite right to claim your arrogance
does battle with a multitude of arms,
since you fuse devil, world, and flesh's charms
within your promises and your insistence.[7]

Now, given the scope and quality of Sor Juana's literary achievements, why, one might ask, is she so little known outside the confines of the scholarly community, and then not even by all scholars of Romance literature? I think the answer is obvious. Not only was this poetry by a woman, but by a nun who—far from confining herself to the mystic postulations of an earlier Santa Teresa—presented strong and unpleasant statements destined to wound the male ego. Nevertheless, in the new climate that has been created for women's literature, one can hope that we will soon see Sor Juana's work completely revived, that we will see her discussed as the literary genius she is, and that a volume of the best of her work will soon be made available to the American poetry-reading public in a competent translation.

NOTES

[1] *Obras,* edited in 4 volumes by A. Méndez Plancarte (Mexico, 1951-57).

[2] The reader who does not know Spanish will find running translations of many of these sonnets in *Renaissance and Baroque Poetry of Spain,* (Dell, 1966), and also in *The Penguin Book of Spanish Verse.* All translations in the present article have been made by the author, Jan Pallister.

[3] In Dell, op. cit., p. 340.

[4] The screech owl.

[5] The olive tree; olive oil.

[6] Redondillas: A fixed poetic form, comprised of 8 syllable lines incorporated into a series of quartets rhyming A B B A.

[7] This translation first appeared in the *Women's Newsletter of the Northwest Ohio Feminist Community* (January, 1978).

Nina M. Scott (essay date 1985)

SOURCE: "Sor Juana Inés de le Cruz: 'Let Your Women Keep Silence in the Churches,'" *Women's Studies International Forum,* Vol. 8, No. 5, 1985, pp. 511-19.

[*In this essay, Scott reviews* La Respuesta a Sor Filotea *as a feminist treaty that reveals Cruz's passion for education and women's equality.*]

'Entréme religiosa, porque aunque conocía que tenía el estado cosas . . . muchas repugnantes a mi genio, con todo, para la total negación que tenía al matrimonio, era lo menos desproporcionado y lo más decente que podía elegir en materia de la seguridad que deseaba de mi salvación;' 'And so I entered the religious order, knowing that life there entailed certain conditions . . . most repugnant to my nature; but given the total antipathy I felt for marriage, I deemed convent life the least unsuitable and the most honorable I could elect if I were to insure my salvation.'[1] So stated Sor Juana Inés de la Cruz in her famous letter *La Respuesta a Sor Filotea* [*The Reply to Sister Philotea*] (1691), a statement of startling frankness, considering that she was answering a letter of censure from the Bishop of Puebla, an ecclesiastical superior to whom she, as a nun, owed humility and obedience.

The autobiographical nature of her letter is extremely important, given the marginality of women in the literary activities of her day and the fact that up until that time most accounts of women in the Church had been recorded by male authors. We are thus dealing with a primary source of great importance, yet critics rightfully caution about accepting all of the *Respuesta* at face value, recalling that autobiographies are self-portraits, the calculated impression an author wishes posterity to remember.[2] Nevertheless, the brilliance of Sor Juana's mind and the enigmatic nature of her personality have fascinated generations of *sorjuanistas,* who have grappled with the elusive prose of the *Respuesta* in attempts to decode the messages left by this supremely intellectual woman who dared to verbalize a radically feminist stance in a time and context most unpropitious to her.

The fact that she was a nun, formed within the ecclesiastical world of viceregal Mexico, is naturally crucial to her life and work. As daughter of the Catholic Church, she found herself alternately supported and censured by an institution whose attitudes towards women had been largely shaped by the internalization of patriarchal ideologies rooted in the earliest days of the Christian faith. The decision to take the veil ultimately forced her into a series of irreconcilable dilemmas which were at once personal, intellectual and spiritual. Her status as a woman and a nun demanded obedience, humility and self-efface-ment, yet during her lifetime Sor Juana was publicly acclaimed for her genius both by the secular and the ecclesiastical world, and was well aware that she was the intellectual superior of many of her male contemporaries. Sor Juana made a calculated decision when she chose the religious life, and from within the confines of her convent dared to challenge the Catholic establishment in ways which became increasingly radical. This study will focus on those aspects of Sor Juana's biography which deal with her decision to profess, and then examine three related works—the **"Primero Sueño"**, the *Carta atenagórica* and the *Respuesta*—to show the skill with which she manoeuvred to achieve maximum personal and intellectual freedom.

Born in 1651, Juana Inés de Asbaje y Ramírez de Santillana was the illegitimate daughter of a middleclass Mexican *criolla* and a Spanish captain. Family circumstances, coupled with her great intellectual precocity caused her to be sent at the age of eight to live with her relatives in the capital; at the age of about sixteen she was appointed lady-in-waiting to the Vicereine. Her status at court was brilliant, earned largely through her intelligence, charm and beauty, but as Octavio Paz points out, Juana had neither legitimacy, a dowry nor the protection of her father, so that she could not hope for an advantageous marriage (p. 152). The Viceroys made much of her, but as each one stayed in office for only a few years, she could not count on their sustained support. For all intents and purposes she was totally on her own. Her professed aversion to marriage was probably sincere, all the more because a husband would most likely have opposed her intellectual pursuits, and since this left her no other viable personal or economic alternatives, entrance into a convent was her best option. In the context of her time becoming a religious was a profession like any other and the convent also held the appeal of being the one place where women could legitimately devote their lives to study, to meditation and, in a limited way, to writing. From a contemporary perspective it is sometimes difficult to appreciate the great attraction which the communal religious life held for women of the past, yet from its inception in the patristic age, the convent had offered women a genuinely liberating choice. According to theologian Ruether, 'Asceticism redeemed woman from the female condition. It gave women license to reject traditional demands put upon them by society; . . . they could withdraw into female communities to engage in intense study and cultivation of their minds and spirits . . . Asceticism allowed women to move from being an object, governed and defined by others, to being a subject, in charge of defining one's life as a spiritual person' (Ruether, 1979: 151-152).

In the text of the *Respuesta* Sor Juana delineated those inclinations of her nature to which she would have given free rein, had she been able: 'que eran de querer vivir sola; de no querer tener ocupación obligatoria que embarazase la libertad de mi estudio, ni rumor de comu-

nidad que impediese el sosegado silencio de mis libros' (p. 446) 'wishing to live alone, and wishing to have no obligatory occupation that would inhibit the freedom of my studies, nor the sounds of a community that would intrude upon the peaceful silence of my books' (pp. 30-32). Given these tendencies, she vacillated in her decision to profess and sought the counsel of Antonio Núñez de Miranda, Jesuit confessor to the viceroys and her own spiritual advisor. According to her letter, Núñez convinced her that such inclinations were 'temptation' and urged her to take the veil. Juana Inés's physical and intellectual gifts, coupled with her uncertain social position were cause for alarm to Núñez and to at least one other cleric. Sor Juana's first biographer, the Spanish Jesuit Diego Calleja, repeatedly mentioned the risk of her being alone during those years, an opinion shared by Núñez: 'solía decir que no podía Dios enviar mayor azote a aqueste Reino que si permitiese que Juana Inés quedare en la publicidad del siglo' (Maza, 1980: 279) 'he used to say that God could not send a greater scourge upon this Realm than to allow Sor Juana to remain in the public eye of the time.'

The fact that at least two members of the religious establishment concurred in their estimation of her as risk and potential threat *as woman* was illustrative of the institutionalized bias against women transmitted to Christianity via Paul and the Pauline communities (Prusack, 1974: 97-98), subsequently to be furthered by Church Fathers such as Augustine and Jerome, for it was during the patristic period and the institutionalization of the celibate life that there developed a dualistic attitude towards humankind which equated woman with carnality and made her ethically dangerous to the more spiritual male (Ruether, 1974: 157). Both Calleja and Núñez were thus profoundly relieved when Juana professed in 1669 and was safely contained by the Jeronymite convent of St Paula.[3] However, profession was neither cheap nor easy and admission to elite nunneries was reserved for the legitimate daughters of the economically privileged white *criollos*. It was probably a combination of Núñez's influence and Juana's fame at court that caused the Jerony-mites to disregard her illegitimacy,[4] but, in a concession to appearances, Juana maintained in her document of profession that she was indeed of legitimate birth. It would not be the last time that she would manipulate the facts to serve her ends.

To a modern reader the *Respuesta* at times conveys a startling lack of vocation, but in her day it was common for many women to profess for decidedly pragmatic reasons without feeling that this contradicted their commitment to a religious life. Sor Juana never doubted her orthodoxy: it was the communal life which made her apprehensive, though a lax order such as hers allowed her considerable leeway. St Paula required perpetual enclosure, but the less-rigorous convents of colonial Mexico were by no means silent retreats of prayer and meditation. The nuns were attended by servants and slaves and enjoyed concerts, plays and other social gatherings. Sor Juana in particular was sought out and lionized by a succession of viceroys who facilitated and encouraged her sustained intellectual involvement in the secular world. The convent was as close as she could come to a room of her own in which to nurture her intellectual life.

Scholars have pointed out that the involvement of nuns in literary pursuits was not uncommon in Spanish America (Lavrin, 1983; Monguió, 1983) but Sor Juana was unique in the scope and direction of her writings, for she did not restrict herself to the religious meditations, lives of saints or reports of mystical visions which formed the literary *corpus* of her contemporaries. Her enlightened mind anticipated a more modern era and she scorned the praise allotted two other nuns for their literary activities: memorization of the Breviary and translations of Jerome's letters from Latin; to her it seemed regrettable that 'tales talentos no se hubieran empleado en mayores estudios con principios científicos' (p. 469) 'such talents could not have been employed in major studies with scientific principles' (p. 80).

The issue of permissible inquiry vs excessive and thus sinful striving for knowledge is the topic of one of Sor Juana's most complex and brilliant works: the **"Primero Sueño"** [**"First Dream"**]. Sabàt-Rivers judges the **"Sueño"** to be a late work and, along with the *Respuesta*, essential to an understanding of the nun as poet and as person (1982: 283). The poem is unquestionably important in revealing to the careful reader the ways in which she managed to question Church doctrine while appearing to remain within approved parameters (Montross, 1981: 39-40). The dream sequence was a common Baroque convention, as was the allegorical dialogue between the Flesh and the Spirit (or the Body and the Soul); in Sor Juana's poem, once she achieves the state of dream-sleep, her body is left totally behind while the soul soars upward, not towards the conventional spiritual union with Christ, but towards an intellectual comprehension of the nature of the Cosmos. Within the linguistic and conceptual labyrinths of her poem Sor Juana hid the transformation of a conventional topic into a controversial one: she converted the soul into pure intellect and addressed the topic of permissible vs sinful striving for knowledge. The soul as depicted in the **"Sueño"** does indeed transgress and is punished for it by a dual failure to reach its goal, all of which safely conforms to Church doctrine. But by simultaneously citing the myths of Icarus and Phaeton Sor Juana implied that the attempt to rise above restrictions and assert one's liberated self constituted success, even though it might provoke a devastating retaliation by the gods. Thus, while Sor Juana appears to endorse established doctrine, the covert message of the **"Sueño"** is quite the opposite.

Sor Juana's most famous religious work also did not conform to the norm. It is openly ambitious, and instead of the hidden agenda of the **"Sueño",** this time her defiance of the Catholic establishment was quite open. In 1690 she wrote a critique of a sermon by the Portuguese Jesuit Antonio de Vieira, acclaimed as a brilliant preacher both in Europe and in Latin America. Sor Juana's cri-

tique was at first in oral form but then someone, almost certainly the Bishop of Puebla himself, was so impressed that he requested her to put her comments in writing (Puccini, 1967: 35-36). Some critics have found it puzzling that Sor Juana should have chosen to comment on a sermon preached some forty years earlier, but upon reading both Vieira's text and her critique of it, her motives seem quite clear: her intellectual ambition fueled a desire to equal or surpass the Jesuit's accomplishments in speculative theology.

Vieira's sermon hinges on the nature of Christ's greatest *fineza,* or act of selfless love towards humankind. Not a little pompously he announced at the onset that he would not only refute the opinions of Saints Augustine, Thomas Aquinas and John Chrysostom on the subject, but that he had conceived of a *fineza* greater than any of theirs: 'Que ninguna fineza del amor de Cristo me darán, que yo no daré otra mayor; y a la fineza del amor de Cristo que yo dijere, ninguno me dará otra igual' (*OC:* 674) 'they will not think of one proof of Christ's love that I will not better, and the *fineza* of Christ's love which I shall state, no one will be able to equal.' Sor Juana began her critique by stating flatly that his undeniably brilliant arguments rested on a framework which was logically unsound. She must have realized her own daring at challenging a male adversary of a very powerful order, but in spite of several *pro forma* statements of humility, one senses that she is enjoying herself: 'que no es ligero castigo a quien creyó que no habría hombre que se atreviese a responderle, ver que se atreve una mujer ignorante, en quien es tan ajena este género de estudio, y tan distante en su sexo . . .' (p. 435) 'it is no small chastisement for one who believed that no man would dare to answer him to see that an ignorant woman dares to do so, to whom these studies are so alien and so little practised by her sex . . .' Sor Juana's critique is written in an informal, conversational style, for she stated in the *Respuesta* that she had no idea that the Bishop would publish her remarks,[5] but in print some of her more flippant statements must have jarred her readers: '¡Válgame Dios! . . . ¿Qué forma de argüir es ésta? (p. 418) 'Good Lord! . . . What manner of reasoning is this?' she asked at one point, and at another, which discussed Christ's presence on Earth, remarked impatiently, 'No gastemos tiempo: ya sabemos la infinidad de sus presencias' (p. 422) 'Let us not waste time: we already know the countless examples of His presence.' By means of copious biblical references she defended the stance of the three Church Fathers, which not only gave her a chance to demonstrate her own facility with Latin and mastery of scholastic methods, but also her profound knowledge of Scripture. However, some of her conclusions are theologically equivocal—indeed almost heretical—and Montross has shown that Sor Juana was not above manipulating the logical premises on which she based her refutations of Vieira (Montross, 1981: 10).

Her published critique unleashed a storm of controversy and criticism, but there were other factors at play besides her precarious theology. The fact that the author was a woman rankled many, and in the conclusion of her statement Sor Juana had also indulged in some unfortunate mythological allusions. Apparently totally deferential to Vieira's stature, she had remarked, '. . . y basta para bizarría en los pigmeos atreverse a Hércules. A vista del elevado ingenio del autor, aun los muy gigantes parecen enanos . . . ¿Pues qué hará una pobre mujer? Aunque ya se vio que una quitó la clava de las manos a Alcides, siendo una de las tres imposibles que veneró la antigüedad' (p. 434) '. . . it is a gallant act of courage for a pygmy to dare to challenge Hercules. In view of the great eminence of the author's ability, even the tallest giants appear as dwarfs. . . . What is a poor woman to do? Although it so happened that a woman took the club from the hands of Alcides, which was one of the three impossible tasks venerated by Antiquity.' Hercules, also known as Alcides, was famous for his strength but not renowned for his intelligence and Sor Juana also chose to mention the episode when Hercules was sent to serve the Lydian queen as atonement for one of his murderous frenzies. Omphale amused herself by making her slave put on dresses and do women's work while she wore the Thespian Lion's skin and appropriated his club, both emblems of Hercules' masculine prowess.[6] That Sor Juana should allude to this kind of role reversal while criticizing a Jesuit of the fame of Vieira was perceived as an act of insolence and impropriety and retribution was not long in coming.

Around the year 1690, a year of famine, pestilence and social turmoil in the viceroyalty as a whole, Sor Juana came under mounting pressure because of her notoriety and her continued activity in secular literature. The new Archbishop of Mexico, Francisco Aguiar y Seixas, was a severe and misogynistic prelate in no way disposed to judge her case favorably. 'A twisted Catholic puritan, he had a pathological aversion to women, to whom he imputed all the evils against which the Church inveighed. . . . If, through some mischance, a woman crossed his threshold, he promptly ordered all the bricks torn up and replaced upon which sacrilegious feet had trod' (Leonard, 1971: 160). The publication in Madrid of a volume of Sor Juana's poetry, much of which dealt with courtly love, could not have been less propitious. The Bishop of Puebla, who greatly admired Sor Juana and knew her well, apparently attempted to head off the wrath of the Archbishop by publishing a religious work of hers: the critique of Vieira's sermon. He gave her text the flattering title **"Carta atenagórica" ["Letter Worthy of Athena"]** but as the Bishop was not on good terms with Aguiar he covered himself by simultaneously drafting a letter of censure to the author; some critics speculate that he may also have wanted to give Sor Juana a chance to defend herself publicly (Paz, 1982: 531; Caudet, 1979: 139). The letter is short and generally kindly in tone, but it also specifically suggested that in order to avoid damnation Sor Juana would do well to curtail her excessive devotion to matters secular in favor of more worthy subjects: 'Lástima es que un tan gran entendimiento, de tal manera se abata a las rateras noticias de la tierra, que no desee penetrar lo que pasa en el Cielo . . . que

no baje más abajo, considerando lo que pasa en el Infierno' (*OC*: 696) 'What a pity that such a great mind should so surrender itself to the base follies of the world that it should not wish to comprehend that which passes in Heaven . . . may it not sink any lower, considering that which passes in Hell'. Perhaps to soften the effect of his letter the Bishop availed himself of the pseudonym 'Sor Filotea' (God-lover'), a polite conceit implying that his was not a letter from a superior but rather from a sister nun.

The receipt of this letter, coupled with the effects of long-standing criticism of her activities by many others, triggered a personal crisis in Sor Juana. Her rational mind had trouble reconciling the mixed signals of praise and censure sent out by her superior, and while the Bishop specifically stated that he did not hold with those who deplored all learning in a woman, the nun knew that the real issues were both her sex and her pursuit of secular knowledge. Her reply is an impassioned, eloquent and anguished attempt at intellectual self-justification.

Of the three works discussed in this study, the **Respuesta** is her clearest and most radical statement, one in which she articulated the many areas where she felt constrained by the convent: her loneliness in always having to work alone, with neither teachers nor peers with whom to discuss her ideas; the times her studies were forbidden by superiors anxious to have her remain in 'holy ignorance'; the constant interruptions of her work by her religious duties and the chafings inherent in a close communal life. On the one hand her status as a nun permitted her the greatest possible opportunity to exercise her intellectual vocation; on the other, her concomitant success coupled with her defiance of the rules put her on a collision course with the ecclesiastical establishment. In the context of her time her superiors felt completely justified in their censure of her excessive involvement in secular literature, but to Sor Juana's rational mind the Bishop's criticism appeared to be a case of monumental inconsistency. How could he publish her critique of Vieira's sermon, praise her Athenalike wisdom and simultaneously censure her publicly? With all due respect Sor Juana pointed out the fundamental conflict of his position: 'De donde se conoce la grandeza de vuestra bondad, pues está aplaudiendo vuestra voluntad lo que precisamente ha de estar repugnando vuestro clarísmo entendimiento' (p. 471) 'By which one knows the munificence of your kindness, for your goodwill applauds precisely what your reason must wish to reject' (p. 90).

Apart from the particular controversy over Vieira's sermon, Sor Juana also addressed other ongoing problems which she had with her church, particularly the restricted parameters within which it was disposed to let her intellect operate. She cited fear of the Inquisition as one factor which deterred her from dealing with religious subjects (Núñez was a member of the Inquisition) and defended her right to express herself in poetry by reminding the Bishop that parts of the Bible (specifically Psalms and the Song of Songs) were also in verse. She had been told to ignore secular subjects and devote herself to Theology, yet she, like the Austrian Jesuit Athanasius Kircher, whose scientific works she knew well, felt the Universe was a universal chain whose parts were intrinsically inseparable. As Sor Juana had already stated in the **"Sueño",** the mind had to proceed step by logical step from one concept to another before attempting to deal with Theology, the Queen of Sciences. The most basic problem, however, remained her sex and the gist of the **Respuesta** is her perception that the Church itself was inconsistent in its treatment of women. As the first step in her defense Sor Juana cited an extensive list of illustrious learned women, culled from mythological, biblical and historic sources. She was also aware that, at least in part, the antifeminist tradition in the Church had its roots in Scripture, specifically in the Pauline Epistles. The Bishop had referred to Paul in his letter, but stated that neither he nor the apostle subscribed to the position that women should be denied learning, 'cuando no sacan las letras a la mujer del estado de obediente' (**OC**: 695) 'as long as learning does not make a woman disobedient.' The Bishop had also mentioned St Jerome, spiritual father of Sor Juana's order and—in spite of his misogyny—the author of a number of celebrated letters which encouraged the education of young girls and women. Sor Juana took the surprising gambit of appealing to precisely these two saints for the authority to defend her own intellectual vocation and to plead for other women with similar inclinations. The method which she used in presenting her arguments provides the reader with significant insights into parts of the **Respuesta** generally ignored by critics: her use of Scripture and of certain patristic texts to support her case.

Given the expanded roles of women in today's Christian churches, scholars have rigorously re-examined those passages from Scripture which deal with the status of women. Most theologians agree that in the context of his time, Jesus's treatment of women was not only liberal but revolutionary; they have also underscored the significant role which women played in the establishment and furtherance of the early Christian church. A close reading of the letters of Paul attests to this fact, but the rules of conduct which he drafted for the Church at Corinth, as well as the later, deutero-Pauline Pastorals (Timothy and Titus), in effect continued the prevailing tradition of the subservience of women and excluded them from the public magisterium. As Parvey notes, Paul's theology endorsed the equality of women in Christ, but, as he was convinced that the end times were near, he kept to the traditional norms of social behavior; thus, what 'Paul had understood as a kind of temporary status-quo ethics . . . became translated two generations later into moral guidelines for keeping things as they are forever. The later Church . . . inherited two seemingly widely divergent messages: the theology of the equivalence in Christ; the practice of women's subordination' (p.146).[7]

Sor Juana was most interested in those passages of Paul which dealt with the issues of a woman's right to learn and to teach, and boldly went straight to 1 Corinthians 14.34, a passage which appears totally detrimental to her

position: 'Mulieres in Ecclesiis taceant . . .' 'Let your women keep silence in the churches: for it is not permitted unto them to speak; . . .' (King James Version). Sor Juana, however, demanded that this verse be interpreted not only according to its meaning within Paul's entire Epistle, but also within the context of its time. She noted that in the first-century Church women did indeed teach each other in the temples and offered the somewhat ingenuous explanation that they were told to be quiet because their voices interfered with the apostles' preaching. She also asserted that the phrase 'it is not permitted unto them to speak' referred to public preaching in church, from which women were barred and with which position Sor Juana agreed. She correctly stated that in 1 Corinthians 14 Paul was addressing the entire issue of the interpretation of Scripture, urging that only those who were truly qualified to carry on exegesis be permitted to speak. Citing Rom. 12.3, Sor Juana ultimately concluded, 'Y en verdad no lo dijo el Apóstol a las mujeres, sino a los hombres; y no es sólo para ellas el *taceant*, sino para todos los que no fueren muy aptos' (p. 463). 'And in truth, the Apostle did not direct these words to women, but to men; and that *keep silence* is intended not only for women, but for *all* incompetents' (p. 72). While on the subject, she addressed the Church's general lack of consistency in this matter. If it endorsed Paul, and all women were to keep silent, why then did the Church praise and encourage the writings of St. Theresa, Sor Agreda and others?

Sor Juana did not restrict herself to Paul's letter to the Corinthians, but cited as well the Epistles to Timothy and Titus, which also deal with rules of conduct for men and women.[8] To prove that Paul had permitted women to study in private she cited 1 Timothy 2.11: 'Mulier in silentio discat . . .' 'Let the woman learn in silence . . .' without, however, giving either the rest of the passage, which reads 'with all subjection' nor the following verse, which deals with the same topic: 'But I suffer not a woman to teach, nor to usurp authority over the man, but to be in silence.' In other words, she used only that part of the verse which supported her case, ignoring the context of the Epistle as a whole and contradicting herself with respect to what she said about the interpretation of 1 Corinthians 14.34. There was good reason for her to suppress 1 Timothy 2.12, for the issue of women as instructors to other women was another topic which passionately concerned her.

To support her arguments in favor of women teachers she quoted Titus 2.3 as: 'Anus similiter in habitu sancto, bene docentes . . .' 'The aged women likewise, that they be in behavior as becometh holiness, teachers of good things'; A look at the original text reveals that here, too, Sor Juana had manipulated her source. First of all she omitted that part of the verse which referred to aged women as prone to gossip and to too much wine and once again she cited out of context. Verses 4 and 5 of this same Epistle spell out what the good things were which the aged women were to teach, which were to exhort young women to be sober and discreet, to love their families, to keep a good home and to be 'obedient to their own husbands, that the word of God be not blasphemed.'[9] All of this Sor Juana suppressed, for she wished to emphasize the words 'bene docentes.' In Latin this phrase has an equivocal meaning, as is shown by the variety of ways modern translations have rendered it: 'teachers of good things' (King James Version); 'teachers well' (Douay-Rheims); 'to teach what is good' (New Oxford Annotated Bible); 'teachers of the right behavior' (Jerusalem Bible). Sor Juana chose to take Paul's charge—that women should teach—one step further and made it the heart of her plea for the education of all young women. She deplored the fact that many Mexican girls were deprived of any education whatever because the close association with male teachers was an invitation to scandal which many families wished to avoid. As her letter to the Bishop progressed, 'bene docentes' gradually became 'una mujer anciana, *docta en letras* y de santa conversación y costumbres' (p. 465, italics mine) 'an older woman, *learned in letters* and in sacred conversation and customs' (p. 76) who would further the education of young girls in reading, writing, mathematics, etcetera. Interpreted in this way and taken to the above conclusion, 'bene docentes' strayed mightily from the intention of the original Pauline text. Was she aware of the liberties she was taking with her Scriptural authority? It seems difficult to believe otherwise but she was so concerned with the lack of suitable women teachers that she would go to any length to prove her point: ' . . . es grande daño el no haberlas. Esto debían considerar los que atados a *Mulieres in Ecclesia taceant,* blasfeman de que las mujeres sepan y enseñen; como que no fuera el mismo Apóstol el que dijo: *bene docentes*' (p. 465) 'Then is it not detrimental, the lack of such women? This problem should be addressed by those who, bound to that *Let women keep silence in the church,* say that it is blasphemy for women to learn and to teach, as if it were not the Apostle himself who said: *The aged women . . . teaching well*' (p. 76).

In her search for another authority to support her position, Sor Juana also turned to the writings of St Jerome, the fourth-century ascetic, missionary and scholar who was in many ways curiously similar to Juana herself. A superb scholar and elegant stylist, he was nevertheless no great theologian (Fremantle, 1892: xxix-xxxiii), and his biographer Kelly points out other contradictory tendencies. Although Jerome's iconography portrays him as a solitary hermit, his stint in the desert was brief and unsuccessful and he felt happiest either in urban society or in his scholarly activities. A man of passion and strong sexual drives, he made the celibate life a condition for holiness and struggled all his life to resolve the conflict between his ascetic ideals and his love for pagan culture and literature. The text of the *Respuesta* attests to Sor Juana's familiarity with Jerome's famous letters, especially the ones written to or about women, which comprise about one-third of all extant epistles. Although overtly misogynistic, Jerome was nevertheless close to a circle of devout, patrician Roman women who gave him not only spiritual, but considerable financial support as well. Sor Juana mentioned the names of a number of these supporters of Jerome in her list of illustrious women of the past, emphasizing especially those of Paula and her two daughters Blesilla and Eustochium. Paula had headed one of the twin monastic

communities which Jerome established in Bethlehem and was also the patroness of Sor Juana's convent. Although Jerome and Paula had exchanged many letters during their twenty-two years of association, only two of these remain, and most of what we know of this woman comes from Jerome's long eulogy, directed to Paula's daughter Eustochium. In this letter (No. 108) he dwelled at length on her modesty, chastity, generosity, and pious nature; however, it was Paula's learning, which Jerome mentioned only in passing, which most interested Sor Juana, and is the one quality she chose to mention to the Bishop: 'Paula, docta en las lenguas Hebrea, Griega y Latina y aptísima para interpretar las Escrituras' (p. 461) 'Paula, learned in Hebrew, Greek and Latin, and most able in interpreting the Scriptures' (p. 66). Actually, Jerome did not refer to Paula's expertise in exegesis so much as to her facility in learning and speaking Hebrew, it being the widow Marcella who excelled in the interpretation of Scripture (No. 127). It is possible that Sor Juana confused the two letters, but given her *modus operandi* up to this point, the slip could just as well be intentional.

Just as she had suppressed Paula's humility and piety to highlight her intellect, Sor Juana also edited Jerome's letter to Laeta (No. 107) to serve her particular purposes. Laeta was Paula's daughter-in-law and this letter, one of Jerome's most famous, contained detailed instructions for the education of her infant daughter, also named Paula. As the child was destined to enter the community in Bethlehem, Jerome was most anxious that she be trained for her role from the start. Paula was to be taught to read and speak both in Latin and Greek and her readings were to be restricted solely to Scripture.[10] Sor Juana quotes at length from this letter, specifically excerpting the command to Laeta: 'And let it be her task daily to bring you the flowers which she has culled from Scripture' (Fremantle, 193). Sor Juana stressed the fact that the child's *mother* was to be her teacher, concluding that therefore both Paul and Jerome had sanctioned teaching by women. However, a comparison of Jerome's text with the passage cited by Sor Juana reveals that she had taken isolated sentences from different parts of his letter and recombined them in her quotation, suppressing Jerome's explicit instructions to Laeta that Paula was to have a male teacher, 'a master of approved years, life and learning' (p. 191) who would not think it beneath him to teach a girl. Read in its original context this passage implies that although Laeta is to listen to her daughter recite scriptural passages, she should above all be a 'model on which she may form her childish conduct' (p. 193). Basically, then, Paul and Jerome agreed that women could teach each other rules of conduct, a far cry from the kind of intellectual training Sor Juana advocated. She, however, continued to insist that both Paul and Jerome backed her position to effect reforms in the education of women: '¡Oh, cuántos daños se excusaran en nuestra república si las ancianas fueran doctas como Leta, y que supieran enseñar como mandó San Pablo y mi Padre San Jerónimo!' (p. 464) 'Oh, how much injury might have been avoided in our land if our aged women had been learned, as was Laeta, and had they known how to instruct as directed by Saint Paul and by my Father, Saint Jerome' (p. 74).

But however much she argued and manipulated all manner of authorities to support her case, Sor Juana realized that her basic problem with her Church remained that of her sex. In the conclusion of her letter she alternates between statements of assertion and humility, which attests to the conflictive position in which she found herself. Chastised for her critique of Vieira she demanded on the one hand, 'Mi entendimiento tal cual ¿no es tan libre como el suyo, pues viene de un solar?' (p. 468) 'My reason, such as it is, is it not as unfettered as his, as both issue from the same source?', then countered her own boldness with more submissive phrases: 'aprecio, como debo, más el nombre de católica y obediente hija de mi Santa Madre Iglesia, que todos los aplausos de docta' (p. 469) 'I esteem more highly my reputation as a Catholic and obedient daughter of the Holy Mother Church than all the approbations due a learned woman' (p. 84). Did she mean this or were such phrases artfully constructed rhetorical gambits designed to placate 'Sor Filotea' and other hostile readers? She had, after all, taken a daring step by refusing to repent when given a chance to do so, and instead took the initiative in voicing the demand for women—in and out of the Church—to have the right to an intellectual life.

But the Church as institution was too formidable an adversary to challenge for long, and in spite of Sor Juana's numerous admirers and supporters, majority opinion still demanded that she bow to the will of her superiors. This she appeared to do, and although she continued a number of literary activities, including revisions of previously published works as well as the creation of some new material, disastrous events beyond her control in the years 1691-1693 caused her to lose confidence in herself, diminish her literary output and abandon a position of public defiance. She recalled Núñez—who had withdrawn his spiritual support of her for two years—as her confessor, renewed her vows and sold off her voluminous library to propitiate the vindictive Archbishop. However, Paz points out that Juana had not given up her worldly goods even at her death (p. 601) and speculates that the renewals of her religious vows were probably *pro forma* admissions of repentance and humility. In his opinion she never totally capitulated. Formula or no, the context of her time still obliged the finest mind in colonial Spanish America to say of herself: 'Yo, Juana Inés de la Cruz, la más mínima de los esclavos de María Santísima Nuestra Señora, debajo de la corrección de la Santa Madre Iglesia Católica Romana' (p. 516) 'I, Juana Inés of the Cross, the most insignificant slave of the Most Holy Mary, Our Lady, under the guidance of the Holy Roman Catholic Mother Church'; 'Juana Inés de la Cruz, la más indigna e ingrata criatura de cuantas crió vuestra Omnipotencia' (p.520) 'Juana Inés of the Cross, the most unworthy and ungrateful creature ever created by Your Omnipotence'; 'Yo, la peor del mundo' (p. 523) 'I, the worst in the world.' She died in an epidemic four years after writing the *Respuesta*.

In *A Room of One's Own* Virginia Woolf, who never knew of Sor Juana, made several observations about women of the past that are curiously appropriate to the Mexican nun. Sor Juana most definitely suffered from a lack of private space, from a life fragmented by obligatory duties

and from the hostility with which many of her contemporaries reacted to her intellectual pursuits. Woolf had tried to imagine the fate of a gifted sister of Shakespeare and concluded that 'genius of a sort must have existed among women. . . . But certainly it never got itself on paper' (Woolf, 1957: 50). In Sor Juana's case it did, but the *Respuesta* documents the price she had to pay for having dared to defy the establishment and to ask the unaskable questions. Mistress of hidden meanings, of paradox and irony in her language, the conscious manipulation of both her sources and her methods of reasoning to serve her own ends reveals the lengths to which she would go in the battle to keep her voice from being silenced.

NOTES

[1] All Spanish quotations of Sor Juana's works (with the exception of the 'Primero Sueño') are from *Obras completas de Sor Juana Inés de la Cruz*, Vol. 4, and will henceforth be indicated in parentheses in the text. The English translations of the 'Respuesta a Sor Filotea' are from Margaret Sayers Peden's *A Woman of Genius* and will likewise be indicated in parentheses immediately following the quotations. All other translations are mine. The material cited here is from *Obras completas* (henceforth *OC*) (p. 466) and Peden (p. 30).

[2] Elías Trabulse, in 'Prólogo' to Francisco de la Maza's *Sor Juana Inés de la Cruz ante la historia* (p. 21). As I will be citing a number of different authors from this compilation, I will henceforth refer to it in the text as Maza (1980).

[3] Sor Juana had originally opted to join the severely ascetic Discalced Carmelites, the reformed order founded by St Theresa of Avila, but fell ill after a few months and withdrew from this community. She subsequently chose the more relaxed order of the Jeronymites.

[4] Núñez also persuaded a rich aristocrat to donate the sizable dowry that Sor Juana needed for admission to St Paula, a common act of charity among wealthy colonials.

[5] Paz is of another opinion: he feels that Sor Juana had prior knowledge of the Bishop's intentions (pp. 538-539) and that her permission to include the critique in the second volume of her works (1692) is proof positive of her initial consent to have this work published (p. 561).

[6] Similarly, in her play *Los empeños de una casa*, Sor Juana departed from the Baroque convention of having women disguised as men and introduced a man (Castaño) in woman's attire.

[7] For a detailed examination of this issue, see Ruether (1979), Fiorenza (1979) and Hewitt and Hiatt (1978: 45-56).

[8] In Sor Juana's time the Church accepted the Pastorals as authentic Pauline texts, but subsequent scholarship has shown that there are substantive variations in syntax and vocabulary in these Epistles and thus place them in the second half of the second century. (See Buttrick *et al.*, 1955: 343-344.) Ruether furthermore believes that the 'deutero-Pauline community that produced the pastorals also edited the original corpus of Paul, i.e. 1 Cor. 14:34' (1979: 143).

[9] With reference to this statement, *The Interpreter's Bible* explains: 'Since Christian women had been granted unusual freedom, it was necessary

that they should be unusually careful not to become insubordinate or neglectful at home. Otherwise their actions would scandalize and alienate pagans. To upset the order of the family would be to precipitate social revolution and bring ruin on the church' (p. 535).

WORKS CITED

Buttrick, George Arthur, *et al.*, gen. eds. 1955. *The Interpreter's Bible. The Holy Scriptures in the King James and Revised Standard Versions with General Articles and Introduction, Exegesis, Exposition for Each Book of the Bible,* Vol. 11. Abingdon Press, New York.

Caudet, Francisco. 1979. Sor Juana Inés de la Cruz. La Crisis de 1690. *Cuadernos americanos* 222 (enero-febrero): 135-140.

Cruz, Sor Juana Inés de la. 1957. *Obras completas de Sor Juana Inés de la Cruz. Comedias, sainetes y prosa,* Vol. 4. Salceda, Alberto G., ed. Fondo de Cultura Económica, Mexico.

Cruz, Sor Juana Inés de la. 1976. *Sor Juana Inés de la Cruz: Obras selectas.* Sabàt, Georgina de Rivers and Elías L. Rivers, eds. Editorial Noguer, Barcelona.

Cruz, Sor Juana Inés de la. 1982. *A Woman of Genius. The Intellectual Autobiography of Sor Juana Inés de la Cruz.* Trans. Margaret Sayers Peden. Lime Rock Press, Salisbury, Conn.

Fiorenza, Elisabeth Schüssler. 1979. Word, spirit and power: Women in early Christian communities. In Ruether, Rosemary and Eleanor McLaughlin, eds, *Women of Spirit. Female Leadership in the Jewish and Christian Traditions.* Simon and Schuster, New York.

Fremantle, W. H. Translator of *St. Jerome: Letters and Select Works.* See below.

Hewitt, Emily C. and Suzanne R. Hiatt. 1978. *Women Priests: Yes or No?* Seabury Press, New York.

Jerome, 1892. *St. Jerome: Letters and Select Works.* Vol. 6 of *A Select Library of Nicene and Post-Nicene Fathers.* Trans. W. H. Fremantle. Wm. B. Eerdmans, Grand Rapids, Mich.

Kelly, J. N. D. 1975. *Jerome. His Life, Writings and Controversies.* Duckworth, London.

Lavrin, Asunción. 1972. Values and Meaning of Monastic Life for Nuns in Colonial Mexico. *The Catholic Historical Rev.* 58 (October): 367-387.

Lavrin, Asunción. 1983. Unlike Sor Juana? The model nun in the religious literature of Colonial Mexico. *Univ. Dayton Rev.* 16 (Spring): 75-87.

Leonard, Irving. 1971. *Baroque Times in Old Mexico.* 1959. Rpt. University of Michigan Press, Ann Arbor.

Maza, Francisco de la. ed. 1980. *Sor Juana Inés de la Cruz ante la historia.* (Biografías antiguas. *La Fama* de 1700. Noticias de 1667 a 1892.) Revisión de Elías Trabulse. UNAM, México.

Monguió, Luis. 1983. Compañía para Sor Juana: Mujeres cultas en el virreinato del Perú. *Univ. Dayton Rev.* 16 (Spring): 45-52.

Montross, Constance. 1981. *Virtue or Vice? Sor Juana's Use of Thomistic Thought.* University Press of America, Washington, D.C.

Parvey, Constance F. 1974. The theology and Leadership of women in the New Testament. In Ruether, Rosemary Radford, ed., *Religion and Sexism.* Simon and Schuster, New York.

Paz, Octavio. 1982. *Sor Juana Inés de la Cruz o Las trampas de la fe.* Seix Barral, Barcelona.

Perelmuter Pérez. Rosa. 1983. La estructura retórica de la *Respuesta de Sor Filotea. Hispanic Rev.* 51 (Spring): 147-158.

Prusack, Bernard P. 1974. Woman: Seductive Siren and Source of Sin? Pseudoepigraphal Myth and Christian Origins. In Ruether, Rosemary Radford, ed., *op. cit.*

Puccini, Dario. 1967. *Sor Juana Inés de la Cruz: Estudio d'una personalità del Barroco messicano.* Edizione dell'Atteneo, Roma.

Richard, Robert. 1951. Antonio Vieira y Sor Juana Inés de la Cruz. *Revista de Indias* (enero-junio): 66-87.

Ruether, Rosemary Radford. 1974. Misogynism and Virginal Feminism in the Fathers of the Church. In Ruether, Rosemary Radford, ed., *op. cit.*

Ruether, Rosemary Radford. 1979. Patristic Spirituality and the Experience of Women in the Early Church. In Fox, Matthew, ed., *Western Spirituality: Historical Roots. Ecumenical Roots.* Fides/Claretian, Notre Dame, Ind.

Sabàt-Rivers, Georgina. 1977. *El Sueño de Sor Juana Inés de la Cruz: Tradiciones literarias y originalidad.* Tamesis, London.

Sabàt-Rivers, Georgina. 1982. *Sor Juana Inés de la Cruz.* In Madrigal, Luis Iñigo, ed., *Historia de la Literatura Hispanoamericana,* Vol. 1. Ediciones Cátedra, Madrid.

Vermeylen, Alphonse. 1976. El tema de la mayor fineza del amor divino en la obra de Sor Juana Inés de la Cruz. In Magis, Carlos H., ed., *Actas del Tercer Congreso Internacional de Hispanistas.* Colegio de México, Mexico.

Woolf, Virginia. 1957 [1929]. *A Room of One's Own.* Harcourt, Brace, Jovanovich, New York.

Frederick Luciani (essay date 1995)

SOURCE: "Sor Juana Inés de la Cruz and Her Worlds: An Exhibition at The Hispanic Society of America," in *Colonia/Latin American Review,* Vol. 4, No. 2, 1995, pp. 3-13.

[*Here, Luciani analyzes the manner in which Cruz's* Respuesta a Sor Filotea de la Cruz *simultaneously conforms to and defies the standards of a true autobiography.*]

The "autobiographical" anecdotes that Sor Juana Inés de la Cruz recounts in her **Respuesta a Sor Filotea de la Cruz** fall into two clusters. The first group relates to her childhood: learning to read at about age three by surreptitiously attending school with her older sister, begging her mother to allow her to attend university dressed as a boy, cutting her hair as punishment for not learning Latin on her self-imposed schedule, and abstaining from eating cheese. The second group relates to the period of about three months during which a conventual superior prohibited her from studying, believing that "el estudio era cosa de Inquisición." Sor Juana tells how she turned to the study of the "Book of Nature," making observations about her physical surroundings, and realizing experiments with everyday things at her disposal: spinning tops, frying eggs, and so on.

It is probably safe to say that these anecdotes are virtually inseparable from the contemporary reader's sense of who Sor Juana was. They possess the virtues of charm and visual clarity. They serve to elicit intellectual admiration for and emotional identification with Sor Juana. They are tantalizing in their brevity and relative scarcity, compelling in their succinct evocation of an entire personality. It is not surprising that they have served prominently as a source of information for biographies and fictional recreations of Sor Juana—and hybrid combinations of biography and fiction—and as material for critical assessments of Sor Juana's thought and work. They have often been granted, implicitly, the status of primary biographical source material, of equal authority to the few formal documents that give evidence of such things as the circumstances of Sor Juana's birth, her financial dealings, her taking and renewing of vows, her renunciation of profane letters, and so on. That authority has been reinforced as the anecdotes have become integrated into other biographical source material that is considered "canonical," beginning with Father Calleja's first biography of Sor Juana in 1700.

Common sense, however, suggests a certain caution when dealing with these anecdotes; it reminds us, as do modern theories of the genre, that all autobiography contains elements of self-invention, that the self evoked is—in varying degrees but inevitably—fictive, metaphorical, a rhetorical construct. A number of Sor Juana critics have sounded this note of caution. Elías Trabulse (1980), for example, observes the following with regard to the **Respuesta**:

> Un documento autobiográfico y escrito como contes-tación a una incitación previa, la **Carta** del obispo Fernández de Santa Cruz, y por una poetisa, es una invitación, sensata y razonable, a la desconfianza y a mantener una prudente reserva. Porque un documento autobiográfico es un autorretrato, en el que las más de las veces, el autor quiere dejarnos la imagen de sí que desea que contemple la posteridad. (21)

Theories of autobiography also remind us that the genre itself is historically and culturally embedded. Elizabeth Bruss (1976), for example, tells us:

> Living as we do in a time and in a literary community which recognizes autobiography as a distinct and deliberate undertaking, it is difficult for us to realize that it has not always existed. We read older texts, or texts of other cultures, and find in them autobiographical

intentions, but it is often our own conventions which inform this reading and give the text this force. . . . What is autobiography for us may have originally been only the by-product of another act . . . (6)

It is in this spirit that Sylvia Molloy (1991, 3) cautions us against a facile classification of the **Respuesta a Sor Filotea,** like other colonial Latin American texts, as true autobiography. Given the circumstances of their composition and their rhetorical goals, these texts are at best, she suggests, tangentially autobiographical.

Another caveat against an ingenuous or anachronistic understanding of the **Respuesta**'s anecdotes is offered by recent work on the genre of spiritual autobiographies of nuns in the sixteenth- and seventeenth-century Hispanic world. Critics like Jean Franco (1989), Kathleen Myers (1990), Stephanie Marrim (1991), and Electa Arenal and Amanda Powell (1994) have considered the ways in which Sor Juana's letter conforms to and departs from such autobiographies. Regarded in this light, the **Respuesta**'s anecdotes are revealed as topoi within a set of generic conventions: the topos of self-mortification, for example, in the anecdote of hair-cutting, or that of the overcoming of obstacles in the road toward the realization of a vocation, suggested by the various anecdotes that deal with Juana Inés'/Sor Juana's impeded desire for formal schooling. The formulaic nature of such topoi serve as a reminder to be wary about reading the anecdotes as historical data. At the same time, their *departures* from the generic norm of spiritual autobiographies—the calling that Sor Juana records is, after all, an intellectual, not a spiritual one—remind us of the essentially rhetorical purpose of the **Respuesta**'s anecdotes.

Rosa Perelmuter (1983) has demonstrated that the **Respuesta a Sor Filotea** is *formally* rhetorical: it conforms to the structure of the forensic speech as prescribed by classical and Renaissance manuals of rhetoric. Specifically, it is divided into exordium, narration, proof and peroration, with the second part, the narration, comprising the anecdotes that are our concern. The boundaries of the narration are clearly delineated: it begins, "Prosiguiendo en la narración de mi inclinación, de que os quiero dar entera noticia . . .", and ends "Esto no ha sido más de una simple narración de mi inclinación a las letras." Perelmuter points out that, strategically, this section appeals to the sympathy of the reader through both *ethos* (an underscoring of the good character of the writer) and *pathos* (a recounting of the various forms of suffering endured by the writer) and, in so doing, prepares the way for the proof that follows, a proof that argues for Sor Juana's right, and the right of all women, to study and teach privately.

Beyond its appeal to sympathy, Sor Juana's "autobiographical" *narración* conjoins with the argumentative substance of the **Respuesta**: that is, the narration supports, reflects, and even illustrates and performs, the letter's proof. One way of conceiving of the way that narration and proof work together strategically is Stephanie Marrim's (1987, 116) suggestion that the **Respuesta**'s anecdotes serve to place the responsibility for Sor Juana's intellectual inclination outside of herself, and with God. Sor Juana can therefore borrow the irrational language of the mystics to mount a "supremely reasoned self-defence, where the estranged *yo,* emptied of will by divine possession . . . relieve[s] Sor Juana of responsibility for either her abilities or inabilities . . ." This enables Sor Juana to "speak as the voice of knowledge by which she is 'possessed'. in its defence."

Another key to the strategic import of the anecdotes may lie in their individual clarity and vividness, their quasi-allegorical coherence, which give them the quality of an emblem or an exemplum. While in one sense, that noted by Merrim, the anecdotes collectively effect a kind of self-effacement—or perhaps, *defacement,* to borrow Paul De Man's (1979) metaphor for autobiography—, they may also constitute a form of self-invention or self-fashioning, a re-shaping of Sor Juana's own fame, a fame that, as Octavio Paz (1982) and Stephanie Merrim (1993) have both argued, Sor Juana consciously cultivated. Thus, the Sor Juana that Sor Juana evokes in her letter, responds to a textual Sor Juana that, by 1691 (the year in which Sor Juana wrote her **Respuesta**), enjoyed a vibrant existence in the imaginations of readers throughout the Hispanic realms.

Accordingly, beyond the idea that the anecdotes in the **Respuesta** serve rhetorical rather than autobiographical purposes, it is possible that they could be fabrications or citations)that is, of textual rather than biographic origin.[1] Such a possibility makes sense for an age in which, as Stephen Greenblatt (1980) has shown, individuals began to see themselves as self-fashionable, including through the medium of literary self-invention. Moreover, as Timothy Hampton has demonstrated, Renaissance "self-fashioning" often was achieved through reference to prior exemplary beings culled from textual sources. In her (at least) re-read life or (at most) re-invented life, Sor Juana may have felt a sense of fascination for the metaphorical or allegorical resonances found between textual exemplars and her earlier selves, and between her earlier selves and her present self as writing subject. Sor Juana's thought was drawn, after all, to the hidden correspondences and connections—"los ocultos engarces"—that, she believed, united all things in a universal chain. Her thought, for all of its capacity for close reasoning, often proceeds metaphorically, and her more explicitly fictional alter-egos, such as Phaëthon in the **"Primero sueño,"** stand in metaphorical (archetypal, exemplary) relation to her lyrical "I."

Such a hypothesis is unprovable, since there is no outside source that can corroborate or refute the biographical authenticity of the **Respuesta**'s anecdotes. But the hypothesis is, at least, sufficiently plausible to merit exploration. That exploration would proceed through the investigation of textual or intertextual references—possible sources for the anecdotes—with the goal of considering what sorts of strategies and meanings might be teased out of the **Respuesta**'s tight rhetorical weave. Such a procedure carries some potential dangers. There is the danger of setting up an either/or proposition (that is, the anecdotes are either authentic or fabricated), when, for writers in particular, historical selves are bound up inextricably with imagined selves and with the textual archetypes that inform both the way people live and the way people remember having lived. There is the danger of assuming that any textual coincidence or antecedent has to be a source. And there is the danger of over-extrapolating from potential textual sources for the anecdotes, of positing meaning or intent where there is only a coincidence or an echo.

But allowing for the unprovability of the hypothesis, and keeping in mind the potential dangers, textual source-hunting at very least opens up new possibilities for a more nuanced understanding of Sor Juana's rhetorical goals in her selection (or creation) of the details of her life story. An example may be found in one of the most vivid and memorable of the **Respuesta**'s anecdotes, one that occurs in the first group of anecdotes in the letter's *narración:*

> Empecé a deprender gramática, en que creo no llegaron a veinte las lecciones que tomé; y era tan intenso mi cuidado, que siendo así que en las mujeres—y más en tan florida juventud—es tan apreciable el adorno natural del cabello, yo me cortaba de él cuatro o seis dedos, midiendo hasta dónde llegaba antes, e imponiéndome ley de que si cuando volviese a crecer hasta allí no sabía tal o tal cosa que me había propuesto deprender en tanto que crecía, me lo había de volver a cortar en pena de la rudeza. Sucedía así que él crecía y yo no sabía lo propuesto, porque el pelo crecía aprisa y yo aprendía despacio, y con efecto le cortaba en pena de la rudeza: que no me parecía razón que estuviese vestida de cabellos cabeza que estaba tan desnuda de noticias, que era más apetecible adorno. (4:446)

Anecdotes like these, that suggest an element of masculinization in Sor Juana's early years, have provided provocative material for psychoanalytical studies of Sor Juana. Ludwig Pfandl ([1946] 1963, 95-96) offers them as proof of Sor Juana's "complejo de virilidad"; Urzaiz Rodríguez (1945, 13) finds "envidia del pene", Arias de la Canal (1988, 130) alleges "adaptación masoquista." Octavio Paz (1982, 122) professes wariness of such psychoanalytical allegations, and asserts, with reference to these anecdotes, "el origen eminentemente social y no psicosomático de la virilización" in the young Juana Inés. Yet the disclaimer—this is a case of *social* virilization—does not quite mask the fact that Paz, too, performs highly speculative recreations of Sor Juana's psyche, as reviewers of his book have pointed out.

The biographical fallacy can be sidestepped, however, by positing a textual antecedent rather than a psychological origin for this anecdote. Such textual antecedents might be sought in the general use of women's hair as a symbol of *vanitas* in literature, or in the hagiographic legends of women who acceded to masculine privilege or adventure through masculine disguise. But a much more direct antecedent for Sor Juana's anecdote is "hiding in plain sight" in St. Paul's first letter to the Corinthians, the very same epistle that furnishes the key passage for the scriptural exegesis that constitutes the most important part of the **Respuesta**'s proof: "mulieres in ecclesia taceant" ("let women keep silent in the churches"). Indeed, this possible textual source for Sor Juana's anecdote is directly related to St. Paul's injunction regarding female silence: both passages refer to proper behavior of women in public worship. As the two most provocative passages relating to feminist concerns in 1 Corinthians, they have been used on both sides of the issue of woman's historical role in the church. The passage is as follows:

> I want you to understand that Christ is the head of every man, and the husband is the head of his wife, and God is the head of Christ. Any man who prays or prophesies with something on his head disgraces his head, but any woman who prays or prophesies with her head unveiled disgraces her head—it is one and the same thing as having her head shaved. For if a woman will not veil herself, then she should cut off her hair; but if it is disgraceful for a woman to have her hair cut off or to be shaved, she should wear a veil. For a man ought not to have his head veiled, since he is the image and reflection of God; but woman is the reflection of man. Indeed, man was not made from woman, but woman from man. Neither was man created for the sake of woman, but woman for the sake of man. For this reason a woman ought to have a symbol of authority on her head, because of the angels. Nevertheless, in the Lord woman is not independent of man or man independent of woman. For just as woman came from man, so man comes through woman; but all things come from God. Judge for yourselves: is it proper for a woman to pray to God with her head unveiled? Does not nature itself teach you that if a man wears long hair, it is degrading to him, but if a woman has long hair, it is her glory? For her hair is given to her for a covering. But if anyone is disposed to be contentious—we have no such custom, nor do the churches of God. (11.3-16)

Scholars regard this passage as one of the most enigmatic ones in all of the Pauline epistles. It is not clear to what the passage is alluding—what specific practices among the Corinthians, what questions or issues referred to Paul by the Corinthian Church. The passage blurs the literal and figurative use of words (especially, "head"), and contains some particularly obscure references (e.g., "because of the angels"). It is not surprising that the passage has given rise to the most diverse interpretations; even today, those varying interpretations are used to argue different sides of the debate over the larger significance of St. Paul's teachings on women (see Fiorenza 1983; Wire 1990; Cobb-Stevens 1992; Bassler 1992). An example of this is the enigmatic declaration that "a woman ought to have a symbol of authority on her head, because of the angels." This has been read both as a statement of woman's subordination, and as an affirmation of woman's authority as prophetess, depending on whether "authority" is regarded as belonging to the male or to the female.

Some things, at least, can be said about the passage with some certainty. The passage recognizes the important role of women in the Corinthian Church, in public worship and prophesy. It seems to respond to some sort of transgression of traditional gender expectations by these women in the realizing of that important role. There is

a clear tension in the passage between a sense of an order of being that puts woman at the bottom of a hierarchy (God-Christ- Man-Woman) and, on the other hand, a sense of equality between the sexes. There is a call for proper male and female behavior, that argues according to custom and according to Nature. And head covering (hair, the veil) is referred to both literally (some particular custom must be referred to here) and metaphorically, to express something about women and the Word, about the relative status of the genders with regard to accession to spiritual insight—although what that something is remains unclear.

If this passage from 1 Corinthians is the source of Sor Juana's anecdote, any explicit or implicit message that it contains would be part of overall strategies of enlightenment and persuasion directed toward Sor Juana's addressee, the Bishop of Puebla (who would be as conversant as Sor Juana with the passage). But what is that message? What meaning, what rhetorical end, can be attached to Sor Juana's recasting of her own life in terms of this scriptural antecedent?

A tempting, but facile answer to this question might be sought in the enticing sentences "For if a woman will not veil herself, then she should cut off her hair; but if it is disgraceful for a woman to have her hair cut off or to be shaved, she should wear a veil." Especially since Sor Juana's anecdote comes immediately before her explanation of her decision to "take the veil," (indeed, with no transition at all, as if a connection were implied), the Pauline passage tempts with its enigmatic words about the connection between head-shearing and head-veiling. It could be read as an encoded disclosure of Sor Juana's motives for becoming a nun, motives that had to do with frustrated self-masculinizing impulses.

Yet even avoiding this temptation, it is not unreasonable to propose that St. Paul's sentence could, somehow, offer a kind of bridge between these two contiguous sentences in the *Respuesta*:

> . . . no me parecía razón que estuviese vestida de cabellos cabeza que estaba tan desnuda de noticias, que era más apetecible adorno. Entréme religiosa porque aunque conocía que tenía el estado cosas . . . , muchas repugnantes a mi genio, con todo, para la total negación que tenía al matrimonio, era lo menos desproporcionado y lo más decente que podía elegir en materia de la seguridad que deseaba de mi salvación . . . (4: 446)

St. Paul's words, at least, seem to set out the options available to Sor Juana, as to the Corinthian prophetesses. For women, accession to knowledge (through language: Latin, prophesy) can involve transgression, an implicit usurpation of masculine prerogative. But accession to knowledge need not be transgressive; indeed, it may even enjoy a kind of privilege, if done in conformity to convention, which involves "veiling," a symbol of authority—whether male authority over women, or (as Sor Juana would undoubtedly prefer) the learned woman's own authority.

More importantly, perhaps, and certainly more strategically, the indirect citation of St. Paul's words would be part of Sor Juana's overall "liberal" reading of his view of the role of women in the Church. That reading, like those of countless others who have taken on this question, would ultimately hark back to St. Paul's often-quoted words from Galatians: "There is no longer Jew or Greek, there is no longer slave or free, there is no longer male and female; for all of you are one in Christ Jesus" (3.28). Sor Juana's "liberal" reading of St. Paul is evident in her exegesis of his "let women keep silent in the churches": she concludes that he recommended this for practical reasons, that he did not forbid and elsewhere even encouraged female study and teaching.[2] In the hair-cutting/veiling passage, Sor Juana would be drawing attention to the implicit equality between males and females in the early Church, not in terms of what is of secondary consequence (proper dress and grooming), but in terms of what is fundamental: the right to worship and prophesy as equals, or indeed, as noted above, a possible sense of special female authority in these areas.

Most importantly, the aphoristic conclusion of Sor Juana's anecdote)"no me parecía razón que estuviese vestida de cabellos cabeza que estaba tan desnuda de noticias, que era más apetecible adorno"—suggests a kind of re-metaphorization of St. Paul's metaphors of the head and head-covering. If St. Paul transforms a statement about customs of head-covering into a statement about the relative dignity or authority of the sexes—he sees a man as the "head" of his wife, and thus implies a subordinate status for women—Sor Juana attributes to the female head the same capacity (and right, and obligation) for reason and self-determination as that enjoyed by men. Knowledge, through language, is the proper adornment for any head, male or female. This could be a direct equivalent of Sor Juana's interpretation of "mulieres in ecclesia taceant," a companion act of exegesis, but exegesis through metaphor—a living metaphor, taken from or imposed upon her own life. This would suggest an element of *performance,* of enactment, in this anecdote, as in other anecdotes in Sor Juana's "autobiographical" narration.

This aspect of performance is augmented by the clarity and reasonableness of this anecdote's "aphoristic" conclusion, which contrasts with the murkiness of St. Paul's meaning. Sor Juana makes her point with the same sort of binary, *conceptista* phrasing that one finds in her analogous sonnet, " . . . sólo intento / poner bellezas en mi entendimiento / y no mi entendimiento en las bellezas" (1:277). She is more concise and more rational than St. Paul himself; her arguments about the proper covering or adornment for the female head proceed from reason, not from custom ("no me parecía *razón* . . ."). And she exemplifies her argument in her own life story, in her very being: she embodies the argument with her own body. Exactly as with her exegesis of "let women keep silence," she thus illustrates the intellectual capacity of women even as she argues it; the *Respuesta* is a self-reflexive act, a giant emblem of the intellectual woman, every one of whose parts, including the anecdotes)lived metaphors—reflects and reproduces that emblem in miniature.

By way of closing, it may be useful to return to Elizabeth Bruss's (1976, 6) observations on autobiography, cited (incompletely) at the outset: "What is autobiography for us may have originally been only the by-product of another act, an apology undertaken in self-defense or a self-exhibition for the sake of selling the man himself, as an instructor in the rhetorical skills exemplified in the text." Changing only the word "man" to "woman," this idea may be seen as directly applicable to the ***Respuesta a Sor Filotea,*** which is "autobiographical" in the limited and period-bound (Baroque) sense of self-exhibition, rather than in the modern (Romantic) sense of self-revelation. Sor Juana "exhibits" metaphorical prefigurations of her writing self in her previous selves. And that writing self is, in turn, a living emblem or metaphor—a "metáfora encarnada," to borrow Octavio Paz's phrase[3]—an embodiment of the accession to knowledge through language, to which exceptional women, like exceptional men, may aspire.

NOTES

[1] I have made this argument with regard to two other anecdotes in the *Respuesta:* that of the young Juana Inés' desire to study at the University in masculine attire (Luciani 1989), and that of Sor Juana's observation that the lines of vision have a pyramidal shape (Luciani 1988).

[2] Nina Scott (1985) has demonstrated that Sor Juana's interpretation involves a tendentious reading and selective citation of St. Paul.

[3] For a further discussion of the "incarnated metaphor" theme (and analytical/biographical method) in Paz's book, see Luciani (1987).

FURTHER READING

Feder, Elena. "Sor Juana Inés de la Cruz; or, The Snares of (Con)(tra)diction." In *Amerindian Images and the Legacy of Columbus: Hispanic Issues, Volume 9,* edited by René Jara and Nicholas Spadaccini, pp. 473-529, Minneapolis: University of Minnesota Press, 1992.

   Explores the symbolic relationship between Cruz's *Primero Sueño* and her autobiographical and *Respuesta a Sor Filotea de la Cruz.*

Sayers Peder, Margaret. "Sor Juana Inés de la Cruz's *Respuesta a Sor Filotea.*" *Latin American Literature and Arts,* Vol. 30 (September / December 1981): 7-9.

   Discusses the events that led Cruz to write the celebrated *Respuesta a Sor Filotea.*

Ward, Marilynn. "The Feminist Crisis of Sor Juana de la Cruz." *International Journal of Women's Studies,* Vol. 1, No. 5 (October 1978): 475-81.

   Analyzes Cruz's defeats and triumphs as an independent female thinker in 17th century Mexico.

Wilkins, Constance. "Subversion through Comedy?: Two Plays by Sor Juana Inés de la Cruz and María de Zayas."

In *The Perception of Women in Spanish Theater of the Golden Age,* edited by Anita K. Stoll and Dawn L. Smith, pp. 28-41, London and Toronto: Associated University Presses, 1991.

    Compares two of Cruz's plays with two plays by María de Zayas.

Additional coverage of Sor Juana de la Cruz's life and career is contained in the following sources published by the Gale Group: *Literature Criticism from 1400 to 1800*, **Vol. 5;** *Poetry Criticism*, **Vol 24.**

José Lezama Lima
1910-1976

Cuban poet, novelist, short story writer, essayist, and critic.

INTRODUCTION

José Lezama Lima is considered one of the greatest twentieth-century Latin American writers. His first and most famous novel *Paradiso* (1966) is the culmination of his lifelong work as a literary theorist and poet. In *Paradiso* and its sequel *Oppiano Licario* (1977), Lezama Lima embraces themes of sexuality, friendship, mythology and religion to create an aesthetic world of his own: erudite, baroque, and rich in symbolism and allusion. When *Paradiso* was first published, Lezama Lima's unorthodox depiction of family life sparked controversy in Fidel Castro's Cuba and led to official efforts to repress the work. However, the praise of other Latin American writers brought Lezama Lima's work to international attention.

Lezama Lima was born on December 19, 1910 in a military camp near Havana, Cuba. His father was a military officer who died at a young age in 1919. This haunted Lezama Lima throughout his life and served as a preoccupation of his writing. Lezama Lima formed an unusually close relationship with his mother and lived with her throughout her life. Chronic problems with asthma led him to spend much of his childhood reading in solitude. He studied Spanish literature before entering the Universidad de la Habana to pursue legal studies. The student protests against the dictator Gerardo Machado awakened his political consciousness and the school shutdowns which resulted from the protests led to a four year hiatus during which Lezama Lima read widely and began to develop his interests in Cuban intellectualism and culture. In 1927 he began to write poetry and in 1937 he published his most important poem, *Muerte de Narciso (Death of Narcissus)*. From 1937 through the 1950s he edited a series of journals devoted to literature, politics, the arts, and culture in Cuba. At odds with the Batista regime, Lezama Lima became director of the department of literature and publications of the National Council of Culture after Castro's rise to power. In 1964, following his mother's death, he married Maria Luisa Bautista Trevino, an old friend of the family. The publication of *Paradiso* two years later brought trouble: authorities labeled the book pornographic due to its homosexual content, and in 1971 Lezama Lima was accused of anti-revolutionary activities. He died in 1976, alienated from his friends and the Cuban culture to which he had devoted his life.

Lezama Lima's two best known works, the novels *Paradiso* and *Oppiano Licario,* build on his early work as an essayist and poet. In poems and essays such as *The Death of Narcissus, Enemigo rumor* (1941; Enemy Rumors) and *La fijeza* (1949; Persistence) he explores themes such as the role of poetry and the poet, life, death, God, and religion. In *La expresión americana* (1957; The American Expression), Lezama Lima claimed that American culture, in contrast with that of Europe, creates an environment where neo-baroque aesthetics, ecstasy, joy, and magical realism converge to produce a uniquely American literary hermeneutic. In *Introdución a los vasos órficos* (1971; *Introduction to the Orphic Vases*) the author contended that the poet is the intermediary between God and humankind and alone can express the unlimited possibilities which exist in life. The somewhat autobiographical *Paradiso* follows the life of José Cemí as he comes of age in pre-Castro Cuba, exploring issues such as the connection between the material and spiritual worlds and the nature of family life. Cemí is taught by his friend and mentor *Oppiano Licario* that he must live his life through the eyes of a poet. *Oppiano Licario* and a collection of poems, *Fragmentos a su imán*, were published posthumously.

Lezama Lima has been labeled a "difficult writer" because of his use of arcane language and obscure imagery. However, many critics praise his aesthetic innovations, both in his poetry and his novels. *Paradiso* sparked negative comments from some critics in the United States—one critic calling the book "less a modern novel than a garrulous, old-fashioned treatise about a modern novel which hasn't been written yet"—but Latin American writers such as Julio Cortazar, Mario Vargas Llosa, and Octavio Paz argue that Lezama Lima's work represents some of the finest of twentieth-century writing and that he deserves to be considered one of Cuba's greatest writers.

PRINCIPAL WORKS

Muerte de Narciso (poem) 1937
Enemigo rumor (poetry) 1941
Aventuras sigilosa (poetry) 1945
La fijeza (poetry) 1949
Analecta del reloj (essays) 1953
El padre Gaztelu en la poesia (poetry) 1955
La expresión americana (essays) 1957
Tratados en La Habana (essays) 1958
Dador (poetry) 1960
Antología de la poesía cubana (editor) 1965
Orbita de Lezama Lima (selected works) 1966
Paradiso (novel) 1966
Los grandes todos (poetry) 1968
Posible imagen de José Lezama Lima (poetry) 1969
La cantidad hechizada (essays) 1970

CRITICISM

Robin Lutz (essay date 1984)

SOURCE: "The Inseparability of Opposites in José Lezama Lima's *Muerte de Narciso*," *Kentucky Romance Quarterly,* Vol. 31, No. 3, 1984, pp. 329-39.

[*In the following article, Lutz highlights the place of friction between opposites, using Lezama Lima's reworking of the myth of Narcissus to examine the fused space between life and stillness.*]

Among the many excellent poems that José Lezama Lima wrote, none has aroused more sustained interest than his first major poem, **Muerte de Narciso**, published in 1937 as a *cuadernillo*.[1] The poem's tangle of metaphors, symbols, and resonance-charged descriptions effectively conveys the contradictory nature of Narcissus' vigil beside the river—his efforts to unite himself with the beautiful creature he sees in his reflection and his knowledge that this endeavor inevitably must end in his death. Lezama captures the ironical aspects of the myth of Narcissus—that to possess what he seeks he must die—through the use of imagery that simultaneously points towards the sensorial beauty of Narcissus in his surroundings and towards his imminent death.

Lezama accomplishes this double thrust by the use of key symbols which possess both positive and negative connotations: the river as a source of fertility and a representation of time's passage, the arrow's flight as search and transience, snow as crystalline beauty and lifeless matter. The development of the central symbols in two directions at once is made possible by the ambiguous syntax, the nonliteral descriptions with several possible referents, and the use of the central images as both metaphors and symbols.[2] The river, for example, serves not only as a symbol of time but also as a sensorial metaphor for the feathers of a heron and as an ominous metaphor for ashes. The interest in fusing rather than distinguishing the physical elements of the landscape finds expression as well in the

merging of the first- and third-person speakers within the poem. Through the use of language, imagery, and speaker, Lezama constructs an evocative reality in which each detail suggests both Narcissus' beauty and his death. The ambiguous and contradictory imagery of **Muerte de Narciso** causes the reader to experience in the myth of Narcissus that inseparability of opposites which forms a major theme in Lezama Lima's poetic work.

From the poem's beginning, the speaker focuses on the simultaneously generative and fatal nature of time. As the title makes clear, the poem deals with the certain death which the future will bring to Narcissus. Time destroys Narcissus' bonds to the past (note the reference to the lotus, a symbol of loss of memory, and the repetition of "olvidar"), imprisoning him in its movement. However, at the same time that the dynamic quality of time hastens Narcissus' death, it also brings him closer to union with his reflection:

> Dánae teje el tiempo dorado por el Nilo,
> envolviendo los labios que pasaban
> entre labios y vuelos desligados.
> La mano o el labio o el pájaro nevaban.
> Era el círculo en nieve que se abría.
> Mano era sin sangre la seda que borraba
> la perfección que muere de rodillas
> y en su celo se esconde y se divierte.
>
> Vertical desde el mármol no miraba
> la frente que se abría en loto húmedo.
> En chillido sin fin se abría la floresta
> al airado redoble en flecha y muerte.
> ¿No se apresura tal vez su fría mirada
> sobre la garza real y el frío tan débil
> del poniente, grito que ayuda la fuga
> del dormir, llama fría y lengua alfilereada?[3]

The immediate identification of time with the flow of the river—"Dánae teje el tiempo dorado por el Nilo"—endows the passage of time with positive connotations. The mythical allusion to Danäe, made pregnant by Zeus in a shower of gold, establishes the river as a source of fertility which engenders or gives form to time. The reference to the Nile, upon whose seasonal fluxes the Egyptian harvests depend, underscores the cyclical aspect of time.

The sense of movement associated with both the river and with time is made more concrete in the image of weaving time. The temporal flow is something which, like the threads of a tapestry, acquires substance in space through its motion. By mentioning snow, whiteness, and silk in such a way that they can refer to Narcissus, the river, or time, the speaker equates certain temporal and spatial aspects with each other and with Narcissus' situation. The white silk can refer to the river's surface, to the marble beauty of Narcissus' limbs, or to time, which gradually envelops and obscures him. Not only are the physical elements of the landscape fused, but they are combined in such a way as to emphasize the union of the positive and negative aspects which each possesses.

Narcissus gives himself over to the inexhaustible, restless flow of images which originates in the contemplation of his reflection in the river. The description of the world as unfolding from its core (Narcissus and his reflection) suggests that the entire natural world is in some sense the reflection or expansion of Narcissus' perception. The desire to merge himself with his image is not expressed as an attempt to attain a physical union but as an effort to open himself to his reflection, to ascend, to assemble the fragmented pieces of his being, and to overcome the blindness and muteness of his double. The repetition of the word "abrir" chronicles the movement outwards from his reflection to the world: "[e]ra el círculo en nieve que se abría," "la frente que se abría en loto húmedo," "[e]n chillido sin fin se abría la floresta" (p. 11). For Narcissus the effort to become one with his reflection is a process of change, the difficulty of which is mirrored in the violence of the imagery. He sees himself as subject to time, bound to his reflection in the river, yet he presses forward toward what he knows will be his death.

The fatal nature of Narcissus' quest is foreshadowed by the predominance of images of sharp or icy things, burial, weapons, wounds, and harsh sounds. The universe which he perceives is hostile and fragmented; in this sense the linguistic difficulties with which the reader must grapple correspond to the amorphous, fluid reflection in the river which Narcissus strives to reach. There is a sense of loss or diminution associated with the contrast between Narcissus' face and his reflection: the firmness of his features becomes pliancy ("blanda") in the watery image, the bloodless mouth in the river moves but is silent ("la abierta boca negada en sangre que se mueve"), breath—the essence of terrestrial life—is absent ("olvidada por un aliento que olvida y desentraña") (p. 11). The effect of describing the reflection negatively in terms of Narcissus' face is to underscore the irony of his position. Passionately drawn to his counterpart, he can yet see in it the premonition of his own death. In attempting to endow the reflection with warmth, speech, and sight he sacrifices himself.

The auditory relationship between Narcissus' voice and his reflection's muteness parallels the visual relationship between him and his fragmented image. Lezama Lima's comparison of the longing to see (the poem describes Narcissus or his reflection as being blind) and the effort to speak has its source in the Greek myth of Narcissus. In that story Echo sadly accompanies him in his vigil by the pool, unable to tell him of her love as long as he remains silent.[4] While Echo does not appear in *Muerte de Narciso*, the frustration she felt in not being able to speak is present in the images of sound and muteness which describe Narcissus' despair. At one point the effort to overcome the silence provokes a metaphoric transformation from the auditory plane to the visual plane: "Espirales de heroicos tenores caen en el pecho de una paloma/y allí se agitan hasta relucir como flechas en su abrigo de noche" (p. 13). The emphasis on sounds, silence, breath, and lips—"silbo enmascarado," "labios destrozados," "timbre ausente"—also suggests that the poem itself is an effort to overcome silence, a reading which is

encouraged by past literary treatments of the story of Narcissus (p. 13).[5]

The speaker emphasizes the irony of Narcissus' devoting his life to a search for a fatal knowledge by means of the many explicit and implicit oxymorons ("llama fría," "blanda muerte," "timbre ausente") and by using symbols which simultaneously point towards life and death (pp. 11, 13). Guillermo Sucre has pointed out that the arrow, one of the central symbols in the poem, is one such image.[6] Its effectiveness as a weapon establishes it as an image of death ("fresco agujero al corazón"), while its shape and movement towards a goal associate it with the river's flow, with fertility, and with Narcissus' endeavor to unite himself with his reflection (p. 11). Thus, while the arrow's trajectory has positive connotations, its arrival is fatal, just as the river's merging with the sea is traditionally a symbol of death, and Narcissus' union with his reflection is possible only in death.

In *Muerte de Narciso* Lezama Lima confers symbolic meaning on those objects or qualities which occur repeatedly and which tie into the other core images of the poem. The arrow is an example of an object which, regardless of whether or not it is literally present in the landscape, acquires conceptual importance in the poem through its frequent use and its association with the river, time, movement, the hunt, and the heron's fishing. Snow is another key image which functions as a premonition of death because of its identification with the river, the heron, Narcissus, and the approaching winter. As with the arrow, which signifies both the search and the resultant death, so the snow has a double referent—approaching death and the crystalline beauty of the river's surface, which is described as icy even when it is not frozen.

The use of symbols such as the arrow, snow, the tapestry, and the flame—each of which are developed in contrary directions—creates an ambiguous effect, adding to the tension in the poem between the beauty of Narcissus' quest and the violence of his death. Whether a specific reference to fire in the poem evokes an impression of beauty or of ruin, the other half of the symbol's meaning is always covertly present since both his passionate dedication to his search and his inevitable destruction are described as flame-like. "[D]espertando el oleaje en lisas llamaradas y vuelos sosegados" gives an impression of a smooth surface of water aroused to activity by the urging of bees and pine trees, but the undercurrents provided by the earlier association of flames with ashes and ashes with snow endows the scene with an ominous note (p. 14).

The emphasis on the passing of time adds a sense of urgency to Narcissus' venture. Images of the coming of winter intertwine with images of the approaching night, stressing the physical changes that time causes and the imminence of even greater changes:

> Granizados toronjiles y ríos de velamen congelados,
> aguardan la señal de una mustia hoja de oro,
> alzada en espiral, sobre el otoño de aguas tan
> 　hirvientes.

Dócil rubí queda suspirando en su fuga ya
   ascendiendo.

Ya el otoño recorre las islas no cuidadas,
   guarnecidas

islas y aislada paloma muda entre dos hojas
   enterradas.

El río en la suma de sus ojos anunciaba

lo que pesa la luna en sus espaldas y el aliento que
   en

      halo convertía.

Antorchas como peces, flaco garzón trabaja noche y
   cielo,

arco y cestillo y sierpes encendidos, carámbano y
   lebrel.

Pluma morada, no mojada, pez mirándome, sepulcro.

                                        (p. 12)

Both a frozen river and a dark night would destroy Narcissus' reflection, making it impossible for him to see himself in the river. The destructiveness of winter and, more generally, of time is linked by images of whiteness, coldness, and iciness ("cristal") to the river and its function as a mirror: "el granizo/en blando espejo destroza la mirada que le ciñe" (p. 12). The use of verbs such as "aguardar," "anunciar," and "convertir"; the repetition of "ya" ("su fuga ya ascendiendo," "[y]a el otoño recorre las islas"); and the overwhelming impression of movement—rivers boiling (perhaps reddened by the setting sun), leaves whirling upwards, autumn approaching—emphasize the transience of the physical world (p. 12).

The inconstant nature of reality increases the difficulty of Narcissus' undertaking: "Antorchas como peces, flaco garzón trabaja noche y cielo, / arco y cestillo y sierpes encendidos, carámbano y lebrel. / Pluma morada, no mojada, pez mirándome, sepulcro" (p. 12). Objects from the shore merge with underwater elements; similarities in shapes and colors suggest a basis for identifying the land and the submarine landscape. The heron's fishing (for his reflection?) is, because of the word play on "garzón" (a great white heron and a youth), linked to a nobleman's hunting ("arco," "lebrel," "faisanes") (p. 12).

Even the distinction between the third-person speaker and Narcissus dissolves when, in the sixth stanza, the speaker refers to Narcissus in the first person: "pez mirándome," "nunca me preguntan" (p. 12). Anthony J. Cascardi explains the fusion of points of view, saying: "We should read the poem as the expression of a state of consciousness in which there is no clear boundary between the self and the nonself: as if the whole poem were dominated by a tacit subject, in whose consciousness these verses occur."[7] The restless shifts in point of view, as well as the variability of the physical reality, mirror the uncertainty and ambivalent emotions which Narcissus feels. The merging of the first- and third-person speakers confuses the reader because it denies him a fixed point of reference, but it also leads him to equate Narcissus' state of being with the world external to him. When in the fifteenth stanza the speaker calls on Narcissus, naming him for the first time in the poem's text, the reader watches

Narcissus with the third-person speaker, observes with narcissus the images of the scenery in the river, and with his reflection stares up at Narcissus on the bank.

As with many of the poem's elements, the "total openness to *lo Otro*" which Cascardi and Sucre note is two-edged.[8] There is a merging of self with the external reality, but it is balanced by the process of separation in which Narcissus attributes his awareness of impending death to the antagonism of the physical world. Narcissus identifies himself with the external world but he also takes pains to separate himself from it. If, as appears to be the case, the imagery reflects the sensorial perceptions that Narcissus experiences, the universe is for him a hostile element, foreshadowing in its violence his approaching death:

Triste recorre—curva ceñida en ceniciento airón—
el espacio que manos desalojan, timbre ausente
y avivado azafrán, tiernos redobles sus extremos.
Convocados se agitan los durmientes, fruncen las olas
batiendo en torno de ajedrez dormido, su insepulta
   tiara.
Su insepulta madera blanda el frío pico del hirviente
   cisne.
Reluce muelle: falsos diamantes; pluma cambiante:
   terso atlas.
Verdes chillidos: juegan las olas, blanda muerte el
   relámpago en sus
      venas.
Ahogadas cintas mudo el labio las ofrece.
Oriental cestillos cuelan agua de luna.
Los más dormidos son los que más se apresuran,
se entierran, pluma en el grito, silbo enmascarado,
   entre frentes y
      garfios.
Estirado mármol como un río que recurva o aprisiona
los labios destrozados, pero los ciegos no oscilan.
Espirales de heroicos tenores caen en el pecho de
   una paloma
y allí se agitan hasta relucir como flechas en su
   abrigo de noche

                                        (p. 13)

The two-pronged imagery describes Narcissus' death as being both a sacrifice caused by his determination to remain at the water's edge and a destruction inflicted on him by forces outside himself. He is thus both the hero and the victim, the hunter and the hunted.[9]

The river, like Narcissus, has both beautiful and fatal aspects. Their dual natures link them—each is sensuous, each is destructive of life. Ambiguous metaphors which can refer to either Narcissus or the river identify both the positive and the negative characteristics that they share. The heron ("curva ceñida en ceniciento airón") serves as a metaphor both for the pale Narcissus bending over his reflection and for the river's curve as it sweeps past him; the final image of the ninth stanza ("Verdes chillidos: juegan las olas, blanda muerte el relámpago en sus venas") equates Narcissus' blood with the river's deadliness; and the river itself is simultaneously a prison of sound which enforces silence on the mute reflection and a vista of sparkling water glimpsed through reeds ("Ahogadas cintas mudo el labio las ofrece. / Orientales cestillos cuelan agua de luna") (p. 13). By making the key features of the physical world, such as the river, both attractive and threatening, the speaker sustains the reader's awareness of the warring forces within Narcissus.

The speaker uses the same key images of the poem as both symbols and metaphors in order to further develop the web of hidden relationships between Narcissus and his environment. The river, for example, is not only a symbol of time but also a metaphor for snow, ashes, the heron's feathers, and white silk, based on the river's physical properties—its color, surface texture, and movement. Even when one of these elements is used in the poem without either the syntax or the perceptible links which would make it a metaphor, a comparison is still implied. "Triste recorre—curva ceñida en ceniciento airón—/el espacio que manos desalojan" is not a metaphor, but it suggests a comparison between the heron and the river which causes the reader to associate the heron's greyness, sadness, and movement with the river (p. 13). Even though the poem appears to digress extensively into descriptions of the flora and fauna along the river, the reader's attention remains on Narcissus and on the river because they are continuously evoked in the images used to describe the landscape.

Another effect of using symbols (the river represents time's flow) as metaphors (the river is a heron) is to give symbolic value to the metaphors (the heron's feathers represent time's flight). Images subsequently become linked to other images through new metaphoric associations (the heron is like silk in that both ascend—"la blancura seda es ascendiendo"), which then suggest additional symbolic meanings (the rising tide connotes the approaching flight—or liberty—of Narcissus) (p. 15). The poem's organization depends upon these metaphoric and symbolic relationships between Narcissus and his universe, rather than upon logical associations and anecdotal details.

The intensity of the poem increases as it moves towards a climax. The ambivalent attitude towards Narcissus continues with the imagery suggesting both a slow death and a coming to fruition: "Narciso, Narciso. Las astas del ciervo asesinado / son peces, son llamas, son flautas, son dedos mordisqueados. / Narciso, Narciso" (p. 15). The relationship between the objects named is in part physical—they can all have the same shape—but the juxtaposition with Narcissus' name makes the series a visionary image as well, linking Narcissus and objects previously associated with death or destruction.[10] The images of death begin to coalesce in metaphors as the poem nears its end: destruction by fire and by water are joined ("llamas tristes las olas"); the sky and the river draw together ("pez del frío verde el aire"); and Narcissus' tears unite him with the river ("espuma colgaba de los ojos, gota marmórea") (p. 15). As the images converge, the focus of the poem narrows to the relationship between Narcissus and the river.

The emphasis on sound and silence increases as the shell, which earlier provided an echo of the blood's rhythm as Narcissus lifted it to his ear, now becomes the buzzing of a swarm of bees, a physical representation of the shattered silence. Ironically, while his reflection remains indifferent to Narcissus' passion, the entire natural world responds to his ardor. The landscape explodes in sound, both beautiful and violent, as it reacts to Narcissus' pleas to his reflection by foretelling his death:

> Desde ayer las preguntas se divierten o se cierran
> al impulso de frutos polvorosos o de islas donde
>   acampan
> los tesoros que la rabia esparce, adula o reconviene.
> Los donceles trabajan en las nueces y el surtidor de
>   frente a su
>   sonido
> en la llama fabrica sus raíces y su mansión de gritos
>   soterrados.
> Si se aleja, recta abeja, el espejo destroza el río
>   mudo.
> Si se hunde, media sirena al fuego, las hilachas que
>   surcan el
>   invierno
> tejen blanco cuerpo en preguntas de estatua
>   polvorienta
>
> (p. 14)

As with every other stage in the poem, Narcissus' death entails both positive and negative aspects. In the classical myth Narcissus was transformed at his death into a flower; here the secret which Narcissus has sought also becomes a flower: "el secreto en geranio convertido" (p. 15). The change suggests Narcissus' dying but also hints at the beauty of the conversion. The river rises, bringing with it the forgetfulness and dreams suggestive of death, but providing as well the flood of water which makes the land fertile. The rising of the river culminates in the last line of the poem with Narcissus' flight at high tide.

> Narciso, Narciso. Las astas del ciervo asesinado
> son peces, son llamas, son flautas, son dedos
>   mordisqueados.
> Narciso, Narciso. Los cabellos guiando florentinos
>   reptan perfiles,
> labios sus rutas, llamas tristes las olas mordiendo sus
>   caderas.
> Pez del frío verde el aire en el espejo sin estrías,
>   racimo de palomas
> ocultas en la garganta muerta: hija de la flecha y de
>   los cisnes.
> Garza divaga, concha en la ola, nube en el desgaire,
> espuma colgaba de los ojos, gota marmórea y dulce
>   plinto no ofreciendo.
>
> Chillidos frutados en la nieve, el secreto en geranio
>   convertido.
> La blancura seda es ascendiendo en labio derramada,
> abre un olvido en las islas, espadas y pestañas vienen
> a entregar el sueño, a rendir espejo en litoral de
>   tierra y roca impura.

Húmedos labios no en la concha que busca recto
  hilo,
esclavos del perfil y del velamen secos el aire
  muerden
al tornasol que cambia su sonido en rubio tornasol de
  cal salada,
busca en lo rubio espejo de la muerte, concha del
  sonido.
Si atraviesa el espejo hierven las aguas que agitan el
  oído.
Si se sienta en su borde o en su frente el centurión
  pulsa en su
    costado.
Si declama penetran en la mirada y se fruncen las
  letras en el sueño.
Ola de aire envuelve secreto albino, piel arponeada,
que coloreado espejo sombra es del recuerdo y
  minuto del silencio.
Ya traspasa blancura recto sinfín en llamas secas y
  hojas
    lloviznadas.
Chorro de abejas increadas muerden la estela, pídenle
  el costado.
Así el espejo averiguó callado, así Narciso en
  pleamar fugó sin alas.

                    (pp. 15-16)

The poem describes the sense of approaching fulfillment both in temporal terms (as awaiting an instant which finally arrives) and in spatial terms (as the penetration of previous boundaries). Just as the arrow represented both life and death, so the images of piercing suggest both the wounding of Narcissus and his transcendence of obstacles, most notably the water's surface:

  Si atraviesa el espejo hierven las aguas . . .
  Si se sienta en su borde . . . el centurión pulsa en su
    costado.
  Si declama penetran en la mirada . . .
    . . . piel arponeada . . .
  Ya traspasa blancura recto sinfín . . .

                    (pp. 15-16)

Narcissus has triumphed, but the union with his reflection brings with it pain and death.

The phrase "fugó sin alas" exemplifies the triumphal tone of Narcissus' death (p. 16). It culminates the series of birds which have been compared with his situation. He has been likened to a dove, pale and vulnerable, to the heron, fishing for its reflection, and to an imprisoned bird ("¿Ya se siente temblar el pájaro en mano terrenal?" [p. 13]). Now he escapes, wingless, and the ambiguous imagery fuses his ascension upwards with his plunge to meet the reflection in the water. A "wave of air," he pierces the whiteness (of the air and of the water's surface) and creates a wake of water, or a trail of fire, behind him.

The final line of the poem, "[a]sí el espejo averiguó callado, así Narciso en pleamar fugó sin alas," stresses the paradoxical nature of his experience (p. 16). Only the mirror remains, a silent witness; the being who was re-

flected in it flees. Time continues and silence reigns in the form of the river, which has incorporated Narcissus' death into its memory: "sombra es del recuerdo" (p. 16). Although Narcissus is no longer present, his existence is remembered by the river. In this sense it is significant that the mirror rather than the river witnesses his passing. Since a mirror witnesses by reflecting, the final lines suggest that Narcissus' reflection may continue in existence as a memorial to him.

The association of Narcissus' death throughout the poem with the coming of night or of winter and, in the last part of the poem, with the rising tide suggests that he in some way lives on. All of these metaphors allude to recurring, cyclical processes in nature; might not, then, Narcissus' death be a change of form (into the flower) which would integrate him with the physical world which earlier had threatened him? This reading is suggested by the emphasis on the golden sunflower near the end of the poem, reminiscent of the gilding of time by the Nile in the first line: "muerden / al tornasol que cambia su sonido en rubio tornasol de cal salada, / busca en lo rubio espejo de la muerte, concha del sonido" (p. 15). Time mirrors death and echoes the lament, bringing about Narcissus' death but also, in the turning sunflower, providing an infinite commemoration of the event in its daily and seasonal cycles.

Muerte de Narciso uses the myth of Narcissus to make certain observations about the double nature of reality. The paradox of Narcissus' search for a fuller life having brought about his death exemplifies the inseparability of contrary forces which Lezama Lima perceives in the world. The poem's emphasis on pairing opposites (nature's tranquility and its violence, Narcissus as hunter and as victim) anticipates the thematic importance of Lezama's later efforts to synthesize positive and negative elements.

The contradictory aspects of Narcissus' circumstances find expression in the poet's use of symbols which simultaneously point towards fulfillment and destruction (the arrow as search and as death). Metaphors forge unexpected ties between dissimilar objects (the heron and ashes, ice and the mirror), suggesting the interconnectedness of everything and the combination of opposites in each physical element. The convergence of the first- and third-person speakers, the absence of concrete anecdotal details, and the ambiguous syntax contribute to the poem's effect by provoking the reader to discover additional associations among the poem's components. These techniques enable Lezama Lima to hint at Narcissus' approaching death even as he embraces the sensorial present. *Muerte de Narciso* is an exaltation of the staggering richness and complexity of the transitory.

NOTES

[1] See Cintio Vitier, "Introducción a la obra de José Lezama Lima," in *José Lezama Lima, Obras completas,* I (México: Aguilar, 1975), xiii-xx for an account of the poem's reception.

[2] For a discussion of the effects of the ambiguous syntax see Anthony J. Cascardi, "Reference in Lezama Lima's *Muerte de Narciso,*" *Journal of Spanish Studies,* 5, No. 11 (Spring 1977), 5-11. Monique de Lope provides an in-depth study of the key metaphors of the poem in "Narcisse ailé, Etude sur *Muerte de Narciso* (1937) de J. Lezama Lima," *Cahiers du Monde Hispanique et Luso-Brésilien (Caravelle)* 29 (1977), 25-44. In it Lope discusses the mechanisms by which Lezama uses the metaphors to create ambiguity.

[3] José Lezama Lima, *Poesía completa* (Barcelona: Barral Editores, 1975), pp. 11-16. Subsequent page references to the poem will be noted in the text. Because of the poem's length, the entire text is not given here.

[4] Edith Hamilton, *Mythology* (New York: New American Library, 1940), p. 88.

[5] In *Muerte de Narciso,* Lezama Lima draws on the literary images and associations which had fastened themselves to the story of Narcissus as well as on the original myth. Several of the motifs which Lezama uses may have been drawn from two poems about Narcissus by Paul Valéry, a French Symbolist: "Narcisse parle," a 53-line poem (1891) and "Fragments du Narcisse," an expansion of the earlier poem (1926). Besides the similarities in the way the two poets use certain images (lips, the river's banks, the coming of night) to create a tone of imminent tragedy, both also depend on paradoxical structures to convey the complex nature of Narcissus' situation. Valéry several times describes Narcissus' ambivalent reaction to his reflection with oxymorons; Lezama Lima uses both oxymorons and the dual development of the poem's major symbols in contrary directions to communicate the thematic paradox of seeking fulfillment in death. Additionally, in several instances in *Muerte de Narciso* Lezama takes an image already developed by Valéry and, eliminating the "descriptive" framework in which Valéry placed it, uses it as a symbol which already possesses certain associations for the reader.

[6] Guillermo Sucre, "Lezama Lima: el logos de la imaginación," in his *La máscara, la transparencia* (Caracas: Monte Avila Editores, 1975), p. 194.

[7] Cascardi, p. 7.

[8] Cascardi, p. 7.

[9] Cascardi, p. 10. Cascardi notes: "He is the hunter, but also the *ciervo herido,* who in a Christian context gains life through death."

[10] The term "visionary image" or "imagen visionaria" is defined by Carlos Bousoño as one in which "el poeta contemporáneo llamará iguales a los términos A y B . . . porque despierten en nosotros, sus contempladores, un sentimiento parejo." *Teoría de la expresión poética,* 5ª ed., Biblioteca Románica Hispánica (Madrid: Editorial Gredos, 1970), p. 143. The basis of the comparison is thus irrational rather than logical.

Julio Ortega (essay date 1984)

SOURCE: "Re-reading *Paradiso,*" *Poetics of Change: The New Spanish-American Narrative,* Julio Ortega. Austin: University of Texas, 1984, pp. 60-84.

[*Here, Ortega centers the most compelling aspects of Lezama's* Paradiso, *his use of poetry as truth combined with images to create each moment's epiphany, as the basis of human connection.*]

I

Any interpretation of **Paradiso**[*] can only be approximative, because this novel cannot easily be reduced to a process or a structure. But perhaps Lezama Lima himself proposes a suitable coherency: the expansion of language, which replaces the conventions of reality. Still, an analysis of the novel must in any case be provisional because this expansion comprehends a complex hierarchy that, beyond or in a reappraisal of literature, organizes a world view whose components are a symbiosis of cultures, a synthesis of Greek and Christian conceptions, and even of Oriental aspects, which acquire form as *poetics.*

Paradiso situates the personal experience of a formative process—in order to elucidate it as poetics—within a reality unified as if by verbal enchantment. In other words, the entire novel becomes the debate and discovery of a means leading to the finding and formulation of a conception of reality based on poetry. The coherency of poetic apprenticeship is what is most secret and also most visible in the book, because while this coherency establishes the novel's *form,* it also establishes the text's progress toward an integrative poetics that comprehends complex levels. On the one hand, it traces the family chronicle (the hierarchy of nobility as a form of human relations and the nucleus of the home as an *axis mundi* defining José Cemí); on the other hand, it follows Cemí's personal literary destiny (based on a metaphorical debate over the complexities of Eros); and, as a consequence of these two processes, the search leads to the peculiar synthesis of the culture in which Cemí lives (also as a form of nature) and the resultant formulation of that synthesis as a poetics, an understanding of reality through words.

These *vases communicants* constitute the internal process of the novel, its historical and symbolic coherency. Lezama's Baroque incorporates zones of all cultures in order to expand the mechanism of the image, and at times this incorporation is only illustrative or comparative (that is, an expansion of the space of the image). But often the incorporation is also allegorical or symbolic because this Baroque is not merely "literary" or literally textual (as Góngora's laborious, gratuitous Baroque probably was); rather, it is a symbolic Baroque. In other words, Lezama creates a "superreality" with a baroque figure, but this figure is not only a signifier but also a new meaning, and, as such, it supposes allegorical expansion and symbolic implication. It should be kept in mind that he speaks in the novel of "the creation of the law of extension by the Tree of Life," which is the reproductive principle of his language as "nature," as a figure and as a symbol.

II

This process of the conquest of reality by poetry is a cycle, a universal epic, that begins in the first image of the novel (the sick child) and concludes in the last image (the poet who recognizes the voices, the hesychastic rhythm, the poetry of totality). These images are intimately related within the poetization of the story. The disease is perhaps an allegory of birth itself, an image of man severed from divinity by his very human nature (although in Lezama there is no explicit metaphysical guilt that would directly suggest the Christian concept of original sin); the final image, that of the man who transforms the world in poetry, also suggests a profound allegory of the word as the recovery of innocence, as the foundation of paradise in verbal creation, as the link in temporality, elucidating experience as a form of created Nature.

It is in dream that the anecdote is recomposed and organized into a symbol; the father's finger is withdrawn from the water, and immediately Cemí's finger finds its own harmonious solution. The fish that recognizes and protects this solitary finger seems to be the figure of Christianity leading him to a new place where his breathing is a "carefully calculated rhythm," that is, the anticipation of poetry, of that rhythm of breathing that is the rhythm of the created universe. The fish finally changes into the mother and then the harmony of integration is closed, the presence of the mother, the order she generates as a transparency of Nature, is also the solution to the origins, because this illness is now part of an origin guilty in its separation from God, but as the emblem of an irrevocable destiny. Because of this the father's death, too, will transmute into an absence that must be sought in the manifestation of poetry itself.

In a conversation with Alvarez Bravo (*Orbita de Lezama Lima,* Havana, UNEAC, 1966), Lezama explains that for him poetry conceives of man's end not in death but in resurrection. It is precisely this Christian principle that is found in the profound unity of **Paradiso**. The final image recalls the first one, and also the death of Oppiano Licario, through whom it symbolically incorporates the previous deaths of Cemí's father and of his uncle Alberto. Licario (Icarus, the adventurer of the word as time and as resurrection) was the strange and solitary witness to these deaths, perhaps a kind of image projected by Cemí himself. In this projection of the allegory, Cemí can witness the deaths of father and his uncle, both of which occurred at night, leaving no trace in his memory. They must, therefore, be recalled for him by Licario, the enigmatic witness who finally surrenders his enigma in the multiple resurrection symbolized by José Cemí as the advance sentinel and the craftsman of rhythm and of poetry.

But let us return to the first image. The child Cemí, who has asthma, is covered with sores, and the servants are in despair because they do not know how to ease his attack, how to assume the ritual responsibility placed on them by the situation, because the boy's father and mother are not at home.

> No comment was passed among them, as if they did not want to face up to this situation that was beyond them. Their thoughts were focused mainly on the Colonel's return and the attitude he would take toward them. Since the strange connection that might exist between their watching and the spreading of the welts was ambiguous, it unnerved them to think that perhaps the connection was quite close and it might appear to be their fault.

There are three servants to take care of the child—Baldovina, Truni, and Zoar. Truni, Lezama notes, is also called Trinidad, and she "defined the ritual and the rite: Zoar as God the Father, Baldovina as the daughter, and Truni as the Holy Ghost." This is one of the configurations reiterated in the novel: the triad as a group of complementaries. The image also suggests another constant in the book: the successive displacements. In this fundamental episode, the parents have been displaced and Cemí falls ill in the presence of the servants, figures who also replace the figures of the Trinity. Moreover, in Lezama's mechanism, Cemí himself is displaced by the trinitarian figure, since the author speaks of "the daughter" and not the son (Cemí), who here is a fourth term of the figure. José Cemí is undoubtedly an alter ego of the author, and his name may represent a radical declaration in this mechanism of displacement, since when Licario meets Cemí for the first time—a meeting that establishes his destiny as a figure in the novel—he recognizes him by the initials J.C. Is this then a parallel between Cemí's poetic destiny and the destiny of Christ the Son? Whatever the answer to that question, the resonant significance of this episode lies in the rituals practiced by Truni and Zoar in their attempts to cure the child. When Cemí awakens he tells Baldovina, "Now these crosses are going to stay etched on me and no one will want to touch me because of Truni's kisses." And Baldovina says to him, "What you've got is the king's evil, which spreads out like streaks, like the red blotches of a royal poinciana tree. Like a little circlet of seaweed that first floats over your skin and then gets inside your body." These images of kisses, of crosses etched on the body, of blotches like internalized forms, are images that the author recapitulates in the episode as expansions of Cemí's own figure.

Thus illness becomes a visible metaphor that on the one hand allegorizes the advent of human nature and on the other hand initiates the specific destiny of one character; and this initiation recognizes the proximity of death ("the Colonel and his wife agreed that it was, purely and simply, a miracle that the boy was still alive") and especially the symmetry that will exist between Cemí's troubled, asthmatic breathing and the discovery of breathing as the integrative rhythm of poetry.

Cemí's illness also generates strange resonances in relation to his father and decisive adjustments in relation to his mother. In chapter 6 José Eugenio Cemí decides to teach his five-year-old son how to swim:

> "I don't think you can learn how to swim by yourself," he said. "So I'm going to teach you today. Now, you jump into the water and hold onto this finger." He held up his forefinger, created for the exercise of authority, strong, like a midget who was an important personage in the Tower of London. The forefinger curled like an anchor and then straightened up like a reed that jumps its moorings but then comes back to root itself in the sand once more.
>
> The child jumps into the water and holds onto his father's finger as the boat moves along.
>
> José Cemí clutched his father's forefinger with his whole hand, feeling the resistance of the water as it tightened like a stone against his panting chest. "You're not afraid any more, now you can learn by yourself," he said. The Colonel withdrew his finger just as a small whirlpool formed.
>
> The child's body then disappears beneath the water and the father, frightened, dives in to rescue him.

The following episodes show the father vaguely troubled by his son's asthma because he wants the officers to see his children as strong and forthright when they wander through Morro Castle. The father—Lezama calls him the Chief—points out a dark, gaping hole in the building and tries to frighten his children by telling them how in colonial times they used to throw prisoners in there; later Cemí will find out that they throw garbage down the hole, attracting voracious sharks in the water below, and the image becomes an obsessive nightmare. The father also has his daughter Violante swim in a pool and the girl runs the risk of drowning; again the father rescues a child from the water, and again the image of the pool and its infernal center becomes a obsession in Cemí's dreams. Cemí's illness worries the father "incessantly," and he decides to attempt a cure, which the novel portrays with relentless terror—he fills the bathtub with crushed ice and submerges the small invalid. "The scene had something of an ancient sacrifice about it. Except that the Colonel did not know to which deity he was making the offering. And the mother, shut up in the farthest room, began to weep and pray." The child counters this confused obsession of his father with a pious and silent reply—he pretends not to be frightened, conceals his dread, and tries to console his father when desperation at wresting the son from this illness leads him to torpor and repentance. The father thus tries to free Cemí from one part of his nature, the asthma that Cemí already accepts as an initial and definitive part of his destiny.

In this account—which does not stress the rich psychic vibrations of the episodes—we must keep in mind above all the references to the father's finger and to the repeated rescue from the water. In a nightmare Cemí sees his own arm covered with sweat:

> Sweat passed along his arm again, and again he experienced the separation from his father's finger. . . . Then a broad fish swam up. . . . The fish eyed the forsaken finger and laughed. Then it took the finger into its mouth and began to afford it protection. Towing him by the finger, it brought him to a patch of floating moss where the carefully calculated rhythm of his new breathing began. Then he no longer saw salvation in the fish, but instead his mother's face.

His mother's face, as a protective solution that prolongs Cemí's new breath, also appears, overcoming the terror of the episodes with his father, resolving them in a model of profound protection. The father's finger seems to repeat, in the symbolic pattern of the beginnings of Cemí's life, that other finger of the Father giving shape to Adam. Actually, the father casts his son into the waters of life, only in this case the son is destined by an illness that confuses the creator, making him despair and dive into the river to save his son and also, curiously, one of his daughters. The gaping hole, through which they throw prisoners and garbage, and which ends in the sea full of sharks, also indicates the obscure and vaguely tenebrous vision of the origins, suggested by the anecdotes, but which Cemí incorporates, eliminating that funereal implication, bringing the origins an integrated harmony; and this discovery of harmonious meaning is explained in dreams, the allegorical region of poetic understanding.

It is in dream that the anecdote is recomposed and organized into a symbol; the father's finger is withdrawn from the water, and immediately Cemí's finger finds its own harmonious solution. The fish that recognizes and protects this solitary finger seems to be the figure of Christianity leading him to a new place where his breathing is a "carefully calculated rhythm," that is, the anticipation of poetry, of that rhythm of breathing that is the rhythm of the created universe. The fish finally changes into the mother and then the harmony of integration is closed, the presence of the mother, the order she generates as a transparency of Nature, is also the solution to the origins, because this illness is now part of an origin guilty in its separation from God, but as the emblem of an irrevocable destiny. Because of this the father's death, too, will transmute into an absence that must be sought in the manifestation of poetry itself.

The last scene of this sequence of relations with the father has the Colonel showing his son two contrasting engravings in an open book:

> The father pointed at two small, square pictures on the right and left pages, with two captions: The Student and The Grindstone. The first was the usual picture seen in study halls, a midnight scholar resting his elbows on a table covered with open books, ribbons marking the pace of his reading. . . . In The Grindstone, the man's shirt is puffed up by a gust of rain, an unstarched handkerchief wrapped around his jaw as if he had the mumps, and the wheel is densely cloaked in sparks, the rosettes of a rain of stars on a full-moon night. His curiosity ran faster than the time it took him to distinguish between

the two pictures, and when José Cemí's forefinger stopped on the picture of the grindstone, he heard his father say: "Student." Thus a warped accommodation of gesture and voice caused him to believe that the student was the grindstone and the grindstone the student.

The father has shown him these opposing emblems in order to suggest, pedagogically, a preference for the student, and so he asks, "When you're older, do you want to be a student?" "What's a student?" But Cemí has inverted the images and responds with metaphors that allude to the grindstone and surprise the father, who "was startled at his son's rare gift of metaphor, his prophetic and symbolic way of understanding a profession."

Prophetic and symbolic because for Cemí, with his maturing destiny, the opposition between the two images is false; he integrates them through language, thus displacing his father's finger with his own.

III

Octavio Paz wrote that Lezama Lima's baroque is a verbal world that is fixed, like a stalactite, and this is quite true; time fixed in a glance, a stalactite fixed in poetic adventure are also recurrent images in **Paradiso**. And the image is the mechanism that amplifies language, based on a syntax that develops in turn a geometric expansion; and the very peculiar punctuation detaches, sometimes obsessively, the zones of this verbal forest. These are tense, unwieldy sentences that intersect each other, that are integrated into the broad framework of detailed evocation.

These baroque reconstructions in the widened space of the phrase correspond also to an oral tendency, but to oral speech as atmosphere, if it can be so called. Lezama's is not a spoken language, not even in the dialogues, but a writing, which veils the warm reverberations of the game of speech. This speech as atmosphere prompts Lezama to avail himself of descriptions of oral language as another image, as an extension of written language; the novel is full of metaphorical descriptions of speech, evocations of orality that also generate that atmosphere. For example:

> Then the Colonel would turn up, and she would become the target of a volley of questions to which she would respond, nervously distracted, with a counterpoint of curtsies, starts, and lies, so that while the Colonel baritoned his laughter, Baldovina tried to make herself invisible bit by bit; and when he spoke to her again, his voice had to penetrate a forest so dark and with so many obstacles that he would be forced to amplify it with echo upon echo until he seemed to be summoning the whole household. And Baldovina, who was only a household fragment, would be reached by such a small particle of his voice that he would now have to reinforce it with a more peremptory tone to carry the force of a command.

Thus the voice is the living pattern that unifies the space of an event in evocation. The voice is also the correlate of a character, his active definition. The unsuccessful

organist Mr. Squabs, for example, defines his destiny in his language; he has to move to a new climate because of an affliction of the larynx and "This move had innocently darkened his destiny, one which he believed to be rich with artistic gift, bringing him to a dense terseness." Florita, his wife, "baritoned, as if accompanying her husband the organist," and also spoke "broadening her vowels." We read of workers who, "devouring the syllables like a ghost who makes a clock run slow, were amusing themselves." Señora Augusta is also described by her language; she says: "I have a lisp, and I've had it ever since I was a small child, when with my little sister I used to make fun of the sibilant sounds made by a funny cook we had." Uncle Luis is "talkative, although with a rich flow of palatals transformed into explosive syllables, incorrectly dividing syllables and swallowing the ends of words"; this character is the center of a detailed description by speech: "If you pronounce the word *horloge* correctly, I'll give you mine, because I intend to buy another."

Lezama also describes the "baritonal density" of a phrase; he says that the use of the diminutive indicates that the speaker is taking the side of the listener and that "reproduction exists by look and shout . . . because a shout can reproduce itself by the conjugation of different things"; he also speaks of "the sexual slowness of conjugation" in a character whose syllables "walked in the smoke like spirals that he would recover with the corner of his eye." And he writes of "syllabification," "monosyllables," "the open hollow of a shout," or someone who speaks "slowly and syllabically," "raking her words with little bubbles of sticky saliva," "muttering syllabic divisions or exploding palatals toward the ceiling." All of this suggests the poetry or the eroticism of oral speech, which is the pattern of time and of the spoken nature of a multiple dialogue with reality. Therefore two bodies embracing and caressing are described as "syllabifying with fruition."

But language can also be the metaphor of a relationship, such as that of José Cemí and Alberto Olaya.

> Alberto did not cast a glance, as on the previous occasion, and as he went up the steps to his apartment, the match dancing now with muscular energy, he said, "It bothers me when I look up and find two legs in front of me." José Eugenio had caught the round impact of the phrase, but Alberto Olaya was already going into his apartment, leaving the syllables bodiless, bringing the body around to collect the syllables.

And immediately afterwards we are told that José Eugenio "felt the syllables again, spoken next to him, but without clearly perceiving his shadowy bulk, his existence resting on an age-old boredom. And yet the phrase, walking like a centipede, tail like a serpent's head, head with the indentations and outcroppings of a key, of a clue to a puzzle, would give him the labyrinths and bays of other years that Chronos would offer him. The key to his first-born and genetrix happiness, a shadow of death to slip along his street"; which connects this metaphor of speech with José Eugenio's marriage, that is, with the birth of Cemí.

But language is essentially the central character of the novel, its pursuit and its conquest formulated as a poetics. Therefore Cemí's experience is developed as a process that comes to constitute the other absolute language of poetry. In chapter 7 we read an episode that clarifies one of the focal points of this process. Demetrio says to Cemí: "Come close so you can hear what your Uncle Alberto wrote, and you'll get acquainted with him and his special ebullience. This is the first time you'll hear language made into nature, with all its artifices of allusion and loving pedantry." This experience of language become nature is but another allegorical anticipation of Cemí's own style, because Alberto's letter is written with a metaphorical, imagistic passion, Lezama's absolute love of the word. The episode also reveals that Cemí's childhood and adolescent experience is a series of initiations into the process of learning that take on the aura of an almost religious destiny opening the way for the advent of Cemí the poet:

> When his grandmother and his mother withdrew as Demetrio began to read the letter, Cemí felt as if he had suddenly risen up into a chamber where what was said would follow an inexorable path to his ears. When he first drew his chair closer to Demetrio's, he thought he was going to hear a secret. As he listened to the succession of the names of submarine tribes, his memory not only brought forth his class in secondary school where he studied fish, but the words themselves rose up, lured up out of their own territory, artificially grouped, and their joyous movement was invisible and ineffable as it penetrated his dark channels. Listening to that verbal parade, he had the same feeling as when he sat on the wall of the Malecón and watched fishermen pulling in their catch, the fish twisting as death overcame them outside their natural habitat. In the letter those verbal fish had been hauled out twisting too, but it was a twisting of jubilation as they formed a new chorus, an army of oceanids singing as it disappeared in the mist. When he drew up his chair and was then the only one in the room listening, since his Uncle Alberto was pretending not to hear, he felt the words taking on substance and he also felt a soft wind on his cheeks shaking those words and giving them movement, how the breeze blew the peplums in Panathenaic processions, as meanings oscillated, were lost, and then reappeared as a mast in the midst of the waves, full of invisible alveoli formed by fish bites.

Cemí moves from the discovery of language in Uncle Alberto's letter to another poetic initiation, this time connected with the sense of orderly adventure which will shape the first discovery—the beautiful encounter with his mother after the disturbances in Upsalón. Experience as a totality, which is the breath and substratum of the novel, is manifested here by the mother, along with the announcement of poetry as the configuring order that harmonizes reality. She tells him:

> "Waiting for you to come home, I was thinking about your father and thinking about you, saying my rosary and asking myself: What will I tell my son when he comes back from that danger? The passing of each rosary bead was a prayer for a secret will to go with you all through your life, and for you always to have a

determination that would bring you to seek what can be seen and what is hidden. A determination that would never destroy, but that would look for the hidden in the visible, and find in the secret what will rise up for the light to give it form."

Rialta admonishes him not to reject danger, but always to try what is most difficult, danger as epiphany:

> "When man throughout his days has tested what is most difficult, he knows that he has lived in danger, and even though its existence has been silent, even though the succession of its waves has been peaceful, he knows that a day has been assigned to him in which he will be transfigured, and he will not see the fish inside the current but the fish in the starry basket of eternity."

This moral of poetry appears dictated by the mother and inscribed on the portals of the most difficult adventure that Cemí must undertake—to pass through erotic hell in order to transfigure it, too, into a moral of creation, into epiphany. The "light" (a recurrent image in the novel) configures what is secret, Rialta observes, and the poetic risk demanded by this configuration is connected to the perpetual instant which marks the identity of creator and created. As in Uncle Alberto's letter, as in the poetic conduct of Oppiano Licario (who pursues "the hare of the instant") at the end of the novel, in this second poetic opening the mother has recourse to the instantaneous, perpetuating image of the fish in poetry and in light. And later on she connects this prefiguring of Cemí's poetic destiny with his father's death:

> "For me the event, as I told you, your father's death, left me with no answer, but I've always dreamed, and those dreams will always be the root of my being alive, that it would be the profound cause of your testimony, of your seeking difficulty as transfiguration, of your answer. Some doubters will think that I never said these words, that you invented them, but when you give the answer and the testimony, you and I will know that I did say them and that I will say them as long as I live and that you will continue saying them after I have died."

The response to the father's death is also the transfiguration of the mother's response, and so poetry is the testimony of this root whose absence acclaims it not as invention but as truth. Poetry is truth, because invention is woven by a verbal presence that reveals an original absence. Thus, for Cemí, the memory of his father will have become visible in his mother's voice through the invocation "look for danger in what is most difficult," and this transfigured search is the truth and the order of poetry as a destiny.

And this entire process takes shape in the formulation of the novel as a poetics when Oppiano Licario meets Cemí at the end. For Licario, a phrase evokes reality because language, magically, precedes and configures it; reality is an extension of the phrase. Here language is nature because the process of learning through initiations has been completed; Licario, the verbal parable of Cemí himself, alter ego of the poetic enigma, dies integrated into the rhythm conquered by Cemí's destiny.

Emir Rodríguez Monegal (*Mundo Nuevo,* No. 24) has established the necessity of an anagogic reading of this novel that, according to Dante's classification in *Il Convivio* (*The Banquet*) corresponds to "the definitive and spiritual meaning of the text." This reading is undoubtedly fundamental in the case of **Paradiso,** and this search for the sublime, in a radically spiritual literature such as Lezama's, is based on that adventure of the poetization of the world, of the poet as the destiny that reveals nature, of man seen as the image of a creation understood within a primordial and total reality. This implicit religiosity orders the extraordinary verbal world of **Paradiso.**

IV

The contrapuntal play of metaphors, which produces the freedom of the analogies, also creates the web of the image. The image is prolonged, in turn, in the hyperbole channeled by the modeling form. "Actually, when a likeness is most elaborated and most approximates a Form, the image is the design of its progression," Lezama has written in an essay entitled "The Possible Images" (*Orbita de Lezama Lima*), and just as in his works "the body upon taking itself as body takes possession of an image," the novel is the body of a materialized Form, a sequence of images revealing a manifested unity and also its other side, the primordial unity. In his conversation with Alvarez Bravo, Lezama stated: "The oblique experience is as if a man, without knowing it of course, by flipping the switch in his bedroom were to produce a cascade in Ontario." This experience is, therefore, the prolongation of poetry, the open method by which to integrate similarities through the word.

The image represents a path of poetic knowledge:

> As they passed by a tomb in which the body of St. Flora was reproduced in wax, Doña Augusta said to her grandson: "That's a saint there, a real dead saint." . . . That it wasn't an image, but a very ordinary wax mold made with no excess of realism, added to the confusion, and Cemí, six years old, could not perceive the objects he was discovering as he lacked the framework that might have helped him to form analogies and group dissimilar objects around nuclei to be distributed and newly arranged.

As a child Cemí still does not recognize the possibility of analogical knowledge afforded by the image, but he is already aware of a sense of form or of the style of one of the formulations of his world:

> The tale at which Cemí had surprised his grandmother, talking about the day her father had been exhumed, disappeared in a sudden whirlwind of invisible dust. The yellowish delicacy of St. Flora's wax, which he already felt to embody the extended, violated shadow of death, began to change into the smile of Doña Augusta and Rialta. His imagination would resurrect that smile

whenever an introduction to the world of magic was needed. The smile that he observed on his grandmother and his mother was not a reaction to pleasant or comic motivations. It was the artifice of an upright goodness governed by delicacy and will, seeming to dissipate errant and sinister spirits. Cemí's approach to other people depended on whether they could produce an imitation of one of those smiles where ancestral artificiality finally poured out goodness and confidence, as if we could penetrate the eyes of animals that watch a train pass, inserting ourselves between an illuminated world entirely free of causality in the golden region of a serene portent.

This passage reveals a private heaven within the family, in other words, the archetypical forms by which reality will later be appropriated; but it also reveals a hierarchy of poetic knowledge. Cemí is still not able to define the analogies in the image because he is just beginning to discover objects. These analogies are based on the dissimilarities that, integrated as similarities by a new order, are transformed into images. This is the highest poetic knowledge, the occupation of the world by the word, the discovery of reality as a modeling of the form. Cemí already recognizes the first levels of this progression: sentiment and imagination. The early sense of death, which is one of the fundamental experiences and the intimate mechanism that poetry transfigures into an absent origin, emerges here from the awareness of an object, the wax figure of St. Flora, and is also linked to the prefiguration of family separations, but this feeling is appropriated by the imagination and is elicited by the noble resource of the smiles of his mother and grandmother, "serene portent." So although in this incident knowledge is not yielded by the image, it is yielded by a familiar and archetypical formula, by the context of the nobility that the family projects. In recapitulating this episode Lezama construes Cemí's initial experience as image, in other words, as knowledge, because although in the novel we witness a process of initiation in the struggle to conquer a poetics, the description of this process is a recapitulation that starts from the image, from the knowledge sought throughout the story. This is true because in Cemí's story, in the poetic process, the total image is a search made with images; in other words, the Form must be made flesh in the form, the Word in the words.

It is within this verbalized world that we recognize the base or the context of the poetic adventure. In the above passage Cemí uncovers these bases in the idea of the family as a form of spiritual nobility, as a sense of the maternal wisdom, as the inexhaustible flexibility of a creole culture. This rootedness in the family is also a rootedness in the land, in secureness and kindness. We have already noted the mother's disclosure of the intimate connection between the death of the father and the poetic destiny of their son in its dimension as response and testimony. This rich and complex creole nobility is, then, the foundation on which Cemí's adventure will rise beyond sentiment and imagination towards the spiritual knowledge channeled by the image through the prism of contemplation.

The image is the signifier of complex significations, a formulation comprised of the freest dissimilarities that

650

in the metaphor burst forth as analogies, creating beyond their terms a new domain. When Cemí's father and mother are married, they are the terms of an image that is just beginning. "José Eugenio Cemí and Rialta, dazzled by the gravity of the symbols, exchanged rings as if the life of one fell upon that of the other through the eternity of the circle. They felt in the proliferation of faces of family and friends a convergence into the unity of image that had begun." In these convergencies the image is the force that succeeds in transposing the space and time of the situation, creating a hyperbole that summarizes the situation in the "eternity of the circle." And like this figure, which has no beginning and no end, the image rescues reality for the idea of absolute poetry.

The image is thus a metamorphosis of time and space: "when the cornucopia of things to come has a tendency to upset itself on top of the stifled moment"; "like the parade of a Chinese military band placed between eternity and nothingness"; "in the living room, every piece of furniture seemed to be stretching, emerging from the dawn." Hyperbole prolongs the object through comparison, and this mechanism is infinite because it can provoke images by discovering analogies through the "poetically unconditioned," through a "hypertelic method" (see conversation with Alvarez Bravo), in a visualization that the word conjures outside its own organized figure. This freedom of conjuring opposing terms and prolonging them in a unity is never gratuitous, however, because with these new relations the image embodies a formal process, a path of knowledge that always refers to the calm but inflexible development of a poetics.

Severo Sarduy has written that Lezama's metaphorical mechanism is actuated by a sort of "unfolding": "Free from the dead weight of verisimilitude, from all exercise of realism—including its worst variant: magical realism—and given to the demon of correspondencies, the Lezamean metaphor reaches a distance from its terms and a hyperbolic freedom that is obtained in Spanish (I disregard other languages: ours is by nature baroque) only by Góngora. In Lezama the distance between signifier and signified, the gap opened between the phases of the metaphor, the scope of the *how*—of the language, since the metaphor implies it in all its *figures* of speech—is at its greatest" (*Mundo Nuevo,* No. 24). This "unfolding," this distance between the subject and its complements is so wide that the decisive part of the metaphorical phrase is frequently not the subject but the predicate adjective. It is even possible to lose from sight the real determining object because it is often absorbed by a proliferation of comparisons which submerge it in another, purely verbal reality. This displacement proceeds without interruption; it is a progression of wonder. The reader, who is being displaced from the subjects or objects toward the terms of comparison, perceives he is being pushed toward the unknown limits of the figure that is being proposed, toward a region in which the pervasive atmosphere is one of wonder. And while the object is being integrated as the element of a broader figure in this baroque space, the reader also reaches the point of integrating himself as the element of another form, of a current that

is unpredictable in its creationist, aleatory movement. The reader thus experiences reading as a naked experience, ascending, along with language, to the luminous realm that sparks these expansions of the image. The act of reading becomes an eroticism of this tactile light, which lingers resolutely in its painstaking discovery of the world.

The breakthrough incited by the contemplative activity of the image and the depth of knowledge achieved through the progression of wonder is revealed in the game of jacks, a truly labyrinthian ritual that evokes the image. Cemí and his two sisters are playing jacks. Their mother, who had been watching them, also joins the game.

> They had reached that point of choral ecstasy that children achieve so easily. Their time, the time of those around them, and the time of the external situation all coincided in a kind of temporal abandonment, where camphor or poppy seeds, in a silent and nocturnal vegetal growth, prepare an oval and crystalline identity, and where the isolation of a group provokes a communication that is like a universal mirror.

This universal mirror may also be an image of the novel itself, since it views language as the germinative growth of a supernature. The interesting point about this episode is that the game, magically and because the mother joins it, reveals the process by which an image is formed:

> The square formed by Rialta and her three children changed into a circle. . . . A rapid animism was transmuting the tiles, and their inorganic world was being transfused into the receptive cosmos of the image. . . . To the four jacks players, the tiles were an oscillating crystal that broke up silently after coming together silently, never losing its tremor, making way for fragments of military cloth, feeling harsh hobnails, freshly polished buttons. The fragments disappeared, reappearing at once, joined to new and larger pieces, the buttons falling into their sequence. The collar of the tunic was precisely starched, waiting for the face that would complete it.

The hallucinating, giddying game reconstructs the figure of the dead father.

> Penetrating that vision, seemingly released by the flash that preceded it, the four inside the illuminated circle experienced a sensation that was cut short as it opened up inside for an instant, and then the fragments and the totality coincided in the blink of a vision cut by a sword. Rialta nestled her head in her arms and let go the anguish that had accumulated that day; she wept until she was sated.

Thus the ritual game is also the labyrinth that reconstructs an image. The image conjugates the episode as a desired form, as wonder. The mechanism—the game—and its process—the conjured vision—are summed up in that instant, which coincides with the totality; and this procedure is also the ritual of the universal mirror that the novel itself represents. In these episodes the extraordinary aspect of the contemplative discovery rests, it seems to me, in its gratuitousness, in its representation of the occult, which in this novel destroys the banal notion of everyday life. Here everything, including the most petty detail, occurs at the incandescent edge of contemplation, where every detail stands out in relief. This is why the labyrinth expands when a door is opened or when two objects fortuitously coincide in a show window. These coincidences create a new space, a different order that discovers the enigma of seeing in the enigma of the object.

The last passage also discloses the part played by Cemí's family throughout his poetic adventure. The mother is the starting point, the manifested form of an unmanifested, unconquered form linked to the father; and the home is the permanent background, the fertile soil of this adventure.

In *Paradiso* the home is the *axis mundi,* the image par excellence, the central fire. It is not an excluding image, however. It is an incorporating image starting from which the world is an unknown house waiting to be inhabited. It is not simply a matter of chance that the last pages of the novel narrate the nocturnal adventure of Cemí entering a three-floor, lighted house in whose center he will find himself. In addition, the home is transformed in the evoked, oozing oralness, thus preserving in its spatial anchor the flavor of a time that has already been lived.

The family context is the common background of the transformations and also the constant mirror against which the characters are defined. In defining Cemí's friends— Fronesis and Foción—Lezama feels that he must define their family "mirrors," in other words, their personal labyrinths. This family context is defined, in addition, by the creole virtues that predominate within it. In this sense Uncle Alberto is probably the most animated character of this virtuous setting:

> All the lordliness of the Cuban bourgeoisie showed in him, the disdain, the domination of their surroundings, in which they came and went at will, accompanied by certain propitious deities that seemed to wave their hands, calling to approach without fear. It pleased his deities to have given him those gifts and a gracious, pleasant manner, which usually responded by shooting a precise arrow at the hare of the instant.

And also:

> For the family dynasty of the Cemís and the Olayas, the small diabolic dose of Alberto was more than enough. The family watched over and cared for that little devil cat as if he were the end result of a classical and robust development, characterized by smiling good sense and allied to the river of time in which that ark floated with alliances intertwined at the roots. Except for certain small features, Uncle Alberto formed an inaccessible and invisible part of this lustrous family tapestry, as if to receive the caress of the generations.

Courtliness is one of those high creole virtues, a form that establishes the standard of nobility in the life of the family and in society.

"Discipline should be accompanied by the grace that the image bestows, for to cut off from oneself the possibility of memory is an act which only mystics can support, living in the ecstasy of Paradise's plentitude," Lezema writes in this novel, stressing in this passage the potentiality of the image, an expanding nucleus of the past reconstructed by the desire to effect a formal process capable of convoking that plentitude.

In the last scene of the book, in which Cemí advances into the night to possess the enigma of poetry, he moves through a series of images: "This transition from amusement park into forest was invisibly assimilated by Cemí, for his hallucinated state kept the range of the image's possibility on its feet." He enters the lighted house where Oppiano Licario's sister gives him the poem that Oppiano had written about Cemí: "Reason and memory by chance / will see the dove attain / faith in the supernatural"; the discovery, therefore, of poetry as unity.

V

If courtliness is an eroticism of family nobility because it conjugates grace and wisdom, friendship is the opening of a world that conceives Eros as the conjugation of opposites, as a center from which nature, reality, is occupied, in the sense of the *occupatio* of the Stoics. As part of the process leading toward an integrating poetics, *Paradiso*'s astonishing eroticism is an uninterrupted debate, an exorcism of its other side: homosexuality. This debate brings together Foción, Fronesis, and Cemí, the three polemicists involved in the verbalization of an Eros that is about to be formulated. In his madness, Foción, who bears a *Neronian* sign, loses the possibility of defining his own eroticism at the level of poetic transmutations. The opposite is true of Fronesis, of *Goethean* sign, and especially of Cemí, who will make of Eros another analogical mechanism for discovering similarities. Thus, this conflictive debate will again be resolved in its poetic prolongation, a true guiding thread in this erotic labyrinth.

This debate is developed in chapter 9, which begins by describing a skirmish between rioting students and the police. The description suggests a battle between the Achaeans and Trojans. Cemí is confused by the turmoil, but suddenly "he felt a hand take his and pull him along from column to column every time there was a pause in the shooting." Like a warrior rescued by a god from the battlefield of Ilium, Cemí is rescued by Fronesis, whom he does not recognize until they have both reached safety. The Greek plot underlying this episode is also the plot of their friendship, and this incident brings together the three friends for the first time. A sort of introduction, this episode leads to another introduction, to Cemí's mother's words about his destiny and the epiphany of danger in the search for what is most difficult. This tortuous, labyrinthine search by means of Eros brings out the family history of the friends in order to disclose the reformulation of a deep-rooted eroticism. Although it would take too long to summarize this debate, it does not involve excluding viewpoints but, rather, different perspectives of homosexuality that eventually conjugate a central point of view; the origin conceived as an androgynous beginning and the end seen as liberation from sin. Toward the end of the chapter Cemí has a magical vision of an enormous phallus leading a strange procession. This image anticipates one of the final images of the novel, when Cemí has entered the "lucifugous house":

> The emblemata of the mosaics were executed in red cinnabar, the lance was transparent like a diamond, a steel gray shaped the sword stuck in the ground like a phallus, and every trefoil showed a key, as if nature and super-nature had been united in something meant to penetrate, to jump from one region to another, in order to reach the castle and interrupt the feast of the hermetic troubadours. A garland tied Eros and Thanatos together, the submersion into the vulva was the resurrection in the Vale of Glory.

The lengthy debate on homosexuality can be understood starting from this type of metaphorization. The androgynous substratum of creation on which the dialoguers insist would thus be the source of the transformation, the matrix that prolongs the similarities, converting nature and supernature into transparent similarity. This duplication of nature through eroticism is also related to the recurring image of the tree of life, which in the novel is allegorically related with the phallus. This explains why the episode (chapter II) in which Cemí listens to Foción's protracted monologue on the anality of the god Anubis and on how the embryo is prior to all sexual dualism (Mercury) is followed by a decisive passage on poetry and its practice. It should be noted that this type of construction is the basis of the narrative structure of the novel: one episode summons another in a successive hyperbolic transformation. The section on the practice of poetry in chapter II—which transforms the exacerbated speech of an inebriated Foción—presents the poetic views of Cemí, who now conjugates in a new space the objects around him:

> That immense populated area, from the alabaster Minerva to the Cuban smokers' engravings, was matched by the two bronze statuettes, the angel and the baccante, on each side of the Pueblan cup. At first with terror, and then with everyday joy, he viewed the coincidence of his navel, his omphalos, with the center of a universal phallic dolmen. Those groupings with an expressed dimension and with a directional waft were thought created, were animals of durable images that drew his body toward the earth so that he could ride them.

It seems to me, therefore, that the complex debate on homosexuality tends to exorcise an erotic point of view at this poetic level: eroticism is the ground on which objects coincide in order to create new objects, new images that expand our vision. The materialization of imagination, the invisible becoming visible, seems to require in this poetic system an eroticism capable of conjugating the poet with creation, with the Form, through an identity prior to sexual dualism; in other words, poetry is born from a totalizing eroticism, from an erotic inception defined by an unrestrained freedom to plot the conjugation of opposites in the essential similarity of reality. Nevertheless, this integrating eroticism, this germinative center, is also an asceticism, because its analogical freedom is guided by the intimate and irreversible march of a destiny whose labyrinths must evoke the "paradisiacal solution" announced by Foción.

The encounter of the *omphalos* and the universal phallic dolmen—axial symbolism—is also the encounter of the word and nature, the mutual creation of the poet and of the universe created by God. Poetry should find the axis of its condition in an intimately religious context, where it acquires its creative dimension, its principal justification. Poised between the descent into Hades (Foción) and the return to the light (Fronesis), Cemí sublimates eroticism through his discovery of the gnostic space, of officiating poetry, of the word as a religious act that leads to the axial encounter.

VI

Poetry has its origin in Eros, which generates its drive toward an incorporating knowledge, and that is why language is a supernature in the new space of its expansion:

> The door to the classroom closed, Cemí looked it up and down as if it were an inebriated Polyphemus who had come out to stop him from dealing with those questions in the Goethean tradition of "precise perceptive fantasy," which was almost the way in which the *intelligere* embraced its Eros, a lustful fanaticism of knowledge that was the shade from the tree of life, not in the antipodes of the tree of knowledge, but in the shade that joins the silent heaven of the Taoists to the Word that fertilizes the city as the supernatural.

The path leading to the unity of poetry is one of apprenticeship, a configuration and integration of different discoveries. Lezama gives us the following insight into the process of poetic formation:

> Like Fronesis, he had been led by the impassioned reading of Plato to polarize his culture. Those great rhapsodies in the *Phaedrus* and the *Phaedo* brought him to that mixture of exaltation and lament which constitutes love and death in the flash of their conjoinment. The hallucinated fervor for unity laid out, perhaps unsurpassably, in the *Parmenides* brought him to the mysticism of the relationship between creator and creature and to a conviction of the existence of a universal marrow which controls series and exceptions. In the *Charmides* he would discover the seduction of the relationships between wisdom and memory. "We know only what we remember" was the Delphic conclusion of that culture. . . . And the unforgettable months of his adolescence, spent with the *Timaeus*, which taught him Pythagoreanism, and the apparent respite offered by the *Symposium*, spawning the myths of primitive androgny and the search for the image in reproduction and in the sexual complementaries of the Topos Ouranos and the Aphrodite Ourania.

A revitalization of the past and a search for the unknown are also dimensions of the poetry conceived by Cemí and formulated as poetics by Lezama Lima. The above passage assembles the substratum of a poetry activated by love-death, mystical and guiding unity, wisdom and memory, Pythagorism and symbolism, the image sought in the original androgyny. The discovery of the image that conjugates these levels is also the discovery of the gnostic space. The practice of poetry is the materialization of the word, an entering into the gnostic space, "which expresses, which knows, which has a density that contracts to bring forth"; "gnostic space, tree, man, city, spatial groupages in which man is the median point between nature and the supernatural." In this poetic convocation, seeing plays a decisive role. It discloses the alliance with incarnations in time, and this is the instant of epiphany.

This way of seeing is outlined in the section of chapter 11 that describes the exercise of poetry in Cemí. The coincidence of a cup between two bronze statuettes evokes a baroque space. The coincidence of objects in a unitary space that prolongs them into an image is a poetic allegory, an exercise of Lezama's poetic system. In this instance it involves creating "cities invented by those groupings" that allegorize the words in this episode.

> He was able to establish that those groupings had temporal roots, had nothing to do with spatial groupings, which are always a still life; for the viewer, the flow of time converted those spatial cities into figures, through which time, as it passed back and forth like the labor of the tides on the coral reefs, produced a kind of eternal change of the figures, which by being situated in the distance were a permanent embryo. The essence of time, which is the ungraspable, by its own movement that expresses all distance, achieves the reconstruction of those Tibetan cities which enjoy all mirages, the quartz doe of the contemplative way, but into which we are not able to penetrate, for man, everything external producing an irradiation which reduces him to a diamond essence lacking walls. The man knows that he cannot penetrate into those cities, but in him there is a disquieting fascination with those images, which are the only reality that comes toward us, that bites us, a leech that bites without a mouth, that by a contemplative method sustains the image, like most of Egyptian painting, and wounds us precisely with what it lacks.

In this passage Lezama has described its limits in the labyrinth it ventures to discover, as well as the proximity or the final convocation that its unitary adventure is able to call forth in its void, in its absence. Thus, "the image in the distance is always contemplative," because it summons the Form in its form, because it repeats as supernature that which exists in the form of created nature. The image provokes an axial relationship, the union of the *omphalos* and the universal dolmen. Poetry is a religious act, the Tibetan city, the gnostic space that evinces the Unity. In an article entitled "Para llegar a Lezama Lima," Julio Cortázar discusses the passages that are central to the poetics of this book. He states that in this novel words are converted into objects and then objects are transformed into words. This is precisely what is involved in the gnostic process, the path from a temporal

vision to a baroque space. In addition, this vision is animated by a "lingering of nature," in the presence of which an observant lingering, "which is itself nature," implies the discovery of rhythm, in other words, the prolongation of the look in the framework of the "hyperbolic memory" (see the dialogue between José Cemí and his grandmother).

Guided by these discoveries, chapter 12 appears to be an allegory of the poetics that Cemí is beginning to formulate. This chapter, which consists of literary exercises written perhaps by Cemí himself, interposes the following four sequences, which will later be conjugated: the story of a Roman general, that of a child and a vase, that of a nighttime stroller, and the curious story of the music critic who prolongs a timeless, grotesque life. The final shuffling of these stories allegorizes the theme of time. Through the intervention of his wife, the music critic appears to be outwitting time by prolonging an artificial life, but in the end his story is a grotesque absurdity. He dies, and the Roman warrior surprisingly appears in his glass casket.

> Instead of a music critic surrendered to sleep to conquer time, the face of a Roman general who moaned, immobilized as the possibility of dying in the whirlwind of battle was obliterated for him. . . . Now the critic can perceive the drops of the temporal, but not as other mortals do, for death, not sleep, begins now to really give him the eternal, in which time cannot be conquered, beginning with the non-existence of that sin which is time.

In the final scene of this chapter, two centurions are rolling dice in the ruins of a Christian temple that had previously been an academy of pagan philosophers. A Greek bust falls and interrupts the game, changing the marks on the two dice to a four:

> The two dice achieved a four, one alongside the other, as if the two surfaces had joined their waters. The four remained under the ruined cupola in the center of the crossing of the nave and transept. The two centurions covered themselves with a single cape, from the neck there arose something like the head of a large turtle, and trying not to stumble, they strode off with the pace of a forced march.

This scene suggests a symbolic synthesis of the four stories developed in this chapter, perhaps in a religious framework, because four is the number of the Ineffable Name, "the fountain of nature that always flows, God." Thus, and although this chapter undoubtedly contains much richer allegories, Cemí is shown developing an exercise of poetry that is resolved in the symbol.

The presence of Oppiano Licario dominates the remaining chapters, and through him poetry is postulated as the final image of *Paradiso*. As we already mentioned, Oppiano is also an allegory of Cemí himself, a projection of him toward the past, toward the decisive moments of his life at which he was not present (the death of his father and of his uncle Alberto), and therefore his encounter with this fulgent Icarus represents the closing of an open cycle, the encounter that links a past and a destiny in the relating of a *Bildungsroman*.

Oppiano and Cemí meet on a bus marked by the sign of the decapitated head of a bull, a multiple image of power. Oppiano's conversation with several girls on the bus could also apply to the rich process of Cemí's discovery of poetry:

> Every instant brings a fish out of water and the only thing I'm interested in is catching it . . . if not for an occasion, whirlwinds of coincidence frozen into sculpture, how would we be able to show wisdom? Life is a web of indeterminate situations, each coincidence is something that wants to speak at our side, if we interpret it, we incorporate a form, we control a transparency. . . . The only thing that can interest me is the coincidence of my ego in the diversity of situations. If I let those coincidences pass, I'll feel myself dying when I interpret them, I'm the maker of a miracle, I've dominated the unformed act of nature.

Here poetry is defining life, prolonging it by the coincidence through which the "I" incorporates nature, sculpturing the instant. From a compelling vision, poetry now becomes the breath of imagination, a new axis of the world:

> That ancestor (his father) had endowed Licario from birth with a powerful *res extensa* which could be watched from his childhood on. The cogitative had begun to burst out, to divide or to perform subtle breathing exercises in the expanding zone. . . . The *occupation* of extension through the cogitative was so perfect that in it cause and effect reworked incessantly in alternating currents producing the new absolute order of the cognitative being. It broke with Cartesian mathematical progression. In the analogy, two ends of the progression developed a third progression, or a march to encompass the third unknown point. At the first two ends, much nostalgia for the expansive substance continued to persist. The discovery of the third unknown point at the moment of recovery, was what visualized and slowly extracted from the extension the analogy of the first two movables. Cognitive being attained its sphere always in relation to the third, errant, unknown movable, before that moment given by the disguised mutations of ancestral evocation. . . . Thus, where that spatial ordering of the two points of analogy intersects with the temporal, movable unknown, Licario situated what he called *Poetic Syllogistics*. . . . Licario nourished himself, in his cogitative extensibility, on those two currents: an ascent of the germ until the act of participation, which is knowledge of death, and later in the poetic awakening of a cosmos that reverted from the act to the germ through the mysterious labyrinth of the cognitive image.

Licario is, therefore, the allegorical realization of Cemí, the mirror that projects him. His definition through poetry, his destiny occupied by poetry is also an anticipation of his disciple, who will incorporate his dead teacher in the center of this verbal ritual. Licario is the key that opens the flaming house from which Cemí will emerge toward a new beginning, toward the recognition

of rhythm, that is to say, toward the unity of his own experience in poetry, in **Paradiso**. The analogy of the terms in a progression that develops the third term of the adventure, creating the image, is also the germinative and nuclear eroticism, and this syllogistics is also an asceticism, a mysticism of total poetry (or a poetry of totality, as Octavio Paz prefers) as an enchanted vision of the world. In the end it is David, not Oedipus, who in his praise reproduces the Creator, the verbal supernature, the unified paradise, the garland which links Eros and Thanatos. This fabulous novel thus formulates a poetics as a multiple adventure, as an amazing metaphor of the world.

NOTES

* José Lezama Lima, *Paradiso,* translated by Gregory Rabassa (New York: Farrar, Straus, & Giroux, 1974).

FURTHER READING

Beaupied, Aída. "The Myth of Narcissus and the Poet's quest for knowledge in Sor Juana Inés de la Cruz and José Lezama Lima." *Romance Notes*, Vol. XXXV, No. 2 (Winter 1994): 111-25.

> Utilizes the myth of the narcissus flower as a means toward enlightenment as the pivot of comparison between two poets' works, Lezama Lima's *Paradiso* and Sor Juana de la Cruz's *The Divine Narcissus.*

Bravo, Victor. "Figurations and Transfigurations of the Image." *The South Atlantic Quarterly*, Vol. 92, No. 3 (Summer 1993): 445-51.

> Offers insight into the poetic process of symbolic and ritualistic metamorphosis, primarily in the text of Lezama Lima's *Narcissus.*

Fazzolari, Margarita. "Reader's Guide to *Paradiso.*" *Latin American Literature and Arts Review*, Vol. 29 (May/August 1981): 47-54.

> Summarizes the importance of the Word in Lezama Lima's life and works.

Levinson, Brett. "Possibility, Ruin, Repitition: Rereading Lezama Lima's 'American Expression'." *Revista Canadiense de Estudios Hispanicos*, Vol. XVIII, No. 1 (Fall 1993): 49-66.

> Explores the process of repetition and rereading as a method toward understanding the layers of meaning in texts, paying particular attention to Lezama Lima's 'American Expression,' and its posits of influence of tradition among three continents: Europe, America, and Latin America.

Lutz, Robin R. "The Tribute to Everyday Reality in José Lezama Lima's *Fragmentos a su Iman.*" *Journal of Spanish Studies Twentieth Century*, Vol. 8, No. 3 (1981): 249-66.

> Tries to evince the unifying force among ritual abstraction and concrete reality simulated in Lezama Lima's use of word play and imagery.

Pellon, Gustavo. "The Loss of Reason and the Sin *Contra Natura* in Lezama's *Paradiso*." *Studies in Homosexuality,* Wayne R. Dynes and Stephen Donaldson, eds., pp. 253-267. New York: Garland Publishing, Inc., 1992.

> Discusses the hinderance placed on the protagonists' enlightenment due to misdirected sexual frustration and confusion in *Paradiso*.

———. "Portrait of the Cuban Writer as French Painter: Henri Rousseau, José Lezama Lima's Alter Ego." *MLN,* Vol. 103, No. 2 (March 1988): 350-73.

> Reveals the relationship between painter Henri Rousseau and Lezama Lima's artistic techniques as necessitated by their place in geography and time.

Pérez Firmat, Gustavo. "Descent in 'Paradiso': A Study of Heaven and Homosexuality." *Hispanofila*, Vol. 59, No. 2 (May 1976): 247-57.

> Captures theories of androgyny and homosexuality as mirrors of Cemí's descent into purgatory and hell, and subsequent ascension into heaven in *Paradiso*.

Additional coverage of Lezama Lima's life and career is contained in the following sources published by the Gale Group: *Contemporary Authors*, **Vol. 77-80;** *Contemporary Authors New Revision Series*, **Vol. 77;** *Contemporary Literature Criticism*, **Vols. 4, 10, 101;** *Dictionary of Literary Biography*, **Vol. 113;** *Hispanic Writers*.

Clarice Lispector
1920-1977

Ukrainian-born Brazilian novelist, short story writer, journalist, essayist, children's fiction writer, and translator.

INTRODUCTION

One of the preeminent Latin American writers of the twentieth century and a revolutionizing force in Brazilian literature, Lispector has been hailed as a brilliantly original prose stylist. Her modernist narratives move away from the regional interests of her predecessors to take up universal themes deeply rooted in the psychological drama of everyday existence. In them are found the purest expression of her major concerns: human suffering and failure; the interrelation of language, life, and identity; the effect of social constraints on individuals; the place of women in male-dominated society; and the subjective nature of reality. Her philosophically oriented stories are often told in a stream-of-consciousness or interior-monologue style, with plot subordinated to the inner experiences of her solitary, sensitive characters. This use of paradox characterizes her fiction, and often in her tales the quotidian and the realm of the fantastic merge, realistic observation is coupled with poetic description, and minor events give rise to extraordinary insight. Her prose style shows a poet's concern with linguistic nuance and the use of symbolism and metaphor. Lispector is also celebrated as an early practitioner of post-structural and feminist writing because of her interest in the problems of language and existence, gender roles, and sexuality.

Lispector was always reluctant to divulge information about her background to critics, so the details surrounding her birth are difficult to ascertain. She was most likely born in the Ukraine in 1920 shortly before her family, of Jewish origin, emigrated to the Americas. She spent her early childhood in economically depressed Alagoas and Recife in northeastern Brazil before moving to Rio de Janeiro. Her mother died when Lispector was nine, and she and her sisters were raised by their father, a man of modest means but with a love of books and music. Lispector took advantage of the cultural and educational opportunities available to her in Rio de Janeiro, reading widely in Brazilian and foreign works, expressing a particular fondness for the fiction of Katherine Mansfield, Virginia Woolf, Herman Hesse, and Fyodor Dostoevsky. She decided early on that she would become a writer, and her earliest efforts from her teenage years, some of which were published posthumously in *A bela e a fera* (1979), show considerable maturity.

In 1943 Lispector married Mauro Gurgel Valente, a fellow law student at the National Faculty of Law in Rio de Janeiro. After graduating with a law degree, she began working for the Rio de Janeiro newspaper, *A noite*. In 1944 she published her first novel, *Perto do coracão selvagem*. It was immediately lauded for its lyrical language and feminine insight into external events. The novel was groundbreaking also because it marked a shift away from the realism and regionalism of traditional Brazilian literature to a modern aesthetic with universal and psychological concerns. Her next two novels, *O histre* (1946) and *A cidade sitiada* (1948) were written while she lived in Europe, where her husband, then a diplomat, was posted. The couple and their two young boys moved to the United States in 1952. That year, Lispector's first collection of stories, *Alguns contos,* was published to little critical or commercial response.

Lispector separated from her husband in 1959 and resettled in Brazil with her two children. In 1960 she gained widespread recognition for *Laços de família,* an expanded version of her 1952 short story collection. The publication of the novel A *maçã no escuro* in 1961 confirmed her reputation as a major figure in Latin American letters. This was followed with several other well-received novels, including the widely read *A paixão segundo G. H.* (1964), a first-person narrative with biblical overtones told by a bourgeois woman of the strange events that lead to her existential awakening. From 1967 to 1973 Lispector wrote short weekly pieces for the *Jornal do Brasil* on a range of subjects, from interviews with other writers to short "chronicles" with fictional qualities. She remarked that her success during this period made her feel as though she was forced to play the role of the "Great Lady of Brazilian Letters," which went against her nature as an intensely private woman. In the 1970s, facing financial difficulties, she reissued many of her earlier works in new anthologies and translated works by Jack London, Walter Scott, Jules Verne, Edgar Allan Poe, Oscar Wilde, and Henry Fielding. With her last novel, *A hora da estrela* (1977), she reached a broader audience as she touched on the theme of social oppression, an element some critics found wanting in her earlier works. She was diagnosed with cancer in the fall of 1977 and died a few weeks later.

Throughout her career, Lispector constantly revised her works, reissuing old stories under new titles, modifying pieces and publishing them under the original titles, and incorporating shorter pieces into longer ones. The six stories in the 1952 collection, *Alguns contos,* appeared eight years later in *Laços de família* together with other stories written and published while she was living abroad. The reissue of these stories in 1960 immediately captured the attention of critics, and they continue to be regarded as the reason Lispector is considered a genius of the short story genre. Most of her best-known stories, acknowledged classics of modern Latin American literature, are included in this volume. Many of the protagonists of these tales are females, young and old, who experience epiphanies regarding their identities: in "Amor," a young woman's encounter with a blind man on a tram forces her to question her regimented existence. Several stories deal with the "ties" of family and community that serve to bind and repress, as in "Feliz aniversario," a sad tale about the strained family relationships made clear during an old woman's eighty-ninth birthday party. Animals also figure prominently in these tales, for example in "O bufalo," in which a woman goes to the zoo in order to experience the purity of emotion that animals enjoy, and "O crime do professor de matematica," about a man's discovery of his humanity through the act of burying a stray dog.

Lispector's novel, *A maçã no escuro* (1961; *The Apple in the Dark*), was praised primarily for its rich use of language and for its investigation of the relation between language and identity. The novel offers a symbolic, psychological portrait of an antihero who undertakes a quest for identity after he has apparently committed a crime. Much of the action takes place in the minds of the protagonist and the two women with whom he becomes involved. *A paixão segundo G. H.* (1964), centers on language and relates a woman's attempts to understand reality. Her failure to transcend her feelings of loneliness contribute further to her sense of alienation.

One of Lispector's later novels, *Água viva* (1973), while rooted in the consciousness of a character searching for meaning and identity, initiated Lispector's more intense, self-reflective experiments in fiction. This feature also forms a major part of her last work, *A hora da estrela* (1978; *The Hour of the Star*), a novella concerning a young woman who moves from an isolated rural locale to Rio de Janeiro. The story is narrated by a man who relates her experiences and comments on how he will present them in fictional form. The adventures of the protagonist and the commentary of the narrator reflect Lispector's life and her ideas about art and language. This work exemplifies Lispector's interest in social issues, as she depicts the experiences of a poor female struggling to establish herself in a male-dominated society. Once again, Lispector was praised for her innovative use of language. In summarizing Lispector's contribution to Brazilian literature, Gregory Rabassa stated: "[Lispector marshals] the syntax in a new way that is closer perhaps to original thought patterns than the [Portuguese] language had ever managed to approach before."

Lispector's potential as a major writer was recognized by Brazilian reviewers with the publication of her first novel in 1944, and critics offered immediate praise for her extraordinary flair for poetic language, intensity of expression, and the psychological complexity of her protagonists, features which critics continued to admire in her later works. Lispector's reputation was established with her short story collection *Laços de família* whose translation into English in 1972 made her one of the most respected writers in the late twentieth century. English language criticism of her work tends to concentrate on

this volume, with earlier commentators remarking on the tales' existential concerns and later critics noting the stories' use of myth, religious symbolism, animal imagery, social parody, and feminist thematics. These elements, it has been pointed out, are echoed in all her stories, and even her earliest tales reveal a young writer concerned with the problems of sexual and social identity, gender roles, and the nature of androgynous existence.

It is generally agreed that Lispector's 1974 collection, *A via crucis do corpo,* marks a transition in her development as a writer. As several critics have noted, the stories in this volume depart from her earlier works in their overtly sexual nature, their lack of focus on characters' inner being; their use of colloquial language; the presence of the lower spectrum of middle-class characters; and their emphasis on the reader's role in conferring meaning to text. Initial reception to the stories was mixed, with many of Lispector's admirers considering they indicated a decline in the quality of her work. However, others have noted that the stories use a new deconstructivist/postmodern aesthetic model to express in artful form many of her most important concerns, including sexual independence, authenticity, absurdity, male/female relationships, consciousness, and self-determination.

PRINCIPAL WORKS

Perto do coracão selvagem [*Near to the Wild Heart*] (novel) 1944

O lustre [*The Chandelier*] (novel) 1946

A cidade sitiada [*The Besieged City*] (novel) 1948

Alguns contos [*Some stories*] (short stories) 1952

Agua viva [*The Stream of Life*] (mixed-genre work) 1960

Laços de família [*Family Ties*] (short stories) 1960

A maçã no escuro [*The Apple in the Dark*] (novel) 1961

A paixão segundo G. H. [*The Passion According to G. H.*] (novel) 1961

A legiao estrangeira [*The Foreign Legion*] (stories and essays) 1964

O misterio do coelho pensante [*The Mystery of the Thinking Rabbit*] (children's fiction) 1967

A mulher que matou os peixes [*The Woman Who Killed the Fishes*] (children's fiction) 1968

Uma aprendizagem; ou, O livro dos prazeres [*An Apprenticeship; or, The Book of Pleasures*] (novel) 1969

Felicidade clandestina [*Secret Happiness*] (short stories) 1971

A imitação da rosa [*The Imitation of the Rose*] (short stories) 1973

Onde estivestes de noite? [*Where Were You That Night?*] (short stories) 1974

A via crucis do corpo [*The Via Crucis of the Body*] (short stories) 1974

A vida íntima de Laura [*The Private Life of Laura*] (children's fiction) 1974

Visão do esplendor: impressoes leves [*Visions of Splendor: Slight Impressions*] (essays and sketches) 1974

A hora da estrela [*The Hour of the Star*] (novel) 1977

Um sopro de vida: pulsações [*A Breath of Life: Pulsations*] (mixed-genre work) 1978

A bela e a fera [*Beauty and the Beast*] (short stories) 1979

A descoberta do mundo [*Discovering the World*] (journalistic essays) 1984

Soulstorm: Stories (short stories) 1989

CRITICISM

Earl E. Fitz (essay date 1988)

SOURCE: "The Passion of Logo(centrism), or, the Deconstructionist Universe of Clarice Lispector," in *Luso-Brazilian Review*, Vol. 25, No. 2, 1988, pp.33-44.

[*In this essay, Fitz analyzes Lispector's fiction as deconstruction of language and action as an attempt to find the meaning therein in three of Lispector's novels and one short story.*]

For those critics who regard it as involving something more than mere nihilistic nonsense, the term "Deconstructionism" has come to refer to that view of literature in which a text—any text—can be shown to be undercutting, or "deconstructing," itself at the same instant that it is working to organize, or "construct," itself into a stable, coherent and verifiable system of meaning. As a literary theory, we know that Deconstructionism owes much to the linguistic model outlined by Ferdinand de Saussure in which all language use necessarily involves eternally fluid systems of arbitrarily connected "signifiers" and signifieds" and in which there are no absolute references external to the language systems themselves. For Saussure, who held, in regard to linguistic signs, that, ". . . il n'y a que des différences sans termes positifs" (". . . there are only differences without positive terms"),[1] meaning, in language and therefore in literature, emerges as an entirely arbitrary function; or, to paraphrase Humpty Dumpty (who may be considered one of Western literature's earliest deconstructionist critics), "Words mean exactly what I want them to mean, nothing more and nothing less!"

Yet in spite of its vast potential for abuse and obfuscation, Deconstructionism offers the literary critic a linguistically based way of explaining why texts generate different meanings and why they elicit different responses in readers. For certain texts, Clarice Lispector's opaque, lyrically meditative novels and stories figuring prominently among them, the question of meaning is not merely a thematic problem but a technical one, a feature of the work that relates to what the "New Critics" tended to describe as a text's "ambiguity," its artistically poised uncertainties. For the deconstructionist, however, this very "ambiguity" or "uncertainty" is shown to be a function not of a text's style or its "literariness" but of language itself, of language's endless self-reflexivity, its semantic instability and its ever-fluctuating relation to the various "realities" that it simultaneously describes, "constructs," and "deconstructs." This essentially poststructuralist sense of language and meaning, I believe, is the fundamental philosophical and psycholinguistic principle that Clarice Lispector develops so brilliantly, as I will now try to show, in the creation of such extraordinary texts as *Perto do coração selvagem* (1944), *A maçã no escuro* (1961), *A paixão segundo G. H.* (1964), *A legião estrangeira* (1964), *Agua viva* (1973), *Um sopro de vida* (1978) and **"A quinta história."**

From her first novel, published in 1944, to her posthumous works, it is clear that Clarice Lispector was a writer whose primary thematic concern was the flickering, ephemeral relationship between words, reality and the ebb and flow of human cognition. Like Hélène Cixous (whose *Vivre l'orange,* 1979, was based upon several of Clarice's texts), the later Barthes (particularly of *S/Z*), Jacques Derrida,[2] Jonathan Culler, Julia Kristeva, and Lucy Irigaray, Clarice was a writer for whom the problem of meaning (how it is generated, how it is mentally processed and how it is reformulated as literary art) lies, restively, at the heart of the human condition.

Consistent with these other "poststructuralist," or "deconstructionist" critics, Clarice and her characters view the human creature as being inescapably locked within a prison house of language, one in which words refer only to other words rather than to what Derrida has called a "metaphysical" referent, a substantiating "first principle" that exists beyond language and upon which a system of perfect and stable meaning can be built. In works like *Perto do coração selvagem*, *A paixão segundo G. H.*, *Agua viva* and **"A quinta história,"** to cite just four examples, Clarice has created not "novels" and "stories" but "texts," a critical term used by poststructuralists to refer to the "web-like complexity of signs" in which the "back and forth, present and absent, forward and sideways movement of language in its actual processes"[3] is highlighted. Joana, for example, the protagonist of *Perto do coração selvagem*, develops as a character in direct relation to her gradual and disquieting discovery of the spurious nexus between language and its referents, between its conventionally understood signs and the supposedly reliable "first principles" of meaning they are believed to express. Gaining steadily in self-realization and strength, Joana, who comes to reject first the "logocentrism" and then the "phalllogocentrism" that has entrapped her, eventually feels the need to create a new, private and, she hopes, authentic language system, one that will truthfully embody and express her as yet inchoate process of self-realization.[4] Her creation of a new, non-"phallogocentric" language system thereby mirrors and sustains her newly achieved sense of self.

One of Clarice's later protagonists, Martim (of *A maçã no escuro*), is also depicted as a human being whose identity is stunted by virtue of being trapped in language. As the omniscient voice of his "text" describes him:

> . . . o que fêz Martim experimentar essa perfeição foi o fato de suas palavras terem de algum modo ultrapassado o que êle quisera dizer. . . . Em algum ponto não identificável, aquêle homem ficara prêso núm círculo de palavras.[5]

Martim, like Joana, G. H. and the voices of *Um sopro de vida* and *Agua viva*, comes to discover that his quest for authenticity of being is inescapably bound up in the essence of language itself. The fluid, open poststructuralist "texts" that give form to the ontological struggles of these characters are, as they and the reader come to discover, composed of structures and patterns of words that refer, endlessly, to other structures and patterns of words. This explains why texts like *Perto do coração selvagem*, *A maçã no escuro*, *A paixão segundo G. H.* and *Agua viva* have no stable "first principles" of semantic reference and no structurally clear beginnings, no unambiguous lines of development and no decisive, conflict-resolving conclusions. Overwhelmingly, Clarice's texts—especially her longer, "novel" length narratives[6]—create fictive worlds in which words, Saussure's "signifiers," continuously reveal themselves to be only arbitrarily linked to their supposed "signifieds," and it is from this poetically rendered tangle of thought and sign that Clarice's famous lyricism and ambiguity derive. From the perspective of a deconstructionist critic, then, the "fictions"[7] of Clarice Lispector are brilliant examples of what Derrida calls "inter" (as well as "intra") textuality," dense webs of semantically destabilized words that refer essentially to themselves[8] and to their "différance," to the superfluities and slippages of meaning constantly generated by them.

A second principle of Lispectorian deconstructionist theory, and one that, like the importance given the self-reflexive "intertextuality" of words, fully characterizes Clarice's writing, is her abolition of the orthodox distinctions between "criticism" and "creative writing." For Lispector, as for Hélène Cixous, Lucy Irigaray, Jacques Derrida, Roland Barthes (at least of *S/Z*) and Julia Kristeva (especially her *La Révolution du langue poétique*, 1974), the concept of "criticism" as "evaluation" gives way to an often creative discourse on "text" or "writing" (what Derrida calls "écriture"), on the interactive mental process that is involved in the writerly creation and readerly deconstruction of a "text." The feminist writer and critic Hélène Cixous, has, in *Vivre l'orange,* called attention to precisely this key post-structuralist dimension of Clarice's work, one which, typified in such texts as *A maçã no escuro*, *A paixão segundo G. H.* and *Agua viva*, she finds to be powerfully demonstrative not merely of Derrida's "écriture" but of "l'écriture féminine," of a uniquely "feminine" way of writing, one often described as the process of "writing the body."[9] Merging her self-conscious preoccupation with words as a viable mechanism for self-creation and growth with this deconstructively hybrid concept of "text" as simultaneously "fiction" and "nonfiction," the voice of *Agua viva* lyrically declares:

> Não sei sobre o que estou escrevendo: sou obscura para mim mesma. Só tive inicialmente uma visão lunar e lúcida, e então prendi para mim o instante antes que ele morresse e que perpetuamente morre. Não é um recado de idéias que te transmito e sim uma instintiva volúpia daquilo que está escondido na natureza e que adivinho. E esta é um festa de palavras. Escrevo em signos que são mais um gesto que voz. . . . refaço-me nestas linhas. Tenho uma voz. Assim como me lanço no traço de meu desenho, este é um exercício de vida sem planejamento. O mundo não tem ordem visível e eu só tenho a ordem da respiração. Deixo-me acontecer.[10]

In an earlier (1964) collection of ostensibly "nonfiction" pieces entitled "No fundo de gaveta," Clarice had also contemplated the fluid nature of writing, here metaphorically equating it to the act of fishing:

> Então escrever é o modo de quem tem a palavra como isca: a palavra pescando o que não é palavra. Quando essa não palavra morde a isca, alguma coisa se escreveu. Uma vez que se pescou a entrelinha, podia-se com alívio jogar a palavra fora. Mas aí cessa a analogia: a não palavra, ao morder a isca, incorporou-a. O que salva então é ler 'distraìdamente'.[11]

Later in this same work, Clarice reiterates what we can now see as a fundamentally deconstructionist concept of writing as process or flow, as "écriture:"

> Não me lembro mais onde foi o começo, foi por assim dizer escrito todo ao mesmo tempo. . . . Escrevi procurando com muita atenção o que se estava organizando em mim. . . . Tinha a impressão de que, mais tempo eu me desse, e a história diria sem convulsão o que ela precisava dizer. . . . infelizmente não sei 'redigir', não consigo 'relatar' uma idéia, não sei 'vestir uma idéia com palavras'. O que vem à tona já vem com ou através de palavras, ou não existe. — Ao escrevê-lo, de nôvo a certeza só aparentemente paradoxal de que o que atrapalha ao escrever é ter de usar palavras. É incômodo (Lispector, *A legião estrangeira,* 251-252).

Clarice's rejection of the old boundaries between "fiction" and "nonfiction" has been a constant in her writing ever since her first published work, the densely poetic, self-reflective and open-ended "novel," *Perto do coração selvagem*. This text, which, in retrospect, can now be seen as having initiated a revolution in terms of the ways narrative would be written in Brazil, received its title from Joyce's *A Portrait of the Artist as a Young Man,* Joyce being a male writer much admired for his "antiphallocentric" texts by such critics as Hélène Cixous and Julia Kristeva, whose own brand of feminist theory owes much to deconstructive analysis.

Integrally related to this deliberate merging of nonfiction discourse and creative writing is a third characteristic of deconstructive "écriture" that is also endemic to Clarice's work, her penchant for utilizing what, in *Allegories of Reading,* Paul de Man calls "rhetoric,"[12] not the art of persuasion but a heavy reliance on interrelated systems of tropes, figuration and etymology. Calling attention to Clarice's philosophical relevance to Heidegger, which many critics have noted, as well as to Joyce and Woolf, this key poststructuralist feature of her texts tends to generate and nurture the "binary oppositions" so typical of classical structural analysis. Within the context of Clarice's work, many of these "binary oppositions" can also be seen as constituting a number of motifs and metaphors that are endemic to her work:[13] language/silence, speaking/thinking, light/darkness, love/hate, writing/speaking, isolation/socialization, and, in a unique way, male/female, to name just a few.

Yet for all that Clarice's work can be said to be structured around systems involving these "binary oppositions," there is also present in her texts a powerful and often self-conscious tendency toward the undermining or "deconstruction" of language and the supposed reliability of its semantically generative systems and structures. Typically, as in *Perto do coração selvagem*, *A maçã no escuro* or *Agua viva*, Clarice's texts generate precisely the sense of linguistic destabilization and unreliability that Derrida expresses in the term "différance," a neologism of his coinage related to the Saussurean concept ("différence") that in language "meaning" is an eternally evolving function of the arbitrary and imperfect connection between signifiers and signifieds. At the moment there is no known evidence to suggest that Clarice was ever directly influenced by either Saussure or such poststructuralist theoreticians as the later Barthes, Derrida or Paul de Man, though, given the dates of their major studies, such influences could have taken place. Yet, as Assis Brasil, Benedito Nunes, Olga de Sá and others have shown,[14] Clarice's work contains unmistakable echoes of such seminal precursors of deconstructionism as Ernest Cassirer (especially his concept of the "thing" versus one's awareness of the "relations" between "things"), the phenomenologists, Husserl and Heidegger (phenomenology itself constituting a revealing approach to Clarice's work), Kenneth Burke (because of his "logological" emphasis on, like Cassirer, "relations" rather than on logically organized substances) and texts like Joyce's *Ulysses*, *Finnegans Wake* and *A Portrait of the Artist as a Young Man*. The point of all this is that in Clarice Lispector we have a writer who, though apparently without being directly, or, at least, verifiably, influenced by the deconstructionists, began in 1944 to create fluid, metafictionally self-referential and linguistically self-conscious texts in which there is clearly evident a rejection of what Derrida would later describe as a "logocentric metaphysic" of presence and structural stability and in which there is a new emphasis on the ontological unreliability of language and on the interplay of differences (Darrida's "différance") between relations. As early as 1944, then, and for years hence, Clarice Lispector was engaged in writing the kinds of ostensibly "formless," lyrical and metacritical texts that, some twenty years later, would be said to typify deconstructionist writing. Because of their constant preoccupation with the ambiguous but crucial relationships between language, meaning, reality and human perception, Clarice's texts continuously undercut or "deconstruct" themselves even as they move toward new levels of knowledge and self-awareness. Thus, a kind of writing usually associated with post-

structuralist and feminist narrative in Europe and the United States was actually being practiced in Brazil in the mid-1940s.

In his analysis of Proust's *Swann's Way*, another deconstructivist critic, Paul de Man, has, without making any direct reference to Clarice, offered a discussion of another revolutionary text, one that clearly has some important parallels with Clarice's work. Focusing on what he takes to be the "grammatization" of Proust's rhetoric (which he defines in terms of Charles Sanders Peirce's distinction between "grammar," a stabilizing force, and "rhetoric," a destabilizing one), de Man argues (in terms easily applicable to Clarice's work) that the constant interplay of such "unresolvable opposites" as the perspectives of inner and outer landscapes, of language versus silence, of presence and absence and of speaking versus thinking (or writing) gradually come to reveal, via a fluid, often ambiguously interrelated system of metonymy, oxymoron and synecdoche, the essential superiority of metaphor as a vehicle for literarily artistic expression. Systematically advanced in even an early 1960s work like *A Maçã no escuro*, this metaphoric, ironically self-inquisitional mode of writing thrives, as does deconstructive analysis itself, on precisely the kinds of unresolved and unresolvable psycholinguistic complexities that, especially in their philosophical context, defy the simplistic assumptions of logocentrism. The constant concern over words, their meanings and the various realities they create, describe and obscure all reflect Clarice's lifelong concern over Derrida's concept of "écriture" ("writing"), the production of language as flowing mental process rather than as static conclusion. For Clarice, the act of writing (like the act of reading) springs from a mental and spiritual quest for identity and authenticity of being, one that in virtually every one of her texts is bound up in a narrator's (or a character's) artistic creativity and, ineluctably, in a reader's reaction to (or deconstruction of) a text. The quest motif, which, as we see in works like *Perto do coração selvagem*, *A maçã no escuro*, *A paixão segundo G. H.*, *Agua viva* and even the posthumously published *Um sopro de vida*, is a constant in her longer texts, and can, perhaps, be best explained from a deconstructionist perspective. One feels this is so because in each of these cases the text—the "écriture" or, as Cixous would have it, Clarice's "écriture féminine"—is never a stable, closed and perfectly knowable construct; it is, to the contrary, an open, fluid and poetically rendered process, one involving the author and reader as well as the characters and one in which the elusiveness of language itself is the primary subject.

Developed in a distinctly antilogocentric fashion, Clarice's texts deal with language in two major ways: as the all too flawed means by which our human quest for self-realization is undertaken and, in a less obvious way, as the ultimate end, or purpose, of that quest. As characters like Joana (from *Perto do coração selvagem*), Martim (*A maçã no escuro*), G. H. (*A paixão segundo G. H.*) and the voice of *Agua viva* struggle with language (with its maddeningly self-referential "différance") in their quests for a sense of ontological stability, they (and the reader) gradually come to suspect that control over language—and not physical existence—is what they must really seek, for as narratives like *A maçã no escuro* and *Agua viva* imply, to control language is to control reality itself. Thus, the ultimate conflict in Clarice's texts, as for such better known deconstructionist writers and critics as Barthes, Cixous, Kristeva, Derrida, Cullers, Lacan and de Man, is over language: do we control it (as the conventional wisdom of logocentrism holds) or, as much poststructuralist theory argues, does it control us? For Clarice Lispector, a writer whose work has long exemplified the theories about language, meaning and human existence that the deconstructionists seek sometimes tortuously to elucidate, human existence is best defined in terms of this immensely frustrating struggle with language, with the problem of communication that derives from out of the ever unstable relationship between signifiers and signifieds, between what we say and what we mean (or want) to say, and between our speech acts and their receptions by other people. Relentlessly advanced and lyrically orchestrated, this is the thematic terrain for which Clarice is so renowned. Because they weave back and forth between the realms of the viscerally personal and the expansively theoretical, the stories of such figures as Joana, Martim, G. H. and the female presence in *Agua viva* all generate a sense of the socio-politically quotidian at the same time that they convey a powerful sense of the cosmic, of the ultimately mystical, even gnostic grounding of existence in language.

Although this dialectic between the corporeal and the cosmic is endemic to Clarice's fiction, it perhaps can be best seen in two of her greatest works, the generically hybrid *A paixão segundo G. H.*, one of the most powerful and overlooked texts to appear anywhere during the 1960s, and *Agua viva*, a lyrical "fiction"[15] par excellence that, due in no small part to what Hélène Cixous has lauded as its prototypical "écriture féminine,"[16] stands as one of the truly outstanding "new narratives" of the 1970s. In the case of *A paixão segundo G. H.* the self-conscious first-person narrator takes the reader from the vicissitudes of a woman's mundane middle-class existence to the harrowing throes of her psychic rebirth (birth and rebirth being motifs that appear throughout Clarice's work). Early in her story, G. H., placing herself in a particular socio-political context (one based on a male/female opposition) declares:

> Para uma mulher essa reputação é socialmente muito, e situoume, tanto para os outros como para mim mesma, numa zona que socialmente fica entre mulher e homem.[17]

At the conclusion of her uncertain tale, G. H. possesses a much more cosmic sense of self and of existence. Referring to this new and unsettling mode of being (one that strongly evinces the essentially paradoxical poststructuralist linkage between existence and language), G. H. declares:

> A realidade é a matéria-prima, a linguagem é o modo como vou buscá-la—e como não acho. . . . A linguagem é o meu esfôrço humano. . . . O indizível só me poderá

ser dado através do fracasso de minha linguagem. Só quando falta a construção, é que obtenho o que ela não conseguiu (Lispector, *A paixão segundo G. H.*, 212-13).

Presented as a character, G. H., like most of Clarice's other characters, comes, via radically different modes of discourse, to view an understanding of language itself as the end of her quest at the same time that she begins to see it as the conundrum-like mechanism by which it is simultaneously found and lost, this realization reflecting the poststructuralist system by which, in terms of deconstructive analysis, the end of the quest is at the same time "present" and "absent." As G. H. and the reader discover, it is only through language that "being" and "nonbeing" can co-exist in the same space and in the same instant of time.[18]

A similar focus on the nexus between language and existence animates *Agua viva*, a 1973 "fiction" in which the unnamed female narrator declares, " . . . é novo para mim o que escrevo porque minha verdadeira palavra foi até intocada. A palavra é a minha quarta dimensão (Lispector, *Agua viva*, 10). Then, invoking an image that exemplifies both Derrida's elusive concept of "différance" and Saussure's belief in the radical discontinuity between the signifier and the signified, the voice of *Agua viva* says:

> Transmito-te não uma história mas apenas palavras que vivem do som.
> Digo-te assim:
> 'Tronco luxurioso'.
>
> E banho-me nele. Ele está ligada à raiz que penetra em nós na terra. Tudo o que te escrevo é tenso. Uso palavras soltas que são em si mesmas um dardo livre. (Lispector, *Agua viva*, 27).

As we see in *Agua viva, A paixão segundo G. H.* and in Clarice's other works, the modes of her characters' discourses vary a great deal. This is especially apparent in the intensely lyrical *Agua viva*, where the style, always analytical and questioning (questing?), continuously vacillates between the sublimely poetic and the frustratingly inarticulate as the narrative voice ebbs and flows between the poles of brave self-affirmation and fearful hesitancy. Of all Clarice's "novels," only *Uma aprendizagem ou o livro dos prazeres* (1969) takes a more definitive stand, suggesting that, if they are able to understand, accept and communicate with each other (and themselves), men and women can (despite its semantic arbitrariness) learn to use language for purposes more liberating than entrapping, more supportive than divisive. This often overlooked work, along with *Um sopro de vida*, offers a guardedly optimistic alternative to the despair and nihilism that are often said to be the inevitable conclusions of a deconstructive view of language and literature. Although it seems true that, if pushed to its logical extremes, a deconstructive view of existence would indeed consign everything to a standard-less level of utter and total relativism, it is also true that, as thinking beings, we are not obliged to live out our lives according to such a bleak vision. And, in fact, we do not, for the supreme ironic truth of language is that for however much it undercuts our efforts to create stability and constancy in our existences, it also serves as the endlessly inventive mechanism by which our actions and moral choices are determined. Even though we may accept the deconstructionist argument that the concept of perfect, stable meaning is a myth, an impossibility, we can and do, through language, conduct our lives as if it were not. In forcing us to confront the confusion and anxiety that result from our discovery of language's self-referential arbitrariness, the questions asked by the deconstructionist critics—like those asked and lived out by Clarice's characters—lead us, as they lead Joana, Martim, G. H., Lóri and Ulysses (from *Uma aprendizagem*), to deal with ourselves and with each other in a more careful, more honest fashion. Thus, as Clarice suggests, the lasting—and surprisingly humanistic—contribution of Deconstructionism may finally be that it leads us to ask yet once again the ancient and still unresolved questions about the relationships between language, reality and being, the questions not merely about what we know (or think we know) but about how we know.

As we see in texts like *Perto do coração selvagem*, *A maçã no escuro*, *A paixão segundo G. H.* and *Agua viva*, another fundamental characteristic of Clarice's open, fluid "écriture" is her constant creation of what deconstructionist critics like Derrida, Kristeva and Barthes call "aporia," those inescapable impasses of meaning when, by both generating themselves a sense of "undecidability" and by calling for a description in similarly ambiguous terms, a text begins to dismantle or challenge itself, to call its own "meanings" into question. Although as Derrida makes clear, this semantic "dissemination" (". . . a continual flickering, spilling and defusing of meaning," Eagleton, *Literary Theory*, 134), occurs in all language use, it is most apparent in what is known as "literary" discourse. My point, however, is that these two decisive features of deconstructive criticism, the nature and function of aporia in a text and, as a corollary, its polysemy (its semantic "dissemination"), working in conjunction with the closely related issues of "l'écriture féminine," logocentrism and intertextuality, do not merely apply to the work of Clarice Lispector but characterize it. By giving these moments of aporia, or impass, a central place in her work, Clarice makes us see that language inevitably turns back on itself, that for whatever "meaning" we may believe a linguistic sign may have, we must also confront the disturbing possibility that it is nothing more than an arbitrary and artificial construct, one that gets its "meaning" from still other signs and structures.

Without knowing the terms themselves, Clarice, who has fomented a revolution in Brazilian literature, made a career out of writing precisely the kinds of linguistically self-conscious and philosophically charged texts that the later appearing deconstructive critics would prize so highly. Clarice, we might say, wrote deconstructive literature without ever knowing what Deconstructionism was; she was, in terms of her preoccupations with the phenomenologically unstable, ever evolving relationships between language, existence, human cognition and meaning, very much ahead of her time.

Close readings of Clarice's novels, stories and "nonfiction" pieces reveal that, as a structuralist critic would note, she develops much of her best material around the tensions generated by certain recurring "binary oppositions," notable among which are conflicts between language and silence, male and female and a variety of ontological questions relating to presence ("logocentrism") and absence ("différance"), and to "authentic" being versus "nonauthentic" being. But, as a deconstructive commentator would rightly point out, what truly distinguishes Clarice's work, what identifies it as being uniquely hers, is the fact that these many motif-like "binary oppositions" are seldom, if ever, resolved. As we see in such works as, *A maçã no escuro*, *A paixão segundo G. H.* and *Agua viva*, these oppositions simply go on, multiplying in their semantic possibilities, generating endless moments of aporia and defying all rationally logocentric efforts to control or even contrast them. For Clarice, as for Barthes, language (in its Saussurean sense of being an arbitrary system of signs based upon difference without positive terms) was the great theme, the one from which all other themes and questions of style and form would derive. Thus, a deconstructive reading of Clarice's texts helps explain why they are so full of aporia, so "vague," "amorphous" and "open ended."

With language itself as her main subject, Clarice creates fictive worlds not of definitive results (which would reflect a "logocentric" world) but one of process, of flux, of "écriture," of "différance." Though her texts ceaselessly generate questions about language, meaning and existence, they do not, with the possible exceptions of *Uma aprendizagem ou o livro dos prazeres* and *Um sopro de vida*, offer much in the way of substantive answers to the dilemmas and complexities of human existence. Rather, they generate questions; they depict human beings as being caught up in a continuum of words, one that, never anchored in anything but other words, simultaneously tantalizes and maddens us. Given her basic themes and techniques, then, one can see that the narratives created by Clarice Lispector between 1944 and 1978 reveal themselves to us with dramatic intensity if approached from a deconstructivist perspective. Epitomizing the profoundly disturbing philosophical, psychological and sociolinguistic issues raised by this often misunderstood and maligned critical school, the powerful and compelling narratives of Clarice Lispector are beginning to receive the international acclaim they so richly deserve.

NOTES

[1] Saussure, Ferdinand de, *Cours de Linguistique Générale* (Paris: Payot, 1931), 166.

[2] In "L'approche de Clarice Lispector," *Poétique* 40 (Novembre 1979): 408-419, Hélène Cixous notes certain affinities between Clarice's work

and that of Heidegger, Rilke and Derrida (409), while "Reaching the Point of Wheat, or A Portrait of the Artist as a Maturing Woman" in *New Literary History* 19, no. 1 (Autumn 1987): 1-21, she compares Clarice to Joyce and declares that, for her, the Brazilian woman " . . . is the greatest writer in the twentieth century" (7).

[3] Terry Eagleton, *Literary Theory: An Introduction* (Minneapolis: University of Minnesota Press, 1983), 132.

[4] Indicative of her (often clumsy) struggle to achieve this goal of authenticity of being via authentic language use is Joana's coinage of the term "lalande," a sign (defined, arbitrarily, by her) she hopes will spur on this crucial development. Cf. *Perto do coração selvagem*, 4th ed. (Editora Sabiá, 1944), 166. "Phallogocentrism" is, of course, a variant on "Logocentrism," one that emphasizes the repressiveness of its masculinist ideologies.

[5] Clarice Lispector, *A maçã no escuro*, 3rd ed. (Rio de Janeiro: José Alvaro, 1970), 34-35.

[6] Clarice wrote nine "novels" during her career. Clarice's longer, "novel" length narratives seem, on balance, to be considerably more lyrical and "deconstructively" oriented than her short fictions, or "stories," which, by contrast, seem somewhat less poetic and more mimetic.

[7] Clarice herself described *Agua viva* as a "fiction"; Cf. Bella Jozef, "Chronology: Clarice Lispector," *Review* 24 (1979): 26.

[8] A number of sections in *Agua viva* appear virtually verbatim in the "Fundo de Gaveta" portion of an earlier work, *A legião estrangeira* (1964). These sections include: "A vingança e a reconciliação," "Lembrança de um verão difícil," "Porque eu quero," "Esbôço de um guarda-roupa," "Africa" and "Os espelhos de Vera Mindlin."

[9] Ann Rosalind Jones, "Writing the Body: Toward an Understanding of L'écriture Féminine," *The New Feminist Criticism*, Elaine Showalter, ed. (New York: Pantheon Books, 1985), 361-377; see also, Sharon Willis, "Mis-transtation," *Substance*, 52 (1987): 76-83. Willis believes that *Vivre l'orange* ". . . is ostensibly a reading of . . . *La passion selon G. H.*" (76).

[10] Clarice Lispector, *Agua viva*, 3rd ed. (Rio de Janeiro: Editora Nova Fronteira, 1978), 24.

[11] Clarice Lispector, "A pesca milagrosa," from *A legião estrangeira* (Rio de Janeiro: Editôra do Autor, 1964), 143.

[12] *Allegories of Reading* (New Haven: Yale University Press, 1979). Deplorable though it is, the recently discovered (1987-88) scandal allegedly linking de Man to Nazi propagandists and collaborators should not prevent us from considering seriously his theories on language and literature.

[13] See my "The Leitmotif of Darkness in Seven Novels by Clarice Lispector," *Chasqui* 7, no. 2 (Feb. 1978): 18-28, and "A Discourse of Silence: The Postmodernism of Clarice Lispector," *Contemporary Literature* 28, no. 4 (Winter 1987): 420-436; see also, in this regard, Naomi Lindstrom's "Clarice Lispector: Articulating Women's Experience," *Chasqui* 8, no. 1 (1978) 43-52, and Marta Peixoto's "*Family Ties*: Female Development in Clarice Lispector," in *The Voyage In*, Elizabeth Abel and Marianne Hirsch, eds. (Hanover, N.H.: University Press of New England, 1983), 287-355.

[14] Olga de Sá, *A escritura de Clarice Lispector* (Petrópolis: Vozes, 1979); Assis Brasil, *Clarice Lispector* (Rio de Janeiro: Editôra Organização,

1969); Benedito Nunes, *O mundo de Clarice Lispector* (Manaus: Edições Governo de Estado do Amazonas, 1966); and Earl E. Fitz, *Clarice Lispector* (Boston: Twayne Publishing Co., 1985).

[15] See, Ralph Freedman, *The Lyrical Novel* (Princeton: Princeton University Press, 1963).

[16] Hélène Cixous, *Vivre l'orange* (Paris: Des Femmes, 1979); see also, Sharon Willis, "Mis-Transtation: *Vivre L'orange*," *Substance* 52 (1987): 76-83.

[17] Clarice Lispector, *A paixão segundo G. H.*, 3rd ed. (Rio de Janeiro: Editôra Sabiá, 1964), 27.

[18] The word "instante" occurs throughout Clarice's work and must be regarded as one of the essential motifs of her work. As a sign, its function is nearly always to suggest this basically deconstructionist sense of "presence" and "absence," of "being" and "nonbeing" and of confusion and understanding that co-exists in the act of human cognition at any moment of time. In trying to show this function, Clarice's texts undercut or destabilize themselves in a continuous process of "deconstruction."

Ingrid R. Muller   (essay date 1991)

SOURCE: "The Problematics of the Body in Clarice Lispector's *Family Ties*," in *Chasqui—Revista de literatura latinoamericano*, Vol. XX, No. 1, May 1991, pp. 34-42.

[*Here, Muller identifies the feminine perspective in Lispector's* Family Ties, *and addresses issues of control and the self in relation to society.*]

Feminist readings of Clarice Lispector's collection of short stories, *Family Ties*, generally focus on the preponderance of women protagonists in the stories and their—mostly short-lived—attempts to assert themselves as autonomous human beings by escaping the narrowly defined roles imposed upon them by a male-dominated society. Thus A. M. Wheeler, in his article "Animal Imagery as Reflection of Gender Roles in Clarice Lispector's *Family Ties*," states that the stories "primarily relate the struggle of women to realize themselves as subjects and to escape their role as objects" (125), and Magda Velloso Fernandes de Tolentino, in a comparative analysis of the story **"The Imitation of the Rose,"** asserts that Lispector "denounces the fact that women cannot indulge in their own search for self-fulfillment, but rather act as instruments of their men's comfort" (75). Marta Peixoto, in a similar vein, affirms that "through the plots of the stories and the inner conflicts of the heroines, Lispector challenges conventional roles, showing that the allegiances to others those roles demand lead to a loss of selfhood. The protagonists' efforts toward recuperating the self emerge as dissatisfaction, rage, or even madness" (288-89). Focusing on the women characters' difficulties in verbalizing their thoughts in the story **"The Daydreams of a Drunk Woman,"** Naomi Lindstrom concludes that "the total result is Lispector's fictional critique of woman's difficulties with verbal expression—a critique that parallels the concerns of feminism" ("Feminist Discourse Analysis" 9).

As Lindstrom's statement implies, Lispector's "feminism" does not express itself in an overt manner in the stories. In her analysis of Lispector's story **"Preciousness,"** Lindstrom recognizes that "many readers have perceived the Brazilian's writing to be essentially feminine, although this quality has been difficult to define critically" ("Discourse Analysis" 187), and Earl E. Fitz, in his study "Freedom and Self-Realization," concedes that "feminism is not present in her work as a clear-cut or easily defined feature" (58).

Although the presence of women characters who are trapped in their domestic roles—all of them, with one notable exception, middle-class women in an urban environment—is a dominant feature in the stories, narratives of feminist criticism founder because of the lack of a villain: the drama is played out largely in the minds of the women characters, while the men who occasionally appear on the scene generally take on the roles of puzzled bystanders witnessing their wives' eccentric behavior rather than representing agents of oppression. Nor does Lispector appear to point an accusing finger at the male establishment as a whole: her women characters generally live in comfortable circumstances and seem to have plenty of time for daydreaming and introspection; many of them cherish the security their social position as married women affords them, a fact which has led at least one critic to term the characters' return to domestic tranquility after a brief period of increased self-awareness as essentially positive in some of the stories (Seniff 163, 165-66, 169).

I suggest that the feelings of frustration and discontent Lispector's women characters experience are only indirectly related to their oppression by a patriarchic society. Instead, I propose that the stories be viewed in a broader perspective, namely, the problematic issue of the mind/body split, one of the fundamental principles of Western thought.

In the binary opposition mind/body, the mind is clearly privileged, inasmuch as it produces meaning and direction, and thus appears to provide a measure of control over one's existence, whereas the body is perceived as out in the world, one object among others, and as such highly vulnerable to outside forces which elude direct control: it is prey to injury, sickness, decay. In his study *Mind-Body: A Categorical Relation*, H. Tristram Engelhardt, Jr., observes that "thoughts and volitions are often set in opposition to the mute, cognitional and volitional opaqueness of the body. . . . With mind, one encounters a cognitional translucency opposed to the opacity and recalcitrance of the body. The experience of sickness and physical limitation present the body as an other which the mind is always endeavoring to make its own" (2).

If his fear of the contingencies of the body makes man's relationship to his body problematical, woman's relation to her body has become doubly problematic. "If the [male] intellectual, the cleric epitomizes the life of the mind," Jane Gallop states in *Thinking Through the Body*, "woman epitomizes the life of the body" (21). Man has projected

the ambivalence he feels toward a body which largely escapes his control upon woman: she becomes the sorceress, the sphinx, the witch; she is, by nature, irrational, treacherous, *unheimlich*, often malevolent. By repudiating his body and the feeling of impotence it inspires in him, man becomes free to perceive himself as an autonomous being, while woman is made to carry the burden of the flesh. As the "representative of the body principle" she enables man to deal with "not only brute nature as it surrounds him, but also brute nature as it exists inside him, in his own mute unfathomable body. That body is in some intimate sense himself; yet it is not himself: it is in many ways the archenemy of his long-range, distinctively human, concerns" (Dinnerstein 125-26).

Colonizers have always felt the need to convince themselves of the inferior human status of the colonized: with woman incarnating all that is disturbing, uncanny and detrimental to the superior life of the mind, she can now, without further qualms, be harnessed to the yoke of a patriarchic system where she is largely reduced to the functions of wife and mother. Jane Gallop, rejecting man's attempt to define woman in terms of her usefulness to man, states that "the sons of a certain Western European tradition of subjugating the secondary body to a disembodied consciousness, are less and less able to maintain that domination, a domination which historically depended on other sexes, classes, and races to embody the body as well as care for the Master's body so he would not have to be concerned with it, so he could consider himself disembodied, autonomous, and free to will" (19-20).

It is not surprising then that, reduced to their physical functions by the narrow specifications of a male-dominated society, women have become profoundly alienated from their bodies. Adrienne Rich affirms in her autobiographical study of *Of Woman Born:* "I know of no woman—virgin, mother, lesbian, married, celibate— . . . for whom her body is not a fundamental problem" (290). Although Lispector's stories are not directly accessible to a feminist reading, the problematic relationship of women to their bodies forms one of the underlying principles in almost all of the stories in the collection *Family Ties*, most obviously in **"The Imitation of the Rose," "The Daydreams of a Drunk Woman," "The Buffalo"** and **"The Smallest Woman in the World."** With the significant exception of the pygmy woman in **"The Smallest Woman in the World,"** the women characters in these stories have recourse to a number of different strategies to deal with their bodies, of which their submission to the traditional female role is only one, albeit the one sought most often.

Woman's alienation from her body is most evident in Lispector's story **"The Imitation of the Rose,"** not only because Laura, the central character, uses a variety of different strategems to rid herself of her body, but because she pursues her objective to its rigorous end: the total denial of the body. The tone of subtle irony which pervades the story reveals the contrast between Laura as she attempts to see herself, a meek, conventional, dull housewife, and her urge to assert herself: she observes the people around her with a critical eye, and she has no illusion about her inferior status as a housewife. After her release from the hospital, where she has undergone treatment during a psychotic episode, she sees herself as "finally returning to play an insignificant role with gratitude" (34). What makes Laura's internal struggle so intense is that her stubborn determination to assert her individuality is matched by an equally strong internalization of the prescriptions of male-dominated society: the daily glass of milk her doctor has prescribed for her becomes a symbol of the conditioning to which she has been subjected. Although, "in her humble opinion," Laura finds the doctor's orders contradictory, she blushes with pleasure when the doctor gives her a friendly pat on the back, and she scrupulously complies with his command to drink her milk, "that glass of milk which had finished up by gaining a secret power, which almost embodied with every sip the taste of a word and renewed that firm pat on the back . . ." (56).

Laura's problematic relationship to her body becomes apparent in her refusal to acknowledge her sexuality. She is unable to deal with the sexual aspect of her body except by using pseudoscientific terms. Embarrassed by her husband's repeatedly voiced admiration of her ample hips, she feels compelled to counter, each time he does so, with the explanation "that this resulted from ovarian insufficiency," while secretly labelling her husband's frank sexuality as "shameless" (60).

Laura's manner of dress is likewise calculated to defuse her sexuality: her brown dress—obviously a favorite—with the demure lace collar gives her "an almost childlike appearance, like some child from the past," and she perceives her "real life" as the time of her girlhood in Tijuca (59). In a similar vein, she takes refuge, in her relationship with her husband, in the sexually safe role of the child who tries to endear herself to the adult by her innocent charms; the sexual act becomes a kind of reward for good behavior: picturing her husband's reaction to her "impulsive" decision to have a bouquet of roses delivered to a friend, she anticipates with pleasure his look of surprise, certain that "Armando would look with kindness upon the impulses of his little wife and that night they would sleep together" (64).

One of the stratagems Laura employs to obliterate her body is camouflage. With her brown dress and brown hair and eyes she effectively blends into the environment. Reflecting upon her appearance, as she pictures herself walking down the street on her husband's arm, she congratulates herself on being "chestnut-haired as she obscurely felt a wife ought to be. To have black or blonde hair was an exaggeration, which, in her desire to make the right choice, she had never wanted. Then, as for green eyes, it seemed to her that if she had green eyes it would be as if she had not told her husband everything" (60-61).

Likewise, Laura appears to measure the excellence of a wife by the degree of her unobtrusiveness. In anticipation of a dinner party at the house of their friends Car-

lota and João, she imagines with pleasure her husband being engaged in a conversation with João without paying attention to her; "a man at peace," she speculates, "was one who, oblivious of his wife's presence, could converse with another man about the latest news in the headlines" (53-54).

By the same token, Laura takes great care to efface all traces of her presence from her personal surroundings. "Laura," the narrator tells us, "experienced such pleasure in making something impersonal of her home; in a certain way perfect, because impersonal" (56).

In view of Laura's ultimate breakdown, the image she tries to create of herself as a busy little housewife "who had never had any ambitions except to be a wife to some man" (57), and her constant attempts to extol the importance of her domestic tasks must be seen in an ironic light. In fact, the bodily exhaustion she feels after doing her housework merely serves her as "a sort of compensation" (57) for the exhilarating feeling of superhuman power and independence she experienced during her illness: "In exhaustion she found a refuge, that discreet and obscure place from where, with so much constraint toward herself and others, she had once departed" (58).

In the end, Laura finds that she can no longer uphold her fiction of domestic bliss: contemplating the "luminous tranquility" of the roses she has bought at the market, she recalls, with mounting excitement, her former state of insanity in which she, like the roses, had become "superhuman and tranquil in her bright isolation" (57). Although she contrives to rid herself of the roses by having them delivered to a friend, she relapses once more into insanity; divesting herself of her body, she again becomes "luminous and remote" (72), a disembodied mind.

As Marta Peixoto observes, "an alert lack of fatigue, clarity of mind, a sense of independence, of possessing extraordinary powers, accompany her returning madness" (295). However, although Laura's escape into insanity effectively ends her internal struggle, it is difficult to maintain that madness, in this story, essentially "takes on a positive value" (Peixoto 299). The tragic loss of human identity Laura experiences after her relapse is conveyed to the reader by a shift of narrative focus to Laura's husband, Armando. As the narrator reports his reactions to his wife's alienation from reality, the reader, with Armando, watches helplessly and with a sense of doom as Laura withdraws to a remote, unearthly realm of existence: "From the open door he saw his wife sitting upright on the couch, once more alert and tranquil as if on a train. A train that had already departed" (72).

"The body," Adrienne Rich writes, "has been made so problematic for women that it has often seemed easier to shrug it off and travel as a disembodied spirit" (22). Laura's state of insanity in which, ironically, she perceives herself as "superhuman," prevents her from living a truly human existence as effectively as her previous reduced state of the dull little housewife. Magda Velloso Fernandes de Tolentino observes that "the irony lies in the fact that the only freedom allowed her is madness, which substitutes one status of marginality for another; closure just takes another form" (76). Moreover, the narrator makes it clear that Laura's escape into psychosis is not an easy cop-out: we are told that Armando watches his wife with "fear and respect," because he knows that "she had done everything possible not to become luminous and remote," before embarking, once more, on the road to insanity (72).

The Portuguese woman in Lispector's story **"The Day-dreams of a Drunk Woman"** may, in some ways, be considered the reverse image of Laura in **"The Imitation of the Rose."** Whereas Laura negates and tries to obliterate her body, the Portuguese woman flaunts it: sensuous, healthy, conscious of her physically, her laughter, the narrator tells us, comes "from the depths of that security of someone who has a body" (32). All is not well, though; as the story progresses, the reader becomes aware that her relationship to her body, for all that, is no less problematic. Although the woman's disgust at what she terms a "degrading and revolting existence" (32) frequently erupts in angry deprecations directed at herself and others, she is at a loss to account for the source of her dissatisfaction. Having internalized society's prescriptions which have reduced her to the functions of child-bearer and sexual object, she seeks the causes of her discontent in herself: "Ah, what's wrong with me! she wondered desperately. Have I eaten too much? Heavens above! What *is* wrong with me?" (36). Only when she is drunk—her drunkenness serving as "a beacon that sweeps through the dawn while one is asleep" (32), does she become dimly aware of the problem, and even then she can express her feelings only metaphorically: "Her white flesh was as sweet as a lobster, the legs of a live lobster wriggling slowly in the air . . ." (32). Disgusted at the thought of being a lobster, a passive object of consumption, the urge to assert herself as an active and autonomous being subsequently produces a different image in her mind: "She was no longer a lobster, but a harsher sign—that of the scorpion. After all, she had been born in November" (32).

In the foreword to her study *Of Woman Born,* Adrienne Rich states that "woman's status as childbearer has been made into a major fact of her life. Terms like 'barren' or 'childless' have been used to negate any further identity" (xiii). In Lispector's story, the Portuguese woman tries to justify her existence and assert her personality by having recourse to society's glorification of motherhood: she is obsessed with the procreative potential of her body.

Imagery related to pregnancy and the proliferation of flesh abounds in the story. The triple mirror in the opening paragraph of the story becomes a symbol of the woman's physical multiplicity: the reader is introduced to her as she is standing in front of the dressing table, combing her hair, while "her open dressing gown revealed in the mirrors the intersected breasts of several women" (27-28). Later, at the restaurant, her drunkenness makes her feel "swollen and rotund like a large cow" (31). Reflecting upon her conversational skills, she speculates that

"the words that a woman uttered when drunk were like being pregnant—mere words on her lips which had nothing to do with the secret core that seemed like pregnancy" (31). The woman despises the "barren" people in the restaurant, while she feels herself to be "plump and heavy and generous to the full" (33). Her contempt finds a welcome target in another female guest who has caught her eye because of her elegant attire; berating, in her mind, the woman's looks and refined manner, which she considers pure sham, her scorn is provoked in particular by the fact that the woman is "flat-chested" and erupts in a spiteful evaluation of the woman's procreative faculties: "And that pious ninny so pleased with herself in that hat and so modest about her slim waistline, and I'll bet she couldn't even bear her man a child" (33).

After returning home from the restaurant, the Portuguese woman undergoes a Kafkaesque metamorphosis, in which she herself and the objects around her suddenly take on the appearance of flesh: "Meanwhile she was becoming larger, more unsteady, swollen and gigantic. If only she could get closer to herself, she would find she was even larger. Each of her arms could be explored by someone who didn't even recognize that they were dealing with an arm, and someone could plunge into each eye and swim around without knowing that it was an eye. . . . Things of the flesh stricken by nervous twinges" (34).

Accustomed to think of herself in terms of the flesh, the woman, as her sense of self is being engulfed by her body, experiences a painful loss of control: "How sickening! How very annoying! When all is said and done, heaven help me—God knows best. What was one to do?" (35).

After the crisis has passed, the woman, in an ineffectual burst of energy, once more tries to prop up her sense of identity by having recourse to the image of herself as a childbearer: "Ah, she was feeling so well, so strong, as if she still had milk in those firm breasts" (36).

The Portuguese woman's efforts to enhance her self-esteem by thinking of herself as a desirable sexual object prove to be equally unsuccessful. Recalling the amorous advances her husband's business associate has made to her under the table at the restaurant, she falsely interprets them as a sign of respect: "When her husband's friend saw her so pretty and plump he immediately felt respect for her. And when she started to get embarrassed she did not know which way to look. Such misery! What was one to do?" (36). In the end, the woman's problem remains unresolved. The fact that she labels herself a "slut" signals her unquestioning acceptance of society's standards of female comportment and her lack of a sense of self as an autonomous human being.

The actions of the woman in the story **"The Buffalo,"** who has been spurned by her lover, must be seen as a last desperate effort to free herself from the bondage of her body and to salvage an identity which, at the beginning of the narrative, is already severely damaged. As Marta Peixoto observes, "the role of the woman in love limits severely the protagonist of **"The Buffalo."** She only senses her deficiencies when her husband or lover abandons her and she is deprived of her source of identity" (296). Having allowed herself to be defined in terms of her usefulness to the male as a compassionate and nurturing female, she tries to recover her self-esteem by learning from the animals in the zoological gardens how to "find her own hatred" (147); instead, she finds that the bodies of the animals she encounters only mirror the sweetness and passivity of her own; the giraffe, perfectly attuned to its environment, is "more landscape than being" (148), the elephant and the camel exude patience and submission, and the hippopotamus is "a round mass of flesh, its round, mute flesh awaiting some other round, mute flesh" (148). The sight of the animals confirms her own status as a passive object, a mere body: "Then there was such a humble love in maintaining oneself only as flesh, there was such a sweet martyrdom in not knowing how to think" (148). The woman's attitude appears to bear out Adrienne Rich's argument in the final pages of her book *Of Woman Born,* in which she speaks out on the necessity of women to "repossess" their bodies. "We have tended either to *become* our bodies—blindly, slavishly, in obedience to male theories about us—," Rich declares, "or to try to exist in spite of them" (291-92).

Frustrated in her attempts to assert her individuality by hating the other, the woman turns her anger upon herself; her excursion becomes an orgy of self-destruction. By taking a ride on the roller coaster and surrendering her body to the play of exterior forces over which she has no control, she symbolically reenacts the humiliation she has suffered at the hands of her lover: "But suddenly there was that soaring of entrails, . . . the deep resentment with which she became mechanical, her body automatically buoyant . . . her humiliation, 'they were doing what they liked with her,' the terrible humiliation . . . the utter bewilderment of this spasmodic game as they did what they liked with her . . ." (150).

The woman's ultimate defeat takes place in her encounter with the buffalo, the only animal which appears to embody the hatred she has sought. However, instead of learning from him how to hate, she is overcome by the buffalo's hatred; in a staring down contest with the animal she falls, unconscious, to the ground. "Fainting," Peixoto observes, "signals, no doubt, her failure of nerve: a traditionally feminine strategy of withdrawal, it obliterates from consciousness her involvement and insights" (297).

The woman in this story employs strategies somewhat similar to those Laura uses in **"The Imitation of the Rose"** in her efforts to deal with the problematics of her body. She, too, attempts to obliterate her body by using camouflage; one of the markers Lispector employs is the brown coat—reminiscent of Laura's favorite brown dress—the woman is wearing, and, the narrator tells us, "she was not the sort of person others might notice" (152). However, whereas Laura seeks refuge in a disembodied mind, the woman in this story opts for a different solution: losing herself in the buffalo's gaze, "without wishing nor being able to escape" (156), she finds at last what

she has come for, the annihilation, albeit temporary, of her self as a thinking and feeling body.

The figure of Little Flower, a pygmy living in the recesses of equatorial Africa, in the story **"The Smallest Woman in the World,"** forms a sharp contrast to the other women characters in *Family Ties.* "With the story of Little Flower," Marta Peixoto observes, "Lispector creates a comic parable of a native female power, sustained against all odds. The jungle inhabitant manages to retain the tranquil independence sought eagerly by city-bred women in their civilized world of enclosed spaces, prescribed behavior, and family ties" (302). Little Flower, as opposed to the other women characters, is the only woman whose self-image is fully intact, and who appears to be living in harmony with herself and her environment. "The pygmy woman's successful retaining of her own autonomy," A. M. Wheeler affirms, "is an achievement not replicated in *Family Ties*" (133). Far from denying her body, Little Flower lives through her body which she perceives as an integral part of her self.

The concept of control—the control of mind over body, the male over the female, the lover over the one he loves—is one of the main principles which underlie the structure of the story. The greater part of the story deals with the reaction of the civilized world to the discovery of the tiny woman who measures only forty-five centimeters in height; a full-size photograph of her minute body in the newspapers evokes feelings of profound unease in the readers. Trying to incorporate the pygmy woman in some way in their own societal system, they variously describe her as an animal or reify her as a sexual object, a plaything, a servant. The French explorer who discovers the pygmy is equally disturbed by the living, breathing presence of the little woman before him. The narrator ironically describes the explorer's attempts to regain control by inscribing her in the narrow categories of the mind: "Certainly it was only because he was sane that he managed to keep his head and not lose control. Sensing a sudden need to restore order, and to give a name to what exists, he called her Little Flower. And, in order to be able to classify her among the identifiable realities, he immediately began to gather data about her" (89).

The act of naming, another attempt at control, is described in a humorous manner. In this incident, too, the pygmy woman effectively eludes control: at the very moment the explorer, "with a delicacy of feeling of which even his wife would never have believed him capable," pronounces her name, "Little Flower scratched herself where one never scratches oneself" (90), causing the explorer to turn away his eyes in embarrassment. The incongruence of the explorer's official statement to the press, in which he describes the pygmy woman as "black as a monkey" (89), and the sentimental image evoked by her name denounces the idealization of the female body, and reveals the arbitrariness of conventional standards of female beauty. Commenting upon Little Flower's untimely itch, A. M. Wheeler remarks: "The explorer ineptly names her 'Little Flower,' romanticizing her in the way in which females are often romanticized and objectified, but that delicate name is immediately contrasted with the woman's actual nature" (130).

The Western concept of romantic love is alien to the little woman. Unlike the Portuguese woman in **"The Daydreams of a Drunk Woman,"** who vents her frustration at being locked into a dull marriage by dreaming about the Prince Charming who will be worthy of her love, Little Flower's idea of love, the narrator tells us, is untainted by the "cruel refinements" of Western culture (94), in which love is often sought as a means of control and self-enhancement. To the pygmy woman, love is a deeply joyous, sensuous feeling which embraces the person of the "yellow explorer" as well as his boots and the ring that shines on his finger. Wheeler points out that "in civilized countries love is too often confused with the desire to be possessed or to possess, it is also often experienced as a validation of the self. . . . Little Flower is deeply interested in herself, but nonetheless she is able to appreciate objects and people outside herself without needing to appropriate them to her own being" (132).

By the same token, pregnancy is experienced by the pygmy woman as a state of profound joy and sensuous pleasure: "If the unique thing itself was smiling it was because, inside her minute body, a great darkness had started to stir" (94). Other than her civilized sisters, Little Flower finds love and motherhood unproblematic; she conceives of her body as an intimate part of her self and as an immediate source of pleasure uncontaminated by the exigencies of the mind. For all that, the pygmy woman is not living in edenic bliss; her small tribe is surrounded by the savage tribe of the Bantus who are in the habit of netting the pygmies for food. Although doubly vulnerable because of her small size and her pregnancy, Little Flower accepts the fact that her existence is largely outside of her control, and is thus able to enjoy life to the fullest: "Little Flower was enjoying herself. The unique thing was enjoying the ineffable sensation of not having been devoured yet. . . . Not to be devoured is the most perfect sentiment. Not to be devoured is the secret objective of a whole existence" (93-94).

In many ways, **"The Smallest Woman in the World"** provides a key to the understanding of the other stories in the collection. It is significant that the central character in this story exhibits, in appearance and behavior, a number of animal characteristics; she is repeatedly referred to as an animal by the members of civilized society, and the narrator flatly informs us that "she looked just like a dog" (90). Yet, none of the other women characters in the stories possesses the kind of disinterestedness and integrity the pygmy woman exhibits: as A. M. Wheeler points out, Little Flower's love is completely nonpossessive (132), and her charms are not calculated to elicit approval and admiration from others to enhance her self-image. It is clear that Little Flower's animal nature is presented as a positive feature in the story; being an "animal," she is uncontaminated by the Western malady of the mind/body split, which makes the other women characters' relationships to their bodies so problematic.

In the article "Excerpts from the Chronicles of *The Foreign Legion*," which includes some of the rare commentaries Lispector has offered on her writing, Lispector states with reference to her story **"The Smallest Woman in the World"**: "I am convinced that this narrative too, stems from my affection for animals: I tend to regard them as the species closest to God, matter that did not invent itself . . ." (Pontiero 41). The tragedy of Western man, Lispector seems to imply in her stories, is that, in the course of "inventing himself," he has strayed from the living source of his existence and has become a victim of his own mental fabrications. Another of Lispector's commentaries, in the same article, is more explicit. "In everything," she affirms, "your body will be your main asset. Our body is ever at our side. It is the one thing that never leaves us to the end" (41).

WORKS CITED

Dinnerstein, Dorothy. *The Mermaid and the Minotaur: Sexual Arrangements and Human Malaise*. New York: Harper & Row, 1976.

Englehardt, Jr., H. Tristram. *Mind-Body: A Categorical Relation*. The Hague, Neth.: Martinus Nijhoff, 1973.

Fitz, Earl E. "Freedom and Self-Realization: Feminist Characterization in the Fiction of Clarice Lispector." *Modern Language Studies* 10.3 (1980): 51-61.

Gallop, Jane. *Thinking Through the Body*. New York: Columbia UP, 1988.

Lindstrom, Naomi. "A Discourse Analysis of 'Preciosidade' by Clarice Lispector." *Luso-Brazilian Review* 19 (1982): 187-94.

———. "A Feminist Discourse Analysis of Clarice Lispector's 'Daydreams of a Drunken Housewife.'" *Latin American Literary Review* 19 (1981): 7-16.

Lispector, Clarice. *Family Ties*. Trans. Giovanni Pontiero. Austin, TX: U of Texas P, 1960.

Peixoto, Marta. "Family Ties: Female Development in Clarice Lispector." *The Voyage in: Fictions of Female Development*. However, NH: UP of New England for Dartmouth College, 1983: 287-303.

Pontiero, Giovanni. "Excerpts from the Chronicles of The Foreign Legion." By Clarice Lispector. *Review* 24 (1979): 37-43.

Rich, Adrienne. *Of Woman Born: Motherhood as Experience and Institution*. New York: Bantam, 1977.

Seniff, Dennis. "Self-Doubt in Clarice Lispector's Laços de família." *Luso-Brazilian Review* 14 (1977): 161-73.

Tolentino, Magda Velloso Fernandes de. "Family Bonds and Bondage within the Family: A Study of Family Ties in Clarice Lispector and James Joyce." *Modern Language Studies* 18.2 (1988): 73-78.

Wheeler, A. M. "Animal Imagery as Reflection of Gender Roles in Clarice Lispector's Family Ties." *Critique* 38.3 (1987): 125-34.

Lorna Sage   (review date 1992)

SOURCE: "Tease on the Run," in *The Times Literary Supplement*, No. 4655, June 19, 1992, pp. 7-8.

[*In the following review, Sage reviews the British release of Lispector's* Discovering the World, *a posthumously published collection of articles written for a weekly Brazilian journal.*]

Clarice Lispector (1925-77) has long been famed, thanks largely to Hélène Cixous's tributes, as an elusive exemplar of *écriture féminine*. She has, however, proved hard to read in English. She said herself that she perversely cherished the recalcitrance of Portuguese—"I love the Portuguese language. It is neither easy nor flexible"—and though some of the fiction has been translated (*Near to the Wild Heart*, 1944, *Family Ties*, 1960, and *The Hour of the Star*, 1977, for instance, also by Giovanni Pontiero, also published by Carcanet), it is not exactly easy to grasp her specialness. All too often her work seems fey or frantic, a slender Latin American variation on familiar experimental themes.

But *Discovering the World* is different. It's a generous selection from the weekly newspaper column she wrote in the *Jornal do Brasil* between 1967 and 1973, a form of "chronicle", conventionally loose, in which she could explore the myriad topics which took her fancy, and be as intimate, angry, bored or whimsical as she pleased. Lispector seems to have found genuine release in escaping literature—or at least, playing around on its margins, and *having* to be aware of her readers. She grouches about her slavery, of course ("I was hoping to give up writing. I am only carrying on because I need the money. I wanted to remain silent"), but revels at the same time in the games she can play with this new first person: *They tell me you bare your soul when you write. Do I really?*"

In fact, it's precisely her restless and contradictory sensibility that sustains the act so well. She can digress *ad infinitum,* it seems, with no need for a plot. She is a Sarraute with a Saturday by-line, writing about writing for newspaper readers:

If I could, I would leave my space on this page blank; filled with the greatest silence. And readers, on seeing this blank space, would fill it with their own desires.

> . . . this can hardly be called a column. It is simply what it is. It does not correspond to any genre. . . .

Lispector, Ukrainian Jewish by birth, Brazilian by culture and conviction, found herself at home in this odd no-man's land of letters. "Life has allowed me", she confided to her readers, "to belong now and then, as if to give me the measure of what I am losing by not belonging." By the time she began writing for the *Jornal,* she had separated from her diplomat husband, and could settle down in Rio with her two young sons and concentrate on imaginative exursions. In January 1972,

when she's been teasing her readers for more than five years, she announces: "I have learned to be elusive". But she had always known how, it was the experience of going public that made sense of her ambivalence—"Paradoxically, there is alongside this need to defend my privacy a burning desire to confess in public, and not to a priest".

Many of her topics, when you filter out the idiosyncrasies of the style, belong with the banalities of women's mags—though you have to throw in an element of time-warp: anecdotes about eccentric, tragic or malicious servants (these are pieces you wouldn't publish if you thought the servants could or would read them); conversations with cab-drivers; stories about her children; pieces about food and flowers and pets. However, she contrives almost always to distort the stuff of bourgeois life into provocation and mystery. Plants "are unconsciousness itself". "Not to have been born an animal", she muses, "seems to be one of my secret regrets". One April Saturday, she does a Dictionary of flowers—"There is nothing more pleasing than to watch the rose flower into womanhood. Try crushing those petals between your lips. They taste so good". This is a set of parody household hints, an outrageous but not untypical example of her polymorphous hedonism. Elsewhere, the traditional Brazilian dish of chicken cooked in its own blood also produces a *frisson* all its own: "We must never forget that we are cannibals. We must respect our cruelty". She specializes in excess, nausea even. Falsity and bad taste are, her whole manner implies, risks worth taking: "There is something of the charlatan in all of us. . . . I can feel the charlatan inside me, haunting me".

She writes about how much she dislikes turning ideas into stories, how redundant conventional scene-setting and word-painting are—"I know perfectly well what makes a true novel. Yet when I read such novels with their web of facts and descriptions, I simply feel bored". One of the charms of the column was obviously that it allowed her to give an image an outing without building a narrative around it. She could let things go, fade them out or focus in *ad lib.* There are, however, set pieces. She starts the new year in 1970 with an autobiographical piece, **"A Mischievous Little Girl"**, that lasts her until February 7, when it culminates with an epiphany about the wolfish nature of love: "Suddenly it became clear why I had been born intransigent, why I had been born without aversion to pain. Why do you have such long nails? All the better to claw you to death and pluck out your fatal thorns, the wolf-man replies. . . ". And there is a memorably crystalline tribute to the architecture of Brasilia ("This is the place where space most closely resembles time"). On the whole, though, she settles for what she calls "intuition" and "instinct", and free-associates her way from one sentence to the next ("I see that I have moved on from mercury to the mystery of wild beasts"). Or to put it another way—"One does not make a sentence. A sentence is born". This is a favourite line, one of the very few she repeats, though with variations.

Always starting again, living and writing in a continuum, Lispector in these vanishing "chronicles" very exactly embodies Cixous's version of a feminine writing. Indeed, she prints one week a letter from an actress friend, Fernanda Montenegro, that spells it out—"Dear Clarice, I am writing to you with deep emotion. . . . The feelings you arouse are so utterly feminine; painful, subdued and discreet, anguished yet concealed." Fernanda, as she herself points out, should know what she's talking about since deception is her profession, her truth. It's this honest dishonesty that Cixous seems to have in mind—"'I am always on the run'". As has often been pointed out, there's more than a whiff of feminine mystique, the eternal feminine—the old essence we're supposed not to believe in any more-about all such strategies. But Lispector, like Cixous, disarms criticism by the simple expedient of going over the top. (For instance, here she is confronting the Sphinx—"I could not decipher her meaning, nor could she decipher mine".) It's a kind of writing that's spiritually sly, nostalgic for a bodiless existence—or a soulless one, for that matter—which can shuck off identity's dimensions altogether. "Even one's own style", she'll say, "is an obstacle that must be overcome." Euphoria and depression seem inextricably mixed in all this, as if the only thing you can build with words is a prison. So: you're always escaping (bliss) but always having it to do all over again, like housework. Clarice Lispector's weekly stint, in fact, was just right for the effect, and *Discovering the World* is a tireless demonstration of her elusive talents.

FURTHER READING

Brower, Keith H. "The Narratee in Clarice Lispector's *Agua Viva*." *Romance Notes,* Vol. XXXII, No. 2 (Winter 1991): 111-18.

   Probes Lispector's use of the narrator in *Agua Viva* as he addresses his subject and the audience.

Daidone, Lisa Casali and Clifford, John. "Clarice Lispector: Anticipating the Postmodern." *Multicultural Literatures through Feminist/Poststructuralist Lenses*, Barbara Frey Waxman, ed., pp. 190-201. Knoxville: University of Tennessee Press, 1993.

Examines Lispector's use of language in *Chronicles* as casual and unpretentious.

Fitz, Earl E. "'A pecadora queimada e os anjos harmoniosos': Clarice Lispector as Dramatist." *Luso-Brazilian Review*, Vol. XXXIV, No. II (1997): 25-39.

   Clarifies Lispector's themes and concepts in early dramatic pieces as indication of her concerns in later works.

Lastinger, Valerie C. "Humor in a New Reading of Clarice Lispector." *Hispania*, Vol. 72, No. 1 (March 1989): 130-37.

   Views different levels of humor in Lispector's short stories.

Mathie, Barbara. "Feminism, Language or Existentialism: The Search for the Self in the Works of Clarice Lispector." *Subjectivity and Literature from the Romantics to the Present Day*, Philip Shaw and Peter Stockwell, eds. London: Pinter Publishers, 1991, 175p.

   An in-depth look at several of Lispector's characters, their lack of identity, and the crises that propel them forward.

Ruta, Suzanne. Review of *Selected Cronicas. The New York Times Book Review* (December 15, 1996): 20-21.

   In-depth review of the American publication of *Cronicas,* mentioning the comprehensive translation and Lispector's influences and background.

Saenz de Tejada, Cristina. "The Eternal Non-Difference: Clarice Lispector's Concept of Androgyny." *Luso-Brazilian Review*, Vol XXXI, No. 1 (1994): 39-56.

   Explores Lispector's use of conflicting issues between male/female and spirit/body that result in a third option, androgyny, as a means to define the self.

_____. "Ecologist and Ecofeminist Awareness in *Agua Viva:* A Brazilian Woman Rereading Nature." *Brazil: A Journal of Brazilian Literature*, Vol. 10, No. 8 (1997): 39-56.

   Applies Robert Goodin's *Green Political Theory* of extracting wholeness from the relationship between two separate parts to Lispector's *Agua Viva* and her images of nature and human existence.

Somerlate Barbosa, Maria Jose. "The Transgression of Literary and Ontological Boundaries According to Clarice Lispector." *Romance Languages Annual*, Vol. II (1991): 327-29.

   Details four of Lispector's texts, and her blurring of boundaries, specifically between fiction/reality and character/reader.

Additional coverage of Lispector's life and career is contained in the following sources published by the Gale Group: *Contemporary Authors*, Vols. 116, 139; *Contemporary Authors New Revision Series*, Vol. 71; *Contemporary Literature Criticism*, Vol 43; *DISCovering Multicultural Authors*; *Dictionary of Literary Biography*, Vol. 113; *Short Story Criticism*, **Vol. 34.**

Leopoldo Lugones
1874-1938

Argentinian poet, short story writer, essayist, and novelist.

INTRODUCTION

Lugones is considered one of the most important poets and fiction writers of the *modernista* movement in Spanish American literature. While his mentor, Rubén Darío, is credited with initiating this revival in Spanish literature, the first since the seventeenth century, Lugones's technical virtuosity is considered even greater than that of his predecessor. His experimental use of metaphors, symbolism, meter, rhyme, and visual imagery in such early collections as *Las montañas del oro* and *Lunario sentimental* displays the influence of such poets as Victor Hugo, Walt Whitman, and Jules Laforgue. Lugones later moved toward more traditional poetic forms, a trend firmly established with the publication of *Odas seculares*, a collection of nationalistic poems commemorating the Argentinian centennial. In addition to his innovations in poetry, influential short stories in Lugones's *Las fuerzas extrañas* introduced science fiction to Argentinian literature and inspired imitation by such writers as Jorge Luis Borges. More than any other writer of the *modernista* movement Lugones strove to establish an independent Latin American form of expression by synthesizing the most unique and expressive elements of Romanticism, Realism, Naturalism, Symbolism, and Aestheticism.

Lugones was born in the village of Rio Seco in the province of Cordoba and as a youth moved with his family to the city of Cordoba. There he attended a Catholic secondary school, which he left in protest against both strict discipline and church dogma. In 1893 he moved to Buenos Aires, where he became one of the dominant figures among the school of *modernista* writers led by Rubén Darío. Darío's high regard for Lugones's first poetry collection, *Las montañas del oro*, insured the young poet's place among the leaders of the avant-garde movement, and after Dario left Argentina, Lugones's leadership was indisputable. As a journalist and a member of the socialist group Centro Socialista de Estudios, Lugones wrote articles expounding political views that sometimes served as the themes of his poetry as well. However, he soon shifted from socialism to a conservatism that grew increasingly reactionary and nationalistic, ending in fascism. He held several government posts, serving as the director of the library of the National Council of Education from 1914 until his death, and also as Argentina's representative to the Committee on Intellectual Cooperation of the League of Nations. Lugones's drastic political changes are reflected in his later works, where nationalism and historical themes are developed. Argentine intellectuals once led by Lugones attacked these later works, accusing him of opportunism, imitation, and even

plagiarism. Even after his style turned to more traditional forms, Lugones continued to experiment with metaphors and imagery. This experimentation has been viewed as Lugones's search for a standard of stability in his work that was lacking in his emotional life. This search culminated in disillusionment and despair, and in 1938 Lugones took a fatal dose of cyanide.

With the appearance of his first poetry collection, *Las montañas del oro*, Lugones's reputation as the most innovative of the *modernista* poets was established. In a grandiose style indicative of youthful vigor and bombast, the poems call for a revolution of poetic conventions, and also define the poet as a prophetic visionary uniquely qualified to lead a social revolution, thus establishing a relationship between the poet's artistic and political goals. The experimental use of free verse in this collection exhibits the influence of the French *vers libre* poets and of Walt Whitman; it also displays elaborately sensual visual imagery that has been regarded as both beautiful and shocking. The tone of *Los crepúsculos del Jardín,* Lugones's second collection, is quieter and more detached, moving from the spacious mountain settings of *Las montañas del oro* to the confines of small gardens. Here the poet is characterized as a loner who is divided by his superior vision from the masses by a gulf of misunderstanding. This detachment is complemented by an emphasis on emotion rather than style and by the use of metaphors that display a mastery of the interplay between sound and meaning. Lugones's final work of his *modernista* phase is *Lunario sentimental*, considered his masterpiece and his most influential work. Metaphors that juxtapose unlike elements and original rhymes in the collection were praised and imitated. Many critics also note the influence of Laforgue on *Lunario sentimental* in the ironic, irreverent humor of the collection.

In *Odas seculares* only vestiges of French influences remain. This epic celebration of pastoral Argentina abandons the explosive virtuosity of the earlier collections, turning to classical poetic models. In the villages and plains, ordinary objects and scenes are illuminated by the poet's observant eye. "A los ganados y las mieses," representative of the poems in the collection, honors the poor minorities who seek refuge in the grassy pampas. This celebration of traditional modes of living praises rural life and displays a growing conservatism that would characterize later collections. In these subsequent works, Lugones warned against the encroachment of industrialization and modernization that threatened the farmlands. Despite the somewhat monotonous nature of the traditional rhymes used in the works, Lugones's imaginative power persists in new manners of expression that some critics have called "Latin Americanisms." *Romancero del río seco*, published posthumously, contains Lugones's most intimate poems, formed from memories of his youth in Cordoba, that extoll the virtues of love, patriotism, and courage embodied in the laborers, artisans, and gauchos of the recent past. The gaucho is also honored in *La guerra gaucha*, a collection of historical vignettes that present romantic pictures of heroism. These patriotic tales depict freedom fighters opposing supporters of Spanish rule. Natural imagery informs the work, symbolising suprahuman support of the gaucho's cause; sunlight in particular, one critic has observed, implies the blessing of an Inca deity.

In addition to his influential poetic innovations, Lugones also affected the course of Argentine fiction. His most well-known short stories, collected in *Las fuerzas extrañas*, introduced science fiction to Argentine literature. By using the names of real scientists and alluding to factual innovations in contemporary science, Lugones made the far-fetched stories more credible, confusing the delineation of fact and fiction. This use of realistic elements and references to current scientific knowledge would be used by other writers, including Borges, an early commentator on Lugones's work who praised this collection as containing some of the best fiction in Hispanic literature. Some critics contend that the maudlin point of view and obsessive concern with death in the tales shows the influence of Edgar Allan Poe, while others note that the two writers chose distinctly different points of view for their work. In contrast to the first-person confessions of Poe's horror tales, Lugones's stories are typically narrated by an observer and often demonstrate the two-pronged nature of scientific discovery—the pleasure of acquiring valuable knowledge and the fear of delving into the unknown. In "El psychon," the recent discovery of the process of liquifying gases is employed by Lugones to depict a doctor who produces pure thought in liquid form. "La lluvia de fuego" depicts the growing horror in ancient Gomorrah as a volcanic rain of incandescent copper particles slowly destroys the city. The confusion and fear of the farm animals, who cannot understand what is happening, is juxtaposed with the terror of the humans, who fully comprehend the situation. Lugones's interest in science fiction eventually waned, but his fascination with the unknown led to stories dealing with the occult, Egyptology, theosophy, and Argentinian superstitions. Most critics argue that these stories, including those in *Cuentos fatales*, do not have the verisimilitude of the science fiction tales. The writer's involvement with his subject is thinly veiled with weak plots, and the stories are longer and more diffuse. Others believe that his entire body of fiction was of secondary importance to Lugones, and therefore not as carefully revised and finely wrought as his poetry, for which he had a higher regard.

Lugones has been praised as a poetic innovator who more than any single poet helped create a uniquely Latin American form of literary expression. His knowledge of world languages and literature aided him in selecting the most modern terms and techniques in poetry, and allowed him to assimilate components from disparate schools of thought in the creation of an individual voice.

PRINCIPAL WORKS

Las montañas del oro   (poetry)   1897
La guerra gaucha [*Death of a Gaucho* (partial translation)]   (novel) 1905
Los crepúsculos del jardín   (poetry)   1905
Las fuerzas extrañas   (short stories)   1906
Lunario sentimental   (poetry)   1909
Odas seculares   (poetry)   1910
Historia de Sarmiento [*Sarmiento the Educator* (partial translation)]   (history)   1911
El libro fiel   (poetry)   1912
* "Como hablan en las cimas"   ["How the Mountains Talk"]   (poem)   1915
El libro de los paisajes   (poetry)   1917
† "A Good Cheese"   (short story)   1920
† "Shepherd Boy and Shepherd Girl"   (short story)   1920
Las horas doradas   (poetry)   1922
Cuentos fatales   (short stories)   1924
Romancero   (poetry)   1924
‡ "Luz" ["Light"]   (poem)   1927
Poemas solariegos   (poetry)   1928
Romancero del río seco   (poetry)   1938
Antologia poetica   (poetry)   1941
"Autumn Sweetness"   (poem)   1942
†† "Death of the Moon"   (poem)   1943
Obras poeticas completas   (poetry)   1948
** "Yzur"   (short story)   1963
Las primeras letras de Leopoldo Lugones   (letters)   1963

* published in journal *Stratford Journal*
† published in journal *Inter-America*
‡ published in newspaper *Christian Science Monitor*
# published in journal *Commonweal*
†† published in journal *Poetry*
** published in *Classic Tales from Spanish America*

CRITICISM

Manuel Belloni   (essay date January 1969)

SOURCE: "Leopoldo Lugones: The Golden Condor," in *Américas*, Vol. 21, No. 1, Janurary, 1969, pp. 15-20.

[*In the following essay, critic Manuel Belloni praises Leopoldo Lugones as the first prominent Argentinian writer and a leader of Modernism, offering a substantial review of his life and writings.*]

Leopoldo Lugones was the first Argentine writer; that is, the first intellectual totally dedicated to letters, the first *homme des lettres* who as such heralded a step forward in Argentine culture. It was not mere coincidence that he should be, at the same time, the torchbearer of Modernism, whose mantle he had inherited from Rubén Darío, and should head the first really independent movement in Latin American literature. This innovation has not been given the revolutionary value it deserves, as it perhaps defines the form of Latin American culture as eclectic and recompilative of all Western culture and, at the same time, the source of a wave of culture from Latin America to Europe that foretold the prominence of the New World in the realm of ideas. Modernism was the first step in the increasing influence of Latin America in Europe, the first conquest-response clearly our own that heralded the dawn of Latin American culture. Lugones' effect on Spain was similar to that of Benjamin Franklin on France a century before, renewing the nation's repertoire of ideas. Nevertheless, he was clearly original in his ecumenical effort of New World gathering, assimilating, ruminating, and creating.

Edgar Allan Poe influenced Baudelaire to create Symbolism. Rubén Darío conquered all Spanish poetry with his golden light. He was thus the precursor of the first intellectual awakening of Latin Europe; Lugones was his brilliant disciple. Lugones was born June 13, 1874, in the inland province of Cordoba, Argentina—the province of the singing tone. He was always a mountain man. His native countryside marked the face of his soul with its rocky style, carved it in petrified slivers of bone. Córdoba was ever a chaste and Catholic province, that of the Jesuit colonial university, of the resistance and the May Revolution, and was the center of the republic in all the rebellions at the immigrant seaside capital, at the head of the bridge to Europe. Córdoba is almost Spain, as its name suggests. The laughing streams, the dry air, the mountain light, the pure sky, the trees along the river banks and the dominant earth define the province, its style of life, and Lugones. He himself says so. *En la Villa de María del Río Seco, / Al pie del Cerro del Romero, nací. / Y esto es todo cuanto diré de mí, / Porque no soy más que un eco / Del canto natal que traigo aquí.* (In Villa de María of Río Seco, / At the foot of Romero Hill I was born. / And this is all I will tell about me, / Because I am no more than an echo / Of the native song I sing.) [*Poemas Solariegos*, Ancestral Poems, 1928].

Let us follow him from his first work, *Las Montañas de Oro* [The Golden Mountains], published in 1897, as it is a poet's glory to live in his works and not in his deeds, above all in as factual an age as ours. Poet means creator. Poets have so much of the divine in them that they act only through their works, like God, who has been resting for millenniums after a week of work. Lugones, too, created his mountain and created it of gold, because its richness would be the stamp of his poetry, a sensational baroque richness, Latin American to the core, full of boiling metaphors, sparkling jewelry like a Crivelli painting, continually Renaissance with the Botticellian luxury of Simonetta Vespucci that marks his perennial search for Eternal Beauty.

Yes, Lugones is the search, through the word, for eternal beauty. And for this search he must master verse technically and language formidably in order to win in this battle of giants. His stylistic signs are metaphor, vocabulary, golden brilliance, the voluptuousness of the baroque movement, sylvan spiral and volute, Latin Amer-

icanism in his great figures of speech, rocky dryness in conceptual synthesis, sparkling jewelry. We would almost say that to read him one ought to wear sunglasses. His sensual rhythm has Whitmanesque swells, and he uses repetition to embed one wave on another, with his nutritive, telluric touch: *Emigre la semilla de la siembra / del genésico horror de las matrices / Emigre la semilla de la siembra.* (Let the seed depart from the sown field / from the generative horror of wombs / Let the seed depart from the sown field.) (*Las Montañas de Oro*).

There is always an agrarian and nourishing tone in his sweeping visions, as we see in his "Oda a los Ganados y las Mieses (Ode to the Cattle and Pastures)," his greatest poem in *Contos Seculares* [Secular Songs], published in 1910, one century after the May Revolution. This deeply-lying patriotic feeling made him the intellectual head of the Centennial, the federal *caudillo*, youthfully attacking everything. He entered the Plaza de Mayo in Buenos Aires with his poems like any other provincial conquistador and soon dominated its literary circles. He boasted of his homeland, was dazzled by big-city ideas, and turned to socialism. He knew his own dignity and did not join the scramble for the top of the pyramid, and his silence, and his poems, made him the leader. He knew Darío, who, leaving for Europe, tacitly named him his heir in the realm of Modernism.

What did Modernism signify? A declaration of independence for Latin American intelligence, without rejecting valuable support from the outside. The brain was liberated in that it made decisions *per se* and without fearing the authority of foreign criticism. Literary activity, which had been sporadic and derivative, surged forward like a sea that had newly acquired the rivers to cover a continent. The River Plate, the sea-river, began to produce notable figures on both banks. All categories were cultivated passionately, fruitfully. Selective eclecticism united the new cosmovision and the emphasis on nature of Romanticism; the search for the concrete truth and avoidance of the unreachable metaphysical of Positivism; the valiant capture of reality as it is, of Realism; the descriptive bent toward the low and the ugly, of Naturalism; the expressive capacity of the particular or the symbol's induction toward the general, of Symbolism; a certain disdain for the commonplace and a search for the rare and strange of Aestheticism (*Los Raros*, The Strange Ones, was one of Darío's key books).

Modernism was a passionate crucible in which all the previous styles were melted and alloyed, adding the influences of music and the plastic arts, molded in neoclassical forms, refining the ironlike stylism that Parnassus desired and adding handfuls of the vibrant light that Impressionism sought. The rhythm, melody, orchestration and *sfumato*, hue and luminosity, of Symbolism and Impressionism. Objective realism and subjective individualism.

Modernism rejected nothing and, without intending to, gave an original and Latin American note to everything. To the antagonistic European world it was the integrative

Latin American reply, and by foreswearing the choice of factions, it inaugurated a new and different world. It wrung the neck of the *purely* romantic swan, but preserved exoticism, orientalism, traditionalism and romantic sentimentalism. It selected from every movement and made a sensational Creole stew that would nourish, even politically, half the twentieth century. The unity of the cultural process was recovered, intuitively forwarding the German historicist discoveries of Spengler concerning cultural cycles.

A great unitive love vibrates in the new message. The concept of the urge behind the form described by Wilhelm Worringer was assimilated along with Gebhardt's axiomatic rhythm, and Weisbach's evaluation of the baroque brought respect for Latin America, which is *intrinsically baroque.* Lugones and Córdoba's stone desert *are* baroque. Life and the mountain are. Wölfflin later discovered and systematized the intercreation of the classic and the baroque in a pendulous movement, or rather, Modernism intuitively took what was in the air at the end of the century and opened new perspectives.

Lugones not only symbolized the Taoist pendulous swing as an aesthetic guide, but he himself, in his own works, showed such a Laotian spiral. The socialist would become aristocratic; the extremist, moderate; the epic, lyric; the traditionalist, futurist; the esoteric, open; the feminine transcendent from spiritual intuition would become the eminently humanist masculine intelligence. And thus the condor would fly over the whole continent with his wings tinted with the solar gold of beautiful truths. All nature would remain at his feet like a visible sign of the word conquered by the heights. All human gambits, even parapsychology, would be frazzled by the unsleeping eye. Epic glory would make our hair curl with the heroism of his stories like *La Guerra Gaucha* [The Gaucho War], a sensational description of Güemes' guerrillas. He was demoniacally baroque and Apollonianly classical, unmeasured and balanced, volcanic and supportive, realistic and numinous, chiaroscuro and luminous, beautiful and supremely ugly. Because Modernism and its chief refused to select and reject, because to choose is to cut something from reality and throw the rest away, and they preferred to synthesize all and fire it in an earthborn and experimental passion.

Uruguay gave the best of its literature in essayists like Rodó and Vaz Ferreira, poets like Herrera and Reissig, Agustini and Vasseur; in playwrights like Florencio Sánchez, short story writers like Horacio Quiroga and novelists like Reyles. Argentina strove forcefully to fill the half-century with the powerful wingbeats of Lugones, in all categories. His condor's wings cover the poem with *Los Crepúsculos del Jardín* [Dusk in the Garden], *Poemas Solariegos*, *El Libro de los Paisajes* [The Book of Landscapes], *Odas Seculares,* and *Romances del Río Seco* [Romances of the Río Seco]. His voice is made complete in an eclectic book, a sentimental Lugonariad of prose and poetry, or in a robust historical exposition in *Historia de Roca* [History of Roca] or *Historia de Sarmiento* [History of Sarmiento] where he sees like a

profound and ontologic poet and carves a masterful and rotund prose, among the most perfect of Argentine literature. He is aware of his mission, and he writes: *El poeta es el astro de su propio destierro. / El tiene su cabeza junto a Dios, como todos, / Pero su carne es fruto de los cósmicos lodos, / De la Vida . . .* (The poet is the star of his own exile. / He has his head next to God, as all do, / But his flesh is the fruit of the cosmic mud, / Of life . . .)

Installed on Parnassus, Lugones occupied it for a quarter of a century with his sacred poet's work. He was gallant and fine, sumptuous and plastic, rigorous and terse, ample in Olympian gesture and language. He had one of the widest vocabularies in Spanish literature and was a renewer of the classics and of words. He was a master of grammar, to the boundary of rhetoric. To be the teacher of generations it was necessary to learn everything and then to forget it when it had become part of one. Thus having mastered technique to its depths, one can be free of constant watchfulness and vacillations.

Lugones was a sculptor whose every stroke was precise. He wrote forty books and expended enough effort on magazines and newspapers for at least another ten. He was never in a hurry and wove his fabric with the tenacity and brilliance of a silkworm in its cocoon. He completed ten books of poetry. A metaphysical investigator who was proud of his origins, he wrote in *Romances*: *esto no es para extranjeros, / cajetillas ni pazguatos* (this is not for foreigners, / wealthy *porteños* or simpletons). Neither did he write for an acquiescent public; he wrote because it was his means of expression and he required the public to mount his stairs of philosophy, history, mythology, language, philology, Latin, Greek, and Spanish to reach him. It was his lofty manner of respecting the public. Everything he did had a Creole flavor to the marrow. He was moved emotionally by the achievements of the Gauchos of Salta Province and he makes us weep with their integrity and humble heroism.

He possessed the sacred destiny of making the daily act transcendent through its inherent symbol and this is the essence of art; to rescue the day from its precariousness and to praise its meaning to eternity. And without meaning to he was to be a democratic knight, as leaders are always men in perfect contact with their people and their best interests rather than those foreign to them. The whole human race passed before him and he powdered the earth and recognized his favorite son. He tamed the language and achieved the supreme skill of saying exactly what he wanted, without cuts or additions. He is comparable in simplicity only to Goethe.

Exhalaban un perfume labriego / De polen almizclado las boñigas. / Su compás hidráulico a la paz macilenta. / Y llena de luna su alma simple como la menta, / A ilusorios pesebres rebuzna un pollino. (Cow dung exhales a rustic perfume / Of musty pollen. / Its hydraulic beat to withered peace. / And its simple soul full of mint like the moon, / The donkey brays at illusory mangers.) Or: *Raza valerosa y dura, / Que con pujanza silvestre /*

Dio a la patria, en garbo ecuestre, / Su primitiva escultura. (Brave and hard race, / Who with wild power / Gave the country, in equestrian gallantry, / Its primitive sculpture.) Dry, down-to-earth poetry that says only what is necessary; but when we try to cut one word from the poem, only one, it plummets, mortally wounded, like a common dove.

There is no one else who can equal Virgil in the description of the countryside, as we see in **"El Buey"** (**The Ox**): *Sobre el estanque en cuya inmovil lastra / Esfumará su muaré la tarde quista, / Con relieve escabroso su silueta / Afirma un recio plomo de pilastra. // Su vasta sed, un agua violeta / Con anhelosa deglución arrastra, / Y la naturaleza, en el madrasta, / No turba su canícula incompleta. // Vuelve los ojos densos de fatiga, / Hacia el fútil juncal donde prodiga / Gárrulo borbollón la esclusa rauda. // Y con la insipidez de la costumbre, / Lo amodorra de paz la servidumbre / Que su sexo monótono defrauda.* (Over the pond in whose immobile boat / Will vanish the quiet afternoon's moiré, / With rough relief his silhouette / Asserts a pillar's leaden strength. // His vast thirst, a violet water / With eager gulps draws in, / And nature, his stepmother, / Does not disturb his incomplete drouse. // He turns his eyes leaden with fatigue, / Toward the futile rushes where is wasted / The garrulous bubbling of the rapid floodgate. // And with customary insipidity, / He drowses with the peace of servitude / That his monotonous sex defrauds.)

How much he says, and how economically; how rich and how severe, the ox rises beyond his inanity and attains a definite place, with the definitive strength of art like a Michelangelesque statue on the hazy pampa. Lugones is one of those traitorous poets whom our spoiled palate often offends, believing them deaf or simple; but if we let their honey fall into our mouths, closing our eyes, we will taste the nectar of Mount Hymettus and will find again the line that comes from Theocritus through Virgil, Greco-Latin to the core. And Lugones knows it. By instinct. *Llevo en mí lo mejor / De mi padre y mi madre, que en mí es vida gloriosa, / Y lo mejor del hijo y de la esposa, / Y así está en mí todo el amor. / Lo que en mi madre fue belleza / y en mi padre vigor y nobleza, / En la esposa fe segura / Y en el hijo ternura, / Ilumina mi corazón / Con esplendor absoluto.* (I carry in me the best / Of my father and my mother, which in me is glorious life, / And the best of son and wife, / And thus in me all is love. / What in my mother was beauty / and in my father vigor and nobility, / In my wife confident faith / And in my son, tenderness, / Illumines my heart / With splendor absolute.)

From such possession by poetry he becomes hearty and countryish and is not frightened of the common side of humanity. *Su brazo era el martillo de una industria divina, / Frío, tenía un solo color, pero este era / El del bronce. Profundo, su gigantesca carrera / ás conmovió las rocas que removió la arcilla, / Su sable era el arado, su sangre la semilla, / La gloria le trataba fraternalmente. El viento / le abría paso. Un vasto*

fulgor de pensamiento / Alumbraba las nubes detrás de su cabeza. / Su vecina más próxima se llamaba grandeza / El cóndor le decía Señor. (His arm was the hammer of a godly industry, / Cold, it had only one color, but / that was bronze. Profound, his gigantic career / moved rocks rather than clay, / His saber was the plowshare, his blood the seed, / Glory was his brother. The wind made way for him. A vast glare of thought / Lighted the clouds behind his head. / His nearest neighbor was grandeur / The condor called him *sir*.) [From **"Gesta Magna,"** or Great Feats].

Thus he passed from anecdote to action, from Virgil to Homer, and he could have been the French poet Banville, or the Ecuadorian Olmedo. All previous poetry met in him; and all subsequent came from him. *Llevo en mí la Patria entera, / que es una dulzura cordial, / Como la miel de panal / Lleva en una gota la pradera.* (I carry in me the entire country, / which is a sweet cordial, / As honey from the honeycomb / Carries in one drop the prairie.) [**"El Tesoro,"** The Treasure].

Only Sarmiento can be compared with Lugones in sweep, with his command of prose that Unamuno admired so much. Thus from his native homeland this rocky man came down to show us the country and to unify the Gaucho wisdom of Hernández and the sweeping power of Sarmiento, to join in a still unrecognized miracle of synthesis, the Aeolian harp with summoning drum, the pastoral flute with the bugle of war, thunder with the blond curls of a pretty girl. Goethe said that the true poet does not describe things but is them. Herein lies Lugones' complicated simplicity in making us fall in love with the pampa: *infinitamente gimen los ejes broncos / De lejanas carretas en la tarde morosa. / A flor de tierra entre los negros troncos, / La luna semeja un hongo rosa.* (Infinitely squeak the hoarse axles / Of distant carts in the laggard evening. / A flower of earth between the black trunks, / The moon appears to be a rosy mushroom.)

Need we say more? From him came Enrique Banchs, Arturo Capdevilla, Alfonsina Storni, Ricardo Güiraldes, Leopoldo Díaz, Ricardo Rojas, regional poets like Miguel A. Camino, Juan Carlos Dávalos, Antonion de la Torre, Esteban Agüero and Manuel Castilla. Macedonio Fernández was to be his follower as philosophical poet; Jorge Luis Borges, as a visionary and metaphoric ultraist; Oliverio Girondo, as a renewer of the language; Francisco Bernárdez as a Catholic poet; Leopoldo Marechal as a mystagogue and, finally, Ricardo E. Molinari as a lyricist of the pampas. A certainty: All poetry has the tint of Lugones, the precursor who opened up all of the paths for spiritual conquest, the golden condor.

Joan E. Ciruti   (essay date 1975)

SOURCE: "Leopoldo Lugones: The Short Stories," *Revista Interamericana de Bibliografia / Inter-American Review of Bibliography*, Vol. XXV, No. 2, April-June 1975, pp. 134-49.

Leopoldo Lugones

[*In the following essay, Ciruti offers substantial evidence to defend her argument that Lugones' short stories are just as important—and are even more insightful—than his poems.*]

The short stories of Leopoldo Lugones have not yet been fully appreciated for what they can tell us of the man and of his contributions to Spanish-American prose fiction. That he wrote short stories all his life is well known, for he published collections at intervals in his career. He is recognized also as one of the originators of the "cuento fantástico,"[1] a type that has flourished in his native Argentina. The collected stories of Lugones, nevertheless, number fewer than half of those he wrote, and even they have not received the critical attention they deserve. Scholars and critics tend to dismiss his short stories with brief comments, as they judge his narrative skill on the basis of the baroque prose of *La guerra gaucha*.[2] The short stories, however, differ markedly from *La guerra gaucha*, and afford insights into the thought processes of the artist from age twenty, in 1894, to his death, in 1938.

Lugones was a journalist by profession, and almost everything he wrote appeared first in a newspaper or magazine. During his lifetime, he compiled four major collections of short stories: *Las fuerzas extrañas* (1906), *Cuentos* (1916), *Cuentos fatales* (1924), and *Filosofícula* (1924), the latter having parables, anecdotes, and meditations interspersed among the stories. These books, to-

gether with four stories that were included with the poetry of *Lunario sentimental* (1909), make available only forty-two of the more than one hundred short stories he published.[3] Almost forty additional stories can be found in *Las primeras letras de Leopoldo Lugones*, published in 1963 to commemorate the twenty-fifth anniversary of his death.[4]

A chronological ordering of the short stories shows that Lugones' most active period in the genre was from 1897 to 1899, twenty-six stories being published in the latter year alone. These are, of course, years that Rubén Darío was in Buenos Aires, and the young *modernistas* gathered around him, Lugones outstanding among them, were extremely productive. Another peak is reached in the years 1906-1909, when Lugones was an active collaborator in the weekly news and literary review *Caras y Caretas*.[5] The remaining years of his career see the publication of isolated stories; on two occasions as many as five years pass in which none appears, and once, 1925-1935, it is ten years. As one would expect from a *modernista* writer, the subject matter of these short stories is varied. Nevertheless, as will become evident, certain themes and preoccupations continue throughout the years.

Love, in many guises, ranging from the innocent to the diabolical, is a recurring motive especially in the stories of Lugones' early years, before he was thirty. More often than not, the plots concern a candid attraction between adolescents who scarcely comprehend the emotion they feel; frequently there is a humorous twist, in which the lovers are protected in their innocence by some higher power. Five of the seven stories in the collection *Cuentos* are of this type, and similar story lines are found in four additional narrations. Typical of the plots is "**Las manzanas verdes**" (1907; *C*),[6] in which Braulio communicates his love for Naira by pasting cut-outs on green apples so that, when they ripen, the skin shows a heart pierced by an arrow. But one apple has a skull and crossbones, representing Naira's guardian, and the insult narrowly avoids detection when the girl bites off the incriminating design. Where love is concerned, innocence, faithfulness and sincerity are apparently of great importance to the author. Even the Lugones version of Don Juan Tenorio emphasizes a certain candor and sincerity. In "**El secreto de don Juan**" (1923; *CF*), the spirit of Don Juan himself appears at the end to confirm that his secret lay in his sincerity: "No te engañó, dulce amiga, la voz de mi amor. Pues según puso en mis labios la única comedia que entre tantas necedades como han escrito de mí, haya sabido interpretarme, y que, por lo mismo también permanece inédita: Es que nunca enamoré sin estar enamorado." (*CF*, p. 96).

In other stories a lack of selfless faith produces tragedy. Such is the case in "**Piuma al vento**" (1903; *C*), in which his sweetheart's skepticism about his feather-balancing act leads a clown to commit suicide. And in "**Los principios de moral**" (1899; *PL*), Lugones goes so far as to present a woman frivolous in her infidelity. In a conversation between two dogs, reminiscent of Cervantes' *Coloquio de los perros*, the satire is biting. Leal, an exemplary greyhound, was suddenly turned into the street after his mistress, an errant wife, saw Leal kissing Fany. The other dog comprehends the expulsion perfectly: "El vagabundo compañero de *Leal* miró poéticamente a la Luna, pues él tenía también una novia, y la Luna lo era; revolvió en una especie de erupto amargo toda su filosofía de miserable, y encogiendo la pata junto a un poste del alumbrado, gruñó con gravedad extraña:—¡Olvidas, mi querido *Leal,* que nosotros los perros somos unos cochinos!" (*PL*, p. 143). These lines, which end the story, suggest both the beauty of pure love and how it may be vilified, as the stray dog, in an implied zeugma, raises his eyes to the moon and his leg to the lamp post.

Love for Lugones, then, is not always untarnished or happy. A number of his stories relate details of an illusive or melancholy love, the unnatural frequently playing a part as in **"¿Una mariposa?"** (1897; *C*), the first story Lugones published in Buenos Aires. And three of the four stories in *Lunario sentimental*—**"Inefable ausencia"** (1903), **"La novia imposible"** (1898) and **"Abuela Julieta"** (1899)—suggest that sadness and suffering may be an integral part of love.[7] Sometimes the torment of love is more than melancholy; it is satanic. The title of **"Amor de nieve"** (1899; *PL*) at first suggests purity, but the story ends by aptly describing a "belle dame sans merci" who finds a worthy adversary. Her honor already tarnished by a subterfuge that makes it appear her cousin has seduced her, Aurelia receives him for one week in a strange, frigid love affair, then cleanses her stained honor with blood, as the code demands. In **"Francesca"** (1909; *LS*), a variant on the story of Francesca da Rimini, it is the male who is diabolical, and he abides by no code of honor. But in the ultimate manifestation of this morbid trend, **"La vampira"** (1899; *PL*), Lugones again portrays the fatal woman: "Sus labios aristocráticamente fatigados, sus ojos verdes en que la pasión relampagueaba fulguraciones de oro, sus mejillas, sus manos, obtenían besos, promesas, despertaban exaltaciones de erótica locura" (*PL*, p. 79).

The range of motives in the stories treating of love already reveals a duality that is present throughout Lugones' short story production. On the one hand, he is attracted by a simple life where goodness prevails, and, on the other, he is fatally drawn to the mysterious, where there is always a hint of evil. This preoccupation with what Lugones himself called "las fuerzas extrañas"—the occult, the inexplicable, the powers beyond man's control or comprehension—predominates in his two best-known collections, *Las fuerzas extrañas* and *Cuentos fatales*, and, consequently it is the tendency for which he has been most recognized. The stories contained in these two collections are, indeed, typical of this aspect of Lugones' short story production, but when seen within the larger perspective, they may be categorized differently and re-evaluated with regard to their importance in judging Lugones as a short story writer.

Perhaps most impressive in *Las fuerzas extrañas* are the five science-fiction stories that make up roughly half of the collection. The procedure in much contemporary

science fiction is to suggest an alternate reality in which the reader becomes enveloped. Lugones, a typical *modernista* spirit that rejected limitations, provides an adventure beyond the usual boundaries of man's reality. The narrator, typically, participates in the story as a knowledgeable observer, which gives him a perspective from which to judge the events, and Lugones has ample opportunity to display his considerable scientific knowledge. He also uses the technique, later so important in the stories of Jorge Luis Borges and others, of mentioning the names of real men of science along with fictional characters, thereby blurring the line between the real and the unreal. These stories can be all the more frightening, as Lugones intends, for having an aura of truth about them.

In order of time, the first was **"El psychón"** (1898; *FE*, *PL*). Suggested by the recent discovery of the process for liquefying gases like hydrogen, the story recounts Dr. Paulin's production, in the laboratory, of pure thought in liquid form. In "La metamúsica" (1898; *FE*), Juan, the narrator's friend, succeeds in projecting on a screen the colors of music and achieves the poet's ideal of being able to interpret the universe. In **"La fuerza omega"** (1906; *FE*), the force so named is a sonic beam of tremendous destructive power. **"Viola acherontia"** (1899; *FE*, *PL*) tells of a diabolical gardener who seeks to produce a deadly black violet through the power of suggestion, including watering with the blood of children. And in **"Yzur"** (1906; *FE*), it is linguistic science that is utilized, as the narrator, convinced that his chimpanzee does not speak because he has forgotten how, tries to teach him.

The one story of this type that was not included in *Las fuerzas extrañas* is **"El espejo negro"** (1898; *PL*), and it, in some ways, holds the key to explain Lugones' fascination with such topics. Here the black mirror, made from pure carbon impregnated with the electricity of thought, reflects the head of a man, and the horror comes from the experience of eternity that is patent in that reflection: "La cabeza no tenía nada de monstruoso, siendo esto precisamente lo más terrible: era una cabeza humana; pero sus ojos entrecerrados, su barba color de polvo, su frente en que galopaban sin duda extrahumanos terrores, sus pómulos verdosos, fosforescentes, como el abdomen de un pescado muerto, su boca inmovilizada en una lúgubre torcedura, y vieja, vieja, de cien, de mil, de veinte mil años—todo aquello aplastaba el cerebro. Un horror de eternidad vagaba en la mirada del aparecido, que me envolvía sin verme; mirada de vidrio cuya fijeza expresaba soledades enormes" (*PL*, p. 87). Lugones, in these stories of science fiction, feels that he has a window looking onto the abyss of more complete knowledge than man possesses, perhaps of total comprehension. This feeling is at once marvelous and frightening. The narrator of **"El espejo negro"** also expresses the hesitation and fear he feels: "Si he de especificar mis sensaciones, diré que esa oscuridad producía una inexplicable impresión de miedo. Era la lobreguez del abismo, el vértigo de las profundidades marinas, la desolación del desierto al mismo tiempo—y algo más todavía, algo que era la desesperación" (*PL*, p. 87). Lugones, like the characters of these stories, is curious to decipher the mysteries of the universe, but he is afraid that man cannot venture into the unknown with impunity. Each of these stories, with the possible exception of **"Viola acherontia,"** ends with the destruction of the invention or the inventor. In **"Viola acherontia,"** where the outcome of the experiment is left in doubt, the mad biologist is described as a criminal and "un perfecto hechicero de otros tiempos," which is to say that he represents evil present in the real world. Lugones maintains a greater distance from him: the narrator is no friend of the experimenter, merely an interviewer.

Lugones' venture into science fiction ends with this group of stories written about the turn of the century, but his preoccupation with the unknown continues all of his life. His attention, from this point on, is concentrated on phenomena that are not empirically verifiable. A number of his stories deal with the occult sciences, particularly as practiced in the Middle East. He was an early disciple of Madame Blavatsky and was well versed in her theosophy. **"Un fenómeno inexplicable"** (1898; *FE*, *PL*) was originally published with the title **"La lycanthropia"**[8] in the monthly theosophical magazine *Philadelfia*. In this story, while traveling in a deserted area of the provinces of Santa Fe and Córdoba, the narrator meets an elderly, solitary Englishman, whose medi-tations had led to an awareness of a dual personality, and a desire to see his double produce the form of a horrible monkey that shadows him continually. Another early story, "Kabala práctica" (1897; *PL*), has a similar plot.

By the early 1920's Lugones' interest has turned to Egyptology, which provides the theme for three of the *Cuentos fatales*, as well as for **"Nuralkamar"** (1936), one of his last stories. **"El vaso de alabastro"** (1923; *CF*) and **"Los ojos de la reina"** (1923; *CF*) form one long tale based on the theory that the ancient Egyptians left guardians in their tombs to punish anyone who disturbed their sleep. **"El puñal"** (1924; *CF*) and **"Nuralkamar"** both concern the mysterious appearance of objects. **"El puñal"** deserves special attention as Lugones himself is a participant in the story, and it contains several biographical references. Early in the narration, as he is chatting with the intriguing visitor who suddenly appeared at his home, Lugones mentions that he was not given the name of the saint on whose day he was born, and this leads to other revelations as the conversation continues:

> —Así tuvo usted en su nombre la doble ele inicial que corresponde a su signo astronómico—Los Gemelos, ¿no es cierto?—y repetida por contenido fonético, la influencia del León, que significa el imperio de la violencia en su destino.
>
> —Confirmada—añadí, tendiéndole la palma de mi mano izquierda con voluble abandono de la jovialidad—por una doble señal de muerte violenta . . .
>
> El desconocido echó una viva mirada sobre mi nítida red palmar.
>
> —¡Y todavía con el signo del puñal en el valle de Saturno! Diablo, señor Lugones, agregó, riendo a su vez, su caso podría ser inquietante.

—¿Por qué interrumpí? Si es realmente la fatalidad, fuera inútil oponerse a lo ínevitable.

(CF, p. 63)

Succumbing to the same facination for the inexplicable that Lugones felt, one immediately remembers that the author died by suicide fourteen years after writing this story. In notes to the *Cuentos fatales* (p. 127), Lugones' son tells us that his father and Rubén Darío shortly before World War I visited the famous French occultist Papus, who, among other things, called to his attention the sign of violent death. He also confirms that his father was sincerely fatalistic. Of less moment is the fact that the dagger described in the story was in Lugones' possession at the time, and it still exists.

As in other stories, but perhaps more intensely here, Lugones wishes to convince his readers that this story deals with reality: "No intento desaparecer en éste [el relato] con la impersonalidad narrativa cuya eficacia reconozco, porque no se trata, a la verdad, de una novela, sino de una historia." That morning, he says, he had discovered the secret word of the Drusean sect, an "order of assassins" that terrorized Moslem territories from the eleventh through the thirteenth centuries. A few minutes later, the mysterious stranger appears, and they discuss the ancient fraternity at length. The stranger shows him a dagger in whose blade, as in black mirrors, one can evoke the image of an absent person. Then he speaks of the attitude of the brotherhood toward women, saying that only those who dominate the attraction for women can achieve immortality. He succumbed to love, and, therefore, has fallen from grace.[9] He has come to Buenos Aires to ask for Lugones' help. Assured of Lugones' aid, he vanishes. Some time later, as the stranger had promised, the dagger suddenly materializes behind the piano.

Of all the short stories Lugones wrote, these on the occult sciences tend to be the longest and most diffuse. The plots are complicated and lack the unity that normally characterizes his narrations. More often than not, the flimsy story line serves primarily as a vehicle for extensive expositions on the history and occult beliefs that presumably form the background for the story. He does not manage, as in *Las fuerzas extrañas*, to create a plausible fictional situation in which to incorporate his erudition. Perhaps in his zeal to pass these off as histories rather than stories, he suppresses the truly fictional. Perhaps his attraction to the occult is so great that he can only conceive of it as reality.

Lugones' liking for the exotic beliefs of distant lands does not cause him to neglect the superstitions of the Argentine gaucho. **"El escuerzo"** (1897; *FE*), originally published as **"Los animales malditos,"** illustrates the belief that a dead *escuerzo,* a kind of toad, must be burned or it will resuscitate and take revenge on the person who killed it. In **"Águeda"** (1923; *CF*), a romantic legend of a bandit, the superstitious beliefs are incidental to the plot, but still of prime importance in the total effect of the story.

Inexplicable appearances and dead people provide the subject matter for a number of stories. In **"Luisa Frascati"** (1907), an oil painting comes to life, and the transference of a young woman's beauty from life to an image on a white wall is the motive in **"Hipalia"** (1907). **"El hombre muerto"** (1907) narrates the tale of a singular madman whose dementia consisted of believing himself dead. In **"El hombre del árbol"** (1935), a dead man, a suicide, reads each day under a certain tree in Palermo Park, in Buenos Aires, then disappears into the tree. A more conventional tale is **"La idea de la muerte"** (1907), in which suspicions that a man killed his wife are confirmed by reactions of the family dog.

With the exception of **"El hombre del árbol,"** all of these stories of ghosts and the dead were published in 1907. This seems to indicate, as was suggested earlier, that Lugones reached a turning point around 1906 or 1907, in which the irrational became more fascinating to him than the science fiction that had occupied him for several years. Further support for this conjecture may be found in three short stories, also published in 1907, which seek to define insanity. In **"El descubrimiento de la circunferencia,"** Clinio Malabar's unique madness, like that of the man who believed he was dead, consisted of maintaining that the circumference was the key to human life and that death could not come so long as he was enclosed in a circle. The protagonist of **"Un sujeto ilógico,"** on the other hand, defines insanity as a lack of concordance between logic and the will. And the third story, **"El 'definitivo,'"** leaves insanity in the realm of the inexplicable: it is something that is at once undefinable and "definitive."

Along the same general lines of treating the unnatural, a substantial block of stories narrates myths. One, **"El origen del diluvio"** (1906; *FE*), bridges the gap between science fiction and myth, and also has elements of the occult. The story has the sub-title "Narración de un espíritu," and the scene, as revealed at the end, is a group of spiritualists in session with a medium. Quite a few of the stories recounting myths have a Hellenic atmosphere. An early one, **"Apolo"** (1897; *PL*), was printed with the heading "Mitología moderna," indicating that Lugones may have briefly contemplated a series. The story, however, is frivolous. Some of the narrations can be very lyrical, as is **"Iris"** (1899; *PL*), in which the fairy Iris is related to the rainbow and the diamond. Similarly, **"La invención del firmamento"** (1908; *F*) tells how the blue sky is created from a drop of dew on Pan's flute as he blows into a huge bubble all of his love for Siringa.

The most outstanding of the Hellenic myths, and one of Lugones' better stories, is **"Los caballos de Abdera"** (1906; *FE*). The proud inhabitants of Abdera, a Thracian city justly famous for its horses, treat their animals so well that the horses begin to humanize: they become vain, fall in love with humans, and develop a conscience. Finally, they rebel, and it takes the divine intervention of Hercules to save the humans. As the inventors in the science fiction stories created machines that killed them, so the inhabitants of Abdera unwittingly produced a beast

that could overpower them. The frightening part is that the horses' destructive desire develops along with their humanization. As happened with the chimpanzee Yzur, acquisition of the power to think was no blessing.

Myth, by its very nature, affords Lugones the opportunity to use his imagination to the fullest, without being fettered by convention or reality. Three narrations with fairytale atmospheres relate flowers and the life of man: **"La muerte de la señorita Clementina"** (1900; *PL*), **"La rosa y la espina"** (1907; *F*) and **"El culto de la flor"** (1909; *F*). Another large category of myths treats of biblical and religious themes. Most were written early in Lugones' career, and in some the sentiment overpowers the artistic value. Several of the stories end with miracles, another version of the strange and inexplicable forces that always interest Lugones. In **"Gemas dolorosas"** ([1899]; *PL*), for example, Sor Inés del Sagrado Corazón offers herself as a sacrifice to obtain the carbuncle she needs for the bishop's chasuble she has embroidered. **"El milagro de San Wilfrido"** (1897; *FE*), one of the earliest short stories Lugones published, is a moving evocation of the Israeli desert in biblical times and in the days of the crusades. In **"La estatua de sal"** (1908; *FE*), Lugones is especially good at capturing the emotional state of his protagonist who, it is strongly suggested, is a reincarnation of one of the principals in the tragedy of Lot's wife.

One of the most interesting stories of *Las fuerzas extrañas* is **"La lluvia de fuego,"** which bears the sub-title "Evocación de un desencarnado de Gomorra." Told from the perspective of an elderly recluse whose only vice now is gluttony, the story manages to capture the progression from curiosity to sheer horror, as incandescent copper particles rain down on Gomorrah. In capturing the horror of the situation, Lugones makes effective use of animals. The first indication that the volcanic rain is not a passing thing comes from the reaction of the birds. And finally, as virtually all life has been extinguished, a pride of thirstcrazed lions is the vehicle for describing the terror of the incomprehensible destruction. The animals' terror is instinctive, from not understanding; man's horror stems from comprehending too well.

Although many of the short stories already discussed at least imply a lesson to be learned, there is a sizeable group that explicitly proposes a standard of conduct or sets forth a system of values. Some take the form of fables; others have modern settings and characters taken from contemporary life. A few present abstract principles, but the majority are, on a personal level, concerned with the moral character of the individual. Of those dealing with the abstract, **"El mal, el bien, la justicia y la ley"** (1909) and **"El espíritu de justicia"** (1909; *F*) express the notion that justice does not depend on the law, but is something that exists between men of good faith. **"La defensa de la ilusión"** (1909; *F*) and **"Cosas de gansos"** (1899; *PL*) take on political overtones as they present plots in which the consequences of the actions men take are unimportant so long as a principle is being defended. Among those stories that are more personal, several comment on human faults, the criticism softened by humor. Egotism is the target in **"Locos . . ."** (1897; *PL*) and **"El hombre ideal"** (1898; *PL*), vanity in **"Aguinaldo sentimental"** (1909) and **"La gavota"** (1909), coquetry in **"Un tierno corazón"** (1906). In other instances, the technique is to praise virtues: generosity in **"El anciano caballero"** (1908), and patience in **"Elementos para una bomba"** (1899; *PL*). **"El mendigo ingenuo"** (1899; *PL*) and **"Tres infidelidades"** (1899; *PL*) carry the message that human companionship and affection are more precious than all the possessions of the world. In **"La burra coja"** (1922; *F*), a philosopher advises his disciples to look after their own moral conscience and not to preoccupy themselves with that of others. And in **"El imperio de cristal"** (1909) and **"Historia del niño tuerto y el diamante milagroso"** (1897; *PL*), the advice is to be content with what you have.

The tone of the stories becomes more serious as Lugones moves from general to more specifically Christian themes. In **"Verano"** ([1898]; *PL*), a monk's devotion before a crucifix produces a new Garden of Eden that is once again destroyed by carnal love. The result of the original fall from grace is the subject of **"El carnaval negro"** ([1899]; *PL*), which makes its point through a dantesque vision. Another dantesque vision is the motive of **"La biblioteca infernal"** (1898; *PL*), important for the insights it gives into Lugones' own moral code. As the narrator turns the last page of a book that has given him a vague impression of fear, a vision begins in which he descends into the library of Satan. In the rooms of Pride, he finds books that glorify suffering and tyranny, all the codes of force. The rooms of Avarice contain volumes that produce money and measure out hunger among the peoples. The shelves of Lust, he says, are the ones preferred in Hell, and he describes them in terms of serpents. Then he mentions some of the books contained there, from Petronius and Apuleius to the moderns: "Y luego, toda la exhuberante librería moderna con su tufo carnal, con sus antojos inauditos, con su exaltada brama precursora de locuras y de suicidios" (*PL*, p. 86). The rooms of Anger, Gluttony, and Envy are crossed rapidly, and he descends to the area of Stupidity, where he finds all the newspapers of the world, all the products of rational philosophy, all the books against God. Finally, the entire library seems to come together to form a gigantic Satan, and he slams shut the covers of the book he is perusing.

The tragedy of succumbing to the temptation of avarice provides the theme for one of a group of stories that may be said to treat of the human condition: **"El aderezo de rubíes"** (1903; *PL*), which is a variation on the theme of Guy de Maupassant's "The pearl necklace." While Lugones sympathizes with the protagonist, and manages a masterful exposition of his crisis of conscience, there is a hint of severe punishment for any moral lapse. Normally, Lugones displays a feeling of solidarity with the poor and suffering of the world, as is evident in **"La careta roja"** (1899; *PL*), in which a poor poet without favor suffers so much that his own face appears to be the perfect mask of

Christ. The lesson is reiterated in **"La máscara olvidada"** (1899; *PL*), which illustrates the traditional theme of the Dance of Death. **"Los dos caminos"** (1916; *F*) contrasts two ways of spending one's life: roaming the world or taking the interior road of meditation, the latter being the one that produces a truly distinctive man.

If Lugones seems to provide answers in the form of moral guides in many stories, there are others in which the motive is clearly a search: for happiness, for beauty, for the ideal. These values in the life of man can be as illusive as was love in some of the first stories discussed, or as mystifying as the forces of the Great Beyond. In **"El talismán de la dicha"** (1909; *F*), a fifty-year search exposes the ineffability of happiness. In **"El secreto de la dicha"** (1925), it is the poet who discovers the secret of happiness: he sends a rose to his sweetheart, which gesture leads to a fruitful marriage. **"El pájaro azul"** (1908; *F*) immediately calls to mind Rubén Darío's short story of the same title, and, in fact, they have the same basic theme of the search for the ideal. In Lugones' story a chimerical youth begins chasing a marvelous bird, but his arrow always misses. As he comes out of the forest, he notes he has learned its language. In each phase of the continuing chase, the bird is larger and the boy turns into a man, and he successively learns the language of new areas. Finally, he reaches the highest peak, where the bird's wings touch the horizons and leave the now aged man dazzled. Some days later, when shepherds find the aged blind man, he can only mumble: "Me extravié persiguiendo un pájaro azul que tenía dentro de la cabeza" (*F*, p. 63). As in Darío's story, the blue bird represents the ideal of poetry. But Lugones gives the added dimension of defining the poet as an interpreter of the world around him, utilizing the knowledge he gains as he continues his search.

In **"El amor al arte"** (1903; *PL*), Lugones makes a further comment on the status of the poet and also displays the admiration for ancient Greece that was common among *modernistas*. The pastoral setting and the names of the characters recall Greece, and, in an aside on feminine beauty, he evokes ancient Greece: "Es imposible no hallar algo griego en el camino de la Belleza" (*PL*, p. 164). The story tells of Arsenio, noted for his physical strength, who is spurned by the lovely Laurencia. Arsenio becomes hostile and seeks the solitude of the forest, where, like Pan, he makes a flute and becomes a musician: "La música encantó su fiera interna, y de huraño se volvió melancólico" (*PL*, p. 164). When he plays for the feast of the Virgin, he enchants everyone, including Laurencia, but he no longer needs her earthly love. Arsenio, as a poet, is divine: "Comprendía que su amor, evaporado en música, no pertenecía ya a la tierra; y si agradecía a la joven el haberle inspirado con él el arte, y hasta se reprochaba su frialdad para con ella, no podía remediarlo" (*PL*, p. 165).

Lugones also is preoccupied with the search for beauty. In **"El hallazgo de la belleza"** (1925), the caliph who lives in a spendid palace is told that he must find beauty within himself. In his youth, however, Lugones was concerned with exterior beauty, as is evidenced by three short stories, all published in 1899 and all notable for their symbolist style. **"Misa de primavera"** ([1899]; *PL*), a symphony of color, is the most lyrical of the three. It is a fantasy of a mass celebrated each spring in which all the characters are birds, and they move in an environment beautifully decorated with flowers. In **"La reina de las perlas"** ([1899]; *PL*), a former pearl diver who lost his sight after a particularly long dive can visualize in his blindness entering the palace of the Queen of Pearls and seeing her in her incomparable beauty. Finally, in **"El paraíso de buen tono"** (1899; *PL*), Lugones treats of what might be described as a *modernista* paradise. Ismenia is a young lady given to traveling through fantastic regions in her dreams: "Soñaba, naturalmente, con jardines de abanico, recorría arroyuelos de soneto, veía príncipes rubios, pajes morenos y damas elegantes—pero menos elegantes que ella. Todo cuanto observaba era distinguido: las cosas estaban siempre 'bien' y las personas, sin excepción, tenían 'maneras'" (*PL*, p. 99).

The depiction of such an elegant, sophisticated society—"de buen tono"—that is so frequently taken as the standard of the *modernista* generation, is not characteristic of the short stories of Leopoldo Lugones. His preference is, obviously, for a simpler, pastoral existence. Nature, especially animals, appears with great frequency in his stories, making many of them like fables or apologues. Born and raised in the province of Córdoba, in the village of Río Seco, Lugones knew and had a healthy respect for natural things. In an early story, **"Los buscadores de oro"** (1899), two adventurers, attempting to collect the gold uncovered by the ocean in Tierra del Fuego, narrowly escape death from an angry sea that takes them on "hombre a hombre." Similarly, **"La ley natural"** (1899; *PL*) illustrates that nature can defend itself against the domination of man.

Taking into account the role of nature in Lugones' stories, and the uncomplicated characters that populate the majority of them, it is not at all surprising that he had in process at the time of his death a series of *criollo* stories, the "cuentos serranos."[10] Animals and gauchos are the protagonists of these eight narrations. Two, **"Cual"** (1925) and **"El perro flaco"** (1937), tell of loyal and courageous dogs. **"El burrito servicial"** (1936) is such a good companion and servant to an archaeologist in the Argentine mountains that the scientist has him retired to an alfalfa field. **"El vecino"** (1937) is the story of an amiable fox whose familiarity leads him into the mistake of eating poisoned meat intended for a puma. In **"La tigrera"** (1936), a young girl earns this nickname by playing with a tiger, which is like a great playful cat with her. In **"La mula negra"** (1937), "el rengo Faustino" maintains his dignity and his usefulness even after his legs are paralyzed. And **"La campana"** (1937) is a simple tale of the emotions of an entire village as their old, cracked bell is melted down and forged into a new bell with a beautiful tone.

"Sangre real" (1938), also one of the "cuentos serranos" and Lugones' last published story, has a majestic condor as its protagonist. Because the drought is bringing out the scavengers, the worst of them the condor, the *patrón* and a youth seek out the bird's nest. At first, Lugones carefully delineates the destructive power of the condor, but, as the male returns to protect his young, the attention is turned to the beauty of his flight, and, finally, the bird's bravery and nobility are so impressive that the gauchos decide to let him live. The description of the condor's flight is as sensitive and the prose as harmonious as anything Lugones had written before:

> Magnífico en su envergadura perfilada sobre el cielo horizontal por la misma línea de la meseta, acudía el cóndor al riesgo de su nidada. Avanzó así de frente, sueltas las patas como si fuera a asentarse, oblicuó instantánea guiñada cuando parecía que iba a tocar el peñón, pasó rozando la grieta en vibrante resoplido de huracán. . . . De una aleteada se explayó hasta el fondo del valle, mientras remontaba un poco a la vez; viró en redondo, derecho hacia el farallón. . . . Fue descendiendo luego más y más, casi hasta el pie del mogote. . . . Soslayó de pronto con cerrada espiral, tomando altura de nuevo. Oíamos, al acercársenos, el zumbido de bordón con que su vuelo venía cortando el aire; resaltaba a pleno sol la cándida gola; sonroseábanse breves toques de luz en el sesgo de las alas cenicientas. (*La Nación,* Buenos Aires, 6 febrero 1938).

If the *criollo* subject matter of these last stories Lugones wrote is, in a sense, a return to his oirgins, the stories themselves reflect the same system of values that has predominated throughout his production. Lugones was a humanist concerned more with the moral than the social. In the "cuentos serranos," as in so many of his earlier stories, he is extolling such virtues as loyalty, faith and courage. The characters, animal as well as human, are unpretentious, and display a warmth of human affection that Lugones, evidently, prized highly. In many of his earlier stories, the Argentine setting is of little consequence; the events could have taken place almost any place in the world. The fact that Lugones now finds in typically Argentine characters and situations the same universal values that he has esteemed all along is simply a confirmation of his *modernismo*. The *modernistas,* although frequently accused of neglecting their own countries and continent in their literature, in truth, never did. They were guilty only of not permitting themselves to be bound by a too narrow nationalism: they viewed America in more universal terms, as part of a larger world.

The style of Lugones' short stories tends to be conversational, although it can vary from the erudite to the lyrical. A frequent structure has the narrator talking to someone, a friend or a disciple, and it is common for the narrator to speak from experience as a participant in, or as an observer of, the action. Lugones, sometimes accused of a lack of intimacy in his poetry, in his short stories strives to achieve the effect of nearness to the action. In stories dealing with the unnatural and the unreal, he tries to convince the reader that the events actually happened. This leads him to be one of the first to use the names of real people in his stories, a technique later much imitated. His writing is spontaneous, without evidence of a lot of polishing. In the album of clippings that was reproduced as *Las primeras letras de Leopoldo Lugones,* he sometimes annotated, with corrections, on stories he intended to publish again. The corrections tend to make changes in language, not in content, and, on the whole, are not extensive. Spontaneity suffers at times, however, when he seems to want to overwhelm his reader and lectures at length. The stories of *Cuentos fatales* are the worst offenders in this respect. For the most part, his stories are very short, and he is adept at creating suspense.

Leopoldo Lugones was, indeed, a man of his time, aware of a broad spectrum of trends and events going on in the world. The distinguishing characteristic of the *modernista* generation is their openness to artistic and philosophical currents and to subject matter from all around the globe.[11] *Modernismo* brought much that was fresh to Spanish-American letters by being an eclectic movement that refused to impose limitations on its artists. Lugones, in his short stories, draws from the principal literary tendencies of the late nineteenth century. In some stories, those treating the love theme being the best example, he is essentially romantic. In the one group that idealizes the attraction between unsophisticated adolescents, usually in a pastoral setting, he is clearly returning to the romantic notion of the *bon sauvage.* But he also writes, in a vein much like the "leyendas" of Bécquer, of an impossible love that produces melancholy, sometimes bordering on madness. And in stories that emphasize a decadent erotic sensibility associated with suffering and death, he represents as well that phase of Romanticism that Mario Praz has called the "Romantic Agony."[12] His divinization of the poet is another romantic trait.

Along with the Parnassians, he admires the classic beauty of ancient Greece, and the lyrical intent of some of his stories, especially those written around 1900, reflects Symbolist tendencies. His sentences are composed of harmonious, rhythmic phrases, and human senses figure largely in his descriptions. Odors are important, and they even provide the main thrust of stories like **"El perfume supremo"** (1910) and **"El vaso de alabastro."** Death is regularly associated with coldness. Colors are used symbolically: blue represents the poetic ideal in **"El pájaro azul,"** and fidelity in **"Dos bellas almas"** (1907)); white symbolizes, variously, infidelity in **"Dos bellas almas,"** fatal madness in **"Hipalia,"** and lack of human warmth in **"Amor de nieve."** But it is not in such elements of style that one must seek the *modernismo* of Lugones, for the majority of examples would come from only a few of the short stories. To be sure, Lugones was consistently conscious of style and careful in his composition, but, as was mentioned before, most of his stories are brief and are narrated in a straightforward, conversational manner, with few adornments.

The broad range of Lugones' themes is the best indication of his openness and curiosity. His stories treat of the real and the unreal, and sometimes the line between the two is blurred. But his interest in the exotic and the fantasmagoric is no attempt to escape from a humdrum existence; he lives in a cosmopolitan epoch and a cosmopolitan city. Lugones does not go to the exotic places; they come to him in Buenos Aires, and, on occasion, as in **"El puñal,"** they are shown to relate to his own life. The narration of **"El secreto de Don Juan,"** a story in which Lugones also figures as a character, is introduced with the following dialog:

> — . . . resulta curiosísimo este etro aspecto de la ciudad: el cosmopolita. Buenos Aires es, por decirlo así, una encrucijada del universo. Por aquí, malos o buenos, pasan todos los tipos interesantes del mundo, desde Lloyd George hasta Bolo Paschá.

> —Todos, en efecto, afirmó Lemos.

> —Y si hubieran existido—sonrió Julio D.—el Judío Errante y Don Juan Tenorio.
>
> (*CF*, p. 82).

It is interesting that the names mentioned cover the legendary and fictional as well as the real: knowledge for Lugones was not to be limited to what he could verify empirically.

In his short stories Lugones is constantly searching for some universal truth to which he can cling. The reality of Argentina and other places, the Bible and church history, legends, the physical and biological sciences, the occult sciences, theosophy, everything comes under his scrutiny. Like the boy/man/old man of **"El pájaro azul,"** Lugones learns many things along his route, and, as in the story, there is the hint that the ideal is unobtainable. He seems to suggest, by the attention he gives in his short stories to unpretentious, good people leading a pastoral existence, that happiness and contentment lie in an uncomplicated life where there is no consciousness of the limitations of man or his status in the universe. Such is the life Lugones seems to long for, but his curiosity continues to draw him to the mysterious in spite of the intranquility of the soul with which it leaves him. The desire to return to his origins that is inherent in the "cuentos serranos" of his last years is perhaps one of the clearest manifestations of the longing he had felt throughout his adult life. It is, as Arturo Ghida says, a return "a través del recuerdo . . . al mundo de la Égloga, a su ingenuidad, a su pureza."[13]

It is now clear that *Las fuerzas extrañas* and *Cuentos fatales*, the collections most widely read, convey a distorted conception of Lugones as a short story writer. *Las fuerzas extrañas*, the better of the two, contains some masterful representations of his talent and illustrates that his interests covered science fiction, the occult, Hellenic and religious myths. But even it gives no indication of the more romantic side of his character, or of the continuing search that is so evident when all of the short stories are considered. Borges, writing more about the man than about his works, sees his lively intellect as a distinctive characteristic: "Por la activa pasión de su inteligencia, por la pluralidad de sus inquietudes, por la constante busca de una verdad que tantas veces lo llevó a contradecirse, Lugones constituye en este país un fenó-meno insólito. Su personalidad excede sus libros; la ima-gen de sí mismo que un escritor dejó en los otros es también parte de su obra."[14] Lugones may not have con-sidered his short stories on a par with his poetry, and, for that reason, may have left so many of them dispersed in journals. Perhaps, for the same reason, he labored less over them, with the result that his personality comes through more easily. In any case, the image of himself that Leopoldo Lugones left in his short stories is clear, and it shows us a multi-faceted man at once a part of his generation and an individual.

NOTES

[1] Nicolás Cócaro, in the only article that takes cognizance of Lugones' entire short story production ("Leopoldo Lugones, cuen-tista," *La Nación*, September 27, 1953), makes the following state-ment: "Precisamente por haber sido escritos estos cuentos en aque-lla época ya señalada 1899, 1906-07, Lugones puede ser consid-erado, por lo menos en la Argentina, como un precursor del relato corto, sobre asuntos de carácter extraordinario que tanta difusión han alcanzado y siguen obteniendo entre nosotros." Jorge Luis Borges ("Leopoldo Lugones," *Inter-American Review of Bibliogra-phy*, 12:2, April-June 1963, p. 145) says: "Yo he sido injustamente elogiado por haber traído al cuento fantástico a las letras de lengua española. Pues bien, la verdad es que en 1906 Lugones publica *Las fuerzas extrañas*, en lo que hay por lo menos tres obras maestras del cuento fantástico: 'Yzur', 'Los caballos de Abdera' y 'La lluvia de fuego.'"

[2] *La guerra gaucha* (Buenos Aires, Arnoldo Moen y Hermano, 1905) is a collection of interrelated historical episodes of epic proportions.

[3] I have identified and located 113 short stories, from "Puede ser cuento . . . (prosa)," *La Libertad* (Córdoba, Argentina), January 20, 1894, to "Sangre real," *La Nación*, February 6, 1939. The results of my own search were corroborated and enhanced by Miguel Lermón, compiler of the excellent *Contribución a la bibliografía de Le-opoldo Lugones* (Buenos Aires, Ediciones MARU, 1969), who has in progress an even more fundamental bibliography of uncollected publications and criticism on Lugones.

[4] *Las primeras letras de Leopoldo Lugones; reproducción facsim-ilar de sus primeros trabajos literarios escritos entre sus dieciocho y veinticinco años.* Guia preliminar y notas de Leopoldo Lugones, hijo. Buenos Aires, Ediciones Centurión, 1963. (Colección Los Pre-cursores).

[5] *Caras y Caretas* was published in Buenos Aires from 1898 to 1939. For an almost complete list of the short stories Lugones published here, see Mary G. Berg, "Para la bibliografía de Lugones," *Hispanic Review*, 36, 1968, 353-357.

[6] As the date of first publication is of interest for tracing trends, it will be cited regularly in parentheses after the title of the short story. The name of the journal in which it appeared, however, will not be given. Sometimes a story was published in more than one journal. When it later appeared in one of the collections which are readily available, this will be given in parentheses within the text, using the abbreviations that appear below. Where appropriate, page numbers will be cited and will refer to the following editions:

C—Cuentos. Buenos Aires, Ediciones Mínimas, 1916. (Cuadernos Mensuales de Ciencia y Arte, 8).

CF—*Cuentos fatales*. Estudio preliminar y notas de Leopoldo Lugones, hijo. 2a. ed. Buenos Aires, Editorial Huemul, 1967. (Colec-ción Clásicos Huemul).

F—*Filosofícula*. 2a. ed. Buenos Aires, Ediciones Centurión, 1948.

FE—*Las fuerzas extrañas*. Estudio preliminar y notas de Leopoldo Lugones, hijo. 4a. ed. Buenos Aires, Editorial Huemul, 1966. (Colec-ción Clásicos Huemul).

LS—*Lunario sentimental*. In *Obras poéticas completas*. Prólogo de Pedro Miguel Obligado. Madrid, Aguilar, 1959.

PL—*Las primeras letras*. . . . See note 4 for complete reference.

[7] Carlos Navarro discusses the duality of true love versus ideal love in the stories of *Lunario sentimental* in his article "La visión del mundo en el *Lunario sentimental*," *Revista Iberoamericana*, 30:57, enero-junio 1964, pp. 150-151.

[8] Lycanthropy is a form of mental illness in which the patient imag-ines himself a wolf or another wild animal.

[9] This reference could also be seen as prophetic, for, according to Jorge Luis Borges (*op. cit.,* p. 145), a similar fall from grace led to Lugones' suicide: "Y creo que no es una indiscreción que yo recur-de aquí las circunstancias del suicidio de Lugones, ya que nadie las ignora en Buenos Aires y ya que prescindiré de nombres propios. A Lugones le había tocado vivir la época de la bohemia. Fue amigo y discípulo de Rubén Darío. Sin embargo, se jactaba de no ser bohemio, en aquel tiempo en que era casi obligatorio serlo para ser un poeta y en que no se concebía un poeta que no fuera un 'poète maudit'. Pues bien, Lugones, burguesamente, puritanamente, se había jactado siempre de ser el marido más fiel de Buenos Aires. Dedica *El libro fiel* a su mujer: 'Tibi unicae sponsae'; pero hacia el fin de su vida conoció a una muchacha, que se enamoró de él, así como él se enamoró de ella. Entonces, al tener amores con esa muchacha, sacrificó la norma de toda su vida. Fue Lugones el que hizo el sacrificio. Al cabo de un año esta mujer lo dejó quizás brutalmente, porque Lugones no se resignaría a ello y entonces se encontró ante esta tragedia: para él, él había pecado y había pecado vanamente."

[10] The stories were published in the Sunday literary supplement of *La Nación* (Buenos Aires), being announced on Saturday always as "otro de los Cuentos Serranos." For a perceptive article on them, see Arturo Horacio Ghida, "Los cuentos criollos de Lugones," *Cultura* (La Plata, Argentina), 2:5, 1950, pp. 73-86.

[11] *Modernismo*, as a generation, is defined on this basis by Cedomil Goic ("Generación de Darío; ensayo de comprensión del modernismo como una generación," *Revista del Pacifico*, 4, 1967, pp. 17-35), and Mario Rodríguez Fernández (*El modernismo en Chile*) en Hispan-oamérica, Santiago de Chile, Editorial Universitaria, S. A., 1967).

[12] Mario Praz, *The romantic agony.* New York, Meridian Books, 1956.

[13] *Op. cit.,* p. 86.

[14] Jorge Luis Borges, *Leopoldo Lugones*. Ensayo escrito con la colab-oración de Betina Edelberg. Bibliografía por Edgardo Cozarihsky. 2a. ed. Buenos Aires, Pleamar, pp. 73-74. (Colección Arquetipos).

FURTHER READING

Fraser, Howard M. "Apocalyptic Vision and Modernism's Dismantling of Scientific Discourse: Lugones's 'Yzur.'" *Hispania* 79, No. 1 (March 1996): 8-19.
  Analyzes Lugones's "Yzur" in the context of its prophecy of *fin de siècle* chaos and doom.

Kirkpatrick, Gwen. "Art and Politics in Lugones's Early Journalism." *Discurso Literario* 3, No. 1 (1985): 81-95.
  Discusses art and politics in Lugones's formative writings.

———. "Lugones and Herrera: Destruction and Subversion of Modernismo." *Romance Quarterly* 33, No. 1 (February 1986): 89-98.
  Discusses Lugones's and Julio Herrera y Reissig's contributions to the Modernist movement.

McMahon, Dorothy. "Leopoldo Lugones: A Man in Search of Roots." *Modern Philology* LI, No. 3 (1954): 196-203.
  Offers a detailed biography of Lugones.

Sanders, Janice. "Silence in the Poetry of Leopoldo Lugones." *Hispania* XLVI, No. 4 (December 1963): 760-63.
  In the following essay, critic Janice Sanders Moreno explores the function of silence in Lugones's poetry.

Additional coverage of Lugones's life and career is contained in the following sources published by the Gale Group: *Contemporary Authors*, Vols. 116, 131; *Hispanic Writers*; *Twentieth Century Literature Criticism*.

Joaquim Maria Machado de Assis
1839-1908

Brazilian novelist, short story writer, poet, critic, dramatist, essayist, and journalist.

INTRODUCTION

Machado de Assis is considered one of the greatest and most complete man of letters in Brazil. He is known as one of the most important writers throughout Latin America. He is particularly noted for the novels *Memorias postumas de Brás Cubas* (1881; *Epitaph of a Small Winner*, 1952) and *Dom Casmurro* (1899). His fiction has been called bitterly pessimistic and sardonic. Machado de Assis often used satire to illuminate trivial human vanities and selfishness, particularly among the white Brazilian upper middle class; he rarely addressed his own mulatto culture. Although his works have not found a large audience outside of Latin America, Machado de Assis was considered one of the most original novelists to appear in the Western hemisphere in the nineteenth century.

Machado de Assis was born in Rio de Janeiro, the son of a black Brazilian house painter and Portuguese mother. After the early death of his mother, he was raised by his mulatto stepmother, Maria Inés, who is credited with introducing Machado de Assis to literature. At seventeen he was apprenticed to a printer and became a proofreader and typesetter. In the course of his work he met many important literary figures, some of whom later helped him get his first works published. After his printing apprenticeship, Machado de Assis joined the civil service and spent most of his life as a middle-level bureaucrat. Popular with readers and critics alike—he was already acclaimed in his native country by the time he was twenty-five—Machado de Assis was made president for life of the newly founded Brazilian Academy of Letters in 1897. He continued to write until his death in 1908.

Machado de Assis began his literary career by writing drama and poetry. Most of these works went unpublished or unproduced, but his poetry collection *Occidentais* which appeared in 1901 in *Poesias completas*, was well received. Critics have noted that while these poems are often stylistically mundane, they consistently reflect Machado de Assis's belief that life is essentially meaningless. These beliefs and attitudes are displayed more extensively and with greater artistic success in Machado de Assis's early novels. His first four—*Ressurreição* (1872), *A mão e a luva* (1874; *The Hand and the Glove*, 1970), *Helena* (1876; *Helena*, 1984), and *Iaiá Garcia* (1878; *Yayá Garcia*, 1976)—are products of the Romantic movement in Brazilian literature and are considered inferior to his later fiction. Like other works of this movement, Machado de Assis's novels, which center on thwarted love or ambition, are often criticized for their unrealistic situations and lack of character motivation. In these works Machado de Assis presented detailed portraits of female characters, examining the moral and social implications of the marriage of convenience. In his later works he abandoned female protagonists as well as his concern for the delineation of class and social distinctions.

Epitaph of a Small Winner is the autobiography of a dead writer—"I am a deceased writer not in the sense of one who has written and is now deceased," writes the narrator, Bras Cubas, "but in the sense of one who has died and is now writing." This often humorous novel explores the effects of egotism, focusing on the extremes of self-love, the absurdity of life, and the inevitability of death. Machado de Assis viewed human nature as fundamentally irrational and described self-love as the only consistent motivating force in human behavior. While characterizing this world view as pessimistic, critics comment that Machado de Assis's fiction conveys amusement rather than bitterness toward the folly of selfish, passion-driven humanity. Throughout his novels, particularly in *Epitaph of a Small Winner*, Machado de Assis mockingly challenged the accepted beliefs of society.

Like *Epitaph of a Small Winner*, *Dom Casmurro* is told by an unreliable narrator. This novel, considered Machado de Assis's masterpiece, is full of deception and ambiguity. The narrator's self-destructive conviction that his wife and best friend cuckolded him, and that his son is in fact theirs, was long accepted as a central fact of the novel. But critics have recently questioned whether the narrator's conclusion was perhaps based merely on suspicion, circumstantial evidence, and unfounded jealousy—all prevalent themes in Machado de Assis's novels. Many commentators agree that the narrator seems to be pleading his case before a jury of readers in an attempt to let them decide if his cruelty toward those closest to him may be justified.

Machado de Assis's last two novels, *Esau e Jaco* (1904; *Esau and Jacob*, 1965) and *Memorial de Aires* (1908; *Counselor Ayres' Memorial*, 1972), are considered extended allegorical interpretations of turn-of-the-century Brazilian social conflicts. The warring twins of *Esau and Jacob*, for example, have been interpreted as symbols of the emancipation period in Rio de Janeiro; they represent conflicts between liberal and conservative factions, between traditional and modern values, and between colonial life and the birth of an independent Brazil. In *Counselor Ayres' Memorial*,

Machado de Assis again metaphorically evoked Brazil, but this time expressing hope for his country, provided Brazilians learn to be guided by selfless love—the force that rejuvenates the jaded ambassador Ayres in the novel. Machado de Assis's affirmations of life and love in *Counselor Ayres' Memorial* are regarded as foils for the total pessimism he expressed in his earlier works.

Although not as successful as his novels, Machado de Assis's short stories are also considered masterful depictions of irony and social criticism. His range as a short story writer was much broader, exploring hidden or unconscious motives as well as human egotism and inadequacy. This is especially evident in Machado de Assis's experimental use of styles and forms as well as in the diversity of his subjects and techniques.

Critics have found Machado de Assis's racial heritage problematic in analyzing his works. One scholar, Raymond Sayers, has commented: "One of the strange paradoxes of literature is that the greatest Brazilian novelist . . .was a mulatto who wrote very little about his fellow Negroes and their lives but instead drew most of his material for his novels from the lives of the upper classes of Carioca society, which were predominantly white." The resulting product is Machado de Assis's analysis of society and social mores as prescribed by the dominant culture. His cynical defiance of the selfishness of the upper classes in Brazil has been confused with accusations of denying his mestizo, or mixed, heritage. Most critics agree, however, that Machado de Assis is one of the greatest writers of Latin America. "I am astonished," wrote Susan Sontag, "that a writer of such greatness does not yet occupy the place he deserves."

PRINCIPAL WORKS

Desencantos (drama) 1861
Teatro (dramas) 1863
Crisálidas (poetry) 1864
Quase ministro (drama) 1864
Os deuses de casaca (drama) 1866
Contos fluminenses (short stories) 1870
Falenas (poetry) 1870
Ressurreição (novel) 1872
Historias de meia-noite (short stories) 1873
A mão e a luva [*The Hand and the Glove*] (novel) 1874
Americanas (poetry) 1875
Helena [*Helena*] (novel) 1876
Iaiá Garcia [*Yayá Garcia*] (novel) 1878
Memorias postumas de Brás Cubas [*Epitaph of a Small Winner*] (novel) 1881
Esau e Jaco [*Esau and Jacob*] (novel) 1904
Memorial de Aires [*Counselor Aires' Memorial*] (novel) 1908

CRITICISM

Alfred J. MacAdam (essay date 1977)

SOURCE: "Machado de Assis: Satire & Madness," *Modern Latin American Narratives*, Chicago: University of Chicago Press, 1977, pp. 11-20.

[*In the following essay, MacAdam examines Machado's* Brás Cubas *as a nihilistic character who, placed within a context of satire, becomes "a kind of everyman," encompassing one vital difference wherein he is unable to save himself from his own destruction.*]

A narrative is the deployment of words to represent the passage of time. It is of no consequence whether the temporal flow is circular or linear; all narratives are committed to time, which is of their essence. But there is also built into narrative, into words used as narration, a contrary activity, one that concentrates the reader's attention on a timeless moment. These two notions, derived from the notions of synchrony and diachrony in Saussure's linguistics,[1] constitute the basic structure of all narratives. Furthermore, they may be seen as identical to the distinctions Jakobson makes between metaphor and metonymy in *Fundamentals of Language*: "The development of a discourse may take place along two different semantic lines: one topic may lead to another either through their similarity or through their contiguity. The METAPHORIC way would be the most appropriate term for the first case and the METONYMIC way for the second, since they find their most condensed expression in metaphor and metonymy respectively" (p. 90). While metaphor (or selection) and metonymy (or combination) are the basis of all discourse, one tends to predominate in the various sorts of literary discourse. As we have already seen in Frye, poetry tends toward "epos" or recurrence, while prose tends toward continuance and flow: what we shall see in the works examined in this essay is the conflict between metaphor and metonymy, between closure and extension, between synchrony and diachrony. When we consider Machado de Assis's **Memórias Póstumas de Brás Cubas** (1881) in the light of this opposition, we find the conflict first expressed as a struggle between the flow of life and the metaphorizing tendency of autobiography. This is the problem of unity in any first person narrative, the one Don Quijote presents to Ginés de Pasamonte (*Don Quijote*, bk. 1, chap. 22): how can a picaresque narrative end—that is, have unity—unless the life of the *pícaro* is over. Machado resolves this difficulty by locating his narrator outside of time, in eternity. From the privileged vantage point of death, to which, presumably, the past conceals no secrets, Brás presents the reader with the events that constitute his life. To prove he will have no difficulty finishing his story, Brás begins by describing his death: "Life was shuddering within my breast with the power of an ocean wave, awareness faded, I sank into physical and moral immobility, and my body became vegetable, stone, mud, nothing" (p. 512/20-21).[2] This passage marks a moment in Machado's literature in which he is consciously liberating himself from the resolutions to certain narrative problems presented to him by his immediate literary tradition. First, the narrator makes us see that it will be impossible for us to identify ourselves with him. That is, he demands that we never forget either his fictional identity or his being "on the other side" of time. All writers of autobiographies, as Olney points out, claim some sort of special point of view with regard to their own lives, and it is one of the standard fixtures of the Spanish picaresque that the hero comment on himself, as he was, as if that other self were dead. Here however we find no such ethical posturing; the difference between the narrator's two selves is the relationship each has to time.[3]

The ramifications of this temporal status for determining the text's genre are serious. An omniscient narrator can tell things about which the characters themselves are ignorant; characternarrators, located simultaneously within and beyond the action they describe, can reveal things they themselves do not suspect. But both of these types of narrator exist primarily as shapers of temporal flow. Their purpose is to organize linear narrative into a particular shape. Brás Cubas, to be sure, does exactly this, but he does it in such a way, from such an alien perspective, that we must consider what he says not only as flow but also as icon, not only as metonymic narrative flow but also as metaphor.

When we say that a text is metaphoric, that it has, in Jakobson's sense, drifted away from metonymic scene linking, we are admitting that the text is discourse à propos of something else. It is of the nature of satire and romance to be accumulations of metaphors: the great problem of interpreting metaphoric texts involves locating the referent, the meaning which would "close" the open gap of metaphor. This, clearly, is impossible, and it is the peculiar nature of metaphor, of all signs in fact, to be eternally elusive, always suggesting something which they can never be.

Brás Cubas, from his first words, knows what he is doing, and he explains why he is doing it by confessing a lifelong desire for fame and glory. He hopes to gain immortality, after death, by writing a text, and in doing so renders ironic a traditional apology for writing. The text will be his life story, his autobiography, but a reading of the book reveals that it can in no way be taken for an exemplary life. The saint's life is a model to be emulated: even Saint Augustine offers himself as an example, implying that what happened to him can happen to the reader. The lives of great men are called "inspirational" precisely because they spur the reader on to imitate the hero's life. Brás Cubas falls into neither category, unless we think of him as we would of Lazarillo De Tormes, as a negative saint whose ironic life is a model to be avoided rather than copied. Of course, Lazarillo, unlike Brás, spends his life trying not to be what he is, trying to find his place in the world. Brás's life is as ironic as Lazarillo's, the difference being one of emphasis: Brás is spiritually dead amidst material comfort, while Lazarillo must die spiritually in order to achieve material comfort.

Brás's tale is certainly as pessimistic as Lazarillo's, but the ethical impetus behind Lazarillo's story, its criticisms of institutions and people, is lacking in Brás's memoirs. The institutions with which Lazarillo collides do not have the same weight in Brás's narrative: he envisions society as composed of greedy egoists, but he does not suggest, as Lazarillo's narrative does, that human affairs might be bettered if institutions were reformed. This concept, common in the didactic satires of the eighteenth century, is alien to the text, probably because the naturalists of the same era—and many texts by Machado's Portuguese counterpart, Eça de Queiroz (1845-1900)—were criticisms of society with an eye toward its regeneration.

Society in Brás's book is a projection of man himself; therefore it contains the same bizarre mixture of ideals and perversities as its creator. If Brás is a pessimist, it is not because he is horrified by man as a social animal, but because he sees life as a series of futile exercises leading to an end identical for the good and the bad, the foolish and the wise. Brás is a pessimist, not on an ethical or social level, but on a biological level. To act, to be idle, to move, or to stand still often turn out to be synonyms instead of antonyms. When Brás strives for something, for Virgília the woman he loves, for example, he loses. Later she becomes his mistress without his having to fight at all. That this is a parody of Augustinian grace may be true, but it is certain that whatever man's plans may be, they lead inexorably to the grave. Anti-existentialist from the outset, Brás's discourse mocks even itself: his is a voice from the grave telling us we have nothing to lose.

In the perspective of the ideologically "committed" literature of the same era, from the point of view of naturalism, for example, Machado's text is reactionary. Its radical skepticism, which discredits all notions of progress and history, and all hopes of altering human nature, runs contrary to the spirit of the age, but not, of course, to the spirit of satire. Just as he had done in his first extended narrative, *Ressurreição* (1872),[4] Machado extracts his protagonist from the "struggle for life," releasing him thereby from any involuntary contact with the world around him. It is in this liberation of the protagonist from the world of contingencies that we see Machado's desire to present his subject as an ethical or psychological type rather than as a "real" person living in a real world.

It is in this attitude that we see Machado turning away from a representation of time as history, metonymical realism (in Jakobson's sense), and turning toward the presentation of time as metaphorical scene. The "free form of a Sterne, or of a Xavier de Maistre," that Brás posits as a model in his first paragraph is in reality not free at all, but an abandonment of plot as an imitation or metaphor of history. Machado's work proceeds by accumulation, in the same way Lazarillo's does, and it is in this subjective sorting that we see the author turning toward satire. We may wonder why Brás thinks of Sterne and de Maistre—he is presumably referring to *Tristram Shandy*, *The Sentimental Journey*, and *Voyage autour de ma chambre*[5]—as utilizing a free form, and we may simultaneously ask what texts he would think of as not being "free." It would seem that freedom for Brás is the ability to digress, to abandon plot, while the opposite, keeping to a linear flow and adhering to a plot, constitutes imprisonment. And yet this seems too vague a distinction. *Tristram Shandy* has a plot, its own particular kind, and it would seem that Brás's story also possesses one. The type of plot neither has is one based on history, on a Hegelian concept of history which postulates a goal in the historical process.

Nothing typifies Machado's attitude toward history better than the celebrated chapter 7, "Delirium." Brás begins the chapter with another "first" (he is already the first dead man to become an author): he will describe his own delirium. But this mental disorder is peculiarly iconic in its development. It begins with a series of metamorphoses by the subject himself: he becomes a Chinese barber and a morocco-bound edition of the *Summa Theologica* before returning to his own shape. Both of these seemingly bizarre transformations may be images of the artist—the barber who shaves a capricious mandarin, who punishes and rewards his servant at the same time, and the text which is the writer once he has died or ceased to exercise any control over it. Neither of these interpretations is far-fetched when we think of Kafka's hunger-artist, who starves himself to entertain his public, or Borges's "Borges and I" (1960),[6] where the living author acknowledges that the Borges whose name appears on the spine of books, who is somehow different from the man who lives in Buenos Aires, is "more real" than he is The portrait of the artist is in fact the most consistent motif in the texts under consideration in this study.

The problem of universal history enters the chapter when Brás, in his own shape, is whisked away to the "origin of the centuries" by a hippopotamus. There would seem to be at least three other literary texts in the background of the scene: the *Divine Comedy*, an influence which pervades all of Machado's work; *Gulliver's Travels*, especially the scenes with the Brobdingnagians; and Camões's *Os Lusiadas*, particularly the Adamastor episode. Machado's relationship with Dante is a complex matter, but in **Memórias Póstumas** the *Commedia* may be seen as an ironic analogue to what Machado's text is. Dante, in life, is granted a trip to the tripartite other world, and is then told to publish his vision. Symbolically, he dies and is resurrected so that he may die and again be raised, this last time for eternity. His text is a message of hope for all Christians, but unlike Saint Augustine's, it gives testimony to a miracle, something more spectacular than an individual's receiving grace.

Brás is mad (delirious) when he has his vision (his madness is the result of illness, however, not divine inspiration), and his experience is a kind of affirmation of the nothingness which awaits him and has awaited all those who came before. There is no hope in Nature's (or Pandora's, the female figure who instructs Brás) message to Brás; the only hope she bears is the one nurtured by all men, a hope which is naturally fatuous. Unlike Dante, who also visits the "origin of the centuries" when he enters the Earthly Paradise

in *Purgatory* 28, Brás is presented with a vision of the centuries in the form of an endless parade of identical beings: all the ages of mankind are one in ethical terms and all pursue a Harlequin-like figure:

> a nebulous and fleeting figure, made of bits and pieces, a bit of the intangible, a piece of the improbable, a bit of the invisible, all sewn loosely together with the needle of imagination; and that figure, nothing less than the chimera of happiness, either fled perpetually or let itself be caught by its skirt, and the one who caught it would grasp it to his breast while the figure would laugh in mockery and disappear like an illusion.

> (p. 521/35)

Both happiness and hope are verbal fictions, like Brás's vision, and exist only as figments of the imagination.

Brás's Nature/Pandora, a colossal female figure combining aspects of the Brobdingnagians, of Adamastor, and of Baudelaire's giantess, is a grotesque. She is a kind of eternal feminine, a parody of both Matelda and Beatrice, anthropomorphic but not human, whose sole function is to show man (Brás) an objective picture of the universe. She gives no explanations, makes no promises, instills no hopes: she *is,* and her existence, together with the spectacle of the procession of the ages, all set in an ice-bound wasteland "beyond Eden" instead of a garden, moves Brás to see the insignificance of human life.

In a sense, Brás's delirium vision, an echo of the Erasmian blend of reason and folly, represents a systematic negation of the transcendental significance assigned to space in the *Divine Comedy*. Dante begins his journey on a plane located above, physically and morally, Hell, and below, in the same senses, Purgatory. In the all-important phase of mediation, Purgatory, his physical and moral motion acquires a certain logic: the past is evil; the present is a removal of the past and a lengthening of the distance from that past. The privileged present from which Dante writes what he has experienced is a metaphoric representation of what his present time will be in the future, the absence of time. Brás's space and time are equivocal, false, because they never go beyond esthetic representation. The Dantesque tripartite division is mocked here in the two metamorphoses and the vision-journey. The transformations, as we have seen, are of an esthetic nature: Brás becomes an artist and then a book. The vision reveals to him what he has always known, that the universe has no human dimension; but it reveals it in such an ironic fashion—the hippopotamus used as magical means of conveyance, for example, even more absurd than Astolfo's hippogriff—that attention is diverted from the content of the vision to the spectacle itself.

Nevertheless, we must note that human history in the vision drifts back into undifferentiated time: as far as man is concerned all centuries are the same. No change is possible, and no moral content is anywhere visible in the cosmos. Dante had something to say after his experience; Brás, very literally, has to talk about nothing. Dante had a vision, Brás has a dream, and if there is any transcendental significance in the dream, it emanates from within Brás's psyche, this scene being the only one in which a visionary, albeit a mock visionary, mode is utilized.

That the function of the dream-delirium is to make a grotesque statement about a grotesque reality may be seen by comparing it with another eschatological episode, the death of Brás's mother. Here we find no dream framework, and it would seem that we are to take the event literally: this is how Brás reacts to his mother's death. The difference between action and metaphoric representation seems to be Brás's inability to comprehend the former: "What? Was it absolutely necessary that so docile, so mild, so devout a creature, who had never caused anyone to shed a tear of grief, die in such a way, tortured, mauled by the tenacious jaws of a merciless affliction? I confess that all of it seemed dark, incongruous, insane" (p. 543/70). Brás's reaction is so "natural," his mediation on death as the end of social conventions is itself so conventional, that we are apt to forget the context in which it occurs. In effect, the scene is highly sentimental, recalling similar passages in Sterne and de Maistre, but we must recall what sort of character Brás is in order to see just what function the ruminations on death fulfill.

If Brás were a novelistic character, we might expect some sort of transformation in his personality. Because he is a satiric character, however, the scene has a different value. Brás's life up until that moment had been a series of egoistic, selfish actions: his childhood greed and cruelty, his ambition to "own" a beautiful courtesan (Marcela), his scapegrace student life, and his adventures on the grand tour. Now the mirror is held up to his face: in his mother's death he sees his own. But does this change him? Only to the extent that he is now incapable of dedicating himself body and soul to any vital project since he knows where it will end. It is a moment comparable to Lazarillo's (or any *pícaro's*) "enlightenment," or the moment of *desengaño* in a Baroque text: the veil of ignorance is torn away and reality presents itself as a mirror. Brás is now ready to become a wounded soul, incapable of taking direct action, incapable of acting on his own desires, wishing for fame and glory but unable to seize them. He is now himself, sick with the incurable malady of nihilism combined with an egoistic incapacity to place himself in any social context.

What seems difficult to grasp is why Machado chose to repeat the same message. It is true that the dream is more applicable to history itself, that an event like the death of Brás's mother provides a cause, an explanation for the narrator's later relationships. It is almost as if the two events were the opening and closing of a life composed of reiterations, of a life which could "go" nowhere. What Brás may have understood, what the reader may also have understood, as a "personal tragedy" is revealed in the text to have been nothing more than the common fate of all men. Brás must be thought of as a kind of Everyman, but with this difference: he exists in a world devoid of metaphysical possibilities where salvation in the Christian sense is impossible. This transforms him into an abstraction camouflaged with personality, a name only, totally devoid of reality. And it is this abstract quality which links him with the character-types of traditional satire instead of making him a novelistic "person."

This same generalized status is manifest in all of the characters in Brás's narration. Abstraction and repetition are the hallmark of the *Memórias Póstumas*. We should remember that Brás is an author "for whom the graveyard was a cradle" (p. 511/19), that beginnings and ends in his life are peculiarly affinal. In chapter 51, Brás pronounces his "law of the equivalence of windows" (repeated in chapter 105), which for him is an ethical posture: "the way to compensate for a closed window is to open another so that one's morals can constantly ventilate one's conscience." This ironic passage may also be taken as a structural postulate: Brás cannot change or develop after his mother's death; his life consists of a number of repetitions. The people around him are really permutations of his own personality, all versions of himself.

That birth and death, creation and destruction, and many other traditionally opposed terms are actually opposite faces of the same process is a commonplace of metaphysical speculation. It is a commonplace taken ironically throughout Machado's work. The very title of his earliest long narrative, *Ressurreição* [*Resurrection*] (1872), points to the hero's inability to be truly reborn, and it is this persistence of character which marks all of Machado's protagonists. In the *Memórias Póstumas* the rebirth is, again, esthetic, and there is no possibility of transcending that category. Brás can never be a part of life because he was always dead. His world too is devoid of real life, locked in a permanent state of flux. Only a few social roles possess a rudimentary sort of identity: people are rich or poor, slaves, beggars, or priests. All are narcissistic; all are either victims or oppressors; and, most importantly, because of this, all are mad.

That the characters are all mad is consistent with the generic identity of the text. There may be a statement about Machado's attitude toward Brazil in this reduction of character to type, and the name of the protagonist here certainly invites an identification of him with the country in which he lives. This may further suggest that the text is in fact a true-to-life representation of life in Brazil in the nineteenth century. All of this is possible; however, it seems more useful, especially after considering the *Memórias Póstumas* in the context of Machado's other satires, where character is reduced to stereotype and society is reduced to a cardboard stageset, to think of Machado as a writer who could produce only satires.

The final cause for this sort of literary output as opposed, say, to the writing of novels may be social in that Machado's act of *mimesis* may actually be accurate for a society devoid of those elements necessary for writing novels (a specific sense of history for example). And if it is so, then one would have to say that the same kind of society is still in existence in Latin America and that the same kind of relationship that exists between Machado's texts and his world exists between the other texts examined here and their worlds. Be that as it may, it may be concluded that the novel as a genre has never manifested itself in Latin America, where writers of narrative have turned either to satire or to romance. A confirmation of this theory, a confirmation based, to be sure, on repetition, may be found in another text by Machado de Assis, **Dom Casmurro**.

Ana Maria Camargo Seara (essay date 1991)

SOURCE: "Embedding as a Vehicle for Metafictionality in Machado de Assis's Later Novels." *Romance Languages Annual: 1990*, Vol. II, 1990, pp.362-64.

[*Here, Camrago Seara identifies Machado's use of the narrative technique of embedding, a process that utilizes each character's language and dialogue as the main construct of their lives and the narrative as a whole.*]

Machado de Assis (1839-1908), Brazil's most distinguished prose writer, is acknowledged as a forerunner of contemporary fiction. Recent studies have reopened the discussion about the modernity of his writings in relation to both form and content. Of his many literary techniques, *embedding*, defined by Greimas and Courtés (1979) as the "insertion of a narrative into a larger narrative" plays a major role in the novels of his co-called "second phase"—i.e., his works from 1881 to the year of his death. The micronarratives (usually disguised in miniplots) inserted in all of Machado's later novels foreground the recurrent themes and motifs of the main narratives. A study of these *metadiegetic* narratives (Genette, 1980) provides a basis for an analysis of each novel, and of Machado's work as a whole. These pieces, once put together, constitute a system of ideas about life and art, which includes Machado's acknowledged humor and irony, his satire of human vices, and his thoughts on the status and relationship between the "real" and the "fictional."

Embedding, a technique as old as literature itself, results from a shift of narrating levels, and sometimes of narrative voices. The device produces an effect of "strangeness" in the reader, who becomes aware of the process of construction of the novel and, in this way, becomes more intensely engaged in the process of decoding it.

An embedded narrative has to satisfy the criteria of *insertion*, *subordination*, and *homogeneity*, according to Mieke Bal (1981, 1985). There has to be a transition from the main narrative and the inserted story; these two units have to be ordered hierarchically, and they must belong to the same class of "complete stories." The embedded narrative can fulfill one of three functions according to Rimmon-Kenan (1983): *actional*, if it maintains or advances the action of the first narrative; *explicative*, if it offers an explanation to the first narrative; or *thematic*, if the relations established between the hypodiegetic level (or second-degree narrative) and the diegetic level (or first-degree narrative) are those of analogy, that is, relations of

similarity or *contrast*. Because the explicative and the thematic function narratives are used to confirm and amplify the main text in which they are inserted, they ultimately become a sign of the main narrative.

Among Machado's most famous embedded narratives are "O delírio" (chapter 7 of **Memórias póstumas de Brás Cubas**) and "A Opera" (chapter IX of **Dom Casmurro**).

"O delírio," structured around the notion of ambiguity, can be seen as a matrix for all of the embedded narratives of Machado's novels. It is made up of a series of intertextual references and contains in itself the major ideas underlying Machado's writings of the second phase. Brás Cubas, the protagonist-narrator of **Memórias,** is seriously ill and about to die. He experiences a "delirium," a series of apparently incoherent images that take place in his mind during a few minutes. The delirium, more than a hallucination, is a disclosure of eternal mysteries, of eternal truths (Machado's ambiguous characters show extreme lucidity of mind when they become deraged). Brás Cubas is in bed, being visited by Virgília, his lover of twenty years before. As he wonders about human nature, Brás Cubas sees himself turned into a Chinese barber shaving a Mandarin, a symbol of the authority of the Law, who pays for his services arbitrarily with pinches and sweets. The situation at the barber shop parallels Brás Cubas's life and his successes and failures that come as a result of his actions but which have no connection with them—they seem to him as absurd as his dream. After that, Brás is turned into St. Thomas's *Summa Theologica* (1265-74), a major theological treaty, and here a symbol of the Church. While many commentators have stressed Machado's lack of concern for the spiritual, this passage contradicts these opinions. It reveals a true understanding of Christian doctrines freed from the apparatus of institutionalized religion (cf. the ironic description of his uncle Ildefonso, p.528). The next sequence of the delirium is the most fantastic: the narrator, back in human form, is taken by a hippopotamus (a symbol of ambiguity due to its dual nature: it lives both on the earth and in the water; cf. Cirlot, 1971) on a trip through the centuries to the beginning and the end of Time. The scene has eschatological echoes of the prophet John's experiences on the island of Patmos as described in the first four chapters of Revelations, and of the poet's descent into Hell in Dante's *Divine Comedy.* The climax of the trip takes place when Brás Cubas has an encounter with Pandora, the figure from Greek mythology equated with Life's principle, the ambiguous sign par excellence ("sou tua mãe e tua inimiga," 421). Machado's philosophical attitude becomes clear in the exchange between Brás Cubas and Pandora. This attitude is marked at first by astonishment and incomprehension. Later, it is transformed to include a profound pessimism and nihilism on the part of Brás Cubas, and cold cynicism and total egoism on the part of Pandora. To Brás Cubas, Pandora signifies the absurdity of life. What this embedded narrative, thematically related by similarity to the main narrative, reveals is that there is no reason for hope in life— a profound sense of nothingness comes to dominate all human existence. Life proceeds in a circular manner, fusing and confusing beginning with end, constantly transforming meaning into nothingness:

> E fixei os olhos, e continuei a ver as idades, que vinham chegando e passando, já então tranqüilo e resoluto, não sei até se alegre. Talvez alegre. Cada século trazia a sua porção de sombra e de luz, de apatia e de combate, de verdade e de erro, e o seu cortejo de sistemas, de idéias novas, de novas ilusões; em cada um deles rebentavam as verduras de uma primavera, e amareleciam depois, para remoçar mais tarde.

> (523-4)

Machado de Assis's skepticism is conveyed through his humor—from the image of the Mandarin who pays for the barber's work with pinches or sweets to the ambiguous image of Pandora as mother and enemy. Human beings are torn between forces they cannot control: the result is pain and destruction. The only escape is Death, which is the absence of suffering, the "voluptuosidade do nada" (522) in Pandora's words. Freed from physical limitations and looking at life in retrospect, Brás Cubas understands that his efforts for achieving Love (or whatever substitutes for it that he searched for) were in vain. His only consolation comes when he can boast that at least he did not have children, that he managed not to transmit to any creature the legacy of human misery.

Another version of the existential undertones in Machado de Assis's work can be seen in the embedded narrative called "A ópera" in ***Dom Casmurro***. In this book, considered his most mature and elaborate work, the embedded narrative at the beginning of the main narrative foregrounds and parallels important motifs. Although the device spoils the suspense a little, it gives the reader guidelines to follow in the interpretation of the main text. After explaining his purpose in writing the book (***Dom Casmurro*** is also a book of memoirs) and presenting some of the characters, the narrator relates a tale he had heard some years before from an old Italian tenor, who believed that "life was an opera." Dom Casmurro begins his narrative by summarizing the tenor's words: "Deus é o poeta. A música é de Satanás, jovem maestro de muito futuro, que aprendeu no conservatório do céu" (817). One day, after being expelled from the conservatory of heaven, Satan appeared before God with a score that he had composed to a libretto for an opera that God himself had written. Satan's idea was that the Lord would hear it and correct it and be so pleased as to admit him with his opera back into heaven. The Lord said no, and it was only after Satan pleaded that He consented to have the opera performed, outside of heaven. God created a special theater for it—Earth—and a whole company for the performance. He also refused to hear the rehearsals. While the conductor's friends thought the composition was a masterpiece, the poet's friends claimed that the libretto was corrupted, and that the performance was in reality the opposite of the original drama. The narrator claims, through the tenor's words, that life is a spectacle controlled by forces superior to humankind; human beings' only option is to accept and perform the roles they are assigned at birth.

Life is a stage, and the cliché works well for Dom Casmurro, who later states:

> Eu, leitor amigo, aceito a teoria do meu velho Marcolini, não só pela verossimilhança, que é muita vez toda a verdade, mas porque a minha vida se casa bem à definição. Cantei um duo terníssimo, depois um trio, depois um quatuor . . .

> (819)

The duo refers to Dom Casmurro's relationship with Capitu, the trio to the birth of their child, and the quatuor to the inclusion of Escobar in their relationship, to the disgrace of the other three.

This embedded narrative and the one found in Chapter CXXXV "Otelo" (an allusion to Shakespeare's play) emphasize the narrator's lack of doubt that he was betrayed by his wife and his best friend. In Shakeapeare's play, Desdemona is not guilty and the plot centers around a misunderstanding. Bento, while watching the play and drawing a comparison to his own situation, cannot accept this possibility regarding Capitu ("e se ela deveras fosse culpada, tão culpada como Capitu?" (935). One of Machado's favorite themes—the ephemeral boundary between reality and fiction—emerges here. By comparing life to an opera and having Dom Casmurro watch *Othello* on stage, the author questions a strict division between the world of fiction and the "real" world. Is the narrator's personal "drama" real or fictitious? Does he control his own destiny or is he simply performing a role assigned to him? As for art, is it detached from reality or is it just another way of looking at reality? These questions seem to loom in both the narrator's and the reader's mind.

The narrator ends the book in a resentful tone saying with certitude that "minha primeira amiga e o meu maior amigo, tão extremosos ambos e tão queridos também, quis o destino que acabassem juntando-se e enganando-me . . ." (944). The turning point of Dom Casmurro is left to the readers once they have gathered enough clues about the unreliability of the narrator. Little by little, mostly through embedded narratives, the reader comes to realize Bento's ability to twist things around to make them conform to his own views. As the narrator says of himself:

> A imaginação foi a companheira de toda a minha existência, viva, rápida, inquieta, alguma vez tímida e amiga de empacar, as mais delas capaz de engolir campanhas e campanhas, correndo. Creio haver lido em Tácito que as éguas iberas concebiam pelo vento; se não foi nele, foi noutro autor antigo, que entendeu guardar essa crendice nos seus livros. Neste particular, a minha imaginação era uma grande égua ibera; a menor brisa lhe dava um potro, que saía logo cavalo de Alexandre.

> (852)

Chapter LVIII "O tratado" is an embedded narrative that portrays the power of Bento's wild imagination. One Monday, going back to the seminary with José Dias, Bento sees a woman fall down on the street, giving him a glimpse of her hose and silk garters. Although he tries to rid himself of the image, it becomes fixed in his mind:

> Dali em diante, até o seminário, não vi mulher na rua, a quem não desejasse uma queda; a algumas adivinhei que traziam as meias esticadas e as ligas justas . . . Tal haveria que nem levasse meias . . . Mas eu as vias com elas . . . Ou então . . . Também é possível . . .
>
> (869)

At the seminary the priests' cassocks remind him of the lady's skirt. At night he dreams of her legs and after a while cannot sleep anymore. He tries praying but that does not work either. In the morning, as he cannot get rid of the image, he decides to make a treaty between his conscience and his imagination: "As visões feminis seriam de ora avante consideradas como simples encarnações de vícios, e por isso mesmo contempláveis, como o melhor modo de temperar o caráter e aguerri-lo para os combates ásperos da vida" (870). From the embedded narrative, the reader learns that since youth Dom Casmurro has been an insecure and imaginative person who cannot control his emotions. His insecurity and wild imagination provoked severe pangs of jealousy.

The function of both the tale of the opera and the incident of the lady on the street is explicative. Both offer an explanation to the events of the main story—i.e., the unsuccessful relationship between Bento Santiago and Capitu. The "desconcerto do mundo" illustrated in "A ópera" accounts for much of the unhappiness in Bento's life, for that sense of the unresolved that persists even after he has written a book. "O tratado" exemplifies the power of Bento's imagination.

The embedded narratives in Machado's novels obey the criteria of insertion, subordination and homogeneity. Insertion is achieved through smooth transitions from the diegetic level to the hypodiegetic one. The embedded narratives are subordinate to the texts in which they are inserted—i.e., the narrative objects of the main narratives (the delirium, the Italian tenor's tale, etc.) become the subjects of the embedded levels. The concept of homogeneity reveals that the criteria used to specify that the "primary" text is a complete narrative applies to the embedded text as well.

The *thematic* and *explicative* functions appear most frequently in Machado's fiction, possibly because they emphasize the text as fictional object by laying bare its narrative devices. The texts become self-reflexive, providing a deeper engagement on the part of the reader in the process of decoding the work, thus, in a sense, constructing the work. The embodded narratives, which are such an integral aspect of Machado's later novels, call the reader's attention to a number of motifs that permeate Machado's work as a whole: the view of life as a cycle, the ambiguity inherent in human behavior, the relativity of truth and reality, the human beings' frustrated quest for unity and perfection, and death as the only absolute.

The embedded narrative in Machado's works does more than reflect the themes of the main text. It reflects the process of construction of the text as a literary work, while exposing the highly creative power of fiction and language. it also foregrounds the notion of the reader as an accomplice in the creative process of text construction. The embedded narrative provides the locus for discussions about the creation of reality and fiction through language. It offers multiple possibilities of interpretation within the same story. In **Dom Casmurro**, for example, a reinterpretation of the total narrative is only possible after Bento's true character is revealed through several embedded narratives. Along with metanarrative discourse—Machado's famous "digressions"—the embedded narratives constitute the main vehicle for commentary and reflection on the main texts in which they appear. Through these devices Machado achieves a perfect balance between plot and technique, a balance that challenges the critic and pleases the reader.

WORKS CITED

Bal, Mieke. "Notes on Narrative Embedding." *Poetics Today* 2, 2 (1981): 41-60.

————. *Narratology. Introduction to the Theory of Narrative.* Toronto: U of Toronto P, 1985.

Cirlot, J. E. *A Dictionary of Symbols.* New York: Philosophical Library Inc., 1971.

Genette, Gérard. *Narrative Discourse. An Essay in Method.* Ithaca: Cornell UP, 1980.

Greimas, A. J. and J. Courtés. *Semiotics and Narrative. An Analytical Dictionary.* Bloomington: Indiana UP, 1979.

Machado de Assis, Joaquim Maria. *Obra Completa.* 6th ed. 3 vols. Rio de Janeiro: Nova Aguilar, 1986.

Rimmon-Kenan, Shlomith. *Narrative Fiction. Contemporary Poetics.* London: Methuen, 1983

José Suarez and René P. Garay (essay date 1992)

SOURCE: "Characterization in Machado de Assis's *A Mão e a Luva,*" *Journal of Evolutionary Psychology,* Vol. XIII, Nos. 3 & 4, August, 1992, pp. 322-27.

[*Here, Suarez and Garay study the two lovers in Machado's* A Mão e a Luva *in their approach to love, life, and each other, revealing Machado's use of characters to engage the reader intimately with the narrative.*]

The setting for **A Mão e a Luva** (**The Hand and the Glove**), [an] 1874 novel by Machado de Assis, is Rio de Janeiro's court during the middle of the nineteenth century. During that period, it is not uncommon to find a romantic plot where love—in this case, that of three men for the principal character, Guiomar—creates a situation of extremes. On the one hand, we have Estevão's "mad and blind" passion, a good example of poetic love à la Byron; on the other, the "puerile and lascivious love" of the Baroness' nephew, Jorge. Luis Alves's feelings lie somewhere in the middle, a fact that denotes an "ambitious heart." We shall soon see how he changes.

The plot's composition is an attempt to underscore the difference between "true love" and the "selfish attachment" that arises from materialistic or carnal desires—being a romantic piece, the carnal is not here a consideration. Both types of attraction manifest themselves in the person of Guiomar who understands that her aspirations to ascend the social ladder are in conflict with her godmother's (the Baroness) desire that she wed Jorge. Consequently, her decision to please the Baronness, to whom she owes much, and her aspirations are continuously at odds throughout the work. Thanks only to Luis Alves's love does she resolve the dilemma satisfactorily at the end.

At the outset, Estevão's role may appear superfluous because it only demonstrates the excesses of romanticism. Nevertheless, though it may be of small significance per se, the character does contribute to the development of Luis Alves's; not only does Estevão become his *"professor do amor"* (teacher of love), but he also justifies the pupil's gradual emotional shift toward Guiomar. The significant number of lines given to his character in the novel denotes this aim.

The plot's organization, in relation to time and space, is monolinear with chapters whose length are appropriately equal. Other than the account of Guiomar's childhood—justified because of its importance in her development as protagonist—there is no chronological deviation. Time passes sequentially with a two-year lapse between Guimoar's first and second encounter with Estevão. The inclusion of the first encounter breaks up the narrative and creates a sort of prologue to the plot. From the beginning, we realize that Estevão is to be a character of relative importance in the novel's ironic denouement. From a contextual viewpoint, his role is justified because it enhances that strong emotion that Luis Alves and Guiomar disregard as absurd, but to which they ultimately succumb. There is also, in the structural design, a repetition of occurrences with some variations (or modulations). We are referring, for example, to the scene in the *chácara* (country estate) where Guiomar's encounter with Estevão takes place, a scene that is later repeated between her and her fiancé, Luis Alves:

> Coincidence willed that that morning she wear the same bathrobe in which Estevao had seen her on the other side of the fence, and she wore at her neck and at her wrists the same pin and the same sapphire buttons. She didn't have the book, but to make up for the missing item, there was another which was the same as on that celebrated morning: there were some eyes that peeked at her lovingly from the other side of the fence. They weren't, however, the same pair; they were her fiancé's eyes which met hers—and the most painful thing is that

not even the fence, nor the other accompaniments—nothing—reminded her of the other man, who was about to die because of her.[1]

The account of Guiomar's childhood breaks up the narrative's temporal and spatial sequence by taking the reader back in time. The justification is that, in the evolution of the story, it is necessary to include appropriate background; it is also related to what years later takes place in the *chácara*:

> As a child, her eyes had followed the silks and jewels of the women she saw on the grounds opposite her mother's modest yard; as a young lady, her eyes followed the brilliant spectacle of social grandeur. She wanted a man who, in addition to having a youthful heart that was capable of loving, felt within himself the necessary strength to place her upon a pedestal where she could be seen by all.[2]

Generally speaking, we may say that the beginning of the story "in medias res" and the inversion of historical time in Chapter V are techniques that highlight the work's content. We begin to see in Chapter I the importance of Estevão on the development of Luis Alves's character. In Chapter V, the detailing of Guiomar's childhood describes her own characterization.

All but the Baronness reason selfishly. Her kindness stands in sharp contrast to the selfishness exhibited by the other characters. For the sake of harmony, her own desires are often subordinated to theirs. She thereby assumes an attitude that is radically different from that of those whose self-interests drag them into intrigues—only at the end, for example, do Luis Alves and Guiomar react without a clear perception of their motive (love). The narrator suggests that they were unaware of this emotion, but the discerning reader knows that, though this may be true, they were in love with one another all along. As Maria Luisa Nunes indicates in the *Craft of an Absolute Winner*:

> If Machado de Assis's narrators give us any advice, is to read attentively. If we are to divine the meaning of Machado de Assis's lapses, subtleties, and teasing, we must understand what he demands of us as readers. He expects us to participate actively in the literary process and not to simply absorb a straightforward story.[3]

Estevão's love is more whimsical than sincere (let us note his obsession, not with the singer, but with the "fuzzy upper lip" at the beginning of the story!). He amuses himself with what the narrator calls the "voluptuousness of pain," i.e., he derives pleasure from Guiomar's rejection. She, on the other hand, sees him as a boy: " . . . your great defect is to have retained something of a childish spirit."[4] But whereas Guiomar "covets" the good life, Estevão "aspires" to such a life. There is a difference here. Estevão, unlike Guiomar, embodies the romantic stereotype. He is gripped by a tragic fatalism that thwarts initiative and leads to sorrow. She, on the other hand, is able and determined to realize her dreams.

Joaquim Maria Machado de Assis

Besides his role and importance as a secondary figure in Luis Alves's character development, Estevão has little or nothing to do with the plot's progression; his character does not noticeably evolve. It is at the end that we understand the primary function of his role: "Whether he is still vegetating in some corner of the capital, or whether he wound up in some village of the interior, is not known."[5] He is included as a pretext to justify Luis Alves's emotional change, a sort of "sacrificial lamb" to expedite the action. Also, as mentioned, Estevão contributes considerably to Luis Alves's "education":

> You trusted me with the pains and hopes of your heart; in doing so, you experienced my friendship and the profound esteem I have always felt for you. But neither you nor I were expecting me to enter the picture; I also have a heart the distinctions of beauty also speak to my soul.[6]

The final irony is dependent on this emotional development. Luis Alves, a "calculatingly ambitious" person, ultimately has a more than "logical" relation with Guiomar: ". . . I am depending on you also; you will be a new source of strength to me."[7] Let us remember Luis Alves's statement to Estevão in the first chapter, "During your last hours on earth, you will teach me a lesson on love, and I shall repay you with one on philosophy."[8] Compare it with the following lines:

The tumult was natural in both of them; there they remained for several moments, quiet, he with his eyes fixed on her, she with hers on the floor. Their hands touched and their hearts beat in unison.[9]

Such a narration conceals their love behind a veil of ambition and willfulness (". . . the protagonists' fulfillment of love based on conscientiously directed will rather than spontaneity would seem to introduce a degree of irony into [Machado de Assis's] character drawing").[10]

Guiomar shares Luis Alves's characteristics: arrogance, ambition, willfulness. She is the best accomplished character in the work.[11] The narrator reveals her thought process much better than that of the other characters. We know, for example, that it was circumstances that led to her selfishness and ambition. Her constant daydreaming as a child appears to have been a manifestation of her frustrated desires. Nevertheless, she manages to conceal her designs to such an extent that hypocrisy becomes the most useful means of fulfilling her desires. Images associated with Guiomar are derived from the classical Greek world—not only her "marmoreal" beauty, but also references to classical entities (Diana, Alcibiades, Helen, Venus). All this intensifies the contrast between "cold natured Guiomar" and "Guiomar in love." It underscores the final irony.

The meddlesome Mrs. Oswald, a secondary character like Jorge, is apparently included to complicate the plot. Behaving like a panderer, the British housemaid takes delight in manipulating the lives of others. She even says that "all's well that ends well," a phrase that links the novel's denouement to Shakespeare's play. Such a view defines Mrs. Oswald as a selfish and venal character. For example, financial reward is the source of her desire to wed Guiomar to Jorge—there is no love lost between the maid and the protagonist. Is it not Guiomar, after all, who ends the privileged position she enjoys with the Baroness? Jorge also belongs to the group of self-serving characters: "to possess was his only profession."[12] At the novel's conclusion, he neither feels dejected, nor she defeated: "Mrs. Oswald also appeared to be happy, perhaps even more so because she had an air of magniloquence, as if wanting to make up for the past mistakes."[13]

Our view of Mrs. Oswald stands counter to that of Mary Huseby Schil who maintains that:

> The pleasure of Mrs. Oswald in the house provided another "mother figure" for Guiomar's development. To make her happy, these two "mothers" deferred to Guiomar the choice of a fiancé, thereby demonstrating a healthy and loving attitude.[14]

As implied, Guiomar perceives Mrs. Oswald as a self-serving intruder who, besides overstepping her social bounds, could not care less about her welfare. A remark made by Guiomar to the Englishwoman partly corroborates this observation: "These are family matters which are none of your business."[15]

The narrator of *A Mão e a Luva* is omniscient. He interprets the characters' action instead of solely presenting them in sequence. Perhaps for this reason, at times, the characters appear sterile, i.e., they become stereotypical figures instead of people exhibiting psychological depth. The lack of dialogue prevents us from knowing what they think about particular situations. *A Mão e a Luva* often gives the impression that it was composed as a play for a puppet show.

This narrator or, better yet, this "storyteller" conveys an ironic attitude denoting the author's approach to his characterization as that of a caricaturist. Estavão is the typical romantic of the period (e.g., he liked Verdi's *Ernani* and Bellini's operas). Description is so exaggerated that it reaches comical levels. That the characters often enter a scene conversing is a mere pretext for the narrator to make comments. His omniscient interpretations lead to an ironic and satiric denouement. We are not only referring to the caricaturing of characters, but also to the presence of what M.H. Abrams calls "romantic irony":

> *Romantic irony* is a term invented by German writers of the late eighteenth and early nineteenth centuries to designate a mode of dramatic or narrative writing in which the author builds up artistic illusion, only to break it down by revealing that he is, as artist, the arbitrary creator and manipulator of his characters and their actions. The concept owes much to Lawrence Sterne's use of a self-conscious and willful narrator in his *Tristam Shandy*. Byron's great narrative poem *Don Juan* constantly employs this devide for ironic effect, letting the reader into the author's confidence, and revealing him as an inventor who is often at a loss for matter to sustain his plot and undecided about how to continue it.[16]

The narrator insists on establishing a direct relation with the reader. Having accomplished this, he, as creator of the story, attempts to impose observations like the following: "I, who am the Plutarch of this illustrious lady, will not fail to point out that in her endeavor there was something of Alcibiades. . . ."[17] The epithet may be interpreted as a barb because we know that Guiomar is not "illustrious."

The attempt to separate the character from the reader accentuates the narrative's ironic structure. It removes the reader from the fictional world and allows the narrator to differentiate between illusion and the awareness that the story is mere fiction. Consequently, any of the narrator's observations may result ironic because we do not always agree with him. The possible discrepancy between his message and what we perceive makes this sentence ironic: "Will and ambition, when they truly dominate, can struggle with other feelings, but they are sure to win, because they are the weapons of the strong, and victory belongs to the strong."[18] It may be considered ironic because earlier, as quoted, Luis Alves confesses to Estevão that he, also having a heart, was overwhelmed by passion.

The above confirms that Luis Alves learned Estevão's lesson well. Machado des Assis attempts to adjust or harmonize his perspective in the novel with the romantic view of some readers: although the "strong" usually win out in the material world, only love can stimulate sincere relations among people.

Thus we are able to observe that, in *A Mão e a Luva*, Machado de Assis begins to demonstrate his capacity for observing individuals in society by developing characters of some psychological complexity who, nevertheless, still exhibit many traits associated with caricatures. In the words of Eliane Zagury:

> Everything revolves around a characterization that subordinates all scenes and descriptive passages to a functional role. It is the action and, primarily, the narrator's commentary that develop the characters. On the other hand, although each character is a separate entity, Machado does not miss the opportunity of abstracting and generalizing, showing their characteristics as "symptoms" of human beings in general, with their weaknesses and deceits.[19]

NOTES

[1] Machado de Assis. *A Mào e a Luva,* 7th Ed. (Sao Paulo: Atica, 1981), 95. Translation by Albert I. Bagby, Jr. *The Hand and the Glove* (Lexington: Kentucky UP, 1970), 114. Henceforth, all translations of the novel will be from this text. Unless indicated, all other translations are by the authors of this article.

[2] Bagby, *The Hand and the Glove,* 82.

[3] (Westport: Greenwood Press, 1983), 11.

[4] Bagby, *The Hand and the Glove,* 49.

[5] *Ibid.,* 116.

[6] *Ibid.,* 89.

[7] *Ibid.,* 116.

[8] *Ibid.,* 6.

[9] *Ibid.,* 90.

[10] Nunes, *The Craft of the Absolute Winner,* 34.

[11] See Penny Newman; "`O lustre do meu nome'; uma leitura de *A Mào e a Luva*," *Luso-Brazilian Review* XX 2 (1983), 232-40.

[12] Bagby; *The Hand and the Glove,* 84.

[13] *Ibid.,* 115.

[14] "Pais e filhos nos romances de Machado de Assis," *Luso-Brazilian Review* XXV 2 (1988), 75-88.

[15] Bagby; *The Hand and the Glove,* 61.

[16] M.H. Abrams; *A Glossary of Literary Terms* (New York: Holt, Rinehart and Winston, Inc., 1971), 83.

[17] Bagby, *The Hand and the Glove*, 83.

[18] *Ibid.*, 102.

[19] See "Amor e Casamento no Folhetim Machadiano," Prologue to *A Mào e a Luva*, 6.

Maria Manuel Lisboa (essay date 1997)

SOURCE: "Machado de Assis and the Beloved Reader: Squatters in the Text." *Scarlet Letters: Fictions of Adultery from Antiquity to the 1990s*, London: Macmillan Press Ltd., 1997, pp. 160-73.

[*In the following essay, Manuel Lisboa illuminates the relationships among characters in the text of* Dom Casmurro, *assessing the strength of the bonds of their relationships.*]

> I was his wife
> But henceforth
> My name from his
> Be freed.
>
> —*Aeschylus*

One of Machado de Assis' critics, John Gledson, has commented that

> Machado presents his readers [. . .] with the choice between two books, the one immensely readable, interesting, amusing, the other much more unsettling, giving uncomfortable insights into Brazilian upper class society, [. . .] its repressiveness and callousness. With immense tact and daring, with a mixture of aggression and politeness which is the hallmark of his style, Machado kept his readers, and was, in his own lifetime, a writer of considerable prestige. The only price he had to pay (and no doubt he was content to do so) was that part of his message went unperceived until long after his death.[1]

I should like to suggest that Machado was more than willing to be misunderstood and possibly delighted to be so, in his capacity as a writer who, in his own words, offered to his resisting and unresisting readers alike 'one utterance but two meanings',[2] a cryptic, Machereyan, gap-ridden posture which nevertheless did not prevent him from occasional unambiguous self-positioning as an author driven, in his own words, by the 'monomania [. . .] for taking art not for art's sake, but rather as [. . .] a social, national and human mission'.[3] It is this delight in the encoded but, paradoxically, intermittently signposted impetus to have a political and ideological impact which will be drawn upon here as informing the present consideration of his most famous novel, *Dom Casmurro*.[4]

Briefly, the plot, a first-person narration retrospectively recounted in old age by Bento Santiago, or Bentinho, concerns his adolescent idyll with the young woman next door, Capitu. The larger part of the novel deals with the adolescent pre-marital period, in the course of which Bentinho, with Capitu's help, must contrive to release himself from his pre-ordained enrolment into the seminary and the priesthood, a destiny originating in a promise made by his mother, Dona Glória. Following the miscarriage of her first child years before Bentinho's birth, Dona Glória vowed to offer up her next son, if vouchsafed one, to the priesthood, and in due course conceives Bentinho. The latter's father dies just before the birth, and Bentinho grows up as an only child.

The priesthood vow is eventually circumvented, largely thanks to Capitu's initiative in finding a solution to the problem, and also through her deliberate arousal of Bentinho's prospective jealousy, by means of her vivid description of the likelihood that if Bentinho does not marry her, someone else will, and beget a child upon her. This episode is possibly crucial since, at this early stage in their lives, Capitu plants in Bentinho's adolescent mind the image of herself as the mother of another man's son. This image will subsequently return to haunt them both. In the event, Bentinho and Capitu marry, and after two childless years, a boy, Ezequiel, is born. For a variety of reasons Bentinho comes to suspect the child of being not his but his best friend's, conceived adulterously and, after the accidental death of this friend Escobar he charges Capitu with adultery and banishes her to Europe where in due course she dies. Dona Glória and Ezequiel also die in quick succession, and Bentinho is left in old age to write his memoirs of these events, which constitute the narrative we read, and in which Capitu emerges as a deceitful temptress, seen, through the optic of the retrospective male character's first-person narration and with the advantage of hindsight and monopoly of speech, to have been corrupt from an early age. Capitu herself is deprived by the nature of the first-person narration of the opportunity to present her case and to defend herself. The adultery itself, moreover, is never unambiguously ascertained, merely stated to be a fact by Bento's narrative, whose primary structuring device is the reorganisation of pre- and post-marital events to the purpose of reinforcing his case. The consequences for Capitu of her continuing silence will be marital separation, exile and death. Less clearly, but no less importantly, however, as I shall argue in the remainder of this paper, the alleged adultery and the ambiguity accruing to the actual likelihood of its occurrence nonetheless become, through a series of coded narrative sleights of hand, the pretext in the course of the novel for the enlisting of, among other unlikely bedfellows, mothers-in-law and daughters-in-law in a larger counterplot, whose objective and effect, as will be argued, is the hijacking of a series of linguistic puns and literary metaphors whereby the previously excluded female voice and presence are forcibly imposed upon the canons of a variety of master discourses, and, in particular, that of the first-person narrator.

The speaking male subject—in this instance the husband self-presented as deceived to a reader whom he seeks to convince of his marital misfortune—resorts for the shoring up of his crumbling subjectivity to a series of literary metaphors and self-affiliations, frequently invoking ancient and modern classics of various denominations for the purpose of self-accreditation in the eyes of the reader. Thus Bentinho, for example, has recourse to, insistently misreads and *is shown* to misread Plato, Socrates, Shakespeare and the Bible, which he uses as backing traditions, only to find, curiously, that the canonical text will in the end insist upon having the last stubborn word, and a last word, moreover, which, by undermining the male in favour of the female voice, would appear sometimes to contravene its own expected orthodoxy. For example, when already to all appearances convinced of Capitu's guilt, Bentinho goes to the theatre to see a production of *Othello*. At the end, remarking upon the audience's furore at the moment of Desdemona's death he remarks: 'how would the public react if she were truly guilty, as guilty as Capitu?' (*DC*, 933). What is omitted from the parallel Bentinho draws between his own and Othello's plight is of course the admission of another obvious possible similarity between Desdemona and Capitu, namely that of their analogous innocence. The omission on the part of a narrator who early on in the exposition of his *are poetica* exhalted the advantages of the gap-ridden text ['livro omisso,' *DC*, 868] and the advantages for the reader of filling in the gaps for the purpose of a full understanding of the whole, allow here for a moment of self-undoing which requires no intervention on the part of either Machado as author or his female characters as objects, but speaks for both. By a curious paradox, furthermore, while the classical plots of Aeschylus, Sophocles and Euripides, and of Shakespearean and Biblical scenarios, reject the obeisances of the male in this narrative and preserve their integrity in the face of his subservience to them, ultimately, in fact, undoing his credibility as speaker, in the hands of the plot-controlled female protagonist they appear willingly to lend themselves to a variety of reversals and distortions of their original plots; and in doing so, they self-defeatingly allow the heroines - Capitu and as will be seen Dona Glória also - to arrive, notably almost entirely without the advantage of direct or indirect speech, at effects which aid and abet a female re-writing of the established canonical fates of a variety of Medeas and Clytemnestras, in the original texts defeated and condemned, but here possibly and surprisingly morally victorious at th e end.

Thus, what the obedience of the male voice to the orthodoxy of the classical text is unable to achieve, namely the purchasing of support for its own version of reality and for the *status quo* which it serves, the contrasting silence of the female character *does* achieve. The deconstructive difficulty at the heart of the male character's first-person narration in the end unwittingly leads to a revision of previously sacred plots which newly redefine the parameters of textual truth. And by the same rationale, the extradiegetic author, Machado, as well as the textual critic, in particular perhaps the feminist critic— his beloved (female) reader ('my dear friend,' 'my lady [. . .] whom I admire'[5]) in contrast with the unqualified male one (*EJ*, 954, 971)—whom he invites into the fictional and fictitious world of his male protagonist's first-person narration, become joint squatters in these multiple texts, that is, in both the narrator's text and in the canonic classical tradition which the latter recruits, but whose territory both Machado as author, his female pro-

tagonists as actors and the critic as reader variously invade, newly to unlock within them hitherto forbidden female textual spaces. In the process, and as regards the issue which specifically concerns us here, the female character, and in particular the machadean mother and mother-in-law, wife and daughter-in-law, may die, but in the words of Machado himself, albeit losing their lives, they win the discursive and literary battle of posterity (*DC*, 863-5).

The male protagonist's penchant for classical allusion, his need to frame his argument within the perceivedly comforting parameters of a tradition of authorship which he sees as complicitious in his own misogyny, leads to the deployment within this novel of an array of intertextual literary cross-references which at first glance appear to encode a gender separation unfavourable to the female protagonist. Thus, Machado's male characters invoke Greek philosophy and world literature, Christian dogma and pagan wisdom in a manner which exludes the woman from language, thought and text, casting her instead as either compulsorily silent within the dominant culture, or as venturing into speech as an act of wary transgression, deprived of a shared tradition of representation, alientated from sources of power and definition, and always guilty *a priori,* whether according to a post-lapsarian, post-edenic or an Aristotelian or Platonic vocabulary of lost Grace. Curiously, however, in antithesis to this project of negative female representation, what emerges beneath the gaze of the mystified male protagonist is a gallery of newly cast, newly cleansed heroines, modern but endowed with an array of lost and regained classical mothers or foremothers, Jocastas, Antigones, Iphigenias, Electras, a recovered tradition which now permits their accession to a right to speech which Machado himself seemingly consciously allows in them, while disallowing in his male would-be heroes.

The classical metaphor persists throughout this author's novels, in particular **Dom Casmurro** and later works, so that at one point Bentinho, admitting that he is 'proficient in Latin but virgin of women' (*DC*, 821), relates an adolescent episode in the course of which, in true biblical fashion, he associates the temptation to sin with his own knowledge or awareness of womanhood and of female sexuality, and desires the generic fall of all women, in an accurate modern replay of Genesis and the expulsion myth (*DC*, 867-8).

Unsurprisingly then in view of this, Capitu, slandered, debarred from the possibility of self-defence, textually and divinely condemned by her blessed lover (his name after all *is* Bento, or 'Blessed One'), and later, indeed, banished and figuratively murdered by him, on a number of occasions experiences a strong desire to learn Latin, the language from which she is particularly and explicitly excluded by masculinity, as embodied in the figures of her husband and her priest, the language of culture and of the *status quo*, and of their associated religion or God. Latin is the language which, if infiltrated, might grant her a platform for self-representation, the power of self-definition and the possibility of acquittal from a charge of adultery which will otherwise silence her and lead to her expulsion and death at the hands of Bento, the representative of the Law of God-the-Father/God-the-Son, a law which Latin articulates (*DC*, 838-40).

Capitu is condemned as an adulteress, excluded from speech, Latin or otherwise, denied the opportunity of self-defence and banned from the hegemony of the masculine universe whose monopoly over language, wisdom and truth she inconveniences. The metaphor for this denial of her rights is the prohibition of her acquaintance with Art as well as the classical languages and other subjects seen as the prerogative of the male, symbolic of his supremacy, and therefore his exclusive sphere. Bentinho, in his adolescence a seminarist vowed into the priesthood by his mother and the recipient of a classical education, has the command of Greek and Latin; furthermore, through his self-identification with Othello the Moor, to whom he variously refers and with whose plight he compares his own (without, however, at any point arriving at the obvious conclusion of Capitu's innocence, analogous to that of Desdemona[6]) he must also be seen to speak Arabic, the language through which the classicals re-entered and influenced Western thought.[7] He can thus be seen to operate from a privileged position *vis à vis* language and knowledge, an advantage from which Capitu as a woman is excluded. Nevertheless, as will be seen, the decodable text of Bentinho's would-be incontrovertible truth (which at another level might be read as Machado's invitingly deconstructible plot), will result in the undoing of the former within its own chosen frame of reference, since it will be by means of enlisting the self-same classical texts, pagan and Christian alike, that the messianic heroine will be revived, reinstated and recast as victorious after death.

The reinstatement initially requires the bonding of the two female protagonists, Capitu and her mother-in-law, Dona Glória. After Capitu's marriage to Bentinho, she is attenuated in the role of *femme fatale* attributed to her by her husband and temporarily reassigned to the roles of virtuous wife and mother, just as Dona Glória's function as mother surrenders to a more obvious narrative necessity as the figure of the loving, protective mother-in-law. The latter event, all the more unusual in a Brazilian nineteenth-century context as forcing the interests of blood and lineage to surrender to those of gender, might be taken as an example of bold feminist alignment on the part of the author. All the more so since it is a ploy which is repeated even more explicitly, in both the novels that followed this one, the last two that Machado wrote before his death.[8] In all these instances, whatever revision the lovers and husbands might bring to their perception of their women, the virtue of the latter, interestingly, and strikingly in the case of Capitu, remains untainted to the end in the eyes of the mothers-in-law, as grudgingly admitted by the accusing males. Early on in ***Dom Casmurro*** it is suggested that Dona Glória's experience of love in marriage was a unilateral one. On one occasion Bentinho contemplates two portraits of his parents which face one another on the walls of the family home, and interprets their gazes as signifying the following, respec-

tively: 'I am all yours, my handsome gentleman' (in Dona Glória's case) and 'See how this girl adores me' (in her husband's) (*DC*, 815). Love, then, originates in the woman towards the man, and results in the death of either one. If Dona Glória guesses that in Capitu's case it will be the latter, not Bentinho, who will die, and in the light of her realigned loyalty (or maternal duty) to gender rather than blood (or to a daughter-in-law rather than to a son now clearly co-opted into the Law of the Father) as suggested above, following the marriage she takes on the established classical guise of the two-faced, Janus woman, two-faced, that is, in the literal sense, since the mother (in-law), like the classical tragic Greek one, here displays two distinct facets. First, the loving, avenging function of a stricken Clytemnestra faced with the sacrifice of her daughter to an exclusively male enterprise of offended marital honour (in the Homer version and in the first play of the Aeschylus trilogy[9]). And second, in the light of her own husband's early demise, the murderous wife/mother whose slaying of her husband is duly punished in the last two plays of the Aeschylus version by the son and heir of the Law of the Father. The revisionary writing, therefore, begins in Machado in apparent obedience to Aeschylus' plot of female fiendishness, with the symbolic disposal of Dona Glória's husband through death, and her assumption of possession over the body (and soul) of her son. This supposition accounts also for the numerous widows elsewhere in this writer's fiction, in which the disappearance of the head of the family signals the coming-of-age of the wife within the family circle, and the transfer of power into her hands following the death of the spouse.

In Dona Glória's case, the death of her husband leaves her effectively in sole control of a household moreover conspicuous by the number of male dependents which otherwise inhabit it: her young son, an impoverished uncle kept by her charity and an even more impoverished *agregado*, an ambiguous combination of servant, errand-runner and unpaid adviser, also kept out of charity. Widowhood in Machado, therefore, introduces a reversal in domestic power relations and an altered *status quo* which vouchsafes women's access to a position of control over a variety of males to whom they were previously subjected. This new order more than once results also in Machado in an alliance between the newly empowered mother and her daughter-in-law.[10] In Dona Glória's case her relationship with Capitu, initially grounded in mutual suspicion, is curiously altered only when the latter is recast from girl-next-door into prospective daughter-in-law. In this new context of marriage and admission into a family in which arguably, in Dona Glória's experience, women either stand as unilaterally loving wives or as powerful widows, the two women are recast as protective mother and vulnerable daughter, in defiance of the actual mother-son blood tie. This new *status quo* will only be undone by Bento when he succeeds in discrediting his wife and bringing about her death—and therefore that of his mother as the latter's functional avatar—through accusations of immorality, and, more specifically, adultery.

The upsetting of the matriarchal household, however, takes place only after the widowed mother has variously attempted to dispose of her male lineage, metaphorically or literally, as a means of safeguarding primarily her own domestic rule, but presciently, as it turns out, the life of her daughter-in-law, threatened by marriage to the son. In *Dom Casmurro*, Dona Glória miscarries one male child, and her next autonomous act, just before her husband's death—one which she conceals from him and which he would almost certainly have forbidden as implying a threat to the male succession within the family—involves the promise of their unborn son to the priesthood, a promise tantamount to castrating and silencing him in a context where the importance of clerical power, however great, must be seen to be eclipsed, in the terms of the novel, by that of the male imperative to beget a son and perpetuate the male secular lineage. By vowing to make her son a priest, Dona Glória deprives him of the possibility of marriage, sexual expression and paternity within a literary paradigm in which sexuality and paternity signal voice, and voice is power. Moreover, she reverses the gender of the burnt-offering in the Aeschylean sacrifice of Iphigenia by Agamemnon, thereby rewriting the classical original.

Her promise defuses the future patriarchal threat which her son will personify to herself and secures her own familial power and dynastic control. In her now matriarchal household only unthreatening males (her submissive adolescent son and a series of impoverished male relatives and economic dependents) are suffered to remain, on condition of obedience to her rule. The sexless, childless, disempowered, ideologically void male relatives are adult versions of the adolescent Bentinho, and Dona Glória, therefore, by miscarrying her first son, emasculating and marginalising the second, becoming a widow and thus technically usurping familial power—in a patriarchal context in which no other trajectory to autonomy outside that of a *coup* is available to the woman—effectively ensures the continued negation of masculine supremacy within the family, and the impossibility of reinstating the male rule. She also, albeit unbeknown to herself at this point, secures for a while Capitu's deliverance from the unforeseen dangers of marriage to Bento. In this instance it is interesting to note that early on in the novel Dona Glória becomes associated, through an allusion made by Bentinho himself, with Pandora, who also appears elsewhere in Machado's fiction as a paradigmatic inimical mother, malevolently intentioned toward her male offspring (*DC*, 814-15).[11] The array of murderous, Medea-like mothers in Machado's novels, indeed, sets up an agenda of monstrous maternity threatening, in classical form, to exterminate or be exterminated by the son in his pursuit of patrilinear rights. In the original myth Pandora did permit control over the fated box, symbolic of contained evil, to slip out of her hands into those of her husband, Epimetheus. In *Dom Casmurro*, too, Dona Glória in the end allows power to revert back to the male line by deciding not to proceed with Bentinho's symbolic castration, releasing him from the priesthood and allowing his marriage and eventual paternity, tantamount to a recuperation by him of masculine power at other levels, and culminating, as we shall see, in Capitu's death and her own in a novel where the continuation of marriage leads to the death of the wife. Her decision thus inaugurates the re-

instatement of the Law of the Father in the person of his son and successor, and, once again, as per the classical strictures, the Oresteian son will rise to power and vindicate the father through a matricide at first glance exculpated by the restored *status quo*. Bentinho's effective murder of his wife, as I shall argue below, is also the murder of the mother who is that wife's alter ago, and their deaths will be seen to become narratively contiguous, contingent and interchangeable.

If Dona Glória's promise of her son as sacrificial victim is a rewritten classical betrayal of offspring by parent (for example a gender reversal of the Iphigenia sacrifice by Agamemnon), Dona Glória's identification with Capitu, echoing that of Clytemnestra and Iphigenia, equally inaugurates a cycle of murder and revenge which will culminate in the deaths of the two female protagonists at the hands of the husband/son. The linking of the two deaths—and the assertion of a common causality, the agency of the son/husband as murderer—relies here upon a chain of similarities and analogies which connect the two women, and in particular the imagery surrounding their deaths, their epitaphs, and the implications of the latter. Dona Glória's death, coinciding chronologically with Capitu's, and identifiable with it through the similarity of their epitaphs, not surprisingly is dealt with even more elliptically than the latter's, since it is matricide, and clearly the more serious of the two crimes in antiquity as in nineteenth-century Brazil, both societies whose conventions condoned the murder by a husband of a wife guilty or merely suspected of infidelity.[12] The downfall of Capitu, moreover, coincides diegetically with the decline of Dona Glória who, until the loss of her younger self, had been insistently described by Bento as someone whom old age did not affect. When Capitu is exiled by Bento, Dona Glória according to him rapidly ages by all the years she had not done before and the two women's deaths follow each other in close succession, concluding the fusion of their two characters. Each woman is dismissed by the narrator in one sentence, Capitu as an afterthought—[Capitu] I believe I have not mentioned, was dead and buried' (*DC*, 939-41).

Their analogous epitaphs, perhaps more clearly than any other aspect of the novel, signal the moment of authorial contradiction of both the narratorial verdict of guilt and the prescriptions of the classical foretexts. In an inversion of the Aeschyllean sequence whereby Clytemnestra's initially understandable murder of her husband, motivated by maternal grief and the desire for vengeance, is quickly reformulated by the Greek playwright as unforgivable homicide punishable by death, Machado begins by presenting us with heroines of seemingly dubious character. Controversially, however, but I would argue consciously and with the deliberation of an intended political purpose, he proceeds to reappraise and redeem them in the moment of their deaths at the hands of the Oresteian son upon whom, in contradiction to the prescriptions of the paradigmatic tragedy, the burden of blame is authorially imposed at the end. In an echo of his male protagonist's own favoured self-accrediting strategy, but clearly with the purpose of the latter's undoing, Machado, like Bento, has recourse to canonical philosophy from both pagan and Christian sources to validate his own authorial conclusions, the two women's analogous epitaphs providing the material clue to the process of apportioning blame or innocence in this novel. If Capitu is Dona Glória's alter ego, the latter's epitaph—'a saint' (*DC*, 937-8)—chosen (significantly and against considerable opposition, by Bento himself, who insists upon its descriptive accuracy), must be seen equally to apply to the former and therefore to confirm the unlikelihood of her adultery and criminal motherhood, since even Machado would presumably balk at the canonisation of an adulteress. Furthermore, Dona Glória's epitaph effectively rephrases Capitu's own—'she died beautiful' (*DC*, 940)—an accolade bestowed, significantly, by her own son Ezequiel, and which, according to the Platonic contingency frequently drawn upon by Bento (for instance when he repeatedly draws the reader's attention to Capitu's eyes, represented as shifty and symptomatic of a general deviousness), equates physical with spiritual worth, and must therefore be seen to assert Capitu's bodily and moral soundness alike, and to acquit her of essential blame. Similarly, the description of Dona Glória by Bento, elsewhere, as being 'candid as the first dawn, prior to the first sin' (*DC*, 73), further reinforces the suggestion of spiritual blamelessness, phrased now not in Platonic but in Christian prelapsarian terms, which, according to the alter ego extrapolation, must be seen to encompass her daughter-in-law too. In the case of both women, therefore, their sanctity and their beauty, according both to Biblical symbolism and to the Platonic strictures which Bentinho himself evokes and then hastily revokes at critical moments, refer also to their moral status and override the possible negative connotations of their disobedience, thereby reaffirming their innocence at the end, and becoming causally linked to the fact of their deaths, here reformulated as martyrdoms.

The two women, therefore, emerge as twinned heroines, their alter ego status and the Oresteian script alike being further echoed through the fact that in both women's case it is the birth (or at least, in the case of Dona Glória, the *fact* of having) a son—Bentinho himself and Ezequiel, the child Bentinho suspects of being conceived adulterously—which leads to their downfall. Motherhood, therefore, kills Capitu as well as Dona Glória, the latter because in her capacity as her daughter-in-law's mirror image she must stand or fall with her at the hands of the same opponent. Bentinho, like Orestes, thus becomes guilty of matricide as well as of the murder of his wife. In the end, nevertheless, Machado is in the business of revising, rather than simply rewriting the classical texts, and the pairing of mother and daughter, or in this case mother-in-law and daughter-in-law which he deploys must be seen to contest the original defeated Clytemnestra/Iphigenia duo, and to rethink the original myth's conclusions. Thus, when Dona Glória releases Bentinho from his priest-in-training status, she may deliver both Capitu and herself to the death which follows Bentinho's suspicions of Capitu's adultery, but the verdict surrounding their deaths remains as problematic as the irresolvable question of Capitu's guilt or innocence.

Finally, therefore, Bentinho, Oedipal son in his love-hate fixation upon the mother, Oresteian in his matricide, is betrayed not by her, nor even by his allegedly adulterous wife, but in effect by his author, who deals with him in the only way in which the speaker of the dominant discourse of the Symbolic Order can be dealt with, that is, through the removal of his voice's transcendental impunity, and the withdrawal also of the various traditions upon which Bento as the mouthpiece of masculinity draws for credibility. Bentinho, therefore, would-be priest, Blessed One, the son of God,[13] rewrites the edenic script in a manner which accentuates the female guilt intrinsic to it, thereby creating a new, aggravated textual truth, but by this act he, like Adam, also partakes of forbidden knowledge and becomes implicated in the enjoyment thereof. Moreover, since as far as Machado's male character is concerned, knowledge is tantamount to sexual initiation, by attempting to become the originator of a new textual truth he becomes sinful, and sees this truth, or his claim to truth, in the end snatched from him not by the earthly mother whom he murdered but by the Divine Father here deployed as agent by the extradiegetic author. Both the Divine and the literary father, therefore, or the former as the means to the latter's narrative end, can be seen to indict Bentinho for his lost innocence and to forsake him at the last.

The possibility of Machado having been able to step outside the sexual political assumptions of his epoch to pose instead the illegitimacy of those assumptions, need not resort for example to a Marxist principle of internal contradiction[14] or to the assertion of an unconscious dimension to the author's text.[15] Already in his early chronicles Machado readily engaged in or pioneered important literary and political debates in Brazil, including his polemics on nationalism in literature, naturalism, and, more pertinently here, his texts on the relations between the sexes in the second half of the nineteenth century in Brazil and the importance of education for women.[16]

In *Dom Casmurro* Machado, as the extradiegetic author of this first-person narration, in the end betrays both his narrator/hero and the classical texts to which the latter has recourse for support, and returns us instead to the untruth of the diegetic texts, as well as to *a* truth in it, a female truth which that narrator originally silenced. Dona Glória and Capitu, therefore, at the end become truly mother- and daughter-in-law, *in law,* acquitted in the eyes of a new, reconstituted tribunal, revisionary of former ones both contemporary and antique. In this way, moreover, a further provocation is enacted, and in this novel, as in others, Machado, glancing retrospectively at the classics, unseats the possibility of the empirical truth of his male speaker. By doing so he simultaneously dislocates the Brazilian Positivist moment which the latter, like other of this author's heroes—for example the pseudo-Darwinian Brás Cubas of *Memórias Póstumas de Brás Cubas*—represent and involuntarily caricature, gesturing instead backwards, to a (now unstable) realist certainty, and forward, to modernist uncertainty, to disturbing lost possibilities in Homer and Aeschylus, in Genesis and in Shakespeare, then and now.

NOTES

1 John Gledson, 'Brazilian Fiction: Machado de Assis to the Present', in *Modern Latin American Fiction: A Survey* ed. by John King (London: Faber and Faber, 1987), 21.

2 Joaquim Maria Machado de Assis, *Obra Completa*, 3 vols (Rio de Janeiro: Editora José Aguilar, 1962), III, 398.

3 Quoted by Astrojildo Pereira, 'Instinto e Consciência da Nacional-idade', in *Machado de Assis*, ed. by Alfredo Bosi (Rio de Janeiro: Livraria São José, 1959), 43-85.

4 Machado de Assis, *Dom Casmurro*, in *Obra Completa*, I, op. cit., 807-942. All subsequent references and quotations from *Dom Casmurro* will refer to this edition and will be indicated by a page reference in the text and the abbreviation *DC*.

5 Machado de Assis, *Esaú e Jacó*, in *Obra Completa*, I, op. cit., 980-1. All subsequent references will be to this edition and will be indicated by a page reference in the text and the abbreviation *EJ*.

6 For a discussion of the links between Bentinho and Othello, and the identification of Bentinho as *being* Othello, see Helen Cald-well, *The Brazilian Othello of Machado de Assis: A Study of Dom Casmurro* (Berkeley and Los Angeles: University of California Press, 1960).

7 Ibid.

8 Machado de Assis, *Esaú e Jacó*, op. cit., 943-1091. *Memorial de Aires* in *Obra Completa*, I, op. cit., 1093-198.

9 As will be discussed later, the second play of the *Oresteian Trilogy* appears to contradict the initial understanding reading of Clytemnestra's murder as the result of a mother's grief, and to re cast her as simply the unforgivable slayer of her husband.

10 For example in one of his early novels, *Iaiá Garcia* in *Obra Completa*, I, 389-507.

11 See also the notorious figure of Pandora in *Memórias Póstumas de Brás Cubas*, in *Obra Completa*, I, op. cit., 509-637. All subsequent references will be to this edition and will be indicated by a page reference in the text and the abbreviation *MP*.

12 For a discussion of Brazilian legislation on crimes of passion see Ingrid Stein, *Figuras Femininas em Machado de Assis* (Rio de Janeiro: Editora Paz e Terra, Coleção Literatura e Teoria Literária, 1984), 29.

13 See Helen Caldwell, op. cit., 32-61 for a discussion of Bentinho's status as Divine Son and Fallen Angel.

14 K. Marx and F. Engels, *On Literature and Art*, ed. by L. Baxandall and S. Morawski (New York: International General, 1973).

15 Both Engels and Marx separately debate the notion of an unconscious dimension to a text. Engels does so among other writings in his letter to Margaret Harkness and Marx in the text 'The Holy Family' on Eugène Sue, both discussed in Terry Eagleton, *Marxism and Literary Criticism* (London: Methuen, 1983), 46-8.

16 Machado de Assis, 'Queda que as mulheres têm para os tolos' in *Obras Completas*, III, op. cit., 965-72. 'Cherchez la femme,' ibid., 1003-4.

FURTHER READING

Haberly, David T. "A Journey Through the Escape Hatch: Joaquim Maria Machado de Assis." *Three Sad Races*, pp. 70-98. Cambridge: Cambridge University Press, 1983.

> A detailed overview of Machado's most influential works, the internal and external metamorphoses in his characters' lives, and the autobiographical influence of Machado's life on his characters.

Larsen, Kevin S. "*Dom Casmurro* and the Elective Affinities." *The Luso-Brazilian Review*, Vol. 28, No. 2 (Winter 1991): 49-57.

> Finds influences and kindred characters of Machado's *Dom Casmurro* in other works with similar themes and plot.

MacAdam, Alfred J. "Machado de Assis: Narrating and Lying." *Modern Latin American Narratives*, pp. 21-28. Chicago: University of Chicago Press, 1977.

> Looks at Machado's use of satire not only as a means to depict his characters' incapacitated efforts to attain true life and language, but also as a metaphor for Machado's presence in Latin American literature.

Pritchett, V. S. "Machado de Assis: A Brazilian." *The Myth Makers*, pp. 158-63. London: Chatto and Windus, 1979.

> Presents psychological portraits of characters manifesting their destinies as shaped by their outlook on life: a study of past, present, and future embodied in three characters in Machado's *Epitaph for a Small Winner*, and the conflicts that arise when they meet outside of a harmonious context.

Weiner, Lauren. "Rediscovering the "espírito" of Machado." *New Criterion*, Vol. 16, No. 2 (October 1997): 18-25.

> Examines two main approaches to character in Machado's writing: the *tolo*, or the sexual/physical, and the *espirito*, the psycho/spiritual. This essay analyzes the connection between the two, placing particular emphasi s on Machado's development of *espirito*.

Additional coverage of Machado de Assis's life and career is contained in the following sources published by the Gale Group: *Black Literature Criticism Supplement*; *Contemporary Authors*, Vols. 107, 153; *Short Story Criticism*, Vol. 24; *Twentieth Century Literary Criticism*, Vol. 10.

Rigoberta Menchú
1959-

(Born Rigoberta Menchú Tum) Guatemalan testimonial writer and activist.

INTRODUCTION

Rigoberta Menchú's work toward human rights in Central America and her writing about the personal and cultural experiences of the Guatemalan Mayans have earned her wide recognition as a political writer and activist. She won the 1992 Nobel Peace Prize because of her timely testimonial *I . . . Rigoberta Menchú*, first published in Spanish as *Me llama Rigoberta Menchú y asi me nació la conciencia* (1983) during the late period of the 30-year Guatemalan oppression of indigenous Mayan communities. She has since established a foundation to further her fight for human rights around the world.

Born in 1959 in the small Quiché village of Chimel in Guatemala, Menchú grew up working with her brothers, sisters, and parents on the coffee plantations of the Guatemalan highlands. Her family eventually became involved in the resistance of governmental land disputes and the forced servitude of the workers on the coffee plantations. Already in a similar dispute among their own people, the Menchú and Tum families were drawn into the Guatemalan tragedy that became the foundation of Rigoberta Menchú's writing. She spent some time in Catholic schools on scholarships, where she received only the equivalent of a middle school education. She was self-taught in a few of the twenty-two Mayan language groups and furthered her education to become fluent in Spanish. The Quiché have espoused, for the most part, a policy of isolationism, so Menchú's adoption of the Spanish language as a tool against her opposition was an important breakthrough in the development of her work. She has witnessed horrifying violations of human rights against members of her community, and while some particulars of her story are questionable, these atrocities occur regularly in Guatemala, El Salvador, Nicaragua, and Honduras. Menchú was forced into exile as a result of her writing, and the torture and execution of her mother. After her receipt of the Nobel Prize she returned to Guatemala, where she was arrested by the government. Under pressure from the international community, she was released.

The controversy over *I . . . Rigoberta Menchú* comes partly from the book's many translations. Menchú herself has called it "fragmentary," and acknowledged that some of the material presented as personal fact is actually the testimonial of others with whom Menchú has sympathized. But for the Guatemalan Maya, as Victor Perera writes in *Unfinished Conquest*, the collective experience is often appropriated by a storyteller as an individual experience. The book, frequently misrepresented as an "autobiography," is actually a testimonial. It has been the subject of some criticism since anthropologists gather conflicting testimonies from Guatemalans who may tell a different story to non-natives. It is important to view Menchú's work as a view of the Guatemalan hostilities and her narrative of conscience, designed to make the world outside of Guatemala aware of the chronic injustices of that government.

Although the Nobel Prize is customarily awarded on the basis of a lifetime of work, *I . . . Rigoberta Menchú* garnered Menchú a prestigious honor. For this the controversy over the book's factuality has sometimes reached a fevered pitch. Menchú declined to dignify the argument in her second book, *Crossing Borders* (1998), instead choosing to focus on the plights of those suffering for human rights around the globe, the changes as a result of her fame, and the state of her family after the violent crimes committed against them. The two books demonstrate the decades of effort and ongoing struggle against native indians in Guatemala and throughout the world. The Indigenous Initiative for Peace, founded with the money she received for the Nobel Peace Prize, flowered into the Rigoberta Menchú Tum Foundation, which addresses education, health care, and civil rights worldwide.

Critics have compared *I . . . Rigoberta Menchú* to Christian mythic plotlines, the Electra myth, the American slave narrative, and the common *bildungsroman* or coming-of-age story, especially by those who see Menchú's work as primarily contrived. But such a complex mix of personal narrative and civil awareness is often oversimplified or misunderstood, and the merits of Menchú's writing are chiefly political, not literary. The prose style is affected by the translator's and editors' decisions; consequently it is fragmentary and repetitive at times. The accomplishment of the book is that it is not dependent upon a specific context and is entirely the result of Menchú's own effort. The result is a combination of personal testimony and social appeal that reaches all people regardless of its course diction, cultural difference, and translation.

PRINCIPAL WORKS

Me llamo Rigoberta Menchú y asi me nacio mi consciencia [*I, Rigoberta Menchú: An Indian Woman in Guatemala*] (testimony) 1984
Crossing Borders (testimony) 1998

CRITICISM

Linda Larson   (review date 1994)

SOURCE: A review of *I, Rigoberta Menchú: An Indian Woman in Guatemala*, in *English Journal*, December, 1994, pp. 105-6.

[*Larson recommends Menchú's book to those interested in the concerns of women in contemporary culture.*]

Rigoberta Menchú's story strikes the reader as significant on several levels: It is a social and political comment narrated by a 23-year-old Guatemalan woman whose Indian heritage, while it places her in the numerical majority, condemns her to the status of expendable political minority. It is a candid story told by a speaker who was forced to learn Spanish in order to break out of the isolation her native Indian language imposed on her. It is also a chance for the rest of the world to glimpse a culture struggling to keep its rituals and identity from systematic extermination.

Menchú derives the courage to speak directly from her family and her community. Every chapter reveals some aspect of her upbringing in El Quiche, a province in Guatemala. From the beginning when the reader finds out that Menchú is from only one group of 22 indigenous Guatemalan Indian tribes, to her exile from her beloved community, Menchú's role in her people's fight to maintain cultural identity serves as a backdrop for her testimony to a beautiful country and a spiritual people seared by political persecution.

Despite the civic brutality, Menchú maintains her optimism. In Chapter I she describes her birthplace as "practically a paradise, the country is so beautiful. There are no big roads and no cars. Only people can reach it. Everything is taken down the mountainside on horseback or else we carry it ourselves. So, you can see, I live right up in the mountains" (2). To understand Menchú's clarity of vision and her unflagging devotion to El Quiche, the reader need only contrast this paradise with a scene from Chapter 24: "My mother went closer to the lorry to see if she could recognize her son. Each of the tortured had different wounds on the face. I mean their faces all looked different. . . . Some of them were very nearly half dead, or they were in their last agony. . . . All the tortured had no nails and they had cut off part of the soles of their feet" (176).

The reader feels a sense of wonder, then awe, that Menchú can feel the same innocent devotion to her country at the end of the book as she does at the beginning. But that's why the book works. It is a testimony to culture tightly woven through its oral traditions, its customs, its rituals, its spiritual beliefs, and its resistance to wholesale murder. The children of such a culture are drenched in their own traditions so thoroughly that they run little danger of being confused. So consistently are the children included

in various ceremonies, and so consistently are they made responsible for maintaining their cultural identity, that they run little risk of being assimilated into the outside *ladino* world. (*Ladino* refers to a Guatemalan who rejects Mayan origins and traditional Indian values; the term may imply mixed blood.)

Menchú explains that as children grow, they fulfill a series of obligations that parents commit them to at birth. These areas of responsibility ensure that tribal secrets are passed on. Parents promise that their children will do everything in exactly the manner as their ancestors. As the modern reader can readily understand, this often leads the *ladino* world to describe the Indian cultures as antediluvian. This lack of political identity further perpetuates the stereotypes that typically characterize the disenfranchised as the Indians themselves speak 22 distinct languages and, therefore, have no means of uniting. Even common employment at the lowland *fincas*, or coffee plantations, provides little common denominator when people cannot communicate. This division is magnified by the Spanish-speaking world in its perception of the Indians as people without power or institutions. Thus, ultimately Menchú is compelled to study Spanish so that she might urge communities to unite in their plight to maintain their ways of life.

The irony is that, without Spanish, Menchú remains mute and powerless. Only with the *ladina*'s words can she tell the story of her people's fight for their cultural identity. Thus, the reader hears her thirdhand. But the unwavering picture of a culture threatened by violent extinction is without distortion. The picture of a brutal government lusting after even the tiniest, most inaccessible plot of mountainous *altiplano* Indian land is startlingly clear. So, too, is the story of the human spirit's ability to rise above degradation and systematic oppression. The ability to bridge a cultural gap so profound that it took two languages, an editor, and a translator to bring us the story, is also a triumph.

This is a must-read for anyone interested in feminist politics; women's cultural roles; the status of the Indian community in Guatemala today; and the incredible power of language to separate people—or to bring them together.

David J. Leigh   (essay date 1998)

SOURCE: "Rigoberta Menchú and the Conversion of Consciousness," in *Christian Encounters with the Other*. New York: New York University Press, 1998, pp. 182-93.

[*Leigh expounds upon three underlying principles he believes are integral to Menchú's work.*]

The awkward but fascinating plot of the Guatemalan autobiography *I, Rigoberta Menchú* has puzzled readers since its appearance in English in 1983. Critics have discussed its use of secrecy to preserve the mystery of the native way of life (Sommer), its use of the testimonial genre and oral-to-written format to show its unique relationship to social movements in Central America (Beverley), and its cross-cultural situation in relation to its third-world origins and its first-world readers (Gunn). No one, however, has made sense out of the awkwardly didactic restructuring of descriptions and events by Menchú's Venezuelan translator, Elisabeth Burgos-Debray. A close analysis of the "plotting" of Menchú's story into thirty-four chapters suggests that three principles are at work beneath the structuring of this autobiography. First, the autobiography can be read as Menchú's encounter with three types of otherness—internal others within herself, external others in the dominant culture, and the "other" of death on the faces of suffering villagers, especially her dying brother, father, and mother. Second, these encounters with otherness lead to a conversion of consciousness, both within the autobiographer Menchú herself and within the minds of her readers. These conversions of consciousness are mediated by the subtext of a theology of liberation, which helps Menchú become aware of the divine suffering Other in the faces of her people, and of her own responsibility to work as a catechist and organizer in the altiplano of Guatemala. Finally, this conversion of consciousness (or "conscientization" as it was called by Paolo Freire) becomes the dynamic form that holds together the double plot of the autobiography. A close reading of the narrative events uncovers a first-stage plotting of Menchú's "cultural story" (Chapters 1-12), which is aimed at raising the consciousness of her readers, and a second-stage plotting of Menchú's "personal story" (Chapters 13-34), which reveals her gradual transformation of consciousness from that of passive traditionalist village girl to active resistance-organizing woman.

Menchú's primary struggle in this story of her life is with several *internal* others—her parental models, her changing self-image, and her linguistic identity. The encounter with her parents provides an underlying motif of the autobiography, as it does for most twentieth-century autobiographies, but for Menchú this encounter becomes a struggle to integrate within herself, as Gandhi did, two quite different models of living provided by her father and her mother. From her father, an orphan who was "given away" by his mother to be a servant to a *ladino* employer, Menchú learns how to cope with life. As his favorite and most intelligent child, she imitates his early initiative, his steady work habits, his ability to resist injustice, and his political strategies. Beneath these personal qualities, she constructs her character on the model of his love of native traditions together with his Catholic faith. From her mother, Menchú derives her love of nature and tradition, but also the need to challenge the limits of women's roles in the villages and tribes of northern Guatemala. Her mother teaches Menchú to express her feelings and not to avoid painful emotional scenes which her father and other men can not face publicly, especially the burial of the dead. More significantly, her mother teaches her the customs and values of her people—marriage preparation, family living, tribal solidarity, sowing and harvesting, predicting the weather, and the rules of gift-giving. However, her mother's own growth as a woman in social awareness is perhaps an even greater legacy to Rigoberta, for her mother shows her how to resist machismo within a marriage and a tribe. From these

double parental models, Menchú internalizes an integrated sense of her identity, including, as both her parents taught her, "to be politicized through her work," for her father was the main political leader in her village and her mother was the first woman in their area to join the struggle for liberation.

From this struggle to integrate these two models within her own self came the search for an adequate directional self-image, a model of self-identity which would sustain her as it has sustained many modern writers of spiritual and political autobiographies from Gandhi to Dorothy Day to Malcolm X to Nelson Mandela. After a childhood in which Menchú sees herself as a timid, fearful, and awkward girl, and then an adolescence in which she is told by the dominant *ladino* overseers that she is a dirty, stupid Indian, and an early adulthood in which she is told by middle-class leaders in the resistance movement that she is only a woman, Menchú, with the inspiration of her parents, eventually creates the self-image that she uses to open her autobiography. She takes on the dynamic identity of a witness for her people to the world:

> My name is Rigoberta Menchú. I am twenty three years old. This is my testimony. I didn't learn it from a book and I didn't learn it alone. I'd like to stress that it's not only *my* life, it's also the testimony of my people . . . My story is the story of all poor Guatemalans. My personal experience is the reality of a whole people.
>
> (1)

This imaging of herself as a witness for a people in a socio-religious struggle from the 1970s to the 1980s embodies the people's coming to awareness through Menchú's personal experience in her first twenty years. Both Rigoberta and her native village in Quiche begin their journey into consciousness as passive childlike victims of an oligarchical social system with power held by *ladino* landowners, government officials, and the Guatemalan army. As Menchú tells her story in the framework of tribal and personal testimony, she and her people transform their self-image from that of passive traditionalists to active revolutionaries. This image, of course, is present from the start in the title, words, and narrative structure of the autobiography, but present as an image created (with more than a little help from her editor) from her final standpoint as a committed Catholic and native liberationist (Berkeley 96).

Finally, Menchú struggles with a linguistic "other" within herself. Her desire to learn to speak and read Spanish, even against the wishes of her more traditional father, is a recurring motif of her story, one that drives her to a more complex level of social awareness. She uses the new language not to substitute for her native tongue and identity but as an enriching otherness that contributes to her usefulness in the liberation movement. Yet she discloses only a small amount of her inner struggle to learn and use Spanish, the language of her people's oppressors but also the language which opens her to communicating her story to the others of the first-world.

These three struggles by Menchú with internal "others" take place, in fact, within the surrounding lifelong struggle of herself and her people with an external other—that of the dominant *ladino* culture. Beyond this encounter, of course, lies the powerful world cultures of the industrialized east and west, engaged during this time in the cold war. This encounter with the dominant *ladino* and world cultures presents Menchú with first a personal crisis and later a literary challenge. The personal crisis forces her to strive to maintain her identity and preserve her culture in the face of exploitation on the fincas, cultural discrimination in the city, and both exploitation and oppression in the altiplano villages. As several critics have noted, Menchú cannot avoid negotiating with these cultural others. Thus, as we shall see, she must learn to distinguish among various persons and classes in the *ladino* culture; she must learn to use its language and ways of organizing resistance; and she must learn to use its Spanish language as a means of communication. In learning these things, she creates the very form of her autobiography. Within the autobiographical form, however, she is presented with a difficult problem of communicating her experience and social situation to the culturally "other" modern world. With the help of Burgos-Debray, Menchú mixes a form of idealized "cultural stories" within her realistic personal narrative. This mixture succeeds in raising the consciousness of her readers, but simultaneously undermines some of her credibility.

These encounters with internal personal otherness and external social otherness are assisted in part by Menchú's positive experience with what Emmanuel Levinas calls encounters with the face of the Other. For Levinas, full human ethical, and even religious, enlightenment is brought about by a compassionate meeting with another person in his or her suffering. This suffering personality is revealed most strikingly in direct encounters with the "face" of the other person. Unlike alienating encounters with internal or cultural otherness, this sort of encounter can be a moment of transformation. As we shall see, Menchú explicitly describes in great detail the crucial moments of her encounter with the disfigured faces of her brother (Ch. 24) and her mother (Ch. 27). These encounters, as both personal and representative of the faces of all the suffering others in Guatemala, confirms her final conversion to become a committed Christian resistance worker.

Contemporary conversion theory sheds light on the structure of Menchú's autobiography. If the autobiography is read as a document aimed at transforming the minds of its readers both by its narrative of the ideal cultural story (Ch. 1-12) and by its subsequent narrative of the realistic personal story of Rigoberta Menchú, then the process of conversion is central to this autobiography's method. According to Wayne E. Oates, conversion stories are expressed in three images—unification (of a divided self), turning (in a new direction), and surrender (in love to another, especially to God or some ideal). Menchú's story fuses all three of these images within its basic structural pattern of conversion of consciousness (Oates 149ff). Menchú unifies the family and cultural conflicts with her internal others; she turns from the old passive direction

of fatalistic flight away from the dominating enemies, and she surrenders herself in total commitment to the community of her native peoples in whom she finds "the kingdom of God on earth" (Menchú 134). According to an expanded version of Walter Conn's model of conversion, the process of radical self-change has five dimensions. As conversion, these changes call for a leap from one level of human awareness to another, a leap that transforms the self and its framework of beliefs (Conn 27). Menchú exhibits the first dimension, affective conversion, when she begins in her early teenage years to move from self-absorption to concern for the feelings of others. She undergoes a second dimension, imaginative conversion, when she first imagines herself as a witness for her people to the world, an image that eventually becomes the title of her story. She undergoes a third dimension, intellectual conversion, when she moves from simple direct awareness of the horrors of her people's suffering to a reflective awareness of the causes of this suffering. She experiences a fourth aspect of conversion, moral transformation, when she commits herself to work for the common good of her village and the entire native peoples. Finally, she brings in a transcendent dimension, a religious conversion, when she learns through liberation theology to see the suffering of her people as also the suffering on the human face of the ultimate Other.

What makes Menchú unique, in fact, among modern spiritual autobiographers is her attempt (mediated by Burgos-Debray) to construct the plot of her life story in accord with the conscientization process of liberation theology. This mixture of social and theological movements that began in Latin America in the 1960s was distinguished, as Menchú's autobiography shows, by its ability to use concrete social situations of oppression (in this case, experiences of her people and their persecution by the Guatemalan army and economy) as the context for religious reflection and growth. As summed up by one current theologian, liberation theology "is an attempt to interpret Christian doctrine in a way that is responsible to the universal problem of human suffering, which is especially manifest in the social oppression of today's world. . . . By uniting theology, ethics, and spirituality, it provides answers to fundamental questions of why one chooses to be a Christian in the modern world" (Haight 276). For Menchú, who chooses to be such a Christian, the portrayal of the contrast between the ideal village life of her culture stories and the realistic pain of her personal stories provides an opening for theological reflection. In response to these conflicts, Menchú applies theological and Biblical teachings to illuminate her situation and to motivate her readers. Since a central term and goal for liberation theology is conscientization (the development of awareness by oppressed people that they are unjustly treated but that they have the moral power and duty to transform their situation), it is no surprise to discover that Menchú's primary plot structure derives from liberation theology's pattern of consciousness-raising.

What is troubling, however, is that the patterns of liberation theology both mask and uncover the struggle within Menchú to find a way to integrate her religious conversion experience of the divine suffering Other (in Christ) with the human suffering others she wants to identify with. Liberation theological patterns mask the struggle insofar as Menchú lacks the creative literary power to convey her religious experience in any but conventional language from her catechetical role in the tribal life. However, despite this limitation, the patterns of liberation theology help her to incorporate a theology of consciousness-raising into the basic outline of her own personal story in Chapters 13-34. The very subtitle in Spanish of the autobiography ("the birth of my consciousness") reinforces the liberation theology patterns beneath the plot. What is theologically most significant is that Menchú, brought up in a traditional and radical Catholicism at the same time, came to realize that the divine Other had identified itself in Christ with the least of the brothers and sisters, precisely the human marginalized others whom Menchú identifies with. The plot of the personal story is primarily a narrative of such conscientization—the step by step realization by Menchú of her converted identity as a worker, a daughter, a native, a woman, a resistance worker, and a Christian believer in a liberating divine Other who is revealed in the faces of the suffering people around her. A closer analysis of the plotting of the autobiography will reveal this conversion pattern to be the main form of her story.

As we have indicated earlier, the overall plotting of this autobiography can be divided into two parts, each with a different narrative genre, purpose, and imagined audience. The first twelve chapters provide primarily a series of culture stories about the customs and values of the native Quiche peoples for whom Menchú declares that she speaks in her opening account as a witness in Chapter 1. In these first chapters, at the urging of her transcriber, Menchú describes the initiation ceremonies (Ch. 2), the animal identity (Ch. 3), the work patterns in the fincas (Ch. 4), the family life in the villages (Ch. 8), the agricultural religious ceremonies (Ch. 9-10), the courtship and marriage customs (Ch. 11), and the social and religious life of the villages (Ch. 12). The form of these culture stories is that of an anthropological ideal model, told in a direct descriptive style by a naive narrator, with the intended effect of winning sympathy from the reader for the values and traditions of the people portrayed. Even the occasional admission of the fatalism, excessive labor, machismo, and alcoholism among the people seems only to contrast with the idealized pictures of this anthropological model (48, 50).

When Menchú begins her personal story, it serves as a violent contrast to the idyllic world of the culture story in which she is raised. For her personal story—as an embodiment of liberation theology—is one of gradual coming to an awareness of the injustices done to her culture by the *ladinos* and a coming to a commitment to take on responsibility for resistance to these injustices. This conscientization process that makes up her personal narrative takes Menchú through her conversion process in five stages:

- Conversion (affective) to direct awareness of problems within her childhood (Ch. 5-7)

- Conversion (naive moral) to direct awareness of the unjust social situation and of her responsibility to change it (Ch. 8-9, 12-13)

- Conversion (intellectual) to reflective awareness of the causes of these injustices (Ch. 14-16)

- Conversion (complex moral) to reflective awareness of and commitment to social, gender, and theological distinctions (Ch. 17-23)

- Conversion (imaginative and religious) to full commitment to personal and social transformation by seeing the human and divine Other in the faces of the suffering (Ch. 24-32)

Menchú's first account of the childhood seeds of her consciousness-raising occurs when at age seven she gets lost in the mountains. As she says, " . . . they lost me for seven hours. I was crying, shouting, but no one heard me. That was the first time I felt what it must be like to be an adult, I felt I had to be responsible, more like my brothers and sisters" (29). As she later acknowledges, her predicament of "being lost" was a symptom of the social "lostness" of her family in their poverty. Even when she is found again, she speaks primarily "of the anger I felt at the way we live" (29). This minor episode of an emotional change prepares the reader for the many small steps into consciousness that Menchú takes during the years leading up to the death of her parents. She also recalls that at age five, "my consciousness was born" from the affective experience of watching her mother work herself to exhaustion on the fincas (34). At age eight, Menchú reacts to her family's being fired for attending the funeral of their child by crying out, "From that moment, I was both angry with life and afraid of it . . . I remember it with enormous hatred. That hatred has stayed with me until today" (41). These instances from Chapters 5 to 7 show the early affective conversion to an emotional awareness of the problems in her life.

When Menchú reaches her tenth birthday, she is formally initiated into the customs and responsibilities of young adults in her village. It is at this point that she begins a moral conversion to a direct awareness of the injustice in her family's situation and of her responsibility to respond to it. As her father tells her, "From now on you must contribute to the common good" (49). When she becomes twelve, she beings to think, as she puts it, "like a responsible woman . . . I joined the communal work; things like harvesting the maize . . . I began taking over my mother's role too" (79). At this point, she also leaves behind her naive childhood faith to take on the task of spreading Catholic teaching as a catechist. As she sums up her inculturated Christianity, "By accepting the Catholic religion, we didn't accept a condition, or abandon our culture. It was more like another way of expressing ourselves. . . . We feel very Catholic because we believe in the Catholic religion but, at the same time, we feel

Rigoberta Menchú

very Indian, proud of our ancestors" (80-81). After she narrates at length her new religious duties, Menchú gives an account of her first direct consciousness of the evils in the plantation system. The catalyst for this moral conversion is the death from poisoning of her best friend, to which she responds, "I was afraid of life. . . . I was mad with grief" (88-89). It is at this point that she first confesses that she wants to learn Spanish, a skill that would help her learn more theology from the circuit-riding priests to help her as a catechist, and would give her greater skills to deal with the *ladinos.*

Menchú soon learns more than she anticipated. As she describes her work at age twelve as a housemaid in Guatemala City, she shows that she is awakening to the causes of her people's problems in the racial prejudices and exploitation of Indian peoples by the *ladinos.* In this vivid account of her humiliations and degradations as a maid for a rich family, her reflective conscientization expresses itself in pure narrative (Ch. 14). Then, in the following Chapter, Menchú recounts the event that is the final stage in awakening her and her village to the systemic injustices of the land reform and the need for united resistance— the mistreatment and imprisonment of her father. She recalls the earlier conflicts with the landowners which led to her father's twenty-two years of resistance. In particular, she gives a detailed description of the event in 1967 when the government threw her village out of their homes in their newly claimed and cultivated land in the

altiplano. As she says, "Those few days confirmed my hatred for those people. I saw why we said that *ladinos* were thieves, criminals, and liars" (106). Admitting that at that date "we didn't have the political clarity to unite with others and protest about our land," Menchú describes her father's awakening to consciousness of the systemic nature of the injustices and the need to form a union, an action that leads to his imprisonment for fourteen months (111). After a second imprisonment in 1977, he is forced to work underground, and Rigoberta herself begins traveling with him. From these events, Menchú tells of the community conscientization: "We began thinking, with the help of other friends, other *campeneros,* that our enemies were not only the landowners who lived near us . . . We started thinking about the roots of the problem and came to the conclusion that everything stemmed from the ownership of the land. The land was not in our hands" (116). At this point, too, the village learns not only the systemic causes of their problems but also learns how to form an organization to resist the government, the Peasant Unity Committee (CUC). As Rigoberta travels around to other villages, she also is shocked to learn of the degraded status of Indians in the minds of even the poorest *ladinos,* who tell her, "Yes, we're poor but we're not Indians" (119). At this point, she admits that she is only partially transformed: "I still hadn't reached the rewarding stage of participating fully, as an Indian first, then as a woman, a peasant, a Christian, in the struggle of all my people" (120). She still has two more aspects of full conversion to undergo—reflective awareness of several crucial distinctions, and then full commitment based on religious and human response to others.

The complex moral distinctions do not come easily to this young unsophisticated village girl. She spends two chapters telling the story of the "painful change in herself and her village" as they decide, after studying their situation and the Bible, that they are justified in using force in self-defence (Ch. 17-18). Beneath her summary of the methods of reasoning within her "base community" (as liberation theology calls it) lay her faith in Christ as resurrected and present Liberator: "For me, as a Christian, there is on important thing. That is the life of Christ . . . there was no other way of defending himself or Christ would have used it against his oppressors, against his enemies. He even gave his life. But Christ did not die, because generations and generations have followed him" (132-33). While this testimony seems to overlook the power of nonviolent resistance which many find in Christ's sermon on the mount, the testimony provides Menchú with some justification for the use of force in defending the villages of the altiplano. She is forced, however, to place most of her rational arguments on examples of Judith, Moses, and David in the Hebrew scriptures. Her motivation in working out these distinctions is largely religious, for, as she says, "as Christians, we must create a Church of the poor . . . we feel it is the duty of Christians to create the kingdom of God on earth among our brothers" (133-34). But her consciousness raising does not stop at her new ability to make theological distinctions. She also becomes radicalized as a woman, especially after learning of the brutal butchering of her friend

Patrona Chona at the hands of a lustful son of a landowner (Ch. 20). She becomes more sophisticated economically when she learns by following her father's example of the need to organize the villages (Ch. 21) and the need to protest against the individualistic plans of the government for isolated family plots (Ch. 22). These new distinctions lead her in 1979 to join the CUC and to learn several native languages in addition to Spanish so that she can become an effective community organizer. The travel in her organizing work also teaches her to make distinctions among the "enemy" *ladinos*: one friend "taught me to think more clearly about some of my ideas which were wrong, like saying all *ladinos* are bad" (165). As she concludes, "So I learned many things with the *ladinos*, but most of all to understand our problem and the fact that we had to solve it ourselves" (167). All of these distinctions are part of her complex moral conversion which also includes, as the praxis-based theology of liberation requires, a commitment to action and to learn from action.

Menchú saves the most dramatic stage of her conscientization process for Chapters 24-34. In these chapters, she gives a realistic account of the violent effects of class and cultural warfare by the government against her family, her people, and especially against native women. She describes in brutal detail the torture and death of her brother, and then the fiery death of her father during the occupation of the Spanish Embassy in Guatemala City in 1980. In describing the torture of her brother, she emphasizes the disfigurement of his face: "They took my brother away, bleeding from different places. When they'd done with him, he didn't look like a person any more. His whole face was disfigured with beating, from striking against the stones, the tree-trunks; my brother was completely destroyed. . . . And his face, he couldn't see any more, they'd even forced stones into his eyes, my brother's eyes" (173-74). This evidence of the suffering on the face of her brother is repeated in her description of her mother's rape and torture: "On the third day of torture, they cut off her ears. They cut her whole body bit by bit. . . . From the pain, from the torture all over her body, disfigured and starving, my mother began to lose consciousness . . . Then they started raping her again. She was disfigured by those same officers" (198-99). When Rigoberta and her family are brought in to view her last agony, they notice that "her face was so disfigured, cut and infected." After her mother dies, Menchú notes with horror that "the soldiers stood over her and urinated in her mouth" (199). This emphasis on the suffering on the faces of her brother and mother, in the light of Levinas' notion of the ethical imperative derived from confrontation with the face of the other, especially the suffering other, suggests that here Menchú has reached the fullness of her moral, imaginative, and religious conversion. For, according to the theology of liberation, she has learned to see the divine Other embodied in the suffering others in her family, especially in their faces as they are dying in disfigurement. This vision of the divine Other in the suffering human other leads Menchú not to withdraw in fear but to commit herself with confidence to reach out to these others in solidarity.

This final conversion to commitment in solidarity includes four important dimensions. First, she learns from the funeral of her father to break through all boundaries of class and race: "People at all levels—poor, middle class, professional—all risked their lives by going to the funeral of the *companeros* from the Spanish embassy" (186). Second, she learns from the treatment and life of her mother to carry on her struggle for a radical change in the position of women in Guatemala, not only in cultural matters such as the fiestas but even more importantly within the resistance movement itself, where she uses her personal authority to teach the macho leaders some respect for women (Ch. 30-31). She also believes that the needs of the people take precedence over her personal happiness, thus leading her to postpone any thought of marriage until after the revolution (225). Thirdly, she learns the need for solidarity among all the various groups working for revolution. As she says in her account of the results of the 1980 agricultural strike: "We came to the conclusion that we had to form a united front" (231). This solidarity is expressed in the 31st of January Popular Front which encompassed six organizations in 1981, including the one to which she belongs, the Vincente Menchú Revolutionary Christians, named after her father. Finally, Menchú learns to live out her religious commitment with sophistication and hope in the face of exile. While recognizing the differences within "the Church of the rich" and "the Church of the poor" (234), she is convinced of her vocation as a leader "practicing with the people the light of the Gospel" (246). As she says on the concluding page of her testimony in words that indicate the deeply religious dimension of her conscientization, "I know that no one can take my Christian faith away from me . . . together we can build the people's Church, a true Church . . . I chose this as my contribution to the people's cause. . . . That is my cause" (246).

WORKS CITED

Beverley, John. "The Margin at the Center: On *Testimonio* (Testimonial Narrative)," in *De/colonizing the Subject: The Politics of Gender in Women's Autobiography*. Ed. Sidonia Smith and Julia Watson. Minneapolis: U. Minnesota P, 1992. 91-114.

Conn, Walter. *Christian Conversion*. New York: Paulist, 1986.

———, ed. *Conversion: Perspectives on Personal and Social Transformation*, New York: Alba House, 1978.

Gunn, Janet Varner. "A Window of Opportunity: An Ethics of Reading Third World Autobiography." *College Literature* 19 (1992): 162-70.

Haight, Roger. *An Alternative Vision: An Interprelation of Liberation Theology*. Ramsey, NJ: Paulist, 1985.

———. "Liberation Theology," in *The New Dictionary of Theology*, ed. Joseph Komanchak, Mary Collins, and Dermot A. Lane. Wilmington, DE: Glazier, 1987. 570-76.

Levinas, Emmanuel. *A Levinas Reader*. Oxford: Blackwell, 1989.

Menchú, Rigoberta. *I, Rigoberta Menchú: An Indian Woman in Guatemala*, ed. and intro. by Elisabeth Burgos-Debray, tr. by Ann Wright. London: Verso: 1984.

Oates, Wayne E. "Conversion: Sacred and Secular," in *Conversion,* 149-68.

Sommer, Doris. "No Secrets: Rigoberta's Guarded Truth." *Women's Studies* 20 (1991): 51-72.

Stoll, David. "*I, Rigoberta Menchú* and Human Rights Reporting in Guatemala," a presentation at the Western Humanities Institute Conference on 'Political Correctness" and Cultural Studies, at the University of California-Berkeley, 20 Oct. 1990.

Doris Sommer   (essay date 1998)

SOURCE: "Sacred Secrets: A Strategy for Survival," in *Women, Autobiography, Theory.* Madison, Wisconsin: University of Wisconsin Press, 1998, pp. 197-207.

[*In this essay, Sommer attempts to determine Menchú's actual relation to and participation in what she has written, based as much on what the author does not say as much as what she does.*]

Rigoberta Menchú's secrets astonished me when I read her autobiographical testimony over ten years ago. Secrets seemed then, as they do now, the most noteworthy and instructive feature of her book, however one judges the validity of the information or the authenticity of the informant. Why should she make so much of keeping secrets, I wondered, secrets that don't have any apparent military or strategic value? The book, after all, is a public denunciation of murderous Indian removal politics in Guatemala, an exposé in an ethnographic frame. Yet throughout, Rigoberta claims that she purposely withholds cultural information. Is she a witness to abuse as an authentic victim, or is she being coy on the witness stand? The difference is significant, even if we will see that the alternatives are irreducibly tangled: Either she is a vulnerable vehicle for truth beyond her control, revealing information that compromises and infuriates the government; or she is exercising control over apparently irrelevant information, perhaps to produce her own strategic version of truth.

In what follows, a reference to Nietzsche will help to negotiate the distance between telling and troping, between relevant and irrelevant data. Then, lessons from Enrique Dussel, Paul Ricoeur, and the shades of Church-affiliated victims of Guatemalan death squads can remind us that bearing witness has been a sacred responsibility throughout Christianity, a responsibility that is related both etymologically and historically to martyrdom. I will suggest that Rigoberta glosses those lessons in her performance of ethically responsible survival. Her techniques include maintaining the secrets that keep readers from knowing her too well. One conclusion to be drawn is that giving and getting information should respect the cultural differences of an exchange that can produce alliances, if we are careful not to collapse positions into single-minded programs. Like the rhetorical figure of metonymy, alliance is a relationship of contiguity, not of metaphoric identification. To shorten the distance between writer and readers is what autobiographies do, in the game of mutual displacements that Paul de Man described as defacement. This invites identifications that make both positions unstable and finally make one of them redundant. Rigoberta is too smart to prepare her own removal, in the logic of metaphoric evaporations of difference. Embattled Indians generally know that reductions are dangerous. Since the Conquest, *reducción* has been the name for violent pacification and for a defeated indigenous community controlled by Spanish masters.

SYMPATHY AND SURVEILLANCE

But first we might notice that the audible protests of silence are, of course, responses to anthropologist Elisabeth Burgos Debray's line of questioning. If she were not asking what we must take to be impertinent questions, the Quiché informant would logically have no reason to refuse answers. From the introduction to *Me llamo Rigoberta Menchú* (1983), we know that the testimonial is being mediated at several levels by Burgos, who records, edits and arranges the information, so that knowledge in this text announces its partiality. The book, in other words, does not presume any immediacy between the narrating "I" and the readerly "you." Nor does Rigoberta proffer intimacy when she claims authorship for the interviews that remain catalogued under the interrogator's name (Britton and Dworkin, 214). Yet some readers have preferred the illusion of immediacy, deriving perhaps from certain (autobiographical?) habits of reading that project a real and knowable person onto the persona we are hearing, despite being told that the recorded voice is synthesized and processed, and despite the repeated reminders that our access is limited. Could the ardent interest, and our best intentions towards the informant, amount to construing the text as a kind of artless "confession," like the ones that characterized surveillance techniques of nineteenth century colonizers? For a recent and typical case of violation by sentimentality, consider the editors of *Autobiographical Essays by Native American Writers* who insisted that their contributors reveal and publish intimate information. "While our presentation of autobiographies of contemporary Native American writers may seem to testify to the congeniality of the autobiographical form to Indians today, the reality is finally much more complex. Thus, a contributor . . . movingly wrote in a covering letter: 'You should realize that focusing so intently on oneself like that and blithering on about your own life and thoughts is very bad form for Indians.'" In response to the reticence, the editors proudly report that they persisted and prevailed (Swann and Krupat, ix). Yet another example are the African American women who increasingly bring their experience more plainly into focus. Barbara Smith explains that part of the process is calling attention to the pain and the personal costs of telling.[1]

Maybe empathy for an informant is a good feeling that covers over a controlling disposition, what Derrida calls "an inquisitorial insistence, an order, a petition. . . . To demand the narrative of the other, to extort it from him like a secretless secret" (87). The possibility should give us pause. Natives who remained incalculable, because they refused to tell secrets, obviously frustrated the controlling mechanisms of colonial states (Bhabha, 99).

Rigoberta probably appreciated and deployed the aggressively passive ruse of leaving the interrogator unsatisfied, while her sentimental readers have missed the point. She too manages to frustrate unabashed demands for calculable confessions. One such frustration is recorded in Dinesh D'Souza's tirade against institutionalizing her testimonial in a required curriculum at Stanford University. He would surely have preferred scientific information about genuine Guatemalan Indians, stable objects of investigation. Instead he gets a protean subject of multiple discourse in Indian disguise (D'Souza, 71-73). Some of us, no doubt, would dismiss his inquisitorial demand for knowable essences. But my concern here is that the demand lingers in what passes for sentimental interest and solidarity. Sympathetic readers can be as reluctant as is D'Souza to doubt the sincerity of a life-story; they are reluctant, as well, to question their own motives for requiring intimate truth, even when they know that the life in their hands is a mediated text.

"What draws the reader to the novel," in Walter Benjamin's scornful observation, "is the hope of warming his shivering life with a death he reads about" (101). But novels seem unobliging today, given the sheer intellectual difficulty of important Latin American fiction since the "Boom" of the 1960s and 70s. Testimonials promise more warmth. In a strong case for the genre's distinctiveness, John Beverley argued that *testimonio* is poised *against* literature: that its collective denunciatory tone distinguishes testimony from the personal development narrative of standard autobiography. Testimonio allegedly erases the tracks of an elitist author who is mediating the narrative. This allows for a "fraternal or sororal" complicity between narrator and reader, in other words, a tighter bond of intimacy than is possible in manipulative and evasive narrative fiction (Beverley, 77, and generally chapters 4 and 5). I have already argued that the projections of presence and truth are less than generous here (Sommer, "Rigoberta's"). Empathy is hardly an ethical feeling, despite the enthusiasm for identifying with Others among some political activists, including some first-world feminists (See for example, Cornell, 97). In effect, the projections of intimacy invite appropriations once the stretch is shortened between writer and reader, in disregard of the text's rhetorical (decidedly fictional) performance of a politically safe distance. To close in on Rigoberta might be to threaten her authority and leadership.

The very fact that I am able to call self-critical attention to our culture-bound appetites is a sign that I have been reading Rigoberta. When I began, her forthright refusals to satisfy my interest woke me to the possibility that she was cultivating my interest so that I could feel the rebuff. Concerns about the text's authenticity—that is, transparency—seemed beside the point, as I began to appreciate its artful manipulations. Perhaps the informant was being more active and strategic than our essentialist notions of authenticity have allowed. The possibility triggered memories of other books that had refused intimacy, perhaps more subtly, so that their distancing tropes came into focus only then, as corollaries to Rigoberta's lesson. The unyielding tropes add up to a rhetoric of particularism that cautions privileged readers against easy appropriations of Otherness into manageable universal categories. Among those rhetorical moves, I remembered El Inca Garcilaso's introductory *Advertencias* about the difficulties of the Peruvian language, Juan Francisco Manzano's refusal to detail the humiliating scenes of Cuban slavery, "Jesusa Palancares's gruff dismissal of her interlocutor, and Toni Morrison's distinction between love and the demand for intimate confession, in *Beloved*. There were white authors, too, who theatricalized their incompetence to narrate colored lives across social asymmetries and cultural barriers: Cirilo Villaverde's *Cecila Valdés* (1882) and Cortázar's "The Pursuer" (1959); later, Vargas Llosa's *The Storyteller* (1987) would fit into the cluster of texts I now read more cautiously.

Why did we assume that our interest in the "Others" was reciprocated? Edward Said asked that question, at the public lecture, as he interrupted a sympathetic colleague who was asking how we could know the Orient better, and avoid the errors decried in *Orientalism*. Did we imagine that the desire was mutual, or that we were irresistible? Could we consider that the sympathy was not bilateral in an asymmetrical world? This possibility of non-requited interest is one lesson to be learned from the kind of textual resistance Rigoberta performs. The problems raised by presuming anything less than political inequality and cultural difference are both episotemological and ethical, problems that ring familiar now that postmodern skepticism has lowered the volume on masterly discourses in order to hear some competing, even incommensurate, voices.

Masterful reading is what some particularist narrators try to baffle. One is Rigoberta Menchú whose secrets can help to cordon off curious and controlling readers from the vulnerable objects of their attention. Secrecy is a safeguard to freedom, Emmanuel Levinas argues against Hegel who ridiculed it; it is the inviolable core of human subjectivity that makes interaction a matter of choice rather than rational necessity. "Only starting from this secrecy is the pluralism of society possible" (78-79). Menchú will repeat with Villaverde's contraband dealer in slaves, "Not everything is meant to be said" (Villaverde, 112). But her discretion is more subtle than his, and far less corrupt, since it is entirely possible that she is hiding very little. Perhaps, as I suggested, Menchú's audible silences and her wordy refusals to talk are calculated, not to cut short our curiosity, but to incite it, so that we feel our differences as frustrated intimacies.

STAGED STANDOFFS

What I find so noteworthy about Rigoberta's testimonial, in contrast to most autobiographies, is that her refusals remain on the page after the editing is done. The refusals say, in effect, this document is a screen, in the double sense that Henri Lefebvre (78) uses the term: something that shows and that also covers up. From the beginning, the narrator tells us very clearly that she is not going to tell: "Indians have been very careful not to disclose any details of their communities" (*I, Rigoberta*, 9; in Spanish, 42). They are largely "public" secrets, known to the Quichés and kept from us in a gesture of self-preservation. "They are told that the Spaniards dishonoured our ancestors' finest sons. . . . And it is to honour these humble people that we must keep our secrets. And no-one except we Indians must know" (13; in Spanish, 50. See also 17, 20, 59, 67, 69, 84, 125, 170, 188; in Spanish, 55, 60, 118, 131, 133, 155, 212, 275, 299). By some editorial or joint decision, the very last words of the testimonial are, "I'm still keeping secret what I think no-one should know. Not even anthropologists or intellectuals, no matter how many books they have, can find out all our secrets" (247; in Spanish, 377).

Readers have generally noticed the inevitable interference of the ethnographer in these transcriptions. And they have been predictably critical or disappointed at the loss of immediacy, perhaps with a resentment born of ardor that chafes at insulating frames that contain explosive life-stories. Most disturbing to many readers is probably Burgos Debray's Introduction, where she presumes to have shared intimacy and solidarity with Rigoberta as they shared nostalgic plates of black beans in Paris. Almost unremarked, however, but far more remarkable for being unanticipated, are the repeated and deliberate signs of asymmetry throughout Rigoberta's testimony. Either the informant, the scribe, or both were determined to keep a series of admonitions in the published text. Uncooperative gestures are probably typical of ethnographic interrogations, but they are generally deleted from the scientific reports as insignificant "noise." Here, however, scientific curiosity turns out to be impertinent, a conclusion we draw from the refusal to respond. And if she did not refuse decidedly and repeatedly, we might mistake her active negation for a passive inability. This contrast between the possibility of speech and an impossibility imposed by others is what Jean-François Lyotard adapts from Aristotle in order to distinguish between a plaintiff (who can attest to a crime against her) and a victim (who is silenced by her fear or is dismissed as irrelevant).[2] Are we being warned, by Rigoberta's active refusal, that curiosity may be an impulse to warm our cold bodies with the fuel of passionate and violated lives? Ironically, in the backhanded logic of metaleptic effects, our curiosity—the cause of Rigoberta's resistance—is a product of her performance. I wonder if she staged even more questions than she was asked, so that she could perform more refusals; this seductive possibility doesn't occur to Lyotard's legal logic.[3] Without refusing our putative interest often enough for us to notice, she could hardly have exercised the uncooperative control that turns a potentially humiliating scene of interrogation into an opportunity for self-authorization.

Nevertheless, the almost 400 pages of the original book are full of information. About herself, her community, traditional practices, the armed struggle, strategic decisions. Therefore, a reader may wonder why her final statement insists, for a last and conclusive time, that we "cannot know" her secrets. Why is so much attention being called to our insufficiency as readers? Does it mean that the knowledge is impossible or that it is forbidden? Is she saying that we are *incapable* of knowing, or that we *ought* not to know? My line of questioning is not entirely original, of course. It echoes the quandary that Nietzsche posed in a now famous posthumous work about the nature of language. If I repeat his dilemma here it is to highlight a particular textual strategy in Rigoberta's testimonial, to notice it and to respect its results.

Nietzsche begins his consideration of the possible truth value of language, including philosophical language that makes claims to truth, by wondering what our general criteria for validity are. The first, he says, is the identity principle: "We are unable to affirm and to deny one and the same thing." But he adds immediately, "this is a subjective empirical law, not the expression of any 'necessity' but only an inability. . . . The proposition therefore contains no criterion of truth, but an imperative concerning that which should count as true" (quoted in de Man, *Allegories*, 119-20). In other words, the identity principle, which at least from Aristotle on has been the ground for logical claims to truth, merely *presupposes* that A equals A as an ethical restriction; it is a necessary beginning, a fiction that constructs a ground for systematic philosophical thinking. If the claims of philosophy are based on a fiction, there can evidently be no categorical difference between one kind of writing and another, between logic and literature. It is rather a difference of degree in self-consciousness. In literature, tropes are obviously constructed and fictional, while non-literary texts presume their tropes to be true. Yet language, Nietzsche argues, cannot absolutely affirm anything, without acknowledging that any affirmation is based on a collective lie. He concludes from this exposition that the difference between truth and fiction, philosophy and literature, constatives and performatives, philosophical persuasion and literary troping is finally undecidable.

How then are we to take Rigoberta's protestations of silence as she continues to talk? Are there really many secrets that she is not divulging, in which case her restraint would be true and real? Or is she performing a kind of rhetorical, fictional, seduction in which she lets the fringe of a hidden text show in order to tease us into thinking that the fabric must be extraordinarily complicated and beautiful, even though there may not be much more than fringe to show? If we happen not to be anthropologists, how passionately interested does she imagine the reader to be in her ancestral secrets? Yet her narrative makes this very assumption, and therefore piques a curiosity that may not have pre-existed her resistance. That is why it may be useful to notice that the refusal is performative; as I said, it constructs metaleptically the apparent cause of the refusal: our craving to know. Before she denies us the satisfaction of learning her secrets we may not be aware of any desire to grasp them. Another way of posing the alternatives is to ask whether she is withholding her secrets because we are so different and would understand them only imperfectly; or whether we should not know them for ethical reasons, because our knowledge would lead to power over her community.

Rigoberta continues to publicly perform this kind of silence, almost like a leitmotif. At an address delivered at the Political Forum of Harvard University, in April of 1994, she opened with some literally incomprehensible words for her audience. It was an incantatory flow pronounced between smiling lips under friendly eyes, words which a student asked her to translate during the question period. "No," was her polite response, "I cannot translate them." They were a formal and formulaic greeting in Quiché, she said, and they would lose their poetic quality in a different rendering. This speech act was not hostile, as I said; but it was distancing.

As in the case of Nietzsche's meditation on the nature of rhetoric in general, the choice between ethics and epistemology is undecidable. Because even if her own explicit rationale is the non-empirical, ethical rationale (claiming that we should not know the secrets because of the particular power attached to the stories we tell about ourselves) she suggests another reason. It is the degree of our foreignness, our cultural difference that would make her secrets incomprehensible to the outsider. We could never know them as she does, because we would inevitably force her secrets into our framework. "Theologians have come and observed us," for example, "and have drawn a false impression of the Indian world" (9, translation adjusted; in Spanish, 42).

DOUBLE DUTY

Guatemalan Indians have a long history of being read wrong by outsiders who speak European languages. From the sixteenth century to the present, the Maya have been "Surviving Conquest," as a recent demographic analysis puts it. If some readers perceive a certain ahistorical inflection in Rigoberta's sense that the Spanish conquest is an event of the recent past, George Lovell might corroborate her sense of continuity in this new period of cultural genocide. "Viewed in historical perspective, it is disconcerting to think how much the twentieth century resembles the sixteenth, for the parallels between cycles of conquest hundreds of years apart are striking. Model villages are designed to serve similar purposes as colonial congregaciones—to function as the institutional means by which one culture seeks to reshape the ways and conventions of another, to operate as authoritarian mechanisms of resettlement, indoctrination, and control" (47; see also Manz). The less comprehension in/by Spanish, the better; it is the language that the enemy uses to conquer differences. For an Indian, to learn Spanish can amount to passing over to the other side, to the Ladinos, which simply means "Latin" or Spanish speakers. "My father used to call them `ladinized Indians,' . . . because they act like *ladinos,* bad *ladinos*" (Menchú, *I, Rigoberta,* 24; in Spanish, 66). This kind of caution has managed to preserve Mayan cultural continuities, and the political solidarity it can activate, beyond the social scientific paradigms that have tried to account for it.[4]

All the theologians could not have been equally insensitive, however. Rigoberta, after all, became a Christian catechist devoted to the socially engaged spirit of liberation theology; and she continued to believe in a God who inspires political commitment, even after marxist comrades objected. Those objections surely underlined her determination to keep an autonomous distance from allies. Testimony itself, the very kind of juridically oriented narrative that she produces for us to read, is a Christian's obligation, as Paul Ricoeur reminds us. He explains that from the moment God appeared directly to human beings, testimony has implied an investment of absolute value in historical, contingent, events (Ricoeur, 119). The Old Testament prophets had prepared the connection, with their divine intuitions of God's will. But it was the New Testament, where eternal truth irrupts into human history, that the juridical act of bearing witness obliged even average people to confront a defensive and punitive world (Ricoeur, 134). "When the test of conviction becomes the price of life, the witness changes his name; he is called a martyr. . . . *Martus* in Greek means witness" (Ricoeur, 129).

The root word also grounds Enrique Dussel's project to Latin Americanize ethical philosophy by way of lessons from theology of liberation: "He who opens himself to the other, is with him, and testifies to him. And that means *martyr*; he who 'testifies' to the other is a martyr. Because, before murdering the Other, totality will assassinate the one who denounced its sin against Otherness" (Dussel and Guillot, 29). One limitation of European, basically Levinasian, ethics, he objects, is that absolute and awe-inspiring Otherness leaves the philosopher paralyzed, too stunned and too cautious to do anything useful (Dussel and Guillot, 8-9). Another limitation is that in order to face Otherness, ethics turns its back to a long tradition of subject-centered ontology that has ravaged difference by reducing it to more of the same. For Levinas, in other words, to identify the Self *as* the subject of history would be self-serving. But, Dussel argues, if an inhospitable First World has always had its back turned to oneself, the discovery of Otherness at home is nothing less than liberating (Dussel and Guillot, 38). A Latin American ethics needs to be actively committed, not cautiously self-effacing. As a corollary, or rather as a precondition for activity, it needs to refocus the Levinasian asymmetry from this side of the relationship between colonial centers and colonized peripheries.

Gayatri Spivak used to quip that if the subaltern could speak, she would be something else (*Post-Colonial,* 158). But more recently and more reflectively in collaboration with subaltern historians, Spivak has appreciated the "subject-effects" of subaltern eloquence ("Introduction," 12). It is the eloquence of what might be called a genre of "speech-acts" that inverts the relationship between tenor and vehicle (just as Self and Other change places from the center to the sidelines) and recognizes the acts of organized resistance as a narrative speech. For Dussel and Guillot, too, violence is the language of a "subaltern" committed philosophy. Liberation means reconstituting the Alterity of the Other in a fallen world where Cain has already murdered Abel (Dussel and Guillot, 27), a violated and violent world. "If there is no reply to domination, nothing happens; but if a reply is made, the war begins" (Dussel and Guillot, 18). At the end of his essay, in a climax after which words are insufficient, he repeats, "The war begins" (43).

From the comments by Ricoeur and Dussel, it would seem that a commitment to absolute imperatives requires physical self-sacrifice, that the discourse of subalternity is written in blood and in the statistics of martyrdom. On the other hand, sacrificial responsibility can be finessed, somehow. Maybe an immobilized posture of awe before so much responsibility can keep philosophy out of the fray; or maybe a purely rhetorical self-defense can slip off the mantle of martyr that witnessing would dress on its vehicles. In terms of Rigoberta's personal comportment, to recall the apparently incommensurable difference between vulnerable testimony and coy control, either she accepts the traditional Christian robe, or she designs disguises.

But Ricoeur confounds the polarity by adding another, mediating, term: it is the incorrigibly compromising term of our fallible human languages. Charged with a communicative duty imposed by absolute truth, language cannot avoid humanizing, not to say debasing, the message by interpreting it. There is no help for it; even sacred testimony passes through the contingency of interpretation. So, Ricoeur concludes, the only possible philosophy of testimony is hermeneutics, an interpretation (143). Testimony is hermeneutical in a double sense: it both gives a content to be interpreted, and calls for an interpretation; it narrates facts, and it confesses a faith during the juridical moments that link history to eternity (Ricoeur, 142).

Rigoberta apparently appreciates the double duty of testifying: the message of liberation pulls in one (ideal) direction, and the (earthly) medium of political persuasion pulls in another. To confuse the two would be worse than simply foolish. It might be disastrous to mistake unconditional demands for justice with what she evidently senses as sentimental interest from interrogators and readers. Their offers of solidarity may not stop to distinguish doing good from feeling good. The double challenge for this Christian leader, as new and as beleaguered as Christ's first witnesses, is to serve truth in ways that make a difference in the world. Testimony to that truth and coyness about how to convey it turn out to be voices in counterpoint. If we cannot hear the complexity, perhaps the inability is simply that, as Nietzsche would remind us, rather than a sign that contradictions cannot exist.

"J'accuse" rings loudly throughout the text, between the provocative, and protective, pauses of information flow.

The pauses work in two directions, because it seems quite clear that Rigoberta's secrets are doubly strategic. They stop avid readers in their appropriative tracks, tracks that threaten to overstep the narrator's authority by assuming an unobstructed textual terrain. We have detoured here from the autobiographical meeting place where one particular life can become the potential experiences of others. Rigoberta Menchú's performance doesn't describe an isolated individual whom we can reproduce through readers who decide to pick her up. Her testimony is "not a personal story," as she makes clear from the first interview session; instead it is communal, grounded in collective memory and practices. The book grips the reader more than it gives. It demands responsibility more than it satisfies curiosity. An autobiography might not have stinted on giving the pleasure of vicarious fears and passions; but Rigoberta evidently understood that frustration has a political purpose. By stinting and explaining why, she can keep us ardently but respectfully engaged.

NOTES

[1] Smith, 158: "It seems overwhelming to break such a massive silence. Even more numbing, however, is the realization that so many of the women who will read this have not yet noticed us missing either from their reading matter, their politics, or their lives."

[2] Lyotard, #14: "Not to speak is part of the ability to speak, since ability is a possibility and a possibility implies something and its opposite. . . . To be able not to speak is not the same as not to be able to speak. The latter is a deprivation, the former a negation. (Aristotle, *De Interpretatione* 21 b 12-17; *Metaphysics* IV 1022 b 22ff.)"

[3] Lyotard, #26. "Silence can indicate my incompetence to hear, the lack of any event or relevant information to recount, the unworthiness of the witness, or a combination of these."

[4] See Nash, 9: "The rebellion attests to the extraordinary durability of distinctive cultures in Middle America. Anthropologists have attributed this persistence variously to indigenous withdrawal into zones of retreat, exploitation in the form of internal colonialism, and Catholic traditions imposed by the conquerors to encumber native groups with debts for religious celebrations. These earlier theories stressed one side or the other of the dominant-subordinate hierarchy, with those maintaining the essentialist position emphasizing primordial cultural characteristics and those arguing domination from above emphasizing that forced acculturation has conditioned indigenous responses. Structuralists attacked the functionalism of those emphasizing the rational basis for distinctive indigenous characteristics, while their opponents challenged economic determinists for failing to recognize the preconquest ideological constructs manifested across wide regions.

"Protagonists on both sides of this older debate have shown that the persistence of distinct beliefs and practices among indigenous populations of the Americas arises from internal resources and from pressures exerted by the dominant group. Current debates are taking into account the combined force of antagonistic but interpenetrating relationships between *indigenas* and *ladinos* as they generate and sustain ethnic diversity . . . By looking inward at 'narrative strategies for resisting terror' (Warren *The Violence Within: Cultural and Political Opposition in Divided Nations* Boulder, Westview 1993), evoking dialogue between ancient and present traditions (Gossen and Leventhal 1989), and assessing the economic opportunities that condition their survival, researchers are constructing a theory that recognizes both the structural imperatives of the colonial and postcolonial systems encapsulating indigenous peoples and their own search for a base from which to defend themselves and generate collective action."

FURTHER READING

Beverley, John. "The Real Thing (Our Rigoberta)." *Modern Language Quarterly*, Vol. 57, No. 2 (June 1996): 129-39.

Appraises Menchú's autobiography as *testimonio*.

Handley, George B. "'It's an Unbelievable Story': Testimony and Truth in the Work of Rosario Ferré and Rigoberta Menchú." *Violence, Silence, and Anger, Women's Writing as Transgression*, Dierdre Lashgari, ed., pp. 62-79. Charlottesville, Virginia: University Press of Virginia, 1995.

Compares and contrasts Menchú's and Ferré's writing as testimonial and historical narratives.

Hunsaker, Steven V. "Exceptional Representatives." *Revista/Review Interamericana*, Vol. XXIII, Nos. 1-2 (Spring/Summer 1993): 7-18.

Compares autobiographies of Harriet Jacobs and Rigoberta Menchú.

Kirkus Reviews. A review of *Crossing Borders: An Autobiography*. *Kirkus Reviews*, Vol. LXVI, No. 13 (July 1998): 951-52.

Summary of the contents.

Additional coverage of Menchú's life and career is contained in the following sources published by the Gale Group: *Contemporary Authors*, Vol. 175; *World Literature and Its Times.*

Tirso de Molina
1580-1648

(Born Gabriel Téllez) Spanish playwright.

INTRODUCTION

Tirso de Molina was one of the four most famous and revered playwrights of Spain's Golden Age. De Molina was a disciple of the first, most famous, and most prolific of these dramatists, Lope de Vega. Although he is supposed to have written nearly 400 plays, not all are assuredly his writings and today, less than 90 are extant. Because de Molina's plays range from the highly comic to the tragic and because he wrote as much to serve principle as to please an audience, comparisons to Shakespeare are common. De Molina's greatest contribution to both life and letters is Don Juan, the character of who first appeared in the very similar plays, *El Burlador de Sevilla y convidado di piedra* (1626; *The Trickster of Seville and the Stone Guest*) and *Tan largo me lo fidis* (1616; *You Give Me Such a Long Time*). Even if de Molina had written nothing else, or created no other character, Don Juan has been a staple of drama ever since, from Moliere's seventeenth-century play, *Dom Juan ou Le Festin de Pierre,* to Mozart's eighteenth-century opera, *Don Giovanni,* to late twentieth-century television's "Don Juan," Sam Malone, the barkeep from *Cheers.*

De Molina was born Gabriel Téllez in Madrid around 1580. His parentage is uncertain, but he was probably the illegitimate son of a duke, a status that might account for de Molina's complaints about his lack of social position, the injustice of certain social conventions, and his dislike of nobility and hierarchy. He studied at the universities of Alcalá and Guadalajara. In 1601 he joined the large and noble Mercedarian Order in which he held high office, winning prestige as a theologian and acting as the Order's chronicler. In 1613, he relocated to Toledo, becoming a friar, and later moved to Santo Domingo. In 1621, de Molina was travelled to Madrid, where he wrote a great many of his plays. He took part in the literary celebration in 1622 for San Isidro—presided over by Lope de Vega—but did not win any prizes for the poetry he submitted. In 1625, de Molina was banished from the Junta de Reformación for alleged obscenities and was transferred to a remote friary in Trujillo where he served as Prior for three years. He was told never to write further plays or poems and it appears he mostly followed this edict, since most of his plays appear to have been written from 1605-1625, the latter date being the year of his reprimand. At Trujillo, he served as official chronicler of the Order. During the thirties he was in Barcelona, Madrid, and Toledo, and was again banished to a friary in Soria where he became its prior from 1645-47. He is said to have written three to four hundred plays in his lifetime. He died in Almazán in 1648.

De Molina believed that the most successful way to write plays was to compose according to public taste. Next to Lope, de Molina is the most prolific of the playwrights of Spanish drama's Golden Age. Like most of Spain's playwrights, de Molina disliked needless restrictions and believed that the dramatist should have total control over his creations. In general, the plots in de Molina's plays are tightly constructed and intense, but when de Molina fails, the result is a plot that can be difficult to follow. Often stories involve manipulations of jealous lovers intent on dominating or deceiving their victims. His characters have tremendous three-dimensionality, frequently subject to psychological, social, and historical forces. While a moral undercurrent is common for the plays written and produced during the counter-reformation, de Molina added a secular element: a critique of decadent nobility, especially in the character of Don Juan, a nobleman described by the peasant, Batricio, as "an ill wind that blows no good." At their sharpest, de Molina's plays call into question the alliance between Spain's theological and social hierarchy. At other times, the plays concentrate solely on social hierarchies to demonstrate the leveling effect on inherited traditions and beliefs. *El burlador de Seville y convidado di piedra* tells the story of Don Juan, a nobleman of bad intent who seems to have little reason to live other than the pursuit of sexual pacification. Juan's seductions are performed for two reasons: his enjoyment of deceit and the delights of sex. After stabbing and killing the father of one of his conquests, Juan must face the ghost of the dead man and is pursued by him until Juan's eventual descent into hell. Juan's sins are less his crimes of passion than those of deceit and murder, sullying his status as a nobleman. In addition to *El Burlador de Sevilla y convidado di piedra,* de Molina's other famous plays are: *El condenado por desconfiado* (1635; *Damned for Despair,* 1986), praised by many as Spain's best religious play; *Le vergonzoso en palacio* (1624), a light comic piece about the adventures of a shy yet ambitious youth at court; and *La prudencia en la mujer* (1634; *Prudence in Women,* 1964), a historical play about the Queen Mother Doña Maria de Molina of the fourteenth century.

Some consider that de Molina's talent as a playwright was greater than that of his mentor, Lope de Vega. His agility with language and resourceful imagination was frequently coupled with his strong sense of irony. He was also a skillful craftsman of plot and comic situations. Although not as subtle as Lope in characterization, de Molina's characters possessed a psychological depth which lended to the sense of reality in his plays. Not only did de Molina create at least one character, Don Juan, who stands with the greatest characters of Shakespeare (Hamlet, Othello, Romeo), but de Molina could create bold female characters, as well. His plots are frequently battles of wits between male and female characters, the latter often winning by being more clever, daring, or ardent than her rivals. Perhaps de Molina might have surpassed all other playwrights if his religious profession and the government's unwanted interference had not undermined his confidence and effort. It is likely that his salacious spirit and wit caused a backlash in his own time, earning him wide acclaim and making *El Burlador de Seville* one of the most influential plays in history.

PRINCIPAL WORKS

Amazonas de las Indias [*The Amazons of the West Indies*] (drama)

El cobarde más valiente [*The Most Valient Coward*] (drama)

La joya de las montañas [*The Jewel of the Mountains*] (drama)

Siempre ayuda la verdad [*The Truth Always Helps*] (drama)

Trilogía de los Pizarros [*The Trilogy of the Pizarros*] (drama)

La vida de Santa María de cervellón [*The Life of Saint Mary of Cervellón*] (drama)

Los lagos de San Vicente [*The Miraculous Lakes of Saint Vincent*] (drama) 1607

El vergonzoso en palacio [*The Shy, Young Man at Court*] (drama) 1611

El colmenero divino [*The Divine Beekeeper*] (drama) 1609

Auto de Nuestra Señora del Rosario: la Madrina del Cielo [*The Play about Our Lady of the Rosary: The Heavenly Sponsor*] (drama) 1611

La mujer que manda en casa [*The Wife Who Rules the Roost*] (drama) 1612

No le arriendo la ganancia [*Much Good May It Do Him*] (drama) 1613

La ninfa del cielo [*The Heavenly Nymph*] (drama) 1613

La mejor espigader [*The Best Gleaner*] (drama) 1614

Santa Juana (drama) 1614

La villana de la Sagra [*The Peasant Girl of Sagra*] (drama) 1614

Los hermanos parecidos [*The Identical Brothers*] (drama) 1615

Don Gil de las calzas verdes [*Don Gil in Green Breeches*] (drama) 1615

Próspera fortuna de don Alvaro de Luna y adversa de Ruy López Dávalos [*The Prosperous Fortune of Alvaro de Luna and the Adverse Fortune of Ruy López Dávalos*] (drama) 1615

El condenado por desconfiado [*The Man Condemned for Lack of Faith*] (drama) 1615

Santo y sastre [*The Saint-Tailor*] (drama) 1615

Marta la piadosa [*Pious Martha*] (drama) 1615

Tan largo me lo fíais [*You Give Me Such a Long Time*] (drama) 1616

El caballero de Gracia [*The Gentleman of Grace*] (drama) 1620

La vida y muerte de Herodes [*The Life and Death of Herod*] (drama) 1620

Tanto es lo de más como lo de menos [*Enough is as Good as a Feast*] (drama) 1620

La romera de Santiago [*The Pilgrim of Santiago*] (drama) 1620

La villana de Vallecas [*The Peasant Girl of Vallecas*] (drama) 1620

Doña Beatriz de Silva (drama) 1621

Averígüelo, Vargas [*Find It Out, Vargas*] (drama) 1621

El mayor desengaño [*The Greatest Disillusionment*] (drama) 1621

Cigarrales de Toledo [*Country Houses of Toledo*] (drama) 1621

Adversa fortuna de don Alvaro de Luna [*The Adverse Fortune of Alvaro de Luna*] (drama) 1621

Antona García (drama) 1622

El malancólico [*The Melancholiac*] (drama) 1622

La prudencia en la mujer [*Prudence in a Woman*] (drama) 1622

La venganza de Tamar [*The Vengeance of Tamar*] (drama) 1623

Por el sótano y el torno [*Through Basement and Hatch*] (drama) 1623

Le vergonzoso en palacio (drama) 1624

Los balcones de Madrid [*The Balconies of Madrid*] (drama) 1625

Mari-Hernández, la gallega [*Mari-Hernández, the Galician*] (drama) 1625

Desde Toledo a Madrid [*From Toledo to Madrid*] (drama) 1625

El burlador de Sevilla y convidado de piedra [*The Trickster of Seville and the Stone Guest*] (drama) 1626

La prudencia en la mujer [*Prudence in Women*] (drama) 1634

Los amantes de Teruel [*The Lovers of Teruel*] (drama) 1635

El condenado por desconfiado [*Damned for Despair*] (drama) 1635

Deleitar aprovechando [*Pleasure with Profit*] (drama) 1632

Laberinto de Creta [*The Cretan Labyrinth*] (drama) 1636?

Las quinas de Portugal [*The Arms of Portugal*] (drama) 1638

CRITICISM

Melveena McKendrick (essay date 1989)

SOURCE: "Tirso de Molina and the Other Lopistas," *Theatre in Spain, 1490-1700*. Cambridge, England: Cambridge University Press, 1989, pp. 115-27.

[*McKendrick discusses honor, irony, and religion in de Molina's plays.*]

Tirso de Molina's world, by contrast with Lope's, is a world peopled by the unusual and the extreme, even bizarre. Tirso de Molina was the pseudonym of a Mercedarian monk called Fray Gabriel Téllez (*c.* 1584-1648).[1] The greatest of Lope's disciples, although their personal relationship was neither close nor particularly good, he was writing plays by the mid-1600s and within a few years had become one of Spain's major dramatists. He more or less dominated the Spanish stage along with Lope in the early 1620s. This period of maximum productivity coincided with his transfer to the house of his order in Madrid at a time of great intellectual activity. Góngora, Quevedo, the ageing Lope and the young Calderón all lived and wrote there and other dramatists gathered from elsewhere—Guillén de Castro from Valencia, Luis Vélez de Guevara and Mira de Amescua from Andalusia, Juan Ruiz de Alarcón from Mexico. Tirso entered with gusto into this exciting literary world with its academies and controversies, its friendships and its animosities. For him, sadly, it was not to last. On 6 March 1625 the Council of Castile's Committee for Reform declared his dramatic activities scandalous in a man of his calling and recommended that he be exiled to a remote monastery. Why Tirso was singled out for this treatment is not clear— there were other men of God involved in the theatre, including Lope who even as a priest more or less openly kept a mistress—and his own order seems not to have taken exception to his activities. Tirso himself thought envious fellow writers were responsible—he even implied that Lope was involved.[2] Whoever his enemies were, he somehow through their intervention managed to attract the animosity of Philip IV's first minister, the powerful Count-Duke of Olivares, who directly influenced the findings that virtually ended Tirso's dramatic career. He wrote few plays after his departure from Madrid.

It is not surprising that Tirso made enemies who saw insults or supposed insults to themselves in his plays, for he is a hard-hitting dramatist who tackled the social and political questions that interested most dramatists at the time in an unusually direct way. Technically all his plays are cast in the mould established by Lope and in the literary and moral controversies that surrounded the *comedia nueva* he was resolute in its defence. In *Los cigarrales de Toledo,* a framed miscellany in prose in which a group of lords and ladies entertain one another with stories and plays, he states that times change and inevitably bring with them legitimate changes in the way drama is written. The new genre is quite as praiseworthy and respectable as the old classical forms of drama, he claims, especially now that it has matured and improved, and contains nothing corrupting. On the contrary it delights and instructs simultaneously.

Tirso brought to the Golden-Age stage an intellectual turn of mind and a psychological range and penetration absent in Lope. He was interested in the extraordinary and possessed a greater tolerance and understanding of human oddity and variety than the other dramatists. Owing perhaps to his observer status, he had a broadness of outlook with regard to women's role in the scheme of things which Lope, for all his passionate interest in women and his sympathy with their problems, lacked. His particular contribution to the Spanish theatre's often vaunted feminism was to allow women something which other playwrights tend to overlook—Lope's women have courage, passion, daring and determination but Tirso's have intelligence. If Lope's women rise to the occasion, Tirso's create it. Their intelligence, furthermore, is invariably greater than that of their men. The heroes of Golden-Age plays habitually pale in comparison with their female counterparts, but in Tirso the discrepancy is striking. In his comedies of intrigue the often mind-boggling complexities of plot are, typically, the way the ingenious heroine contrives to get herself out of trouble and on to the happy-ever-after path. Except that Tirso's comic vision is not that complacent. The selfishness and ruthlessness exhibited by seemingly nice people in pursuit of their own ends are embedded in the humour of the plays like a gently gnawing toothache, and their endings have an astringency which stays with us and subtly subverts the plot's conventional unravelling.

The controlled complexity and ingenuity, the wit and unique sparkle of his comedies of intrigue have rightly led to his acknowledgment as a master of this genre which was so popular in seventeenth-century Spain. In *El vergonzoso en palacio* (*The Shy Man at Court*) one of the three main characters, the wayward, narcissistic Serafina, falls in love with a picture of herself dressed as a man, not recognizing it as her own. *Don Gil de las calzas verdes* (*Don Gil of the Green Breeches*) is a hilarious romp so complex that in the final scene, in spite of the fact that no real don Gil exists, no fewer than four turn up, all in green breeches. In *La celosa de sí misma* (*Jealous of Herself*), don Melchor falls so passionately in love with an unknown lady's hand at Mass that he refuses to go ahead with his arranged marriage to Magdalena, whose hand it is. Mysteriously depersonalized, the hand attracts him, openly attached to his betrothed's arm it loses its mystery and therefore its appeal: Tirso is almost certainly sending up the neo-platonic cult of an ideal love that leaves the body and reality behind in its pursuit of perfection. In *Marta la piadosa* (*Pious Martha*) the eponymous heroine pretends to have a religious vocation to avoid an unwelcome match and once out of the marriage stakes is allowed to roam around the streets at will— an ironic comment on contemporary attitudes to women. The quirkiness of Tirso's imagination, his fascination with role play and illusion, and his uncompromisingly realistic view of human nature will be immediately apparent. Human vanity and gullibility, the capacity of human beings to deceive themselves and others, the lack of honesty and realism in the way man and society conduct their affairs, are all strongly predicated in Tirso's comedies, but the attractive thing about them is that they never preach and rarely judge. Tirso manages to establish that perfect equilibrium between exposure and understanding which we expect of the best comedy, provoking an ambivalence of response that is entirely satisfying. We warm to Serafina's non-conformity but laugh at her self-preoccupation; the notion of falling in love with a hand appeals to our sense of the absurd, yet its attraction for a man faced with an arranged match strikes a chord with our belief in the legitimacy of romance; we can accept the logic of allowing a prospective nun to do as she likes, yet deplore the hypocrisy of the rationalizations used to prevent marriageable girls from doing the same.

The originality in these comedies lies in their ingenious or unusual treatment of themes and situations already introduced by Lope and this is true of much of Tirso's theatre. But he is not always successful in his use of established motifs, tending to pack too much too breathlessly into his plays which can then end up seeming rather hasty and predictable. His trump card was his ability to produce memorable characters. Thus his enthusiastic adoption of the type of the forceful woman produced heroines like *La gallega Mari-Hernández* (*Mari-Hernández from Galicia*) and *Antona García*. Mari-Hernández is a fusion of two distinct *comedia* types: the rumbustious country wench and the quick-witted miss who for the sake of love poses as a dashing gallant (a particular favourite of Tirso's). Hers is a double image: the hoyden looks into the mirror but it is the charming Galician aristocrat who gazes back and only Tirso could have successfully synthesized the two. Antona García, based on a woman who in 1476 conspired to oust the Portuguese from the Spanish city of Toro, is reminiscent of certain East European shot-putters with her herculean strength and fondness for horseplay. But in this dominating, idealistic peasant woman, compounded as she is of masculine and feminine qualities, Tirso almost succeeded in creating a masterpiece. He fails because, once again, he embarks on something more complex than he has time for—he allows his attention to be divided between historical theme and protagonist. Indeed Tirso often strikes one as a dramatist interested above all in characterization but trapped by historical accident within what was primarily a theatre of action.

His most memorable heroine and without a doubt the noblest female figure on the Spanish stage is María de Molina in the historical play *La prudencia en la mujer* (*Prudence in Woman*). María was regent of Castile during the minority of her son and Tirso portrays her fighting to protect her son's interests from unruly nobles who, because she is a woman, think she is easy prey. Here the combined emphasis on character, historical events and moral idealism works because all three are inseparable. María proves to be a supremely able ruler and Tirso with the utmost care draws her in her threefold majesty as perfect wife, queen and mother in an age and society dominated by men. It is a characterization both grand and nuanced. Tirso shows the human doubts and misgivings beneath the Queen's surface control and at the same time reveals in her an astuteness, a realism, an intelligent sense of strategy which nicely leaven her sublime virtue and nobility. In spite of the disadvantages of having a model protagonist, therefore, the play is entirely gripping and believable. It is essentially a *de regimine principum* in dramatic form in that it has direct relevance to the situation created in Spain by the death of Philip III in 1621.[3] The accession of a sixteen-year-old boy to the throne of the world's largest empire at a time when its future was seen by Spanish intellectuals to be in the balance understandably intensified Spanish concern with the concept of kingship and delegated authority. It is a concern that

informs many Spanish plays of the period. Tirso repeatedly chose to dramatize this preoccupation using woman rulers, though I doubt whether this has any particular significance in terms of sexual politics. The Empress Irene in *La república al revés* (*The Republic Turned Upside Down*) is a lesser María de Molina, the very model of the wise and just monarch by which her son Constantine is measured and found wanting; but in the character of the biblical Jezabel in *La mujer que manda en casa* (*The Woman who Rules the Roost*) he depicts a female tyrant. Tirso could readily conceive of woman as possessing the qualities necessary for leadership, but essentially he was tackling a contemporary preoccupation in a way which was congenial to him, which was theatrically attractive and which at the same time diplomatically deflected the plays' overt relevance to the Spanish king.

The importance of the seventeenth-century political background for our understanding of many Golden-Age plays is only gradually emerging, but it is already clear that Tirso was probably the most politicized of the Spanish dramatists of the age. In the years before his banishment he wrote a number of plays, *La prudencia en la mujer* and *Privar contra su gusto* (*The Reluctant Favourite*) amongst them, which are critical of government and corruption at court and which pointedly reflect contemporary misgivings about the new reign and its *éminence grise,* Olivares.[4] It has recently been persuasively argued that even his Pizarro trilogy, apparently fairly run-of-the-mill plays written between 1626 and 1629 while Tirso was head of the Mercedarian convent in Trujillo founded by Francisco Pizarro's daughter, is an audacious indictment of the failings of centralized government and delegated power.[5]

Some of the most successful of Tirso's plays are those which dramatize biblical events. *La mujer que manda en casa* is one of the most memorable, in spite of its structural weaknesses, because of the explosive and beguiling presence of its protagonist, Jezabel, an incarnation of the medieval Vice figure. The sexual relish she exudes, her unexpected inhibitions, her rages, her unquenchable belief in her own attractions, give the play a sexual charge which threatens at times to swamp its exemplary aspects. The best of these plays, however, is *La venganza de Tamar* (*Thamar's Vengeance*) which is closely based on the account in Samuel II of Thamar's rape by her half-brother Amnon and the latter's murder by her full brother Absalom. No hasty craftsmanship here—the play is an extremely accomplished piece of writing. Structurally Tirso makes three memorable additions to the familiar story. First is the charade scene where Amón, feigning to be mourning a lost love, persuades his unsuspecting sister to 'cure' him by acting the part of his mistress in a courtship scene. The sinister discrepancy between Tamar's understanding of the situation and the obsessed Amón's intentions in this play within the play is dramatically very potent. The flower scene in Act III where the peasant girl Laurela presents the brothers Amón, Adonías, Salomón and Absalón with a lily, a larkspur, a saxifrage and a narcissus is rich in dramatic irony and prophetic symbolism. While the pathetic hallucination scene where old King David, fearing for his beloved first son Amón who is in fact already dead, goes to embrace him, is extremely moving. The outstanding feature of the play, however, is its characterization. The disintegration of Amón's self-control, his disgust for Tamar after the rape and his outrageous shrugging off of responsibility after he threatens to rape her a second time when she is disguised as a peasant girl—a betrayal of his vow to behave that is crucial to our judgement of him and his father—these are magnificently portrayed. Explained as melancholy in terms of the medical theory of humours of the age, his obsession is in fact presented as an integral part of a characterization which is convincingly all of a piece. Absalón too—narcissistic, urbane, plausible and self-justifying—is drawn with care and consistency, while Tamar is superb in her anger and her scorn. Through her verbal quickness and the consistently witty and metaphorical language she uses to convey her predicament she dominates the play intellectually.

As the play proceeds, however, it is the old King who emerges as the tragic figure, torn between his love for his children and dismay at their behaviour, incapable any more of exercising either his judgement or his authority. We are left at the end with the poignant image of the once great and powerful king lamenting the murder of his beloved first son, a murder precipitated by his own partisan compulsion to put mercy before justice. The last line of his speech, invoking as it does the murderer Absalón, reminds the audience that the full course of this tragedy is not yet run.

It has been suggested that the action of *La venganza de Tamar* unfolds against a contemporary political background characterized by the upheavals that surrounded the succession of Philip IV to the throne of Spain in 1621; Tirso undoubtedly saw the death of Philip III as marking the end of stability and prosperity for Spain.[6] But a contemporary audience's interest would have been captured mainly by its powerful handling of a particularly gripping, familiar biblical story. The full-length plays on biblical and doctrinal themes by seventeenth-century Spanish dramatists constitute a significant proportion of the theatre's total output. Lope proved their popularity and other dramatists followed his example in providing the *corrales* with plays which could unequivocally boast of providing instruction along with entertainment. The theatre as a result became in a way a self-appointed instrument of the faith, providing an extra dimension to the religious life of Spain that at once reflected and stimulated popular devotion and afforded the theatre some protection from the attacks of ecclesiastical and moral reformers. This allowed churchmen to become enthusiastic patrons of the *corrales* and of course a significant number of dramatists were themselves men of God: of the three major playwrights both Lope and Calderón became playwright-priests, while Tirso was from the start of his career a friar. Technically the religious plays they wrote do not constitute a category apart. They were performed in the *corrales* before the usual audiences and were written to the familiar *comedia* pattern. They speak the standard language of love and honour, they are full of action, excitement and passion, with *graciosos* who provide touches of comedy, and they employ all the conventions and devices of the secular plays. They even use sexual excitement as a legitimate channel of moral instruction, as can be seen in Tirso's ***La mujer que manda en casa*** and Calderón's *La devoción de la cruz* (*Devotion to the Cross*). To all intents and purposes they take place in a world whose ethos is recognizably that of seventeenth-century Spain. The liberties they took with their material often attracted the opprobrium of the theatre's critics but their audiences, of course, loved them.

The *comedias de santos,* saints' plays, form a coherent group within this larger body. These normally portray, with considerable artistic licence, the conversion or martyrdom of famous figures from hagiographic history and legend, but the special dramatic potential inherent in the theme of conversion inspired bolder, freer creations as well. There are as a result a number of very striking plays which depict not only the conversion and salvation of criminals but conversely the descent into crime of men and women who have been travelling the road to sainthood. This chiastic movement between the two poles of criminality and sanctity baffled, even shocked commentators until A. A. Parker convincingly argued that the plays present problems which are in fact psychological and social (in the widest sense) rather than religious, and therefore essentially moral not dogmatic.[7] Banditry in the Golden-Age drama is unquestionably a means of personal self-assertion and not of sociopolitical reform as it tends to be in other literatures. The psychological and philosophical justification of the apparently melodramatic plots, Parker claimed, is to be found in the proverb 'The greatest sinners make the greatest saints', which implies that temperamental energy is a prerequisite both of great good and great evil, and in the aphorism 'Corruptio optimi pessima' which encapsulates the Thomist principle that evil follows from the inversion or distortion of good.

The most famous and the finest of these plays is Tirso's magnificently grim ***El condenado por desconfiado*** (***Damned for Despair***),[8] a complex play which seems to confirm Parker's interpretation of the psychology of the saints and bandits plays but which has in addition an important contemporary theological dimension. Tirso uses the psychology of sin and repentance to confront in an unusually direct way for the theatre two of the dominant religious problems of the age—the question of justification by faith or good works and the related question of free will and divine grace. Even within Catholicism there was such fierce disagreement between Jesuits and Dominicans over the relationship between free will and divine grace that in 1611 the exasperated Inquisition forbade the publication of any more works on the subject of grace. In 1607 the Pope's pronouncement that both sides were free to defend their opinions had been jubilantly greeted in Madrid with fireworks and bull-fights. When Tirso dramatized these problems some years later he was dealing not with some technical squabble over abstractions but with a topic of still passionate concern.

The play tells the story of two young men. Paulo is a hermit who to save his soul has spent ten years of penance and prayer in the wilderness. One night he has a terrifying nightmare of Hell which impels him to beg God to reveal his spiritual fate. Seeing his chance, the Devil appears in the guise of an angel to tell him that his fate will be that of a certain Enrico. Paulo complacently assumes that Enrico must be a saintly man and is horrified to discover that he is a dyed-in-the-wool villain. Overwhelmed by bitterness and despair he avenges himself on God by becoming a murderous bandit himself. Unable to believe that either Enrico or he himself can now be saved he meets a violent death at the hands of the law and goes unrepentant to Hell. What he did not know was that Enrico himself has never lost faith in the possibility of redemption; just before Enrico's execution his ailing father, whom he loves, respects and supports, prevails upon him to repent and he is saved. The Devil's ambiguous prophecy has proved both true and untrue; whether or not the Devil himself knew that Enrico would in fact escape his clutches remains an intriguing question mark.

The play's theological position *vis-à-vis* the *De auxiliis* controversy is elusive, perhaps intentionally so; in a way it compromises by emphasizing both faith and responsibility. Its practical message of faith, hope and charity, however, is clearly spelt out. So, too, are Paulo's sins: doubt in the efficacy of repentance, arrogance in trying to preempt his own fate and lack of charity in his judgement of Enrico. The power of the play comes from Tirso's masterly ability to give dramatic life to these ideas by showing us two men gambling for the highest stakes of all—eternity. Even for us now the play succeeds in making this issue as dramatically real and immediate as any threat of physical death; its impact on an audience of seventeenth-century believers is not difficult to imagine. The work's fascination lies partly in the startling outcome,[9] partly in the understandable uncertainty and confusion generated in Paulo, and in Act III in Enrico as well, by the difficulty of telling the real from the counterfeit, of distinguishing between false voices and true. There is fascination too in the contrary characters of Paulo and Enrico, both psychological adolescents, the one rebelling against an apparently unjust God, the other against all restraints upon his own will. Our reactions to each are complicated. In Paulo we recognize the rational intellectual, eager to know, incapable of blind faith and irrational hope, believing in fair and logical connections between crime and punishment, effort and reward. We understand the insecurity, self-doubt and almost pathological fear which lead to his calculating attempt to buy himself salvation and then erupt into the fateful nightmare. At the same time we lose patience with his meanness of spirit, his wilful over-interpretation of the Devil's prophecy,[10] his obdurate rejection of hope in the face of all encouragement and, above all, his refusal throughout to accept responsibility for himself and his fate. As for the presumptuous Enrico, we detest his mindless violence and bully-boy ways, but we respect his spiritual courage and are moved by his tenderness towards his father and most of all we admire his complete accep-

tance of responsibility for what happens to him. He recognizes that forgiveness is there, that it is up to him ask for it or not. Paulo, on the contrary, is guilty even at the end of a crucial failure of understanding: when assured that Enrico has been saved he sees no need to repent, confident that he will automatically share the same fate.

The abdication of control over his own destiny, together with his incapacity for love—love of God, his neighbour or himself—makes of Paulo the lesser man, for all Enrico's wickedness. Not only theologically but psychologically and dramatically as well, the play's outcome is entirely convincing and consistent. The fact that it leaves us harbouring more sympathy than we probably ought to feel for the pessimist, the man temperamentally incapable of faith, is a reflection of Tirso's tendency to create characters which overflow the containing ideas of the age. It is certainly the inadequate, anguished Paulo, unable to the last to see that the salvation he hungers for lies all along within his own grasp, who remains most vividly with us; the scene in Act III in which he dons his hermit's garb once more and desperately tries to persuade an impatient Enrico to repent has a quite extraordinary intensity.

As becomes its subject the play is sparely written. Dramatically and theatrically it operates entirely through the stark power of its parallel enactment of two conflicting ideologies and two opposed temperaments in a situation where Hell's flames await the one who has misunderstood the nature of redemption. There are virtually no concessions to public taste. Both men are in their different ways insufferable and apart from the stricken Anareto, Enrico's father and for him a sort of God-figure, the play is full of objectionable individuals. There is no real love interest—Enrico has a sharp but unsavoury moll who plays a minor role. Apart from a few intense speeches of Paulo's, more elaborate as becomes his intellectual and contemplative nature, the play's language is correspondingly pared down and direct. The work has as its structural basis an elegant symmetry, the symmetry of its protagonists, each with his servant, the symmetry of its supernatural adversaries—the Devil and the Good Shepherd—or inner voices, and the criss-cross symmetry of the saints and bandits theme. Its final theatrical effects are appropriately awe-inspiring and balanced: Enrico's soul soars heavenward supported by angels, Paulo disappears in flames through a trapdoor in the stage. The popularity of doctrinal drama in Spain was due in no small measure to such spectacular climaxes.[11]

The play that makes truly magnificent drama out of Christian ideas and reveals the eternal human preoccupations they contain was Spain's distinctive contribution to European drama. Tirso's most famous play *El burlador de Sevilla o El convidado de piedra* (*The Trickster of Seville or The Stone Guest*) is another masterly example.[12] Less openly dogmatic than *El condenado por desconfiado,* it is, for all that it gave Europe one of its legendary lovers, don Juan, another eschatological work. Here, however, presumption, bombast, and over-confidence end up not in Heaven but in Hell. The don Juan of popular imagination—compulsive, irresistible lover, intellectual and social rebel—is a composite figure, the result of many subsequent versions and variations. Tirso's original is very different—a brothel-creeper, a trickster, a predator, a betrayer of promises, friends and hospitality, a murderer even—who delights not in seducing women but, more sinisterly, in dishonouring and humiliating them. He wins their favours either by bribery or outright deception. He is not a rebel but a criminal within the system, exploiting his social privileges to further his own ends, believing in divine retribution but foolhardy enough to think that youth is an insurance against it. He prates about his honour when in fact he is everything that is dishonourable; he believes in the rules but regards himself as above them.

As the alternative titles of the play indicate, the work has two main strands which converge in don Juan's consignment to Hell: that of the trickster and that of the stone guest. We are shown four of don Juan's sexual japes. He makes love to the Duchess Isabela in the King's palace by pretending to be her fiancé; he seduces a fishergirl, Tisbea, under solemn promise of marriage (regarded as binding by the conventions of the theatre); he tries to take his best friend's place in his mistress doña Ana's bed when the lovers arrange a tryst to consummate their passion, and finally he desecrates a sacrament by seducing the bride, Aminta, on her wedding night under promise of marriage to himself—'the choicest trick of all'. This essentially episodic plot is given cohesion and sustained tension by don Juan's obliviousness to the gravity of his actions. His catchphrase whenever he is warned that he will one day be called to account for his crimes, 'Tan largo me lo fiáis' ('You certainly allow me extended credit'—*fianza* being a financial and legal term meaning credit or bailbond) becomes the play's leitmotif, reminding us that while don Juan thinks time is on his side (penance, he thinks, is for the infirm and the aged) it is in fact rushing him onwards towards his doom. The time bomb is triggered when don Juan scornfully invites to dinner the sepulchral statue of doña Ana's father, don Gonzalo, killed while defending his daughter from don Juan's predations. That night a thundering on the door announces the arrival of the terrifying guest, who sits at the table but remains silent in the face of don Juan's flippant bravado and his servant Catalinón's hysterical attempts at conversation. Only when he and don Juan are left alone does he speak, to invite don Juan to dine with him in return the following night in his chapel and only after the statue has left does don Juan collapse into terror. Persuading himself that it was all a figment of his imagination and that not to turn up the following night would be a sign of cowardice, don Juan decides to go. After a meal of vipers and scorpions, vinegar and gall, during which don Juan remains defiant to the end, the statue offers don Juan his outstretched hand. He takes it, only to be fatally overpowered by its burning, crushing grip, refused the absolution he begs for and swallowed up into the tomb, never to re-emerge. As he disappears, the statue booms out, 'This is God's justice: as man sows therefore shall he reap.'

While Tirso took don Juan's catchphrase and the idea of the stone guest from oral tradition (the exchange of invitations between a living man and a corpse belongs to European folklore),[13] don Juan was his own creation. Tirso's conception of the character has a moral and ethical emphasis absent from don Juan the myth figure, symbol of sexual energy and individualistic self-assertion. There is undoubtedly an incontrovertible fascination in don Juan's brazen recklessness in the play, in his refusal of fear in the face of the supernatural, in his sense of himself as archetypal man; when he refuses to let Isabela light a lamp to see his face and she cries out in alarm '¿Quién eres, hombre?' ('Who are you, man?'), his answer is 'Un hombre sin nombre' ('A man without a name?'). And herein the seeds of the myth lie. Tirso's don Juan, however, as bringer of chaos and confusion, with his sinister arrogance, his delight in power and control, his cynicism and slippery duplicity, assumes an aura that is more than human. When he appears in Aminta's bedroom and she remonstrates '¿En mi cuarto a estas horas?' ('In my bedroom at this hour?'), he replies 'Éstas son las horas mías' ('These hours are mine'). Night is his element; it is no coincidence that the play opens in the dark and that, like some earlier Count Dracula, don Juan resists the light. It is not only we who catch a whiff of the Devil: described by his uncle as a snake—the Devil's symbol—he is explicitly called Lucifer by that man of judgement and conscience, his servant Catalinón, when he commiserates with the wretched Aminta. Defiant to the end, he is greater in death than in life; it is in defeat that he commands our admiration. He is one of the few Golden-Age characters who swamp the action that contains them. He is too big for the play and hence has had to leave it behind.

His ultimate sin is Lucifer's own—he challenges God himself, unaware that he is playing with hell-fire. Fire consequently provides the play's dominant imagery, linking as it does the ideas of sexual lust and destruction. Don Juan uses vocabulary of fire to describe not only his passions but his contempt for the world—'que el mundo se abrase y queme' ('Let the world burn and go up in flames')—and significantly he uses the same words in reverse when he is crushed by the statue—'¡Que me quemo! ¡Que me abraso!' ('I am in flames! I burn!'). When he disappears the whole chapel goes up in flames; the destroyer is destroyed, the consumer consumed; Hell has claimed its own. It is a cataclysmic ending to a cataclysmic struggle. Don Juan has defied God's law as well as man's, pitting the power of youth and noble birth against the power of time and divine retribution. He has scoffed at death and it is therefore a dead man who calls in the debts he thought he could pay at his own convenience. The relationships he has violated are, with a little manoueuvring and papering over the cracks, re-established in a socially acceptable way. But there is no complacency in this ending. Few characters emerge with honour from the events the play portrays, and peasantry and aristocracy alike are depicted with a pervasive irony.

This gives the play a unity of tone and vision which, together with the themes of deception and deferred payment, and the metaphors of the bailbond, fire and personified death, knits the four episodes into a dramatic whole. The work has not the structural perfection of *El condenado por desconfiado*. Of the women, the proud self-assertive Tisbea is the only one in whom any dramatic conflict takes place, and even so the thematic parallelism between her character and don Juan's—she delights in making men suffer as he does women—is never developed. Once more we see Tirso's imagination straining against the discipline of the *comedia* form. For all this, the work is a magnificent achievement, thematically and poetically tightly coherent, theatrically stunning, with a larger than life protagonist of extraordinary potency who was to step out of the work and capture the imagination of the world in a way unrivalled by any other dramatic creation. In consigning don Juan to Hell, Tirso ironically gave him the gift of immortality: the theologian in Tirso would have disapproved but the artist would certainly have rejoiced.

Tirso is the only seventeenth-century dramatist who compares with Lope and Calderón in terms both of sustained achievement and outstandingly memorable individual plays. Distinctive as their typical creations are, they habitually combine theatrical impact, thematic weight and mastery of language in a way not matched consistently by any other dramatist. Nonetheless, Lope's lessons were successfully applied and developed by a number of other gifted dramatists capable of producing plays of the first order. It must be emphasized that the drama during Lope's theatrical hegemony did not stand still. Not only was there a general move, led by Lope himself, towards greater artistic control, but there were as the years went by certain developments from which Lope remained aloof: a marked growth in the satirical content of plays, and the visible influence on some dramatists (not Tirso) of the complex, Latinate language of Góngora's major poetic works, the *Fábula de Polifemo y Galatea* (1613) and the *Soledades* (1614). There was a certain tendency, too, to sensationalism, exaggeration and stylization, a move away from realism into the fantastic and mannered. Satire apart, Lope's followers were walking the path that would lead to Calderón.

NOTES

[1] See David H. Darst, *The Comic Art of Tirso de Molina* (Chapel Hill, 1974); I. T. Agheana, *The Situational Drama of Tirso de Molina* (New York, 1972); Ruth L. Kennedy, *Studies in Tirso de Molina, I: The Dramatist and his Competitors, 1620-26* (Chapel Hill, 1974); I. L. McClelland, *Tirso de Molina: Studies in Dramatic Realism* (Liverpool, 1948); S. Maurel, *L'univers dramatique de Tirso de Molina* (Poitiers, 1971); Henry W. Sullivan, *Tirso de Molina and the Drama of the Counter Reformation* (Amsterdam, 1976); and Margaret Wilson, *Tirso de Molina* (Boston, 1977).

[2] In his *Los cigarrales de Toledo* and in a scene interpolated for the purpose in his play *Antona García.*

[3] See Ruth L. Kennedy, '*La prudencia en la mujer* and the Ambient that Brought it Forth', *Publications of the Modern Languages Association,* 63 (1948), 1131-90.

[4] J. C. J. Metford, 'Tirso de Molina and the Conde-Duque de Olivares', *BHS,* 36 (1959), 15-27; and Ruth L. Kennedy, 'La perspectiva política de

Tirso en *Privar contra su gusto,* y la de sus comedias posteriores', *Homenaje a Tirso de Molina* (Revista Estudios, Madrid, 1981), 199-238.

[5] Marie Gleeson Ó Tuathaigh, 'Tirso's Pizarro Trilogy: A Case of Sycophancy or Lèse-Majesty?', *BCom,* 38 (1986), 63-82.

[6] See A. K. G. Paterson (ed.), *La venganza de Tamar* (Cambridge, 1969), 28.

[7] In an essay first published in Spain in 1949, republished as 'Bandits and Saints in the Spanish Drama of the Golden Age', *Critical Studies of Calderón's Comedias,* ed. J. E. Varey, vol. 19 of *The Comedias de Calderón,* ed. D. W. Cruickshank and J. E. Varey (London, 1973), 151-68. See also Melveena McKendrick, 'The *bandolera* of Golden-Age drama: a symbol of feminist revolt', *Critical Studies of Calderón's Comedias,* 169-90.

[8] Authorship has been disputed but the play is now generally accepted as Tirso's. For the background to the play, see Daniel Rogers' introduction to his edition (Oxford, 1974).

[9] Tirso anticipates the audience's surprise, referring them at the end to two theological sources for the events he describes.

[10] Paulo consistently holds that what the 'angel' said was that if Enrico were damned he would also be damned, whereas if Enrico were saved then that would be his fate too. This is in fact his own reading of the Devil's words, born, like the Devil's appearance itself, of his own obsession.

[11] In addition to Parker's article, among the many studies of the play are I. L. McClelland, *Tirso de Molina: Studies in Dramatic Realism;* C. V. Aubrun, 'La comédie doctrinale et ses histoires de brigands. *El condenado por desconfiado',* *BHisp,* 59 (1957), 137-51; T. E. May, *El condenado por desconfiado.* I. The enigmas. II. Anareto', *BHS,* 35 (1958), 138-56; C. A. Pérez, 'Verosimilitud psicológica de *El condenado por desconfiado',* *Hispanófila,* 27 (1969), 1-21.

[12] The play has a complicated textual history and may not in fact be Tirso's although it is generally accepted as his. For a discussion of the play and bibliography see Daniel Rogers, *Tirso de Molina: El burlador de Sevilla,* Critical Guides to Spanish Texts (London, 1977).

[13] See Dorothy McKay, *The Double Invitation and the Legend of Don Juan* (Stanford and London, 1943).

Alan K. G. Paterson   (essay date 1993)

SOURCE: "Tirso de Molina and the Androgyne: *El Aquiles* and *La dama del olivar,*" in *Bulletin of Hispanic Studies,* Vol. LXX, No. 1, January, 1993, pp. 105-14.

[*Paterson assesses sexual dichotomy as evidenced by cross-dressing and other devices in* El Aquiles *and* La dama del olivar.]

Tirso de Molina's play **El Aquiles** has two memorable transformations. In one, Ulises, reluctant to leave Penelope to serve with his Greek allies against Troy, feigns madness. 'Medio desnudo y loco', he associates with the archetype of fury, Hercules in the shirt of Nessus. From the poison of the Centaur, administered by Deyanira, he passes to the Minotaur, conceived in bestial intercourse with Pasiphaë. He offers mocking condolences to her husband Minos and creates a playful, bitter pun between 'cama' and 'toro'. In his absence, he predicts, his own bull-bed will notoriously confirm the etymology when Penélope consumates her adulterous desire:

¿Hércules está en camisa?
Deyanira le pegó
la ponzoña del Centauro.
Creta encierre el Minotauro
que Pasifé le parió;
pobre Minos, ¿qué dolor
de cabeza os atormenta?
Toro se llama la cama
del matrimonio en latín,
etimología ruin
sacará de ella la fama;
díganlo los adivinos
mientras yo mi ausencia lloro, . . .

(1909)[1]

Other quick-changes follow. Ulises plays both the *verdugo* and the criminal he flogs, the one publicizing the sentence passed on absent husbands careless of their honour, the other receiving the imagined lashes. Then he enters scattering salt, first yoking two characters to an imagined plough and then with spade digging the salt into the ground, so sterilizing his house to ensure that there will be no fruit to harvest while he is away. The series of transformations is handled to effect. On the one hand, the madness has method to it ('locura cautelosa' he calls it), to deceive those who would deprive him of the domestic bliss of wife and child. On the other, the make-believe gives voice to another and opposed set of feelings expressed in images of disturbed sexuality: a male fear of the female's animal lust and his intent to sterilize her unlawful desire. It is this other self, the misogynistic Ulises, revealed in acted madness, who later will determine that Aquiles leave the effeminate pleasures of love for the duties of war. The transformation is a prelude, too, to a second and more dangerous one that provides the play's basic narrative: that is the motif of Aquiles disguised as a woman. From Tirso's exploitation of male to female cross-dressing in *El Aquiles,* I will move to the general notion of androgyny in his work, whence to *La dama del olivar* in an attempt to locate an origin for variants of the androgyne in his theatre.

Female to male cross-dressing was of course stock dramatic business in the *comedia. La mujer vestida de hombre* no doubt offered the opportunity to expose basic issues about female status. But instances of male to female transformations do not come readily to mind in the *comedia.* The contrast between the frequency of female transvestite roles and infrequency of the male equivalent is enough to suggest a censoring mechanism in the anthropology of that society; maleness implied an essential security (legal, civil, religious) which was not to be exposed to enquiry on the public forum of the stage. (The case-history of the Madrid *esterero* who dressed as a female in his amateur theatrical group reminds us that

male cross-dressing for entertainment's sake caused authorities to take offence.)[2] As so often, Tirso de Molina proves the exception, for *El Aquiles* not only gives a rare example of *el hombre vestido de mujer,* but through its central transvestite role the play enters with a rare audacity into matters of bisexuality and the semiotics of gender. As a quick-change role, Aquiles contains extreme opposites of virility and femininity. The role of the manly Aquiles draws on the familiar dramatic figure of the Wild Man, and when he fells the corktree that hides the *gracioso* Garbón he recalls that other unstable hero Orlando, maddened by love into wreaking violence on trees, and in particular that model play which tapped the magic of Orlando as the antic rogue and sentimental lover, *Un pastoral albergue.*[3] Out of love for Deidamia, the Wild Man takes on the dress of woman. Initially he is a figure of fun who stumbles on high heels and fights against lace frills as he rehearses curtsies before his mother:

¡Que prender puedan a Aquiles
corchos y telas sutiles,
y en vez de maromas, randas!

(1921)

Inevitably, such comedy is not abandoned, for it contains an irresistible fund of theatrical energy, but the woman's role receives progressively surer focus as Aquiles enters into deeper complicity with his feminine other self. He traces a biological aetiology for this new combination:

También ha habido mujeres
belicosas; iba a hacer
la Naturaleza en mí
un varón, y arrepintióse;
hizo medio hombre y quedóse
lo que en mí faltaba; así
acabó lo que quedaba
en mujer.

(1928)

Here we are being brought into the presence of the Tirso androgyne, who slips to and from the poles of his/her bisexuality. The agreement between Nereida/Aquiles and Deidamia to act out a scene of love (one that echoes the equally dangerous performance between brother and sister in *La venganza de Tamar*) weakens further the boundary that separates real from feigned identity. As Nereida, the androgyne finds an eloquence denied to him as Aquiles the warrior, yet it is an eloquence that gives the woman who is seen to speak it and use it the privileged lyric of male sensuality.

In this provocative sequence, one defiant quick-change remains that will confirm the androgyne's status: Deidamia is invited by Nereida/Aquiles to a closing spectacle:

(Aquiles, *desde dentro*) Abra esa puerta y verás
espectáculos funestos
de una fe menospreciada.

and there, in the inner stage, is the transformed Nereida, now Aquiles in male garb: *Tira una cortina y halla a Aquiles de hombre con calzas y jubón, bizarro,* dressed, as it were, to kill. This discovery by no means dissolves bisexuality by restoring the normal gender dichotomy; on the contrary, it is further proved, for Aquiles now frankly asserts an epicene identity in answer to Deidamia's anxious enquiry:

> (Deidamia)   ¿Eres Nereida o Aquiles?
> Aquiles   Uno y otro, que no quiero
>   con amorosos engaños
>   tener tu temor suspenso.

It has perhaps been mischievous to withhold until this point the detail that gives the androgyne a theatrical immediacy: the part of Aquiles was almost certainly to be played by a woman.[4] This sustained exploration in Act II of *El Aquiles* of *el hombre vestido de mujer* is done with a haunting and subversive energy that derives from more than a conventional switch of sexual identity. The relationship of bodies on stage is strikingly at once both lesbian and heterosexual, the first existing at the level of theatrical artefact (there are two actresses) and the second at the level of narrative (the male gains proximity and intimacy by feigning to be female). The sexual dichotomy is deeply disturbed as the male progressively merges his masculine self with the feminine and forms a dual self within which male and female tend towards undifferentiation. In this process, the normal semiotics of gender mutate, as we see female sensitivity become the source of potency and the male gain by submitting to his feminine other self. In Act III, Tirso can replay this magic, either in language which sharpens the simple male and female signifiers into a robust and memorable paradox:

> (Aquiles)   si de mujer disfrazado
>   vengo esposa a poseer,
>   lo que de hombre he de perder
>   mujer mi dicha me nombre,
>   pues nunca he sido más hombre
>   que después que soy mujer.[5]
>
> (1937)

or in the erotic stage-image when Aquiles/Nereida lies in the skirts of Deidamia who combs his hair. But in Act III, basically the quick-change processes are put into reverse; the warrior Aquiles is progressively restored by the wiles of the misogynist Ulises, to keep his appointment with destiny in the male world of honour, law and war. Nevertheless, before that 'real' world of male relationships is imposed, the magic of performance has allowed other possibilities of desire and fantasy to materialize and prevail.[6]

If the androgyne is imagined as a metamorphosis, then the original may be indifferently male or female. Yet it is unusual that one of Tirso's finest works on gender transformation should deal with the male, for his theatre is noted for the women who, one way or another, stretch the limits of their gender stereotype. From the margin, they seem to exercise an independence that interrogates

and challenges the forces that would draw them back to their conventional centre. The variations on the Protean woman in Tirso's dramatic world are too many to detain me here. Some simply occupy the other, masculine role (*la mujer varonil*) in such a way that while the generic attributes are exchanged for those of the male, the dichotomies remain: they act, basically, as men. Others approach the strange duality of Aquiles but without attaining it to the full. One, however, does and even surpasses him. I refer to Santa Juana of Tirso's eponymous trilogy, a figure who clearly held a deep and lasting fascination for the dramatist. The heroine was, of course, modelled from a life, and indeed the trilogy has been shown to fit with a series of events, celebrations and negotiations spanning the years from about 1609 to 1620 and whose purpose was to promote the canonization of Sor Juana.[7] That programme formed part of a greater campaign to establish the doctrine of the Immaculate Conception of the Virgin Mary. The recent study of Sor Juana de la Cruz by R. Surtz takes us back a century to the actual life and writings of this remarkable visionary, whose career he sees as characterized by a sustained spiritual assault on patriarchal authority.[8] Surtz's study makes essential reading if Tirso's interest in Sor Juana is to be understood, there being no doubt that the shockwaves from this life were still active into the following century. (There can be few cases in which a subject is on the one hand denounced for sorcery by a doctor of the church and the hagiography put on the Index and on the other hand upheld by most eminent divines as the vessel that was fit to receive the vision of Our Lady's Conception.) In Surtz's view (which I am sure is right), Sor Juana's commitment to sexual politics had led her to make radical corrections to key orthodoxies in her recorded visions and the sermons to her sisters: Genesis is retold to relocate guilt in Adam, woman is shown to be spiritually superior to man etc., texts which reform the nature of womanhood and in turn impute a similar feminist motive to Juana's vision of the Virgin's Immaculate Conception. But a significant part of Sor Juana's rewritings deals with the motif of androgyny; she who claimed to have been conceived male and only at God's intervention emerged female at birth, suffered in rapture the crucifixion, body to body as one flesh with Christ—a variant on a Christomimetic pattern, says Surtz, that occurs obsessively in Sor Juana's biography. These are clues, boldly scattered in the banned hagiography, which Tirso collects and reassembles into a character whom he initiates through *la mujer vestida de hombre* into the dual role of the New Eve who re-enacts the passion of Christ: the redemptive androgyne. In that abbreviated reading of *La Santa Juana* lies a reminder that Tirso was a friar before he was a playwright. If we ask what was instrumental in ordering Tirso's dramatic perceptions of gender, then his religious experience was preeminently the foundation upon which his outlook on identity was raised.

One passage corroborates this with great force. It is found in Tirso's account, as his Order's historian, of the founding of the Order of the Mercy of Our Lady. When the narrator focuses on the beginning, it is dress that he selects, the white robe of the Order, subjecting it to a usual inversion. For if clothing represents inner qualities, in this case the robe of St Peter Nolasco is white because an inner purity has transfused the visible garment, fusing together the outer, male Nolasco and the inner, female Mary in a manner of mystical union:

> Quedó nuestro Nolasco vestido el cuerpo de la cándida limpieza que siempre le comunicó el alma. Quedó adornado exteriormente de la librea religiosa de María, como transformado en ella, dentro de sus entrañas, por lo virgen, por lo puro, lo piadoso y lo celeste, que si las propiedades de el amor fino son unir y reciprocar al que ama y al amado, pudieran dudar las atenciones de el espíritu, en esta unión, quál fuese María y quál fuese Nolasco.[9]

Clothing being, among other things, an indicator of sex, it is of great significance that the habit worn by Tirso should be thus invested in his mind with the function of conveying a duality of gender, externalizing an interior femininity and combining it with the virile and heroic conduct to which the friars of Mercy were vowed in the exercise of their mission. (The organization and terminologies of the Order drew on the military model, reflecting how its ransom operations were closely associated from the beginning with warfare. A military/pacific duality is expressed, too, in the emblematic laurel and olive branches that decorate the Order's shield.) Tirso's bold attribution of this special spiritual androgyny to the founder of his Order and archetype Mercedarian, suggests that a conscious religious-anthropological outlook towards gender was formed in the Order. The primordial cult of the Virgin Mary in an exclusively masculine fraternity can be assumed to have been a key element in this ideal duality. Indeed, a seventeenth-century woodcut offers a striking iconological corroboration of this sexual and spiritual nexus; it shows the Virgin, with the traditional emblems of her Immaculacy, holding open her robes under which friars of the Order of Mercy gather, like chickens under the wings of a mother hen.[10] It is not surprising that when the dramatist makes theatre of the origins of The Order of Mercy in *La dama del olivar*, he should create in the process one of his complexly Protean images of woman.

La dama del olivar tells of the founding of the Mercedarian monastery at Estercuel, in Aragón. This monastery had special status. It was built in a remote spot where in the early years of the Order Our Lady of Mercy had appeared in an olive tree. So important strands in Mercedarian historiography combine in the memory of this special location: local origins; primordial Marianic devotion; Mercedarian virtues bred from familiarity with remoteness and solitude. That the place provided roots for a Mercedarian culture comes across in Tirso's evocation of it in his *Historia general*:

> ... antiquíssimo monasterio de el Olivar, cuya soberana y milagrosa ymagen, aparecida en los primeros años de nuestra fundación sobre un olivo, que asta el presente día se conserva en sus ramas y ojas, vivo y verde, y no con menos fructo que el de la que nos le produxo eterno,

le hace devotíssimo y ylustre. Está fundado en un casi desierto, bien acomodado para los desahogos espirituales y todo lo caduco.[11]

In the invented plot that supplements the story of the Virgin's appearance, the recurrent motif is marriage, addressed by the rustics with an earthy humour. In a scene of acerbic male solidarity against the tribulations caused by wives, the case is put by the rustic menfolk for the parish priest to receive a tythe of ten days per month of a wife's company. This leads into a more serious misogyny; Laurencia, the rustic protagonist, is abducted and raped by the noble Don Guillén, who first flaunts his intentions before his own betrothed, doña Petronila, reassuring her that a rehearsal in intercourse with the peasant girl will guarantee a good performance with her:

> El que no fue buen galán
> no puede ser buen marido;
> quien cañas ha de jugar,
> primero ha de ensayar;
> sólo a ensayarme he venido
> en Laurencia; si os molesta
> la osadía que en mí veis
> consolaos con que seréis
> de aqueste ensayo la fiesta.
>
> (1193)[12]

The brutal inversion of chivalresque values, the most obvious association of violent penetration carried in the metaphor of the lancer spearing his target and the cold, literal explicitness about the sexual act conveyed by the reflexive in 'ensayarme' and the preposition 'en Laurencia', these are designed to repel. And so too does the post-coital rejection of Laurencia, who is handed over, now as a despised object of possession but still possessed, to the servant, who explains his right to shared property in the homely and thus deeply debasing image of cast-off shoes:

> Estaos, Laurencia, quedita;
> los zapatos que se quita
> mi señor son siempre míos;
> y así, por mía os acoto,
> pues después que os ha calzado
> venís a ser del criado,
> porque sois zapato roto.
>
> (1195)

Wounded and humiliated, Laurencia swears revenge; to do so, she will become a man. Her role-revolt leads her to occupy the extreme androcentric position, from which she turns upon the men of her class and hurls at them the ultimate insult of being women. In an act of total revenge, she will submit them all, dressed as women, to a public humiliation:

> hizo medio hombre y quedóse
> hombres sólo en la apariencia,
> en conversación infame,
> que no sentís vuestra afrenta?

[. . .]
Guárdese de mí mi tierra
que en vosotros los primeros
he de vengar mis ofensas,
y, vestidos de mujeres,
sacaros a la vergüenza.

(1197)

And abandoning her class, indeed her society, she enlists with the marginalized, the robber gang of Roberto. Laurencia bears comparison with another *comedia* victim of rape turned brigand, Gila in Vélez de Guevara's *La serrana de la Vera,* and with the recent important reading of that character by J. A. Drinkwater.[13] In this reading, which acknowledges directions given by Hélène Cixous' views on 'marked writing', the female rebel against her treatment by men occupies a marginal position which is that of the hysteric; from that impossible position, where her victimization is complete, the inevitable movement of sexual politics forces her reintegration 'into the mainstream', in Gila's case through her punishment. Thus the spectator learns 'that women who defy the established order face social marginalisation and death' (83). There are points of contact with Tirso's *La dama del olivar,* but the tone is profoundly different. Tirso locates his action in an unequivocally androcentric culture. The scene where Niso, Laurencia's father, negotiates with a prospective son-in-law (1175-76), praising the physical merits of the daughter even to suggesting slyly the promise of sexual satisfaction, and concluding with the most obvious acknowledgement of the dowry as a deal between men in the trade of women, observes familial androcentricity with great anthropological acumen and even suggests an awareness of psycho-sexual mechanisms of the kind referred to as 'the Father's seduction'.[14] The marked characteristic in this male culture is its misogyny. Laurencia's intended, Maroto, his imagination fired by bachelors' nightmares, has learned from the priest not to expect maturity from a daughter of Eve ('porque, al fin, es de costilla', 1184), though his authorized and patriarchal view of woman's inferiority coexists absurdly with his devotion for Our Lady, who he trusts will spare him the trials of matrimony. The absurdity is quickened by virtue of his misogynist's diatribe being a gloss on 'Ave Maria gratia plena' (1184-85); as he tells his beads, he sends up his bachelor's prayer to be saved from matrimony and thus slips in blithe contradictoriness to and from vituperation of all women and all praise for the one. The sinister, violent side of misogyny is made manifest in the rape and then the humiliation. These scenes reconstruct a flawed patriarchal culture that reaches crisis-point and propels its female victim to take a stand as *la mujer varonil* that magnifies and mocks its own psychic disorder. Laurencia's androgyny is at once an expression of failure as well as an accusation, for in order to effect her resistance she abandons her female self, resorting to a male paradigm of power and authority through violence. This point could bring me close to J. A. Drinkwater's account of Gila, *La serrana de la Vera,* but I maintain that our reading of Tirso's text is conditioned by our knowledge of its religious orientation, signalled at an early stage in Act I by the account of the miraculous

discovery of an image of Our Lady near Valencia and the subsequent founding of the Order of Mercy. The immanent religious motif prompts the possibility of reading a symbolic order in the text that is opposed to the gender-relations characterizing the world of Estercuel: don Guillén's rape of Laurencia reorders the mysogynistic view (Maroto's, the priest's) of woman as the source of transgression and relocates the original sexual guilt in man. At any rate, the triumph of the New Eve in Act III manifests a perfect androgyny which effectively alters the previous androcentric order.

The olive tree dominates the stage image of Act III. The tree opens to reveal an image of Our Lady of Mercy. The effigy will be acted, for it speaks and also must at one point reach out and turn Maroto's head back to front (1212). There is no gender-switch in Act III to figure forth sexual duality with the immediacy we see in *El Aquiles.* On the contrary, the androgyny of *La dama del olivar* is spiritual, free from uneasy associations with hermaphrodeity and built from the conceits provided by the olive-tree. The tree embodies androgyny, but it is of a botanical and not a corporeal kind; accompanying Our Lady in the branches are figures of Mercedarian worthies (Pedro Nolasco, Pedro de Armengol, Serapión, Ramón Nonato), forming together with Mary the fruit and sprigs common to the one tree. The variations on the botanical trope include grafting, in reference to the Annunciation:

Aquel injerto divino
que de dos naturalezas
en un supuesto da fruto
que sana el que comió Eva

(1206)

Here the grafting of two natures applies aptly to the dyadic union ('un supuesto') of male and female attained in Mary. It is consistent with the extended trope of luxuriant growth in this key address by Our Lady in Act III (1207-08) that the identities it refers to should be merged and confused in a way that does not belong to properly logical and orderly discourse; so, if God the Father is the trunk that sustains the branch, then he is one with Mary, for she is herself the olive-tree. The interfolding nature of this discourse reflects the topic it carries throughout, the oil of the tree, which is at once the Virgin and Christ, spilling throughout the Church and lighting the faithful. While the liquid imagery of this speech and the circulation and exchange of meaning between its parts impart a feminine quality to the text, it contains authority, too, for Our Lady instructs in the three vows of monastic obedience and the fourth Mercedarian vow of love.[15] If androgynous modes of writing exist, this text merits inclusion. Of course, the end of the play celebrates common devotion and reconciliation that could be construed as a restoration of conservative verities. This is not the reading proposed here. On the contrary, the spiritual androgyne presents Tirso's radical strategy for liberation from the androcentric order empowered in Acts I and II. For full measure, in a zany and memorable way that order is duly and aptly humiliated when Maroto, arch representative of its misogyny, is turned into the back-to-front man, *el hombre al revés.*

Tirso's theatre, it has often been observed, is marked by a proclivity for plots dealing with unusual sexual conduct. His audacious treatment of sensational behaviours raises questions of critical method, as seen in Henry Sullivan's recent article where he relates the dynamics of incestuous desire in Tirso's theatre to Lacanian psychoanalysis.[16] In the case of androgyny, a psychoanalytical method could also doubtless operate, perhaps starting from Freud's views on the bisexuality of males and females. But although language and occasional concepts in this article show inevitable borrowings from the psychoanalytical motifs in today's gender-related writing, nevertheless it is the historical model that I believe holds the key to Tirso's outlooks on gender and sexuality. They derive from his intellectual formation. That source is most clear in the case of androgyny, though I avoid the broad view taken by R. Kimbrough[17] of a central myth of androgyny that diffuses throughout Renaissance education. It is to Tirso's formation within his own Order that I refer. There is much to learn about the Order of Mercy and its relation to Tirso's theatre, but the liminal image from his ***Historia general*** of the heroic Pedro de Nolasco transfigured into the perfect Virgin and Man suggests not only a bond between Tirso's two professions, but a strong one.

NOTES

[1] Tirso de Molina, *Obras dramáticas completas.* Edición crítica por Blanca de los Ríos, Tomo I (Madrid: Aguilar, 1946), 1909. All quotations are from this edition.

[2] María José del Río, 'Representaciones dramáticas en casa de un artesano de Madrid de principios del siglo XVII', in *Teatros y vida teatral en el siglo de oro a través de las fuentes documentales,* ed. Luciano García Gómez y J. E. Varey (London: Tamesis, 1991), 245-58. This fascinating piece of social history deals only marginally with acting and cross-dressing, but the cue is worth taking up.

[3] Thus *El Aquiles* shares a repertoire with Calderón's *La vida es sueño;* for greater detail on Orlando and the Wild Man as types, see my article 'The Traffic of the Stage in Calderón's *La vida es sueño*', *Renaissance Drama,* New Series IV (1971), 170.

[4] The proof for this rests in the stage-direction to Aquiles' first entrance, as the Wild Man: '*Salen Aquiles, que ha de hacer la mujer vestida de pieles, y Quirón, viejo, también de pieles, y Tetis, bizarramente vestida de campo*' (1912). There are no extra-textual documents about this play, as far as I know.

[5] In his *Shakespeare and the Art of Humankindness* (New Jersey/London: Humanistic Press International, 1990), 40, Robert Kimbrough reminds us of Dustin Hoffman's lines to his girl at the end of *Tootsie,* when Hoffman is no longer dressed female: 'I was a better man with you as a woman than I ever was a man with a woman as a man'. Tirso achieves a similarly epigrammatic effect, though the conundrum is deepend; whereas Tootsie does not make love with his/her partner, Aquiles/Nereida does. Thus Deidamia enters into complicity with the bisexuality of her partner. Tirso

does not abandon this feature for, at the end of Act III, Deidamia cross-dresses *de hombre* in pursuit of her now male Aquiles. The promised second part, which presumably took up the sequel, does not exist.

[6] The question of what these 'other possibilities of desire and fantasy' are is left open. But one answer may lie in Cristina Peri Rossi's 'Nochevieja en el Daniel's', the preamble to her *Fantasías eróticas* (Madrid: Temas de Hoy, 1991). There the coincidence of aesthetic, histrionic and erotic experiences in the presence of a female couple cross-dressed to appear heterosexual is described. The social and moral distance between Peri Rossi and Tirso de Molina is great, but the other elements are comparable.

[7] A. K. G. Paterson, 'Teatro para canonizar: Tirso de Molina y Sor Juana de la Cruz', in *Tirso de Molina. Immagine e Rappresentazione.* Segundo Coloquio Internacional, a cura di Laura Dolfi (Napoli: Edizione Scientifiche Italiane, 1991), 53-63.

[8] Ronald E. Surtz, *The Guitar of God. Gender, Power, and Authority in the Visionary World of Mother Juana de la Cruz (1481-1534)* (Philadelphia: Univ. of Pennsylvania Press, 1990). My own article on the posthumous identity of Sor Juana in the seventeenth century was unable to take advantage of this important study on the life of the Sister. I extend my views on the posthumous Sor Juana in the light of Surtz's biographical account in an article due to appear in *Cuadernos de Teatro Clásico.*

[9] *Fray Gabriel Téllez (Mercedario) (Tirso de Molina). Historia general de la orden de Nuestra Señora de las Mercedes* (Madrid: Colección 'Revista Estudios', 1973), I, 36.

[10] The title-page of *Bvlla Smi. D. N. Pavli Divina prouidentia Papae V. Confirmacionis et Innovationis Privilegiorum, et Bvllarum Ordinis Beatae Mariae de Mercede Redemptionis captiuorum . . . Ad preces Philippi III . . .* [no place, no date]. The British Library has a copy, 4783.e.1.

[11] *Op. cit.,* Vol. II, 546.

[12] Tirso de Molina, *Obras dramáticas completas,* edición crítica por Blanca de los Ríos (Madrid: Aguilar, 1946), I, 1173-1218. All quotations are from this edition.

[13] J. A. Drinkwater, '*La serrana de la Vera* and the "Mystifying Charms of Fiction" ', *Forum for Modern Language Studies,* XXVIII (1992), 75-85.

[14] Jane Gallop, *Feminism and Psychoanalysis. The Daughter's Seduction* (London: Macmillan, 1982), in particular the chapter entitled 'The Father's Seduction'.

[15] In the general poetics of gender, the notions of liquid, liquefaction, flow, etc. can be said to characterize the feminine textual economy. See V. A. Conley, *Hélène Cixous: Writing the Feminine* (Lincoln/London: University of Nebraska), 1984, throughout.

[16] H. W. Sullivan, 'El motivo del incesto en el drama de Tirso de Molina: una orientación lacaniana', *Tirso de Molina. Immagine e Rappresentazione,* 207-17.

[17] R. Kimbrough, *Shakespeare and the Art of Humankindness* (New Jersey/London: Humanistic Press International, 1990).

Amado Nervo
1870-1919

(Born José Amado Ruiz de Nervo) Mexican poet, novelist, short story writer, dramatist, and essayist.

INTRODUCTION

Along with the Nicaraguan poet Rubén Darío, Nervo is considered the most important poet of the *Modernismo* movement. His novels and short stories place him among the movement's leading fiction writers, although his works are less typical of the writing style associated with *Modernismo*. The Spanish-American *modernistas* sought to free Spanish poetry from its strict adherence to fixed poetic forms. These poets were directly influenced by the experimentalism of the French Symbolists, whose formal innovations, including *vers libre,* had earlier deviated from a long-established tradition of poetic forms in their own country's literature. Nervo's early collections, such as *Perlas negras* (1898) and *Poemas* (1901), display particular influence of the Symbolist poet Paul Verlaine. Later in his career, Nervo adopted a more philosophical and spiritual approach, removing his works from the typical aesthetic principals that define *Modernismo*.

Nervo, the oldest of seven children, was born in Tepic on the Pacific coast of Mexico, a rugged area where his Spanish ancestors had settled. In his youth he received religious training, and it seemed likely that his pious temperament and enthusiasm for the traditions of the Church would lead him to the priesthood. While he went as far as entering a seminary, an experience which provided the background for his novel *El bachiller* (1895), Nervo eventually elected to follow literary pursuits which had developed alongside his religious aspirations. He moved to Mexico City, where he worked on various newspapers. He also wrote for the *Revista azul,* the *modernista* literary journal which took its name from Darío's *Azul,* a collection of poetry and prose often regarded as the inaugural work of the *Modernismo* movement. It was through the editor of the *Revista azul,* poet Manuel Gutiérrez Nájera, that Nervo was introduced to the work of Paul Verlaine. Nervo later helped found the *Revista moderna,* which succeeded Gutiérrez Nájera's publication as the leading journal of *Modernismo.* In 1900 Nervo traveled to Paris, where he lived with DarRo and associated with many writers involved in the French Symbolist movement. In 1905 Nervo took the examination to enter the Mexican diplomatic service and for the next thirteen years worked in Madrid as secretary to the Mexican legation. He ended his diplomatic career as minister to Argentina and Uruguay, dying in Montevideo not long after assuming his post.

In many of Nervo's major works, the influence of a specific literary figure or movement is clearly visible.

His earliest publications were the novels *El bachiller* and *Pascual Aguilera,* both of which remain his best known works of fiction and each of which is modeled on the French Realist and Naturalist novels of Guy de Maupassant and Émile Zola. While Nervo employed the technique of these literary schools, he did not share their social designs or materialist ideology, and his first two novels exhibit a distinctive thematic concern of his work: the obstacle of physical desire in the search for spiritual transcendence. The title character of *Pascual Auguilera* destroys himself and others by force of an unregulated passion and a temperament devoid of spirituality. In *El bachiller,* a seminarian's sexual awakening undermines his intentions for a religious vocation. He finally overcomes his sensual nature by means of self-castration. A later novel, *El donador de almas,* also explores themes of physical versus spiritual love in a fantasy that recalls the ethereal romantic affairs common in the stories of Edgar Allan Poe. Nervo's literary kinship with the American author can be noted in their mutual concern with death, abnormal psychology, and both scientific and supernatural explanations of life.

Like his fiction, Nervo's poetry displays his assimilation of various artistic styles and reflects his studies in philosophy and mysticism. The early collections *Perlas negras* and *Poemas* express his affinity for Verlaine and demonstrate the definite traits of much Symbolist poetry: mysticism, melancholy, and the musical quality of words above their meaning. Following his Symbolist phase, Nervo harkened back to the Parnassian poets of the early nineteenth century, to create poems in the highly formalized manner of this movement. Nervo's pursuit of religious concerns is preeminent in his works. Critics have commented that Nervo eventually reached a stage of artistic development that defied any schools or sects of classification. Nervo himself wrote: "I support only one school, that of my deep and eternal sincerity."

Nervo's later poetry, similar to his prose in works like *Plenitud* (1918; *Plenitude*), reflect various spiritual and intellectual conflicts which the poet attempted to resolve throughout his life. While he had left behind much of the dogma of traditional Christianity, he struggled to reconcile the basic beliefs in God and life after death with the spirit of scientific materialism that emerged in the nineteenth century. Challenged by French intellectualism and the sceptical *Cientificos* that dominated the Mexican intellectual life at the time, Nervo sought to broaden his understanding of both natural and supernatural existence by intense study of philosophy and mysticism. He was especially receptive to the theory of "creative evolution" and the belief in a transcendental realm of being, which gave Nervo hope for a personal existence beyond the confines of the physical body. Nervo also incorporated the doctrines of the Hindu and Buddhist religions, especially focusing on renunciation of the material world.

In 1912, after the death of the woman whom Nervo deeply loved, the author intensified his search for a divine plan of existence which could be both rationally and emotionally accepted—a quest which motivated much of the mystical poetry and prose of Nervo's last volumes. Most critics agree that he never settled into a fixed doctrine of belief, and his works are variously read as Christian or Hindu or humanist in their essence. It is more the intensity of his spiritual quest and the quality of his poems that appeals to Nervo's admirers, rather than the coherence of his thought. Nervo, as Esther Turner Wellman has written, "stands or falls, not as a philosopher, but as an intense lyric artist who has emotionalized philosophy.

PRINCIPAL WORKS

El bachiller (novel) 1895
Pascual Aguilera (novel) 1896
Místicas (poetry) 1898
Perlas negras (poetry) 1898
Poemas (poetry) 1901
El éxodo y las flores del camino (poetry and prose) 1902
El donador de almas (novel) 1904
Las voces (drama) 1904
Los jardines interiores (poetry) 1905
Almas que pasan (short stories) 1906
En voz baja (poetry) 1909
Ellos (short stories) 1912
Serenidad (poetry) 1914
El diamante de la inquietud (novel) 1917
Elevación (poetry) 1917
Plenitud [*Plenitude*] (essays) 1918
El estanque de los lotos (poetry) 1919
La amada inmovil [*Confession of a Modern Poet* (partial translation)] (poetry) 1920
Obras completas. 28 vols. (collected works) 1920-22
Cuentos misteriosos (short stories) 1921
* "Leah and Rachel" (short story) 1963
† "Let's Speak of Writers and Literature" (essay) 1965

* Published in *Spanish American Literature since 1888*
† Published in *The Modern Mexican Essay*

CRITICISM

G. Dundas Craig (essay date 1934)

SOURCE: "Amado Nervo," in *The Modernist Trend in Spanish-American Poetry: A Collection of Representa-* *tive Poems of the Modernist Movement and the Reaction,* Berkeley: University of California Press, 1934, pp. 276-81.

[*In this excerpt, Dundas Craig provides an overview of several of Nervo's poetry collections critiquing many of his major themes.*]

[Nervo's] long association with Darío was due to a deep sympathy with Darío's aims and ideals, a sympathy which finds expression in the poem, **Homenaje**, written on the occasion of Darío's death. . . . What Amado Nervo most admired was evidently the clear-cut imagery, the precision and delicacy of [Darío's] workmanship, such that each poem

> twinkled with diamond sparks,
> Myriads of topaz-lights, and jacinth-work
> Of subtlest jewellery;

and this delicacy of workmanship he was eminently successful in reproducing in his own work.

Thus we find in Amado Nervo the same fondness for experimenting with new metrical effects as in Darío, the same sensitiveness to the musical quality of words and rhythms, the same felicity of phrase, and the touch of melancholy characteristic of the Modernist school—though he wears his rue with a difference.

Yet there are elements in the work of Amado Nervo that are hardly perceptible in that of Darío. For example, his early poems display a certain pantheistic sentiment, as in **La hermana agua** and **Viejo estribillo**. . . . Later, in **El puente**—the fanciful title reminds one of *The Pulley,* by George Herbert, another mystic—he comes very close to the thought of Wordsworth. (p. 277)

Parenthetically we may note that this mention of Wordsworth is somewhat remarkable, as it would seem from the writings of other poets that almost the only poetical work in English known in Spanish America is that of Walt Whitman or of Edgar Allan Poe. It is also an evidence of the broad culture of Amado Nervo. . . . Nervo, however, did not attain to this power of mystic absorption without struggle. Like Darío, like Verlaine, he experienced the seductions of the flesh and the torments of a stylite; but the combat between the soul and the body, the spiritual and the material, Christ and Pan, which in Darío ceased only with death, had in the Mexican poet an earlier and happier ending. In 1914, he wrote:

> Siento que estoy in las laderas
> de la montaña augusta de la Serenidad;
>
> ["I feel that now I stand
> On the slopes of the stately mounts, Serenity . . ."]

and, having attained this peace of mind, he was able at last to comprehend the meaning of things. . . . (p. 278)

[The poem **"El día que me quieras"**, from the posthumous collection **El arquero divino**] is, I think, unique in modern Spanish-American poetry, for if there is one thing more remarkable than another in the poetical work of this period, it is the note of melancholy, tending usually to become morbid. Here there is nothing of that kind. Instead, we have the spontaneous welling up of a spirit at peace within itself, and able to look out upon the world and find all things good. This is the happiest poem of the period under consideration.

This, however, is not the prevailing tone of Nervo's work. Dominating its transparency of form and its almost overpowering sweetness is the note of an ascetic melancholy. This is not the melancholy of Milton, austere and majestic, . . . nor yet the melancholy of Darío and Burns, which found its source in a pained reflection over the past and an equally painful anticipation of the future, . . . nor even the whimsical melancholy of Jaques. Nervo's melancholy is a wistful and expectant longing for the great revelation that is to come. . . . (p. 279)

Closely allied to this melancholy is the sense of mystery in outward nature and in human life. Something of this power of suggesting the mysterious is found in the poem, **"Tel qu'en songe"**, where the reiteration of the phrase, "en los sueños" ["in our dreams"], has a very curious effect. So in nature he finds secret meanings which he attempts to interpret to men. (pp. 279-80)

As has been already hinted, Nervo's life was not without its struggle. In **"Delicta carnis"** . . . he portrays the conflict of the flesh and the spirit with a vividness and power of introspection in which, I think, he excels Darío. **"La montaña"** . . . shows a marked difference of feeling. By force of will he has gained a serene outlook upon life. . . . In this mood his insight into the heart of things is deepened; he finds God everywhere, in nature and in his fellow-men; and from this springs a well of sympathy for all mankind.

For some years before his death Nervo was attracted by the teachings of Buddhism, and some of his later poems show this influence very strongly. . . . In complete renunciation of desire of every kind he has found Nirvana. Yet not quite. . . . (p. 280)

The whole struggle is figured forth allegorically in **"La conquista"** (in **El estanque de los lotos,** the last volume published in the poet's lifetime). In this poem, the hero, Miguel, whose love has been rejected by Helena, at first determines to win her, come what may; later, counseled by "una voz augusta, nunca jamás oída" (the voice of the "dios interior"), that fortifies him with a strange mixture of the philosophies of Buddha and Schopenhauer, he reaches the point where all desire is quenched, love's power over him ceases, and he finds his real happiness in the single life devoted to contemplation. One feels, however, that the scales were rather unfairly weighted against the lady, who was only eighteen while her lover was forty. Had Miguel been twenty years younger, one doubts whether either Buddha or

Schopenhauer would have counted for more than two grains of sand in the balance. (pp. 280-81)

Esther Turner Wellman (essay date 1936)

SOURCE: *Amado Nervo: Mexico's Religious Poet,* Hispanic Institute of Columbia University, 1936, 293 p.

[*Wellman's critical study of Nervo analyzes the artistic and philosophical influences of his work.*]

Amado Nervo might be reduced to three words, *scepticism* and *mysticism* finally swallowed up in *love*! In fact his final philosophy might be synthesized into a single word, for in Nervo all values were eventually transvaluated by *love*. To him love was an absolute which made all other values subservient to it. A generalization that eventually overmasters his emotion, his thought and his form. Here is the only string upon which the scattered beads of his art may be strung. Love is the organizing idea—and the only idea under which he was ever able to handle the chaos of experience.

The simplicity of design is almost beyond belief. His philosophy of life is little more than a set of directions for living, with love as the simplifying principle. Nervo wonders why it is that after Jesus untangled us once, we are forever getting all tangled up again. (pp. 217-18)

It might be urged that his oversimplification of life is pathetically naïve. For instance, he never doubted but that a pure love ethic would solve all the problems of the universe. And once the center of his philosophy was fixed, it radiated in all directions and he took it to apply everywhere. He never anticipated the slightest difficulties— neither in its application nor in its content. The infinite amount of problems which Jesus did not face directly never occurred to him. That Jesus does not define the specific duties in the content of love never bothered him. Everything to Nervo proceeded from a feeling more powerful than rules—from love. Jesus' teaching placed the emphasis upon the motive of an action, not the action itself. Therefore the outward act was less significant than the inward attitude. Nervo followed by driving sharply into motives. And a statement of the motive was a statement of his whole philosophy. (pp. 218-19)

Yet for all the disadvantages of oversimplification, this interiority of love gave to Nervo's philosophy such plasticity and powers of adaptation, that it was capable of almost indefinite renewal. Its applicability to everything was characteristic of Nervo's personal demand for universality. His transcendental talent swept everything off into the infinite. And whatever he accidentally picked up with his baggage which was incapable of such flights, he finally dropped along the way. Whatever passes through Nervo's thought becomes universal. The same thing happened to Christianity that happened to everything else. He blew off all the dust which had accumulated upon the original essence. Frankly Nervo refuses to accept from Christianity all the paraphernalia which it has accumulated throughout the ages. He will accept only those universal aspects of Christianity . . . which are the same in other religions. . . . (pp. 219-20)

Anything that is true anywhere, Nervo felt, must be true everywhere. That is to say that truth is not truth unless it is grounded in the laws of the universe. And that like sunlight it cannot be kept in one little town, and shut off from the rest of the world. And he was convinced that the only universal truth that we know, so far, at least in the realm of spirit is love. That love is at the heart of the universe. That it is the unifying cosmic force. That love, at least in the realm of spirit, like radiant energy in cosmic space (whether both are the same he does not know) is more universal than any known force. That love, the integrating force in all relationship, is God permeating the entire world. (p. 220)

Love is the first clear step in Nervo's ultimate philosophy. And although it might be urged that like Pragmatism his teaching was a method and not a philosophy, nevertheless there are moments such as in the above quotation, when his ethical art is on the point of passing over into a cosmic creed. Undoubtedly Nervo found rest from his own uncertainty in this universal conception of love. And this is where he finally satisfied his life-long hunger and thirst for belief. (p. 221)

Nervo's vast human sympathies had brought his philosophy down from the clouds. His scepticism and mysticism were drowned in his humanism. He went a step further, however. The fundamental law of love was universal in its application. And his philosophy passed over from a way of life into what amounted to an actual program for humanity. He was caught in the social consciousness of our epoch. He would not leave the world to stew in its own juice. His place was in the thud and surge of life. For he was consumed with the conviction that the revolutionary principle of Love must be unflinchingly applied to the whole tangle of social and economic problems. He believed that love should widen itself to the full limit of its possibilities. That every field of human experience should be brought under its dominion. This drew him on and on toward horizons of which he had no previous idea. It was a practical philosophy to be applied to the constructive tasks of humanity. In all his later books he is frankly out for a new world wherein dwelleth righteousness. He was rethinking the world. Creating it in his own image. His imagination could not be contained within the goals of history. And he dreamed of War, Race, and Industry merged in a higher synthesis—the kingdom of pure love. (pp. 274-75)

Three words—Scepticism, Mysticism, and Universal Love—sum up the whole of Nervo's philosophy. But the greatest of these is Love. Could Nervo have been a thorough-going sceptic, or a through-going mystic, he might have been satisfied. But he was caught in a tragic impasse and would give himself to neither. He ultimately satisfied both these warring tendencies within himself, as he did everything else, by transcending into another realm. Scepticism and Mysticism were taken up into a higher synthe-

sis which contradicted neither. His Humanism never interfered with his Scepticism. And he ultimately satisfied his life-long hunger for Reality by accepting truth on the human level, which was the only place where he could scientifically test it. This led Nervo to distrust both intellect and emotion and gradually he came more and more to proclaim the force of the will. In this mysterious region where the experts are at war—how can a poet know? It may be, however, that one of the tragedies of Nervo's thought was the old traditional psychology that dissected man into the Platonic compartments of thinking, feeling and willing, instead of seeing him as a whole. Possibly his great error was in thinking it possible to separate the human spirit, and to set emotion to war against thought, without disintegration. Possibly his tragedy may have come from separating what should never have been separated. Possibly he should have trusted the totality of his spirit, and have distrusted either emotion, or thought, or will, whenever divorced from each other. Who can tell? One thing is certain, that Nervo's life was one of mortal anguish over the puzzling contradictions which he found in life. And what could be more puzzling to a student than the paradox to be found in Amado Nervo himself? His dominant intuition of unity which saw the universe as a whole, and yet at the same time feeling his own spirit chopped up into parts. . . . [He] was ultimately forced to the position of a Humanist.

It is not only a final philosophy which emerges from out the welter and mass of Nervo's contradictions. Certain steadfast attitudes toward the totality of things also appear often enough to be typical. For instance, in Nervo's Humanism, as well as in his Mysticism, and his Scepticism, his genius is essentially spontaneous. The "soul vomiting" of a subjective poet is always there. One feels that intensity of an artist. He cannot look at things with detachment. He was a meteor (he himself confesses it), rather than a star. And it is because of a lyric heart laid bare that outlines so clearly emerge of a Nervo always and forever concerned with mystery. We traced this through his Scepticism and through his Mysticism. But he was finally forced to accept truth on the only level where he could scientifically test it—on the human level. And this represents his most definitive and ultimate thought. He never stops seeking, however. For Nervo was a Bergsonist who hoped and waited for whatever emergent evolution might evolve in the future. He lost all interest in the past. His search, therefore, though never carried on in any systematic way, was nevertheless consistent in one aspect only. His contemporary consciousness always pounced upon the *dernier cri*. His conviction that truth was universal, made him receptive to every philosophy. But he drank from so many contradictory sources that he suffered from intellectual indigestion. This situation was met in the way characteristic of his peculiar genius by his trick of transcending what could never be solved. His whole philosophical pilgrimage was one of wider and wider integrations until he finally reached the extreme limit of his final philosophy. A code of ethics which contradicted neither his Scepticism, nor his Mysticism, and yet which in a measure satisfied both. A way of living which was universal enough to admit all religions and all philosophies. Such was the life of Mexico's poet-philosopher. He could not give himself entirely to philosophy because he was born a poet. And he could not give himself entirely to poetry because his whole life was consumed with a passion for Reality. This was the distinctive stamp of his personality. This was the essence of all his work. . . . Nervo, like Spinoza was a "God-intoxicated man." (pp. 277-80)

Such outstanding professors as Pedro Henríquez Ureña, Antonio Caso, and Julio Jiménez Rueda—all have named Amado Nervo as one of the six greatest poets in Mexican literature. The six are: Nájera, Othón, Nervo, Díaz Mirón, Urbina, and González Martínez . . . But Nervo transcends Mexican literature and must be classified with such names as Nájera, Casal, Silva, Darío, Herrera y Reissig, Chocano, Valencia, Lugones, Gonzáles Martínez, and Jaimes Freyre, as one of the leaders of the Modernista Movement in Spanish literature (p. 280) . . . . But Nervo, again, not only transcends Mexican literature. He also transcends Spanish literature. Something in Nervo refuses to be classified anywhere. (pp. 280-81)

There are two Amado Nervos. In his first manner he epitomizes his period. In the second he transcends it. The first Nervo belongs to Spanish literature. The second to the Universe. In the first, Nervo the poet swallows up the mystic. In the second, the mystic swallows up the poet. The first Nervo is an artist. The second one a saint.

Now it is illuminating to follow the shifting of public opinion regarding these two Amado Nervos. During his life-time Nervo's fame in the Republic of Mexico rested almost entirely upon the first Nervo. Mexican anthologies frankly chose from the artist. And the Mexican intellectuals preferred the Modernista lyrist. . . . But the Modernista Movement was largely taken up with form, and Nervo's interest . . . shifted from form to philosophy. Here his emotion, thought, and form became universal. His philosophy of universal love not only led him to the intellectual internationalists. Nervo could not even be contained in this world and his cosmic consciousness led him to proclaim himself a citizen of the Infinite. The same thing happened to his thought. He exercised the same weakness toward all philosophies which he did toward people. He was far too kind to all. The same thing happened in form. Like his French master, Francis Jammes, another Franciscan after his own heart, he would belong to no literary schools in order that he might belong to all of them. It is universality which characterizes Nervo in his second manner. . . . Nervo did not even publish in Mexico. (pp. 281-83)

The opposite was true of the first Nervo. Of Nervo the artistic and literary artist. He wrote for Mexico. Was published in Mexico. And his prestige and irradiation rested almost entirely upon his Modernismo. Outside of the few who knew his writings in the Southern Continent, the Republic of Mexico was largely unconscious of the fact that one of her poets had conquered the whole Spanish-speaking world by his Franciscan universality. The first Nervo had many followers because form is easy to imitate. The

second had few because such lofty ideals of purity and renunciation are too difficult to follow. And yet the legend of Amado Nervo is based almost entirely upon the second. After 1919, Nervo was lifted up into what has amounted to an apotheosis. It was the year when the Spanish-speaking nations of the new world went "Nervo mad."

There are two Amado Nervos. In his first manner he epitomizes his period. In the second he transcends it. The first Nervo belongs to Spanish literature. The second to the Universe. In the first, Nervo the poet swallows up the mystic. In the second, the mystic swallows up the poet. The first Nervo is an artist. The second one a saint. . . . Now it is illuminating to follow the shifting of public opinion regarding these two Amado Nervos. During his life-time Nervo's fame in the Republic of Mexico rested almost entirely upon the first Nervo. Mexican anthologies frankly chose from the artist. And the Mexican intellectuals preferred the Modernista lyrist. . . . But the Modernista Movement was largely taken up with form, and Nervo's interest . . . shifted from form to philosophy. Here his emotion, thought, and form became universal. His philosophy of universal love not only led him to the intellectual internationalists. Nervo could not even be contained in this world and his cosmic consciousness led him to proclaim himself a citizen of the Infinite. . . .

"Can a pacifist come out of Mexico?" is perhaps just as natural a question as, "Can any good thing come out of Nazareth?" Over and over Nervo has been accused of being unpatriotic. Whether he was or was not depends entirely upon what content is given to the word "patriotism." If by "patriotism" is meant the love of one's country, then Nervo of all Mexicans was most patriotic. But if by "patriotism" is meant a chauvinistic hatred of all the rest, then Nervo was not patriotic. (p. 284)

Nervo in his final and universal self was a travelled man, and much too intelligent for hate. He had read too much philosophy from all the nations and from all the ages for ethnocentrism to take root. He sought truth rather than victory. History passed before him as a rosary of hatreds, and Nervo's cosmic consciousness transcended history. During the Mexican Revolution and during the World War he was a lonely figure, lean, ivory, aloof, like a towering gargoyle brooding over a ghastly abyss where humanity had reverted to cannibals and men were tearing each other to pieces below. Nervo did not fall in submissively behind any of the Revolutionary "istas" of Mexico. Not a word can be found in his twenty-nine volumes in favor of any of them. Before the endless divisions of Mexico, Nervo held up his nightly journeys through his telescope from one star to another, for he had always been a Don Quijote of the heavens. He was at home both on earth and in the sky. It would not even be accurate to say that Nervo was more cosmopolitan than Mexican, for in speaking of Nervo one must take into consideration the whole universe. And this is the central and overshadowing fact of Nervo in his second manner. What he actually did was to take transcendentalism from world philosophíes and world literature and implant it in the soil of Spanish America.

He projects all his sentiments against a timeless background. This is why his work does not bear a distinctive Mexican hallmark, and why he is so quietly appropriated by the most bitter and contradictory camps as one of their own number. While he lived, humanity was his province and he suffered for it. But now that he is gone it is by all humanity that he is claimed. Nervo has woven the most contradictory material into one amazing texture. *E Pluribus Unum*—one out of many, might be his universal theme. This has made him one of the most quotable of Mexican poets, because every one can find himself reflected somewhere. He is regarded as something of a secular Bible, with the same advantage and disadvantage that Nervo in his universality can be made to say almost anything simply by suppressing certain passages and focussing the spotlight on others. For instance, I have before me on my desk three works. One by a Mexican Catholic, one by a South American Theosophist, and another by a North American Presbyterian, each claiming Nervo exclusively as their own. In certain aspects they are all correct. In others they are all wrong for

> Truth is always polychrome.
> One fact taken all alone
> Isolated from its home
> Is often false. Remember this:
> It must be told in synthesis!

The same thing is true of all the *páginas de devoción,* proclaiming Nervo either as a sceptic or mystic, depending upon the temper of the writer. The truth is neither the one nor the other but includes both. (pp. 285-87)

G. W. Umphrey (essay date 1949)

SOURCE: "Amado Nervo and Hinduism," *Hispanic Review,* Vol. XVII, No. 2, April, 1949, pp. 133-45.

[*The author of several critical essays on Nervo, Umphrey here examines the influence of Hindu philosophy on the Mexican poet. A later essay by Roderick A. Molina (excerpted below) emphasizes his Christian, specifically Franciscan, themes.*]

Amado Nervo's approach to Hindu philosophy was slow, and was not due, at first, to any conscious thought of finding in it the solution of the spiritual problems that

were besetting him. During his Modernistic period, he, like his fellow craftsmen, sought the strange and exotic wherever he could find it; and apparently the rich imagery and symbolism of Oriental literature appealed to him more than the better known mythology of Greece and Rome. As early as 1898, in *Perlas Negras,* he made reference to the favorite flower of Buddha, the lotus; but since the symbolism is still that of the Homeric legend, the reference has slight significance when compared with the many later references to the *flor del loto* as the Buddhist symbol of spiritual purity uncontaminated by materialism. Six years later, in *Místicas,* he gave to one of the poems a title, *Transmigración,* the importance of which could easily be exaggerated; the Hindu doctrine merely serves as a literary device for the expression of the poet's fictitious experiences in faraway times and places. The exoticism is that of other Modernistic poets who played with the idea of reincarnation: Rubén Darío, for example, in *Metempsicosis;* or José Santos Chocano, in *Avatar.*

Nor should we consider the Pantheism of the best of his early poems, **"La Hermana Agua"** . . . , as proof of Hindu influence. It is true that Pantheism tings almost all Oriental religions; but it is not, of course, exclusively Oriental, since many of the poets and mystics of Western civilization are decidedly Pantheistic. The Pantheism of **"La Hermana Agua"**, the exaltation of self-abnegation and sacrifice as symbolized in the joyous, humble service of Sister Water, differs little from that of Saint Francis, that saintly man of Assisi who held in the heart of Amado Nervo a place not much lower than that of Christ. **"La Hermana Agua"** is no more pantheistic than the still small voice of *Thanatopsis.* or the speaking stars of David's *Nineteenth Psalm,* or a dozen Biblical texts which are intended to teach submission to divine will and guidance."

In another poem, **"Implacable"**, written at about the same time, there is stronger evidence of Hindu influence. In the spiritual crisis through which he was passing, brought about by a more worldly mode of living, a new scientific curiosity and a more persistent questioning of religious doctrines, he called upon Doubt . . . to cease pursuing him or to give him some consolation for his lost faith; but Doubt, the implacable, had little consolation to offer him. . . . Unwilling to become the victim of implacable Doubt, he turns for aid to the Supreme Being, whoever it may be. . . . (pp. 133-34)

Just as the Hindu theory of reincarnation is used in **"Implacable"**, not merely as literary ornamentation but as an essential part of the main theme, so in **"Las Voces"** . . . the Buddhist doctrine of the attainment of spiritual happiness through complete renunciation of human desire. In this dramatic poem the poet Angel (Nervo), weakened and saddened by youthful excesses, goes to Nature for consolation; but she, speaking with the *voices* of birds, flowers, stars, fountains, has nothing to offer him but hostility and contempt. Later in life, after he has gained serenity of spirit by renunciation, detachment from worldly joys and sorrows, self-abnegation and charity, he returns to Nature; and the same voices that had been so antagonistic give him now a glad welcome. . . . Here we have the very essence of Buddhism, the suppression of desire as the only way to final peace and serenity; and the philosophy underlying the whole poem is Buddhistic rather than Christian. The Pantheism upon which the mechanism of the poem is based is not necessarily Oriental; it is, however, entirely in accord with the Buddhist doctrine that pervades the poem. (pp. 134-35)

From 1904 until his death in 1919 the spiritual life of Amado Nervo oscillated between Hinduism and Christianity. Several volumes of his poetry and prose are permeated with the spirit of Christianity (**Serenidad, La Amada Inmóvil, Elevación, Plenitud** . . .); and various literary critics, by carefully selecting their evidence, have presented him plausibly as the Christian poet *par excellence* in modern Spanish-American literature. But scattered through these same volumes and in the volume entitled **El estanque de los lotos** . . . , there is a sufficient number of poems to prove that he was decidedly Hinduistic in the eclectic religious philosophy that finally gave him the spiritual serenity that he desired. (pp. 135-36)

The first of the Hindu teachers to absorb the attention of Nervo and the one who exerted the greatest influence upon his personal philosophy and mode of living was the Buddha Siddharta Gautama. The great love and compassion of Buddha for his fellow men and the idealism of his doctrines of morality were in harmony with the Christian virtues that were gradually changing the pattern of Nervo's own life. The Middle Path that Buddha taught was, moreover, the kind of life that Nervo was trying to follow; in public, he was an efficient diplomat, an active journalist and a poet of distinction; in private life, he chose solitude and meditation. He did not become an ascetic, and his love of humanity and deep yearning to give moral and spiritual aid to his readers still remained the inspiration for much of his poetry and prose; but his growing detachment from worldly affairs and his faith in renunciation as the only means of attaining peace of mind and serenity drew him closer to the central doctrine of Buddhistic philosophy.

In the first of the four sections of **El estanque de los lotos**, *La Conquista*, Nervo tells the story of a middle-aged poet scholar who falls in love with a young woman; his love unrequited, he listens to an inner voice, that of Krishna; and, unlike Faust, decides to seek serenity and happiness through suppression of desire. When finally the young woman offers him her love, he discovers that it is merely an illusion of Maya and no longer desirable; knowing reality, he attains Nirvana. (pp. 136-37)

The fifty-eight poems of the second section of **El estanque de los lotos**, entitled *Los Lotos*, composed over a period of four years and therefore contemporary, many of them, with the Christian poems of **"Elevación"** . . . and the prose aphorisms of **Plenitud** . . . , are mainly Buddhistic in tendency. His conception of Nirvana varies from poem to poem and seldom reaches that of complete repose through personal annihilation. At times, when

meditation fails to give him the desired serenity, he goes so far as to seek emancipation from thought itself, as well as from sensation and desire. . . . Usually, however, Nirvana becomes synonymous with serenity attained through meditation; and in several poems he makes the Buddhist doctrine less repugnant by combining with it the Brahmanic theory of identity of the human spirit with that of the Supreme Being, the happy emancipation of the individual spirit from the need of reincarnation and its final absorption in Brahma (God). (pp. 137-38)

The enigmas of life and death are the ever-recurring themes of the prose and poetry of Amado Nervo and in few of the thirty volumes of his **Obras Completas** do we fail to find some reference to his tireless quest for spiritual reality. During his early provincial life, at home or in a seminary, he found spiritual satisfaction in the Christian doctrine; when wider acquaintance with modern thought began to weaken his religious faith, he decided that the priesthood was not his true vocation. In Mexico City and in Paris success soon came to him in journalism and literature, and for a few years he tried to take life as he found it, refusing to heed the inner voice that kept telling him that without spiritual growth and some religious belief there could be no real satisfaction or happiness. He then probed more deeply into the natural sciences that had made him skeptical of his religious beliefs; they gave him much information about the material world; they afforded him no help in his quest for spiritual truth. Then he turned to the great religious philosophers, particularly the mystics of all ages and countries; they could not answer all his questions, but they did convince him that spiritual reality should be sought only by spiritual means. (pp. 142-43)

Western civilization has produced many notable mystics; their influence and his own conviction that the mystic approach to spiritual problems is the only one possible would account for the mysticism that modified the poetic content of Nervo's writings during his last fifteen years. Nevertheless, in view of the fact that his favorite philosophers of the last hundred years were Emerson, William James, Schopenhauer, Maeterlinck, Bergson, all of them inclined toward mysticism and all sympathetic to Hindu philosophy, and in view of the fact that this philosophy did influence him in some of its other aspects, it may safely be said that the intuitive cognition that is so characteristic of the monistic religions of India confirmed, at least, Nervo's belief in meditation and intuition as the only means of discovering spiritual truth. (p. 143)

There are two extreme points of view regarding the religious life of Amado Nervo. Orthodox Roman Catholics would have us believe that his life consisted essentially of a spiritual evolution from the religious faith of youth, through the skepticism of his middle years, to the restored orthodox Christianity of his later years. They cannot ignore entirely the numerous references to Hindu philosophy and the scores of poems suffused with Buddhist and Brahmanic doctrine; these they explain away as a poet's use of exotic material for literary purposes. On the other hand, some critics find in these same references and poems proof of their contention that there was in his last years a definite turn from Christianity to Hinduism.

There can be no doubt that Hindu philosophy penetrated his life and writings much more deeply than the orthodox Christians are willing to believe; that through its influence his religious creed was simplified by the elimination of non-essential precepts of Roman Catholicism. His admiration for the idealistic life and teachings of Gautama Buddha was great; but it did not lessen his intense love of Christ. He was inclined to accept the Hindu doctrines of Maya, Identity of the human soul and the Supreme Being, Karma and Reincarnation; but only in so far as they did not conflict too seriously with what he considered to be the essential principles of Christianity. The religious philosophy that he finally formulated for his own guidance and that became the source of much of his later poetry was religious eclecticism, essentially Christian, a Christianity based on love of God, of Christ, and of humanity; a Christianity freed from non-essential dogmas and strengthened by the spiritual truths that he had learned from the religious mystics and teachers of India. (p. 145)

Roderick A. Molina, O. F. M. (essay date 1949)

SOURCE: "Amado Nervo: His Mysticism and Franciscan Influence," *The Americas,* Vol. VI, No. 2, October, 1949, pp. 173-96.

[*In this overview of Nervo's works, Molina explores the relevance of Catholic mysticism in the author's works.*]

Amado Nervo's affection for religious themes is projected so frequently and so intimately in all his work that literary critics have constantly classified him among the number of the mystical poets—those privileged beings who aspired to union with God through love, and who expressed their sublime thoughts in poetic form.

From his very youth, Amado Nervo was characterized by an ascetical seriousness—almost that of an El Greco portrait—a nostalgia, as it were, for the supernatural, that surrounded all his person and activities and permeated his work. This hunger for the divine is evinced in a very special manner in his *Serenidad* and *Elevación,* and above all in *Plenitud.* These works have made Amado Nervo an almost legendary personage, whose brow is crowned with the aura of sainthood.

The religious theme is found so frequently in the literary work of Amado Nervo that one considers it to be autobiographical. Now that thirty years have passed since his death, it is fitting to analyze his art—so easy to classify and so difficult to analyze—in order to find a better explanation of it for ourselves and to determine more exactly whether or not Amado Nervo was really a mystical poet and if he actually found his inspiration in the school of Saint Francis of Assisi.

The tremulous sobbing and weeping of Amado Nervo have been interpreted in very different ways. For us, they are only the revelation of a soul who abandoned the path that had been traced out for him by his vocation, and who, engaged in the battle with life's passions, succumbed for a while, until, like another prodigal son, he returned in the maturity of his faculties, that were by now tempered by suffering, to his Father's house.

Love is the principal *motif* in the work of Amado Nervo. The tender emotions aroused by a smile, a perfume, or a prolonged glance are for him the occasions for sentimental memories. They are like flowers found along the wayside and treasured among the pages of a book. One day, paging through the book after long years, they have the power of evoking again the almost forgotten emotion. But love in Amado Nervo is also like a tranquil and fraternal sentiment, possessing a depth of gravity and a religious emotion that reminds us of the strophes of St. Francis' "Canticle of the Sun".

The literary career of Amado Nervo began without loss of time. His first writings appeared at the period when the work of Gutiérrez Nájera marked the beginning in Mexico of a reaction, both intellectual and artistic, that was to have a decisive influence upon Hispanic American literature. From Gutiérrez Nájera, Amado Nervo learned to appreciate the poetry of Verlaine, acquiring from the symbolists and the decadents the sense of color and of shading and a more profound sensitivity to the musical possibilities of words, which he later poured forth in his *Perlas Negras* and in *Místicas.* In 1900, Nervo went to the World's Fair in Paris as correspondent for the Mexican newspaper *El Imparcial,* and there he became an intimate friend of Rubén Darío. (pp. 173-75)

During this period of companionship with Rubén Darío, Amado Nervo's poetry began to shine forth with new beauty, enamored of the French poets. His poetry of that epoch is unforgettable; it was authentic; it was embellished, moreover, with expressive and musical forms, with graceful rhythms that combine with the turns of a dance, with a pleasant arrangement of metrical structures, and with an air of sadness, elegantly hidden and reserved. If he could have chosen his own career—Nervo himself tells us—he would have chosen that of organist. In a poem dedicated to the King of Bavaria, entitled **"Un Padre Nuestro"**, he manifests his great admiration for Wagner. Perhaps we must understand his words in this sense when he says that he has not invented any new metric form; but he, as well as Darío and the Argentine, Lugones, by the application of clever fluctuation and the use of new registers, obtains the effect of delicate musicality and a new sensitiveness that are captivating. In *Místicas,* his art is one that is in perpetual flow and continual transformation. The Alexandrine verses of **"La Hermana Agua"**, in *Poemas,* lend an exquisite musical tone to the theme treated therein with esthetic devotion and a fervent, ecstatic adoration before the beauty of nature, which make his song flow like a spring of enchanting freshness. . . . The imitative harmony of the poem **"El metro de doce"**, from *Jardines*

Interiores, where the verses enumerate the syllables as he describes the dodecasyllabic form, achieves the effect of dancing joyfulness. Nervo obtains this effect by breaking up the trochaic rhythm native to the Spanish language by the use of anapests. (pp. 176-77)

Nervo gives a very modernistic and extraordinarily vibrating effect to the strophes of **"Mi Verso."** . . . This aristocracy of style, the selectness of thought, the novel manner of developing his themes, the rich variety of rhyme—all of these make Amado Nervo a profoundly original poet. These qualities change him into a prince of the "blue country" of fantasy, into a magician who weaves into fans of silk and lace the forms of delightful figures and landscapes.

About the year 1910, the poetry of Nervo undergoes a strange transformation. He ceases, for the most part, to pay homage to his own century—the century of confusion—and begins to speak in a lower tone, or, in the words of the title of his outstanding work of this period, *En voz baja.* (pp. 177-78)

All those who have written about Amado Nervo have considered him to be a mystic poet. It must be admitted, however, that the spiritual path of the poet is not as clearly marked nor as precisely outlined as that of his literary development. The latter is crystal clear; the former often deviates off on tangents and detours. Attempting to clarify this difficult problem, one must not forget that Amado Nervo was forced to earn his own living early in life, because of the death of his father. And for lack of training in a clear and solid philosophy, his work often suffers from a confusion of thought. His youthful study of philosophy is the bitter fruit of a spoiled vocation, which was ruined by indiscriminate and undigested reading, as well as an excessively lyrical temperament incapable of mental serenity and scientific objectivity. When Amado Nervo attempts to explain the intricate problems of philosophy, he is beyond his depth. If to all this is added the great admiration and devotion the poet had for the world of his day, it explains, quite possibly, the waves of confusions and the sea of contradictions that overwhelmed Amado Nervo's thinking. A recent writer [. . .] finds that the poet drank from such contradictory fountains of thought "that he suffered from intellectual indigestion." Amado Nervo undeniably sought to be a man of his own century, the century of philosophical confusion, the century of the fusion of the most diverse schools of religious fashions and fads. "In modernness, no one gets ahead of me. I live with my feet placed solidly in my century and my eyes firmly sighted on the future." But those years toward the end of the nineteenth century and the beginning of the twentieth were ones of feverish intellectual activity. Nervo described this restless movement as follows: " . . . all of us who read have a new philosophical, cosmogonal or religious system at breakfast every day, with another one still newer for lunch, and the newest of all at dinner." Engulfed in this mental whirlpool, Nervo began to devour all the writings of Taine and Renan. He came to accept Bergson's opinion that sci-

ence would evolve the religious formula of the future, and he thought that perhaps the present century might see the dawn of a universal religion that would be eminently scientific. In his poem "Al Cristo", he describes his feelings at this period of his life, when he was drifting about in the darkness, without any sure guide, because the faith of his forebears no longer cast its peaceful glow over his path. In this intellectual confusion he had recourse to all the errors of those times—to Darwinism, spiritism, theosophism and pragmatism. This, however, was only a transitory stage in his spiritual orbit. Grown weary of living far from his Father's house, he returned after ten years of restless seeking, "like the sad prodigal", to the peace of his true spiritual heritage.

Nervo's was, in every way, a religious temperament. He was one of those men so intent upon the divine that they can only find their happiness when they have solved for themselves, both theoretically and practically, the problem of God. It is difficult to distinguish in his literary work that which is authentically and truly autobiographic from that which is merely literary artifice. We believe that there is a great deal of this latter in Nervo's works. There are many places in his works wherein he seems to be posing, projecting himself in his poems in a striking and attractive manner, as it were, allowing himself the pleasure of seeing his own reflection in the echo of the popular applause.

Nevertheless, the greater part of his work is the sincere expression of the heart-rending struggle going on within his very soul. *La Amada inmóvil* is the story of this painful, interior conflict, of an illicit love which, having been lost by death, results in the author's return to realities that are not perishable. Only after the poet's death have we come to know how deeply Nervo was affected by the death of Anne Cécile Louise Dailliez, the young French maid of extraordinary delicacy and beauty, whom he loved so much. She of the golden hair, white skin, blooming complexion and the dignity of a princess—for so does Nervo describe her for us in his *Gratia plena*. . . .   (pp. 178-81)

From *La Amada Inmóvil*, which is a poem composed in the form of a diary, only one logical conclusion can be deduced, if one leaves aside the artistic surface of its construction and the moments of confusion that agitated his mind: Amado Nervo had found his way through suffering and he was turning back, after the tragic search for his lost faith, back to his Father's house. Master Eckhardt, who Nervo cites in this work, had said: "Suffering is the swiftest steed to ride to perfection". The suffering poet's dedication of *La Amada Inmóvil* is a trust-worthy testimony of the transformation that had taken place in his soul. . . . (pp. 181-82)

The richest and deepest chord, the one which Amado Nervo has played with the greatest confidence and with the greatest feeling, in all the succession of his songs, is the one he found in suffering and sorrow at the loss of his earthly love on January 7, 1912. The masterpieces which he wrote after that tragedy, *Serenidad* . . . , *Elevación* . . . and *Plenitud* . . . , glow with moments of authentically mystic poetry, for now the poet is ardently striving to reach and possess God, through love. (p. 182)

Toward the end of his public life he published *El estanque de los lotos*, which shows the strong attraction that doctrinal analogies had for him and the seduction of symbolism that he had noticed in his reading of Hindustanic literature. After a reflective reading of this work, we are convinced, as was the noted Mexican critic, Alfonso Junco, that in it Amado Nervo seems to have been touched with the same affectation for Buddhistic fantasies as were so many other writers of his day, not that they, or he, really believed in these Oriental doctrines, but rather in a spirit of literary romanticism and to give their work a certain poetic emphasis and interpretation of hazy aspirations of the soul. Nervo made these excursions in the field of religions as he had done with a succession of philosophies, very much in a passing way. (p. 184)

If we may compare the literary compositions of Amado Nervo to a great symphony made up of many diversified themes, literary, religious and social, then we may also say that throughout this symphony there vibrates, repeatedly, sweetly and harmoniously, the Franciscan note. It would be difficult to explain the origin of Nervo's marked affection for Franciscanism with any precise historical data. Dr. Wellman, who has carefully assembled all possible facts bearing on the development of the poet's human and artistic personality, suspects that he did not become acquainted with St. Francis in the Church, but that he "discovered" his favorite Saint in the works of Renan and in the Parnassian literature which he read so avidly in those days at the turn of the century. It seems more logical and more natural to the present writer to suppose that for psychological reasons, his early background, family-life and education, Amado Nervo first found his Franciscan inspiration in Mexico itself, without its having been necessary for him to recur to later and more exotic sources, although admitting that these may well have confirmed and enlarged his acquaintance with matters Franciscan. (pp. 185-86)

This interest in Franciscan themes is very evident in all the work of Amado Nervo. But it is in his **"La Hermana Agua"** that we find the best expression of the poet's Franciscan sentiments and it is here, more than in any others of his works, that Nervo's poetic genius reaches its peak. In his introduction to this poem, he says:

> A trickle of water that falls from an imperfect spout; a trickle of soft, clear water that runs happily all through the night and every night near my bedroom, that sings of my solitude and accompanies me in it; a trickle of water—what a simple thing! And, nevertheless, these ceaseless and resounding drops have taught me more than books.

"The holy soul" of Sister Water spoke to him, and he learned her lesson in loving meditation and he pointed it out in his poem, a lesson which might be summed up thus: "to be docile, to be crystal-pure."

I know that whoever reads it ["**La Hermana Agua**"] will feel the gentle pleasure that I felt in hearing it from the lips of Sister Water, and this will be my guerdon in the contest, until my bones rejoice in the grace of God.

The poem finds its inspiration in that crystalline strophe of St. Francis' "Canticle of the Sun." . . . (p. 189)

This work of Nervo's in 234 verses, is true poetry, in which the Mexican author sought to sing the praises of Sister Water in lyric commentary. It is completely saturated with the Franciscan spirit, which he herein proves to have understood. The form of the poem, although it does not lack technique and polish, is notable for its purity, and rests on a basis of religious emotion and mysticism. Its literary vestiture has an immediate purpose. Like one who is not in a hurry, he tarries to listen to the pleasant message of the water "which flows under the earth", and of that which flows upon it, as well as that of the snow, the ice, the hail, the steam, the mist. And from all its forms he hears the query: "Poet, you who by the grace of heaven has come to know us, will you not sing with us?" And he replies: "Yes, I'll sing, sister voices." Thus, in an authentically Franciscan way, he has caught sight of the divine irradiation of created things, clear reflections of the beauty of God, as a means of perfection and of elevation to the Creator of all being.

Nervo shares in the tendency of Mexican poets to give a sort of pantheistic flavor to his development of the theme; but his religious and Franciscan sentiment recognizes the worth of humble things and magnifies them, recognizing their spiritual dimensions as things that have come from the hand of God by an express act of His will. This clarity of view is one of the secrets of St. Francis' soul. And for Nervo, too, the various transformations of Sister Water are so many fundamental characteristics whereby one may reach back to the beneficent Hand that created them. For this reason, amid the sea of doubts in which his spirit is tossed, the poet turns to God to ask, as did St. Paul on the road to Damascus, "Lord, what wilt thou have me do?" (p. 190)

Variety is not the outstanding note in Nervo's philosophy—it is rather monotonous and without originality. It is limited to a repetition of the ideas of confused intellectuals, with no precise distinction between what is orthodox and what is unorthodox. His model is the Archer, Apollo, constantly winging arrow after arrow at any and every cultural mark that presents itself to his view. But never, not even in the darkest days of spiritual prostration, does he lose sight of the profound beliefs of the Catholic faith that he learned in his childhood and early youth.

The aphorism, "Every one writes as he is", is usually true only when the one who writes really has a personality of his own. Amorphous and apathetic people have no style of expression—they can only state facts. But in the case of Amado Nervo there is no doubt; as soon as we begin to read his works, we are aware of his very individual personality, with its qualities of sweetness and aspiration for good. (pp. 194-95)

Dorothy Bratsas (essay date 1968)

SOURCE: "The Problem of Ideal Love in Nervo's Novels," *Romance Notes,* Vol. 9, No. 2, Spring, 1968, pp. 244-48.

[*In this excerpt, Bratsas probes the shortcomings of the human condition in its quest for love in Nervo's fiction.*]

Much consideration has been given to Amado Nervo, the Mexican Modernist poet, but relatively little has been given to his prose fiction. Many critics have pointed out the numerous themes used by Nervo but little has been done to demonstrate Nervo's use of psychological character study as a means of exploring a specific idea. In Nervo's three earliest novels, [*El Bachiller*, *Pascual Aguilera*, and *El donador de almas*], . . . he used the techniques of the psychological novel to describe the conflicts arising between wordly and spiritual love.

The three protagonists represent distinct psychological types. Felipe of *El Bachiller* is hypersensitive, pensive, religious, and lives in a subjective world restricted to his fantasies, illusions, prayers, and books. His excessive idealism contributes to his feeling of displacement in society. His fear of being disillusioned, of never being able to attain an ideal love in secular life, and his obsessive desire for solitude contribute to his decision to study for the priesthood. Felipe's intense neurotic personality feeds on his self-introspection and soon inhibits the little semblance of normality left to him. His religious zeal contributes to his development of a morbid fear of physical gratification. He even denies himself food and water in his mortification of the flesh. Chastity becomes an obsession. This morbid fear of sex results in his self-emasculation when he is confronted with making a choice between worldly and spiritual love.

Felipe's rejection of life represents the extremist position to the one maintained by his uncle and Asunción. They represent the life force and point out that salvation and union with God may be attained in other ways as acceptable as entering the priesthood. Felipe's inability to see the intrinsic difference between worldly and spiritual love contributes to his commiting a crime more offensive to God by not following his natural desires and by not accepting life's responsibilities.

Pascual Aguilera is Felipe's antithesis. He is brutal, crude, unsophisticated, and salacious. All of his interests are physical and material rather than spiritual, intellectual or artistic. He personifies primitive man whose physical needs motivate every action. His entire life has been preoccupied with gratifying his morbid sexuality. Pascual is as pathologically obsessed as Felipe, and his neurosis contributes to his death. His frustrations and anger precipitate an hysterical outburst, because he is thwarted in his attempts to possess Refugio. Her marriage to Santi-

ago precipitates a psychotic episode culminating in his attack on his stepmother. Pascual dies from the excesses of his hysteria.

The principal point Nervo makes in *Pascual Aguilera* is that the hero is not only depraved because of heredity but that his and man's destruction is because of sex. Nervo feels that sex impedes man's progress and the ideal state is one based on intellect rather than physical contact. The basis for humanity's ills and human suffering is mankind's great sin, "espíritu de fornicación".

The two protagonists destroy themselves because they are emotionally incapable of handling their problems. The other characters, representing normal society, in the two novels are directly affected by the problems created by the two disturbed heroes. Asunción in *El Bachiller* and doña Pancha in *Pascual Aguilera* represent the normal, healthy world in which the pathological does not function. Yet, these normal members of society suffer and are victimized by man's selfishness. Nervo is sympathetic to the problems of the Mexican woman and her role in marriage. He laments the treatment she receives from the male, while selfishly pursuing his gratification of the flesh without giving her the consideration she deserves.

In *El donador de almas* Nervo continues the development of his thesis that worldly love is not possible because of man's intrinsic shortcomings. The hero, Rafael, is the most stable protagonist of the three novels although he shares some characteristics with Felipe: he is refined, cultivated, sensitive, and somewhat neurotic. Rafael is also possessed of the monomaniacal desire to find the perfect woman for a perfect relationship. He remains frustrated in his search until he is given a soul, Alda. The novel is a fantasy describing the psychological interplay of the two protagonists, one representing the flesh and the other the spirit. The ensuing conflicts and crisis arising between the two produces some fascinating dialogues on worldly and spiritual love.

Through his characters Nervo states that the soul is a sexless, immortal entity fortunately not governed by the emotional problems of the organism housing it. Therefore, spiritual union can be realized—but a physical manifestation of love is not successful because it is motivated by self-love. . . . (pp. 244-46)

Love creates many conflicts, and love between the sexes is no more than an enchanting form of hate that has existed since time immemorial and will continue to exist. . . . (p. 246)

Rafael and Alda maintain an ideal relationship as long as she remains a free spirit not restricted to living on earth, and is permitted to experience and see the beauties of the universe. Alda refuses to remain with Rafael. She says that if man on earth would develop a love for his fellow man as strong as the one for himself then she might consider returning, for utopia would then exist.

The primary theme of all three works is love, worldly and spiritual. All three protagonists are neurotic, and their neuroses are of varying degrees of severity. Pascual is primitive man always motivated by his physical needs. Felipe and Rafael are idealists in search of perfect love. Neither can achieve a satisfactory relationship on earth, because neither is capable of establishing a relationship compatible with their standards. Therefore, one turns to religion and the other to developing an intellectually perfect cerebral relationship with his captive soul, Alda. Two succeed in destroying themselves and the third in losing his captive spirit because of their human frailties.

The various ideas expressed by Nervo through his characters in these three novels are repeated in his non-fictional prose and in his poetry. Wordly love, because of its physical manifestations, prevents the complete union of man and his loved one. It is a primitive and destructive emotion as seen in a person like Pascual Aguilera. Man is imperfect because of this sexual drive or *espíritu de fornicación* as Nervo calls it. It causes man's destruction. Felipe exemplifies this view. He cannot separate his love for God from his love for a terrestrial being. His conflict precipitates him into committing a crime against nature, graver than the one committed by Pascual. Be-

cause of his intrinsic self-centeredness, man cannot love unselfishly. A perfect relationship must be completely reciprocal, and this condition can never exist because man is hindered by his physical desires. Nervo's ideal state is a sexless one. The best possible relationship is an intellectual marriage between individuals as seen in *El donador de almas*. Only after death can one expect to achieve this *camino de perfección* or *escala de perfección* as Alda calls it. In life after death, when two beings are not bound by their physical selves, they can enjoy a perfect union. (pp. 247-48)

FURTHER READING

Peters, Kate. "*Fin de Siglo* Mysticism: Body, Mind, and Transcendence in the Poetry of Amado Nervo and Delmira Agustini," *Indiana Journal of Hispanic Literatures,* No. 8, Spring 1996, pp. 159-76.

> Notes themes of mystical realism in this comparison between Nervo's metaphysical expressions and Delmira Agustini's spiritual dilemmas in their poetry.

Additional coverage of Nervo's life and career is contained in the following sources published by the Gale Group: *Contemporary Authors*, Vols. 109, 131; *Hispanic Writers*; *Twentieth Century Literary Criticism*, Vol. 11.

Juan Carlos Onetti
1909-1994

Uruguayan novelist, short story and novella writer.

INTRODUCTION

Onetti is widely considered among the finest and most innovative novelists and short fiction writers of Latin America. Commenting on the alienation and dissatisfaction of modern life, his works feature such novelties as self-referentiality, nonlinear representation of events, emphasis on subjectivity, multi-layered narrative, characters invented by other characters, and the creation of a fictional milieu called Santa María. Onetti achieved international distinction with the publication of *La vida breve* (1950; *A Brief Life*), hailed as one of the most original novels to emerge from South America in the 1950s. He remains, as James Polk of the *New York Times* noted, "probably the least-known giant among modern Latin American writers."

Juan Carlos Onetti was born in Montevideo. His education was interrupted frequently as a result of numerous relocations by his family, and he eventually dropped out of high school to pursue a bohemian lifestyle, supporting himself with a variety of jobs. Though his formal studies ended, Onetti was an avid reader, favoring particularly the works of Knut Hamsun. In 1931 he completed *El pozo* (1931; *The Pit*), though this novella was not published until 1939, after having been reworked. An early publication of his won a prize from the journal *Prensa* in 1933, and Onetti was subsequently encouraged by the appearance of the stories "El obstáculo" and "El posible Baldi" in *Nación* in 1935 and 1936, respectively. He served as the managing editor of the influential weekly magazine *Marcha* from its inception in 1939 until 1941. The magazine lasted as an important voice within the Uruguayan cultural world for more than three decades, with Onetti as a notable contributor of essays and articles. In 1962, after the success of the novels *El astillero* (1961; *The Shipyard*) and *Juntacadáveres* (1964; *Junta, the Bodysnatcher*), Onetti was awarded the Premio Nacional de Literatura by the Uruguayan government for his body of writing. In the following years, his schedule included the travels and conferences typical of an internationally renowned author. However, in 1974 the government sentenced him to a three-month-long prison term for having served on the jury of a contest that honored a book deemed subversive. Frustrated by the country's dictatorship, Onetti abandoned Uruguay for Europe the following year, settling in Spain. In 1980 he received a nomination for the Nobel Prize in Literature from the Latin American PEN Club and was awarded the Premio Miguel de Cervantes Prize by the Spanish Ministerio de Cultura y Información. Onetti remained in Madrid until his death in 1994.

Creating an atmosphere of moral, physical, and psychological decay, Onetti wrote about characters who are isolated, disenchanted, and lonely. They mourn squandered opportunities, live in fear of death, or seek to escape the monotonous routine of their daily lives. These people are often pushed to the edge by society and live in a nightmare world of ruin and corruption that they try to escape through their imagination or the creation of dream worlds. Seldom given proper names by Onetti, these characters are identified by their occupation, psychological characteristics, or a particular aspect of their appearance. Usually little action occurs in Onetti's fiction. Plots tend to center on an event or decision, followed by testimonials from various characters whose observations relate to the preceding anecdote and simultaneously elucidate and muddle the story. Most of Onetti's fiction is open-ended: he offers no neat conclusions and some mysteries remain. The novella *El pozo* is the story of a man alone on the night of his fortieth birthday, writing his memoirs. He recollects his rape of a girl, his moral degradation, and torturous nightly self-analysis. This confession signals the potential for choosing a different way of life, but at the close of the narrative the man's direction remains unknown. Onetti's dramatization of the protagonist's internal, subjective state in *El pozo* is regarded as the beginning of existential fiction in Latin America.

Praised for their imaginativeness and originality, Onetti's works have been described as fundamentally ambiguous, fragmented, and complex. John Deredita noted that "critics reproach Onetti's thematic insistence, the lapses into rhetoric, the minute descriptive style that serves as the imitative form of boredom and that sometimes reproduces it in the reader." Furthermore, critics have accused Onetti of misogyny because his fictional women are almost always presented in an unflattering light, often as prostitutes or unfaithful wives. Despite these defects, Onetti's works have been favorably compared to those of Jean-Paul Sartre, James Joyce, Samuel Beckett, and especially William Faulkner, whose interest in layered narratives and imaginary settings was shared by Onetti. Referring to the arrival of modern society in the twentieth century, Carlos Fuentes has stated that civilization, "far from providing happiness or a sense of identity or the discovery of common values, was a new alienation, a more profound fragmentation, a more troublesome loneliness. No one came to see this better or sooner than the great Uruguayan novelist, Juan Carlos Onetti."

PRINCIPAL WORKS

El pozo [*The Pit*] (novella) 1931
Tierra de nadie [*No Man's Land*] (novel) 1941
Para esta noche [*Tonight*] (novel) 1943

La vida breve [*A Brief Life*] (novel) 1950
Un sueño realizado y otros cuentos (short stories) 1951
*Los adioses [*Goodbyes*] (novella) 1954
Una tumba sin nombre [*A Nameless Tomb*] (novella) 1959
La cara de la desgracia [*The Face of Misfortune*] (novella) 1960
El astillero [*The Shipyard*] (novel) 1961
El infierno tan temido [*Dreaded Hell*] (short stories) 1962
Juntacadáveres [*Junta, the Bodysnatcher*] (novel) 1964
Jacob y el otro; Un sueño realizado y otros cuentos [*Jacob and the Other; A Dream Come True and Other Stories*] (short stories) 1965
La novia robada y otros cuentos [*The Stolen Bride*] (short stories) 1968
La muerte y la niña [*Death and the Girl*] (novel) 1973
Tiempo de abrazar [*Time to Embrace*] (novella) 1974
Réquiem por Faulkner y otros artículos [*Requiem for Faulkner, and Other Articles*] (essays) 1975
Tan triste como ella y otros cuentos [*As Sad as She Is, and Other Stories*] (novella and short stories) 1976
Dejemos hablar al viento (novel) 1979
Cuando entonces [*When Then*] (novel) 1987
Cuando ya no importante [*When It Doesn't Matter Anymore*] (novel) 1993

*This work is translated in *Goodbyes, and Other Stories,* 1990.

CRITICISM

Luis Harss and Barbara Dohmann (essay date 1967)

SOURCE: "Juan Carlos Onetti, or the Shadows on the Wall," in *Into the Mainstream: Conversations with Latin-American Writers,* Harper & Row, 1967, pp. 173-205.

[*Harss is a Chilean-born novelist, journalist, and critic. In the following essay from a study by Harss, originally published in 1966 as *Los Nuestros *and subsequently translated with Dohmann, the critics provide a thorough survey of Onetti's fiction. Observing the miserable state of Onetti's characters, they conclude that "his pessimism seems to have become almost genetic."*]

Montevideo, the capital of a welfare state fallen on hard times, has become a drab gray city. When we were there in July—the middle of winter in the Southern Hemisphere—the weather was unseasonably muggy. Heavy clouds hung overhead, the depressing remnants of a long heat wave. A strike of public employees, utility workers, etc., had added paralysis to bureaucratic blight; drought had brought power rationing; the streets were dark. Garbage strewn on doorsteps blew about in a listless wind. There was a general feeling of glumness and apathy. As usual in times of economic crisis, the accompanying devaluation was not only monetary but human as well. Life goes on, but in an atmosphere of unreality. The wear and tear shows in the worried glances of people hurrying into offices lost in the interiors of old buildings with stalled elevators.

In the slow drizzle, trudging down the street in a bulky coat, stooped under the weight of the city, is a sleepwalker on a sleepless night. Like the city, he looks tired and middle-aged. He is tall, gaunt, with splotches of white in his gray hair, insomniac eyes straining behind horn-rimmed glasses, painfully grimacing lips, a high professorial forehead, and the slouch of an aging clerk. His grandfather was a stockbroker, his father a customs official, and he, the protagonist of an unfinished book he has been writing for years and publishing in installments, under different titles, is "a lonely man smoking somewhere in the city . . . turning toward the shadow on the wall at night to dwell on nonsensical fantasies." He seems friendless, idle, and absent, and has always been that way, because of some flaw of nature, some inner lack dating at least as far back as adolescence, when he already "had nothing to do with anyone." He lives in solitary confinement, withdrawn and practically unattached. It was this physical and emotional isolation, he has said, that turned him into a writer in the first place, in spite of himself, for unknown reasons, out of a habit that became his "vice, passion, and misfortune." He bears his cross as if atoning for some nameless guilt that can never be expiated or forgiven. Such is the picture we have of Onetti, the lone wolf of Uruguayan letters, whose habitat, according to the critic Mario Benedetti, is the disaster area of those fated to suffer "the basic failure of all bonds, the general misunderstanding and miscasting of lots in life."

Onetti, an ardent Arltian, belongs to a "lost" generation that came of age around 1940, when the intellectual life of the country was being reassessed against a background of demagoguery and political disenchantment, of totalitarianism in Europe, and nationalism—with pro-Axis sympathies—in Argentina. In Uruguay a reactionary government ruled the country from 1933 to 1942, eroding faith in democracy as the corruption lurking under the monotonous surface of bureaucratic stability became daily more obvious. There were many broken lives in those days. Onetti speaks of the nihilism of his generation—portrayed in massive detail in his second novel, **Tierra de Nadie (No Man's Land,** 1941)—as a delayed echo of the epidemic malaise of the twenties. But, of course, Onetti lived it as an endemic phenomenon. For him, it was the disillusionment and resulting individualism of an era in which he was one of those who fell by the wayside.

In Uruguay, as in its next-door neighbor Argentina, the thirties and forties marked a period of great literary ferment. Until then Uruguayan culture had flourished in circles that followed European fashions and had been eclectic and cosmopolitan. By some curious but significant quirk of fate, Uruguay contributed Jules Laforgue and Lautréamont, and later Jules Supervielle, to French literature. At home in the nineteenth and early twentieth centuries it had nourished the usual schools of academicians and traditionalists. Toward 1915 or 1920, disquieting underground movements had begun to be felt in the work of Quiroga, where an era's neurasthenia had suddenly turned introspective and touched somber depths. But Quiroga was something of an anomaly in his day—when no one wanted to fish in troubled waters—and his work remained exceptional. At the turn of the century—the heyday of Modernism in all of Latin America—the general mood, in spite of literary agonies imported from Europe, was hopeful and optimistic. The first decade of the century, balancing the stresses created by the vast wave of immigrants that reached the shores of the River Plate between 1880 and 1910, saw the rise of a middle class that found its truculent but whimsical spokesman in the person of Florencio Sánchez, our singlehanded inventor of the theater of social realism. It was a period of economic development for the River Plate, which prospered through the First World War. Symptoms of the age were political commitment and social reform, literary experimentation and radicalism in government. The euphoria, as we know, lasted until about 1930. The climate of the period was put in a few words by the Argentine poet Carlos Mastronardi, who, looking back on it wistfully across the years some time ago, said: "We were the last happy men."

The thirties, with the coming to power of nationalist groups, changed all that. There was the beginning of panic and collapse in intellectual circles. Isolated figures at first—an Arlt, who discovered unsuspectedly disruptive behavioral patterns in the humdrum and the commonplace—started to draw a bleakly pessimistic picture of their society. With the usual lag in time, the River Plate, reflecting worldwide insecurity, was caving in under the dislocations of the twentieth century. The atmospheric distress contaminated regional literature—for instance, the works of Uruguay's grim soul-searcher, Francisco Espínola. But it was essentially an urban phenomenon. Toward 1940 it was widespread. It throbbed with poetic splendor in the essays of our great "agonist," Ezequiel Martínez Estrada, who bared a continent's inherited ills mercilessly in his belligerent sociological mural, *Radiografía de la Pampa* (1939). His *La Cabeza de Goliat (The Head of Goliath)* was to give an incisive diagnosis of the ravages of urbanization. Suddenly, it seemed, the battle call of the thirties, "Here and now," had issued in the age of debunking, of violent indictments and denunciations of a system already in crumbling decline. Our novel, still suffering from upper-class nostalgia—therefore threatened with becoming an extinct species—had to catch up with the times to survive. Which was easier said than done. Adapting, for it, meant not only getting reorganized but shifting its foundations. It was a slow process, a timid growth, but far-reaching in its effects. As literary "schools," once active but never very cohesive, broke up, for the first time our writers, living in exacerbated isolation in anonymous big cities, turned their eyes inward, to build subjective worlds. In this they were part of a pattern that reflected not only the fall of established values but the facts of daily life. A new type of human being, a creature of twilight, rootless, rancorous, frustrated, displaced, populated our big cities. He was not so much the Marxist underdog as the spiritual outlaw, the moral discard. Arlt had aleady drawn his prophetic

portrait. Now Onetti followed suit, with the dour shrug of a man shouldering the burden of a sad responsibility. In a prefatory note to *Tierra de Nadie,* whose action takes place in the Buenos Aires of 1940, Onetti has said: "I paint a group of people who may seem exotic in Buenos Aires but are nevertheless representative of a generation. . . . The fact is that the most important country of the young South American continent has started to produce a type of morally indifferent individual who has lost his faith and all interest in his own fate." He adds, defining a bankrupt attitude conditioned by the surrounding indigence: "Let no one reproach the novelist for having undertaken the portrait of this human type in the same spirit of indifference."

In his first published work, *El Pozo (The Pit,* 1939), the gloomy protagonist, Eladio, a thinly veiled projection of the author, had already recorded his skepticism in regard to personal commitment, his phlegmatic unconcern for anything resembling direct action or involvement. With sad irony Eladio confesses his total lack of social consciousness, of "popular spirit." The tone, as in most of Onetti, is confessional. Why even bother to put pen to paper? wonders Eladio, thinking out loud for the author. The willful answer is in a kind of militant argument for self-expression. "It's true I don't know how to write," he admits. "But I write about myself." Eladio, with his apoplectic inhibitions, is the classic Outsider. He lives disconnected from the world, stranded within himself, adrift in his tiny corner on the borderline of humanity, without any possibility of joining the mainstream. He begins and ends in himself. Which is why his single ambition is "to write the story of a soul, all by itself, without any of the events it had to mix in whether it wanted to or not." Though, of course, whether he "wants to or not," he forms part of the unconscious community of the lonely, the diaspora of the estranged. Even in his alienation, or because of it, he is the representative of a time and place, a frame of mind, an epoch. It is this fact that gives his experiences relevance and validity. To have realized this is Onetti's merit. In a literary scene still too often made up of inflated social canvases, painters of the soul like Onetti are a rarity. But, if only because in the last years they have been producing much of our best work, they have begun to seem inevitable. That our literature is gradually shifting its focus from object to subject, in appearance, perhaps, narrowing its perspectives, is actually a clear sign of our growing self-awareness and, of course, the price in pain and distress that we are paying for it. The price may be high, but, then, who can deny that the stakes are, too? Meditating on the world of solitary inner lives he has created out of what might pass for superfluous materials in the age of industrial waste, Onetti, a man who has never bargained, said in an interview in 1961, without immodesty: "All I want to express is the adventure of man."

For Onetti, who seems to suffer from permanent pangs of conscience over his life, the adventure has been a dismal one. We are trying to piece it together with him, up in a small hotel room in the shabbiness of downtown Montevideo, overlooking an expanse of limp rooftops

Juan Carlos Onetti

and cluttered back yards. Perhaps the rain, which is sprinkling hot splinters outside, makes him take a particularly dim view of things. With its drone in the background, the conversation, like a worn record, progresses in fits and starts. Onetti is a man of few words, most of them mumbled or swallowed entirely. He sits slumped, chain-smoking, hunching his shoulders every now and then, looking miserably uncomfortable.

"To think someone has come all the way out here just to talk to me," he says in his usual slightly bored and vaguely deprecating tone, but perhaps with a little inward smile, in which it seems to us we can detect a trace of coquetry.

We met the night before at a party, where we listened to a needle in a tired groove churning out tangos by the immortal Gardelito, who, though dead many years, was, as the saying goes among his devotees, sounding better than ever; and after a sentimental drink or two Onetti, an old fan, became harsh, ponderous, mournful, and finally sullen.

Now he has come in with a heavy shuffle, a sign of chronic exhaustion. In periods of insomnia he does not eat or sleep for a week. He smokes, drinks, and fidgets; then he collapses for days. He has left his post at a branch of the municipal library to come speak to us, and he has been with us for no more than a few minutes when the phone rings. His wife is worried about him. He has wandered

out of work without warning her. Soon she arrives, startling us: a tall blonde of Anglo-Austrian descent, brisk, witty, pink-cheeked, with charmingly puckered lips and a fretful look. At the sight of her he hangs his head guiltily over some imaginary or remembered offense he has committed. But on the whole he seems more relaxed with her around. She jollies him along, occasionally prompts him. And he takes heart, and opens up a bit. But it is difficult for him to talk about his work. He does not believe in the possibility of true communication. "The deeper experiences are intransmittable," he says. He is obsessed with the notion that the things he says are misinterpreted, the jokes he cracks turned around and held against him. "The misunderstanding is so frequent." He hates to look back. He never rereads his books. They would upset him. "The sensation of the past is painful to me," he says. His immersion in his work is so extreme that it acquires terrifying proportions in his mind. He is afraid to "abandon" himself to his writing. Remembering his books afterwards seems to affect him in the same way. He has left them behind, forgetting them as he has forgotten his own life— they are so much a part of it. "I am not a writer except when I write," he says. Like Proust or Faulkner—especially the latter, with whom he identifies in more ways than one; we think of Faulkner's legendary shyness—he inhabits a world of his own, outside literary currents. When he is done with his books, they tend to get scattered or lost, he never knows exactly how or why. The case of *Tiempo de Abrazar* (*Time for Embracing*), an unpublished novel—his first, begun around 1933, when he was twenty-four years old—was typical. Shortly before the war, four copies of the book were submitted to a contest in Buenos Aires. Eventually—in 1943—some loose fragments appeared in the Uruguayan magazine *Marcha,* but the rest of the manuscript seems to have been mislaid and he has never taken the trouble to recover it. Perhaps out of his own carelessness and neglect, it was years before his work began to be published. He forgets how long *El Pozo* gathered dust on his desk before it saw the light of day. Then it was ignored. In his time Onetti knew all the difficulties of a literary career without "connections" in an inhospitable environment with an unreceptive public: the lack of incentive, the impossibility of financial independence. The first of his books to attract attention was *Tierra de Nadie,* which won a prize in a contest organized by Losada, a publishing house then newly founded by a Spanish exile who, like so many of his countrymen, had set sail to seek fortune across the ocean, far from the Civil War. But that was of little help to Onetti. His books have always lost money; which is why almost every single one of them has been put out by a different publisher. The idea was "to spread the damage," he says. He almost gave up on *Los Adioses* (*Goodbyes,* 1954). It was all set up for printing—even the type was cast—when the house that had bought it went broke and shut down. The loss might have gone unnoticed but for a friend who fortunately rescued the manuscript and passed it on to a guardian angel of the arts, Victoria Ocampo—her famous little magazine *Sur* had by then given its name to a publishing house—who generously published it at her own expense. But it was something of a flop, and Onetti soon lost track of it. Whether there have been any more editions after the original one he does not know, though he heard somewhere—probably one of those false rumors that keep plaguing him—that the book had been reprinted in Havana. He wonders—perfunctorily—whether they will split the losses with him. At least now he is beginning to receive his share of critical recognition at home and abroad. Which seems only fair. Though of uneven quality, his work has provided our postwar literature with some of its finest moments. Perhaps because he has never had the money for the classic Latin-American pilgrimage to Europe—the farthest he has ever been from the River Plate, until a recent visit to the United States, is Bolivia—there is something genuinely home-grown about him that goes a lot deeper than the strident feelings or protestations of self-conscious literary nationalism that characterize so many of his countrymen. He is perhaps the closest thing we have to a truly autochthonous writer. Years of commuting between Buenos Aires and Montevideo have made him one with the soul and character of the area. He did not invent the urban novel in Uruguay; the genre already existed, in a somewhat high-minded form, in the days of Reyles. But at a time when Europeanized circles did not consider local settings grand enough to be of universal concern he set himself the job of going beyond the purely picturesque or physiognomic to explore the city's hidden face. Uruguay's lack of epic or heroic themes or burning issues—exploited Indians, hardship zones such as mines or oilfields, military dictatorships—has not bothered him. He has devoted himself to a more intimate task: the imaginative re-creation of a spiritual landscape. Santa María—his Yoknapatawpha County—is a mythical town; but its feel, its mental features, the psychological traits of its inhabitants, are distinctly Uruguayan. In Onetti accuracy of observation combines happily with insight and intuition. In the apparently incidental or anecdotal he finds the key to what is authentic and important. In this he is in the direct line of descent from Robert Arlt, the first to discover the metaphysical in the microscopic. Onetti's emphasis is on minute states of mind, "intensities of being," as he calls them, in the gray continuum that surrounds him.

It all began in Montevideo, in 1909, where Onetti spent his youth through secondary school. He speaks of it in a dwindling voice, as if he were trying to remember a lost version of some forgotten story. An attitude which is of the essence of the man and the writer. "I was born with it," he says of his writing. He was a child who told tales about people—"lies," he calls them harshly. And he means it. Perhaps the word indicates a qualm inherent in those who inhabit a fantasy world subject to slanderous and freakish twists of the imagination. If anything can be said about his work, it is that it is hypothetical in outlook, more shading than substance. It is made of half-thoughts, interrupted gestures, statements stealthily proposed, examined, denied, contradicted. He is less interested in arriving at the truth of a situation than in isolating its components—its alternatives—which are likely to yield as many falsehoods as facts. The variants are inexhaustible. The reader looking for a final authoritative version is disappointed. Nothing ever quite works out or adds up

in Onetti. We have a hard time finding out who he is. His family seems to have little or nothing to do with him. The name is of British, probably Irish, descent; originally it was spelled O'Nety. In the mid-nineteenth century his great-grandfather was the private secretary of General Rivera, the leader of the insurgent forces that fought against Argentina's bloody dictator, Rosas, who was trying to extend his influence to Uruguay.

"He became Rivera's secretary under very curious circumstances," says Onetti with the shadow of a smile. Great-grandfather O'Nety ran a general store in a small town in the interior of the country. "And one day Rivera went by on his way to one of the ten thousand revolutions there were in those days, and spent the evening with the old man. They played cards—General Rivera's great passion. And the idiot was so overcome with admiration for the personality of General Rivera that he picked up right then and there, loaded all his possessions into a horse-cart, and since he knew how to read and write, unusual talents in the back country, he was named Rivera's secretary. According to some very old letters preserved by an aunt of mine, I've seen that the name was O'Nety. I've dug up some information, and it seems that my great-great-grandfather, the first to come here, was an Englishman born in Gibraltar. My grandfather was the one to Italianize the name, probably for political reasons, environmental reasons—I don't know." By then the family lived in Montevideo. Onetti touches on the subject, but immediately glosses over it. As for his mother, she was Brazilian, the offspring of landed gentry—"slaveowners," says Onetti gloatingly—in Rio Grande do Sul.

We find out little about Onetti's early years. After high school, when he was about twenty years old, he moved to Buenos Aires, the promised land, where he took random courses in the university and held innumerable odd jobs—which he refuses to name, bored or ashamed of them—before eventually making a career of journalism. He was with Reuter's News Service, became their Buenos Aires bureau chief in the early forties. At the same time he was associated with and helped edit *Marcha* in Montevideo. After Reuter's, he was editor in chief—up to about 1950—of an Argentine magazine, *Vea y Lea*. Then he was in charge of a publicity magazine called *Ímpetu*. It was a very small magazine—subsidized, or owned, by the Walter Thompson advertising agency—that came out once a month and paid him enough to scrape by on.

He says, not particularly gleeful: "It was restful work, because all I had to do was make up an editorial, a lot of blah, blah, public relations, and all that sort of stuff. The rest was translations stolen from *Printer's Ink* and *Bertelsmann*."

He was in Buenos Aires until about 1954, when vaguely political aspirations brought him back home. It was the time of the electoral triumph of Luis Batlle Berres in Uruguay. Friends in the ruling party had him drop everything to come and join them. He took over the party paper, counting on an optimistic promise that he might be given a consulate somewhere (a promise that never materialized). He remained with *Acción*—to which he still contributes occasionally—for two or three years. After which he moved to his present library job at the Institute of Arts and Letters.

Better than his external career, his inner course can be traced in his books, which contain no direct references to personal—or worldly—matters but are, more than with most authors', an almost complete spiritual autobiography of their creator. It took his some time to find his way into his fictional world. But he was busy mapping himself out from the beginning. He tells us about his first attempt, *Tiempo de Abrazar.* It was an adolescent love story involving a virginal vamp—a Lolita-type compound of seductiveness and false innocence—whose perishable youthful bloom the protagonist struggles to rescue from the devastation of time and age. The girl is the first of a long series of pseudo-virginal female adolescents that populate Onetti's books, high priestesses of erotic love usually endowed with a combination of morbid sensuality and bitter misanthropy that makes them at once devastating and inaccessible. The physical contacts they grudgingly submit to are a sorrowful and desultory affair symptomatic, in Onetti's scheme, of the forces of disintegration at work in all human relations. In Onetti's ordinarily middle-aged protagonists—his other selves—there is a desperate yearning for vanished youth, innocence and purity, corroded images to which they cling, rusted by time and undermined by memory. They live in the nonexistent past, in the shambles of approaching death and decay, as life passes them by. They have grown old without ever growing up, barely surviving or subsisting through the years, after some distant—and more or less nebulous—fall from grace into the sordid facts of life. Thus, we have Ana María in *El Pozo,* a joyless little sexpot who inspires a sad lust in the protagonist. His absurd love for her, which exists entirely in the sublimated realm of reverie, is a cynical front behind which he disguises feelings of guilt and remorse. It is nothing but an exorcism—an alibi. The fact is that he has once raped or in some way humiliated her—an impulse that in Onetti functions as a form of wish fulfillment—after which, for understandable reasons, their relations were discontinued. But in his vagaries the climactic act of violence repeats itself indefinitely with a high poetic charge, as if it had been an act of love. The switch is an attempt on Eladio's part to trick himself out of the trap he has set for himself. But it is too late. In Onetti a single moment of bad faith—or bad luck—derails a life forever. Perhaps because "love is marvelous and absurd, and incomprehensibly visits all kinds of souls. But absurd and marvelous people do not abound; and even those gifted with those qualities retain them only for a short time, in their early youth. Then they start accepting things and that's the end of them."

For Onetti, growing out of adolescence into adult life means compromising with impotence and despair. Hidden somewhere in the process is a loss that can never be made up. Says Onetti: "I think that happens to everybody." The sense of having strayed, of things left undone, opportunities missed, chances overlooked, is universal, says Onetti. He has always been haunted by it. The feeling is

vague—a sort of chronic uneasiness. "Each person, out of convenience, even intellectual convenience, tries to pinpoint the cause of the trouble, to find something concrete and say: 'This is it.' Even if it isn't." The effect is numbing. But numbness is the human lot. Onetti defines his characters in terms of their omissions. "Because that's the way I am." In fact, in his early work—*El Pozo, Tierra de Nadie, Para Esta Noche* (*For Tonight,* 1943)—the characters are little more than episodes in his own mental processes. They are passing fancies that flicker in and out of existence like dream figures. Their sole reality is their subjective charge. And that defines their function. They are dreams dreamed by an author who in turn is dreamed by them. They have only a shadowy secondary—subsidiary—existence and no dramatic substance.

Passing himself off as his narrator is a favorite Onetti device. "I feel freer, more like myself, working this way," he says. Thus Eladio, an inchoate writer, is doubling for the author when he sits down to compose a page of his journal reflecting, as he puts it with heavy irony, that "a man ought to write the story of his life when he reaches the age of forty, especially if interesting things have happened to him." The point is, of course, that nothing has ever happened to him worth mentioning. And what little has happened is a lot less real or interesting than what he has imagined. Reality is tedious and destructive, never up to the high standards of fantasy. Perhaps in this notion lies the source of the narrator's sense of inferiority which his dreams compensate for, providing him with a means of working off his obscure grudge against the world. Because "facts are always empty." It is out of this sense of inadequacy that the author invents surrogate characters who in turn perpetuate themselves in an endless succession of other invented characters that are all his mirror images. "For the writer," says Onetti, "his world is the world. Otherwise he is cheating." What this amounts to in practice is that reading an Onetti book is a schizophrenic experience. The reader is in constant flux between the mind or perceptions of the narrator-protagonist and those of the author, the two being practically indistinguishable. Onetti's figments would cease to exist the moment no one looked at them. They are in the mind's eye and gain access to their borrowed reality only in so far as there is an onlooker to bear witness to them. That is why Onetti says he writes "for his characters." They are his inner inventory. Exposing and outlining himself in them is his way of offering himself through them. Even in their spuriousness, the subjective load they carry is a sign of his abiding affection for them. He has been accused of emotional poverty. The charge is not unfounded. He is not versatile with his emotions. But he says: "The characters don't function unless you love them. Writing a novel is an act of love."

Nowhere is this more visible—or more relevant—than in what may well be his masterpiece, *La Vida Breve* (*A Short Life,* 1950), a book that is all chaos and ferment, a monument to evasion through literature. "An open book," he calls it fondly. An appropriate term. It is a plotless series of imaginings that unfold in the mind of a viewer—one of the author's delegates into the shadow world—

in the form of gestures and situations. The title, deliberately ambiguous in its allusiveness, was taken from the words of a French song quoted in the book. Says Onetti: "I wanted to speak about several short lives, to show different persons leading these short lives." Sharing them, transferring them to each other, might be more exact. As he says: "The end of one would be the beginning of another, and so on indefinitely." Of course, the "several" lives are really one life, multiplied, relayed many times. It appears in the form of certain types of scenes that repeat themselves at odd intervals, like cyclic rites, in which certain shapes of persons recur, are transformed into others that resemble them, and die to be born again. Every chapter provides a choice or option within the limited possibilities available. Seen from another angle, *La Vida Breve,* which contains the germ of everything that followed in Onetti's subsequent work, is a long pregnancy that ends in the birth of a subject and a fictional world. Onetti seems to have caught a sudden—incomplete but ultimately lucid—glimpse of the whole road that lay ahead of him. Here, for the first time, we encounter Santa María, "a small town extending between a river and a settlement of Swiss laborers." Here, in the narrator's overactive imagination, we witness the birth of Díaz Grey, himself the narrator and central intelligence in later works. *La Vida Breve* is a dreamworld that later becomes the real world. Dreams used symbolically, says Onetti, are a cheap device. For him they are not transparent Freudian metaphors subject to pat clinical interpretation but an added dimension of reality.

The protagonist, or figurehead, of *La Vida Breve,* Bransen, is a colorless minor employee in a publicity firm who, attempting to find a way out of the dreariness of his life, dreams himself into the person of Díaz Grey, a doctor he conjures up out of some vaporous literary reminiscence, presumably for a film script he has been commissioned to write for his friend Julio Stein. A chance meeting in the hallway of the rooming house where he lives supplies him with a third identity. A fourth—the author, multiplied, occasionally dissolved, in the roles he shares—complicates the strange cast of characters. Bransen's various split personalities are in constant tension, nourishing and starving each other as they compete for supremacy. There is doubt up to the end as to which will impose itself at the expense of the others. The center of the whirlpool—the eye of the storm—is a static tableau, a set piece of décor in which Bransen, in suspended animation, stages the drama: his room. The immutable setting, says Onetti, was "stolen" from a still life by Ivan Albright that depicts objects on a table, among them a pair of empty gloves that retain the shape of the hands that have been in them. Bransen inhabits this unchanging picture. From there he spins out his fantasies, which branch off in all directions in an intricate pattern of criscrossing lines in which each intersection is a new starting point. The author, hovering over his shoulder, is an active participant in every story. In each, there is a woman who is all women and enacts the standard parts in the female repertory, appearing under the different guises of sister, wife, mistress, prostitute. The protagonist, in vicarious raptures, escapes from one life into another,

improvising as he goes. But every apparent escape leads to a dead end.

Of all Bransen's surrogate creations, it is the doctor Díaz Grey (Dorian Gray?) who acquires the most depth and substance and gradually gains the upper hand over the others, finally supplanting the author himself. Bransen simply—and arbitrarily—places him in the nondescript Santa María "because I had once been happy there, years before, for twenty-four hours and for no particular reason." Bransen is referring to the usual Onettian moment of truth and beauty in his life, now gone forever. He searches for it everywhere, particularly in an old blurred picture of his wife, Gertrudis, with whom he has broken up. He finds a semblance or duplicate of her as she was in the days of her bloom in the image of her younger sister, who occasionally replaces her in his fantasies. Gertrudis suffers from his same aging pangs, and the consequent desire to impersonate herself in her previous roles. Her symptoms are physically portrayed in a typical Onetti sequence: she is seen in the shifting postures that mark the steps of her mental retreat, reviving old gestures and attitudes in a regressive order that leads back through time to what we assume will end in fetal position. Like Bransen, she is in search of "the only faintly glimpsed and as yet incomprehensible origin of everything that was happening to me, of what I had become and what cornered me." To break the irreversible pattern of his life is the compulsive need of every Onetti character. The solution—if one can call it a solution—that Bransen finds is to lead a phantasmal existence outside time. He is a sort of calamitous Walter Mitty. At times he thinks he can assume his condition. He tells himself that perhaps "if I cherished and deserved my daily sadness, if I coveted it, longed for it, steeped myself in it until my eyes and every last syllable I uttered were full of it"—in other words, if he accepts and installs himself in it—then "I would be safe from revolt and despair." But that is just another false comfort, a final snare.

The single nightmare theme is orchestrated in every pitch and key. There is no real chronological sequence; all actions and events are simultaneous. They take place in a sort of eternal present which is the time of the mind that is breeding them. There is a minimum of plot. Or, rather, there are many bits and strands of different plots forming an aimless patchwork that would be completely incoherent were it not sustained by a single even tone as hypnotic and inexorable as the senselessness of reverie. Bransen is a case beyond repair. He lives in "the unforgettable certitude that there is no woman, no friend, no house, no book, even no vice anywhere that can make me happy." Little keeps him alive: "the awareness I have of myself, misunderstandings. Nothing else. . . . Meantime, I remain what I am, an unalterable, timid little man married to the only woman he seduced or who seduced him, incapable at this point, not only of being anyone else, but even of wanting to be someone else." He is resigned to the slow torture of "a short life" that has declined into living death. So is everyone else; for instance, his friend, Lagos, whose whole life is a sham that no longer fools anybody but which he maintains "because he is afraid, because he is old, because every Lagos he invents is a possibility—ultimately, a possibility of oblivion."

What is left, under such desolate circumstances, are small deaths and resurrections, such as the act of love, an "imposed exercise" in the performance of which Bransen becomes a "manipulator of immortality." At least passion is "personal," a situation in which he can "be myself once and for all and then immediately forget myself." But of course this is no real release from the surfeit of self. Because the partner remains elusively out of reach. Besides, each new woman is a reincarnation of the women who preceded her and a premonition of the ones who will follow, ad infinitum. Instead of being annualled, Bransen is reproduced in her. His predicament is not a matter of the weariness of age, or decadence, Bransen stresses, but simply of the way life is. His last and only hope is that even the damned are not condemned to a particular life or course of action, but only to "a soul, a certain disposition." Therefore, he reasons, "one can live many times, many different, longer or shorter, lives." However devoid of faith a man may be, he can still "enter into many games," pretend to others in order to convince himself, to keep the farce going. Because "any passion or faith contributes to happiness in so far as it keeps us entertained or helps us forget." The lines already drawn cannot be effaced, but perhaps the original terms could be modified or restated, the beginning forced "to occur again, differently this time." And if "the memory of the first beginning" could be altered, then perhaps the new beginning would be strong enough "to alter the memory of what followed." Except that, however hard Bransen tries, "neither my hands nor my memory could hit on the right clue" to get the wheel turning. Nevertheless, the search, which is like "a quiet madness, a melancholy rage," as if he were being called somewhere for no purpose and yet could not refuse to answer the call, goes on. He continues to "suppress words and situations," in hopes one day of coming upon "that single moment that will express everything: Díaz Grey, myself, and therefore the whole world." It will be a moment of plenitude, containing all things, among them the key to life's lost paradise, "the days cut to the size of our true self."

Behind the search—for order, serenity, impossible perfection—one suspects is a nostalgia for an experience of the divinity in a godless world. There is a Kafkaesque bishop who expounds at one point, as a spokesman for an unseen and paradoxical God, that man must understand that "eternity is now" and that he—man—is "the only end." Therefore, the bishop recommends—curiously arguing, not for Hedonism but stoicism—man must put all his enterprise into being himself, if only for the sake of argument, at all times and against all obstacles. Since he was not consulted on the rules of the game or invited to give his opinion on whether or not he wanted to play it, the only way for him to beat it is to enter into connivance with it. Says Bransen, echoing these words of wisdom: "The whole science of living . . . consists in the simple expedient of being flexible enough to fit into the gaps between the events we have not provoked, not forcing things, always, simply, being." The road to salvation, if there is one, is to "keep the consciousness of death alive in every cell of our bones." The dismal alternative, into which most of Onetti's people fall, is the habit of accepting "what one sees of oneself in the eyes of others," adopting the fraud as the genuine article, and acting accordingly. Better to "despise whatever must be obtained through effort, whatever does not fall into our hands by miracle." Then we will be "free of the past and the responsibility of the future, reduced to an event, strong in proportion to our ability to dispense with things." The prescription is not merely utilitarian but ultimately mystical. It proposes an aesthetic method as well as a form of mental accommodation. Communing with his fictions is the author's way of resolving his conflicts. The hypostatic existences born out of him in the act of writing are his temporary liberation from his inner stalemate. Their adventures take him through a mirror to the far side—the outer edge—of ordinary experience, where answers precede questions and he can, as he says, relax and drag his feet for a while, having found inner leeway. The author lives through the lives of his characters. The trouble is that their lives are short. Prolonging and sustaining them requires a huge imaginative effort. The creation, via Bransen, of Díaz Grey and his world committed Onetti to a task of years and heroic feats of concentration. It has always been a tenuous and unstable fiction that a moment's absentmindedness could obliterate. Already in *La Vida Breve,* says Onetti, "there are several attempts on the part of the narrator to keep Díaz Grey alive." The ubiquitous but incurably ephemeral doctor keeps slipping away from Bransen, who "sets him back up again, shelters him, damns him, puts him by the window to look out at the river. At a certain moment he says: 'So many days have gone by since I was last able to see Díaz Grey.' He has to bring him back to put him on his fated course again." A lot is at stake. Like God and His creatures in some eminently symbiotic scheme, Onetti and Díaz Grey depend on each other.

Evidence of this is *Un Sueño Realizado y Otros Cuentos* (*A Dream Fulfilled and Other Stories,* 1951), written between 1941 and 1949—or more or less simultaneously with *La Vida Breve*—and first published in the course of the years in the Buenos Aires newspaper *La Nación.* Here, amid a lot of peripheral stage machinery, we can see Onetti assembling and dismounting the props that support his framework. *Un Sueño Realizado* is setting and background for *La Vida Breve.* Onetti is projecting antecedents, plotting case histories, feeling his way into attitudes, customs, and habitats. People and faces are in uncertain suspense, shadows flashing on the screen and flickering off in the blink of an eyelash. We have no clear concept, no over-all view, of the situation yet; but Onetti's main themes are all present. The hypocritical idealism of adolescence is exposed in **"Bienvenido, Bob"** (**"Welcome, Bob"**). The shabbiness of false hope—in this case a man who swindles his boss to fulfill his Danish wife's ruinous yearning to return to the land of her childhood—is portrayed in **"Esbjerg, en la Costa"** (**"Esbjerg, on the Coast"**). Again, there is the death of illusion on contact with reality, in the title story, **"Un**

Sueño Realizado." And, most notably, there is our friend Díaz Grey—grown independent of his progenitor, Bransen—in a familiar dilemma: the recollection, from the unfathomable depths of age, of the one moment of possible redemption in his life, which he threw away when he betrayed the trust of the woman who had offered him her help and love (**"La Casa en la Arena"**—**"The House on the Sand"**). The retrospective view of Díaz Grey ties up some loose ends in his story, but actually raises more questions than it solves. The past, in Onetti, is mythologized. Remembrance is a distant vantage point in which old scenes recur full of problematic variations. In **"La Casa en la Arena"** we are told what actually happened, what the protagonist imagined had happened, what he wished had happened, and what may, for all we know, still be happening, all of these different phases of the experience superimposed as time holds still around them. Onetti does not want to crystallize his world; he wants it to remain fluid. Therefore his various accounts of events, even when they cover the same grounds, may not coincide. Facts in one book may contradict those given in another, or even elsewhere in the same book. Inconsistencies need not be accounted for. What remains unchanged is the atmosphere of loss and drift, resentment and cynicism, that absorbs his creatures with their vague urges, their flashes of hate toward others, their perverse fantasies and obscure qualms and regrets. They are fixtures in a closed circuit that seals off all escape routes and makes all conclusions foregone. The town is little more than an extension of their boredom, staleness, and misery. Everywhere there are "fat and badly dressed people." The settings are grubby bedrooms, sweaty bars, fetid back streets, or "any smelly office." The detailed description—sometimes ad nauseam—of the gestures and movements of minor characters thickens the paste, adding to the cumulative agony. Every twitch and contortion has its place in the system. Even as the protagonists reflect the author, the secondary characters enact the moods of the protagonists. They form overlapping images that act as objective correlatives of a single state of mind. "That's the way I am. The small detail in persons or situations is enormously important to me," says Onetti. The traits scattered among the surrounding human specters belong less to individual persons than they do to the ensemble, to the repertory of the book as a whole. Personifying the décor is a way of rendering it dynamic, humanizing it. Onetti's figments are never rounded persons; they are choreographic figures. He says he could never create the complete psychology of a Babbitt. Nor would he want to. He deals with a single emotional—almost abstract—type: the stranger. Often his characters are actually out-of-towners of vaguely foreign genealogy; there is a predominance of Nordic or Germanic names that enhance this effect. They lead an erratic existence, "a grotesque life," married to flabby women, too big for their small lives, too small for their fantasies, straitjacketed by their past, eroded by "the quiet underhanded work of time."

A somewhat painful subject must be brought up in relation to Onetti: his style. Over the years it has gone through subtle but steady changes that throw considerable light on Onetti's intentions. In *El Pozo* the language was careless, straightforward, almost journalistic, in the Arltian manner—decidedly antiliterary. In *La Vida Breve* it had become more elliptical, but without taking on any added syntactical complications, retaining its aura of artlessness. In *Un Sueño Realizado*—as in *Tierra de Nadie* and, increasingly, in *Para Esta Noche*—there is more artifice. Onetti is echoing a master who has had an enormous influence on him: Faulkner. The influence is conscious and deliberate, and Onetti sees no reason to apologize for it. But it is sometimes embarrassing to the reader. *Un Sueño Realizado* is made of tortuously long and graceful Faulknerian sentences that contribute to the cloistered atmosphere of the book but, because of an excess of imitated mannerisms—intricate modifiers, pleonastic subclauses, redundant adjectival expanses—sometimes seem affected. Onetti loves the circular and static, perfectly suitable devices in a world of fates settled in advance, where every life is a sentence served backward, predestined and therefore in some sense tautological. The reiterative style is an integral part of the manic-depressive atmosphere. But in strong doses it can begin to seem like a noisy contrivance, more hysterical than inherent. In Faulkner accumulations of words add force and momentum to the story; in Onetti they too often merely distract and diffuse. Onetti admits and does not attempt to justify, his Faulknerian variations. He merely points out the obvious difference between his and Faulkner's conceptions of the world. Faulkner is a tragedian; Onetti, if one can coin a term, is a pathetician. He shares with Faulkner the use of a fictional site as his setting, a preoccupation for inner architectures with metaphysical overtones. Otherwise—above all, temperamentally—they have little in common. Their respective frames of reference are entirely different. And perhaps that is where the trouble lies. Faulkner's characters live outside him, in time and history; they are endowed with independent means of action and individual consciences. Onetti's characters are at once more intimate and more abstract. Living at such close quarters with their creator, they have become disembodied. The more said about them, the less real they seem. They are floating essences. Words bury them. Whether or not Onetti has overcome this danger is a matter we leave unresolved. The Faulknerian trance has had such a lasting hold over him that even today he claims that the best thing he ever wrote was a translation he did years ago of a story from *These 13.*

One of his works most damaged by contact with the Faulknerian mode was *Los Adioses,* an involuted chronicle of futility that ends in suicide. A moribund athlete—one of Onetti's melancholy maniacs—retires to die in Santa María. He rents a house on a knoll outside town, where he secludes himself, alternately receiving two apparently rival women who have an agreement to visit him separately. Letters, in the possession of the narrator (in this case not one of the protagonists but the owner of the general store, who keeps the refugees in supplies), subsequently reveal the women to be his wife—and a daughter by a previous marriage. The loneliness and essential selfishness of the suicidal impulse are the subject of the story. The protagonist, reduced to the last imaginable extreme, clings to the forlorn hope of privacy in death, because "he had only that, and did not want to share it." The language overloads a thin plot which, typically, unfolds at second hand, progressing through gossip, rumor, and indirection. The effect is somewhat hazy. The surprise ending—based on withheld information—does not seem implicit. Yet in a sense *Los Adioses* represents an advance over *La Vida Breve,* or at least a new phase in Onetti's work. The narrator, though not dispensed with, has been relegated to a secondary plane. The protagonists—whose impenetrable mystery ultimately remains intact—have at least a semblance of an objective existence outside him.

A considerable improvement in this vein, and one of Onetti's most readable books, because of a skillfully handled element of suspense in it, is *Una Tumba sin Nombre* (*A Nameless Tomb,* 1959), an enigma without a complete solution that generates some of the excitement of a good detective story (a genre the author is much addicted to; he says he wishes he could plot as well as Raymond Chandler). The setting, as usual, is Santa María. The subject is the moral corruption and consequent compunctions of an errant adolescent, Jorge Malabia, who pours out his guilt to a sympathetic listener, and chronicler: Díaz Grey. As Díaz Grey records it with bloodthirsty relish—picking up odds and ends to complete the picture from Tito Perotti, Jorge's roommate at the university, and spicing the racy mixture with his own acid speculations—it is a gory tale. It involves an amoral young woman, Rita, an ex-maid in the Malabia household, once the mistress of Marcos Bergner, the brother of Jorge's sister-in-law, Julita. Exploited, then abandoned, by Marcos, Rita has taken to whoring for a living in Buenos Aires, where Jorge meets her while studying at the university and sets up house with her. *Una Tumba sin Nombre,* with all due allowances for its Onettian vagaries, is a Bildungsroman. The occasion for Jorge's growth is his enslaving passion, which is at least partly self-imposed. As a child, the commentator reveals, Jorge used to spy on Marcos and Rita through the keyhole, fascinated by their love-making. It is his tormenting memories of Rita in intimate postures, become obsessive with time, that somehow make him feel entitled to possess her now, as if she had been destined for him. He picks her up, installs her among his belongings, and although he has a generous allowance of his own and he knows she is dying of tuberculosis, lives off her for months, completely abandoning his studies. A curious twist is the motivation Onetti provides for the melodrama. Rita, bound from the beginning to occupy the unmarked tomb of the title, attracts disaster and thrives on humiliation; she is one of the insulted and injured of the world. Jorge turns out to be a sort of minor Raskolnikov. He acts out of gratuitous malice, pleased to imagine himself in the shoes of Rita's ex-pimp, Ambrosio, whose identity he borrows on the theory, as he tells Tito Perotti, that "I can never regret anything because whatever I do will have to be within the limits of human possibility." Of course—as we gather from the distortions and refractions out of which the story gradually takes shape—he learns better. His intellectual arrogance, his middle-class smugness, have led him into

some of the cardinal sins on Onetti's list: hypocrisy, cynicism, and above all, the false pride that tempts the gods. His righteousness is a disguise for cowardice, his rebelliousness for conformity. Onetti—or Díaz Grey—does not blame him. He merely exposes him. Jorge has tried to find a way out; he has failed. His crime—the crime of phoniness—was in pretending he could win in the first place. Covering up his failure compounded it. The author's—or narrator's—verdict is dispassionate. Such is life. Jorge's defeat is everyone's defeat. As they filter through to us, the facts of the case remain somewhat enigmatic. We have to sift shifting points of view. Here Onetti has hit on a compromise formula he uses with varying success in his later books. Díaz Grey, the seeing eye, is only a partial witness. Sometimes there is none. Certain passages are told straight. Others are once, twice, or even three times removed behind layers of lenses. Díaz Grey, not quite emancipated from his creator, has become a sort of universal conscience, a father confessor and faceless guilt-bearer for others. His independence is strictly putative, conditional—a convenient assumption for narrative purposes, pending the author's suspension of belief in him, whereupon his fickle autonomy will instantly vanish. Which is what happens once he has provided the necessary angles and insights. Suddenly slight differentiations are abandoned. The author becomes the actor. He is directly involved when he qualifies his—or Díaz Grey's; here the two fuse—account of Jorge's adventures as a liberating experience for him, who, in living it down or, more precisely, writing it out, has gained the upper hand over at least one of life's "daily setbacks."

In *La Cara de la Desgracia* (*The Face of Misfortune,* 1960) we find Onetti making a clean breast of the things he will obviously never be entirely rid of. Written in an unusually polite and slick style for him, told directly in the first person, with its share of ambivalences and blackouts, it is another story of guilt and noncommunication. The setting is a resort somewhere in the coastal area of Santa María, where the protagonist, in retreat, searches his conscience over the recent death of his brother, declines responsibility for the brother's widow, and on the side conducts an intermittent love affair on the beach with a deaf girl—another nymphomaniac virgin—who pays for their love (a scandal against the order of things: the rules of mourning, human solidarity in suffering) with her life. The germ of *La Cara de la Desgracia* was a story called "**La Larga Historia**" ("**The Long Affair**") that Onetti had written many years before (in 1944). The lighter accent, the more flippant tone, cannot hide the fact that his standard themes appear in a more muddled form than usual. There are too many blind spots. But we strike a new note here. The narrator-protagonist is another of Onetti's dreamers; but, though as usual mortally wounded by life, he is no longer entirely the helpless victim of circumstance. He has begun to develop a strategy with which to fight back. He is an embryonic ancestor of the saintly sinner that appears in Onetti's later work, for whom criminal intent miraculously becomes a twisted form of faith and inner harmony.

The novel that comes closest to fulfilling this paradoxical scheme is *El Astillero* (*The Shipyard,* 1961). The hero, or central figure, of *El Astillero* is Larsen—who took his first bow, in a minor role, in *La Vida Breve*—one of Onetti's Scandinavian-sounding outsiders. The name is not misleading. Larsen is a man with a shady background; he was expelled from Santa María five years before for running a house of prostitution. Now he is back in town to take a job in a dilapidated shipyard owned by a bankrupt tycoon, old Petrus. The shipyard is a carcass, and has been for ages; it functions only on paper, with a shadow board and a couple of superannuated administrative employees who while their time away in empty offices, busying themselves to keep up a pretense of work as they sell the useless machinery out from under Petrus' nose. In spite of which Larsen makes a grand entry. He has himself named general manager, spends his time going over old inventories and moth-eaten documents of forgotten shipwrecks, blatant in his imposture, drawing an imaginary salary while old Petrus is presumably maneuvering in the summits of bureaucracy to get his business back on its feet. For Larsen the musty shipyard is a last chance of doing something significant with his life; a chance in which he does not believe, of course. It is all an act and show—a flagrant hoax. He preys with predatory aplomb on the situation. He courts the pregnant wife of one of his employees while at the same time fanning a flame in Petrus' idiot daughter, whom he hopes, or purports to hope, to marry in order to inherit the nonexistent business. The whole action is made up of meaningless ritual motions leading nowhere. The shipyard will never be rehabilitated. Eventually documents come to light revealing an ancient fraud Petrus had perpetrated in better days. The old man is denounced to the police and arrested. All plans collapse. Everyone disowns everyone else. The whole scheme is discredited. But not before Onetti has made his point. Better to gnaw at an old bone than to have none at all.

Speaking of the atmosphere that prevails in *El Astillero,* Onetti, shivering, says: "It's like wearing a wet coat on a rainy day." He speaks of "the closed world in which unfortunately I live nowadays when I write. Also in general. I have many periods of absolute depression, of a sense of death, of nonlife. Maybe if I changed my habits, if I went on a diet—a good doctor might be able to cure me," he adds wryly. But perhaps, he reflects with a wisp of a smile, the doctor would turn out to be as impotent and ineffectual as Díaz Grey. In any case, he would arrive too late for Larsen, who has driven himself into a last hermetic solitude that finally leads to suicide.

Larsen, as do all Onetti characters, suffers from advancing age, an obsessive fear of death, a hopeless longing to rescue his wasted life, and a compulsive need to retreat through time to recuperate that moment of truth presumably buried somewhere in the lost blitheness of childhood. But there is a new element—the one just barely hinted at in *La Cara de la Desgracia*—that distinguishes him from his predecessors. The seed was planted in that passage of *La Vida Breve* where Bransen thinks of assuming his condition, installing himself in it, hopeful

that perhaps in sitting it out he will be relieved of it. So it is that we find Larsen accepting the inevitable, taking it for granted, actually entering into partnership with it, becoming its accomplice. Since there is no chance of breaking the rules of the game, he must master them. "If they're mad," he says to himself, "then I must be, too." Alone in his game, he had distrusted it. But since others seem to accompany him in it, "it must be the real thing." The decrepit shipyard is a reduced model of an absurd and godless world made of senseless routines, where living is a gamble with deadly risks: a "concerted lie." Old Petrus knows it. "Years back he had stopped believing there were any profits to be derived from the game; he would continue to believe, with violence and joy, unto death, in the game itself." Larsen, an old hand at deception, decides to follow suit. He knows the odds are stacked against him. Outwitting the intelligence behind the game, if there is one, is impossible. What counts is to go through the motions. His management of the shipyard is an act of defiance, a challenge—and a prayer—thrown in the face of the deity. It glows with the splendor of a Faulknerian grand design. There are also distinct Dostoevskian undertones in it. Larsen is a sort of diabolic, and at the same time strangely phlegmatic, weaver of absolutes—a Stavrogin. His gesture is symbolic. It is an open provocation. The shipyard is an antichurch with its reigning apostle, Larsen, the high priest of despair, officiating daily at its uninhabited altar. Starting out as a pimp to the prostitution of life, he has ended up as a theologian building his pointless architecture in the face of the incriminating evidence of his condition, out of the stuff of his defeat.

After *El Astillero,* which can be said to culminate the second phase of Onetti's work, we have a pause which he fills with a mortuary exercise in Faulknerian craftsmanship, a collection of stories called *El Infierno tan Temido* (*The Hell We Dread,* 1962). We are back in a Santa María now so intensely felt that it is almost lost in the glare. Somehow it seems less credible than before. The verbal flood has become more convoluted as the author's backstage maneuverings become more devious and remote. Díaz Grey, Petrus, and other staples reappear, but in residual form. The foreground is occupied by marginal characters, sometimes outlandish visitors on their way through town, who flare into existence for a second, then recede into the surrounding vacuum. The language is of no help. The compliment of imitation Onetti pays his master sometimes verges on parody. Nevertheless, the characteristic Onettian mode is present. The best of the stories deals with the sad predicament of an aging lecher infatuated with a frivolous actress who succumbs to extracurricular temptations, elopes with one of them, then tortures her admirer for the rest of his life mailing him obscene photographs she has posed for in compromising postures, as if to get back at him for saddling her with his charity and forgiveness, intent on blaming him for her inability to atone for her own weakness and treachery.

Shifting the blame is also the topic of the rather careless and superficial *Tan Triste Como Ella* (*As Sad as She Is,* 1963), "a sketch that didn't quite come off," as Onetti says himself, recognizing its poverty, which gives it the distinction of being probably the worst thing he ever wrote. He committed the mistake, he says, of describing something—a marriage on the rocks—that had actually happened (to him? He has been married three or four times) and that therefore enslaved him to the facts, dampening his inventiveness. The story reads like a self-conscious love letter that soon dwindles into radio drama. A curious slip for a writer at such a late stage in his work. But Onetti has too little distance from his work to take an objective view of the results. He lacks judgment and perspective. His latest work, *Juntacadáveres (The Corpse Collector,* 1964) has also been disappointing. It seems like a rehash of *El Astillero,* made of leftover materials that amount to little more than a poor duplicate of the original. Says Onetti, more or less subscribing to the verdict: "The trouble is that I'd already started to write *Juntacadáveres* when one day, going down a corridor, I had a vision of the end of Larsen. That's in *El Astillero.* So all of a sudden I left off writing *Juntacadáveres.* Perhaps when I returned to it I couldn't get into it properly any more." Or perhaps *El Astillero* spilled over into it, contaminated it. In a sense, they are both the same book.

Yet *Juntacadáveres* is an interesting and important addition to Onetti's theologic architecture: another cathedral built in the ruins. We are no longer in the shipyard; we have been flashed back to the days when Larsen ran a whorehouse. But the whorehouse is also a sort of visionary construction raised against the absurdity of life. The book chronicles the town's reaction to the whorehouse: the political interests involved, the opposition from the church, civic circles, and ladies' action groups. Larsen, the great sinner, the saintly cripple, presides at his Black Mass amid sacrilege and anathema. Born a diehard, handicapped from the start, he will dip into his depleted stocks until he reaches the bottom of the barrel. Founding the house has been an old ambition. And that is his advantage. He has waited so long for his chance that when it finally comes it is like a posthumous favor, "like marrying on one's deathbed, believing in ghosts, acting for God." Therefore, in a sense, he is invulnerable. In any case, his utopian construction is no worse than any other: a house of worship comparable to the church inhabited by the local priest or the ragged remnants of the phalanstery founded on the rim of town by one of his most bitter enemies, Marcos Bergner (righteous in his condemnation of Larsen though he is a veteran of communal orgies and squalid love affairs). In fact, the various forces that line up against him under the guise of high moral purpose all derive from the same premise: the simple human need on the part of each person to impose his individual order on the surrounding chaos. The opposing points of view, by any measurable standards, are all equivalent, and cancel each other out. It is a conflict not so much of personalities as of inner priorities. The language, calculated to hold tensions in delicate balance, quotes itself to the point of plagiary, falling into a sort of rhetoric of numbness that has an almost parasitical effect on the action. But perhaps that is fitting and proper. It sets the tone. The town is deep in the doldrums. Dead faces roam the streets. Even the physical world seems to languish. The days are

bleak and windless. Time drifts by like a whisper. Travestied intentions dissolve into vacant pantomimes. We have Díaz Grey, whittled down by time; and Jorge Malabia, here aged sixteen, a sensitive boy who secretly writes poetry and is on the verge of straying into the abysmal perversities of manhood. Jorge's respectable family, invoking its traditions of civic decency, inveighs against the whorehouse, while actually conspiring with it: Jorge's father, making the best of a bad deal, is the man who has rented out the land for the house. Jorge himself ripens and blooms in the throes of a sickly lust for his brother's deranged widow, Julita. But he is no more at fault than anyone else. In Onetti's scheme, those who stand for law and order—to save face—are at bottom the most hollow and corrupt. By contrast, those who struggle against the order of things, however crookedly, are at least worthy of a pitying respect. Such is the case of the abominable Larsen. In an aberrant world where raising a glass, getting out of a chair, going through a door are gestures that require almost superhuman effort, he is a man with a vocation, touched by a divine madness—an unheroic rebel fired by weakness, anguish, his fear of solitude and death. Little matter if he draws a blank at every turn. He has leverage. The contest of wills that takes place between him, on the one hand, and the priest or Marcos Bergner, on the other, may be nothing, says the author, but a form of artistic rivalry. The author is one of the rivals. So is his double, Jorge. And so is Díaz Grey, who again, as in *Una Tumba sin Nombre,* has been cast in the role of the informed witness and scapegoat, perhaps one of the elect destined to carry the burden of human sorrow. There is a moment when Jorge confronts him—as he might confront the author—and blames him for everything that has happened in town, for seeing it, understanding it, permitting it. It is, says Onetti, as if the boy were blaspheming against God. We remember that the ageless Díaz Grey was born as a god in *La Vida Breve,* fully grown, to live and be lived by others. Now, going down a staircase one day, he suddenly feels, as he has many times before, that he may kill himself. It is as if the supreme Master of Ceremonies, summoned out of nothingness for a moment, had leaned out and breathed His blessing on him.

Juntacadáveres, the ultimate in Onettian scope and structure, seems like a last stop on a long road leading back where it started from. One wonders where Onetti can possibly go from here.

Putting the question to him is like asking for a weather forecast. He has an image he is brooding over. What will become of it depends on meteorological conditions. Meantime he is taking notes, sketching situations. He grabs his ideas where he finds them. He has been remembering the time of Eva Perón's death in Argentina, when crowds of worshipful admirers lined up for days outside the Ministry of Labor to snatch a glimpse of her embalmed body, which had been put on display in a glass case. It was a time of national mourning, of mass necrophilia, says Onetti. There was talk of having the venerable corpse canonized. The collective cult of the dead, one of life's most sacred rituals, is a subject that appeals to

Onetti. He knew Eva Perón well because he had frequent access to her when he was working for Reuter's.

He says: "We were in contact with a Catalonian embalmer who was installed in the Presidential Palace in Olivos. We called him every night to find out whether or not the moment had come yet. 'No, unfortunately not,' he'd say. 'Nothing yet.' He used to distribute a pamphlet on the method he'd developed in his specialty. He didn't reveal the method—it was secret. But he gave examples of people he'd treated. There was an incredible photograph of a five- or six-year-old child in a sailor's suit. He'd been dead for years. The family kept the corpse in the closet and for every birthday and every anniversary of the child's death they took it out, put it on a chair, and had a family reunion around it." One can imagine the scene—or a similar one based on it—laid in Santa María. We are already familiar with the cast of characters. "The narrator will be Jorge Malabia, twenty years later. There will be the line of mourners. Of course the whole thing will be turned around to bring out its absurdity." Onetti recalls the historical events involved. "When Eva Perón died, the line for the wake lasted a week or ten days, or more." Eva had been pickled and preserved by the Catalonian expert. But the treatment had to be constantly renewed. "They kept locking up all the time to take her out. Because the doctors at Eva Perón's bedside had been Catholics. They knew of the plans to embalm her, and the Catalonian doctor wasn't notified in time. She'd died in the morning, I think, and the news wasn't released until eighty-thirty in the evening, when all the clocks in town were stopped. By then the corpse had started to rot. To keep it in shape, it would have had to receive its first injection at the moment of death. So the work failed. . . . Now, what I want to do is this: The way the line was organized . . . In reality, at first, it was spontaneous. The people were devoted to Eva Perón. For the working classes she was a saint. She gave away thousand-, ten thousand-peso bills, houses, automobiles; all photographed, of course, for propaganda. There was the Eva Perón Foundation, her Cities for the Young, which functioned exclusively when there were important visitors from abroad. . . . But then the wake was put in the hands of a publicity firm. The line was organized so five persons could go in at a time. Then the doors were closed, or blocked by soldiers. The idea was to have the line move at the rate, let's say, of half a meter every fifteen minutes. So it would be there permanently. . . . So the trick I have in mind is simple: to slow the rate down even further. To have the line advance, say, a tile a day. Then take someone standing in the line and have him live it: fall in love with a woman, marry her, all while standing there. I'm exaggerating; but that was what happened up to a certain point. People had to knock on the doors of houses to use the toilet. They ate in the street, slept and made love there. The Ministry of Labor was full of floral crowns. In the early mornings there were orgies, while the soldiers stood by, watching. That's an important factor in my book: the sensation of death, its connection with erotic behavior."

What will all this lead to? Onetti is sure to erect another of his temples of despair out of it. If anything, he regards the prospect with detachment. His pessimism seems to have become almost generic. He is resigned, as Jorge in *Juntacadáveres,* to furnish his empty world with the shapes of his fictions, to create faces and gestures, needs and ambitions, and appropriate roles to which they can be appointed, the better to be sacrificed. The fate assigned each man is impersonal, he wrote in *La Vida Breve.* It can be fulfilled only in so far as it is the fate of all men. It does not allude to his true self, which is elsewhere, out of sight and circulation, a humble offering waiting to be put before the gods, who may choose to regard it as a small masterpiece or a penny dreadful.

Yvonne Perier Jones (essay date 1971)

SOURCE: "Plot and Meta-plot: Variations on a Theme," in *The Formal Expression of Meaning in Juan Carlos Onetti's Narrative Art,* Centro Intercultural de Documentation, 1971, pp. 1-17.

[*In the essay below, Jones focuses on the recurring "pattern of effort and failure" in Onetti's major novels.*]

Onetti's novels, like those of many modern writers, are characterized by a significant lack of traditional, active plot. Because of the static vision he protrays, he has even been described as an anti-novelist.[1] This term, however, implies that he has abdicated the novelist's responsibility of telling a story, while, in fact, he has merely displaced much of the story from plot to other levels of meaning. The shift from surface action—plot as anecdote—began with the psychological novel, whose concern with presentation of character necessarily restricted external plot development. The drama of these novels derives from conflicts within characters. Their battles are fought within the mind; their foes are demons nourished by the mental process.

In contrast to this subjective view, many writers, among them the existentialists and objectivists, have been concerned with an external view. While in some ways continuing the realist and naturalist tradition, these writers seek to portray not the social reality of a particular milieu, but the universal reality of individual human experience. Their interest in specific events—the anecdotal aspect of plot—is secondary to their efforts to reveal the nature of that experience. They emphasize the surface impressions surrounding events or characters in order to recreate a situation rather than to report it. Plot is a device that shapes these impressions, a means of transforming them into universal terms. Frequently this transformation depends on mythic and symbolic elements. The real plot emerges from the relation between these elements—the story of the novel—and the manner in which it is told.

Onetti combines objectivist and existential techniques and vision while presenting a plot that functions on several levels. The dilemma of twentieth century man—alienated from his traditional spiritual, physical, social, and psychological frame of reference—has been discussed didactically, but has been most eloquently communicated in art forms. Juan Carlos Onetti expresses this dilemma in his novels through the vehicle of minimal plot. But this level of interpretation becomes clear only after plot has been understood as the representation of deeper meaning.

The events of his novels are minor expressions of human activity, mere sketches of life that only suggest the real story. He is often more concerned with the situation surrounding an event than with the event itself. While the emphasis on surface detail and small things creates a studiedly objective tone, this transcription of surfaces communicates only the immediate story in Onetti's novels. At this level the plots can be described as the effort of common men to deal with some very common human problems: love and communication, growing old, success, productivity, the need to feel self-respect, and the need for a sense that one's life matters. The repeated failure of their efforts reveals the modern sense of alienation from such traditional values.

The tragic inevitability of man's failure to resolve the problem of alienation is so constant that it forms a "meta-plot" for all of Onetti's novels. The author has commented on this aspect of his work, saying:

> . . . todos los personajes y todas las personas nacieron para la derrota. Claro, uno puede interrumpir la trayectoria del personaje en un instante de triunfo. Pero si continuamos el final siempre es Waterloo, Martinelli o Lázaro Costa.[2]

This meta-plot of effort and failure also has a mythic identity with the story of Sisyphus. Once the pattern is clear, dramatic interest is deferred to the nature of the landscape through which the stone must pass and to the techniques that the characters use to approach the peak.

Introducing his first major novel, *Tierra de nadie,* Onetti describes his purpose as the creation of a portrait. He says, "I paint a group of people . . . representative of a generation . . . , a type of morally indifferent individual who has lost his faith and all interest in his own fate."[3]

The static image he employs to describe his novel suggests the lack of vitality in its plot and in the individuals he portrays. The effect is not quite a portrait, but, rather a repetitive series of slow-motion film clips. While there are several characters in the novel, each presented in a series of situations, the sum of their activity always reduces to a variation on the pattern of effort and failure. Jaime Concha observed the similarity between the experiences through which the characters pass, viewing it as the "homogeneidad espesa . . . de las situaciones."[4] In terms of novelistic development, the major character is Diego Aránzuru, a young lawyer who rejects his legal practice and his circle of friends to go in search of some meaning for his life. But his search, sometimes so passively expressed that it is scarcely visible, describes the action for all of Onetti's characters.

Aránzuru's quest procedes along two paths. One is determined by the hope of relating to others, principally women. His goal is love or even mere communication; neither is attained. The plot describes his repeated failures. His efforts are directed toward four characters, each representing a different kind of femininity. The first, Nené, is a young, attractive women. She is ready to give herself to love if she can find it. But she, like the other women in the novel, is cut off from such a relationship by Aránzuru's unwillingness or inability to commit himself to another person. The second is a very young girl, Nora. Nora represents an enduring type in Onetti's novels; the adolescent, innocent girl—woman before she has begun to grow old. She suffers a symbolic death that is the fate of all love objects in the novel. Aránzuru " . . . tuvo la seguridad de que Nora había muerto un momento antes. No estaba metida en una caja, sino estirada en una cama de un lugar desconocido" (*Tierra,* p. 221). Nora also experiences another kind of death typical of Onetti's vision of women. She becomes pregnant, physically deformed, and polluted by life.

The third woman with whom Aránzuru attempts to relate is also a common Onetti type, the aging prostitute. She is a warm, loving person with whom he has a rather extended but one-sided affair. He accepts her affection and her gifts passively. She eventually asks him to leave her, not only because of his passivity but also because of her own sense of unworthiness, and her awareness of the degeneration of her body. She describes herself as "podrida."

This situation forms a transition in the development of Aránzuru's search. Following his rejection by Katy, the prostitute, he begins to talk more seriously of going to the fantasy island of Faruru. Rolanda, the fourth woman in his life, enters at this point. She is unique among the novelistic characters in that she appears to have become reconciled to a world without meaning beyond her own feelings and actions. She says of the people she sees around her: "Son estúpidos, todo lo ven al revés y tienen un modo total, terrible, de ser insensatos, de no acordarse de que tienen que morirse y tomarse semejantes inmudicias, en serio" (*Tierra*, p. 77). Her vision has an ironic distance denied the other characters: "Basta removerles el hormiguero para que se muestren más frenéticamente absurdos." She is self sufficient: "Es feliz estar sola y darse el calor necessario sin la ayuda del prójimo puerco espín" (*Tierra*, p. 77). She is the one woman with whom Aránzuru would share his dream of the island, but she is too realistic to be able to participate in his fantasy.

Each of these relationships reflects themes in this and the other novels. The first, that with Nené, is symbolic of the character's inability to relate to each other, of their sense of alienation and their lack of communication. The second, with Nora, represents the degeneration and death of ideals and naive dreams. Katy personifies the theme of decay and the aging process. She portrays what all the other characters avoid admitting to themselves; they too are subject to decay and putrefaction. Aránzuru's failure with Rolanda reflects the failure of all the characters to accept reality when it conflicts with their dreams.

The other major story line in the novel is determined by the pursuit of a fantasy goal. The search for a love object is in a sense, a fantasy. At least it is an abstract goal pursued to give some value to an otherwise meaningless existence. The ideal aspect of love is best expressed for Aránzuru, as for the others, through Nora's character. She is revealed as being subject to the same corruptive, degenerative influences that have touched them all. But the ideal goal is also represented by Aránzuru's dream of the south-sea island of Faruru. The essence of the goal depends on its separateness from the negative influence of every-day reality. It forms an ideal retreat from the elements that corrupt men. Aránzuru has a real retreat, the "molino de la Alemana," which has failed to take him far enough from the world. He offers to share his *molino* with several others. He even spends a few days there with Rolanda. Yet he is unable to draw her on to his dream retreat, Faruru.

Even though he knows, intellectually, that Faruru does not exist, he chooses to make reaching the island his chief preoccupation in life. As with the love situation, he is shown not just once, but several times, trying to lure others toward his dream. Although none of them reaches it, not even Aránzuru, his forced faith in the island attracts others to him like a magnet. Early in the novel someone remarks that there is no honor except that derived from having hope. Perhaps this thread of hope—the search for a place where a man might live with honor and dignity—forms the island's allure. But the frustration experienced in the search for love repeats in the ill fated search for a mythical retreat from human degradation.

This novel thus establishes the failure pattern that dominates later works. It also suggests the principal ways in which Onetti's characters approach their search. Aránzuru typifies one of these in action orientated behavior motivated by the dream image that he seeks. He keeps moving: from woman to woman, from place to place. For another character, Llarvi, suicide is the only answer. Llarvi is a highly intellectual figure, so much so that he finds it impossible to believe in the myth of the island or any other dream goal. But intellectual answers, because they are too simple, are also unsatisfactory. Llarvi, having neither faith nor logic to guide him in his search, is forced to renounce it. The one challenge to his lack of faith is a love object from his past, a woman named Labuk. Although she really existed, nothing remains but her memory and this, like other love objects in the novel, dies. The story of Casal, an artist, suggests another approach. While the object of his love, Balbina, also suffers a symbolic death when he destroys his portrait of her, Casal can survive because he has faith in art as a way of life.

These modes of confronting life establish the formula for action in Onetti's novels, just as failure forms the design for their plot. The plot of *Tierra de nadie* has been discussed in considerable detail to reveal how this pattern repeats within the novel to form a "meta-plot." But this meta-plot also applies to Onetti's other major novels. The notion of repetition will be treated in the following chapter, which deals with structure. For the

present these novels will be considered with a view of revealing their fictional plots as representations of the effort-failure pattern.

Onetti's second major work, *La vida breve,* is the complex expression of survival through creation. The main character, Brausen, seeks a replacement for a love that has been sullied by his wife's physical deformity, the result of breast surgery. He attempts to provide alternatives to his own destroyed life by creating fictional lives in which he can rediscover love and form a new identity. At one level this is accomplished by his living a fantasy existence in his dealings with the real world. He creates an alter-ego through whom he relates to new acquaintances who are not tied to his past. Going even further in the creation of fictional alter-natives, he comes to identify with Díaz-Grey, the main character in a movie script that he is writing. The plot of *La vida breve* is the story of testing these alternative identities and of their failure to provide any improvement on his real life. The alter-ego loses love and is frustrated in his one effort at an affirmative act when another man commits a murder that he has planned. Díaz-Grey also fails in love. While at the end of the novel there is some possibility that he has found a new love, this is only suggested and, at that, on the level of still another identity—the *torero* role he has assumed for carnival.

In the third major novel, *El astillero,* the action alternative is tested and found lacking. Junta Larsen, a minor figure from *Tierra de nadie,* reappears, now as the central character. He is a solitary, middle aged man who is trying to lend some meaning to his life. At the fictional plot level, he does this by returning to the town of Santa María to assume the position of bookkeeper in a major industry, a shipyard. From the beginning it is clear that the shipyard is only a vestige of its former financial strength. Nonetheless, Larsen, like the two men with whom he works, is obsessed with its survival, because his own depends on it. During the course of the novel Larsen realizes how ineffectual his efforts are, yet he decides to continue to act *porque sí.* Only when the owner of the business is definitively revealed as a fraud, and when Larsen has lost the supportive faith of his co-workers, does he finally admit failure. While he can no longer maintain the myth of the business, he is forced, by his nature, to continue the life of action.

Defeated in his struggle with the shipyard he moves on toward new efforts. Two endings are posited, both telling of his death. In neither case does he surrender the struggle by taking his own life.

In Onetti's most recent major novel, *Juntacadáveres,* Larsen again appears as a central figure. The Santa María setting and most of the other characters are familiar to those who have read the previous novels. In many ways Larsen, like Aránzuru in *Tierra de nadie,* undergoes the kind of failure which all the characters experience. The central situation deals with the brothel that Larsen establishes in Santa María, with the approval of the town council. The action, and there is significantly more action in this novel than in earlier works, evolves from the town's response to the presence of the brothel. However, another situation comes to dominate the affective center of the novel. It develops young Jorge Malabia's first exposure to love through his relationship with Julita, his older brother's widow. Mario Benedetti has criticized *Juntacadáveres* for its apparent ambivalence in presenting these two situations.[5] He feels that the situation between Jorge and Julita overshadows the conflict between the town and the *prostíbulo.* But if this relationship is viewed in terms of the Onetti blueprint of effort and failure it is but another expression of the same story. Larsen is forced to leave the town and abandon the project of the *prostíbulo,* thereby renouncing his dream; Jorge loses his love when Julita commits suicide. Seen in this way, the situation between Jorge and Julita forms a highly concrete counterpoint to the rather depersonalized representation of the Larsen/town conflict. It also serves a comparative and contrastive purpose by showing the first disillusion of youth against the repetitive pattern of loss and failure in the older generation. Other characters support the failure theme. Marcos, Jorge's cousin, is a generational intermediary who in the past had failed in an attempt to create a utopian farming community. The town druggist, the agent for securing Larsen's dispensation to open the *prostíbulo,* was forced to compromise his ideals in order to gain approval from the town council.

This novel develops the trend that was suggested in *El astillero,* where the vision of alienation changed slightly. Instead of defining the situation of isolated individuals, alienation began to encompass small groups of souls who sensed a common bond in the similarity of their condition. This might even be traced back to Aránzuru's efforts to share the dream of the island in *Tierra de nadie.* In *Juntacadáveres* the trend continues, expanding to reveal a group rather than an individual conflict with society. Larsen, and those who appear with him in the final scene, are individuals whose activities conflict with the *status quo* of the town. Once again the ending is open. While Larsen and the prostitutes, having lost their battle against a reactionary society, leave the town, they are in a position to move on to renewed efforts. Still—as always—the implication is that these too will fail.

Onetti has made a statement that illuminates the question of plot in his novels. He describes his intentions in a typically paradoxical way: "Yo quiero expresar nada más que la aventura del hombre".[6] Nothing more, he says. But this is what the novel, beginning with the epic form, has always attempted. In order to understand Onetti's conception of this statement, the terms "man" and "adventure" must be examined. At the level of fictional plot, Onetti's man is far from heroic. He is not dashing, is seldom young, and reveals little nobility in thought, word, or action. He is imperfect, far from any romanticized ideal. Yet, in the context of "meta-plot", his man acquires the stature of a tragic hero whose flaw consists of clinging to hopes and dreams. His heroic action derives from accepting their loss and constantly renewing his effort to attain their realization. As Harss says, "to break the irreversible pattern of his life is the compulsive need

of every Onetti character."[7] Onetti's man becomes a hero precisely because of this compulsion, as he continues to operate in full knowledge of the absurdity of his efforts.

The nature of man's adventure also appears to be anti-heroic. This is increasingly true in the evolution of the novels. Some heroic stature might be attributed to Arazuru's quest. Even Brausen's effort to live through fiction has dignity. But Larsen's faith in the *astillero* is, at the immediate denotative level, foolish and mundane. The dream of the brothel in *Juntacadáveres* is an even less heroic goal. However, the fictional plot forms only one stratum in Onetti's novels, one that suggests a more comprehensive meaning. The failure motif in their plots is merely a superficial expression of deeply symbolic failure.

A symbolic interpretation of these novels will be considered in depth later. For the present, the concern is with the repetition of patterns at various levels. At the symbolic level the failure blueprint can be applied to some of the major philosophical and psychological quandaries of twentieth century man: his alienation from traditional concepts of love, truth, and God. In *Tierra de nadie,* love and the possibility of communication are repeatedly put to death. The objects of the character's efforts to find love all die, symbolically or otherwise. In *La vida breve,* objective truth—reality as knowable—is denied. Brausen not only creates an alter-ego but also a fictional character who eventually replaces him. Fiction becomes the equivalent of truth; it may even become its master. In *El astillero* God is put to death. There is a remarkable scene in which Larsen finally confronts the old man who has sustained his hope, and has been the means for his salvation. With Larsen as witness, the old man dies.

Having denied such transcendent values as love, truth, and God in the previous novels, it scarcely seems possible that Onetti would allow them to survive in the various situations of *Juntacadáveres.* They do, in fact, suffer their usual fate. However, through its presentation of social conflict, this novel introduces a new dimension. The individuals who challenge the town are concerned with social progress. For men like Barthé and Díaz-Grey, the prostíbulo is a symbol of that challenge. While the effort for social progress is frustrated, the confrontation between these people and the town's reactionary forces reveals that they have acquired some independence from traditional values. It is almost as though they have accepted the notion that man is alone and his own agent. By sharing this new attitude they are capable of establishing a very tenuous mutual identity and sympathy with a man like Junta.

The central theme of failure and the meta-plot of *fracaso,* evolve through the four novels. At the beginning, in *Tierra de nadie,* the story negates all values, especially those bound to the possibility of meaningful human relationships. In *La vida breve* the very lack of values leads to an effort to form new ones through fictional lives and adventures created by a fictional character. Later, in *El astillero,* fiction as a way of living takes new form. Fiction, or fantasy reality, was no more than a dream to be shared in *Tierra*. In *La vida breve* it becomes a potential mode of existence. With *El astillero* fiction and dream are reduced to the notion of game. This game is the only means of surviving in an existential sense. Life's only significance derives from the individual's rebellion against its absurdity and thus most obviously suggests analogies with the modern existential Sisyphus.

In *Juntacadáveres* the game and the various hopes and dreams crushed throughout previous novels are again posited and destroyed, though with a more humanized vision. There is a new compassion, a possibility that man may find some meaning, if only in himself. The situation of *Juntacadáveres* represents the conflict between this apparent amorality and traditional Christian bourgeois ethics. But it develops that man alone is not amoral; Larsen formulates an ethical position in the sanctuary of the *prostíbulo*. This ethic may be related to the enduring theme of creation as a meaningful way of life, for Larsen's dissatisfaction with a life based on sin depends not on a traditional religious concept, but on his awareness of its lack of productivity.

> Junta había llegado a descubrir que lo que hace pecaminoso al pecado es su inutilidad, aquella perniciosa manía de bastarse a sí mismo, de no derivar; su falta de necesidad de trascender y depositar en el mundo, visible para los demás, palpables, cosas, cifras, satisfacciones que pueden ser compartidas
>
> (*Juntacadáveres*, p. 149)

Junta wishes to leave tangible evidence of his existence not only as a means of transcending his personal finitude but also in order to share his life more fully with those around him. His attitude thus reflects the novel's increased concern with man's relation to other men. Significantly, the novel ends not with a man alone but with men divided into groups defined by common aspirations.

However, this concern does not alter the pattern of existence. Like the other novels, *Juntacadáveres* repeats the meta-plot cycle of effort and failure. This pattern appears in the denouements of the stories told and in the resolution of the philosophical questions they suggest. It even attains a symbolic value that extends it beyond our immediate time and place by its identity and the myth of Sisyphus. In Onetti's novels the plot exists simultaneously on anecdotal, symbolic, mythic, and generic planes and so acquires much greater complexity and drama than is apparent at the surface level. The unity of these planes and the mutual reinforcement of the same pattern intensify the impact of Onetti's story of the anguished adventure of man.

NOTES

1. Mario Benedetti, *Literatura uruguaya siglo XX* (Buenos Aires: Alfa, 1965), pp. 76-79.

2. Interview by María Ester Gilio, "Onetti y sus demonios interiores," *Marcha*, Jul. 1, 1966, p. 25.

3. Luis Harss and Barbara Dohmann, *Into the Mainstream*, (New York: Harper and Row, 1967), p. 178.

4. "Sobre *Tierra de nadie*," *Atenea*, CLXVI, 417 (Jul.-Sept., 1967), 174.

5. "Juan Carlos Onetti y la aventura del hombre, "*La Cultura en México*, No. 342, supplement to *Siempre!*, Sept. 4, 1968, p. VI.

6. *Ibid.*, p. III.

7. *Into the Mainstream*, p. 188.

Michael Wood   (essay date 1993)

SOURCE: "A Faint Sound of Rust," *London Review of Books*, Vol. XV, No. 20, October 21, 1993, pp. 20-1.

[*In the following evaluation of Onetti's career, Wood discusses Onetti's major novels, including* El astillero (The Shipyard), Juntacadáveres (The Body Snatcher), *and* La vida breve (A Brief Life).]

Juan Carlos Onetti, 84 years old and now a Spanish citizen, living in Madrid, is one of the most distinguished and most neglected of Latin American writers. He was born in Montevideo, but takes the idea of being an important Uruguayan author as something short of a compliment, even as a kind of joke. He hasn't sought his neglect, but he has cultivated the neglect he found, made it part of his story. He boasts of failing to get literary prizes in the way other writers casually mention that they've got them. His neglect began early, almost as soon as he was discovered, with his harsh and jagged short story **"El Pozo"** (**"The Pit"**), 1939; and when he did get a major literary prize, the Cervantes, it was in 1978, late enough for the legend of neglect to be maintained.

We get a recent picture of Onetti in Ramon Chao's book (*Onetti*, 1990), although not an entirely reliable one perhaps. Partly because he behaves a little too much like everyone's idea of an old-style Latin American intellectual, drinking endlessly and making dark epigrams by the score ('Critics are like death: they may be late but they always get there'); and partly because Chao has cobbled lots of these epigrams from Onetti's novels, so that he seems, in casual conversation, to be talking like his most literary self. Perhaps this is how Onetti talks, but the uneven texture of Chao's book suggests otherwise: that the speaking Onetti and the writing Onetti are quite different. Still, it's a good performance, however stage-managed. We meet a man who has read enormously, is generous about other writers, has not grown old mentally, is often very funny and has what seems to me an unfailingly accurate view of the qualities of his own work —not the most common capacity among neglected or unneglected writers.

Early in Chao's book, Onetti recounts the visit of a young man who tells him that his best book is **Los Adioses**

(*Farewells*), 1954. Onetti says this is his own favourite too, but critics have preferred *El Astillero* (*The Shipyard*), 1961. 'No, absolutely not,' the young man says. '*Farewells* is the best.' Later Onetti says he likes *Farewells* the most, has 'a special tenderness' for it; but thinks *The Shipyard* is 'a more perfect narrative', and regards *La Vida Breve* (*A Brief Life*), 1950, as 'richer in literary content'. Glossing these casual but lucid discriminations, we might say that *Farewells* is perhaps the best introduction to Onetti, the place where we meet his odd curiosity and his distinctive tone, both clinical and kindly, in their most undisguised form; that *A Brief Life* best shows the range of Onetti's interests and talents but also his faults as a writer; and that in *The Shipyard* he found the absurd and compelling metaphor he had been looking for all his life, so that he was able to become something like a Conrad who had soaked himself in Beckett, or a Dashiell Hammett who had been reading Camus and Ionesco.

These are wild approximations, of course. Onetti's voice and subject-matter are his own, and their very elusiveness has played a part in his neglect. The other part was played by accident. Onetti was too late for some fashions and too early for others. He was an existentialist before he had read Sartre, but everybody else had read Sartre before they read Onetti. He invented and peopled a Latin American town like García Márquez's Macondo, but he filled it with obliquities and ironies rather than miracles. Onetti owes a lot to Borges, as almost all contemporary Latin American writers do, but a hardboiled manner borrowed from North American detective fiction conceals many of the more dizzying conceptual moves he makes. Onetti's work is always on a knife-edge: it could lapse at any moment into sententiousness or bathos, and quite often does. But the edge itself makes it like no other writing we are likely to meet.

It's not easy to say what Onetti's fiction is about, and perhaps not entirely appropriate to try. It centres not so much on plot or theme or character as on an erratic but insistent inquisitiveness about the stories people step into or trail behind them. These stories can be lifted from life or frankly invented; sometimes they are pursued at length, sometimes merely held up for us to look at, like slides or title-cards or icons. What matters is their shape or implications, their power of suggestion, what they say without meaning to say anything. 'An anecdote,' Onetti has one of his characters think, 'can contain life but cannot alter the sense of it.' One way of describing this would be to say that what looks like a narrative device is one of Onetti's major subjects. Everything is perspective, guesswork; people tell tales, of themselves and of others, read clues and hints, listen to gossip, put pieces of history together. *The Shipyard* opens with a joke about a hundred days, as if the seedy central character were a sort of Napoleon, and the mode in which we keep hearing about him ('Many people swear', 'Others on the contrary remember', 'In all likelihood', 'It is almost certain', 'According to reports', 'Everything points to') ironically shunts him into legend, as if his very seediness was fabulous.

The narrator of *Farewells* is the owner of a bar and shop in a small town close to a sanatorium. He prides himself on knowing more about the patients than they know about themselves, on being able to read whole histories in their faces and gazes and hands and gestures. What seems to be the main story concerns a former basketball star who is resisting the idea of his encroaching death—he finally defeats his illness by committing suicide—and the two women who visit him. More deeply, the work explores the power the narrator thinks he has over people through his knowledge or fore-knowledge of their condition, the consolation he finds in this power for the loneliness and abjection of his life; and above all his rage when he finds he is wrong about the women who visit the basketball player: not younger and older mistress, as he thought, or wife and young mistress, but his daughter and mistress, who finally make peace with each other. The narrator says, probably correctly, 'that death was all the man had left and he hadn't wished to share it'; but he says it 'with contrived pity and a note of contempt', as if what he calls the man's 'final avidity' could compensate for the narrator's own error and arrogance.

'I don't know how to write badly,' Chao reports Onetti as saying. This is not an empty boast, but the remark needs interpreting. Onetti writes wonderfully well, indeed never writes badly; but he often overwrites, his work is full of moments of old-fashioned fine writing, bids for easy lyricism or philosophy. His characters, so dedicated to perspective, are always trying to find out where they are, and they often lecture us about it. It is on these occasions that we read of 'an unproud enemy to pity', or 'the pale silent frenzy of putrefaction', or the 'apocryphal evocations' of 'the aroma of jasmines'; or that a character tells us, 'I examined my bravado, I began to doubt the sincerity of my hatred.' More often, Onetti's language is not easy but brilliantly risky, moving very suddenly from the laconic to the expansive, with an almost Joycean lift from the shabby into the poignant. 'It was surprisingly dark as he made his way cautiously down the three steps and swayed his rolling walk across the empty lot. No sign of the women or the dogs. A light-hearted wind was sweeping the sky clear; by midnight it seemed certain the stars would be out.' The laconic tone has its effects too, of course; more like Tom Waits than Joyce. We see a woman give 'a small smile of despair', hear of another who 'may prefer catastrophes to explanations', another who has 'memories that stuck to her like bandages, yet another from whom 'happiness continues to flow . . . like a bad smell'. We learn of a man's 'implacable cordiality', and of the 'cretinous haste' of passing time; or are told that 'Our faces have a secret, not always the one we try to hide.' 'The delicate administration of pity' is not exactly laconic, but it shows ironies within sorrows within ironies.

It helps to look at *Juntacadáveres* (*Body Snatcher*), 1964, and *The Shipyard* together, since Onetti interrupted work on the first to write the second, and since both novels recount the sombre and ludicrous travails of one Larsen, an ageing pimp of the River Plate. He is called Body Snatcher, more literally a collector of corpses, because 'bodies', 'mortuary', 'skeleton' and associated terms are Onetti's playful language for brothels and those who work in them, and because Larsen specialises in picking up fading women, listening to their stories, making them feel better and taking their money. In **Body Snatcher** his exploit is to set up the first brothel in Santa María, a ramshackle town that has just become a city— a place built, as Emir Rodríguez Monegal says, out of 'pieces of Buenos Aires, Montevideo, Rosario and Colonia do Sacramento', that is, out of cities in Argentina, Uruguay and Brazil situated on the banks of the Plata or the Parana. Onetti has invented this place in the way Flaubert invented his Normandy: imagined it as an intricately specified reality. Santa María, like Macondo and Faulkner's Yoknapatawpha County, doesn't exist, but you can find its twin all over Latin America.

> It's easy to draw a map of the whole area and a plan for Santa María in addition to giving it a name. But you've also got to put a special light in each store, each doorway, each corner. You've got to give form to the low clouds that drift over the church steeple and the flat roofs with their cream and pink balustrades; you've got to dole out disgusting furniture, accept things you hate, bring in people from who knows where so that they can take up residence, dirty things, move us to tears, be happy, and waste themselves. And during the game, I have to give them bodies, the need for love and money, different and identical ambitions, a never-examined faith in immortality.

The brothel is a lamentable, half-hearted affair but the source of great scandal, and Onetti treats it, through his various narrators, as a sort of deviant, heroic innovation—as if Larsen were a decrepit Mack the Knife aggrandised by the sheer distaste others feel for him. He's a man with an ideal, Onetti says in Chao's book: of the perfect brothel. The ideal is disreputable, and the brothel is a dump, but that's what makes them into a sly commentary on other ideals and achievements. Larsen is a small-time philosopher, *un petit philosophe*: 'he knows that our daily reality gives us no weapons for the struggle against time.' Larsen thinks of his brothel as anyone may think of a project: as a way of staving off failure, or rather the acceptance of failure, the final renunciation of what Onetti elsewhere calls the 'sin' of believing that 'what's unavoidable needs our consent.' Larsen represents Onetti's suspicion that all ideals are parodiable (many of them are parodies already), although to think of the brothel as only the parody of an ideal is to condescend to it more than Onetti would want. His humour is not only deadpan here; it will turn into seriousness at the slightest sign of pomposity on our part. Larsen has 'a vocation or mania', he understands 'the need to fight for a cause without having real faith in it, and without considering it an end in itself'. It's true, as Mark Millington has written, that Onetti's novels focus on the individual consciousness rather than the community—except in so far as the community is the enemy of such consciousness—but it's also true that Onetti's individuals often acquire a weirdly satirical even allegorical aura, as if whole cultures had been caught up and had found their emblems in them.

Massive stories of emigration and loss lurk in Onetti's books: we may think of the character in *A Brief Life* who seeks to justify himself 'above all to some corpses he could imagine lying, more severe in death, beneath the earth of some cemetery in some Austrian village'. Or of Larsen, in **Body Snatcher,** refusing to look at the vision he might have of himself.

> If he'd had the slightest suicidal impulse, the courage necessary to stop in front of a mirror, interrupt his siesta and examine his conscience, he'd have found he was exactly like the image of a long-haired, threadbare violinist playing medleys and waltzes from operettas without the permission of the owner in second-class cafés located in third-class cities. There he'd be, his head held high, variously scornful, his large mouth fixed in a smile that could withstand any interpretation, confident that something essential was safe as long as he didn't pawn the greasy, darkened violin, as long as he didn't play tangos, as long as he protected his music from the accompaniment of drunks and disgusting women, as long as, every three numbers, he could make the rounds of the tables and hold out a tiny metal tray onto which fell the coins he could empty into the pockets of his black jacket without having the skin on his hands participate in the joy and humiliation. Sometimes showing a yellowed concert programme, worn out in the folds, hard to unfold, with his still-recognisable photo on it, with the word *Wien* underlined in red by himself so that it could be found rapidly among the others, which were incomprehensible, and pursued by diaereses and curves devoid of sweetness.

In the end, when Catholicism and civic dignity get their act together, Larsen is run out of town on the order of the governor of the province—his hundred-day return to power, five years later, is recounted in **The Shipyard.** **Body Snatcher** offers an edgy comment on the vanity of human wishes, memorably mingles sarcasm and pathos, but it is a slow and sometimes cumbersome book, its deadpan often hardening into ponderousness or rigidity. What Onetti needed was an image so rich that he and his readers could circle round it for ever, and Larsen's brothel was not quite that. **The Shipyard,** the novel and the place within the novel, is. This book is frankly phantasmagoric, a detailed report on an extraordinary folly, but it is written with the bemused intimacy we all have with our own moments of craziness. It is, to evoke Conrad again, like *Heart of Darkness* in slow motion, and irreparably cut off from anything resembling mundane or practical reality. A man steps into a fantasy which others play along with, and which nothing, strictly, contradicts or confirms.

Larsen, now described as 'a heavy, small, aimless man' with 'tiny, calm eyes', becomes general manager of a derelict shipyard just upriver from Santa María. There are no boats, no work, no contracts, the place has been disused for years. The owner, Jeremias Petrus, is engaged in Dickensian legal disputes which he dreams will bring activity back to the yard; there are two employees, who make a living by selling off bits of rusting junk from time to time. Larsen and Petrus have important business meetings; Larsen and the employees show up for work, stare at old files, send each other memos, make sure the inter-office buzzers are working, go home—which for Larsen is a run-down hotel and bar called The Belgrano. Larsen is fully conscious of the madness of what he is doing, as indeed are the others, but he prefers the madness to what he might be doing instead. The triumph of the book is the agility and ingenuity and wry sympathy with which Onetti evokes this astonishing and desperate game, this story of a 'fat, obsessed man' in 'a ruined, unlikely office'.

Onetti denies having had any conscious allegorical intention in this work, any idea of picturing or prophesying the fate of Uruguay or Latin America, and I think we should take him at his word. But *The Shipyard* brilliantly catches a quite particular mentality, not confined to Latin America, but not peculiar to Larsen either. It involves what Larsen calls the acceptance of a farce as if it were a job, and there are many farces, public and private, that we go on playing out because we can't bear the thought of what's beyond them. If Larsen in the shipyard is not an allegory, he does set in motion something like a fable, or parable. He is like a character in Kafka, only far shabbier: his life is not ours, but we can't disavow him entirely, we have been in parallel places.

When one of the employees defects from the game, fear settles on Larsen like an illness ('like the nagging, gentle, companionable pain of a chronic illness, one you are not going to die of, because it is only possible to die with it'); fear not that the game is over but that it is going on without him, that it doesn't depend, as he thought, on his choice: what's unavoidable doesn't need our consent. Larsen is last seen leaving Santa María with some boatmen, to whom he gives his watch as payment for his passage. He is so attuned to the ruin of the shipyard that he can hear 'the faint sound of moss climbing over the piles of bricks, of rust eating at the iron'. Or—there is an alternative version, as is fitting for a legend, however squalid—the boatmen find Larsen sick, delirious. They refuse to accept his watch. Larsen can still hear the ruin of the shipyard, 'the hiss of corrosion and collapse'; but he dies of pneumonia, in Rosario.

At one point in *The Shipyard,* sitting in the main square of Santa María, Larsen contemplates the statue of the city's founder, and the narrator treats us to a short excursus on the discussions the good citizens had about the statue when it was first put up, the 'arguments over: the poncho, seen as too Northern; the boots, as too Spanish; the jacket, as too military; the hero's profile was criticised as being too semitic; his features were said to be too cruel, sardonic, and the eyes too close-set; some said his body was so tilted it looked as though he was a novice on horseback.' This is funny as it stands, but it takes an interesting extra twist when you realise that the founder, in this case, is a character in another Onetti novel, and that 'founding' means inventing and fleshing out as a fiction. Juan María Brausen, the founder of Santa María, is the narrator and chief character in *A Brief Life,* and Santa María a place he inhabits in his mind, an escape from the pain and confusion of his broken marriage, his failed career and his

entanglement with the prostitute next door. The title of the novel is borrowed from de Falla, and also glances at a sentimental French song which keeps cropping up in the text:

> La vie est brève
> Un peu d'amour
> Un peu de rêve
> Et puis bonjour

More concretely the phrase alludes to Brausen's brief lives in Buenos Aires and Santa María, and to a further life he has as a man called Arce, the persona he adopts for visiting the prostitute and her world. These lives are all impersonations, and Brausen comes to feel he is finally no one, or only a 'bridge between Brausen and Arce', or only the gloomy demiurge of Santa María.

For Santa María is no less painful and confused than Brausen's reality—and no less real in the end, since he goes there at the conclusion of the novel—but in Santa María he has a creator's rights, he can make corrections, he can come and go in his mind, and above all, he can live out the sorrows of other people instead of his own. Having a statue of him in a later novel solidifies Brausen's act of imagination into a fictional history strongly analogous to the history we are living; and also, more mischievously, makes most cities and founders in Latin America look like Santa María and Brausen, dreams and dreamers that have crept on to the historical map and stayed there.

The same eerie joke appears, in another key, in Onetti's most recent work, *Cuando ya no importe* (*When It Doesn't Matter Anymore*), published earlier this year. Díaz Grey is a doctor through whose eyes much of Santa María is seen, in a number of Onetti's novels. He is about forty when Brausen conjures him up ('feeling my growing need to imagine and to draw close to me an indistinct doctor of forty years, the laconic and despairing inhabitant of a small city located between a river and a colony of Swiss farmers'). In the new novel Díaz Grey, now considerably aged, and married to the mad daughter of Jeremias Petrus, is a quiet accomplice in a flourishing drug traffic on the Brazilian border, and in love with and then abandoned by a very young girl, who may be his daughter. He confesses that he has no memories of his earlier life, of anything before his appearance in Santa María, when he was already qualified as a doctor. He says he was then 30, but this means that Onetti either didn't check on the age he had given Díaz Grey in *A Brief Life* or doesn't care about consistency. It may be 'a very strange case of amnesia', the doctor thinks. He must have had, like everyone else, 'childhood'. adolescence, friends and parents, the inevitable'. He doesn't quite arrive at the suspicion that he is a character in a novel, but he does say, in one of those Borgesian twists which are so easy to miss in Onetti, that 'only a novelist can put a creditable past into writing'—he means he would have to be a novelist to provide himself with a satisfactory past, but there is the same mischievous idea at work here as with Brausen's statue. What if our real past is just the fiction we prefer, a fiction supported by documents and corroborating evidence, and therefore not so openly imaginary as Díaz Grey's past would have to be?

Cuando ya no importe is a casual, untidy but engaging work. It consists of the 'notes', the *apuntes,* of an unnamed narrator—he has false papers identifying him as John Carr, an engineer, but we never learn his real name and he doesn't appear to have a profession. His notes are dated but scrambled—he tells us at one point he dropped them all, and couldn't be bothered to put them back into chronological order: a handy device. The narrator is also involved in the Brazilian drug traffic, and in love with the doctor's nymphet; but he is new to Santa María, which allows Onetti to show us his old haunts through fresh, sceptical eyes. The tone, again is that of the philosophical private eye, although the narrator is not a detective. He is, like Onetti, a great reader, and has the appealing habit of referring to fictional characters—Kirilov, Almayer—as his friends.

Needless to say, things end badly, in loneliness and drizzle; and with thoughts of death, and the suggestion that in Montevideo there is a *cimetière marin* more beautiful than the poem, 'un cementerio marino más hermoso que el poema'. This, I take it, is Onetti's idea of elegy and farewell, and it is entirely in keeping with his work, and with the image he presents of the writer: laconic, elegant, literary, yet convinced that people, even dead or disgraceful people, could have homes more handsome than literature.

Fernando Ainsa   (essay date 1994)

SOURCE: "Juan Carlos Onetti (1909-1994): An Existential Allegory of Contemporary Man," *World Literature Today,* Vol. 68, No. 3, Summer, 1994, pp. 501-04.

[Below, Ainsa examines the universal qualities of Onetti's protagonists.]

Now that Juan Carlos Onetti has left us—when we had already come to believe that he was immortal—we ask ourselves, from where within a country in which narrative is traditionally polarized between rural realism and modest urban incursions did this writer emerge? What was his literary heritage? And, most important, how could he establish, based on a "territory of the imaginary," Santa María, a fictional tradition in which a good many Uruguayan and many other Latin American writers can recognize themselves, an exclusive world that today is the inheritance of universal literature?

If going from the regional to the universal is the privilege of good literature, then in Onetti's case everything began in 1939, in the unkempt room of a tenement house, where a man smokes and paces incessantly through a hot and humid summer night, after a day of celebration. Bored with lying in bed and with smelling alternately one armpit then the other while grimacing in disgust, the man takes stock of his life on the eve of his fortieth birthday: he

has no work or friends, he has just divorced, and his neighbors seem "more repugnant than ever"; it's been more than twenty years since he lost his ideals, and, according to news he has heard on the radio, "it appears that war is imminent."

Any human being confronted with a similar life circumstance could not avoid the most somber of reflections. Nevertheless, Eladio Linacero, the protagonist of *El pozo* (1939; Eng. *The Pit,* 1991), Juan Carlos Onetti's first novel, succeeds in evading his sad reality. For him, it is enough to begin writing a dream ("the dream of the log cabin"), although to do so he feels obliged to recognize that, in his words, "I am a solitary man who smokes anywhere in the city," a confession with which he ends his monologue. In the space of fifty-six pages, narrated in the first person throughout that insomniac night, he not only frees himself from the most menacing ghosts of solitude but also establishes another reality, thanks to his simple formula of acceptance: "I am a man who turns toward the shadow on the wall at night in order to think of foolish and fantastic things."

This salvation through writing portends a destiny that Onetti would fulfill with exemplary precision. Twelve years later, in 1951, another man also paces while suffering insomnia in a small apartment in the San Telmo district of Buenos Aires, "a small and timid man" who has said "no to alcohol, no to tobacco" and that there is "nothing like women." José María Brausen, the protagonist of *La vida breve* (1951; Eng. *A Brief Life,* 1976), appears to be the direct descendant of Linacero. Like the latter, Brausen maintains a mediocre existence and, after five years of marriage, comes to discover the end of his relationship, ruined by indifference. The pretext of this sudden revelation has been the mastectomy which his wife Gertrudis has just undergone, but the reality of his solitude appears much more profound than the scar that cruelly marks her amputation. Without feeling compassion or affection and while listening to her moan as she dreams, Brausen accepts his failure with "the expected resignation that comes with being forty."

Nevertheless, within the four walls of his apartment and through successive nights during which, plagued by insomnia, he paces between the kitchen, the bedroom, and the bathroom, Brausen is capable also of freeing himself from his present circumstance. "Any sudden and simple thing was going to happen, and I could save myself by writing," he says the night he decides "to do something." He sits at a table where, by his own account, "I had under my hands the paper necessary to save myself, a blotter, and a fountain pen." Unlike Linacero, for whom it sufficed "to tell a dream" with the "event" that preceded it, Brausen simultaneously undertakes a twofold escape. On the one hand, he doubles as Arce, a makeshift *macró* (pimp) who bursts into the apartment of his neighbor, a prostitute whose noises he has heard through the thin partition walls that separate their bedrooms, as if the two beds were end to end. At the same time, he assumes the identity of a character he has created (Díaz Grey) in a city (Santa María) imagined with such perfection that at the end of the novel he is able to flee to it without forcing the ambiguous reality of the fiction he invented. Beginning with *La vida breve,* this mythical city with recognizable archetypes of the River Plate region—synthesized by Onetti as a true paradigm—becomes the setting for the rest of his work. Brausen, its "founder," will have a monument erected in his honor in the principal plaza in **"La novia robada" ("The Stolen Bride";** 1968), and in *Cuando ya no importe (When It No Longer Matters*; 1993) his name will be invoked during religious processions.

Through the evasion of the sad personal circumstances of Eladio Linacero and José María Brausen, Onetti establishes a formal, tense universe, a world enclosed existentially on itself, rigorous in style and without concessions yet saved by the act of writing placed at the disposal of its antiheroes. Disoriented beings (when not frustrated), uprooted noncomformists, *outsiders,* and marginal figures face the difficulty of communicating with others and feel that authenticity is repressed by society. They take refuge with their anguish in the space of a small room and carry out a solitary, intense "descent into themselves," having been preceded by the first *outsider* in modern literature, the protagonist of Dostoevsky's *Notes from Underground.*

Born 1 July 1909 in Montevideo, Uruguay, Onetti is a member of a kind of lost generation of the River Plate that reached maturity in the 1940s and could be characterized as somewhat nihilistic. To the extent that he was able to create characters who were authentic spiritual pariahs, morally banished and politically disenchanted, his total rejection of the ruling values is among the most radical. His anti-heroes go much further in their forsaking all belief. Abandoned beings, "amoral, indifferent" men "without faith or interest in their destiny," as he would define them in his foreword to *Tierra de nadie (No Man's Land;* 1941), they are depicted, Onetti admits, "with an equal spirit of indifference," although in reality he has always been empathetic to their sadness through an expressive pity and has discovered with them that the freedom such characters as Linacero or Brausen attained only served to make their isolation more obvious.

In Onetti, solitude is the result not of a deliberate calling for independence but rather of a kind of paralyzing lucidity. All impulse to "action" is denied by a thoroughgoing introspective analysis. In this position there is an inevitable failure, a negation of all that could become delightful, vitalistic enthusiasm, a call to analyze and reflect instead of openly enjoying life. Protagonists who are confined to their rooms like Linacero and Brausen, uncommitted observers of other people's business like Díaz Grey or Jorge Malabia, impresarios destined for defeat like Larsen, eternal planners of projects that are never carried out like Aranzuru—all seem to have come to the conclusion that, as H. G. Wells said, "there is no escape or getting around it or getting through it."

In Onetti's work there is no place for a man of universal values, even if these values appear to be threatened, problematic, or alternative. His disillusionment is total and absolute; there is no possible faith, no imaginable response to crisis, no question worth posing. His dispossession brings him close to the essential dead-end truths of Samuel Beckett's characters. Linacero is, in effect, not unlike Molloy.

Onetti's characters, moreover, live "marginalized" on the muddy banks of the River Plate, "expelled" from Europe, and "fallen" into "an uncharted land, void of spirit." H. A. Murena defines the situation of the River Plate in *El pecado original de América* (America's Original Sin): "America is made up of exiles, is the land of exile, and all who are exiled know profoundly that in order to live, one must be done with the past, must erase memories of this world to which one's return is forbidden, for to do otherwise is to remain suspended from memories, unable to live." Therefore, Onetti ironically asks himself, "Why here? Preceding us there is nothing. One gaucho, two gauchos, thirty-three gauchos," making a clear, irreverent allusion to the Uruguayan national myth, historically founded on the landing of the "thirty-three gauchos from the east bank of the River Plate."

Onetti not only affirms the lack of a perceptible historical past, but he also disavows the expression of traditional culture. In a weekly newspaper column, symptomatically called "La Piedra en el Charco" (The Rock in the Puddle), he severely criticizes his era for lacking originality, for the sterility into which regionalism, *costumbrismo,* and social realism have fallen. Devoid of all rhetorical weight, history is transformed into a tabula rasa, where everything remains to be written, but where, in reality, nothing is worth writing.

Onetti's antiheroes proclaim that "nothing can be done," or, what seems more serious still, that "nothing is worth doing." Far from anguish, nausea, and even *détresse,* one can speak only of fatalism and resignation. Onetti himself declared as an elemental philosophical principle that "the whole art of living lies in the simple ease of accommodating ourselves within the hallow of events that we have not provoked by our own will; not forcing anything; simply being each minute."

In conclusion, it is not worth struggling for some other future, since "An enlightened man should do nothing. Look at construction workers, at any number of things. It breaks your heart. All life wallowing in misery. Look at politics, literature, or what have you. All is false, and the autochthonous is the falsest of all. If there's nothing to do here, don't do anything. If gringos like to work, let them break their backs. I don't have any faith; we don't have faith. Some day we'll have a mystique, for sure; but in the meantime, we're happy."

The formulation of a philosophy of existence in Onetti can, consequently, seem weak. One must wade through sundry isolated paragraphs of his works in order to construct a scheme that surprises by its simplicity and its coherence. For the moment, one discovers that, like a good inhabitant of the River Plate region, Onetti understands that synonymous with virility is a certain contentiousness, a certain obligatory terseness of emotional expression and its mysterious reasons—a constant that appears in the works of authors as diverse as Macedonio Fernández, Jorge Luis Borges, and Julio Cortázar, as well as in many tango lyrics.

In essence, more than a form of deracination, Onetti translates the profound frustration of the inhabitants of the River Plate region, maladjusted as a result of expectations and legitimate aspirations and the sad proof of their surrounding reality, a reality which he judges with a severe, hypercritical focus. His is a criticism that opens its doors to the skepticism of "withdrawn men who shun the masses with taciturnity," about whom Juan Carlos Ghiano has written. In this self-reflection one recognizes not only a single esthetic stance but also a generalized attitude, even at the popular level, where one vacillates between denunciation and acceptance, the confirmation that "things are as they are and there is no recourse but to accept them as such."

One reality Onetti himself had to face came in 1973, when, during the coup d'état of 27 June, he was forced to leave Uruguay and take refuge in Spain, where he resided until his death. In Madrid, far from the Buenos Aires where he had worked as a correspondent for the Reuters news agency, or from his native Montevideo, where he had written for the weekly *Marcha* and the daily *Acción* and where he was director of the municipal library, he received the 1978 Cervantes Prize and, thanks to numerous translations, international recognition.

The fame that was to arrive late did not change Onetti's view of life at all, that vision that Díaz Grey outlined in *El astillero* (1961; Eng. *The Shipyard,* 1968): life "is nothing more than this: what we see and what we know." There is no transcendence or philosophical meaning worth insisting upon. The important thing is that "nothing makes sense." The meaning of this view of existence is quite simple: men are beings who, refusing to accept clarity, complicate everything with "words and anxieties." Resignation, not at all anguished, must lead to admitting death itself as part of a routine.

Onetti's fatalism seems to lead to a certain passivity. Here we are far from all demonic existential anguish; we are close to a kind of beatific, transcendent understanding of all human and earthly anxieties, an attitude that could be religious had it been nurtured by faith. This insistence on the precariousness of existence, which provides the basis for the title of one novel, *La vida breve,* and is implied by the title of another, *Los adioses* (*The Goodbyes;* 1954), makes one recall the lyrics of a song which points toward maturity: "Las marionetas, dan, dan / dan tres vueltas y se van" (The marionettes turn, turn, / turn three times and are gone).

From the impersonal rooms or boarding houses the evasion projected by solitary men has led to boredom or sadness, the expression of a resigned fatalism, far from all anguish and despair. At the end of the dream there is nothing left but to "watch oneself parsimoniously, calmly, growing old without drawing conclusions," or perhaps to "bore oneself smiling," as Díaz Grey suggests with a certain sadness—a sadness which can also be a "state of love" that assures a balance between hopelessness and rebelliousness and foretells a possible individual salvation.

And for what purpose is one saved? The answer rests in literature alone, that form of writing which frees Linacero and Brausen and which Onetti makes his own with a rigorous vocation, for what matters is to write, but not in any old way. In Onetti, beneath the guise of anti-intellectualism, one discovers a compendium of many of the techniques of the best contemporary narrative: the ambiguity of Herman Melville, the multiple points of view of Henry James, the interior monologue of James Joyce, the collective characters of Sherwood Anderson (Does *Winesburg, Ohio* influence Santa María?), the rounded perfection of a story by Stephen Crane, the atmosphere of William Faulkner. The lack of faith in any philosophical, religious, or political dogma does not keep Onetti from believing in the essential condition of the writer. As Lucien Goldmann would say of Jean Genet, one could also say of Onetti: "Only art and appearance can constitute the esthetic compensation of a deceptive and insufficient reality." The exaltation of the powers of imagination through literature would, therefore, constitute more than escape; it would constitute authentic liberation. One could add, from a gnostic point of view, that if to tell a story is to understand, then to understand is to create—an understanding and a creation that, in Onetti's literary praxis, has been translated into a brief yet intense saga. If his work appears to be an enterprise of evasion, made acute with mechanisms that go along with the able management of the best techniques and procedures of writing, it does not constitute an easy escapism, for to escape from one specific reality does not imply abandoning man's essential reality, to let fall into "moral indifference" his existential problematic, which is valid in all time and space.

Herein lies the true meaning of Onetti's work: to arrive at the crux of the individual's intimate solitude, at the metaphysical sadness of the human condition, through the progressive awareness of the uselessness of most human action and through the stripping away of all the trappings that surround us and create for us false dependencies on our surrounding reality; and, in arriving at this crux, to grasp the essence of the human condition in order to distill in an original and solitary way a true existential allegory of contemporary man, not just of the River Plate region or of Latin America but of universal man.

FURTHER READING

Adams, M. Ian. "Juan Carlos Onetti: Alienation and the Frangmented Image." In *Three Authors of Alienation: Bombal, Onetti, Carpentier,* pp. 37-80. Austin: University of Texas Press, 1975.

> Addresses the theme of alienation in Onetti's fiction, arguing "Onetti's artistic manipulation of the schizophrenic experience

. . . produces a unique imagery and an unusual sensation for the reader of participation in an alienated world."

Jones, Yvonne Peier. *The Formal Expression of Meaning in Juan Carlos Onetti's Narrative Art.* Cuernavaca, Mexico: Centro Intercultural de Documentacion, 1971, 162p.

An interpretive study of Onetti's fiction.

Kadir, Djelal. *Juan Carlos Onetti.* Boston: G. K. Hall, 1977, 160p.

Discusses Onetti's major works, focusing on the author's aesthetics.

Millington, Mark. *Reading Onetti.* Liverpool: Francis Cairns, 1985, 345p.

Provides detailed analysis of each of Onetti's major works.

Additional coverage of Onetti's life and career is contained in the following sources published by the Gale Group: *Contemporary Authors,* Vols. 85-88, 145; *Contemporary Authors New Revision Series,* Vols. 32, 63; *Contemporary Literary Criticism,* Vols. 7, 10; *Dictionary of Literary Biography,* Vol. 113; *DISCovering Authors: Multicultural Module; DISCovering Authors: Novelists Module; Hispanic Writiers; Major Twentieth Century Writers,* Vol. 1; and *Short Story Criticism,* Vol. 33.

Luis Palés Matos
1898-1959

Puerto Rican poet, essayist, and novelist.

INTRODUCTION

Palés Matos's influence in Puerto Rican literature is most often felt in the essays and novels which followed him, rather than his own medium of poetry. His *negrista* movement began a controversy in Puerto Rico concerning nationalism and cultural pride which has continued long after his death.

Palés Matos was born on March 20, 1898, in Guayama, Puerto Rico. Guayama, a small town on the southeastern coast, is surrounded by sugarcane plantations and has a large black population. Both the geography of his home and its black culture made a tremendous impact on Palés Matos and would influence his later poetry. Palés Matos had a literary family: his father, Vincente Palés Anes, and his mother, Consuelo Palés Vicil, were both poets. Palés Matos's father and two of his brothers, Vincente and Gustavo Palés Matos, served as poet laureates of Puerto Rico at one time or another, and his sister, Consuelo, also wrote verse. The literary influence of his family inspired him to begin writing poetry at the age of 13. When Palés Matos's father died in 1913, he quit school and began a series of odd jobs. In addition to writing poetry, he worked as a journalist, a secretary, and a bookkeeper. He published his first volume, *Azaleas* (1915), when he was 17. The times in which Palés Matos grew up also influenced the themes of his poetry. The United States took possession of Puerto Rico from Spain after the Spanish-American War in 1898, crushing the burgeoning political autonomy Puerto Ricans had begun to feel under Spanish rule. This led to a period of pessimism which can be seen in Palés Matos's poetry through the themes of despair, futility, and self-doubt. Throughout his poetic career, Palés Matos held various bureaucratic positions with Puerto Rico's government, until he became poet-in-residence at the University of Puerto Rico in 1944. Palés Matos died of a heart attack on February 23, 1959.

Palés Matos's early work, though written while he was still a teenager, shows a great poetic maturity. The poems from the first part of his career, including those collected in his only published collection of this phase, *Azaleas*, were in the *modernista* tradition of such poets as Ruben Darío, Leopoldo Lugones, and Julio Herrera y Reissig. This work shows Palés Matos's use of clear poetic diction and attention to detail that would characterize his work throughout his career. Palés Matos's wrote two collections of poetry that were never published, *El palacio en sombras* and *Canciones de la vida media*, although several of the poems were included in a later anthology. Again the influence of the *modernista* poets are felt, but these collections also are filled with strong imagery evoking the tropical landscape of Puerto Rico and the alienation felt by the poet. The next phase of Palés Matos's career was short-lived; in 1921 he developed the *diepalismo* movement with José I. de Diego Padro, which featured the extensive use of onomatopoeia. The two wrote a manifesto and a jointly written poem entitled "Orquestacion diepàlica." Palés Matos is most famous for his celebration of black themes and rhythms in the poetry from his next phase. He was the originator of the movement in Puerto Rican poetry known as *negrismo,* which is a celebration of the contributions and culture of blacks in Puerto Rico. The movement was simultaneous to the same movement in Cuba. His *Tuntun de pasa y grifería* (*Drumbeats of Kink and Blackness,* 1950) is his most important *negrista* work, and it is credited with cementing his reputation. The premise of the poetry from this volume is that the Hispanic Caribbean is a result of the mixing of European and African cultures in Caribbean nations such as Puerto Rico. The work caused great controversy from Hispanophiles in Puerto Rico who were resistant to Western influences. Many literary critics have also complained that Palés Matos, a white man, stereotyped the black experience in Puerto Rico. Others argued that the use of stereotypes can be useful in conveying an image and that the charge was only leveled because Palés Matos was white. In the final stage of his career, Palés Matos turned away from black themes to write more personal love poetry which he devoted to a woman only identified as "Filí-Melé."

Palés Matos has been called one of the most sensory poets in the Spanish language, with critical praise for his ability to evoke an atmosphere using all of the senses. Beyond his lyrical contributions, however, Palés Matos will be most remembered for his contribution to the history and culture of Puerto Rico. Although critics disagree with different aspects of Palés Matos's poetic assertions, his celebration of black culture in Puerto Rico depicted the uniqueness, strength, and diversity of its history and culture with a fluid and sensual sound.

PRINCIPAL WORKS

Tuntún de pasa y griferia: Poemas afroantillanos (poetry) 1950
Poesía, 1915-1956 (poetry) 1957
Luis Palés Matos: Vida y obra, bibliografía, antología (collected works) 1959

Luis Palés Matos (1898-1959): Vida y obra, bibliografía, antología, poesías inéditas (collected works) 1960

Poesía completa y prosa selecta (poetry and prose) 1978

Obras (1914-1959), two volumes (selected works) 1984

Azaleas (poetry) 1915

Pueblo negro (poetry) 1925

CRITICISM

Julio Marzán (essay date 1995)

SOURCE: "Images of the Numen," in *The Numinous Site*, London: Associated University Press, 1995, pp. 96-114.

[*In this excerpt, Marzán heralds the sensual, spiritual imagery present in Palés Matos' poetry, highlighting his affinity with nature and music.*]

In the pre-Afro-Antillean poems, we recall, the speaker submerges, leaps or flies to the superior reality beyond the surface mundane reality to an atemporal destination that as yet Palés did not call "numen." That atemporal destination was invariably depicted in several recurring images, some of which foregrounded the destination itself (the moon, the distant star) and others of which foregrounded the medium (the distant land, the dream) through which one passed. In *Tuntún de Pasa y Grifería*, however, the destination/passage images gave way to the "numen," which fused the medium and the destination, epitomizing Palés's vision of the physical realm as always in contact with the spiritual one. The "numen" in *Tuntún,* then, is an explicit rendering of the subdued numinous function of the destination images of the pre-Afro-Antillean poetry. Otherwise, the Palesian poetry structure remains unchanged: a passage, whether instant or slow, through the medium of the poem, to an encounter with the numinous. Both stages of numinous images are semantically synonymous. This parallel accounts for Palés's carrying the numen concept over to the post-*Tuntún* metaphysical poems and argues once again that the ostensible diversity in the stages of Palés's poetry is merely a surface variety that enriches his style as he consistently reiterates his discourse.

LUNA/ESTRELLA LEJANA

Although not always explicitly an imagistic destination of a flight or passage, the moon is variously foregrounded as an enchanting object. **"Las Torres Blancas"** to which the speaker flies are bathed in a moonlight medium that causes "monstruos sublunares" to rise in the night air. In **"Candombe"** the warriors must elect someone to travel to the moon that telescopes into a metaphor of a silver tortoise releasing an evil spell as it swims in the black waters of the night (both water and night also being numinous images):

La luna es tortuga de plata
nadando en la noche tranquila.
¿Cuál será el pescador osado
que a su red la traiga prendida:
Sokola, Babiro, Bombassa,
Yombofré, Bulón or Babissa?
Tum-cutum, tum-cutum,
ante la fogata encendida.

Mirad la luna, el pez de plata,
la vieja tortuga maligna
echando al agua de la noche
su jugo que duerme y hechiza . . .
Coged la luna, coged la luna,
traedla a un anzuelo prendida.
Bailan los negros en la noche
ante la fogata encendida.
Tum-cutum, tum cu-tum,
ante la fogata encendida.

[A silver tortoise is the moon
swimming in the placid night.
Who'll be the daring fisherman
to bring it caught in his net:
Sokola, Babiro, Bombassa,
Yombofré, Bulón or Babissa?
Tum-cutum, tum-cutum,
round the blazing bonfire.

Look at the moon, the silver fish,
the old, malignant tortoise
oozing in night's water
its lulling, bewitching broth . . .
Catch the moon, catch the moon,
bring it dangling from a hook.
Black men dance in the night
round the blazing bonfire,
Tum-cutum, tum cu-tum,
round the blazing bonfire.]

In **"Claro de Luna,"** the speaker's heart, a frog, leaps into the night "de luna clara y tersa." Here the moonlight provides the conditions for the heart's passage to (and among) the stars:

¡Ah, que no llegue nunca la mañana!
¡Que se alargue esta lenta
hora de beatitud en que las cosas
adquieren una irrealidad suprema;

y en que mi corazón, como una rana,
se sale de sus ciénagas,
y se va bajo el claro de la luna
en vuelo sideral por las estrellas!

[Ah, let morning never come!
Never end the languor
of this blessed hour when things
assume a supreme unreality;

and when my heart, like a frog,
emerges from its swamp,

and takes off in the moonlight
on a star's flight among the stars!]

By foregrounding the moon's enchanting powers, these poems give the impression that the moon inspires or causes flights to distant points that are presumably distinct from the moon itself. In the early poem **"Luno-manía,"** for instance, a prefiguration of **"Claro de Luna,"** we see how the purity of the moon prompts the speaker to desire to travel heavenward so he may become a celestial body. The speaker relies on a synonymy between the moon's purity and the "vivas / claridades" found in the heights of the "escala luminosa":

> Luna que haces soñar en bailarinas
> vaporosas, aéreas, diamantinas . . .,
> dame la leche de tu jarra llena:
> quiero ser de la altura, alba y serena.
>
> Ser de los azahares que cultivas.
> Quizá volverme estrella que dé vivas
> claridades. ¿Entiendes? Deseo irme . . .
> por tu escala lumínica subirme.
>
> Le tengo mucho miedo a esta bajura.
> ¡Es tan impura. Y tú, ¡eres tan pura!
> que quisiera escurrirme por tu vientre . . .
>
> [Moon that makes me dream of dancers,
> vaporous, aerial, diamond-bright . . .,
> give me the milk of your full pitcher:
> I want to be of sky, dawn and serene.
>
> Be of the orange blossoms you grow.
> Maybe turn into a star to impart
> bright clarity. Understand me? I want to depart . . .
> up your luminous ladder.
>
> I'm so afraid of this lowliness.
> It is so impure! And you, you are so pure,
> how I would slide into your womb . . .]

To take the argument one step further, the lunar influence to which the speaker in **"Claro de Luna"** attributes his heart's desire to fly among the stars (in other words, write a poem) in **"El Destierro Voluntario"** is credited exclusively to the star:

> Quiero purgar ¡oh montaña pagana!
> sobre tu roca mi lírico estigma,
> bajo la estrella escultora y lejana
> que le da al verso su forma y su enigma.
>
> [Upon your rock, oh pagan mountain,
> I want to wash off my lyrical stigma,
> under the distant, sculptor star
> that gives the poem its form and enigma.]

The star's inspiring poetry here makes explicit the semantic synonymy between the effects on the poet of any celestial body and that of the moon, a synonymy between celestial bodies that in **"Lunomanía"** is expressed im-

plicitly and in **"Claro de Luna"** is completely absent from the surface text.

This synonymy also operates in two poems that, on the surface, employ completely unrelated images. In **"El Pozo,"** the moon's influence causes the toad in the water's depths to croak, an act that fills the soul with "a remote sense of eternity." This feeling of being submerged in eternal waters is but a surface variation on the metaphorical flight through the heavens. **"Canción de la Vida Media,"** as discussed in a previous chapter, employs an image of flight, with the star image as the destination, but before that flight the soul starts out compared to a tree, which must be pruned of the leaves of excess rhetorical devices. After the pruning, the tree is erect, clean and light, allowing the poet to telescope the tree into a pointed prow poised to set sail towards the heavens to the "estrella lejana":

> Así estás, alma mía, en tu grave hora nueva,
> toda desnuda y blanca,
> erguida hacia el silencio milenario y profundo
> de la estrella lejana.
>
> [So you stand, my soul, at your solemn new hour,
> completely bare and blank,
> erect toward the millenary, fathomless silence
> of the faraway star.]

Despite the surface impression that in **"El Pozo"** and **"Canción de la Vida Media"** the speaker is being transported to different destinations and in diametrically opposite directions, in both poems that destination is described as deep ("profundo") and timeless ("eterno") or virtually endless ("milenario"). Furthermore, in neither poem is the destination a fixed point: in **"El Pozo"** the destination is the water's depth, which suddenly becomes metaphorically open-ended, and in **"Canción"** the speaker's soul is bound for the "silencio milenario y profundo"—in other words, the space surrounding the distant star and not the star itself. Both images therefore are merely variations of the same limitless medium evoked by all the numinous images.

SUEÑO

Synonymous with the soul or dream world, the "sueño" image is Palés's most explicit medium image. Through the "sueño" the poet is transported to the eternal. The importance of the "sueño" as both image and experience is explained by the poem **"El Sueño,"** discussed in a previous chapter, which avows that "El sueño es el estado natural" ["The dream is the natural state"]. But "sueño" is amorphous stuff, an abstraction, which generates more abstraction. Thus we frequently encounter the "sueño" image embodied in another, more concrete image, such as water in **"El Sueño"** above:

> ese ras de agua inmóvil perennemente mudo,
> muy allá de los límites del espacio y el tempo.
>
> [that stagnant water surface, perennially mute,
> far beyond the shores of space and time.]

"**Lullaby**" resorts to a subdued allusion to water, as the speaker travels submerged in dream. On the other hand, in "**Lunomanía**" the "bailarinas" evoked by the moon are really *sueños*.

One underlying numen feature of the "sueño" image, whether explicit or subdued, is that it evokes both a sense of place and of being transported to another place. This dual sense operates in both "**Pueblo Negro**" and "**Las Torres Blancas,**" in which the "sueño" is simultaneously medium and the encountered dream object. The "Pueblo Negro" is described as being "de sueño" and "caserío irreal de paz y sueño," where "irreal" refers to a superior unmundane reality. "**Las Torres Blancas,**" the black town's parallel, is a dream city in a nocturnal countryside indistinguishable from the dream itself.

This capacity of "sueño" to evoke simultaneously a changed state or the medium to that state is also demonstrated in "**Canción de Mar,**"[1] a poem that employs a numinous water image to provide a depth that telescopes into a dreamscape cluttered with dream images that are encountered in other changed media in Palés's poems. The sea depths, referred to as the "imperio fabuloso," becomes a metaphor of "sueño":

> Abajo es el imperio fabuloso:
> la sombra de galeones sumergidos
> desangrando monedas de oro pálido y viejo;
> las conchas entreabiertas como párpados
> mostrando el ojo ciego y lunar de las perlas;
> el pálido fantasma de ciudades hundidas
> en el verdor crepuscular del agua . . .
> remotas ulalumes de un sueño inenarrable
> resbalado de monstuos que fluyen en silencio
> por junglas submarinas y floras de trasmundo.

> [Below is the fabulous empire:
> shadows of submerged galleons
> bleeding old, faded doubloons;
> conches half-open like eyelids
> revealing blind, moon-bright pearl eyes;
> the pale ghosts of sunken cities
> in the water's twilight green . . .
> remote Ulalumes of an indescribable dream
> slimy with monsters soundlessly weaving
> through submarine jungles and afterlife flora.]

AGUA, MAR, NOCHE

As "**Canción de Mar**" also demonstrates, the passage to the nether or distant world is frequently depicted as a movement through water or a watery substance. We have also seen the speaker in "**Lullaby**" refer to his being "submerged" in the dream and, in "**El Sueño,**" to mundane existence as a light splash on the water's surface. In "**Pueblo,**" a water image is at first suggested, with the mayor "dabbling" in his life, and later expressed explicitly, as the poet urges some scoundrel to come to the town and throw a stone against "el agua muerta de sus vidas."

One of the most complex constructions in Palés's imagistic repertory is the series of images telescoped from the simple image of water as the medium to the soul-world. The prototype of this series is found in "**El Pozo,**" a poem that compares the soul to the "pozo" ("well") in whose depths a toad croaks. Taking the "pozo" as one element (the toad being the other), we notice that in some poems the "pozo de agua" is compared to the night, as occurs in "**Voces del Mar**": "bajo la noche hueca como un pozo infinito" ["under the hollow night like an infinite well"]. And that same "pozo infinito" drips down on mundane reality from overhead in "**Nocturno**" ("**Nocturn**"), in which the insomniac poet contemplates the stillness of the night with its "luna acuosa" ("watery moon"):

> El silencio es tan hondo y las cosas están
> tan sensibles, tan vagas, tan aéreas, tan frágiles,
> que si yo diera un grito caerían las estrellas
> húmedas sobre el parque.

> Hay que estar quieto, quieto, pues cualquier ademán
> tendría una alargada repercusión unánime . . .
> —Como una gota densa y profunda, en la noche,
> la hora, remota, cae.

> [So abysmal is the silence and things feel
> so tender, so vague, so aerial, so fragile,
> that if I were to let out a scream, stars would rain
> wet over the park.

> One has to keep still, still, lest any movement
> cause a protracted reaction all at once . . .
> —Like a dense, huge drop, in the night,
> somewhere distant the hour falls.]

Similarly, the toad submerged in the "pozo" appears in several poems. In "**Topografía**" a toad is submerged in the metaphorical "pozo infinito" of the night:

> La noche cierra pronto y en el lúgubre
> silencio rompe el sapo
> su grito de agua oculta que las sombras
> absorben como tragos.

> [Night shuts down early and in the gloomy
> silence, toads blurt out their croak,
> gurgling an underground water
> the shadows gulp like drinks.]

In this region, the toad's "grito de agua oculta," which only emerges at night, is one of the few sources of water, which semantically signifies spiritual vitality. During the day, the only water around is shallow and stagnant:

> El sol calienta en las marismas rojas
> el agua como un caldo,
> y arranca del arenal caliginoso
> un brillo seco y áspero.

> [The sun in the red marshes heats
> the water like a broth,

and from dark sandy patches extracts
a cragged, dry shine.]

The toad in the well is also the prototype of the reptilian drums in the night of **"Intermedios del Hombre Blanco"** (**"White Man's Interludes"**):

La noche es un criadero de tambores
que croan en la selva,
con sus roncas gargantas de pellejo
cuando alguna fogata los despierta.

[Night is a breeding ground of drums
whose hoarse throats of skin
croak throughout the jungle
when awakened by a bonfire.]

Knowing that the night, like a huge well, also has the attributes of a huge soul adds to our evoked sense of spiritual weight on the shoulders of the white man lost in the jungle (from which, nightly, the Afro-Antillean numina, demons to the white man, emerge). Like the toad's croaking in the water or the black woman's sensual body-song dissolving in the atmosphere of **"Pueblo Negro,"** the sound of the "tambores" pervades the night air:

Con soñoliento gesto de batracios
alzan pesadamente la cabeza,
dando al cálido viento la pringosa
gracia dc su cncrcgía tuntuncca.

[With drowsy amphibian faces
heavily they lift their heads,
lending the warm breeze the oily
grace of their drumming energy.]

Steeped in the night, the white man is chased by the "tambores" that, although reptilian, have stingers that can get into his interior self and contaminate his soul with their contagious musical "cró-cró":

¡Ahí vienen los tambores!
Ten cuidado, hombre blanco, que a ti llegan
para clavarte su aguijón de música.
Tápate las orejas,
cierra toda abertura de tu alma
y el instinto dispón a la defensa;
que si en la torva noche de Nigricia
te picara un tambor de danza o guerra,
su terrible ponzoña
correrá para siempre por tus venas.

[Here come the drums!
White man, watch out they don't reach you
to nail you with their music-making stinger.
Cover your ears,
close every opening in your soul
and ready your reflexes in defense;
for in the fierce Blackland night
should a war or dance drum prick you,
its savage venom
will flow in your veins forever.]

The three-element telescoped metaphor made up of alma-pozo-noche—along with other numinous images—operates in **"A Luis Lloréns Torres"** to create both the medium in which a *coquí,* the tiny Puerto Rican tree frog, whistles in the night and the medium through which the poet Lloréns submerges to reach the heavenly spheres and the "origen de las primeras cosas":

Y más allá, en el fundo, en la paz anchurosa
y vegetal del campo, cuando la soledosa
voz del coquí, goteando de la nocturna calma
bajaba hasta el hondón elemental de tu alma . . .

[And farther off, in your country space, in the wide,
vegetal rural peace, as the *coquí*'s
solitary voice, dripping from the night's calm,
fell to the elemental bottom of your soul . . .]

Another key recurring water image, as noted earlier, is the sea. In **"El Dolor Desconocido"** (**"The Unknown Pain"**), for example, like the water in **"El Pozo,"** the sea is a metaphor of the soul:

A veces, de sus roncos altamares ocultos,
de esas inexploradas distancias, vienen ecos
tan vagos, que se pierden como ondas desmayadas
sobre una playa inmóvil de bruma y de silencio.
[A times, from their hoarse, unseen seas,
from those unexplored reaches, arrive echoes
so dim they dissolve like waves that flatten
against an immovable shore of mist and silence.]

As a metaphor for the soul, the sea is also portrayed as being influenced by the numinous moon, as the well-water was in **"El Pozo."** This effect of the moon on the water-soul-sea is seen in **"Voces del Mar"**:

A medianoche escuchan gritos, y se levantan
medrosos. De la luna baja un silencio astral;
el mar se tiende vasto y azul; las aguas cantan;
cunde el retumbo de la armonía sideral . . .

[At midnight they hear shouts, and rise from bed
trembling. From the moon descends a star's silence;
the sea extends vast and blue; the waters sing;
everywhere a starry harmony resounds.]

Different from the "pozo," the sea image contributes its capacity to evoke a sense of horizontal infinity that provides the medium for the image of a long sea voyage. In a few cases, however subdued the metaphors, this sea voyage image is obvious. In **"San Sabás,"** for instance, the subdued metaphor of the night as a sea obviously becomes the medium across which the "peñón colosal" ("colossal rock") will travel into the heavens "como una proa espiritual" ("like a spiritual prow"). But a subdued long sea voyage image is also central to **"Elegía del Duque de la Mermelada,"** in which the Duque in a former life is depicted as being transported by his ritualistic dances on the banks of the Pongo river through the wet night to the "farthest shores" where he encounters his numinous "great-great grandfather."

This subdued voyage parallels the explicit one referred to in **"El Llamado,"** in which, no matter where the speaker turns, he encounters the call to voyage across a sea. At first, he is looking at a real sea:

> Estoy frente a la mar y en lontananza
> se va perdiendo el ala de una vela;
> va yéndose, esfumándose,
> y yo también me voy borrando con ella.

> [I'm facing the sea and in the horizon
> a wing-shaped sail fades from view;
> it continues to dissolve, turning to smoke,
> and I erase myself as it does.]

Later his lover's eyes also become a metaphorical sea calling the called one inexorably "allá":

> Mas de pronto, despierta,
> y allá en el negro hondón de sus pupilas
> que son un despedirse y una ausencia,
> algo me invita a su remota margen
> y dulcemente, sin querer, me lleva.

> [But suddenly she awakes,
> and far in the black fathoms of her pupils,
> at once a departure and an absence,
> something invites me to her distant shore
> and, helpless, I am lovingly taken there.]

Finally, resigned—or sounding resigned—to his fate, he describes the sea he will sail:

> Un mar hueco, sin peces,
> agua vacía y negra
> sin vena de fulgor que la penetre
> ni pisada de brisa que la mueva.
> Fondo inmóvil de sombra,
> límite gris de piedra . . .

> [A hollowed-out sea, fishless,
> a vacant, black water
> with no brilliant ray to enter it,
> nor breeze's step to ripple it.
> Motionless floor of shadow,
> gray limit of stone.]

LEJANO PAÍS (DISTANT COUNTRY)

On the surface, the "lejano país" is one of the destination images at the end of the speaker's long voyage. In **"A Un Amigo,"** he arrives at the "lejano país" by way of the sea. In **"Voz de lo Sedentario y lo Monótono,"** the speaker in a wheelchair imagines himself travelling to it in a landau. An earlier version of **"Voz,"** titled **"Tic-Tac,"** however, demonstrates that, on a semantic level, the "lejano país" is actually a metaphor for the envisioned dreamsoul world and, by extension, for eternity. In that early poem,[2] the speaker not only has a vision of the "lejano país" but of the dream city found in it, the same city encountered in **"Las Torres Blancas."** Also, as in the later poem, in **"Tic-Tac"** the speaker spiritually flies there:

> Y otear en los confines la ciudad prometida;
> el lazareto blanco para las penas malas,
> y previvir la vida dormida de esa vida
> más puro el sentimiento y más firmes las alas.

> [And envisage in the horizon the promised city,
> the white quarantine for harsh sentences,
> and imagine the sleepy life in that life,
> purer my perceptions and firmer my wings.]

Only after waiting a long time for that vision, when the speaker is virtually convinced that the vision will be a failure does **"Ella"** (a prefiguration of the Diosa-Poesía) arrive from the dream city in the "lejano país."

But unlike the other pre-Afro-Antillean numinous images, the "lejano país" rarely appears in the surface text of the mature poems, in which this image appears subdued in other images. In **"El Llamado,"** the "lejano país" is pointed to by the adverb "allá" ("far-off"). In **"El Dolor Desconocido,"** it is the "ciudad dormida" ("sleeping city"). In **"A Gloria Madrazo Vicens,"** it is the ultimate destination of the speaker's own "último viaje sin regreso" ["final trip without return"]. In **"Puerto al Tiempo en Tres Voces"** (**"Entrance to Time in Three Voices"**) that place is alluded to as "ribera" ("shore").

Also, every instance of the "lejano país" image, whether explicit (in early poems) or subdued (in the mature poems), is part of an extended image that evokes a sense of passage. That "país" only exists as an unattainable destination or vision whose very impossibility makes the dream or poem necessary as a medium to it, and only the numen, the dead and the poet experience the journey. Hence in **"A Luis Lloréns Torres,"** the "lejano país" is the "cósmico imperio" ("cosmic empire") to which the dead poet used to travel when pondering metaphysical questions and now will reach in death. In **"Boceto,"** the antecedent of "tú" is really the Essence of Poetry, described as "vuelo hacia país flotante" [flight to a floating country"]. In **"Majestad Negra,"** the goddess Tembandumba is from the "Quimbamba," an African-derived word meaning "país lejano" (see Alvarez Nasario, 231), which in popular speech signifies a remote unspecified place, into whose realm the Antillean street has semantically been transported by means of the "*rumba, macumba, candombe, bámbula.*"

NUMINA, DEITIES, ATMOSPHERE

The "numen," as indicated earlier, replaced the manifold spiritual and medium (to a spiritual encounter) images in the pre-Afro-Antillean poems. This shift to the numen concept changed the emphasis of Palés's vision: whereas in earlier works one experiences a sense of passage to the spiritual realm, a voyage that came about either under the spell of celestial bodies or from a desire that emerges from the nether-soul world, in *Tuntún* what is emphasized is the process of *return* to origins or an *immediate contact* with that numinous source.

To illustrate, in **"Falsa Canciíon de Baquiné"** (**"False Child's Wake Song"**) the baby's death is depicted as a return across a superficially unimaged sea to the beach where the maternal Tembandumba awaits:

> Pero que ahora verá la playa.
> Pero que ahora verá el palmar.
> Pero que ahora ante el fuego grande
> con Tembandumba podrá bailar.

> [But now he will see the beach.
> But now he will see palm trees.
> But now round the great fire
> he can dance with Tembandumba.

Tembandumba and Bombo are the two most frequently invoked numina in *Tuntún*. Tembandumba also appears in **"Ñam-Ñam,"** a poem that explodes by exaggeration the former Western racist convention that depicted "Dark Africa" as a chomping mouth devouring a meal of white missionaries and explorers:

> Quien penetró en Tangañica
> por vez primera—ñam-ñam;
> quien llegó hasta Tembandumba
> la gran matriarca—ñam-ñam.

> [Who was the first to penetrate
> to Tanganyica—*ñam-ñam*
> who reached Tembandumba,
> the great matriarch—*ñam-ñam.*]

Consumed by the natives, the white man's penetration therefore extended to the great goddess and matriarch Tembandumba.

In **"Majested Negra"** (**"Black Majesty"**), Tembandumba personifies the totemic Antillean dances. Invoked by the "rumba, macumba, candombe, bámbula," Tembandumba descends on the hot Antillean streets. As an anthropomorphism, she is sensuality incarnate and her dance movements are rendered in a metaphor of a sugar mill grinding out sugar and molasses:

> Culipandeando la Reina avanza,
> y de su inmensa grupa resbalan
> meneos cachondos que el gongo cuaja
> en ríos de azúcar y de malaza.
> Prieto trapiche de sensual zafra,
> el caderamen, masa con masa,
> exprime ritmos, suda que sangra,
> y la molienda culmina en danza.

> [Curvaceous behind, the Queen advances
> as down her huge rump drip
> sexual jiggles the conga curds
> in rivers of cane juice and molasses.
> Blackened sugar mill for a sensual harvest,
> her great thighs, mass against mass,
> squeeze out rhythms, sweat clear blood,
> and the grinding culminates in dance.]

In this poem, Tembandumba from the **"Quimbamba"** (**"Farplace"**) exists as both a surface image of an earthy black woman and a semantic image of the goddess.

In **"Falsa Canción de Baquiné,"** the great god Bombo escorts the dead baby's "zombi," or resurrected corpse, back to Guinea:

> Y a la Guinea su zombí vuelva . . .
> —Coquí, cocó, cucú, cacá—
> Bombo el gran mongo bajo la selva
> su tierno paso conducirá.

> [And to Guinea his zombi returns . . .
> —*Coquí, cocó, cucú, cacá*—
> Bombo the great god of the jungle
> will lead his baby steps.]

Bombo also lends his name to the title of the poem **"Bombo,"** in which he is instantly invoked by the dance "la bomba," used here by Palés as a totemic word (see chapter 5) that evokes both the original drum and the dance it inspired. Ambiguously, both meanings of "bomba" invoke the great numen **"Bombo"**:

> La bomba dice:—¡Tombuctú!
> Cruzan las sombras ante el fuego.
> Arde la pata del hipopótamo
> en el balele de los negros.
> Sobre la danza Bombo rueda
> su ojo amarillo y soñoliento,
> y el bembe de ídolo africano
> le cae en cuajo sobre el pecho.
> ¡Bombo del Congo, mongo máximo,
> Bombo del Congo está contento.

> [The *bomba* says:—Timbucktu!
> Shadows crisscross before the fire.
> Leg of hippo roasts
> at the black tribe's feast.
> Above the dancing, Bombo rolls
> his yellow, dreaming eyes,
> and his African-idol lip
> thickly sags over his chest.
> Bombo of the Congo, highest god,
> Bombo of the Congo is now happy.]

Besides God, other Western deities are invoked in Palés's work. Three poems employ the image of the Valkyrie, the handmaiden of the Nordic god Odin, who carry off the slain warriors to their rightful place in the Valhalla, another "lejano país." In **"Walhalla,"** the poet imagines himself in a Nordic setting superimposed over his own Antillean town. Speaking to himself, he acknowledges that his song resurrects the ancient Nordic myth, an acknowledgment that the poem, on the semantic level, opens a door to the myth's spiritual dimension. Similarly, the Valkirie is mentioned in **"Sinfonía Nórdica,"** which consists of five stanzas each composed of Nordic images evoked by the music of five different European composers, a process that culminates in the chant of the Valkyrie, which transports the poet once again to the spiritual realm. Finally, it is to the Valkyrie that Palés compares his own Antillean myth, the *mulata-antilla*:

En potro de huracán pasas cantando
tu criolla canción, prieta walkiria,
con centelleante espuela de relámpagos
rumbo al verde Walhalla de las islas.

[On a hurricane colt you ride by singing
your creole song, dark Valkirie
with lightning spurs flashing,
bound for the green Valhalla of the islands.]

(Observe the ambiguity created by the omission of a comma after "relámpagos." Both the Valkirie and the "lightning" are "bound for . . . ," the latter's destination being the islands praised as heavenly and the former's being the heaven that watches over the islands. Thus the image operates on both a mundane and spiritual level simultaneously.)

Other numina-gods in *Tuntún* are given less auspicious treatments: the warrior numen papá Ogún is invoked in **"Falsa Canción";** Ecué, Changó, papá Abasí and papá Bocó in "Lamento"; the unnamed "gran bisabuelo" of the Duque de la Mermelada in the **"Elegía."** Along with Tembandumba and Bombo, these numina compose the pantheon of ancestral African spirits that are invoked by the Caribbean music, dance and language. They are also the unspecified "demonios" that, invoked by the "tambores" in **"Intermedios del Hombre Blanco,"** descend upon the white man:

A su conjuro hierven
las oscuras potencias:
fetiches de la danza,
tótemes de la guerra,
y los mil y uno demonios que pululan
por el cielo sensual del alma negra.

[At their conjuring
the dark powers swarm;
fetishes for the dance,
totems for war,
and the thousand and one teeming demons
across the black soul's sensual heaven.]

A major juxtaposition of theistic conventions occurs in **"Ñáñigo al Cielo,"** in which a *ñáñigo,* a member of a secret society of black Cubans, rises to the heaven of the Western God. An excellent example of Palés's antipoetic aesthetic, mixing humor with seriousness, on the surface **"Ñáñigo al Cielo"** is like a graphically spectacular cartoon of heaven's celebrating the event by turning itself into a Caribbean paradise. Behind the wit and imagery, however, the poem inquires about the fate of black souls in a white heaven. Besides the surface anthropomorphic goings on, stylistically what takes place is that the Western God, implicit in Palés's non-Afro Antillean allusions to eternity and the soul, now joins his pantheon of myth and imagistic numina, a white tribal counterpart to the great Bombo:

De pronto Jehová conmueve
de una patada el espacio.
Rueda el trueno y quedan solos

frente a frente, Dios y el ñáñigo.
—En la diestra del Señor,
agrio foete, fulge el rayo.

[Suddenly Jehova quakes
the cosmos with one kick.
Thunder rolls, and face to face,
God and the ñáñigo are alone.
—In the Lord's right hand,
a sharp whip, lightning flashes.]

The speaker admits that God's utterances to the *ñáñigo* are in a language that "no es música / transportable a ritmo humano" ["isn't a music / playable to a human rhythm"]. All he can claim to know are the signs perceived by his senses. His sight does see them embrace and his sense of smell detects that their embrace emits an odor of Antillean rum that engulfs the pair and evokes a festive air:

Pero donde el pico es corto,
vista y olfato van largos,
y mientras aquélla mira
a Dios y al negro abrazados,
éste percibe un mareante
tufo de ron antillano,
que envuelve las dos figuras
protagonistas del cuadro,
da tonos de cumbancha
al festival del espacio).

[But where the beak is short,
sight and smell go farther,
and while the former sees
God and the black man hugging,
the latter smells a dizzying
whiff of Antillean rum,
which engulfing the scene's
two principle players,
adds a tone of good times
to the cosmic get-together.]

The result, of course, is a spiritual communion that mythically defines the Caribbean, the same *mulatez* celebrated in **"Mulata-Antilla"** and **"Ten con Ten."**

The product of that embrace is also a telescoped metaphor of perhaps the most subtle of the images of the numinous presence: *atmósfera*. A transformation of the water image, the dense humid atmosphere—etymologically a "sphere of vapor"—threads all the phases of Palés's work by evoking throughout his work a sense of a dreamsoul state. In the non-Afro-Antillean poems we encounter both explicit and subdued examples in **"Walhalla," "Humus," "Las Torres Blancas,"** and **"Los Animales Interiores,"** to name a few. In *Tuntún*, the "atmósfera" becomes the collective Caribbean medium charged with African ancestral numina, an air that Palés perceived as spiritually haunted. As in the non-Afro-Antillean poems, the image is often used explicitly as itself and other times is transformed into images of sound, smell or heat, as is illustrated above in **"Ñáñigo al Cielo."** Other examples were previously discussed in **"Pueblo Negro," "Canción Festiva para Ser Llorada," "Intermedios del Hombre Blanco,"** and **"Mulata-Antilla."**

As with all the other numen images, the "atmósfera" is quite literally another *sphere,* an "allá" inhabited by a spiritual source, the object of Palés's recurring poetic encounter. Satisfactorily naming or defining or possessing that object is, of course, impossible. The quest generates the poem, the altar on which we fleetingly understand the enigmatic and see the unseeable. Through the poem Palés can only recreate a sense of the encounter with this "irrealidad," a sense recreated not only through imagery. For the numen images also come to our consciousness as predicate nominatives of an impersonal and undefined "es," which give them the quality of a causeless existence, an emergence, an apparition.

NOTES

[1] Federico de Onís placed this poem among Palés's later, post *Tuntún* works; Arce de Vázquez strangely grouped it among the Afro-Antillean poems.

[2] The Arce de Vázquez edition has two poems by that title. The one cited here is grouped under "Otros Poemas (1917-1918)," 99. An earlier version "Tic-Tac" and even earlier version of "Voz" is included among the poems of the unpublished book "El Palacio en Sombras (1918-1919)."

Gus Puleo (essay date 1997)

SOURCE: "'Los Dos Abuelos': Nicolás Guillén and Luis Palés Matos," in *Revista Hispanica Moderna*, Vol. L, No. 1, June, 1997, pp. 86-98.

[*Puleo attests to the commonality between Guillén and Palés Matos in terms of the unity and diversity in Caribbean societies.*]

> Al ritmo de los tambores
> tu lindo ten con ten bailas
> una mitad española
> otra mitad africana.
> —Luis Palés Matos **"Ten con Ten"**
> in *Tuntún de pasa y grifería*.

When speaking about the Negritude Movement and the image of blacks in Latin American literature, inevitably the names of the Cuban poet Nicolás Guillén and the Puerto Rican Luis Palés Matos are mentioned. Most comparisons, however, tend to value Guillén's poetry more highly than Palés'. Often literary and cultural theory are a labyrinth of prejudice, preference and ideological motivations, such as this opposition of Guillén/Palés Matos. For example, Robert Márquez in his "Introduction" to Guillén's *Patria o Muerte! The great zoo and other poems* (1972) presents the Puerto Rican poet as just another white man who went "slumming" under the guise of writing "black poetry." Many critics have exalted Guillén's poetry as being more "authentic" than Palés' because Guillén is a mulatto

and Palés Matos is considered "white." Not to mention that the Cuban critic Gustavo E. Urrutia wrote in a letter to the African American Poet Langston Hughes, author of "blues poetry" found in *The Weary Blues* (1926),[1] that Guillén's poetry in *Motivos de son* (1930) is "truly authentic poetry with verses that are the exact equivalent of your blues." Since then, some ideologists have elevated Guillén to the status of "people's poet" as detailed by Martha E. Allen in her article "Nicolás Guillén, poeta del pueblo", while Palés Matos' political views have gone completely ignored. Until now, scholars have not read and studied the works of these two poets with an appreciation of their diversity and complexity, and in fact continue to view Guillén and Palés Matos as a "black" poet and a "white" poet respectively, and therefore somehow as antagonists. It is time that the works of these two poets are carefully examined and analyzed within a common Hispanic-Caribbean framework so that their similarities and differences come into sharper focus without diminishing each one's contribution to his own national literature and Latin American letters.

> **Palés . . . has long been considered an important writer in Puerto Rican letters . . . Not only was his purpose aesthetic, but his beautiful Spanish verses must be considered a form of anticolonial "attack" on the then increasing North American encroachment in Puerto Rican culture. His poems, celebrating Puerto Rico as a hybrid culture of African and Spanish influences, were a reply to the violent and brutal attempt by the United States to "americanize" the island. Even if Palés did not create a school of poetry, he did have a tremendous influence on Puerto Rican culture since he changed the way Puerto Ricans view their own society and heritage . . . It is noteworthy that for a time during the 1940s and 1950s, the Puerto Rican government deliberately suppressed Palés' new ideas of a mixed culture in order to stress social harmony on the island. . . . Palés' legacy is evident not in poetry, but in the prose of [the next generation of Puerto Rican] writers.**

Sidney Mintz describes the Caribbean in his article "The Caribbean Region" as follows:

> This region is defined as a patchwork quilt of societies, each one a patchwork itself . . . Whether one examines the Caribbean region from a racial, a demographic, or a socio-cultural perspective, it is a differentiated as it is complex. Any attempt to evaluate the Afro-Caribbean people must lead the generalizer to despair.

As seen in Mintz's definition of this geographic region, this area is very diverse and therefore complicated due to distinct historical events and influences that have affected the many different islands. The work of Guillén and Palés Matos show their interest in this problematic question of unity versus multiplicity in the Caribbean, which by the way does not arise from mere curiosity nor philosophical speculation, but rather from an important need on the part of both poets to understand and define national identity and cultural heritage within the context of the Caribbean. As a result, the two poets were active in the Negritude Movement in the Caribbean in order to participate in the defining of each respective island's national identity within the context of the Caribbean, but more specifically the Afro-Caribbean. *Negrismo* in the Caribbean was not merely an imitation of the European "Africanism" in vogue during the 1920s and 1930s, nor a carbon copy of the Harlem Renaissance of the 1920, but rather a movement that was influenced by these European and North American trends, and also a part of the broad search for roots of national identity taking place at that time in Latin America. In many ways Palés Matos's early poems and Guillén's *Motivos de son* (1930) and *Sóngoro Cosongo: Poemas mulatos* (1931) more closely parallel the essays of identity writen during the second and third decades of this century by the Mexican José Vanconcelos' *La raza cósmica* (1921), the Argentinean Ezequiel Martínez Estrada's *Radiografia de la pampa* (1933), and the Puerto Rican Antonio S. Pedreira's *Insularismo* (1934). Their poetry is definitely forged within the question of national identity, but at the same time it is fraught with contradictions about this same theme.

One important difference between the two Caribbean poets is that Palés Matos, as not in the case of Guillén, had begun writing poetry before the publication of his Afro-Caribbean poems. His early verses are found in his books *Azaleas* (1915), *El palacio en sombras* (1918), and *Canciones de la vida media*, the latter written during the twenties, but published much later. These early collections followed the pattern of Latin American modernista poetry at that time which is defined as a lyric, harmonious, and highly introverted poetry dealing with topics favored by the late nineenth-century "decadent" writers, who consider the themes of solitude, boredom, exoticism, and mysticism. Palés adopted some of these same themes, but also tried to unite disparate elements of this poetry into a coherent whole.

Only after briefly experiment with avant-garde verse forms did Luis Palés Matos begin writing "identity poetry." Before the appearance of this "black poetry", Palés Matos along with J. I. de Diego Padró founded Puerto Rico's first literary avant garde movement in 1921. The short-lived *diepalismo* (which took its name from the last names of the two founders) provided the opportunity for Luis Palés Matos to experiment with the possibilities of onomatopoeia. 1921 was special year for the innovative and literary adventures of Luis Palés Matos and J. I. de Diego Padró. For example, in poems like **"Orquestación diepálica"** (1921) and **"Abajo"** (1922), Palés Matos experimented with form and sounds with the intention of substituting logic for phonetics. In a verse of **"Orquestación diepálica"** found in Federico de Onís' collection of Palés' poetry, this Puerto Rican poet rebels with sounds against the conventional meaning of words:

> ¡Guau! ¡Guau! Au-au, au-au, au-au . . . huuuummm . . .
> La noche. La luna. El campo . . . huuummm . . .
> Zi, zi, zi-zi, zi-zi, co-quí, co-quí, co-co-quí . . .
> Hierve la abastrusa zoología en la sombra.
> ¡Silencio! ¡Huuuuuummmmmm!

With these poems, Palés Matos introduces *"poesía vanguardista"* to Puerto Rican letters. The Puerto Rican critic José Emilio González affirms that for Palés "la mayor parte se escribió durante el período de Vanguardia, entre 1925 y 1937" (41). Traces of such early *"vanguardista"* experimentation are evident in many of Palés Matos' Afro-Antillean poems, such as the refrain in **"Danza negra"** (1926) in *Tuntún de pasa y grifería*: "El Gran Cocoroco dice: tu-cu-tu. / La Gran cocoroca dice: to-co-tó."

1921 was also the year during which the two Puerto Rican poets Palés Matos and J. I. de Diego Padró discussed the literary possibilities of including "lo africano" in Puerto Rican literature. During that important year, José I. de Diego Padró published a series of poems known as "Fugas diepálicas" in the Puerto Rican literary magazine *El Imparcial*. The poet de Diego Padró describes one of these poemas as "un cuadro evocador de los bailes y ritos de la Hotentotia, en el que rige un tucutún de tambores rebotante y monótono."

The same year, Palés wrote a poem in prose titled **"El pueblo negro"** also found in *Tuntún de pasa y grifería*. He exalts "el pueblo negro" as he visits it one evening. With this poem "lo africano" started to be tied to the spirit of *vanguardia* in Puerto Rico poetry. This was perfectly natural since during those years after the First World War artists of the *"vanguardia europea"* started to look to Africa to help them discover new and innovative ways of expressing themselves. Books written by León Frobénius about African peoples and nations during that time had great diffusion and readership. In the field of art, painters such as Cendars, Matisse, and Picasso were influenced to include "lo africano" in their works. André Gide and René Maran traveled to Africa and began to include Africans in their books. In the United States Vachel Lindsay and Langston Hughes wrote about the lives of blacks in Africa and in the diaspora. In Puerto Rico during these years while de Diego Padró rapidly abandons the African influences in his poetry and even the poetry of the *"vanguardia."* Palés Matos persist with his experimentation and eventually creates "un auténtico proyecto literario in the words of José Luis Vega. For Palés Matos, as with other Latin American writers of that time, their works serve as the base of inspiration for the creation of a new national "art" form. In the case of Puerto Rico, this art form was manifested in the verses and themes of Palés Matos' Afro-Antillean poetry.

Many of Palés Matos' poems with an Afro-Caribbean theme began to appear in newspapers and journals during the twenties and thirties, more than a decade before the publication of the first anthology of his works *Tuntún* in 1937. "'**Danzarina africana**' de 1918, constituye el primer acercamiento de Palés al tema negro" (93) as documented by Mercedes López-Baralt in her edition of *Tuntún*. In *Otros poemas* (1917-1918) where "**Danzarina africana**" was firts published, Palés employs themes of Africa and African influences in his poetry. However, in his verses he also calls attention to the stereotypical sexuality of "la mujer negra": "Oh negra densa y bárbara: Tu seno / esconde el salomónico veneno." According to the Onís' *Luis Palés Matos,* this poem is "anterior a *El palacio en sombras,*" whose publication was dated between 1918 and 1919. Thus, it is very possible that Guillén read, or heard recited, Palés Matos' Afro-Caribbean poetry since the Puerto Rican poet's poems were disseminated throughout the Hispanic Caribbean during the twenties and thirties by many *readers/reciters,* such as the Cuban woman Eusebia Cosme, the Spaniard José González Marín, and the Puerto Rican Leopoldo Santiago Lavandero. Guillén in the chronicle "Regreso de Eusebia Cosme" about the *declamadora* Eusebia Cosme alludes to Palés in passing and his contribution to *negrismo* (156). Consequently, many of Palés' Afro-Antillean poems were familiar to readers and other poets in the Caribbean by the time *Tuntún* was published in 1937. For this very reason, many critics have often read Palés' poems out of context and have only considered them as a collection written in the latter years of the 1930s. This, in turn, has contributed to the numerous misunderstandings and the great confusion surrounding the Puerto Rican writer's Afro-Caribbean poetic enterprise.

It is documented that as early as the beginning of the third decade of this century, Palés Matos was well-known as a *negrista* poet in Puerto Rico and in the Caribbean. For example, on November 13, 1932 in an important interview with Ángela Negrón Muñoz for the Puerto Rica Newspaper *El Mundo,* Palés Matos openly opposes the then accepted *"jibarismo hispánico"* of the Puerto Rican Luis Lloréns Torres. In the interview, Palés affirms:

> Nosotros, en las Antillas . . . como punto de partida podríamos tomar a Lloréns Torres y a los poetas cubanos Guillén y Ballagas. Estos poetas, con manera personal y distinta, han levantado el andamiaje ideal de una poesía típicamente antillana y están llevando nuestro verso a sus cauces lógicos y naturales. Lloréns, sin embargo, se limita a la pintura del jíbaro, campesino de pura descendencia hispánica, adaptado al trópico, y hace abstracción de otro núcleo racial que con nosotros se ha mezclado noblemente y que por lo fecundo, lo fuerte y lo vivo de su naturaleza, ha impreso rasgos inconfundibles en nuestra psicología dándole, precisamente, su verdadero carácter antillano. Me refiero al negro. Una poesía antillana que excluya ese poderoso elemento me parece casi imposible (10).

When read as a book, along with essays by Palés such as "**El arte y la raza blanca**" (1927) and "**Hacia una poesía antillana**" (1932) and his interviews with various jour-

nalists such as Angela Negrón Muñoz, *Tuntún* displays Palés' thesis that the Hispanic Caribbean is the birthplace of a new culture arising from the fusion of European and African cultures on Antillean soil. The new *mulatto* culture, postulate by Palés, is thus a synthesis in which "white society and history" meshes with "black history and culture." Palés probably derived his idea of cultural fusion from the Cuban ethnographer Fernando Ortiz's book *Los negros brujos* (1917). Additionally, following the Cuban historian Ramiro Guerra y Sánchez's observation in *Sugar and Society in the Caribbean* (1921), Palés was influenced to accept the sugarmill and the processing of sugar as the common ground for the contact and the creation of a hybrid culture. Aníbal González Pérez in his article "The Ballad of the Two Poets: Nicolás Guillén and Luis Palés Matos" describes in detail how the sugar mill for Palés is a metaphor for the "meeting and melting of cultures" (288). González Pérez asserts how the meshing of cultures lies in music and dance since "music marks the beat of the liturgical, sacred time of the black, while dance mimics in its gestures the movement of the body at work in the process of sugar production" (289). Some verses of "**Majestad negra**" in *Tuntún de pasa y grifería* are an excellent example of the way in which Palés represents the fusion of dance with production, of rituals with work, and of music's tempo with the time of the sugarmills.

> Culipandeando la Reina avanza,
> y de su inmensa grupa resbalan
> meneos cachondos que el gongo cuaja
> en ríos de azúcar y melaza.
> Prieto trapiche de sensual zafra,
> el caderámen, masa con masa,
> exprime ritmos, suda que sangra,
> y la molienda culmina en danza.
>
>   (114-115)

In an exhaustive study of this same poem, Diana Ramírez de Arellano affirms that Palés restores his African themes to "lo pristino del hombre, al instinto primordial" (309). With regards to the use of language in the poem, the critic asserts that Palés returns it to "su potencia virgen" (309).

Other poems within this collection, such as "**Tambores**" (143-144) and "**Ten con ten**" (139-140), find a unity in the theme of cultural synthesis or fusion. For example, in "**Tambores**" the poetic narrator warns: "Ten cuidado, hombre blanco, que a ti llegan [los tambores] para clavarte su aguijón de música" (143). In "**Ten con ten**" the theme of the mulatto is obvious in the last verses as: "Al ritmo de los tambores / tu lindo ten con ten bailas, / una mitad española / y otra mitad africana" (140). Here, Palés proclaims the existence of various cultures that together comprise a Caribbean identity. For example, "**Canción festiva para ser llorada**" in *Tuntún* paints this region as "Antilla, vaho pastoso / de templa recien cuajada. / Trajín de ingenio cañero" (123). For Palés, this hybrid culture has always existed in the Caribbean as further demostrated in the verses of "**Placeres**" (144) of *Tuntún*. In "**Placeres**" a "pabellón francés entra en el puerto";

two verses later "la bandera británica ha llegado" along with "el oriflama yanki". As all of these ships arrive displaying foreing flags, the narrator advises "el negrito y la palmera" of the Caribbean to prepare yourselves. For Palés, this poem portrays scene of the Caribbean, a calm and peaceful "patchwork" of many cultures and peoples.

Tuntún then culminates in the poem **"Mulata-Antilla"** (146-147) in which Palés symbolizes the future harmony of a racially mixed Caribbean in the lyrical form of a mulatto woman. As proposed by this poem, Palés seeks to produce a utopian vision of a harmonious future for the Hispanic Caribbean, a harmony produced by the reconciliation of opposite races and cultures in the mulatto. This final poem is the coronation and the message of the entire collection. If we reflect on this poem, we realize that the first five stanzas, which comprise the first part of the poem, celebrate the sensuality and the plastic arts of the Antilles. This region is depicted as an earthly paradise filled with colorful plants and flowers, and people living in harmony. The second part of the poem consists of only two stanzas; however both are very significant. In this part the mulatta is described in the following manner: "Eres inmensidad libre y sin límites, / eres amor sin trabas y sin prisas; / en tu vientre conjugan mis dos razas" (147). The idea of freedom in these verses is linked to the unlimited power that this mulatta possesses. Her beauty is overwhelming and described in biblical terms "contra pestes, ciclones y codicias". However, the last stanza of the poem is the apotheosis of this culture—la mulatta is "la libertad cantando en mis Antillas" (147). This final verse is the declaration of faith and love for the mulatta as the author expresses his sentiment of her indestructibility and her important role to help liberate this geographic area. With this poem, Palés not only proclaims and defends the validity of an Antillean culture, but also he considers that its pillars are *"el/la negro/a y el/la mulato/a."* Since *"el negro y el mulato"* embody freedom, they are not only liberators and guardians of their own cultures, but they are also examples of freedom fighters for all people. Many Caribbean nations are mentioned at the end of this poem, such as Jamaica, the Dominican Republic and Haiti. Antillean unity, one of the projects of such Caribbean intellectuals of the ninteenth century as the Puerto Rican Ramón Emeterio Betances, his fellow countryman Eugenio María de Hostos, and the Cuban José Martí, is now the banner taken up by Luis Palés Matos as he postulates a common Antillean culture based on the commonality of Africa and African influences.

Africa and blackness are prominent thems for Palés Matos in his poetry. In his evoking of this continent and its people, Palés creates an imaginary, geographic space where African and African peoples live. They move within this world of misery without destination. This theme of pain and sorrow is most obvious in the short poem **"Lamento"** (104-105) found in *Tuntún*: "Hombre negro triste se ve / desde Habana hasta Zimbambué, / desde Angola hasta Kanembú / hombre negro triste se ve . . ." (105). The verses in this poem express geographical locations in Africa and the New World and its traditions

help describe Caribbean peoples in the context of an Afro-Antillean reality. His intentions are pan-African and also pan-Caribbean in nature. Thus, it is evident that Palés' vision of an Afro-Antillean culture has within it the inherent quality of emancipation and freedom, along with unity.

Read as a book, *Tuntún* produces the impression of a vast fresco of the diverse Caribbean, like the pictorial representations of Mexican culture painted during those same years by muralists Diego Rivera and José Clemente Orozco. Palés "painted" the Caribbean with his Afro-Antillean poems and his view of the Hispanic Caribbean as an ethnic mixture of races and cultures, theories which troubled many "European-based" Puerto Rican intellectuals. The controversy sorrounding the themes of negritude and Africans in the poetry of Palés began as early as November, 1932 when Luis Antonio Miranda published an article in the Puerto Rican newspaper *El Mundo* titled "El llamado arte negro no tiene vinculación con Puerto Rico" (21) as cited by Mercedes López-Baralt in her edition of *Tuntún*. The following year Gracián y Miranda Archilla wrote an article "La broma de una poesía prieta en Puerto Rico" in the literary magazine *Alma Latina* denying the African influence in Puerto Rican culture and letters. Palés Matos in an interview with Ángela Muñoz on November 13, 1932 in *El Mundo* answered these critics by defending himself with these words: "Yo creo . . . en la necesidad de una poesía antillana . . . El poeta tomará asunto para su arte de su propio ambiente . . . y estilizándolo a golpes de gracia, de ironía y selección" (10). During that same year, Palés wrote the article **"Hacia una poesía antillana"** for *El Mundo* date November 26, 1932. In that article he affirmed and repeated that: "Yo no he hablado de una poesía negra ni blanca ni mulata; yo sólo he hablado de una poesía antillana que exprese nuestra realidad de pueblo en el sentido cultural de este vocablo". These words echo the sentiments of the Cuban revolutionary José Martí, who at the turn of the century characterized Caribbean societies in his essay "Nuestra América": "No hay odio de razas, porque no hay razas" (100).

If Palés's Afro-Caribean themes in his poetry have bothered Hispanophilic Puerto Rican intellectuals, his treatment of his black subject has elicited negative criticism from critics who feel that Palés, as a "white man", could hardly speak for or understand what it means to be black in the Caribbean. Ivo Domínguez in "En torno a la poesía afro-hispanoamericana" states that the poet adopts "la postura del observador que mira y nos habla con simpatía no sólo del negro puertorriqueño, sino de la raza negra en general" (127). He is viewed as a poet who provides the perspective of an outsider since he is categorized as "white". As a result, critics have often criticized Palés Matos by pointing out how he frequently depicted blacks as caricatures by portraying them through the use of demeaning exaggerations and stereotypes. For example, his conception of Africa is dominated by his vision of this continent as "un jardín edénico, de una Edad de Oro" (53) as described by the critic José Emilio González. Palés' stereotypical vision of African follows the characterization of blacks found in Spanish classics written in the sixteenth and seventeenth century when Africans were depicted as superficial and even buffoons. Often they would be characterized as speaking and acting in childish ways. Some examples are found in "Zalambú" and "Morenica del Congo" by Góngora; "Boda de negros" by Quevedo, and "El capellán de la Virgen" by Lope de Vega. Being a Puerto Rican, Palés composes poems that fit within the tradition and discourse of Spanish and Latin American poetry. Thus, it is typical that Palés' work is filled with bourgeois stereotypes and the mystification of African ancestors; however, it is important to keep in mind, and reiterated by Alba Lía Barrios in "Ese negro fantasmal de Palés Matos" that Palés' poems advanced the "descubrimiento del negro" (72) in Puerto Rico culture.

Literary critics, more specifically, have singled out the male oriented, racist stereotyping of the Caribbean woman with Palés' poem **"Mulata-Antilla"**. Of course, these are valid points. In fact, the Puerto Rican poet generalizes in other poems too, such as **"Bombo"** in *Tuntún*. The mulatta in **"Bombo"** is represented mystically as "el numen fabuloso / cuyo poder no tiene término" (182). Her animal sexuality is portrayed in **"Candombe"** (101-103) also found in *Tuntún* in the following way: "con dientes feroces de lascivia / cuerpos de fango y melaza / senos colgantes, vaho de axilas" (101). Critics should always be aware of pointing out gross generalizations and false stereotypes; however, most avant-garde writing during the time Palés wrote used caricatures and stereotyping to depict characters and thems. Even Nicolás Guillén resorted to racial stereotyping, especially in his collection *Motivos de son* (1930). While literary critics blame Palés Matos for his racial generalizations, they often overlook Guillén's similar treatment of Caribbean women. For example, the Cuban poet's poem "Búcate plata" (15) in *Sóngoro cosongo* presents a "stereotypical" Afro Caribbean woman who threatens her man with "sex". In her monologue she tells him to find her money or she will leave him. The mulatta ends the poem by speaking to her lover candidly if you get me some money, you can then "bucamé pa gozar!" Another Guillén poem in this same anthology "Negro bembón" (39) is an obvious caricature of blackness. In the following poem "Mulata" (41), a black woman is defined in stereotypical terms. For example, her African nose is described by the metaphor "un nudo de corbata."

If Guillén used stereotypes freely, Palés was in fact impartial in his use of caricature. If he referred to some blacks (especially those who deny their blackness) as "monos", he also spoke of the U.S. as a "dark bull-dog". He also depicted Puerto Rican politicians as "loros tropicales en la selva", and himself in various poemas as "un sapo", "caballo viejo". As Juan Antonio Corretjer has emphasized, rather than blaming Palés for being a "white" man, the positive elements of his Afro-Caribbean poems should he stressed especially his vindication of the Caribbean's black heritage and the idea of Pan-Caribbean unity.

What is interesting is that critics have read and praised Guillén's poetry, but they have overlooked the impor-

tant theme of the first sonnet "El abuelo" (86) of Guillén's anthology *West Indies Ltd.* (1934). This poem's title is ironic, since its verses describe a "white" woman, rather than an "old grandfather". The narrator of this poem accompanies us on a journey to describe "esta mujer." At first, she is described in the third person, and then the narrator concludes the poem by addressing her directly as "mi señora". The poem abandons the catalogue of physical charms to provide an intimate description of her state of mine; and finally poetic voices end the poem with a glimpse into her soul. Guillén leads us into the innermost recesses of her being; from top to bottom, from the lady's skin to her soul, from her physique to her psyche. However, this movement inward is then accompanied by an outward movement, as we are given a retrospective glance in history at the end of the poem. In sum, the perspective of the poem shifts from inspection to introspection, then to retrospection. These changes are present in the vision of the woman presented since she is first described in great detail from her "snowlike" skin to her heart of darkness, and then onto the dark shadow of her 'cimarrón' fugitive grandfather.

> ¡Ah mi señora! Mírate las venas misteriosas; / boga en el agua viva que allá dentro te fluye, / y ve pasando lirios, nelumbios, lotos, rosas; / que ya verás inquieta junto a la fresca orilla / la dulce sombra oscura del abuelo que huye, / el que rizó por siempre tu cabeza amarilla. (71-72)

By the end of the poem the earth-angel of the opening lines, described as "Esta mujer angélica de ojos septentrionales" (71), has been transformed into a real woman. This woman of "carne y hueso" has a heart that pounds to the "ritmo de su sangre europea" (71), and also beats to the "ritmo que golpea un negro el parche duro de roncos atabales" (71). What is crucial to the understanding of this poem is the imporant theme of *mestizaje,* not only because it symbolizes Cuban culture, but also Antillean culture. Therefore according to Guillén's thesis, it would be unfair to categorize the Puerto Rican Palés Matos as a "white" man since he is a Caribbean person who most likely comes from a family of mixed heritage.

Even more surprising is that intellectuals have often mistakenly attributed one of the first poems written by Palés Matos **"La danza negra"** to Guillén and not to the Puerto Rican poet due to its theme of Negritude and style of the poem. To help render some of these misconceptions, recently the Haitian scholar Jean-Claude Bajeux has written "Luis Palés Matos, ou le poéte de la danse", published in his *Antilia retrouvée. Claude McKay, Luis Palés Matos, Aimé Césaire,* which includes Luis Palés Matos in the company of two prominent Black figures—one from the Harlem Renaissance and the other one famous for founding the Negritude Movement in the Caribbean. As early as 1917 or 1918, Palés Matos wrote the short poem **"Danzarina africana"** in which he describes "La belleza de la negra que es profunda y confortante como el ron de Jamaica." Here, not only is the theme of the poem of great significance, but also the date of it. Chronologically, it precedes the *"negrismo"* de Guillén, and even the "Black" poetry of African American writers such as the celebrated *Harlem Shadows* (1922) written by Claude McKay, and *The Weary Blues* (1926) by Langston Hughes. It is written during the beginning of the Negritude Movement in the Caribbean. The record should be set straight, Luis Palés Matos was one of the first poets to include the theme of *"negrismo"* in his poetry.

Like Guillén's Afro-Cuban poetry found in *Motivos de son* and *West Indies, Ltd.*, these early poems of Palés perform a cultural catharsis, a public purge that shows Puerto Rican society its black component, and integral part of *boricua* culture. This influence is visible everywhere in Puerto Rican culture, but generally unacknowledged and almost always undervalued. Palés Matos y Guillén both celebrate the African element in Caribbean culture, but they also profess a strong anticolonialism in their works along with a utopian vision of Pan-Caribbean unity. Whereas, Guillén's Pan-Caribbeanism is postulated on the common sociohistorical experiences suffered by the peoples of the Caribbean, especially the commonality of colonialism; Palés' unity is based on the notion of *mestizaje* as a common link between nations. Guillén's more pragmatic approach to the question of the Hispanic-Caribbean has provided him with a more "modern" appearance to his poetry, and more importantly the Cuban poet's activism permits him to easily enter into the twentieth-century anticolonialist discourse found in the works of such prominent modern writers as Fanon and Memmi. The purpose of Guillén's poetry is not to undertake an abstract investigation of a utopian vision of the Caribbean, as in Palés' poems, but to achieve social justice and racial harmony as seen in his "committed" poetry and his continuous participation in Cuba's contemporary historical evolution. This Cuban writer's poems fulfill an active role in the revolutionary process in Cuba. On the other hand, Palés Matos often experimented with poetry's linguistic nature and struggled constantly to try to make poetry pertinent to the "real" world. For these reasons, Palés Matos never became known as an anti-colonialist thinker.

Also, it should be remembered that Palés Matos died in 1959 on the threshold of the Cuban Revolution. Guillén, on the other hand, continued to write during this time of dramatic, sociopolitical changes in the Caribbean. Perhaps, one can speculate that if Palés Matos had lived longer, he might have become more overtly political, like his Cuban counterpart Guillén. This assumption is not so improbable since as late as 1953, Palés Matos wrote the poem **"Plena del menéalo"** found in *Obras 1914-1959*, which shows that he once again summoned his themes of *"negrismo"* to denounce U.S. imperialism.

> Bochinche de viento y agua sobre el mar,
> está la Antilla bailando—de aquí payá, de ayá pacá.
>
> Dale a la popa, mulata,
> proyecta en la eternidad

> ese tumbo de caderas
> que es ráfaga de huracán,
> y menéalo, menéalo,
> de aquí payá, de ayá pacá,
> menéalo, menéalo.
> ¡para que rabie el Tío Sam!

(526-528)

Written when the repression of the Puerto Rican independence movement was at its peak, **"Plena del menéalo"** links the twin strands of the themes of Palés: the African influence in the Caribbean and the denunciation of colonialism in this geographic area. One can not help but hear the echoes of Guillén's own combative spirit in these verses, but the more obvious influence of this Cuban poet is in Palés' choice of the Puerto Rican *plena*—an Afro-*boricua* popular, musical form—in structuring his poem. The use of the *plena* here parallels Guillén's uniform use of the *son* in his poems dealing with the Afro-Caribbean. Obviously, Palés' first book **Tuntún** is rhythmic throughout; however, this anthology does not utilize any specific musical style. Despite the many differences between these two Caribbean poets and their poetry, this final poem by Palés Matos demonstrates where the two merge since here they both share the same concern for the destiny of the Caribbean in the face of U.S. imperialism.

Of course, Nicolás Guillén is best known as an anti-imperialist poet who has had a considerable and direct influence on the direction of contemporary Cuban literature. As poet an president of Cuba's National Union of Artist and Writers (UNEAC), Guillén has served as a link between the Afro-Cubanism of the 1930s and the impetus provided by the Cuban Revolution to artistic creation and research dealing with Cuba's African heritage. Guillén's poetry filled with colloquialism and dialogues has clearly paved the way for a great deal of post-revolutionary Cuban poetry, and his constant evocation of Africa is clearly seen in the contemporary prose and poetry of the Cuban writers Miguel Barnet and Nancy Morejón.

Palés, to the contrary, has long been considered an important writer in Puerto Rican letters; however, he has no significant poetic imitators. This might be attributed to the fact that few Puerto Rican poets have understood Palés' intentions of creating a sensuous and meticulously crafted verse, which incidentally achieved a brilliance reminiscent of Spanish Golden Age poetry. Not only was his purpose aesthetic, but his beautiful Spanish verses must be considered a form of anticolonial "attack" on the then increasing North American encroachment in Puerto Rican culture. His poems, celebrating Puerto Rico as a hybrid culture of African and Spanish influences, were a reply to the violent and brutal attempt by the United States to "americanize" the island. Even if Palés did not create a school of poetry, he did have a tremendous influence on Puerto Rican culture since he changed the way Puerto Ricans view their own society and heritage. Before Palés Matos, Puerto Rican culture was defined as a purely Hispanic entity by its traditional "Afro-phobia", Hispanophilic insular elite. Blackness in this culture was viewed as a foreign and often and exotic element. Palés' insistence on the Afro-Hispanic essence of Puerto Rican identity helps unmask the class and racial prejudices that have supported this narrow view of Puerto Rican culture and society, and consequently his poetry has led many Puerto Rican intellectuals to reconsider and reflect on the perpetual, problematic relationship between politics and culture for *boricuas*. It is noteworthy that for a time during the 1940s and 1950s, the Puerto Rican government deliberately suppressed Palés' new ideas of a mixed culture in order to stress social harmony on the island. As documented by Arcadio Díaz Quiñones, the Puerto Rican government tried to foment the view that there was "no racial prejudice on the island" (16) in order to serve their express interests at that historical moment. During the 1960s and 1970s, Puerto Rican writers, spearheaded by the playwright and novelist Luis Rafael Sánchez with his *La guaracha de Macho Camacho* (1976) embraced Palés' vision of Puerto Rico within the context of the Caribbean. In order to delineate his theory more carefully, these new writers had to separate Palés' theory of culture from his crafted verse. Consequently, Palés' legacy is evident not in poetry, but in the prose of such writers as José Luis González, Edgardo Rodríguez Juliá, Sánchez and Ana Lydia Vega. These contemporary authors have incorporated his vision of a multi-cultural and multi-racial Puerto Rican identity in their essays, short fiction and novels. However, these intellectuals have transcended Palés' ideas by utilizing them to not only define a Puerto Rican identity, but to also critique modern Puerto Rican culture and society. González's *El país de cuatro pisos* (1980) attempts to characterize *el pueblo puertorriqueño* by using the metaphor of a nation/house of four floors. Of course, this house has a foundtion or first "floor," upon which the nation rests. This important first floor is postulated by González as the Afro-*boricua* one. His conviction is that "los primeros puertorriqueños fueron en realidad los puertorriqueños negros" (20). Of course, it is obvious that Palés' work influenced this essayist. The PanCaribbean theme of Palés is seen in Sánchez's novel *La guaracha,* in Rodríguez Juliá's many *crónicas,* and in Vega's collection of short stories *Encancaranublado* (1983). These heirs, or grandchildren, to "los abuelos" Nicolás Guillén and Luis Palés Matos seek to understand their nation in the broader regional context, defining Puerto Rico as part of the Caribbean, Latin America, the U.S., and the African diaspora.

As a final observation, critical reappraisal of Palés Matos' work reveals Palés' affinities with Guillén. This new perspective postulates a "new" Palés Matos who resembles Guillén in that he is one of the founders of the Negritude movement in the Hispanic Caribbean, and that he is also radically anticolonial. It is time to rediscover Luis Palés Matos and his work; however, this time without preconceptions and prejudices since his *negrismo* in poetry prefigures the increased social and cultural visibility of *mulatos* in contemporary Puerto Rican and Caribbean society.

NOTES

[1] A letter from Gustavo E. Urrutia to Langston Hughes dated May 1, 1930. From the Langston Hughes Papers, James Weldon Johnson Collection. Beinecke, Comprising mainly correspondence (General, family, fan mail, miscellaneous, etc.) and Manuscripts.

WORKS CITED

Allen, Martha E. "Nicolás Guillén, poeta del pueblo". *Revista Iberoamericana,* 136 (febrero-julio 1949): 36-40).

Bajeux, Jean-Claude. "Luis Palés Matos, ou le poéte de la danse". *Antilia retrouvée. Claude McKay, Luis Palés Matos, Aimée Césaire, poétes noirs antillais.* Quebec: Agence de Coopération Culturelle et Tehnique, 1983.

Barrios, Alba Lía. "Ese negro fantasmal de Palés Matos". *INTI: Revista de Literatura Hispánica* 29-30 (primavera-otoño 1989): 65-67.

Corretjer, Juan Antonio. "Lo que no fue Palés". *Revista del Instituto de Cultura Puertorriqueña* 3 (abril-junio 1959): 35.

Díaz Quiñones, Arcadio. "Tomás Blanco: Racismo, historia, esclavitud". *El prejuicio racial en Puerto Rico.* Río Piedras: Ediciones Huracán, 1985.

Diego Padró, José I de. *Luis Palés Matos y su trasmundo poético.* Río Piedras: Editorial de La Univerrsidad de Puerto Rico, 1973.

Domínguez, Ivo. "En torno a la poesía afro-hispanoamericana". *Cuadernos Hispanoamericanos* 319 (enero 1977): 125-131.

González, José Emilio. "El negro en la poesía de Luis Palés Matos". *Kentucky Romance Quarterly* 18 no. 1 (1971): 37-63.

González, José Luis. *El país de cuatro pisos y otros ensayos.* Río Piedras: Ediciones Huracán, 1980.

González Pérez, Aníbal. "Ballad of the Two Poets: Nicolás Guillén and Luis Palés Matos". *Callaloo* 31, vol. 10 no. 2 (Spring, 1987): 285-301.

Guillén, Nicolás. *Motivos de son.* La Habana: Rambla Bouza y Cía, 1930.

———. *¡Patria o muerte! The Great zoo and other poems.* Ed. and trans. by Robert Márquez. New York; Montly Review Press, 1972.

———. "Regreso de Eusebia Cosme". *Prosa de prisa. Crónicas.* Las Villas: Universidad Central de las Villas, 1962.

———. *Sóngoro cosongo.* Buenos Aires: Editorial Losada, 1992.

Hughes, Langston. *The Weary Blues.* New York: Alfred A. Knopf, 1926.
Martí, José. "Nuestra América". *José Martí. Antología.* Ed. Andrés Sorel. Madrid: Editora Nacional, 1975.

Mintz, Sidney. "The Caribbean Region". *Daedalus* 103 (1974): 45-46.

Negrón Muñoz, Ángela. "Una entrevista con Luis Palés Matos". *El Mundo,* 26 de noviembre, 1932: 10.

Onís, Federico de. *Luis Palés Matos.* San Juan: Ediciones Ateneo Puertorriqueño, 1960.

Palés Matos, Luis. *Obras: 1914-1959 Tomo I: Poesía.* Ed. Margot Arce de Vázquez. Río Piedras: Universidad de Puerto Rico, 1957.

———. *Poesía (1915-1956).* Ed. Federico de Onís. Río Piedras: Editorial de la Universidad de Puerto Rico, 1992.

———. *Tuntún de pasa y grifería.* Ed. Mercedes López-Baralt. San Juan: Editorial de la Universidad de Puerto Rico, 1993.

Ramírez de Arellano, Diana. "'Majestad Negra' de Palés Matos". *Homenaje a Andrés Iduarte.* Ed. Jaime Alazraki, Roland Grass and Russell O. Salmon. Clear Creek, Indiana: The American Hispanist, 1976: 301-310.

Vega, José Luis "Luis Palés Matos: Entre la máscara manierista y el rostro grotesco de la realidad". *Revista de Estudios Hispánicos* 12 (1985): 189-203.

FURTHER READING

Cumpiano, Ina. "The 'ten con ten' of Abjection: A Kristevan Reading of Luis Palés Matos's *Tuntún de pasa y de griferia.*" *Revista/Review Interamericana*, Vol. XXIII, Nos. 3-4 (Autumn/Winter 1993): 51-65.

Supports Julia Kristeva's belief that literature is "a signifier for abjection," exemplified in *Tuntún de pasa y de griferia.*

Johnson, Lemuel. "*El Tema Negro*: The Nature of Primitivism in the Poetry of Luis Palés Matos," *Blacks in Hispanic Literature: Critical Essays,* Miriam DeCosta, ed., pp. 123-36. Port Washington, N. Y.: Kennikat Press, 1977.

Surveys Palés Matos's poetry in terms of the *tema negro*, one of the artistic and literary "poses" of the 1920s.

Teresa de la Parra
1898-1936

(Born Ana Teresa de la Parra Sanojo) Venezuelan novelist.

INTRODUCTION

Teresa de la Parra was Venezuela's first major female writer. Her small body of work consists mostly of short stories and two novels due to her battle with the tuberculosis that eventually took her life. Her first novel was *Ifigenia: diario de una señorita que escribió porque se fastidiaba* (1924; *Iphigenia: diary of a young lady who wrote because she was bored,* 1993). The novel, according to critic Mariano Picón Salas, "pinpoints the modern problem of the Latin American woman who has entered into a negation of the Arab-Spanish concept of femininity, and analyses it, shakes it up, and affirms the values of her own life in struggle against a society that is satisfied with the routine."

The Venezuelan author was born on October 5, 1890, in Paris where her wealthy father worked as a diplomat for the Venezuelan government. When de la Parra was still an infant, her family returned to Venezuela following a change in the country's leadership. She lived on her family's sugar plantation in Caracas until she was seven years old. It is that period she nostalgically recalls in her second novel, *Las memorias de Mamá Blanca* (1929; *Mama Blanca's Souvenirs,* 1959). De la Parra's father died when she was eight years old, and she was sent to Spain for seven years to study at a Catholic school near Valencia. When she returned to Caracas as a young woman, de la Parra had intellectual and literary aspirations. De la Parra's earliest short fiction was published in 1915 in newspapers. These early works include "Historia de la señorita Grano de Polvo Bailarina del Sol" ("The Story of Miss Speck of Dust Dancer of the Sun"), "El genio del pesacartas" ("The Genie of the Letter Scales"), and "El ermitaño del reloj" ("The Hermit of the Clock"). All of these belong to the literary genre of fantasy and allude to her position in society, particularly as a female artist.

In 1922, de la Parra won a contest run by a newspaper for her story "La mamá X." The same year, a Caracas newspaper printed "Flor de loto," and another publication, *Lectura Semanal*, published two chapters of a novel that eventually became part of *Ifigenia: Diario de una señorita que escribió porque se fastidiaba.* De la Parra submitted *Ifigenia* to the Instituto Hispano-americano de la Cultura Francesca in Paris, winning first prize. The 523-page book presents a panorama of Caracas society, analyzing the author's existence as a rebellious soul constricted by the social mores of her generation and the patriarchal attitude of the world in which she lived. *Ifigenia* made de la Parra

famous, suddenly placing her in demand for lectures and conferences—most of which were about the roles of Latin American women in society. Some of these lectures were printed as *Tres conferencias inéditas* (1961; *Three Unedited Conferences*). In 1927, after beginning her second novel, de la Parra moved to Switzerland and completed *Las memorias de Mamá Blanca.* Although the novel was published in Paris in 1932, much of the work had already appeared in Caracas newspapers.

Las memorias de Mamá Blanca unfolds through the "manuscript" of a mature Blanca Nieves (Snow White) inherited by a woman writer after Blanca's death. The manuscript is a commentary on the disappearing countryside falling to capitalist encroachment, as well as a treatise on the nature of a love that transcends bloodlines. The novel also explores and affirms the necessity of relationships between women. Blanca's authoritarian father is a distant figure. Her mother, however, is close and influential, inspiring in Blanca a love of language, stories, and narrative. Scholar Ana García Chichester sees *Las memorias de Mamá Blanca* as part of a Latin American feminist tradition. "As in many feminist fictional narratives that have followed," Chichester said, "it is the inner world of women, the daily concerns of domestic life, and the interrelationships within the female members of the family that become the main subject of the novel."

While her first novel broke new ground, it is de la Parra's second novel that showed marked progress in the author's stylistic abilities. Nobel Prize-winning Chilean writer, Gabriela Mistral, considered that de la Parra's work showed the most progress between a first and second novel she had ever seen. If *Ifigenia*'s well-groomed characters are in a position of uncertainty, oppression, or broken by their ideals, *Mamá Blanca*'s disorderly characters are assured, persistent, and undaunted in pursuit of them. Themes, however, remain consistent: both feature the female point of view as well as examples of older women guiding their younger counterparts. The novels illustrate life's ironies, the hypocrisies of social mores and conduct, the clash of differing codes of honor, and a marked relationship with nature. In *Mamá Blanca*, de la Parra's anti-intellectualism intensifies. Predominant in this novel is her belief that value is to be found in obscure, sometimes metaphysical, places. *Ifigenia* is born of the author's restless longing to escape from a conservative Latin American home and a constricting past. *Mamá Blanca*, on the other hand, comes from de la Parra's yearning to return, to travel into older knowledge, and to delve into her childhood memories of her serene home in the Venezuelan countryside.

Throughout her life, de la Parra remained interested in Simón Bolívar, the Latin American liberator, but was unable to write his biography because of her tuberculosis. It was while giving a lecture on Bolívar that de la Parra established her lifelong friendship with Cuban writer, Lydia Cabrera. Sometimes in the company of Cabrera, de la Parra began conducting research on Bolívar during extended trips throughout Europe and South America. After 1931, however, de la Parra no longer wrote because of her tuberculosis—an illness that placed her in several Swiss sanatoriums. In 1936, fed up with inactivity brought on by her illness, de la Parra traveled to Paris and Barcelona. In Barcelona, the illness progressed and de la Parra sought relief in a Madrid sanatorium. On April 23, 1936, de la Parra died with Cabrera at her side.

Critics either praised or disdained *Ifigenia* for its potential subversion of young women. The novel's narrator, María Eugenia Alonso, is modeled after de la Parra. In the book, María is educated in Europe and returns to conservative Caracas where she is pressured to relinquish her liberal ideas. Though she is initially outspoken and rebellious, María is soon tamed. Her politico-personal fissure is reinforced by love interests, Gabriel (younger and liberal) and Leal (older and conservative). Though Leal berates or ignores María's intelligence and individuality, she consents to marry him out of a sense of duty. Like Iphigenia, the Greek mythological daughter of Agamemnon, María allows herself to be "sacrificed" for "the greater good." While the Iphigenia of Greek mythology consents to being sacrificed to the gods for the sake of winds and war, María allows herself to be sacrificed in marriage.

De la Parra's second novel, *Las memorias de Mamá Blanca*, is a superior work, according to critic Elba Mata-Kolster who says the novel has "a more solid structure and a greater maturity in the descriptions of color and movement." Author Naomi Lindstrom has said that de la Parra exhibits "a preference for intimate and domestic subject matter, a mannered style of somewhat whimsical, teasing humor, and, broadly, a chatty, gossipy mode." De la Parra's style, however, has led some critics to undervalue her work. Her novels, however, have received critical praise for her fiction as the first "women's novels" written in the Spanish language.

PRINCIPAL WORKS

Diario de una señorita que se fastidia (prose) 1922
La Mamá X (prose) 1923
Ifigenia: Diario de una señorita que escribió porque se fastidiaba (novel) 1928
Las memorias de Mamá Blanca [*Mama Blanca's Souvenirs*] (prose) 1932
Cartas (letters) 1951
Epistolario íntimo (testimony) 1953

Cartas a Rafael Carías (letters) 1957
Tres conferencias inéditas [*Three Unedited Conferences*] (speeches) 1961
Obras completas (collected works) 1965
Obra (selected works) 1982

CRITICISM

Doris Sommer (essay date 1991)

SOURCE: "'It's Wrong to be Right': *Mamá Blanca* on Fatherly Foundations," *Foundational Fictions*, Berkeley: University of California Press, 1991, pp. 290-321.

[*In this essay, Sommers reflects on the characters in de la Parra's* Mamá Blanca *and their incapacity to relate to each other on an immediate and emotional level.*]

Fortunately, the mother of six little girls in *Las memorias de Mamá Blanca* (1929), by Teresa de la Parra (1889-1936), was wrong most of the time, wrong especially about the names she chose for her daughters. More demiurge than New World Adam, this mistress of a controlled plantation paradise finished her own creations with names that just wouldn't fit, as if to laugh at the pretense of forcing bonds between a system of arbitrary signs and her flesh-and-blood, delightfully unpredictable, referents. "Poetic" and impractical, this mother took advantage of the whimsical opportunities for finishing touches: she "scorned reality and systematically endeavored to rule it by pleasant and arbitrary laws" (27; 15).[1] In the very first paragraph of Mamá Blanca's memoirs, a series of vignettes and evocations that never really add up to a coherent story about Venezuelan plantation life at the turn of the century,[2] the eccentric old lady recalls how absurd—almost perverse—her mother's choice of names seemed to the girl of five:

> Blanca Nieves, la tercera de las niñitas por orden de edad y de tamaño, tenía entonces cinco años, el cutis muy trigueño, los ojos oscuros, el pelo muy negro, las piernas quemadísimas del sol, los brazos más quemados aún, y tengo que confesarlo humildemente, sin merecer en absoluto semejante nombre, Blanca Nieves era yo.
>
> (27)

> Blanca Nieves (Snow White), the third of the girls in order of age and size, was five years old at the time, dark of skin, dark-eyed, black-haired, legs tanned to the color of saddle leather by the sun, arms darker still. I must blushingly confess that, wholly undeserving of such a name, Blanca Nieves was I.
>
> (15)

By referring to herself in the third person, which inexplicably coincides with the first, Blanca begins by dramatizing the liberating distance between the child referred to and the linguistic referent that cannot, or should not, catch up to her. The mother dictated absurd connections, not because that would change reality ("reality never submitted") but because reality didn't matter. So, far from fostering the kind of nominalism that would challenge unexamined facts on higher epistemological ground, this linguistically irresponsible mother knew that her prodigious hand was simply "sowing a profusion of errors that had the double property of being irremediable and absolutely charming" (27; 15). Throughout this surprising little book, the distance between the child and her name, a distance repeated already in the dis-encounter between the narrator's third-person voice and her autobiographical subject, and in the unstable difference between error and charm, will provide a space and a mandate for the conciliatory work of time-honoring tolerance and of love.

The narrator and her name, that inseparable companion, were one mismatched couple, "a walking absurdity." And if that was a joke at her expense, she puts it into a mitigating context on the same first page of the memoirs, comparing it to an even better (or worse) joke: an older tomboy of a sister named (what else?) Violeta. "She and the modest little flower, were two opposite poles" (56; 37). Violeta was so rough and ready, she was more like a brother in disguise than a sister (56; 37). And of the six little girls who saw themselves at the center of the universe, a plantation called Piedra Azul, this was the only one who almost satisfied their father's insistent desire for a son. "I believe that Violeta's body lodged the spirit of Juan Manuel the Desired, and this was the reason he had never been born: for six years he had walked the earth disguised as Violeta. The disguise was so transparent that everyone recognized him. Papa first of all" (56; 37). The jumble of sexual identities and gender roles, where the terms are not so much mismatched as available for mix-and-match permutations, is not only a recollection of the old lady's dynamically "disordered and pantheistic soul" (17; 7); it is also the entire plantation's acknowledgement of normally missed encounters between one system of signification and another. Everyone in Piedra Azul could see that a person's gender did not necessarily coincide with his or her sex. The father's second daughter was also his son. And this liberating mistake is, as we will see, part of a general phenomenon here in which the sign doesn't quite manage to describe its referent but rather leaves a space for interpretation; that is, for empowering play.

Before we follow many more playful moves, we should put this sort of irreverent linguistic freedom into a different context from that of Violeta, this time more stark than extenuating. ***Las memorias de Mamá Blanca*** was written in the same country and in the same year as Rómulo Gallegos's *Doña Bárbara*. And, focusing for the moment on Violeta, both novels are about women who are also men. For Gallegos, of course, this jumbled identity is literally a mess, a monstrous transgression of neat social constructions of nature, a threat and obstacle to the oppositional logic that positive progress depends on.[3] He measured Bárbara's hatred for men and the fear she engendered by a criterion of inviolable nature in which those feelings amount to depravity, even though he must have been aware of the arbitrarily—almost legalistical-

ly—drawn distinctions between legitimate and illegitimate sentiments.[4] But here, by conspicuous contrast, virile Violeta is loved by everyone: her admiring sisters, her amused mother, and not least of all by her gender-lonely father. And if Mamá Blanca could have met Doña Bárbara, it is possible that she would have loved her too. At the very least, she would have perceived Bárbara's uncontrollable energy and a certain pride in womanly independence as evocations of her beloved Violeta. As for Mother Nature, she loses all authority to real mothers in this book, because her work is sometimes unfeeling and almost always unfinished. A fatherly text, like Gallegos's may take nature to be a sacred ground; but mothers seem to take her as a challenge to their own creative authority. Blanca Nieves here is more amused than disappointed about her mother's nominal mistake, an innocent joke that brought laughter but never malice from other people. But she is furious with that false mother, Nature, for giving her straight hair, a cruel joke that had to be corrected each day at her own and her mother's expense. Nature was merely a "cruel, heartless stepmother. But as Mamá was a mother, she defied her in a struggle without quarter, and the stepmother was defeated and thwarted" (43; 27).

Juxtaposing the novels by Gallegos and de la Parra is hardly arbitrary. A comparison practically forces itself on the reader who notices the coincidence of time and place, as well as the thematic similarity between two books about women who occupy the center of their rural worlds until they are deposed by men who dispute property and propriety.[5] Through these disputes, and the changes they announce, both novels comment on the process of social modernization. By every other comparison, though, the books could hardly be more different. The one Gallegos wrote continually forces itself into a straight line—with possibly compromising flashbacks about Santos and about Bárbara clearly marked off as prehistory—aimed at positive, economically rational change. Proper language and legitimate propriety are two sides of the same civilizing coin whose purchase is never at issue. If the relationship between language and legitimacy is admittedly allegorical here, it is not attributed to metaphoric leaps from one system of representation to another, the kind of moves that predictably fall short of a close fit. Instead, we saw that the allegory here is generated metonymically and dialectically (perhaps tautologically), from the legal implications of authoritative language and from the authority conferred by a linguistic construction called law. By contrast, so much of Teresa de la Parra's novel seems to take place in one single moment, a single and sonorous moment that exchanges time for space and gives room to the most diverse and equally legitimate codes in a world that is doomed by positive and rational change. The mother's aristocratic disdain for referential language, the father's incontestable but also inconsequential pronouncements, the English-speaking governess' absurdly ungrammatical insistence on being proper, Vicente Cochocho's popular archaisms, Cousin Juancho's pleasing and pointless monologues, cowherd Daniel's precisely modulated calls to each of his bovine wards. Finally, there are the little girls whose indiscriminate imitations produce a democratizing effect among these codes and whose permutations construct flights beyond the linguistic pluralism. It is something like a playfully postmodern instability, inspired perhaps by the mother's genteel disregard for "reality," far more inclusive than hers and as irreverent about the signifier as about the signified.

This kind of contrast between the novels' narrative trajectories and their linguistic strategies, even their ideological implications, probably has some relevance for what may broadly be called literary criticism. But I am moved to leave that ground for a moment when I imagine the two books in terms of a possible confrontation between the "personifications" of barbarous dissemination in one book and of playful permutations in the other. My own feminist longings and readerly desire for poetic justice make me unable to resist a temptation to shift the discursive ground from criticism to intervention. Instead of analytical categories, the two female protagonists begin to loom independent from their texts, like participants in a very intimate, unscheduled but unavoidable, consciousness-raising session. Deposed and displaced, Bárbara would surely have found an empathetic interlocutor in Mamá Blanca, the exile from paradise where she had learned how to listen to everyone. Their hypothetical conversation, as I choose to imagine it, would manage to get beyond the inevitable racial and class differences, although Bárbara's resentment toward the sheltered aristocratic breeding of the white woman—white to her very name—would surely make her wary of sharing indiscreet confidences. But Blanca's unaffected tone, the nostalgia for Violeta that this exorbitant guest would evoke, and especially the discreet but knowing questions with which Blanca would make room for Bárbara, would soon generate a friendly dialogue. They would tell each other about their respective stories, stories already written and, perhaps, those they might still write. Bárbara's resistance to this sort of intimacy would necessarily falter as she considered the self-legitimating possibilities of the narrative strategies developed by the author of her own memoirs. Incredulous, she would ask how Blanca managed to organize her chapters so unsystematically, or how she could side with Vicente and Daniel over her father, the legitimate authority of the place. "What, you? A five-year-old authority? Don't make me laugh . . . You're right; why not laugh?"

If my mind wanders from time to time along the conciliatory and syncretic narrative paths where Doña Bárbara could meet up with Mamá Blanca, it is probably because Blanca taught me to meander there. And if I needed any justification for imagining the meeting, I could quote her own (un)reason, not so much a lack of reason as an awareness that there was no need to be reasonable. The only excuse she gives for letting herself combine, distort, and reframe the stories her mother told her is, "Nobody told me I couldn't" (51; 33). Guided by her intertextual lead, I can hardly be expected to keep the stories about Bárbara and Blanca straight. And even if that were possible on my reading, I am convinced that she would have experimented with a dialogic (con)fusion between the two, had she heard the tale of the nostalgic old lady and the one about

the despoiled cattle-boss. I am persuaded that the same five-year-old girl would have imagined them as I do: sitting together in the garden, sipping coffee, chatting and remembering a Venezuela "tan relejos," long, long ago (15; 5). The girl's own habit of blending and twisting her mother's stories is so contagious that it becomes useless for me to refrain from the narrative mixes that she herself prepares. How else can we listen to these compatriot and contemporary books after Blanca Nieves shows us the charm of listening actively?

Now the scene of her deceptively passive activity hardly seems promising. She is sitting in front of the big mirror in her mother's bedroom, this and every morning, getting her hair curled. Like a penitent for the sin of having straight hair, or like a convict for esthetic crimes with an insistent parole officer, Blanca Nieves suffers the daily humiliation of being only temporarily improved. But the Hegelian intuition of the ward hints to her about the power she exercises over the warden. If curls were the mandate, since curls are beautiful and "a woman's first duty is to be beautiful" (42-43; 27), Blanca's black head of hair would have to remain absolutely still in front of that disciplinary mirror; any lack of cooperation would frustrate the process. So her captive captor was forced to concede to a coterminous demand: to captivate the girl with stories as long as the curling process lasted. And just as the result of the curling would produce a pleasing excess, so the telling would be excessive, because Blanca Nieves sometimes insisted that the stories be repeated with unprecedented borrowings from other stories, with tragic endings required by some caprice and comic endings by another. The girl dictated, unpredictably, and the mother dutifully narrated. While her mother curled her straight hair, adjusting stepmother Nature to higher esthetic standards, the daughter was also stamping her creative will on the stories that she demanded for entertainment. Like her hair, those stories were mere raw material, the pretexts for supplements that never achieved stable or definitive shapes. In front of the great mirror that conspired in the daily ritual, mother and daughter supplemented all they wanted. This is certainly not the mirror that some female autobiographers complain can only frame them in the male gaze; nor is it Luce Irigaray's penetrating speculum, an instrument that promises to reflect on feminine interiority.[6] It is a screen for aimless projections, a compensatory diversion, a forced freedom to recount without being held accountable to models, or to nature.

We may also want to read this scene of manipulation as a figure for the primal scene of Hispano-American creativity, akin to Sarmiento's self-arrogation of authority every time he saw a hint of himself in an imperfect model. Contemplating themselves in the mirror of European and North American art, Latin Americans create specular distortions that return very different images or "identities" from that of putative models. The difference is not always parody but quite often represents a "correction" or an improvement of the adoptive parent culture, as we have seen in Latin American rewritings of Rousseau, Chateaubriand, Scott, Stendhal, Cooper, Balzac. Along with the acknowledgment of foreign authority comes the greater measure of local authority that can respect models and supersede them at the same time. Blanca's straight hair is evidently acknowledged in the curling process, but the rectilinear matter is returned with pleasing twists every time Blanca's mother wins her battle against nature. And the European stories come back from the mirror equally transformed, domesticated and perfected in various and contradictory ways. Far from being content with the foreign stuff, or from repeating it in servile imitations, the childish narrator was learning from her mother how to tangle, tie, and adjust the malleable matter in ways that kept giving it new life. There was no reason why established plots always had to coincide with their traditional developments, as little reason as there was to make names identify with their subjects or to make genders coincide with sexes.

Frustrated, bored, or offended by the ending of Bernardin de St. Pierre's *Paul et Virginie*, for example, where the chaste girl prefers to die in the storm at sea rather than expose her limbs enough to swim safely to her lover, Blanca Nieves sometimes demands a happy reunion. Although at other times she makes all the characters die together in a final cataclysm. On hearing "Beauty and the Beast," to mention another example, she decides that the metamorphosis at the end is an extraneous concession to those who cannot truly love. So, she has it omitted, charging that it is an offense to the noble Beast, and to her dog, Marquesa, whom she identified with the hero. "How wonderful!" Bárbara would interrupt, slapping her thigh and throwing her head back to laugh outloud. "You cast the bitch as hero!" "Of course," Blanca would giggle, "it was the only thing I never changed in that story."

> —Pero ya sabes, Mamá, que la Fiera se quede Fiera con su rabo, su pelo negro, sus orejotas y todo y que asimismo se case con la Bella. ¡Que no se vuelva Príncipe nunca! ¿Ya lo sabes?

> Mamá tomaba nota.

> Es inútil decir que Pablo y Virginia acababan a veces muy bien. Virginia salvada milagrosamente de las aguas caudalosas se casaba a menudo con Pablo y eran muy felices. Si dadas las circunstancias mi alma sentía un vago, voluptuoso deseo de bañarse en la tristeza, dejaba entonces que las cosas siguieran su curso normal:

> —Mamá, que llueva muchísimo, que crezca el río, que se ahogue la niñita y que se muera después todo el mundo.

> Mamá desencadenaba los elementos y la escena quedaba cubierta de crespones y cadáveres.

(54)

["You remember, Mama, the Beast is to remain Beast, with his tail, his black hair, his ears and everything, and he is to marry the Beauty like that. He is never to become a Prince. You won't forget?"

Mama took due notice.

Naturally, *Paul and Virginia* at times had a happy ending. Virginia, miraculously saved from the flood waters, married Paul and they lived happily ever after. But if it so happened that my soul felt a vague, voluptuous desire to immerse itself in grief, then I let things take their course.

"Mama, let it rain terribly hard, and the river rise, and the little girl drown, and then everybody die."

Mama unleashed the elements, and the scene was covered with crepe and corpses.]

(35-36)

Little Snow White is infectiously willful, with her requirements for stories to fit her childish moods, and with the liberating lack of discrimination that lets her daydream about her mother's wedding on hearing *El Cantar de Mío Cid* (96-97; 65-66).

Reading her extravagant or extraneous demands, and watching them take pleasing shapes in the makeup mirror, goads me to reflect back on another possible narrative twist and to wonder what Bárbara and Mamá Blanca might have said to each other with their first introductions. "Good afternoon, I am Bárbara. I mean, I am called Bárbara and that's been a problem." "Oh, names are so absurd," Blanca would say with soothing levity, "it took me all these years and all these white hairs to fade into mine." Doña Bárbara, trained to recognize the indelible mark of barbarity in (or as) her calling, would be surprised to learn that, in Piedra Azul, names didn't announce characters with some supposed allegorical immediacy; instead, they alluded indirectly, almost against the grain, in the same way that the stories Blanca Nieves demanded were hardly self-identical but rather capricious misrepresentations. As for the visual language of faces and physical features (so expressive of Santos's superiority, Marisela's unwashed nobility, and Bárbara's unnatural appeal), it was no more reliable a code than other words in Piedra Azul. Marquesa was one incongruous example, another was the gentle peon nicknamed for a stinging bug: "Vicente Cochocho, who was a giant in kindness of soul, could hardly have been smaller in physical stature" (101; 69). These representational disencounters, multiplied throughout the memoirs, are instances of a general (and merciful) crisis of authority here. So, perhaps it will suffice to mention only one more emblematic failure to find transparent correspondence between expression and experience: the evident authority that the father wields is hardly a controlling force, since Vicente Cochocho and cowherd Daniel can both lord it over the master's "absolute power" (114; 78). Like Blanca Nieves under her mother's beautifying authority, the master's underlings understand his dependence on them. Daniel leaves graciously when Don Juan Manuel fires him for his scandalously personal treatment of the cows, because the employee knows long before the soon-desperate employer that he will be called back. And the patriarchal outrage caused by Vicente's multiple marriages or his occasional leadership of regional revolutions do little more than humiliate him and the master who is caught between principled pronouncements and his inability to let Cochocho go. By contrast, we saw Gallegos forcing the hierarchy, and the supporting verbal correspondences, into a tidy construction. That Santos is meant to rule, Altamira to command an encompassing vision, Bárbara to be banished, and El Miedo along with her, are all announced by their names. Hardly insensitive to verbal and narrative waywardness, Doña Bárbara is determined to erect a tight allegorical defense against surprises.

But in Piedra Azul, the end of verbal surprises is quite literally a discursive dead-end, death itself. As if to underline the paradoxical reasonableness of irrational and anti-allegorical naming—and of the generally liberating gap through which referents can escape, finally unnamed and unmanageable in any allegorical system—Blanca Nieves tells what happened once, by "mistake." It was the only time that her mother forgot her disdainful precaution against reality while naming her little girls. Tragically, she named one Aurora, the one who would die just as her life was beginning.

> El geniecillo exquisito y mal documentado que aproximando su boca al oído de Mamá le dictaba atolondrado nuestros nombres, acertó una vez. Su acierto fue funesto. No hay que tener razón. Para segar dichas no es indispensable sembrar verdades. Tú lo supiste, pobre Mamá, tú lo llevaste tatuado en lo más sensible de tu corazón. El haber acertado por casualidad una vez, debía costarte raudales de lágrimas . . . Aurora fue la aurora.
>
> (157)

> [The charming, whimsical genie that carelessly whispered our names into Mamá's ear happened to be right in one instance. His accuracy proved fatal. It's wrong to be right. To reap happiness it is not necessary to sow truth. Poor Mamá, you knew it, you bore it tattooed on the tenderest fibers of your heart. This having been accidentally right once was to cost you floods of tears. Aurora was the dawn.]
>
> (114)[7]

The self-identical sign, like a simple-minded equation too redundant to repeat, closes up all the space between the girl and the controlling symbolic order. By reaching its goal so directly, her name fixes her as an immobile sign; and she suffers the same fatality that dooms Bárbara. "Poor Aurora," Bárbara would agree, "and poor Mamá," because by now she will have caught on that, thanks to the fissured nature of language, and to the desire that language cannot (and perhaps refuses to) satisfy, words usually fail to name adequately. Luckily, the effort to name can become a continual game of hide and seek, frustrating for a "positivistic soul" such as the Governess Evelyn (55; 36), but hilarious in the disordered and aimless affections of Mamá and Mamá Blanca. If, by a paradoxical disfunction, the symbolic order occasionally functions the way it pretends to, it can produce a glimpse of what Lacan called

imaginary harmony—a postulated, prelinguistic, immediacy between child and mother before spoken interventions by the father teach a rhythm of cleavages. That preconceptual, even prehuman, harmony is the rapport that some fathers imagine the mothers to foster; but mothers may choose to evade this dubious and debilitating honor, preferring to play in the gaps that the "order of the father" (of Gallegos, for example) dreams of closing up.[8]

Hardly discursive obstacles, the linguistic failures and maladjustments between desire and experience describe a playing field where Blanca Nieves and her mother enjoy re-creation. It was also the space enjoyed by María Eugenia, the young lady who wrote a diary out of boredom in Teresa de la Parra's first novel and who was sacrificed to convention like the Ifigenia of her title.[9] Certainly in this second novel, those disencounters constitute no communication crisis between mother and daughter, presumably exiled into a linguistic diaspora from which there is no going home. They no doubt understand each other very well, precisely because of their shared disappointments with a symbolic order in which, for example, hair should mean curls although it cannot always mean that. The current and future mothers make themselves accomplices in covering over the difference between reality and desired ends. But the process of curling, shaping, and deceiving becomes more than a compensatory process; it becomes a series of willful, creative impositions that inevitably reinscribe the gap. If, in Lacan's terms, that order belongs to "Poor Papa, . . . [who] took on in our eyes the thankless role of God" (31; 18), it may be because he demands that it work. He yearns to reconquer the supposed originary harmony by insisting that desire be satisfied, that signifiers *mean* their signifieds, without stopping to take creative advantage of the disappointments. He yearns, for instance, to reproduce himself perfectly in a male child who could carry on the legitimating name of the father. Each year, his renewed insistence would send his wife off, heavy with child, to Caracas where she would deliver another daughter. The mother, evidently, was taking her own sort of control of the paternal order, enjoying the annual and irremediable slips between intention and issue, the intention to introduce a son and the consecutive debuts of six little girls, an excessive production that nevertheless could not satisfy the father's unmovable desire. "The truth of the matter is that we never disobeyed him but once in our life. But that single time sufficed to disunite us without scenes of violence for many years. This great disobedience took place at the hour of our birth" (33; 20). Being born female was the original sin that had them expelled, not from maternal harmony but from the divine order of paternal paradise; yet thanks to the exile, these little women were also let loose in a fully humanized world where the constitutive distance between desire and realization, language and experience, gave them room to play. If they had been born male and fully legitimate for the father, perhaps their unauthorized games would have taken longer to develop.

A study in contrast is Primo Juancho, the girls' aging uncle who demonstrates better than anyone the mechanisms of verbal misfirings. But he seems stubbornly to delay any acknowledgment of a systemic difficulty. The impoverished old gentleman shows all the intellectual disorder these memoirs associate with great spirits, but he resists calling it that, because he worships positive programs even if they don't work. When one scientific scheme fails him, another quickly takes its place; the value of scientific thinking is never at issue. Juancho's verbal aim was as far off the mark as Mother's, but not by a choice that would make the best of an impossible system. He wanted to *make* a difference, not just to play with it. He would dream, for example, of being appointed to powerful government positions, but he "could not govern or direct anything, not for lack of ability, but because of too much thinking. His learning was his ruin" (73; 48). This is one unmistakable hint that at the end of the novel, after the plantation is sold to appease the father's family, the successful modernization of the new owner (let's call him Santos) is accomplished thanks, precisely, to the modernizer's limited knowledge. To organize anything rationally one has to make choices, to exclude, to resolve debates in favor of one speaker, in favor of one code of conduct, just as "Santos" would do in Piedra Azul and in Altamira. It was a narrowness that could not contain Juancho. (Dis)ordered arbitrarily, like an unbound dictionary (74-75; 50), which includes everything in scattered juxtapositions and metonymical relationships that need no hierarchy, and composed also like this almost static novel that recognizes Juancho's particular brand of purposeless heroism, and like Mamá Blanca herself, with her noisy failures in every practical venture (19; 8), cousin Juancho's exorbitant humanity gets in the way of his own positive projects.[10] In equal measure, his un-self-conscious flair for traitorous language manages to articulate, not the desired projects, but rather his loyalty to "the idealistic soul of our race" (86, 58). English-speaking Evelyn, for example, was brought by his insistence so that the girls would learn her "sane mentality and indispensable language." What happened instead was that Evelyn learned creolized Castilian, and spoke it badly, without definite articles. So the diametrically opposed result of Juancho's efforts to "Europeanize" the plantation was to instill there a love for indolent tolerance and for "Mamá's dulcet, affected, lilting Spanish" (85; 58).

Juancho would even trip himself up quite literally when his ideal code (alternately and conflictively positivist and chivalric) might fail at the moment of the communication he yearned for. This happened, for instance, when he slipped on a fruit peel and fell on top of the very lady to whom he was preparing to bow on the street. The indignant woman made an inappropriately insulting remark, because she could never have understood this "master of etiquette" (77; 52). If we understand Juancho, and love him, perhaps it is because by now Blanca Nieves has taught us how admirable linguistic (verbal and gestural) misfires can be, especially when they attempt to respect a disinterested code of behavior out of date and dear to the same degree. Juancho lives from one disaster to the next without admitting that a quixotic pattern trails behind, a weave of idealized notions repeatedly surprised in their encounter with reality. And reality here is, by contrast,

nothing more than a discourse that refuses to be surprised, exiling whatever is unpredictable as, by definition, unrealistic. It is a fatal discourse for Cousin Juancho whose ingenuousness amounts to an ethical posture. As if to insure our empathy, or at least to dramatize his almost helpless sense of wonder, these memoirs continually confront us as readers with the impossibility to predict anything, or to hold on to the stereotypes that might make our reading less hazardous, and perhaps less rigorously ethical.

It should not come as a surprise, therefore, that the young woman and friend who "edits" Mamá Blanca's posthumous memoirs criticizes herself for organizing, clarifying, and polishing what the old lady called, aware of how writing distances what it brings into focus, the "portrait of my memory" (23; 12). The young professional writer might have defended herself, nevertheless, by noting how Blanca Nieves loved to put her mother's stories in order, giving "unity to the whole" (51; 33). But the editor surely recognized a difference in the two procedures. Blanca Nieves would weave her stories together and take them apart, without worrying about achieving a final form or about the reception by an anonymous public. Her future friend deviated by submitting Blanca's loose pages to the kind of logical *Nachträglichkeit* that the vogue for biography imposes on diffuse material. The difference comes into relief against the background of continuity between these characters, since the old writer's pains to cultivate the young one suggest a transfer of mantle. Their contiguous relationship (literally at the piano or at the table) accounts, in fact, for much of the charm of their friendship. But the editor could not have forgotten that her indiscriminate transfer of text to a faceless public violates the old woman's confidence.

—Ya sabes, esto es para ti. Dedicado a mis hijos y nietos, presiento que de heredarlo sonreirían con ternura diciendo: "¡Cosas de Mamá Blanca!," y ni siquiera lo hojearían. Escrito, pues, para ellos, to lo legaré a ti. Léelo si quieres, pero no lo enseñes a nadie. . . . Este es el retrato de mi memoria . . .

Siendo indiscreción tan en boga la de publicar Memorias y Biografías cortando aquí, añadiendo allá, según el capricho de biógrafos y editores, no he podido resistir más tiempo la correinte de mi época y he emprendido la tarea fácil y destructora de ordenar las primeras cien páginas . . . a fin de darlas a la publicidad. . . . Mientras las disponía, he sentido la mirada del público lector, fija continuamente sobre mí como el ojo del Señor sobre Caín.

(23)

[Now you know, this is for you. It is dedicated to my children and grandchildren, but I know that if it came into their hands they would smile tenderly and say: "One of Mamá Blanca's whims," and they wouldn't even bother to read it. It was written for them, but I am leaving it to you. You read it if you want to, but don't show it to anybody . . . This is the portrait of my memory . . .

Since the publication of Memoirs and Biographies has become one of the more fashionable indiscretions, cutting here, padding there, according to the taste of biographers and publishers, I have been unable to resist the trend of the times, and so I have undertaken the easy destructive task of arranging the first hundred pages . . . to bring them to the public . . . While I have been arranging them I have felt the eye of the reader fixed upon me like that of the Lord on Cain.]

(12)

We readers, titillated by the illusion of conspiracy, read on; but this rather conventional ploy of arousing voyeuristic interest is more than that here. It is also a staging of the forced displacement narrated in the following pages, a proleptic loss of privacy with the sale of the plantation and the move to Caracas, which also amounts to the loss of a pointless freedom to make and unmake texts. By extending the continuity from Mamá Blanca, through the editor, to a general readership that can identify with the story, the introduction frames the impersonal process of modernization that will end Blanca Nieves's private haven and her narrative. And after her irresistible decision to bring the memoirs out, the modernizing agent reinscribes her fatal, Cain-like, guilt every time she transcribes (or invents) Mamá Blanca's own objections to fixing words in writing. "As many times as I have attempted to explain to you how Vicente talked and how Mamá talked, those two opposite poles, one the essence of rusticity and the other of refinement or preciosity, one in which the rhythm predominated, the other the melody, I have sadly realized the uselessness of my endeavor. The written word, I repeat, is a corpose" (111; 75). For the price of that guilt, however, the editor gains the purchase of a conflicted—modern—freedom. It allows her to resist a traditional and maternal authority by submitting to the contemporary sway of market and fame. It is as if she had learned from Mamá Blanca herself how to perform inside the contradiction between codes. Writing is a death that, paradoxically, assures the memory of what it has killed, not the death of "meaning" that might concern a more rigorously deconstructive reading so much as of musicality and gesture, always an impoverished, but also a repeatable, representation.

Far less tortured or coyly self-deprecating, the narrator of *Doña Bárbara* sees things differently. For this modernizer, the flatness and public visibility of writing are great advantages, not lamentable losses. They are the preconditions for distinguishing written and generally binding law from oral tradition, which amounts to distinguishing civilization from barbarism. This mandate to draw neatly demarcated terms of opposition would have been dangerously impatient with the plurivalent heteroglossia that survived in Piedra Azul. Blanca Nieves would find out that, after a while, Bárbara was left with no space between signifier and signified in which the feminine subject could enjoy re-creation. On the contrary, that space for enchantments, interpretations, and seductions was the measure of Bárbara's abnormality. The same kind of verbal and gestural freedom that made the naughty little girls of Piedra Azul charming, made Bárbara the target of a linguistic cleanup campaign. Her independence

and power were interpreted as the wages of hatred, perversions of her female nature. By wedging a space between the word woman and her aggressive, virile persona, Bárbara had dared to untie the bond between virility and virtue, father and fatherland, and had sent the entire rationally demarcated system into motion. Obviously she had to be eliminated.

In Piedra Azul, by contrast, nothing is eliminated; all the rational and irrational discourses cohabit in common-law polygamy if not altogether legally, like Vicente and his two wives. Ancient and noble traditions, together with popular practices, eccentric superstition, races, generations, all occupy the same inclusive and static space. Everything coexists and each element enriches Piedra Azul, although the adults don't see it that way.

Ni Evelyn (en su intransigencia inglesa y puritana), ni Mamá, ni Papá, ni nadie eran tampoco capaces de apreciar el buen sabor a español noble y añejo del vocabulario que empleaba Vicente. Nosotros sí, y porque lo apreciábamos lo copiábamos. Evelyn nos corregía asegurando severa que hablábamos vulgarmente; también Mamá nos corregía, pero ellas no tenían razón: la razón o supremo gusto estaba de parte de Vicente y de parte nuestra. Sólo muchos años después pude comprenderlo bien. Fue leyendo a López de Gómara, Cieza de León, Bernal Díaz del Castillo . . .

Vicente decía, como en el magnífico siglo XVI, *ansina,* en lugar de así, *truje,* en lugar de traje; *aguaitar,* en lugar de mirar; *mesmo,* por mismo; *endilgar,* por encaminar; decía *esguazar,* decía *agora,* decía *cuasi,* decía *naide,* . . .

(107-108)

[Neither Evelyn (with her British and Protestant intolerance) nor Mama nor Papa nor anyone could appreciate the flavor of the noble, vintage Spanish that comprised Vicente's vocabulary. We could and because we appreciated it we copied it. Evelyn corrected us, assuring us that we were talking vulgarly; Mama corrected us too, but they were both wrong. Right, or supreme good taste, was on the side of Vicente and us. Only many years later did I realize this. It was when I came to read López de Gómara, Cieza de León, Bernal Díaz del Castillo and other authors of the period who came to America and generously bequeathed us the Spanish which Vicente used, just as one uses a strong, solid, comfortable piece of old furniture inherited from one's ancestors. Vicente's Spanish was that of the Golden Age.]

(72-73)

These very archaisms, which Harriet de Onís wisely decided not to translate and which are preserved by Teresa de la Parra as a precious inheritance of the original "American" language, were being presented at the same time in *Doña Bárbara.* And just consider the difference in presentation. Coming from Marisela, they really do seem to be the vulgarities that Evelyn and the girls' parents thought they heard in Piedra Azul. For Santos Luzardo, a man obsessed by the ideal of a centralizing and efficient language, variations are disturbances, or they are reduced to the opposition between correct and incorrect usage, and always, ultimately, between civilization and barbarism. By contrast to Sarmiento's pampa and to Gallegos's llano, Piedra Azul knows no barbarism. The narrator doesn't perceive it because her memoirs don't represent a fight to the death between two cultural-linguistic systems where the "other" is almost by etymological definition barbarous, or foreign. Bárbara is, of course, the "other," the one who competes with the Father.

It is possible that while she listens to Doña Bárbara's story, Mamá Blanca may come to the same conclusion about "other" being unfairly coded as evil, because there is abundant reason for thinking that the apparently ethical difference between civilization and barbarism is, as I have said, also a proprietary difference between mine and yours. In my imagined epilogue for their books, the two women would certainly develop a profound friendship based on their common and rending experience that made them "excentric." They are already absent from their ideal contexts, an absence that both allows for and obliges them to write. In one case, it is in order to supplement the emptiness that nostalgia leaves; in the other, writing is the caricature of another writer that banishes Bárbara and makes her absent. Long before she sat down to write her memoirs, Mamá Blanca evidently knew the value of distances, between names and people, between experience and the "portrait" of a life that she was writing. Her editor is no less sensitive to the calculus of loss and gain when she describes "my hands touching the places where now absent hands had lingered" (13; 3).[11] By extension, she is also describing how our hands caress the same pages and occupy an analogous position to hers in the chain of absences that paradoxically make our association possible. But Bárbara would only begin to conceive of absence as an opportunity now that she was far from the llano and planning to write her own story. Her version might take advantage of Mamá Blanca's appreciation for what was missing, her flair for narrative mismatches and contempt for absolutely binding signification, because in the other version, his version, Bárbara's history seems to terribly present. It pretends to be as coherent as if a person could signify anything so categorical as evil.

Gallegos declares the immediacy of his writing in the very first words, "Who goes with us?," where present tense and first-person plural interpellate the reader as participant. He writes as if interpretation and slips of meaning were entirely conquerable. And when he appeals to literary subtexts, as in the case of "Sleeping Beauty," it is not to remark on a literary continuity that may be affecting his own production. It is rather to enlist an apparently transparent allegory for didactic purposes, where Beauty is a figure for Marisela or Venezuela. But now that Gallegos has put us on the track of the allegorical possibilities of using fairy tales, Bárbara, or Blanca, or we, may continue to experiment where he stopped. Minds that lack the necessary discipline may wander beyond Gallegos's demarcations. We may think, for one obvious example in this epilogue, about the fairy tale of Snow White while we reread his Sleeping Beauty. And perhaps by this path of associative reading, as well as

through the writerly leads given by Parra's heroine, we can imagine a feminist rereading of *Doña Bárbara* through Snow White. In the fairy-tale version, the heroine is a good little girl, good fundamentally because she is a little girl. That is, she is innocent because, at her prepubescent age, she lacks the maternal power to reproduce herself in daughters. The mother (stepmother here, in order to underscore their discontinuity) is necessarily evil, basically because she exercises power that challenges the father. Sandra Gilbert and Susan Gubar offer these provocative observations and add that the supposed real mother in the story had died shortly after giving birth, as if that very demonstration of maternal power somehow annulled her validity as mother.[12] This apparent absurdity, and the radical separation of mother and daughter (Bárbara and Marisela) in this story so basic to our Western narrative habits, represents a kind of Oedipal struggle between parent and child in which father is the prize. It is a construct of familial relationships that has by now been shaken by tools in feminist psychoanalysis that describe female development as a process of continuity and extension with the mother and by a feminist literature that disarticulates inherited models.[13] There is probably no better example of the literary assaults on the Oedipal model than *Las memorias de Mamá Blanca*, where the spatial figures of extension and metonymy become the very principles of narrative organization. Here the bedroom mirror is no magic mirror on the wall to judge competing women's worth, no determining voice of the absent and desired father as in the fairy tale, but the projection screen for a mother's hands entwined in her daughter's hair while they become accomplices in creative daydreaming.

If Bárbara had the chance to write her own story, inspired as much by the "evil" (enterprising) Queen as by that other Snow White, the naughty, oxymoronically dark one, perhaps she could have extended her entrepreneurial plotting to include literary plot-making in the demonic reflections of her own witch's conjuring table. There she would surely have enjoyed the twists she could give to some of the neat lines of the patriotic "epic" named for her. The heroic genre, always told with the suffocating self-respect of the victor, was no place for a woman's willful tangles. Perhaps, in the untidy novelized result that her literary conjuring might produce, there would have been more room for mothers to be accompanied by their daughters.[14] In Gallegos's version, mother and daughter get together too, but as antagonists, when Marisela barges into Bárbara's bedroom to confront the "witch" who is casting a spell on Santos. The women fight (over him) and Santos overturns Bárbara's advantage by breaking in to save the girl.[15]

It is entirely possible that my rereading against the grain of *Doña Bárbara* may seem a bit perverse, and short of perverse it may be at least anachronistic or irresponsible.[16] No one should forget the importance that Rómulo Gallegos had as figurehead for the Generation of 1928 that opposed dictator Juan Vicente Gómez. And of course it is true that his 1929 novel did much to build bases for the victorious populism of Acción Democrática. The educator, author, and president was, without a doubt, "progressive," advocating as he did a binding legal system as well as economic development that would promote general prosperity and welfare. To a great degree, modernization did, in fact, equal social improvement. And there is no question that it was preferable to Gómez's outmoded authoritarianism that organized the state as if it were his personal estate. Perhaps the one, halting worry that I would like to voice in the dialogic pause that Bárbara would give to Gallegos's epic flow is an observation about a certain rhetorical and emotive continuity between populism and personalism. Both kinds of political culture tend to be centralizing under the leadership of a practically cultlike figure. And although the centralizing project in a populist novel like *Doña Bárbara* grounds itself in a legal and apparently impersonal system, the victorious result seems suspiciously like the problem it has conquered. With even more clarity than the novel, the movie script that Gallegos later prepared, dramatizes the coincidence. The problem that Santos has come to resolve is the absolute power that Bárbara wields on the llano. And the solution celebrated at the end of the movie is the almost equally absolute power that Santos has wrested from her. By then his cousin and possible rival for real estate has conveniently died, Marisela has learned to speak correct Spanish, and Bárbara has taken the lady's way out, disappearing into the background. First she and then he are in control. Between them is what might be called a metaphoric relationship; a semantic substitution that, however radical, does not destabilize the verbal organization. The invariable is the protagonist's position as leader. This simple observation suggests the possibility that some authoritarian habits might survive in a populist project that, say, could not satisfy the popular demands it helped to formulate.

It seems hardly promising, by contrast, that Teresa de la Parra was never really concerned about progressive or popular demands. Even her feminism was, in her own words, quite moderate and never went so far as suffrage.[17] For many readers she tended to be rather conservative, even reactionary in the strictest sense of the term, given her pride in illustrious forebears, the charm and refinement that distinguished her in elegant society, and her alleged nostalgia for colonial life.[18] Born in Paris and raised on the family's sugar plantation outside of Caracas until she was ten, when her father died and the family moved to Spain, Parra's short life of shuttling back and forth between Spain and France—with short stays in Venezuela and visits to Cuba and Colombia—was given to the re-creation of a lost world. More poignantly absent from Venezuela (and from her truncated childhood) than la Avellaneda was from Cuba, Teresa de la Parra knew just as well how to turn distance to literary advantage. One might call her compensatory writing project reactionary, in terms of literary as well as political history, because it reverts to the episodic, loosely articulated, "costumbrista" literature that produced static "portraits" of rural life, the same word Mamá Blanca used for her memoirs. This characterization, though, is excessively simple; it comes from the kind of political imagination that reduces everything to left and right, to good and

bad, to a binarism as proper and constraining as Santos Luzardo's language. Instead of forcing her into one pole or another, one might place her more commodiously on an anarchic tangent. If her persona Mamá Blanca is conservative, it is because she wants to conserve everything, from the most archaic practices to the most unpredictable variations on the modern, like the special brand of Spanish without articles that Evelyn perfected. Blanca refuses to thoughtlessly equate new with improved and thus leaves room for those whom history, and even her adored mother as well as her "all-powerful" father, would marginalize and finally erase. What is more, she orchestrates a rhythmic and melodious polyphony from the equal linguistic marginality of each inhabitant of Piedra Azul, a concerted simultaneity of sound supported by the contiguous and metonymic mapping of the place, where it would be impossible to substitute anyone (metaphorically) without sacrificing the general effect.

With an analogous and imitative gesture, I might find a tangent from which to preserve the politically promising aspects of this novel: its tolerance, flexibility, and the merciful "incoherence" of its multiple voices.[19] If one cared to extract a moral from all this, it could be suggested, perhaps, that marches of progress might take note where and on whom they step; otherwise, progress may turn into something else, as it did for some critics of Acción Democrática when it "progressively" silenced internal voices that challenged party leadership. To step (or sidestep) gingerly might be preferable, and not necessarily utopian. The Nicaraguans, for example, were learning this lesson in the wake of trespassing on too many Misquito settlements. After the surprisingly effective resistance of the Indians, whose refusal to submit to Nicaraguan centralism had identified them merely as obstacles for some time, the state questioned the political virtues of insisting on a centralized, Spanish-language culture. A linguistically and culturally diverse polity no longer seemed an impossibly complex alternative to unattainable uniformity. One real concession was that the constitution ratified in 1987 made provisions for locally legislated education in which a Spanish-speaking teacher could no longer take the place of one who speaks Misquito, or English, or Rama. The polity was beginning to understand itself by metonymic accretion rather than by metaphoric substitution.

Teresa de la Parra's reluctance to assign definitive meanings to words, and her framing of what might be called a feminine lineage by an introduction that stages a transfer of text between two women, makes my mind wander in another direction from where Bárbara meets Blanca. Besides the literary confrontation with foundational fathers like Gallegos, Parra's book invites us—and her three lectures on "The Influence of Women in Forging the American Soul" direct us—on a trail of continuity with other women writers. In these talks, which she was invited to deliver about her life and work in Cuba and Caracas, Parra prefers to put herself in good company rather than to make a tokenized spectacle of her female self. She mentions Delmira Agustini and Gabriela Mistral as admirable contemporaries and then arches back to America's beginnings, with Queen Isabel's humanizing influence and Doña Marina's multilingual agility, to linger on the accomplishments of Sor Juana Inés de la Cruz, quote whole poems by the pseudonymous "Amarylis" ("How many Amarylises have lived since then behind our latticed cities watching life go by!"),[20] and remember her own grandmothers and aunts to whom the nation is indebted. This catalogue of foremothers arouses a speculation on the possibility that finding and pausing at imperfect meanings may be a common feature among the most interesting women writers of Spanish America. I cannot help thinking that it is because their keen sense of irony comes from being over- (or under-) whelmed before a verbal system that cannot correspond to their lived experience. By dramatizing the incommensurability between experience and expression, they keep pointing to a gap between available words and the world, a valuable pointer for rereading male Latin American writers as well. Perhaps the women's obsessive discourse of disencounters derives, in part, from a certain feminine distancing, either reticence about public scrutiny or playfulness, from a language of stable authority.[21] In that case, being a woman and therefore marginalized may be, how ironic, a real esthetic advantage, somewhat like Eve's fall and expulsion from paradise (followed by Adam), a transgression that makes women creatively compensatory. This is the way Blanca Nieves, at least, understands her humble superiority over her "brother" Violeta.

> Yo admiraba a Violeta en las mismas proporciones en que Violeta me desdeñaba a mí. Era natural. Yo podía apreciar la puntería de sus pedradas y la elegancia de sus maromas, mientras que a ella no le era dado contemplar aquellos brillantes cortejos de príncipes y hadas que tras de mi boca abierta asistían con magnificencia a las bodas de Pablo y Virginia. Era yo respecto a ella lo que es en nuestros días cualquier poeta respecto a cualquier campeón de football, de la natación o del boxeo: es decir, nada. Pero mi humilde superioridad aplastada y oscura tenía su encanto. Mis ensueños limpios de todo aplauso, asaetados por Violeta y desbaratados por Evelyn, al igual de un arbusto después de una poda, reflorecían a escondidas con más abundancia y mayor intensidad.

(57)

> [My admiration for Violeta was in inverse ratio to her contempt for me. It was only natural. I could appreciate the accuracy of her stone throwing and the elegance of her acrobatics, whereas she could not see those brilliant corteges of princes and fairies which, behind my gaping lips and ecstatic eyes, attended the marriage of Paul and Virginia. In her eyes my status was that of a poet as compared to a football, swimming, or boxing champion; that is to say, negligible. But my poor trampled, cowed superiority had its charms. My hidden dreams, transfixed by Violeta's arrows, rudely shattered by Evelyn, like a pruned tree, only flowered with greater lushness and intensity.]

(37-38)

If women, more consistently than men, are exiled from the athletic paradise where signifiers reach their signifieds, it is possible that their conscious frustration may become an incitation to play with possible miscombina-

tions. In other words, thanks to our disobedience and our deterritorialization, we already remark on the arbitrariness of authority.[22]

It may easily, and correctly, be objected that this kind of distancing or defamiliarization is constitutive of all writing, and that language, by its allegorical nature, necessarily dramatizes the absence that it hopelessly strives to fill in. Nevertheless, differences matter among the many possible ways to manage that tension between desired but unattainable presence (of truth, of authority, nature, etc.) and the absence left in the short fall of words that don't reach their referents. Indifference to the variations would be strangely to lose sight of the same deconstructive terms that bring the absences into focus. Gallegos, for one, may be as keenly aware as Parra that his language can be treacherous; but his punitive policy for traitors is quite unlike her amused benignity. Faced with the restlessness that makes writing run away with lived experience, she manages, not by consigning them both to closer quarters, but by acknowledging the futility of authorial discipline.

This is not the first time we have noticed a woman's bemusement or complaint about an uncooperative language. We saw it in Gertrudis Gómez de Avellaneda's *Sab*, where an entire glossary of racially identified color categories was unequal to the description of Cuba's most typical resident. Signification was an indirect process in which, for example, black, white, and yellow couldn't quite describe Sab and yet suggested him by a doubleplay of composite and default. Signification was as indirect as Sab's letter writing to Teresa, while Carlota was the ideal but unreachable destination. Like Mamá Blanca's memoirs, written for her sons and yet delivered to an adoptive daughter, Sab's authoritative letter was handed over to a sympathetic accomplice. On the same tangent of women's circuitous communications, I am tempted to add that soon after Avellaneda's novel, three Argentine women took advantage of the political indeterminacy following Rosas's defeat to clear some discursive space for themselves in the journal they published, anonymously, a journal called *La Camelia* and dedicated to "Liberty, not license: equality between both sexes [secsos]" (April 11, 1852).[23] One strategy was to introduce themselves, indirectly of course, in their anonymity, with analogously (in)appropriate signs to those Avellaneda used for Sab: "Without being pretty little girls, we are neither old nor ugly." In that same generation, writers like Rosa Guerra, Juana Manuela Gorriti, Mercedes Rosas de Rivera, and Juana Manso were taking issue with their Unitarian fathers and husbands over the unitary and limiting language that was sure to reproduce some of the same abuses they opposed in Rosas. In its stead, the women cultivated a heterogeneous national discourse, in which Indian languages, Italian, Gallician, English, and gaucho dialects made a heteroglossic mix with standard Spanish.[24] At the same time, they staged complaints about specious associations that particular words force, associations like family and fatherland, or feminine and frivolous. If home was the site for establishing civilized social relations, as the male Generation of 1837 never tired of saying, then the women demanded consistent and balanced foundations for the new national family. Wives had to assume equal responsibility and equal rights; otherwise the celebration of an unexamined domesticity would backfire and mire the country in feudal, barbarous habits.

From this tangent, it is easy to note the unmistakable difference between their straining for consistency and Parra's straying. Her almost aggressive defense of incoherence is the other side of their demand for fits between family and state. Where they and perhaps Avellaneda may feel their marginality to authoritative language as an exclusion, she feels it as a liberation. This constitutive distancing from absolutes may be common to all literature, but it is not always as self-reflexive or as promising as in Parra, and to other degrees in Avellaneda and her Argentine contemporaries. It doesn't always provide, as it does for them, a negotiating point from which to wrest a furlough from the prison-house of language, or at least an account for redecoration.

From her particular cell, disobedient Sister Juana Inés de la Cruz (1648-1695), the model for generations of naughty novice writers including Teresa de la Parra, had time to reflect on her own relationship to language. The prospect of strategically manipulating the impossibility of language obviously appealed to her, and never so much as when she was preparing her famous response to Sor Filotea. The superior had just instructed her ward to desist from debating with church authorities and also from pursuing secular studies of literature and science. These were unauthorized activities for a woman who had joined a religious order. But the feminized signature on the strident reprimand reveals some reserve, because Sor Juana's superior and confessor was a man, the bishop of Puebla. Signing as "Sister Friend of God," he was probably attempting to cover over his requirements by casting them as appeals to the nun's sense of common decency. Earlier, the bishop had encouraged his spiritual charge to be more daring, when he urged her to dust off a forty-year-old provocation by the Portuguese Jesuit Vieyra about the nature of Christ's virtues and then had her criticism published and circulated. Sor Juana's brilliant casuistry—in the critique the bishop published and called "Carta Atenagórica" (after the goddess of wisdom)—was more proof of women's ability than he would later want. As candidate for archbishop of Mexico, competing with a Spanish Jesuit who was Vieyra's personal friend, and also as a man whose ecclesiastical career boasted special attention to the education of women, it had been important for the confessor to demonstrate his special contribution to Mexican society through women's accomplishments. But once he lost the competition to the Spaniard, an incorrigible misogynist, the Mexican bishop chose to make amends by making Sor Juana repent of her presumption to argue with men.[25] She was, however, hardly the pious pawn to be moved forward and backward as he pleased. Sor Juana's response to his reprimand is to heap one self-legitimating argument on another, to overdetermine her right to write.

Many readers remember the scant autobiographical details about her irrepressible, God-given intelligence (antholo-gized time and again): how she would steal off behind an older sister to learn to read and write; how she would punish herself with unwanted haircuts and dessert deprivation for not learning fast enough; how she dazzled the doctors at court with her wit and erudition; and how she entered the convent as a sanctuary for learning, free from the responsibilities of marriage and children. Other readers are beginning to value the impressive tradition of foremothers Sor Juana constructs (mixing and matching Catholic saints with pagan and heretical victims of the church) in order to license herself in their company.[26] This kind of self-celebration through other notable women evidently appealed to Parra, who repeated the scheme in her talks. But I would like to call attention, in the present context, to her literary critical arguments (hardly ever acknowledged as far as I know) about the instability and the infinite interpretability of any text, including those called sacred texts. When her confessor suggested that the dedicate herself to the exegesis of sacred scripture, he seemed to have forgotten that the terrain would be as slippery as that of the profane letters in which she dabbled. The effort, she feared, would distance her more than ever from the authoritative doctrine of the church. If Virgil, Homer and all the great poets and orators are subject to (mis)inter-pretation, Holy Scripture is no less so, according to her. It is fraught with grammatical difficulties, such as using plurals for singulars, switching from second to third persons, giving adjectives a genitive rather than an accusative case, and replacing feminine for masculine genders.[27]

This last category calls special attention to itself by its boldness and baldness; it is the only one that appears without examples. Certainly not because examples of gender slippage don't exist in the Bible; Sor Juana must have known some to conceive of the category at all.[28] Instead, it is likely that she omitted the target examples because her target here was the confessor himself, the male authority, disguised in the epistolary crossdressing of Sor Filotea, who was hoping to simulate an identification with the (in)subordinate nun and to gain her confidence. Sor Juana, of course, has no choice but to let him have it, his way. At the same time, though, she takes advantage of the transparent fiction to dramatize how unstable and flexible attributions of gender can be. And so, excusing herself, with a wagging tongue barely contained in her cheek, she ends her response by reminding her confessor that if she has been transgressive of gender proprieties, it is because he taught her how it is done. She begs "forgiveness of the homely familiarity, and the less than seemly respect in which by treating you as a nun, one of my sisters, I have lost sight of the remoteness of your most illustrious person; which, had I seen you without your veil, would never have occurred."[29] To be sure, it would have been less strategic for the bishop to have attempted a more naked intervention, because it would have insured his absence from the convent. In order to feign his presence there, he absents himself as a man by covering over the difference. It's not that his game fails to convince his ideal reader, but that the bishop himself is reluctant to play it to the logical end. Sor Juana, by comparison, has no hesitations and forces him into the next move. The confessor may have been criticizing her for presuming the kind of ecclesiastical authority reserved for men, but what he acts out is his equal flexibility as a gendered sign. To enter into debate with her, he had to "(a)veil" himself of a female identity, neither superior nor inferior to his opponent.

I will not insist on many more examples, primarily because this chapter might become far too long and also because it may not be necessary. Nevertheless, Sor Juana's inspiration, the catalogue of matriarchs that she and then Parra prepared in their self-presentations, lead me by an irresistible mimetic desire for remembering good company to mention some works that dramatize what might be called a feminist distancing in language. One favorite is *Balún Canán* (1957) by Rosario Castellanos, a novel narrated by a seven-year-old girl who can't seem to make the racial and sexual codes in conflict around and through her coincide with the scenes she puts together. Her initial ingenuous confusion never clears up; it becomes fixed, repeating the fragmentation of a Mexico that never manages to congeal into a society and repeating also the national language that excludes, more than it includes, Indian territory. By way of the discursive clashes in the book, between Indians and whites, women and men, workers and landowners, Castellanos writes an anti-*Bildungsroman,* a personal history without development or goal. Another favorite writer is Clarice Lispector (1926-1977), that ingenious narrator of the domestic uncanny, who makes perfectly quotidian situations gnawingly grotesque by the same kind of static focusing and disturbing repetitions that can make women's lives unbearably familiar. With her, I also remember Luisa Valenzuela, whose best stories in *Cambio de armas* (1982), defamiliarize a politico-linguistic system that doesn't correspond with her logic of loving.

But perhaps the most dramatic example of what I would like to call an esthetic tradition of feminine estrangement is the testimony given by Rigoberta Menchú, the young Quiché woman of Guatemala who learned Spanish in order to organize a multi-ethnic resistance to government expropriations and violence. She, even more than the childish narrators or the social pariahs, is a newcomer to the system of language in which she must defend herself. Her special treatment of Spanish is often a reminder of her social marginality, not a marginality to one particular ideological code from a sense of belonging to another, but a repeated posture of the linguistic *bricoleuse* who combines native traditions of the Popol Vuh with Catholicism, ethnic exclusivity with national struggles and with marxism, because she has learned that no one code fits or contains her. The lack of fit is also the mark of her advantage as a new speaker, one who maintains her distance from and in language, who translates unheard-of expressions to express unheard-of experiences. Not all those experiences are meant for a Spanish-speaking readership, though. And Rigoberta's most telling reminder of her difference is a cautious reluctance to get everything right, as cautious as Mamá's deceptively irresponsible habit of naming little girls. It is surprising, I think, to come continually upon passages in the testimonial where Rigoberta purposely withholds in-

formation. Of course the audible protests of silence may well be responses to anthropologist Elizabeth Burgos—Debray's line of questioning. If she were not asking particular questions, the informant would logically have no reason to refuse answers. But what is noteworthy here is the way Rigoberta's refusal to tell secrets remains on the page after the editing is done. Either the informant, the scribe, or both were determined to keep a series of admonitions in the published text. From the beginning, the narrator tells us ever so clearly that she is not going to tell: "Indians have been very careful not to disclose any details of their communities."[30] By some editorial or collective decision, the very last words of the testimonial are, "I'm still keeping secret what I think noone should know. Not even anthropologists or intellectuals, no matter how many books they have, can find out all our secrets."[31] Yet the almost 400-page book is full of information: about Rigoberta herself, her community, traditional practices, the armed struggle, strategic decisions. A reader may therefore wonder what she means by referring to secrets that "cannot be known," and why so much attention is being called to our insufficiency as readers? Is she saying that we are *incapable* of knowing or that we as subjects of a centralized and centralizing culture *ought* not to know (just as Mamá *ought* not to have announced Aurora's name), for reasons of ethnic safety?

Paradoxically, perhaps, the writer who most cleverly keeps us (and herself) at a safe distance from a hegemonic Hispanic culture was the one who seems to have fit in most effortlessly. I am referring again to Teresa de la Parra, writing though a childish narrator who knows, without bragging, that she and her sisters were at "the center of this Cosmos" (30; 17). That's why she explains, defamiliarizing the familiar form of address, everyone referred to them in the royal second-person singular. "Thou" (110, 75). Defamiliarization here doesn't suppose a lack of familiarity with the modern world, as in Rigoberta's case, or a grotesque decomposition as in Lispector's. It assumes a virtually divine sense of security that turns everything into raw material available for manipulation, an absolute security that recognizes with more humor than horror the space between, say, regal and familial appeals for attention. It is also a security that authorizes simultaneous linguistic differences, holding them together with the loose bonds of indulgent love, since, as Avellaneda, Castellanos, Menchú, and many others would discover too, no one code is entirely adequate to the narrative.

Those horizontal bonds, dramatized by the *Memorias'* episodic organization, by the scene of writing and rewriting in the proliferating mirror, and finally by the narrator's caution against confusing change with progress, may remind us of one of the promises that, according to Benedict Anderson, novels made to their first Latin American readers. It was to open their imaginations to the idea of an inclusive national community by including them all, horizontally, in one flexible and secular concept of calendrical time. If the foundational fictions of the nineteenth century and the populist romances that revised them for anti-imperialist projects tended to take the inclusions for granted and to strain forward rather than laterally, pulling time into straight, rational lines that go from barbarism to civilization, and if the recurrent pattern of Boom novels can be visualized as a vicious circle that reaches the end of patriotic history to find out that end no longer means goal, this feminist novel stops the dynamic or the dizzying movement. Instead of a straight line or a circle, the shape of **Las Memorias de Mamá Blanca** is fanlike. It unfolds a bit wider with every page to make room for the next speaker, only hinting that the central fulcrum is being manipulated by one who was born in the center. But the design she produces is hardly the hegemonic or pyramidal structure of founding fictions. It is an acknowledgement of the mutual dependence of every fold on the others.[32] Anything less would fail to capture the polyphonic airs of a society so admirable for its complexity.

NOTES

[1] Teresa de la Parra, *Las memorias de Mamá Blanca* (Caracas: Monte Avila Editores, 1985). References will be made to this edition. Second page numbers refer to Teresa de la Parra, *Mamá Blanca's Souvenirs,* trans. Harriet de Onís (Washington, D.C.: Pan American Union, 1959), which I cite here with an occasional adjustment.

[2] Luis Sánchez-Trincado, a Spanish critic, called *Mamá Blanca* a "novela-album," explaining that these "viñetas folk-lóricas" are typical of children's literature with which Parra's work is often associated. "Teresa de la Parra y la creación de caracters," in *Revista Nacional de Cultura* 2, 22 (Caracas, September 1940): 38-54; 47.

[3] For an excellent study of *Las memorias,* which includes a suggestive comparison with *Doña Bárbara,* see Elizabeth Garrels, *Las grietas de la ternura: Nueva lectura de Teresa de la Parra* (Caracas: Monte Avila Editores, 1986). Another perceptive comparison, more generally between feminism and "mundonovismo," appears in an essay by Francine Masiello: "Texto, ley, transgresión: Especulación sobre la novela (feminista) de vanguardia," *Revista Iberoamericana,* nos. 132-133 (July-December 1985): 807-822.

[4] If a case had to be made for the prevalence of stereotypes like Gallegos's, many writers could be mentioned, among them the very popular José Rafael Pocaterra. The heroine of his aptly and allegorically titled novel *Tierra del Sol amada* is described like this: "she encarnates the great spiritual *patria,* which gives herself over, offers herself entirely, whose body flourishes and then disintegrates, self-denying, like the dark roots of a race." Quoted in Pedro Díaz Seijas, *La antigua y la moderna literatura venezolana* (Caracas: Ediciones Armitano, 1966): 494. Of Teresa de la Parra's work, the same critic will say it is less objective, more inductive and feminine.

[5] Their literary "collaboration" dates at least from 1920, when Parra published "Diario de una caraqueña por el Lejano Oriente" in the magazine *Actualidades,* edited by Gallegos. See the Chronology at the end of Teresa de la Parra, *Obras completas "Narrative, ensayos, cartas"),* "Selección, Estudio Crítico y Cronología by Velia Bosch" (Caracas: Biblioteca Ayacucho, 1982): 696.

[6] For the contrast see Bella Brodzki and Celeste Schenck, "Introduction" to *Life/Lines: Theorizing Women's Autobiography* (Ithaca, N.Y.: Cornell University Press, 1988): 7.

[7] de Onís translates, more literally, "No hay que tener razón," as "There is no need to be right."

[8] See Luce Irigaray's discussion of the imaginary as a male "Blindspot," that space that separates the boy from his mother while positing a primal unity. "The Blind Spot of an Old Dream of Symmetry," in *Speculum of the Other Woman,* trans. Gillian C. Gill (Ithaca, N.Y.: Cornell University Press, 1985): 87-89. Also "Questions," in *This Sex Which Is Not One* (Ithaca, N.Y.: Cornell University Press, 1985): 164: "I am trying, . . . to go back through the masculine imaginary, to interpret the way it has reduced us to silence, to muteness, to mimicry . . ."

Also Patricia Yaegar, *Honey-Mad Women* (New York: Columbia University Press, 1987), on playful strategies as against a French feminist idea that language is always alienated.

[9] Teresa de la Parra, *Ifigenia: Diario de una señorita que escribió porque se fastidiaba,* published in 1924. For a fine reading, see Julieta Fombona, "Teresa de la Parra: Las voces de la palabra," in de la Parra, *Obras completas:* ix-xxvi; but I evidently quibble with the contrast she suggests between this first novel (where words are obstacles to meaning) and *Memorias* (where words fit meanings perfectly): xxii.

[10] Arturo Uslar-Pietri appreciated Parra's writing for similar reasons. His essay called "El testimonio de Teresa de la Parra" begins, "There was a time, marvelously imprecise and static."Although, to judge from his quick overview, he misses much of the slow-motion detail: "In *Mamá Blanca* Teresa painted the portrait of our grandmothers. A world devoted to security, resigned to pain." See *Letras y hombres de Venezuela* (Mexico: Fondo de Cultura Económica, 1948): 148-153.

[11] This is my more literal translation of "el roce de mis manos sobre las huellas de las manos ausentes."

[12] Sandra Gilbert and Susan Gubar, *The Madwoman in the Attic: The Woman Writer and the Nineteenth-Century Literary Imagination* (New Haven: Yale University Press, 1979): 37. "The real story begins when the Queen, having become a mother, metamorphoses also into a witch—that is, into a wicked 'step' mother: '. . . when the child was born, the Queen died,' and 'After a year had passed the King took to himself another wife.'"

[13] Nancy Choderow, *The Reproduction of Mothering: Psychoanalysis and the Sociology of Gender* (Berkeley, Los Angeles, London: University of California Press, 1978). The relationship is not always a happy one, of course, because the daughter's only recourse for limiting her mother's consuming power is to submit to paternal authority.

[14] I refer to the distinction made by M. M. Bakhtin in "Epic and Novel," in *The Dialogic Imagination,* trans. Caryl Emerson and Michael Holquist (Austin: University of Texas Press, 1981): 3-40.

[15] Gallegos, *Doña Bárbara*: 178-179.

[16] For a more developed discussion, see my *One Master for Another.*

[17] Teresa de la Parra, "Influencia de las mujeres en la formación del alma americana," in *Obras completas*: 474. She defends women's rights to careers, "fitting for women with fair pay. . . . I don't want, as a conse-

quence of my tone and argument, to be considered a suffragist. I neither defend or object to suffragism for the simple reason that I don't understand it. The fact of knowing that it raises its voice to win for women the same attributions and political responsibilities that men have frightens and disburbs me so that I could never manage to hear out what suffragism has to say. And this is because I generally believe, in contrast to suffragists, that we women should thank men for resigning themselves to take on all the political work. It seems to me that, next to that of coal miners, it is the most difficult and least cleanly work that exists. Why demand it?

"My feminism is moderate."

[18] In the second of three talks she gave on the "Influencia de las mujeres en la formación del alma americana," Parra corrected, or responded defensively to, a common (mis)perception: "My affection for the Colony would never bring me to say, as some do in lyrical moments, that I would have preferred being born then. No, I am quite happy in my epoch and I admire it." *Obras completas*: 490.

For a lovingly written evocation of de la Parra, the creole Circe, see Mariano Picón Salas's review of her published letters in *Estudios de literature venezolana* (Madrid: Ediciones Edime, 1961): 265-270— ". . . so beautiful a woman, who could be seen at all the parties with her splendid eyes and her bearing of a young Spanish Marquise who dressed in Paris, could tell us about episodes and anecdotes that dated back a century, because she had heard them from grandmothers and from old servant women": 266-267.

[19] Of course, one may choose to draw connections between Teresa de la Parra's idcological position and the bald manipulations justified by the socialist rhctoric that she admires in Daniel (148):

> En el corralón, sobre la república de las vacas, por elección y voluntad soberana de ellas . . . todo sabiduría y buen gobierno, imperaba Daniel, Daniel era el vaquero . . .

> El orden reinante era perfecto: era el orden de la ideal ciudad futura. Al pleno aire, pleno cielo y pleno sol, cada vaca estaba contenta y en su casa, es decir atada a su árbol. . . . Nadie se quejaba ni nadie se ensoberbecía, nada de comunismos. Satisfecha cada cual con lo que se le daba, daba en correspondencia cuanto tenía. Por todas partes conformidad, dulzura y mucha paz.

(142-143)

[The rule of the republic of the cows, by their choice and sovereign will—do not laugh, you will see that this is true—, all wisdom, all good government, was Daniel, the cowherd.

When we made our appearance in the city of the cows, Daniel, who had been up since four in the morning, had already, with the assistance of a stable boy, filled many buckets of milk. The order which existed was perfect: the order of the ideal future city. In the open air, under the sky and sun, each cow was happy and in its house, that is to say, tied to a tree or a post. . . . Nobody complained and nobody was resentful; there was no class warfare. To each according to her needs, from each according to her ability. All was peace, all was light.]

(102)

But this praise occurs in a novel where other systems of organization or disorganization receive equal applause. And if one thinks of the liberties the girls take with everyone, or of Juancho's flagrant failures and the other's anachronistically poetic posturing, among other practices, it may be seen that Daniel's government represents one point of this portrait, if not a delicate scoffing at the "future city."

[20] Parra, *Obras completas*: 503.

[21] Although Julia Kristeva assumes woman's challenge to symbolization differently from Parra's performance (as a presymbolic "semiosis," an "archaic, instinctual, and maternal territory" of language that challenges meaning by cultivating meaningless phonic and rhythmic, poetic, excesses), Mamá is subversive, not because she's indifferent to meaning, but because she competes by exaggerating its opacity. Nevertheless, Parra's evocation of Cochoco's style does respond to Kristeva's celebration of semiosis. "From One Identity to Another," in *Desire in Language: A Semiotic Approach to Literature and Art* (New York: Columbia University Press, 1980): 124-147. For a useful review see also Deborah Cameron, *Feminism and Linguistic Theory* (New York: St. Martin's Press, 1985).

[22] Regarding "author-ity," the editor of the memoirs comes "to the melancholy conclusion that this compelling need to sign a book may not be the manifestation of talent, but perhaps, a weakness of the auto-critical faculty" (24; 12-13).

[23] This and other references to Argentine women's claims for sexual equality come from Francine Masiello's very informative essay, "Between Civilization and Barbarism: Women, Family, and Literary Culture in Mid-Nineteenth-Century Argentina," in *Cultural and Historical Grounding for Hispanic and Luso-Brazilian Feminist Literary Criticism,* ed. Hernán Vidal (Minneapolis: Institute for the Study of Ideologies and Literature, 1989): 517-566; 530.

[24] Masiello, "Between Civilization and Barbarism": 535.

[25] For the best narrative I know of this fascinating triangulated power play between two men over an apparently defenseless woman, see Octavio Paz, *Sor Juana Inés de la Cruz: Las trampas de la fe* (Barcelona: Seix Barral, 1982), trans. Margaret Sayers Peden (Cambridge, Mass.: Belknap Press, 1988).

[26] There is Saint Paula, for example, whom Jerome, the patron of Juana's Carmelite order, repeatedly honors for her sanctity and her learning. On the next page is Hypatia, the Alexandrine mathematician and astrologer whom the church fathers ran out of town for improprieties of doctrine, and perhaps of gender too.

[27] Sor Juana Inés de la Cruz, *Respuesta a Sor Filotea,* translated in a bilingual edition as *A Woman of Genius: The Intellectual Autobiography of Sor Juana Inés de la Cruz* by Maragret Sayers Peden (Lime Rock, Conn.: Lime Rock Press, 1982): 80-81.

[28] See P. Paul Jouon, *Grammaire de l'ebreu Biblique* (Rome: Institut Biblique Pontifical, 1923). On pp. 148-149 there are several examples: e.g., Gen. 31: 5, 6 is feminine and Gen. 31: 9 masculine. Ruth 1: 9*a* and 1: 9*b*. See also *Journal of Biblical Literature* 105 (1986): 614.

[29] Sor Juana, *Respuesta*: 98-99.

[30] *Me llamo Rigoberta Menchú* (Havana: Casa de las Americas, 1983): 42. *I, Rigoberta Menchú: An Indian Woman in Guatemala*, edited and

introduced by Elisabeth Burgos-Debray, trans. Ann Wright (London: Verso, 1984): 9.

[31] Menchú: 377; trans., 247.

[32] Irigaray, in "La mechanique des fluids," *Ce sexe* (108), where she turns around Lacan's privileging of metaphor over (continuous) metonymy.

Naomi Lindstrom   (essay date 1993)

SOURCE: An Introduction to *Iphigenia,* in *Iphigenia,* Austin: University of Texas Press, 1993, pp. ix-xiii.

[*Lindstrom places* Iphigenia *within the context of the upper-class women of her day, and presents the critical reception of de la Parra's novel.*]

The novel *Iphigenia* by Teresa de la Parra (Venezuela, 1889-1936; real name, Ana Teresa Parra Sanojo), popular with readers since its first appearance, scandalous in its day, has increasingly won the respect and attention of literary critics. Its author was a well-read, socially prominent young woman whose wit, winning presence, elegance, and above all her powers of verbal expression had placed her in demand on the Caracas scene as a speaker at social, diplomatic, and cultural events. She possessed a talent for writing pieces on demand for notable occasions. As was typical for a woman of her time, place, and social class, she had had to pursue on her own the extensive literary learning that she later put to good use in her celebrated novels.

From the outset of her career, the public was very insistent in attributing special qualities of femininity to de la Parra and her speech and writing. At the same time, the author often appeared to invite such an attribution by employing a type of writing that her public would tag as feminine. She exhibited in her work a preference for intimate and domestic subject matter, a mannered style of somewhat whimsical, teasing humor, and, broadly, a chatty, gossipy mode. Her first publications, the journalistic pieces she began publishing in 1915, were certainly in this vein. A critic dubbed her "Miss Frivolity" and her choice of a pseudonym, Fru-Fru, is a good clue that she had reached a similar judgment about her own work.[1] The issue of a discourse certain to be perceived as feminine is an important one in her first full-length novel, *Iphigenia.* (Between her early journalism and her famous novel, de la Parra had pseudonymously published two short narratives with Oriental themes and backdrops.) *Iphigenia* makes a more purposeful use of a hyper-feminine discourse. The heroine, María Eugenia, is given to gushing, and her themes frequently run to personal adornment, household decor and entertainment, domestic intrigues and politics, and amorous involvements. This time, though, there is an important shift: the heroine's speech is utilized to make a critical examination of women, their role, and their ability to speak of important issues. The author had witnessed the spread of feminism in European intellectual circles and had considered how this movement might apply to the Spanish American context, particularly among women who had little if any chance to study progressive social thought.

She found especially worrisome the case of young women who had, through travel or hearsay, glimpsed the possibility of greater freedom for women, but remained in a cloistered, sheltered environment. These concerns appear in *Iphigenia (The diary of a young lady who wrote because she was bored),* a novel whose five hundred manuscript pages were begun in 1922 and completed in less than a year. As de la Parra finished chapters, they appeared serialized in both Spanish- and French-language literary magazines. *Iphigenia* appeared in its entirety as a book in 1 924. When the first completed chapter appeared in the Caracas *La Lectura Semanal* (Weekly Reading), the magazine sold out its print run of six thousand on the day of publication,[2] and *Iphigenia* has often been reprinted in book form.

Encouraged by the book's first-person form (the early pages are an immensely lengthy, soul-baring letter to an intimate friend; those that follow are a diary), the public tended to view *Iphigenia* as the direct, confessional outpourings of its author, unmediated by artistry or by critical, satirical awareness. Many readers of the novel without hesitation identified the author with her excitable, daydreaming heroine, María Eugenia Alonso. The linkage of the two is not entirely rational, since the author, who was much in the public eye, was known as an accomplished literary intellectual who could find the right words for any occasion. Her heroine, in contrast, is a half-educated young woman, confused by personal vanity and romantic fantasies, often floundering in her efforts to express a critical outlook on society and personal relations. De la Parra was well aware of the wide-spread perception of her work as a "confession"and complained that her readership was insensitive to its strong ironic component.[3]

María Eugenia is a young woman of the upper class, though she has been despoiled of her fortune and now is seen as needing a wealthy match. She inhabits almost exclusively the personal and private sphere and has only the most tenuous notions of the feminism developing in the world at large. When, in her long letter, María Eugenia reminisces to a schoolmate about her education, *Iphigenia* offers a sharply satirical look at the options for learning open to the daughters of good families of Caracas. Despite her sketchy intellectual background, María Eugenia is intelligent and independent-minded enough, and eager enough to attain pleasure in life, to begin to develop her own version of feminism based on her experiences and observations. She can draw upon these insights to analyze, sometimes rather ingenuously and sometimes with surprising sophistication and humor, the situations in which she finds herself. María Eugenia's ability to set her new insights down in effective words fluctuates widely throughout the novel. In some passages she melodramatizes her own plight and falls into a self-indulgent lyricism; in others, she is a sharp observer of individual and collective behavior, as able to mock herself as to satirize those around her. From time to time she bursts into a stiffly didactic speech on society and morals; the reader must sympathize with her ardor even while cringing at the awkwardness of her expression.

For all María Eugenia's intelligence, it is a difficult task for her to generate a critical feminist analysis out of the scanty materials she has at hand. One of the fascinating aspects of the novel is that the reader frequently observes María Eugenia faltering and blundering in her efforts to think and act with a new freedom. In her mind, liberation is often confused with simply getting her own way. At various times in the course of the novel, the heroine appears to associate personal liberation with the wearing of low-necked gowns, dancing "American dances" in public, associating with worldly friends, and coming and going at less restricted hours and unchaperoned. María Eugenia persists in her reading despite the disapproval it raises in her household; yet, she reads only for pleasure and it never occurs to her to undertake a program of study.

The limited range of María Eugenia's aspirations not only has made this heroine seem frivolous to readers, as indeed she often is, but has at times brought the same judgment down on the entire book. Amaya Llebot, for instance, complains in 1974: "What's regrettable is that Teresa de la Parra, an intelligent and well-educated woman, raised in Europe, should limit herself to showing that oppression and only fight it in the name of banal and superficial motives."[4] To state a perhaps self-evident point, readers of *Iphigenia* need to keep in mind that the heroine's thoughts and writing, which range from romantic effusion to petty gossip to stilted attempts at serious analysis, are all intended as the expression of a very young woman not well prepared to understand and comment upon the events surrounding her.

María Eugenia is partially successful in learning to articulate her concerns, but she finds no opportunity to create change. By the end of the novel, she faces only a choice between marriage to a family-approved candidate certain to make his spouse unhappy and life as the mistress of an appealingly imaginative and romantic, but married, man. In the sacrifice prefigured in the title, she must weigh her aspirations for freedom and personal pleasure against her need for security. Readers who have built up their hopes that María Eugenia will break free of her constricting environment will be especially horrified by those pages in which the heroine expresses satisfaction over her own domination by her stodgy fiancé, although María Eugenia quickly recovers from this paroxysm of submission. In the final passages, de la Parra has no scruples about resorting to melodramatic twists and turns as the heroine swings back and forth between her alternatives.

The link between the Greek myth of Iphigenia, particularly as Euripides elaborated it in his *Iphigenia in Aulis,* and the story of María Eugenia is charged with more of de la Parra's ironies. In an obvious contrast, Iphigenia's sacrifice gives her heroic stature, while María Eugenia's turns her into a figure of capitulation. Iphigenia offers herself to be sacrificed in order to bring justice and glory to Greece, while María Eugenia's motive is a desire for comfort and security. But even so, parallelisms emerge: in both Iphigenia's story and María Eugenia's, there is a comment on a society's willingness to sacrifice the well-being of its

daughters. María Eugenia is a disappointing Iphigenia, but the reader is supposed to experience disillusionment over the outcome of the heroine's conflict. The important point is that the disappointment be aimed, not at the protagonist who was struggling spiritedly in an unsupportive environment, but at the society that headed her toward surrender.

While de la Parra was the object of a widespread public fascination during the time she was writing and serializing *Iphigenia*, she became the target of negative criticism after the book was published. While the complaints were many and varied—some local readers felt that Caracas was not described in its proper beauty—the dominant objection was that the novel was immoral and might harm young female readers. A number of readers were offended that the heroine considered her respectable marriage a defeat in life and criticized her as a light-minded creature obsessed with showing off her beauty and seeking pleasure. De la Parra vigorously defended her book; among other arguments, she stated that the book's detractors were men, while women readers recognized the accuracy of *Iphigenia*'s vision of society.

Teresa de la Parra has been coming in for a rediscovery in recent years, principally for *Iphigenia* but also for her 1929 *Las memorias de Mamá Blanca.* Translated into English as *Mama Blanca's Souvenirs* (1959), the later novel offers a more lyrical and celebratory treatment of the culture of traditional upper-class women. Here a household full of women, with their feminine occupations and their intimate conversations, is nostalgically recalled by a narrator now well into adulthood.

Perhaps because of its genteel setting, upper-class heroine, and the subtly ironic way it presents ideas, *Iphigenia* was not fully perceived as a work of social criticism until after the 1960s-1970s resurgence of feminism, which affected the reading of many existing literary texts. The novel is now especially prized for its early recognition that Latin American women living in conservative environments, while no less in need of change than their counterparts in fast-moving European and U.S. cities, would necessarily approach the issues of women's role and status from a different background and perspective and face a different set of obstacles.

NOTES

[1] The source of this information is Louis Antoine Lemaître's biography *Between Flight and Longing: The Journey of Teresa de la Parra* (New York: Vantage Press, 1986), p. 60.

[2] Ibid., p. 65.

[3] Laura M. Febres, *Cinco perspectivas críticas sobre la obra de Teresa de la Parra* (Caracas: Editorial Arte, 1984), p. 14.

[4] Amaya Llebot, cited in Febres, *Cinco perspectivas,* p. 15.

Richard Rosa and Doris Sommer (essay date 1995)

SOURCE: "Teresa de la Parra: America's Womanly Soul," *Reinterpreting the Spanish American Essay*. Austin: University of Texas Press, 1995, pp. 115-24.

[*Rosa and Sommer show the vital role that women play in the evolving history of Latin America, characterized by doña Marina in* Mamá Blanca].

Invited to talk about herself, Teresa de la Parra (1889-1936), in a series of lectures written for Bogotá and rehearsed in Havana, preferred to talk about her venerable lineage of intensely verbal and efficacious women. Rather than tokenize her female self, Parra located her accomplishments in a long line of accomplished women, all Spanish American women, in fact, from the Conquest on. **"Influencia de la mujer en la formación del alma americana" ("The Influence of Women in the Formation of the American Soul")** is the general title for her three lectures of 1930 (***Obra*** 471-528). They are Parra's only production of anything like formal essays, perhaps because her life was short and so strained, in the last decade, by fatal tuberculosis. The talks were apparently an enormous success, with crowds spilling over the balconies and into hallways and with enthusiastic coverage from the press. Enormously entertaining to read, they must have been even more delightful to hear, given Parra's personal charm and her lament—through the narrator of *Las memorias de Mamá Blanca* (***Mama Blanca's Memoirs***, 1929)—that the written word kills the musical spirit of language.

Evocations of doña Marina's (Malinche's) flair for negotiations and forgiveness during the Conquest of Mexico, the genre of oral epistles that includes, for example, Sor Juana's occasional sonnets to the vicereine, long quotes from anonymous "Amarilis" who represents so many unpublished and unknown colonial women poets screened from view and from the corrupting heat of the tropics, are all memorable, thanks to Parra's delivery. But one wonders if the crowds came away with any substantive information or result that was not already announced by the apparently benign title of the lectures. Perhaps these performances were merely occasions for dwelling on loving detail, a talent that Parra's fans knew how to appreciate when they invited her to speak.

This harmless hearing will, however, miss a radically female, if not feminist, departure from standard essays and histories. It will miss the provocation in the very title of the talks. Women's "influence" for Teresa de la Parra is no meek intervention; it is definitive in the history of the Americas. Influence here carries something of Harold Bloom's meaning, so strong that it provokes unconquerable anxiety. Quoting Oscar Wilde on the problem, Bloom worries about it: "Because to influence a person is to give him one's own soul . . . He becomes an echo of someone else's music, an actor of a part that has not been written for him" (6). In their charming, apparently frivolous and inoffensive review of Latin America's history from the Conquest to independence, Parra's essays

in fact perform an outrageous occlusion of the men who have been giving themselves credit for forging history. Parra leaves them behind as she foregrounds female fashioners. History's men occupy the same laughably dignified space that the authoritarian but ineffectual father inhabits in ***Las memorias de Mamá Blanca***: "the thankless role of God." The presumed superiority of Cortés over doña Marina, for example, or of Lope de Vega over the "Amarilis" who sent him pseudonymous poetry, is chastened in Parra's rereadings. And the pattern of reducing male presumption in the face of female agency repeats so consistently throughout the lectures that by the last one, when Simón Bolívar himself turns out to be the product of female creativity and the beneficiary of female valor, the reader has been trained to wink at the text with more complicity than skepticism.

Probably one of doña Marina's earliest apologists,[1] Teresa de la Parra credits her with the most difficult and crucial maneuvers accomplished during the Mexican campaign. She mediated, mitigated the conflict, and set the tone for a truly catholic conciliation, figured by the scene of her own forgiving conciliation with the mother who sold her into slavery.

> *There is no mission that she fails to perform, no peace proposals that she does not preside at along with Cortés. She goes about sweetening the bitterness as she translates everyone's discourse. This faith in her intervention, as if it were a secret Providence, guides us continuously through the countless crises that Bernal Díaz narrates.*

> (482)

If only she had been in his story of "la noche triste" (a major defeat by the Aztecs), Parra's ideal reader might lament, that night would have been less calamitous. But her very real presence in Díaz's book is what Parra finds most noteworthy. As a simple man attentive to detail and to surprise, unlike the official historian Gómara whose writing was more prescribed by bureaucratic form, Bernal Díaz writes in a popular vein that Parra identifies with her own. Being "so full of trivial detail!," his book never hesitates to dwell on Marina in the midst of heroic history. "She will be the polestar of his story, which is not really a history but something loftier and more beautiful: a prose ballad" (484).

Marina's epoch-making words are reported, not recorded. This is true also for El Inca Garcilaso's mother, and for the numberless passionate patriots who fueled independence in their kitchens, bedrooms, and sometimes in unconquerable movement from one liberated point to another. It is as if women's work, performed consistently, efficaciously, quietly, had no need of self-glorifying signatures, a sure sign of (male) insecurity. Garcilaso signs his own name to his mother's stories, "the highest pinnacle," in Parra's estimation, of his *Comentarios reales*.

> *Memoirs of his childhood, memories of memories that others told him, converge there and unite through love the two main currents that will form the future*

American nation. . . . It is the echo of the maternal voice, which, under the stars at night, used to tell him the legends of the Incan tradition.

(489)

By recording them in Spanish, Garcilaso evidently appropriates Incan lore into his Spanish (patriarchal) code. But underneath the legal language, Parra points out, lies the organizing rhythm and music of a mother's world.

That unaffected musicality, and the patient repetition of narrative lines, sets the tone for the entire colonial period, according to Teresa de la Parra. It is a quintessentially feminine period that drew time in reassuring circles. For her, the colony transpires in the chronotope we associate with traditional, anonymous fiction; it is a matrix of stories without a particular subject or signature. Anonymity is the decisive sign here. To refuse to identify oneself as a singular subject leaves the discursive space open, accommodating, ironically democratic. Said otherwise, history is beside the point in colonial life: "Naive and happy, like peoples who have no history, the Colony closes itself off entirely behind the Church, the home, and the convent" (490).

And yet anonymity itself, even the cloistered life of convent and kitchen, would—by a paradox of male politics—marshal colonial women for history. When Spain expelled the Jesuits from America in 1767 in an effort to police partisans for independence, it simultaneously closed America's women off from their repetitive, cloistered lives and produced more local patriots than it imagined. Unhappy, but also unfettered, women would wonder about the future. On the one hand, since the Crown had shown that it held nothing to be holy, the Crown could not presume any legitimate authority. On the other hand, with their "spiritual dictators" gone, women met the "emotional catastrophe" by adjusting Catholicism to the tropics, feminizing it, which amounted to paganizing Christianity (512). Once they reduced mortal sin to a vague abstraction, and once the terrible God of the Inquisition began to look more and more like the lord of a plantation whose paternalism extended to financing and presiding over African dances, the vacancy left by old authority would welcome such revolutionaries as Voltaire and Rousseau. For Teresa de la Parra, it was not the famous men, celebrated in histories, who really won independence; instead, political freedom was an anonymous and collective confection of their more modest mates (513).

The most dramatic example of official overestimation, as already mentioned, was Simón Bolívar himself. He was not merely influenced by women, even in the strong sense Parra intends here; he was practically created by them. Bolívar appears on Parra's pages as a blank figure on whom others—mostly women—inscribe their desire, their fiction. His mentor, Simón Rodríguez, is another mercurial figure whose significance comes from presiding over those women. Rodríguez is one of those men, Parra taunts, who have "gotten too close to genius without ever reaching it, and go mad." In one of his transports, he cast Bolívar in the role of Rousseau's Emile. But it was Bolívar's cousin

in Paris, Fany de Villars, who would bring the role to life on the stage of her elegant salon. Influence, here (remembering Wilde's worry), is literally giving "an actor . . . a part that has not been written for him." "Fany sized him up with one glance and decided to open up the doors of success to him" (522). But in translating Rodríguez's enlightened desire to Fany's feminine fantasy, the featured actor of American freedom will have changed from educable Emile to Chateaubriand's romantic René. Fany is the one who anoints Bolívar's brow, like the Old Testament prophet who turned goatherd into king, before she launched the liberator's fateful journey home. Like Cortés' Marina and Garcilaso's mother, Bolívar's cousin is the voice that conditions American history.

The point in all three essays seems to be consistent, and almost predicts the fashion for social history that would develop alongside contemporary feminism: women make history just as (or because) they make homes. But beyond affirming the decisive and salutary influence of women, the essays show a marked indifference to coherent argumentation, unless, of course, the argument is simply that women have been making the decisive differences in history. Whether those differences seem restrictive or revolutionary from the perspective of official history, Parra's point is that women's work is always a balm and a blessing. Like Walt Whitman, that other defender of Americanism in its multifarious forms, Parra might have responded to criticism of ideological inconsistency with, "Do I contradict myself? Very well, I contradict myself." (It is tempting to speculate that their same-sex eroticism freed both writers, in some measure, from simple hierarchies and defensive preferences.) Still, there seems to be no contradiction at the meta-ideological level of theme: women have civilized the continent through the virtues of unconditional love and self-sacrifice, the very virtues that Catholicism worships in a feminized God and in his virginal mother.

I had begun to prepare, in these three lectures, a kind of historical overview of feminine abnegation in our countries, that is, of the hidden but happy influence that women have exercised during the Conquest, the Colonization, and Independence. . . . I have kept, then, to my selfless women. Frankly speaking, I will tell you that down deep in my heart I prefer them: they have the charm of the past and the infinite poetry of voluntary and sincere sacrifice.

(474-475)

Here the reader will notice that Parra is *reinscribing* or reaffirming the theme, admitting that second thoughts intervened between the formulation and the conclusion. In fact, on the previous page of this first lecture, two minutes earlier for the listening public, she had said, "The crisis that today's women are confronting cannot be resolved by preaching submission, submission and more submission, as was the practice during the time when a quiet life could be confined entirely behind doors" (473).

Rather than noting what might be—and no doubt has been—taken as woman's generic failure to be consistent, we may choose to read the contradiction as Parra herself thematizes it. She offers two reasons for simultaneously praising and resisting female self-sacrifice. One is the chronological and developmental differences that separate modern women from their foremothers of the Conquest through independence.

> *My affection for the Colony will never bring me to say, as some do in lyrical moments, that I would have wanted to be born then. No. I feel very well in my own time and I admire it. As far as it concerns me, I should say that almost all of my childhood was colonial and that the need to react against it, at a moment in which we are all revolutionaries—as much because of a spirit that demands justice as because of a spirit that practices petulance—that need was the cause that made me into a writer.*

(490)

The self-attribution of petulance, then, allows Parra the irony of traveling alone in short skirts and stylish hats to celebrate female confinement, whether in the nunnery ("Inside the peaceful cell, intelligence was cultivated harmoniously along with virtue, those two closed and neighboring gardens" [496]) or the equally cloistered home where Amarilis wrote unrequitable love poems to Lope de Vega. A year after Teresa de la Parra's amorous outing with Lydia Cabrera to Italy, the cosmopolitan and fiercely independent woman reflects on the splendid spiritual flights of women who found freedom from prohibitions only with their imagination.

The other reason for contradiction coyly justifies those who expect women to be confused. In Parra's version, though, the confusion is purposeful, peaceloving, perhaps prescient of feminist and deconstructive moves away from antagonistic polar oppositions. It is the loving "irresponsibility" that characterized Mamá Blanca's "disorderly soul" and resonates with her forebears:

> *I believe that as long as politicians, military men, journalists, and historians spend their lives putting antagonistic labels on things, the job for young people, simple people, and above all women, since we are many and quite disorderly, is to shuffle the labels in order to reestablish cordial confusion.*

(477)

The labels do not disappear for Parra, but they no longer distinguish between correct and incorrect, mine and yours. For example, she reviews the struggles for independence through two equally admirable, literally familial, foremothers: Great-Grandmother Panchita, a stubborn royalist, and Great-Aunt Teresa Soublette, a passionate patriot. Nevertheless, Parra's preference for peace and for the privilege her family enjoyed during "indolent" times (as if no one really slaved on plantations) amounts to preferring colonial continuity over revolutionary change. Revolution brought intolerance; "When a fight to the death came, it finished off anyone in the middle" (505). In any case, Great-Aunt Teresa's dedication to independence had more to do with love

for an illustrious father (general and president) than with love of country. Parra repeats her critique of revolution in letters from her tuberculosis sanatorium, letters to Lydia Cabrera about plans to write a novel about Bolívar: "I am now convinced," Parra writes in 1932, "that with Bolívar in control of that poor Caracas of one hundred thirty years ago, with its forty thousand inhabitants, the city left the Colony behind, along with all the enchantments, virtues, and graces that any city in history might have had. That's why I'm not anti-Spanish, Cabra" (Hiriart 152).

Fans of Teresa de la Parra will find downright embarrassing other expressions of privileged conservatism in both her essays and the letters. Black slaves are commended for their loyalty (one would never guess at the history of rebellions throughout the Americas), and Spaniards fomented revolutionary resentment by strategically favoring *pardos,* or mulattoes, who were the "natural enemies" of the white criollos (510). Miscegenation is evidently at the root of political confusion, as are the peevish complaints of students in Machado's contemporary Cuba and Gómez's dictatorial Venezuela. "I say, just as Goethe used to say, that `I prefer to suffer the injustice of tyranny over the injustice of disorder.' That's why I'm a Gómez supporter, to a certain point, and I would have been for Machado too, if only to oppose the false apostles" (Hiriart 155).

The panegyric to long-suffering maternal mitigators of conflict in the third essay comes as no surprise, given this preference for stability, any stability, which amounts to a horror of politics. It underlines the general moral about female fostering announced in the title of these talks and repeated throughout.

> *During more than three centuries they had worked in the shadow, like bees; without leaving a name, they left us their creation of wax and honey. They wove, with their abnegation, the patriarchal spirit of the criollo family. And by caressing the language with their voices, they worked into its fabric all the cadences and sweetness of their daydreams.*

(513)

What may be surprising, though, are the final pages of accolades for the gutsy woman who thrived precisely on social and military conflict, Manuelita Sáenz, "La Libertadora." Like other commentators, Parra remembers her for saving Bolívar's life in 1828, and for her progressively more military and provocative outfits. But she also remembers Manuelita for blasting the very conventions that made other women so admirably submissive: "Manuelita is interesting in the extreme, for more than just her picturesque flair. She also represents, if one considers the case well, a violent protest against woman's traditional servitude, and against a future that promised only the not-always-open door of marriage" (524).

Where in this conclusion is the praise of mitigation, of a bias toward conserving and tolerating apolitical neutrality? Men do us the favor, Parra had said in the first essay, of soiling their hands in politics so that we can remain true angels of our national and continental houses. Military service, suffragism, and public debate were all thankfully beyond the protective limits of domestic spirituality (474). And yet the essays end in a defiant and sustained embrace of military and combative Manuelita. Is this because the female "liberator" prepares a future in which woman and wife are no longer synonymous in Spanish, a future that Teresa de la Parra can freely inhabit, intimately with Lydia Cabrera, for example? To this loving friend, forty-three-year-old ailing Parra would complain that her own traditional mother and sister threatened to infantilize her.

> *A plan to reduce me again to a minor, under an iron tutelage where they would have the deciding voices. I'm about ready for such a plan! Although I understand that I'm being ill mannered, and that I should be grateful for their efficiency, the business about arranging the house has made me furious. . . . I'd be more likely to kill myself doing foolish things, given my contradictory nature, and make them see that they can't dominate me.*

(Hiriart 147)

Of course it is possible that Teresa de la Parra's liberating embrace of Manuelita is neither proleptic nor programmatic of rebelliousness. It may be simply another, outlying example of Parra's inclusive gesture in these essays about women. She includes them all, whether it takes nostalgia or utopian projections to do so. Meek Amarilis merits inclusion for her meekness, proud Panchita for her pride, and manly Manuelita for her transgressive *vir*-tues. The point is that everything fits into a woman's soul, and by extension into the feminized soul of America celebrated in Parra's essays. Like ***Las memorias de Mamá Blanca***, the essays are structured like a fan, opening a new fold with each page. Reading them becomes an unfamiliar but deliciously dizzying exercise in following the folds as they zigzag in and out of apparent contradictions. The folds would ideally add up to a conflicted but inclusive history. And even where some wrinkles are evidently stuck, as in the forgotten or purposefully excluded heroines of ethnic struggles (since Catholic Hispanism here is universal by definition), the gift of Parra's accommodating form is that it has the potential to fan out more fully in other hands.

NOTES

[1] See more recent revisions of la Malinche, for example the work by Enríquez and Mirande.

WORKS CITED

Bloom, Harold. *The Anxiety of Influence.* Oxford: Oxford University Press, 1973.

Enriquez, Evangelia, and Alfredo Mirande. "Liberation, Chicana Style: Colonial Roots of Feministas Chicanas." *De Colores* 4:3 (1978), 7-21.

Hiriart, Rosario. *Cartas a Lydia Cabrera: Correspondencia inédita de Gabriela Mistral y Teresa de la Parra.* Madrid: Ediciones Torremozas, 1988.

Parra, Teresa de la. *Obra: Narrativa, ensayos, cartas.* Selección y estudio de Velia Bosch. Caracas: Biblioteca Ayacucho, 1982.

FURTHER READING

Fox-Lockert, Lucia. "Teresa de la Parra." *Women Novelists in Spain and Spanish America,* pp. 156-65. Metuchen, N. J.: Scarecrow Press, Inc., 1979.

> Critiques *Iphigenia* as a picture of ambivalence and despair, clinging desperately to the men in her life, to her grandmother, and to her concepts of what life holds for her in dreams.

Krieger Gambarini, Elsa. "The Male Critic and the Woman Writer: Reading Teresa de la Parra's Critics." *In the Feminine Mode,* Noel Valis and Carol Maier, eds., pp. 177-94. Lewisburg: Bucknell University Press, 1990.

> Studies the variable between a traditional feminine literary structure of dualism as observed by male critics.

Nance, Kimberly Ann. "Pied Beauty: Juxtaposition and Irony in Teresa de la Parra's *Las memorias de Mamá Blanca.*" *Letras Femeninas,* Vol. XVI, Nos. 1-2 (1990): 45-49.

> Explores social class, the use of names, and de la Parra's development of plot and theme with the use of action.

Parra, Teresita J. "Feminist Ideas in the Works of Clorinda Matto de Turner, Teresa de la Parra, and Maria Luisa Bombal." *Multicultural Literatures through Feminist/Poststructuralist Lenses,* Barbara Frey Waxman, ed., pp. 152-72. Knoxville: University of Tennessee Press, 1993.

> Compares three South American writers and their personal afronts against patriarchy as it presents itself in their countries.

Schade, George D. "*Las Memorias de Mamá Blanca*: A Literary Tour de Force." *Hispania,* Vol. XXXIX, No. 2 (May 1956): 157-60.

> Praise *Las Memorias* for its fresh style and truthful depictions of life viewed through the eyes of a child.

Carlos Pellicer
1899-1977

Mexican poet and historian.

INTRODUCTION

Carlos Pellicer is lauded as one of the most original voices in Mexican poetry. Known for his rich visual imagery and depth of emotion, Pellicer is a poet of inspiration who faithfully records the life and culture of his native Mexico.

Pellicer was born on November 4, 1899, in Villahermosa, Mexico, to Carlos and Deifilia Camara de Pellicer. After graduating from Escuela Nacional Prepatoria, Pellicer entered the School of Electrical and Mechanical Engineering at the Polytechnic Institute in Mexico City, upon the urging of his family. Realizing the he wanted to be a writer, Pellicer left the school and traveled to Europe to study literature. He published his first two collections, *Colores en el mar y otros poemas* (1921) and *Piedra de sacrificios, Poema iberoamericano* (1924) and gained almost immediate recognition in the artistic community. In addition to his work as a poet, he was variously a member of the diplomatic corps in Colombia and other countries; a university professor of modern poetry; the director of the Ministry of Fine Arts; the founding curator of the Museo-Parque de la Venta; and the director of the Palacio de Bellas Artes. Pellicer had a profound love of Mexico, its people, and its history, and he was very involved in the creation of several archaeological museums throughout Mexico, including one in his home region of Tabasco. Mexico also figured prominently in Pellicer's poetry. Later in Pellicer's life, he underwent a religious conversion to Roman Catholicism which had a profound effect on his work. He turned to more spiritual concerns and to an exploration of the sacred. In 1964, Pellicer was awarded the National Prize for Literature and the following year he became the president of the Congress of Latin American Writers. In the years just before his death, Pellicer served as a senator representing Tabasco. He died of a heart attack on February 15, 1977, after undergoing surgery for peritonitis.

Pellicer is from a group of Mexican poets known as the *Contemporaneos*, but unlike other members of the group, he lacks pessimism and despair. Although an important part of his work is an expression of the tragedies inherent in American life, Pellicer's poems maintain a sense of the pure joy of existence. He is primarily a visual poet, and his poetry is filled with images of the countryside and the tropics. In his book-length study, *Carlos Pellicer*, Edward J. Mullen stated that Pellicer's work is characterized by a "dazzling and sensuous tropicalism." His poetry speaks for mankind and is concerned with humanity and social justice. Raul Leiva argued that Pellicer's "social lyricism escapes any narrow preoccupation; it is rather the pure expression of a man who knows how to live fervently in his time." Beginning with *Hora de junio* (1937; *June Hour*), Pellicer's naturalism becomes more restrained and he tackles the themes of desolation and love. In *Practica de vuela* (1956; *The Practice of Flight*), Pellicer's religious conversion becomes apparent in his work through his treatment of sacred themes. The religious poetry is not mystical in nature, but rather a celebration of God's creation of the world and the beauty and wonders it contains.

In discussing Pellicer's style, Octavio Paz said, "Pellicer is not a writer of poems but rather of poetic instants." Most reviewers praise the sense of poetic inspiration behind Pellicer's work, and the naturalness and almost inevitability of his verse. Critics laud his faithful representation of the richness of Mexico and its people, culture, and history. Most critics believe that his *Subordinaciones* (1949) represents Pellicer at his finest, exhibiting the poet's gifts of rich visual imagery and depth of feeling which set his work apart from his contemporaries.

PRINCIPAL WORKS

Colores en el mar y otros poemas (poetry) 1921
Piedra de sacrificios (poetry) 1924
6, 7 poemas (poetry) 1924
Bolívar (history) 1925
Hora y Veinte (poetry) 1927
Camino (poetry) 1929
Esquemas para una oda tropical (poetry) 1933
Estrofas del mar marino (poetry) 1934
Hora de junio (poetry) 1937
Recinto y otras imágenes (poetry) 1941
Exágonos (poetry) 1941
Subordinaciones: Poemas (poetry) 1949
Sonetos (poetry) 1950
Julio Castellanos, 1905-1947 [with Salvador Toscano] (history) 1953
Práctica de vuela (poetry) 1956
Museo de Tabasco: Guía Oficial (history) 1961
Material poético, 1918-1961 (poetry) 1962
Con palabras y fuego (poetry) 1962
Teotihuacán, y 13 de agosto: ruina de Tenochtitlán (history) 1964
Simón Bolívar, Secretaria de Educacion Publica (history) 1965
Geopolítica de Tabasco [with José Vasconcelos and Manuel R. Mora] (history) 1965

Anahuacalli: Museo Diego Rivera [with Ruth Rivera and Dolores Olmedo de Olvera] (history) 1965
Leonardo Nierman (history) 1967
Mexiko [with Max Mittler] (history) 1968
Noticias sobre Nezahualcoyotl y algunos sentimientos (history) 1972
Los manos del mexicano [with Justino Fernández and Gonzalo Obregón] (history) 1975
Esquemas para una oda tropical (history) 1976
Reincidencias (history) 1978
Cosillas para el nacimiento (history) 1978
Práctica de vuela (history) 1979
Cuaderno de viaje (history) 1987
Es un país lejano [with Negrete Martinez] (poetry)

CRITICISM

Andrew P. Debicki (essay date 1973)

SOURCE: "Perspective and Meaning in the Poetry of Carlos Pellicer," *Hispania*, Vol. 56, No. 4, December 1973, pp. 1007-13.

[*In this essay, Debicki delves into Pellicer's fusion of dual image and idea in his poetry.*]

Carlos Pellicer has gained recognition as one of the most important Mexican poets of the century. Several critics have noted his skill in portraying the vividness of nature through sensorial images, his ability to convert abstract themes into concrete experiences, and his whole-hearted commitment to poetry as a way of seizing the beauty of life.[1] Pellicer has been called the first really "modern" poet of Mexico; his work has been considered a prime example of the new life and the artistic success brought to Mexican letters by the generation of the "Contemporáneos."[2]

At first glance Pellicer's reputation may seem a little unjustified. The dominant themes of his verse, after all, echo those of an earlier poetry; a sense of wonder at the order of nature, a feeling of participation in the life of the cosmos, and the relation of nature to poetry and to religious belief—all elements which can be found in many romantic and *modernista* works. Pellicer's poetry is filled with metaphors; most of them, however, are based on reasonable and objective likeness between the two planes being compared (frequently a natural scene and a human situation). Hardly ever do we find the "new" imagery said to be typical of Pellicer's era: unusual correspondences, "visionary images," oneiric allusions, or metaphors which construct a whole new reality, different from the one that surrounds us.[3] Our poet's metaphors often recall those of nineteenth century "modernistas." Also evocative of the modernistas is Pellicer's frequent use of personified nature; his creation of mood by delineating landscapes; and his dependence on a rich descriptive vocabulary. His constant effort to capture emotions in verse also fits into a tradition of

the nineteenth century. Where then does the originality and the contemporary nature of his poetry reside?

A detailed look at Pellicer's works reveals that they often set up a very conventional scene, mood, or image; but that having done so, and having in this fashion evoked certain expectations in the reader, they dramatically shift tone or perspective. This allows them to undercut an initially complacent attitude and to produce a very original experience—without making use of "visionary images" or unusual metaphorical techniques. Some of Pellicer's poems achieve similar effects by different means: without violently changing their perspective, they nevertheless counterpose or alternate several viewpoints, scenes, or attitudes. In this manner they transcend a conventional view of their subject and offer us a new outlook. In several somewhat different ways, then, Pellicer manipulates perspective to give new life to old images and subjects and turns his admiration of the natural order into a compelling experience for the reader.

In the following untitled poem originally published in *Colores en el mar y otros poemas*, the theme of Man's longing to join nature is first presented conventionally and then modified:

> Como un fauno marino perseguí aquella ola
> suelta la cabellera y el talle azul-ondeante.
> Como un fauno marino nadé tras de la ola
> que distendió sus líneas como hembra jadeante.
>
> El Sol estaba ya viejo, pero era un rey
> que aburrido aquel día de bañarse en el mar,
> se embarcó en una nube
> y apenas si tenía algo que recordar . . .
> Yo perseguí la ola pensando que la hora
> miedo haría en la ola musculada y sonora.
>
> Pero como avanzara yo sobre el litoral,
> la ola arqueando ímpetus se retorció en la arena
>
> dejando en mi lascivia tres algas por melena
> y una gran carcajada de espumas de cristal.[4]

The beginning seems hardly original. Pellicer compares a cresting wave to a woman with flowing hair, and the speaker attracted by the wave is likened to a faun pursuing the woman. The use of similes rather than metaphors makes the comparison explicit rather than implied—and all too obvious. The images themselves echo *modernista* commonplaces, and the stanza strikes us as both blatant and worn.

The image of Sun as king (stanza two) also seems conventional. Yet we note a shift in tone and technique. By likening the sun to a king bored with swimming, Pellicer evokes a more matter-of-fact setting. (This is reinforced by the vocabulary; words like "fauno marino" and "azul ondeante" have now given way to "aburrido," "bañarse," "se embarcó.") And by using metaphor rather than simile he obtains a tighter link between planes: we are faced by a single scene rather than by the labored set of correspondences of stanza one.

Though stanza three returns to the image of the faun, it differs considerably from the beginning of the poem. Here, too, we see metaphor rather than simile: the speaker now *is* a faun, the wave a sinewy girl. The metaphor, the word "musculada," and the direct tone produce a new sense of immediacy. In this stanza even more than in the second the speaker seems to be trying to vivify the conventional scene with which the poem started.

The last stanza differs even more clearly from the first one. The basic image, true enough, remains the same. But the highly stylized beginning has given way to the specific metaphor of the wave as a lithesome, elusive and mocking girl who tricks the lascivious (and inept?) speaker. Pellicer does continue to develop his one basic image by means of visual correspondences: the movement of waves is the nymph's escape, the crashing noise is laughter. But in the process he has moved from a conventional stereotype to a sharp vignette, as human as it is unexpected. The subject of man trying to establish communion with nature and failing—hardly an original one—acquires new life.

Clearly there is humor in the last stanza, which almost seems to parody the basic image of the poem. By contrasting with the nebulous solemnity of the beginning, this stanza makes us realize how Pellicer has first set up and then completely modified a conventional image, and how he has infused life into an old theme. The whole poem illustrates beautifully the difference between a trite and an original handling of a traditional subject. The conventional portrayal of a man seeking to join nature which begins the poem is modified in the middle section, and we are shown how it can be made immediate and then turned around even more to highlight the difference between cliché and effective image.

Pellicer achieves a similar effect in **"Scherzo,"** beginning with a standard portrayal of the sea's beauty and then jarring us with some very modern allusions:

> Y el mar dorado
> que coloridas olas serpentea
> bajo los vinos suaves de la aurora.
>
> . . . . .
>
> Y las nubes llenas de semejanzas
> familiares.
> Y la alegría sin esperanza
> destas horas sin pares.
> Y el ave que halla su tono
> en el verde glorioso de la palmera.
> Y el encanto siempre desconocido
> de las olas nuevas.
>
> . . . . .
>
> Y un grito.
> Y una mujer desdibujada que lleva un pez
> y así parece anuncio de joyerías.
> Y la destreza imponderable de las olas
> que bien merece ya el premio Nobel
> por cultura física y dos o tres más cosas . . .

> Y mi juventud un poco salvaje
> que sienta bien al paisaje.
> Y el poema que nunca se canta
> pero que siempre se adivina. .
> Porque está en mi cabeza y en mi garganta
> el elogio habitual de las marinas.
>
> (***Material poético***, pp. 121-22)

The first series of images effectively reflects the beauty of the seascape; the anaphora creates a measured effect; each sentence begins with "y," underlining the tranquil happiness evoked by the scene. The reader, however, long accustomed to "poetic" representations of idyllic seascapes, may treat the poem as yet another conventional praise of nature's glories and pay scant attention.

Almost lulled by the chain of conventional vignettes beginning with "y," he is brought to an abrupt stop by the brief sentence "y un grito" and by the images that follow. The joking allusion to the Nobel prize, the personification of waves as athletes, and the modern image of a jewelry store advertisement call attention to themselves and break the previous mood. They also help the reader accept the viewpoint of the speaker; the latter turns out to be not a sentimental admirer of conventional seascapes, but a modern man possessed of a sense of humor, who can perceive unusual correspondences and who can even parody his previous outlook.

The shift in perspective does not negate the positive view of nature which has been developed. The "modern" images, like the earlier ones, point to the surprising beauty of the scene and underline the sense of elation which it evokes in the speaker. But the change does make it easier for us to accept the view offered, to judge it tenable rather than sentimental, and to agree with the speaker that such a scene has poetry in it. Thanks to this change, the man has become more credible and more exciting.

An obvious change of perspective occurs in the following poem, one of a group entitled *Exágonos*:

> Cuando el transtlántico pasaba
> bajo el arco verde oro de la aurora,
> las sirenas aparecieron coronadas
> con las últimas rosas
> pidiéndonos sandwiches y champagne.
> Se olvidaron las islas, y se hundieron las costas.
>
> (p. 315)

Even though a modern ship is mentioned, the first four lines constitute a rather standard evocation of nature coupled with a conventional mythological allusion. The last two lines then startle us and break the impression of a stylized world.

Although this last poem ends up destroying the idealized vision with which it began, while the two previously analyzed merely modify their initial outlooks, all three employ a similar technique and achieve similar effects. By setting up a conventional vision and then shifting to a more ironic perspective, each one saves itself from triteness and from sentimentality.[5] Each illustrates how Pellicer's poetry transcends a cliché praise of nature.

Although **"Grupos de palomas"** does not surprise us by undercutting a conventional view, it nevertheless uses diverse viewpoints to embody successfully an important theme. The first stanza of the poem portrays a stylized natural scene:

> Los grupos de palomas,
> notas, claves, silencios, alteraciones,
> modifican el ritmo de la loma.
> La que se sabe tornasol afina
> las ruedas luminosas de su cuello
> con mirar hacia atrás a su vecina.
> Le da al sol la mirada
> y escurre en una sola pincelada
> plan de vuelos a nubes campesinas.
>
> (p. 162)

The initial image already stresses the aesthetic effect of the scene rather than its literal presence: the doves relate to the hill as notes and sections of a musical composition relate to the whole. Pellicer again stresses the artistic effect and leaves behind the concrete scene by describing the characteristic head-turning of the dove as a way of "tuning" its neck. He does so once more by linking the dove's flight to a painter's brush stroke (line 8). These images do more than stylize the scene; by introducing references to several artistic disciplines, they also invite us to consider the relationship between diverse artistic disciplines and perspectives. The scene has served to suggest how the arts handle and enhance reality.

Stanza three of this poem seems very different from the first one:

> Hay una casi negra
> que bebe astillas de agua en una piedra.
> Después se pule el pico,
> mira sus uñas, ve las de las otras,
> abre un ala y la cierra, tira un brinco
> y se para debajo de las rosas.
> El fotógrafo dice:
> para el jueves, señora.
> Un palomo amontona sus *erres* cabeceadas,
> y ella busca alfileres
> en el suelo que brilla por nada.
>
> (pp. 162-63)

Again the images are what stands out. But instead of stylizing the doves and making them catalysts for an artistic perspective, these images now evoke a pedestrian reality. Basing himself on the restless motion of the dove and on the visual resemblance between its pecking and a woman's gestures, Pellicer conjures up caricatures of overly fussy ladies, primping for a photographer and nervously hunting pins.

In its other stanzas the poem offers yet other images and perspectives. One dove is likened to a traveller in a gray dress who adds an element of surprise to her surround-

ings; another, a white one, is identified with a clean perfection; a group of doves taking flight becomes a geometric figure. The work ends by repeating again its second line, now with full stops between words (creating a frame around the poem), and by adding a whimsical allusion to its composition, to song, perhaps to poetry:

> Notas. Claves. Silencios. Alteraciones.
> El lápiz se descubre, se inclinan las lomas,
> y por 20 centavos se cantan las canciones.
>
> (p. 163)

Although they differ from each other, all the perspectives adopted in **"Grupos de palomas"** transform an ordinary scene into something quite different from itself. Throughout the poem the doves have become a means of recalling and projecting many realities and attitudes found in the world. By bringing forth these diverse realities from a single everyday scene, Pellicer makes us realize how such a scene can be a catalyst for a poet and how a poet can make rich meanings out of his materials.

Had this poem limited itself to one of its perspectives, it would have remained a rather good example of conventional metaphor. By combining and counterposing them all, it becomes a dramatic embodiment of the power of poetry. The theme of artistic expression is of course introduced directly in the first stanza. But the value of poetry and the arts becomes much more meaningful to us as we observe all the different visions which the poet Pellicer here weaves out of his one ordinary scene.[6] (The whimsical ending, making us notice the presence of a speaker-poet who has been remaking reality in this work, underlines this subject one more time.)

A similar effect is achieved in another poem alluding to several artistic perspectives:

> En negro se desafina
> la penumbra de la tarde.
> ¿Y el corazón? Tarde a tarde
> a la muerte se encamina.
>
> Árbol negro. La silueta
> torna el paisaje elegante.
> Una tarde sin poeta,
> un amante sin amante.
>
> Aguafuerte inacabada.
> La postrer ola en la arena
> como una larga pisada.
>
> (p. 31)

The first image is based on music; lines five and six make us see the scene as a sketch; line nine defines it as an etching. These references to different artistic media stylize the poem, helping differentiate it from a romantic lament. They provide a detachment needed when dealing with the traditional subject of a landscape which evokes a nostalgic mood. They also take the emphasis off this mood and off the romantic scene itself; they direct us instead to a more general topic, the ways in which nature can be transformed into art in order to embody human emotions.

Somewhat different references to the arts appear in **"Estudio."** Here a city observed by the poet is first treated as a subject for poetic transformation. Later on, allusions to Monet and to Rembrandt connect the scene to an impressionistic painting and to the Flemish artist's work:

> Jugaré con las casas de Curazao,
> pondré el mar a la izquierda
> y haré más puentes movedizos.
> ¡Lo que diga el poeta!
>
> . . . . .
>
> Por la tarde vendrá Claude Monet
> a comer cosas azules y eléctricas.
> Y por esa callejuela sospechosa
> haremos pasar la Ronda de Rembrandt.
> . . . pásame el puerto de Curazao!
>
> (p. 29)

Allusions to various artistic perspectives again make us view the scene recalled—and reality in general—as a reservoir of possibilities for the creative artist.

Pellicer quite clearly uses multiple perspectives—frequently those of the different arts—to transcend mere description, or even the creation of vivid metaphors. By offering several viewpoints within a poem, he invites us to note the artistry involved and to perceive how the creative impulse can transform reality. Just as in the first three poems discussed he shifts from a conventionally "poetic" view to a matter-of-fact one in order to transcend a routine praise of nature, so in these last four he has combined perspectives in order to transcend description, to create unique visions, and to suggest the power of art and poetry over reality.

In other poems, Pellicer works together evocations of different places and times. "Concierto breve," for example, is based on remembrances of Bruges. The city is described as it might appear to a modern traveller. But a reference to a fifteenth-century Flemish painter leads to memories of Mexican landscapes and artists:

> Hans Memling me pregunta:
> ¿Cómo están mis discípulos de Pátzcuaro?
>
> —Maestro: todos los detalles te saludan,
> tus discípulos pintan . . .
>
> (Venado azul de Pátzcuaro que corres bajo el
>   sorbo
> de agua que en la jornada me dio mano silvestre;
>
> (p. 244)

The initial perspective of the poem, that of a city as observed by a traveller, is altered by these references to different times and places. At the same time the allusions to artists again bring in the theme of creation.[7]

The poem moves beyond the literal and the descriptive and suggests the timelessness and universality of the arts. In another poem, a vignette of Cyprus motivates allusions to Greek myths, to historical events, and to modern elements, and again brings in the theme of poetry:

> Chypre. El buque cruza frente a Paphos.
> Una boya flotante dice en portugués:
> "Aqui nasciou Aphrodita."
> Restos de espuma, de jabón, de esplendor y de fe.
>
> 4, 5, 6, 7 poemas
> para estas aguas de nadadora coloración,
> para los finos cambios que las montañas sesgan,
> los soles corridos y el aire del sol.
>
> En la divina isla, la luz alerta
> caza nubes. Volad
> brisas de Napoleón, hidroaviones-sirenas,
> Paphos cuaja su perla sobre el mar.
>
> (p. 187)

The changes in perspective that so frequently appear in Pellicer's poetry do differ from each other: some consist of dramatic shifts which undercut conventional outlooks; others are formed by a gradual accumulation of viewpoints. Several are caused by references to various arts, while the last ones we have seen are based on allusions to different times and places. All these changes, nevertheless, force the poems out of conventional molds: they eliminate the possibility of our seeing these poems as realistic descriptions, they undercut routine visions of nature, they destroy the appearance of traditional "modernista" metaphors. They can all be considered examples of what Carlos Bousoño has called "superposiciones": combinations of different planes which intrude on each other and destroy the limitation of a conventional outlook.[8] Very often these changes are used by Pellicer to highlight the value of poetry. They help him not only assert but demonstrate how an artistic vision transcends the boundaries of literal reality and creates original experiences.

Even in poems which do not contain shifts in perspective Pellicer often achieves the same results which we have been noting. The following lines are taken from another poem entitled **"Estudio"**:

> La sandía pintada de prisa
> contaba siempre
> los escandalosos amaneceres
> de mi señora
> la aurora.
>
> . . . . .
>
> ¡Estamos tan contentas de ser así!
> Dijeron las peras frías y cinceladas.
> Las manzanas oyeron estrofas persas
> cuando vieron llegar a las granadas.
> Los que usamos ropa interior de seda . . .
> dijo una soberbia guanábana.

. . . . .

Salían
de sus *eses* redondas las naranjas.

(p. 168)

The picture drawn seems delightfully unusual. Yet on examining the images we realize that these are based on objective characteristics of the fruit. (The haphazardly varied colors of a watermelon suggest fast painting, the smooth and sculptured appearance of a pear corresponds to cool smugness, the soft white interior of a *guanábana* recalls silk underwear.) The personifications also have an easily understandable basis: a dawn of several sharp colors creates an impact, as does a woman causing a scandal. These techniques-objectively based metaphors and personifications—cannot of themselves account for the impact produced.

The ways in which Pellicer develops likenesses between the fruit and human characters does help explain this impact. We admire the ingenuity with which a human vignette or caricature is constructed on the basis of each object's appearance. Several times Pellicer uses double meanings to stress the connection: "fría" describes the feel of the pear, but also alludes to the icy disposition of a smug woman; "soberbia" refers both to the fruit (here it means "great") and to the snobbish lady (who is "arrogant"). The poet makes the pears and the *guanábanas* speak set phrases-really clichés-which evoke caricatures of smug, arrogant people. The objective tone of the poet himself contrasts with these clichés and with the exclamatory tone in which they are uttered, stressing even more the absurdity of the human types represented by the personified fruit. (In the first lines, the speaker adopts a playful tone which prepares us for the caricatures that follow.) It seems as if every detail were used to dramatize the human situation which has been derived from the images of the fruits.

All this makes the poem an eye-catching combination of two different planes. Though the metaphoric techniques used here may not be so innovative, the linking of these planes to create sharp human vignettes is most effective. Pellicer has used poetic art to relate the world of inert vegetables with that of human personalities, and to make life look very different-and more interesting-than the way it appears to our everyday point of view. (He has even used sound to heighten this creation of a new perspective. We note repeated alliterations in *s* throughout the poem, which produce a soft effect and remove us further from any matter-of-fact description. The visual image of oranges emerging from s-shaped peels connects with this alliteration, and helps underline the imaginative transformation of reality which has been taking place.)

Something similar occurs in **"Grupos de palmeras"**:

Los grupos de palmeras
—edad de 20 a 30, estado célibe,
libre oficio-secundan el poema.

Ceñir la brisa o desnudar el viento,
inaugurar el mundo cada día,
esas palmeras son Río de Janeiro.

Una tarde en avión las vi bañarse
entre aguas repentinas que surgían
del fragmento de tierra de las alas.

Los grupos de palmeras
-idénticos detalles
siguen las curvas altas del poema.

. . . . .

Palmera real, cintura luminosa, rodeos de la
    danza,
final de todo viaje
a cielo azul. ¡Se pierde la esperanza
y una palmera real es el paisaje!

(p 275)

The metaphor of palm trees as young girls has a recognizable visual basis: a cluster of similar palm trees can easily call to mind a group of graceful females. But again Pellicer goes beyond the mere comparison. He adds details to the characterization of the trees, making them carefree twenty-year olds and constructing a vignette of human life. Later he identifies the graceful shapes of the personified trees with poetry and with dance; this not only underlines the vignette constructed before, but also brings in the larger theme of beauty (natural and human) as a source of art.

Again Pellicer has established a correspondence between a natural and a human plane, developed it beyond the initial metaphor, and used it to embody a constant theme of his work: the wonderful beauty of our cosmos and its value as a basis for art. In this poem, as in the one previously discussed, a metaphor expands into a counterposition of planes in order to develop a new perspective and capture an important theme.

These last two poems, like all the others we have seen, balance off different planes to trascend a routine vision and a conventional experience. This procedure, so common to Pellicer's work, is excellently fitted to the prevalent subjects of this work: the beauty and excitement offered us by the natural world and the value of poetry in portraying this beauty and this excitement. The form and the content fit perfectly together to create a unique experience, making Pellicer's work first-rate poetry.

NOTES

[1] See the excellent study by Frank Dauster in his *Ensayos sobre poesía mexicana: asedio a los "Contemporáneos"* (México: Ediciones de Andrea, 1963), pp. 45-57; Luis Rius, "El material poético de Carlos Pellicer," *Cuadernos americanos*, 21 (Sept.-Oct. 1962), 239-70; and Luis Monguió, "Poetas postmodernistas mexicanos, *Revista hispánica moderna*, 12 (July-Oct. 1946), 254-55.

[2] See Octavio Paz, *Las peras del olmo* (México: Imprenta Universitaria, 1957), pp. 95-104. Pellicer, born in Villahermosa (Tabasco) in 1899, has

published many books of poetry since the first one appeared in 1921. His work previous to 1961 is collected in *Material poético (1918-1961)* (México: Universidad Nacional, 1962); in 1969 a brief *Primera antología poética* of his was published by the Fondo de Cultura Económica in Mexico.

The dominant characteristics of Pellicer's work can be found in all his books. The use of varying perspectives seems to be one of the constant traits of his work; I will use examples from different eras. The themes treated by Pellicer do change in time: at one point love poetry gains great importance, and at another a religious view of nature.

³ This has been perceptively pointed out by Octavio Paz (*Las peras del olmo*, pp. 101-02). For a discussion of "visionary images," see Carlos Bousoño, *Teoría de la expresión poética*, 5th ed. (Madrid: Ed. Gredos, 1970), vol. I, 140-51.

⁴ Pellicer, *Material poético*, p. 18; later references to this volume will be made in parentheses in the text. All quotations in this study are taken from this volume.

⁵ Robert Penn Warren has discussed the way in which irony can protect a work from sentimentalism in "Pure and Impure Poetry," published in the *Kenyon Review* in 1943 and reprinted in *Criticism: The Foundations of Modern Literary Judgment*, ed. Mark Schorer (New York: Harcourt, Brace & Co., 1948), pp. 367-78.

⁶ Merlin Forster has very effectively discussed Pellicer's handling of the theme of poetry in "El concepto de la creación poética en la obra de Carlos Pellicer," *Comunidad* [Mexico], 4 (1966), 684-88.

⁷ Forster has indicated that Pellicer sees a great connection between poetry and painting, which is reflected in his own work; he quotes a letter of Pellicer's in which the latter states that music, painting, and written poems are three ways of expressing poetic insights. See Forster, pp. 684-85.

⁸ Bousoño, op. cit., pp. 303-336.

George Melnykovich   (essay date 1974)

SOURCE: "Carlos Pellicer and *Creacionismo*," *Latin American Literary Review*, Vol. 2, No. 4, Spring-Summer 1974, pp. 95-111.

[*Malnykovich presents Pellicer as an example and arbiter of* creacionismo *in his sensuous fusion of abstraction and reality.*]

The first two decades of the twentieth century shaped the artistic avant-garde in Europe and the Americas and gave birth to a multitude of *isms*. Cubism, Dadaism, Expressionism, Imagism, Futurism, Surrealism, and Ultraism are some of the major movements that formulated modern aesthetic theories. In Latin America the most influential *ismo* during the burgeoning years of the avant-garde was *creacionismo*.

Creacionismo, whose chief exponent was the Chilean poet Vicente Huidobro, is clearly an avant-garde movement in the full sense of the word. In *The Theory of the Avant-*

Garde Renato Poggioli characterizes the avant-garde as an "activist movement" which is "formed in part or in whole to agitate against something or someone."¹

In addition avant-garde art implies a spirit of futurism in the broad sense of the word and not merely in the limited sense given to it by Marinetti. Poggiolo contrasts this futurist consciousness of the modern avant-garde period with the consciousness of the past of a classical epoch.

These attitudes are expressed on numerous occasions in Huidobro's manifestos and in his poetry. His program is in direct opposition to what preceded him and clearly outlines a plan for the future.

While there have been some disagreements as to Huidobro's originality, recent criticism points to the undeniable fact that the Chilean's verse and essays reflected the latest European achievements in poetry and aesthetics and initiated corresponding trends in Latin America. Although there was no formal school or banner for *creacionista* poets, its influence was manifest in poets such as Pablo Neruda, Jorge Carrera Andrade, Oliverio Girondo, and, as we will demonstrate later in this study, Carlos Pellicer.

The influence of Huidobro on the modern poets of Latin America is made obvious in an interview with the Ecuadorian poet, Jorge Carrera Andrade, by William J. Straub:

> W.J.S. With whom, among the *ultraístas*, do you feel most affinity as a writer?
>
> J.C.A. I do not believe that I have affinity with any *ultraísta* poet. I feel closer to Huidobro and *creacionismo*. Someone has said that I occupy a place equidistant and equinoctial between the intellectualism of Borges and the intuitive expressivism of Vallejo.
>
> W.J.S. Do you believe that the *creacionismo* of Huidobro marks a radical and fundamental dividing line in American poetry?
>
> J.C.A. Yes. In Latin American poetry, the *creacionista* movement manifests itself with strong outlines. In Mexico, Venezuela, and Peru many followers of Huidobro appear. The aesthetics of Huidobro can be identified in some poems of Carlos Pellicer, Villaurrutia, Queremel, Parra del Riego, Alberto Hidalgo and others. There is no poet of the second quarter of the XXth century who does not owe something to *creacionismo*.²

The influence of *creacionismo* was paramount in the development of avantgarde poetry in Mexico. The theories of *estridentismo* owe much to Futurism and *creacionismo*. The "Contemporáneos", especially Ortiz de Montellano and Salvador Novo, reflect in their poetry the aesthetic doctrine of *creacionismo,* but it is Pellicer who is the chief exponent of *creacionismo* in Mexico. One critic contends that: "Without doubt, Carlos Pellicer's was one of the first to attempt adopting *creacionista* airs to a simple and vernacular poetry."³

As early as 1913 the Chilean poet began to realize the uniqueness of the modern epoch. In a letter to the literary editor of *El Mercurio* of Santiago de Chile (Nov. 15, 1913), he writes: "We are now in other times, the true poet is he who knows how to vibrate with his epoch or move ahead of it, not he who looks back."[4]

In a manifesto entitled *Non serviam* read in the Ateneo of Santiago de Chile in 1914 he states his desire to liberate art from nature and to create autonomous realities: "We have sung to Nature (a thing which matters little to her). We have never created our own realities, as she does or did in times past when she was young and full of creative impulses".[5]

In 1916 Huidobro travels to Buenos Aires where he delivers his theories of *creacionismo* to the Ateneo there. He states that a work of art "is a new cosmic reality that the artist adds to Nature . . ."[6] Later in the same discourse he contends that "the history of art is no more than the evolution of manmirror towards man-god." In other words he traces the development of art from the Aristotelian concept of mimesis to his own aesthetic theories expressed in the poem "Arte poética" [Poetic Art] where "The poet is a little God."

A sythesis of *creacionista* principles is found in this poem, where in free verse form Huidobro outlines the technique of the new poetry and the role of the *creacionista* poet:

ARTE POETICA

Que el verso sea como una llave
Que abra mil puertas
Una hoja cae; algo pasa volando;
Cuanto miren los ojos creado sea,
Y el alma del oyente quede temblando.
Inventa mundos nuevos y cuida tu palabra;
El adjetivo, cuando no da vida, mata.

Estamos en el ciclo de los nervios.
El músculo cuelga,
Como recuerdo, en los museos;
Más no por eso tenemos menos fuerza:
El vigor verdadero
Reside en la cabeza.

Por qué cantáis la rosa, ¡oh, Poetas!
Hacedla florecer en el poema;

Sólo para nosotros
Viven todas las cosas bajo el Sol.

El Poeta es un pequeño dios.[7]

[Poetic Art]

[Let verse be like a key that opens a thousand doors. A leaf falls; something passes flying; whatever the eyes see, let it be created, and the soul of the listener tremble. Invent new worlds and take care with your words. The

adjective, when it does not give life, kills. We are in the cycle of nerves. The muscle hangs as a memory in the museums. It is not only for this that we have less strength: True vigor resides in the mind. Why sing to the rose, poets. Make her bloom in the poem. All things under the sun live only for us. The poet is a little god.]

The "Arte poética" and other *creacionista* doctrines were not to fall on deaf ears in Latin America. Earlier in this study we cited specific poets who recognized the importance of Huidobro to the development of the avant-garde in Latin America. Let us now examine specific instances of *creacionismo* in the poetry of Carlos Pellicer.

The reader will note that some poetic elements introduced here as *creacionistas* have been discussed in other studies on avant-garde poetry and attributed to different sources. This is not to deny Huidobro's contributions, but to suggest a simultaneous creativity. For Huidobro was only one of hundreds of poets who were seeking a new poetic that would be capable of responding to the challenge of language and reality in the modern world. His theories are similar in many ways to those put forth by other *isms*, but in as many ways Huidobro shows original thought in postulating guidelines for the poet of the twentieth century. Modern poetry has no one hero, no one school, and no fixed point in time. Philosophers and poets, together as well as other artists, have all fashioned an aesthetic, a view of reality and man's role within that reality, which falls into a general category of "the modern." Thus the poetic elements we term *creacionistas* are those that are consistent with Huidobro's manifestos and his poetry, as well as with the works of other artists of the age

I

The *creacionista* poem, as we have seen earlier in this chapter, is a creation in and of itself. It needs no external, *a priori* reality to give it veracity or validity. It creates situations which could never exist in any reality other than of the poem. Or as Huidobro put it so succinctly: "A poem is a poem, in the same way that an orange is an orange and not an apple."[8]

Where in Huidobro this is a statement of aesthetic doctrine, in Pellicer it rises above a formalistic principle and characterizes a unique, personal vision of reality that is inherent and natural.

Pellicer's relationship to the world surrounding him has never been a passive one. In an interview with this writer he spoke of his first encounter with the sea: "When I was six years old, my mother took me, for the first time, to the sea. This trip by way of the Tabasco River to the seashore was my first contact, which I would call violent, with Nature."[9]

The experience was not one of mere contemplation; but rather the "violent" act of interiorizing that aspect of external reality.

In *Colores en el mar* [*Color in the Sea*], his first book of poems, the sea is not copied or described in accordance to an *a priori* adherence to an exterior reality, but undergoes a transformation, a creation to use Huidobro's terms, in the imagination of the poet. At times it is a great orchestral arrangement:

> Sonata alternative de adelante y andantino
> Las notas que no surgen en perlas se cuajaron.
>
> Y el mar se desmelena tocando su diurno,
> concierto matinal en sus gloriosos pianos.[10]

[A sonata alternating in movement and andantino. The notes which do not surge forth as pearls are coagulated. And the sea disarranges itself playing its diurnal, matutinal concert on its glorious pianos.]

Later the sea is children bathing:

> Pareció que en el mar
> se bañasen mil niños
>
> (13)

[It seemed that a thousand children were bathing in the sea.]

>   . . . . .
>
> Las olas se estaban bañando.
>
> (15)

[The waves were bathing themselves.]

But ultimately it is an object over which the poet has complete control.

The use of *creacionista* techniques is found in many poems and isolated images throughout the early production of Pellicer. Most notable among these are a group of poems entitled **"Suite Brasilera"** [**"Brazilian Suite"**] and a poem which we will transcribe in its entirety, **"El sembrador"** [**"The Sower"**]:

> El sembrador sembró la aurora;
> su brazo abarcaba el mar.
> En su mirada las montañas
> podían entrar.
>
> La tierra pautada de surcos
> oía los granos caer.
> De aquel ritmo sencillo y profundo
> melódicamente los árboles pusieron su danza a
>   mecer.
>
> Sembrador silencioso:
> el sol ha crecido por tus mágicas manos.
> El campo ha escogido otro tono
> y el cielo ha volado más alto.
>
> Sembrada la tierra.
> Su paso era bello: ni corto ni largo.
> En sus ojos cabían los montes
> y todo el paisaje en sus brazos.
>
> (134)

[The sower sowed the dawn; his arm reached the sea. The mountains could enter his vision. The earth lined by furrows heard the grains fall. The tree began to dance to that simple and profoundly melodic rhythm. Silent sower: the sun has grown by your magical hands. The countryside has chosen another tone and the sky has flown higher. The earth is sown. His step was fair: neither short nor long. The mountains filled his gaze and all the landscape in his arms.]

Here we have many of the characteristics of *creacionista* verse: destruction of spacial concepts; "en su mirada las montañas / podían entrar" also; "En sus ojos cabían los montes / y todo el paisaje en sus brazos"; the joining of two disparate elements in one image as in the following example where the noun "tierra" is joined with the verb "oía": "La tierra pautada de surcos / oía los granos caer"; and most important the concept of the poet (here represented as the "sower") as creator of reality: "El sembrador sembró la aurora."

II

As Huidobro states in "Arte poética" the poet "is a little god." Hugo Friedrich refers to this attitude as the "dictatorial imagination", that is, a poetic imagination that assumes complete liberty in recreating reality according to the laws of the poet and not some external absolutes.[11] In Pellicer the poet's autonomy is proclaimed early in his literary career in a poem from *Colores en el mar* entitled **"Estudios"**: [**"Studies".**]

> Jugaré con las casas de Curazao
> pondré el mar a la izquierda
> y haré más puentes movedizos.
> ¡Lo que diga el poeta!
>
> (29)

[I will play with the houses of Curazao. I'll put the sea on the left and will make more moving bridges. Whatever the poet says!]

And in the fourth poem of **"Suite Brasilera"** [**"Brazilian Suite"**] he writes:

> Profundamente oblicuo, el aeroplano
> se retorcía y el paisaje entero
> era un acto glorioso de mis manos.
> Sin un solo recuerdo ni un deseo,
> como un dios, desdoblé los panoramas,
> ataviado de luz, leve de vuelo.
> ¡Y juré entre las nubes alzar una montaña!
>
> (80)

[Profoundly oblique, the airplane twisted and the entire landscape was a glorious act of my hands. Without a single remembrance nor desire, as a god, I unfolded the panoramas, adorned with light, airy with flight. And among the clouds I promised to raise a mountain!]

In **"Las colinas"** [**"The Hills"**] the poet-creator-god is a painter whose will it is to:

> ¡Dibujar las colinas!
> Repartirles los ojos

y llevarles palabras finas.
Mojar largo el pincel; apartar neblina
de las nueve de la mañana,
para que el vaso de agua campesina
se convierta en alegre limonada.

(165)

[To draw the hills! To give them eyes and bring them
fine words. To dip the brush slowly; to divide the fog at
nine o'clock in the morning, so that a country glass of
water becomes a happy lemonade.]

This theme is again repeated in **"Elegía"** [**"Elegy"**]:

Si yo fuera pintor
me salvaría
con el color
toda una civilización yo crearía.
El azul sería
rojo
y el anaranjado
gris:
el verde soltaría en negros estupendos.

(119)

[If I were a painter I would save myself with color. I
would create a whole civilization. Blue would be red and
orange, gray; green would leap out in stupendous blacks.]

In the poetic world of Pellicer the wind possesses the
ability to change the color of the landscape:

Y el viento que mesaba las ágiles palmeras
le cambiaba al paisaje el color.

(15)

[And the wind that plucked the agile palms changed the
color of the landscape.]

The day becomes a celestial gambler:

El día jugó su as de oro
y lo perdió en tanto azul.

(16)

[The day played its golden ace and lost it ni so much blue.]

And night is depicted as:

la selva de vidrio en agua abierta

(221)

[the jungle of glass in open water]

The sky is water that has decided to fly:

El cielo de los Andes
es una agua divina que se ha echado a volar.

(69)

[The sky of the Andes is a divine water that has begun to fly.]

His poetry creates a world of fantastic events and autonomous images that defy literal interpretations:

Por la tarde vendrá Claude Monet
a comer cosas azules y eléctricas

(29)

[In the afternoon Claude Monet will come to eat blue
and electric things.]

. . . . .

La desnudez os ilumina
como un poco de piano en la noche

(107)

[Nudity illuminates you like a little bit of piano at
night.]

III

Although the method of formulating a *creacionista* image is limited only by the imaginative powers of the poet,
we have found four constants in the *creacionista* imagery
of Pellicer: 1) the combination in one image of two disparate things; 2) destruction of normal limitations; 3)
representation of the abstract and intangible by the concrete; and, 4) the creation of unreal sensuous imagery.

CREATION OF UNREAL SENSUOUS IMAGES[12]

If one were to catalogue the most repeated phrases used
by critics to describe the poetry of Pellicer, they would
most certainly be "sensuous," "visual," and "plastic."
Speaking of the early period of Pellicer's production,
Octavio Paz states: "Many of his poems of that period
are no more than a prodigious succession of metaphors
and visual and sonorous impressions."[13]

Pellicer's poetry abounds in visual imagery which subordinates intellectual expression. His poetry is involved with
the world of things rather than with metaphysical ponderings. It is not our purpose to reiterate here all that has
been written about this aspect of Pellicer's poetry, but
we will, however, stress an aspect of this imagery that
pertains to the modern era as a direct inheritance from
Baudelaire, the creation of unreal sensuous imagery in
its most common form, synesthesia.

We have frequent examples of synesthesia in Pellicer's
"Ruido oscuro" [**"Dark Noise"**] for example. Sound to
describe other senses, appears with far less frequency
and is characteristic of modern incursions into synesthesia. Thus in Pellicer we have examples of the visual given
in terms of the audible:

Nubes en *sol* mayor
y las olas en *la* menor.

(13)

[Clouds in *sol* major and the waves in *la* minor.]

El oleaje finge rumores de gacela
perseguida

(17)

[The waves feign the sound of a pursued gazelle].

Desde el avión
la orquesta panorámica de Río de Janeiro
se escucha en mi corazón

(78)

[From the airplane, the panoramic orchestra of Rio de Janeiro is heard in my heart]

La bahía, dirigida como una orquesta
toca las luces

(81)

[The bay, directed as an orchestra, plays the lights]

La luz, rota en el ritmo de la hélice,
humeaba de furor entre mis ojos
y se oía pasar.

(79)

[The light, broken in the rhythm of the propeller, smoked in fury between my eyes and was heard passing].

In the last image light is not only described in terms of sound, but it is also given physical mass by virtue of the verb "rota" [broken].

A quite uncommon use of synesthesia is found in "Mi sed amarga que alzó gritos" ["My bitter thirst that raised shouts"] where the sensation of taste is expressed in terms of sound, or the combination of smell and sight in:

Es la bolsa de semen de los trópicos
que huele a azul. . . .

(257)

[It is, the pocket of semen of the tropics that smells of blue. . . .]

In **"amarillenta voz de radio"** (125) [**"yellowed radio voice"**] he joins two sensations with a similar attitude, the feeling of brightness, linked in an audio-visual experience. The practice of joining two sensations sharing a common attitude is repeated in: "Y ardimos en la sed del Helesponto." (150) ["And we burned in the thirst of the Helespont"].

Other sensuous images are created by describing sound in terms of touch which in turn is described in terms of light which is then qualified by the word "ámbar" [amber] which has properties of smell and light: "Tu voz tenía el tacto de las luces del ámbar." (221) ["Your voice had the feel of lights of amber"]. One can appreciate the ingenuity of combining four sensations within an image, but its effect is limited by the obvious strain of the relationships.

The unreal sensuous image is not limited to synesthesia. For example, movement is described in terms of color:

El agua se mueve en semitono

(79)

[The water moves in semitones].

An important use of sensory images in Pellicer is attaching sensory qualities to emotive or physical states. Solitude is given both dimension and sound in the following image:

ruido de las vastas soledades

(258)

[the noise of the vast solitudes]

Absence is described in terms of taste and given a characteristic of physical mass:

tu dulce ausencia me encarcela

(335)

[your sweet absence imprisons me]

Thus the effect of sensuous imagery in Pellicer is multiple: it can expand the sensuous limits of a given object by the introduction of new senses; it can assign sensuous qualities to abstracts and intagibles; or create what Friedrich calls "irrealidad sensible" [sensuous irreality][14] in which real objects of nature become unreal through attachment to a sensuous image.

DESTRUCTION OF NORMAL SPACIAL AND TEMPORAL LIMITATION

Perhaps the single most important technical advancement of the twentieth century which altered man's vision of reality was the invention of the airplane. The once massive and imposing reality of nature was now seen in miniature from above. Tall mountains were now lumps of rocks, huge rivers were now but mere lines, large cities were but quadrangles on the terrain. The poet in capturing this new vision of reality certainly felt himself to be "a little god."

Very early in his poetic career Pellicer made a trip through Latin America and viewed this continent from a plane for the first time. The result of this trip was his second book of verse entitled *Piedra de Sacrificios* [*Sacrifical Rock*] which contains a series of aerial poems entitled **"Suite Brasilera."** In images from these poems we can experience the new perspective of reality which is a result of aviation and the consequential destruction of normal spacial limitations:

El cielo en mi frente
cambiándome el mar.

(77)

[The sky in my face, changing my view of the sea.]

Tu mar y tu montaña
—un puñadito de Andes y mil litros de Atlántico.

(79)

[The sea and the mountain—a handful of Andes and a thousand liters of Atlantic.]

El mar se baña entre mis brazos.

(80)

[The sea bathes in my arms.]

Canción de las palmeras sobre la colina
y de la colina junto al corazón.

(82)

[A song of palms on the hill and of the hill next to my heart.]

This technique is not only used in the poems of aviation but is also effective in expressing the closeness of two lovers:

Tan cerca estás de mi
que la estrella del ángelus nace entre nuestras manos.
(221)
[You are so near to me that the evening star is born
between our hands.]

Or it can express the strange perspective of a ship sailing
at night:

El buque ha chocado con la luna.
(320)
[The ship has collided with the moon.]

Once the borders of normal special confines are crossed
the poet is free to attack even a more sacred absolute:
time. Pellicer lives in two temporal worlds: one which is
modern and western in which time and history are linear
thus constantly moving to some end. The other is of his
native tropical Tabasco and a circular concept of time
characteristic of the pre-Columbian cultures of that region. In **"Estudios"** from *Hora y 20* [*Hour and 20*] he
captures the essence of timelessness:

Relojes descompuestos,
voluntarios caminos
sobre la música del tiempo

. . . . .

La juventud se prolonga diez minutos

. . . . .

las horas se adelgazan;
de una salen diez.
Es el trópico,
prodigioso y funesto.
Nadie sabe qué hora es.

. . . . .

No hay tiempo para el tiempo.

[Broken watches, free roads on the music of time. . . .
Youth is prolonged for ten minutes . . . the hours are
stretched, from one come ten. It is the tropics, prodigious
and mournful. . . . Nobody knows what time it is.
There is no time for time.]

He ends the poem with an image of time which is not
speeding to some conclusion, but rather moves slowly in
a circular path:

Y en una línea nueva de la garza,
renace el tiempo,
lento, fecundo, ocioso.
creado para soñar y ser perfecto.
(193)
[Time is reborn in the new line of the heron, slow,
fecund, idle, created to dream and be perfect.]

COMBINATION OF TWO DISPARATE ELEMENTS

Through the combination of two existing elements of
reality, the modern poet creates a situation that is unlike
any that can exist outside of his poem. Thus a sky can be
filled with automobiles:

El cielo se llenaba de automóviles
(77)
[The sky was filled with automobiles].

Palm trees can go shopping:

Las palmeras desnudas
andaban de compras por la Rua D'Ouvidor.
(77)
[The nude palms went shopping on the Rua D'Ouvidor.]

And a city seen from an airplane is "un libro deshojado"
(79) ["an unbound book"].

Pellicer's combination of disparate elements in one image has various effects. It can be humorous as in:

El Pao de Assucar era un espantapájaros
(71)
[The Pao de Assucar was a scarecrow],

or by the use of a single verb the commonplace is converted into a fantastic event:

El maíz en la mazorca
reía de buena gana

. . . . .

El cielo de Tilantongo
vuela en un pico de garza
(352)
[The corn in the cornfield laughed heartily. . . . The sky
of Tilantongo flies in the beak of a heron.]

Through combination of disparate elements the poet
makes a statement about modern reality as an element
composed of both the natural and the mechanical coexisting equally:

Bajo las ruedas de las montañas
el mar moderno y resonante
rueda lentamente sus antiguas máquinas

. . . . .

Y el puerto suntuoso,
liberal y tropical
entre grúas y palmeras en reposo
(81)
[Under the wheels of the mountain the resonant and
modern sea turns its ancient machinery slowly. . . .
And the sumptuous port, liberal and tropical between
cranes and palms in repose].

And:

Bajaron las palmeras
de las trescientas olas automóviles
(262)
[The palms descended from the three hundred automobile waves.]

By combining words of the modern technical world such as "wheels," "machines," "cranes," and "automobiles" with traditional natural elements the technical terminology is lifted to poetic heights, expanding both its meaning and the limits of poetry as well.

Although these images are delightful in their own right, they have the power to describe an object beyond the limits of normal adjectivation. To express his awe of an airplane motor he states:

> El motor que perfora el aire espeso
> algo tiene de bólido y de toro.
> 　　　　　　　　　　　　　　　　(77)
>
> [The motor that perforates the thick air has a little of a shooting star and bull.]

or:

> El aire está en soprano ligero
> 　　　　　　　　　　　　　　　　(79)
>
> [The air is a light soprano]

and:

> la voz, la silenciosa
> música de callar un sentimiento
> 　　　　　　　　　　　　　　　　(268)
>
> [the voice, the silent music to quell a sentiment].

At times, however, the combination of disparate elements creates an obscure and personal image that defies any attempt at interpretation:

> Aquella luna del pueblo
> con su piano y su esquina
> donde acabó la aurora
> 　　　　　　　　　　　　　　　　(124)
>
> [That village moon with its piano and its corner where the dawn ended].

And:

> la luz es un fruto que devora el paisaje.
> 　　　　　　　　　　　　　　　　(124)
>
> [the light is a fruit that devours the landscape.]

Pellicer's early involvement with this technique is manifest in a poem from his first book, *Colores en el mar* [*Colors in the Sea*], in which the body of the poem constitutes a series of arrangements of disparate elements:

> Ayer se hundieron
> un barco holandés y el Sol.
> La medianoche ha quedado estancada
> en los astros mayores y en los pechos de amor.
> En la playa hay preguntas y luciérnagas.
> En el puerto sólo yo soy feliz.
> ¡Tu nombre me salva del mundo!
> ¡Divina palabra!
> 　　　　　　　Silencio y abril.
> 　　　　　　　　　　　　　　　　(37)

[Yesterday a Dutch boat and the sun were sunk. Midnight has become stagnant in the larger stars and in the breasts of love. On the beach there are questions and bats. In the port I alone am happy. Your name saves me from the world. Divine word. Silence and April].

Through this seemingly chaotic arrangement one can sense the utter frivolity, the youthful exuberance that Pellicer brings to poetic creation. Nothing is too sacred or too commonplace for his imaginative manipulations. Octavio Paz captures this sense of joy in Pellicer when he states: "His poetry is a vein of water in the desert; his joy returns to us the faith in joy."[15]

The final category, representation of the abstract and the intangible by the concrete, could easily be discussed here but its frequency of appearance in Pellicer's poetry merits its own section.

ABSTRACT AND INTANGIBLE BY THE CONCRETE

As we have stated before, the poetry of Carlos Pellicer is a poetry of things. He is a man fascinated with every aspect of the world that surrounds him. Pellicer's command of his circumstances goes beyond personifying objects of nature to making concrete and visible the abstract and intangible. Hugo Friedrich contends that this stylistic technique is not uncommon among many modern poets: "Another stylistic law," says Friedrich, "that has almost become topical consists of situating on the same level the tangible and concrete and the abstract."[16] This technique in Pellicer, however, was not simply a borrowed innovation, but an act which demonstrated his natural desire to express himself in visible or other sensual terms. His poetry is not about things, but rather about the things created in a reality all his own.

In **"Elegía"** he writes "Yo tendría ojos en las manos / para ver de repente." ["I would have eyes in my hands in order to see suddenly"]. Here he expressed the desire to see by touching and feeling and not through a conceptual process. This desire is again repeated in **"Estudios Venecianos"** [**Venetian Studies**]:

> (Como Santa Luía,
> llevaba yo los ojos en las manos
> para ver de tocar lo que veía.)
> 　　　　　　　　　　　　　　　　(226)
>
> [(As Saint Lucia I carried my eyes in my hands in order to see by touching what I saw.)]

In this poetic reality his personal emotions are given physical dimension—solitude: "es olvido esférico de mi soledad"; (234) ["it is the spherical oblivion of my solitude"], "Vuelvo a tí, soledad agua vacía, / agua de mis imágenes, tan muerta, / nube de mis palabras, tan desierta"; (267) ["I return to you, solitude, empty water, water of my images, so dead, cloud of my thoughts, so empty"], "ausencia/ manzana aérea de las soledades";

(340) ["absence, aerial block of solitudes"], "veo tu soledad cárcel abierta"; (212) ["I see your solitude, open jail"], or this personification: "la soledad está pensando / junto a la ventana." (157) ["Solitude is thinking next to the window"].

Note how in the second example solitude is not only given a concrete representation through its metaphoric relationship to water and clouds, but the intensity and immensity of the emotion is heightened as well through its attachment to elements which are vast and unfathomable.

Another emotion which is made concrete is happiness: "por el rincón de un sollozo / pasó la felicidad." (224) ["happiness passed through the corner of a sob"]; here not only is happiness personified by the use of the verb "passed," but "sob" is given physical dimension in the metaphor "corner of a sob." No emotion or concept is free from Pellicer's poetic sculpture: sound; "tu voz . . . de perfil," (221)) ["your voice . . . of profile"]; the afternoon is capable of being cut, "El segador con pausas de música / siega la tarde." (135) ["The reaper cuts the afternoon with musical pauses"]; and night is personified in "La noche, lentamente se desnuda / para dormir sobre mi corazón" (72) ["Night slowly undresses itself to sleep on my heart"]. Even the inverse is possible as in the following image where two tangible objects are described in terms of an abstract: "ventanas y puertas de alegría" (29) ["windows and doors of joy"].

This then is the body of the poetic work of Pellicer. A world of things, visible and invisible, but all transformed to correspond to his unique vision of reality. Although, as we have demonstrated, Pellicer had adopted many of the *creacionista* techniques, philosophically there stretched a distance between him and Huidobro. Where in Huidobro there is a tendency to reject nature, Pellicer's relationship to nature is one of harmonious coexistence. It is an interchange by which the sun, the sea, and the wind provide him with inspiration, and he in turn dresses them in imaginative colors and forms.

Thus we come to the problem of classification—is Pellicer a *creacionista* poet? To the extent that he adopts many of the *creacionista* techniques we would answer yes. However, Carlos Pellicer is clearly not an avant-garde artist. While he adopts many of the devices and attitudes which originate in avant-garde movements, he is not disposed to the avant-garde mentality. His poetic production begins at a time when the avant-garde frenzy of the first two decades of the century had subsided. His modernity is manifest most of all in the attitude that all advances in poetry are his own. He is at once a *contemporáneo*, a *creacionista*, an *ultraísta*, but most of all he is Carlos Pellicer.

NOTES

[1] Renato Poggioli, *The Theory of the Avant-Garde* (Cambridge, Mass.: Harvard University Press, 1968), p. 25.

[2] William J. Straub, "Conversation with Jorge Carrera Andrade," *Latin American Literary Review*, I, 1 (Fall, 1972), p. 73.

[3] Antonio de Undurraga, "Teoría del creacionismo," in Huidobro, *Poesía y prosa*, p. 37. [All translations from Spanish text are mine.]

[4] Vicente Huidobro, *Poesía y prosa: Antología*, 2nd. ed. (Madrid: Aguilar, 1967), p. 20.

[5] Vicente Huidobro, *Obras completas de Vicente Huidobro*, Vol. II, ed. Braulio Arenas (Santiago de Chile: Zig-Zag Editores, 1964), p. 261.

[6] *Ibid.*, p. 661.

[7] *Ibid.*, p. 255.

[8] *Ibid.*, p. 697.

[9] Unpublished interview, February, 1969.

[10] Carlos Pellicer, *Material poético: 1918-1961*, 2nd ed. (México: Universidad Nacional Autónoma de México, 1962), p. 14. All further quotes of Pellicer's poems will be from this edition with the page number given in parentheses.

[11] Hugo Friedrich, *Estructura de la lírica moderna* (Barcelona: Seix Barral, 1959), p. 311.

[12] We use the term "unreal" to refer to images which are not attached to any consideration of an *a priori* exterior reality.

[13] Octavio Paz, *Las peras del olmo*, 2nd ed. (México: Universidad Nacional Autónoma de México, 1965), p. 100.

[14] Friedrich, p. 309.

[15] Paz, *Las peras del olmo*, p. 107.

[16] Friedrich, p. 315.

Edward J. Mullen (essay date 1979)

SOURCE: "The Early Poetry of Carlos Pellicer," *Revista de estudios hispanicos*, Vol. XIII, No. 1, January 1979, pp. 29-44.

[*Here, Mullen explores Pellicer's early works for his use of reverie to explore time and space, human nature, and civilization.*]

In her introduction to *The Literary Origins of Surrealism*, Anna Balakian makes a seminal observation on the art of poetry when she writes: "Fortunately, in the case of poetry, whether one writes it or philosophizes about it, youth is an asset rather than a detriment."[1] This observation which runs counter to the popular theory that a writer's work matures at an exponential, chronological rate has particular meaning when applied to the poetry of the Mexican writer Carlos Pellicer. The latter, unlike many of his contemporaries (Pablo Neruda, Jorge Carrera Andrade), is a writer of individual poems and not of integrated books of poetry. His career as a poet is marked by a series of artistic high points which bear little or no relation to the general quality of the books in which they were published. While it is true that Pellicer has been the object of limited critical interest,[2] it is doubly true that a number of key poems from his early period (*Colores en el mar*, 1921; *Piedra de sacrificios*, 1924; and *6, 7 poemas*, 1924) have been subject to the least critical scrutiny.[3] It will be the purpose of this essay to examine some of Pellicer's earliest poems in an effort to identify the major stylistic and thematic motifs which emerge as the underpinnings of his work as a whole.

I. COLORES EN EL MAR

Pellicer's earliest published poems, **"Grecia"** and **"Sonetos romanos"** were published in the review *Galdios* in 1916 and clearly evince a debt to the Modernists in their emphasis on chiseled, exotic detail. The poet's first book-length collection of verse, **Colores en el mar y otros poemas** (1921), however, represents a departure from his early dependence on Modernist models. Illustrated by his friend Roberto Montenegro, it bore a dedication to the recently deceased poet Ramón López Velarde. The book is largely a collection of landscapes, seascapes, and travel poems, the fruition of his journey to Colombia and Venezuela as a member of the Mexican Federation of Students and his later travels to Brazil with José Vasconcelos. In this brief edition of thirty-three poems, Pellicer initiated a number of basic thematic concerns which were to recur throughout his later poetry. There is a certain aptness in considering it germinal to Pellicer's entire career as a poet, for although his work grew in terms of thematic variety and technical complexity, he never substantially veered from the basic poetic orientation established here. One is at once struck by the poet's debt to the plastic arts. The first twenty-five selections, which present definite pictures and colors, call to mind the works of Claude Monet, George Braque, and Rufino Tamayo.

Almost all these initial poems are efforts to represent the multifaceted pictorial possibilities of the tropical sea. The sun emerges as the dominant image in the first poem, which is a collage of six separate but complimentary images related to the power of the tropic sun—a symbol which for Pellicer often achieves almost archetypal proportions:

> ¡El Sol! ¡El Sol! ¡El Sol! . . .
> Detrás de un arrebol
> llegó aquel joven Sol . . .
> Nubes en *sol* mayor
> y olas en *la* menor.
> La vida era tan bella como el amanecer.
> Pareció que en el mar
> se bañasen mil niños; así las olas eran
> infantiles y claras de gritar.
> Y una mujer pasaba
> toda dominical.
>
> (p. 13)

"El Sol" is a telling poem inasmuch as it typifies not merely the technical aspects of Pellicer's early poetry but sheds some light on his attitude towards reality as well. At first glance, it may seem to be a traditional, descriptive poem. A closer examination reveals that it is not a transcription in normative poetic terms of some external visual phenomenon but rather an attempt to recreate a mental image of something experienced by means of juxtaposing separate but connected impressions, all of which attempt the re-creation of the single impression of dawn breaking on a seaside morning. Pellicer moves from a simple personification in the first stanza, where the sun is presented as a young man, to a comparison of waves and clouds in terms of notes on the musical scale in the second, to a strikingly elemental simile in the fourth. The last verses suddenly shift back to the terrestrial and the mundane by evoking a somewhat conventionalized image of a well-dressed woman. In effect the poet seems to be manipulating several different types of poetic conceits on simultaneous planes; hence reality appears not to be described but created.

Another feature of these early poems is the attention given to certain dominant colors, above all, aqua, blue, and green. In particular, three poems attempt a color transcription in which Pellicer establishes a link between color and emotion:

> Azul.
> Pintado el cielo en azul.
> El mar pintado en azul.
> El alma suelta en azul.
> Azul.
> Azul.
> El día jugó su as de oro
> y lo perdió en tanto azul.
> Y el silencio dijo en coro:
> «Ya mañana no hay azul!»
>
> (p. 16)

This first short piece betrays a structural pattern which was to be repeated often in Pellicer's poetry: an initial descriptive allusion (here a reference to the blueness of the sky) followed by a startling shift in perspective, as in this case where the day becomes a card player. Pellicer demonstrated in early poems such as this a marked ability to play with the reader's sense of anticipation, since he often began his poems with a diction well within the bounds of the established formulaic poetic language of his day, only to intercalate an image clearly at odds with such preconceived conventions.

In a great number of these poems, Pellicer creates the impression that he is describing the scene to the reader, somewhat like a critic might point out the color lines and geometric shapes of a painting, and thus achieves a degree of poetic objectivity. These selections show the same basic architectural plan as others—a series of relatively independent strophe-images linked by similarity of tone or mood. In the three-strophe **"Noche sin sombra,"** for example, a solitary ship at sea is first equated to a bird in flight over the vast sea. This is followed by a description of light playing off the waves which culminates with a more objective portrait of a vessel:

> Noche de terror y de gloria . . .
> Solos, en el misterio cristalino del mar,

viendo vivir la Luna y contando una historia
desolada y sombría de un buzo singular.

(p. 24)

As the critic Luis Rius has pointed out,[4] there is a certain childlike candor and freshness in the imagery of **Colores en el mar** because it is derived chiefly through elemental personifications of the natural world: "las olas se estaban bañando" (p. 15); "El sol ya estaba viejo, pero era un rey" (p. 18); and unusual linkages such as "Como fauno marino perseguí aquella ola / suelta la cabellera y el talle azul-ondeante" (p. 18).

At times, the poet appears to stand back and comment on his own propensity to play optical games with color, air, and light. **"Estudio,"** dedicated to the critic Pedro Henríquez Ureña, is one of Pellicer's first autocritical moments as well as one of his most often quoted poems. Unlike many of the poems in **Colores en el mar**, it is written in the first person as an uninterrupted block of poetic narrative:

> Jugaré con las casas de Curazao,
> pondré el mar a la izquierda
> y haré más puentes movedizos.
> ¡Lo que diga el poeta!
> Estamos en Holanda y en América
> y es una isla de juguetería,
> con decretos de rena . . .

(p. 29)

"Estudio" is very important in understanding the esthetic principles which underlie Pellicer's poetry. This poem, much like **"El sol,"** proves that his early verse was neither particularly traditional nor descriptive. While it is true that many of the images employed are essentially visual, their arrangement, disposition, and structural focus reveal an attempt by the poet not to reproduce reality in the manner of the Modernists, but to evoke impressions of an independent and personal "poetic" reality. In this sense, a poem like **"Estudio"** places Pellicer closer conceptually to the Vanguard writers of the twenties who had proposed a radical departure from descriptive poetry in favor of the creation of a new poetic reality rooted in, but independent of nature.

The poem's opening lines, while casual and almost conversational in tone, contain an important statement which is essential to the poem's elucidation: the explicit assertion by the writer that he will manipulate the reader's perception of reality. I shall "play" he declares. Immediately in the second line Pellicer establishes a kind of optical-spatial relationship with his audience as he explicitly directs the eye around a poetic bas-relief map of Curaçao. The impression that this is a world freed from the normative laws of the physical world is reinforced in lines 6-8 where we are told that this is a "tyshop isle," where "the laws are a queen's" and where even doors and windows "smile." The reference to the Dutch painter Rembrandt and the French artist Monet underscores the poet's intention of evoking through words a set of visual-emotional impressions much like those captured by the

master artist. The poet clearly shifts from description to fantasy and wish-fulfilling in the last four lines where he yearns aloud to be carried to the world of his own poetic creation.

Apart from the poem's somewhat innovative narrative structure, the total effect of its reading creates a unique impression. A first scanning of **"Estudio"** may evoke the feeling that it is a descriptive poem, but a closer study of the component lines shows that the poet has gone beyond the realm of description and the metaphor of analogy: it is a world of anthropomorphic doors and windows, where ships sail to nowhere, and artists consume "blue and electric things." It is a poem of childlike exuberance in which the poets' sense of discovery is conveyed through the deliberate distortion of the ordinary.

Similar to the imagistic tension of **"Estudio"** is **"Recuerdos de Iza."** Here again, the poet demonstrates his skill at assembling multiple, independent images and fusing them into a poetic whole:

> 1. Creeríase que la población,
>   después de recorrer el valle,
>   perdió la razón
>   y se trazó una sola calle.
> 2. Y así bajo la cordillera
>   se apostó febrilmente como la primavera . . .

(p. 53)

"Recuerdos Iza" is composed of ten stanzas, each two lines in length with the exception of the first which is four verses long. The typographical arrangement by which each strophe is numbered suggests that Pellicer was consciously trying to stress the poetic independence of these two-line strophes. The title "memories" serves as a thematic matrix for the poem, conferring an organic unity on what might otherwise be labeled disparate impressions. The poem almost seems to be a parody of the landscape poetry which flourished after the decline of Modernism. In many ways **"Recuerdos de Iza"** is a deceptive poem inasmuch as it plays with the reader's sense of anticipation. The poet does not evoke a set of predictable visual images, but instead builds a rather gradual montage of synesthetic impressions. Its total effect is powerful: the memory of the village is presented as a multi-sensory experience rather than a lineal one-dimensional recollection. The poet's desire to capture and express a sense of newness and wonder is effectively conveyed through a "newness" of structure and form.

II. *6, 7, POEMAS*

Pellicer continued and refined many of the techniques he had begun in **Colores en el mar** in the collection **6, 7, poemas**, which was published in 1924. As in his earlier verse, Pellicer continues the tendency to elaborate visual images. In **"Aurora"** the poet addresses the personified morning light with a series of flashy color conceits. Dawn is not depicted as the classic goddess of the morning sun, but rather as a uniquely Mexican deity through a series of chromatic impressions. The poem begins with a simile in which the arrival of dawn is related to personified areas of the Mexican landscape in lines 1-3. This is followed in lines 4-5 by an enumeration of Mexican place names: Pátzcuaro, Chapala, Jalisco, Tzintzuntzan, Uruapan, and Oaxaca.

In line six, the poet-narrator directly addresses the personified dawn, thus latering the poem's narrative perspective. What had begun as a description of Dawn's arrival now becomes a kinetic portrait of the Mexican landscape. It is a world of dancing palm trees and flying clouds where the moon has become Dawn's "white umbrella." As the poem draws to a close, the reader is left with a multifaceted portrait of Dawn based on unusual linkages and associations. This abstract picture is concretized somewhat in the last seven lines of the poem with specific references to the "knees of springtime," Dawn's "tinted feet" and "smile." **"Aurora"** is an unusual variation on a very traditional theme.

There area a number of nature portraits like **"Aurora"** which manifest a repeated tendency to depict man infused with nature: **"Motivos," "Scherzo," "Sembrador,"** and **"Segador"** are among the most outstanding examples of this technique. **"Motivos"** exemplifies Pellicer's ability to evoke a complex series of visual images within a controlled poetic framework. Here the central thematic and imagistic motifs imaginatively call forth a feeling of reverent wonder as the poet gradually constructs a portrait of the pleasures of the bucolic life. The poem is composed of two stanzas of irregular length. In the opening lines Pellicer makes an immediate association between man and nature through a tripart visual image linking a plowman to his oxen, who in turn are related to the dawn. Thus the level of metaphoric illusion becomes more gradually abstract as the poet moves from man to animal to nature concretized. This interpenetration between man and nature is further heightened by a series of fertility images in which the plowman is depicted as an archetypal figure of creation. His hands are "red" and "potent," his sweat "sacred" and he is capable of sowing "faith" in the furrows he plows. The poem comes full circle in the last stanza where the impressions of creativity are replaced with allusions to completion. The plowman who cast the spores of life in the first stanza emerges here as the biblical shepherd and symbolic guardian of life.

"Segador" and **"Sembrador"** are two tightly constructed visual poems. In both cases, the central poetic image is derived from a linking of two levels of reality: the world of man and the greater physical universe of which he is a part. Both poems caught the eye of the poetess Gabriela Mistral, who reproduced them in an early note on Pellicer's poetry first published in *El Mercurio* in Chile and then reprinted in the prestigious *Repertorio Americano*. **"Segador"** exemplifies well this interplay between man and nature. The poem, dedicated to José Vasconcelos, consists of four stanzas. Similar to **"Motivos,"** it is developed around a central metaphoric image: here the comparison between man and nature with an implicit analogy between reaper and poet. There is also evident a clear attempt to describe one medium in the

terms of another. Thus the opening of the poem depicts the reaper rhythmically cutting the golden stalks of grain which are compared to the afternoon sun:

> El segador, con pausas de música,
> segaba la tarde.
> Su hoz es tan fina,
> que siega las dulces espigas y siega la tarde.
>
> (p. 135)

In the second stanza the auditory and musical dimension is stressed again as the sickle becomes the reaper's "sharpened noise":

> Segador que en dorados niveles camina
> con su ruido afilado,
> derrotando las finas alturas de oro
> echa abajo también el ocaso.
>
> (p. 135)

In the final two stanzas the reaper emerges as a figure of cosmic proportions whose physical stature now has been fused with the optical forces of daylight and sunset. There again appears a reference to music which may perhaps be thought of in terms of the rhythmic forces of nature.

> Segaba las claras espigas.
> Su pausa era música.
> Su sombra alargaba la tarde.
> En los ojos traía un lucero
> que a veces
> brincaba por todo el paisaje.
>
> (p. 135)

The **"Sembrador"** is an almost parallel development of the same theme. Here, however, the central metaphor of sower as poet may be more easy to perceive. The sower here clearly achieves messianic attributes as we are told that he sows the dawn and that the sun grows from his magical hands. The poem climaxes with a forceful intermixture of man and nature:

> Sembraba la tierra
> Su paso era bello: ni corto ni largo.
> En sus ojos cabían los montes
> y todo el paisaje en sus brazos.
>
> (p. 134)

In several poems in this collection, Pellicer meditates about his own involvement in the act of writing poetry. More than philosophic poems, they are stylized impressions of his art. In **"Elegía,"** for example, he underscores his desire to express himself with colors rather than words. It is an excellent example of Pellicer's virtuosity as a poet, for here as opposed to his purely visual poems he is able to establish a link of tone and mood between poet and reader. Dedicated to "nadie," the poem builds to a gradual dramatic climax. In the first fifteen lines Pellicer heaps staccato images of ennui one upon the other in an effort to emphasize his sense of futility and boredom. The poet stares into empty streets, thinks of his absent lover, his hatred of books and sunless days. Even here in a seemingly conventional, confessional framework, unusual images and associations appear. The poet muses that the cathedral looks "mortgaged" and that he feels as if he has eaten "Yankee apples." From line 16 to line 39, however, passive reflection, erupts into an extended exclamation as the poet passionately voices a desire to express himself with color rather than words:

> Si yo fuera pintor,
> me salvaría.
> Con el color
> toda una civilización yo crearía . . .
>
> (p. 119)

This autocritical tendency culminates in **"Deseos,"** one of Pellicer's best known works and the quintessential poem of *6, 7, poemas*. Here Pellicer laments that he is merely a colorist poet and requests that he be allowed to write more introspective verse. The poem is a short one (20 lines) in which the narrator directs his voice to a personified embodiment of nature (the tropics) and regrets that he is unable to express deeply felt emotions, that he is merely a superficial colorist poet. Structurally, **"Deseos"** is a good example of Pellicer's tendency to make adaptations or shifts of focus within seemingly conventional forms. The initial use of an apostrophe is of course not of itself a startling device and may set up in the mind of the experienced reader of poetry a degree of anticipation for traditional tropes and stylized poetic diction. This initial question elicits no answer from personified nature but rather is gradually transformed in the closing verses of the poem into a soulful cry. There are important imagistic and thematic links here with poems such as **"Elegía."** The first four lines, in particular, call to mind the recurrent association between the senses (above all tactile and visual) which seem to be ever present in Pellicer's verse. In short, the opening lines have a dual importance: they demonstrate a very effective way of establishing a bond between narrator and reader (achieved here through the almost auditory intimacy of the second person form) and show how adept Pellicer is at translating an emotional experience through the medium of a graphic, visual image:

> Trópico, para qué me diste
> las manos llenas de color.
> Todo lo que yo toque
> se llenará de sol.
>
> (p. 123)

In lines 5-16 the poet continues to stress the synesthetic nature of poetic experience with images such as "sound of a glass sunflower." More importantly, however, he alludes to a process of transformation by which the narrator is described in terms usually applied to flora and fauna. Thus the persona declares that he will travel through distant lands like a sunflower, that he will soak up light, and that he yearns to be strewn about like the petals of a flower. Similarly significant is the parallel use of the interjection (déjame) in lines 7-8 to underscore the building dramatic tension of the poem.

"Deseos" climaxes with a four-line exclamation in which the poet returns to the initial question which began the poem. Quite apart from the obvious structural unity which this technique bestows on the poem, it should be pointed out that **"Deseos"** is among the shorter, more carefully constructed poems in this book. Esthetically, it represents a balance of theme and form, for there is a feeling of symmetry and balance present which is lacking in many of the other compositions. As we have seen, **"Deseos"** begins with a question (lines 1-2) which is gradually transformed in the closing verses into a soulful exclamation. On a metaphoric level as well, Pellicer has been more successful in controlling his use of poetic language since the central poetic image remains clear and intelligible.

III. *Piedra de sacrificios*

The same year in which ha published *6, 7 poemas*, Pellicer brought out **Piedra de sacrificios**, a collection of Americanist poems which signaled a strong attraction for the pre-Columbian past.

The second poem in the book, **"Uxmal,"** is singularly important since it marks one of Pellicer's earliest comments on the importance of pre-Hispanic civilization and illustrates the initiation of one of his most characteristic techniques of treating indigenous motifs. Simply stated, **"Uxmal"** is a poetic evocation of the ruins of an ancient Mayan city located in the Yucatan peninsula. Instead of merely describing the physical, chromatic attributes of the ruins (as he does elsewhere in many "portrait poems"), Pellicer narrates a cluster of experiences related to the central image of the city from the perspective of an omniscient poet-seer. The poem assumes some of the characteristics of an epic hymn or vision in which the narrator's voice is blended with a variegated pattern of exotic images of pre-Columbian life. Thus, the central metaphorical structure of the work appears to be associated with a subconscious or archetypal level of creation. In the terminology of the critic Northrup Frye, we are dealing here with that which "we vaguely describe as instinctive, intuitive, inspired or involuntary."[5]

Francisco Pabón,[6] who has carefully studied indigenous motifs in Pellicer's poetry, considers **"Uxmal"** a key poem to the understanding of Pellicer's world view. In a lengthy and carefully done analysis of the poem, Pabón finds a pre-Columbian prototype for **"Uxmal"** in the *icnocuícatl,* or "songs of sadness" of the ancient Nahuatl poets. Similar to these ancient ballads, the basic structure of **"Uxmal"** is related to the dramatization of a ritual act (sacrifice) and is carried out in a form of implicit dialogue.

A study of the poem appears to corroborate Pabón's theory. In the first ten lines, the sight of the ancient ruins initiates a sort of poetic revery in which the persona is gradually swept back through space and time. The poet responds to the physical stimulus of the view of the city by gradually moving deeper in his own consciousness until he becomes the embodiment of the spirit of Uxmal.

The transition from present to past is achieved by the sixth line which contains a reference to ritual dance:

> Uxmal,
> desde las rocas de mi corazón.
> Y danzó en la ruda mañana estival,
>   sacerdotal
>   tu antigua voz.

>   (p. 65)

The poet then enumerates a series of emotions linked to the city and its role in the sacrificial rites of pre-Columbian Mexico. The empty temples and gigantic platforms call to mind the sacrificial aspect of Mayan religion, an idea which is furthered strengthened by the repetition of the blood images a few lines below. Of particular importance is the fusion of the poet-narrator with the physical world of Uxmal:

> Como árboles sobre el fondo de la tarde,
> mis brazos se levantaron,
> profundos, de tu sangre.
> Y fue el arquitecto sinfonizante
> de melodías y rumbos de astros

>   (p. 66)

Lines 21-24 present three allusive images which draw in and focus on the concept of divinity on successively smaller things: an "architect" of the heavens, a snake charmer, and a sacred flower jar. The last sentence (lines 25-27) is a description of the city's plaza, the site of the mystical experience of the poet presented in the next part of the poem (lines 28-41).

Approximately from lines 34-41, the narrator shifts from describing the magnitude of the city to a depiction of the effects of the temple on his own poetic sensibility. Past and present fuse in a moment of poetic truth, an instant of suspended time.

The poet is also aware of his own smallness and unimportance in the universe when he represents his soul as an atom (line 33) and an ant (line 34). This suspension of time is a productive period (line 31), because it gives rise to this poem, which the poet's soul sings.

> Hormiga entre bloques de siglos,
> alma mía que suspendiste
> la quietud trágica de tus movimientos
> entre el instante alegre el momento triste.
> Desde la casa del adivino
> disfruté de todas las religiones
> como de una copa de vino.

>   (p. 66)

The allusion to suspended animation reinforces the extra-visionary posture of the narrator, making the poem more plausible to the reader. It was as if Pellicer, the poet of the twentieth century, had for a moment seen the ruins of Uxmal through the eyes of his ancient counterpart. The poem concludes with approximately the same lines with which it began, an indication that the dream is over and the poet has returned to the present.

> Tú tocaste la puerta de mi corazón,
> Uxmal;
> se alza una voz,
> se oye otra voz.
> Uxmal,
> es tu divina sensación.

>   (p. 67)

"Uxmal" is a key poem in the development of Pellicer's poetic vision, for it points to a concern with an entire constellation of ideas and feelings related to Mexico's pre-Hispanic past.

In summary, it should be pointed out that an examination of Pellicer's early poetry shows that he is a paradoxical figure in twentieth-century Mexican letters. He is, on the one hand, the quintessential Spanish American poet, a writer of hymns to tropic splendor. On the other, he is an extremely difficult, modern poet, deeply concerned with language and form.

NOTES

[1] *The Literary Origins of Surrealism* (New York University Press, 1947), p. vii.

[2] Two important exceptions to this statement are: Andrew Debicki, "Perspective and Meaning in the poetry of Carlos Pellicer," *Hispania,* 56 (December 1973), 1007-1013; and George Melnykovick, "Carlos Pellicer and Creationism," *Latin American Literary Review*, 2 (Spring-Summer, 1974), 95-111.

[3] All references to the poetry of Pellicer will be made to the *Material poético 1918-1961* (México: Ediciones UNAM, 1962) with the page number in the text.

[4] See Luis Rius, "*El material poético* de Carlos Pellicer," *Revista Iberoamericana*, 124 (September-October 1962), 239-270.

[5] *Relations of Literary Study*, ed. James Thorpe (New York: Modern Language Association, 1967), p. 40.

[6] Francisco Pabón, "Gravitación de lo indígena en la poesía de Carlos Pellicer," Diss. Rutgers, 1969. See especially, pp. 61-65.

Additional coverage of Pellicer's life and career is contained in the following sources published by Gale Group: *Contemporary Authors*, **Vols. 69-72, 153;** *Hispanic Writers*.

Benito Pérez Galdós
1843-1920

Spanish novelist, dramatist, essayist, and journalist.

INTRODUCTION

Galdós is considered the most important Spanish novelist since Cervantes and is one of the few Spanish writers to have achieved international recognition. Applying the techniques of the European schools of Realism and Naturalism, he created a portrait of Spanish society that critics find both accurate and comprehensive. A prolific writer, Galdós wrote over seventy novels, the majority of which are divided into two groupings, the *Episodios nacionales* (*National Episodes*) and the *Novelas españolas contemporáneas* (*Contemporary Spanish Novels*); the latter are considered his best works and form the basis of his critical reputation.

Born in Las Palmas in the Canary Islands, Galdós was the youngest of the ten children of a retired military officer and his wife. Galdós's mother hoped that her youngest son would emulate her favorite brother, a respected and wealthy attorney in Cuba; when it was time for the young Galdós to begin his secondary education it was she who decided he would study law at the University of Madrid. Galdós, however, had already decided to make writing his career and had in fact been publishing articles in Las Palmas journals for some time. Galdós enrolled at the university but seldom attended classes; instead, he spent his time discussing politics in student cafes, familiarizing himself with the street life of the city, and writing essays for leftist journals. Within three years he had abandoned the facade of university studies altogether and was making a nominal living as a journalist.

Galdós completed his first novel, *La sombra* (1870; *The Shadow*), early in 1867, but he was so dissatisfied with the work that he did not attempt to have it published. Later that year, however, inspired by Honoré de Balzac's novel *Eugénie Grandet*, he wrote two historical novels, *La fontana de oro* (1870) and *El audaz* (1871), and conceived the plan for the historical series *Episodias nacionales* or the *National Episodes*. Galdós worked at a feverish pace throughout the next decade, producing a total of twenty *National Episodes*. He also continued his journalistic activities during this period, and his acerbic attacks on the Bourbon monarchy and the Spanish Catholic church earned him the respect of the republicans, who responded by electing him to the Spanish congress in 1880.

While the *National Episodes* were a huge popular success and made Galdós a national celebrity, they failed to satisfy the author's artistic ambitions. As a result, in 1879 he announced his intention to abandon the series in order to concentrate on the creation of "contemporary types" in his fiction. One year later, he began writing his *Novelas Españolas contemporaneas* (*Contemporary Spanish Novels*). Working steadily and rapidly, he completed twenty of the twenty-four *Contemporary Novels* within a nine-year period. Although this series is today acknowledged as Galdós's crowning achievement, it was not well received during his lifetime, and he was forced by economic necessity to return to the production of *National Episodes*. Despite these concessions to financial exigencies, Galdós remained insolvent throughout the rest of his life.

Galdós continued to work on the *National Episodes* even after he became partially disabled by a stroke in 1905. His writing career ended only with onset of total blindness in 1912. That same year, several of Galdós's colleagues attempted to gain the Nobel prize for him, but their efforts were blocked by civil and academic authorities who had been offended by his republican sympathies. Galdós remained active in politics throughout his final years. Although he was unable to continue his journalistic activities, he frequently appeared at rallies for various liberal causes, where his presence often inspired a strong show of support. He died in 1920.

Critics find in Galdós's fiction the direct reflection of his liberal political ideology. In the *National Episodes*, which recount the events of Spain's turbulent history from 1805 through 1880, he attempted to show that the monarchy had proven itself unfit to rule the Spanish people, thus implying the inherent rectitude of the republican cause. Similarly, he revealed what he considered the moral bankruptcy of the Spanish Catholic church in the hope that such a revelation would help to decrease the enormous influence of the church in Spanish society. The narrative plan of the *National Episodes*, however, was necessarily shaped by the constraints of historical accuracy, and it was in the *Contemporary Novels* that Galdós was able to fully realize his didactic aims.

In creating the *National Episodes*, Galdós had been influenced chiefly by Balzac's *Comédie humaine*, attempting to vivify historical periods through the use of accurate detail. Before beginning work on the *Contemporary Novels*, though, Galdós read Emile Zola's *Rougon-Macquart* series and was deeply impressed by the French author's Naturalist theories. Like Zola, Galdós believed that fiction should frankly portray all aspects of human existence, whether pleasant or distasteful, noble or ignominious. Galdós further believed that honest depictions of social ills could serve as the pretensions of the Spanish middle class. In *Miau* (1888), for example, Galdós exposes the greed and corruption of minor bureaucrats, while *La desheredada* (1881; *The Disinherited Lady*) satirizes the aristocratic prejudices of an orphaned girl. Critics note, however, that the primary achievement of the *Contemporary Novels* is not their accurate identification of social evils, but their perceptive portrayals of the subtleties of human psychology and social interaction. Most notable in this respect is the novel *Fortunata y Jacinta* (1887; *Fortunata and Jacinta*), in which Galdós explores the fierce rivalry of two women from drastically different social backgrounds who share the same man, one of them as his wife, the other as his mistress and the mother of his son. Critics agree that while *Fortunata y Jacinta* provides a comprehensive and realistic portrait of the manners and customs of nineteenth-century Madrid, the primary interest of the novel is in the characterization of the two women, and this work is universally acknowledged as Galdós's finest.

Although Galdós's contemporary Marcelino Mendenez y Pelayo called the *National Episodes* "one of the most fortunate and timely creations in Spanish literature," most critics today find them prolix and lacking in narrative coherence. Galdós's current reputation rests primarily on the *Contemporary Novels*, with critics citing *The Disinherited Lady*, *El amigo Manso* (1882), *Tormento* (1884; *Torment*), *La de Bringas* (1884; *The Spendthrifts*), *Miau*, *Fortunata y Jacinta*, and *Angel Guerra* (1891) as the best of the twenty-four. Considered a major artistic and intellectual achievement, the *Contemporary Novels* are internationally esteemed by readers and critics, while their author is recognized as the most accomplished Spanish novelist of the nineteenth century.

PRINCIPAL WORKS

La fontana de oro (novel) 1870
La sombra [*The Shadow*] (novel) 1870
El audaz (novel) 1871
*El 19 de marzo y el 2 de mayo (novel) 1873
*Bailen (novel) 1873
*La corte de Carlos IV [*The Court of Charles IV*] (novel) 1873
*Trafalgar [*Trafalgar*] (novel) 1873
*Cadiz (novel) 1874
*Gerona (novel) 1874
*Juan Martin el Empecinado (novel) 1874
*Napoleon en Chamartin (novel) 1874
*Zaragoza [*Saragossa*] (novel) 1874
*La batalla de los Arapiles [*The Battle of Salamanca*] (novel) 1875
*El equipaje del Rey Jose (novel) 1875
*Memorias de un cortesano (novel) 1875
*El 7 de julio (novel) 1876
Doña Perfecta (novel) 1876
*El Grande Oriente (novel) 1876
*La segunda casaca (novel) 1876
*Los cien mil hijos de San Luis (novel) 1877
Gloria, 2 vols. (novel) 1877
*El terror de 1824 (novel) 1877
Marianela (novel) 1878

*Un voluntario realista (novel) 1878
*Los apostólicos (novel) 1879
*Un faccioso mas y algunos frailes menos (novel) 1879
La familia de Leon Roch, 3 vols. [*Leon Roch: A Romance*] (novel) 1879
**La desheredada [*The Disinherited Lady*] (novel) 1881
**El amigo Manso [*Our Friend Manso*] (novel) 1882
***El doctor Centeno*, 2 vols. (novel) 1883
**Las de Bringas [*The Spendthrifts*] (novel) 1884
†*Tormento* [*Torment*] (novel) 1884
†*Lo prohibido*, 2 vols. (novel) 1885
†*Fortunata y Jacinta*, 4 vols. [*Fortunata and Jacinta*] (novel) 1887
**Miau (novel) 1888
**La incognita (novel) 1889
***Torquemada en la hoguera* (novel) 1889
†*Realidad* (novel) 1890
**Angel Guerra, 3 vols. (novel) 1891
***La loca de la casa* (novel) 1892
†*Tristana* (novel) 1892
†*Torquemada en la Cruz* (novel) 1893
La de San Quintin [*The Duchess of San Quentin*] (drama) 1894
***Torquemada en el purgatorio* (novel) 1894
†*Halma* (novel) 1895
†*Nazarin* (novel) 1895
†*Torquemada y San Pedro* (novel) 1895
La fiera (drama) 1896
**El abuelo (novel) 1897
**Misericordia [*Compassion*] (novel) 1897
*De Onate a la Grandma (novel) 1898
*Mendizabal (novel) 1898
*Zumalacarregui (novel) 1898
*La campana del Maestrazgo (novel) 1899
*La estafeta romantica (novel) 1899
*Luchana (novel) 1899
*Vergara (novel) 1899
*Los ayacuchos (novel) 1900
*Bodas reales (novel) 1900
*Montes de Oca (novel) 1900
Electra (drama) 1901
*Narvaez (novel) 1902
Las tormentas del 48 (novel) 1902
*Los duendes de la camarilla (novel) 1903
El abuelo [*The Grandfather*] (drama) 1904
*O'Donnell (novel) 1904
*La revolucion de julio (novel) 1904
*Aita Tettauen (novel) 1905
Barbara (drama) 1905
*Carlos VI en la Rapita (novel) 1905
**Casandra (novel) 1905
*Prim (novel) 1906
*La vuelta al mundo en la Numancia (novel) 1906
*La de los tristes destinos (novel) 1907
*Espana sin rev (novel) 1908
***El caballero encantado* (novel) 1909
*Espana tragica (novel) 1909
*Amadeo I (novel) 1910
*De Cartago a Sagunto (novel) 1911

La primera republica   (novel)   1911
Canovas   (novel)   1912
**La razon de la sinrazon*   (novel)   1915
El tacano Salomon   (drama)   1916

* These novels comprise the historical series *Episodios nacionales.*

† These volumes comprise the series *Novelas españolas contemporaneas.*

** These volumes comprise the 6-volume series *Obras completas*

CRITICISM

Sherman H. Eoff   (essay date 1961)

SOURCE: "The Deification of Conscious Process," *The Modern Spanish Novel,* New York: New York University Press, 1961, pp. 120-47.

[*In this essay, Eoff studies the positivist aspect of Perez Galdós's spiritual and psychological assessments in reference to popular philosophies of his day.*]

Contemporaneous with the somber view of life so stoutly exemplified by Zola, there was an equally virile manifestation of optimism. It is an attitude that must not be confused with "Victorian complacency," for it was characterized more by determination than by placid contentment. Evidencing respect for but not fear of scientific developments, it was the expression of a frank effort to incorporate the biological, social, and moral sciences in a meaningful whole. The philosophical outlook is appropriately called "spiritual naturalism," a term in wide use in the late nineteenth century.

This "other side" of naturalism finds an unusually vigorous exponent in Benito Pérez Galdós, foremost novelist of modern Spain and one of the most truly representative personalities of the nineteenth century. Although very much a product of his age, Galdós was an independent and poised thinker who occupied a firm middle ground in which he evinced neither a worship of science nor a worship of religion and yet respected both. Like Zola, he was interested in man as a product of nature and of society, but his attention was directed more to the upper reaches of the evolutionary slope and hence showed a greater interest in psychology than in physiology. Moreover, in his conception of man as a social being, however deeply entangled in relations with others, he saw always an individual character rather than a fragment of group consciousness at the mercy of a mysterious vital force or "will." Much more of an intellectual than Zola, he persistently tried to harmonize all knowledge, exact and speculative, in an interpretation of human nature within a comprehensive view of total Nature. At times, especially in his early works, his antagonism to certain excesses of static society, such as religious and social prejudices, led him into the emotionalism of an evangelistic progressive. In his mature and most characteristic posture, however, he contemplates studiously and often with quizzical amusement the relationship between individual personality and its social environment. He thus constructs a novel of character, which typically is a psychological story of struggle, adjustment, and growth.

The age in which Galdós attained his professional maturity—roughly, the twenty years following his arrival in Madrid in 1862 from his home in the Canary Islands—was for Spain a period of intellectual invigoration contrasting with the dull mid-century period of staticism. The age was marked by the growth of liberalism and a lively interest in ideas from other European countries. The major orientation for the Spaniards continued to be France, as it had been since the advent of the Bourbon dynasty in 1700. Paris was, in fact, not only a source of French ideas but a kind of clearinghouse, by way of commentary and translation, for the intellectualism of other lands, notably Germany and England. Of these two major sources of ideas, in addition to France, German thought is especially to be noted in the second half of the century. This influence is no doubt partly to be explained by the personal stature and leadership of Julián Sanz del Río, who took the chair of philosophy in the University of Madrid in 1854 after several years of study in Germany and soon became one of the most influential figures of modern Spain—not so much for the philosophical system (Krausism) that he espoused as for his liberalizing and stabilizing effect on the youthful intellectuals of the 1860's.

In the decade 1870-1880, particularly, there was much controversy between traditionalists and liberals on literary and philosophical subjects, but there was also a widespread attitude of conciliation, which, incidentally, was one of the earmarks of Sanz del Río's philosophy.[1] The attitude was a continuation of the desire manifest in Europe throughout the century for co-operation among science, philosophy, and religion. With some the spirit of conciliation was scarcely more than a willingness to accept a state of peaceful coexistence of independent fields of thought in a compartmentalized world where science could go its own way without intruding on the domains of another discipline. Thus an orthodox religious believer, while trying to keep abreast of intellectual activity, could remain comfortable by dividing the human being, as of old, into body and soul and assigning the parts to different and actually disconnected areas of study.[2] The kind of conciliatory attitude, however, which has special relevancy to our subject is the determination to find within a unitary system of being a co-operative activity that is at one time a natural and a spiritual process. What this intention amounts to is the incorporation of science into philosophy. In the intellectual climate of Spain in the last two decades of the nineteenth century the science most amenable to the merger was psychology. The psychological viewpoint referred to may, in broad terms, be described as a combination in which the physical and the psychical, though apparently independent, are mutually dependent and open to synthesis at a higher level of consciousness.

The subject of psychology seems to have acquired particular importance in Spain around 1880. The Spaniards, who in general rejected any kind of scientific materialism, welcomed a psychology that made room for philosophical idealism. This is one reason why it is worthwhile to look for indications of German ideas in philosophical and fictional literature, and the German psychologist whose natural philosophy would seem most at home in the liberal Spain of 1880 is Wilhelm Wundt. In so far as Galdós is concerned, the way of thinking represented by Wundt has greater interest for us than the systems of other leading European philosopher-psychologists, such as Spencer and Taine.

Spanish acquaintance with Wundt apparently was very superficial at first, coming about indirectly, probably through the French. U. González Serrano, prolific writer of philosophical and psychological treatises, opposed the German psychologist in 1879 on the grounds that he was a mechanist who treated the physical and the psychical as one. Referring to Wundt's *Physiological Psychology* (1874), he mistakenly identifies him with the school of contemporary psychologists who place greatest weight on sensation and molecular movement, thus producing a "psychology without a soul."[3] Actually, Wundt was as much opposed as González Serrano to the mechanistic materialism of the eighteenth-century sensationalists and the "psychophysical materialism," as he calls it, of the nineteenth century; and he makes this clear in the Introduction to his *Physiological Psychology*. He refuses to believe that there is any such thing as mind substance—for he believes that mind is process—but he just as quickly rejects any thought of material substance. He makes use of physiology as a necessary basis in experimental science, but he keeps it subordinate by arguing that mental life holds the key to its true interpretation, and he accordingly gives much value to voluntary activity, which is found at the highest levels of life.[4] González Serrano, in some of his statements of later date, shows himself to be in agreement with Wundt in several important respects: the belief that necessity and freedom are complementary rather than contradictory,[5] the belief that the body possesses an unquestionable psychological value,[6] and the contention that will, the most complex and superior manifestation of life, which reaches its height in the form of human personality, must be examined in terms of reason.[7]

It is unnecessary—and it would probably be difficult—to prove that Wundt as either scientist or philosopher had a specific and direct influence on Galdós. The latter partook of many fountains, combining them at will and no doubt depending upon popularized presentations of well-known works more than upon primary sources.[8] The important thing, then, is to point out certain ideas prevalent in the novelist's intellectual environment that help to account for his interpretation of character and personality. Wundt and González Serrano represent a psychological-philosophical outlook with which Galdós was in large degree compatible. In broad perspective, it was a mixture of philosophical idealism and scientific realism, which in novelistic art may be aptly termed *idealismo realista*.[9]

Psychology was the medium by which this particular outlook was most concretely understandable. "The psychological system," as one writer declared in 1885, offered new hope in the realm of philosophy, for it provided for a synthesis of empiricism and idealism.[10]

In connection with the marked desire to reconcile nature and reason by way of philosophy, the rise of social psychology must be kept in mind and with it the increasing inclination to emphasize the relationship between the individual and society. Sociologists early in the century (Comte and Spencer, for example) had recognized the close relationship existing between the social and the biological sciences, but it took time for the crystallization of the concept of an active interdependence in which heredity as the natural agent and society as the environmental agent share responsibility in the creation of an individual. The concept of such a creative relationship, however, did assert itself gradually in the field of psychology, and personality came to be regarded as a process of becoming: "personality is not a phenomenon but an evolution, not a momentary happening but a history, not a present or a past but both of them."[11] A viewpoint that visualizes a continuously active combination of natural and environmental factors as an explanation of personality tends to de-emphasize the passive states of evolutionary development, in which man appears to be more or less at the mercy of a nature that looks only to the interests of the species. It allows, rather, for a process of give-and-take, in which the individual uses environment for his own good while being molded by it. A combination of the social and the psychical is thus made to provide a constructive basis for the human situation.

In so far as Galdós is concerned, there is perhaps no more significant phase of nineteenth-century scientific thought than the rise of social psychology; and, as we shall see later, the subject takes on special interest when viewed in conjunction with the spiritual evolutionism of Hegel. The social and psychological synthesis of competing yet co-operative forces, which was a rather common topic of discussion in Galdós' day, is actually suggestive of Hegel and raises the question of his possible influence in the late nineteenth-century novel. Hegelianism had lost ground with the raise of positivism but it regained some of its popularity in the last third of the century and, curiously enough, at a time when Schopenhauer's star was definitely in the ascendancy. Von Hartmann testified in 1878[12] that the two philosophies most fruitful and decisive in Germany in a period of several years preceding that date were those of Hegel and Schopenhauer, and he himself drew on both in constructing his own system. In the 1870's and 1880's in Spain a number of prominent intellectuals were Hegelians, among them Emilio Castelar, who declared in 1874 that "the real philosophy of progress is the philosophy of Hegel."[13] In the periodical literature of the epoch Hegel is mentioned at times in a general way only, and at times with reference to the harmony of opposites; and occasionally one finds statements that definitely recall the philosopher without any allusion to him as a source. Such statements give prominence to the idea that progress toward truth is a step of transcendent movement achieved in the synthesis of opposites. For example:

> To rise above the objects that experience presents, to dominate this world of oppositions and struggles, of contradictions and antitheses, and to find the truth in which those oppositions disappear, negations are erased, and everything comes together in laws of unity and harmony; such is the science of the essential; such is the object and the usefulness of philosophy.[14]

Or again:

> In order that there may be a perfecting, it is necessary that there be limitation; in order to weigh the truth, it is also necessary that there be an opposition of contradictory ideas, and to this conclusion those people will come who allow themselves to be puzzled by the force of antithesis.[15]

Discourses about the necessity of conflict, the transcending of antithetical situations, and the resultant expansion of human personality as an evolutionary expression of Mind are pretty definite indications that certain fundamental Hegelian ideas formed a part of the intellectual subject matter with which the youthful Galdós, alert to ideas of every kind, would certainly have been familiar.[16] When adapted to social psychology, Hegelian theory provides a view of evolution that focuses attention on the later stages of man's history and shifts the emphasis from the past to the future. It is precisely this perspective that becomes evident in Galdós' novels of contemporary social life once he has expended some of his pent-up rebelliousness against the severe Spanish traditionalism that he opposed both publicly and privately. By 1886 he seems to have developed a firm philosophical outlook; and it was at this time, the most vigorous stage of his career, that he composed *Fortunata y Jacinta.*

FORTUNATA Y JACINTA (1886-1887)

This massive novel is one of the richest and most elaborate examples of nineteenth-century realism. Deeply set in local milieu, it is a broad social record of Madrid life around 1870-1875, and a veritable depository of national types. With all its local color, however, it is an outstanding study of an individual personality and the vital expression of a positive philosophy. Because of the novel's detail and its leisurely tempo, the present-day reader may wish that Galdós had condensed his story into half the space. Yet much of the material that might be classified as background is actually a necessary part of a novelistic method that makes character portrayal the first duty of a novelist and makes social environment an indispensable basis for the portraiture. No better example could be found of a novelist who is also a social psychologist observing the formation and growth of personality in its contact with surroundings. In Galdós' world environment consists primarily of ideas and personal relationships, as compared to the heaviness of physical surroundings found in Zola. Out of a rich background of social relations, the characters emerge slowly, as the author, with a narrative rhythm befitting his leisurely biographical plan, follows

the course of personal vicissitudes over a comparatively long period of time. The reader, therefore, cannot expect to find in *Fortunata y Jacinta* a concentration of dramatic action centering on a specific set of circumstances such as Zola presents in *Germinal*. He should look, instead, for a story of gradual psychological development in one or two of the principal personages, and he may expect these sometimes to retreat from view within a large network of friends and relatives, whose activities and speech form a kind of historical record of contemporary Spanish life.

For purposes of a quick introduction, the story of *Fortunata y Jacinta* may be defined as the progress and outcome of a rivalry in which two women, one from the *pueblo* or proletariat (Fortunata) and one from the upper middle class (Jacinta), vie for the love of a man (Juanito Santa Cruz) who belongs to a wealthy merchant family. The outcome of the rivalry, however, when defined in terms of surface events, will prove to be of less interest than the psychological portraiture of Fortunata's efforts to compensate for her inferiority.[17] The feeling of inferiority, which is actually a creative motivation in the central character, is not so much attributable to her social class as to her fall in society's respect after being seduced and abandoned by Santa Cruz. As the author follows Fortunata's psychical agitation and the regenerative development growing out of it, he is deliberately dealing with the problem of morality, viewing it in the light of conflicting demands of natural and social laws. The two women rivals in fact—the author makes clear by repeated allusions to the subject—are meant to be representatives of two great forces, nature and society; and in their relationship, particularly as evidenced in Fortunata, there are definite philosophical implications that will have to be considered an integral part of the story. These have to do especially with the subject of individuality.

The philosophical quality of *Fortunata y Jacinta* will perhaps seem remote to one who begins the novel for the first time, because it is deeply submerged in character and situation as these are handled by an enthusiastic follower of realistic technique. The Spaniards of 1887, themselves, were undoubtedly less moved to philosophical reflection than to enjoyment of a picture of life in Madrid in 1870 revived with the humor and informality of a sympathetic onlooker. Galdós unquestionably took pride in the role of social historian, which he enacts quite openly in volume one of his novel. But he was also concerned with society as a formative influence on personality, and his attention to background must be considered partly as preparation of the medium in which the main characters are to be observed. Thus, when *Fortunata y Jacinta* is viewed in its totality, volume one is hardly more than a setting for the narrative situation and an exposition of the milieu in which the heroine is to perform.

In this introductory volume Fortunata remains almost altogether out of sight, like the protagonist of a play who comes on stage only after the way has been thoroughly prepared. The reader's attention meanwhile is directed to various minor characters, whom the author treats in a manner reminiscent of Charles Dickens. For Galdós also has the spirit of an amused spectator watching some of the curiosities of the big broad world; and with him, as with Dickens, the most striking curiosities in all nature are people. Purely as an artistic activity the author enjoys describing people, giving us "More and more particulars relating to this illustrious family" (chapter heading, I, vi). Consequently he uses much more time in this pursuit than is strictly necessary for narrative purposes, though he has the incidental characters justify their presence by performing mechanical roles in advancing the central narrative action. One such personage is Estupiñá, a friend of the Santa Cruz family, a former clerk, now eking out a humble existence doing odd jobs and living in one of the poorest sections of Madrid.

It was on a visit to Estupiñá's place, once when he was ill, that Juanito Santa Cruz first met Fortunata, coming upon her as she stood sucking a raw egg on the steps of the apartment where she lived with her aunt, a poultry dealer. This is the only time in all of volume one that the reader sees Fortunata, but the brief glance at an uninhibited, vital, and beautiful girl is sufficient to leave an indelible image of the wholesome primitiveness that was continuously thereafter to exert a magnetic attraction on Juanito Santa Cruz. Juanito is a pampered only son who usually does as he pleases, though the general course of his life is pretty closely watched by his mother, Doña Bárbara. Soon after he meets Fortunata, Doña Bárbara detects signs of waywardness in her son and hastens to arrange his marriage to his cousin Jacinta, a model of respectable middle-class society who carefully observes the approved social and moral standards. On their honeymoon Jacinta's curiosity gets the best of her professed indifference concerning her husband's past, and she finally elicits his confession that he had seduced and abandoned Fortunata. Generous enough to overlook this stain on Juanito's record, she soon realizes that she will have to be even more forgiving during her married life; for after a short time she faces the necessity of competing with another woman for her husband's love. Her longing for a child, attributable partly to a desire to hold her husband, increases when she learns that Fortunata had borne a son to Juanito. She even tries to locate the child and adopt it, invoking the aid of her spinster friend Guillermina, whose charitable activity has led her to an acquaintance with various families of the slums. Jacinta's hopes are thwarted when Juanito tells her that his son has died and her father-in-law asks her to give up the small boy whom she has mistakenly thought to be her husband's. She thus feels with double sharpness the unpleasantness of her competitive position when she detects evidence of her husband's recurring waywardness and suspects that he is seeing Fortunata again.

The first volume, which closes with attention to Juanito's persistent search for Fortunata, has been largely devoted to his part in the triangle and is the one section of the novel in which his characterization has real psychological solidity. His is the case of a young man conditioned in the static ease of middle-class society feeling the attraction of a representative of the virile *pueblo*, intelligent enough to recognize the value of an intermixture of

social classes, and yet reacting with the mediocrity of his insignificant companions. Repeatedly he shows this vacillation between two forces (symbolized by Fortunata and Jacinta), between revolution and order, between spontaneity and conventionalism, but he accepts more and more cynically the prejudices of the privileged group and solves his personal problem easily by way of an indifferent, laissez-faire attitude. His characterization is firmly grounded in the general ideational content of the novel having to do with the relative validity of reason and natural impulse and the role of individuality as a medium of interaction between the two. But in so far as our interest in an individual is concerned, Juanito's portrait quickly recedes into the background, becoming of importance only as a mechanical object of reference in the Fortunata-Jacinta relationship.

In all of the novel after the first volume, the rivalry between the two women is presented primarily from Fortunata's viewpoint, and the narrative action records the course of a changing sense of values as Fortunata turns gradually from Juanito to Jacinta as her main orientation. The course is marked off in major steps, in which decisive psychological shifts of emphasis follow climactic happenings, with each new stage being an extension of ideas already at work in the preceding stage. This view of the novel's principal impact, of course, is an interpretation of the story as a psychological development, in which personality change is the most meaningful aspect of the narrative action. It is based on the conviction that Galdós should first of all be understood as a socio-psychological novelist.

When Fortunata comes actively into the story at the beginning of the second volume, some three years have passed since she was abandoned by Santa Cruz. In this time she has drifted from one man to another, and now, temporarily unattached, rests in a rather low trough of indifference. In this state of dulled consciousness a period of reactivation begins, which will become both a process of socialization or adaptation of the individual to the social whole and a moral regeneration or growth in self-respect and sympathetic attitude toward others, including eventually her "enemy" Jacinta. First, the motive of social respectability is stimulated when she meets Maximiliano Rubín and after much persuasion prepares to marry him. Maximiliano is one of the numerous unfortunate specimens of the human race portrayed with humor and sympathetic understanding by Galdós and occasionally, as now, elevated to a major supporting role in the narrative. Physically insignificant, suffering from a chronic nervous illness, held in low esteem by people in general, and dominated by his officious aunt, Doña Lupe, Maxi sees in Fortunata not only a beautiful woman but an opportunity to assert himself and, by reclaiming her, to accomplish something in his own right. Enthusiastically he sets about his plans, gaining with some difficulty the co-operation of his aunt. Fortunata accepts the proposal of marriage halfheartedly, submitting to a transitional period of "moral cleansing" in a convent for fallen women. But, despite all her seeming indifference, she sincerely desires the security of a home and honestly believes that she may someday be able to love the unattractive Maxi.

Even as Fortunata prepares for the marriage, however, certain disturbing thoughts begin to complicate her social reclamation. Through Mauricia *la Dura,* a derelict whom she meets in the convent and who will repeatedly encourage her to return to Juanito, she hears of Jacinta's virtuous reputation and her unfulfilled desire for children. She then learns that Juanito is looking for her. The temptation to rejoin the man whom she has never ceased to love reaches a climactic point on her wedding night when Juanito comes to the door of her apartment and she paces the floor in debate with her conscience as her husband lies sick in bed. Her sense of fair play with respect to Maxi maintains the upper hand on this occasion, bearing eloquent testimony to a restimulated strength of character; but the temptation has been too great, and she soon deserts the Rubín family to live in an apartment provided by Santa Cruz.

Fortunata's attempted readjustment thus appears to be a failure, as the second volume of the novel comes to an end. Pride of possession in a competitive struggle and natural love unmixed with complicating social motives triumph over concern for what people think. "You are my husband," she tells Juanito, defiantly ignoring society, "everything else . . . piffle!" (288)[18] Nevertheless, the seeds have been planted that will cause Fortunata to modify her untamed individualism. Thoughts of Jacinta's spotless reputation will never leave her, looming up first as a cruel obstacle, then as a challenge, and eventually as an object of admiration. Angry when Juanito abandons her a second time, she walks over to the Santa Cruz home, feeling the savage impulse to engage her rival in combat though giving in finally to passive dejection and a liaison with Feijoo, a man three times her age. What follows in volume three is essentially a groping for orientation on the part of one who is bewildered by the conflict between natural, honest impulses and the demands of conventional society. Feijoo himself, acting partly as lover and partly as father, contributes toward Fortunata's stabilization. For, although he discusses the subject of compromise between nature and society with the cautiousness of a tightrope walker and the flexibility of one who must justify his own situation, he supplies much-needed kindness and sympathetic understanding. Fortunata, however, is less concerned with Feijoo's moral philosophy and the expediency of social conventions than she is with her relative standing with respect to Jacinta. To be *honrada* like Jacinta, even though she doesn't know exactly what the word means, becomes for her a necessity. For a while she follows a calm, routine existence, showing an acquired veneer of conventionalism, especially after rejoining her husband when Feijoo, because of his age and bad health, urges her to do so and persuades the Rubíns to take her back into the family. A period of intense psychological activity and uncertainty arises again when by chance and for the first time she finds herself in Jacinta's presence, on the occasion of Mauricia *la Dura*'s illness. Here Fortunata again feels the impulse to hurt her enemy and does in fact aggressively reveal who she is.

The conflict now is clearly more than a battle between two persons, one a representative of nature and one a representative of society. It is a psychological conflict between the primitive and the social within the same person, which may also be described as the struggle between a life force that is always surging forward in raw instinctive action and a restraining and directive force that compels halts and periods of stabilization. More important, both elements of the conflict are indispensable to the individual. The "natural" impulse tells Fortunata that the man she first loved belongs to her and that Jacinta "stole him from me" (401). Social motives become gradually more intense, as evidenced by the increasing desire to be accepted in the small circle to which Jacinta belongs. Trapped in a conflict between natural and social interests, like a child groping for understanding, Fortunata climbs a ladder of changing values bearing on self-respect and the respect of others.

The climb, however, is slow and faltering. While in an emotional state of confused aspirations following her unexpected meeting with Jacinta, Fortunata is drawn into the second major climactic happening of the narrative, which proves to be a decisive turn of events and a decisive development in the heroine's personality. Looking for guidance and encouragement, she turns to Guillermina, who has taken a tolerant, even friendly attitude toward her, recognizing that an inherent soundness underlies the rough primitive surface of this representative of the *pueblo,* this "uncut stone." With sincere respect for her "friend's" saintly reputation, Fortunata calls on her one day, nursing the rather astonishing hope that she can gain the gratitude of the Santa Cruz family by contributing a son to Juanito. Jacinta, she argues, may be "as much of an angel as you like; but *she doesn't have any children,*" and a wife who cannot have children is not a wife (421). Guillermina is less bewildered by this strange idea than she is embarrassed by the fact that Jacinta had dropped in unexpectedly shortly before Fortunata's arrival and is now concealed in a bedroom. For once in her life the resourceful "virgin and founder" (of charities) finds herself unable to dominate a situation and remains almost completely helpless when Jacinta, at a remark of her rival's, furiously rushes out of her hiding. The hand-to-hand combat and the battle of words that follow end with Fortunata physically the victor and emotionally the loser, at least temporarily; for in an aftermath of despondency she feels more keenly than ever her inferiority. Instrumental in her recovery from this momentary defeatism is her determination to carry out her idea, her *pícara* idea of having a son by Juanito. Volume three thus ends with a reestablishment of relations with her lover in what seems to be another moral relapse: a rebellious defiance of social regulation and the triumph of natural love.

It is quite clear, however, that Fortunata is now merely using nature (the capacity for bearing children) as a means of compensating for a feeling of inferiority caused by society; that Juanito, in contrast with his position earlier in the story, is important to her primarily as a stepping-stone to a more favorable relationship with Jacinta; and that defiance of moral rules is in reality an expression of the value attached to approval by others, which brings the ever-increasing need of a more respected moral status. Here is illustrated the paradoxical appearance of life, which Galdós is fond of portraying. Paradox, it should be emphasized, is fundamental in the novel's structure, and apparently so through deliberate design. The turning to Juanito is in reality a turning from Juanito to Jacinta; the attainment of superiority is the expression of inferiority; the desire to triumph over an enemy is a desire to win her respect and friendship; the ascendancy of natural forces is a concession to social forces. In short, Fortunata's seeming reversion to a former state is really an advance to a higher state. The firmness and decisiveness noticeable in her action after the violent meeting with her rival are in themselves an indication of self-direction and self-respect. But the major consideration continues to be her self-enlargement by way of social relations, which is directly attributable to her competition with Jacinta.

The heroine's psychological journey, it must be noted, is a succession of stages, some of which are periods of repose following moments of intense agitation. Her portrayal is characteristic of Galdós' method, by which a protagonist is allowed to rest on a plateau of psychological consolidation after a decisive turn of events. The method is very much in accord with our present-day conception of personality growth as being a fluctuating movement of advances, halts—and retrogressions at times—and consolidations of slowly changing tendencies, rather than an even, uninterrupted flow. Thus in the case of Fortunata there is a quiet period of relaxation and even a display of conventionalistic veneer as she resumes relations with her lover while maintaining appearances as a member of the Rubín family. The author meanwhile devotes a great deal of attention to various secondary characters, especially to Maximiliano, whose bad health and suspicions concerning his wife are driving him nearer and nearer to madness. Some of the personages who receive lengthy attention are altogether minor. Such, for example, are the tragicomic and wretched José Ido del Sagrario and the lonely Moreno Isla, who is hopelessly in love with Jacinta and would have been a much more suitable husband for her than Juanito Santa Cruz. These and other incidental characters contribute to a general impression of tangled and unhappy lives and thus, collectively, give the novel a certain pessimistic coloring, though not enough to obscure the dominant mood of charitable humor on the author's part. Collective human experience, moreover, never assumes a major role in the narrative development. It is, rather, a supplement to the portrayal of a few leading characters, who sometimes appear in harmony with the mass synthesis but are just as likely to present a marked contrast. The explanation is to be found in the author's focus on individuality. Even the mass picture seems to the reader to be an assembly of individual aspirations rather than the fusion of an unconscious urge to live, such as one often finds in Zola. The total picture may be darkened by the shadows of failure and distress, but these only heighten the effect of individual accomplishment; and so it is that Fortunata's struggles and attainments stand out in bold relief amidst a seeming morass of twisted hopes and wasted lives.

As the long narrative approaches its conclusion, the most prominent motive in Fortunata's behavior is her desire for friendship and equality with Jacinta. After a period of quietness she is again drawn into turbulent psychological activity because of accepting as true the assertion of her friend Aurora that Jacinta is unfaithful to her husband. When she tells Juanito what she has heard, he uses the occasion as an excuse for dismissing her, cruelly throwing in her face the lowliness of her moral status as compared to that of her impeccable rival. The fact that she is again abandoned by her lover concerns her much less than her relative moral position, and her desire to attain virtue now becomes a veritable drive to attain partnership with her rival. Formerly she would have delighted in knowing that Jacinta was immoral. Now she begins to have pride in her rival's virtuous reputation, which stands before her like an ideal whose attainment is absolutely necessary to her own happiness. Her preoccupation with this ideal overshadows all other interests, including her domestic situation, and after a quarrel with her husband's aunt she makes a final break with the Rubín family and returns to her childhood home. There she awaits the birth of her child (by Juanito), while Maximiliano, now calm after a period of intense nervous disorder, engages in a long and patient search to discover his wife's whereabouts.

The richest dramatic episode in Fortunata's life and the peak of her psychological journey follows soon after the birth of her son, itself a meritorious accomplishment in her opinion. This contribution of a son is the concrete evidence she has needed to establish her superiority over her rival, but even before the actual event the self-assurance deriving from it by anticipation has already resulted in a feeling of magnanimity toward Jacinta, which she expresses after the birth of her son with a mixture of pride and charity: "now that I have won the dispute [*pleito*] and she is down, I pardon her; I am like that" (524). The "accomplishment" has, of course, a special importance for her as a claim to being accepted, in spirit at least, within the Santa Cruz family circle. She does indeed have the respectable Santa Cruz family in a corner; for, as she muses to herself, "Yes, Señora Doña Bárbara, you are my mother-in-law over and above the head of Christ our Father, and you can jump in any direction you like, but I am the mother of your grandson" (524).

On the basis of this assumed inclusion in the Santa Cruz family, Fortunata takes upon herself the responsibility of the family honor. She is furiously disturbed, therefore, when she learns that Aurora is Juanito's lover, the news coming to her from Maxi, who has found her after a supreme display of logical deduction, of which he, as a person lightly esteemed, is extremely proud. There is in the heroine's reaction an element of anger at Aurora's deception and a good portion of jealousy with regard to the man on whom she has always honestly believed that she held first claim. Juanito as a person, however, is no longer necessary either to Jacinta or to Fortunata. The latter's major motivations are a sense of protectiveness toward her rival and a purely personal need of security; for she sees in Aurora not only a danger to her "friend" Jacinta but a threat to her own hold on the Santa Cruz family. Rising from bed prematurely and fighting for the sanctity of her own and Jacinta's family relationship, she engages Aurora in a violent struggle, which leaves her mortally weakened but one step closer to complete partnership with the woman whom she had once considered her enemy.

The narrative impact of the novel is at its strongest as Fortunata, having willed that her child be given to Jacinta, lies on her deathbed filled with a magnanimity toward everyone, with the possible exception of Aurora. Her desire to be accepted is partially met, because Guillermina, acting in the capacity of friend and counselor, openly recognizes her essential goodness as she tries patiently to prepare her charge for a correct departure from this world; while the author, himself opposed to formalistic religion, mischievously complicates matters by allowing his heroine to die without following the ritual of words pronounced by the priest. Even Jacinta is able finally to admire her rival, and indirectly (through Guillermina) she expresses her gratitude for the gift of the child. The focus of attention in the conclusion nonetheless remains, as it has been through the greater part of the narrative, on Fortunata's preoccupation with her relative position when compared with Jacinta; except that now the standards of comparison reside in a spiritual realm where the approval of God is a necessity. "Both of us are angels," the heroine declares as she nears death, "each in her own way" (545). With the simplicity of a child seeking the warmth of an intimate group, she reaches out in complete sincerity to those around her, at the same time trying desperately to talk herself and everyone else into believing that she, like Jacinta, is a "darling of Heaven" (*mona del Cielo*). The grandeur of spirit that she attains before her death is sufficient to convince a number of her acquaintances, including the author, that she has a good chance of winning God's approval.

The reader who wishes to enjoy the full strength of Galdós' novel must look beyond the situational plot—first to the psychological development that takes place in the leading character and then to the attendant implications of a moral-philosophical nature. The elaborate social background and the large array of secondary characters are not to be disregarded. The portrait of Maximiliano Rubín, who ends up in an insane asylum, is a psychological study that commands a great deal of interest in its own right. But the major significance of **Fortunata y Jacinta**, most critics will surely agree, rests in Fortunata herself, whatever be the method by which the novel is judged. From the standpoint of situation, we have witnessed a shifting course of emphasis within a triangle, where a woman turns gradually from enmity to friendliness toward her rival, virtually forgetting the man involved in the relationship. The final episode, in which Fortunata makes the sacrifice of giving her son to her former enemy, carries a strong dramatic effect when judged purely as situation. The rich emotional quality of the drama, however, derives primarily from the psychology of the heroine, a child of nature, a primitive woman of the *pueblo*, who is increasingly drawn toward ideals of the social whole which opposes her. Fortunata's natural soundness, with all her insistence

on the honorableness of natural love, lies at the heart of the characterization; but it is brought to the surface and developed by way of a process in which the socially important (respectable reputation) becomes personally important and growth results through response to challenge. Almost to the last the heroine maintains, verbally at least, that "when that which is natural speaks, men have to keep their mouths shut" (501). But there is no mistaking the value that she places on a sympathetic relationship with those of unquestioned moral and spiritual standing. The Fortunata who in the end is capable of giving her son to her rival is not only far removed from the castoff who had passively agreed to a plan of social regeneration; she is morally and psychologically far beyond the childhood stage where the reader first glimpsed her. Most important of all, perhaps, the advance derives from a contest in which individual impulse and the restraining force of collective humanity continuously counterbalance each other.

The psychological progress, then, may be described as a transcending development arising from the meeting of antagonistic forces. Such a statement naturally brings Hegel to mind, and indeed the developmental process evident in Fortunata's psychology can appropriately be compared to the Hegelian interpretation of self-realization in so far as this is applicable to an individual life. Three aspects, especially, recall Hegel's theory of self-consciousness as set forth in his *Phenomenology of Mind*: the dependence of self upon an otherness (a specific person, for example) for the attainment of its own reality, the necessity of conflict, and a transcending movement in which self emerges from the conflict to rise above its former state. The succession of upward steps by which Fortunata expands her sympathetic attitude toward her antagonist, reverting sometimes to former levels and yet ever acquiring a new and more refined consciousness, could be used as a concrete illustration of Hegel's theory of spiritual evolution. Moreover, Galdós' optimistic contemplation of the paradoxical aspects of experience suggests Hegel's determination to bring meaning into the paradoxes of life. Fortunata's moral rise is a continuous course of elevation by way of seeming defeat and moral relapse, and the most dramatic and significant episode in her personal history is a triumph by way of surrender (in the gift of her son to her adversary). Maxi's case also is paradoxical. Though destined finally to an insane asylum, he is serenely confident of his philosophical and spiritual rise; and the author, who looks on in smiling fantasy, would grant that Maxi may be right, because he is willing to look for wisdom and spiritual grandeur in seeming madness. "The Reason of Unreason" (*La razón de la sinrazón*), the title of one of the late chapters in the novel, is a favorite theme with Galdós.

There is, further, an unmistakable symbolic meaning, apart from the psychology of the characters, in the author's contraposition of nature and society as beneficially antithetical. The representative of nature (Fortunata) and the representative of society (Jacinta), the one dominated largely by impulse and the other by the discipline of social regulation, are mutually dependent though constantly engaged in a tug of war. Society may seem victorious in the end, but Jacinta is no more the winner than Fortunata; for she must accept the contribution (a son) of nature's champion. The social woman and the natural woman (and symbolically, too, the middle class and the *pueblo*) are each incomplete without the other and by their very conflict come to realize this fact. Jacinta, whose thoughts are much less in evidence throughout the novel than Fortunata's, finally admits that she would like in some ways to be like her rival. Undoubtedly the author meant the two women, when symbolically viewed, to be mutually complementary in a moral sense; but the moral import can easily be extended to harmonize with a philosophical concept of universal law. From a comprehensive viewpoint, then, including the psychology of the main character along with plot situation and symbolism, the story of **Fortunata y Jacinta** is the account of a co-operative activity on the part of natural and social forces working itself out in individual psychology along a line of moral invigoration. The personality of Fortunata is the heart of the process, and the picture of Spanish society is its framework.

In an earlier study the present writer went to some length in arguing for Hegelian content in a number of Galdós' novels written after 1885.[19] There seems to be no reason for a change of opinion, especially in the light of further evidence that Hegelian thought, though by no means attaining the proportions of a major movement in Spain, constituted at least a fairly prominent part of the novelist's intellectual environment. Still, we must not overemphasize any one specific influence. Galdós was stimulated by various philosophers, and artists as well, among them Cervantes, with whom he evinces a broad compatibility. But whatever the sources of his philosophical ideas, we can be sure that his outlook is firmly grounded, by way of psychology, in the natural world, which is also a social world. For this reason, while looking for metaphysical meaning in his novels we must look to contemporary developments in the field of psychology. From his viewpoint, nature presents two fundamental aspects which reveal a process of competition and co-operation. In a realistic, practical sense, the process is best described as socio-psychological, since the human being is seen as an interaction of personal impulses and determination from without. The most important consideration, however, is that the psychological process is creative. To borrow a term from Wilhelm Wundt, it may be called "creative synthesis," for it could be used to illustrate the trend in the late nineteenth century in the direction of creative evolution. It is therefore worthwhile to include in our discussion of **Fortunata y Jacinta** the psychological viewpoint of which Wundt is representative.

Briefly, Wundt's concept of creative synthesis visualizes the generation of something new from the combination of distinct elements. It is, in the words of Harold Höffding, "a collection and composition, the product of which possesses properties which neither of the moments possessed of its own account."[20] As early as 1863 Wundt lays the foundation for his theory when he says, "Every remembered idea is really a new formation, composed of numerous elements of various past ideas."[21] By this he is saying that the remembered idea does not exist on its own account like a material substance, but arises out of the act of putting two and two together. In a way, of course, this view may be considered an extension of associational psychology, and one should not forget that J. S. Mill, and perhaps others before Galdós' day, had observed that the compounding of parts psychologically often results in a new product. It should be added, however, that Wundt's emphasis rests upon the creative activity in the process of synthesis rather than upon the mere combination of different elements.

For a writer like Galdós, who was inclined always to reflect seriously on current ideas from the field of scientific endeavor, it was almost inevitable that he should give philosophical coloring to the notion of psychological synthesis; and at a time when the theory of evolution was much discussed in both scientific and philosophical circles, it would not be at all surprising if he arrived at a philosophy of creative synthesis independently of Wundt.[22] The process can be seen in operation in the novel under consideration if we think of Fortunata's *pícara* idea of contributing a son to the Santa Cruz family in order to gain their good will. A creature of nature and very much subject to it, Fortunata nevertheless takes charge of her natural heritage for a purpose that produces psychological results quite different from the initial motives. Reacting to her feelings of inferiority, she uses nature (the capacity for bearing children) to satisfy her desire to surpass her rival and actually achieves magnanimity in the process. From either a moral or a psychological viewpoint, there has been a creative synthesis, arising from the meeting and combination of self-centered impulse and social opposition.

Without trying to establish a direct line of influence from Wundt to Galdós, it is profitable to compare their ideas, because the comparison shows how the Spanish novelist reflected in creative art a major contemporaneous development in psychology. Wundt, while maintaining the objective attitude of a scientist, not only conceived of nature as a psychical self-development but considered social psychology the anteroom of ethics.[23] Without the obligations attaching to a scientist's stand, Galdós held essentially the same views. Moreover, both the German and the Spaniard adopt a middle road in regard to the subject of necessity, recognizing that freedom and constraint are reciprocal concepts and both necessarily connected with consciousness.[24] Of special interest is the great emphasis placed by psychologist and novelist alike on individual personality. Wundt looks upon character as the "inmost nature of personality" and, though admitting that we cannot prove that character is not a product of external influences, refuses to assign it to a place in the chain of natural causation:

> It has been said that a man's character is a resultant of air and light, nurture and climate, education and destiny; that it is pre-determined by all these influences, like any other natural phenomenon. The assertion is undemonstrable. Character itself helps to determine education and destiny; the hypothesis makes an effect of what is

to some extent also a cause. And the facts of psychological inheritance make it extremely probable that if our investigation could penetrate to the very beginnings of the individual life, we should find there the nucleus of an independent personality, not determinable from without, because prior to all external determination.[25]

Compare the following statement from *Fortunata y Jacinta*, made in reference to the effort on the part of the Rubín family to re-educate Fortunata by placing her in a convent for fallen women:

> In these matters it is necessary to take into account the (particular) disposition, the spiritual skeleton, that internal and lasting form of the person, which is usually stronger than all the epidermic transfigurations produced by instruction (257).

This assertion can hardly mean that Galdós discounts the effect of environment on personality, for he clearly demonstrates its influence in his portrayal not only of Fortunata but of numerous personages throughout his many novels. What he wishes to stress is his belief in a natural "given," the core of individuality, which escapes determinism from without. In this respect he was in line with contemporary psychologists, among them some of the positivists as well as Wundt, who recognized in the individual a germ of original character, a primitive "given" containing *l'idée directrice.*[26] The significance of this viewpoint lies not so much in the relative importance of heredity and environment as in the fact that individuality is given a conspicuous place in nature's process; for in conjunction with the outer world it provides the basis for creative activity, which at its best is manifest in the development of human personality.

Nature and society, or natural drives and social restraint, thus are visualized by Galdós as two aspects of a larger whole that depends upon their interaction for its own continuity. The life impulse (nature in a strict sense) that aims always at forward movement is individual, egoistic; the restraining force, necessary as a stabilizer for what otherwise would be chaotic activity, is collective. This is a view almost directly the opposite of what we find in Zola (and Schopenhauer), where the life force is aligned with an unconscious mass entity which uses individuation for the purposes of continuity but otherwise denies it recognition. The comparison between the two viewpoints can better be understood if under the banner of individuality we group the following: life, instinct, love, progress; and under the banner of collective phenomena: mass weight or inertia, discipline, reason, stabilization. In Galdós' case, the role of life and forward movement falls to the individual, and deviation from the collective pattern—or mutation by way of individuation, if you will—is the factor of newness. The fact that there are numerous examples of failures and retrogression does not invalidate the general principle of individual potentiality manifest in some of the main characters. In Zola's case, the two groups mentioned above are merged in one and the responsibility for forward movement falls to a total mass force. As manifest in the form of human species, this force is divided against itself in a destructive way; for the conservative, preservative pull toward the past (heredity and atavism, for example) is stronger than the individual deviation that results in change.

The evolutionary view in Galdós, therefore, as compared to that in Zola, reveals a radical shift in emphasis in which the individual deserts the position of servant to the species and becomes the leader. The leadership, however, though providing the indispensable impulse toward newness, is possible only in co-operation with the challenging and determining force of the environing world of nature and society. From a social-moral viewpoint, it is effectuated by living example and not by words. Fortunata unconsciously plays the role of leader, because she not only draws all eyes to her, eventually winning the admiration of all, but she demonstrates a constructive process in her personality itself. Compare this version of the individual's place in the total scheme of things with that in *Germinal,* where Etienne Lantier, having (on the basis of the novel's philosophical implications) no rights in his capacity as individual, finds himself trying to control mass humanity, which theoretically has all the rights.

Considerable interest attaches to the fact that Galdós regards reason as a static aspect of the total life process. For him intuition is the true creative factor in life and is to be found perhaps in its highest state of sensitivity among simple folk who, like Fortunata, are more spontaneous than rational. In a fundamental way, therefore, he exemplifies the nineteenth-century tendency to glorify the instinctive. But there is no indication that he was attracted to the philosophy of the unconscious, of either the Schopenhauer or the Von Hartmann kind. His emphasis falls, rather, on the emotion of love, whose biological expression he sublimates in a mysticism which is more suggestive of Bergson's exaltation of creative intuition than it is of Zola's awe before animal instinct. For he makes love the agency for a plunge forward in evolution,[27] rather than a destructive sacrifice of self to an impersonal life force. At the same time, the fact that he allows reason the role of an organizing and directive force clearly shows that he does not disregard its importance. The most accurate view of Galdós, therefore, must underscore his sense of balance rather than his exaltation of one aspect of experience over another. His intellectual outlook embraces probably the most positive and constructive contributions of nineteenth-century thought: the concept of life as change and growth, the co-operative interplay of self and otherness, the belief that obstacles are but a challenge that leads to progress, and faith in the value of the individual human being. His is unquestionably an optimistic philosophy, but it is free of sentimentalism and complacency. The surface view, in fact, presents much savagery and unhappiness, but the waste and contradictions in nature's total process are not regarded as too high a price for the crowning achievement reached in the creation of an individual personality.

Fortunata y Jacinta is a high mark of the "spiritual naturalism" which was very much a part of the public consciousness in Europe in the 1880's (the author calls one of the chapters in volume four "naturalismo espiritual"). The novel leaves us with a vision of natural law, manifest primarily in the realm of psychology, co-ordinated with, actually incorporated in, spiritual law;[28] and it does so with the indirectness of artistic subtlety. The firm, clear image of frictional though orderly advance transmitted to an imaginary record of human experience in an almost casual way is sure evidence of Galdós' ability to keep his intellectual perspective subordinate to his function as artist. The psychological structure of his story is so deeply submerged in the record of events and the philosophical message is so thoroughly woven into the texture of the whole that the reader can very easily overlook the novel's essential substance. The author's equilibrium, in fact, has contributed to an impression of serenity that lulls rather than excites the reader's emotions. On the other hand, in Zola, whose intellectual perspective is much less equilibrated, emotional turmoil makes itself felt in a great surge of energy, which is directed by artistic sensibility into an organized scheme of dramatic action, the essential drama resting in the sacrifice of the individual to the mass. In Galdós' novel the drama, less spectacular, consists not in the sacrifice of individuality but in its accomplishment within a process that is more psychological than biological. If the Spaniard's view of life had been more terrifying, perhaps he would be more widely known today than he is.

Whatever the comparative storytelling ability of these two novelists, there is no question that they are outstanding representatives of two of the most prominent phases of nineteenth-century thought. Just as a Schopenhauerian outlook combines with Darwinism in *Germinal* to produce a retrospective view of evolution, so a spiritual perspective of Hegelian color combines in **Fortunata y Jacinta** with a Darwinian look toward the future. Of the Spanish novelist it can be said, as it has been said of Hegel,[29] that he makes the Absolute play a double role: the artificer-deity of the eighteenth century and the organism of the nineteenth century. As to the ultimate destiny of the individual, Galdós does not venture a precise opinion. In a sense he is more scientific in his attitude than Zola, for he examines life as a truth at hand unclouded by fear of the hereafter. Stopping short of the extreme consequence of Hegelianism, which would find individuality absorbed in Spirit or personality lost in Personality, he is willing to leave the question to the imagination, fascinated and perhaps amused rather than frightened by the mysterious unknown. Meanwhile he concentrates on immediate life and produces justification for a belief in individual immortality by creating a personality that has earned it.

NOTES

[1] This general conciliatory attitude is possibly the most important consideration in regard to Sanz del Río's influence on Galdós. For a discussion of more specific aspects of the Krausist influence on Galdós, with attention primarily to the novelist's early stage, see Walter T. Pattison, *Benito Pérez Galdós and the Creative Process* (Minneapolis: University of Minnesota Press, 1954), pp. 37-58.

[2] "Las dos filosofías, la que se ocupa de los cuerpos y la que estudia

los espíritus, son en sí buenas, útiles, necesarias," declares Nicomedes Martín Mateos ("Las corrientes filosóficas del siglo," *Rev. de Esp.*, LVIII [1879], 232), a defender of "la filosofía espiritualista," which conceives of an objective spiritual (religious) Law independent of the individual seen as an organism.

[3] "La psicología contemporánea," *Rev. de Esp.*, LIX (1879), 206-20.

[4] See *Principles of Physiological Psychology,* trans. Edward Bradford Titchener (London: S. Sonnenschein & Co., 1904), I, 211, and *Lectures on Human and Animal Psychology* (1863), trans. J. E. Creighton and E. B. Titchener (London: S. Sonnenschein & Co., 1901), pp. 3-10, 409. Cf. also Alfred Fouillée ("La Sensation et la pensée selon le sensualisme et le Platonisme contemporains," *RDM*, LXXXII [1887], 422-23), who observes that Wundt seeks the unity of mental composition in the act of thinking itself instead of in something more *vital* than thought.

[5] "La psicología novísima," *Rev. de Esp.*, C (1884), 747-71. Cf. Wundt's *Lectures . . .* , p. 426.

[6] For which opinion he cites Wundt, Lotze, Ribot, and others: "Valor moral del cuerpo humano," *Rev. de Esp.*, CIV (1885), 27-36.

[7] *Estudios psicológicos* (Madrid, 1892), p. 11.

[8] As far as I know, there were no Spanish translations of Wundt's works in the nineteenth century and no French translations before 1885. There were, however, numerous treatises on contemporary psychology from which a general view of Wundt's ideas could be had. For example, James Sully, "La psicología fisiológica en Alemania," *Rev. contemporánea*, II (1876), 329-57 (trans. of an article in *Mind*); and Th. Ribot, *La Psychologie allemande contemporaine (école expérimentale)* (1879).

[9] González Serrano uses this term based on the German *Realidealismus* (as he calls it), while approving the fact that contemporary art draws on the natural sciences: "El arte naturalista," *Rev. de Esp.*, CV (1885), 41.

[10] Mariano Amador, "El fatalismo de Hartley," *Rev. de Esp.*, CVII (1885), 23.

[11] Th. Ribot, *Les Maladies de la personalité* (1885), as quoted by González Serrano in *Estudios psicológicos*, p. 100.

[12] Preface to the 8th edition of *Philosophy of the Unconscious.*

[13] "La filosofía del progreso," *Rev. Europea,* I (1874), 1. Cf. also: "Síntesis entre la filosofía y la historia," *Rev. de Esp.*, LXXX (1881), 433. For a brief survey of Hegelianism in Spain in the nineteenth century, see Mario Méndez Bejarano, *Historia de la filosofía en España hasta el siglo xx* (Madrid, n.d.), pp. 457-61.

[14] Luis de Rute, "Breves indicaciones sobre filosofía a los matemáticos," *Rev. de Esp.*, VII (1869), 241.

[15] Jaime Porcar, "Observaciones psicológicas," *Rev. de Esp.*, XXV (1872), 266.

[16] Such ideas, of course, could be an indirect reflection of Hegel, through Sanz del Río; but Hegel's personality itself was definitely felt in Spain. His *Logic* was translated into Spanish in 1872.

[17] The essential content of my interpretation of *Fortunata y Jacinta* has been expressed elsewhere: "The Treatment of Individual Personality in *Fortunata y Jacinta*," *Hispanic Review*, XVII (1949), 269-89; and,

rather fragmentarily, in *The Novels of Pérez Galdós* (St. Louis: Washington University Studies, 1954). I feel justified in repeating the main ideas in order to give a comprehensive picture of the novel in relation to its thought background.

[18] Quotations (translated) are from Galdós' *Obras completas* (Madrid: Aguilar, 1942), V.

[19] *The Novels of Pérez Galdós*, pp. 138-50.

[20] *Modern Philosophers*, trans. Alfred C. Mason (London: The Macmillan Co., 1915), p. 6.

[21] *Lectures on Human and Animal Psychology*, p. 452.

[22] The possibility of Wundt's influence, however, cannot be dismissed, since his psychological theories were discussed in Spanish periodical literature before Galdós wrote *Fortunata y Jacinta*. For example, Teodoro [Théodule] Ribot, "La psicología alemana contemporánea. Guillermo Wundt," *Revista Europea*, IV (1875), 293-304, 339-49. The article is a translation from *Revue Scientifique*.

[23] Cf. Höffding, *Modern Philosophers*, pp. 7, 11.

[24] See Wundt's *Lectures . . .* , p. 426.

[25] *Ibid.*, p. 434.

[26] See E. Caro, "Essais de psychologie sociale," *RDM*, XLVII (1883), 530-34.

[27] The view is comparable to that of Bergson set forth in *Les deux sources de la moralité et de la religion* (1932). Cf. my study *The Novels of Pérez Galdós*, pp. 123-24.

[28] Henry Drummond's *Natural Law in the Spiritual World* (New York, 1883), though having no specific likeness to Galdós' novel, is typical in title and content of the general effort at the time to bring the natural sciences into harmony with man's religious impulses.

[29] William Caldwell, *Schopenhauer's System in Its Philosophical Significance* (Edinburgh and London, 1896), p. 55.

Gerald Gillespie   (essay date 1966)

SOURCE: "Reality and Fiction in the Novels of Galdós," *Anales Galdosianos*, Vol. I, No. I, 1966, pp. 11-31.

[*In this essay, Gillespie studies reality in various connections both familial and worldly in Galdós's novels.*]

These words, which the guards speak in piety to comfort their broken prisoner, the priest Nazarín, serve as a fitting epigraph. For no discussion of Benito Pérez Galdós' mature realism is, of course, complete without reference to the impact of Cervantine wisdom upon it. The question of truth and illusion has been standard in the European novel since *Don Quixote,* which became the revered model for English "humor" and German "romantic irony." Cervantes' haunting suggestion that, in addition to the opposites reason and unreason, there was a paradoxical "reason of unreason" also undermined any neat distinction between re-

ality and fiction—perhaps in spite of his own intention of separating them. Through the interaction of Quixote and Sancho, through the treatment of literature as a subject, even the very same mock romance in process of being created, and through the mingling of aspects of the creative personality, was born the "reality of fiction." Nineteenth-century naturalism applied the by then considerable body of psychological theory in its examination of humankind's mental life and tried to effect a clear scientific definition which classified all impulses of the brain as sound or unsound. Two major these were held, both connected with the "facts" of evolution: the physiological or deterministic, and the developmental or organic. Because of its older realism in the picaresque genre, Spain could not be as impressed by the inroads of naturalism. The nation was more receptive to a developmental view (Hegel, Wundt, et al.) which salvaged its Christian faith. As Sherman H. Eoff has shown, Galdós absorbed the fundamental tenets of the post-romantic organic concept of man.[2] But it was through the Cervantine tendency to transcend his own subject, that Galdós achieved genuine universality and renewed the mission of the Spanish novel.[3] From his more clinical case histories (*La desheredada*) to his depictions of sublime self-deceiving (*Angel Guerra*), Galdós tirelessly ascended from the wry irony of naturalistic truth to indulgent meditation, progressing along a pathway analogous to that of his great predecessor from Part one to Part two of the *Quixote.*

It is appropriate to affirm this pattern before we focus too exclusively on late works imbued with the spirit of primitive christianity (*Nazarín*, *Misericordia*) on the lofty plane of Dostoevski's *Idiot.* Otherwise we will fail to take seriously the ending of symbolic works like *La loca de la casa,* which asserts that the "good" cannot live without "evil" (V, 1721). "Mad" Victoria is actually not simply a pious fool, but rather in the Cervantine *loco-cuerdo* tradition. She wins her struggle with her beloved "monster," but out of it grows mutual reconciliation; brute strength of nature in her *nouveau riche* husband and spiritual grace in her womanhood, with its aristocratic pride, achieve a synthesis. If the story of their marriage is a metaphor for mankind's development, it is only more obviously so than Angel Guerra's quest to commune with his beloved, the mystic Leré. When Victoria decides to save her family and offers herself to Cruz, she is virtually a martyr challenging the world for recognition; her imperious demands are answered in kind; and the dramatic contest of wills forms our fable set in reality. While Victoria gives up becoming a nun, Guerra moves in the opposite direction toward fulfillment, drifting from his early activity as a radical and original love to a religious vocation that keeps him close to the woman he believes is a true saint. Guerra's "foolishness" ends in a disillusionment without rancor, when "the blow of reality" both clarifies his mind and brings him to death (V, 1573). Simultaneously, he confesses his own self-deception, understands that he has only been sublimating his nature, and declares "que la única forma de aproximación que en la realidad de mi ser me satisface plenamente, no es la mística, sino la humana, santificada por el sacramento" (1573). No rejection occurs except the banishment of illusion; led by his

Beatrice, Laura, and Dulcinea in Leré, Guerra's soul has climbed to heights of noble acceptance.

Guerra penetrates to the "reality of his being" in a process of growth toward self-discovery, not toward bitter disappointment. If we compare Galdós treatment of the "real" and the "illusory" with that of Balzac and Stendhal, what distinguishes the Spaniard's realism is its Cervantine consciousness. In *Le rouge et le noir*, for instance, the fundamental contest is between the power of the individual heart and the tyranny of an already debunked world. The established order, wearing many masks of splendor, is a very traditional realm of hypocrisy. Hollow secular and religious glory continually threatens to debase the "happy few," those noble souls who live from the knowledge of their own existence in enmity to everything shallow and corrupt. Sorel literally mortifies himself in order to progress through the several spheres of society to high position; his deepest experience of bliss occurs, correspondingly, in prison under sentence of death. In extremity, he at last lives with sincerity. His execution represents the martyrdom of the heart, and Madame de Renal's beatific passing confirms the unassailable validity and absolute commitment of love. Balzac still renders isolated tributes to an élite of romantic individualists in his *Comédie humaine*, as, for example, in the case of Madame de Beauséant. But, generally, his more sensitive figures go rapidly up or down in the harsh, money-dominated society which he depicts. All destinies proceed over the crossroads of finance, and those who do not capitulate fall by the wayside. Balzac reinterprets many "virtues" as maladies, tragic but pathological, and unfortunately on a par with many "vices" in a purely abstract, "scientific" sense. All drives and ideals which do not further worldly success rank as obsession. When Balzac's fuller characters like Rastignac "awake," their sardonic consciousness of the incompatibility of noble aspirations and survival under the laws of nature still generates considerable pathos. Galdós does deliberately create similar tensions, but never *externalizes* the problem to the same extent. For Galdós "fiction" and "reality" are not dichotomous, but interacting, aspects of human existence.

That Galdós fuses the nineteenth-century theory of man as a creature in evolution and another heritage from the romantics, an elaborate psychology, is clear throughout his works. What provides cohesion is not, however, any particular doctrine that sunders fact and fancy. Rather, the Cervantine interplay of various "fictions" and "realities"—the *personaje's*, his world's, the reader's, the author's—binds together a complex realism. Returning to our epigraph, we note that even the guards are aware of some puzzling relationship between saint and madman, but certain only of the fact that folly is everywhere causing things to happen. Yet how carefully they phrase this, clinging to their realism which is a comforting surface order—with loopholes. The real trouble for Nazarín comes when he tells the judge what actually went on, because he cannot keep it to himself. Naturally, the judge thinks he is crazy, since the truth, which is much simpler, may not be accepted without certain "revisions" of reality. The confrontation

with established reality includes, of course, paradoxical inversions, as when villagers (Part three, ch. three) claim that Nazarín worked a miracle on a child, whereas he claims only that he prayed to God; Nazarín actually believes in scientific medicine, after the exhaustion of whose remedies, one then turns in humble supplication to the All-Mighty. Galdós' fascination for scientific discoveries is alive still, in spite of his attempt to portray a mystic sympathetically. For example, he follows the naturalistic vogue by equating neurosis and unfulfilled desire in Nazarín's disciple Beatriz; as soon as she has met someone who can polarize her in another direction, her symptoms become pleasant and she has visions of angels instead of devils. Galdós nevertheless shows no commitment to Nazarín's or his questioners' opinions, when he is handed from the *alcalde* to a judge in Madrid. The parallels to Christ are presented typologically, without a breath of dogma; and yet, Galdós introduces himself into the novel as an eyewitness in order to give all the objections to the reporter's accusations, on a rather materialistic level, against Nazarín as anti-social, escapist, parasitical, and so forth (Part one, ch. five).

Galdós' objectivity is subtle and gratifying in comparison with the usual partisan writings of the nineteenth century. Indeed, it is through this objectivity that he can suddenly overwhelm us with the intensity of "prophetic" statement—a term to which we shall again refer. Nazarín's dream, closing the novel, both expresses his piteous state and removes him from the terrestrial limitations it has imposed. In his own mind, Nazarín reverently is celebrating mass and, when he takes the Host in his hands, he hears Jesus speak to him:

> —Hijo mío, aún vives. Estás en mi santo hospital padeciendo por mí. Tus compañeros, las dos perdidas y el ladrón que siguen tu enseñanza están en la cárcel. No puedes celebrar, no puedo estar contigo en cuerpo y sangre, y esta misa es figuración insana de tu mente. Descansa, que bien te lo mereces. (V, 1814).

The divine voice asks him not to be discontent and promises that he has "much more" to do, whereby the author, of course, prepares us for Nazarín's career in *Halma*. The intimacy of this message avoids any question of veracity—a feat which we can compare only with Ivan's vision of the devil in Dostoevski's *Brothers Karamazov*. By allowing Nazarín to hear in his own thoughts, from the highest authority, that his experience is hallucination, Galdós *demonstrates* convincingly both the priest's sincerity and his probable recovery. This is a moment of crisis that is transcended by profound growth—a mysterious "disillusionment" which occurs through dream in the brain of a visionary, a prime example of the reality of fiction on the highest level of storytelling. Objectively considered as a "message" of his own mind reaching the plane of consciousness, the poignantly subjective dream by Nazarín conveys *truth*. The priest's genuine holiness is deepened and enhanced when his mind integrates his experiences of outside "reality." The validity of his mission is guaranteed by pious acceptance of his natural state.

The general tone of Galdós' novels is so literal that whenever the fantastic is introduced, it produces a very special effect on us. Galdós completely deglamorizes stereotyped romantic situations such as the life of prostitutes. In *Nazarín*, for instance, he introduces the ugliness of one downtrodden woman by having her nicknamed "Camella" from "Camelia," for her tall, bony frame (ch. two). This rather sympathetic humor may strike us as cruel or sublime, according to our conception of Galdós' role as narrator, in a work like **Miau**, whose title derives from the insulting sobriquet with which the Villaamil women have been dubbed. Sáinz de Robles ably argues that "generalmente el satírico y el irónico no son creadores" (IV, liv); in defending Galdós against the charge of impassiveness and cold isolation, he explains the author's non-cohabitation "ni para el bien ni para el mal a sus criaturas" (xxxii) as transcendental humor, in analogy to God's role. While one cannot quarrel with this interpretation, it still avoids a puzzling and intriguing aspect of Galdós' artistry in particular cases. How should we accept the strange interplay of stark realism, vision, and nightmare in a book like **Miau**, through which even the title runs as a motif of the ludicrous, as a whimsical apprehension of harsh truth. No warm humor of late Dickensonian variety can explain away the commingling of the grotesque and sentimental, as in the "oracular" utterances of little Luis—a sweet boy, who tells his grandfather to commit suicide. A contemporary European phenomenon may be reflected in this novel: the upsurge of a phase of late realism which we can well term "sentimental naturalism." As the strictures imposed by doctrinaire determinism loosened and writers had already grown aware of the new spheres which the novel could explore, their interest in the mental life of the masses increased. Psychology was brought to bear on the condition of the lower classes of society, with the result that hitherto stereotyped figures could be analyzed spiritually. An example would be Gerhard Hauptmann's play *Hänneles Himmelfahrt*, which contrasts the wretched death of the abused girl in a barren poorhouse with her childish dreams of apotheosis. The dream episodes, fading in and out of reality, integrate materials from Hanna's environment and experiences, including her juvenile crush on a sympathetic teacher, who is transformed into a heavenly redeemer.

Galdós was in many respects in advance of this wave, as we shall indicate below. Likewise, because of his Cervantine heritage, he was independently in the vanguard of a closely associated movement: psychologistic impressionism and symbolism. Let us examine these two related sorts of realism, which have in common a considerably developed psychology, now expanded to all reaches of society. The fundamental naturalistic trait of the novel **Miau** is its depiction of several generations in one family with related, and presumably, inherited mental illness. Luis' visions of God, so filled with pitiable rationalizations about the course of his own and his family's life, are brought on by epileptic fits. His own mother, now dead, had gone berserk and tried to kill him before the time of the novel. His dignified grandfather, driven to his wits' end by the women in his household and constant,

debasing rejection by the bureaucratic machine for which he formerly worked, chooses release. The boy's aunt shows the same weakness for his reprobate father, a sexual adventurer, and conceives a similar compensatory hatred for her poor nephew. The night she almost murders him in his troubled slumbers is a ghostly scene, in which the reality of her action is scarcely distinguishable from nightmare, for with terrifyingly irrational logic, she slips back into normal behavior. Our realization that daytime and the waking state are only a patina over horror lifts this story from the ordinary level of naturalism toward symbolic drama, but not quite all the way. The meaningful center of motivation is never shifted fully to external agencies, such as the complex of offices which old Villaamil clings to desperately. There is no monstrous symbol to which people are subordinate that compares with the mine in Zola's *Germinal*. Rather the pathological symptoms are identified with psychic pressures in a kind of chronicle that represents with continuity the adjustment or failure of a living strand of humanity in the larger fabric of Madrid. Thomas Mann's *Buddenbrooks* exploits this kind of realism more extensively. We might distinguish Galdós by noting that he tends to favor a more horizontal examination of society in a collection of casas in several novels, as does Balzac. Mann follows the fraying life-line through several periods of history, encompassing thereby also many features of the development of European bourgeois civilization.

The symbolic implications of settings and moments are perhaps clearer in the earlier novel of naturalistic bent, Galdós' **La desheredada**. In the chapter, "Entreacto en la Iglesia," idle, deluded Isidora finds herself staring at a dark, unknown man because she has felt his insistent gaze. Galdós relates—

> Mientras Isidora hacía estas y otras observaciones, notaba que algunas de las elegantes cofrades eran miradas tenazmente por los caballeretes, y que ellas solían mirarlos también con afectada distracción, de donde vino a considerar que si tanto flechazo de ojos dejase una raya en el espacio, el interior de la iglesia parecería una gran tela de araña. ¡Mísera Humanidad! (IV, 1071)

The social theme of the secret religion of the magdalenes would be ordinary in itself, were it not for the sinister evocation that springs from the woman's own brain of the very web in which she will perish. This fleeting prefiguration is less a naturalistic statement than an "impression." The author's outcry sharpens our sense of the danger, but also makes us aware of the sickly thought processes of the protagonist, briefly coming to the surface. There are many similar moments in which external appearance and internal pattern merge in an impression that is revelatory, as, for example, when Isidora masquerades as a Carmen type at festival time in the chapter "Flamenca Cytherea," foreshadowing her descent into low life. The metamorphoses of the public squares of Madrid occur so subtly that we may not at first notice how unfixed, how lacking in hard classical edges they are. When Miquis and Isidora first contemplate the swirling spectacle of society in ostentatious motion, she is rapt in contemplation of its patches of color, whereas Miquis vainly unmasks the phenomena for her, a "believer" in the aristocratic system headed by the queen. But, after Isidora has failed to convince the marquise, her imagined grandmother, of her noble identity, she equates the external scene upon the banishment of the royal household with her own "transition." Her switch to a dishonorable but effective party is associated with the power to topple established authority, i.e., the marquise.

Galdós' imposing talents as an impressionist transform the novel from a harsh analysis of human ills into a great book with depth and breadth. The chapters entitled "Beethoven" and "Sigue Beethoven" are, of course, a deliberate *tour de force,* two moods in analogy to major and minor key. they surely rank alongside Mann's depiction of little Hanno Buddenbrooks evoking through the piano the music of his own languishing soul and Tolstoy's "Kreutzer Sonata." And the sheer beauty of these passages painting the marquise's anguish furnish, by aesthetic proof, as it were, all the knowledge we require to grasp what true nobility of spirit is. Among the number of chapters on Isidora's sleeplessness through mental disturbance, "Insomnio número cinquenta y tantos" should be singled out for its brilliant treatment of interior monologue—again an impressionistic technique. Galdós skillfully weaves together, in a compressed simulation of hours of reverie, the train of thoughts stimulated or deflected by minute occurrences. Acutely perceptive, Isidora hears the bells, scratching, and so forth, details which elicit the whole range of her consciousness and reveal to us the roots of mania under the surface. Although Galdós has not yet gone as far as Joyce in creating a stream of consciousness by (artistically contrived) totally free association, he ought to be recognized for his rather astonishing proximity to Arthur Schnitzler, the master of psychological impressionism and first great exponent of the associative technique (*Leutnant Gustl*, etc.).

The rather obvious analogy to Flaubert's *Madame Bovary* would be exaggerated, if one took no account of the greater variety of techniques in Galdós' novel. To be sure, Galdós too pursues ironically the romantic type who lives "farsas estudiadas o capítulos de novelas" (IV, 1050) and seeks to "encontrar armonías entre su estado moral y la Naturaleza" (1051); who through this sickly pride would be "mala . . . si se quiere; pero ordinaria, jamás!" since "mejor es soñar que ver" (1116). But since the naturalistic analysis is set in a framework, the Quixote tradition, a more specific irony reigns over Galdós' story. The region of La Mancha remains throughout the author's works a Spanish hinterland which is the breeding ground for deluded souls and extravagant idealists. A census of the Madrid of Galdósian novels would show a rather extraordinary migration of these types to the capital. To underscore his thematic adaptation of Cervantes, Galdós divides Isidora's history into two parts, the first of which ends with the humorously mad letter from her uncle the canon, Quijano-Quijada, on his death bed. It is filled with superficial, vain advice, a shallow conception of things religious, opinions on side issues that rankle Spanish pride, such as French cooking, and

unconsciously ironic literary reminiscences, such as his assertion, "Yo tengo gran fe en la fuerza de la sangre" (IV, 1056). Galdós accomplishes much with this reiteration of the context of his narration. He summarizes the illness, points to its roots in the influence of environment, refers to the naturalistic thesis of inherited characteristics, and establishes a parallel for Isidora's case, her foreseeable finish, while temporarily raising our spirits with a comic piece.

The literary context is supremely important, for we note that—unlike Don Quixote—the canon dies *sans* disillusionment. Thus the scientific realism of Galdós' times, which his careful documentation through Isidora's father at the madhouse, her criminal brother, her macrocephalic son, and touched uncle reflects, also makes sense in "classical" Spanish terms. For her history is not a copy but an inversion of the knight-errant's idealism. Isidora's obsession does not ennoble anything nor lend enchantment to our world. That point is made as an opening statement with consummate irony, when Galdós depicts the delicate beauty of nature which the inmates of the insane asylum ignore in their frenzied self-occupation, in the "Final de otra novela." Isidora's typical statement—"¡Qué feísimo es esto!" (1051)—reveals this "cierta hostilidad contra la Naturaleza." She demeans the ordinary inn which Quixote would have transformed into an enchanted castle (986). She wastes a chance to marry a good man, Juan Bou, and the sound advice of Miquis, who generously elaborates the serious implications of *desengaño* for her. She finally dies when her illusion is destroyed, but in vileness contrasting with the sober dignity and salvation of Quixote. In a corroborative inversion, her loyal Sancho, the meek gallant Don José de Relimpios, perishes of a broken heart. Galdós uses the Cervantine tradition to show us what a non-poetic obsession is. Not divine madmen, but wretched creatures lacking any true inspiration, fill the asylum and the prison.

La desheredada is a carefully constructed book which conveys through the rigor of its formal repetitions a sense of tragic dissolution under the pressure of given forces. For, unmistakably, Galdós emphasizes the analogies between collective manking in his city and the above institutions. In the chapter "Navidad," the symbolic season of rebirth, man's activities offer ironic counterpointing to the meaning of the holiday. "Madrid parece un manicomio suelto. Los hombres son atacados de una fiebre que se manifiesta en tres modos distintos: el delirio de la gula, la calentura de la lotería y el tétanos de las propinas" (1037). Galdós' vision of the frenetic upsurge of "pleasures" is more than clinical; the gross appetites, passions, and manias are presented with moral asperity as in the medieval fool tradition. Folly has broken out in an entire population, giving rebirth to thousands of lesser and greater tragedies. Isidora is busy at this sacred turning of the year first getting her brother from jail, and second acting the role of a story-book heroine at the marquise's palace ("Anagnórisis"). Miquis, who in this novel demonstrates lively wit and intellectual control over life, explains to Isidora:

> La vida toda es cárcel, sólo que en unas partes hay
> rejas y en otras no. Unos están entre hierros y otros
> entre las paredes azules del firmamento. (1123)

Galdós is scrupulous and unrelenting in this more severe
mood, even while joking. The motif of the carnival and
its masks, the motif of collective folly, the motif of the
world as prison and hospital (favorites of the *siglo de
oro*) support a fundamental proposition that man must, of
necessity, pass through darkness in his progress toward a
higher state:

> . . . el error tiene también sus leyes y . . . en la marcha
> del universo cada prurito aspira a su satisfacción y la
> consigue, resultando la armonía total y este claroscuro
> en que consiste toda la gracia de la Humanidad y todo
> el chiste de vivir. (1145)

On the one hand, the above words spoken by the author
evoke the grand outline of seventeenth-century theodicy,
the tension of a drama in which our lives are roles and
over which hovers a benign Creator, enacting and beholding what to us is largely confusion. On the other hand, it
suggests a *process* toward some higher synthesis; even
man's "dark urge" (as in Gothe's *Faust*) contributes to
the evolution of this "claroscuro." The organic view, which
was predominantly a product of late eighteenth-century
German thought, dovetailed neatly with the Christian
conception of a world theatre—an affinity which the
romantics thoroughly exploited.[4] The distinctive romantic ingredient added to this literary marriage was, then, a
developmental view of psychic processes.[5] We shall discuss Galdósian traits which are analogous further below.
For now, let it suffice to point out the considerable literary consciousness behind the tiniest details in *La desheredada*. This book, in a positive sense only, is contrived. If, for example, we take too seriously the above
quoted reflection, we are missing one of the principal
joys in reading the story—an aesthetic delight in form.
For the same sentiment appears originally in the mouth
of the amanuensis at the insane asylum: "Consolémonos
todos pensando en que la grandiosa armonía del mundo
consiste en el cumplimiento de la voluntad soberana"
(986), and so on. Unknown to us, Isidora, the listener,
will disintegrate too. Unknown to her, the philosophizing
secretary is about to blow up in a psychic explosion; he
is subject to cyclic fits connected with his pondering of
the imponderables. With choice self-irony, Galdós as
author cites another "writer-philosopher" inside of his
own novel. Such self-quotation in altered circumstances
is a technique for which perhaps Thomas Mann is best
known (e.g., *Tonio Kröger*); it pertains to the overall
"scientific" objectivity which discovers purely abstract
patterns behind vital phenomena. But in the case of Galdós,
it derives also from the Cervantine irony of being now
involuted in one's own fictions, now hovering over them.

Galdós' reworking of Cervantine themes raises questions about man's reality and freedom long before Unamuno. The novel *El amigo Manso* is appropriately, like
Tonio Kröger, an autobiographical relation by an intelligent, sensitive self-observer. Manso, a professor of
philosophy, like Mann's artist, possesses full competence to speak for the mind painfully aware of its own
laws in separation from life, nasty life, of which, however trite and shallow it may be, the intellectual is jealous. Indeed, so bitter is Manso as narrator that he begins by declaring, "Yo no existo," and tells his story
from the "other world" with sardonic disillusionment;
looking back and down from the clouds in his last words,
he sees reality as a puppet play:

> ¡Dichoso estado y regiones dichosas estas en que puedo
> mirar a Irene, a mi hermano, a Peña, a doña Javiera, a
> Caligula, a Lica y demás desgraciadas figurillas con el
> mismo desdén con que el hombre maduro ve los juguete
> que le entretuvieron cuando era niño! (IV, 1283)

Since Manso is one of the most lovable *personajes* created by Galdós, we cannot comfortably ignore his quirks—
or the abstraction of reality as a grotesque fiction. Manso's ability to so envision life is bound up with his destiny to suffer deep anguish. His alienation finally passes
the mark of "neurotic failure" in life and enters a new
realm, the problematic metaphysics of modern forlorn-
ness. Even in his "real" or fictionally real supernatural
state, Manso remains forever alienated. The scope of
Galdós includes both the estrangement of an Isidora from
sane living and the alienation of disabused intellect from
the ridiculousness of life. Manso does not blindly de-
grade nature; however, he cannot help perceiving that
there is something "unreal" about reality, its factual "in-
verosimilitud" (1259). An important question which
Galdósian criticism must ask is whether the author conceives of such understanding as Manso commands as a
kind of "liberation." When Isidora loses her dream, she
falls apart too. Manso begins in disillusionment, but does
this set him free?

Late figures like Nazarín attain spiritual freedom, yet lack
the visible signs of any cerebral dissection of human
existence in search of its key. Rather they appear to share
something of the instinctive impulse which asserts, against
all logic or illogic, life itself. We have noted this reconciliation with existence in the dream through which Jesus
tells Nazarín of his insanity. Dreams in Galdós are the
first manifestation of psychic forces which, flowing from
the darkness of human nature, shape character in the
dynamic process so ably expounded by Eoff. Galdós seems
to agree—probably by general intellectual osmosis—with
the post-romantic formulation of human mentality as an
organism, whose evident layers interact with hidden layers in a continuum of growth or "unfolding" (*Entwick-
lung,* development). The hidden nucleus of the mind never is dormant, even though it is impossible to witness its
activity, and we only learn about its operations when, on
the surface of consciousness, thoughts happen. Manso is
quite aware of the pressures of the mind—in fact, he is
a nascent "psychoanalyst" at moments, and his probing is
connected with his doubts and malaise about the "fiction
of reality"; for example:

> No es puramente arbitrario y vano el mundo del sueño,
> y analizando con paciencia los fenómenos cerebrales

que lo informan, se hallará quizá una lógica recóndita. Y despierto me di a escudriñar la relación que podría existir entre las realidad y la serie de impresiones que recibí. Si el sueño es el reposo intermitente del pensamiento y de los órganos sensorios, ¿cómo pensé y vi? . . . ¡Pero qué tontería! Me estaba yo tan fresco en la cama, interpretando sueños como un Faraón, y eran las nueve, y tenía que ir a clase, y después . . . (1219)

An estimate of the measure in which Galdós reproduces dreams with the stamp of authenticity, as we understand it in the light of modern science, or "contrives" them for romanesque effects is not to the purpose of this essay.[6] More important here is the consistency of his use of dreams and reflections about dreaming with his art.

Galdós' novels belong to the dawning period of "analysis," in which art becomes self-conscious to the point of ambiguous self-denial and fastens on "absurdity" for both its aesthetics and metaphysics. But his faith in the integral "occurrence"—whether human personality or work of art—still prevails. This confidence in the *creative action* whose model is nature knits together the amazing variety of his own productions. Doubtless the observable "reason of unreason" in the instinctual pathway of evolution intrigues Galdós as much as anything negative or pathological. The novel *Tormento* offers us a vibrant example in the earlier Galdós of a positive utterance of inner needs. Amparo, a mere underling in a petty bourgeois household, has emerged from a grisly affair with a priest by the end of the story; she has an opportunity to marry an older man, Agustín, who has made money and seems to crave placid respectability. A deep need to confess overwhelms her, and she experiences the agony of growth in telling him about her life, at the price of rejection. But Agustín is strong enough to develop reciprocally in this confrontation. He rebels against the pretenses of society, religion, the unauthentic "¿qué dirán?" which is not his own voice. To be sure, his heart is not entirely free of prideful lie; however, under the dominant "rules" of life then in force in Spain, his decision to accept Amparo in a common-law marriage, though disgraced, and rescue her by going away to France is a human triumph. The seemingly anarchic impulses of nature deny the "fiction" of our world and proclaim healthy "reality":

> Sal ahora por el ancho camino de tu instinto, y encomiéndate al Dios libre y grande de las circunstancias. No te fíes de la majestad convencional de los principios, y arrodíllate delante del resplandeciente altar de los hechos . . . Si esto es desatino, que lo sea. (IV, 1556)

The complexity of Galdosian art prohibits any simple tragic dualism from usurping the larger Reality, which encompasses both the historical milieu and the myriad intrahistorical dramas within it. The success of Agustín is not canceled out by the failure of Isidora; nor do Manso's own discoveries about himself and his world negate its independent validity. There is no easy formula for a Reality that is not classically fixed, but in flux— very like a Story. Hence Galdós' maturest vision offers us not statuesque, representative "truths" wrapped in the

mask of a personality as *persona,* but organically "happening" personalities who appear to be polarized around basic drives and ideas. His Cervantine framework proves to be exactly that: a matrix of storytelling, through which we learn something also about the nature of a "story." This can be demonstrated by a comparison of *La familia de León Roch*, a novel which marks a turning point in Galdós' own development, and his acknowledged masterpiece *Fortunata y Jacinta*. Superficially, they have in common obvious elements of a very traditional plot arrangement. Disregarding the considerable differences, we might name the type after Goethe's famous novel, *Die Wahlverwandtschaften,* whose title is borrowed from older chemical theory of the "elective affinities" of primary substances. Since only the plot type is of concern, we may over-simplify and define it as an exposition of natural laws which operate when "molecules" (i.e., couples) encounter and, through inner forces or needs, break apart and their "atoms" (i.e., individuals) either form new molecules, or separate. To the compassionate "scientific" eye, such an encounter in the turbulent "solution" of society has "tragic" implications, because it may set loose events which gainsay established morality.

The significant point is the recognition of "atoms" which need to "elect" other atoms for reasons of inner nature and can be subsumed in a molecule, or synthesis, whose bond varies in strength according to that fateful involvement in the flow of existence known as fate. Galdós, however, only makes a half-hearted try at a configuration of lives in an aesthetic pattern in *La familia de León Roch*. He appears to initiate the lines of an "hour glass" when he allows the childhood friends Pepa and León to diverge. León, the idealist, is drawn to María Egipcíaca, one side of whose life is dominated by religious fanaticism. Pepa drifts to the cynic Cimarra. The first couple are both deluded as to their total needs and motives; the second couple are both more truthful, Pepa in a vital way, Cimarra as a decadent. Emotionally, we hope for a repolarization of León and Pepa, who do again come together but do not quite meet, because of the separation forced on them by her family for its own selfish reasons. Galdós does not seek symmetry, however, and any formal design is secondary to the dynamics of the tragedy. The forces are internal—mainly in the self-deceivers María and León. León is less interesting, for Galdós obviously wishes to make him, as the noble champion of liberal idealism, virtually invulnerable to criticism from bigoted quarters. María's case is more dramatic, because she is split between her suppressed sensual drives and religious obsessions; she is, as León aptly puts it in anger and disappointment, not his dream of "una esposa cristiana" but "una odalisca mojigata" (IV, 799). In part one, María falls under the malign influence of her brother, who would dominate her in a "spiritual" marriage of twin souls. This polarization to the sickly mystic effectively splits her from León, whose relationship with Pepa and her daughter occupies most of part two. But through wounded pride, María reorients to her love for León and, changing her habits of mortification for a stunning outfit, she sets out to win him back. Her failure entails devastating consequences for her; she pines away, appearing to the innocent eyes of Pepa's daughter to be a "muñeca muerta" (887).

The death of Luis Gonzaga, ending the first third of the novel, generates new events—the passing of León into Pepa's orbit, and the wrongheaded isolation of María. The near death of Monina draws together her mother and León, who worships this image of Pepa. María's dying, which is a major section of part three, leaves León, at least in his own mind, morally isolated and bereft. For when Cimarra intervenes to enforce a pact of mutual separation of those left in a triangle, León's principles prevent him from escaping with Pepa into an illicit union outside society. The novel opens and closes with letters, by María and Fúcar, which exude the hypocrisy of a blind and greedy aristocracy that holds sway over Spanish mores. We may think of the novel as three unwieldy acts, conflict, climax of doomed happiness, and dénouement, with distinct raisings and lowerings of the curtain. But these external parallelisms do not grip us with the same intensity as Galdós' revelations, mostly through his characters' dreams, of the course of the *hidden* drama in the depths of their souls. For example, though largely prevailing in her stubborn campaign against her own husband, María's suppressed anxieties bubble to the surface (Part one, ch. fifteen):

> —¡Qué sueño! . . . ¡Figúrate . . . , soñé que te habías muerto y que desde lo más hondo de un hoyo negro me estabas mirando, mirando, y tenías una cara . . .! Después aquello pasó . . . Estabas vivo; querías a otra . . . Yo no quiero que quieras a otra. (799)

This "message" occurs right after León's angry charge that she is "una odalisca mojigata." María's suppressed desire is manifested in her nightmare of the viper nesting in her (Part two, chapter thirteen). The conflict in her soul is brilliantly exposed through her vision of hell, which integrates scenes from a visit to the Krupp works in Germany (Part three, ch. one). Despite her need to see León punished in fires of damnation, she cries out to save him (889).

These various disclosures of psychic happenings are not just planted like flags on certain high points in the terrain of the book. In María's case, for instance, the seeds of all future mental development are present in part one. Even the possibility of her own love—death is prefigured in the sudden reversal of the above quoted dream:

> —¡Qué horrible visión! Ahora me he visto a mí misma muerta, y mirándote desde el fondo del hoyo negro y profundo . . . Estabas abrazando a otra, besando a otra . . . ¿Pero es ya de día? (801).

Galdós' considerable reliance on, and talent for, dream sequences doubtless indicates that he is not the kind of writer in love with plot. His moments of dreaming, such as the outstanding chapter "Batiéndose con el ángel" (Part one, ch. twenty-one), do not really interrupt the book but give it a "substitute" for the missing drama of outward

facts. The briefer announcement of dreams reminds us off and on that this hidden drama is continuously at work under the surface. To state that Galdós does not manipulate outward facts in a dramatic configuration implies no criticism, for the ghostly "reality" of León's struggle with his "adversary," just after contemplating the splendor of the night heavens, lifts this book above successful artificiality to the poetic plane. Galdós here approaches the realm of the great masters of prose who have time for fantasy and prophecy, because they also have the ability for it. Our standard of comparison, to which Galdós may not measure up, must nonetheless be Mann and Dostoevski: Hans Castorp's watching the constellations (*Der Zauberberg*) and Dimitri's visionary ride through a lugubrious, wasted steppeland (*Brothers Karamazov*).

Fortunata y Jacinta has been extensively treated elsewhere, and is mentioned now only to corroborate that Galdós is more concerned about characterization than plot. His interest in the individual lives occupies him so thoroughly that he "allows" their story to develop out of the given materials of their existence, and often devotes great attention to "secondary" figures. If some critics object that Galdós is diffuse, rambling, lacking in style, they mean precisely that he is not out to offer us neat narrative shapes. The book *Fortunata y Jacinta*, for example, is really a tetralogy of unwieldly acts. Fortunata is actually off-stage throughout part one, except for a single glimpse. Then part two recapitulates the earlier beginning (Ch. one, "Juanito Santa Cruz") by introducing the male half (Ch. one, "Maximiliano Rubín") of a new "molecule" and its particular chemical history. But parts three and four no longer pursue the very ready possibilities of "pattern," and are concerned, rather, with the psychological unfolding of the principals. As Eoff has shown, both of the women "grow" in the measure that each approaches the nature of the other and their characters interact in the depths of the mind and heart; so much so that, with the consciously symbolic exchange of the child, we may be tempted to interpret their essence as some sort of allegory in motion. True, plot too demands a certain interdependence of protagonist and external history, parallels between individual reality and visible happenings in his world, a degree of subordination to the unity of the work. But the requirement of "unity" never curtails the validity of Galdós' treatment, because he does not need to set events in relief according to their *causality* by means of plot.

Causality is buried in the seeds of character; it unfolds within the circumstances of the story, which thus appears to be a relation according to simple time sequence, close to the most primitive mode of story telling dominated by a "voice." This recognizable tone, no matter how faint it may be at moments, runs through every utterance about what is "happening" and keeps us captive, waiting for the next detail. Of course, in switching back and forth among locales—or minds—Galdós actually operates on the simpler level of plot as well, in the sense that we must suspend our knowledge about some things while proceeding with others, must ponder, relate, anticipate. Yet, as Eoff emphasizes, Galdós never falls back on "static" character to bring about confrontations. This Galdosian preference for *life* rather than *style* (in its limited sense) is the core of his artistry, and criticism has rightly concentrated upon his convincing portraits with their palpable substance. But this judgment is only a partial explanation for the fact that Galdósian novels have ample proportions, without having the titanic sense of space and history which, for instance, Tolstoy's *War and Peace* commands. And the matter of Galdós' expansiveness is not resolved by pointing to his borrowing of the Balzac "panoramic" technique for the purpose of achieving vast scope. The totality of Galdós' creations exhibits a nation and society, of course, but the particular works after the *Episodios nacionales* usually dilate upon the "ordinary" in various corners of Madrid. The romantic writers had discovered that one could write about a single room because it contained a "story," then that one could examine a building whose inhabitants offered a microcosm, finally that the city was a universe with its own laws. Galdós moves about mainly in interior spaces, secondarily over streets and squares. The royal palace in *La de Bringas*, a symbolic city within the city, is a visible complex not far removed from Mann's sanatorium in the *Zauberberg*. But even the latter gives way to the spaciousness of the enveloping landscape of the mountains in many an excursion.

Except for dream passages, Galdós' novels are cut off by their own kind of realism from the universals of Heaven and Hell, lack the vastness of God's arena, and reach few epiphanies as transcendent as those in the great Russian works of the nineteenth century. The Spaniard may occasionally suggest the shadows of "myth" in the complementary questing of two beings like Fortunata and Jacinta for intangible wholeness in their femininity, but he generally bypasses the enormous for the local and limited sphere. Yet Galdós is exciting, because we sense that he is performing an amazing anatomy, baring the skein of "reality," without reference to any pre-existing Galenic chart. He gives us the simulated experience of being observers, simultaneously, on the informed, scientific level and on the more obtuse, involved level. The Galdósian method of characterization is also a distinct statement about reality.

Our world is not peopled by "round" characters alone. Indeed, most individuals of the human race are in our vision quite limited to a few exaggerated traits and features. We cannot see anything but their "flatness" until we learn about their inner life—and even then, we remain to one another and to ourselves largely hidden. From chapter to chapter and novel to novel, Galdós bridges the way as do our own minds. After fleetingly perceiving, we may discover more profoundly. Fortunata, for example, appears briefly in part one in a stark encounter with Juanito. The attractive woman is sucking a raw egg on the doorstep of her aunt's poultry shop. She possesses all the qualities of an artistically achieved "flat" character, because she radiates meaning and implications like an intense apparition. In the back of our minds, we keep waiting impatiently to discover the secrets under the surface vanished from direct view. A similar moment is when María Egipcíaca receives a sudden visit in *La familia de*

León Roch from the mysteriously "ignored" figure called Doña Perfecta. The blood of those who have already read the novel by that name freezes, for they at once sense the *meaning* of an entire human existence approach; that destiny is fully attested elsewhere in the annals of reality. The complexity of life converges in a *symbol,* and that is what Galdós' "flat" characters make us feel upon first encounter as well. The ability to expand into three and four dimensions his own stereotypes, or to see his formerly "round" figures as accessory shadows on the fringe of a tale, permits Galdós to use the so-called panoramic technique without the introduction of burdensome doctrines to govern or explain their behavior. Naturally, the author sheds his polemical commentary step by step during his career, and not all at once; however, we may point to his achievement as a definite trend after 1880, with the *serie contemporánea*.[8]

Galdós' ability to convince us that we experience not shaped art, but life shaping itself, is, of course, the power to conjure illusion—which brings up several subjects for later discussion: his turning to pure dialogue, and his very modern examination of the *relativity* of "reality." The linkages between clusters of personalities do give us the feeling of experiencing mankind at large in social context. But Galdós does more than depict customs or exposit naturalistic tenets; he is not the secretary listening to Spain's unvarnished dictation, or to any "spirit" which determines and directs our lives. Because his figures develop organically, the creative process is always flowing from the particular to the universal, and institutions are composite products of lives interacting. The energies emanate from within his individuals, and not from any "world spirit" that impinges on humanity; the world is co-existence and nothing more. The *rhythm* of the psyche informs the individual in reaction to its bodily, social, and intellectual environments. Galdós doubtless conceives his obligation as a realist not merely to record the external, historical "facts," but to listen to the pulse of the secret generator, the flow into consciousness of creative and harmful desires. Because he does not believe in a determinant physical environment, we should not conclude that his interest is solely the "complex of social and moral ideas." Galdós does not penetrate into the intrahistorical flux just for "confessional" glimpses; he is out to capture the symphonic simultancity of humankind.

Individual lives are allowed to sound, fade, interact, now dominate in variations upon themselves, cede to other passages in the music. This musical analogy touches again on the fundamental contrast between pictorial and psychological realism, between "classically" fixed patterns and organic rhythms. In this regard, Galdós' collection of novels should not be associated with Balzac's *La comédie humaine*, but with Proust's continuum held together by the musical threads of interior existence. Let us not exaggerate the relationship. Galdós is not conscious, as are Proust and Mann, of the literary leitmotif principle based on Wagner's operas. The connection is rather through the artistic affinity of Galdós' developmental characterization and the late nineteenth-century trend toward impressionism—the capturing of moments in their peculiar subtlety which depended on *subjective*, as well as objective, "reality." Imitation of nature cedes to the orchestration of vital continuity. Galdós must have felt the pull of this creative urge to achieve what Wagner called "total art"—a favorite romantic term. The romantics had already postulated at the start of the nineteenth century the possibility that the *novel* might become the vehicle for "universality"; also, that every work of art is merely a "fragment." Considering this typical paradox, we can understand that Galdós' period had several choices for the direction it would take in developing romanesque form. The novel did not need to be a sealed unity, in order to avoid being chaotic; it did not have to present a microcosm, in order to reflect an established macrocosm.

Cervantes directly, and not the romantics, taught Galdós about subjectivity. His tendency to shift the "point of view" is evident in his earlier novels. Now he catches the secret revery fading from a character's mind, now he describes persons from without in a context of history, now he projects three-dimensional figures in a scene, with stage directions and dialogue, now he meditates, withholds comment, merely smiles. It is a river fed from many sources. That is why Galdós' interesting experiments in form are not actually complete departures from his predominant method. It may be that the urge to espouse a thesis induces him to move toward pure drama. Dramatization helps tighten form into clear configurations, principle contending with principle. But it also flattens out Galdós' *personajes*, since their being is concentrated into the explicit words, gestures, motions, the mainly surface phenomena of events subordinated to "plot." Unless mixed in as scenes in the body of a narration, dialogue tends to make figures more opaque and symbolic. What makes Galdós' best creations great art is the third dimension of the mind. A serious objection may be raised that Galdós infrequently treats persons of intellect, or blunts their consequence by making them ineffectual in the management of their lives (e.g., León, Manso. The charge is justified, with the reservation that the author does, nevertheless, demonstrate the possibility of human success on *all* levels of intelligence. Both a Dr. Centeno and a Benina can redeem life from the powers of decay and despair. Naturalism was in many regards a bad influence on Galdós, keeping his attention too often on human weakness and vice. But since great artists are our only witnesses to reality, except for the chronicle of outward happenings which historians record, we are obliged to accept the Galdósian visión of a "disappointing" era. Artists are not good or bad according to the quality of the parade which passes before their eyes, but according to the sharpness of their eyesight. Hopefully, the time is past when chauvinists *or* hispanophobes will fasten on Galdós personally as "hero" or "villain" for his contribution.

Galdós does not belong to Spain any more than Mann does to Germany or Tolstoy to Russia. Galdós belongs to a great tradition whose standards were established by Cervantes. As an artist, dealing with reality through fiction, he is—in a different context from Nazarín's—"un árabe manchego" (V, 1729), a Benengeli and indulgent critic of him, a strange mixture of different layers of consciousness. Galdós' modernity is seen in his matching of two novels about the same subject. *La incógnita* is his only fully epistolary work, and tells its story through the exchange between two friends. Manolo writes to Equis about the strange events which are the talk of Madrid and with which he has intimate connection, yet the lowest level of understanding. Even in observing himself, Manolo can but dimly see through the opacity of the living persons whose relationship—a love triangle—he explains only obliquely to Equis. Equis and the reader must probe and construct hypotheses through the agency of the distant viewer on the spot, and through his reports of the numerous theories current in Madrid. ***Realidad (novela en cinco jornadas)*** brings the principals and Manolo on stage; now we witness directly the dramatic action whose surface was reported. Much of the play consists of internal monologues with many analogies to O'Neill's technique in *Strange Interlude*, except that Galdós' figures, especially Federico, often ponder the enigma of their relationships and the problematic aspects of "deception." Augusta, his lover, seems impelled to recreate ordinary life as a higher, exciting "reality": "Yo apetezco lo extraño, eso que con desprecio llaman novelesco los tontos, juzgando las novelas más sorprendentes que la realidad" (V, 851). Orozco, her husband, is attempting to discover "ultimate reality by and within himself," elevating himself through spiritual discipline and abstractly observing his own reactions, with increasing alienation from the world he pretends to serve.[9] If we follow the detective work of Manolo as a figure inside of the drama and accept his conclusions about the participants, it is only to find out he is wrong.

Introspection dominates the being of these uncommon personages in quest of reality—and certainty. But in their world truth is not fixed; it changes with their groping, and in a sense, they are producing it as they move along the pathways of the psyche, rather than "discovering" it. No one character possesses it, nor by implication do we have more than a partial view as audience to the spectacle of our own existence. Galdós seems to foreshadow the modern theatre's theme of inexorable loneliness within the walls of one's own mind: "No hay simpatía espiritual" (924). Only the symbolic perceptions and occurrences such as Orozco's vision of the suicide's image, have convincing intensity; and yet, these we understand to be not supernatural, but psychological epiphanies. They too are not final guides. For all the differences in possible philosophic intent, the writing of two works, one about the other, foreshadows the twentieth-century "novel of a novel"—as done, for instance, by Mann for *Doctor Faustus* or by Gide within *Les faux-monnayeurs*. Galdós does not revive the old romantic technique of purposeful, ironic disruption of the simple "illusion" of fiction by constant commentary upon the work of art itself. Nevertheless, his separation of the same story into two generic presentations forces upon us the task of reflecting about such an "illusion" and relating it to the human condition. Federico puzzles over the fact that "fictions" of the mind have their own strange validity: "La realidad del hecho [a talk with "la sombra de Orozco"] en mí la siento; pero este fenómeno interno, ¿es lo que vulgarmente llamamos realidad?" (899).

These paired "novel" and "novela dialogada" offer us many insights into Galdós' artistry, for in one respect they are an analysis, i.e., a "taking apart," of his realism. On the one hand, there is the *historical* method. In *La incógnita*, a "witness" interprets and records somewhat as would a Jamesian obtuse narrator. Characters are introduced, described according to visible traits, and their known statements about one another, as well as reportable observations of other parties concerning them, are given. Our task is to assess all this information for what it may be worth; we too become "historians." On the other hand, there is the *psychological* method. By a direct intrusion into the intrahistorical mind processes, we learn what it is ordinarily impossible to know. In this regard, *Realidad* is "unreal"; it goes so far beyond the limited asides and glimpses of dreams in older drama that it is part of the symbolic "realism" of a new age in art, when distinctions between hard fact and meaningful fantasy dissolve. These distinctions are only a further subject for profound meditation, but no longer divide the realms of our experience into that which is "false" versus that which is "true." In dialogue passages set within his novels, Galdós does not use this fuller revelation of psychic truths but simply portrays an action which we must look at from the outside. In *La desheredada*, for example, or in *Miau*, he is only affording us a close-up experience of actual scenes, tiny documentaries still part of outer, historical reality. Just as dramatization of stories can suddenly force us to change our perspective, so now in *Realidad* omniscient peering into the hearts of *dramatis personae* jolts us from any complacent projections into the artistic illusion's mere surface. Basically, the Galdósian method of narration comprises several points of view; the author's "reality" is multidimensional, in keeping with his Cervantine heritage.

Our theme has been limited to one aspect of Galdós, his ability to move back and forth with multiple vantage points. This was not a kind of intellectualism that could enfeeble the Spanish novel of the nineteenth century, which was in the rut of simply describing habits and customs, and only rarely motives.[10] While one may admire the aesthetic accomplishment of a writer like James in maintaining a unified point of view and perfect plot, that order of mastery is at a price too. Jamesian characters are usually so subordinated to the beautiful pattern of his books that their lives are held in check; lives are nasty, uncooperative, always threatening to go off on their own with the "reason of unreason" that impels them, and must be "domesticated" to conform to his pattern. Galdós is quite aware of himself as a creator, with his own way of doing things. The subject matter of which he wants to speak—life in Spain—seems paramount to him; the subject itself suggests the shape of a plan.

> Ya sé que mi estilo no parece estilo a muchos que buscan . . . ; buscan otra cosa. Creen que lo mío es fácil. Yo les entiendo; comprendo que trabajen. Pero

sería demasiada inocencia si yo me entretuviera en esos perfiles con *tantas cosas que tengo que contar.* Para mí el estilo empieza en el plan . . . Comprenderá usted que dando tal extensión al estilo, ya puedo despreocuparme un poco de lo que para ustedes es esencial y casi cínico . . . En general, los arrepentimientos que yo tengo no son por errores de estilo, sino por precipitaciones de plan.[11]

Galdós does not eschew practicing any tricks of the trade, but they are secondary. Considering him as one of that breed of writers of mammoth appetite, the hearty digestion which absorbs life without too many qualms or finickiness, we must, however, also ask whether Galdós is merely robust or indeed has a sensitive palate.

We may apply his own standard here to the theme of man's many-layered world of dream and waking, illusion and reality. For purposes of illustration, one example must suffice of the growth of his artistry. In the chapter "El deshielo" in *León Roch*, María is traveling in great perturbation of soul by coach to reclaim her husband. The moment is masterfully portrayed. Her anxiety that is nigh to blindness, the internal ruminations as she rehearses and worries over her encounter to come are put in compact relief in this paragraph:

> No se fijó en ningún accidente del camino ni en nada de lo que veía. Para ella, el coche rodaba por una región vacía y oscura. No obstante, como acontece cuando en el pensamiento se embuten ideas de un orden determinado y exclusivo, María, que no observaba las cosas grandes y dignas de ser notadas, se hizo cargo de algunas insignificantes o pequeñísimas. Así es que vió un pájaro muerto en el camino y un letrero de taberna al que faltaba una *a*; no vió pasar el coche del tranvía, y vió que el cochero de él era tuerto. Esto, que parece absurdo, era la cosa más natural del mundo. (IV, 880)

This passage already reveals the greatness of a maturing novelist. The veracity of his pinpointing of salient details, the successful impression of vague psychological time, while a large measure of external time must be flowing by, and the irrational suggestiveness of the "things" of a peculiar reality which her mind isolates all combine convincingly. There is also the virtually "surrealistic" quality of her journey that makes it into a "sign," like appearances of the balloon-man as a "herald" in Flaubert's *Madame Bovary.* Yet Galdós is so taken with his own achieved "truth" and the theory behind it that he cannot refrain from interpreting for us. Or perhaps he is eager that we not miss the point, because it is important.

In chapter thirty of *Miau*, Galdós portrays a similar traumatic moment when Abelarda, meeting Victor in church for what she thought was an amorous tryst, is fathoming the scoundrel's smooth speech—and needing to look at the statue of the saint by his name with the question "si aquello era verdad o sueño" (V, 669). Victor has cruelly toyed with her and now is breaking their relationship. Abandoned, in a state of shock, Abelarda kneels at the altar unable to pray.

El Cristo, mucho mayor que la imagen de su madre, extendíase por el muro arriba, tocando al techo del templete con su corona de abrojos, y estirando los brazos a increíble distancia. Abajo velas, los atributos de la Pasión, exvotos de cera, un cepillo con los bordes de la hendidura mugrientos, y el hierro del candado muy roñoso; el paño del altar goteado de cera; la repisa pintada imitando jaspe. Todo lo miraba la señorita de Villaamil, no viendo el conjunto, sino los detalles más ínfimos, clavando sus ojos aquí y allí como aguja que picotea sin penetrar, mientras su alma se apretaba contra la esponja henchida de amargor, absorbiéndolo todo. (669-f.)

The dream-like reality of her emotional crisis simply *happens*. The outer "facts" and the inner pressure interact. Instead of explaining what is occurring and why, Galdós demonstrates it with immediacy. And the fundamental human experience of desolation flows naturally into the symbolism of the environment itself. The author still intervenes to a certain extent, by speaking about her "soul," but since we have already submitted with Abelarda to the moment, this statement only lifts us gently onto a slightly higher plane, from the intensity of inner truth to a conscious paradigm.

Not many hours later, Abelarda conceives a strange antipathy toward her nephew Luisito, whom she has hitherto treated affectionately, and it develops steadily into an urge to murder him. Here Galdós slips back into "scientific" explanation, because he may fear that the reader will balk at the next events. He links her insane desire with the already violent hatred for her own father, "hostilidad contraria a la naturaleza, fruto, sin duda, de una de esas auras epileptiformes que subvierten los sentimientos primarios en el alma" (671). But such naturalistic asides do not very much upset us, for they are less frequent and more and more offset by the penetrating veracity of what he narrates. The scene in the bedroom which aunt and nephew share is uncanny, a plunge into the grotesque region of human mentality from which tragedy springs, and yet a sublime moment of insight into the affinity of "dream" and "reality." Little Luisito cries out in his sleep:

> —Le veo las piernas negras, con manchurrones de sangre; le veo las rodillas con unos cardenales muy negros, tiíta . . . , tengo mucho miedo . . . ¡Ven, ven! (671)

Even while his aunt is on the verge of killing him, Luis' thoughts turn to the "other God," a dignified grandfathergod who does not frighten him like the image in the chapel. Galdós weaves together the motifs of divine immolation and human agony. Thus Luis' nightmare assumes a quality of truth, becomes as it were oracular. The ominous linking of the two figures, the victim Son-of-Man and the Father, is later confirmed when grandfather Villaamil kills himself. Luisito translates the vibrations of other minds into his own distorted dreams; however, these specters have validity in analogy to the evident symbolism of our world, notably the "mythic" pattern in Christian belief.

Not patterns of plot, but patterns of reality come forward in Galdos' novels. They are clearest in a novel like *La de*

Bringas, with its odd beginning—a thorough description of a picture made of bits and pieces of hair. This frivolous composition progresses parallel to the Galdósian relation of events in the life of a government employee's family up to the revolution; a space of months, during which we explore the ever more ramshackle "inner city" of the palace, until the evanescent reality there established is swept away, like the hair-picture. It is a fitting "cenotafio" (IV, 1562) for the period coming to an end, and in it we sense Galdós' powers of whimsical irony over our transitory show. Likewise, the fevers and vomiting fits of the little Bringas girl are not just arbitrary local "color," but hint at a pattern in the larger world—which we first understand fully when the nation has its fever and casts out its tokens of indigestion (including Bringas, hair-artist). Rosalía de Bringas is also cast out, economically, or rather, must expel any unrealistic moral principles: "El tiempo ahogaba; la situación no admitía espera" (1645). Galdós could have ended his novel here and earned the reputation of constructing a neat plot shape. But he cannot resist continuing with several confrontations which Rosalía now has to experience. The meeting with Refugio really forms a short story in itself. But Galdós does not believe that a pat fiction can be superimposed on reality; fiction ultimately subserves realism. And he knows, as he often enough says in his chapter headings, that where one story ends another begins. All these stories together first suggest the story of humankind, for the telling of which great patience and lofty irony are required.

NOTES

[1] All quotations will be cited by volume and page numbers from the Aguilar edition under the care of Federico Carlos Sáinz de Robles, *Obras completas de don Benito Pérez Galdós* (Madrid, 1942).

[2] *The Novels of Pérez Galdós; the Concept of Life as Dynamic Process* (Saint Louis, 1954), the best book overall, takes up at length, for example, possible Hegelian influences (pp. 147 ff.); but its argument that Galdós "integrates environmental influence with personality development" (p. 34) and that is "aware of the unevenness of psychological growth" (p. 59) can stand on its own merits; Eoff carefully shows that "at no time, however, does Galdós use a particular case to generalize upon the inability of the human species to rise above its surroundings" (p. 38), though he must be "regarded as a historian of society in movement" (p. 111).

[3] Without very much interpretation of his materials, J. Chalmers Herman, *Don Quijote and the Novels of Pérez Galdós* (Ada, Oklahoma, 1955), has nevertheless complied an impressive catalogue of quotations, allusions, themes and motifs from Cervantes.

[4] Shakespeare *and* Calderón were the favorite dramatists of the German romantics, and as a result of their being well translated, they became standard poets in the German repertory—and still are. The romantics associated their own concept of creative freedom, i.e., "romantic irony," with the complex illusory reality of the seventeenth-century theatre and its sense of transcendental irony. The romantics themselves never created great drama, however, but rather analyzed it "ironically" in virtuoso demonstrations of the (if necessary, irrational) "spirit" controlling "matter." Thus plays like Tieck's *Der gestiefelte Kater* actually are forerun_

ners of Pirandello and the art of "absurdity," rather than continuations of the world-play of theodicy. The organic view, whose roots are in the late-Renaissance (Böhme, Bruno, et al.), seemed to offer a parallel principle of freedom, in contrast to mechanistic views (French rationalism, English empiricism).

[5] Many psychologies existed after the considerable impetus given by late Renaissance thinkers like Richard Burton in his *Anatomy of Melancholy.* But the developmental theory received its stamp at the same time the German *Bildungsroman* originated, a novel of education that included psychic processes; e.g., Moritz' *Anton Reiser, ein psychologischer Roman,* which followed a case history in analogy to natural growth, showing the interrelationship of early experience and later drives, psychosomatic factors, education, wish-fulfillment and illusions, etc., in the biography of a superior personage. Romantic scientists like C. G. Carus then codified such knowledge in accordance with the theory of biological evolution of the race; the "mind" of the individual grew organically during the history of its vessel, just as "spirit" developed organically during the entire story of humanity from unconsciousness in the primitive animal state through various levels of fulfillment. The romantics made the evolution of spirit into a vitalism.

[6] Joseph Schraibman, *Dreams in the Novels of Galdós* (New York, 1960), catalogues the author's numerous instances of dream, revery, hallucination, vision, etc., according to storytelling functions, which are conceived of only as "devices"; the study is more a handbook of references and statistics, than an interpretation.

[7] Anthony Zahareas, "The Tragic Sense in *Fortunata y Jacinta," Symposum,* XIX (1965), brings out the developmental interaction, "the mystery of human life in its clash between the 'inner' and 'outer' forces," by which Galdós "succeeds in destroying the formulas of human relationships given by some philosophers and many naturalists"; according to Galdós' presentation, "the spiritual life of man can at times be deformed, but not easily rationalized," as "man's position in the universe is first, to suffer, for it is a tragic position, and then, to understand" (p. 47).

[8] This study is limited to what is described as "the second phase" and "apogee" by Robert Ricard, *L'évolution spirituelle de Pérez Galdós* (Paris, n.d.), pp. 6-8. The upper boundary line is roughly *Misericordia.* The upsurge of fantasy in the late works such as *El caballero encantado* (1909) does not indicate a revolutionary change in Galdós, but only the assertion of already latent and dormant traits, first notable in *La sombra*

(1870). These traits will be touched on as they appear in *El amigo Manso* and the *novela dialogada, Realidad* within the "high" period.

[9] Eoff, *The Novels of Pérez Galdós,* p. 143.

[10] For an examination of Galdós' historical position, consult H. Chonon Berkowitz, *Pérez Galdós: Spanish Liberal Crusader* (Madison, Wisconsin, 1948); the tolerant humanity of Galdós' intellect so far as his stands on politics, moral issues, etc., are concerned is, of course, also an important contribution to Spanish literature, made through remarkable tenacity against the pressure of criticism, indeed an achievement of magnitude.

[11] Luis Bello, "Aniversario de Galdós: Diálogo antiguo," *El Sol,* 4 de enero, 1928. Quoted in Angel del Río's *Estudios galdosianos,* Zaragoza, 1953, p. 13, n. 4.

FURTHER READING

Becker, George J. "Benito Pérez Galdós," *Master European Realists of the Nineteenth Century,* pp. 239-77. New York: Frederick Ungar Publishing Co., 1982.

> Determines Galdós's philosophical stance of the essence of reality as order beneath chaos, and relates it to city dwelling and poverty in his novels.

Elliot, Leota W. and Kercheville, F. M. "Galdós and Abnormal Psychology." *Hispania,* Vol. XXIII, No. 1 (February 1940): 27-36.

> Presents Galdós's adept perceptions and analyses of psychological conditions in his novels, predating Freud's psychoanalytic theories.

Miller, Stephen. "Galdós and the Theory and Practice of Epic in Spain (1805-1914)." *Essays on the Interpretation and History of a Genre,* Steven M. Oberhelman, Van Kelly, and Richard J. Golsan, eds., pp. 289-309. Lubbock: Texas Tech University Press, 1994.

> Pursues Galdós's influence and contribution to the revival of the epic poem in Spain during the nineteenth-century.

Cristina Peri Rossi
1941-

Uruguayan short story writer, poet, essayist, and novelist.

INTRODUCTION

Cristina Peri Rossi is an Uruguayan essayist, poet, short story writer, and novelist who once said she works on three typewriters at the same time. Her fiction has received some of the most important prizes in Uruguay: the 1968 Premio de los Jóvenes de Arca (Arca Publisher's Prize for Young Writers) for the short prose volume, *Los museos abandonados* (1968; *The Abandoned Museums*), and the 1969 Premio Biblioteca de Marcha (March Library Prize) for the novel, *El libro de mis primos* (1969; *My Cousin's Book*). While writing, Peri Rossi was politically active in the left-wing Frente Amplio (Broad Front) coalition against the government but was forced to leave the country just before Uruguay's 1973 military coup, taking up residence in Barcelona. In 1975, Uruguay's military junta denied her a passport and she became a Spanish citizen. Peri Rossi's exile and the exile of many other Latin American writers helped inspire her view of humanity itself in exile, cut off from nature, sexuality, and political and personal freedoms ever since Colombus sailed the seas. Peri Rossi has been recognized internationally with awards and grants for both her short stories and her poems.

Born in Montevideo, Uruguay, on November 12, 1941, under simple circumstances, Cristina Peri Rossi was inspired by her mother with a love of literature and music at a very young age. As a child, Cristina was sent to live with her maternal grandmother because of the discord between her mother and father. At her grandmother's country house she learned her love of animals and plants. Peri Rossi described herself at this age as a "quick learner, given to fantasies." She was a good student in subjects she liked, but garnered her real education in her uncle's library, where her reading "list" rambled from Shakespeare to Freud, Woolf to Schopenhauer, Wilde to Faulkner to Pavese. When she turned eighteen, she studied music, biology, and comparative literature. She began writing, concentrating on sexual identity within cultural confines, calling herself a "cultural-constructionist." In a word, the cultural-constructionist approach to sexuality or gender is characterized by freedom to be comfortable in acknowledged sexual "roles" without the constrictions of predetermined social mores. For Peri Rossi, such a revolution in sexual thinking is more political than social. Another concern explored in her writing, language, is also a matter of national politics and politicized sexuality.

At the age of twenty-two, Peri Rossi wrote her first work for which she had aspirations, *Viviendo.* The book was not only published but highly praised, and she became the youngest writer published in Uruguay. At twenty-three, she received her license to teach literature and taught in various high schools and at the city's university, an occupation she maintained for ten years. During this time, she began working for the independent leftist movement and was a frequent contributor to the well-known newspaper, *El Popular* of Montevideo and the cultural weekly *Marcha* (March). From *El Popular*, she won a prize for the poem, "Ellos, los biennacidos." From the latter, she won first prize for her novel, *El libro de mis primos.* In 1971, her first book of poetry, *Evohé,* was published. In 1972, exiled from Uruguay and forced to settle in Barcelona, she began working for a publishing company. Three years later, she applied for an Uruguayan passport and was denied. She was also denied asylum in Franco's Spain and had to reside in Paris where she arranged a marriage with a Spaniard in order to gain citizenship. Meanwhile *Descripción de un naufragio* (1974; *Description of a Shipwreck*) was published in Barcelona and she won the Gran Canarias for *Diáspora.* While in Spain, Peri Rossi wrote and lectured against the Uruguayan dictatorship, and also worked as a journalist and a translator, publishing the works of Baudelaire and Cocteau, as well as other Latin American authors such as Clarice Lispector and Gracilano Ramos. From 1979-80, Peri Rossi was on fellowship in Berlin and continued working for Spanish publications. Her works have been translated into Polish, English, French, Italian, German, Swedish, and Dutch.

Two concerns overarch and interweave in Peri Rossi's work: first, nonconformism in regard to both sexual and governmental practices and means, and second, a continuous preoccupation with the meaning and use of language. In terms of the political, Peri Rossi denounces oppressive regimes and societal expectations. Her collection of short stories, *El museo de los esfuerzos inútiles* (1983; *The Museum of Useless Efforts*), recounts the story of a national runner expected to beat a speed record but stops shortly before the finish line to watch the dance of light in the treetops. In Peri Rossi's fiction and poetry there is a sustained rejection of heterosexuality and monogamy as the constitution of normal forms of sexual relation. In a subset of works, her homosexual perspective is somewhat more pronounced. For example, in her volume of poems *Diáspora* (1976), one poem makes explicit reference to the beauty of two women engaged in a sexual act; it emerges as a poeticized liberation of masturbation and of principles. In *Fantasías eróticas* (1991), one essay discusses the gay fantasy of St. Sebastian's martyrdom in relation to his sadomasochism. Fantasy in Peri Rossi's poetry and fiction is actually a reality developed through metaphorical profusion, digression, and the accumulation of information and meaning, all signs of a total experience intolerant of boundaries, "boundaries only an exile could detest."

Peri Rossi's vast literary output, numerous prizes, and commitment to personal, sexual, and political freedoms makes her one of the most outstanding of the maturing generation of new Latin American writers. No less committed to freedom of technique than politics, Peri Rossi is known for her peripatetic fiction that floats between, and incorporates, various genres into a folding of events and circumstance.

PRINCIPAL WORKS

Viviendo (short stories) 1963
Los museos abandonados (short prose) 1968
El libro de mis primos (novel) 1969
Indicios panicos (poetry and short prose) 1970
Evohé: poemas eroticas (poetry) 1971
Descripción de un naufragio (poetry) 1975
Diáspora (poetry) 1976
La tarde del dinosaurio (short stories) 1976
Lingüística general (poetry) 1979
La rebelión de los niños (short stories) 1980
El museo de los esfuerzos inútiles [*The Museum of Useless Efforts*] (short stories and essays) 1983
La nave de los locos [*The Ship of Fools*] (novel) 1984
Una pasión prohibida [*A Forbidden Passion*] (poetry) 1986
Europa despues de la lluvia (poetry) 1987
Solitario de amor (poetry) 1988
Cosmoagonias (poetry) 1988
Babel Bárbara (poetry) 1990
Fantasías eróticas (essays) 1991
La última noche de Dostoievski [*Dostoevsky's Last Night*] (novel) 1992

CRITICISM

Psiche Hughes (interview date 1984)

SOURCE: "Interview with Cristina Peri Rossi," *Unheard Words,* Mineke Schipper, ed., pp. 255-274. London: Allison & Busby, 1984.

[*In this interview, Peri Rossi answers questions about the dynamics of literature and gender in Latin American culture, as well as her personal stance on language and the cultural misconceptions and boundaries that shroud its use.*]

[PSICHE HUGHES]: *Why do you think there are so few women writers in Latin America in comparison with the number of male writers of international reputation?*

[CRISTINA PERI ROSSI]: One of the reasons why there are less women writers than men in Latin America is the enforcement of the traditional female role which still occurs in our countries, especially in the least developed ones whose social customs are still those of the last century. In many cases, the Latin American woman is still limited to the domestic and family world with a specific set of duties. As such, she is the victim of circumstances which have prevented her from developing a personal cultural life and a specific space around herself, what Virginia Woolf called a "room of her own".

Do you know whether women writers active now in Latin America are writing more prose, drama or poetry?

I believe that the general tendency so far has been for women to write more poetry than prose. In Mexico and Argentina, for example, there have been and there are many women who have written poetry of high quality. The reasons for this are many and complex. The principal one is that poetry, whilst it is a rigorous and exacting discipline as far as expression and language use are concerned, needs less time and less space than a long term project like a novel. Also, traditionally, lyrical poetry (and I mainly refer myself to the poetry which has been written by Latin American women) deals principally with emotions, sensitiveness and affection, all of which have been traditionally the private lot of women, attributed to women. The world for men, emotions for women. . . . To write a novel, on the other hand, almost always implies a worldly vision and a rich vital experience of life, neither of them generally within the reach of the Latin American woman.

Do women writers in Latin America form an intellectual élite or do they integrate with the rest of the population, try to communicate with them and interpret their desires and amibition?

It is difficult to generalize and see the Latin American countries at the same level of economic, political and social development. In fact, Latin America is a series of countries of different races, different origin and in many cases with a different history. I am not happy talking of Latin American writers in general when their countries are so different, without distinguishing between the one who lives in a large industrial town in Brazil or in Buenos Aires and the one from a village in Peru or in Ecuador.

My personal experience is very limited because I only know Uruguay, and Argentina a little. I do not know the rest of Latin America, even though I know the work of many of its women. Up to say 1950, there was a series of women writers, particularly Argentinian writers, belonging to a class which may be described as an intellectual élite. But from 1950 onwards, during the period of great economic and social crisis in Latin America, I believe that women writers have been as politically committed as their male colleagues and have reflected the great conflict of our countries as much as men have done.

In general, the work of women in Latin America has great difficulty in crossing national frontiers. There are some Mexican women writers, for example, who are very much in touch with the questions of their country and yet they are only known in Mexico. It is very hard for a writer who has not travelled and has always lived in her own country to have her works known outside the geographical context in which she lives. In Latin America the frontiers are real barriers against communication among the various nations, in spite of their common language. Also, publishing houses in Latin America are on such tight budget that that in itself prevents books from being known outside their countries of origin.

How are Latin American women writers received by the society to which they belong? Are they admired, criticized, or ignored? Are they treated with the same respect with which men writers are treated?

The very existence of the word "poetess" which has a pejorative connotation, reflects the fact that society does not treat a man and a woman writing poetry the same way. In general, female poets (and I use this term to avoid the word "poetess") are considered capable of writing poetry within the terms of what I would call "official literature", a decorative literature. Certain Central American politicians, for instance, considered it to be a matter of good taste to have wives who could write occasional verse, at public occasions. As a toast, during a banquet, it was not uncommon for the wife of a particular minister to get up and recite four or five lines of homage to the national flag or to the dictator in power. Within what is considered "official literature" in Latin America, the attitude towards women has been ambiguous: on the one hand it is considered proper for them to write decorative, incidental (and accidental) poetry; on the other hand we see how the very application of the word "poetess" carries slighting connotations.

With regard to what is not "official literature", that is real literature, the attitude towards women cannot be generalized. In some cases, and I am thinking particularly of the biography of the Latin American woman poet *par excellence* the Brazilian Clarice Lispector, we see the struggle she had in order to write within the social context in which she operated, in order to write. In other cases, there has been admiration but it has been ambivalent. I know of instances of people praising the beauty of a woman writer, who deserves to be praised for her work. Elsewhere, they criticize women when they no longer accomplish the traditional feminine literary role and instead compose literature of a more liberated or ambiguous kind. There is no doubt that the attitude towards women writers in Latin America is permanently ambivalent and that at the same time it reflects the uneasiness of men in the face of a woman who performs an activity which until then has been the exclusive purview of the male sex.

In Latin America who writes radio serials, the text of soap operas, the novelettes and short stories of magazines? Is it men or is it women? And, as far as you know, does this kind of writing reflect the influence of the European and or North American culture or is it based on the Latin American scene?

I confess that I am not in a good position to answer this question. First, I have been away from Latin America for twelve years. Secondly, my disregard of commercial literature has made me not pay too much attention to its manifestations. In order to answer you I must say this. I believe that the commercial literature on the radio, television and magazines has been created by both men and women but destined principally for feminine public. It seems to me that the writer is of less interest than the public at which the work is aimed. The programmes, both on radio and television, have been for several years even in countries of a higher cultural level like Uruguay and Argentina, the daily nourishment, a permanent form of escapism and alienation for women of all social classes.

As for the world which these programmes and this kind of commercial literature reflect, I believe it is a fictitious world, specially created to compensate for the poverty of reality, the conflicts of reality. The problems they present are generally of a sentimental nature. Hardly ever of a social or political one. Moreover they reflect a universal model. There is no difference in the style and content of North or South American serials and there is not much difference between those made by men and women for the daily consumption of housewives of any social class. In all cases it seems to me that this kind of art accentuates the most trivial, the most banal aspects of life and in general deforms the expression of sentiments and emotions and creates a sort of sentimental mystification of life totally removed from the real conflicts of existence.

Do you think that Latin American writers of today intend to break the moral and sexual taboos which have been imposed on women and society for thousands of years? If so, do you believe this is done more by women than by men?

Once again, one cannot generalize because men and women writers of different Latin American countries obviously reflect different realities. Your question can only be answered by analysing one by one the case of each individual writer. On the whole, I do not know whether most writers have been consciously aiming at breaking social and sexual taboos. One must not forget that many of them have lived during the 1970s, through a process of great political and social conflicts. The exacerbation of these conflicts in the face of the great dictatorships of the Southern Cone for example, has produced some specific consequences for literature causing it to give priority to social and political problems. Therefore, all the revolutionary and subversive intents of the writers have been directed towards certain fields, neglecting others. All the same, I think that there are some instances, mine among them, of authors who have realized that it is not only a matter of denouncing political problems, but also of denouncing the fixed roles and all the forms of social oppressions which still apply in Latin America.

Among Latin American intellectuals what is the general opinion about feminism and what attitude do critics assume faced with a feminist writer?

Feminism has been problematic in Latin American countries. First, for the reason I gave in my previous answer: the priority writers have given to the political struggle, justified by political tyrannies and by the economic crisis which the continent has suffered and is still suffering. This has pushed other struggles, equally justified, in the background.

Feminism has appeared only very recently in Latin America and in a very tentative form. All the same it has created great problems and embarrassment for men, generally quite satisfied and complacent when watching women accomplish the role allotted to them. This embarrassment has manifested itself in attitudes of great ambiguity among intellectuals faced with women writers who assume a positively feminist attitude. In some cases what has happened is that men have superficially accepted the revindication of feminism. This is a false and dangerous way of adopting feminist ideas. What I mean is that men continue being *"machistas"* and only consider it necessary to change some gestures and some forms of behaviour towards women. I think this is what has happened with many male writers and intellectuals in Latin America who have realized that they could not go on with the traditional manifestations of machismo. All they have done is to change for the time being some of their attitudes, but in the daily contact with their wives or sweethearts, I do not think their sexual and social behaviour has changed at all. These changes of course cannot occur suddenly. Machismo is a form of alienation, I'm sure of this. The process of integration is slow and needs a lot of deep thought.

My personal experience tells me that, faced with a feminist writer or even just a woman writer who does not play her habitual role, that is, for example, the poetess who writes occasional verse for toasts and ceremonies, male writers feel uncomfortable. They feel confronted with a person out of her natural place. A person who calls into question their own position, who makes them feel unhappy by just being there. This is of course a permanent source of a dialectic process of conflict. I believe that a feminist woman writer, even though she is not necessarily so in a militant way, creates a kind of bad conscience in men and therefore their relationship with this kind of woman is generally awkward.

As for the critics, I believe that they can be similarly classified. Although it is easier to analyse a text without having to refer to the author, I have observed that when the text breaks with a traditional scheme both in its content and in its form, it creates a very embarrassing situation for the critic who would of course prefer that the author of this text were either already dead or someone with no apparent sex. Someone who is just a mind and an abstraction.

Is there any difference in the form of criticism which men and women write in Latin America?

Only recently have women had access to critical activities in Latin America. Principally because these activities require a formation which women did not have.

Also because the language, the apparatus necessary to exercise criticism, had already been chosen by men. One had to learn it as one learns any other form of knowledge. This explains the fact that there are less women than men involved in critical work in Latin America. The few women critics in existence, however, have shown deep sensitivity and a perception which in my opinion reflect a richer, deeper and more flexible understanding of literature.

What do you think and what do Latin American women writers think of European women and of their position in relation to men and to their society?

I am glad you have asked me this question because it is a subject on which I have reflected a lot. Having lived both in Latin America and in Europe, I have been able to observe the curious and different relationship established between women writers of the two continents. I would say there is a phenomenon of reciprocal admiration and at times, of course, also of reciprocal interests. Admiration because the conditions in which Latin American and European female writers work are different. For a European a Mexican woman writer, for example, is the object of great admiration because, in order to publish a poem or a book of poems, she has had to fight against a quantity of hostile factors which in Europe have already been overcome. She has had to break with her traditional role and make a place for herself in the intellectual world exclusive to men. All this requires great courage and energy and provokes the admiration of European women who have lived and succeeded in another context.

On the other hand, Latin American women writers in contact with their European colleagues have realized to what extent it is easier in Europe for women to write and to create. Women here have already been accepted. This has caused a deeper awareness of our situation in Latin America. It has made us understand that it is not only a matter of improving the economic and political conditions of our countries but also of effecting a social revolution. Personally, I have felt as much at home with European women writers as with Latin American. From them I have understood that the personal effort I had made in order to be able to write and publish, and free myself of the myths and taboos involved in my feminine role, is something that they had already done. This put me on a level of sisterhood with all European writers whatever language they used.

Do many Latin American women writers leave their countries and, if so, why?

The case of Latin American women writers living outside their country or even in other Latin American countries is not frequent. The insecurity of the social and material position in which women find themselves in Latin America, their dependence on their social role and in many cases their economic dependence on men prevent them from leaving their homes. On the other hand, of course, they all share the dream of travelling to Europe, of knowing Europe. But this does not mean wanting to establish themselves there. There are writers in exile, of course, a much more dramatic condition in which some Latin American intellectuals and artists have lived in the last ten years, but, as you know, they are a minority.

The greater majority of women have preferred to remain in their countries, even if this limits their chance of writing and being published because their work might be forbidden there, rather than facing that option. They have decided against having to start life afresh in another country and having to find an opening in other societies which, as well as proving protective towards them, might exact a higher level of intellectual performance. Therefore there are very few women writers in exile and very few artists by profession who at present live in Europe.

I would now like to ask you some questions concerning your own work. I have noticed that, in spite of the inevitable changes and developments, there are some recurring constants. As with many Latin American writers I think that you feel a strong preoccupation with language and are urged by the necessity to renovate it. This is noticeable in the use you make of syntax, punctuation, images, word-associations, neologisms and "genres". The position of the writer vis-à-vis the language she uses and her continuous frustration is something which you express in many of your poems. I am thinking of some poems from **Diáspora**. *May I quote? "If only language were the way of making love, of wrapping myself in your hair . . ." or: "You loved children because their language flies freely, ignoring the fundamental laws. . . ." And elsewhere: "You stopped talking out of sheer prudence, then out of annoyance, finally to punish the words." Would you like to comment on this, please?*

It is a complex question which involves a certain amount of clarification. My work has been constant, preoccupied with language not only in the poems but also in the stories. I refer in particular to the book **The Rebellion of the Children**, in which I often refer to language as a manifestation of social oppression, being institutionalized and posing a permanent dialectic relationship between its official and personal usage.

Many Latin American writers who have contemplated a literary revolution, as well as social and political, have believed that to change a society implies also a free and more creative use of language. Accordingly they have set out to make frequent breaks with the traditional linguistic structures and, above all, with literary genres and these have undertaken a total transformation in contemporary literatures. Novels in our countries are much less formal, much less along the patterns of nineteenth century novels than they were at the beginning of the century. In the same way, short stories, which are in great supply in Latin America, have broken the conventional rules and often been converted some into aphorisms, others into a kind of prose poem or into a vignette. There is a tendency not to accept the conventional patterns of "genres" as a symbolic way of breaking with the limitations of reality.

I too have felt the same necessity of forcing literary forms, of utilizing a quantity of personally imaginative and creative techniques to establish my own identity outside the norm. Any kind of norm. I think this has been the great contribution of contemporary Latin American literature: the freedom that it has achieved. I imagine that literature has been the only territory of real freedom that we Latin Americans have had for a long time. We, especially the exiled, who have been able to publish all we have written. Personally, I consider myself a rebel against all laws. Literature has been the space which has permitted any transgression. I think this is the key word which explains most of the work of Latin American writers: transgression, the desire to break with norms and create a proper time and space.

Latin American reality is so complex and so rich in landscapes which change rapidly from one place to another in the same country that it has been too difficult to enclose it in forms. In spite of the wealth of language, we still lack the words to name the enormous number of nuances and shades of this reality, accounting for the fact that the imaginary is also a form of it. These poems of mine from which you quote are no more than a way of expressing exactly the poverty of traditional inherited language in the face of this multiple, complex, contradictory reality. I believe that almost all Latin American writers have felt on the edge of the genesis. Neruda's poetry, for example, is a way of giving a permanent name to this multiplicity of Latin America. The task, of course, is almost impossible. We have to be like gods to be able to name all that exists. In the poems which you mentioned I reduced this challenge to circumstances purely personal.

Museums feature in your first collection of stories of 1969 and also in the last collection of 1983, and these museums are always old, deserted, abandoned, and have succumbed to dust and disorder. Am I correct in attributing to them a symbolic function? Do they constitute a reflection of the society in which we live?

I am aware that the title of my last book in relation to my second one creates a certain confusion. But this confusion does not bother me. I have deliberately played with it. In actual fact your interpretation is correct. Both in poems and in prose I have used museums as allegory, more than as a symbol, because they are a complex symbol. Museum is an image which I have tried to enrich as it returns in a dialectic form in the various books I have written. It constitutes for me an allegory of the culture, society and world in which we live. The content of this allegory is multiple and only with an analysis of the term in relation to the context in which it appears can one visualize exactly what it means. I don't think it is difficult. Museums are in the first case a symbol of an old society which retains old values, principally aesthetic ones, and enters into contradictions with modern ideas and with life and death.

In other cases museums are a symbol of exactly the opposite. They indicate the dream of crystallizing time and space. What attracts us when we enter a museum is exactly the fact that we are confronted by the most positive aspect of humanity: its creativity. In fact a picture always fixes a time and a space and at the same time it eliminates the anxiety which arises in man when in conflict with time, which means death, and with space. The crystallization involved in a work of art, a painting or a poem is a way of comforting, of protecting us from the essential anguish which is created by the sense that all is transitory, all is ephemeral. It has been very important to me to emphasize this element of museums. Because I believe that the fundamental drama of life, of personal existence, is the struggle against the ephemeral; we die but also die all the things around us. They are changing. The permanent process of life and death is a source of the anguish which, it would seem, the work of art manages to suppress by presenting us at the same time with something which is permanent. Be it in the words of a writing, the colours and shapes of a picture, or the sounds of a piece of music. The great merit of art is, banal though it sounds, that it triumphs over time, and finally over death.

In many of your stories one notices traces of cruelty and in those landscapes of surrealistic nightmares which you describe one senses a feeling of alienation, anxiety and persecution. Is this the reflection of your particular position, or is it also an expression of the predominant political situation in Latin America?

El museo de los esfuerzos inútiles, my last book of 1983, begins with a series of quotations among which there is one by the German poet Gottfried Benn which goes: "The category in which the universe manifests itself is that of hallucination." I was very happy to find this sentence, which expresses something I have felt during most of my life: hallucination, the paranoiac hallucination of persecution is a way of interpreting and understanding the world.

Your observations are very accurate. For me literature is a vision, a creation of symbols to interpret and understand reality. This reality is nightmarish not only for those political elements to which you refer and which exist in Latin America. Not only because, for instance, in Argentina thirty thousand people have disappeared and one out of five Uruguayans have suffered cruel torture and persecution, but also because when it is not the military, the totalitarian regime in power, who persecute us, there often remain our internal phantoms, our own hallucinations.

My literature is one of a disturbing and paranoic nature. I believe that paranoia is one of the most real ways of understanding the world. I remember an anecdote, which I will tell you. I have a friend in Uruguay who is a psychoanalyst. Once, when she was attending a paranoiac patient trying to convince him that life was not persecuting him as much as he thought, six soldiers armed with machine-guns broke into her clinic to inspect her files. They lined up against the wall and handcuffed her patients and held her captive for various hours.

Paranoia is not just a fantasy. It often reflects the tension and the struggle of life. On the other hand my literature is generally symbolic. Therefore I often start by writing my own nocturnal nightmares. I believe that there are a few writers (and Kafka is one of them) who have succeeded to give literary form to their internal visions and fantasies, to that nightmarish world where all is symbol. I often start writing from my dreams knowing perfectly well that dreams are symbolic constructions whose task is to interpret reality. If the writer is a creator of symbols, man in his dreams is also one.

Psychoanalysis—for which I feel great respect—and literature are similar in this: both work with language trying to discover the meanings contained in language. I am well aware that these dreams, which are often a source of inspiration for a writer, are not the property of the individual. By this I mean that a large number of our nightmares are part of a collective unconscious. We dream what others have already dreamt years and centuries ago and we dream with the same fears that men have had, faced by a reality which pursues them. The theme of my stories is in fact fear. Fear of all forms of exterior life, fear of freedom, as well as the fear which produces in us the daily acts of aggression of the world. Be they spiritual or concrete. I think that this fear exists in all of us in different forms. At times it takes the appearance of euphoria, at other times it is simply the horror of death. Finally, it is fear of the rest of the humanity which appears to consist of potential aggressors and persecutors.

You have been away from Uruguay a long time, some twelve years. Do you miss it and do you miss your own people?

Exile is always a form of tearing oneself away, a loss, a breakage. In this sense I think it is the final experience in which one's whole identity crashes. When I arrived in Barcelona in '72 I was 30, had published five books in Uruguay and so was relatively known in my country. Besides I had a career, I was professor of literature, had a circle of friends and ample contacts within the context in which I lived. The change was a violent uprooting and therefore had consequences which I could not foresee. I was living in Barcelona but of course I was merely existing there.

What we must realize when talking of exile is that we have to start living afresh, being in a place where nobody can name us, in a place where nobody knows us. Identity is to have a name in relation to others. To exist for the rest of the people, to see that their look reflects us, recognizes us. Exile is to lose this context, this look which others give us, and therefore exile sets a challenge. We have to be reborn in a place where nobody knows us yet and can share our past. All those things which until then had been part of our identity. I believe that this challenge puts in question the whole of our personality.

The first years of exile are the most dramatic. One's heart and emotion are elsewhere. One becomes a ghost. One has stopped existing for one's country and for the people with whom one was living and one is still not in the place to which one has arrived. This ghost-like existence of being in exile makes us less real even in front of ourselves. The city we left appears in our dreams, in our nightmares, yet we still do not know the city to which we have come. All this causes anguish, but also makes for deep reflection. I believe that all those who have lived in exile can talk of the grief, terror and separation of their experience.

At the same time, one can talk of the stimulus, painful though it may be, created by having to live suddenly at the age of 30-35 in a place where we have no past, only a present (because often we don't even have a future). For me Montevideo has become a city remote in time and space. I am completely aware that the Montevideo I knew and where I lived the first thirty years of my life no longer exists. The present Montevideo is another. Twelve years have elapsed during which I have not been there and in which the city did not exist except as a memory for me. My main fear, in fact, is to feel a stranger the day when I return to Montevideo, even if it is only for a visit. I prefer to feel a stranger in a country where I know I am a stranger because I know I was not born there.

I believe that the exile is victim of certain fantasies. One is that of time: the exile lives in an unreal time which is static. It is the time in which she left her country. This staticness, immobility of time, is like a delirium. It is also a delirium of space. The exile mentally lives in a geographic space which is not the city to which she has come to live but the one in which she has lived her fundamental experience, the one which she has left behind. These two deliriums of time and space provoke that permanent sensation of unreality, of floating, which the exile feels.

I have understood in a very dramatic way that exile is something more than leaving one's country, being torn away from the place of one's birth. It is a great metaphor of the human condition. We have been exiled from almost everything. We have lost childhood, innocence, friends, loves. Above all for me to be exiled symbolizes that space in which writers, those who interest me anyway, write. The writer is the person who looks on from a certain distance (which of course does not at all imply lack of emotion), the distance which is the one of the person who observes and judges. In other words I mean that the writer is the person who entirely complies with the sentiments of Adamow, who said that the duty of the writer is to describe the horror of the time in which he has had to live. I think that this defines perfectly the condition of the writer. She is an exile because not only she "suffers" the time in which she has to live, but also because she has to create a space, a distance which will allow her to reflect the time in which she has to live.

In your work there are many allusions to sex and to love but they are almost always of a rather bitter nature. I am thinking for instance of how you describe the deterioration of a love relationship when the two lovers are incapable of ending it, and also of the destructive element present in a situation in which two people *are compelled to be together for life. A character of one of your stories says: "We have the sex that they impose upon us; at the most we accept it." Do you think that your attitude is in part a consequence of the sexual conventions and of the stereotypes which society forces upon us?*

First of all I would like to say that there certainly are many references to love in my books and in particular in my poems. I don't, however, think that in most cases the destructive aggressive element of love is what I have emphasized, on the contrary.

There is a book which you will of course not know, a book which I published in Uruguay in 1971 and which is now out of print and forbidden. It is a book of poems called **Evohé**. **Evohé**, as you might know, is a Greek word transferred into Spanish. It is a call of the Bacchantes during Dionysiac ceremonies. I was in fact writing a book which I would describe as dionysiac. It is a book about the pleasure of love, in which I celebrate the joy of the human body. It belongs to my youth, it is an erotic book, in fact its other title is **Erotic Poems**. In it I compare the pleasure of physical love to the sensual pleasure which the use of words gives to the writer and to the reader of poetry.

Erotic action and the action of writing hold for me something in common which is the ludic element. The element of play. In the same way in which a body has density, colour, light and shape, so words have texture, density, and there are bodies which I love and words which I love in the same way in which there are bodies and words which repel me. Eroticism is very similar to the creating activity.

This is however only one of the aspects of love. It is true that in other texts (and you refer particularly to the story **"Punto Final"** in my last collection) I have accentuated the destructive element of love, because love is not only one thing. It is sensual pleasure, communication, but it is also a terrible struggle between two identities which lose their individualities and enter into conflict. The only way out of this situation is the survival of one of the two. This double-headed monster, as at times married couples have been described, implies the fight between two individuals in a state of osmosis and it implies also the predominance and the power of one or the other.

It is true also that our concepts of love are historic and therefore reflect the ideology of social and sexual classifications. In Latin America they have almost excessively caricatured the element of power in heterosexual couples.

Power relations are always ambivalent. This I wish to point out because between the master and the slave one finds multiple types of relationship where sometimes power is not total but partial. At times slavery possesses the expedients of power so that I would not want in any case to fall into the category which affirms that heterosexual relationships in Latin America are purely relations of power. It is true that these relationships are that of the master and the maid. But it is also certain that they are subject to all the contradictions which are proper of any struggle for power. In this sense I think that when I describe the destructive element of love, I refer fundamentally to the appearance. That is, in many cases, love relationships, so-called love relationships, enclose other elements which are not specifically of love. For example, envy; power provokes envy and envy leads in many cases to attitudes which are not just, which betray and therefore destroy. Love is not, or hardly ever is, Christian love based on compassion such as a whole tradition has assumed throughout the centuries. Love is often destruction, fight and triumph on one side and defeat on the other.

As for sex, I believe we do have the sex which is socially imposed upon us, first by our parents and next by society. Sex for me is not the simple result of biological elements and of genetic characteristics. These genetic characteristics impose a social role (and this in Latin America is felt in very strong terms), a social role which is almost always an imposition on our sentiments and on our free behaviour. In this sense we don't have the sex we would like to have for in many cases this would be a multiple sex. And in this sense I am convinced that to limit this multiple sex to one sex only involves a limitation of our freedom. Of course I understand the social reasons for this limitation but I also believe that they are a source of neurosis and of pathological conditions. If only we could all have various sexes and use them at liberty without society feeling attacked and upheaved by this!

What do you think of the role of women? In your poems woman is described as "filling the world" but at the same time as "looking and destroying". Perhaps it is not fair to take sentences out of their context. What seems to be most relevant at this point is your poem which says: "You are here as the result of twenty centuries of predestination in which men of the past made you so in order to love you according to their needs and their rules, and this tradition, though injust and offensive, is not after all the least of your attractions." The end of this poem is for me very interesting because it turns an argument which could be feminist in a banal way into something much more thoughtful, complex and ambiguous.

Talking of women's role and also of men's role, I think that the problem is to have a specific role generally imposed on us by our education, tradition and by the people around us. What is terrible about roles is that they limit our freedom of choice and even our freedom to make mistakes, to misunderstand ourselves. Therefore I rebel against traditional roles both in my personal life and in my writing, which means that I have to break away from the conditioning of society which sets definite and predetermined ways both for men and women.

I believe that just as it would be better if we had various sexes during the course of our life and if we could enjoy

them all, it would also be better for each of us to elect our role. This would not have to be predetermined and unchangeable and above all would not be a role imposed in social or historical terms by the functions which we have to perform in society.

It is true that I have played extensively in my poems with the role traditionally attributed to women particularly in the field of literature and art. It is a role full of ambiguities from the poetry of the troubadours to the portraits of the Renaissance. The way of presenting women has always been complex and contradictory. On one hand, woman has been turned into an object of veneration, into a myth. On the other hand she has been sold and prostituted. By tradition woman has played different and multiple parts. We all write by this tradition and base ourselves on the dialectical interplay with it.

Woman in my poems and in my books is made up of many, not just one. I often place myself in the position of those who look at her and watch her birth and are fascinated by the multiple aspects within one person. Ambiguity, which is for me a source of poetry, is also a source of love and therefore, perhaps, in some of my poems the image of woman is not only based on the aspects which previous poets have given her, but also undergoes a process of mythification, counterbalanced by a vision which is ironic up to a point and also critical of woman.

What I am sure of is that each woman must look for the role which corresponds to her in each individual stage of her life and must not yield to the conditioning to which society submits her because of tradition or because of man's needs. This role must at once be highly flexible and must be able to evolve constantly.

Cynthia A. Schmidt (essay date 1990)

SOURCE: "A Satiric Perspective on the Experience of Exile in the Short Fiction of Cristina Peri Rossi," in *The Americas Review*, Vol. 18, No. 3-4, Fall-Winter 1990, pp. 218-226.

[In the following essay, Schmidt explores Peri Rossi's reorientation/identification of the self upon the approach to new worlds of thought, consciousness, and experience, and her subsequent and deeper rejection of the same in her short stories.]

Cristina Peri Rossi's work was already well-known in her native Uruguay when she went into exile in Spain in 1972. Her years in exile have been highly productive. In addition to literary translations and journalistic writing, she has published four volumes of poetry, five collections of short stories and two novels. If we were to single out a common thematic thread unifying her works before and after exile, it could be her criticism of oppressive social structures. CPR explains the sense of continuity in her writings: "Escribo contra la realidad. Empecé a hacerlo porque la realidad que veía a mi alrededor—en mi casa, primero; luego en mi país—no me gustaba. Y sigo escribiendo, me parece, por la misma razón . . . En este sentido, poco importa cuál sea la realidad geográfica."[1]

Exile, a reality which CPR has been forced to experience, is a frequent target of her satiric vision of social ills. Two highly imaginative short stories, **"La tarde del dinosaurio"** and **"La influencia de Edgar A. Poe en la poesía de Raimundo Arias"** focus on the psychological trauma and social margination of the Uruguayans who were ideologically opposed to the military coup of 1973. The former is about exile within the limits of the country, while the latter tells a tale of extraterritorial exile. Imagination, fantasy, a keen sense of the absurd, irony and humor all come into play in CPR's vision of a reality which is other than the desired. In these stories, as in all of CPR's fiction, allegory serves as a structuring principle, linking the singular case to its abstract, universal meaning.

Both stories recount the events from the perspective of a child, and in both cases the loser of the local "war" is the child's father, represented as a worn-out small-time intellectual. No one escapes the critical vision—both the victors and the defeated are demystified. Far from attempting to detail a sweeping portrait of the Southern Cone diáspora, Peri Rossi's families are at once a microcosm of Uruguayan society and human society. Social catastrophe is interpreted in individual terms—defeat in politics is equated to loss in love, and loss of social esteem is reflected in the lucid uncompromising scrutiny of a young son or daughter.

"La tarde del dinosaurio" encompasses multiple levels of reading. On the literal level it is the story of a child of divorce who lives with his remarried mother and stepfather. The child feels sympathy for his real father, a social misfit, and resents his adoptive father, a highly successful businessman. Within this reading, the child's recurring nightmares of a huge brontosaurus can be interpreted as the result of the anguish and confusion caused by his family situation. On an allegorical level, the story depicts the fissures within Uruguayan society created by repressive military rule. The broken and re-formed family represents Uruguay after the coup of 1973. The natural father and the adoptive father are metaphors for the state, the mother embodies Uruguayan civil society and the child is at once the innocent victim of the fractured country and its future. Within the double articulation of the allegory, the regional situation is a reflection of Peri Rossi's vision of the human condition, permeated with millenary fears brought on by our own irrationality. My analysis will focus on how the story blends historical fact and free imagination to depict the alienating effect of social upheaval in Uruguay.

The narrator provides a brief historical allusion to account for the contrasting lifestyle of his two fathers: "ellos habían tenido . . . una guerra pequeña, no de las grandes guerras internacionales, . . . una guerra dentro de los límites del país, pero guerra al fin" (84)[2]. This reference undoubtedly corresponds to the period immediately before the coup when the Tupamaros assassinated several government officials, and President Bordaberry responded by declaring "internal war."[3] The narrator tells us the results of the war: "De la guerra había surgido un sentimiento de seguridad para unos y un sentimiento de inseguridad para otros"(84).

The boy's real father, to whom he refers as Father no. 1, is one of those who suffered adverse effects from the internal war. Father no. 1's situation and personal characteristics seem to parallel the liberal faction of the constitutional government in exile. The son's observation: "Le era muy difícil no preocuparse por todos los hombres y mujeres que encontraba en su camino"(98) hints at the socialist concept of a welfare-oriented polity. Father no. 1 lives in a state of internal exile. The child's description of him reveals both the causes and effect of his failure. Besides having lost the custody of his child, he is nearly indigent, and the reader is first introduced to him in terms of lack: "—¿No tendrás un cigarrillo para darme?—le había pedido su padre, el primero, el que no tenía oficina, ni casa en la ciudad, ni otra casa en el mar o en la montaña, ni auto propio, ni tenía televisor ni nevera ni mocasines de piel ni cigarrillos ni nada"(82).

This father is a journalist. One day he decides to show his articles to his son, but he has to look in drawers of unmatched socks and other unlikely places to gather them together. The articles run a gamut of topics from growing roses to sailing to instructions for preparing a delicious rice pudding. The narrator reflects: "Se ve que su padre era un tipo muy capaz. De escribir cualquier cosa"(85). In reality, he had never planted roses, he was afraid to sail and he hated rice. Despite the shortcomings he recognizes in Father no. 1, the child feels genuine sympathy for this tender and inept fellow: "Era más amable y más suave, vivía dando explicaciones de todo. A él le parecía que las explicaciones las usaba para sí mismo, porque le debía resultar muy complicado vivir"(84). Although kind-hearted and well-meaning, Father no. 1 is too weak, too reflective, and too beaten-down by life's problems to try to take control. He prefers to make peace. Thus, Father no. 1 echoes the bankrupt liberal faction which proved itself incapable of overcoming Uruguay's economic crisis and lost the capacity to articulate an alternative political response.[4] Although it produced convincing rhetoric, it could not systematize a program and put its words into action.

Father no. 2, his mother's second husband and a winner of the war, represents the military dictatorship. He is depicted as if he were part of the *Junta de Comandantes,* the self-proclaimed builders of the nation: "Tenía una oficina toda para él. Parece que no se trataba de un empleado cualquiera, sino de un patrón algo así. Daba órdenes por un dictáfono y le mostraba la oficina como si toda fuera suya, como si él mismo, con gran esfuerzo, hubiera colocado piedra sobre piedra, ladrillo sobre ladrillo . . ."(82). The most salient characteristic of Father no. 2 is his authoritarianism: "daba órdenes con la aparente seguridad de que sus órdenes respondían íntimamente a los deseos ajenos"(85).

Peri Rossi's satiric picture of the military regime's vision of the future finds its symbol in "la máquina." Father no. 2 insists his son accompany him to the office to admire "el último modelo de calculadora que hemos adquirido"(89), which the father proclaims to be "símbolo del futuro, símbolo de la unidad familiar, símbolo de esfuerzo y del genio del hombre"(94). When the father exhorts the child to think up an appropriate name for the machine, the boy reflects on its meaning: "la máquina parecía . . . un soldado que sólo cumplía órdenes, sin discutir, sin pensar, . . . un soldado exento de reflexión, pero adoctrinado, programado, útil para servir y para callar. Obediencia." *Obediencia* thus encapsulates Peri Rossi's vision of the regimes' plan for its citizenry. The machine represents its impersonal and alienating rule as well as the sterile and unimaginative future to be created in a country where intellectuals were considered subversives, and the most talented and creative people were censored, imprisoned, tortured and exiled.

Although he has two fathers, the boy continues to have only one mother. The mother resembles Uruguayan civil society, weak and subordinated to a paternalistic state. His mother married young, and later found she was married to "un loco." The way the child refers to her seems to disclose an attitude between resentment and resigned disgust: "su madre. O sea la esposa de su padre, que ya no era su esposa, aunque seguía siendo su madre. ¿Por qué uno no podía divorciarse de las madres, como había hecho su padre?"(83). Even though he disapproves of her fickle behavior he cannot disown his mother, just as one cannot disown the people of one's country. She is the average Uruguayan who initially supported the Left's demands for a restructuring of the economy to later reject them in favor of middle-class security. Turning against the liberal factions and succumbing to the military's gradual takeover, this sector acquiesced to the erosion and destruction of the constitutional government.

The boy is the country's youth who must grow up under the dictatorship and will inherit its legacy. He embodies the tension of living in a country divided by a civil war: he retains a feeling of loyalty to his real father, but he must live with and obey his adoptive father, the man his mother married. The boy's haunting oneiric vision—his recurring dream of a dinosaur emerging from the waters—is a pervasive and enigmatic symbol. When the monster first appears, the boy is afraid of it, but it gradually becomes familiar: "Se acostumbró a verlo aparecer, a nombrarlo, a caminar con él por las calles, a tenerlo por compañero y amigo. . . . Dino, monstruo ingenuo, y familiar"(99-100). The boy is aware that one day the dream creature will burst into his waking life and carry out the terrible threat of his dreams. When this happens, he realizes he must mediate between the dinosaur and the other people: "Su tarea consistía en detenerlo. Apaciguarlo. Domesticarlo. Evitar la destrucción. . . . También debía impedir que alguien lo matara al descubrirlo"(110).

The story draws to a close as the child witnesses the portentous emergence of the huge brontosaurus from the sea. It walks like a baby trying out its first steps in a fragile, watery territory. It looks toward the house and calls out "¡Papá!" In this final cry for help, for recognition or of warning, we realize the child has fused with his oneiric vision. This dinosaur is a paradoxical creature: he is babylike but prehistoric, fearful yet familiar. He opposes Father no. 2's vision of the future as a supercomputer—the irruption of this irrational nightmare was not calculated in Father no. 2's meticulous plans for obedience, order and progress.

Explaining her use of nightmarish landscape, Peri Rossi provides important clues for the meaning of this symbol: "[S]omething I have felt most of my life [is] hallucination, the paranoic hallucination of persecution is a way of interpreting and understanding the world. . . . For me literature is a vision, a creation of symbols to interpret and understand reality. This reality is nightmarish not only . . . because, for instance in Argentina thirty thousand people have disappeared and one out of five Uruguayans have suffered cruel torture and persecution, but also because when it is not the military, the totalitarian regime in power, who persecute us, there often remain our internal phantoms, our own hallucinations."[5]

With the insight afforded by this statement, we can see Dino as an oneiric representation of paranoia of persecution at both a personal and political level. The prehistoric dinosaur represents the repressed horror at the torture and abuse of the regime which had accumulated gradually behind the boy's submissive daytime facade. The dinosaur is the revelation of the future, suggesting an apocalypse when the youth rise up against the absurd and alienating structures of the military dictatorship.

"La influencia de Edgar A. Poe en la poesía de Raimundo Arias" deals with the trials of extraterritorial exile. The story is centered around a father and his young daughter who go into exile after the father is accused of professing "la fe marxista-leninista." The mother had left them previously to join the guerillas. These characters do not correspond to specific political entities as in **"La tarde"** but rather represent the plight of exile in general.

The story develops through constant shifts between the two spaces created by the experience of exile: the "here and now" as opposed to the "over there and then." The "here and now" is a European country, unnamed, but obviously Spain. The father returns home after a hard day trying to sell *jabones-Maravilla* in the streets of a bustling city. His daughter, Alicia, informs him that they have no money. Continuing what seems to be a daily ritual for the pair, the father studies his address book and admits there is no one they can ask for money. The story ends as Alicia, dressed as a Charrúa Indian, goes out the door to beg for money in the streets. This story line is constantly interrupted with extended flashbacks relating the experiences of the father and daughter in their country of origin, their ocean voyage and their arrival.

The "over there and then" is their non-European country where there was a revolution. Paradoxically, an element of differentiation between the country of origin and the country of refuge, according to Alicia, is their common language: "Ella comió . . . pan con mantequilla y mermelada de melocotón, que era como en este país llamaban a los duraznos. . . . las frutillas eran fresas, en el país donde habían decidido ir, por hablar el mismo idioma." (51)

The characters' displacement results in disorientation, humiliation and loss of identity. The humiliation of the father is a leitmotif of the story. Life seems to be nothing but a series of indignities for him, in his own country as well as in the country of refuge, and in his relations with both his wife and his pre-adolescent daughter. In Europe, the humiliation begins at the moment of disembarkment: "nadie les recibió, mas bien fueron mal-recibidos"(48). The narrator provides an endless list of all the documents they were required to present. An absurd situation is created when the Spanish functionary insists the presence of the mother is necessary in order for the girl to enter the country: "—Deberá venir la madre a confirmar que la niña es fruto del matrimonio con usted— . . . Usted puede ser un delincuente, un raptor, un violador de menores, y esta niña, su rehén" (49-50). They decide to perform a blood test to verify his paternity. Here we see a literal translation of the figurative expression as the Spanish authorities extract blood from the father-daughter couple: "un cuarto de litro de sangre más de lo necesario, como se hacía con los extranjeros, porque eran extranjeros" (50). In exile, the father suffers daily humiliation to survive as he fights his way down the jammed sidewalks, peddling soap.

The indignity he suffers in exile is a variation of that which he experienced in his own country. Through the contrast between the father, a literary critic and would-be novelist, and his revolutionary wife, Peri Rossi satirizes the perceived superfluousness of the academic at a time of political upheaval. The title of the story is a paper the father is writing. He runs into his wife's sister, a screen for a clandestine revolutionary group, in a grocery store. He is attracted to her and would have liked to show her his paper, but he tells himself "ella no tenía tiempo para esas cosas." As if to confirm the father's imagined belittlement in the eyes of his sister-in-law, the reader is given access to her thoughts: "Ella pensó que era una lástima que él fuera un intelectual pequeño-burgués, tal como le había dicho su hermana antes de abandonarlo"(46). He was working on a novel about the revolution at the time his wife joined the guerila.

Heaped upon his feelings of disparagement as an intellectual, is his sexual emasculation. To cover up when his wife goes underground, they say she went to Czechoslovakia with another man; thus he meekly assumes the public image of a man betrayed by his wife. We note the reversal between the traditional male and female roles—when she becomes a warrior, he must become the caregiver for their daughter. It seems he is ill-equipped for violent tasks: when they are taking his blood for the paternity test in Spain, he faints as he always does when he sees blood. At this moment he recalls his wife's admonition: "Así no se puede hacer la revolución"(50).

Finally, he must endure disapproval from his young daughter. He is expulsed from the country for having written "artículos que eran verdaderos panegíricos a la turba guerrillera que pretendía socavar la patria y el prestigio de las instituciones nacionales. Muy dignamente asió a su hija de la mano—no soy objeto, para que me lleves en brazos, dijo ella—"(47). Precisely in the moment when he wanted desperately to summon up all his self-respect, he is forced to face insubordination from a child. The reader does not fail to see the irony of the dangerous subversive intentions the government attributes to a man who is seen as a useless intellectual by his wife and sister-in-law. At the moment of disembarkment, Alicia observes that no one has come to meet them, to which the father replies, "Bien sabes que no soy un jugador de fútbol." Alicia looks at her father's skinny legs in his only pair of pants, "y reflexionó que como hija no había tenido demasiado suerte" (47-48).

With the repatriation comes a loss of identity. On one hand, the father and daughter feel isolated from and misunderstood by the Europeans, and, on the other, their presence in Europe makes them aware of their lack of knowledge regarding their own cultural heritage. As Alicia dons her Indian costume, the father and daughter realize how little they know about their country's original inhabitants because they were destroyed by the Spaniards and reelaborated by Hollywood. Alicia's disguise is a creative and cynical solution to their economic problems. In order to survive in this hostile land, she exploits the Europeans' ignorance regarding Latin America, projecting a false image of an indigenous population which bears correspondence to neither the reality of her country nor her own cultural identity.

The transition between the home land and the country of refuge—the sea voyage—creates a third space, both in the surface of the narrative and in psychic dimensions. This passage is characterized by loss, symbolized by the loss of time as they sail from west to east. Alicia is incensed by the fact that they have stolen four hours from her. She imagines traffickers in stolen time: "Pensó en barcos . . . que atravesaban el mar con su carga secreta de tiempo . . . robado . . . a involuntarios emigrados, como su padre y ella"(53). Her image creates a metaphor for the exiles' divestment of their inalienable rights. "—Putaquelosparió a los barcos—" Alicia cries out. This emotional outburst expresses her feeling of impotence in the face of cosmic injustice. Her father does not know how to comfort her about the lost time, nor has he any consolation for the even greater injustices of which he has been victim: "le habían robado mucho más de cuatro horas, y no había podido hacer casi nada para cambiar el orden de las cosas" (52).

In the new country, Alica becomes her father's parent. She assumes control and treats him like a child, and he, in turn, behaves childishly and is submissive to her. The role reversal symbolizes the overwhelming psychological effects of exile. So debilitating is the exile, and so incapable is the father of reconciling himself to it and facing up to the continual humiliation that he experiences infantile regression. The shock of violent times and sudden change has had the opposite effect on Alicia, causing her to mature overnight.

The father attributes his daughter's resilience and ingenuity to the idea that her generation is a new breed: "Esta era otra raza, provista de una singular resistencia . . . habían asimilado las enseñanzas de íntimas, oscurísimas derrotas . . . Concebidas en noches amargas"(58-59). However, since Peri Rossi's vision of a disharmonious and fractured world allows for no heroes, Alicia's final words serve to demystify this elevated vision of the country's youth: "—Estoy segura de que lo que piensas acerca de nuestra generación es completamente falso" (59).

In these stories, CPR uses free imagination to dramatize the dehumanizing effects of civil war, the implantation of an authoritarian regime and exile. In addition to her criticism of the practices of the military regime, CPR implicates the reasons why liberal intellectuals—persons like herself—failed to prevent the military take-over and had to go into exile. The self-mockery we glimpse behind the satirization of tired, impotent journalists and literary critics allows no room for self-indulgent pity. The unrelenting and unforgiving child observer will accept no justification or rationalization for this failure. CPR's intuitive creatures, surely first cousins to the child who cried out, "The emperor has no clothes on," do not hesitate to expose the perversity and falsehood which surrounds them. Their creative and unexpected self-transformations serve to both defy and parody the alienating structures of which they are victims. While the ominous dinosaur is a paranoic response to life under the dictatorship, Alicia's Indian disguise calls attention to the humiliation and incomprehension which the Latin American exiles must endure in Europe.

NOTES

[1] Interview with Ana Basualdo, "Cristina Peri Rossi: Apocalipsis y paraíso," *El Viejo topo* 56 (1981): 48.

[2] Cristina Peri Rossi, *La tarde del dinosauro* (Barcelona: Plaza & Janés, 1985). Page numbers following all quotations from the stories correspond to this edition.

[3] Martin Weinstein, *Uruguay. Democracy at the Crossroads* (Boulder: Westview Press, 1988): 41.

[4] Ibid, 47-49.

[5] Psiche Hughes, "Interview with Cristina Peri Rossi," *Unheard Words.* Mineke Schipper, ed. (New York: Allison & Busby, 1984): 267-68.

Christine Arkinstall   (essay date 1992)

SOURCE: "Desire and Difference in the Poetic Work of Cristina Peri Rossi," in *Love, Sex & Eroticism in Contemporary Latin American Literature*, Alun Kenwood, ed., pp. 35-48. Madrid: Voz Hispánica, 1992.

[*Here, Arkinstall extols Peri Rossi's vocal and poetic embodiment of the "other" in lesbian love and the desire for the oneness of being.*]

The work of Cristina Peri Rossi constitutes a devastating critique of a Western philosophical tradition founded on the privileging of masculine difference. In Myriam Díaz-Diocaretz's words, the Uruguayan-born writer stands with those contemporary women poets whose "emancipatory project is a vast polemic against colonialism, and the traditional position of woman, as well as a rejection of the corresponding myths and mythologizations."[1] This article will explore how Peri Rossi develops the theme of difference with relation to desire in three of her poetic works. In *Descripción de un naufragio*,[2] she analyses how patriarchy attempts to limit meaning to preserve female difference and masculine hegemony, while at the same time her own use of language bears witness to the word's inherent ambiguity. In *Lingüística general*,[3] she examines and subverts certain patriarchal myths which confine woman to the position of desired object and passive muse. Finally, in *Babel Bárbara*,[4] she develops the theme of woman's desire and creativity as channelled through the female body, and not through a forced identification with the male.

Although on one level *Descripción de un naufragio* deals with the breakdown or shipwreck of Uruguayan society on the rocks of fascism,[5] Peri Rossi presents this political event as a symptom of patriarchal politics in general, with hegemony dependent on the colonisation and exploitation of another individual or collective body, perceived as different and valued as inferior. As the symbol *par excellence* of patriarchy's other is "woman," the cultural construction of female sexuality and desire becomes synonymous with all other forms of socio-political subjection.

The equation between otherness and female sexuality may be seen in the following poem. The meeting between hitherto unknown worlds is presented in terms of the sexual act, with the ship that enters an exotic territory a metaphor for the male sexual organ exploring the female body:

> Toda esta parte está compuesta de subyugante
>   geografía
> islas de vellones, muslos que embisten como olas,
> dos piernas,
> una al lado de la otra,
> en concupiscente intimidad,
> y entre ellas,
> un riachuelo que clama por las noches.
> Por el riachuelo puede pasar la pequeña
>   embarcación.
>
>   . . . . .
>
> y recorrí las veinticinco leguas de tu cuarto
> hasta el puerto donde hallé refugio.
> Detrás dejá navegación,
> puentes claros,
> asechanzas,
> el general y la prisión.

(*DN*, 33)

Here, however, the poetic explorer is a dissident fleeing from the oppressive socio-political order embodied in "asechanzas, / el general y la prisión" and, as such, he places himself outside patriarchal ideology and in a position to rediscover a repressed nature, symbolised by nature's feminised desire: "un riachuelo que clama." The rejection of patriarchy, with its rigid hierarchical distinction between "male" and "female," enables the resurgence of other forms of self-expression—a concept reinforced by the fact that the site of the sexual act, the bed, is also the page or place of poetic creation—"En la cama, / desde el extremo blanco de la página."

This poem may be fruitfully contrasted with another, where the unknown other is now perceived from the patriarchal perspective. In **"Carta del navegante"** (*DN*, 53-57) the male poetic voice, the captain of a ship, addresses his Queen in the form of a letter to relate his discoveries of other lands in her name.[6] In his description of the native people encountered, it is relevant that cultural difference becomes the grounds on which the oppression of the other race is justified:

> ni construían barcos como nosotros
> ni sabían leer ni escribir
> con lo cual demostraban ser un pueblo de salvajes.
> Por todo ello decidimos tomarlos como esclavos.

Difference is also considered to characterise the language of the natives. Based on so-called natural sounds—"compuesta de ruidos a mar y viento, ramas, pájaros y animales"—it threatens the unity of the colonising body by reminding the sailors that their most natural allegiance is to the family, displaced under patriarchy by allegiance to the State:

> que con ser hombres valientes y muy entregados a
>   Dios
> y al servicio de Vuestra Majestad
> solían apesadumbrarse de los sonidos aquellos
> añorando padre y madre, hijos y familia.

Patriarchy's fear of a civilisation that emphasises natural laws over political ones, together with its preservation of a rigidly defined "masculine" identity at the expense of any other, is evident in the fact that the indigenous people's subjugation is symbolised in the savage rape of its women:

> Siguiendo vuestro consejo,
> a las mujeres las tomé a todas,
> haciendo posesión de ellas por Vuestra Excelencia y
>   por mí mismo
> con lo cual comprenderá, Señora, que hube de
>   poseerlas dos veces
> a cada una de ellas:
> una por Vos,
> una por mí.

The equivalence established by patriarchal thought between the other culture, a feared nature and woman is again made clear when the colonisers attempt to suppress the native language by brutally torturing and killing twelve pregnant women: "di autorizatión para someter a tormento a doce mujeres preñadas / que les faltara poco tiempo para la parición." Since patriarchy has traditionally considered reproduction to be the only legitimate form of female creativity, the implicit linking of woman with both human and linguistic creation speaks the truth that patriarchy endeavours to suppress: the fact that differences are not naturally present but culturally created to maintain hegemony and exclude the other. It is significant that the poem ends, not with the closure desired by patriarchy, but with the triumph of the repressed; unable to successfully silence the native tongue and the questions it raises regarding their own nature, the colonisers are forced to depart.

If, according to Lacanian theory, the establishing of meaning in a specific context is due to the anchoring of signifier to signified,[7] it is clear from a series of other poems pertaining to nautical definitions that in the context of patriarchal discourse the dominance of the paternal metaphor depends on the anchoring or pinning down of the signifier "woman." In **"Relente,"** for example (*DN*, 61), the night dew that falls on coastal areas becomes a symbol for the perspiration covering the sexually aroused female body: "Humedad que cubre el cuerpo de la mujer, / una vez que la hemos empezado a amar." Now the sexual act, elsewhere seen as a life-giving force, becomes a matter of life and death, in which the "mar agitado" and "aguas revueltas" that threaten to drown the unwary are metaphors for the woman's sexual fluid emissions. The danger that patriarchy perceives in female desire is evident in the description of the woman's beckoning thighs as singing sirens and of her vagina as a fishing net: "No escuches el canto de sus sirenas / varadas en las piernas" and "No dejes que su humedad te cubra / conduciéndote al fondo de la red." That such a portrayal of female sexuality is characteristic of a misogynist tradition intent on preserving male hegemony through restricting woman is revealed in the reference to the "canto de sus sirenas / varadas en las piernas," where the connotations of the past participle "varadas" point to woman's real lack of free movement and expression within such a conceptual system. Similarly, patriarchy's objectification of woman is implicit in the allusion to the "intersticios de un cuerpo que yace."

With each successive definition, the images associated with the sexual relationship between man and woman become progressively more violent, revealing the violence that must be used to keep woman in her place. In **"Armador"** (*DN*, 64) the title, meaning shipowner and shipbuilder, also contains the word "arma" or weapon. As the poem defines "armador" as "[a]quel que construye un barco, una mujer," woman is thus seen as private property, a man-made sexual vessel contained within patriarchal desire. The supposed softness and sweetness of the lover's caresses are quickly shown to be the mere lip-service of a sadist whose process of "construction" inflicts atrocious pain on the body or matter: "suavemente lo va descortezando, / con dulces tirones arrancándole la piel." The blow that opens and splits the tree-trunk, clearly suggestive of the male penetration of the female body, is a stunning reference to the fragmentation of woman by the imposition of patriarchal gender codes: "con el hacha le abre / una herida profunda que lo parte en dos / —por donde toda virginidad fluye—."

This enforced assimilation of woman into the patriarchal order is further emphasised by the conversion of the tree into the man-made "arboladura" or masts and spars. However, as is evident in the following verses, where the mainmast or "palo mayor" stands for the male sexual organ, patriarchy presents itself as supporting the "arboladura," as protecting woman: "el palo mayor, / aquel que sostendrá la arboladura." Significantly, it is the other meaning of "palo"—a stick that inflicts blows—that allows such protection to be read as a process of colonisation involving the definition of gender boundaries and the marking of difference:

> erige el palo mayor,
> aquel que sostendrá la arboladura
> izará banderas
> señalará la mujer.

The violence inherent in woman's objectification and subjection, socially reinforced by being eroticised, continues to be stressed in **"Aferrar"** (**DN**, 67-68), which relates a sexual history of male domination and female bondage.[8] The pleasure of the male coloniser is due to the subjection of the woman or other, as it is her enforced immobility and inability to resist—"irresistible inmovilidad"—that constitutes the real and inadmissible source of her attraction:

> Atarla con mástiles y palos
> al borde de la cama.
> . . . . .
>
> Una vez que está sujeta
> en irresistible inmovilidad,
> arriarla de golpe.

Similarly, in the first of two poems entitled **"Arbolar"** (**DN**, 70-71), the living woman is converted into patriarchy's figure-head, a lifeless object fixed in place for show:

> poner de pie a la mujer
> sobre cubierta,
> . . . . .
>
> la cubierta llena de sangre,
> . . . . .
>
> difícilmente la he erigido
> . . . . .
>
> Como si fueras
> una muerte muy blanca.

As the following verses state, the patriarchal social edifice and representation of woman depend on a figurative,

if not physical, sexual mutilation: "Bosquejar una ciudad. / Circuncidar una mujer."

In the second poem of the same title (**DN**, 72-73) woman's sexual space, symbolised by "bosque" and "cuevas," is defined according to patriarchal parameters as a natural wilderness that must be tamed: "En ese bosque cazar los salvajes animales / refugiados en sus cuevas." At the same time as the verbs "cazar," "registrar," "relevar" and "penetrar" reveal the male narrative subject engaged in an activity hostile to woman, his control of her sexuality, symbolised by "vientre," is suggested in the reference to the astrolabe: "derrotadas tus defensas, / montar sobre tu vientre un astrolabio / para que por el cuerpo te mida las distancias." As a scientific instrument that studies the heavenly bodies, the astrolabe becomes an excellent symbol of the patriarchal signifier that measures woman's distance or difference from man.

In **Lingüística general**, Peri Rossi's point of reference for evaluating woman's difference is Saussure's *Course in General Linguistics*.[9] Linguistics aims at the scientific study of the "natural," and thus irrefutable, grammatical laws that govern linguistic expression.[10] Defined as a metalanguage or "space of hierarchized reflection" in which language is both the object and means of analysis,[11] linguistics is shown to be founded on the same principles of difference as patriarchy; as Elizabeth Grosz explains, "[a] language that considers itself . . . capable of being formalized in the terminology of logic . . . and aims to limit the play of multiple meanings so that only one clear, precise meaning exists is analogous to oedipalized male sexuality (which puts in place of the pleasures of the whole body/language system, the primacy of one organ/meaning)."[12] In her **Lingüística general** Peri Rossi subverts patriarchal discourses of difference that present man as the grammatical, creative subject and woman as his created object. In this way, her stance admits comparison with that of Luce Irigaray, concerned with "breaching the boundaries between fictional and theoretical texts, asserting one in the face of demands of the other," and with "showing that those discourses which present themselves as universal and neutral, appropriate to all, are in fact produced and maintained according to male interests."[13]

In **Lingüística general** authoritative discourse is breached by the poetic metaphor, a linguistic body of love which sees the one in terms of the other, displacing conceptual limits and challenging given identities. For Peri Rossi, the alchemy of both poetry and love is engendered by the "distancia" or difference that separates the dream from a lost reality:

> En la nostálgica distancia que va
> del sueño a lo real
> se instala la alquimia del poema
> y del amor.[14]

(**LG**, 27)

Given that the dream is a consequence of unconscious desire being barred from linguistic expression, it is relevant to the revolutionary purpose of Peri Rossi's **Lingüís-**

tica general that it is not expressed by the logical and grammatical relations proper to the preconscious, but instead by a metaphoric condensation.[15] It is by means of the poetic metaphor or dream that female desire—the repressed other of the patriarchal unconscious—can express itself in images forbidden to a Symbolic where the values are those determined by men.[16]

In **"Dolce Stil Nuovo"** (*LG*, 55) Peri Rossi takes up the metaphor of the literary convention of the same name. In this tradition the adoration of the male poet for the unattainable noble woman constitutes a secular version of Marianism: the cult of the Virgin Mary. However, far from occupying the position of power she appears to be elevated to, woman is thus cast in the mould of passive virtue, the silent muse of the male creator, the object of desire but never desiring subject. Both virgin and mother, she fulfils patriarchy's ideal, but contradictory, representation of femininity.[17] In Peri Rossi's poem, the poetic voice addresses the loved woman or word as her God, adhering to the norms of the *Dolce Stil Nuovo;* made in His image, the created woman/word receives the love that should be due to the Father. If she reflects him, however, it must also follow that her imperfection or lack originates from her Creator and, it is implied, from the entire patriarchal tradition.

> Si has sido hecha
> a imagen y semejanza de Dios
> he de decir
> que mucho más que al Padre,
> amo a la hija imperfecta.

In this way, Peri Rossi works within established images to highlight their ideological paradoxes and create a new style, her own *Dolce Stil Nuovo*, that will represent woman more realistically.

With its reference to Haendel, **"Haendeliana"** emphasises that poetry is a "water music": a fluid element that will reflect woman's image by defying excluding barriers. As in the previous poem, Peri Rossi continues to subvert patriarchal tradition by rewriting the Biblical story of Christ walking on the lake in terms of the passage of the beloved poetic muse and word over her own linguistic kingdom. Now the miracle that challenges all logic is not due to Father and Son, but mother and daughter: the woman poet and her recreated image:

> Largo movimiento el de sus pies
> como si caminara
> sobre un firmamento líquido
> como si al caminar
> las aguas del lago se movieran
> a cuyo movimiento
> lo denomináramos el paso que ella da
> sobre mi reino.
>
>   (*LG*, 53)

Similarly, in a series of poems entitled **"Fosforescencias,"**[18] Peri Rossi indicates that metaphor or change in the image of the loved one or word has the power to transform the known, "natural" order of the world:

> Las mutaciones de tu rostro
> que precipitan catástrofes
> siderales
> terremotos
> eclipses.
>
>   (*LG*, 51)

In **"Fosforescencias III,"** metaphor alters the perception of heaven and earth. Now the creative force is not the Father, but the poet's pregnant hand or "palmas redondas"—a literary matrix or "cava" through which the sky may be contemplated: "Lleva, en sus palmas redondas, agua de todos los lagos / Invierto su cava, para mirar el cielo" (*LG*, 52).[19]

In **"Incesto"** (*LG*, 58), the poetic metaphor again becomes the means of reordering patriarchal premises. To the extent that metaphor unites two linguistic bodies conceptually separated by difference, it is an ideal procedure for the representation of incest: the taboo which regulates society's desire.[20] The type of incest envisaged by Peri Rossi is doubly subversive, as it not only challenges the concept of a kinship founded on difference, but the very institution that kinship depends on: heterosexuality.[21] In the poem, the sea—"mar" and "agua"—which the loved poetic word enters becomes a "playa" or border situation,[22] which is in turn transformed into a house or "casa," symbolic of the mind—the metaphoric bed or "lecho" of a female desire that flouts difference:

> Entrabas al mar
> con mansedumbre
> como si toda aquella agua
> fuera una playa
> la playa fuera una casa
> y la casa
> el tibio lecho de tu hermana.[23]
>
>   (*LG*, 58)

Consequently, whereas in a universe based on differentiation the subject is constructed according to a "phallocentric system of meaning" and desire is bound by the rules of gender,[24] in Peri Rossi's poetic world female desire transgresses social sanctions in order to express its eroticism freely.[25]

Lesbian love continues to be the major theme in the final section of *Lingüística general*, **"Travesía."** It is pertinent that its four poems take as their titles the names of stations situated in Venice: both a woman's name and a city constructed on water,[26] and thus a symbol of a female culture founded on fluid principles. In **"3ª Campo de San Barnaba,"** the crossing of the linguistic barrier or bridge that separates signifier from signified, the one from the other, may be metaphorically read as woman's abandoning of prescribed gender norms and her socially illicit reunion with her own image:

Esta noche, entre todos los normales,
te invito a cruzar el puente.
Nos mirarán con curiosidad—*estas dos
    muchachas*—
y quizás, si somos lo suficientemente sabias,
discret as y sutiles
perdonen nuestra subversión
sin necesidad de llamar al médico
al comisario político o al cura.

(*LG*, 69)

Similarly, in the following poem, **"4ª estación: Ca Foscari,"** love between women is perceived to annul all socially created hierarchies: "Te amo como mi semejante / mi igual mi parecida / de esclava a esclava" (*LG*, 70).

In Peri Rossi's most recent book of poetry, **Babel Bárbara**, the principal theme is that of woman's desire for a valid representation. Here the demand for a rich heterogeneity of word and experience, outside the differences imposed by patriarchal culture, is revealed in the title. While the word "Bárbara" is both a woman's name and an adjective—the very connotations of which oppose the concept of civilisation in any exclusive sense—, the reference to Babel challenges authoritative history as represented by the Bible. If the Bible presents the confounding of tongues as the punishment of a people whose creative power threatened the Father's hegemony,[27] in **Babel Bárbara** such a diversity of language and perspective is seen as positive because it challenges the monolithic power structure of patriarchy.

These concepts are evident in **"La extranjera"** (*BB*,10), where the poet's naming of the loved woman and word constitutes a counter-culture founded on an exiled multiplicity of meaning: "Contra su bautismo natal / el nombre secreto con que la llamo: Babel."[28] Here the receiving of the name does not imply, as within a Lacanian framework, woman's identification with the paternal Symbolic and her representation as lack. On the contrary, it restores to her a lost (het)erogen(e)ous image and reflective space: "Contra el desamparo de sus ojos primarios / la doble visión de mi mirada donde se refleja."

In **"La transgresión"** (*BB*, 12), Babel is associated with a former linguistic tradition—"mezcla lenguas diversas / declina los verbos muertos / y apostrofa en occitano"—, with a culture foreign to the city or patriarchal edifice: "En la ciudad, hay una consigna: / 'No amarás al extranjero.'"[29] Again, in **"Abalorio"** (*BB*, 19), Babel represents an outlawed linguistic code—"el código de una civilización perdida"—synonymous with a feminine sexuality covered up by consolidated laws: "oculta entre las piedras / o en los bordes salados de su sexo." Such images are clearly reminiscent of Freud's comparison of his discovery of the pre-Oedipus—a buried history centred not on the paternal figure, but on the mother—, with that "of the Minoan-Mycenean civilization behind the civilization of Greece."[30] Likewise, in **"Babel, la ambigüedad"** (*BB*, 20), reference is made to a maternal language disfigured by the definitions imposed by patriarchal culture in its mapping of a "hierarchical social geography":[31]

las palabras que te convocan
primigenias en la lengua antigua y materna
se vuelven obscenas en la segunda piel del uso,
la cultura,
ancha geografía.

As has already been discussed, one way in which woman's repressed desire may be expressed is through the metaphoric condensation of the dream. In **"Babel, el despertar"** (*BB*, 26), Babel is described as her own desired creation, that will be brought to term in the womb of her dream: "La membrana arcaica del sueño / la envuelve, amniótica." This figure of female self-representation is likened to a planet that has no name within the already-created conceptual universe: "Como si—innominado planeta— / estuviera rotando en el cosmos lejano / después de la explosión inicial."

Again, in **"Babel, la noche"** (*BB*, 32), the dream expresses Babel's hope of self-recreation. Here the "himen membranoso" of desire symbolises not only the linguistic barrier erected by patriarchy's censorship, but also the threshold to a buried female creativity. Its breaching by words from past civilisations will enable the reproduction of an image which eludes a differentiation privileging masculinity—"la otra de sí misma"—and which thus successfully expresses female subjectivity and desire:

y en el regreso al pasado
de la noche abisal
las palabras rompan la cripta
atraviesen la membrana
y la penetren
            osmosis de la cual
Babel despertará
como la otra de sí misma.

In **"Babel rival"** (*BB*, 59), the "himen membranoso" of the previous poem becomes the "vallas" or linguistic barriers that Babel defies—"salta vallas"—in order to free language from the sexual and social conventions engendered by patriarchal history: "y en su libre gramática / hay más de dos sexos—Alejandría— / más de tres tiempos." As is evident in **"Babel, las analogías"** (*BB*, 33), such a recreated language would establish a culture in which previously dichotomous terms would be equally present, thus restoring to woman her rightful wholeness:

Si fuera una ciudad,
Babel sería la múltiple Babilonia,
poblada y confusa,
            virgen y pública,
sagrada y profana.

The theme of woman's self-representation is further developed in the final poem entitled **"El parto"** (*BB*, 66-67). As in **"Babel, el despertar,"** here Babel stands for a heterogeneous language and psychic space engendered by her hidden desire: "Babel torre, Babel casa escondida. / 'Es largo esconderse nueve meses', dice Babel, henchi-

woman is both the subject and object of her desire, both creator and created: ". . . Guardada / como una ostra. Ensimismándose." Now expression—fulfilled desire—is seen as the product of a female body in which maternity is no longer separated from woman's voice, but intrinsic to it: "Y de pronto, súbitamente, el grito. / Descendiendo por las piernas abiertas, el grito."[32] It is significant that the embodiment of desire is the scream, "midway between silence and speech"[33]—a polivalent sign that escapes literal meaning but is nevertheless inscribed in the Symbolic. For Peri Rossi such expression is the other linguistic body, excluded from patriarchy's official texts: "voz de la víscera, / palabra sin lugar en el diccionario." Consequently, the function of desire in the poetic work of Peri Rossi could well be described in the following terms: "Desire opens the subject to a broader world of signification . . . a world in which it has access to systems of meaning unregulated by any individual or group, and unrestricted in the range of its possible messages. Desire thus institutes a new relation to and in language."[34] As the position of **"El parto"** in the symbolic order of Peri Rossi's text indicates, female desire need not signify the end of woman's creativity, but its rebirth, the point of departure for a new cultural beginning.

NOTES

[1] See Díaz-Diocaretz, "'I will be a scandal in your boat': Women poets and the tradition," *Knives and Angels. Women Writers in Latin America,* ed. Susan Bassnett (London & New Jersey: Zed Books, 1990) 101.

[2] *Descripción de un naufragio* (Barcelona: Lumen, 1975). All quotations from this work will be indicated by the letters *DN.*

[3] *Lingüística general* (Valencia: Prometeo, 1979). All quotations from this work will be indicated by the letters *LG.*

[4] *Babel Bárbara* (Caracas: Angria, 1990). All quotations from this work will be indicated by the letters *BB.* Although Peri Rossi is perhaps better known for her novels and short stories, she has produced an extensive poetic body. Apart from the books of poetry already mentioned, she has also written *Evohé* (Montevideo, 1971), *Diáspora* (Barcelona: Lumen, 1976) and *Europa después de la lluvia* (Madrid: Fundación Banco Exterior, 1987). Her work is also included in several anthologies, such as *Palabras de escándalo—Textos en el aire 1973-1974* (Barcelona: Tusquets, 1974); Víctor Pozanco and José Santamaría, *Nueve poetas del resurgimiento* (Barcelona: Linosa, 1976); and Mari Pepa Palomero, *Poetas de los 70. Antología de poesía española contemporánea* (Madrid: Hiperión, 1987).

[5] As a militant political dissident in the leftist coalition "Frente Amplio," Peri Rossi was forced to leave Uruguay in 1972, shortly before the military coup. See Ana María Moix, "Encuentro con Cristina Peri Rossi," *Camp de l'arpa*, no. 82 (December 1980): 59.

[6] According to Jacques Lacan's psychoanalytic framework, the position of power and prestige, symbolised by the phallus, may be theoretically occupied by either sex. However, as Elizabeth Grosz argues, "although Lacan's account is directed to the phallus as signifier, not to the penis as an organ, it is committed to an *a priori* privilege of the masculine that is difficult, if not impossible, to dislodge" (*Jacques Lacan. A Feminist Introduction* [London & New York: Routledge, 1990] 123).

[7] See Grosz, 95-96.

[8] As Catharine MacKinnon comments, "[s]exual objectification is the primary process of the subjection of women." ("Feminism, Marxism, Method, and the State: An Agenda For Theory," *The Signs Reader. Women, Gender and Scholarship*, eds. Elizabeth Abel & Emily K. Abel [Chicago & London: The University of Chicago Press, 1983] 253).

[9] See Ferdinand de Saussure, *Course in General Linguistics*, trans. W. Baskin (London: Fontana, 1974). Although Saussurean linguistics is supposedly based on the concept of "pure" difference, where there can be no privileged term, it also creates a series of hierarchical binary oppositions in which relations are "based on one rather than many terms." Fundamental for a patriarchal linguistic framework is the binary opposition of male/female, taken up by Lacan's materialist account of the Saussurean system in his privileging of the phallus as the "signifier of signifiers" (See Grosz, 124-25, respectively).

[10] See Deborah Cameron, *Feminism and Linguistic Theory* (New York: St. Martin's Press, 1985) 10-11.

[11] See Grosz, 177.

[12] See Grosz, 177-78.

[13] See Grosz, 168 and 177, respectively.

[14] In these verses I interpret "lo real" in the sense of the Lacanian Real where, as Elizabeth Grosz puts it, "the vagina, clitoris, or vulva have the same ontological status and functional utility as the penis and testicles. . . ." Grosz adds that the Real "must be displaced and recoded if women's bodies are to be categorized as *necessarily* incomplete" (Grosz, 117). Another poem in which the relationship between poetic metaphor and love is established is "Navegaciones": "Nuestro amor fue metáfora" (*LG*, 49).

[15] See Grosz, 86. It is pertinent that, in Lacanian theory, difference not only defines desire but also determines, as sexual difference, the socially-sanctioned forms in which desire may be expressed: "Lacan assumes a concept of desire as the difference or gap separating need from demand" and "the subject is thus fundamentally a sexed subject, one whose sex is crucial to the kind of subjectivity, desire, and position it is granted in culture" (Grosz, 64 and 73, respectively).

[16] As Elsa Krieger Gambarini points out, "just as the unconscious infiltrates the conscious mind, the body of critical analysis—representing conscious activity—is penetrated by its own unconscious, which it contains within itself as the possibility of its own subversion" ("The Male Critic and the Woman Writer: Reading Teresa de la Parra's Critics," *In the Feminine Mode. Essays on Hispanic Women Writers*, eds. Noël Valis and Carol Maier [London & Toronto: Associated University Presses, 1990] 177).

[17] Myriam Díaz-Diocaretz maintains that Marianism "creates the moral and social paradigms shaping the image of the virtuous woman, the one to be admired, a type which includes the representation of women in courtly love" (Díaz-Diocaretz, 88).

[18] It is significant that in *Babel Bárbara* Peri Rossi associates the concept of "fosforescente" with the female sexual lips: "La vulva, húmeda y violeta, / a veces, fosforescente" ("El parto," *BB,* 66).

[19] Another similar poem is "Pavesiana" (*LG,* 46-48), where the state of expectancy that accompanies the production of the word is symbolised by a maternal image: "la redondez de tu vientre." Here the woman's body is both the text in whose image the world is read and the poetic writing subject: "Cómo amaba los manuscritos de tus manos / en la alfombra / en la mesa de todos los días."

[20] As Judith Butler indicates, "the paternally enforced taboo against incest is foundational to language itself. . . . This system of linguistic differentiation is understood to be based upon the differentiated relations of kinship, and differentiation itself is said to characterize language in its inception. Indeed, the process of differentiation itself is a consequence of the prohibition against incest . . . [which] not only regulates and forbids certain kinds of behavior, but also generates and sanctions other kinds of behavior, and thus becomes instrumental in giving a socially sanctioned form to desire." (*Subjects of Desire. Hegelian Reflections in Twentieth-Century France* [New York: Columbia University Press, 1987] 201-2).

[21] As Catharine MacKinnon states: "Women and men are divided by gender, made into the sexes as we know them, by the social requirements of heterosexuality, which institutionalizes male sexual dominance and female sexual submission" (MacKinnon, 245).

[22] The idea that the lover who contravenes heterosexuality must live on the border of society, marginalised by a hostile environment, is also apparent in other poems in *Lingüística general*; for example: "La amé sólo en el margen alucinante / en que las cosas empiezan a ser la memoria / que tenemos de las cosas" ("Poética," *LG,* 37) and "Raro amor este / de fines de un siglo / peligroso como ningún otro" ("Ella," *LG,* 40).

[23] It is pertinent that in "La argonauta" (*BB,* 24) the word "incesto" is unknown.

[24] See Butler, 202. As Elizabeth Grosz explains, "[woman's] earliest homosexual attachment must be given up so that she is able to enter the circuits of sexual exchange, her pre-history is erased and her relation to the primal love object, to a body similar to her own, is lost" (Grosz, 182).

[25] In her book of essays entitled *Fantasías eróticas* Peri Rossi declares: "Bataille lo ha expresado con absoluta claridad al decir: 'La transgresión difiere de la vuelta a la naturaleza: levanta el interdicto sin suprimirlo.' Ese es el resorte del erotismo: la transgresión" (Madrid: Ediciones Temas de Hoy, 1991) 123.

[26] In an earlier poem Peri Rossi states that "Venecia tiene nombre de agua / de mujer y de vidrio" ("Itinerario," *LG,* 43).

[27] See Genesis, 11: 4-8.

[28] In relation with exiled languages see also, for example, "Babel, la maldiciente" (*BB,* 31).

[29] The connection between linguistic heterogeneity and the subversiveness of repressed love is apparent in the following verses from "La ofrenda": "celebra los cultos sediciosos del amor / en lenguas diversas" (18).

[30] Sigmund Freud, "Female Sexuality" (1931), *The Standard Edition of the Complete Psychological Works of Sigmund Freud,* ed. and trans. James Strachey, vol. 21 (London: Hogarth, 1953-74) 226.

[31] See Grosz, 121.

[32] The neo-Freudianism of Julia Kristeva envisages maternity as a vacant space which "*women* as such can never inhabit" (Grosz, 162). As Marianne Hirsch remarks, within such a psychoanalytic framework "the mother's desire can never be voiced. . . . And since the phallus (as lack) is the tool of representation, and since the mother does not have it . . . any other articulation of her own becomes an impossibility" (*The Mother/Daughter Plot. Narrative, Psychoanalysis, Feminism* [Bloomington & Indianapolis: Indiana University Press, 1989] 168).

[33] See Butler, 199.

[34] Grosz, 66.

FURTHER READING

Antolin Cochrane, Helena. "Androgynous Voices in the Novels of Cristina Peri Rossi." *Mosaic*, Vol. 30, No. 3, September 1997, pp. 97-114.

Undertakes Peri Rossi's use of ambiguous or androgynous characters as representative of Latin American gender identification and liberation.

Arkinstall, Christine. "Fabrics and Fabrications in Cristina Peri Rossi's *La Nave de Los Locos.*" *Travellers' Tales, Real and Imaginary, in the Hispanic World and Its Literature*, pp. 150-58. Madrid: Voz Hispanica, 1992.

Extracts Peri Rossi's comprehension of myths of death and creation in *La nave de los locos.*

Castillo, Debra A. "(De)ciphering Reality in 'Los extraños objetos voladores.'" *Letras Femeninas*, Vol. XIII, No. 1-2 (Spring-Fall 1987): pp. 31-41.

Critically disseminates the symbols represented in Peri Rossi's short story "Los extraños objetos voladores" to define the levels of alienation and anxiety experienced by the characters.

Chanady, Amaryll B. "Cristina Peri Rossi and the Other Side of Reality." *The Antigonish Review*, Vol. 54 (Spring 1983): pp. 44-53.

Explains *Los museos abandonados* as a collection of stories about failed attempts and inherent cowardice toward motion.

Geisdorfer Feal, Rosemary. "Cristina Peri Rossi and the Erotic Imagination." *Reinterpreting the Spanish American Essay: Women Writers of the 19th and 20th Centuries*, Doris Meyer, ed., pp. 215-206. Austin: University of Texas, 1995.

Delves into Peri Rossi's erotica, critiquing its values on various levels from basic to the purest levels of love.

Kaminsky, Amy. "Gender and Exile in Cristina Peri Rossi." *Continental, Latin-American and Francophone Women Writers*, Eunice Myers and Ginette Adamson, eds., pp. 149-59. New York: University Press of American, 1987.

Compares the alienation of exile with lesbian status as a process of regeneration in Peri Rossi's works.

Kaminsky, Amy K. "Cristina Peri Rossi and the Question of Lesbian Presence." *Reading the Body Politic: Feminist Criticism and Latin American Women Writers*, pp. 115-133. Minneapolis: University of Minnesota Press, 1993.

   Amplifies the lesbian presence in Peri Rossi's works, and expresses feelings of growth and pleasure.

Mora, Gabriela. "Enigmas and Subversions in Cristina Peri Rossi's *La Nave de Los Locos* [*Ship of Fools*]." *Splintering Darkness: Latin American Women Writers in Search of Themselves*, Lucia Guerra Cunningham, ed., pp. 19-30. Pittsburgh: Latin American Literary Review Press, 1990.

   Examines the fragments of chaos Peri Rossi's *La Nave de Los Locos* [*Ship of Fools*] to find the common thread of harmony among the inhabitants of the ship.

San Román, Gustavo. "Fantastic Political Allegory in the Early Work of Cristina Peri Rossi." *Bulletin of Hispanic Studies*, Vol. LXVII, No. 2 (April 1990): 161-64.

   Provides an overview of Peri Rossi's life in exile and its effect on her fiction.

Additional coverage of Peri Rossi's life and career is contained in the following sources published by the Gale Group: *Contemporary Authors*, **Vol. 131;** *Contemporary Authors New Revision Series*, **Vol. 59;** *Dictionary of Literary Biography*, **Vol. 145;** *Hispanic Writers*.

Alfonso Reyes
1889-1959

Mexican essayist, critic, poet, and fiction writer.

INTRODUCTION

An extremely prolific and versatile writer, Reyes is acknowledged as one of the finest Latin American essayists of the twentieth century. His works have been especially praised for their consistent originality of theme and graceful clarity of expression. Demonstrating his conviction that human values are universal, Reyes's writings often explore the relationships between classical and modern cultures and between Old World and New World cultures. He has been described as a "Renaissance man," whose humanist ideology found expression in poetry and fiction as well as in works of literary theory and history.

Reyes was born in Monterrey, the capital of the state of Nuevo León, in 1889. His father, General Bernal de Reyes, was a prominent politician in the national government of General Porfirio Diáz and also served as governor of Nuevo León. In 1905, Alfonso entered the Escuela Naciónal Preparatoria in Mexico City, where he first began writing poetry. He continued his education at the Facultad de Derecho, where he studied law and classics and published his first work, the collection of literary essays *Cuestiones estéticas* (1911). He was also involved in the intellectual life of Mexico City, becoming the youngest member of a group of writers and philosophers known as the "Generation of the Centenary." These intellectuals, rebelling against the largely imitative nature of Mexican culture, sought to stimulate renewal and growth in Mexican thought and society in order to establish a culture that would be uniquely Mexican. Members of this group, including Reyes, later founded the Ateneo de la Juventud (Athenaeum for the Youth) with the goal of providing a forum for new ideas. The Athenaeum came to be considered representative of the social and cultural conscience of the times and is credited with playing an important role in the Mexican cultural renaissance of the early twentieth century.

After graduating with a law degree in 1913, Reyes entered the diplomatic service and departed for France as the second secretary of the Paris Legation; however, when the Mexican delegation to France was disbanded as a result of World War I, Reyes went to Madrid. There he lived in what he described as "happy poverty," earning a meager living by translating and editing while writing prolifically and associating with Spain's leading intellectual figures. Ramón Menéndez Pidal, a prominent figure in Hispanic scholarship and president of the Centro de Estudios Historicos, asked him to join the philology department at the Centro, which was known for its critical method rejecting subjectivity in favor of objective philological and historical analysis. While associated with the Centro, Reyes studied sixteenth- and seventeenth-century Spanish literature, becoming an acknowledged expert on the Spanish Golden Age. During this period, **Jos**é Ortega y Gasset invited Reyes to contribute to *El sol* (*The Sun*), often described as Spain's foremost intellectual newspaper, and Reyes was also involved with the Residencia de Estudiantes, considered one of the most influential cultural centers of the period. In 1920 Reyes resumed his diplomatic career, being named second secretary of the Mexican delegation in Spain.

The years Reyes spent in Madrid, from 1914 to 1924, are considered fundamental to his literary development. Barbara Bockus Aponte has suggested that his involvement with Menendez Pidal was especially important, as the discipline and rigorous scientific method of scholarship practiced at the Centro significantly influenced the evolution of Reyes's own critical writing as well as providing a foundation for many of his purely creative projects. Some of his most important works appeared during this period, including *El suicida* (1917), a collection of essays which was the first of his books to receive widespread critical attention; *Visión de Anáhuac* (1917), a description of the ancient city of the Aztecs as first seen by a Spanish conquistador; *Cartones de Madrid* (1917), a collection of impressionistic essays; *Ifigenia cruel* (1924), a tragic poem; and many of the essays that appeared in later collections, most notably in the series *Simpatías y diferencias* (1921-26). The relationships he formed during this time with other intellectuals were important professionally and personally for the rest of Reyes's life. By the time he left Madrid, Reyes had received wide acclaim as a writer.

For fifteen years after he left Madrid, Reyes continued to write while occupying a variety of diplomatic posts, including ambassador to France, Argentina, and Brazil. Upon returning to Mexico in 1939, he was named president of the Casa de España en México ("Spanish House in Mexico"), which later became the Colegio de México, the country's most distinguished institution of higher education as well as an important center for scholarly research and publication. He was also elected to the Mexican Academy of Languages, which he served as director from 1957 to 1959. In 1945 he was awarded the National Prize for Arts and Letters and was a candidate for the Nobel Prize. He spent the last years of his life writing voluminously, encouraging younger scholars, and organizing the extensive library he had accumulated. He died in 1959.

Of the various genres in which he wrote, Reyes's essays received the most critical acclaim, praised for both their thematic depth and stylistic artistry. The tone of his essays is often described as conversational rather than academic, characterized by insight, subtlety, and wit. While he addressed a wide range of subjects in his essays, from metaphysical questions to discarded razor blades, some consistent themes are evident. Perhaps the most prominent of these is the theory that America has the potential to provide an important cultural synthesis combining values of the Old World and the New, an idea most effectively expressed in the essays "Notas sobre la inteligencia Americana" and "Posicion de America." As one who moved easily between Mexico and Spain, Reyes was interested in the possibility of a cultural reconciliation between Spain and Spain's former colonies. His sense of the relationship between the two societies is reflected in *Visión de Anáhuac*, which describes an encounter between an Old World explorer and native American culture. Reyes's early studies of classical Greece and Rome had a continuing influence, as he attempted to explore connections between the cultures of Europe and America. In *Discurso por Virgilio* (1931), for example, he used motifs similar to those in Virgil's *Georgics* to explain a plan by the Mexican government to develop local viniculture industries.

Critics suggest that Reyes's training as a classicist is also evident in his creative writing, most notably in *Ifigenia cruel,* a tragic poem in which he re-created the legend of Iphigenia in Taurus. Although he wrote few poems, many critics view his poetry as an important facet of his development as a writer. Reyes modeled his early poems on traditional verse forms, while in his later poetry he experimented with a variety of forms and techniques. He wrote: "I prefer to be promiscuous / in literature," "the popular ballad / of the neighbor / with the rare quintessence / of Gongora and Mallarme." His varied subjects include friendship, love, death, Mexico, episodes from his life, and gourmet food and wine. Indeed, as Enrique Anderson Imbert has stated, "nothing was outside the pale" of Reyes' poetry. Reyes also wrote short fiction, which often relied on suggestive detail to capture the reader's imagination instead of the traditional plot structure. In *El testimonio de Juan Peña* (1930), for example, subtle changes in the protagonists' points of view, rather than development of plot, provide the suspense of the story. Given the quality of this story, which has been described as a "masterful tale," several critics have questioned why Reyes did not write more fiction. Other critics, however, have criticized his longer fictional writings — each of which he referred to as "arranques de novela" ("beginnings of a novel")—for structural inadequacy, maintaining that these works create intriguing atmosphere and characters but fail due to their lack of narrative development.

Reyes also wrote works of literary criticism and theory. *La experiencia literaría* (1942), a collection of essays written over several years, is thought to most clearly reveal the enormous scope of his literary knowledge which ranged, in the words of Walter Bara, "from Aristotle to Zola, from Chaucer to Chaplin," encompassing classical, modern, and contemporary literature of Europe and America. *El deslinde: Prolegómenos a la teoría literaria* (1944), an ambitious attempt to systematize literary theory and to determine what qualities distinguish literature from other types of writing, is often considered his masterpiece. In this work, he examined such aspects of literature as aesthetic problems, style and expression, semantics, philology, and the philosophy of language. Much of the success of the book has been attributed to his skill in explaining abstractions clearly and vividly by using poetic images and familiar expressions. Reyes was also instrumental in the critical rehabilitation of the seventeenth-century Spanish poet Luis de Gongora, a development that is considered equivalent to the rediscovery of John Donne in English literature.

Reyes is remembered for his original and eloquent essays, his lasting contributions to literary theory and criticism, his commitment to the exaltation of Mexican culture, and his dedication as an educator. He is considered to have trained, by example and instruction, an entire generation of Mexican intellectuals. Reflecting on Reyes's long and varied career, Federico de Onis has called him "the most successful example of a citizen of the international world of letters, both ancient and modern."

PRINCIPAL WORKS

Cuestiones estéticas   (essays)   1911
Cartones de Madrid   (essays)   1917
El suicida (essays) 1917
Visión de Anáhuac   (essay)   1917
El plano oblicuo   (fiction)   1920
Retratos reales e imaginarios   (essays)   1920
El cazador   (essays)   1921
Simpatías y diferencias. 5 vols.   (essays)   1921-26
Huellas   (poetry)   1922
Ifigenia cruel   (poem)   1924
Cuestiones gongorinas   (criticism)   1927
El testimonio de Juan Peña   (fiction)   1930
Discurso por Virgilio   (essay)   1931
Tren de ondas   (essays)   1932
Capítulos de literatura española [first series]   (criticism)   1939
La crítica en la edad ateniense   (criticism)   1941
Pasado inmediato, y otros ensayos   (essays)   1941
La antigua retórica   (criticism)   1942
La experiencia literaria   (criticism)   1942
El deslinde: Prolegómenos a la teoría literaria   (criticism)   1944
Norte y sur   (essays)   1944
Capitulos de literatura española [second series]   (criticism)   1945
Letras de la Nueva España   (criticism)   1948

The Position of America, and Other Essays (essays)
  1950
Trayectoria de Goethe (criticism) 1954
Quince presencias (fiction) 1955

CRITICISM

Tomas Navarro (essay date 1945)

SOURCE: *Books Abroad,* Vol. 19, No. 2, Spring 1945, pp. 116-17.

[*A Spanish philologist, educator, and critic, Navarro was one of the most important figures in the development of modern philological studies in Spain. In 1945, with the goal of encouraging North American readers to examine the works of Reyes,* Books Abroad *published a series of letters about the Mexican author from eleven critics and friends of Reyes. In the following letter, Navarro discusses certain characteristics of Reyes's style and language.*]

A salient characteristic of the style of Alfonso Reyes is the agile and obedient flexibility with which the author's words respond to his turns of thought. The great Mexican writer has constantly and steadily perfected the clarity of expression, rich in nuances and reflections, of which he is today an acknowledged master. And paralleling his linguistic advance one notes the development of that delicate combination of serenity and disquiet, of equilibrium and movement, which Reyes has the secret of infusing into his writing.

Even in conversation Reyes makes occasional use of rising inflexions, rapid and varied, which contrast with the usual medium pitch—perhaps a little lower than medium—of his speaking voice. The proportion and measure of the elements of articulation and accent in Alfonso Reyes' speech reveal prosodic habits which do not, it is true, hide his Mexican origin, but which clearly correspond to the essential tradition of good Spanish "usage," a good usage which Reyes brought with him from his native country before he had lived in Madrid and traveled about among the village of Castile.

There is an admirable example in the achievement of this great linguistic acclimatizer who shows us how it is possible to inhabit the most different regions without ever succumbing to the perils of offensive pedantry, affectation or verbal acrobatics. The note of discretion which is always evident in Reyes' manner is also the wise and solid basis of his literary procedure, whether he sketches his keen *Cartones de Madrid* or lays the grave and ample foundations of his *Visión de Anáhuac.*

About this steady axis play the most varied rhythms. If there is any fault from which the speech and writing of Reyes are entirely free, it is the fault of monotony. One perceives in his language, not the artificial symbolism of a more or less conventional acoustics, but the flawless discrimination of an ear which appreciates the immanent expressiveness of sound. Reyes, who has always written verses and has tried his hand at numerous metrical forms, often evokes the most intimate impressions with the aid of auditory images, as when, in *Huellas,* he recalls the song of the servant and the zestful gatherings at which even the music of the young friends' thoughts was audible.

Reyes is never heedless of his language, not even at those moments when he chooses to write with the most carefree abandon. He has spent a large part of his life in the study of Spanish literature, and has followed the development of the language from its earliest beginnings. That is exactly why this writer's style builds its vigilant modernity on so secure a foundation. The word surrenders completely and obediently only to him who knows and feels its past.

The international scope of Reyes' writing has not diluted the genuinely Hispanic characteristics of his style, nor has his command of the literary language eliminated from his writing the atmosphere and accent of his native country. Reyes' Mexicanism visibly consists, like that of his compatriot Alarcón, in the fostering and selection of traditional elements which become more genuinely Spanish as they grow more cleanly and essentially Mexican. (pp. 116-17)

Antonio Castro Leal (essay date 1945)

SOURCE: *Books Abroad,* Vol. 19, No. 2, Spring 1945, pp. 120-21.

[*In the following excerpt from a letter included in the* Books Abroad *collection, Leal offers a brief description of the phases of Reyes' career and praises his range and versatility as a writer.*]

[Alfonso Reyes] inaugurated his literary career with a beautiful book called *Cuestiones estéticas* (1911), in which one feels the subtle force of expanding life, the intelligent curiosity of youth, and a palpitating humanism in which there was as much divination as doctrine. Then the Madrid period, the most fortunate and fruitful epoch of his early period. From that epoch date the articles and essays which form the first three volumes of *Simpatías y diferencias* (1921-1922), the *Retratos reales e imaginarios* (1920), and a series of important works of erudition and criticism, the *Cartones de Madrid* (1917), intense and rapid pictures of Spanish life which, like the inspired "studies" of the painters, represent a state of pure emotion which is often diluted in their completed works, and the *Visión de Anáhuac* (1915), an essay which attains perfection in the purity and precision of its lines, in its balanced power of evocation and synthesis. In this same period he published *El plano oblicuo* (1920) and *El cazador*

(1921), much of which was written in Mexico: *cuentos* and fanciful sketches in which he has succeeded in expressing situations whose reality merges with forgotten dreams and irreversible moments of spiritual autobiography. To the Spanish period belongs also his dramatic poem *Ifigenia cruel* (1923), which has the severe and noble elegance of old Greek sculpture, and whose lyric current stirs the waters of classic mythology.

After Madrid came a well earned vacation. It was like a general's reorganization of his army after a victorious battle. Reyes found it more effective and more agreeable to adopt a pleasanter and freer rhythm, and he brought into the world without haste but without interruption, books of such charm that they scarcely fatigued the presses. (p. 120)

And finally, back in Mexico. . ., he inaugurated with admirable vigor and lucidity the third epoch of his career. In the last few years he has published books whose method, matter and manner are far above anything to which we Hispano-Americans have been accustomed. *La crítica en la edad ateniense* (1941) and *La antigua retórica* (1942) are two masterful books whose penetration, special competence and ideological elegance give new meaning to the problems which he treats. In amplitude and profundity their treatment of these phases of Greek culture is fully worthy to set beside the work of Professor J. W. H. Atkins [*Literary Criticism in Antiquity*]. . . . In *El deslinde* (1942) and on many pages of *La experiencia literaria* (1942) he has gone more deeply into various fundamental questions of the technique and philosophy of literature than has perhaps ever been done before in our language.

But such investigations do not entirely occupy or satisfy this choice and multiple intelligence. He still turns at times to poetry and to the other forms of personal expression in literature. For this superman of letters moves about in the field of writing as the great artists of the Renaissance turned hither and thither in the world of forms, finding, like them, delight and necessary inspiration in the lines of the flat sketch, in three-dimensional relief, in the architectonic flight of the cupola and the dentate outline of the battlemented wall. (p. 121)

Bertram D. Wolfe   (essay date 1950)

SOURCE: "A Shining Mind from Modern Mexico," *New York Herald Tribune Book Review,* December 24, 1950, p. 7.

[*In this excerpt, Wolfe assesses the essays collected in* The Position of America.]

[The essays in *The Position of America*] have been selected to give the discursive, wide-ranging thought of the author a special unity around the problems of America: "**Vision of Anáhuac**" (Ancient Mexico); "**Thoughts on the American Mind**"; "**The Position of America**"; "**Epistle to the Pinzons**" (the three brothers who piloted Columbus' ships); "**Columbus and Amerigo Vespucci**"; "**Social Science and Social Responsibility**" (with special reference to America's use of European culture); "**Native Poetry of New Spain**"; "**The Tenth Muse of America**" (the Mexican poetess, Sor Juana [Ines de la Cruz]); "**Luis G. Urbina**" (elegy to a Mexican poet); and "**Virgil in Mexico**." Reyes' thought, like the chronicle of his life as intellectual, diplomat and traveler, moves out in a series of widening circles from its Mexican center: he is Mexican, Latin, Ibero-American, Continental American, European of the transplanted Europe of the New Continent, Citizen of the Republic of Letters and of the World, and practiser of "the profession that is superior to all others, the profession of being a man." He has been at home in Buenos Aires, Rio de Janeiro, New York, Madrid, Paris, Rome; he would have been at home no less in the Rome of Virgil and in ancient Athens. His thought moves in transparent, widening, overlapping, concentric circles from its Mexican center. The color grows more intense as we move toward that center, so that the best and most vivid essays are the most specifically Mexican: the "**Vision of Anáhuac**"; "**The Tenth Muse**"; "**Virgil in Mexico**." All the essays are suggestive, little spots of light shine from them as from fireflies in a wooded night; but those with the largest titles like "**Thoughts on the American Mind**" have the thinnest density and precisely because of their large promise leave us aroused but disappointed.

"**Vision of Anáhuac**," on the other hand, with which the volume opens, is a veritable poet's vision of the world of wonder of Aztec-Maya civilization as beheld by the first Spaniards when they broke into it. "Traveler," cries its epigraph, "you have come to the most transparent region of the air." The picture has the profusion of detail, the complex organization, the sense of analogy between hills and objects and men and all the lyricism that characterizes Rivera's murals of the same pre-conquest world. "From the barren, alkaline earth the plants raise the thorns of their vegetable claws, defending themselves against drought . . . the air glitters like a mirror . . . it is like autumn the year round . . . the brilliant humming bird, the emerald trembler . . . the rocks replying to the sweet songs of the flowers." . . . In this setting man has organized a life full of splendor, passion, cruelty and "exotic" wonder. It is a world in which Dionysius would be more at home than Apollo, yet this Apollonian writer feels linked to it by the "common effort to master our wild, hostile natural setting" and by "emotions aroused by the same natural objects," emotions "without whose glow our valleys and our mountains would be like an unlighted theater."

No less characteristic is the closing essay which begins with the celebration of the two-thousandth anniversary of Virgil in Mexico, goes on to an analysis of

Mexico's Latinity and ends with thoughts on the "Geor-gics" as the healing "program" of Mexico's agrarian revolution.

Walter Bara (essay date 1951)

SOURCE: "Aspects of Alfonso Reyes," *Hispania,* Vol. XXXIV, No. 4, November 1951, pp. 378-80.

[*In the following excerpt, Bara compares Reyes's accomplishments as a poet and essayist, and extols the breadth of Reyes's literary knowledge.*]

Twenty-five years ago, more or less, when he was already firmly established as one of the greatest Hispanists of modern times, Pedro Henríquez Ureña registered a literary judgment which the passage of time has proven quite conclusively to be inaccurate. He wrote that the eminence of Alfonso Reyes as a man of letters was most keenly reflected in his poetry. This may have been true in 1927, but surely very few people today would agree with this opinion, since, in the score of countries where the name of Reyes is revered by anyone familiar with contemporary Spanish American letters, Don Alfonso is regarded as one of the finest essayists ever to have written in the Spanish language, and the most outstanding humanist that Mexico, or perhaps any other Castilian-speaking country, for that matter, has produced in this century. It is true that the tone and tempo of many of his shorter prose pieces is imbued with the same inspiration that nourished some of Spain's finest lyricists, and that the color and wealth of Indian pageantry in his *Visión de Anáhuac* is not very far removed from poetry itself. However, over and above his superior accomplishments in the field of poetry, Alfonso Reyes is today rightfully recognized as a true descendent of Montaigne and Bacon and those who, after them, enriched the world's literature through their cultivation of the essay form.

Although his poetic output in volume is insignificant when compared with his prose writings, Alfonso Reyes nevertheless has studied and evaluated this genre with extraordinary ability. *De poesía Hispano-americana,* written in 1941, is a remarkable feat of conciseness and thoroughness in summing up the salient aspects of the modern period in Spanish American poetry. Equally compact and rich in facts, information, and recondite details—qualities characteristic of all his critical studies—is his summary of pre-Columbian letters, written as an introduction to his *Letras de la Nueva España*. . ., published in 1948. Its section on the indigenous poetry of the new world is probably the finest review of the maya-quiché culture to have been condensed within the boundaries of a literary study. In this book, Alfonso Reyes, with consistently enviable clarity of thought and language, offers a truly exquisite literary panorama of Mexican literature in its three centuries of colonial times.

La experiencia literaria, published in Argentina in 1942, may in many respects be considered Reyes' literary biography. In this anthology of essays, written at random over a period of several years, the author reveals more fully perhaps than in any other of his single volumes the infinite scope of his literary knowledge—classical, modern, and contemporary—of France, England, Germany, Iberia and Latin America, as well as the United States. Every one of the more than two hundred pages of this book contains at least one allusion to a foreign author; in some instances, there are as many as ten on a single page. Alfonso el Sabio shares honors with Mark Twain and Valery Larbaud in **"Aduana Lingüística,"** one of the most delightful essays on language barriers that has ever been written. . . . (p. 378)

From Aristotle to Zola, from Chaucer to Chaplin, the literary experience of Reyes is so broad that it defies comparison with the personal culture of any living writer. Undoubtedly, a great many of these allusions are meaningless to all but the best informed in international literature, ancient and modern; and since Alfonso Reyes almost never resorts to explanatory footnotes or biographical glossaries, a large portion of his writings cannot be fully appreciated by most people until they are made available in annotated editions. (p. 379)

Octavio Paz (essay date 1960)

SOURCE: "The Rider of the Air," *The Siren & the Seashell and Other Essays on Poets and Poetry.* Austin: University of Texas Press, 1976, pp. 113-22.

[*A prolific Mexican man of letters, Paz is considered one of the greatest Spanish-American writers of the twentieth century. Although he is known primarily as an experimental poet, he is also a respected essayist, critic, and social philosopher. In the following excerpt, Paz explores characteristic themes in Reyes's work, analyzing in particular the poem Ifigenia cruel.*]

Reyes, the lover of measure and proportion, a man for whom everything, including action and passion, had to resolve itself in equilibrium, knew that we are surrounded by chaos and silence. Formlessness, whether as a vacuum or as a brute presence, lies in wait for us. But he never tried to put instinct in chains, to suppress the dark side of man. He did not preach the equivocal virtues of repression, either in the realm of ethics or in that of aesthetics, and even less so in politics. Wakefulness and sleep, blood and thought, friendship and solitude, the city and women: each part and each one must be given its own. The portion of instinct is no less sacred than that of the spirit. And what are the limits between one and another? Everything communicates. Man is a vast and delicate alchemy. The human action par excellence is transmutation, which makes light from shadow, the word from a cry, dialogue from the elemental quarrel.

His love for Hellenic culture, the reverse of his indifference toward Christianity, was something more than an intellectual inclination. He saw Greece as a model because what its poets and philosophers revealed to him was something that was already within him and that, thanks to them, received a name and an answer: the terrible powers of hubris and the means of controlling them. Greek literature did not show him a philosophy, a moral, a "what should be." Rather, it showed him being itself in all its welter, in its alternately creative and destructive rhythms. The Greek norms, Jaeger says, are a manifestation of the inherent lawfulness of the cosmos; the movement of being, its dialectic. On several occasions Reyes wrote that tragedy is the highest and most perfect form of poetry and ethics because, in tragedy, lack of proportion finds at last its strict measure and is thus purified and redeemed. Passion is creative when it finds its form. To Reyes, form was not an envelopment or an abstract measure, but rather the instant of reconciliation in which discord is transformed into harmony. The true name of this harmony is liberty: fatality ceases to be an imposition from without and becomes an intimate and voluntary acceptance. Ethics and aesthetics are intertwined in Reyes's thinking: liberty is an aesthetic act, that is, it is the moment of concord between passion and form, vital energy and the human measure; at the same time, form and measure constitute an ethical dimension because they rescue us from excess, which is chaos and destruction.

These ideas, scattered through many of his pages and books, are the invisible blood that animates Reyes's most perfect poetic work: *Ifigenia cruel* (*Cruel Iphigenia*). Perhaps it is not necessary to remark that this poem is, among many other things, a symbol of a personal drama and the answer that the poet meant to give it. His family belonged to the *ancient régime*. His father had been minister of war and his elder brother, the jurist Bernardo Reyes, was a university professor and a renowned political polemicist. Both were enemies of Madero's revolutionary government. His father died in the attack on the National Palace and his brother, when the revolutionaries triumphed, fled to Spain and constantly attacked the new regime from there. Hence Alfonso Reyes's situation was not very different from that of Iphigenia: his brother reminded him that vengeance is a filial duty and that to refuse to follow the voice of the blood is to condemn oneself to serving a bloodthirsty goddess—Artemis in the one case, the Mexican Revolution in the other. The poem is something more, of course, than an expression of this personal conflict; as a vision of woman and as a meditation on liberty, *Ifigenia cruel* is one of the most complete and perfect works in modern Spanish American poetry.

Reyes chose the second part of the myth. At the moment when Iphigenia is to die at Aulis, Artemis, to placate the wrath of the wind, exchanges her body for that of a wind and takes her to Tauris. There she consecrates her as a priestess of her temple: Iphigenia is to immolate every stranger who arrives at the island. One day she recognizes Orestes among the strangers whom a shipwreck has cast up on the shore. Destiny, the law of the breed, wins out: brother and sister flee, after robbing the statue of the goddess, and return to Attica. Reyes introduces here a fundamental change in the story, one that does not appear in either Euripides or Goethe: Iphigenia has lost her memory. She does not know who she is or where she comes from. She only knows that she is "a mass of naked rage." As a virgin without origins, who "sprouted like a fungus on the stones of the temple," bound to the bloody stone from the beginning of beginnings, a virgin with neither a past nor a future, Iphigenia is blind movement without self-awareness, condemned to repeat itself endlessly. The appearance of Orestes breaks the enchantment; his words penetrate her petrified consciousness and she passes gradually from recognition of the "other"—the unknown and delirious brother, the always remote fellow human being—to the rediscovery of her lost identity. Reyes seems to suggest that, in order to be ourselves, we must recognize the existence of others. When she recovers her memory, Iphigenia recovers her self. She is in possession of her own being because she knows who she is: the magic virtue of the name. Memory has given her back her consciousness, and, in so doing, it has granted her her freedom. She is no longer possessed by Artemis, no longer "bound to the trunk of her self," and can now choose. Her choice—and here the difference from the traditional version is even more significant—is unexpected: Iphigenia decides to remain in Tauris. Two words—"two words that are empty shells: I refuse"—are enough to change the whole course of fate in one vertiginous instant. By this act she renounces the memory she has just recovered, says "No" to destiny, to her family and origins, to the laws of the earth and the blood. And, beyond that, she renounces her own self. That negation engenders a new self-affirmation. In renouncing her self, she chooses. And this act, free above all others, an affirmation of the sovereignty of the spirit, a shining of liberty, is a second birth. Iphigenia is now the daughter of her own self.

Reyes's poem, which was written in 1923, not only anticipates many contemporary preoccupations but also contains—in code, in a condensed language that partakes of the hardness of stone and the bitterness of the sea, skillful and savage at one and the same time—all the later evolution of his spirit. All of Reyes—the best, the freest, the least trammeled—is in this work. There are even a secret wink, a malicious aside for the delectation of the knowing, and anachronisms and a pointing of the intelligence toward other lands and other times. There is erudition, but there are also grace, imagination, and a painful lucidity. Iphigenia, her knife, and her goddess, an immense stone fashioned by blood, allude simultaneously to pre-Columbian cults and "the eternal feminine"; the sonnet in Orestes's monologue is a double homage to Góngora and to the Spanish theater of the seventeenth century; the shadow of Segismundo sometimes obscures Iphigenia's face; at other times, the virgin speaks enigmas like the "Hérodiade" ("Herodias") of Mallarmé or gropes with her thoughts like "La jeune parque" ("The young Fate"); Euripides and Goethe, the Catholic concept of free will, the rhythmic experiments of Modernism, even Mexican themes (universalism and nationalism) and the family quarrel, all are brought together here with admirable naturalness. There is nothing too much because there is nothing lacking. True, he never again wrote a poem so solid and so aerial in its architecture, so rich in meanings, but the best pages of his prose are an impassioned meditation on the mystery of Iphigenia, the virgin liberty.

The enigma of liberty is also that of woman. Artemis is pure and cruel divinity: she is moon and water, the goddess of the third millennium before Christ, the tamer, the huntress, and the fatal enchantress. Iphigenia is just barely a human manifestation of that pallid and terrible deity, who runs through the nocturnal woods followed by a blood-thirsty pack of hounds. Artemis is a pillar, the primordial tree, archetype of the column as the grove is mythical model of the temple. That pillar is the center of the world:

> The stars dance about you.
> Alas for the world if you weaken, Goddess!

Artemis is virgin and impenetrable: "Who glimpsed the hermetic mouth of your two vertical legs?" Eye of stone, mouth of stone—but "the roots of her fingers suck up the red cubes of the sacrifice at each moon." She is cliff, pillar, statue, still water, but she is also the mad rush of the wind through the trees. Artemis alternately seeks and refuses incarnation, the meeting with the other, the adversary and complement of her being. The carnal embrace is mortal combat.

Eroticism—in the modern meaning of the term—is always veiled in Reyes's work. Irony moderates the shout; sensuality sweetens the mouth's terrible grimace; tenderness transforms the claw into a caress. Love is a battle, not a slaughter. Reyes does not deny the omnipotence of desire but—without closing his eyes to the contradictory nature of pleasure—he seeks a new equilibrium. In *Ifigenia cruel* and other writings desire wears the armor of death, but in his more numerous and more personal works his cordial temperament—melancholy, tenderness, *saudade* ("nostalgia")—calms the blood and its hornets. Reyes's epicureanism is neither an aesthetics nor a morality: it is a vital defense, a manly remedy. A pact: no surrender, but also no war without quarter. In one of his youthful poems, much more complex than it seems at a first reading, he says that in his imagination he identifies the flower (which is a magic flower: the sleeping poppy) with woman and confesses his fear:

> I tremble, let the day not dawn
> in which you turn into a woman!

The flower, like woman, hides a menace. Both provoke dreams, delirium, and madness. Both bewitch—which is to say, paralyze—the spirit. To free oneself from the virgin Iphigenia's knife and the menace of the flower, there is no known exorcism except love, sacrifice—which is, *always,* a transfiguration. In Reyes's work the sacrifice is not consummated and love is an oscillation between solitude and companionship. Woman ("bound up in the hour—free, although she gives herself, and alien") is ours for only an instant in reality. And, in the memory, forever, like nostalgia:

> Thank you, Río, thank you,
> Solitude and companionship,
> Smooth water for all anguish,
> Harbor in every storm.

Pact, agreement, equilibrium: these words appear frequently in Reyes's work and define one of the central directions of his thought. Some critics, not content with accusing him of Byzantinism (there are criticisms that, on certain lips, are really eulogies), have reproached him for his moderation. A spirit of moderation? I refuse to believe it, at least in the simple way in which simplistic minds want to see it. A spirit in search of equilibrium, an aspiration toward measure, and also a grand universal appetite, a desire to embrace everything, the most remote disciplines as well as the most distant epochs. Not to repress contradictions but to integrate them in broader affirmations; to order particulars of knowledge into general—but always provisional—schemes. Curiosity and prudence: every day we discover that there is still something we need to know, and, if it is true that everything has been thought, it is also true that nothing has been thought. No one has the last word. It is easy to see the uses and risks of this attitude. On the one hand, it irritates people with categorical minds who have the truth clenched in their fists. On the other, an excess of knowledge sometimes makes us timid and weakens our confidence in our spontaneous impulses. Reyes was not paralyzed by erudition because he defended himself with an invincible weapon: humor. To laugh at one's self, to laugh at one's own knowledge, is a way of growing lighter.

Góngora says: "The sea is not deaf: erudition is deceptive." Reyes was not always free from the deceptions of that sort of erudition that causes us to see yesterday's madness in today's novelties. Besides, his temperament led him to flee from extremes. This explains, perhaps, his reserve when considering those civilizations and spirits that express what could be called sublime exaggeration. (I am thinking of the Orient and of pre-Columbian America but also of Novalis and Rimbaud.) I will always lament his coldness toward the great adventure of contemporary art and poetry. German Romanticism, Dostoevsky, modern poetry (in its more daring forms), Kafka, Lawrence, Joyce, and some others were territories that he traversed with an explorer's valor but without amorous passion. And even in this I am afraid of being unjust, because how can one forget his fondness for Mallarmé, one of the very poets who most clearly embodies the modern artist's thirst for the absolute? He was blamed for the mildness of his public life, and some said that on occasion his character was not of the same stature as his talent and the circumstances around him. It is true that sometimes he kept still; it is also true that he never screeched as did many of his contemporaries. If he never suffered persecution, he also never persecuted anyone. He was not a party man; he was not fascinated by force or numbers; he did not believe in leaders; he never published noisy statements of support; he would not renounce his past, his thoughts, or his work; he did not confess nor employ autocriticism; he was not "converted." His indecisions, even his weaknesses—because he had them—were changed into strengths and nourished his freedom. This tolerant and affable man lived and died a heterodoxist, outside all churches and parties.

Reyes's work is disconcerting not only in its quantity but also in the variety of the matters it deals with. Yet it is the farthest thing from being a scattering. Everything tends toward a synthesis, including that part of his literary work made up of his annotations and summaries of other people's books. In an epoch of discord and uniformity—two faces of the same coin—Reyes postulates a will for harmony, that is, for an order that does not exclude the singularity of the parts. His interest in political and social utopias and his continuous mediation on the duties of the Spanish American "intelligence" have the same origin as his fondness for Hellenistic studies, the philosophy of history, and comparative literature. He seeks in everything the individual trait, the personal variation; and he always succeeds in placing this singularity in a vaster harmony. But harmony, agreement, and equilibrium are words that do not define him clearly. "Concord," a spiritual word, fits him better. He is more worthy of it. Concord is not concession, pact, or compromise, but a dynamic game of opposites, concordance of the being and the other, reconciliation between movement and repose, coincidence of passion and form. The surge of life, the coming and going of the blood, the hand that opens and closes: to give and to receive and to give again. Concord, a central, vital word. Not brain, not belly, not sex, not caveman's jaw: heart. (pp. 115-22)

Enrique Anderson-Imbert   (essay date 1963)

SOURCE: "1910-1925: Authors Born between 1885 and 1900: Authors born between 1885 and 1900," *Spanish American Literature: A History,* Detroit: Wayne State University Press, 1963, pp. 327-420.

[*Anderson-Imbert has published more than twenty books of essays and criticism, including his major work,* Historia de la literatura hispanoamericana (*Spanish-American Literature: A History*). *In the following excerpt from that work, Anderson-Imbert presents an overview of Reyes's poetry, essays, and fiction.*]

[Reyes] groups his poetry under three headings. The first is a "Poetic review," then the topical verses, and finally, those books of poetry which have a certain unity: *Cruel Iphigenia* (*Ifigenia cruel*), *Three Poems* (*Tres poemas*), *Day's Sonnets* (*Jornada en sonetos*), and *Deaf Ballads* (*Romances sordos*). His first poems, from around 1906, were Parnassian. Having learned respect for verse forms in this school, Reyes struck out for himself. Like other Modernists, he penetrated the obscurities of his own being, sometimes to bring color to it, sometimes to question, and even in order to touch its dark and silent depths. Serious symbolism alongside of which, after the first World War, rhythms and images of juvenile vanguardism begin to play. There were even poems describing sensual African dances. Actually, nothing was outside the pale of his poetry which was "fickle in theme and style." His themes were as varied as the turns of his own life: autobiographical evocations, the homeland, friends and loves, works, and death. His styles come and go between the laboratory in which the hermetic poets distill their verse and the clear, open road where the people walk. Reyes was not afraid to prospect along dangerous trails: for example, along the prosaic trail (in case they "jumped him" he was well armed—see his **"Prosaic Theory,"** where he declares "I prefer to be promiscuous / in literature," "the popular ballad / of the neighbor / with the rare quintessence / of Góngora and Mallarmé"). Difficult or simple he always demands the attention of the reader, because earlier, he was demanding of himself and gives only essences.

His poetry is concise, sober, insinuating. His prose is beaten gold. The virtues of intelligence and esteem that tend to come separately in people in Alfonso Reyes are integrated in gracious and subtle light. He is erudite in the field of philology and sparkling in witty sallies; he writes stories, chronicles, sketches, and penetrating critical glosses. His prose is impish and prying. The multiplicity of Reyes' vocations (a man of the Renaissance) is not only measured by the vast repertory of motifs, but also by the stylistic richness of each turn. Reyes' restlessness transmits to his style a zigzagging, jumpy, prankish, and sensual movement. Before leaving Mexico in 1913, his writer's hand was already educated: from this period, with a single exception, are the stories and dialogs of *The Oblique Plane* (*El plano oblicuo*, 1920), a most original book in the Spanish language because of its rapid shifts from the real to the fantastic (**"The Supper"**—**"La cena"**) and because of its expressionist procedures. From 1914, except for a brief stay in France, he was to live in Spain until 1924, probably the most productive period of his career: *Vision of Anáhuac* (*Visión de Anáhuac,* 1917), *The Eves of Spain* (*Las vísperas de España,* 1937), *The Suicide* (*El suicida,* 1917), *The Hunter* (*El cazador,* 1921), *Real and Imaginary Portraits* (*Retratos reales e imaginarios,* 1920), and the five series of *Sympathies and Differences* (*Simpatías y diferencias,* 1921-1926). This is a consummate work that links on different pages, and at times on the same page, impressionist sentences, fantasies, elegances, narrative flights of fancy, biographical sketches, notes, and reflections. His norms appear to be these: to express himself in miniatures; to not lean too much on actual things; to subjectivize everything, whether it be through his sensibilities or through his imagination; to intermingle life and culture; to address himself to a sympathetic reader who possesses the same qualities that the writer possesses, and to converse with him; to watch each word. . . . Characteristic of his fictional work is its preference for exciting the imagination of the reader with suggestive details rather than satisfying his curiosity with a plot or a denouement. It is fantasy for sharp readers, already accustomed to and perhaps tired of reading so many novels. His essays are always lyrical, even those of didactic or logical themes, because the manner in which he treats his object is personal, not public. In **Sundial** (*Reloj de sol*, 1926) Reyes confessed: "The historian I carry in my pocket will not allow me to waste a single datum, a single document." But it is not so much a desire to recoup a past public as it is to reconstruct an intimate diary whose leaves had fallen out along the road of life. Like Echo, the quartered nymph, the diary that was buried here and there by Reyes throughout his work lives on in a constant murmur. No matter how impersonal a Reyes theme may appear, one can always perceive the vibration of a confidence about to be revealed. Even though he was one of our most exquisite, most original, most surprising writers, Reyes founded his work on healthy experiences. Others would like to look at the world upside down, to see if a world askew will tell them something new: they mutilate themselves or give value to their mutilations; they give themselves over to sophistic frenzy or to lethargy; they corrupt honor, deny light, betray the heart. Not Reyes. Alfonso Reyes is a classical writer because of the human integrity of his vocation, because of his serene faith in intelligence, in charity, in the eternal values of the soul. The uniqueness of Reyes' poetic universe is not extravagance, but the refinement of the normal directions in man. Each one of his volumes is a collection of unsurpassed pages. To date, the Fondo de Cultura Económica of Mexico City has published thirteen thick volumes of **Complete Works**. On contemplating this grandiose monument to his effort, a literary critic states a bundle of problems that should be studied carefully: the problem of a writer who fails in spite of being extraordinarily equipped for success; that of a secret sterility that is disguised by incessant labor; that of an intelligence which, because of its propensity for dialog, remained with its face toward the best spirits of its time, but with its back to its own works; that of a classic of our literary history who, nevertheless, left no great books. Is there in the air of Hispanic-America something lethal to literary creation? Why did not the author of **The Testimony of Juan Peña** give us the novel he promised? Why did not the author of **"The Supper"** give us the collection of stories he promised? Why did not the author of **Cruel Iphigenia**, of **Footprints**, give us the drama, the book of poems he promised? Indeed, the fruits yielded are sufficient. But for those of us who had the privilege of being his friends, it is clear that Alfonso Reyes could have given more, much more than that, to the great genres of literature. Where he did succeed was in the essay. Alfonso Reyes is without any doubt the keenest, most brilliant, versatile, cultured, and profound essayist in our language today. (pp. 412-15)

Arturo Torres-Rioseco (essay date 1964)

SOURCE: "Diogenes of Anáhuac," *Mexico in a Nutshell and Other Essays,* Berkeley: University of California Press, 1964, pp. 1-13.

[*In this excerpt, Torres-Rioseco discusses Reyes' essays, literary theory, and fiction.*]

Alfonso Reyes will remain in the history of Hispanic literatures mainly as an essay writer. He is, perhaps, only a popularizer of scientific principles, a commentator on history, a definer and a systematizer. But, of course, in our America these are noble activities. Strict disciplines hold him firm at the roots of all problems discussed, and his logical mind establishes a rational balance between fact and fancy. He is always elegant and imaginative, evanescent and logical. In the selections presented in [**Mexico in a Nutshell and Other Essays**], especially on America's themes and Columbus's ventures, one does not know whether to admire more the factual interpretation or the ironic sequences of the author.

In his first important book of literary essays, **Cuestiones estéticas** (1916), Reyes reveals an unusual knowledge of classic and modern European literatures and at the same time of literary theories from the Aristotelian system to contemporary techniques. Studying the poetry of Góngora and Mallarmé, he defends the right of the poet to create his own vocabulary according to the needs of his inspiration, and argues that the world of these two poets could not have been translated into poetic experience except by the creation of a new language. Later on, during his residence in Spain, Reyes wrote some of his best essays, which were collected later in his books **Cuestiones gongorinas** and **Capítulos de literatura española**. Besides these essays on erudite matters Reyes wrote books of impressions, **Cartones de Madrid** (1917), of philosophical themes, **El suicida** (1917) and, of especial importance, **Visión de Anáhuac** (1917), a poetical description of the Mexican plateau.

His collection **Tren de ondas** (1932), written in a lighter vein, has an unsophisticated charm. Here we find the delightful short essay **"Diego Rivera Discovers Painting"** and the meaningful **"Los motivos de la conducta,"** an exercise in Semantics which every starchy philologist should read. The definition of "caballero" and "gentleman" is a jewel: to the theory that "caballero" is romantic and "gentleman," classic, Reyes adds his own: "gentleman" is rather dry, "caballero is humid, rather foamy." In this little volume we find the essays on flies, discarded shaving blades, onions (**"Dignity of the Onion"**), humble topics lifted later to an artistic level by Pablo Neruda in his *Odas elementales* and by Camilo José Cela in his novel *Mrs. Caldwell habla con su hijo.*

Four short essays [**"Discurso por Virgilio"** (1931), **"Atenea política"** (1932), **"En el día americano"** (1932), **"Homilía por la cultura"** (1938)] are, according to Manuel Olguín [in his *Alfonso Reyes, ensayista*], of importance because they contain his first attempts to formulate a social and cultural philosophy. The purpose of these essays is to define the philosophical nature of culture and the duties imposed by it on the intellectual. Reyes wishes to solve the main problems of his social philosophy: to find the formula to raise Spanish America to the level of universal culture, without abandoning the fundamental human values of its Latin and Hispanic tradition.

"Culture," according to Olguín, is defined in these essays as the product of intelligence in its most characteristic function: that of unifying, of establishing regular systems of connections. This function is realized in the horizontal order of "space," or communication among neighbors, and then it is called "cosmopolitism," and in a vertical order of "time," communication among generations, and is called "tradition." Cosmopolitism represents the effort of intelligence to unify man spiritually, to place the principle of fundamental human unity above racial or class iniquities, to distribute equitably the material and spiritual benefits of culture, to make of this planet a more just and happier dwelling place for everybody. Tradition signifies the effort of the intelligence to unify itself, to establish the continuity of its action through time, to consolidate the new generations' enjoyments of its previous conquests. As a servant of intelligence, mother of culture, the intellectual, no matter from what country, has the duty of struggling to impose the cosmopolitan ideal, to improve relations among men. This duty is particularly pressing for the Latin American intellectual, since the progress of Latin America, its ascension to a universal level of culture, depend largely on its union, on its democratization, and on the wise use of the mixture of races and cultures which is now being realized throughout the world.

The natural vehicle to achieve this solution in our continent is that of the fundamental human values of its Latin and Hispanic tradition. These are the values—and not those of the aboriginal cultures—that constitute the real nucleus of its culture. From here it must start, then, to realize its destiny: the creation of a cosmic race, of a closer, happier, fairer New World.

Here, then, we have the expression of the social philosophy of Alfonso Reyes, a philosophy that we find in later books such as *Norte y Sur* (1944) and *Los trabajos y los días* (1945).

Finally, among his strictly literary works of later years, we must mention *Pasado inmediato* (1941), *El deslinde* (1944), *Letras de la Nueva España* (1948), *Grata compañia* (1948), *Trayectoria de Goethe* (1954).

El deslinde, a treatise on literary theory, is considered the masterpiece of Reyes. (pp. 5-7)

An extensive knowledge of Greek literature is evident in Reyes's basic books, *La crítica en la edad ateniense* (1941) and *La antigua retórica* (1943). His books of essays, *Junta de sombras,* also showed this preoccupation. Of real significance in this field are also *Panorama de la religión griega* (1948), *El horizonte económico en los albores de Grecia* (1950), and *En torno al estudio de la religión griega* (1951).

His main sources of inspiration for the first two works are the theories of Plato (Reyes is baffled by Plato's duality, his belief in the divine origin of poetry, and his disdain for the poet), and the theories of Aristotle. Reyes gives us a detailed biography of Aristotle and a condensation of his philosophy. Reyes was also familiar with the aesthetic ideas of the peripatetic school, especially of that of Theophrastus.

La antigua retórica is described by Reyes himself: "We devoted the second book to rhetoric, centering it on its great organizers—Aristotle, Cicero, and Quintilian—in order to free ourselves of the immense oratorical bulk, passing from Greece to Rome and coming close to the dawn of the Christian era."

El deslinde marks the most ambitious attempt to systematize literary theory: it is a philosophic and aesthetic study of literature. Reyes tries to establish a demarcation between literature and non-literature, in three sections: 1. Demarcation between pure literature and service literature; 2. A demarcation between history, science, and literature; and 3. A demarcation between mathematics, theology, and literature.

In a very penetrating study of Alfonso Reyes: (*Dos estudios sobre Alfonso Reyes,* 1962), the distinguished Swedish scholar, Ingemar Düring, says that the Mexican author is able to capture in his short stories old images and past experiences, with the vision of a great poet. According to him Reyes shows his capacity as a fiction writer when he sees the heroes of great literature—Achilles, Don Quixote, Hamlet, Peer Gynt—more real than many historical heroes. "Reyes has felt and lived with those heroes the highest form of poetry." Some of these heroes appear in imaginary conversations, in which we find a subtle joke on Landor and his singular conception of Greece. In these pages we perceive Reyes' *lentus risus,* his Horacian virtue of laughing somewhat ironically at himself. Through the light and spiritual dialogue we hear another voice, that of the philosopher and the critic: an intellectual game of the highest level.

There is, then, in this essayist a potential fiction writer. Greek mythology is for him a rich field where his imagination may frolic; the landscape of his native country tempts the descriptive capacity of his talent; the beings or ghosts that he carries in his subconscious are eager to become protagonists of his near-novels. Thus we see them in his *Quince presencias*, and in his poem *Los siete sobre Deva*, which is a prelude to a novel.

His favorite theory is that the landscape can serve as inspiration for the novelist and that in the memory of all human beings there are many elements of fiction. To bring these creatures into the artistic world is the role of the novelist. Therefore, Reyes is a very modern novelist. He does not deal with plots, dramatic developments, or narrations: he creates climates, he analyzes situations very much like a surrealist. It is for this reason that he speaks of his "arranques de novela" ("beginnings of a novel"), novels that are never completed, such as *El testimonio de Juan Peña* (1930).

A good "arranque de novela" is *Los dos augures*. Two Mexican émigrés meet in Paris and in a brief dialogue they tell of their past experiences and reveal their inner thoughts. One is a descendant of Spaniards; the other a half-breed. The two friends give promise of being the two main characters of a novel that never develops. A pity!—to judge by this beginning characterization: "Domingo was a courteous Mexican, discreet, patient, gentle, full of Mexican reserve. If he had not been good, Do-mingo would have furnished the best wood from which to carve the statue of a traitor . . . but he was good." Reyes gives a few more psychological touches to round out his character, and then he stops short. The reader is disappointed and frustrated. We have the protagonists, we know their reactions and their experiences, but nothing happens. The same is true of his *Arbol de pólvora* (1953), *Los siete sobre Deva* (1942); but he shows more structural ability in the surrealist short story **"La cena"** (1920) and in his short novel *Los tres tesoros* (1955).

Reyes is one of the most logical thinkers of his time. His exposition is clear and well balanced. Since he has said that the *word* is the essence of the extension of the poet's world, he is extremely careful in his use of words. His phrase is brief, synthetic, epigrammatic. He uses sometimes an elegant and perfect form, or a light, graceful expression, according to the subject matter. His language is rich and alive, strictly literary or robustly vernacular, classic, without disdain of the use of the Mexican idiom; in short he is the outstanding cultivator of the artistic style in modern Mexican literature. (pp. 8-10)

Martin S. Stabb (essay date 1967)

SOURCE: "America Rediscovered," *In Quest of Identity: Patterns in the Spanish American Essay of Ideas, 1890-1960.* Charlotte: University of North Carolina Press, 1967, pp. 58-101.

[*Stabb is an American educator and critic specializing in Spanish-American literature. In this essay, he evaluates Reyes's ideas on New World nativism, the polarity between city life and country life, and the synthesis of Old World and New World culture in America.*]

To attempt to isolate one theme—or even one cluster of related themes—in the work of Mexico's most prolific essayist [Alfonso Reyes] is no simple task. Some of Reyes' most penetrating views on broad matters of *novomundismo* are found in rather unlikely places, as in his *Discurso por Virgilio* (1933). True to the classical tradition, Reyes is quick to point out that man's social and individual nature show a remarkable constancy across vast realms of time and space. Thus, he can relate a plan of the Mexican government to develop local viniculture and cottage industries with similar motifs in Virgil's *Georgics*. It is in this essay on the Virgilian theme that Reyes expresses his own broad Americanist faith, born of a profound love for classic literature and for his native Mexico. The great literary works of the western European tradition— and especially those of Greece and Rome—are not "foreign" or "exotic" to the American scene, he tells us. Properly appreciated, they are means by which our own indigenous world can be better revealed: "I wish that the Humanities (be) the natural vehicle of expression for everything autochthonous." In the context of Mexico's vigorous but often superficial indigenism of the 1920's, Reyes' comments on the relationship between nativism and Old World culture were extremely timely. First of all he wisely observed that what is genuinely autochthonous will manifest itself in the work of a writer, painter, or thinker of its own accord. Since *lo autóctono* is part of the very make-up of the person one need not be deliberately "nativist": "this instinctive tendency (nativism) is so evident that to defend it with sophisms is to deprive it of its greatest virtue: its spontaneity." He then warns his countrymen not to deceive themselves, for although "the autochthonous element (is), in our America an enormous lode of raw material, of artifacts, of forms, of colors and sounds," only the barest fragments of the world of the pre-Columbian is known today. Therefore Reyes holds that any return to the primitivism of the Aztec would be unthinkable. By contrast, he stoutly maintains that "until now the only waters which have bathed us are . . . Latin waters." Though Reyes does not carry his metaphor any further, it is not unreasonable to view these "Latin waters" as the agent by which the gold of the autochthonous mineral lode is revealed in all its purity, washed clean of its dross. Reyes' view of what he calls "the hour of America" is decidedly ecumenical: he frequently states that the mission of the New World is to overcome the divisive effects of racism and of cultural jingoism. Support for such a program may be found, he notes, in Vasconcelos' vision of an amalgamated "Cosmic Race" and in Waldo Frank's deep humanistic faith.

In the *Discurso por Virgilio*, Reyes touches upon a theme which has figured prominently in a number of Spanish American essays—the city as opposed to the country. He finds the basic terms of this polarity to be quite simple: in the city the "social act" dominates, the fundamental relationship being that of man with man; while in the country the relationship involves man with the land. Reyes feels that human life, virtually by definition, is "a continuous reference to the natural ambience, an unending journey between man and external nature." City life, though not actually attacked, is viewed as a kind of artificial creation, a setting up of barriers against the natural order of man's life. Country life, particularly that of the modest, hardworking landholder, is seen as "The balsam (that) soothes the wounds of politics." More concretely, it is a means for the absorption of immigrants into the national life. Throughout Reyes' discussion of the city versus country theme, this Virgilian attitude toward the land dominates; it distinguishes his telluricism from that of many of his Spanish American contemporaries who view the "force of the land" in terms of the mystical, romantic adoration of nature's primal forces. In one of Reyes' earlier works, the beautifully wrought essay *Visión de Anáhuac* (1917), he notes that this more romanticized feeling toward nature may be justified in much of the New World, (in the jungle, for example) but that his own Mexican plateau is characterized by "sparse and stylized vegetation, an organized landscape, an atmosphere of extreme clarity. . . ." In short, he finds a distinctly "classic" spirit pervading the countryside of his beloved Aná-huac. Although it would be misleading to consider Reyes a believer in rigid geographic determinism—the very antithesis of the classically humanist view of nature—we have seen him speak of man's "continuous reference to the natural ambience." Thus, in the *Visión de Anáhuac* he suggests that there is a real link, disregarding all questions of blood, between the Mexican of today and the pre-Columbian Indian. This link exists since both peoples had the same natural environment with which to contend, and since "the everyday emotion produced by the same natural object" engenders a common spirit. As we have seen, substantially the same view was professed by Reyes' Argentine contemporary, Ricardo Rojas, and by Waldo Frank when he wrote of "the forming life of our land."

Reyes has developed his idea of what I have called the New Americanism in an impressive number of essays, historical studies, articles, and speeches. Two of these, **"Notas sobre la inteligencia Americana"** (1937) and **"Posición de América"** (1942), merit special attention in that they present Reyes' profoundest meditations on the important theme of the relationship of the Old World to the New. In a sense the second essay is a clarification of the first. In 1936 Reyes participated in a series of conferences, held in Buenos Aires under the auspices of the *Instituto Internacional de Cooperación Intelectual*, dealing with the theme "Present-day relations between European and Latin American cultures." George Duhamel initiated the meeting stating the European viewpoint; Reyes presented the first statement for Latin America. In the **"Posición de América"** he notes that this paper, **"Notas sobre la inteligencia Americana,"** was in part misunderstood by some of the distinguished Europeans present. Reyes spoke of an American cultural synthesis which would involve two elements: "a unique balance between our understanding of intellectual activity as public service and as cultural responsibility," and a fusion of autochthonous elements with the "intellectual instruments" of Europe. The product of such a synthesis would be, moreover, greater than the mere sum of its parts. At the Buenos Aires conference Reyes expressed the hope that this distinctive American culture would fulfill the utopian dream of a New World—a dream which formed part of Europe's literature and folklore even before Columbus' voyage. Referring to the Europeans' misunderstanding of his term "cultural synthesis" at this meeting, he states:

> Some of those present remained sadly convinced that we were trying to reduce the function of the American mind to the mere organizing of compendiums of European culture. Above all, we would not have recourse only to the European tradition, but to the entire human heritage. . . . Lastly, in this synthesis we do not envision a compendium or resumé just as hydrogen and oxygen on combining in the form of water do not produce a mere sum to the parts but a new substance, possessing, as does any true synthesis, new powers and qualities.

In these two essays Reyes constantly emphasizes that the fulfillment of the American destiny is a responsibility to Europe ("If the European economy has come to have need of us, so ultimately will the European *inteligentsia* have need of us") or, in broader terms, a responsibility to humanity. Retaining the fervent activism of his early association with the *Ateneo de la Juventud* group, Reyes has been more concerned with the ability of the New World to meet this obligation than with the problem of "choosing" between universalism and nativism. As we have seen, for Reyes there is really no problem of a choice here. Whether he employs the metaphor of the "autochthonous mineral lode" noted previously, or the interesting analogy of culture and a series of concentric circles—as in the **"Posición de América"**—his message is clear: the Universal and the Particular have a complementary relationship; they "nourish" each other; and a society based solely on what he terms "alternatives and peculiarities" would be unthinkable, just as would be a purely "Universal" culture. A final note regarding Reyes' concept of the American cultural synthesis is in order. Several times in these essays he states that although he is restricting himself to Latin America, there are broad grounds for cultural fusion with Anglo-Saxon America: "We do not feel that one may speak seriously of unsurpassable barriers to cultural synthesis. . . ." At the conclusion of the **"Posición de América"** he looks upon the American synthesis in broad philosophical terms. Drawing from the rich thought of one of the Spanish American intellectuals' favorite sources, Max Scheler, Reyes notes that one of the great problems to be resolved before this synthesis may be achieved is that of reconciling three basic types of knowledge: the Hindu knowledge of salvation through psychic and bodily self-control; the wisdom (*saber culto*) of ancient Greece and China; and finally the scientific, practically motivated, knowledge of the western European tradition. Citing Scheler directly he notes, "the time has come to open the way towards an assimilation, and at the same time, towards an integration of these three partial tendencies of the human spirit." The "integration" called for by Scheler is precisely what Reyes would wish America to achieve. The continent, if it is to accomplish its mission, must not develop one of these types of knowledge at the expense of the others:

> Pure knowledge of salvation will convert us into prostrate peoples, into thin, mendicant friars; pure knowledge of culture, into sophists and mandarins; pure knowledge of technique, into scientific barbarians which, as we have seen is the worst kind of barbarism. Only a balance of all these will insure our loyalty to heaven and earth. Such is the mission of America.

(pp. 82-6)

Additional coverage of Reyes' life and career is contained in the following sources published by Gale Group: *Contemporary Authors*, Vol. 131; *Hispanic Writers*; *Twentieth Century Literature Criticism*, Vol. 33.

Tomás Rivera
1935-1984

Chicano novelist, short story writer, poet, and critic.

INTRODUCTION

Tomás Rivera was a novelist, short story writer, poet, literary critic, and educator, born in the U.S. to a family of migrant farmworkers from Mexico. His output is relatively small because he became increasingly concerned with education, rising rapidly through the ranks of academia, and eventually becoming a chancellor at the University of California. Some say that his major work, *. . . y no se lo tragó la tierra* (1971; *. . . and the earth did not part*, 1991) is a novel, while others claim it is a collection of short stories and vignettes. It is a collection of short pieces depicting a life of hardship and desperation among poor Mexican-Americans. In most of his fiction, Rivera shows the emotional deterioration of Chicanos and their search for a solution through spiritual means.

Tomás Rivera was born to a family of migrant farmworkers in the south Texas town of Crystal City, on December 22, 1935. His mother and her family immigrated to Texas in 1920. Rivera's maternal grandfather had been an officer in the Mexican army and a union organizer in the mines of northern Mexico. To avoid reprisals from political enemies, Rivera's grandfather fled to Dallas, then moved to Houston, and finally settled in Crystal City where he bought a truck and became an agricultural crew leader. From childhood until his early twenties, Tomás Rivera was a nomadic migrant worker travelling north to Michigan and Minnesota for work in April and returning to Texas in November. Years later, in his *. . . y no se lo tragó la tierra*, he would write about these experiences. In 1958, Rivera graduated with his bachelor's degree in English Education from Southwest Texas State University, and began teaching high school English and Spanish in various Texas cities. He returned to school, receiving his degree in administration, and then began study at the University of Oklahoma to earn his Ph.D in romance literature in 1969. Rivera's career in academia progressed quickly, acting as an Associate Professor of Spanish at Sam Houston State University, a Professor of Spanish and Director of Foreign Languages at the University of Texas, San Antonio, and then, in 1976, becoming Vice President for Administration at the same institution. In 1978 he left to become Executive Vice President at the University of Texas, El Paso. Finally, he became Chancellor of the University of California, Riverside. He held this position for five years until his death on May 16, 1984. Rivera's relatively modest output (about 250 pages) reflects the immense amount of effort he put into his educational career. After the publication of *tierra,* he published five short stories—two of which were episodes

omitted from *tierra*—a chapbook containing thirteen poems entitled *Always and Other Poems* (1973), and also thirteen other poems, including the epic, "The Searchers" (posthumously published in 1990). It is thought that Rivera was working on a novel when he died of a heart attack in Fontana, California. The works mentioned above and others previously unpublished, are collected in *Tomás Rivera: The Complete Works* (1991).

. . . y no se lo tragó la tierra is a collection of fourteen short narratives tied together by the main character, a nameless Chicano child, who is a migrant worker like the rest of his family. Except for the first and last stories that serve as the frame for the stories in between, each of the narratives is preceded by a very short untitled vignette. In the "Children Couldn't Wait," a boy deprived of water while working in the fields steals water from a tank meant only for cattle. The farm owner shoots and kills him, meaning only to scare him. Though the owner is acquitted, he ends up crazy and penniless. "A Prayer" is the poignant story of a woman who desperately appeals to higher powers to bring her son home alive from the Korean War. *tierra* presents the migrant's life as it is lived in the United States and the deadening effect on Latin Americans—especially Chicanos—caused by the poverty and powerlessness foisted upon them by an Anglo regime. Critic Ralph Grajeda sees *tierra* performing "the significant function of discovering and ultimately appropriating and embracing the past in all of its sometimes painful authenticity," that is the history of the exploitation of the migrant worker in the U.S. In the short story, "The Salamanders" from the collection, *The Harvest*, the narrator is also a young boy forced to sleep with his family in a tent pitched in a wet field filled with salamanders that invade the tent: "What I remember most about that night was the darkness, the mud and the slime of the salamanders and how hard they would get when I tried to squeeze the life out of them. . . . What I saw and what I felt is something I still have with me, something that is very pure—original death." The abject conditions of farmworkers under the thumb of American control drives the migrant worker to acts of uncontrollable violence directed not at the hand that exploits, but at nature and their surroundings. Rivera's characters are generally those whose anonymity reflects their universality. While the stories invite readers to sympathize with the characters, Rivera has drained them of all melodrama, all excessive expressions of passion. Their bondage is to the earth, and education is seen as a way to escape their servitude beneath outside forces of oppression which conspire to keep them struggling from one moment to the next.

Tomás Rivera began writing because he was a Chicano: "I wrote *tierra* because I was a Chicano and am a Chicano. This can never be denied, obliterated or reneged from now on. I chose to create and yet I had no idea of the effect of that creation." Furthermore, Rivera wrote because he never saw the Chicano in American literature and questioned their lack of representation. But Rivera knew that he was able to remedy the situation by depicting the lives of Chicano migrant workers, their ethnicity, and their economic struggle. Rivera, as both writer and educator, began the much-needed task of bringing Chicanos from the fields that could not be seen, into the more visible lines of the published page.

PRINCIPAL WORKS

. . . y no se lo tragó la tierra/And the Earth Did Not Part [*The Earth Did Not Part; This Migrant Earth*] (novel) 1971
Always and Other Poems (poetry) 1973
The Harvest—La Cosecha (poetry) 1989
The Searchers: Collected Poetry (poetry) 1990
Tomas Rivera: The Complete Works (collected works) 1991
Chicano Literature: A Dynamic Intimacy (nomograph)
La Casa Grande (novel)

CRITICISM

Ralph F. Grajeda (essay date 1979)

SOURCE: "Tomás Rivera's *. . . y no se lo tragó la tierra*: Discovery and Appropriation of the Chicano Past," in *Hispania*, Vol. 62, No. 1, March, 1979, pp. 71-81.

[*Grajeda develops the idea that Rivera's work evidenced substantial progress toward the establishment of an authentic Chicano literature.*]

Like two other Chicano novels—*Pocho* by José Antonio Villarreal and *Chicano* by Richard Vasquez[1]—Tomás Rivera's *. . . y no se lo tragó la tierra* is the author's first published book. Unlike *Pocho* and *Chicano,* however, Rivera's book was originally written in Spanish, and it was published by a Chicano publishing house, Quinto Sol Publications[2]—two extra-literary facts that only upon reflection acquire significance. If Villarreal's and Vasquez' works can be said to mark the first attempts by Mexican American writers to give literary expression to the experience of La Raza, it is Rivera's book that marks a progression from those initial efforts toward the creation of a literature which, through the authentic rendering of the Chicano experience, can be considered a literature of liberation.

. . . y no se lo tragó la tierra is difficult to describe structurally. It is not a novel in the conventional sense,

but then neither is it a mere collection of stories and sketches. The book contains a set of twelve thematically unified stories—symbolic of the twelve months of the year—framed by an introductory selection **"El Año Perdido"** and a summarizing selection **"Debajo De La Casa."** Preceding each of the stories except **"El Año Perdido,"** is a brief and usually penetrating anecdote, directed backward (echoing or commenting on the thematic concerns of the preceeding story) or sometimes pointed forward (prefacing the story that follows). In some instances the anecdote does not relate directly either to what immediately precedes or follows, but instead echoes or re-echoes values, motifs, themes, or judgments, found elsewhere in the book. The effect is incremental. Through the reinforcement, variation, and amplification provided by the twelve stories and the thirteen anecdotes, the picture of the community is gradually filled. At the end, the entire experience is synthesized and brought to a thematic conclusion through the consciousness of the central character.

This central figure—presumably the author's alter ego—is the unnamed hero of the two frame-pieces who believed in the beginning that "aquel año se le perdió," and at the end discovers "que en realidad no había perdido nada." It may be conjectured that this central figure is the same one who moves through some of the other selections in the book. Direct and explicit identification between the characters in the stories and the central figure is of minor importance. What is of the utmost importance is that the various persons of the stories, and the experiences and the landscape of their lives, are all a very real part of the hero's past, i.e., of his being. The emphasis falls on the general experience, communal and social rather than individual and personal.

In his introduction to the book, Herminio Ríos observes that "*el pueblo* becomes the central character. It is the anonymous and collective voice of the people that we hear" (p. xvi). He is correct, and we, the readers, hear the voice of the people as the central figure hears it. Structurally this central character has some importance as an individual; thematically, however, this importance is de-emphasized—it is no accident that he remains nameless. The experience of the book is finally a general one. Many of the selections have an uncanny emblematic tone to them; some of them—particularly the frame-pieces—emphatically invite an allegorical or a symbolic interpretation. The voice that we hear does not ring of the individually introspective, existentially or psychologically isolated and alone, but rather of the communally active and enduring. Even in the two frame selections, at the beginning and at the end, as we hear the protagonist contemplating his situation, the voice we hear is not that of an individual hero intent on discovering and expressing his own subjective reality, but of a Mexican American—a *pocho*—in the significant process of discovering and embracing representatively his community's experience and culture. The end toward which the narrative is directed is a social identity. The hero of the frame-pieces plays no explicitly active part in the book. He serves merely as the "rememberer," the central figure—however unrealized he may appear as a rounded character—around whom Rivera weaves his thematic tapestry. At the beginning he is confused, alone, frightened and disoriented. He is the one for whom the year is lost. The succeeding twelve stories and thirteen anecdotes comprise the memory-content of the hero, el que "veía y oía muchas cosas . . ." (p. 1) in his effort to reclaim a part of his past. At the end of the book he is the synthesizer and commentator, the one who discovers his lost year, *el que quisiera tener "unos brazos bien grandes" para "abrazar a todos."*

The form of the book is thus cyclical. Though there is no attempt at shaping a strict correspondence between specific months and particular stories, the twelve stories in a general sense are symbolic representations of the year that the protagonist attempts to recapture. The first story, **"Los Niños No Se Aguantaron"** is set in early April, and the last anecdote—the last selection, that is, before **"Debajo De La Casa,"** the final part of the frame—is set in December. This cyclical movement functions effectively to delineate the cyclical and repetitive nature of the migrant framworkers' lives as they yearly retrace the same roads to the same fields, from Texas and cotton in the winter months, to Utah, Minnesota, Iowa, and Michigan in the spring and summer. It is, therefore, appropriate that the first story, **"Los Niños No Se Aguantaron,"** treat a family already working in the Texas fields, and that the twelfth story, **"Cuando Lleguemos,"** concern a truckful of workers as they journey north to the beetfields of Minnesota.

Throughout the book some tension is created between the opposing values of resignation and rebellion as the people are shown enduring the repetitive hardships of the present, and as they anticipate their future. Usually, but not always, these differing values break down along generational lines. The older people—parents and grandparents—are usually resigned to their situation as is. Theirs is a stoical, at times pessimistic, position learned after years of suffering, best expressed by the grandfather of the seventh anecdote who calls his twenty-year-old grandson *"bien estúpido"* for wishing *"que se pasaran los siguientes diez años de su vida inmediatamente para saber lo que habia pasado con su vida"* (p. 81); by the older speaker of the fourth anecdote who advises the young student not to even bother with going to school, *"que al cabo de jodido no pasa uno"* (p. 37); by the father out in the fields who, in fear of being fired by the *patrón,* urges his children time after time to endure their thirst "un ratito más" (p. 6); and by the father who, knowing little English, and fearful of the schools, is incapable of responding to his son's plea that he accompany him to the principal's office the first day of school (p. 22). These are the parents who through years of deprivation and all of the self-denying effects of colonialism have learned to stay in their place. Again and again in Rivera's book we see them encouraging their children to stay in school, hoping that their children might be able to escape the treadmill of migratory field labor.

The children are in many instances the victims. But so also are they the ones who question their parents' values and who rebel against a situation to which others acquiesce. There is the boy in **"La Noche Estaba Plateada"** who tests the superstitions of his parents and learns that the devil does not exist. The boy in . . . *y no se lo tragó la tierra* who in anger, and hatred of the suffering of his family curses an uncaring God and learns that, contradictory to what his parents have taught him, the earth does not devour anyone. There is the young man in **"Cuando Lleguemos,"** who—in the middle of the night in a broken-down truck loaded with people on their way north— vehemently curses his life and his own stupidity: *"pinche vida, pinche vida, pinche vida, pinche vida, por pendejos, por pendejos, por pendejos. Somos una bola de pendejos. Chingueasumadre toda la pinche vida. Esta es la ultima vez que vengo así como una pinche bestia parado todo el camino. Nomás que lleguemos me voy a mineapolis, afuerza hallo allí algo que hacer donde no tenga que andar como un pinche huey"* (pp. 150-151). In the privacy of his anxiety, he utters a threat (*"un día de estos me la van a pelar todos"*)[3] which, however idle it may actually be, gains its full force and strength in juxtaposition with the mild thoughts of a concerned wife and mother. She, with child in her arms, thinks only of possibly helping her husband in the fields when they arrive.

The affirmation in this book, however, is not dependent on any final resolution of the tension created by the two differing stances of resignation and rebellion generally conceived. Rivera's work, after all, is not a simple, descriptive book of protest, but an artistically important *book of discovery.* The question, therefore, of "proper" or "improper" responses to social conditions is a false one, inappropriate to the premises upon which the work is created. The substantial affirmation of this book rests on the reality discovered and depicted by the author. And this process of discovery is given artistic form through the use of the central character within the frame-structure of the book and the cyclical movement of the narrative.

The overall scheme of the book is laid out in the four brief paragraphs comprising the introductory selection, **"El Año Perdido."** There Rivera uses the language of the dream—or at least a language suggestive of a deeper reality than what is ordinarily accepted as objective fact— to suggest the sense of psychological and social disorientation in which the hero lives. The impetus is to discover the self. The origin and cause of that impetus is perhaps outside the artistic concern of Rivera's book; it is enough to state the truism that personal and social identity is never a "problem" until it is threatened. As Frantz Fanon writes, the native's affirmation of his own culture, and his attempts at recovering a usable past are symptomatic of the "realization of the danger that he is running in cutting his last moorings and of breaking adrift from his people." Unless the native moves culturally in the direction of his true self, "there will be serious psycho-affective injuries and the result will be individuals without an anchor, without a horizon, colorless, stateless—a race of angels."[4]

Tomás Rivera's metaphor for this felt sense of breaking adrift is "el año perdido." The confusion and general disorientation brought on by the sense of "aquel año [que] se le perdió" began for the protagonist

> . . . cuando oía que alguien le llamaba por su nombre pero cuando volteaba la cabeza a ver quién era el que le llamaba, daba una vuelta entera y así quedaba donde mismo. Por eso nunca podía acertar ni quién le llamaba ni por qué, y luego hasta se le olvidaba el nombre que le habían llamado. Pero sabía que él era a quien llamaban. Una vez se detuvo antes de dar la vuelta entera y le entró miedo. Se dio cuenta de que él mismo se había llamado. Y así empezó el año perdido".

(p. 1)

It all begins in a confusion—and a fear—that has its source in the realization that it is he himself who has been "calling." The full implications of that realization, though, are not clearly understood by the hero until the end of the book. In his beginning confusion he thinks that he thinks, and he determines not to think, but he does nevertheless. It is his "thinking"—what Rivera describes as the hero's *seeing* and *hearing*—that the twelve stories and sketches and the thirteen anecdotes reveal. The cumulative effect is a felt sense of struggle.

"¿Por qué es que nosotros estamos aquí como enterrados en la tierra?" (p. 67) asks the young protagonist of the title story, upon hearing the moans of his father who has suffered a sunstroke in the suffocating heat of the fields. And that sets much of the tone of the book. The full-length stories, the impressionistic sketches, and the brief anecdotes that fall within the two frame pieces are quick but lasting glimpses into the lives of these characters. There is no attempt to relate them all realistically and explicitly in time and space. That only generally are they related in time and space—time, through the book's central metaphor ("el año perdido"), and in space by the fields and colonias in Texas and in the unspecified north—suggests, again, Rivera's interest in discovering and giving expression to the general and social, not the specific and individual reality. The same spirit informs all of the "framed" selections: a desperate clinging to life in the midst of deprivation and suffering, and the seemingly ever-present hope that if not for themselves, at least for their children, life will not exact such a heavy toll.

The suffering begins with childhood, as in **"Los Niños No Se Aguantaron,"** where a child is accidently shot and killed by a boss who, because he is paying the workers by the hour, does not want them "wasting" time drinking from the water tanks that he keeps for his cattle. The story is told from an objective and detached point of view, a technique common to many of the other stories and sketches. Rarely does Rivera-as-author intrude; hence the understanding, the judgments and the emotions must be generated out of the narrative situation itself. **"Los Niños No Se Aguantaron"** is quite brief: it consists of an introductory paragraph, some dramatic dialogue between father and child; two brief paragraphs matter-of-factly describing the child drinking water and being killed;

and at the end, another fragment of dialogue between two unidentified field-workers, inhabitants of the barrio, members of what, through the book, quickly assumes the forms of a *colonia* chorus—a collective Chicano voice that, standing at times off at a distance, describes and judges the actions that are being enacted on the stage.

In this story the chorus discusses the fate of the boss after the killing. One speaker affirms the consequences of human guilt feelings; he wants to believe that the boss almost went insane, that he is drinking heavily now and that he tried to commit suicide. The other voice denies the boss even the dignity of remorse. He wants to say: "they are such brutes that with absolute impunity they can kill us and our children." The first speaker says: "A mí se me hace que sí se volvió loco. Usted lo ha visto como anda ahora. Parece limosnero." The other voice answers, "Sí, pero es que ya no tiene dinero." And his *compadre* says "Pos sí" (p. 7).

At the end, the story does not affirm either of these two positions. The chorus's function in this sketch is to articulate the two points of view as part of the book's reality. Part of that reality—in all of its harshness and brutality—is expressed through the routinely dispassionate manner of presentation. The child is shot and "ni saltó como los venados, sólo se quedó en el agua como un trapo sucio y el agua empezó a empaparse de sangre . . ." (p. 7). Such matter-of-fact tone outweighs paragraphs of "concerned" and "committed" prose describing "the lot of the underdogs." In this selection it succinctly intensifies the horror of the situation. In other selections this same tone adds generally to the stark quality of the lives lived by these people.

Equally stark and despairing is the lot of the parents and children in **"Los Quemaditos."** Hoping that one of his children will become a boxing champion and earn thousands of dollars, a father buys boxing gloves for his children and teaches them to rub alcohol on their bodies the way he saw boxers do in a movie. Alone in their shack while the parents are working in the fields, the children accidentally start a fire while playing with the boxing gloves and two of the three children are burned to death in the shack. The chorus that enters at the end provides necessary information, and dispassionately comments on the cruel irony of the burning of everything—even the children—with the exception of the boxing gloves. One speaker, in respect if not in awe of Yankee ingenuity, says "Es que esta gente sabe hacer las cosas muy bien y no les entra ni la lumbre" (p. 96).

In this story, the chorus speaks with convincing authority. Responding to a question about the parents' reaction, one of the speakers expresses an essentially tragic point of view, one that acknowledges the uncertainty of human existence and the profound sense in which one has little control over what will be: "Pues ya se les esta pasando la tristeza aunque no creo que se les olvide. Dígame usted qué más puede hacer uno. Si no sabe uno cuándo le toca, ni cómo. Pobrecitos. Pero no sabe uno" (p. 96). And the reticent "Pos no" that conclusively ends the sketch affirms that point of view as a community reality.

"La Noche Que Se Apagaron Las Luces" is a love tragedy about two young people who are temporarily separated by their families' journeys in the migrant stream and vow to be true to one another until they return to Texas where they plan to marry. Rumors reach Ramón about Juanita's "cheating" in Minnesota, and when they meet again, they quarrel; heart-broken and in despair Ramón kills himself by grabbing onto a transformer at the electric power station. Distance and objectivity are achieved here by Rivera's focus on one tangible effect of Ramón's suicide at the power station: The lights go out throughout the community! And it is in reference to this manifestation that the community thereafter speaks of Ramón and Juanita: "Es que se qerían mucho ¿no crees?" "No, pos sí" (p. 109).

The attempt to hide from a harsh reality becomes frantic among people who are continually forced to struggle for their self-hood and dignity. That attempt—as it is lived by a youth—is the subject of **"Es Que Duele"**: a young man is expelled from school for defending himself against the physical attack of an Anglo student, and now faces the painful duty of telling his parents that he cannot return to that school. This story is written with the same kind of restraint and understatement typical of Rivera's style. The youth's experience involves the shame, anger, hatred and degradation that he is made to feel by a school nurse who forces him to undress and stand naked in her presence while being inspected, and by an Anglo American student who tells him to his face that he does not like Mexicans "because they steal" (p. 24). The main part of this story is told by a first-person narrator thinking in the present as he walks home from school the day of his expulsion. On his way home he wrestles with the problem of telling his parents who have high hopes that he will remain in school and become a telephone operator like the one who they saw as the leading character in a movie. Throughout the narrative there are brief flashbacks that fill in the context of this narrator's shame and anger, and provide ironic point and pathos to his desperate desire to disbelieve the reality of his situation "¿Y que no me hayan expulsado?" he thinks repeatedly throughout his walk home. Reality, however, is too severe and too sharply insistent in this boy's experience to be denied. Ultimately he must accept it: *"N'hombre, sí"* (p. 27).

The children in this book, like the adults, are victimized by that which exists outside of them—the often invisible social and economic forces that govern their lives, the institutions, and the physical environment in which they live and work. But their victimization does not stop there. So also are they prey to that which is within. As the narrator of the title story says, either "los microbios nos comen o el sol nos asolea. Siempre alguna enfermedad" (p. 67). Rivera traces not only the "Chicano" and the "farmworker" contours of his characters' lives, but the universally human as well. In the fields, in the barrios, in their shacks or in the trucks moving north for the summer, the young people, particularly, are shown struggling with the "problems" inherent in their tentative moves into life

generally. Of the twelve selections included within the frame, four—**"La Mano En La Bolsa"**; **"Primera Comunión"**, **"La Noche Estaba Plateada"**; and . . . *y no se lo tragó la tierra*—can be described as "initiation stories."

Guilt and the curious mixture of good and evil in the same person are major themes in **"La Mano En La Bolsa,"** a story about a young man who is made to feel a debilitating guilt over his innocent role in a macabre crime. A youth—the naive first-person narrator of this story—is sent by his parents to live with don Laíto and doña Bone, an elderly couple in the barrio who steal in order to sell or give away: "cuando no podían venderlo a los vecinos, lo daben. Casi repartían todo" (p. 40). Understandably, the couple are well liked by the people, and have a good reputation in the community, even among the *americanos*. The narrator, however, notices the rotten teeth that surround the gold in don Laíto's mouth, and quickly begins to wonder about his hosts' goodness, for not only do they admit their stealing to him, but they even try to persuade him to join them in their pilfering. During the boy's visit, the couple murder a wetback drifter for his money and possessions, and force the boy to help them bury the body and keep their secret. At the end of the story the boy is given a ring that belonged to the murdered victim and the ring becomes a symbol of his guilt. He tries to throw it away but cannot. He wears it, "y lo peor fue que por mucho tiempo, nomás veía a algún desconocido, me metía la mano a la bolsa" (p. 42). Time compassionately repeals his "crime," but the habit of putting his hand in his pocket, he says, "me duró mucho tiempo."

Guilt is again a major theme of **"Primera Comunión."** On the morning of his first holy communion—after spending a restless night memorizing all his sins—the narrator, while walking to church, looks through a tailorshop window to see what was causing the noises that he hears, and sees a naked man and woman having sexual intercourse on the floor. Torn between fear and the strange attracton to see more, he intently remains until discovered by the couple and told to go away. He cannot forget what he has seen, but neither is he willing to share his experience with his friends. He is bothered by the feeling of himself having "cometido el pecado del cuerpo" (p. 84). He keeps his "sin," even from the confessional priest, and when, after his communion, he arrives home with his padrino for the traditional sweetbread and chocolate, "se [le] hacía todo cambiado." He imagines his father and mother—and even the priest and the nun—naked on the floor. "Casi ni pude comer el pan dulce ni tomarme el chocolate," he says, "y nomás acabé y recuerdo que salí corriendo de la casa. Parecía sentirme como que me ahogaba" (p. 85). Alone outside, he recalls the scene at the tailor-shop and soon begins to derive some pleasure from his memory, and forgets even that he had lied to the priest. Then, he says, "me sentía lo mismo que cuando había oído hablar al misionero acerca de la gracia de Dios" (p. 85). The ambiguity at the end of the story enriches its meaning. When the boy says "tenía ganas de saber más de todo. Y luego pensé que a lo mejor era lo mismo," he expresses both an extraordinary resiliency that enable him to take his experience in stride and a propensity to put aside that which is "bothersome."

"La Noche Estaba Plateada" and . . . *y no se lo tragó la tierra* are companion pieces which represent, on one level at least, the young heroes' metaphysical rebellion and their testing of religious and superstitious notions that their elders accept.

In **"La Noche Estaba Plateada,"** the protagonist, after hearing his parents tell of people who have summoned the devil, becomes curious and decides to see for himself whether or not the devil actually exists and in what form. He carefully plans his approach and, according to the traditional formula learned from his parents and others in the community, issues his summons. Nothing happens. "No salió nadie. Todo se veía igual. Todo estaba igual. Todo en paz. Pensó entonces que lo mejor sería maldecir al diablo. Lo hizo. Le echó todas las maldiciones que sabía en distintos tonos de voz. Hasta le echó de la madre. Pero, nada. No se apareció nada ni nadie ni cambió nada" (p. 56). The devil does not exist, he thinks; but if the devil does not exist, then neither does . . . , and at that moment he cannot follow through with the inexorable logic of his discovery. Later on, however, as he reconsiders his experience of the evening, he accepts the existential implication of his discovery: *"No hay diablo,"* he thinks, *"no hay nada.* Lo único que había habido en la mota había sido su propia voz" (p. 56). And this brings him to the realization that the people whom he had heard about going insane after summoning the devil, did so not because the devil appeared to them, but on the contrary, because he did not appear. There is nothing but one's own voice in the dark. His logic forces on him the realization of his own existential solitariness, a conclusion that has an empty sky as its premise.

The hero-narrator of . . . *y no se lo tragó la tierra* tests God's existence, not in the deliberate manner in which the protagonist of the preceding story attempts to verify the devil's existence, but in the full passion of his hatred, protesting against and cursing a God who would allow the illness and the death of his aunt and uncle, the suffering of their children, the illness of his own father and the fate of his small brothers and sisters who seem destined to feed the earth and sun "sin nigunas esperanzas de nada." Frustrated by his own powerlessness "to do anything," he is incapable of taking solace in his mother's religion, refuses to resign himself to the will of God, and rebels against the notion that there is no rest for them until death. He finds, that is, his humanity on this side of the weariness, despair and hatred which he feels. Having been conditioned by historical and cultural forces, however, he is at first incapable of seriously considering the absence of any transcendent and determinant final cause. After his father suffers a sunstroke in the fields, he reviles his mother for clamoring for the mercy of God. He says "¿Qué se gana, mamá, con andar haciendo eso? ¿A poco cree que le ayudó mucho a mi tío y a mi tía? . . . si Dios no se acuerda de uno. . . . A Dios le importa

poco de uno los pobres" (p. 67). But at this point his subservience and dependence—wrought out of fear—prohibit him from cursing God and especially from considering His absence. "Yo creo que ni hay . . . ," he begins, but cannot go on with this thought: "No, mejor no decirlo, a lo mejor empeora papá" (p. 67).

The next day his nine-year-old brother has a sunstroke, and as the protagonist carries him home from the fields he cries in despair and out of anger and hatred. At every moment of the emotion that he feels he draws from it his humanity. Without knowing when, he starts to swear; "y lo que dijo lo había tenido ganas de decir desde hacía mucho tiempo" (p. 70). Unthinkingly he curses God and immediately "al hacerlo sintió el miedo infundido por los años y por sus padres" (p. 70). He imagines the earth opening and swallowing him—but nothing happens! Instead, he begins to feel the solidity of the ground: "Se sintió andando por la tierra bien apretada, más apretada que nunca" (p. 70). His discovery is existential and—in the context of his former despair, dependence, and sense of powerlessness—it is affirmative. Recognizing the emptiness of the heavens he does not fall into the despair of the existential anti-hero who finds himself in the midst of a meaningless and absurd universe. Rivera's character embraces his freedom, and that very evening experiences a sense of peace—and detachment—"que nunca habia sentido antes." The following day, as he leaves for work, he feels himself, for the first time in his life, "capaz de hacer y deshacer cualquier cosa que él quisiera" (p. 70).

La mujer y *la madre* are at the center of traditional Chicano culture. Though in many ways *la madre* is subservient to the father, she remains the nucleus and the predominant mainstay of the *familia.* This importance is reflected by her omnipresence in Rivera's book. Her presence is felt throughout the work. In the majority of the selections she exists in the background, particularized only to the extent that she is placed in her concrete social and cultural milieu. She is the typical Mexican mother caring for her family, gossiping with her *comadres,* hoping for her children, and praying—incessantly—in the background. It is, particularly in her representation in this work that the detachment of the author's point of view wavers, and the book borders on the maudlin.

"Un Rezo" and **"La Noche Buena"** are the only two selections in which the mother emerges from the background to play the major role in the narrative. **"Un Rezo"** is simply that: a first-person narrative rendering of a mother's personal and remarkably concrete prayer to God and *La Virgen de Guadalupe* that her son the soldier be protected from the bullets of the communist Koreans. In **"La Noche Buena,"** the mother plays a more active role. She persuades her husband that this Christmas they get store-bought gifts for their children so that they do not continue to ask why *Santo Clos* never brings *them* any gifts. She leaves the seclusion of her house and timidly undertakes a short excursion to the local Kress. She becomes lost, confused, is accused of stealing and finally collapses in the midst of the crowd and noise (a repetition of a similar experience she had previously in

Wilmar, Minnesota). Back in the safety of her home, she worries that she is insane, and that they will confine her in an asylum, away from her children. Yet life goes on, the story says, and the people accommodate themselves to their condition. In one sentence—another example of Rivera's mastery of the meaningful small touch—the author tells what it means to be among the dispossessed: the children have another Christmas without presents, and after awhile, Rivera writes, "no preguntaron nada" (p. 125).

Rivera has a clear eye for the cruel ironies of life. In the world which his characters inhabit, people are often victimized by the very hopes that they nurture, hopes that spring from the positions in life which they endure. In such a world, attempts at alleviating one's situation often serve merely to reinforce one's deprivation. In such a world even anger is preempted. This is the theme of **"El Retrato,"** one of the better stories in Rivera's book. The door-to-door salesmen from San Antonio—those who thrive on the innocence and misfortune of the powerless—converge on the barrio like vultures when the people arrive from the north with a few dollars in their pockets. In this story it is the portrait salesman who promises Don Mateo that "solamente por treinta pesitos," (paid immediately), they can enlarge—and, in color, inlay—the photograph of his son, who is missing in action in the war, so that he looks "como que está vivo."

Don Mateo and the others in the barrio who have been "sold" wait week-after-week for their portraits. As they wait, they hopefully rationalize the delay that gives them intimations of having been duped. The community speaks:

"—Ya mero nos traen los retratos, ¿no cree?"

"—Yo creo que sí, es que es trabajo muy fino. Se lleva más tiempo. Buen trabajo que hace esa gente. ¿Se fijó cómo parecían que estaban vivos los retratos?"

"—No, sí, sí hacen muy buen trabajo. Ni quien se lo quite. Pero, fíjese que ya tienen más de un mes que pasaron por aquí."

"—Sí, pero de aquí se fueron levantando retratos por todo el pueblerío hasta San Antonio, de seguro. Y se tardarán un poco más."

"—Es cierto. Es cierto." (p. 138)

The photographs that the people had given the salesman are finally found dissolving in a tunnel leading to the dùmp, and Don Mateo, in full anger, goes to San Antonio to search out the salesman who took the only picture he had of his son. He finds the salesman and forces him, upon threats of violence, to do the inlaid enlargement of his son. "Tuvo que hacerlo de memoria," Don Mateo tells his neighbors afterward. "Con miedo, yo creo uno es capaz de todo," he explains as he shows off the finished portrait of his son. Justice is done. Don Mateo receives what he paid for. "¿Usted dirá? ¿Cómo se ve m'ijo?" he asks the admiring *compadre*: "Pues, yo la mera verdad ya no me acuerdo cómo era Chuy. Pero ya se estaba, entre más

y más, pareciéndose a usted, ¿verdad?" Complacently and with some pride, Don Mateo says "Sí. Yo creo que sí. Es lo que me dice la gente ahora. Que Chuy, entre más y más, se iba a parecer a mí y que se estaba pareciendo a mí. Ahí está el retrato. Como quien dice, somos la misma cosa" (p. 139).

In their simplicity and in the powerlessness of their impoverishment, Rivera's characters live by illusions that acquire the force of necessity. Half-heartedly one of Rivera's characters says "Yo creo que siempre lo mejor es tener esperanzas" (p. 125), and—in its various forms—that precisely is the attitude that informs the people's lives throughout the book. In **"Cuando Lleguemos"** these *esperanzas* are emphatically represented through the thoughts of the various characters who find themselves stranded in the middle of the night in a broken-down truck going north for the season. In the privacy of the night, each of the characters is encouraged by the hope that when they arrive things will be "better" for them. The hopes and the dreams that Rivera depicts are indeed those of the oppressed. There is the anticipation of the experienced, which reality has distilled down to a modest *"a ver si consigo una cama buena para mi vieja, ya le molestan mucho los riñones. Nomás que no nos vaya a tocar un gallinero como el del año pasado con piso de cemento"* (p. 152). And there is the radical resolve of youth, to escape altogether the rattrap of the dispossessed.

The impact of Rivera's book is cumulative. Though the sketches and stories can be read individually and out of context, it is as particular parts of a whole which is greater than the sum of its parts that Rivera's work can best be understood and appreciated. All of the experiences, the characters, the themes, and judgments contained in the twelve selections and the thirteen anecdotes are finally summarized and "fixed" into a context by the consciousness of the central character of the book, who reappears in the concluding selection, **"Debajo De La Casa"**—the piece that in combination with the introductory selection, **"El Año Perdido,"** constitutes the finished frame of the work.

In **"Debajo De La Casa"** the collective voice of the community is predominant, but now it speaks explicitly to, and through, the central character—the *pocho*. Throughout the book the voices have been the cumulative result of what the *pocho* brings up out of the depths of his memory, but so readily do the stories and sketches acquire an independent life of their own, that the fact that they constitute mere elements of the protagonist's "lost year" is forgotten. At the end, the reader is reminded of the literary device being used, and, like the *pocho*, he is brought full circle to the beginning—but now with the accumulated experience rendered by the voices through the book. There is, in other words, an analogy between the reader's experience and the protagonist's.

For the latter, the total experience is ultimately regenerative and affirmative, capped as it is by his realization that rather than losing anything, "Había encontrado. Encontrar y reencontrar y juntar. Relacionar esto con esto,

Tomás Rivera

eso con aquello, todo con todo. Eso era. Eso era todo. Y le dio más gusto" (p. 169).

As a "book of discovery," *. . . y no se lo tragó la tierra* is a variation on the *Bildungsroman,* for the focus of Rivera's work is not on the forging of the individual, peculiar and subjective identity; it is rather informed by a concern for the development of a social and collective self-identification. It is not the particular and idiosyncratic which is revealed but the general and the typical. The characters in the *pocho*'s recoverable past—the *pelado* father, the Mexican revolutionary grandfather, the devout mother, the *gachupín* priest, the kindly Cuquita who is everyone's grandmother, the quarreling lovers, the exploitative *patrón,* as well as all the *comadres, compadres,* and *padrinos*—all are recognizable not through personal quirks in their particular character, but rather because they assume—at least within the context of the Chicano experience—archetypal dimensions.

In including **"los nombres de la gente del pueblo"** (p. 163), Rivera's book—like Bartolo's poems performs the significant function of discovering and ultimately appropriating and embracing the past in all of its sometimes painful authenticity. The importance of looking closely and hard at the colonial experience of the *pocho* is assumed. The first step in the *pocho*'s liberation begins with an understanding of his position within a social and economic context. Presumably it is the

kind of understanding—however felt or perceived—that leads the *pocho* of Rivera's book, as well as the author himself, towards the re-identification with that which is his own, i.e., with himself as a member of a people. The movement in the book is inward collectively toward an understanding of the barrio experience as it is—in its pain and in all of its suffering, assuredly, but also in its essential sense of strength, vitality and human celebration.

The language of Rivera's book—the Spanish idiom unique to the Chicano cultural and historical experience—is of no slight importance. It serves, not only to identify the audience that Rivera must have originally had in mind, but so also does it reinforce the immediacy and authenticity of the experience. The language of the book, therefore, legitimizes itself as the essence of the cultural past being embraced. The non-committal reticence of the *compadres'* "pos sí," and "pos no"; the strong, even coarse and vital, phrases unique to the *colonia* experience, like "para acabarla de fregar" ("to boot"), "el que le entra parejito" ("he who really knows how to work"), "Hijo, está caro, oiga" ("hey, that is expensive"), and "Qué padre se mira éste" ("this is really fine-looking")—all of this ultimately constitutes, con "los nombres de la gente del pueblo," la voz que (como dice Bartolo), es "la semilla del amor en la oscuridad" (p. 163).

There are, finally, some comparisons between Rivera's literary effort and the efforts of his fictional character in the framepieces of the book. Besides being a significant artistic effort within the Chicano Renaissance, *. . . y no se lo tragó la tierra* performs a valuable function in that it uses "the past with the intention of opening the future, as an invitation to action and a basis for hope."[5] Criticism of Rivera's work because it does not more directly perform the function of social protest is short-sighted. The reality discovered and depicted by this author contributes to the Chicano act of self-discovery in a manner more profoundly effective, aesthetically as well as socially, than more explicit literature of protest. The vitality of the Chicano social movement depends on the development of a deep understanding of Chicano reality. Rivera contributes notably to this end.

NOTES

[1] *Pocho* (New York: Doubleday & Co., 1959); *Chicano* (New York: Doubleday & Co., 1970).

[2] Tomás Rivera, *". . . y no se lo tragó la tierra"* (Berkeley: Quinto Sol Publications, 1971). Rivera's book was awarded the first Premio Quinto Sol, National Chicano Literary Award for 1969-70. In its bilingual edition (1971), the English translation was done by Herminio Ríos C., "in collaboration with the author, with assistance by Octavio I. Romano-V." Quotations cited in this essay are from the original Spanish.

[3] As in all translations, much of the cultural connotation is diminished or altogether lost in the English version of this book. The translation of the threat and the curse above is extraordinarily mild sounding compared

to the original. There simply is no English "equivalent" for *pinche, chinguesasu madre,* or to *me la van a pelar.*

[4] Frantz Fanon, *The Wretched of the Earth* (New York: Grove Press, 1968), pp. 217-18.

[5] Fanon, p. 232.

Joseph Sommers   (essay date 1979)

SOURCE: "Interpreting Tomás Rivera," in *Modern Chicano Writers: A Collection of Critical Essays.* Englewood Cliffs, N.J.: Prentice-Hall, Inc., 1979, pp. 94-107.

[*Sommers contends that examination of the formal aspects of Rivera's texts will clarify the historical and cultural implications for the reader*].

I

In an introductory article in this volume,[1] I attempted to set out the assumptions and the methods of three critical approaches to Chicano literature. I have called them the formalist, the culturalist and the historical-dialectical. What follows below is an effort to test these approaches by applying each one to a given text— *. . . y no se lo tragó la tierra (. . . and the earth did not part)* by Tomas Rivera. This effort to separate the approaches will seek to avoid the merely mechanical, for we all realize that in published criticism such neatly and conveniently delimited distinctions are rare. Further, it will seek to demonstrate as objectively as possible the critical rewards which derive from each of the first two critical modes, even as it will be clear that my own preference is for the third.

What would lie at the center of a formalist approach to the text? In the first place, there would be a relatively minor concern for historical and social information, though attention would be paid to Rivera's experience in achieving the doctorate, and the extent to which he acquired familiarity with Hispanic literary traditions and with the landmark authors of Europe and North America. This type of information would be useful in examining how the writer achieved his "personal voice," so that his work might be seen in the individualized terms stressed by formalist critics.

A more important formalist concern is usually to situate the text in the larger framework of western literature. A prime critical goal is the identification of literary influences, for two reasons. On the one hand, the degree to which they are assimilated and transformed is an index of the valued quality of "originality." On the other, the presence of literary influences and indirect references to recognized authors or narrative techniques is evidence of the equally valued quality of "universality." Specifically, the formalist critic would identify traces in the text of four major authors: Faulkner, Joyce, Dos Passos and Rulfo, in order of ascending significance.

In formulating and presenting much of the narrative from the first-person perspective of an innocent boy, Rivera can be said to have had recourse to the classic narrative strategy of Faulkner in *The Sound and the Fury.* The interior monologue which closes the book and constitutes a unifying re-examination of the experiences of the preceding chapters, may be a modest reminiscence of Joyce's technique in the ending of *Ulysses.* And the influence of Dos Passos can be identified in the central structural device of prefacing each major narrative unit with a brief passage comparable to the camera-eye segments of *Manhattan Transfer.* These serve to provide thematic resonance, introduce remembered experience, and extend in more general terms the particularized experience of the narrative unit.

But it is Juan Rulfo, the Mexican master-narrator, whose novel *Pedro Páramo* and short stories are most apparent as influences in *. . . y no se lo tragó la tierra.*[2] This affinity has been noted by critics, but rarely analyzed.[3] In a general way, the two authors are linked by a spareness of narrative and a focus on rural themes. More precisely, the innocent first-person narrative voice is even more closely anticipated in Rulfo's story "Macario,"[4] which has likely derivations from Faulkner, than in Faulkner s own work. The innocence of Rulfo's narrator is closer to that of Rivera's, sharing with him an iconoclastic reaction to sexuality and to the phenomena of the natural world. Like Rulfo, too, in *Pedro Páramo,* although much less radically, Rivera ruptures his narrative sequence and interposes unexplained fragments to jar the comfort of a reader accustomed to revelations of cause and effect through linear narrative sequences. Furthermore, in both Rulfo and Rivera a central fundamental irony is generated by the contrast between apparently direct, . . . uncomplicated folk-language and the deep thematic overtones of violence and passion which inform the lives of their characters.

At the center of the formalist approach is rigorous textual analysis. Here issues of genre, language, structure, and theme come into question. In this case the problem of genre is indeed important, for the tendency has been to see the volume as a collection of short stories. The formalist would examine the arguments for seeing the text as a novel (arguments with which I agree) and thus would adduce definitions of the novel, distinctions between realism and modernism, and especially questions of structure. Language explorations, already referred to above, would include the role of rural folk lexical terms, syntactic patterns, linguistic symbols, and English loan elements penetrating the Spanish text. Interesting distinctions could be made between the characters' language, that of the young narrator, and that of the narrator or *persona* closest to the author. An important area, as yet untouched, is critical analysis of the English version, which clearly lacks the linguistic coherence of the original Spanish.

A formalist critic would no doubt devote extensive analysis to questions of structure.[5] He would note that underlying the sequence of narrative units is an understood linkage in time. Despite internal inconsistencies (for example the references to seasons are contradictory), the chapters correspond approximately to the passing of a crucial year in the boy-protagonist's life.

Structural likewise is the scheme by which each experience narrated becomes in some sense a rite of passage, displaying the delicate and complex growth by which a young boy comes of age. This scheme is also evident in the prefatory sections, which function as magnifiers extending the scope and depth of the boy's experience with the quality of typicality, so that they acquire a representative Chicano character. Lastly, there is the thematic framing provided by the introductory section, which introduces the notion of the "lost year," and the final section, which in effect recapitulates and integrates the twelve intervening units, thus impelling the reader to understand that there has been a cumulative process marked by a beginning and an end, a questioning and an answering.

Another area of formalist analysis is likely to be that of thematics, linking the literary idiosyncrasies of a text to systems of meaning within it. One such system might be psychological, involving issues of personality formation and maturation, such as the boy's self-contemplation in the early scene, his encounters with both sexuality and social taboos, and his symbolic emergence, at the end, from a womb of isolation and hiding beneath the house.[6] Another possible thematic system originates in the existentialist formulations of Octavio Paz in his essay on the dialectics of solitude.[7] Applying this, Luis Dávila identifies the crucial process in the novel as the search for the other, for in this view (closely related to early Sartrean thought), being can be defined only in relation to otherness.[8]

What is important here is that formalist criticism stresses the identification of meaning as an index of the "literariness" of the work. The goal of this criticism is not to integrate the literary experience into larger frames of cultural, social and broadly political experience, but to distinguish literature and its aesthetic from other modes of experience.

Formalist analysis, then, can tell us much about the richness, the complexity, and the generic identity of . . . *y no se lo tragó la tierra.* However, we must understand that the formulae of this analysis are a stress on the individuality of the work and the writer, the compatibility of the text with those of established authors, and the definition of internally distinguishing structural and stylistic features which are seen to set the "literary" work apart from other modes of linguistic discourse and from the apprehension of social meaning and historical knowledge.

II

Several objectives would be apparent in the way a culturalist critic approached . . . *y no se lo tragó la tierra.* One would be to understand the work as a product of Chicano culture, and to see in it a reflection of this culture.

For example, the critic would present instances of expressive language which demonstrate the special capacities of Chicano speech patterns to communicate the nature and the significance of Chicano experience. One such instance is the ironic use of the negative, elliptically, to render more vehement the positive. The laconic three-word sentence, "No pos sí" which ends the narrative unit entitled **"The Night the Lights Went Out"**, exemplified this effect superbly. The story is recounted in part by an omniscient third-person narrator who is close to the scene, in part by conversational fragments or interior monologues of the two protagonists Ramón and Juanita, and in part by dialogue between two anonymous people of the community. What emerges is the early love between Ramón and Juanita, her momentary interest in another man during the family's migratory travels, Ramón's possessive jealousy and Juanita's insistence on independence, and finally Ramón's dramatic suicide after Juanita defies him by dancing with the other man. Once the narrator has chronicled Ramón's death (by self-electrocution at the electrical plant, inducing a power failure which stops the dance), the chapter ends with a two-line exchange between the anonymous community people, who throughout have been piecing events together and evaluating them. One voice concludes, "The fact is that they really loved each other, don't you think?" The powerful response to this is couched in a popular idiom that in its very form parallels and reinforces the narrated irony (that too much love brings about its own destruction, that what appears good can be bad, that appearance is the reverse of reality, that what may be voiced as negative can in fact signify the positive) and compresses with remarkable brevity an affirmation: "No, pos sí." (Roughly translatable as, "No, of course they did.")

A comparable example is the deployment of a similar linguistic construction, "N'hombre, sí" in the chapter, **"It Really Hurts."** It functions as a *motif* throughout the text, which takes the form of an interior monologue by a boy protagonist whose family had immigrated north from Texas. He meditates upon his expulsion from school, obviously for racist reasons, and the impact it will have upon his family's aspirations for him. As he feels the hurt and the injustice, he keeps hoping to fend off reality by convincing himself that perhaps it has not really happened. Each time, his relentless sense of realism brings him back to truth and pain as he tells himself that the school authorities did in fact expel him. And the story ends with this final realization, "N'hombre sí." ("No, man, they sure did.") Once again, powerful because the "sí" ironically reverses the "no," the very form of expression echoes and underlines the theme—yes, one must face the concrete reality of injustice rather than retreat to the fantasy of Utopian imagination.

The culturalist critic would affirm, based on analyses such as those cited, that the essence of the narration derives directly from distinctive cultural features, many of which are imbedded in the language itself. Furthermore, it is the migratory experience, itself a matrix of Chicano culture, which gives shape and meaning to the experience narrated in the text.

Another culturalist tendency is to examine the text for the cultural profile it generates, and to validate it if this profile is extensive and detailed. Here the critic would identify many features of Chicano traditional culture which are integral to the make-up of the characters' attitudes and behavior. For example there is both dependence upon religion and incipient critical awareness of conflict between religious orthodoxy and natural human impluse. Thus the critic would affirm that the novel spans the range of impact which Catholicism has had upon Chicano consciousness.

The critic would also stress that the novel projects a view of the Chicano world from within, and would focus on the aspects of Chicano existence which make up the narrative texture: family life, the migratory cycle, attitudes toward love, marriage, religion, school and work. These have special characteristics among Chicanos, and taken together reveal the coherent patterns of Chicano culture. Particular scenes would be singled out and identified as unique to the Chicano experience: the mother's prayerful offer to sacrifice herself to save her son fighting in Korea; the boy suffering from thirst as he and brothers and father stoop to labor in the field; the mother panicked at the prospect of venturing into the center of the strange English-speaking city to shop at the dime store; the fathers aspiring that their children be prizefighters or telephone operators; the boy being refused a haircut or insulted racially by other school children in a strange town in which his family are transients.

In singling out these scenes the critic would stress that Rivera conveys both the particularity and the coherence of Chicano culture. Since it is in culture that the critic sees what characterizes the Chicano, he is concerned with uncovering it in its "purest" form. As a consequence he gravitates logically toward its most traditional manifestations. If he is also influenced by ethnopoetics, he may argue that, because "original" Chicano culture still survives, authors like Rivera are not cut off from their roots, and can enrich their works with the authenticity of themes, characters, and language free from contamination or assimilation. By contrast, he would point out that modern Anglo culture suffers from an *ersatz* quality deriving from loss of the past, urbanization, artificial and elitist sophistication, corruption by the manipulative mass media, and a voguish stress on the mental, the imaginary, and the irrational. The Chicano may live outside the mainstream, this critic would say, but his very exclusion has permitted the retention of traditional culture.

For the culturalist critic the central unifying theme of Rivera's novel is the search for identity, a search which enables the boy to discover that he has rich cultural resources upon which to draw, resources tempered by suffering and endowed with the strength of humanism. In developing this thematic argument the critic might refer, with Ralph Grajeda, to the notions of Frantz Fanon in tracing the development of cultural awareness and the process of cultural identification by which the "colonized" *persona* throws off psychological acceptance of the mask improsed by the colonizer.[9]

In essence, then, the objective of this approach is to show that the work is distinctive because it emerges from the Chicano experience, and valid because it embodies an authentic view of Chicano culture. Its consequent difference from non-Chicano narratives will make it a healthy cultural reinforcement for Chicano readers, who will see themselves and their culture projected in the text with dignity, as compared to the degraded images packaged and transmitted daily by the mass media.

The richness of linguistic variation, the distinctive features of Chicano life style, both rural and urban, and the dramatic nature of Chicano historical experience, all serve to guarantee that embedded in most literary texts will be much material for the culturalist critic to work with. On the other hand, the limitations of culturalist criticism deserve spelling out. Here I refer to the "pure" form of this approach as outlined in the introductory essay. In placing culture (and by implication, race) at the center of Chicano experience, the critic underestimates the all-important factor of class, a factor which shapes and influences the process by which cultural expression is generated.[10] For example, the experience of the migratory cycle is fundamental to the cultural content of *. . . y no se lo tragó la tierra*. Because the structures of the food and textile industries in the United States require special seasonal forms of agricultural production, the migratory labor system is imposed on a large segment of the Mexican-descended population. Were this system of exploitation to disappear, new forms of cultural expression would soon manifest themselves, as has been the case when rural Chicano population has gravitated to urban areas in search of an improved life.

One limitation, then, of culturalist criticism is its failure to show how cultural manifestations are part of a total system of social relations at the base of which are economic structures shaping these relations. A second limitation is the general view of culture as adaptation rather than as a complex of responses to the total set of life conditions which a people faces. The adaptive view tends to be acritical, all-inclusive, and descriptive. The latter view attempts to be critical, to see cultural expression as an area of struggle, and to distinguish between those elements of culture which are adaptive (such as the ideology of organized religion) and those (such as satirical humor) which evolve out of the need to analyze reality, to criticize oppressive institutions, to affirm a people's sense of worth, and to facilitate structural change.

III

A critic working in the third mode, concerned with a historical and dialectical approach, might well begin an analysis by situating the text.

While the narration itself is set in the 1950s, the perspective from which it was conceived reflects consciousness of the 1960s. The end of the decade—the time of composition of the novel—was an important historic juncture. In the first place, coincident with deepening official commitment to the brutal war in Viet Nam, there had been a critical questioning of national policy and of the very assumptions on which United States society was structured. This questioning had come in part from the younger generation which to an unprecedented degree resisted the war and made many tenuous attempts to forge a counter-culture.

Deeper blows to social complacency had been dealt by black people, whose demands for change, heard first during the Montgomery bus boycott, spread throughout the North, from Harlem to Watts. To the humanist ideas of Martin Luther King were added the more radical formulations of Malcolm X, Angela Davis, and The Black Panthers, which analyzed the origins and nature of racism, took account of its economic roots and connected it to the history of Western imperialism. Black consciousness, the reexamination of black history and culture, the ideas of Frantz Fanon, the works of LeRoi Jones, Richard Wright, Ralph Ellison, James Baldwin, Langston Hughes and Claude McKay—all formed part of the nation's cultural atmosphere at the turn of the decade.

A comparable social ferment was felt throughout the Southwest during the years immediately prior to the composition of Rivera's novel. Although the black movement clearly influenced the Chicano upsurge of the 1960's, this did not, as is sometimes simplistically stated, derive basically from the black movement. Rather it continued and renewed long established patterns of struggle for change and justice, whether social or economic, urban or rural. By the end of the 1960s Chicano activity was at a high point in all phases. Land seizures had occurred in northern New Mexico. Chicano urban movements were organized in Denver and Los Angeles. Chicano students initiated national meetings at Denver in 1969 and 1970 which were notable for inspiring student publications, most of them placing a heavy emphasis on cultural nationalism.

For their contribution to the literary coming of age of Tomás Rivera, two elements of the national upsurge were particularly important. The first was the movement in Crystal City, Texas, to take power from the hands of the Anglo minority and transfer it democratically to the Chicano majority. Many constituents of this majority were Chicano farmworkers who annually embarked on migratory treks to Michigan, Wisconsin, Minnesota and Illinois. Indeed, Rivera's family had resided in Crystal City in the 1940s, and had participated in the migratory cycle, traveling to the Midwest and returning. For this reason, the Chicano political movement in Crystal City in the 1960s contained a special personal meaning for him. A second important element was the organizing efforts of the farmworkers' union, renewing the struggles which had begun in the 1920s and had echoed again and again in succeeding decades. The modern union, led by César Chávez, was launched in 1965. By 1970 it had won historic victories in California and had established an organizing committee in Texas. These efforts served to focus national attention on the situation of the migratory farmworker.

While there was no unified national leadership of this many-faceted Chicano movement, there was a widely shared sense of the need to challenge established social structures, and to demand significant change. The cultural nationalism which peaked in the Plan de Aztlán of 1969 began to be supplanted by a more politically and socially based militancy stemming from the hard political realities of Crystal City, the brutalities of the Los Angeles moratorium, and the class consciousness engendered by the farmworkers' struggles against agribusiness. All this experience generated a rich diversity of cultural activity: newspapers, journals, art exhibitions, poetry festivals, and drama performances. Of key importance, a Chicano publishing house, Quinto Sol Publications, proved able to sustain a critically oriented journal, El Grito (launched in 1967), to provide an independent forum for Chicano writers and scholars, and to announce a literary prize based on norms respecting the language and the artistic integrity of Chicano creative authors.

The purpose of this schematic effort to situate Rivera's novel is not to arrive at a simplified equation of cause and effect assuming that the literary work is a mechanically predetermined product of given historical conditions. Rather it is to identify the issues and conflicts of the historical experience to which the author responded, and to analyze the quality and the content of the cultural atmosphere in which he was active at the time of literary productivity.

Turning from context to text, problems of structure and of narrative point of view demand attention. Here our point of departure is serious textual analysis. The formalist's arguments that there are structural and narrative patterns which justify treating the text as a novel are indispensable to this analysis. They need not be repeated but they serve to show that precisely *because* the text has novelistic scope and unity, it embodies a complex system of values and can be analyzed in terms of meaning and ideological contradictions. In brief, then, a close reading of the text uncovers an experiential process narrated across time in such a way as to refer both to the protagonist's personal life and to the common realities shared by Chicanos.

Of crucial importance is the particular *way* in which the narration reaches the reader. Whether by means of first-person passages in which the boy himself conveys his account of events, or through a third-person limited omniscient point of view, the narrative perspective remains largely that of the protagonist. The reader perceives events through the boy's eyes as he undergoes the trials of that crucial year and observes how others act and react. The larger cognitive process for the reader is shaped by a fundamental ironic movement in the narrative—the boy's change from innocence to awareness, from the idealism inherent in unformed human nature to the realism shaped by exposure to the difficult contradictions of the social condition.

The question of whether the same boy figures in each of the narrative sections is not crucial, for ambiguities in this regard are cleared up in the final section, when the central figure assumes knowledge of and responsibility for each of the scenes narrated. We can conclude that his role was that of either protagonist or witness. What is literarily more significant is that the reader in effect looks over the boy's shoulder or listens to his voice as he first encounters the realities of his cultural and social circumstances: the stifling omnipotence of an observant and demanding God; the sense of sinfulness associated with the natural arrival of puberty; the cruel racism of the educational system; the mendacity of some figures who prey upon fellow Chicanos, figures like doña Boni and the portrait salesman. Each encounter embodies elements of irony, for they reverse the hopes and expectations of the reader, who would prefer to see growth and maturation in the boy parallelled by increased education, social mobility, personal freedom, and access to the fruits of modern society.

This ironic contrast between innocence and awareness, accentuated by the reader's identification with the boy from whose point of view the story is narrated, is the basis for the critical perspective of the text, as we shall see below. Thus narrative technique is fundamental to the shaping of meaning and of ideological emphasis.

Another distinctive formal feature of *. . . y no se lo trago la tierra* is its extreme compression. The various narrative units have the intensity of focus of the short story with its insistence on brevity. This has the advantage, on the one hand, of creating tight endings which enrich the text because of the semi-autonomous, self-contained quality of its component parts. On the other hand, in its bare-bones narrative quality, with an almost complete absence of landscape, the text displays a lack of the texture and the detail of experience which can be novelistic virtues in fleshing out human experience. To be specific, excessive laconism contributes to ambiguities in meaning, which will be discussed below. Remarkably, the reader realizes, upon looking back, that the total narration spans no more than sixty-odd pages.

A final aspect of the text, correctly singled out by culturalist criticism, is the casting of much of the narration in popular language. The directness and expressiveness of common people's speech patterns pervade the text and endow it with deeper authenticity than could ever be attained by a distanced voice closer in tone to the Mexican or North American novel.

The important critical observation here is that the expressiveness of folk language functions not merely reflectively, to provide an authentic view of traditional culture, but actively to show how people respond to each other and to the harsh realities of their existence. The total narrative process, which shows the boy finding sustenance in his cultural identity, implies the fusing of this identity with awareness of the need to change the surrounding reality. And this critical awareness, frequently expressed through language, applies not only to the larger societal structures, but also to aspects of traditional culture itself, such as orthodox religious attitudes toward sexuality and guilt.[11]

An example, conveyed in popular language, of the interaction between traditional cultural values (acceptance of social norms, hope that the children will achieve success) and a critical realism (albeit tinged with cynicism) based on actual experience, much of which has to do with social class, can be seen in this brief anonymous interchange, which serves as *introito* and thematic preface to the unit concerning the boy's education:

"Why do you go to school all the time?"

"My dad says it will prepare us. In case some day a chance comes up, he says maybe they'll give it to us."

"Hell, man. If I were you, I wouldn't even worry. The one on the bottom always stays there. We can't be more screwed over, so I don't even think about it. The guys who really have to play it smart are the ones on top who have something to lose. They could be forced down to where we are. But us, what do we have to lose?"

(p. 26)

Taken together, the formal qualities of the text—a hidden but tight novelistic structure, a narrative point of view which precipitates irony, an emphasis through language on popular culture, and an insistence (probably excessive) on narrative compression—must be seen as fundamental to its total literary nature. Indeed the novel is rich in meaning and values as it goes beyond describing the Chicano experience to interpret it. This becomes especially clear in the final section entitled, **"Under the House,"** in which the protagonist takes shelter in a solitary hiding place in order to think over the events of his year.

This recapitulation of his thoughts, reordering and reviewing events which flow through his mind in a jumbled sequence, is meaningful in three separate but interrelated ways. In the first place, he goes through the process of interrelating discrete experiences, as he himself realizes: "He had discovered something. To discover and rediscover and connect. To relate this thing with that, and that with still another, to put it all together. That's what it was all about" (p. 127). As he realizes this and vows to repeat the effort each year, he consciously assumes the intention to grapple with his own and his people's experience, to review, relate, analyze and understand.

The second aspect of this synthesizing process is the feeling of solidarity it produces: "I'd like to see all those people together. And if my arms were big enough, I could hug them all" (p. 125). Here he identifies with all those whose lives have intersected with his during that *lehrjahr:* the people huddled in the migrants' truck, the praying mother, the children burned while their parents worked in the field, all Chicanos who have shared the details of his experience.

Finally, in his recall of events and conversations, he does more than reconstruct. In many instances there are additional fragments, extending what had earlier been narrated. These fragments indicate that the participants in the various scenes have themselves responded to experience analytically and critically, and that the boy, in singling out for recall precisely these qualities, is assimilating their critical perspective. One example occurs in **"It Was a Silvery Night."** The prefatory paragraph tells of a boy who is refused a haircut repeatedly and finally realizes it is because he is Chicano. The paragraph ends, "Then he understood it all and went home to get his father" (p. 37). The equivalent section at the novel's end adds only a fragment of a sentence, but it extends the scene, adding new meaning as it conveys the father's reactions upon learning of the incident: ". . . those bastards are going to cut your hair or I'll tear them apart" (p. 121). An analogous example can be seen in your section, **"And the Earth Did Not Part,"** in which the boy's mother seems tolerant of misery as she tries to cushion her son's resentment at injustice. The fragment at the end of the novel, however, shows that the boy recalls her in an amplified light, in which she understands the injustice and shares her son's resentment: ". . . I think my old man won't be able to work in the sun any more. The boss didn't say a thing when we told him he had a sunstroke. He just shook his head. All he cared about was that the rains were coming on strong and he was losing his crop. That's the only thing that made him sad" (p. 121). Both these fragments, which show understanding of oppression and the disposition to resist it, cast light on the boy's final synthesizing process. (Other examples could be cited.) The clear indication is that "recollection" has led him to understanding and resistance.

The dominant literary features of the text, taken together, highlight the larger experiential process of the protagonist. This process is one of coming of age, of discovery, of passage to awareness. The reconstitution, at the novel's end, of the year which in the introduction had been called "the lost year," in effect signifies the beginning of recuperation of historical experience.

The boy's discovery of self in the experience and the suffering of others is the antithesis of individualism and the affirmation of the value of collective identity. Thus the novel ends as he waves his hand in symbolic confidence, openness, and friendship to the other being he thinks may be watching him. Whether this being is a part of the boy's self—a sort of *alter ego*—or an imagined representative of the outside world, the boy no longer fears him. This act contrasts dramatically and ironically with his feelings at the beginning of the year. At that point he was alone, uncertain of his words, unsure of what was real in life, and fearful that the cause of all his uncertainty might be lodged in his own imperfect self.

Furthermore, the road to critical awareness is laid out in potential for both protagonist and reader. While the boy's is only a beginning step, the critical reader can see beyond it to the sources, instruments, and techniques of exploitation, beginning with those relations of production which determine the very style and rhythm of Chicano lives. The reader, if not the boy, can see how rural agriculture promotes the use of migratory labor in the first place, and how it squeezes from men, women, and children the last drop of production before casting them back into the ever-moving stream without being obliged to pay wages out of season.

Rivera examines the facilitating institutions of oppression, ranging from the system of usury to the method of labour transport at high cost under dangerous conditions. He details the social and cultural mechanisms which function as ideological supports of the institutions of oppression. One is the racism which in school, barbershop, and shopping center isolates and marks its human target, dividing him or her from others, withholding knowledge and education, keeping a man or woman psychologically on the defensive. Another is that aspect of organized religion which inculcates a sense of guilt, sinfulness, and imperfection, upholding as virtues passivity, self-sacrifice, and respect for the authority wielded by growers, school principals, and the omnipresent state with its power to conscript for whatever military endeavor it chooses.

This is not to imply there are no contradictions or shortcomings in the text. One has to do with the sense of history. The novel indeed does narrate the protagonist's coming to grips, personally and socially, with his own immediate history. And while the fragment concerning Bartolo, a folk poet who names the returned migrants in his songs, suggests a form of oral chronicling, the bulk of the narration tends to present both characters and narrator as lacking awareness of the historical past. In the way people speak and think, there are almost no references, direct or indirect, to earlier experiences. Symbolically, the final collage of the boy's memories contains a brief dialogue, extending an earlier interchange between grandfather and grandson. The old man mournfully states: " . . . since I had that stroke, I can't remember too well what I used to tell people. Then the Revolution came and in the end we lost. Villa came out all right, but I had to come over here, where no one knows the things I did. Sometimes I try to remember, but to tell the truth, I really can't any more. Everything gets blurred" (p. 123).

This particular fragment, coming as it does at the story's end, tends to reinforce the effect mentioned above, suggesting that to a great extent people have been cut off from their past, and in particular have lost touch with the rich and complex historical heritage of the Mexican revolution. On the whole this effect is secondary in the novel, but it does stand in contradiction to the main narrative thrust, the coming of the boy to a stage of maturity, self-confidence, and critical awareness.

A final limitation, also tending to counter the novel's value system as a whole, lies in its treatment of female character. With the noteworthy exception, cited above, of critical awareness on the part of the boy's mother, women tend to be presented either as passive prisoners of traditional culture in its most static form, or as tempters whose charms provoke men to tragedy. Thus one mother prays in total self-sacrifice for her son's survival, another panics at having to confront Anglo hostility while shopping. Likewise, dona Boni in **"His Hand in his Pocket,"** and Juanita in **"The Night the Lights Went Out,"** bring tragedy to their men. Granted that Juanita is constrained by a male value system which places burdensome restrictions on her young temperment, her motives in challenging the code of absolute fidelity are frivolous, related to a need to provoke jealousy in the other girls. As a consequence, the novel lacks the depth which might have been created had there been more sharing by women, even on a secondary level, of the boy's experiential process.

Two observations concerning Rivera's response to literary traditions may serve to extend the earlier discussion on influences. A thematic cluster found in Borges posits the inseparability of the subjective from the objective, the difficulty of finding truth in empirical data when the causal explanation is located in the mind of the investigator, and the vulnerability of logic and reason to the more profound categories of the subconscious and the instinctive. This position also is the point of departure of Rivera's novel. The boy, like a character in Borges, is confronted by the mystery of self-consciousness, the origin of the thought process, and the fallibility of memory. The answers, it seems to him, are locked up in his own being, in his own incapacity to separate dream from reason and to order the past. But the process of the novel, which is the narration of experienced Chicano reality and the struggle to recover fragmented time, is Rivera's solution of the perplexities and the labyrinthine dilemma posed by Borges.

Similarly there is an assimilation from Juan Rulfo of literary qualities and techniques, as noticed earlier. But Rivera's novel, in its critical confrontation with social reality, and in its protagonist's passage to a new stage of consciousness, departs from the cosmic pessimism and despair which saturate Rulfo's narratives. Without question, Rivera's text is richer for its connections with literary traditions. Equally without question, it is a novel in which the author's sensitivity to popular culture, social issues, and historical reality enable him to avoid both imitation and derivativeness.

Clearly, then, *. . . y no se lo tragó la tierra* is a text which challenges the critical reader to analyze its formal characteristics and thus to decipher the cultural and historical meanings which lie beneath its surface. The work stands as a major contribution to Chicano narrative, but also must be seen simultaneously as part of North American literature and most certainly as a response to Latin American techniques and themes. Only a multi-leveled and totalizing critical approach, capable of addressing itself to both text and context, to form, meaning and values, without glossing over the considerable shortcomings of the novel, both formal and ideological, can do it the critical justice it deserves.

NOTES

[1] "Critical Approaches to Chicano Literature," pp. 31-40.

[2] References throughout the article are to the second edition (Berkeley: Editorial Justa, 1976). Page numbers will appear in the text. Translations are my own.

[3] An exception is Charles Tatum, who begins such an analysis in "Contemporary Chicano Prose Fiction: Its Ties to Mexican Literature," *Books Abroad,* 49, no. 3 (Summer, 1975), 432-38.

[4] This story is part of the collection *El llano en llamas* (Mexico City: FCE, 1953).

[5] Interesting observations on structural patterns are offered by Ralph Grajeda, "Tomás Rivera's Appropriation of the Chicano Past" which appears in this volume, and by Francisco Lomeli and Donald Urioste, in their *Chicano Perspectives in Literature* (Albuquerque: Pajarito Publications, 1976), pp. 46-47. The latter critics support the argument that the text is indeed a novel.

[6] The case for the central thematic thread being that of personality formation, although not in specifically psychological terms, is argued by Frank Pino, Jr., in "The 'Outsider' and 'El Otro' in Tomás Rivera's *. . . y no se lé tragó la tierra,*" *Books Abroad,* 49, no. 3 (Summer, 1975), 453-58.

[7] *El laberinto de la soledad,* 3rd ed. (Mexico City: FCE, 1972), pp. 175-91.

[8] "Otherness in Chicano Literature." Paper presented at IV International Congress of Mexican Studies, Santa Monica, California, 1973.

[9] "Tomás Rivera's Appropriation of the Chicano Past."

[10] After the present study was completed, the article by Juan Gómez Quiñones, "On Culture," was published in *Revista Chicano-Riqueña,* V, no. 2 (*primavera* (Spring), 1977), 29-47. It contains a lucid, developed analysis of questions such as theory of culture, culture and class, culture and domination, and culture and race. I believe its positions to be consistent with those expressed here. A slightly condensed version of this article, entitled, "Toward a Concept of Culture", appears in this volume.

[11] An insightful analysis of the boy's critical encounters with religious doctrine or belief is offered by Juan Rodríguez, "Acercamiento a cuatro relatos de *. . . y no se lo tragó la tierra,*" *Mester,* 5, no. 1 (November, 1974), 16-24.

FURTHER READING

Cárdenas de Dwyer, Carlota. "Cultural Regionalism and Chicano Literature." *Western American Literature,* Vol. XV, No. 3 (Fall 1980): 187-94.
> Discusses how the Chicano way of life has been incorporated into the art of its people.

Fernández, Salvador C. A review of *The Complete Works. Hispania,* Vol. 76, No. 4 (December 1993): 741.
> Positive review with brief descriptions of contents.

Fredericksen, Brooke. "Cuando lleguemos/When We Arrive: The Paradox of Migration in '. . . y no se lo tragó la tierra'." *The Bilingual Review/La revista bilingüe,* Vol. XIX, No. 2 (May-August 1994): 142-50.
> Examines the issues of migrancy in Rivera's novel.

Pino, Frank, Jr. "The Outsider and `El otro' in Tomás Rivera's '. . . *y no se lo trago la tierra*'." *Books Abroad,* Vol. 49, No. 3 (Summer 1975): 453-58.

   Applies the Chicano image of the outsider in interpreting Rivera's work.

Ramírez, Arturo. A review of *This Migrant Earth,* Rolando Hinojosa, trans. *Hispania,* Vol. 72, No. 1 (March 1989): 166-67.

   Discusses Hinojosa's treatment of Rivera's writing.

Rivera, Tomás. "Chicano Literature: Fiesta of the Living." *The Identification and Analysis of Chicano Literature,* Francisco Jiménez, ed., pp. 19-36. New York: Bilingual Press, 1979.

   Discusses the writing process as it relates to the development of Chicano literature.

Rodríguez, Alfonso. "Time as a Structural Device in Tomás Rivera's *. . . y no se lo trago la tierra.*" *Contemporary Chicano Fiction, A Critical Survey,* Vernon E. Lattin, ed., pp. 126-30. Binghamton, New York: Bilingual Press/Editorial Bilingüe, 1986.

   Supports idea of time as both theme and structural device in *. . . y no se lo trago la tierra.*

Rodríguez, Joe. "The Chicano Novel and the North American Narrative of Survival." *Denver Quarterly,* Vol. 16, No. 3 (Fall 1981): 64-70.

   Demonstrates how ethnic identity can be used to interpret Chicano writing.

Saldívar, José David. "Chicano Border Narratives as Cultural Critique." *Criticism in the Borderlands, Studies in Chicano Literature, Culture, and Ideology,* Hector Calderon and José David Saldívar, eds., pp. 167-80. Durham, North Carolina: Duke University Press, 1991.

   Examines political, ideological, and cultural rhetoric in Chicano border literature.

Testa, Daniel P. "Narrative Technique and Human Experience in Tomás Rivera." *Modern Chicano Writers, A Collection of Critical Essays,* Joseph Sommers and Tomás Ybarra-Frausto, eds., pp. 86-93. Englewood Cliffs, N.J.: Prentice-Hall, Inc., 1979.

   Demonstrates how Rivera's narrative style permits blending of internal and external elements in his stories.

Vallejos, Tomás. "The Beetfield as Battlefield: Ritual Process and Realization in Tomas Rivera's 'Las salamandras'." *The Americas Review,* Vol. 17, No. 2 (Summer 1989): 100-09.

   Discusses symbolism, ritual process, and class struggle in the short story.

José Enrique Rodó
1871-1917

Uruguayan essayist and philosopher.

INTRODUCTION

With the publication in 1900 of José Enrique Rodó's *Ariel*, the contemporary Latin American essay was born. In that first year of the new century, *Ariel* helped to foster and popularize a new Latin American identity grounded in a more indigenous, "American" democratic element, combined with the intellectualism that the world of letters was accustomed to. His work is variously characterized as a transformation of Rubén Darío's version of Shakespeare's play, as a tool for *Modernismo*, and as an attempt to use the bourgeois culture to elevate more specific socio-political agendas in the modernization of Latin America. Rodó's tone was either criticized as pompous and bombastic, or praised as lofty and eloquent. The *Motivos de Proteo* (1909), Rodó's other major work, reaffirms his profound Hellenic spiritualism and somewhat naïve certainty that social transformation is the result of human will. Yet this work descends, at least partially, from its mountaintop of oratory to produce a more down to earth, tighter, and more reflexive prose style. These two works alone established Rodó as the most eclectic of the three Latin American literary leaders of *modernista* (Rodó, José Marti, and Rubén Darío), eclectic because he attempted to synthesize the best of various traditions: the creative leisure of ancient Greece, the positivist goal of perfectibility, the symbolist cult of beauty, etc. But what makes Rodó relevant even today is less the eclecticism of his ideas than his early understanding that democracy is strengthened by ethnic diversity. Latin America, Rodó hoped, would become home to that new democratic configuration.

Born in Montevideo, Uruguay on July 15, 1871, Rodó was the youngest of seven children. His father was a prosperous Spanish businessman and his mother, the daughter of an upper-class Uruguayan family. By 1883 José's father, suffering business losses, transferred his son from a prestigious private school to a tuition-free public school where José continued to study history and literature. In 1885 the father died, forcing his fourteen-year old son to take a job as a part-time clerk. In 1895 Rodó published his first poem and first book review in the periodical *Montevideo noticioso*. With three others, he founded the journal *Revista nacional de literatura y ciencias naturales* in which appeared his first piece garnering critical attention, the essay "El que vendrá" (1897; "Our Redeemer"). In this work, Rodó predicts the advent of a cultural prophet: "We wait, but without knowing for whom. A voice calls from a dark and distant mansion. We too have raised in our

hearts a temple to the unknown god." The inflated oratorial rhetoric evident in this early essay would become a hallmark of Rodó throughout most of his career. Another essay, "La novela nueva" ("The New Novel"), denounced an essay by fellow Uruguayan Carlos Reyles for his rebuke of the contemporary Spanish novel. These two early essays would made up the entirety of the first *opúsculo* of Rodó's three-part *La vida nueva*. The second *opúsculo, Rubén Darío* (1899), was eponymously named for Rodó's contemporary and one of Latin America's most acclaimed writers. Rodó's most famous and influential work, *Ariel*, became the third *opúsculo*, named in honor of the sprite in Shakespeare's *The Tempest*. In 1894 Rodó quit school before graduation but through his publications he was able to secure a job as an adjunct professor in literature at the University of Montevideo in 1898, a position he held three years. During this time he developed the ideas for his two best-known works, *Ariel* and *Motivos de Proteo*. Rodó joined the liberal Colorado Party in 1901 and when he was elected to the House of Representatives the following year, he resigned from the university. Rodríguez Monegal writes that Rodó "scrupulously avoided indulging in petty politics; he always strove to present a broad, strictly legalistic view of national life, placing the interests of State above those of his own party; he gave special support to cultural projects." Though elected for another three year term, Rodó resigned from the House in 1905. Between 1904 and 1907, Rodó would write all 158 chapters of *Motivos de Proteo*. In 1907, he began writing for Latin America's most prestigious newspaper, *La Nacíon*, and the pieces he produced were collected, revised, and combined with other miscellaneous pieces into *El mirador de Próspero* (1913; Prospero's Balcony). In this work, Rodó showed his perspicacity as a literary critic. Finally, in 1916, Rodó took his much-awaited trip to Europe, a trip he would not be able to finish. He did, however, reach his cultural destination, Italy. There he became ill, and in 1917, died in Palermo of abdominal typhus and nephritis.

In *Ariel*, a professor, nicknamed Prospero, calls his students to his study, seeking to plant in them the seeds of wisdom at the close of the school year. Ariel, of whom he has a large statue in his office, becomes the figurehead of the professor's moving and somewhat grandiloquent speech, the pivot of the story. In his speech, Prospero implores his students to follow the example of Ariel as sprite and muse, and avoid its opposite, savage brutality. Some critics have implied a political overtone to *Ariel*, finding the brutality Rodó seeks to avoid is capitalized by the U.S. and its pervasive materialism, something which Rodó considers an impediment to the aspirations of true democracy. The professor, in one of his more inspiring moments, exhorts his students "to be militant in preventing your spirit from being mutilated by the tyranny of a single, or a self-interested, objective. Never devote more than a part of yourselves to utility, or to passion. . . . Do not use the excuse of commitment to work or responsibilities to justify the enslavement of your spirit." For Rodó, Latin America must become ruled by aristocratic democrats elected by an educated populace on the basis of moral and spiritual integrity. Writer Carlos Fuentes criticized *Ariel* for failing to be as diverse as it aimed to be, stating that Rodó simply adopted a character and situation that fit Rodó's preexisting prose style, a style Fuentes has called "supremely irritating" in its grandiloquence and distracting from its point. Few readers align themselves with critic Havelock Ellis who in 1970 found *Ariel* possessing "a style which, with its peculiar personal impress of combined gravity and grace, rendered him . . . the greatest contemporary master of the Castilian tongue." Rodó's next major work, *Motivos de Proteo*, is concerned with change and evolution after the example of Proteus, the god of futurity who could assume unimaginable shapes to avoid capture, but once seized would tell the truth in prophesy. *Motivos de Proteo* is a book of wisdom made up of 158 short chapters. Beginning with the statement that "Life is constant renewal," Rodó explores the tools of self-transformation, through unconscious forces, vocation, and travelling, love, hope, and willpower. His message is not merely to be ready and accepting of change but to be its agent in order for humanity to remake itself in the image of Proteus: a creature of continual progress.

Though Rodó has been justifiably criticized for his sometimes inflated prose and urban elitism, Rodó's arguments have not been substantially engaged and met at the level of his own critique and aspirations. There is no compelling reason why Rodó's desire for esthetic and moral education, espoused in his essays and books, is not usable to improve life universally, however his most notable works remain mostly unrecognized outside of Latin America. As stated by critic C. C. Bacheller, "his purpose and fulfillment in stimulating and directing lie in bringing to our attention and developing the vast potential which exists in each one of us." Perhaps today his influence will render itself more accessible to both his readers and fellow writers.

PRINCIPAL WORKS

"El que vendrá" (essay) 1897
"La novela nueva" (essay) 1897
Rubén Darío (biography) 1899
Ariel (novel) 1900
Liberalismo y jacobinismo (letters) 1906
Motivos de Proteo [*The Motives of Proteus*] (testimony) 1909
El mirador de Próspero (essays) 1913
Obras completas, 7 vols. (collected works) 1917–1927
Ultimos motivos de Proteo (testimony) 1932

CRITICISM

C. C. Bacheller   (essay date 1963)

SOURCE: "An Introduction for Studies on Rodó," in *Hispania,* Vol. XLVI, 1963, pp. 764-69.

[*In the following essay, Bacheller offers an impersonal yet thorough critique of Rodó's life and writing career.*]

In an atmosphere of pessimism and negativism in the western world at the end of the last century, there appeared in Uruguay a spokesman for new optimism and affirmation, José Enrique Rodó. Critic, essayist, thinker, and humanist, and the embodiment of his own highest ideals, he manifested an unusual faith in the potential within the inherent, spiritual nature of man.

He made his first impression on Hispanic American intellectuals in 1896 with such penetrating articles as **"El que vendrá"** and **"La novela nueva,"** which heralded the evolution of thinking of the new generation of men whom he was to call "new idealists." In the former work he describes the vacuum in which his generation found itself with the fall of Positivism as a scientific explanation of the universe and with Naturalism's inadequate conception of human existence, a vacuum filled with doubt, hope for guidance providing the only weapon for escape. In **"La novela nueva"** he speaks of new directions which seek to sound the realities of life and the profundity of consciousness.

These represented only two of several articles contributed by Rodó and his three fellow founding editors to the *Revista Nacional de Literatura y Ciencias Sociales*, evolutionary in bringing together forerunners and moderns. Although the magazine naturally reflected the positivistic background of its young editors, such anti-positivist names as Verlaine, Mallarmé, Ibsen, Nietzsche, Tolstoy, and D'Annunzio were appreciatively cited.

"El que vendrá" and **"La novela nueva"** were republished the next year as the first of three volumes under the auspicious and indicative title *La vida nueva*. The second of the series two years later, 1899, contained a masterful critique of Rubén Darío's *Prosas profanas* and provided an insight into Rodó's thinking at that moment. He declares himself a part of the reaction in thought at the end of the century which, while departing from literary Naturalism and philosophic Positivism, led, without detracting from what these had of worth, to higher conceptions. He sees Darío's art as one example of contemporary anarchical idealism.

Appropriately the third, *Ariel*, connoting anticipation, appeared in 1900, precisely at the turn of the century. It predicted a renaissance in thinking for Spanish Americans individually and collectively and, although diversely interpreted by the populace, it, in itself, accomplished that renaissance. While indirectly bringing in Europe and the United States, Rodó, through his venerable *raisonneur* Próspero, who was bidding farewell to his students, places his own hopes ostensibly in Spanish American youth, where, in turn, he envisions hope for the future. He exhorts these youths to recall the traditional idealism of their culture, to think optimistically and freely and in terms of classic values, and to avoid seduction by the material progress of the positivistic-thinking example to the north.

His active spiritual tolerance, plus his concern for *lo cotidiano,* next called him to write a series of articles opposing a move to abolish crucifixes in the hospitals. His reasons were collected in 1906 under the title *Liberalismo y jacobinismo*. While demonstrating a superior capacity for debate, he pleads for a *human* approach to reality and illustrates the complexness of individual and social sentiments, appreciation of which would always be the basis of education or reform.

Between 1904 and 1909 he created, in all that word implies, his most thoughtful and mature work, *Motivos de Proteo*, a book, like life and ideas, in perpetual evolution. If *Ariel* were a conch on the beach, then *Motivos de Proteo* would be what the shell sings when put to the ear. Here Rodó, the humanist, attempts to fathom nature's most nearly perfect work, man, who is constantly reforming himself and being reformed in time. The basis for study is the individual's calling or vocation, and the point of departure is the importance of exploring one's inner self, this last in order to conquer one's self and to form and perfect the personality.

Three citations from Carlos Real de Azúa's special study of the work merit inclusion here:

> Sobre la ondulosa vida psicológica de la *movilidad, la multiplicidad,* la *vocación* y la *voluntad* tres operaciones (cada vez más ceñidas, cada vez más exigentes), *renovación, reforma, conversión.*
>
>   . . . . .
>
> La tónica esencial es (seguramente) la del *humanismo* . . . apoyado en una profunda convicción, en una fe casi religiosa en la grandeza, la profundidad, la diversidad del hombre. . . .
>
> La nota esencial de este humanismo rodoiano es, sin duda, el *inmanentismo.*
>
>   . . . . .
>
> Clásica majestad y levedad moderna lo filian—dualísticamente—en dos líneas bien visibles: el academismo, el modernismo.[1]

Much of Rodó's own personality can be seen through the diverse works contained in *Mirador de Próspero* (1913), a collection of the products of about two decades of literary activity, which constitutes something like a diary of his spirit. Here are purely literary essays, historical essays, social, moral, and critical essays, as well as some on purely Spanish American themes. Particularly outstand-

ing then for its contribution to Spanish American criticism was an essay of literary history, **"Juan María Gutiérrez y su época."**

Some of Rodó's best in style comes forth as he finds himself in 1916 on his cherished trip to Europe as a traveling correspondent for *Caras y Caretas*. As would be expected, his insight is much deeper than that commonly found in travel literature. His articles, including such titles as **"Una entrevista con el Presidente de Portugal"** and **"Una impresión de Roma,"** were posthumously collected in 1918 under the title *Camino de Paros*.

Following the author's death in 1917 members of his family and a friend, Dardo Regules, attempted to organize the manuscripts left in his library. These were published in 1932 under the title *Últimos motivos de Proteo*. Emir Rodríguez Monegal, who has had available to him these manuscripts, Rodó's correspondence, and other miscellanea in the Archivo de Rodó, shows errors of classification and placement in the family's edition. From the correspondence and from a similarity of thought, he shows that Rodó probably originally intended some of this work to be included in the earlier *Motivos de Proteo*. Study of manuscripts which were included in the *Últimos motivos de Proteo* is still under way, and Rodríguez Monegal concludes that no definitive statement of Rodó's intentions is possible now.[2]

Besides these principal works, letters, prologues, and miscellanea, there exist diverse articles from such periodicals as *El Telégrafo, Diario del Plata,* and *La Nación;* discourses in parliament; speeches such as those before the Club Libertad, the Club Vida Nueva, and the Círculo de la Prensa; and such major addresses as the one at the centennial of Chilean independence, in which he advocates harmony among nations of his continent based on common inheritance and environment.

From these and from comments of those who knew him, Rodó, the man, emerges, a very human personality and a humanist, an intellectual aristocrat with a consistently elevated appreciation of this life. He has been called critic, *maestro,* thinker, philosopher, and poet. To a degree he was the incarnation of all of these. To separate him into such categories is to dismember him. Rodó himself would be the last to take an abstract and divine creation such as a personality and reduce it to ordinary terms. He would attempt to fathom and re-create it in its essence, perhaps, again, abstractly and divinely. Those who would attempt to delimit the nature and morality of an individual are missing one of Rodó's own main points: that a man, a critic, an artist are entities of diverse facets or vocations. To operate on man without proper awareness and concern for the body's fullness and complexities is to kill him.

As a poet, in the strict sense of the word, Rodó wrote only a few pieces which have been published. (Others exist in his private papers.) In the larger sense, his was certainly a poetic spirit. His practices and his theories go to the depths of a lyric poet with language, images, metaphors, and parables as exterior manifestations. As a worthy critic of poetry, of necessity he shared the feelings, stresses, and joys of his subject.

If mere quantity of production were not enough to make him a critic, then quality would. He is capable of panoramas such as **"Juan María Gutiérrez y su época,"** of particularizations such as **"Los 'Poemas cortos' de Núñez de Arce,"** and of mixing the two, as in *Rubén Darío.* He embodies his own prescription for a critic, containing such ingredients as tolerance, fullness of background, and subjective and objective balance. He recognizes the historic and aesthetic value of criticism and his own is one of the early steps in his land in carrying forward and molding it. Perhaps one of the best ways to exemplify his type of criticism would be to compare him with Francesco De Sanctis, using Croce's praise as a base:

> Gustave Flaubert wrote to George Sand: 'In your last letter you speak of criticism, and say you expect it soon to disappear. I think, on the contrary, that it is just appearing over the horizon. Criticism to-day is the exact opposite of what it was, but that is all. In the days of Laharpe the critic was a grammarian; to-day he is a historian like Sainte-Beuve and Taine. When will he be an artist, a mere artist, but a real artist? Do you know a critic who interests himself whole-heartedly in the work itself? They analyse with the greatest delicacy the historical surroundings of the work and the causes which produced it; but the underlying poetry and its causes? the composition? the style? the author's own point of view? Never. Such a critic must have great imagination and a great goodness of heart; I mean an ever-ready faculty of enthusiasm; and then, taste; but this last is so rare, even among the best, that it is never mentioned nowadays.' Flaubert's ideal has been worthily reached by one critic only (that is to say, amongst critics who have given themselves to the interpretation of great writers and entire periods of literature) and that one is De Sanctis.[3]

Rodó was that type of critic. Therefore, other evaluations become secondary. It has been stated that his contribution to literary criticism was not sufficiently original and important to continue calling him the indisputable critic of America[4] and, in the opinion of some, perhaps it was not. In the opinion of others, however, someone else would have to be found to supersede him. It would have to be proven that his work was not original or important and that it has not been used as a basis by later critics; also whether, finally and after all, the limited title of "critic of America" is even sufficient.

As a philosopher, if that title connotes the delineation of a fixed system, he cannot be given it. His friend Victor Pérez Petit advises against thinking of Rodó as such.[5] Alfredo Colmo attacks his philosophic thought as "truisms."[6] On the other hand, Rodó's name has been thought of in relationship with Schopenhauer, Nietzsche, Boutroux, and Bergson.[7] Certainly he touches on philosophic matters and possesses philosophic insight.[8] Our appreciation of Rodó as a philosopher endorses the synthesis most properly stated by Rodríguez Monegal: "Rodó no podía pensar conrígida continuidad filosófica; su pensamiento desconfiaba íntimamente de la sistematización que canaliza el fluir natural de la vida; aunque intelectual, no era meramente razonador y se apoyaba en un sentido intuitivo de la vida como realidad superior."[9]

As for his thought in general, those who delight in the impossibility of finding something new under the sun have classified Rodó as not being original. Again, if "originality" limits itself to something new in the absolute, then Rodó was probably not original. Nor does he pretend to be. He lived a life of observation, meditation, self-education, and broad reading, a background which he recommends for mankind in general, and artists in particular. Important to him, as to the men of the Renaissance, whom he admired, was what newness could be given to assimilated knowledge, a spontaneous but disciplined type of originality. It is questionable whether where he obtained his knowledge is more important than what he chose for consideration and the use he made of it. Much of what he says is at least known to mankind in general. His purpose and fulfillment in stimulating and directing lie in bringing to our attention and developing the vast potential which exists in each one of us. To do this he may rely on someone else for the initial thought but the method is original for him as it must be for every mind except that of a plagiarist. (One feels that the opinion of Alberto Zum Felde is a bit extreme: Rodó was not a thinker but a literary glosser.)[10] Gonzalo Zaldumbide most aptly states that what Rodó did was "actualizar lo eterno, desentrañar de lo cotidiano la originalidad constante, que se renueva en el seno de la multitud.... Si sus ideas no son nuevas, el sentimiento que las templa, la convicción que las reanima, la forma en que se encarnan bajo su pluma le son peculiares e inalienables."[11] Another accurate evaluation comes from Pedro Henríquez Ureña:

> Ha hecho prorrumpir en su elogio las voces del solar clásico de España, con hipérboles no tributadas á ningún otro pensador americano. Como pensador, posee, si no la originalidad que cree un sistema filosófico, sí la del eticista; en vez de dejarse arrastrar por la corriente que lleva á la ciencia fácil, á hacer libros con libros ajenos, vuelve á la clásica tradición que enseña á buscar en la propia experiencia, íntima y social, las verdades morales que deben darse al mundo como fruto acendrado de la personalidad, como aportación real al tesoro de la sabiduría humana. Es, en suma, un maestro, con la aureola de *misticismo laico* y el ambiente de silenciosa quietud que corresponde á los pensadores de su estirpe.[12]

Since the late 1940's and particularly in the late 1950's the "real" Rodó has been emerging in criticism, following periods of exalted praise and exaggerated adverse criticism. His early successes had been immediate. The literati observed a new brilliance in his scholarly articles in the *Revista Nacional. . . .* and the general public, exceedingly enthusiastic about the message it interpreted in *Ariel,* eagerly awaited his next book. Already in 1910 Pedro Henríquez Ureña classified him as perhaps the first in Spanish American culture to influence with only the written word.[13] *Ariel* underwent numerous reprintings, both in Spanish America and in Spain where its author was praised by Leopoldo Alas, Salvador Rueda, and Unamuno.

The Spanish Americans who grew up in close association with the teachings of Rodó, however, became his severest critics in their maturity. Representing this post World War I group were Zaldumbide, who began an attack the year after Rodó's death, Zum Felde, Luis Alberto Sánchez, Colmo, Alberto Lasplaces, and Ventura García Calderón. Their reflections on his work convinced them that his teachings were not adequate for the rapid social progress they desired, and they attacked him for lacking the very things he extolled—action, for example. They warned that actually Rodó's thoughts were not close to life or to the Spanish American need, and that following him would sterilize action in youths and make them discreet conservatives. They wanted precise rules of conduct, whereas Rodó put forth general ones, and they sought outside direction in renovation, whereas he felt each man should map his own course. They found his suggestions enigmatic, "too literary," and decorative but not profound. Worst, from Rodó's point of view, they referred to him as dilettante.

José P. Massera, Uruguayan philosopher and a contemporary of Rodó's recognized the limitations of such criticism, and, as early as 1920, wrote of Rodó's critics,

> Todas las críticas que se le han dirigido, y las que concebimos por ahora, como posibles, han partido de abajo: de una escuela, de un sistema, de un sectarismo, de algo que puede ser noble y sincero, pero que, por su naturaleza misma, obra dentro de los siempre estrechos límites de un aspecto de las cosas, de una faz de lo real, y no tiene acabada conciencia de su imperfección, por ser una paralización del tiempo y una limitación que se pretende definitiva de lo indefinido.[14]

The ultimate value of the exaggerated adverse criticism was that it brought Rodó down from the heights of being adulated into a light where he has been considered more impartially in Spanish America since World War II. Articles by Roberto Ibáñez showing a true understanding of Rodó appeared in the 1940's, but vastly more far-reaching was his organization of the Archivo, which brought into focus the suffering and other aspects of the life of Rodó not pronounced in the latter's published works. Next, Rodó was situated in the history of his nation's thought by Arturo Ardao, particularly in a history of Uruguayan philosophy of the second half of the nineteenth century, published in 1950, and another on the twentieth century, 1956. Finally, in 1957 there appeared studies by two of the finest, sincerest, and most impartial scholars of Rodó, Rodríguez Monegal and Real de Azúa, both of whom had published works on him previously. In that year, Real de Azúa, who pays tribute to earlier studies by Luis Gil Salguero and José Gaos, brought forth a prologue to an edition of *Motivos de Proteo* in which he analyzes originally and learnedly not only the book itself but also the import of the various circumstances surrounding it. Rod-ríguez Monegal's contribution was the first *scholarly* edition of Rodó's complete works and to it he added—all equally competent—an introduction, notes, and prologues to the diverse offerings included. Both Rodríguez Monegal and Real de Azúa are more concerned with authoritatively analyzing Rodó and his works than in judging him, but the judgments they do make merit citation here at some length. Real de Azúa explains:

> Rodó ganó su fama con opiniones, con ideas vertidas en ensayos, en artículos, en manifiestos y en su discurso ariélico, sobre todo. Ganó su fama con opiniones vertidas en una forma hermosa, consciente y deliberadamente hermosa, en una prosa que buscaba la armonía expresiva, el movimiento y el número, el relieve de la imagen, de la parábola, de la comparación. Me parece que refleja Rodó un momento muy especial de la evolución literaria, . . . un momento en que las técnicas de la poesía y la prosa poemática (ya invadida por la primera) irrumpen en todos los géneros literarios, en todos los modos de la expresión de las ideas.
>
> No creo que hoy un escritor pudiera llegar a la altura de Rodó con una obra de su tipo . . . porque esa obra no responde a una necesidad, a una demanda profunda.[15]

Rodríguez Monegal thinks **Rubén Darío** and **Ariel** "sirvieron para fijar el nombre de Rodó . . . como el del primer crítico literario del habla y uno de sus más perfectos ensayistas."[16] His respectful, well-founded opinion of Rodó is:

> Visto en su totalidad, el balance de su obra y de su acción le sigue siendo favorable. . . . Lo que da estatura a Rodó y lo levanta sobre sus coetáneos de habla hispánica y confiere inigualada perdurabilidad a su obra es esa perspectiva que se alcanza desde su obra. Escribiendo en un reducido puerto del mundo occidental, en una ciudad que tenía poco más de un siglo, en la nación más pequeña de la América del Sur, ensangrentada aún por guerras civiles, Rodó alzó su vista por encima de los accidentes y proyectó su palabra sobre todo el mundo hispánico. Lo que pensó y dijo estaba pensado y dicho a esa escala. Esa fué (es) su hazaña.[17]

Four decades after the death of Rodó it becomes possible to consider him impersonally and, employing a critical attitude which he helped further, to weigh what he did represent, rather than what he did not. In a geographical region and in an intellectual and artistic atmosphere ripe for new thought at the turn of the century, his messages became prophecies to be approached with almost divine respect. When the men nurtured in his thoughts began to consider them as doctrine, however, they reacted strongly against him, largely from the point of view of personal prejudices. Nowadays, thanks to recent scholarly impartial studies, to the Archivo de Rodó which reveals his private life, and to a new tolerance in criticism, one considers him dispassionately, yet appreciatively.

NOTES

[1] Carlos Real de Azúa, "Prólogo," *Motivos de Proteo* de José Enrique Rodó (Montevideo: Ministerio de Instrucción Públic y Previsión Social, 1957), Vol. 1, pp. xl, xli, cxv.

2 Emir Rodríguez Monegal (ed.), *José Enrique Rodó: Obras completas* (Madrid: Aguilar, 1957), pp. 867-873.

3 Benedetto Croce, *Aesthetic,* trans. Douglas Ainslie (New York: Noonday, 1956), p. 368.

4 See William J. Berrien, "Rodó, biografía y estudio crítico" (unpublished Ph.D. dissertation, University of California, 1937), pp. 219-220.

5 Victor Pérez Petit, *Rodó, su vida, su obra,* 2d ed. rev. (Montevideo: Claudio García y Cía., 1937), p. 288.

6 Alfredo Colmo, "La filosofía de Rodó," *Nosotros,* XXVI (May, 1917), 173-184.

7 By Leopoldo Zea. See Arturo Ardao, *Espiritualismo y positivismo en el Uruguay y filosofías universitarias de la segunda mitad del siglo XIX* (México: Fondo de Cultura Económica, 1950) p. 288.

8 Cf. Monelisa Lina Pérez-Marchand, "José Enrique Rodó, escritor de signo filosófico," *Asomante,* XIII (Oct.-Dec., 1957), 51-67.

9 Rodríguez Monegal, *José Enrique Rodó: Obras completas,* p. 109.

10 Alberto Zum Felde, "José Enrique Rodó," *Crítica de la literatura uruguaya* (Montevideo: Maximino García, 1921), p. 154.

11 Gonzalo Zaldumbide, *José Enrique Rodó, su personalidad y su obra* (Montevideo: Biblioteca Rodó, 1944) pp. 35 and 44.

12 Pedro Henríquez Ureña, "La obra de José Enrique Rodó," *Conferencia del Ateneo de la Juventud* (México: Lacaud, 1910), p. 83.

13 Ibid., p. 65.

14 José P. Massera, *Estudios filosóficos* (Montevideo: Artigas, 1954) p. 53.

15 Real de Azúa, "Rodó y su pensamiento," *Marcha,* May 7, 1954, p. 15.

16 Rodríguez Monegal, "El caso ejemplar de Rodó," *Marcha,* May 6, 1955, p. 21.

17 Rodríguez Monegal, *José Enrique Rodó: Obras completas,* p. 136. To that quoted from Real de Azúa and Rodríguez Monegal might be added an opinion by Ermilo Abreu Gómez which appeared in 1950.

"José Enrique Rodó es uno de los escritores de mayor capacidad polifacética que ha producido la América moderna. Pero esta diversidad que, en algunos, podría revelar, precisamente, falta de hondura en el pensamiento, un como querer deslizarse sobre los temas, rozándolos con la palabra y el sentir, en Rodó es la expresión más firme, más arraigada, de su preocupación espiritual. Las diversas materias de que trata son—bien miradas—tan sólo aspectos externos, contingentes, de la substancia humana que anhela aprisionar con claridad y sentido." ("Dos notas críticas inéditas: José Enrique Rodó y Andrés Bello," *Armas y Letras* [Nuevo León] VII, no. 3 [March, 1950], 1.)

Arthur P. Whitaker   (essay date 1977)

SOURCE: "*Ariel* on Caliban in Both Americas," in *Homage to Irving A. Leonard: Essays on Hispanic Art, History, and Literature,* edited by Raquel Chang-Rodríguez and Donald A. Yates, Michigan State University, 1977, pp. 161-70.

[*In the following essay, Whitaker studies the influence of Rodó's most famous work,* Ariel, *and examines the intention of the author's political stance toward the United States as well as Latin America.*]

Rodó specialists generally agree that *Ariel* is its distinguished Uruguayan author's best-known book, and it seems clear that the best-known portion of *Ariel*, at least in the United States, is Part 5, which portrays the United States—by implication, though not by name—as Caliban. Yet writers in Latin America as well as the United States have often misunderstood or misrepresented this part of Rodó's classic. The following passage in Hubert Herring's excellent and widely-read *A History of Latin America* illustrates the point admirably:

> [By 1953] Uruguayans were fast forgetting the harsh appraisal of the United States in which they had been tutored by their greatest writer, José Enrique Rodó. In 1900 that brilliant essayist wrote *Ariel*, which has been sacred writ for generations of youth in Uruguay (and elsewhere in Latin America), and which relegated the North Americans to the unflattering role of Caliban—symbol of base materialism—in contrast to Latin America's Ariel—symbol of spirituality. Rodó assailed the United States for its efforts to win a "moral conquest" of the Americas. But by 1954 it became clear that as between the United States and Perón's Argentina, it was safer to trust the northern power[1].

An example of Herring's influence was provided in 1971 by a promising young historiam of the foreign relations of the United States, David Green, who enlivened his book on the Good Neighbor policy, *The Containment of Latin America* (Chicago, 1971, p. 6), with the aid of the above passage. The story lost nothing in the retelling, for *Ariel* now won "instant acclaim" by portraying the malevolent United States as "a misbegotten Caliban bent upon the spiritual and cultural destruction of Latin America", and, as in Herring, remained "sacred writ for generations of [Latin American] youth".

Two propositions stand out in both of the foregoing passages: one, that Rodó pinned the Caliban syndrome on the United States alone; the other that *Ariel* remained the Bible of Latin American youth "for generations". The present article undertakes to show that in fact Rodó, with good reason, aimed his fire at Calibanism not only in the United States, but also among Latin Americans; that he represented its "conquest" of them as proceeding without effort on the part of the United States; and that, far from remaining holy writ for generations of Latin Americans of any age group, *Ariel* came under increasingly heavy counter fire from Rodó's fellow Latin Americans when hardly a single generation had passed since its publication, and less than a decade and a half since his early death. Their attacks still continue; they have spread to other works of his, but *Ariel* remains the chief target. Presumably unaware of these developments, Secretary of State Henry Kissinger in 1974 climaxed a notable address to a meeting of the Organization of American States by quoting with approval a passage from *Ariel* which, with a gloss, will conclude the present article.

For the benefit of any reader who may be distressed by my taking a political approach to this most famous work of a great humanist, it should be pointed out that Arturo Ardao, the leading intellectual historian of Uruguay, lays similar emphasis on politics in his account of Rodó's passion for Americanism in the exclusively Latin American sense. His *Rodó. Su americanismo* (Montevideo, 1970) contains selections from the essayist's writings on the subject, arranged under four headings. The first three of these are literary, cultural, and political, and in the introduction Ardao writes (p. 30): "If in the work of Rodó literary Americanism leads naturally to cultural Americanism, the latter in turn leads no less naturally to political Americanism". He underlines this point by placing his selections from **Ariel** (Parts 1, 5, and 6) under the cultural heading and bringing out clearly the ultimately political purpose of the essay.

A knowledge of the Uruguayan political, economic, social, and cultural background of **Ariel** in the generation preceding its publication in 1900 should contribute to an understanding of the controversial questions raised by the essay. Limitations of space make it impossible to do more than sketch a few salient features of the background. Far from being devastated by its Wars of the Roses between Colorado and Blanco caudillos, as outsiders are tempted to imagine, little Uruguay set the pace for South American growth in the late nineteenth century, outstripping even Argentina, whose increase in population and wealth since 1870 had been phenomenal. Between 1850 and 1900 the populations of the two countries grew from 132,000 to 915,000 and from 1.1 million to 4.74 million, respectively; Uruguay's rate of increase, 7 to 1, was nearly twice the 4.1 rate of Argentina. Immigration, very largely from Italy and Spain, was mainly responsible. In Uruguay it began so early and was so heavy that the proportion of foreign-born in the country's population reached its all-time peak of 35 percent in 1860. That figure had been cut in half by 1908, whereas in Argentina the corresponding peak figure, 30 percent, was not reached until 1914.

In the generation that closed out the nineteenth century Uruguay's population explosion was matched by an almost equally rapid economic expansion. This took place on a broad front, in pastoral production, banking, insurance, and foreign commerce, and in the means of transportation (railways and shipping) and of communication (telephones and mail service). Agricultural production lagged, for the soil of Uruguay could not compare with the rich pampa of Argentina, and manufactures were mostly small-scale and largely confined to food processing and light consumer goods. *Frigorificos,* which were large-scale refrigerated meat packing plants, did not supplant the smaller and simpler salt meat plants, or *saladeros,* until after 1900, but by that year the big Liebig meat extract plant not far from Montevideo was a generation old.

Uruguay, like Argentina, had a boom-and-bust, "Gilded Age" period in the 1880s and early '90s. The central figure of both phases was a Spanish lawyer, promoter, and man-about-town, Dr. Emilio Reus, who became for a brief time the busines tycoon and social lion of Montevideo, only to die bankrupt the year after the crash of 1890. Economic growth was resumed soon after the crash. In both periods, as these bare facts suggest, its most striking feature was its dependence on the stimulus provided by European capital investments (which were mainly British) and an expanding European market for Uruguay's products (mainly pastoral). A result was the incorporation of Uruguay in the European economy. In the 1890s, Uruguayan historian Alberto Zum Felde tells us, foreigners owned more than half the country's productive land and nearly all of its commercial and industrial firms. Great Britain, prominent in River Plate affairs since the dawn of the century, played the leading role in this whole process; much of the financing for it, for instance was provided by Baring Brothers of London, who, with splendid impartiality, performed the same service for Uruguay's trans-Platine competitor, Argentina. The United States, on the other hand, played a very minor role as trading partner and almost none as investor until several years after 1900.

Given the importance of Britain's role in Uruguay, James Bryce naturally included it in the tour of South America in 1910 so perceptively described in his *South American Observations and Impressions.* In most respects Bryce was very favorably impressed by the country and its people and paid them what he surely regarded as a high compliment by saying: "In no part of South America, except perhaps southern Chile, would a European feel more disposed to settle down for life". Yet he was also struck (although, as a historian, not greatly surprised) that Uruguay had continued to grow in wealth and population despite its uncomfortable buffer position between two much larger and very meddlesome neighbors and despite the fact that, according to him, from 1810 to 1876 it had seen more incessant fighting than any other part of the world in the last hundred years, and that even since 1876 conflicts had been frequent. But, reflected Bryce, recalling precedents as far back as the sixth century B. C., as some countries are ruined by war, others thrive on it, and Uruguay was one of the latter. Bryce was right about this, and it might be added that Uruguay's own historians regard the prosperity brought to Montevideo by the Paraguayan War of 1865-70 as a major factor in initiating the country's rapid economic growth during the rest of the century.

Uruguay was more peaceful in the last quarter of the nineteenth century than might have been inferred from Bryce's account. A few minor uprisings occurred and the most serious conflict was a short-lived civil war in 1897. That led to partition of the country between Blancos and Colorados and a restoration of peace, which still reigned in 1900. In all but two years from 1876 to 1890 the country was ruled by military dictators, the first of whom gave a strong impulse to its economic development with the aid of foreign capital, while the third and last carried it on into the boom period of the late 1880s. Civil government was restored in 1890 and continued without a break for many years. Liberalism found expression in the anticlerical measures adopted in the 1880s and the social reform movement that began in the 1890s. Young Rodó (he was born in 1872) considered himself a liberal, but was called a conservative by leftwingers. He supported both anticlericalism and social reform in moderation and was a political ally of José Batlle y Ordóñez until several years after 1900; why they then drifted apart does not concern us here.

Culturally, the upper-class Montevideo to which Rodó belonged was cosmopolitan. As early as 1846 Domingo Sarmiento found it so, in contrast to Buenos Aires, which seemed to him thoroughly Spanish. That was a consequence of the presence in Montevideo of many French, English, and Italians, among them Giuseppe Garibaldi, who had come there to fight in the Great War ("la Guerra Grande") provoked by the armed intervention of the Rosas government of Argentina. The immigrant flood set in motion at that time continued past the end of the century, and the rapid growth or foreign trade and investment heightened the cosmopolitan appearance of the capital city and chief seaport.

The strongest cultural influence from abroad was that of France. Theodore Child, a North American journalist, who visited the city during the economic crisis of 1890, found striking evidence of it even then. The shops of Montevideo, he wrote, impress the traveler by the number and value of the luxury articles they have brought together from various parts of Europe and Asia, but the publishers borrow everything from France and most of the foreign books that crowd the bookstores are French, including the latest works of such authors as Maupassant and the Goncourt brothers. On the other hand, he observed, the Spanish classics, even *Don Quijote*, can be found only with great difficulty, if at all. At the close of the century, according to Juan Pivel Devoto, a leading historian of Uruguay, the men of letters of his country and the rest of Latin America were still suffering from an infection of *fin de siècle* decadence from which France had already recovered. For a time, he continued, Rodó was one of the sufferers, but he too recovered and in *Ariel* found a cure for all Latin Americans, which was to remain faithful to their glorious humanist tradition.

In view of the very minor part taken by the United States in the economic as well as the cultural and political life of Uruguay at that time, one naturally wonders why Rodó chose to present the North American republic, which he never visited, as the epitome of the Caliban spirit of materialism. To answer this fascinating question with any assurance would require a much more exhaustive study than is possible here. One or two clues to the answer may be found below, but first let us see what he had to say in *Ariel* about the Caliban spirit, first in Latin America and then in the United States.

The United States, he wrote, could be considered the incarnation of English utilitarianism; the utilitarian gospel was spreading everywhere, thanks to the material miracles of its triumph, and Hispanic America was no exception. "The powerful federation [the United States] is carrying out a kind of moral conquest among us. Ad-

miration for its greatness and strength is a sentiment that is advancing by giant steps among our leading men and even more rapidly, perhaps, among the masses . . . and nothing is easier than the transition from admiring to imitating it . . . It is thus that the vision of an America *delatinized* by its own will and then made over again in the image and likeness of the archetype of the North floats even now through the dreams of many concerned for our future . . . We have our own *nordomanía;* it must be contained within the limits that reason and sentiment together prescribe"[2]. I do not intend utter exclusion, he explained, for intelligent borrowing from abroad can be highly beneficial to peoples, such as ours, who are still forming their national identity; but I see no glory in denaturalizing our own character by slavish imitation of a foreign model; the cosmopolitanism we must accept excludes neither fidelity to our past nor the guiding force of the genius of our race (*raza*) in shaping the future of America.

Obviously, then, the "moral conquest" by the United States was no conquest at all, but in Rodó's own opinion, voluntary, even eager, surrender by Latin Americans who craved the material rewards it would yield. Perhaps because he presented the threat from the United States in this light, and certainly because he identified it as a moral and spiritual, not an economic conquest, he provided the principal grounds for the attacks made on him in later years by his fellow Latin Americans, namely, his silence about the greatest "Yankee peril" of all, that of economic imperialism. The charge was based on an anachronism, for when he wrote *Ariel*, the economic interest and influence of the United States in Uruguay (and indeed in all South America) were very small and, in comparison with those of Britain and other European countries, microscopic. Even in the Caribbean, its "conquest" had barely begun.

What is more, Rodó did not fail to note a potential economic threat from the United States. When he went on, in *Ariel*, to discuss the merits and defects of that country, he wrote directly and forcefully about ominous economic developments within its borders; presumably, he did not regard them as constituting a threat to Uruguay. Among the many merits he recognized in the North Americans were their leadership in establishing the modern concept of liberty and the dignity of labor, their retention of a religious feeling that provided a tight moral rein on utilitarianism, and their "prodigal generosity". He admitted that he was impressed by the "titanic greatness" of the United States and by its people's "formidable will power", their "school of will and work" (or, in the cant of a later generation, the "Puritan work ethic")[3].

In his estimation, however, the North Americans' merits were far outweighed by their defects. Among these he counted a false democracy, which was based on numbers, not quality, and deficiency in the poetic spirit that tempered utilitarianism in England. Formerly, in the days of Emerson and Poe, he continued, that spirit had existed precariously in the United States, but since then it had all but disappeared, along with the civic virtues of Washington and Hamilton. Worst of all, and one of the most striking features of society in the United States, he said, was the growing political influence of a plutocracy represented by the all-powerful allies of the trusts, which were "masters of the economic life" of this "great people". In this connection he recalled the advent of a rich and haughty class in the last days of the Roman republic, which was an antecedent of the tyranny of the Caesars, and went on to warn that the people of the United States, now drunk with material prosperity, fancy themselves predestined to a *magisterio romano* and to a primacy in universal culture; they even aspire to revise the Book of Genesis, so that they can occupy the first page.

This was certainly not flattering to the United States, but besides recognizing that country's many merits, Rodó conceded that good might come of its utilitarianism. Just as the aristocratic idealist Ernest Renan, whom he venerated, had found moral and spiritual benefits accruing from utilitarian achievements in nineteenth-century Europe, and as the mercantilism of the Italian cities had paid the expenses of the Renaissance, so, he predicted, would the results of North American positivism in the last analysis "serve the cause of Ariel". For its great material gains would be used for higher purposes by other peoples—or, he graciously added, by the United States itself at some time in the future, though not yet.

Rodó was an ardent Americanist, but, as noted above, his was an Americanism from which the United States was excluded. Ardao makes this clear from the outset in his book on the subject[4]. From first to last, he tells us, Rodó used América, América Latina, Iberoamérica, Hispanoamérica, even América Española interchangeably to designate the "same continental community", except that he reserved Iberoamérica for use in certain (unspecified) circumstances. Ardao does not state explicitly that Rodó excluded the United States, but his equivalents for América make that a necessary inference.

For other writers, Pan Latin America would have been still another equivalent term. It has a stronger political connotation than the unity Rodó had in mind, but the difference is only one of degree or, better, of timing. He did not by any means leave political unity out of account; he merely thought it would be so difficult to achieve that it would come last, whereas the cultural unity of "nuestra América", Latin America, already existed, at least in latent form, and needed only to be activated by forming closer ties among its widely scattered members.

Rodó's Americanism was essentially European, in the sense that the ideas, values, and traditions that he espoused were European, as were the vast majority of the authors cited and persons discussed by him. To be sure, three of the latter—Bolívar, Montalvo, Artigas—were the heroes of the "heroic" section—the fourth—of his Americanist writings as arranged by Ardao, and all three were born in America and lived there all their lives. Yet all three were European in their basic ideas and attitudes towards life. Artigas was a great admirer of the political system of the United States, but the core of that system

too was European, since it was based mainly on English precedents as modified by colonial experience. As regards Rodó himself, Samuel Ramos, the distinguished Mexican *pensador,* put the case for Europe in a nutshell when he described **Ariel** as a work of Christian as well as Hellenic humanism.

The same orientation still stands out in one of Rodó's last writings: his **"Testamento americanista"**, written in Rome in December 1916, only a few months before his death. In the opening sentences of this brief (4 1/2-page) essay, he says that all Spanish America is "a single entity, a single image, a single value". A little later he observes that contact with European thought (*juicio*) animates the notion of "continental [Hispanic American] unity"—a goal to which he would give top priority if his advice should be sought by the youth of Hispanic America. Towards the close he declares that the influence of Europe arouses in the (Hispanic) American heart still another sentiment: "profound faith in our destinies, creole pride, and the invigorating energy of our social conscience". As evidence of the effect of this sentiment he cites the building up, amidst the tumult of "our political formation", of such cities as Buenos Aires, Santiago, and Montevideo—all of them, it will be noted, the Latin American cities in which the European imprint was strongest.

Rodó closes his Roman testament of Americanism with a passage to which no English translation could do justice and which must have been inspired by Edward Gibbon's *The Decline and Fall of the Roman Empire.* "Esto pensaba", the passage begins, "al subir las gradas del Capitolio, cuna y altar de la latina estirpe. El sol de una suavísima tarde doraba aquellas piedras sagradas . . ."; continues with references to the "guerrera imagen de Roma", Marcus Aurelius in bronze, the trophies of Marius, the statue of Rienzi, "the last tribune", and the cage of the she-wolf who suckled Romulus; and links all this to the theme of Americacanism by concluding: "Y me parecía como si, en su presagiosa quietud, la nodriza de la raza mirase a donde el sol se pone, y buscara, de ese lado del mundo, nueva libertad y nuevo espacio".

Given Rodó's settled conviction that the achievement of the political unity of Latin America was remote, there may be some exaggeration in Ardao's assertion (in his *Rodó,* p. 31) that in Rodó's mind, the idea of such political unity was inseparable from his "preoccupation with saving our nationalities from imperialist absorption by the United States". Concern seems a better word than preoccupation, and Rodó's concern over that danger seems clearly to have developed after 1900, along with the unfolding of the so-called "protective imperialism", of the United States in the Caribbean. Yet, even then he took comfort in the thought that at some future time *the magna confederación* dreamed of by Bolívar might come into being with strength enough to defend Latin America from depredations like the one at Panama in 1903. In the next ten years his concern mounted as North American encroachments continued, in Mexico as well as the Caribbean. By the outbreak of World War I in 1914 he had reached the point of declaring, in a newspaper article captioned "The Cause of France is the Cause of Humanity", that, although Latin America's sympathies must be with France and England, nevertheless it must not be forgotten that the victory of any national imperialism in Europe would create an even greater and more immediate danger (to Latin America) by facilitating the further extension of the "protective shield" of the United States. If Rodó had written *Ariel* in 1914 instead of 1900, he might well have spoken of the United States in terms as harsh as those often attributed to him.

Several decades have passed since *Ariel* was holy writ to the youth or any other age group in Latin America. The reaction against Rodó was under way by 1930, and from the start it concentrated on his outstanding work, *Ariel*. It spread throughout Latin America and by 1973 it had built up so formidable a *leyenda negra* about him that an admirer, Hugo Torrano, felt called upon to rehabilitate him in a book subtitled "restoration of his image"[5]. The opening chapter deals with Rodó's "political and intellectual ostracism"; the titles of two later chapters are "La escuela detractora de Rodó" and "Balance de la crítica detractora"; and there are frequent reference to his critics throughout the book. Torrano deals mainly with those who are Uruguayans and Marxist, though he also discusses those of other kinds, chief among whom are José Luis Romero, Argentine Socialist, and Luis Alberto Sánchez, Peruvian Aprista. Two main charges against Rodó stand out in Torrano's account: one, that his elitism and traditionalism played into the hands of the oligarchy and strengthened the already formidable barriers to political, economic, and social progress in Latin America; the other, that he was blind to economic imperialism and far too soft on the United States.

Readers who wish to examine the broad picture more closely are referred to Torrano's account of it. Here we can only take brief note of three works that are not mentioned in it and which relate in some way to *Ariel* and the United States. The earliest of the three and a pioneer work in this genre is Juan Zorrilla de San Martín's *Detalles de historia* (Montevideo, 1930), especially the chapter on "Ariel y Calibán americanos" (pp. 195-224), in which the author asserts that Rodó is esteemed more for the beauty of his Castilian style than for the substance of his "ideas and doctrines" and that not a few Hispanic Americans think it would be a good thing if we could get rid of Ariel, the "cause of our inertia", and acclimate Caliban, "forger of Anglo-American progress".

The other two works are much more recent: a book by José Luis Romero[6], and a substantial article by Juan F. Marsal and Margery J. Arent[7]. According to Romero, Rodó sounded, in *Ariel*, the first alarm over the immigrant flood and stimulated an aristocratic *arielismo* and right-wing nationalism throughout the continent—a sentiment also expressed some years later by Ricardo Rojas. This nationalism, notes Romero, was aimed not only against the Uniter States, but also against Latin American admirers of utilitarianism and detractors of Spanish tradition. Marsal and Arent, writing about what they call the "ver-

dadero *boom*" in right-wing thought in Argentina in the late 1960s, declare that Rodó's *arielismo,* with its Catholic-traditionalist spiritual values, was characteristic of that country's counter-revolutionary ideology, which the authors then link with the "anticapitalist and anti-Yankee position" of the right wing in Latin America at large[8].

On April 20, 1974, Secretary of State Henry Kissinger closed an important address before the General Assembly of the Organization of American States in Atlanta, Georgia, with the following quotation, in English translation, from what he called Rodó's "classic *Ariel*":

> To the extent that we can already distinguish a higher form of cooperation [between the two Americas] as the basis of a distant future, we can see that it will come not as a result of unilateral formulas, but through the reciprocal influence and skillful harmonization of those attributes which give our different peoples their glory.

The translation is inaccurate in some respects[9], but the passage was appropriate both to the theme of the address, hopefully described in the State Department's news release as "*Good Partner* policy for the Americas", and to the effort the secretary was making at that time to repair an inter-American relationship badly battered by the exposure of contributions of the United States to the recent overthrow of the Allende government of Chile and by Latin American defections to the Third World group in the United Nations. There was, however, a touch of irony about the affair. This seems to have been the first time that an American secretary of state ever quoted *Ariel* with approval, at least publicly, and yet the time was now long past when any U.S. official could reasonably hope to gain favor with the new breed of Latin American rulers by invoking the authority of Rodó. It was more likely that official Washington's *abrazo* of Rodó would (to use a metaphor he would have abhorred) drive his stock among his fellow Latin Americans lower than ever before[10].

NOTES

[1] 3rd ed. (New York, 1968), p. 798. The passage was identical in all three editions, except that the first, 1955, had read "judgment upon" instead of "appraisal of". For two Latin American writers who state Rodó's position correctly and clearly, see note 8.

[2] My translation. It is from the *Ariel* excerpts conveniently reproduced in Ardao, cited above in the text, pp. 105-106. All other passages from *Ariel* cited below are from the same source. As explained below in the text, Rodó included only Latin America, not the United States, in the term "America".

[3] The exaggeration of Rodó's animus, in *Ariel,* against the United States is illustrated by the common mistranslation of " . . . ya veis que, aunque no les amo, les admiro" (following a three-page explanation of why he admired the North Americans), as, "I admire them but I do not love them" (Ardao, *Rodó,* p. 113, from the Spanish original).

[4] Ardao, *Rodó,* p. 7, note.

[5] Hugo Torrano, *Rodó: acción y libertad. Restauración de su imagen* (Montevideo, 1973). The book won UNESCO's prize in a Rodó centenary competition, 1971.

[6] *El desarrollo de las ideas en la sociedad argentina del siglo XX* (Buenos Aires, 1965), pp. 48, 58, 59. Without explanation, Torrano, *op. cit.*, bases his attack on Romero on an earlier article by the latter in the well-known but not widely circulated Uruguayan weekly journal *Marcha*, September 1, 1961, which he denounces as a compendium of the unjust *leyenda negra* built up by Rodó's detractors (p. 22 and note 11).

[7] "La derecha intelectual argentina . . .", *Revista Latinoamericana de Sociología*, 5, No. 3 (November 1969), 486, 519.

[8] Romero and the Marsal-Arent team could have profited by Enrique Anderson Imbert's excellent analysis of *Ariel* in his *Spanish American Literature. A History,* English translation by John V. Falconieri (Detroit, 1963), especially p. 316, and by the sound but less detailed one by Pedro Henríquez Ureña, a pioneer champion of Rodó and *Ariel,* and himself a distinguished man of letters, in *Literary Currents in Hispanic America* (Cambridge, Mass., 1945), pp. 179-180.

[9] For example, in the original (Ardao, *Rodó,* p. 109), the prospect held out is of *concordia,* not cooperation, and is conditional and remote; "unilateral formulas" is *"imitación unilateral"*, which is followed by a qualifying phrase, omitted in the translation, "que diría Tarde", a reference to Gabriel Tarde that is significant of France's influence on Rodó; and in the translation, redolent *raza* becomes colorless people. The text of the address is contained in Department of State, News Release, April 20, 1974, and the translation in question is on p. 8.

[10] For further reading, see the works cited above and the following: Arturo Scarrone, *Bibliografía de Rodó,* 2 vols. (Montevideo, 1930); Víctor Pérez Petit, *Rodó. Su vida. Su obra* (Montevideo, 1937); Rodó, *Obras completas,* 2nd ed. (Madrid, 1967), and *Ariel* edited with introduction and notes by Gordon Brotherston (Cambridge, England, 1967).

Raymund Paredes (essay date 1988)

SOURCE: "Such Stuff as American Dreams Are Made On," in *L.A. Times Book Review,* May 29, 1988, p. 13.

[*Here, critic Paredes offers a favorable assessment of* Ariel *and Margaret Sayers Peden's translation of it.*]

In 1900, a young Uruguayan teacher and literary critic aroused readers from Mexico to Argentina with a small book proposing a plan of cultural development for Latin America. José Enrique Rodó called for a culture that would preserve traditional European standards of morality and beauty while rejecting North American values. *Ariel* was hardly a work of great originality; the sources of its enormous influence lay instead in its passion, its calculated elegance, its erudition and, perhaps most important, its timeliness.

When Rodó published *Ariel*, Latin America was still suffering the aftershocks of the Spanish American War of 1898. Intellectuals were deeply and often bitterly divided. One faction viewed the war's outcome with alarm and despair, the spectacle of the United States possessing Puerto Rico and occupying Cuba regarded as one more experience of humiliation and loss of sovereignty for the region. But another group saw the easy victory of the United States over a former world power as indisputable evidence of political, economic and even cultural superiority and so rushed to imitate North American institutions. In either case, Latin Americans were ready for the infusion of pride, optimism and vision Rodó provided.

Very quickly, *Ariel* became the subject of tireless discussion not only in print but in the numerous literacy societies that sprang up expressly to weigh its merits. For exhorting his brethren to forge a distinctive cultural identity, Rodó was proclaimed, in a delicious piece of irony, "the Latin Emerson." Meanwhile, *Ariel* went on to attract generation after generation of readers. With the present English translation, it has now reached its 16th edition.

The title of Rodó's essay comes from Shakespeare's "The Tempest," which features not only the "airy spirit" Ariel but two other characters who captured Rodó's imagination, Prospero and Caliban. Rodó regarded all three as cultural archetypes, much as the French scholar Ernest Renan had in 1878 when he brought out "Caliban," a *drame philosophique,* which depicted the decline of aristocratic French culture. An admirer of Renan, Rodó essentially elaborated the Frenchman's formulations of Shakespeare's characters and gave them varying degrees of emphasis. Primary, of course, was Ariel, a representation of "the noble, soaring aspect of the human spirit . . . the superiority of reason and feeling over the base impulses of irrationality." The "base impulses" were embodied in Caliban, a symbol, as Rodó put it, of "brutal sensuality." Finally, there was the noble Prospero: a lover of books, a possessor of magical powers and the master of Ariel. In Rod ' mind, these figures represented the major cultural forces in motion across Latin America.

Ariel consists of six sections presented in the form of an extended address by a teacher to his students at the end of the school year. The opening of the essay is heavy with symbolism. The book-lined classroom in which the "venerable, old" teacher meets his students conveys a distinctly classical quality, as if Socrates himself might feel comfortable there. Dominating the room is a bronze statue of Ariel, wings unfolded and poised for flight. The teacher, dubbed "Prospero" by his students for his fine character and devotion to knowledge, assumes his customary place beside the statue. Once seated, Prospero calls upon Ariel for divine inspiration and begins.

For Rodó, the most fundamental of classical values was "the sense of the beautiful," which he regarded as the indispensable precursor of the ability to distinguish good from evil. Rodó went so far as to insist that an exact correspondence existed between good taste and morality in both individuals and societies; as he did throughout *Ariel*, Rodó cited an impressive array of European thinkers and artists to support his contention.

Rodó made his plea for Latin American idealism and spiritualism so fervently because he considered them to be under sustained attack, primarily from the forces of utilitarianism, materialism and democracy. Rodó believed the first of these to be one of the great sources of corruption in the modern world, encouraging behavior in which "every action is determined by the immediate ends of self-interest." Materialism led to standards of well-being that ignored morality; furthermore, it turned everything, even human life, into a commodity. Democracy was dangerous because it naturally destroyed excellence and encouraged mediocrity.

Unlike Ernest Renan, however, Rodó believed that democracy could be reformed to allow "human superiorities" to develop through a Darwinian process of natural selection. As Rodó looked about, he could hardly help but notice that his three evils were flourishing most conspicuously in the United States. Consequently, he entreated his readers to resist influences from the North. It is important to emphasize that Rodó's attitude toward the United States was disapproving but not hostile; as he himself wrote about the *norteamericanos:* "Although I do not love them, I admire them."

A decade or so after its publication, *Ariel* began to decline in influence. Its florid *modernista* style fell out of favor, and the rise of indigenous art and values created a cultural climate in which Rodó's worship of European culture was not widely admired. In time, the once-sensational *Ariel* became just a literary curiosity. The death blow to Rodó's status as a cultural visionary came in 1971, when the Cuban critic, Roberto Fernandez Retamar, published his own "Caliban," an essay that brilliantly argued that Rodó's symbol of "brutal sensuality" was in fact heroic, an exemplar of Third World endurance and resistance.

Despite its decline, *Ariel* remains a valuable book for American readers, representing a major episode in the evolution of Latin American consciousness. The present translation by Margaret Sayers Peden softens many of Rodó's stylistic excesses; the volume also contains useful annotations and bibliographical sections and a provocative prologue by Carlos Fuentes.

FURTHER READING

Bacheller, C. C. "Rodó's Ideas on the Relationship of Beauty and Morality." *The Canadian Modern Language Review,* Vol. XIX, No. 2 (Winter 1963): 19-22.

Explores Rodó's aesthetic of beauty and virtue.

Castells, Ricardo. "Fernández Retamar's 'The Tempest' in a Cafetera: From Ariel to Mariel." *Cuban Studies,* Vol. 25 (1995): 165-82.

Compares Rodó's and Fernández Retamar's manipulation of Shakespeare's *The Tempest* as commentary on Latin American relations with the United States.

Langhorst, Rick. "Caliban in America." *Journal of Spanish Studies Twentieth Century,* Vol. 8, Nos. 1-2 (Spring and Fall 1980): 79-87.

Analyzes Rodó's comparison of the Shakespearean character Caliban to North American greed and insensitivity.

Van Aken, Mark. "Rodó, *Ariel,* and Student Militants of Uruguay." *Homage to Irving A. Leonard: Essays on Hispanic Art, History, and Literature,* edited by Raquel Chang-Rodríguez and Donald A. Yates. pp. 153-60, East Lansing: Michigan State University Press, 1977.

Analyzes the impact of Rodó's *Ariel* on Uruguayan students and the spiritual quest that it represented.

Fernando de Rojas
c.1465-1541

Spanish novelist and playwright.

INTRODUCTION

Fernando de Rojas is known for writing one of the most famous and influential pieces of literature to come out of the Spanish Golden Age, *La Celestina*, also known as *(Tragi)comedia de Calisto y Melibea* (1499). Considered second in importance only to *Don Quixote* in the history of Spanish literature, it was one of the first works ever to present romance in everyday life as the subject of a play, or more properly, a novel in dialogue. It is also famous for its extremely skillful delineation of character. As one of the most groundbreaking plays in history, it depicted erotic episodes and created characters never before utilized on the Spanish stage, particularly that of the go-between. Critics believe it not only influenced subsequent drama in Spanish, but in Dutch and English, including Shakespeare's *Romeo and Juliet* and *Othello*.

Little is known about Fernando de Rojas. He was born in Puebla de Montalbán or in Toledo, Spain. His father was condemned by the Inquisition for being a Jew, arrested, and executed by firing squad in an auto-da-fé when Rojas was about twelve years old. The family was forced to convert to Christianity. Rojas studied law in Salamanca and was induced by religious discrimination to move to Talavera where he became mayor and where he lived out the remainder of his life. It is known he was a property owner, was married, and had at least one daughter. It is also known that his father-in-law was investigated by the Inquisition in the 1520s and that at least five of his cousins were forced to undergo the ceremony of voluntary public penitence and humiliation euphemistically termed *reconciliación*. This ritual amounted to open admission of false conversion and of secret Jewish practices, often with the penitents forced to march through the streets barefoot to the jeers of a crowd. Rojas's status as a *converso* forced him to keep a low profile and is believed to be one reason why information about his life is scant.

La Celestina has a contested past because of missing dates, discrepancies in the earliest extant manuscripts, and uncertainty as to authorship of subsequent interpolations and additions. As a result, a vast body of scholarship has accreted around the play. Three main editions of the play survive: the first preserved edition was published at Burgos in 1499 and contains sixteen acts; the second earliest edition, published in 1501, contains twenty-one acts; and an edition of 1526 contains twenty-two acts. The 1501 edition contains some acrostic verses stating that the author was "El Bachiller Fernando de Rojas," lending credibility to Rojas's authorship of the second

edition, as well. At least sixty more manuscripts appeared within the sixteenth century alone, not to mention innumerable translations in French, Italian, German, and English. The central plot of *La Celestina* turns on the overwhelming desire of Calisto for Melibea. It is her initial hostility and indifference towards Calisto that prompts him to hire Celestina, a go-between, madam, witch, and repairer of maidenheads, to convince Melibea to respond to Calisto's pursuit. After finally meeting at Melibea's window, Calisto falls from a ladder and is killed. Melibea then throws herself from the tower to join her lover in death. It is thought that Rojas's status as a *converso* had a profound influence on *La Celestina*: religion is accorded the most cursory of mention, and none of the Christians try to live a good life, though all attempt to live *the* good life. Fate and selfishness rule as if Christianity in the time of the Inquisition can garner no respect. The play, or novel-in-dialogue, can be taken as an orthodox and exemplary sermon against lust and greed, and a satire on courtly and romantic love. Its satire is thought to reflect a disintegration of Medieval certainties, with the shift towards urban secularism where values and loyalties are displaced by a quest for material gain. Rojas's acclaim grew due to his mastery of character and dialogue. Calisto's obstinate folly, Melibea's passion, Pármeno's shiftiness and insecurity, and Celestina's scheming and incredible loquacity were complex and thorough characterizations of the quandaries of Golden Age Spain. The play is a masterpiece of entertainment, of ironically didactic speeches and misheard asides, and of what could be the most furious unspooling of maxims in theater history.

La Celestina had enormous influence on Western theater, from Lope de Vega in plays like *Dorotea* to modern day works by writers like Ramón María del Valle-Inclan. It might be that *La Celestina* is not more known by English audiences because of its length and volubility. Despite this, the play employs witty dialogue with occasionally bawdy reference, and clever situations as if enjoying its status of being simultaneously one of the most entertaining and important plays in Western theater.

PRINCIPAL EDITIONS

*Comedia de Calisto y Melibea (novel) 1499
†Tragicomedia de Calisto y Melibea (novel) 1501
‡Calisto and Meliboea: A new commodye in English, inmaner of an enterlude ryghte elygant and full of craft of rethoryk wherein is shewd and dyscrybyd as well the bewte and good propretes of women as theyr

*vycys and evyll condicions with a morall conclusion
and exhortacyon to vertew* (drama) 1526
§*La Celestina* (novel) 1569

*Parts or all of this edition may have been published at an earlier date.

†It is not known when the first *Tragicomedia* appeared; editions dated 1502 are now believed to have been published years later.

‡This translated adaptation of part of the *Tragicomedia* by John Rastell is believed to have been privately performed and published in England in 1526.

§This edition marks the first time that *La Celestina* was used as the novel's title.

CRITICISM

Stephen Gilman (essay date 1962)

SOURCE: "Rebirth of a Classic: *Celestina*," in *Varieties of Literary Experience*, Stanley Burnshaw, ed. New York: New York University Press, 1962, pp. 283-305.

[*Gilman reevaluates the importance of* Celestina *and its place in international literature, speculating on the reasons for its renewed appeal to modern readers.*]

In the last few years, the *Celestina*, a fifteenth-century Spanish dialogue novel, has shown signs of undergoing an international revival. There have been three new translations in English,[1] a revision in five acts of the classic Mabbe rendering, as well as new translations in French, German, and Russian. Scholars in a number of countries and languages have shown increased interest in the text, the author, and the artistry, and performances have been attempted with increasing frequency, particularly in French. The *Celestina* has long been a classic, second only to the *Quixote*, in its own language, but in view of its return to the international exchange of literary values, it is appropriate to estimate anew the nature of its importance. Perhaps, this may also illuminate from within something of the *Celestina*'s appeal to our time.

A provisional spectrograph of the importance of the *Celestina* divides it into three areas or aspects. It is, in the first place, a central landmark in the history of Western literature. In it we can see, as perhaps in no other work, not merely how the novel and drama began but also what they had to overcome in order to begin. At the frontier between the didactic and allegorical forms of the Middle Ages and the modern genres, the *Celestina* is a triumph of literary discovery as startling and in its own way as important as any geographical or technological discovery. To think of its author—a man not so much forgotten as never yet remembered—as a literary Gutenberg or Columbus may seem farfetched, but that is exactly what he is. In the second place, the *Celestina* is a masterpiece in its own right, which is to say that it eval-uates human life in a way that is lastingly significant. Its vision of man at home, in society, and in the universe, of the individual in perilous encounter with himself, with others, and with the dimensions of time and space, has increased in relevance over the centuries. Finally, in the area of imaginative creation, it presents not so much a literary experience as direct immersion in an acid bath of life. The over-used word of book reviewers, "unforgettable," is misleading for the *Celestina*. Indelible would be better. Knowing Celestina herself as intimately as the reader comes to know her is something more than unsettling; the shock waves can penetrate far beneath the surface of mind and habit.

When the first reader opened to the first page of the *Celestina* in 1499 (or possibly the year before)[2] and began to read the summary put at the beginning by the printers (these "arguments" were the jacket blurbs of the time),[3] he was probably somewhat disappointed. Here was a commonplace plot of love and seduction, one used in the Middle Ages and based on types inherited from Roman comedy. Calisto, a hot-blooded young gentleman, badly advised by his corrupt servants, employs Celestina, a professional go-between, to seduce Melibea, whom he had met by accident and with whom he had fallen violently in love. Gentleman, servants, and go-between all succeed in doing what they want to do. And then, by way of retribution for their immorality and imprudence, they all meet sudden and violent deaths. So far there was nothing to surprise that first reader, yet when he began to leaf through his new purchase, he was surely disconcerted. The outward sign of the inner uniqueness and originality of the *Celestina* was its twenty-one acts of unbroken dialogue. A book looking like this had never been printed or seen before. The familiar story had been strangely reshaped. And it is with an examination of this reshaping into dialogue that we may best begin.

Dialogue had, of course, been used before. Boethius in his *Consolations* had left a model of didactic and exemplary dialogue which had been imitated by countless mediaeval writers. In the face of anarchy, the anarchical surging forth of raw human life, the Middle Ages took refuge in order and doctrine. And debates in dialogue—between philosophy and the self, water and wine, the soul and the body, and so many others—were favorite devices for explaining order and teaching doctrine. Whatever illusion of speech the dialogue could give served (like the brilliant colors of church windows) as a pleasant coating around a less tasty core of moral instruction. Even when mediaeval readers encountered such a delightful and often playfully cynical playwright as Terence, they worked hard to convince themselves of his strict moral intentions, as is demonstrated by the elaborately annotated editions which were printed over and over again in the time of the *Celestina*. As for the mystery and miracle plays, their speeches were mostly spoken doctrine embedded in traditional characterizations and rôles. There were a few exceptions, of course. There were moments of tense face-to-face encounter in some of the epic poems and, above all, in a few of the most moving episodes of the *Divine Comedy*.[4] But before the *Celestina* there had been no systematic use of dialogue for its own sake, nothing resembling the two major dialogue forms today so taken for granted, the drama and the novel. Mediaeval writers, in other words, could not produce, or were not interested in producing, sustained interchange between individuals each speaking to the other from his own point of view and from within his own life.[5]

The *Celestina* in one stroke changed all this. After the *Celestina*, literature was to be of a sort more familiar to us; before, it was much more alien. Not that all dialogue as we know it today stems from the *Celestina*, but that in its pages dialogue was perfected and used systematically. For the first time in centuries a work had been written in which an "I" from inside himself speaks to a "you" whom he hopes to sway in thought, action, or feeling. For the first time we can hear[6] lives impinging on each other, living together and struggling with each other in sustained oral interchange. Once this is achieved, of course, the creation of full characters (as distinct from types who serve only to entertain, to reach and make the story-teller's point) becomes a possibility. Even more, that mysterious living independence, that capacity for breaking away from the author, which is the privilege of literature's great character creations is aided by mastery of dialogue. Specifically the *Celestina* furnished Cervantes with the dialogue tradition he used in the *Don Quixote*, the first true novel precisely because of its conversations between knight and squire. It lay also—just as decisively—at the headwaters of the drama, providing a flow of dialogue which was still running strong in Spanish theaters when Lope de Vega (a fervent admirer of the *Celestina*) perfected his definitive formula. Writers, it is more fashionable to admit in our day than it was in that of our grandparents, don't create out of whole cloth. They work with and in a tradition, and the *Celestina* is a central root of the European tradition of dialogue.[7]

As I suggested previously, it is interesting to note that dialogue was for the first time consciously discovered and explored during the same decade that America was given the same treatment. This may or may not be coincidental, but it does at least indicate another suggestive coincidence. When Columbus came from Italy to Spain, as is well known, he Hispanicized himself and severed all connections with his past. He even gave up his own language for another. It was an indication of the shift of the creative center of history at the end of the fifteenth century from Italy to Spain, where it was to rest until it swerved northward in the second half of the sixteenth. And in a similar way, the new interest in the inner life of the individual, so audible in the dialogue of the *Celestina*, seems to have emigrated from Italy to Spain. Preoccupation with inwardness, self-conscious exploration of one's own psyche, found its first concentrated literary expression in Petrarch's lyrics and its first extensive exposition (after Saint Augustine) in his Latin treatises. It was these latter that influenced the *Celestina* so strongly. In them Petrarch, using and renovating the educational dialogue of his time, revives the Stoic notion of man's inwardness besieged from without by both temptations and misfortunes. Man is a sub-

ject, "sub-jected," that is to say the target of all the slings and arrows that are launched at it—the *-jected* is, of course, from *jactare*—from the objective world. We are most immediately and vividly familiar with this sense of consciousness as a state of warfare (besieged consciousness) from our experience of Shakespeare. And if the Italians think of it in Petrarchist terms, the French know it from Montaigne. The *Celestina* is very different from the works of any of the three (it is not tragic, not lyrical, and certainly not essayistic) but, nonetheless, the same Neo-Stoicism is present in almost its every speech and scene. Its version of Stoic warfare is primarily verbal, an incessant oral aggression of one life against another both in argument and appeal. This is the built-in advantage of the *Celestina*. Precisely because collision of lives in dialogue is all that happens in it, it can show consciousness at work without killing or freezing it, not only in depth but at length as well.

What was found in the *Celestina*'s initial sounding of this queer and enormous place? The question is best answered by reading the text, but it is my business here to give at least a schematic reply. Luis Vives, the Spanish philosopher, humanist, and professor at Oxford (while in semi-exile), says in his *De anima et vita* (1538):

> It does not now concern us to know *what* the soul is but rather *how* it is and what are its operations . . . and it is impossible to define in an absolute way everything relative to its operations, because they make themselves manifest to our intelligence little by little, in bits and pieces.[8]

This is precisely the way the *Celestina* presents its souls. It is unconcerned with the "what" of their virtues or vices. Instead it pursues the "how," the change of each soul as it adapts to ever new circumstances, its dynamic advance and retreat in spoken warfare with other souls. Through dialogue we see the soul alive in time, changing from one vital situation to another, remembering backwards, proposing forwards, and constantly forgetting—as life goes on.[9]

The formal model for the dialogue of the *Celestina* was Roman comedy, a genre which was being "reborn"—that is to say, being re-read in a somewhat inappropriate way—in the latter half of the fifteenth century. One can sense the presence of Terence and to a less extent of Plautus in both the names and the plot. But whereas their comedies used dialogue for amusing interchange and verbal display of theatrical types, the *Celestina*, in the tradition of Petrarch, converts it into a means for the expression of inwardness. Let us put sources and their combination into parentheses and sum matters up in this way: by focussing intensely not on the "I" in a state of immobile isolation but on the "I" talking to the "you," engaged in a process of conscious verbal living. The *Celestina* gave the first major literary answer to Luis Vives' fearfully simple question, "How does life work?" Each of its sentences is devoted to only one thing: communication of the transitory inwardness of the moment. We are used to this now. Ever since the *Celestina*, this has been the New

World of the greatest author-explorers, that is to say, the novelists and dramatists of after centuries. But then, we also are used to living in America.[10]

What kind of a man undertook this literary expedition into the unknown? It would be unsuitable to discuss here the incredibly complex arguments regarding the *Celestina*'s authorship. In any case, more and more of us are coming to believe what is stated in the prologue material:[11] that the long first act was by an unknown writer and that the other twenty were completed in two successive stages by a law student at Salamanca. His name, Fernando de Rojas, was revealed in a strange and awkward way, in the initial letters of verses appended to the second edition (1500). But why this acrostic and why the caution and hesitancy which an acrostic would seem to imply? Here we are helped by certain documents turned up in recent years, especially the record of the trial of Rojas' father-in-law before the Inquisition. The author of the *Celestina* belonged to that numerous class of converted Jews which was so intellectually and creatively active throughout the whole of the sixteenth century and so frequently victims of the Inquisition. Only in recent years[12] have we begun to realize fully the enormous contribution to Spanish culture made by these forced converts. Not only were there Rojas and that same Luis Vives whose remarks on the "soul" are significant for the *Celestina*, but also a whole roster of the greatest writers, jurists, theologians, humanists, and even Saints. It is not tactful to mention this in today's Spain, but new documents have appeared establishing beyond doubt that St. Teresa of Avila herself was of a distinguished family of "conversos."[13]

The point to be made in the case of Rojas is a simple one. He belonged not to a class but to a caste[14] which was at once a functioning element of society (it would be very close to the truth to say *the* functioning element) and at the same time was excluded from it, looked upon with suspicion and dislike. He and others of his kind were at once in and out, at once fully aware of everything that went on in the social structure—hypocrisies, intrigues, power mechanisms, corruptions—yet, at the same time, removed from them, at an intellectual distance. Moreover, having abandoned one faith and not yet (in many cases) fully gained another, the "converso" found it hard to share the structure of beliefs which a fully accepted member of society could use to render harmless all awareness of social injustice or failure. He lived on the margin: he observed from without; he had a perspective and a capacity for cynical evaluation of motives that were unlikely in persons born to full membership in their society.

I would, in other words, relate the caustic irony of the *Celestina* and its refusal to accept face values to the ambiguous "converso" existence of its author. On one level the work can be thought of as a kind of confidential exposé, an "inside" story. As a worthy forerunner of the novel, it shows us what went on inside a Spanish town—or as Fielding phrased it, scandal from the "holes and corners of the world." But this is not all. Rojas' mental aggressiveness and axiological nihilism went so far as to deny everything that everyone around him believed was

important, even the great epic event of his age, that climax to Spain's mediaeval history, the conquest of Granada. All is subject to time, all is eroded or swept away in its flow. As Sempronio says:

> Good and evil, prosperity and adversity, glory and grief, all lose the strength they start out with. Wondrous events awaited with high hopes are forgotten as soon as they're over with. Every day we see new things happen or hear about them, and then we pass them by and leave them behind. Time makes them small, even makes them doubtful. Would you be so awestruck if you were told there had been an earthquake or something like that, that you would not soon forget it? I mean things like the river is frozen over, the blind man can see again, your father just died, a lightning bolt has struck, Granada has been taken, the king is coming today, he has won a battle against the Turks, the bridge has been washed away, so and so has become a bishop, Pedro has been robbed, Inés has hanged herself, Cristóbal got drunk. You can't tell me that three days later or the second time he hears about it, anyone will still be amazed. Everything is like that; everything passes on in the same way; everything is forgotten; everything stays behind as we go on.[15]

The precaution of the acrostic and this half-gleeful elegy to the fragility of meaning combine in a single pattern, the pattern formed or set by the consciousness of a man exiled in his own country.

But time does not merely pass externally in the *Celestina*. It is not satisfied with washing away with its days and years all that men care about in the world around them. It also flows ceaselessly within the soul. Rojas does not bring to his examination of his characters' minds any sort of psychological theory or method. Rather, through dialogue, he allows the characters themselves to betray ironically the contrast between their pretenses and rationalizations and what we judge from our reading to be the truth. He has a perverse and resentful urge to touch root motivations and, beneath them that subsoil of the soul, time. His characters pretend to fixed purposes and virtues; they attempt fixed characterizations for each other's benefit. But as Luis Vives knew, they really have no essence, no "whatness" at all. They exist in a series of states changing and shifting all along the temporal course of the dialogue and for each of which the question "how?" is the only appropriate one. Thus each character has a succession not of masks but of masked faces, selves and projected selves, each dependent on the situation of the moment. The most obvious example is Calisto, who thinks of himself as an ideal, true lover and yet has no scruples in using or even in worshipping Celestina, "the oldest whore of them all who has rubbed her back in the dirt of every brothel in the land." In general the characters can go from good to bad, from virtuous to vicious, and back again, without being troubled by the inconsistency. Like the things they hold to be important, they are true creatures of time.

Rojas was, thus, a man engaged in a corrosive assessment of life at every level. Yet he was not a satirist—at least in terms of John Middleton Murry's standard definition, as condemning "society by reference to an ideal."[16] For just as Rojas had no base for his life, so his "criticism" had no ideal basis. He was an anatomist engaged in an autopsy of human life, or, perhaps it would be better to say, a vivisectionist probing man in his innermost intimacy, in his social self-projection, and ultimately in his helpless relation to the cosmos.

What I have just done is to paraphrase what I believe to be the theme of the *Celestina*. Ostensibly I have tried to relate its peculiar presentation of man in the world to a possible biography of the presenter, Fernando de Rojas. But we know so little about him that such a relationship is imaginary. I believe in what I have said about Rojas, and at the same time I recognize that, instead of explaining the book in terms of the author's life (as does the biographical critic), I have reversed the usual direction and imagined the life as the book suggests it might have been. As a result, all that has been said about the life of Fernando de Rojas as a converted Jew can be considered as a kind of illustrative device for getting at the theme of the *Celestina*. In any delineation of a thematic vision, the critic can be helped a great deal by reconstructing (or even imagining) the existence and outlook of the viewer. On this level, biographical criticism cannot be dispensed with. But it is now time to abandon this device and plunge directly into the *Celestina*, the only place where the theme and vision are important or can really be said to exist.

The basic situation of life in the *Celestina* is domesticity. Life is lived at home in close company. The principal action takes place in three houses: Calisto's bachelor household, with its over-familiar servants; Melibea's family residence; and Celestina's home, brothel, and infernal warehouse "half falling down at the edge of the city near the tanneries along the river bank." Each of these domestic establishments is conceived as a kind of cell of human intimacy. But as we read, we quickly discover that the loyalty of the servants to Calisto is either shaky or feigned, and their affection hypocritical. As for Melibea and her mother, the secret adolescent meditations of the one and the superficial social preoccupations of the other (how well Rojas arranges for Alisa to betray herself in a few short sentences as a heedless bourgeoise!) prevent real communication between them. Only Celestina and her companion, Elicia, exhibit any sort of domestic harmony (in this Rojas displays the full bite of his irony), a weird and violent harmony which is maintained cynically by both of them.[17] Domesticity, then, is not only a series of deceits but also a situation of pseudo-companionship. The individual is without company yet never alone. Petty intramural wars and bickerings, ignorance of the state of mind of the nearest and dearest, characterize the daily solitude of all who live within walls. And when Melibea at long last pours out her inwardness to her father, it is from a tower where she stands alone, connected with him only by a fragile bridge of words. She leaps, and he, in his turn, is left alone. Throughout this last scene the word "solo" occurs and recurs as a kind of final résumé of the theme of domesticity. If human life is only an inner flow, only the time of its own consciousness, a true touching

of another person is brief and cannot be taken for granted. And domesticity is precisely this taking companionship for granted.

As far as that larger company called society is concerned, there is no direct criticism or satire.[18] Instead of social observation and indignation, we are given insight into the total moral corruption of the community. All the inhabitants pretend to despise and fear Celestina, yet all go to her secretly. She is the mayoress of a counter-society of sensuality, what Mann in *Felix Krull* calls "the hot inarticulate realm of nature" organized by cosmetics, glances, exclamations, gestures, beneath the covering of the "lukewarm" words of social intercourse. Celestina is, in fact, the only person in town who can bring these antithetical kinds of dialogue together. It is not that Rojas is a moralist who thinks of erotic compulsion as evil (although he pretends to in parts of the prologue material). Rather he observes with unremitting irony the spectacle of human beings living together in society, living together as falsely and unauthentically and artificially as they live at home.

Although the concept of social class as it appears in the realistic novels of the nineteenth century or in the sociological textbooks of the twentieth is misleading for the *Celestina*, there are at least two social categories in the cast. On the one hand: the masters and mistresses, Calisto, Melibea, and the latter's family, who are wealthy, well mannered and dressed, and of high lineage. On the other: all the rest who, possessing none of these advantages, live lives which are at times brutal but more often inept or bitter caricatures of the lives of their betters. Sempronio's reflected passion for Melibea or the banquet scene in Act IX are only two of many examples. There is a kind of sardonic humor in the documenting of such parallel but deviant behavior. But when all is said and done, the two so-called classes really amount to the same thing. Manners and money are realities which channel human relationships in special ways. They may even result in a very special variety and level of rationalization (as in the case of Melibea's surrender to Celestina in Act X). Nevertheless the problems of all members of the cast are not different in kind, and their solutions to them no more dignified or important in the one case than in the other. They all—Celestina excepted—invariably choose the easiest way out. As for love, in spite of all the elevated language and special mutual awareness of Calisto and Melibea, its requirement and its practice are as unashamedly physical for them as for their servants. Rojas' social mathematics always returns to the same negative equation: there is no essential difference between categories of people. It is a notion which in this case has nothing to do with democratic ideas or the dignity of man. Calisto and Sempronio are equal in their indignity, as is so corrosively manifested in Calisto's soliloquy in Act XIV—a revelation of moral cowardice as despicable as Sempronio's physical cowardice in Act XII. Read carefully, the *Celestina* betrays as much scorn for class pretensions as it does for social pretense—that is to say, the organized hypocrisy of society taken as a whole.

It is, to be sure, not in society but face to face with the cosmos that the inhabitants of the *Celestina* discover the full extent of their insignificance, their vulnerability, and their loneliness. Rojas stresses such pessimism explicitly in Pleberio's final soliloquy, a kind of thematic epilogue and résumé. But for all the historical interest of this bitter *planctus* (so revealing of Rojas' feelings as a "converso"), most readers have been more interested in the *Celestina*'s expression of the human condition in the course of its dialogue. As readers we are less concerned with pessimistic ideas than with their representation in the flesh and blood of life. But in such a statement there is an assumption which should be turned around. The notion that ideas are put into literature, first thought out and then shaped poetically, is a misleading one for a work as profound and enduring as the *Celestina*. Rather, pessimistic ideas emerge at the end as a kind of self-conscious conclusion, a final flat schematization of a tragic sense or vision of life which was previously an inseparable element in the creative act.

What is this tragic sense or vision? Specifically, the *Celestina* is a work in which all the major characters die suddenly, first Celestina, then Parmeno and Sempronio, and finally Calisto and Melibea. Even Alisa, Melibea's mother, it is hinted, dies of grief in the last scene. Furthermore, at the moment of death, there is an instant of consciousness, of recognition that they like all mortals are about to encounter the cosmos head on. How does this come about? I think it is worthy of surprised remark that four of these five deaths are the result of falls. All throughout the preceding acts physical space is a determining factor in the characters' existence. They are barred from fulfilling their desires by doors and walls. They see each other approach and depart down long perspectives of vacant streets. They listen to each other's conversations at a safe distance, as in Act XII. They worry continually about tripping in haste or in the dark. And at the end their situation in space proves fatal to them; they are killed by space and in space. Melibea, a moment before her fatal leap from the tower, notices ships and a river stretching out to the horizon as in a Renaissance painting. The only landscape in the work, it accentuates the pathos of her death just as Breughel's immense sea, far promontories, and setting sun set off spatially the fall of Icarus.

What has happened is that the traditional and allegorical fall of Fortune is here presented as an actual fall in space purely by chance. The usual reenactment of this fundamental mediaeval myth—perhaps it would be better to call it a pattern of expectation and comprehension—is that reflected in the proverbial "pride goeth before a fall." A being of high estate, merchant, prince, pope, or angel, becomes proud and heedless and is tumbled down and destroyed—to the delight and moral improvement of all about him. But in the *Celestina* there is no suggestion of moral retribution or even of malicious fatality. Man lives in space (the work has all the verticality of the Gothic art of its time but lacks the closed arch of faith). Man is accident prone. Nothing more. A chance misstep from a ladder or a miscalculation of height in the dark and his brains are splattered on the cobble stones. The universe,

like Melibea's seascape or that more elaborate picture of height and sea painted verbally in *King Lear* by Edgar for his blind father, may be beautiful but it is careless of human concerns. The air around man is *ajeno y estraño* (alien and strange), Rojas tells us in his preliminary verses, and in it we are exposed to destruction. Instead of the covered and vaulted-over mediaeval world, where man was cared for if he kept to his rôle of creature, the world of the *Celestina* is one of exposure and moment-to-moment danger. It is characterized by that rooflessness or shelterlessness which Lukacs sees as the basic situation of the modern novel.[19] Or as Camus puts it in *The Rebel*, in referring to Lucretius, "Already the great problem of modern times arises, the discovery that to rescue man from destiny is to deliver him to chance."

Actually I don't believe that Rojas was an intellectual rebel in Camus' Promethian sense or that he proposed to rescue man from anything. In the text of the *Celestina* there exist hints of a coming fall of Fortune, implicit promises of retribution, and other sorts of moral foreboding. But by the time the characters have unwound their lives, Rojas has created a world in which sheer space takes the place of fortune. The initial moral and exemplary intentions have been absorbed into an artistic organism of a more complex and less comforting significance. Rojas was not a rebel but an ironist, an ironist outside the realm of accepted values and explanations, who watched his characters from a distance and allowed them to betray their own rationalizations and corruptions. Fortune, as it were, was changed into space by being portrayed in a world viewed with astringent irony. Rojas, in creating, followed out his own non-conformism not to an idealogical but to a vital conclusion, which is to say to the point of death. And when he did so he saw Fortune in a new and unfamiliar way. In other words, Rojas did not change or revise the traditional and moral fall of Fortune any more than he interfered with the commonplaces on virtue or friendship as mouthed by his characters. What he did was to dig a pit under them, to portray them in an unexpected and disconcerting state of surrounding vacancy.

Wolfgang Kayser has defined the world of the grotesque as "our world—and at the same time not our world. Horror mixed with amusement has its basis in the experience that our trustworthy and familiarly ordered world has become alien in the face of the abyss and its powers."[20] And if we accept his definition, what we have just said about the *Celestina* classifies it as a masterpiece of the grotesque. Indeed I would maintain that it is the masterpiece, the epic of the grotesque, and precisely because it avoids the spooky, the caricaturesque, and the distorted. In it in an almost pure form, dimensions themselves, the newly perceived dimensions of time and space, are applied to a traditional moral universe. We can suddenly see under, through, and around that universe and seeing thus, we perceive the one thing society and culture itself want us least of all to perceive: that our highest aspirations and our meanest absurdities, our horrors and our amusements, are as close as the two sides of a coin, that they are in fact aspects of each other. It is this that is grotesque, and it is this that Cervantes meant when he said that the *Celestina* would have been a "divine" book if it had only known better how "to veil the human."

We in our time are hardly in a position to be as demanding as Cervantes. We can only admire Rojas for discovering so well how to balance the sublime and the ridiculous in close and complex cohabitation, not as polar possibilities of existence. For by doing so, he brought together inwardness and outwardness, seeing in one light the characters' sharp consciousness of self and the great mindless dimensionality to which they (and we) are all exposed. Separating the sublime from the ridiculous confines a character to a representative and exemplary posture from which he cannot change: "I am ridiculous" or "I am sublime." Putting them together creates a problem of self (what I pretend to be contradicting what I am) surrounded, diminished, more aware, and in the end destroyed in its struggle with the newly recognized nonself.[21] By portraying our weaknesses and chronicling our helpless struggles, Rojas was surely the first to express the full dilemma of man in modern times: existence in a world drained of meaning. Thus, when Melibea commits suicide, there is no mention whatsoever of the mortal sin for which she must answer. The nature of the deed isn't even referred to in Pleberio's lament. Nor does he seem to imply that time has passed, shrinking the importance of such a major event as the conquest of Granada and such a minor one as the prophetic "Inés hanged herself." What is involved in Melibea's uncensured deed against herself is a tacit assertion that we are unjudged. Or even worse, as Pleberio (like Gloucester with his "wanton boys" and "flies") implies at the end, we may have been put here to be tormented.

The third aspect of the *Celestina*'s importance is that of imaginary creation, its power to immerse the reader in what I called an "acid bath of life." But the word "life," with its novelistic overtones, is misleading. The *Celestina* gives us less a portrait of Spanish (or human) life in the novelistic sense than it does of a series of interwoven lives, a texture of lives of which the warp is the lovers and the woof, the rogues and prostitutes who further their love, who plot against it, who envy it, who fear its consequences, and who in general cross it in many different ways and directions. The comparison with the weaving of a piece of cloth must be insisted upon. It helps to free us from dramatic modes of imagination, modes fully as misleading as those pertinent to the novel. To read the *Celestina* as it should be read, one must be prepared for its generic peculiarity. The acts are not really acts (in Act XI nothing "happens" whereas in Act XII everything does). The climax is not really a climax (Rojas made no mistake in inserting into the first sixteen-act version five new acts separating love from death). And the motives are not really motives (although we are shown the psychological preparation for certain deeds at length and with great subtlety, Rojas is not concerned with setting up a coherent structure of cause and effect). Each state of consciousness interests him for its own sake. For example, the servants' inner humiliation and shamed realization of their own cowardice during Act XII help explain their unexpected and apparently uncharacteristic murder of Celestina. But Rojas is far more interested in witnessing the growth of these sentiments and listening to their expression than he is in setting them forth as motives for the homicide. In the same way he doesn't worry about explaining why marriage is out of the question for his lovers. He feels no need to fabricate a Montague-and-Capulet situation with the result that he has puzzled almost twenty generations of readers, trained motive-hunters all.

Let us sum up the generic strangeness of the *Celestina* in this way. Made exclusively of dialogue, it cannot present a narrative world, that fully textured and contoured reproduction of life which we expect of the novel. But at the same time it is undramatic. The drama necessarily imposes a geometry of motive, plot, and climax upon the process of living. Rojas is not interested in such geometry; he prefers to trace the vine-like twistings and growth of each consciousness through its multiple spoken encounters with others. Each life is a temporal path of words heard ironically until it is emptied out into space, silenced in death. And if Calisto and Melibea believe for a moment that erotic companionship has provided a culmination for their existences, they are quickly undeceived by the fatal misstep on the ladder. Even Melibea's suicide, so oratorically justified and prepared, is an empty gesture, a fatal posturing more than a catastrophe. These two may want to be Tristram and Iseult just as Don Quixote wants to be Amadis of Gaul, but the draining of myth from their universe has left them stranded. That is why their rhetoric sounds at times exaggerated and artificial.

This unique attention paid to conscious life following its own course through ramps of space and avenues of time may help explain an apparent weakness of the *Celestina*: the failure to endow its lives with sympathy—that is, the work does not elicit pity for the characters nor full recognition of them as fellow human beings. Rojas' ironic objectivity is so merciless, his malice so unhindered, and his skill so uncanny that we come to know his characters (as we know most of our colleagues) too well to care for them. As we listen, we understand them ever more deeply; we become ever more fascinated with their misguided prudence and their heedlessness of real danger. But they never touch us as human beings who suffer. Their weaknesses are ours, but, in spite of all their preoccupation with love and hate, they are neither lovable nor detestable. They would be out of place in tragedy yet they are not comic types. Why do they fail in this way? Because they are only lives, not persons. Bonds of sympathy between man and man depend ultimately on what we *are*. And the *Celestina*'s inhabitants *are* nothing; they merely exist. They are independent, psychically intricate, pulsating lives, but they are not men and women. They are not in the sense that Don Quixote, or Achilles, Macbeth, or even Huck Finn are men, men who for good or ill, in one way or another, with doubt or confidence, pull themselves erect from out of the time of their lives and say, "I am."

There is one exception, and it is great enough to lift the *Celestina* above the ranks of the world's near-masterpieces—

that is to say, works of intense poetic cohesion and striking originality of theme (for example, *Tamburlaine, Fiammetta,* the *Satyricon*) which have nonetheless lost contact with succeeding generations. Celestina herself is the exception, and, at the human center of the literary world in which she lives, she, unaided by her fellow citizens, triumphs over history. Celestina begins as a type, the go-between, and when Pármeno describes her for the first time, he sets movement, sheer "going," at the foundation of her life:

> If she walks through a crowd of a hundred women and one of them calls her "Old Whore," all unembarrassed she'll turn her head and answer with a cheerful look. Everyone knows her at receptions, parties, weddings, guild meetings, funerals, and everywhere people get together. Why, if she happens by a pack of dogs, they'll bark the same thing at her.

We too are permitted to witness her movement. Through the eyes of the other characters we see her skirts fly, or at other times, her bent-over figure trudging along as she calculates her next move. And they not only see her; they frequently interpret for us the sentimental significance of her changes of pace: triumphant jubilation, hesitancy in the face of danger, or physical caution as she maneuvers her aged body among the stones and pitfalls of the mediaeval pavement. As we follow her along, however, we quickly realize she is more than a go-between, a mere carrier of disruptive messages. She also serves, wheedles, suggests, influences, and, ultimately, directs all the lives around her. Her movement has a human force which distinguishes her from all the others. Except for her own murder, everything that happens in the *Celestina* is instigated by her. She is the dictator of nature's avid republic, the puppet mistress not only of her clients but of all the lives that impinge upon her vital horizon. It does not matter that she is corrupt and corrupting, infinitely calculating, or cold to everything except the physical stimulations of alcohol, danger, and sex. It doesn't matter that she is old, scarred, corporeally grotesque, scuttling like a spider around her broken-down old house, taking inventory of her batwings, cosmetics, and gallows-teeth. It doesn't matter that socially she is the core of the city's infection. What ultimately comes to matter is her courage, her mental fierceness (in Stendhalian coexistence with her talent for cold logic), her belief in herself and her way of life—a vital confidence which all the others in their momentary desires and anxieties never begin to approach.

Let us listen to Celestina herself expressing her basic stamina, her vocational density of being, in one of her last speeches: She has just been threatened by Sempronio with exposure to public shame:

> Who do you think I am, Sempronio? [she asks sarcastically] When did you save me from whoredom? Hold your tongue; don't shame my gray hair. I'm an old woman such as God made me and not the worst of the lot. I live by my profession as untarnished as any other professional. I don't seek out clients. They send for me at home, or they come to my house and ask my help. Whether my life be good or bad, God alone stands as

witness to my heart. And don't try to bully me in your anger! Justice is equal for everyone, and all can appeal to it. Although I'm a woman, they'll listen to me just as much as they will to you, all sleek and combed. Leave me alone in my house to my own fortune.

Much earlier she had talked about "maintaining her honor," just as if she were a knight. And in her marvelous soliloquy of doubt and decision in Act IV, she made up her mind to brave entrance into Melibea's house by asking herself the same proverbial question Cortés was to use when he persuaded his men to follow him on the fearful march inland: "Where shall the ox go if he leaves the plow?" All this is, of course, ironical on Rojas' part. With supreme cynicism he imputes to a sink of human degradation the centrally admired trait of the Spanish world (the one trait shared by the Cid and Don Quixote): integral maintenance of the self in the face of all adverse circumstances. Yet this very imputation, this granting of a firm core of being to Celestina's life, awakens in the reader a special feeling—a kind of intense human involvement—for her. At the lowest level this amounts to appalled admiration as we watch her at her infernal work. But beyond that, and in spite of whatever moral principles the reader may adhere to, there is set into operation that basic sympathy lacking for the other characters.

As we have seen, Rojas was a master artisan of life, both a discoverer and a conqueror of the inner world where life becomes aware of itself. But life in words, as in flesh, is tricky stuff; it doesn't hold still and it is hard to rule. In the case of Celestina he made a life that got away from him, that set up its own being—for all of us to come to, as she herself might have said. Thus it was that before many editions had been printed, the *Tragicomedia of Calisto and Melibea* came to be called simply the *Celestina*. Celestina was the center of its human appeal and of its human repugnance, so much the center that, aside from affirmation or negation, she took over the literary world in which she lived. Like Don Quixote or Lazarillo of Tormes, or Don Juan Tenorio, Celestina stepped out beyond her author's intentions and began to live an authentic and ever-renewed life in the imagination of century after century of readers. Through this heroic antiheroine, they (we in our turn) have not only relived viciousness and sheer degradation but have done so as a human experience. In this, I think, lies the superiority of Celestina over the great villains, the Iagos and Agrippinas, of world literature. It is in this unique, incredible, seemingly impossible coexistence not of human beings but of full humanity with evil, that the final importance of the *Celestina* is to be found.

NOTES

[1] By Mack Singleton, (Madison, Wis., 1958), L. B. Simpson, (Berkeley, Cal., 1955), and P. Hartnell, (London, 1959).

[2] The first known edition is dated 1499, and there has been much speculation about lost earlier editions. Internal evidence recently uncovered indicates 1497 as the earliest possible date of composition.

[3] The first printers, the author himself tells us, added a summary of the whole as individual summaries for each act—the standard practice of the time for the printing of dialogue.

[4] Characteristically Dante's dialogue is based on a static situation, to which the principal speaker is irrevocably chained and which he explains *after the fact*. The *Celestina*'s dialogue, on the other hand, moves with the "action" of a series of constantly changing situations. In this sense it is much more dramatic than narrative.

[5] The *Decameron* and the *Libro de buen amor* (the *Conde Lucanor* is an even more extreme example) show a relative lack of interest in dialogue despite their utilization of spoken language. The narrator's rôle is paramount. This is much less true of the Chaucer of the *Troilus*, but, taken as a whole and excepting the oral epics, I believe my generalization to be valid.

[6] The first "editor" of the text (a humanist named Alonso de Proaza) appended to the 1500 edition some closing stanzas. In them, among other things, he indicates that the *Celestina* was written for reading aloud with appropriate mimicry. The work represents a moment of transition in reading habits. The introduction of the printing press was also an introduction to a new world of silent reading. But the *Celestina* had not yet fully entered this world and often needs actual declamation for its full comprehension.

[7] Such claims are, of course, dangerous, but "defenders" of Spanish literature see the novel both in France and England as stemming from the *Don Quixote*. With respect to the theater, they point with pride to the Spanish origins of *Le Menteur* and *Le Cid*. Surely the French would have mastered dialogue without these Spanish examples (just as the English developed their own theater), but these are nonetheless facts of literary history.

[8] From *Liber primis* (p. 39, first edition).

[9] Unique in its age is the *Celestina*'s systematic attention to remembering and forgetting. Events are witnessed and told again from memory with imaginary embellishment; reminiscence from the long past is observed clinically; and the forgetfulness of old age is contrasted with the significant mental lapses of younger minds (e.g., Alisa's forgetting of Celestina in Act IV).

[10] The reader should not be fooled by the unfamiliar and seemingly artificial rhetoric of some of the speeches. Rojas knew how to use it for dialogue purposes. Just as Shakespeare preserved and used the "high astounding terms" of Marlowe's monologue in his own intense dialogue, so too features of past language remain in the *Celestina*. But read rightly—with awareness of what each character has to reveal and wants to convey—the text contains hardly a word (after the apprenticeship of Act I is completed) that does not find its *raison d'être* in the new art of dialogue.

[11] I refer to the introductory "letter to a friend" and verses, first included in the sixteen-act edition of 1500, as well as the prologue which was added to the twenty-one-act edition of 1502.

[12] The first person to see the full significance of the converted Jews to Spain's peculiar history was Américo Castro in his epoch-making *España en su historia* (Buenos Aires, 1948). Later discoveries have abundantly confirmed his insight. An English translation in revised form, *The Structure of Spanish History* (Princeton, N. J.), appeared in 1954. An expanded Spanish edition is in preparation.

[13] This is not said with the idea of provoking doubts as to the saint's saintliness. Saint Teresa remains herself, but this new knowledge of her background helps explain aspects of her fundamental differences with the society of her time (however much she came to be accepted by it afterwards). As for race, many "conversos" were only remotely Jewish. It is much more a question of a variety of acute and often fecund consciousness of self in relation to society than of inherited characteristics or even of an ideological climate. In this sense the Inquisition, representing mass opinion, may be thought of as an instrument for provoking individual self-awareness in addition to repressing ideas and eliminating lineages.

[14] This fundamental distinction was introduced by Castro.

[15] Translation by Edmund L. King; others are my own.

[16] *The Problem of Style* (London, 1922). Murry points out that if the writer of comedy chastises deviation from a social norm, the satirist makes more radical demands. But Rojas, proposing neither norm nor ideal, goes beyond this venture at classification.

[17] See the two brief homecoming scenes at the ends of Acts VII and XI. There is also a fourth house, in which Areusa lives alone and attempts to maintain a sterile and often desperate rebellion against domesticity as well as society.

[18] Exceptions: the usual mediaeval attacks on cosmetics and on the promiscuous behavior of the clergy. There are also one or two veiled and bitter references to Inquisitional justice.

[19] His word is *Obdachlosigkeit*. See his *Die Theorie des Romans* (Berlin, 1920).

[20] *Das Groteske* (Oldenburg, 1957), p. 38. My translation is not literal, but it represents fairly Kayser's interpretation of the grotesque.

[21] Perhaps it would help at this point to think of King Lear, Tom, and the Fool in the storm, surely the finest grotesque scene in literature. There with extreme poetic intensity a limitless and raging universe (Kayser's "abgründige Mächte") is brought to bear on three variant combinations of human ridiculousness and sublimity. Rojas is prosaic and sardonic (rather than poetic and pathetic), but it is this same encounter that is thematically central to the *Celestina*.

Times Literary Supplement   (review date 1965)

SOURCE: "The Status of Lechery," in *Times Literary Supplement*, February 25, 1965, p. 149.

[*The critic recounts the story in* Celestina, *explaining the social implications of the characters' status and behaviors.*]

The Spanish Bawd is Celestina, a central figure in the ***Tragicomedia de Calisto y Melibea***. This is a tale of fatal and illicit love, written in the late fifteenth century by Fernando de Rojas, in the form of a prose dialogue with brief rubrics explaining the action. Of classical and medieval descent, Celestina is the epitome of all bawds, with a relish for her occupation and the degradation it brings. She serves the hero Calisto by engineering the seduction of Melibea, who has greeted his insolent advances—made all of a sudden, when he appears in her garden in pursuit of a hawk—with a contemptuous reply. Celestina has trimmings of witchcraft and prays to Pluto, but her great weapon is psychology. She allows Melibea to play the *grande dame* and insult and trample upon her, certain that this triumph of pride will breed another deadly sin; she has only to suffer a little, strong and humble as a true apostle of evil, and the victim is hers.

The end of the affair comes when Calisto falls from a ladder as he leaves Melibea and is killed. She jumps after him to her death. The work closes with a long lament by her father Pleberio. Celestina has already been murdered in a brawl, shrieking vainly for confession. All are helpless victims of passion and fortune, illustrating with beautiful simplicity the evils against which the Stoics sought to provide a discipline; and the very wisdom of the Stoics is put into their mouths as they go about their folly. This is simply a direct and essentially witty reflection of the truth that we see the better but do the worse; the didactic value of the work thus belonging to moral vision, not exhortation or censure.

Considering its brevity, Mr. Cohen's introduction gives a good survey of the state of criticism of Rojas's extraordinarily forceful and original work; but he is rather undiscriminating in his appreciation of Señor Garrido Pallardó's book, *Los problemas de Calisto y Melibea*. Señor Garrido is attractive for his commonsense appreciations of character, especially in the case of the jackanapes Calisto, whom some earlier critics had astoundingly succeeded in seeing as standing for Platonic love. But his good sense and humanity are put at the service of a laboured and bewildering thesis.

In the nineteenth century Calisto and Melibea were romantically assimilated to Romeo and Juliet. These two would have married, but were prevented by a family feud. So the question was put, why does not Calisto marry Melibea? Such a question is essentially frivolous. The obvious answer is that the story just is not about a young man who wants to marry Melibea, otherwise he would have been numbered among the suitors her parents mention. Instead he appears in her garden invoking his secret passion, God and the saints. If some additional reason for this behaviour is to be sought not in his character but in circumstance one would have thought it enough to observe that he is not Melibea's equal in estate. He is of noble descent but moderate fortune, whereas she is the sole heir to great wealth, and of the very bluest blood ("muy generosa, de alta y serenissima a sangre". The present translation reduces this to "an honourable young lady of pure blood"). After he has been rejected, Calisto tells his servant Sempronio that he despairs of obtaining her. Sempronio cynically replies that the highest of women have given themselves to muleteers or worse—and what about your grandmother's goings-on with the ape?—so he ought to look to his honour as a man and climb high: "it's better for a man to aim above his merits than to fall from the place where he rightfully belongs."

This is plain enough. But for Señor Garrido it must be turned inside out. Whatever her author may tell us, Melibea is really beneath Calisto and quite unthinkable as a bride. Here is the secret reason why. There is a document in which Fernando de Rojas is described as a *converso*—a convert from Judaism. *Conversos* were looked down on by Old Christians. So Calisto cannot marry Melibea because she belongs to a *converso* family. The Christian Calisto is the contemptuous exploiter of a social inferior. The **Tragicomedia** is a bitter social protest. But the protest must be covered up so that the Inquisition will not be able to detect it.

So begins the game of looking for the three-legged cat. Melibea's ultimate submissiveness before Calisto is a sign of low status; the fact that she is a very haughty young lady indeed at the beginning is brushed aside, as is Sempronio's opinion that all women prove shameless and brainless once you get past their guard. Celestina gains easy access to the Melibea household and is treated with good humour by Melibea's mother Alisa; so Celestina must be of the *conversos* too. But Celestina goes all round the town on her missions, peddling powders and lengths of yarn, exploiting the servant network. She keeps a register of all the girl-children born in the place, to see how many escape her clutches. In her great days she was much sought after by the very best people. And Alisa does not invite her to tea. She hears her maid Lucrecia talking to a caller, and laughs when she is told who the caller is. She knew Celestina long ago. But who did not? Alisa is a woman too, and a silly one, so why should she not have something of a past to match her daughter's present? For that matter, her husband Pleberio sowed his wild oats through a youth stretching into middle age, and must have heard of Celestina too. Again, it is held to be very significant that Alisa speaks in a plain and humble style. Her husband does not, but let that pass. The truth is that Alisa has very little to say at all, and speaks plainly when she is giving simple instructions in her house; on the one occasion when she has anything of emotional depth to say (in the last act) she can compose a period as elegantly as anybody; and faint like the most delicate of ladies after it.

If we are told Pleberio is of noble lineage, this is dust in the Inquisition's eyes. Really he made his money by ungentlemanly means. The grounds for this seem to be a passage in the long rhetoric of his despair as he looks at the body of his dead daughter: "For whom did I build towers? For whom did I acquire honours? For whom did I plant trees? For whom construct ships? O hard earth . . . ." This is taken to mean that he has been in shipbuilding and the like. Why not the fruit trade? Surely he is simply a gentleman who has added to his patrimony and now finds that it will all go for nothing? But no; Señor Garrido says that to be a true Spanish gentleman of the times he would have to say "Why did I conquer towers, why did I usurp trees, why seize ships" (the honours are conveniently forgotten); and he would not weep over a dishonoured daughter but would be in a rage to avenge her. Poor Christian gentleman with his code of honour like tin about his soul! The joke is that the servants who assist Calisto in his amours do not seem to realize that they have to deal only with the family of a despised Jew in a ghetto. To Parmeno, for example, they seem people of arrogance and power. He fears that Melibea may well be laying a trap for them all: "with all her servants she could take master and men at one sweep".

So we reach the conclusion that the author has foxed even his own characters about who they are and what they are up to. Such cunning must have driven more than one Inquisitor out of his mind.

Some things are not worth arguing about. Other critics have given the *converso* thesis greater attraction and depth by arguing that as a *converso* Rojas would be a man between two worlds, without a clear faith. There must have been many such. Hence the anguish and tension of the work, its lack of consolation. There is nothing in the text to show any doubt of the specific revelations of Judaism or Christianity; and all argument on this point is fogged by the plea that it would be necessary to fog the Inquisition. But one important consideration appears to have been overlooked. In the period, morals were normally inseparable from religious belief. It might be expected therefore that any radical and chronic disturbance of faith would reflect itself in some disturbance in the field of moral judgments; yet no one was ever more orthodox and definite in his moral judgments than Rojas. Right is right and wrong is wrong; and the wicked come to a bad end. His work owes a good deal of its impact to its combination of a youthful trenchancy of moral idealism with disillusion about life as it is generally lived.

Dare one suggest that his anguish is in any case exaggerated? Melibea, Calisto, Alisa and Pleberio are lifesize fools, commonplace and sad enough. The marvellous thing is that trivial souls should have such eloquence that they become tragic. But Celestina, who dominates the work in the popular mind, is of larger dimensions. She has her realistic side, but she escapes altogether from reality by her great generosity of evil, pouring it out happily as if mean age and corruption flowed like a spring in Arcadia. She is really a bad fairy for older children. There is a more nagging sense of desolation in the *Guzmán de Alfarache* than in the **Celestina**.

Mr. Cohen's translation has much to commend it, though there are a few oddities. An eater of roast eggs becomes a hawker of boiled ones; "your grandfather's knife" becomes "your cuckold of a grandfather". It is understandable that when Calisto says Melibea is God the translator should write "goddess"; but it spoils the blasphemy. An occasional word drops out. On page twenty-six thirteen lines of the original have been mislaid; another sixteen on page twenty-eight. The translation of the opening rubric removes the difference in status between Calisto and Melibea, and gives the impression that Calisto has been pining for Melibea for a long time before the story opens. This impression is shared by others besides Mr. Cohen. But they could all be wrong; Calisto's subsequent conversation with Sempronio might rather suggest that his infatuation is new and sudden.

Points such as these are not vital. The **Celestina** is hard to translate; and while Mr. Cohen's efforts have not produced a really reliable crib, they will give the general reader as true an impression of it as he can reasonably expect. He has justifiably toned down some of the rhetorical extravagance of the original; to try to be faithful to it these days leads too easily into the fustian-rumbustious.

Olga Lucía Valbuena (essay date 1994)

SOURCE: "Sorceresses, Love Magic, and the Inquisition of Linguistic Sorcery in *Celestina*," in *PMLA*, Vol, 109, No. 2, March, 1994, pp. 207-24.

[*Valbuena demonstrates how Rojas integrates the sacred and the profane—commerce, religion, sex—to form the core drive of society.*]

> *Brujería y literatura son una sola cosa, responden a una única receta: el propio cuento, literalmente, es un hechizo.*
>
> Francisco Rico, "Brujería y literatura"
>
> *Witchcraft and literature are one and the same thing; they respond to a single formula: the tale itself is, quite literally, a spell.*

Since the sixteenth century, Fernando de Rojas's **Celestina** has been accorded one of the highest places in world literature, and to this day Hispanists consider it second only to *Don Quixote* in literary merit.[1] While both works have been called the prototype or the first instance of the modern novel, Cervantes's longer and more intentionally narrative work has taken precedence for its contribution to modern realism. Yet as critics have noted, *Celestina*, first published in 1499 and reissued a couple of years later in an expanded version titled **Tragicomedia de Calisto y Melibea**,

> surpasses in tragic strength and realistic conception everything that went before it in Spanish literature of this class; it was the first book in Spanish to spread throughout Western Europe and to enjoy universal popularity during the sixteenth century. Rojas . . . gave literary embodiment to popular speech and inaugurated the artistic renascence in Spain.[2]

Celestina's realistic and modern character emerges in part from the text's exposure of religion, sex, and commerce as interwoven and fundamentally constitutive forces of urban life.[3] Equally compelling to readers has been the eponymous heroine's seemingly diabolical ability to conjure the devil and to manipulate obscure necromantic substances as part of her complex mediations between the material and spiritual worlds. Although other characters and many critics think of Celestina as a witch, traditional necromancy, with its invocation of diabolical power and manipulation of fetishes, is neither her most dependable skill nor the reason for her success in inciting Melibea's passionate love for the lovesick Calisto, who hires Celestina as his procuress.[4]

Rather, as I argue, Celestina's "linguistic sorcery" overlaps and extends a particular type of popular sorcery called love magic that has been practiced surreptitiously in Spain since the early Middle Ages.[5] Using as a point of departure Rojas's depiction of linguistic and sexual transgression within a Catholic regime, I examine the text of a *philocaptio* conjury as well as the trial record of two New World "sorceresses" whose heretical amalgam of religious, magical, and sexual discourses in one *philocaptio* prayer brought them before the Holy Tribunal of New Granada in 1568. Representative of a large body of *philocaptio* conjuries before and after Rojas's age, these texts specifically place Celestina's linguistic sorcery within the sociohistorical context of other sorceresses of language. The juxtaposition of *philocaptio* texts with the **Tragicomedia** also gives verbal specificity to the class of language Celestina uses and demonstrates her exploration of that linguistic field. Focusing on the materiality of Celestina's language allows for an examination rather than a description (the rhetorical approach) of her discursive practice and provides an alternative to ascribing Celestina's verbal prowess to external sources—diabolical power and intervention. Yet the issue of the diabolical is far from irrelevant to a discussion of dissident voices in imperial Spain during the period of inquisition and conquest. For persecution of heretics and deviants—and the ascription of diabolism to these subjects—proceeded from the Inquisition's first order of business, the pursuit of unconverted or dissimulating Jews:

> Because Judaism at the end of the fifteenth century was completely proscribed in Spain and Portugal and Jewish heresy carried the threat of death at the hands of the Inquisition, the situation of crypto-Jews was more extreme than that of some dissenting and heretical Christian groups that faced persecution in this period.
>
> (Zagorin 61)

THE INQUISITION OF THE JEW AND THE WOMAN

If, as the historian María Helena Sánchez Ortega suggests, witchcraft and love magic were not severely punished in Renaissance Spain, the reason may have been the Inquisition's preoccupation with its initial mission of eliminating clandestine Judaism. Perhaps, as Stephen Haliczer argues, for most of Spain, "the converted Jew substituted for the witch as a pariah, reflecting through antithesis and projection society's most ingrained fears and repressed longings" (154). Christians who perceived the *"converso* as a nefarious dissembler and secret enemy of Christianity" analogously viewed women in general, and accused witches in particular, as treacherous and deceitful enough to drive men to madness or perdition.[6] Thus, the popular imagination could conflate the threat of the secretive Jew, the diabolically empowered witch, and

the proverbial lustful woman. Joshua Trachtenberg relates an anecdote that links the three threatening figures:

> In Castille a legend arose that Pedro I (1350-69) had been victimized by a jealous mistress, Doña Maria de Padilla, who presented him with a waistband that his Jewish treasurer, Simuel Halevi, had bewitched; when Pedro wore it at a court reception, "It turned into a great serpent in the sight of all the court, and coiled itself around all his body, to the great terror of all present and also of the king himself."
>
> (75)

As a Christian of *converso* origin, Rojas understood and experienced firsthand the inquisitorial terror practiced on Jews.[7] In his time, religious Jews who remained in Spain either adopted or simulated belief in Catholicism. But many old Christians distrusted the authenticity of the recently converted, tending to associate them with the suspicious gender (and with witches), in keeping with Catholic antifeminine tradition.

Indeed, the Inquisition expanded its mission from the pursuit of Judaism to the punishment of other nonconforming practices, as Bartolomé Bennassar explains:

> [La Inquisición] persiguió otras creencias y otros cultos. Encarceló, despojó, arruinó, deshonró a millares de hombres y mujeres. . . . Por extensión, la Inquisición persiguió y castigó los comportamientos que parecían poner en entredicho, directa o indirectamente, los dogmas y la disciplina de la Iglesia romana, ya se tratara de palabras, gestos o comportamientos sexuales que conculcaban las reglas del celibato eclesiástico o del matrimonio cristiano.
>
> (338)

> [The Inquisition] persecuted other belief systems and cults. It incarcerated, exiled, ruined, and shamed thousands of men and women. . . . By extension, the Inquisition persecuted and punished those behaviors that appeared to put in question, directly or indirectly, the dogmas and the discipline of the Roman church, whether in words, gestures, or sexual behaviors that contravened the rules of ecclesiastical celibacy or Christian marriage.[8]

The pursuit of female subversion that permeated witch trials in continental Europe found much of its authority in the widely read inquisitorial handbook *Malleus Maleficarum* ("Hammer of Witches"), written by the inquisitors Heinrich Kramer and James Sprenger in 1484.[9] Providing the indispensable link between female carnality and male spiritual death, the authors of the *Malleus* assert that "all witchcraft comes from carnal lust, which is in women insatiable," and that

> though the devil tempted Eve to sin, yet Eve seduced Adam. And as the sin of Eve would not have brought death to our soul and body unless the sin had afterwards passed on to Adam, to which he was tempted by Eve, not by the devil, therefore she is more bitter than death.
>
> (47)

The *Malleus* links witchcraft to carnality and both to the Fall, stating that "God allows more power of witchcraft over the genital functions, on account of the first corruption of sin which came to us from the act of generation" (58).[10] The text even ascribes the serpent's nefarious powers to its contamination by woman instead of viewing the serpent as the instigator of sin. Far from being idiosyncratic to the *Malleus*, this notion is widespread in the Judaic and Christian traditions, as Beryl Rowland notes in *Animals with Human Faces*:

> [T]he malign female power anciently symbolized in the snake was curiously reflected in the sin of the Fall. As in the Hebraic tradition, Christian myth held that the serpent caused sin to enter the world. The symbolism is somewhat confused, as *this serpent was also a woman*. In the Talmud myth, Lilith, the former wife of Adam, became a serpent and gave Eve forbidden knowledge. In ecclesiastical art and architecture this myth was frequently *superimposed* on the Christian myth, and the serpent twining around the tree of knowledge was often given a woman's face.
>
> (144; my emphasis)

Kramer and Sprenger envision female sexuality contaminating male flesh and soul and in a continuous extension finally leading to death.[11] Maintaining that "just as sexual intercourse provides for the replenishment of physical life, it also ensures the continuation of death," Gnostic Christian thinkers at their most vituperative implicitly charged women with perpetuating mortality and sin through reproductive power (Bugge 11). This view had long since found mythical-historical articulation in ancient texts such as Hesiod's *Theogony* and Herodotus's *Histories*. In these texts, the myth of the *echidna*, a voracious female serpent that devours her mate at the peak of her pleasure, anticipates the horror of the female body with its sexual-reproductive power, a horror that the authors of the *Malleus Maleficarum* absorbed from, and gave back to, their culture.[12] The Jewish sorcerer's enchanted serpent-waistband; the Hebraic story of Lilith, who is destroyed after refusing to lie under her husband, only to reemerge as the serpent speaking to Eve; and the *echidna* viper—all associate female knowledge and sexuality with the specific threat of emasculation. Insisting that "the word woman is used to mean the lust of the flesh" (47), the *Malleus Maleficarum* is suffused with anxiety over impotency and castration—fears that ensue in part from the church's avoidance of self-contamination with the "impure matter" that is woman. Thus, Kramer and Sprenger recount the story of a young man who "was bewitched in such a way that he could never perform the carnal act with any woman except one" (118). Rojas, a product of his time, inscribes such gynophobic sentiments in *Celestina* by introducing the myth of the voracious *echidna* viper in the prologue. But as the following pages show, he subverts this gynophobia by insisting that the primary source of corruption in the community is men's avarice and lust.

ROJAS AND *CELESTINA*: ON FEMALE VORACITY AND LOVE MAGIC

There are three things in nature, the Tongue, an Ecclesiastic, and a Woman, which know no moderation in goodness or vice.

Heinrich Kramer and James Sprenger (42)

In the prologue to **Celestina** Rojas cites Heraclitus's assertion that in nature creation occurs through conflict and violence (14-19).[13] From this aphorism Rojas develops an elaborate account of antagonistic behaviors observable among the elements, animals, and humans that culminates in a characterization of the entire process of generation as replete with violence and death. Using the *echidna* viper of Herodotus's *Histories* as a paradigmatic example, Rojas invokes the image of the impassioned female strangling the male at the moment of sexual climax and conception:

> La víbora, reptila o serpiente enconada, al tiempo del concebir, por la boca de la hembra metida la cabeza del macho y ella con el gran dulzor apriétale tanto que le mata. . . .
>
> (16)

> The viper, a crawling creature and venomous serpent, at the time of engendering, the male puts his head into the mouth of the female, and she, through the great sweetness of her pleasure, strains him so hard that she kills him. . . .

Rojas invokes this image in the preface to demonstrate the destructive effects of bestial lust; the serpent faces destruction on submitting to its biological destiny just as Calisto is sentenced to death by his desire for Melibea.[14] But in fact, while Calisto's death is accidental if not farcical, Melibea chooses suicide as the tragic end to the intensified repression and constriction that await her as a fallen woman. Indeed, Melibea eventually complains, "[C]omen este corazón serpientes dentro de mi cuerpo" '[S]ome serpents within my body . . . are gnawing upon my heart' (248). So although Rojas invokes both the Catholic and the mythic antifeminine traditions in **Celestina**, he confronts the vision of female sexuality as serpentine and voracious with the realistic depiction of an exploitative sexual marketplace lurking at the edge of a repressive culture. Presided over by Celestina, this market prostitutes lowerclass women and thrives on the patronage of lecherous clerics, dignitaries, and other citizens.

The women who traded in love conjuries, generally poor, meagerly educated, and, like Celestina, old and unaccompanied, had little to gain from the church's strict teachings on virginity, chastity, and the virtues of self-abnegation. For many, love magic was a vocation of last resort. As the historian Sebastián Cirac Estopañán explains:

> Las mismas hechiceras no creían en la eficacia de los hechizos y en la necesidad de los sortilegios; pero con

ellos remediaban su miseria, porque sacaban algún dinero . . . . Todas las curanderas, y santiguadoras, y encomendadoras, lo eran por remediar su necesidad con lo que les daban.

(216-17)

The sorceresses themselves believed neither in the efficaciousness of their spells nor in the need for incantations; but by these means they remedied their poverty, for their skills earned them at least a little money . . . . All the female quacks, faith healers, and go-betweens engaged in these activities to remedy their penury with whatever they were paid.

And yet the sorceress's ability to explore her victim's belief in the effective power of religious language, iconography, and ritual afforded both practitioner and client at least a modicum of power neither might otherwise have had. Indeed, far from denying God and church, the linguistic sorceress developed her incantations within the parameters of Spanish Catholicism, with its ample catalog of saints, martyrs, and devils.[15] The clients themselves evidently embraced both Catholic doctrine and the short-hand method of ensnaring a resistant lover. The sexual frankness of the conjuries makes clear, however, that the users understood that their methods undermined the church's doctrinal position on chastity and procreative monogamy and the correlative modesty expected of women in Catholic Spain. As Sánchez Ortega explains, "'Love magic' was also extramarital magic, one in which erotic relations always carried a sinful, condemnable connotation for the zealous priests and inquisitors" (83).

Like other users of love magic, Celestina regularly composes conjuries of verbal materials from high and low culture (philosophy, prayer, adages). On occasion she complements these love philters with conventional fetishes (an article of the lover's clothing, a heart of wax stuck with broken needles) meant to work by metonymy or contagion, according to the individual client's needs (Rojas 56-57). But when approaching the sanctimonious Melibea, Celestina shuns this less subtle form of material sorcery in favor of the incipiently erotic passion in the language of Christian martyrology. She ultimately prevails on Melibea by infusing religious pieties about benevolence toward neighbors, specifically Calisto, with sadomasochistic suggestions that Melibea's malady, her "burning" and suffering (*pasión*), can be alleviated only by submission to Celestina's "invisible needle" of language, the induction to physical penetration by Calisto (260-63, 254-57). Celestina refines the vulgarism of love magic into a quasi exorcism, allowing Melibea to participate in her own "enchantment" and sustaining the fiction that in surrendering to Calisto Melibea complies with the highest ideal of Christian charity and self-sacrifice. Celestina's accommodation of conventional love magic to the desires of an ambivalent victim demonstrates her superior interpretive skill, her linguistic sorcery.

Eroticized prayers and spiritual "cures," not straightforward diabolical intervention, assist Celestina in her "enchantment" of Melibea. Still, love magic explores three of the culture's fundamental tenets regarding physical desire and pleasure: the categorical sinfulness of nonmarital, nonprocreative sexuality; the wrongfulness of inducing desire by external agency (whether that of a saint or that of a devil); and the covalence of ecstasy and misery, together with the power of redemption through suffering. Widespread belief in the affective influence of saints, of the devil, and of Catholic dogma in general provides the inducement to mingle saints and devils, pleasure and suffering in the process of the erotic conquest afforded by love magic. Yet critics like P. E. Russell and Javier Herrero, who maintain that "the world of *La Celestina* is dominated by the devil" (Herrero, "Aging Prostitute" 33), remove the agency of individual, willful characters to a supernatural sphere where "desordenado apetito" 'disorderly appetites' are reduced to manifestations of the ongoing Manichaean conflict between forces of good and evil (Rojas 20). These critics downplay Celestina's rhetorical skill, her parasitic ability to read the desires and limitations of her clients and to ensure for herself that "[m]ío era el provecho, suyo el afán" 'mine was the profit and theirs the pains' (240).

Like the charms of all sorcerers and witches, Celestina's threads, serpent oils, and other nefarious substances require affective power to work for her clients (or to subdue her victims). Consequently, the element of rhetorical manipulation in Celestina's "magic"—not the authenticity of her fetishes and diabolism—is central to an understanding of the tragicomedy.[16] As Malcolm K. Read has noted of Celestina:

> [S]killful though she is in drawing upon supernatural aid, her confidence stems from a belief in the possibilities of her unaided humanity, and her manipulation of the supernatural power of the word is more than matched by her purely rhetorical skill. Her greatest art is that of controlling others not with witchcraft but with her own linguistic ability.

("Rhetoric" 85)

Although Celestina has resigned her sexuality, she takes voyeuristic pleasure in arranging the sexual affairs of others and routinely does so for her own titillation and, especially, for money (Rojas 234-35).[17] Her continued success as a go-between proceeds from her ability to mediate between the desires of her clients and the physical or moral obstacles that would prevent the fruition of those desires. When she reissues a patched "virgin" or a lover's message into the community, her creation invariably mimics an "authentic" or ideal state that, for whatever reason, does not exist in the present. Her "sorcery," then, amounts to manipulation of a fetish or idea whose aspect hoodwinks her clients or their dupes.[18] Thus, if a girl has lost her hymen, Celestina stitches in a new one; if Calisto cannot arouse Melibea's sexual desire directly, Celestina importunes the girl with a cunning blend of discourses that transforms Melibea's religious passion into sexual passion. Creating and communicating the experience of something that is not discernible, Celestina proves herself a master of metaphor.

CELESTINA'S LINGUISTIC SORCERY AND THE *PHILOCAPTIO* CONJURY

In act 3, Celestina takes considerable care in preparing the thread for Melibea's "enchantment." While steeping the thread in serpent oil, Celestina recites an incantation replete with figures from classical mythology, a reminder that she borrows from and corrupts the world of masculine learning (Maravall 42). Like much of Celestina's speech, the conjury contains the characteristic language of magic. As D. J. Gifford points out in his study of verbal *facinatio* in *Celestina*, "the incantation, as used by the wise woman or medicine man, is essentially hypnotic." Following Robin Skelton's writing on "spellcraft," Gifford notes of incantations that "the tone, whether quiet and lulling or vatic and oratorical, is consistent in its appeal to the subject to be receptive to rhythm and image and overall intent rather than to anything more precise" (31). Celestina's linguistic sorcery, like that of her historical counterparts, makes use of "rhyme, hidden alliteration and rhythm," elements of any successful incantation.[19] The entire text of *Celestina*, not just the "enchantment" of Melibea, attempts to work a protracted spell on the auditor:

> Yo, Celestina, tu más conocida cliénta, te conjuro por la virtud y fuerza de estas bermejas letras, por la sangre de aquella nocturna ave con que están escritas, por la gravedad de questos nombres y signos que en este papel se contienen, por la áspera ponzoña de las víboras de que este haceite fue hecho, con el cual unto este hilado. . . .
>
> (104)
>
> I, Celestine, thy best known and most noted client, conjure thee, by the virtue and force of these red letters, by the blood of this bird of the night, wherewith they are charactered, by the power and weight of these names and signs, which are contained in this paper, by the bitter poison of those vipers, whence this oil was extracted, wherewith I anoint this clew of yarn. . . .

Despite the rhetorical force and sensory overload of Celestina's language, Pármeno's deflationary comment on completing his catalog of her substances and methods in act 1, "Y todo era burla y mentira" 'And all these were mere mockeries and lies' (56), intrudes on the reader's willingness to believe in the authenticity of her "diabolical magic" (Chevalier 142-43). It is not until Celestina begins to use a specifically Christian discourse in her "enchantment" of Melibea in acts 4 and 5 that she enjoys any success with her victim. Celestina's historical counterparts indeed preferred the sympathetic power of Catholic saints and rituals for their conjures. As Cirac Estopañán explains in his collection of inquisitorial proceedings, "el fondo de las hechiceras castellanas, por su educación, por el ambiente, es totalmente cristiano" 'the essence of Castillian sorceresses, owing to their education, their milieu, is totally Christian' (106).

Most love conjures are poetic compositions discursively grounded in orthodox Catholic belief. Their very existence exposes the rhetoric—and the aesthetic—of erotic violence already operative in the institutional vehicles licensed to displace (celibate) pleasure: religious discourse and the inquisitorial process, the complete surrender to passion and to discipline.[20] Moreover, sacred and profane ecstasy become one in the *philocaptio* conjury, which effectively destabilizes the Catholic attempt to devalue unsanctioned physical pleasure while exalting the agony of martyrdom. The following characteristic love philter, which conjoins the disparate elements of hagiography, sexual intercourse, travail, torture, and even the assistance of the midwife attending the saint's birth, returns to the primal scene of the saint's conception and yokes his purifying physical martyrdom into the service of worldly pleasure:

> Herasmo, herasmo,
> Obispo y Arçobispo, e confesor en Roma,
> bienaventurado señor santo herasmo,
> yo te conjuro con el padre que te hizo.
> Arasmo, Arasmo,
> yo te conjuro por la madre que te parió:
> yo te conjuro por la partera que te rresçivió;
>
> . . . . .
>
> Bienaventurado señor Sant erasmo,
> por aquellas tres oras de ardor y erbores que
>   tuvistes,
> enbieys tales ardores y erbores
> al corazón de Fulano. . . .
>
> (Cirac Estopañán 135-36)
>
> Erasmus, Erasmus,
> bishop and archbishop, and confessor in Rome,
> fortunate lord Saint Erasmus,
> I conjure you on the father that made you.
> Arasmus, Arasmus,
> I conjure you on the mother that bore you:
> I conjure you on the midwife that received you;
>
> . . . . .
>
> Blessed lord Saint Erasmus,
> for those three hours of fervent burning that you
>   suffered,
> send the like burning and fervor
> to the heart of so-and-so. . . .

This conjury, like many of its kind, is predicated on harnessing, and releasing onto a different subject, the psychological impact of a given saint's miraculous power or a martyr's exquisite pain. All love conjures based on the lives of saints share two crucial elements: first, the ritualistic form and cadence and even the suppliant tone of orthodox prayer and, second, the transformation of the canonical account of a saint's torture and suffering into an incantation that exploits metaphor. As Francisco Rico explains, when a sorceress prepares a love potion and heats it over fire saying, "así como hierve esto, llerva el corazón de fulano" 'just as this boils, thus enflame the heart of so-and-so,'

> se da ahí, naturalmente, una estricta correspondencia entre causa y efecto. Pero, además . . . esa correspondencia es en sí misma metafórica: la *idea* de un corazón que hierve cumple perfectamente el requisito del des-

plazamiento significativo, la "translatio" de que hablan los teóricos, que caracteriza la metáfora.

(112; my emphasis)

a strict correspondence between cause and effect is established. But moreover . . . that correspondence is in itself metaphorical: the *idea* of a heart boiling with fever conforms perfectly to the prerequisite of displaced signification, the *translatio* of which theorists speak, characteristic of metaphor.

In a typical love philter words lifted from the martyrology of saints' descriptions of their torture and suffering, such as *quemar* ("burn" or "scorch"), *ardor* ("ardor," "heat," "fieriness," or "fervor"), and *erbor* or *hervor* ("boil"), convey the burning of erotic passion as religious rapture. The conjury asserts the Catholic belief in the supernatural power of saints while profaning the experience of those who "burn" in defense of the religion. Thus Saint Erasmus's legendary "tres oras de ardores y erbores" `three hours of fervent burning' in a vat of fiery pitch becomes the profane metaphor for the burning with desire that the victim is to experience for the user or client. That this kind of incantation circulated among women in medieval and early modern Spain and later in Spanish colonies demonstrates less than monolithic church control of religious discourse.[21]

Celestina cannot proffer such a conjury to the heartsick Calisto. As Celestina well knows, Calisto would like to believe that Melibea has become enamored of him without magical intervention. Celestina also understands herself as an outright bawd for Calisto will repel Melibea. Thus, Celestina conceals the seduction in a shroud of religious and mortal urgency, which nonetheless conveys the power of love magic. She implores Melibea, "Yo dejo uno enfermo a la muerte, que con solo una palabra de tu boca salida . . . tiene por fe que sanará, segun la mucha devoción tiene en tu gentleza" 'I come lately from one, whom I left sick to the death, who only with one word, whcih should come from your noble mouth . . . [believes he'll be cured, so greatly does he prize your courtesy]' (122).[22] Although Celestina names neither the infirm nor his malady, she excites Melibea's curiosity by remarking that God has endowed only special beings with uncommon beauty and grace and that those chosen by God are to be his "almacén de virtudes, de misericoridia, de compasión, ministros de sus mercedes y dádivas" 'magazines of virtue, of mercy, compassion, ministers of [his] blessings and graces' (122). Celestina protests that if there exists a modicum of gentleness toward the weakened adversary even among beasts, humans should display the same compassion freely toward one another:

Por qué no daremos [los humanos] parte de nuestras gracias y personas a los próximos, mayormente, cuando están envueltos en secretas enfermedades y tales que, donde está la melecina, salió la causa de la enfermedad?

Why should we that are men, be more cruel? Why give we not part of our graces and of our persons to our neighbours? Especially when they are involved in secret infirmities, and those such that, where the medicine is, thence was the cause of the malady?

The language of this appeal is grounded in Christian commonplaces that would obscure the hidden agenda if Melibea were not receptive to the sexual connotation.[23] But in the context of Melibea's seduction, the idea of giving "part of our graces and of our persons to our neighbours" clearly exceed strict religious altruism. Instead, as Melibea knows, the words mean that she should give that "part" of herself—her maidenhead—to the one whose "secret infirmities" issue from his unanswered lust for her. Instead of responding to the denotative meaning of the word *enfermedad* 'malady,' Melibea siezes on its association with the passion (torture-suffering-sex) of the love conjury. In so doing, she signals to Celestina her willingness to take part in the exchange of medical-religious for sexual signification and activity. For it is Melibea who first introduces the word *pasión* into the dialogue, when she pleads with impatience to Celestina, "Por Dios que sin más dilatar, me digas quien es ese doliente, que de mal tan perplejo se siente, que su pasión y remedio salen de usa misma fuente" 'For God's love, without any more dilating tell me who is this sick man, who feeling such great perplexity, hath both is sickness [*su pasión*] and his cure, flowing from one and the selfsame fountain" (124).

On witnessing Melibea's violent response to the naming of Calisto, Celestina immediately reverts to a mutually acceptable discourse, one that nonetheless transmits the crucial innuendo.[24] She reintroduces the "necessitated cause" of her visit as a plea for Calisto (120-21), who she claims suffers from a life-threatening toothache that can be healed only by

[u]na oración, senora, que le dijeron que sabías de Santa Apolonia para el dolor de las muelas. Asimismo tu cordón, que es fama que ha tocado todas las reliquias que hay en Roma y Jerusalén.

(128)

a certain charm, madame, which, as he is informed by many of his good friends, your ladyship hath, of St. Appollonia, which cureth the toothache; as also that same admirable girdle of yours: for the report goes that it hath touched all the relics that are in Rome and Jerusalem.

Saint Appollonia is the patron of toothache sufferers, her particular torture having been the forcible extraction of all her teeth, but in the late fifteenth century, as Javier Herrero has shown, toothache was a common metaphor for lust.[26] Although this prayer would belong to the well-known subgenre of the love conjury, its text does not surface in the *Tragicomedia*. Rather, Celestina says Calisto has been "informed" that Melibea has the prayer, when the reader knows the entire "toothache ruse" to be an impromptu fabrication necessitated by Melibea's initial obduracy (Shipley 327). Because Melibea understands the double meaning of *toothache*, *girdle*, and *prayer* in this context, she may appear to respond only to the literal, innocuous meaning of the words. Thus Melibea sustains the pretense that by surrendering her girdle she is helping to save a Christian, while Calisto thinks that Melibea has knowingly and willingly offered him the symbol of her virginity. From this point forward, Celestina and Melibea's exchanges are organized around Melibea's initiation into the uncanny language of symbolic penetration.

The exchanges are also somewhat inquisitorial, for Melibea is to confess the exact cause of her pain and to submit herself to the rigors of the "cure" prescribed by Celestina.[27] As Celestina tells her, "Por ende cumple que al medico como al confesor se hable toda verdad abiertamente" '[I]t is very fit and convenient that you should open the whole truth, as well to your physician, as to your confessor' (250). While Melibea insists that the "cure" should not touch her honor, Celestina succeeds in persuading her to abjure her highborn sensibilities. Melibea ultimately pleads for relief from pain "[a]gora toque en mi honra, agora dane mi fama, agora lastime mi cuerpo; aunque sea romper mis carnes para sacar mi dolorido corazón" 'though it touch upon my honour, though it wrong my reputation, though it afflict my body, though it rip my flesh, for to pull out my grieved heart' (252).

Celestina knows that Melibea's suffering proceeds from her wish to have intercourse with Calisto and still remain a virgin. Recognizing this impasse, Celestina transforms her usual method of patching the hymen into a figurative cure that contains the transgression and its repair in one economical therapy. In contrast to the many young women for whom Celestina has literally stitched up a hymen with "unas agujas delgadas" 'fine small needles,' Melibea undergoes a figurative defloration in which Celestina uses the "invisible aguja" 'invisible needle' of language as an instrument that both penetrates Melibea and leaves her intact, that is, one that prepares her physically and psychologically for sex with Calisto (56, 254).[28] Melibea accedes, sensing that her virginity is as good as lost once she has confronted her desire in language: "Quebróse mi honestidad, quebróse mi empacho, aflojó mi mucha vergüenze" 'It is my honesty that is broken, it is my modesty that is broken' (256). But the most striking feature of the "cure" will actually increase Melibea's suffering and leave a "greater scar," that is, a palpable sign of her loss of wholeness:

> Sufre, señora, con paciencia, que es el primer punto y principal. No se quiebre; si no, todo nuestro trabajo es perdido. Tu llaga es grande, tiene necesidad de áspera cura. Y lo duro con lo duro se ablanda mas eficazmente. Y dicen los sabios que la cura del lastimero médico deja mayor señal y que nunca peligro sin peligro se vence. Ten paciencia . . . .

> Madame, I pray to be patient. That which is the chief and principal point must not be broken, for then all our labour is lost .Your wound is great, and hath need of a sharp cure, and hard with hard doth smooth more effectually. And wise men say that the cure of a lancing

surgeon leaves behind it the greater scar, and that without danger no danger is overcome. Have patience . . . .

Having persuaded Melibea that her sickness and cure, like Calisto's, flow from one "selfsame fountain," Celestina rehearses in language what Bronislaw Malinowski has characterized as "expression of emotion" that replicate the desired end of the sorcery. Malinowski notes that in love magic, the sorcerer vents the powerful feeling of the frustrated lover: "All these spontaneous acts and spontaneous works make man forecast the images of the wished-for results, or express his passion in uncontrollable gestures, or break out into words which give vent to desire and anticipate its end" (213).

To rehearse the penetration, Celestina enjoins Melibea to stifle her voice and senses, not to inhibit but rather to sharpen and focus her imagination on the anticipated deflowering:

> Pues si tú quieres ser sana y que te descubra la punta de mi sotil aguja sin temor, haz para tus manos y pies una ligadura de sosiego, para tus ojos una cobertura de piedad, para tu lengua un freno de silencio.
>
> (252)

> And therefore, if you be willing to be cured, and that I should discover unto you the sharp point of my needle without any fear, frame for your hands and feet a binding of patience and of quietness; for your eyes a veil of pity; for your tongue a bridle of silence.

With the "sharp point" of her needle (and perhaps by guiding Melibea's fingers) Celestina introduces Melibea to the language of sexual desire and surrender, an act of stimulation and linguistic sorcery culminating in Melibea's climactic loss of consciousness.

LINGUISTIC SORCERY AND THE INQUISITORIAL TEXT

[The products of an auditive culture] will be characterized by a high level of rhetorical fabrication. Although orally delivered, such a text does not seek to establish a dialogical relation with the audience but instead to leave the audience dumbfounded: [con la] boca abierta. The audience does not participate, nor does it internalize the arguments: it is conquered, subjugated, carried by the persuasive flow of the rhetoric.

Wlad Godzich and Nicholas Spadaccini ("Popular Culture" 47)

Both the inquisitors and the conquerors in the New World paternalistically viewed themselves as the spiritual and political guardians of ignorant and morally lost peoples (Elliott 51-64). And not surprisingly, both groups described their subjects in feminine terms in various New World chronicles. In one instance, a priest writes to the crown of the need to "pacificar, reducir, y poblar" 'pacify, reduce, and populate' "el seno mexicano" 'the breast of the Mexican land.'[29]

This same priest depicts recent converts as weak vessels that require paternal supervision:

> Y por su natural inconstancia y desordenado apetito a su Barbarie, necesitan de immediatas Poblaziones de Españoles, que con su respecto los *contengan, dociliten, y protejan.*
>
> (*Indiferente General* 137v; my emphasis)

And because of their natural inconstancy and disorderly appetite for barbarity, there is need of immediate Spanish settlements, that respect of these will *contain, render docile, and protect* them.

As Colin M. MacLachlan observes in *Spain's Empire in the New World*, the crown and the church authorized each other's colonial exploits:

> In the American empire, monarchs directed the Church as an instrument of conquest and consolidation. . . . Theoretically, the Church asserted its temporal authority to override the rights of pagan societies so that missionaries could freely preach, as well as judge rulers according to the laws of the New Testament and the Church, and then conveyed such rights to the monarchy along with the obligation to carry them out. The Crown eagerly accepted both the theory and the charge to undertake the task because it justified displacing Indian rulers. Moreover, it implied a benevolent intent behind the seizure of political power in the New World.
>
> (30)

Although an independent tribunal of the Inquisition was not established in New Granada until 1610, the suppressive functions of the Holy Office were carried out in the American colonies as early as 1522 (Greenleaf 8). Accordingly, in 1568, Diego Jimenez, a priest, arrived in the city of Trinidad, in what was then New Granada, as a *visitador* ("inspector" or "special investigator") to preside over an adultery investigation involving a woman known simply as la Espinosa. As Jimenez gathered testimony against her, a series of related narratives eventually displaced the original one and yielded further allegations of adultery, pandering, and sorcery that he could not have anticipated. While attempting to determine what or who had led la Espinosa astray, the priest learned that María de Medina and her daughter Elvira de Medina not only had promoted the adultery of la Espinosa and others but also had given themselves to "muchos excesos y pecados asy en yerbas como en hechizos e otras supersticiones que han thenydo de malas Xyanas [Cristianas]" 'many excesses and sins in evil herbs as well as in sorceries and other superstitions that they have had from bad Christians' (*Justicia* 146r).[30]

The trial record indicates that Elvira de Medina was charged with starting altercations during the Mass, with cross-dressing for nocturnal wanderings, and with disobedience toward her parents and husband (148v, 162v). It was further alleged that,

> como mala Xyana [Cristiana] a procurado tener hechizos y usar de yervas malas y en el cofre de la susodicha tener ciertos hechizos enbueltos en un papel en que tenía ciertos cabellos y uñas cortadas y otras cosas malas para con ello dañar al dicho su marido e otras personas.
>
> (162v)

bad Christian that she is, she has attempted to work spells and to make use of evil herbs, and in her trunk has kept certain fetishes wrapped in paper in which she had certain hairs and nail clippings and other evil things with which to do harm to her husband and other persons.

Despite the severity of the Medinas' alleged adulteries and sorceries and even a claim that they had induced abortions with herbs (151r), Jimenez showed more immediate concern over the women's knowledge and dissemination of a prayer crafted to enthrall a male victim. María de Medina claimed to have learned this prayer or philter from la Espinosa, the woman whose adultery and later accusations brought the Medinas under ecclesiastical scrutiny. Yet even the witness who ultimately denounced the Medinas before the *visitador* betrayed her fascination with the idea of winning a lover through these unusual means. Thus, "aviendo sido persuadida por esta testigo muchas vezes [dijo María de Medina] que la oracion que rrezaba en la tablilla hera para que la quisiese bien un don Francisco Lopez que en aquel tiempo andaba con ella" 'after having been importuned many times by this witness, [María de Medina told] her that the prayer and the little box she prayed on [were used] so that she would be well loved by a don Francisco Lopez who went with her at the time' (147r).[31] The witness then revealed part of the prayer shown her by María de Medina:

> Señora mya Santa Marta digna soys y santa de my señor Jesucristo fuystes querida y amada de my senora la birgen maria fuystes huespeda y conbidada y en el monte de Talarcon fuystes y a la serpiente biba la hallastes y con vuestro ysopo de agua la rrosciastes y con vuestra bendita cinta la atastes y al pueblo la entregastes asy como esto es berdad vos me traygais a fulano que hera la persona a quien queria ella que binyese quedo, ledo, y atado de ojos y manos y coracon y me quiera y ame y senora me llame y con otra no pueda holgar sy no fuere conmigo.
>
> (147v)

My Lady Saint Martha, worthy you are and saintly. By my Lord Jesus Christ you were cherished and loved; by my Lady the Virgin Mary you were hosted and welcomed. To the mount of Talarçon you went and beheld the live serpent; with your hyssop of water you sprinkled it and with your holy girdle you bound and delivered it unto the people. Just as this is true, bring so-and-so unto me, who was the person she desired to come to her, calm, placid, and bound of hand and foot and heart so that he should love me and call me his lady and take pleasure in no one, if not me.[32]

According to legend, Saint Martha delivered the village of Talarçon, in Provence, from a dragon, a symbol of voracity and lust. She accomplished this feat by subduing the creature with the power of her girdle and hyssop, the anointed symbols of her chastity and virtue. Acknowledging the religious significance of this exploit, the speaker nonetheless appropriates the saint's victory while also exploring the metaphorical potential of the privileged symbols. Inscribing sexual meaning in the purificatory hyssop and the girdle (a belt that either holds or releases the garments, thus, a marker of the threshold between repression and release of sexuality), the speaker calls on Saint Martha to assist in rather than to defeat the fulfillment of the supplicant's desire.

Two features of this *philocaptio* conjury coincide with the practice of sorcery in *Celestina*. First, like Saint Martha's girdle, Melibea's is believed to contain magical-religious properties, because it has supposedly come into contact with certain icons kept in Jerusalem and Rome. Next, Celestina urges the exasperated Melibea, "[H]az para tus manos y pies una ligadura de sosiego, para tus ojos una cobertura de piedad, para tu lengua un freno de silencio, para tus oidos unos algodones de sufrimiento y paciencia" '[M]ake for your hands a binding of patience and of quietness; for your eyes a veil of pity; for your tongue a bridle of silence; for your ears the stuffing of sufferance and bearing' (252). This incantatory patter, with its images of conquest and submission, indeed leaves the auditor "dumbfounded: [*con la*] *boca abierta*" and finds a virtual echo in the Medinas' love philter: "Just as this is true, bring so-and-so unto me . . . *calm, placid, and bound of hand and foot and heart*" (my emphasis). If the girdle is to alleviate Calisto's toothache (sexual desire), Melibea must unwind it from her body and give it to Celestina, who in turn must give it to Calisto. This removal certainly prefigures Melibea's loss of virginity, but the girdle also functions as the ligature that binds Calisto and Melibea to each other and, through the dramatic economy of this text, to sexuality and death. The spiritual death or loss of grace Calisto suffers when he commits idolatry in Melibea's name ("Melibeo soy, y a Melibea adoro y en Melibea creo y a Melibea amo" 'I am a Melibean, I adore Melibea, I believe in Melibea, and I love Melibea') parallels Melibea's virtual material death when she loses her virginity and thus her value in the marriage market (32).[33]

Through the power of the holy girdle, the speaker of the unauthorized Medina prayer attempts a metaphorical binding of male desire to female control. Like Calisto, whose desire for Melibea is all-consuming, the speaker in the Saint Martha conjury intends for the victim to "take pleasure in no one, if not me." And to this end, the speaker appropriates the sprinkling device "with which the Roman Catholic missionaries were wont to scatter the holy drops whose mystic virtue could cleanse the soul in a moment from the foulest stains of infidelity" (Prescott 143).[34] The speaker seizes the church's particular fetish and corrupts the objective of purification through the magical properties of the "holy drops" when, through those hallowed words and symbols, she renders a man incapable of choosing on whom to bestow his powers of insemination. The speaker's use of the hyssop as an instrument

of mastery over the "dragon" secures for her the power over what is both threatening and desirable, namely, the male's culturally endorsed prerogative of initiating and regulating sexual relations.

The Medinas' will to assume dominance in sexual relations, especially by their love magic, undermined the church's prerogative of supervising the content of its subjects' desires through dogma and standardized prayer. In the eyes of the Catholic Church, the women's insinuation of a personal sexual quest into the privileged code of religious discourse evinced a dangerous will to influence the love relations formalized in the institution of matrimony or to inflame uninterested or married men. Furthermore, to make "filthy lucre" (1 Pet. 5.2) from the misuse of religious symbols debased the church's claim of their authenticity and transcendent meaning. As the summary charges against the defendant state:

> Yten que la dicha maria de medina como mala Xyana [Cristiana] que es y sintiendo mal de la fe a usado de oraciones malas y supresticiosas la qual no contenta con usarlo sino como dañada y mala Xyana lo a enseñado a otras personas para que usen de las supresticiones.
>
> (*Justicia* 162r)

> Item[:] that the aforesaid María de Medina like the bad Christian that she is, and resentful of the faith, has used evil and superstitious prayers and is not content to use [them] herself, but as a bad and spiteful Christian she has instructed other persons in [their use] so that they, too, will make use of these superstitions.

Although María de Medina could recite the Saint Martha philter perfectly, to her further detriment, she could not recall under oath "las oraciones que la yglesia manda rrezar" 'the prayers commanded by the Church' (162v).

For the Medinas to use "superstitious" objects and means of prayer amounted to disdain for Catholic discipline, and the *visitador* did not overlook the exemplary value of turning their punishment into a public spectacle. Jiminez's closing remarks include the determination "de conden[ar] a las dichas maria de medina y elvira de medina en las mas y mayores penas que hallare en el derecho bajo quales sean executadas en sus personas y bienes porque a ellas sea castigo y a las demas sea exemplo" '[to] condemn María de Medina and Elvira de Medina to the greatest and severest penalties allowable by law, and to proceed in such a way against their persons and goods that it will serve as a punishment for them and an example to others' (163r). Although the church ultimately showed restraint in punishing the Medinas, it nonetheless reimposed the primacy of Catholic symbols and rituals over those of the "superstitious" women: before exiling the Medinas for the period of one year, the *visitador* ordered them to attend mass on Christmas Day, barefoot and with their heads lowered in humility, while holding tapers in their hands (166r).

Like the Catholic Church, for whom even the documentary record of transgression and retribution ought to serve a didactic end, Rojas, in an epilogue containing a collection of poems, exhorts the reader not to forget that the **Tragicomedia** was written to admonish, not to encourage immodest desires. Similarly, the trial document's self-validation through a profusion of signatures, rubrics, and flourishes parallels Rojas's effort to authenticate his faith, to disavow complicity with his worldly characters:

> No dudes ni hayas vergüenza, lector.
> Narrar lo lascivo, que aquí se te muestra;
> Que siendo discreto verás que es la muestra
> Por donde se vende la honesta labor.
>
> · · · · ·
>
> Y así no me juzgues por eso liviano
> Mas antes celoso de limpio vivir;
> Celoso de amar, temer, y servir
> Al alto Señor y Dios soberano.
>
>   (404)
>
> Do not doubt, nor be ashamed, reader,
> to read out the lascivious matter which is shown
> you here, for being discreet you will see
> that it is the sample from which honest
> work is sold.
>
> · · · · ·
>
> Thus do not judge me loose
> on account of this, rather jealous of
> clean living, jealous of loving, fearing
> and serving Sovereign God on High.

And yet the sacred elements in **Celestina**—like those in the *philocaptio* prayer contained in the trial document— are irremediably compromised in their symbolic and spiritual integrity by the coexisting profane elements. Thus, even as the *visitadores* forcibly dissect the appropriation of an orthodox, spiritual text for a manifestly heterodox, sexual end, their interpretive vigilance effectively vitiates its avowed purpose: purging Catholicism's assumed symbolic integrity of contamination by woman. Indeed, the Medinas' alleged corruption of Catholicism's spiritual purity is compounded by their concomitant evolution from the strictly virtual or allegorical function (traditionally accorded to women by the Catholic teachings) to the radically modern position of symbolically and sexually free agents. Consequently, an intrinsically secular and empirical inquisitorial process—though meant to eradicate and suppress any heterodox appropriation of Catholic symbolic practice— can only further erode the putative stability of Catholicism's origins; for the church to legitimate, *post festum factum* 'retroactively,' its coercive and frequently violent practice, its "exegesis" of heresy must invest officially suspect representations with the symbolic cohesiveness the church claims for its own spiritual agenda. The moment of heresy, then, lies not merely in some willful misappropriation of Catholicism's spiritual symbolism but also in the production through such heterodoxy of a simulacrum whose circulation—alter-

natively dramatized by the social and literary practice of the Medinas and Rojas—causes the assumed fixity and authenticity of Catholicism's spiritual tenets to become permanently inscrutable and undemonstrable.[35]

NOTES

[1] For a discussion of the influence of *Celestina* and its sequels and imitations, see Pavia 30-46. See also Lida de Malkiel (572-93).

[2] Martí-Ibáñez 236. For a discussion of narrativity in *Celestina*, see Severin, *Tragicomedy,* esp. ch. 1; Rank.

[3] For a discussion of moral corruption and economic greed in *Celestina*, see Lihani; Round; Deyermond, "Divisiones," "Lost Investment."

[4] On Celestina's uncertainty, see Rojas 106-09. For a discussion of Celestina's "enchantment" of Melibea, see Handy, who writes that "the psychic deflowering" of Melibea "is accomplished with words and ideas, logic and persuasion. Here as elsewhere in the work, rhetoric is the chief instrument used to bring all plans into fruition" (17). For a discussion of formal rhetorical features in *Celestina*, see Morgan, who argues that Celestina's modes of persuasion "have been acquired by experience and cunning and bear witness to the fact that quick wits are just as important as technique" (8).

[5] Sánchez Ortega 59. I also refer to these heterodox texts as love philters, conjuries, and *philocaptio* prayers, the last term being the most traditional.

[6] The connection between the dissimulation of authentic purity among women and that among Jews has proved so powerful that some critics view concerns about female chastity in golden age drama as a metaphoric staging of anxiety about the statutes of *limpieza de sangre* (the condition of being untainted by Jewish blood). On the parallel between female unchasteness and Jewish blood, see McKendrick. On Jews and dissimulation, see Zagorin. On the medieval Christian penchant for conflating Judaism, sorcery, and witchcraft, see Trachtenberg, esp. chs. 4, 15.

[7] The Inquisition investigated Rojas's father, father-in-law, and cousins for crypto-Judaizing; in 1488 Rojas's father may well have been condemned to death for his beliefs. In 1525, when Rojas's father-in-law was brought before the Holy Office, Rojas, a lawyer, was disqualified as a potential advocate, for he, too, was not *sin sospecha* 'beyond suspicion' (Gilman 44-45, 68). One must consider inquisitorial pressure in order to understand Rojas's ironic and satiric turns on Christian duplicity in reading the prologue, epilogue, and *Tragicomedia.* For further discussion of Rojas's ironizing use of *limpieza*, see da Costa Fontes 27-29.

[8] Translations of Spanish quotations are my own unless otherwise indicated.

[9] As Russell suggests, the *Malleus Maleficarum* may not have been published in Spain, but it was in all likelihood known there during Rojas's lifetime (341n10; see also J. Herrero, "Celestina's Craft" 343, 350n2). Haliczer cites its use in seventeenth-century anti-Semitic tractates (147); see also Caro Baroja 30-31. The *Malleus* still provided the formal precepts for trying suspected witches three centuries after its first printing.

[10] It would be pertinent to determine how many *converso* women were accused of being sorceresses or witches as well as crypto-Judaizers, for as Ranke-Heinemann observes, "It is interesting that Tacitus [a pagan] criticizes the Jews for their boundless sexual appetite, just as the Church Fathers, in promoting the ideal of virginity, would later attack the 'carnal' Jews for rejecting celibacy" (64; see also 59).

[11] For an explanation of this belief, see Bugge, esp. ch. 1, in which he traces the development of the notion that Adam's "physical union with Eve is to be read allegorically as the confusion of the spirit with matter, reason with sense" (13). Bugge goes on to explain that "the force of the allegorical reading of Genesis was evidently sufficient to associate the spiritual fall of man with sexual intercourse itself," a belief that effectively locates the origin of the spiritual Fall into materiality and death with Eve (15).

[12] Hesiod 295-306; Herodotus 3.109. See also Burke, who argues that "very often the libido is presented as negatively seductive, as a force actively attempting to lure the individual toward those inner depths from which he may never be able to escape. In this form it appears frequently in myth and literature as some form of dragon or monster, an enormous fish waiting to engorge the unwary" (141). For a psychoanalytical interpretation of Celestina as a "figura materna y manipuladora" 'figure of maternalism and manipulation,' see El Saffar.

[13] All quotations from *Celestina* are from the 1987 edition of Rojas's work, a parallel translation that prints the original Spanish on even-numbered pages and a corresponding English translation on facing pages. English translations of *Celestina* are also from this source.

[14] Sempronio expresses this sentiment in his antifeminine diatribe in act 1 of *Celestina* (esp. 34-39). For a discussion of the perceived danger of mad desire, heresy, and feminine sexuality, see Gossy.

[15] Kramer and Sprenger emphasize that devils "nearly always instruct witches to make their instruments of witchcraft by means of the Sacraments or sacramental things of the Church, or some holy thing consecrated to God" (115).

[16] Though much interesting work has appeared on Celestina's magical arts, my arguments depart from the line of criticism that accepts Celestina's magical arts as in themselves effective and diabolical. For a recent study of Celestina's laboratory and the role of magic in the "enchantment" of Melibea, see A. Herrero; for an interpretation that takes Celestina's magic as diabolical and independently effective, see J. Herrero, "Stubborn Text" and esp. "Celestina's Craft" and "Aging Prostitute." In the last two articles, he makes numerous fruitful and enabling observations about the symbolic import of Celestina's language and instruments but maintains, "[T]he fact that religious activities are replaced by fornication (although keeping the religious ritual as a cover for it) goes beyond rhetorical subversion; it is, in fact, a sign of diabolical activity" ("Celestina's Craft" 344). The following passage demonstrates the critical line drawn from Eve to witches to women: J. Herrero speaks of the *Malleus Maleficarum* as "the textbook that served as the doctrinal bases for the brutal persecution of witches" but then conflates women and witches by adding, "The root, then, of Satan's corruption of humankind is found in lust, and *witches* are usually his chosen instruments because, as we know from the history of the Fall, *they* are more likely to commit the sins of the flesh than men are ('all witchcraft comes from carnal lust, which is in *women* insatiable')" ("Stubborn Text" 142; my emphasis). Also of interest is Russell's influential essay.

[17] See Rojas 192-93, 200-01, 202-03 for instance of Celestina's voyeurism. Round observes that "love, then, is never the lovers' unmixed posses-sion. It belongs in some part to eavesdroppers like Lucrecia [Melibea's servant] or the servants in the street, or to voyeuristic onlookers like Celestina in Auto VII" (44). See also J. Herrero, "Aging Prostitute" 41-43.

[18] In one instance, after Celestina patches a hymen with a "bleeding" onion skin, "tres veces vendió por virgen una criada que tenía" 'she [makes] sale of one of her wenches three several times for a virgin' (56), while in another, a girl's father participates in the sale and reissue of his daughter as a virgin before her marriage (202-03). It is fitting that if both girls are exploited, so are the buyers, who believe that they have purchased the genuine article, an intact hymen.

[19] Gifford 31. Gifford also remarks that "the words that go to make up the charm are part of the deliberative irrelevancies, distractions, references to authority, which go to lull the patient, stop him from thinking or reasoning" (35).

[20] See Sáenz-Alonso, who states, "El hechizo era, en última instancia, un milagro. Y los milagros estaban en boca de los clérigos que dispensaban gracias para salvar las almas" 'The philter was, in the final analysis, a miracle. And miracles were on the lips of clerics who dispensed grace for the saving of souls' (336).

[21] Gifford notes that "during the Middle Ages, incantations and charms were written down in huge numbers. They are among the best documented of any folkloric or anthropological material of their kind, and can be found in the *receptae et orationes medicae,* or medical recipe books, in compilations of prayers, treatises, missals and the fly-leaves of MSS. A large number of them are quite *indistinguishable from ordinary popular prayers*, centering as they do on a repetition of verbal formulae" (32; my emphasis).

[22] I have adjusted the translation: "tiene por fe" implies that Calisto has faith in the healing power of Melibea's words.

[23] Morgan observes that "the abundance of references to God is an attempt to appeal to Melibea's apparent piety, and seems to succeed" (11). See also Shipley; J. Herrero, "Stubborn Text"; Handy; Hartunian 49-53.

[24] On the magical properties attaching to the naming of Calisto, see Gifford, esp. 34-37; Handy 24. Also of interest is Read: "For Melibea the word is a sexual organ that threatens her virginity . . . to the extent that she is penetrated by words . . . and looks upon the tongue as the most harmful of human organs. In particular, the word 'Calisto' assumes sexual overtones . . .' (75). The importance—and danger—of the tongue can be understood in connection with language, taste, and sexuality as simultaneous experiences.

[25] The translation of "una oración" (literally, "a prayer") as "a certain charm" acknowledges the link to the *philocaptio* conjury.

[26] See Severin, *La Celestina* 164n50. See also J. Herrero, "Stubborn Text"; Alzieu, Lissorgues, and Jammes 170-71, 198-99. Shakespeare, too, uses this metaphor, most notably in *Othello* 3.3.414, *Much Ado about Nothing* 3.2.21, and *Winter's Tale* 4.3.7.

[27] See Dudley for a discussion of the inquisitorial tendencies of *tratados* ("treaties" or "transcripts"), among which he places *Celestina.*

[28] The following stanza from a shoemaker's rhyme attests to the availability of the needle-phallus metaphor:

El cuero ablando primero
que la costura se junta,
y encero después la punta
porque atiña al agujero
y pase el hilo ligero,
blando, suave, amoroso.
Señora, coso, coso.

                (Alzieu, Lissorgues, and Jammes 131)

The fur I make supple before
The parts better to join
And then I wax the tip
So it'll fit the goal
Right there through the needle hole
Soft now, lovingly, gently.
Madam, I sew now, I sew.

Melibea's maidservant, Lucrecia, also speaks to her in the language of erotic torture when acknowledging Melibea's desire both to have sex with Calisto and to preserve her virginity. Lucrecia uses *llaga, deseo, fuego, quemaba,* and *llamas* ("wound," "desire," "fire," "burn," and "flames") to characterize Melibea's physical and spiritual condition in act 10 (260).

[29] *Indiferente General* 135r. Interesting analogues to this feminine metaphorization of land are Shakespeare's *Tempest* 2.1.35-58, and Donne's "Elegy XIX." See Kolodny, esp. ch. 1. Also of interest with regard to "female body maps" and the English explorer Raleigh's vision of Spanish conquerors is Montrose.

[30] The trial took place in what is now Colombia. The *visitador's* presence in Trinidad, New Granada, and his use of the term *mala Cristiana*, a common expression in inquisitorial proceedings, indicates the seriousness of this case and its affinity with inquisitorial trials. Thus, although the Dominicans, not the Franciscans, conducted the Inquisition in Spain and in the colonies, the *visitador* and tribunal dealt with this case of sorcery and "superstition" in the same way that the Inquisition would have dealt with similar heresies. For the *visitador's* function in the Spanish colonies, see *Enciclopedia universal ilustrada* 69: 461-62. I wish to express my gratitude to the historian Diana Bonnett Vélez for directing me to *Justicia* while she and I were research fellows at the Archive of the Indies, in Seville.

[31] This type of little box or *tablilla*—a "tabladillo . . . en una cajuela pintada"—is mentioned in act 1 of *Celestina* in the context of the sorceress's magic and restoration of maidenheads (56). Often used as part of a malevolent spell, the *tablilla* was a small tablet or box made of lead that could be inscribed with messages or conjuries and placed at a grave site; it was believed that a message so placed would be carried to the underworld by the spirit of the dead person (*Enciclopedia universal ilustrada* 58: 1436). Such boxes and tablets were evidently used by sorceresses in Athens as early as the third to second century BCE; see Lefkowitz and Fant 296, 298.

[32] This incantation displays the rhyme, alliteration, and distractions discussed earlier in this essay. On the question of feats such as Saint Martha's, see Rowland, who writes that "combats with dragons which were part of ancient folklore were taken over by the saints. At first, such combats symbolized the destruction of paganism; then they were incorporated into the archetypal legend in which a hero, such as St. George, delivered an entire populace from a devouring dragon" (69).

[33] Not unlike a linguistic sorceress, Calisto (re)sexualizes and debases the traditional religious signification of a particular saint. He implores the unredeemed (i.e., adulterous) Mary Magdalene for success in the seduction of Melibea while praying at the church bearing that saint's name. See Thompson 25.

[34]The hyssop, a plant whose twigs were used in rites of purification in Hebrew biblical practice, becomes the aspergillum, "a kind of brush used to sprinkle holy water" in the Roman Catholic Mass (*OED*, s.v. "hyssop"). See *New Oxford Annotated Bible*: "Because of its presumed magical powers, [hyssop] was used for ritual purposes" (Exod. 12.22n). For evidence of the clergy's use of hyssop during the age of Spanish exploration and conquest, see Prescott 143. It is perhaps significant that in the Catholic Church the twigs of the hyssop are replaced by a conspicuously phallic device with a wooden handle. See J. Herrero's excellent reading of a Góngora poem in which the speaker exploits both the religious and sexual significations of the hyssop ("Stubborn Text" 133-34).

[35]I wish to express my gratitude to the Fulbright Foundation and the governments of the United States and Spain for supporting the archival research that led to this essay. I am also grateful to Barbara J. Bono for her invaluable perceptions and support. This essay is for Thomas Pfau, who saw me through all of it.

FURTHER READING

Barrick, Mac E. A review of *The Spanish Bawd. Modern Language Journal*, Vol. L, No. 5 (May 1966): 293.
    Positive review of Cohen's translation.

Brocato, Linde M. "Leading a Whore to Father: Confronting *Celestina." La coronica*, Vol. 24, No. 1 (Fall 1995): 42-59.
    Looks at the treatment of the text in P. E. Russell's edition of *Celestina*.

Burke, James F. "The Innocent Reader and the Failure of Memory in *Celestina." Critica Hispanica*, Vol. XV, No. 1 (1993): 35-46.
    Contends that the text of *Celestina* is a series of misreadings of mental images, or memory.

Corfis, Ivy A. "Celestina and the Conflict of Ovidian and Courtly Love." *Bulletin of Hispanic Studies*, Vol. LXXIII, No. 4 (October 1996): 395-417.
    Demonstrates how *Celestina* ridicules traditional literary treatments of love and their ultimate failure.

Del Cueto, Sandra E. "The Role of the Fourth Deadly Sin in the *Tragicomedia de Calisto y Melibea." Mester*, Vol. XXII, No. 1 (Spring 1993): 1-7.
    Discusses the use of envy in Rojas's *Calisto y Melibea*.

Fraker, Charles F. A review of *Celestina. Comparative Literature*, Vol. XXVII, No. 4 (Fall 1975): 374-77.
    Describes Guadalupe Martinez's editing in James Mabbe's translation.

Larsen, Kevin S. "Bed and Board: Significant Parallels between Plato's *Symposium* and Rojas' *La Celestina." Neohelicon*, Vol. XXI, No. 1 (1994): 247-68.

Points out classical influences in *La celestina* and notes points of comparison with Plato's *Symposium.*

Lawrance, Jeremy. "On the Title *Tragicomedia de Calisto y Melibea.*" *Letters and Society in Fifteenth-Century Spain*, Alan Deyermond and Jeremy Lawrance, eds., pp. 79-92. Llangrannog, Wales: The Dolphin Book Company, 1993.

Explains the use of the term "tragicomedy" as it applies to *Celestina.*

McGrady, Donald. "Calisto's Lost Falcon and Its Implications for Dating Act I of the *Comedia de Calisto y Melibea.*" *Letters and Society in Fifteenth-Century Spain*, Alan Deyermond and Jeremy Lawrance, eds., pp. 93-102. Llangrannog, Wales: The Dolphin Book Company, 1993.

Regards the motif of falconer who has lost his bird as instrumental in a possible dating for the first act of *Calisto y Melibea.*

Quinones, Harry Velez. "Cruel and Pathetic Dissonance: The Grotesque and the *Celestinas. Revista de Estudios Hispanicos*, Vol. XXIX, No. 1 (January 1995): 51-72.

Observes the "textual cohabitation" of contradictory elements which form the grotesque in *Celestina.*

Round, Nicholas G. A review of *Celestina. Modern Language Review*, Vol. 87, Part 3 (July 1992): 773.

Stylistic review of the Severin/Mabbe edition.

Weber, Alison P. "*Celestina* and the Discourses of Servitude." *Negotiating Past and Present: Studies in Spanish Literature for Javier Herrero*, David Thatcher Gies, ed. Charlottesville, Virginia: Rockwood Press, 1997.

Discusses the function of servants in conveying Rojas's social and moral attitudes.

Whinnon, Keith. A review of *Celestina. Modern Language Review*, Vol. 70, No. 1 (January 1975): 202-03.

Mixed assessment of Mabbe's translation.

Additional coverage of de Rojas's life and career is contained in the following sources published by the Gale Group: *Literature Criticism from 1400-1800.*

Gonzalo Rojas
1917–

Chilean poet and essayist.

INTRODUCTION

Gonzalo Rojas is known throughout his native land as one of the most lyrical and genre-bending poets of his generation. Critics of Rojas's work often include him in the group known as the Generation of 1938, writers and artists who applied surrealist asthetics and principles to their work; however Rojas's poetry is marked by a heightened sense of individual rhythm and philosophical and political awareness. Rojas has contributed to literature with weighty volumes of abstract and musical verse, and a steadily increasing output of poetry and essays. His collections of poetry have garnered considerable praise and admiration from critics and students of poetry in Latin America and throughout the world.

Little is known about Rojas's childhood and personal life. He was born the son of a miner in the Lebu region of Chile in 1917. Considered a "late-starter," Rojas learned how to read at the age of 8. He was educated at the University of Santiago, graduating with a degree in the Arts. Upon completion of his studies, he taught at various universities throughout the country, and in the early 1940s taught English to miners in the Atacama desert region in Chile. Rojas began experimenting with poetry, the arts, and writing, and became an early affiliate of the Chilean surrealist group known alternately as the Generation of 1938 and *Mandrágora*. He left the group due to their overarching concern with maintaining a set style of writing, something that Rojas felt inhibited the creative process. Rojas maintained an interest in national politics and served as a diplomat in Chile's foreign service until 1973, when President Salvador Allende was forced to step down. A communist in practice, Rojas was forced into exile, living and teaching in various countries for the remainder of the militarist regime of Augusto Pinochet. Rojas currently resides in Concepción, a city in the southern part of Chile. His poetry has earned him several prestigious awards, including the Premio José Hernandez Award in Argentina. He was also the first recipient of the Octavio Paz Award for Poetry and Essays.

To date, Rojas has published over twenty volumes of poetry and essays. His most prolific period began after he turned sixty with the publication of *Oscuro* (1977; *Obscure*). Before that time, Rojas published infrequently, and has been called "a poet's poet" due to his insistence on precision and a consciencious fusion of rhythm and philosophical content. Rojas's breakthrough publication of *Oscuro* contains poems selected from his first two books of poetry, along with several new poems. The collection expresses the author's thoughts on love, politics, and language in a dignified and humorous way. He analyzes the conflicts of existence in universal terms, evoked through the presence of conflict in his own personal and political views. Rojas has stated that he considers himself more of an observer, a "political witness . . . of maximum awareness."

Rojas's early works, *La miseria del hombre* (1948; *Misery of Man*) and *Contra la muerte* (1964; *Against Death*) were published sixteen years apart, more for reasons of self-censorship than for a lack of poetic proficiency. These works have been criticized for following a tradition of standard set by the known literary masters in Latin America of this century: Neruda, Paz, and Vallejo. Rojas's poetry shows a similar concern with a developed sense of poetic perfection to explore themes that are complete and deeply intuitive, most often expressed with a natural sense of syntax and rhythm. One of his most acclaimed works is *Del relámpago* (1981; *From the Lightning*), a volume containing 177 poems. The collection is an affirmation of Rojas's status as a poet of agility, his verse full of thoughtful reflection on the world around him and the current structures within society. Rojas's poetry has been translated into several languages, although his testimonies and essays have not received a similar level of critical attention. These works focus on similar themes of language and politics, and often discuss other poets and the importance of poetry in society. "De donde viene uno" ("Where One Comes From"), the introduction to his poetry collection *Materia de testamento* (1988; *Testimonial Material*), is a self-reflective piece that describes his personal regeneration through art and writing.

Rojas's development of theme and rhythm has become a hallmark of his personal style, an immutable synthesis that defies classification within any of the numerous movements with which he has been linked during his life. Critics have esteemed his work and he has received many international awards for his poetry. As his career continues to unfold, Rojas consistently attracts the praise of critics and scholars. Although his prolific output has received international acclaim, his work is still relatively unknown outside of the academic community. Rojas's poetry, bold and objective as well as intenstly personal, suffers from a lack of worthy translation, a fact that will hopefully be overcome with the future publication of his works.

PRINCIPAL WORKS

La miseria del hombre (poetry) 1948
Contra la muerte (poetry) 1964

Oscuro   (poetry) 1977
Transtierro   (poetry) 1979
Del relámpago   (poetry) 1981
Críptico y otros poemas   (poetry) 1984
El alumbrado   (poetry) 1986
El alumbrado y otros poemas   (poetry) 1987
Antología personal   (poetry) 1988
Materia de testamento   (poetry) 1988
Schizotext and Other Poems   (poetry) 1988
Antología de aire   (poetry) 1991
Las hermosas: poesías de amor   (poetry) 1991
Cinco visiones: selección de poemas   (selected works)
   1992

CRITICISM

Carlos Cortínez   (essay date 1977)

SOURCE: A review of *Oscuro*, *World Literature Today*, Vol. 51, No. 4, Autumn 1977, pp. 596-97.

[*In this review, Cortínez favorably assesses Rojas's breakthrough volume of poetry,* Oscuro.]

If you were a poet, would you wait until you were sixty to publish your third collection? That is just what Gonzalo Rojas, a Chilean writer who does not indulge himself in fiction, criticism or journalism, has done with *Oscuro*. Only poetry, and not too much; not out of laziness but rather self-censorship. He does not believe in publishing every year or in writing every day. Indeed, sixteen and thirteen years respectively separate his publications.

Oscuro is—and is not—an anthology. The collected and new poems have been arranged not chronologically but thematically according to three main subjects: poetry and language, eroticism and historical and political events. The unity that poems written in different times and circumstances keep with each other is remarkable. The all-powerful presence of death contrasts with the vital— meaning mostly sexual—forces which oppose it. This conflict is the main theme of the book. Life is mysterious and should be lived with vulnerability to the dark and the invisible. It is also a serious matter, which explains the lack of humor in these lines. Anger? Yes, against the social injustice, the corrupting power of money, the bourgeois, frivolity and, in the most recent poems, the military junta which governs his country.

The Western cultural tradition does not win Rojas's confidence. He trusts instead the instincts and cosmic fate. But his range of inspiration is wide and varied (Catullus, Louis Armstrong, Huidobro, Vallejo, Dylan Thomas, San Juan de la Cruz, Breton, Quevedo, Pound, Sartre, et al.), and his mockery of the Academy should not mislead anybody. He is a professor himself but one who seems to believe in the old saying that he who *does* is superior to him who *teaches*.

Only a minority of the poems succeed completely in reaching the reader. Hermeticism, fragmentation and private allusions tend to cripple some, whereas in others the author finds the exact tone and language to suit his theme, and the forceful message gets across. Rojas is a poet with strong roots, one who reveres ancestors and descendants more as a recognition of the sacredness of life than as a reflection of narcissism. His region, Lebu, in the south of Chile, also attains a mystical importance. Birth and death are events that unleash his poetical powers. In the tradition of Quevedo, Rojas is metaphysically disturbed by time ("los días van tan rápidos"), but he does not give up to the absurd. Lucidity and courage are his answers.

> Estemos preparados. Quedémonos desnudos
> con lo que somos, pero quememos, no pudramos
> lo que somos. Ardamos. Respiremos
> sin miedo. Despertemos a la gran realidad
> de estar naciendo ahora, y en la última hora.

If we are to judge *Oscuro* by the best poems—as we should—we must recognize the presence here of some of the most accomplished Spanish poems of this century (**"Carbon," "Al Silencio," "Cítara mía," "¿Qué se ama cuando se ama?"**). To lament that these are too few in the large collection would be petty. The others serve as a frame of reference, as fragmentations of a privileged vision; if they cannot always crystallize with the same splendor, they normally have enough mystery or passion at least to sustain the search of the reader.

Rene de Costa   (essay date 1978)

SOURCE: "Gonzalo Rojas: Between the Poem and the Anti-Poem," *Latin American Literary Review*, Vol. VI, No. 12, Spring-Summer 1978, pp. 15-25.

[*In this article, de Costa deems Rojas's poetry in* Oscuro *beyond classification in its complexity of meaning, unusual rhythm, and light-hearted word play.*]

Borges once referred to poetry as a kind of writing that is printed with only one margin. An interesting notion, and one that tells us much about the textual conventions of literature. After all, how a text is printed does influence how it will be read. The single margin tells the reader that a given series of lines purports to be "poetry" and obliges that he react to its as such. There is a problem with this convention though: not everyone these days is willing to read what is so ostentatiously billed as a "poem." The fact is that the readers of poetry are relatively few. They have always been few of course. In different literary moments they were merely a different few: other poets in the Renaissance, academics in the Enlightenment, a so-called "select minority" in the Modernist period. And today, still few, they are more often than not literary critics, professional readers of a sort.

Now, some modern poets like Neruda have been successful in pleasing these professionals while reaching out for a more general public as well, but most have been content to write just for the predictable few. Only more recently, with the advent of "anti-poetry," has a new avant-garde begun to appear, treating the form and content of poetry somewhat irreverently. For Parra, the anti-poet is a kind of *enfant terrible* whose importunities serve to bring down the conventional: "Durante medio singlo / la poseía fue / el paraiso del tonto solemne. / Hasta que vine yo / y me instale con mi montana rusa." ["During a half century / poetry was / the paradise of the solemn fool. / Until I came along / and moved in with my roller-coaster."] Literature as a new kind of thrill-ride.

Yet there is another kind of poetry situated somewhere between the respectful solemnity of the orthodox and the zany posturing of the new. And it is there, between the poem and the anti-poem that we find the writing of Gonzalo Rojas. His is a sober kind of expression though; when he mocks literary convention it is usually through example rather than statement. A case in point is rhyme:

> He comido con los burgueses,
> he bailado con los burgueses,
> con los más feroces burgueses,
> en una casa de burgueses . . .
>   **("Sátira a la rima")**

[I have eaten with the bourgeois, / I have danced with the bourgeois, / with the fiercest of the bourgeois, / in a house of the bourgeois . . .]

At other times whole sentences are put together differently, even incorrectly, but always without any trace of affectation. In a sensuous lyric poem like **"El fornicio"** [**"Fornication"**], a slightly garbled syntax can have a powerful authenticating effect, making the statement more real and less literary:

> Te besara en la punta de las pestanas y en los
>   pezones, (te turbulentamente besara,
> Te oyera aullar,
> te fuera mordiendo hasta las últimas
> amapolas, mi posesa, te todavía
> enloqueciera, allí, en el frescor
> ciego, te nadara
> en la inmensidad
> insaciable de la lascivia . . .

[I would kiss you on the tip of your eyelashes and on your nipples, you turbulently would i kiss . . . , / I would hear you howl, / I would be biting you up to the last / hickeys, my possessed one, you still / would I drive crazy, there, in the blind / coolness, would I swim you in the insatiable / immensity of lasciviousness . . .]

Rojas, a Chilean of the same generation as Parra and an early participant of the Mandrágora group of Surrealists has retained nothing of the programmatic in his writing. He has made no manifestoes, nor does he make any special claims for what he does. His poetry is both within the tradition and somehow apart from it. This is perhaps because he does not write for the professional readers.

Indeed, in his writing, he comes out rather vigorously against them:

> Lo prostituyen todo
> con su animo gastado en circumloquios.
> Lo explican todo. Monologan
> como máquinas llenas de aceite.
> Lo manchan todo con su baba metafísica.
>   **("Los letrados")**

[They prostitute everything / with their minds worn out on circumlocutions. / They explain it all. They monologue / like well-greased machines. / They muck everything up with their metaphysical drivel.]

In his view, the professional critics, like a chorus of broken records, go on and on, repeating themselves endlessly. In another poem, **"Victrola vieja"** [**"Old Victrola"**], he further elaborates this critique of the erudite:

> Siempre vendrán de vuelta sin haber ido
> nunca a ninguna parte los doctorados.
> Y eso que vuelan gratis: tanto prestigio,
> tanto arrogante junto, tanto congreso.
> Revistas y revistas y majestades
> cuando los eruditos ponen un huevo.

[They're always coming back without ever having gone / anywhere ever those doctors of philosophy. / What's more they fly free: so much prestige, / so much arrogance all together, so many congresses. / Reviews and journals and pomp / when the erudite gather to lay an egg.]

The criticism is strong, yet the tone is not shrill. This is one of the more engaging qualities of Rojas' writing: its serenity. In a language more colloquial than literary, with a repertory of themes drawn from everyday experience, it is only the format, the printed layout of the compositions that tells us this is "poetry" and demands that we react to its as such, reading it with a special consciousness. And, when we do so, we are then able to appreciate another unique quality of Gonzalo Rojas' work: each poem, read through, becomes a kind of event; its words are there not to fill out the measure of a line or to balance off a stanza, but rather to perform, to engage the reader's attention with something that is being made to happen on the printed page. A short poem like **"Acorde clásico"** [**"Classical Harmony"**] nearly illustrates the performance aspect of this kind of writing. And reading:

> Nace de nadie el ritmo, lo echan desnudo y llorando
> como el mar; lo mecen las estrellas, se adelgaza
> para pasar por el latido precioso
> de la sangre, fluye, fulgura
> en el mármol de las muchachas, sube
> en la majestad de los templos, arde en el número
> aciago de las agujas, dice noviembre
> detrás de las cortinas, parpadea
> en esta página.

[Rhythm is born from no one, it is tossed out nude and crying / like the sea, the stars rock it, it slims itself down / in order to pass through the delicate pulse / of the bloodstream, if flows, it flashes out / in the statuesque marble of young girls, it rises up / in the majesty of temples, it flames in a fateful / number of steeples, it says November / behind the curtains, it winks / on this page.]

This is the kind of poetry that flirts with the reader, that triggers his imagination.

Rojas' poetry is also unique in that it seems as though it was not written to be interpreted, to be decoded by those greased machines of literary criticism, but rather only to be read, to be experienced by an attentive reader. This is the arrogant charm and subtle challenge of **Oscuro** [**Obscure**], a comprehensive collection of Rojas' earlier books (**La Miseria del Hombre** [**The Misery of Man**], 1948; **Contra la Muerte,** [**Against Death**], 1964) and from his latest work alternate with others from his youth, many never before published. They are not ordered chronologically; instead there is a three-in-one thematic arrangement reflecting certain basic concerns of the author. Writing, loving and living are the constant themes of the sections titled *"Entre el sentido y el sonido"* [*"Between sound and sense"*], *Qué se ama cuando se ama* [*"What you love when you love"*] and *Los dias van tan rapidos* [*"The days go by so quickly"*]. It is truly Rojas' own book, his personal testimony as a man and as a writer. In this sense its layout follows a kind of internal logic of assembly: an early poem and a more recent one on the same theme will appear on facing pages; even the *"Proyecto del libro"* [*"Project of the Book"*], is found at the end, perhaps as a testimony to the fact that the author's explanatory words, justifying the edition, were written, as is logical, after book had been put together. Gonzalo Rojas, unperturbed by what the critics might say, need only be faithful to himself. The purpose of his writing is to make his experience public, to recreate it for whomever happens to be reading the poem. Thus in a composition about poets and poetry the author revises a 1964 text and updates it so as to include his more recent acquaintance with the work of a new generation of younger writers like Oscar Hahn and Millan:

Los poetas son ninos en crecimiento tenaz.
                                        Arenas,

Anguita,
Cáceres,
Cid.
Quién más?

El desarrollo
es
la arteria
de la realidad.

Tantos
los

pocos
dedos
de
una
sola
mano!

Por eso
Nicanor
dice
que hay que tocar
de una vez
todas las cuerdas
de la razon
en la guitarra.

Ahora
Lihn
tiene la palabra, Hahn,
Millan; ¿ dónde,

por donde
vienen
los otros?

                              (**"Al fuego eterno"**)

[Poets are children in relentless growth. / Arenas, / Anguita, / Cáceres, / Cid./ Who else? / Development / is / the artery / of reality. / So many / the / few / fingers / of / one / hand! / That's why / Nicanor says / you have to play / all at once / all the strings / of reason / on the guitar. / Now Lihn / has the floor, Hahn, / Millán; where, / from where / are the others / coming?]

                              (**"To the Eternal Flame"**)

Where do all these poets come from? Why do they write? Why does Gonzalo Rojas write? The answer is found in a poem on Vallejo:

Ya todo estaba escrito cuando Vallejo dijo:—Todavía.
Y le arrancó esta pluma al viejo cóndor
del enfasis. El tiempo es todavía,
la rosa es todaviá y aunque pase el verano, y las estrellas
de todos los veranos, el hombre es todavía.

Cada cual su Vallejo doloroso y gozoso.
                    No en París
donde llore por su alma, no en la nube violenta
que me dio a diez mil metros la certeza terrestra de su rostro
sobre la nieve libre, sino en esto
de respirar la espina mortal, estoy seguro
del que baja y me dice:—Todavía.

                              (**"Por Vallejo"**)

[Everything was already written when Vallejo said:— Still. / And he plucked this feather from the old condor / of emphasis. Time is still, / the rose is still and even though summer may pass, and the stars / of all the summers, man is still . . . / To each his own sad and happy Vallejo, / It wasn't in Paris / where I wept for his spirit, nor in the violent cloud / that gave me at ten-thousand meters the terrestial certainty of his face / on the clean snow, but rather it is in this matter / of sucking in the mortal spine, that I am sure / that he comes down and says to me:—Still.]

("**For Vallejo**")

Poetry, as such, has nothing important to say. The value of a text is not in its abstract content or even in the formal elements of its composition, but rather in its becoming, its ability to become something, first in the mind of the poet, then in the mind of the reader. For Gonzalo Rojas, poetry is not communication, but creation. In this endeavour, his true mentor is Vicente Huidobro, whose portrait, incidentally, serves as an allusive backdrop to one of Rojas in the frontispiece of *Oscuro*. For Huidobro, poetry was a kind of word-game, a marvelously creative "sport de los vocablos." And so it is for Gonzalo Rojas. Consequently, there is much sport and playfulness in these pages. In **"Juguemos al gran juego"** [**"Let's Play the Big Game"**], for example:

Juguemos al gran juego de volar
en esta silla: el mundo es un relámpago.

Entro en Pekín, y caigo de cabeza en el Támesis.
Duermo en la tumba etrusca de Tarqüinia.

Me troncho el pie en Caracas si te busco en París
y despierto en un muelle de Nueva York sangrando.

Pero me sale a abrir la muchacha bellísima
de Praga, cuando el viento me arrebata en Venecia.

Arcangeles y sputniks saltan el frenesí
y me estallan los sesos. Déjame en Buenos Aires.

Todo y todo es en México lo que empieza en Moscú
y en la rueda, de un trago, llego a Valparaíso.

[Let's play the big game of flying / in this chair: the world is a lightning flash. / I enter Peking and I fall head first into the Thames. / I sleep in the Etruscan tomb of Tarquinia. / I sprain my ankle in Caracas if I look for you in Paris / and I wake up bleeding on a dock in New York. / But the door is opened for me by the beautiful girl / from Prague, when the wind bowls me over in Venice. / Archangels and Sputniks leap all over / and bombard my brains. Let me be in Buenos Aires. / It's all going on in Mexico City what begins in Moscow / and in one roll, in one shot, I arrive in Valparaiso.]

The word-game is evidently fun. The poet is not preaching any message to us; he is making words perform for us. The shifts of scene and image that we have in this poem are only possible in the realm of the imagination. Rojas' poetry consistently transports the reader to that realm, even if the reader happens to be one of those despised professionals. The trick is to engage the reader. The procedure is simple, yet subtle: a few words, com-

bined on a sheet of paper. But combined so as to trigger the imaginative faculty. In the above composition it is the orchestrated arrangement in couplets that gives an added thrust to the reading. Each strophe propels us further into the spatial fantasy.

Words are the stuff of poetry, and in one poem, **"La palabra"** [**"The Word"**], a couple of words are repeated over and over until a typographic break serves to catapult us from a seemingly trivial dimension into one more vital:

Un aire, un aire, un aire,
un aire,
un aire nuevo:

              no para repirarlo
              sino para vivirlo

[An air, an air, an air,/ an air / a new air: / not to be breathed / rather to be lived.]

The closure is exceptionally forceful, aided as it is by the typographical disposition. Borges and the writers of the avantgarde were right: the layout of the poem does determine how we read it. In *Oscuro*, the blank page is a sort of frame for the words, whose arrangement is varied according to the way Rojas makes them perform. In **"La farsa"** [**"The Farce"**], for example, one of many poems dealing with the underside of life's rituals, Rojas springs a mordant ending out of a text that begins as a series of light observations:

Me divierte la muerte cuando pasa
es su carroza tan esplendida, seguida
por la tristeza en automoviles de lujo:
se conversa del aire, se despide
al difunto con rosas.
              Cada deudo agobiado
halla mejor su vino en el almuerzo.

[Death amuses me when it passes by / in its splendid carriage, followed / by the sadness of luxurious automobiles: one talks of nothing, one says farewell / to the corpse with roses. / Each tired mourner / finds his wine tastes so much better when he sits down to lunch.]

Rojas is rarely a metaphysical poet. He does not consistently offer us an interpretation of the world, but rather makes us experience odd facets of reality in each of his poems. Much of his writing seems to derive from his personal experiences, from his chance encounters with the extraordinary. In this way, the thematic repertory of his poetry is constantly widening. Anything can become the subject of a poem. Thus, the delightfully amusing **"Cama con espejos"** [**"Bed with Mirrors"**], derives from an official trip to China made in 1971. A sumptuous mirrored bed is the pretext for a series of reflections on the ambitions of the mandarin who had it made. Experience is the point of departure for the creative fantasy of the poet. As early as 1939 we find this same principle at work in **"Perdi mi juventud"** [**"I Lost my Youth"**], a moving story-poem of sexual initiation:

Perdi mi juventud en los burdeles
pero no te he perdido
ni un instante, mi bestia,
máquina del placer, mi pobre novia
reventada en el baile.

Me acostaba contigo,
mordía tus pezones furibundo,
me ahogaba en tu perfume cada noche,

y al alba te miraba
dormida en la marea de la alcoba,
dura como una roca en la tormenta.

Pasabamos por ti como las olas
todos los que te amábamos. Dormíamos
con tu cuerpo sagrado.
Salíamos de ti paridos nuevamente
por el placer, al mundo.

Perdí mi juventud en los burdeles,
pero daría mi alma
por besarte a la luz de los espejos
de aquel salón, sepulcro de la carne,
el cigarro y el vino.

Allí, bella entre todas,
reinabas para mí sobre las nubes
de la miseria.
A torrentes tus ojos despedían
rayos verdes y azules. A tórrentes
tu corazón salia hasta tus labios,
latiá largamente por tu cuerpo,
por tus piernas hermosas
y goteaba en el pozo de tu boca profunda.
Despues de la taberna,
a tientas por la escala,
maldiciendo la luz del nuevo dia,
demonio a los veinte años,
entré al salón esa mañana negra.

Y se me helo la sangre al verte muda,
rodeada por las otras,
mudos los instrumetnos y las sillas,
y la afombra de felpa, y los espejos
que copiaban en vano tu hermosura.

Un coro de rameras te velaba
de rodillas, oh hermosa
llama de mi placer, y hasta diez velas
honraban con su llanto el sacrificio,
y allí donde bailaste
desnuda para mí, todo era olor
nupcial, nupcial
a muerte.

[I lost my youth in the bordellos / but I haven't lost you / not even for an instant, my beast, / machine of pleasure, my poor lady / wiped out in a dance. / I would go to bed with you, / I would bite your nipples furiously, / I would drown myself in your perfume every night, / and at dawn I would look at you / sleeping awash in the bedroom, / hardfast as a rock in a storm. / We passed through you like waves / all of us who loved you. / We used to sleep with your sacred body. / We came out of you newborn / through pleasure to face the world. / I lost my youth in bordellos, / but I would give my soul / to kiss you in the light of the mirrors / of that salon, sepulcher of flesh, / cigarettes and wine. / There among them all, / you reigned for me over the clouds / of misery. / In torrents your eyes gave off / green and blue flashes. In torrents / your heart would leap up through your mouth, / it would beat throughout your whole body, / in your beautiful legs / and it would drip in the depths of your mouth. / After the tavern, / carefully up the stairs, / cursing the light of the new day, a devil at twenty, / I went into the salon that black morning. / And my blood froze on seeing you mute, / surrounded by the others, / everything was mute, the chairs and furnishings, / the carpet, and the mirrors /that used to copy in vain your beauty. / A chorus of hookers was watching over you / on their knees, oh beautiful / flame of my pleasure, and ten candles / honored the sacrifice with their sobs, / and there where you danced / nude for me, everything smelled / nuptial, nuptial / like death.]

From the ordinary and from the extraordinary, from the daily round and from the extreme event Gonzalo Rojas has been making his poetry for some forty years now. Even his most recent experience with the harrowing Chile of Pinochet has become a part of the record:

Entonces nos colgaron de los pies, nos sacaron
la sangre por los ojos,
         con un cuchillo
nos fueron marcando en el lomo, yo soy el número
   25.033,
           nos pidieron
dulcemente,
casi al oído,
que gritáramos
viva no sé quién. Los demás
           Lo demás
son estas piedras que nos tapan, el viento.
           ("Desde abajo")

[Then they hung us from our feet, they took / blood from our eyes, / with a knife / they were marking our backs, / I am number 25.003, / they asked us / nicely, / practically whispering / to shout / long live I don't know who. / The rest / are these stones that cover us, the wind.]

           ("From Below")

The writing of Gonzalo Rojas is a record of his experience as a poet and as a man. In this volume, containing all of his work to date, old poems are juxtaposed with new ones; texts react and interact. The result is a vitalization of the printed word. Rojas, in putting together this volume has not tried to be consistent. Unlike some modern poets who have spent a lifetime preening their self-image, constantly updating their work in endless revisions as though to stop time and erase change, Gonzalo Rojas is comfortable with the multiplicty of himself and is at home in every one of his many poetic voices. In **"Aparicion" ["Apparation"]**, characteristically, he gives voice to this recognition of self:

> Por un Gonzalo hay otro, por el que sale
> hay otro que entra, por el que se pierde en lo áspero
> del páramo hay otro que resplandece, nombre por
>   nombre, otro
> hijo del rayo, con toda la hermosura
> y el estrépito de la guerra, por un Gonzalo veloz
> hay otro que salta encpma del caballo, otro que vuela
> más allá del 2000 otro que le arrebata
> el fuego al origen, otro que se quema en el aire
> de lo oscuro: entonces aparece otro y otro

[For every Gonzalo there is another, for the one who goes out / there is another who comes in, for the one who gets lost in the wild / highlands there is another who is resplendent, name for name, another / son of a flash, with all the beauty / and the din of war, for running Gonzalo / there is another who leaps on a horse, another who flies / beyond the year 2000, another who knocks / fire back to its remote beginnings, another who burns up in the air / of darkness: then there appears another and another.]

Rojas is a writer who knows that reading is a pleasure. *Oscuro* brings that pleasure to all of us.

Ted Lyon (essay date 1983)

SOURCE: A review of *50 Poemas*, *World Literature Today*, Vol. 57, No. 4, Autumn 1983, pp. 611-12.

[*In this review, Lyons compares Rojas's* 50 Poemas *with other Chilean poets of his generation and offers particular praise for his later poetry.*]

Love, sex, time and death; so what's new in Chilean literature? I was prepared to abandon reading after the first twenty poems, knowing that I had "heard it all before." I was sick of sex, sheets and shipwreck, abandonment, aloneness and anguish. The debt, indeed direct loan, from Neruda's early poetry is transparent. Words and images particular to Octavio Paz's poetry also light up many of the early poems—knives in the night, two bodies that are one body, lightning, naked volcanoes, et cetera. Cesar Vallejo knits his brow and pains through several poems, not only the one written *for* him, but many others. The last half is played much better than the first. Beginning with **"Contra la muerte,"** and including **"Carbón," "Los días van tan rápidos," "Celia"** and **"Numinoso,"** Gonzalo Rojas is original, deep-feeling, even exciting at times.

The author published a thin volume of poetry in 1948 (**La miseria del hombre**), a second one in 1964 and four since 1977; advancing years have awakened the muse of a poet now sixty-six years old. Rojas left Chile in 1973, residing for a time in Venezuela and later trav-

eling the world. The poems reflect love and life in Asia, the United States and Germany. Many of the pieces in **50 Poemas**, most tediously unoriginal, were written in the late 1930s and 1940s, supposedly unpublished previously. Roberto Matla has illustrated the present volume with a few Aztec-appearing line drawings depicting death and sacrifice.

Man in Rojas is usually unhappy and unsatisfied. Chilean *angurrientismo*, stemming from the Generation of 1938 (Godoy, Guzmán), pervades the early pages. Man attempts to live fully, using up food, drink and love as fast and frenetically as possible. Frustration is the only result. Later poems in the book project a calmness, even a peace with the world. God makes frequent appearances in the poetry, at first maligned for unconcern, finally desired and accepted as purveyor of **"Aire y Tiempo,"** of immortality and a more joyous existence beyond the present. The metaphysical realms of Borges's recent verse creep in; **"Poietamancía"** even sounds like Borges's well-known substantive enumerations. Life is fleeting for the poet ("Days go by so quickly in the dark current"), yet in older age he tranquilly exults in beauty and love: "I touch that rose, kiss its petals, adore life, never cease to love women: I take nourishment by opening the world through them." In his work the poet's parents, children, family and friends give meaning to an otherwise unfulfilling world; the best poems are these personal pieces.

Gonzalo Rojas with Estrella Busto Ogden (interview date 1984)

SOURCE: "An Interview with Gonzalo Rojas," *Poesis: A Journal of Criticism*, Vol. 6, No. 1, 1984, pp. 1-11.

[*Here, Rojas specifies his need for and use of poetry as an element to penetrate reality, and divulges his approach.*]

[ESTRELLA BUSTO OGDEN]: *To start, I would like you to tell us about your participation in the generation of 1938 and your relationship with the different groups.*

[GONZALO ROJAS]: The question is perfectly valid because although I am regarded as a part of this period (I don't dare call it a generation), I don't feel that I really belong to it except very marginally. What is the reason for this? Because I became what they call a writer later in life. That doesn't mean that as a child I didn't have a poetic impulse. That is a different story. But the poets of 1938, who spread out in different groups in my country, as occurs in other countries when one movement has different literary beliefs because of aesthetic, political and social affinities, sometimes came up with projects that did not coincide with my way of thinking and feeling.

But anyway, I got very close to a group of poets who were most irreverent toward the small national Chilean and Latin American tradition. These, the most irreverent ones at that time, were the Chilean Surrealists. They were only a small group of young artists who were following more in Breton's footsteps than accepting a concrete situation that would interpret or reflect Chilean reality and therefore they said that more than *being* poets, they should *live* as poets, that they repudiated that worthless fame, and that they would, above all, practice poetry (consider poetry as life, as conduct). But very soon I realized they were tricky, dishonest, because they also wanted to shine in style. And for that reason, I got angry and left. That's why I don't totally consider myself a real part of this group called "Mandrágora," which was a small branch of Chilean Surrealism.

Is there a connection between Surrealism and politics?

Definitely. Surrealism and politics have been closely interrelated since Breton's first great manifesto; but after the second manifesto, we can verify a tie between political and poetic surrealist thought. What I've always loved about Surrealism, especially at the height of French Surrealism, was its freedom, its concept of freedom, that was never related to any strict ideology.

It is true that Surrealist poets were closer to Marxist thought than to liberal or conservative thought but their point of view concerning freedom was that of Charles Fourier's Utopian Socialism or the greatest utopian philosophers of the late eighteenth or early nineteenth century such as Claude Henri Saint-Simon. They were more utopian socialist than Marxist socialist. I believe that my adhesion to Surrealism was due to the defense of freedom, somewhat anarchist, utopian, if you will, but never at the service of political parties.

Which one of the French Surrealist poets do you admire the most or which one identifies most closely with your poetry?

Primarily I was a reader of Breton. I was more interested in him than in anybody else. There are a lot of good poets but they lack the vivacity and liveliness of Breton. The same is true of Benjamin Péret with whom I was able to talk in Paris because he spoke Spanish and this fact made direct and spontaneous conversation possible. In general, I'm interested in the poets of the earlier Surrealism and I especially admire Louis Aragon, author of "Le Paysan de Paris," who deserted the movement very early. He was "my poet," but around 1930, he became a Marxist and joined the Communist Party and abandoned the realm of free creative imagination to join orthodox socialism; he then wrote mostly novels, but he also continued to write some good poetry.

This may have been touched on before, but if Surrealism has roots in the unconscious, is there an interplay between the unconscious sources of the imagination and the consciousness which controls technique in the poem?

This is an especially valid question because at first, it seems that there is no connection between the two; however, they are so interrelated that we could say they are a single entity. And of course the oneiric imagery is essential in a poet who accepts Surrealism. They say the poet should free his hand to write without thinking; in other words, it is automatic writing. However, this idea was only partially accepted by the poets, including the Surrealists, because even though they tried to liberate imagery totally, they had to face the fact that the poetic world is given only in the form, and form implies reflection, thinking, because the words in a poem are unchangeable, necessary, to the point that it is impossible to substitute or change even one syllable in a given poem. If this is true, it is not possible to rely on automatic writing. As Baudelaire says, there should be some control, some rigidity to the rapture of this impulse, and I think that all the Surrealist poets, even those who seem to be more liberated, were working with some control, with some degree of rigidity. I remember Breton's beautiful poem, "L'Union libre." It is a poem that seems to be totally free from reflection, but there is a game of counterpoint, of reflections between different things—the eyelashes, the woman, etc. To conclude, I can't see any disparity between what is called the great free imagery and the fulfillment or coherence of that imagery of the world in words. Of course, you can't get confused when it comes to Valéry, who believes only or mainly in reflection, but don't forget that the same Valéry said: "The first line is dictated by the gods," or it is given to the poet; afterward the poet starts his work to indicate that the starting point is truly a point of subconscious liveliness, but further on, one must weave his verbal space as a spider weaves his web. To summarize, technique or form is not prison for the imaginative freedom; it is the release.

The fact that the first line is given to the poet by the gods or by the all-powerful unconscious could be compared, in the reader's case, to intuition at his first encounter with the literary work.

Yes, certainly, the reader's first step, his first encounter, is unquestionably intuition and, I would not hesitate to say, impression. Presently, there is much reserve, too much, surrounding the word "impression." Remember, at first, everything is impression; I'm thinking about the reader because you've asked me about the reader. In this case, the first thing is an answer of an intuitive nature, but combined with what we could call impression—the first impression; thereafter, with a very rational and coherent analysis, one can make the connections to discover the meaning as reader and critic. But a true critic and a good reader should be always sensitive to the signal that comes from the text itself. This means that the impression is very decisive. Today there are some people who, in their desire to be sharp and precise when interpreting the literary work, refuse to receive passively this influence we call impression. But to me this seems to be an error.

*In the prologue to **Del relámpago**, you say that this book is addressed to the listener. Could you explain what you mean?*

Yes, reader and listener are the same for me in this case, because I've already told you that one reads not only with the eyes, but also with the ears. Now, since poetry is composed of words and words have a zoom, a sound, vowels, breath, and especially since it first started as music, it is natural that the poet can and must be concerned with a word as related to its sound. But this must be understood very carefully. I believe that Pound clarified this idea a great deal when he spoke of language as "speech" and language as "sound." He wrote both types of poetry and surprisingly, his great book, which is still very much rejected by so many people, and quite complicated as it is, he entitled *Cantares* because he liked the Spanish word. Not Cántico or Cantos, but *Cantares*. That's interesting.

What can you tell us about rhythm in your poetry?

There is a lot I can say about this topic and about how I receive it. I think that rhythm is so necessary, so fundamental that if I didn't breathe the words rhythmically, poetry would not be given to me. Since I was a child, I was a defender of the spoken word and of the communication that results from the zoom of vowels, from the sense and meaning of the vocalic and syntactic inner sense. I believe in a breathed, written poetry in which sonorousness operates at the stratum of sound, the meaning operates at the semantic level and there is a level of silence in which the ineffable is almost touched for what cannot be said. I know that you measure rhythm, verses, differently in English, but when I talk about rhythm, I'm not referring to metric measure or metronome. I'm saying that in my poetry, rhythm is similar to imagery itself, even to the point of establishing an equation between the two.

As far as rhythm is concerned, it has been said that when Gabriela Mistral was a young girl living in Montegrande, she used to sit at her doorstep to watch the wagons of hay passing through, and the noise of the wheels, the squeaking wheels, produced within her the need to write poetry. And according to an unregistered anecdote, Pablo Neruda once said that when he was young and very poor, they didn't have rain spouts in his house, so the noise of the rain through the shingles multiplied, making each shingle sound like a spout, a fountain. This noise produced in him the impulse to write poetry. Is there any external stimulus that makes you feel the need to write poetry?

If we consider rhythm in the realm of sound, I can say that also in my case, being from the same country, Chile, natural phenomena such as the rain, or the whisper of the falling snow, or the intense noise of a torrent, or a river, or the waves of the ocean exert influence to the point of producing very intense poetic thought. This is true, but I also want to consider the other rhythm, a visual rhythm, a rhythm that, even though it seems unusual, is given to you in space. Sometimes I look at something and from that glance I obtain data that are rhythmical. For instance, I can't write, as so many writers can't, where there is an accumulation of objects. I need space. I need to see the objects and that opens in me a spatial rhythm. So the rhythm can be related not only to sound but also to space. I hear the words and I also play the game of substitution creating an imaginative space which permits me simulta-

neously to approach and separate myself from reality as the spider makes his space.

All senses are related; as Shakespeare said, one hears with the ears, but one can also see and touch with the ears. All senses are in communion. To give an example, when I was a child, I had a habit of throwing a knife on a table in such a way that the point would stick in the table, and the knife could vibrate. If the knife vibrated (and let's consider that vibration is also rhythmical), it would communicate to me an element of rhythmical liveliness that enabled me to be part of a game. It may have been a mechanical exercise, but it was useful to me. I think rhythm should be considered in all its multiple sensorial aspects. I'm very much interested in space in poetry. That doesn't mean that I'm a concrete poet or that I write concrete poetry. But since I was a child, poetry was given to me in that manner. Let's insist on this subject of rhythm!

Is there something very special in this game of throwing the knife?

Yes, in a way, it is perhaps the concentration that the knife penetrating the wood afforded me, because I would throw it on the table and it would dig into it, which is similar to penetrating poetic matter. It was like looking for the meaning of a reality or an ultra-reality.

Insisting on the rhythm, to show the erotic game in the poem **"Fornix"** *why do you begin the poem with one single, long line: "I'd kiss you on the tips of your lashes and nipples, would turbulently kiss you"?*

To answer, let's take a look at this text, **"Fornix,"** which has an inarguably ironic title with regard to the erotic, because this word "fornicio/fornix" is not used in Spanish. It was used in the Middle Ages to indicate fornication. Therefore, I entitle the work **"Fornicio/Fornix"** so that the reader or the listener isn't too greatly shocked but at the same time, I want him to be stimulated by this reading so that he'll continue reading. This matter concerning the aesthetics of titles could be discussed as well, but since we're talking primarily about rhythm, I'll answer by reading, because this must be read, and the first interpretation is the reading: "I'd kiss you on the tips of your lashes and nipples, would turbulently kiss you." And here ends the first verse. Next it says "My bashful one," referring to the woman. Actually, the bashful one should be the speaker, but that's something else. Notice how the speaker, the poet, begins here, how he cuts the air, we should say, how he creates the imagery of the attraction that one would feel toward a beautiful woman, a beautiful creature.

Here we have something very singular which resembles the knife that I threw on the table when I was a child, when I tried to enter the reality that I was interested in showing. Do you understand? The tip of the knife is involved here and is even similar because there is an allusion to tip in the first line of this poem: "I'd kiss you on the tips of your lashes and nipples." This I see for the first time with you, I had never seen it before. Lashes, of course, are an inoffensive and beautiful part of the body. On the other hand, nipples are an undeniably aggressive and erotic element for a lover. Now, tip, of course, is aggressive, like the knife I threw onto the table and the tip dug in when I was a child. "I'd kiss you" but not "I did kiss you"—it is a possibility, but it is a possibility that at the same time is a reality. This is the gracefulness, one should say, the virtue of the poetic word that always has at least two, if not several meanings. In addition, here we're playing with the sounds of t's—turbulently. And why does the speaker put his adverb in front of the verb? Because he is going to possess the loved person, the creature of his erotic enchantment, he thrusts himself like a shot on top of the creature and says to her: "I'd kiss you on the tips of your lashes and nipples, would turbulently kiss you." One single stroke of rhythm. And then the game begins. I would say that if you open the book to any page (I'm referring to **Del relámpago**, which is the richest of my books), you will always find that rhythm is the center of the very meaning.

*Let's take a look at another poem, **"Tower of the Renegade." ** The manner in which the nature and rhythm are given to us is one and the same. Can you explain the idea of rhythm as a function of meaning, significance?*

Of course, this is the issue. As I've already said in my poetic work, rhythm is identified with the image of the world, with the "imago mundi." I think in rhythm. This doesn't mean that rhythm must be measured in syllables or in feet, but I do think in rhythm. Perhaps you must see this and I'm going to explain it a bit from within my inner workshop, my personal workshop. Perhaps it has to do with something I once said in a lecture. When I was a child, I was a stutterer. Therefore, I couldn't get all the words out, and this made me consider the word a live creature I had to conquer. This is an explanation that can help in part. But my thought process is rhythmical, and I know that even when a person speaks, or at least when I speak, the way the words come out creates the rhythm. This particular poem is not an easy one to explain, or in which to explain the rhythm, because it has a lot of things together, because there's a lot going on in it. It's a work, it's a lively text, yes, it's my return to . . . how shall I put it? . . . to my roots. After many years of absence from my country, I returned and I found a spot there; it was waiting for me. And this is where I have a house today. So, as the poem says:

> To this I came, to the Tower
> of the Renegade, to the raucous
> knife of water that doesn't write
> in the most free
> water or petals, but peaks,
> writes and unpeaks, howling snow, transparent,
> over there below, the stones.

Here what the speaker, the poet, wanted is to establish a permanent link between this place and his word: "To this I came, to the Tower / of the Renegade, to the raucaus /

knife of water." Do you see?—"to the Tower, to the raucous knife." "I came" is the verb. Tower of the Renegade is the name that I gave to my house. The name of the river is "the Renegade" and my wife and I wanted to build a little house on it that would look like an old tower. Now, what's unusual is the use of the neuter. I know that the neuter doesn't have the same power in English as it has in Spanish; "this" or "that" has nothing to do with "this specific thing" or "that specific thing," absolutely nothing. It's the intensification of reality. For example, looking at Rome, I can say, as I have said before, "And this was the world." Do you see the ironic connotation of this? "This" means, "And these were all the things, all the places, all the air of old imperial Rome. Look at what remains." "This" has extraordinary power in Spanish. You don't have a neuter, a neuter like that in English. "This" is the entire world, all of reality. "I was born for this. This is the sum of everything." That's the power of the neuter. Let's see: what do I call the river? "raucous / knife of water that doesn't write / in the most free / water." That is to say that the river is the raucous knife of water—I am taking apart the sentence or the poetic thought—the river is the raucous knife of water. The raucous knife of water should write in the water "river" but it doesn't write "river." It isn't difficult to understand when one thinks about it. I am going to repeat, then I am going to answer your question within the framework of the poetry, which is the only way that I have to answer; I can't answer unless I use the framework of the poetry:

> To this I came, to the Tower
> of the Renegade, to the raucous
> knife of water that doesn't write
> in the most free
> water or petals

That is to say I, myself, the speaker, am the raucous knife that doesn't write in the most free, doesn't write water or petals. "Petals" means that which is delicate. I am the river. We're now involved in an identification game concerning raucous river, raucous knife of water and the speaker, who doesn't write in the most free "water" or "petals." Water is the beauty of the water, petals is the beauty, the enchantment of the delicateness of the flowers, but peaks it writes, the river writes peaks because river and I are the same in this poem. And it continues:

> . . . that doesn't write
> in the most free
> water or petals, but peaks,
> writes and unpeaks

This is a very interesting invention of mine, and I would say it's original, because "unpeaks" doesn't exist. When I write, I write peaks, which is the highest. I write peaks and unpeaks at the same time. When the river writes "water," or writes whatever it writes—it writes peaks and unpeaks—because it falls head first, the river is running. It is unique. The river is the snow that is in the mountain peaks, the river is made of snow and it comes down very rapidly, running: "howling snow." River and speaker fall howling. And the poem continues: "howling snow, transparent, / over there below, the stones." What does that mean? It means that the river writes peaks and unpeaks when it runs. The speaker, the one who sees the world in the river, I, write peaks and unpeaks because I also am falling. But it's always the same in the river as in myself; the stones, that means the foundation, what is beneath the waters, is transparent. Here you have an ethical defense, an ethical position vis-à-vis the world.

A structuralist would break down this poem to the following formula:

1) The river writes, but it doesn't write water, as it could, but peaks and unpeaks.

2) The poet or the speaker writes but doesn't write smooth water or petals but peaks and unpeaks.

3) And both the river and the poet at the very bottom have transparent stones. It means that they have a clear foundation.

Is there something national in the speech of the people and thereby in the speech of the poet of that people? Something distinctive in the rhythm, something distinctively national in the rhythm of the people?

Of course, there is a national character, a national language, a national poetry and, in general, a national art. For instance our art reflects our surroundings and, arising from the depth of our soul, is therefore Chilean. This is a very interesting point you've raised, and I feel that the proper treatment of this issue would be a suitable topic for another interview.

José Saramago
1922–

Portuguese novelist, poet, essayist, and playwright.

INTRODUCTION

While he has written poetry, plays and essays, Saramago is known primarily for his novels, which are distinguished by their mixture of historical plots and the supernatural. Saramago's novels have been admired for their social commentary and critique of human nature as well as for their attention to Portuguese culture. Concerning the latter, Saramago has expressed his concern for the viability of his native language, remarking that "there have to be ways and means of protecting the [Portuguese] language so that it does not become a museum" and that "the writer's role is to protect it and work with it." The universality of his work was noted by the Swedish Academy when they awarded Saramago the 1998 Nobel Prize in literature, observing that "with parables sustained by imagination, compassion and irony, [Saramago's work] continually enables us once again to apprehend an elusory reality."

Saramago was born into a farming family in the village of Azinhaga in the province of Ribatejo, Portugal, north of Lisbon. Financial difficulties obliged him to give up his education while he was still in high school in order to earn his living as a mechanic. He was later employed in a variety of jobs, including civil service work, publishing, and journalism. In 1969, he defied Portugal's military dictatorship by joining the Communist Party. Commentators have remarked that Saramago's connections with the working class are reflected in his sensitive treatment of the human condition in such novels as *Todos os nomes* (1997; *All the Names*), which focuses on the actions and obsessions of a civil servant in a Portuguese census office. In the 1970s Saramago worked as a translator; he achieved literary success relatively late in life and did not gain international recognition until the 1980s with the publication of his surrealistic love story, *Memorial do Convento*, published in English in 1987 as *Baltasar and Blimunda*. Saramago has since been awarded numerous literary awards, including the Prémio PEN Club Português (1983 and 1984) and the Prémio Camoes (1995), and his work has been well-received in Europe and Brazil, but until he won the 1998 Nobel Prize for literature, his work was little known in the United States.

In his first novel, *Manual de pintura e caligrafia* (1977; *Manual of Painting and Calligraphy*) Saramago presented many of the issues which continue to preoccupy him, including the nature of artistic and literary talent, and of narrative itself; the themes of love and politics; the fate of the individual within society; and the power of history and tradition. Thus *O ano da morte de Ricardo Reis* (1984; *The Year of the Death of Ricardo Reis*)—a dialogue between the dead Portuguese poet Fernando Pessoa and one of his poetic personas—has been described in part as a narrative about narrative. Love is the overriding theme in *Baltasar and Blimunda*, a novel which relies on magical realism and satire to tell the story of two eighteenth-century lovers who hope to use a flying machine to avoid the plague and escape the Inquisition in Portugal. Saramago also puts magical realism to use in *A jangada de pedra* (1986; *The Stone Raft*). This novel describes the reactions of the inhabitants of Spain and Portugal when the Iberian Peninsula breaks off and floats away from Europe; in addition, it satirizes the political maneuvering of other nations trying to cope with the newly created island nation. *Ensaio sobre a cegueira* (1995; *Blindness*) is regarded as one of Saramago's most powerful political statements. It depicts the deterioration of a society whose members fall victim to a mystifying blindness. Saramago's own explanation of this novel reveals his assessment of humanity and its ills: "This blindness isn't a real blindness," he explains, "it's a blindness of rationality. We're rational beings but we don't behave rationally. If we did, there'd be no starvation in the world."

Saramago's novels have been described as fables, not simply by virtue of their fantastical content or their surreal style but also because of the repetitive, musical quality of their prose—a quality which elevates the works, some critics argue, to the stature of epic recitation. Thus *Historia do cerco de Lisboa* (1989; *The History of the Siege of Lisbon*), for example, uses the elements of fable as it tells how Portuguese history is changed by a proofreader who purposely inserts the word "not" into a sentence in a book on twelfth-century Lisbon; what is more, commentators have pointed out that the absence of quotation marks and paragraph breaks in the novel's dialogue gives the work a rhythmical, chant-like quality reminiscent of the fable form. This unconventional dialogue format also appears in *O evangelho segundo Jesus Cristo* (1991; *The Gospel According to Jesus Christ*), a novel which has caused controversy with its unorthodox portrayal of the life of Jesus. Ultimately, what unites commentators in their assessment of Saramago's work is their acknowledgment of his imaginative and compassionate view of humanity even as he satirizes it, and his ability to identify and connect with a variety of readers.

PRINCIPAL WORKS

Os poemas possiveis (poetry) 1966
Provavelmente Alegria (poetry) 1970

Deste mundo e do outro (drama) 1971
A bagagem do viajante (drama) 1973
O embargo (drama) 1973
Os opinioes que o D. L. teve (drama) 1974
O an de 1993 (poetry) 1975
Os apontamentos (drama) 1976
Manual de pintura e caligrafia (novel) 1977
Objecto quase (drama) 1978
Levantado do chão (novel) 1980
A noite (drama) 1979
Que farei com este livro? (drama) 1980
Viagem a Portugal (drama) 1981
Memorial do convento [*Baltasar and Blimunda*]
  (novel) 1982
O ano da morte de Ricardo Reis [*The Year of the Death
  of Ricardo Reis*] (novel) 1984
A jangada de pedra [*The Stone Raft*] (novel) 1986
A Segunda vida de Francissco de Assis (drama) 1987
Historia do Cerco de Lisboa (novel) 1989
Entre a historia e aa ficcao, uma saga de Portugueses
  (drama) 1989
Blimunda (opera libretto) 1990
O Evangelho Segundo Jesus Cristo [*The Gospel Ac-
  cording to Jesus Christ*] (novel) 1991
In nomine Dei (drama) 1993
Ensaio sobre a cegueira [*Blindness*] (novel) 1995
Todos os nomes [*All the Names*] (novel) 1997

CRITICISM

Richard A. Preto-Rodas (essay date 1977)

SOURCE: "A View of Eighteenth-Century Portugal: Jose Saramago's *Memorial do convento*," in *World Literature Today,* Vol. 61, No. 1, Winter, 1977, pp. 27-31.

[*Preto-Rodas notes that* Memorial do convento, *according to its author, is intended to investigate recurring characteristics of Portuguese culture.*]

In a recent interview José Saramago stressed that his novel **Memorial do convento** (1983) represents an attempt to examine certain persistent traits in Portuguese culture.[1] According to the author, the plot's eighteenth-century setting has had far greater impact on his nation's current status than has the more-studied sixteenth century. The results of his portrayal of the roots of contemporary Portugal are hardly flattering, but his attempt certainly has produced an extraordinary work. **Memorial do convento** won the first prize of the PEN Club of Portugal in 1983, it has already been issued in a Brazilian edition, and it further consolidates Saramago's place in Portuguese letters. The following commentary is intended to suggest why Saramago's most recent contribution to the Portuguese literary scene is a major one.

The central event in **Memorial do convento** is the construction of an enormous monument to religious and royal pride, the Convent of Mafra, comprising several wings

housing a basilica, a palace, an abbey, and other *dependências*. For Saramago, as for other like-minded predecessors who have commented on Dom João V's grandiose project, the convent represents the triumph of obscurantism and its attendant forces of waste, ignorance, corruption, and religious fanaticism. No less persistent in Portuguese history, however, has been the kind of critical outlook and independence of spirit which account for a lesser-known event of the period: the experiments of the Brazilian-born priest Bartolomeu Lourenço de Gusmão with the idea of an airborne vehicle. Saramago contrasts these two enterprises throughout his novel, so that the convent becomes the expression of the dead weight of reactionary absolutism while the flying machine embodies the aspirations of a few to soar above the limitations of their time.

The author has not written a traditional historical novel with the genre's pretensions to creating the illusion of a self-contained era. Rather, his intention is to underscore the oppressive limitations of eighteenth-century Portuguese society by assuming the voice of the self-conscious narrator who tells his story with an eye cocked on the twentieth century. Throughout **Memorial do convento** the author strikes a mocking tone as he subjects the foibles and vanities of Dom João V's court to the caustic vision and ironic wit of a modern-day rationalist. The mockery is not one-sided, however, for we are frequently reminded that recent history in Portugal betrays uncomfortable similarities to the time that Saramago has recreated. It is the society described by Voltaire as one where "festivities were religious processions, palaces were monasteries, and the king's mistress was a nun."[2] For all their patronage of operas and harpsichord recitals, the absolute monarchy and the Church had created a world which another French contemporary describes as "tout à fait triste."[3] Saramago's success in providing a fascinating literary experience despite his subject's unrelieved grim sadness is a tribute to his skill.

The author gains our acceptance of his ironic point of view by assuming the voice of a genial and cordial raconteur who tells his tale with frequent asides, digressions, and comments, all of which blend with the narrative proper and the characters' dialogues. Saramago attributes his technique to a brainstorm which revealed that *oralidade* or the stance of a storyteller would best allow the narrator to be everywhere heard, now in his own words and now in the dialogues, which are not set off or distinguished by punctuation.[4] The reader is thus obliged to read "aloud," thereby recreating the oral character of **Memorial do convento**. Considerable effort is required to "listen" to an account which shifts without signals from one focal point to another while one character's speech merges with another's and with the narrator's own voice.

The opening chapter provides the inciting moment, sets the scene, and sounds the tone which accompanies the reader to the very end. The august personages that are Dom João V and his Austrian queen Dona Maria Ana are introduced in all their splendor. In emulation of his model, France's "Sun King" Louis XIV, Dom João lives a life of high theatre, where even his regular conjugal visits to the chamber of his childless consort take on the solemn character of a sacramental ritual. Reality of a lesser order is suggested by references to the bedbugs which infest the imposing four-poster, whose regal occupants sweat and reek in royal rutting.

The king's desire for an heir is perhaps second to his wish for a Portuguese equivalent to the basilica of St. Peter in the Vatican, a model of which he frequently assembles and dismantles before the reverential admiration of his court. A vow to construct an even greater monument in Mafra should an heir be conceived is followed one night by an especially promising coupling. The king then drifts off to dreams which meld his sexual prowess with visions of soaring ecclesiastical towers—all, of course, to the greater glory of God. The narrator concedes that an association of sex and piety is unusual ("Such a personality is not common among kings"), but he reminds us that "Portugal has always been well served with the like" (18).

The startling juxtaposition of religious fervor and royal pomp with crude sensuality and squalor is central to the late-baroque atmosphere of Portugal as shown in **Memorial do convento**. Lisbon, the seat of the empire, is a pigsty whose inhabitants suffer from bad water and wretched social conditions. We are reminded of the technique of a Quevedo as Saramago describes a capital of shocking disparities.

> This city, more than any other, is a mouth that chews too much on one side and too little on the other, there being as a consequence no happy mean between an abundance of double chins on the one hand and scrawny necks on the other, between rosy noses and consumptive nostrils, between the ballerina's buttock and the droopy behind, between the full paunch and the stomach which sticks to one's back.

(27)

The constant religious processions afford ladies on balconies with strange thrills ("which only much later will we learn to regard as sadistic," 29) as they watch their lovers below flagellate themselves in bloody penance. The ubiquity of religious observance is matched only by the total absence of any kindness, sympathy, or charity. Commenting on an instance of a father's savage revenge to defend his honor, a veteran of military combat observes that "there is more charity in war" (47).

The veteran is Baltasar Mateus, a penniless twenty-six-year-old from Mafra who has returned from the Spanish frontier, where he lost a hand in defense of his country's impossible causes. His arrival in Lisbon coincides with an auto-da-fé, a lavish spectacle which vies, we are told, with bullfighting in popularity. The narrator releases a torrent of description to convey the excitement and anticipation as throngs flock to the Rossio to witness the Inquisition's grandest show of might in the name of religious right. Alongside Baltasar stand Bartolomeu Lourenço de Gusmão and a comely young woman, Blimun-

da, who mournfully watches as her mother passes with other penitents about to be exiled to Angola. Mother and daughter are endowed with powers that expose them to the suspicion of orthodoxy's guardians. As the older woman draws abreast of the three young people, who fail to share the mob's excitement, she entrusts her daughter to the maimed veteran with a mere glance and passes on. The young couple recognize in each other kindred souls. Like the priest Gusmão, they are also freethinking skeptics, in but not of their time. Their mutual dedication is immediate and complete, and the three depart the frenzied scene as friends and confidants.

Bartolomeu de Gusmão enlists his fellow dissidents in his experiments to construct a flying machine, a daring venture that would bring him before the Inquisition, were it not for royal support. Even so, he is the target of jibes and satire,[5] and even the king's interest is tenuous, since it rests less on scientific curiosity than on a childish infatuation with the possibility of a new toy. The three, then, decide to conduct their work in a secret workshop on an abandoned estate. Their decision is made as the queen gives birth and the king prepares to fulfill his vow. The antithesis is thus established: on one side we find a daring new invention built by a trio of independent spirits; on the other there is the projected convent-palace which will further consolidate state and Church, thereby driving an already impoverished society even deeper into debt.

Saramago departs from the historical record, which tells of Bartolomeu de Gusmão's experiments with hot-air balloons. Instead, the narrator speaks of a far more marvelous gondola in the shape of a bird, a *passarola*, which will be lifted by two thousand human wills and all their desires and aspirations. As the faculty whereby man hopes to transcend limitations, the will allows one to aspire to soar into space. Thus, by ringing the *passarola* with tiny amber spheres containing such hopes and aspirations, the contraption will be lifted by the sun's rays. The task of harnessing such an elusive power falls to Blimunda, the seer who, when fasting, can see in others the small dark cloud which is the will. She is to capture in small amber phials the principle of flight at the moment when an individual expires, a common occurrence in a city as plagued by epidemic as is eighteenth-century Lisbon.

The narrator occasionally refers to flight heavenward as the only relief from the wretched realities of the time. One such instance concerns a bloody bullfight attended by an audience of court drones. Part of the festivities includes releasing doves banded with poetic conceits. Although most of the birds fall into the clutches of shrieking ladies-in-waiting, a few "escape . . . and climb, climb . . . until they reflect on high the sun's light, and when they disappear above the rooftops, they are birds of gold" (99-100). Not every instance of flight from grim reality, however, involves birds or supernatural powers. The narrator tells of several brief interludes of happiness when the intrepid inventor and his friends are joined by a fourth dissenter, the musician Domenico Scarlatti. The Italian is grateful for some enlightened company and brings his harpsichord to the workshop, where he plays while his friends prepare the sails, bellows, and rudder for the *passarola*. His musical skill enchants and uplifts their spirits, and Blimunda observes that if the contraption flies, then "all heaven will be music" (178).

The project is finally completed after a hiatus during which the priest studies physics in Holland and the lovers reside with Baltasar's parents in Mafra, where everyone works on the convent. One afternoon, however, the Inquisition is alerted to the priest's heretical inclinations, and the trio flee in the *passarola,* soaring toward the sun. On the ground is their only witness, Scarlatti. The narrator captures the exhilaration of the experience, which includes flying over the construction site at Mafra before landing at sunset in a mountain thicket a day's walk from the convent. Deranged with fear of the Inquisition, Bartolomeu flees the scene, leaving Blimunda and Baltasar to conceal their invention and return to the poverty and drudgery of living and working on the convent at Mafra. Two visionaries in a land of mean-spirited religiosity, they lead a secretive life. Their coconspirator has fled to Spain, and a dejected Scarlatti returns to his more-tolerant homeland. Better times are a long way off, the narrator reminds us: "Before movie films become a reality, two hundred years must yet pass, to a time when there will be motorized *passarolas*; time weighs heavy while one waits for happiness" (219).

The years pass, the convent nears completion, and the couple guard their secret, occasionally returning to the *passarola* to keep it in repair and under cover lest the sun attract the amber spheres into new flight. On the day in 1727 that the king's monument is to be dedicated, Baltasar returns to the hidden site alone and, while mending the sails, stumbles, tearing away the cover. The sun's rays flood the spheres, and he is lifted to the skies. A desperate Blimunda later comes in search of her lover and immediately surmises what has occurred. The last chapter relates her travels across Portugal in vain search of her Baltasar. Blimunda's quest ends one afternoon in Lisbon when she arrives as an auto-da-fé is in progress. There in the Rossio among eleven victims at the stake— including the playwright Antonio José da Silva, "O Judeu"—she spies the blackened shape of Baltasar. With his expiring breath his will takes flight and finds refuge in the bosom of his beloved Blimunda.

In a brief summary of **Memorial do convento**, little can be said of such pertinent aspects as characterization and style. Thus, much could be written about the inventor-priest's progression from cautious skeptic to freethinker in constant dread of the Inquisition, and the portrayal of Blimunda and Baltasar is remarkably free of any sexism. Also, the author's extraordinary lexical nuance deserves future analysis. No account of the novel, however, can omit the constant presence of the great construction at Mafra. The *passarola* and its hapless builders acquire their full significance thanks to the opposing forces which are synthesized in the fulfillment of Dom João's vow. The author succeeds admirably in suggesting the staggering sacrifices so blithely ignored by the typical guidebook. For Saramago, Mafra symbolizes a crucial moment in his country's

history and presages its subsequent unhappy development to our own time. His perspective, then, rests firmly on the tradition of the Cavaleiro de Oliveira, Oliveira Martins, and others who lament the monkish character of traditional Portuguese officialdom and its indifference to reality and the crying needs of Portuguese society as it pursues extravagant follies in defense of outmoded ideologies.[6]

Even in the court of Dom João some voices questioned official values and indifference to sound national policy. Thus, the British ambassador Lord Tyrawley observed that, because of Mafra, national life was paralyzed for a generation as half the country's revenues were expended on the construction (*P,* 184). Tens of thousands of men from all areas of Portugal were pressed into service to work night and day so that a king's vow might be fulfilled and a queen might present her confessor with a new abbey. Others noted that the riches of an empire, primarily the gold of Brazil, were transformed into the stone and mortar of Mafra (*P,* 185). What little remained went to developed European countries, primarily England, which, as Oliveira Martins noted, fed and clothed a Portuguese society unable to see to its own needs. The Portuguese historian quotes the royal secretary as complaining, "Monkery absorbs us, monkery drains everything, monkery is our ruination."[7] With a few exceptions, life outside the court and ecclesiastical circles was a daily struggle "in depopulated provinces which are brutalized and wretched" (*H,* 437).

The narrator of **Memorial do convento** often employs the technique of enumeration to express just how the construction absorbs the wealth of an empire, from Macao and Goa ("silks . . . tea . . . rubies . . . cinnamon") to Mozambique and Angola ("blacks . . . ivory . . . hides") and Brazil ("sugar . . . emeralds . . . gold," 227-28). Since Portugal itself lay in abject backwardness ("this poor land of illiterates, rustics, and crude craftsmen"), Dom João's project is entrusted to the rest of Europe, which commands a handsome price.

> The architect is a German . . . Italians are the foremen for the carpenters . . . businessmen from England, France, Holland . . . sell us on a daily basis . . . imported from Rome, Venice, Milan, and Genoa, and from Liège and France and Holland, the bells and the carillons, and the lamps, the chandeliers, the candlesticks, the bronze candleholders, and the chalices . . . and the statues of saints.

> (228-29)

The enumeration becomes a torrent and a veritable inventory of Mafra's monument. Every entry becomes an accusation, and wit and caustic irony do not always transform the narrator's anger.

From poor Portugal "let the only requests be for stone, bricks, and wood to burn, and men for the heavy work, not much science" (228). Lord Tyrawley's reference to thousands of toilers often forceably separated from their families suggests none of the courage and simple heroism that Saramago attributes to the real builders of the convent. Indeed, the British observer dismisses the populace's docility with references to a general indifference to reality, as half the country awaits the return of Dom Sebastião and the other half, descendants of Jewish forebears, bides its time until the coming of the Messiah (*H,* 444).

Saramago's sympathies are clearly with the ignored *povo* in his portrayal of the period. Throughout **Memorial do convento** there are names and capsule biographies for the otherwise anonymous thousands who fought in the wars and labored on the royal project. To be sure, their stories vary little, since for the most part they are unschooled peasants, from Minho to the Algarve, already accustomed to physical labor in primitive conditions. Their meager salary and poor diet are small compensation for leaving home and crops in service to Church and Crown. They are shrewd critics of their time and cut through official clichés with a lucidity that provokes admiration in the narrator, who comments, "How such thoughts occur to these rustics, illiterates all, . . . that is something we don't understand" (238). Their female counterparts are similarly inclined toward a spirit of quiet rebellion. Whereas others may flock to the convent's dedication, at least one worker's wife, mindful of her husband's suffering, curses the monks en route to their new home with "Damn the monks!" (325). Blimunda's own independence of spirit is dramatically revealed when she kills a friar who attempts to rape her after Baltasar's disappearance.

The heroic character of the *povo* is underscored by Saramago's occasional use of epic style. Indeed, the construction itself provides grist for epic parody, and Camões is paraphrased when courtiers congratulate Dom João on the occasion of the convent's inauguration: "You will tell me which is the greater glory, to be the king of the earth, or the king of these people" (289). There is little ironic humor, however, in another borrowing from *Os Lusíadas,* where we hear the women lament as they watch their men marched off to forced labor: "One of them, her head uncovered [cries], 'Oh sweet, beloved husband,' while another protests, 'Oh my son, my only refuge and sweet succor for my weary old age,'" and an old peasant becomes a second Velho do Restelo, who cries, "Oh, glory of power, oh empty greed, oh infamous king, oh unjust fatherland," until a guard lays him low with a blow to the head (293).

Epic themes and technique especially abound in the seventeenth chapter, which recounts how four hundred oxen and six hundred men transport a gigantic piece of granite to serve as the abbey's veranda. For several miles along twisting mountain trails the workers push, pull, sweat, and curse as they guide the thirty-one-ton slab. One loses a foot, another his life. Today the stone simply serves as a source of statistical pride for guides to impress tourists before passing on to the next attraction: "Ladies and gentlemen, let us now proceed to the next room, for we still have lots to cover" (245). Not a word is said of the Herculean efforts expended so that a king could fulfill his vow: "Here go six hundred men who impregnated no queen with a son, and yet they're the ones who fulfill the vow; they get screwed, if you'll pardon the anachronistic expression" (257).

The narrator acknowledges that the ragged, sweaty crowd —many, like Baltasar, with one handicap or another— hardly measure up to typical heroes, who are "comely and handsome . . . trim and straight . . . whole and sound" (242). He is no less moved, however, to sing the glory of these valiant wretches: "For this do we write . . . to render them immortal." He proceeds, therefore, to compose an ABC of heroic-sounding names like Alcino and Juvino and Marcolino in order to immortalize all the Antónios, Josés, and Manuéis. As always, Saramago avoids falling into facile sentimentality or rhetorical bombast by maintaining a perspective filtered through wry humor and irony. The reader-listener is hardly surprised to encounter an occasional echo of reference to Fernando Pessoa, the Portuguese era's master of literary irony in the modern era.[8]

Saramago's experiment with *oralidade* as found in **Memorial do convento** is eminently successful in conferring unity upon an extraordinarily dense work. The narrator's presence never falters, and the bite and insight of his wit, coupled with a lively style and understanding of a period and its consequences, provide an experience which enriches in every way. The author blends the realism of historical re-creation and the rationalism of a critical perspective with a wealth of cultural references and a fertile imagination open to magic and marvel as antidotes to misery and folly. For the reader-listener the result is a literary tour de force and wonderfully exemplifies the Horatian ideal of profitable pleasure through artistic creation.

NOTES

[1] "Nosso hoje se radica muito mais no século XVIII do que no século XVI," as quoted in *Viagem à literatura portuguesa contemporânea* by Cremilda de Araújo Medina, Rio de Janeiro, Nórdica, 1983, p. 264. For a review of *Memorial do convento,* see *WLT* 58:1 (Winter 1984), p. 78.

[2] See Hellmut and Alice Wohl, *Portugal,* New York, Scala, 1983, p. 183. All subsequent references use the abbreviation *P.*

[3] As quoted in Oliveira Martins, *História de Portugal,* 14th ed., Lisbon, Guimarães, 1964, p. 444. All subsequent references use the abbreviation *H.*

[4] "Precisava escrever como se tivesse de contar a história. Percebeu em um instante de lucidez plena, que aquele era um projecto de oralidade." See Araújo Medina, p. 265.

[5] Bartolomeu Lourenço de Gusmão's most vociferous detractors were the poets Tomás Pinto Brandão and Pedro de Azevedo Tojal. The latter especially satirizes "O Voador," as the would-be flier was called, in the mock epic *O foguetário.* See Hernâni Cidade, *Lições de cultura e literatura portuguesa,* Coimbra, Coimbra Editora, 1959, vol. 2, p. 298.

[6] See Aquilino Ribeiro, *O Cavaleiro de Oliveira,* Porto, Lelo, 1935, and Oliveira Martins, pp. 436-57 ("As Minas do Brasil"), where one finds

many references to incidents and data which are incorporated into *Memorial do convento*.

[7] Alexandre de Gusmão (no relation to Bartolomeu Lourenço), as quoted in Oliveira Martins, p. 440.

[8] On p. 184 Saramago evokes a night scene by quoting from Pessoa's "Vem, noite antiquíssima," and on p. 227 the author refers to the poet's portrayal of Prince Henry the Navigator as seen in *Mensagem*.

José Saramago with Giovanni Pontiero (interview date 1989)

SOURCE: "Interview with José Saramago," in *Poetry Nation Review*, Vol. 16, No. 4, pp. 38-42.

[*Pontiero queries Saramago about his evolution as writer, and Portuguese writer, particularly regarding style, themes, genres, and inspiration.*]

[Giovanni Pontiero]: *Sr. Saramago, you started publishing your major novels late in life, at least relatively late for a writer of your stature and output. Were there sporadic publications before the appearance of your novel* Levantado do Chão [Raised From The Ground], *first published in 1980?*

[José Saramago]: Leaving aside my first book, a novel, which appeared in 1947 when I was only twenty-five years of age, and which I do not include nowadays in my list of works, my literary activity started in 1966 with the publication of a book of poems *Os Poemas Possíveis* [*Possible Poems*]. But by 1980 I had published nine more books (two books of poetry, two collections of chronicles, two collections of political essays, a novel, a collection of short stories and a play). It's true that I started to write late in life, but less late than you imagine if you start counting from the first of my more important novels.

How would you describe your initial development as a writer?

I was eighteen years of age when, during one of those conversations between adolescents which are one of life's greatest pleasures, I told the friends I was with that I should like to become a writer. By that time all I had written were sentimental and dramatic poems typical of the poetry young people wrote at that time. Probably the most important thing for my future as a writer was my love of reading from an early age.

Your major novels seem to take us back to the tradition of classical fiction in terms of scope, thematic richness, wealth of ideas and associations.

That might be claiming too much and I'm certainly not the best person to reply, since I'd have to be my own judge and advocate. It is true, however, that for me the novel is inseparable from a certain sense of breadth and comprehensiveness, rather like a tiny universe which expands and starts gathering and assimilating all the er-

rant 'bodies' it encounters, sometimes contradictory, but finally capable of being harmonised. From this point of view, the novel, as I understand and practise it, should always tend towards the 'excessive'. Now then, 'excess', at least in principle, should be incompatible with the 'classical' if the facts weren't there to prove otherwise: 'classical' novels are, as a general rule, 'excessive' . . .

While your books are vastly entertaining, they make real demands on the reader in terms of knowledge and curiosity.

It pleases me to know that my novels make the reader think. As for me, I thought a great deal while I was writing them. I thought as best I could and knew, and I should be disappointed if readers didn't find something more than the entertaining narrative I've also provided. If the entertainment has some value in itself, that value is greatly enhanced when the story becomes a passport to reflection.

You exercised various professions, mechanic, technical designer, literary editor and journalist before becoming a professional writer. Have these had any influence on your formation as a writer?

I don't think any of the various professional activities I have exercised have helped with my formation as a writer. They certainly helped to make me the man I am, along with many other factors, some perhaps identifiable, others of which I'm no longer aware. Who knows, perhaps simply by being a child sitting on a riverbank and watching the water flow past. That child will one day become a writer without ever knowing why.

At one point in A Jangada de Pedra [The Stone Raft] *you state that 'the objectivity of the narrator is a modern invention'. Could I ask you to comment on this concept, given your own clear preference for a non-objective stance?*

I shouldn't call it a concept, merely the formulation of the attitude adopted by the author when he identifies with the narrator and who, more often than not, deliberately takes his place. I'm opposed to a certain idea, which is fashionable nowadays, of an absent, impartial and objective narrator, who limits himself to registering impressions without reacting to them himself. Probably all this has to do with my inability (unpardonable from a theoretical point of view) to separate the narrator from the author himself.

The writer and critic Irving Howe in his review of Memorial do Convento (*translated into English under the title* Baltasar and Blimunda) *described you as 'a connoisseur of ironies'. Undoubtedly, there is a strong vein of satire in your writing. I suspect that you enjoy being provocative especially where you refer to politicians and plutocrats.*

Irony, let's face it, is a poor safeguard against power and its abuses, whether that power be political, economic, or religious, just to give some examples. A great Portuguese novelist of the last century, Eça de Queiroz, once wrote that one way to overthrow an institution was to go round it three times with howls of laughter. I'm much less optimistic. Irony is like whistling as you walk through a cemetery at night: we think we can ignore death thanks to that tiny human sound which ill conceals fear. But it's also true that if we should lose the capacity of being ironic we should find ourselves completely disarmed.

How do you view the relationship between text and subtext in your novels, with the frequent parentheses and cross-references?

That's a difficult question. As difficult as asking a tennis player, for example, how he executes a particular move. In reply, he would most likely repeat the move in slow motion before our eyes while explaining it step by step, breaking down, as it were, into fixed images what had previously been only one fluent and effective movement. The writer, I suppose, cannot observe himself as he is writing, nor do I believe that, once confronted with the written page, he is capable of analysing a relationship as complicated as the one your question raises. Molière, on bringing his 'bourgeois gentilhomme' to the conclusion that he was speaking prose without knowing it, wasn't merely presenting us with a situation, comic to the point of absurdity. There is more knowledge in the not-knowing than we imagine.

Your novels take us into a number of different worlds where we meet an impressive range of characters both real and fictitious. Your narratives are peopled by monarchs, poets, priests, artists, musicians, the professional classes, workers and peasants. Yet in the final analysis, for you, as for writers like Colombia's García Márquez and Russia's Solzhenitsyn 'the poor are the salt of the earth'. I refer to the 'poor in spirit' rather than those who are simply poor in material terms.

I don't think that the positions of García Márquez and Solzhenitsyn coincide on this point. I even believe they're referring to quite different things: whereas the Colombian writer would look for a primary and immutable innocence in his characters, the Russian, after establishing an implacable inventory of evils and crimes, would try to restore that innocence to those who had definitely lost it. As for me, who was born poor and am not rich, what drives me is to show that the worst waste is not that of consumer goods, but that of simple humanity: millions of human beings trampled underfoot by History, millions and millions of people who possessed nothing other than life itself, which was of such little use to them, yet much exploited by others, the clever, the strong, the powerful.

Your technique as a novelist is quite distinctive. On the one hand, you have a marked preference for austerity: punctuation limited to commas and full stops without any dashes, colons, semi-colons, interrogation or exclamation marks. You rarely use the conjunctions and *or* but. *On the other hand, you betray a*

penchant for baroque structures, circular oratory and ornate symmetrical patterns.

All the characteristics of my technique at present (I'd prefer to use the word style) stem from a basic principle whereby everything *said* is destined to be *heard*. What I am trying to say is that I see myself as an oral narrator when I write and that the words written by me are intended as much to be read as to be heard. Now, the oral narrator doesn't use punctuation, he speaks as if he were composing music and uses the same elements as the musician: sounds and pauses, high or low, some short, others long. Those tendencies which I acknowledge and endorse (baroque structures, circular oratory, symmetrical patterns), I suppose stem from a certain idea of an oral discourse accepted as music. I ask myself if there may not even be something more than a simple coincidence between the disorganized and fragmentary nature of spoken discourse today and the 'minimalist' expression of modern music.

Critics have commented on the amount of detail in your novels. How do you set about controlling so much detail as the narrative evolves?

I have no special method or discipline. Words emerge, one after another, in strict sequence, out of a kind of organic necessity, to put it loosely. But there is inside me a scale, a norm, which permits me to control, one might almost say intuitively, the 'economy' of detail. In principle, the logical *I* is open to all possibilities, but the intuitive *I* governs itself with its own laws which the other *I* has learnt to obey. All of this is clearly unscientific, unless as part of another involuntary and inherent science, impossible to define by someone like myself who simply practises the craft of writing.

Comparing the three major novels with which I have been closely involved as a translator, like all your readers I am impressed by your powers of invention, **Memorial do Convento [Annals of the Convent], O Ano da Morte de Ricardo Reis [The Year of the Death of Ricardo Reis]** *and* **A Jangada de Pedra [The Stone Raft]** *are all three·vintage Saramago, yet each of these novels constitutes a fresh adventure, a new direction, a different perspective. Is there some point of unity here which you yourself judge to be important?*

It's generally said (and so many people say it that there must be some validity) that the author is the person least qualified to define what he has written, that the intentions which moved him to write are one thing and the final result another, where the so-called intentions (which the author nearly always insists on defending as being paramount in his work) end up by becoming secondary because of the emergence of the subconscious, the aleatory, the humoral, through which he has come to express his deep desire. It is in this domain of intentions (perhaps unfulfilled) that I should look for this point of unity: the attempt to reconcile two opposites—compassion and radical scepticism.

*In **A Jangada de Pedra**, in one of the most poetic and poignant passages in the entire novel, an anonymous voice reminds us that: 'Each of us sees the world with the eyes we possess, and our eyes see what they want to see'.*

The phrase would be more precise if written as follows: 'Each of us sees the world with the eyes we possess, and our eyes see what they can'. Wanting to, as we know, is not the same as being able to.

Could I ask you to comment on one recurring image, that of the journey—either in the form of a pilgrimage, exodus, migration or private journey in search of one's past?

Perhaps something of my own nature is expressed in this. In fact, as a person I'm really somewhat sedentary, and the proof of this is that for me to make a journey is rather like pursuing the path that will lead me back to the point of departure. On arriving at any place, I immediately begin to feel the need to get away from there. I'm convinced that the characters in my novels travel a lot because they want to return to where they were, that place where, in the final analysis, *they are.*

Your use of topography intrigues me. On the surface there are carefully researched locations, landmarks and itineraries. Beneath the surface these are unmistakably linked to states of mind and feeling.

If in the **Memorial do Convento** Blimunda kills the friar who tried to rape her, it was because in that part of the sierra the author found the ruins of a convent; if in **Jangada de Pedra** the lands of Orce are described in great detail, that's because the author travelled more than a thousand kilometres to see them with his own eyes. And there is also the fundamental question of names: of inhabited places, of rivers, of mountains. They are the names, the words, that clothe the world of the spirit.

Gabriel García Márquez once observed that every author, however prolific, in fact only writes one book. He then went on to say that his was the book of solitude. Would you agree? And how would you define your own books collectively?

I believe authors write because, to put it very simply, we do not want to die. Therefore I would say that the book we persist in writing, one in many or all in one, is the book of survival. Needless to say, we are fighting a lost battle: nothing survives.

Jorge Luis Borges has also left us a much-quoted maxim in which he states that: 'Any great and lasting book must be ambiguous'. I find a strong current of ambiguity running through your novels.

Key phrases uttered by famous authors always leave me somewhat cold. Taken out of context, isolated from the work as a whole, they become somewhat contentious and intimidating, and somehow paralyse our own thinking.

Ambiguity in a book, if not a defect, should not be considered a virtue to the extent of making it a condition of lasting value. I see things as being much simpler: the ambiguity of authors is what makes the ambiguity of books. And most likely ambiguity is really something inherent in the act of writing. In which case we really ought to look for other factors before deciding whether a book is important or not.

Sex and religion are examined from every possible angle in your fiction. But I want to ask you more specifically about your interest in supernatural forces, in things prodigious and mysterious; one critic even speaks of mysticism in your work.

Things supernatural, prodigious, mysteries, are simply the things I ignore. One day the supernatural will become natural, the prodigious will be within everyone's grasp, the mystery will cease to exist. The problem is solely between me and the knowledge I possess, and, from this point of view, the computer on which I write my books strikes me as being every bit as enigmatic as life after death. I am not a mystic. If I speak so much about religion, it's because it exists, and above all, because it conditioned and still conditions my moral being. But, being an atheist, I always say that one needs a fair dose of religion in order to make a coherent atheist.

Looking at Portugal's fortunes from the days of mighty empire to dwindling power and influence, you would appear to regret not so much her loss of importance and influence in the political sphere as the danger of losing one's national identity.

The Europe of the Common Market is a holding company with large and small shareholders. Power is in the hands of the rich, the small countries have no choice other than to abide by and fulfil the policies which are, in fact, decided by the large countries, even if there is the appearance of democracy. Today, being in the right means having money. The recent gathering of the Seven Richest Countries In The World is, in my opinion, an obscenity, all the more flagrant insofar as it took place during the commemorative celebrations of a revolution which launched an ideal of liberty, equality and fraternity throughout the world, but which has now become nothing more than a tragic mockery. To give but one example, seventy per cent of the forestation area of my country will be used to plant eucalyptus, not because the Portuguese people want it, but because it has been decreed by the E. E. C.

Portugal looms large in your writing. Your country's history and destiny, her people and their aspirations are evoked with a degree of passion and genuine concern.

If I were North-American, Russian or British, or German or French, perhaps I'd feel proud of my country's power and wealth, even if I reaped no benefits or compensations from that wealth and power. As a Portuguese, I feel it would now be idle to take pride in the power and influence which Portugal once enjoyed. Our present is what confronts us: supranationality, limitation of sovereignty, diverse acculturation. I should like at least to preserve my difference, because, frankly, if the World and Europe are not interested in knowing who I am (I, Portuguese, We, Portuguese), I'm not particularly interested in being a citizen of the World or even a European.

In your essay published in the TLS *(December, 1988) under the title "A Country Adrift", there was one sentence which made a deep impression. I refer to those arresting words: 'Every manner of crime has been committed in the name of patriotism'. An accusation inevitably linked to your open distrust of Eurocentrism.*

I think these words are self-evident. When you send thousands or millions of people to their death with the pretext that the *Fatherland* is in danger—although what's really in danger are the individual interests of those who, directly or indirectly, hold power—that is a crime committed in the name of patriotism. People go to their deaths thinking they know why, and they are deceived to such an extent that they accuse of being unpatriotic anyone who tries to tell them the truth.

After absorbing your intimate portrait of Portugal and her people, I'm almost persuaded that 'small is truly beautiful'.

Small is not beautiful simply because it's small. It's beautiful if it enjoys justice and happiness. But small countries cannot, in fact, be as ambitious as big countries nearly always are. A small country, by dint of much effort, can only hope to get closer to achieving happiness and justice. The worst thing is that there are plenty of small countries in the world which are deprived of both justice and happiness.

At one point in **A Jangada de Pedra** *you write: 'Life itself enjoys cultivating a sense of the dramatic'. Does this account for your own keen sense of the dramatic in your writing, whether farcical or tragic?*

I don't have a dramatic concept of existence, or rather, I have it, but I de-dramatize it through irony. I try as hard as possible to avoid turning life into a Wailing Wall: to have to die is misfortune enough, but even that has its hour.

Have any of your own plays been performed on the stage?

Yes, I have written for the theatre, although I don't see myself as a playwright but rather as a novelist who occasionally writes for the theatre on request. I have written three plays to date, and all three have been performed on stage: *A Noite* [*The Night*] (where the action takes place in a newspaper office during the night of 24th to 25th April 1974), *Que Farei Com Este Livro?* [*What Shall I Do With This Book?*] (in which the protagonist is Luís de Camões after his return from India, when he was looking for a publisher for his epic poem) and *A Segunda Vida de Francisco de Assis* [*The Second Life of Francis of Assisi*] (the hero is, and is not, the saint).

In May, 1990, an opera entitled Blimunda, *based on your novel* **Memorial do Convento,** *will be given its première at La Scala, Milan. Can you tell me something about Azio Corghi, the composer of the opera?*

Azio Corghi is one of Italy's most prominent contemporary composers. He has mainly composed music for opera and ballet. His opera *Gargantua*, based on Rabelais and staged several years ago, caused quite a stir in musical circles.

Have you been involved in the preparation of the libretto?

The libretto of *Blimunda* was prepared by Azio Corghi and based on the Italian translation of **Memorial do Convento.** Any intervention on my part was limited to a general exchange of ideas and helping to find solutions for the dramatic expression of certain situations in the novel once adapted for the opera.

Who would you cite as important influences on your work?

Although this statement might sound absurdly pretentious, I don't recognise any significant influences on my work, except perhaps of certain affinities with Portuguese writers of the seventeenth century.

Who are the writers with whom you feel a certain affinity of temperament and outlook?

Gogol, Montaigne, Cervantes, all of them pessimists, and Padre António Vieira, who was a practical Utopian.

In your contribution to the B.B.C. television series of programmes about Portugal and the Portuguese, you expressed certain fears about literacy and culture. Could I ask you to elaborate on the crisis as you see it?

I suspect that this concern is not confined to Portugal. The number of illiterates in the world is growing. And in this day and age, there exists a very large number of people who have been taught to read and write but who, because of lack of continuity in reading and writing, effectively end up with the illiterate majority. This state of affairs probably suits the super-powers wherever they may be, for all they require to maintain and extend their predominance is to rely on the services of highly specialized minorities who monopolise the skills and means which permit a global vision, without which tactics cannot be defined, let alone strategies.

In recent years, a considerable number of talented Portuguese writers have come to the fore. Worldwide interest in the centenary celebrations to mark the birth of your great poet Fernando Pessoa may have helped to focus greater attention on Portuguese literature in recent years. But perhaps there are other reasons for this sudden interest abroad?

One cannot deny the influence Fernando Pessoa has exerted and continues to exert in the recent projection of Portuguese literature abroad, but it would be a mistake to imagine everything begins and ends with Pessoa. What is interesting to note, within proper limits, is that the Portuguese writers who came after Pessoa have matched up to the expectations aroused by Pessoa's writing. In other words, while no contemporary Portuguese writer aspires to the greatness of a Pessoa, their works nevertheless appear to the outside world as being worthy of attention. It's also possible that a certain crisis in creative writing in some countries has also contributed to this tiny discovery of a peripheral literature: the principle of communicating vessels is not the exclusive domain of physics.

I suspect that even you must be surprised at the ever increasing interest in your fiction abroad. Your novel **Memorial do Convento**, *for example, soon to be appearing in as many as twenty-five different languages.*

Frankly, I don't know. One day, conversing with my German publisher, I asked him why he had become interested in the books of an author hitherto unknown in the Federal Republic of Germany, an author originating from a small, remote country with a literature virtually ignored by the rest of Europe. He replied by explaining that he was looking for unconventional novels to publish and that he had found them in my work. I can only offer you this explanation for what it's worth and which isn't mine.

Your latest novel **O Cerco de Lisboa** [**The Siege of Lisbon**] *looks like equalling the success of your other novels. Is there any other novel on the way?*

The title of my next novel will be *O Evangelho Segundo Jesus Cristo* [*The Gospel According to Jesus Christ*]. I leave the rest to the reader's imagination.

John Butt (review date 1993)

SOURCE: "The Crimes of God," in *Times Literary Supplement*, No. 4725, October 22, 1993, p. 22.

[*Butt reviews* The Gospel According to Jesus Christ, *Saramago's version of the life of Jesus.*]

This is not a magical realist version of the Gospel story; a relief, since the original is beyond compare in this respect. Nor is it the run-of-the-mill realism of some conventional Portuguese *esprit fort* dutifully explaining the material and psychological bases of a myth, although one might have expected as much from one of the last supporters of the Portuguese Communist Party. José Saramago instead offers us a novel which, although formally not particularly modernist, is no doubt more intriguing than anything written in those genres would have been: an idiosyncratic, satirical, bitter and frequently comical account of Jesus' life, written from a viewpoint that is as sympathetic to the man and his family as it is hostile towards the

God that meddled to such disastrous effect in their lives. As one might expect, *The Gospel According to Jesus Christ* is most likely to antagonize Catholics, although it will surely unite all denominations in disapproval. Jesus is born of Joseph, an incompetent carpenter, and Mary, who falls somewhat short of the ideal by later having eight more children. Whether he is God's son is in doubt: apparently His seed was mingled with Joseph's, and the Angel of the Annunciation knows of no foolproof tests of paternity (such heavy-handed humour is an occasional blemish on the book). Nor is Jesus the cherubic babe of legend: from an early age he resents his parents for having run from Herod's massacre of the innocents without first warning their neighbours. Mary is a sympathetic victim-mother: her censorious and high-minded teenage son is a trial.

Abandoning his widowed mother and siblings, Jesus sets out with no certain goal, only to end in bed with the delightful Mary Magdalen; their passionate affair is moving in its tenderness. Saramago does this woman justice as a gentle and supportive companion to a young man tormented by his past. But no human being can save him from his fate: to fall foul of God, who is all too existent and oppressively busy in this novel.

A full description of Saramago's God would exhaust the vocabulary of obloquy. He is a villainous, remote, power-mad, cynical, manipulative, impatient, cold and facetious bureaucrat, cheerfully disposed to extend his influence by founding on the blood of an innocent a religion that will bring pain, death and intolerance to mankind—an outcome that He, as a timeless being, has already witnessed but is unable or unwilling to prevent. This monster bestows mixed blessings on his favourite. Even the fruits of many of the miracles are ambiguous: he causes a disastrous fish glut in Galilee and gets writs from the owners of the Gadarene swine. He can also misuse his powers, as in the unpardonable withering of the fig-tree, although he is surely right to spare Lazarus from resurrection on the grounds that no one should have to die twice. But this uncertain progress reflects a Jesus who is quintessentially human in lacking clear information about his mission, God having been alarmingly unable to give a full explanation of why He needs to found a church.

Up to this point the novel is amusing, sometimes outrageously funny, occasionally cryptic, but usually rather uncertain in its direction and tone—the latter, a curious mixture of provocative insight, banter and indignation, is elusive. But as Jesus' life approaches its terrible climax, the narrative acquires dignity and authority. The last chapters contain pages of great power, everywhere enhanced by an elegant and limpid translation; Saramago is a very fine writer indeed. Jesus in his final days emerges as a complex reluctant Messiah, lonely, well-intentioned, ill-informed, a deeply hurt creature condemned to inspire the foundation of an institution of predictable and foreseen characteristics.

The other important character is the Devil, who gains from comparison with his traditional enemy. He is a troublesome but not altogether unlikeable imp of un-

certain loyalties who obviously attracts Saramago's admiration as an underdog and rebel and also as a friend
of the earth: the Fiend is a zoophile, in every sense of
the word. Since the novel seems to adopt the Catharist
view that the world is the creation of an intelligence
that is not benign, God and the Devil are to some extent
aspects of a single principle, with the Devil having the
advantage of not being a hypocrite.

This complex Satan-Jehovah is the novel's central image,
and Saramago perhaps under-exploits its potential by making God's chief crime the foundation of a religion: given
the events of the novel, Saramago really could have preferred more serious charges, (eg, creating existence as we
know it), but his anti-clericalism may have got the upper
hand. It is also curious that a writer who is presumably a
historical materialist should blame a non-existent being
for the triumph of reaction. But even more paradoxical is
the fact that he should write such an original, wild and
beautiful book that will surely soften the heart of the most
obdurate infidels in favour of the figure of Christ.

David Frier (essay date 1994)

SOURCE: "Ascent and Consent: Hierarchy and Popular
Emancipation in the Novels of José Saramago," in *Bulletin of Hispanic Studies*, Vol. LXXI, No. 1, January, 1994,
pp. 125-138.

[*Frier examines the physical activity in Saramago's
novels and its political implications.*]

The title of José Saramago's second novel, ***Levantado do
Chão***, published in 1980, indicates a metaphorical rise from
the ground, which represents increasing control by ordinary people over their own lives. This idea is central to the
development of the novel as a whole. My intention is to
explore the relationship between such spatial imagery and
political ideology in this and other works by the novelist,
and thus to suggest that the physical movements of their
protagonists should not be regarded merely as events in
the plot, but also as significant indicators of maturity and
responsibility, at a national as well as at a personal level.

It is my contention that the author's political beliefs, in
some shape or form, are a significant element in all of
his works. The experiences recounted in ***Levantado do
Chão*** leave little doubt as to its essentially revolutionary
ideology: the Holy Trinity of Christian tradition finds
itself parodied here in the unholy alliance of Church,
landowners and state, whose repressive character has
served to keep the people of Monte Lavre in submission
for generations.[1] To reinforce this point the author depicts a number of subordinate power-structures which
indicate a whole hierarchy, extending down from the ruling classes and their institutionalized allies to a number
of disadvantaged groups. Thus, for example, as Marie-
Eve Letizia has illustrated at length, there is a particularly marked growth in the consciousness of women who
move from an initial position of willing submission to
prevailing social structures—and, in particular, to male

José Saramago

dominance—to a situation where, by the end, the young
Maria Adelaide is seen as the symbol of hope for further
gains in the future.[2]

The power-structures which operate within the traditional
community of Monte Lavre in the early part of ***Levantado
do Chão*** are, therefore, not based on a simple opposition
between oppressor and oppressed. Rather, as is indicated
early in the novel by the potential conflict between the
local labourers and the cheaper workforce brought in from
the Beiras to take their place, there is a concerted attempt
made by the authorities to enforce a system of 'divide-
and-rule'. They seek thus to create a hierarchy of oppressors who are in turn oppressed by others, all of them ultimately under the control of the ruling classes, whose
influence is evident in the arrival of the 'patrão' to give his
silent approval to the work of the factor and the police
sergeant (37-38). So Letizia's account of the gradual
emancipation of women fits into a broader vision, a vision
of the need for solidarity amongst all of the oppressed
against the true oppressor. In this way a social order could
be created which would be more just for all, reconciling
differences between black and white (323) and between
father and son (334-36), and also bringing an end to the
specific problem discussed by Letizia, that of the exploitation of woman by man.

It is, therefore, the threat of conflict amongst brother-
workers—suggested in the text itself by a casual refer-

ence to Cain and Abel (197)—which is seen to stand in the way of progress for the workers of Monte Lavre. As long as the divisions amongst the rural workers can be preserved, the privileged minority will remain invulnerable, as Father Agamedes insinuates, through archaic language and biblical echoes, in his words on seeing João Mau-Tempo in prison. These words suggest a divinely ordained and therefore immutable social hierarchy:

> Assim estaremos no céu, eu no centro como convém ao múnus espiritual que exerço desde que me conheço e me conheceis, vós tenente à minha direita por serdes protector das leis e de quem as faz, vós agente à sinistra minha por fazerdes o resto do trabalho, cujo não quero saber nem que me obriguem.
>
> (159)

And yet there are suggestions that this power-structure is not as impregnable as it might seem at first: most notably, Father Agamedes' very name is an allusion to the classical legend of Agamedes, who, along with his brother Trophonius, constructed the treasury of King Hyrieus of Boeotia in such a way as to ensure that they could obtain access and steal its treasures in secret, only to be trapped inside and beheaded. The implications for Monte Lavre are clear: Father Agamedes has been acting in complicity with his brothers in crime (the landowners) to defraud the legitimate owners of the land (the workers), who need only become aware of the crimes being perpetrated against them to be mobilized into protecting what is legitimately theirs: 'A grande e decisiva arma é a ignorância', as Sigisberto concedes (72).

Gradually the people do achieve emancipation, and it is significant that this development is linked repeatedly to physical movement upwards: in the earlier stages of the text, the landowners, who observe events from their castle atop the hill which gives Monte Lavre its name, seem impregnable, and this sense of security is linked not only to the idea of height, but also to that of breadth of vision, which at first is the exclusive property of the ruling classes:

> Quando Lamberto Horques Alemão subia ao eirado do seu castelo, não lhe chegavam os olhos para tanto ver . . . Ele próprio, ali com sua mulher honrada e já seus filhos, haveria de espalhar semente anonde lhe aprouvesse.
>
> (26)

Only the landowners have a broader perspective, and only the landowners therefore can take a place on top of the hill in the sun, as João Mau-Tempo dreams of doing (96), and this advantage permits them to take all decisions as they see fit:

> De Monte Lavre, alto lugar, olham os donos do latifúndio as grandes vagas amarelas que rangem sob a mansa rajada do vento, e dizem para os feitores, É tempo de ceifar.
>
> (138)

Immediately, however, this decision is questioned by the refusal of the workers to labour for less than thirty-

three escudos per day (138). The ordinary man and woman have thus begun their gradual ascent towards their ultimate position of control of their own destiny, so that by the latter part of the text, for example, when António speaks of going up to Montemor to demand a living wage, he does so after a symbolic climb to the heights which traditionally have been beyond the reach of his class (308); and from there, it is said (309), he may survey the whole earth, as his brothers and sisters grow in awareness of one another and of their common struggle.

The climb is not without its setbacks. Each step is a dangerous one, and, when the workers go too far, there is a price to be paid. When João Mau-Tempo and his comrades Sigismundo Canastro and Germano Vidigal withhold their labour in the small community of Monte Lavre, the result is that they are taken up to Montemor (literally 'the larger mountain'), where Germano is said to be thrown back on the ground as he is tortured and ultimately killed (173-75). Significantly, the next time that João and Sigismundo meet, the narrator points out that they are on the Atalaia hill, but 'não no alto'—some retrenchment and consolidation is needed before the next upward steps can be taken (207). These come when João is arrested and taken to Lisbon for interrogation on the third floor of a building which must seem like the Tower of Babel to a peasant accustomed to the single-storey architecture of the Alentejo (241); Father Agamedes' comment on João's arrest is to accuse him of sinful pride, which he describes as the worst of the mortal sins, 'porque é ele que levanta o homem contra o seu patrão e o seu Deus' (243). Clearly João is climbing to dangerous heights, and, as he is interrogated and maltreated, he can hardly continue to keep himself upright, whereas 'tudo quanto era igreja estava de pé e triunfante' (251).

The transition to more recent times and more dramatic changes is marked by the birth of Maria Adelaide to Gracinda Mau-Tempo and Manuel Espada. As a preliminary indication of the symbol of hope which her daughter is to become, Gracinda raises her from the ground as the menfolk discuss their plans to go to Montemor to demand their living wages (308). When they go there—in a procession which is presented ironically in terms of a Moorish siege of a Christian castle (310-11)—they are first thrown to the ground by the forces of the local authorities, but they then rise once more, like the irresistible force of the sea (313). On this occasion, although the powerful landowners search for the protesters, they cannot prevent António from remaining in Montemor, and, indeed, on the slopes of the castle-hill itself (317). Significantly, only four pages later we read that 'são os tempos novos que estão a vir muito depressa' (321).

Predictably, the old guard is less than delighted with these developments. Father Agamedes, faced with the loss of his traditional privileges, sees these events as a downward movement from his perspective (321), in terms of a rock rolling downhill out of control, while the ordinary people, long accustomed to accepting his word, react in the opposite way. Suddenly, 'há vozes que se põem de pé' (334), prepared to talk openly of rising from the ground (336), and the narrator writes of 'dois milhões de suspiros que se ergueram do chão' (364). The Revolution has come, and now, at last, it is the people themselves who can make their own new reality.

What is important, is that there has been a *collective* rise amongst the people of Monte Lavre and of Portugal as a whole, as indicated by the image of dogs barking in defiance of their masters—a metaphor which is sustained at regular intervals throughout the text and which could be related to the recovery of the long-lost bark of the dogs of Cerbère in the opening section of *A Jangada de Pedra*:

> Em todo o latifúndio só se ouve ladrarem cães. Ladraram quando entre o Minho e o Algarve, entre a costa do mar e a raia do levante se agitaram as populações ao nome e verbo do general, e ladraram um ladrar novo que em linguagem de gente significava, Se queres aumento de ordenado, vota no Delgado.

(305)

The change in people's lives has been led by individuals such as João Mau-Tempo and Germano Vidigal, who have been prepared to move upwards into personal danger for their ideals. But the rise which ultimately is successful here is a gradual, collective effort. All of the workers involved in it must keep their feet on the soil of the community. This image, which recurs several times in the text, I would suggest, is intended to indicate the importance of remaining in contact with their legitimate base, that of the popular will. Thus, for example, Sigismundo Canastro in prison remains proudly and defiantly 'sentado no chão' (152). The decision taken by José Calmedo to abandon the police force out of shame after arresting João Mau-Tempo for being a communist comes after the former has seated himself on the ground and has laid down his arms (233). This desertion fulfils the earlier prophecy by the narrator:

> Um dia . . . entregará ao comandante do poste de Monte Lavre . . . o seu pedido de demissão, e irá com a mulher e os dois filhos para longe dali, aprenderá a assentar o pé no chão como um civil e levará o resto da vida a esquecer que foi guarda.

(231)

Levantado do Chão, therefore, sums up the entire process of a growing political consciousness and emancipation in Monte Lavre and, by extension, in Portugal as a whole, over several generations. Amongst Saramago's novels this work is unique, being the only one which does not have a specific protagonist or protagonists, but instead—and, some might be tempted to say, in keeping with its ideological inspiration—a whole class of rural labourers as its focus. Moreover, the more recent novels concentrate on restricted moments in history. This concentration would seem to preclude the possibility of the type of broader analysis offered by the earlier work. Should we, then, see the later works, with their focus

upon the individual protagonist and the snapshot in time, as an indication of retreat from earlier ideological purity? Such a view would surely seem difficult to reconcile with Saramago's recent reaffirmation of his loyalty to the Portuguese Communist Party.[3]

I would prefer to explain this development differently, seeing it as a retreat from the *aesthetic* ideology of the neo-Realist movement which undoubtedly influenced the conception of *Levantado do Chão*. The seductive flights of fantasy which are evident in texts such as *Memorial do Convento* simply could not co-exist easily with the predominantly social documentary tone of *Levantado do Chão*. In fact, in view of the prominence which the element of fantasy and the narratorial voice develop in Saramago's more recent works, one might say that his conception of political commitment in writing has moved from a Realist to a Brechtian model, where it is precisely the implausibility of the plot of a work such as *A Jangada de Pedra* which allows it to function effectively at an allegorical level.

In terms of content, however, whereas *Levantado do Chão* presents a complete process of popular emancipation, the other works which I intend to discuss (principally *Memorial do Convento* and *A Jangada de Pedra*) are not a denial, but a development of the same ideas which informed the creation of the earlier work. In other words, although the later texts may be read separately, they should be considered as different panels on something like a medieval triptych, visions of humanity which complement one another—through the recurrence of symbolism and imagery—to form a whole which is greater than the sum of their parts.

At least with *Memorial do Convento*, which takes an unorthodox and rather irreverent view of the construction of the great convent at Mafra, it is not difficult to see traces of the author's ideological commitment. The very opening section unambiguously sets out to ridicule the pretensions of the court and to suggest a monarchy which is morally bankrupt, while, as the text develops, it becomes increasingly apparent that fiscal bankruptcy is avoided only through the exploitation of overseas colonies and the poor at home. Yet I believe that the political implications of this work extend beyond the mere reflection of social inequality which is immediately apparent. For *Memorial do Convento*, like Saramago's other novels, is not only fiction; it is also an exploration of the ways in which popular advancement may—and may not—be achieved.

The author's intentions are surely revealed in the way that he concentrates on the history of the humble couple Baltasar and Blimunda, treating the nobler classes as an object of ridicule and leaving the construction of the convent as merely a part of the background to the novel. In spite of its ideological implications, this preference cannot in itself indicate any specific means for bringing change to the lives of ordinary people. I would suggest, rather, that these matters are explored by Saramago through the sub-plot concerning the couple's involvement in Father Bartolomeu Lourenço de Gusmão's obsessive plans to construct a flying-machine. This machine—whose ability to rise off the ground allows it to reach altitudes which dwarf even the megalomaniacal towers of the convent—seems at first to contrast with the royal project in that it is fuelled by the wills of ordinary people, for Blimunda possesses extraordinary powers of eyesight which permit her to 'see' human wills as dark clouds inside the bodies of other people and to 'collect' them in globes provided for this purpose, as Bartolomeu explains to her:

> o éter não se compõe das almas dos mortos, compõe-se, sim, ouçam bem, das vontades dos vivos . . . Tirou do alforge um frasco de vidro que tinha presa ao fundo . . . uma pastilha de âmbar amarelo. Este âmbar, também chamado electro, atrai o éter, andarás sempre com ele por onde andarem pessoas . . . e quando vires que a nuvem vai sair de dentro delas . . . aproximas o frasco aberto, e a vontade entrará nele.
>
> (123-24)[4]

The 'passarola' (as the machine is known) takes this otherwise ordinary couple on a flight in which they rise to dizzying heights at a speed which was impossible for the peasants in *Levantado do Chão*, and, like Christ tempted by the Devil, they see the world tantalizingly spread before them before they have to come back down to earth (196-203).

After the priest's disappearance, Blimunda will never again journey in the 'passarola', which seems likely to be left to decay. But Baltasar does make one further journey in it. When he goes to check on the condition of the machine several years later, he slips and it breaks free from its moorings to carry him up into the sky. After that we know nothing more of him until the very end of the text, when his lover finds him being burnt at the stake. Even then we are not told the reason for his execution, although it is presumably for witchcraft (356-57). It might seem surprising that, during the period of the couple's separation, Saramago chooses to follow the life of Blimunda on earth rather than what might be thought to be the more obviously attractive story of Baltasar in the skies. The fact that Saramago makes this choice indicates his preference for Blimunda's course of action. The real reason why Baltasar dies is that his flight is a symbolic one, indicating a loss of contact with everyday reality. He takes his example from Father Bartolomeu, who displays considerable 'hybris' as he exclaims during the maiden flight of the machine:

> . . . se me visse el-rei, se me visse aquele Tomás Pinto Brandão que se riu de mim em verso, se o Santo Ofício me visse, saberiam todos que sou filho predilecto de Deus, eu sim, eu que estou subindo ao céu por obra do meu génio, por obra também dos olhos de Blimunda . . . por obra da mão direita de Baltasar, aqui te levo, Deus, um que também não tem a mão esquerda.
>
> (196)

Significantly he then goes on to describe himself as God, Baltasar as the Son and Blimunda as the Holy Spirit (197), a claim whose presumption is instantly evident, given the difficulty which the three have in controlling the machine. Bartolomeu has already compared Baltasar to God on their first meeting, because, he claims, God too has no left hand—the hand which often, of course, is associated with evil (68)—a claim of which we are reminded by the narrator on various occasions (87, 169 and 185).

At a literal level, Baltasar is led to his doom by his carelessness in going back up in the flying-machine on his own, without the aid of Blimunda, who can perceive the wills which power it. Moreover, through repeated references to the classical legend of Icarus, who flew too close to the sun and fell back to earth to his death as a result, Saramago insinuates that Baltasar's fate is in some way a punishment. Even before the flying-machine is constructed, this legend is mentioned as Blimunda sees the irresistibility of rising to the maximum height possible:

> Se o sol atrai o âmbar, e o âmbar atrai o éter, e o éter atrai o íman, e o íman atrai o ferro, a máquina irá sendo puxada para o sol, sem parar.
>
> (92)

Later she repeats the same warning in mid-air, while the inventor is still preoccupied entirely by his own achievement: 'Se não abrirmos a vela, continuaremos a subir, aonde iremos parar, talvez ao sol' (197). A further allusion to Icarus lies in Baltasar's own nickname 'Sete-sóis', which prompts him to remark:

> eu não sei desde quando e porquê nos meteram os sete sóis em casa, se fôssemos sete vezes mais antigos que o único sol que nos alumia, então devíamos ser nós os reis do mundo, enfim, isto são conversas loucas de quem já esteve perto do sol e agora bebeu de mais.
>
> (236)

The intoxication here mentioned is not only the result of alcohol.

Yet, one feels bound to ask just why Baltasar is subjected to this punishment. The answer lies in a contrast, indicated earlier, which now turns out to have been apparent rather than real. For both the construction of the convent and the operation of Bartolomeu's flying machine involve upward movement, and both involve the enslavement of others. In the king's project, workmen are literally brought from all over the country to realize the monarch's insane plans. Baltasar and Blimunda allow themselves—at first quite innocently—to be hoodwinked into capturing people's wills and imprisoning them in Bartolemeu's globes. Bearing these facts in mind, then, Baltasar is seen to be as guilty of 'hybris' as Bartolomeu himself. In spite of the latter's apparent sympathy for the couple who help him—telling a white lie about their marital status, for example (119)—he functions as a Mephistophelian figure in that he attempts to lure them into giving their support to his insane plans, which ultimately lead Baltasar (as Faust) to his downfall. Significantly, when Bartolomeu abandons him after their first flight, Baltasar suspects that the priest may have been whisked away by diabolical powers (206), but he none the less continues his involvement in what is now clearly a doomed project.

Baltasar has been guilty of 'hybris' in two ways. Firstly, of course, he and Blimunda have chosen to live outside the accepted structures of their society by choosing not to marry, long before such practices became acceptable. Perhaps what is more significant, however, is that, after Bartolomeu's disappearance, they presume to maintain control of his flying machine, which is powered by the wills of two thousand people. Blimunda questions the legitimacy of this, but Baltasar dismisses her concern, ultimately for reasons of personal vanity:

> Baltasar perguntou, Foste ver as vontades, Fui, respondeu ela, E estão lá, Estão, Às vezes penso que devíamos abrir as esferas, e deixá-las ir, Se as deixarmos ir, será como se não tivéssemos nascido, nem tu, nem eu, nem o padre Bartolomeu Lourenço, Continuam a parecer-se com nuvens fechadas, São nuvens fechadas.

(271)

Baltasar has been seduced by the temptations of glory—just as the king is—and he no longer regards the wills as wills, but merely as what their physical appearance indicates that they are, dark clouds; Baltasar is guilty of taking the owners of these wills for granted as much as the king is in requisitioning labour for the construction of the convent. Moreover, even granting his goodwill, he is simply not capable of controlling the flying machine. IIis stump of an arm does not, in fact, indicate divine status as Father Bartolomeu wrongly suggests. Rather it indicates his inadequacy for flying. In reaching this interpretation one is influenced by the description of the withered arm of the submissive Marcenda as 'uma ave doente, asa quebrada, chumbo cravado no peito' in *O Ano da Morte de Ricardo Reis.*[5] In common with his Old Testament namesake, then, the writing is on the wall for Baltasar because of his presumption, as the narrator himself insinuates:

> . . . esse Baltasar não é o Mateus que conhecemos, mas sim aquele outro que foi rei de Babilónia, e que, tendo profanado, num festim, os vasos sagrados do templo de Jerusalém, por isso veio a ser punido, morto às mãos de Ciro, que para a execução dessa divina sentença tinha nascido.

(288)[6]

Baltasar's final journey in the 'passarola' is matched by another, the journey made by João Elvas to accompany that of the court to the Spanish border to celebrate two arranged Royal marriages. Interestingly, just as the efforts to raise the 'passarola' match the king's extravagant project at Mafra, so here the commoner's journey is said to be matched by the erection of an elaborate building specially for the occasion (304-05). The word 'erection' is perhaps particularly appropriate here, since shortly afterwards the forthcoming marriage is explicitly presented to one of the enforced brides in terms of brutal male domination (307).

The difference is that, whereas Baltasar's journey is vertical and solitary, João Elvas moves across the surface of the country, speaking to his compatriots, listening to them and learning from them wherever he goes. Baltasar, on the other hand, has been tempted by the spectacle shown to him by the priest. He presumes to keep the human wills imprisoned, thinking that he is capable of taking care of the ship on his own. To give further support to my negative interpretation of the meaning of the 'passarola', I would point to its successor, the Nazi airship which looms menacingly over Lisbon in *O Ano da Morte de Ricardo Reis*, representing a political doctrine which presumed to know the will of the people better than did the people themselves. In *Memorial do Convento* João also contrasts with Baltasar in that he is seen to be contributing to what will one day be a successful change—for the area which he passes through is precisely the area where *Levantado do Chão* is set, and one of the people to whom he speaks is a certain Julião Mau-Tempo, who is even said to have blue eyes, one of the distinguishing marks of the Mau-Tempo family in the earlier novel (236).

Blimunda, in her turn, also undertakes a journey throughout Portugal in the latter stages of the book in search of her lost man. In the course of this journey she experiences many adventures, meets many people, defends herself valiantly against an attempted rape by a friar (345-46), and talks to the people wherever she goes, raising new questions and questioning established hierarchies:

> Por onde passava, ficava um fermento de desassossego, os homens não reconheciam as suas mulheres, que subitamente se punham a olhar para eles, com pena de que não tivessem desaparecido, para enfim poderem procurá-los . . . Nunca entrava em igreja se havia gente lá dentro, apenas para descansar sentada no chão ou apoiada a uma coluna, entrei por um momento, vou-me embora já, esta não é a minha casa. Os padres que ouviam falar dela mandavam-lhe recados para que viesse à confissão, curiosos de saber que mistérios se ocultavam naquela romeira e peregrina . . . A esses mandava dizer que fizera promessa de só confessar quando se sentisse pecadora, não poderia encontrar resposta que mais escandalizasse, se pecadores todos nós somos, porém, pensativas, afinal, que faltas são essas nossas . . . se nós somos, mulheres, verdadeiramente, o cordeiro que tirará o pecado do mundo.

(354)

She has avoided taking the easy upward route. It is people like Blimunda, and João Elvas, who are slowly, painstakingly carrying out a gradual change in the circumstances of the society in which they live. Significantly, when she does finally find her Baltasar again, he has been raised on the stake in punishment for his past. But he has at least learnt from his mistake, for at the last moment, when Blimunda calls his will from his dying body, he chooses not to ascend into Heaven as the Church would wish, but to remain on the horizontal plane:

> E uma nuvem fechada está no centro do seu corpo. Então Blimunda disse, Vem. Desprendeu-se a vontade

de Baltasar Sete-Sóis, mas não subiu para as estrelas,
se à terra pertencia e a Blimunda.

(357)

At the last, then, Baltasar is united with Blimunda. 'Sete-sóis' has been incorporated into 'Sete-luas', perhaps signifying a long-term approach, rather than a short-term one. Instead of tempting fate by soaring to the sun, Blimunda sees just enough in the moonlight to defend herself against the friar who attempts to rape her (345), an action which at a symbolic level indicates resistance to the institutional weight of the Church, as also represented by the huge stone intended for the convent which crushes the innocent Francisco Marques to death (259). Blimunda's way of less spectacular, but more meaningful, action offers raised awareness in the community at large and increased hope that one day a truly just, a truly classless society will be built.

A vision of the kind of solution which the novelist envisages in the longer term is perhaps evident in another of his works, *A Jangada de Pedra*, whose publication in 1986 coincided with the admission of Spain and Portugal into the EEC. Unlike the other novels examined here, this work has a contemporary setting, and there is no vertical axis immediately evident. The movement is wholly concentrated on the horizontal plane, as a small group of Portuguese and Spaniards take the opportunity of the changed circumstances of their Peninsula to engage in a journey of internal discovery. There are here, however, brief instances of what has been seen to be represented by the vertical axis in other works: the elimination by the authorities of the lone sailor who finds himself unexpectedly sailing into a deserted Lisbon (234),[7] and the interrogation of Joaquim Sassa and Pedro Orce (116). But one of the most striking features of this work is the extent to which the traditional hierarchy has been thrown into confusion by the unpredictable movements of the Iberian Peninsula: the poor and homeless take over holiday hotels in the Algarve in spite of the efforts of the police and the army to evacuate them (102-05); even the most powerful governments on earth are seen to be hopelessly incapable of reacting to the events which they cannot control (281-84); and the government of Portugal cannot even find any of its usual hollow words to react to the apparent crisis (223).

The crisis is, however, only an apparent one, for the dominant tone of the latter parts of the text is one of opportunity and hope for the future. The suggestion is made that it is the Iberian Peninsula, which is itself presented as being like a foetus approaching birth (319), which has impregnated all of the fertile women on its soil (319) in what is described as being an 'explosão genésica, uma vez que ninguém acredita que a fecundação colectiva tenha sido de ordem sobrenatural' (321). This statement would seem to be an allusion to the Virgin Birth, suggesting that the real route of Redemption lies in achieving one's own development rather than trusting in any hierarchical order. Further reinforcing this impression is the implicit equation of the Peninsula with an alternative Christ. On their peregrinations around the

horizontal plane of Iberia, the five travellers decide to go up together and see the breach in the Pyrenees which has effectively placed them in control of their own destiny:

Ao menos, estes viajantes sabem que se quiserem ver
os Pirinéus terão mesmo de lá chegar, pôr-lhes a mão
emcima, que o pé não basta, por ser menos sensível, e
os olhos, muito mais do que se julga, deixam-se enganar.

(268)

These modern-day doubting Thomases have thus to put their hands into the wounded side of their homeland. The vision when they look down over the edge to behold their new-found status as an island will give them faith in following their own path, and not one set out for them by the more distant powers of Europe. At the very same moment, the Peninsula finally comes to a halt (296), with its new location between Africa and America reflecting its past history of exploration (322).

Once again, much of the enlightenment gained by the protagonists of *A Jangada de Pedra* is gained from discussions amongst the travellers, frequently while seated on the ground, in contact with the soil of Iberia: 'Estão sentados à sombra de uma árvore' (241), 'Estão sentados, felizmente numa sombra de árvores' (123). Earlier we see Joaquim, José and Pedro Orce seated in the shade of an olive tree, symbolizing peace and understanding (47), just as Jesus is seen twice in *O Evangelho Segundo Jesus Cristo*.[8] The significance which Saramago attributes to discussions of this kind may be deduced from other sources such as his *Viagem a Portugal*, where he writes: 'O viajante viajou no seu país. Isto significa que viajou por dentro de si mesmo, pela cultura que o formou e está formando'.[9] Travelling on the horizontal—not so much in a literal sense, but more in the metaphorical sense of promoting a fruitful exchange of ideas and offering mutual cultural refreshment—is what Saramago sees as being the future for the two Iberian nations. He indicates this same view more explicitly in an article in the journal *Vértice*, where he proposes new ideas of cultural contact to supersede nineteenth-century notions of 'Iberismo' and late twentieth-century plans for European union.[10] The countries which once led European overseas expansion and colonialism—a political system which existed on a clearly hierarchical basis—now have the opportunity to lead the way in showing popular emancipation as a viable alternative to the existing order. No wonder then that in *A Jangada de Pedra* the people of Europe show their solidarity with their erstwhile Iberian neighbours through the necessarily underground medium of graffiti which declare in a multitude of languages the message: 'We too are Iberians' (162-63).

The work closes with the death and burial of Pedro Orce, who has made love to both Maria Guavaira and Joana Carda, so that he too could be regarded as the father of the children which they now expect. In a sense, however, this amounts to the same thing as parentage by the Peninsula, for old Pedro Orce, the man who shares his name with the site of the oldest human remains to be found in the Peninsula, is surely intended to be a specifically Iberian representation of the old man as the Jungian archetypal representative of wisdom.

When Pedro Orce is buried, the staff of Portuguese willow, which throughout has been associated with Joana Carda, is placed in Spanish soil to mark his grave, and the novel closes with a positive allusion to the biblical rod of Aaron which marked his tribe out as having a special duty towards God:[11] 'Os homens e as mulheres, estes, seguirão o seu caminho, que futuro, que tempo, que destino. A vara de negrilho está verde, talvez floresça no ano que vem' (330).

This is, of course, a statement of hope, but like Camões in *Os Lusíadas*—a work which in many ways is paralleled and parodied by the Iberian odyssey of *A Jangada de Pedra*—Saramago does not turn a statement of faith in his people into a simplistic declaration of easy achievement, for the word 'talvez' figures strongly. To conclude, I turn to a quotation from José Saramago's television interview with Carlos Cruz in July 1993, where the novelist declared:

> O que nos faz falta talvez mais do que uma carta dos direitos humanos hoje é uma carta de deveres humanos, proque disso ninguém fala. O Comunismo para mim seria sempre (ou será quando for) um sistema social de responsabilidade colectiva, de interresponsabilidade em que cada pessoa é responsável por todas as pessoas.[12]

In the course of this interview José Saramago rejected categorically the hierarchical practices of Communism in the former Soviet Union and its satellites. What remains clear, however, is that he sees Communism as a means not of restricting, but of empowering the individual. I would suggest, therefore, that, while some of his novels concentrate on the negative course which, as he sees it, Portugal, and Western society in general, have followed until now, his work also outlines a more positive path forward. To take that path, the people themselves must not only be liberated but also be emancipated to assume responsibility, that is, they must be made ready to take on responsibility for the good of others. Baltasar's apparent liberation through the 'passarola' in **Memorial do Convento**, because it benefits only Baltasar himself, is seen to be as inadequate and fruitless as the king's construction of the convent. Along with liberation, therefore, the people must also accept responsibility.

In his vision Saramago sees the former colonial powers of Spain and Portugal, with their cultural links with Africa and Latin America, as having a special responsibility, in international terms, to bring about the development of this more emancipated community. The novelist's view is reflected in the external journey of the Peninsula itself in *A Jangada de Pedra*, while, internally, the greatest discovery made by the protagonists of this novel is the potential of their own voice—their ability to create change in their own lives. José Saramago sees his alter-

native vision of an emancipated Iberian society as being feasible—not in terms of specific political structures but rather in terms of a general culture of democracy—if the Portuguese and Spanish people are prepared to make it happen. The opportunity is there to be grasped, but Saramago emphasizes, in his reference to 'deveres humanos', that the people of Iberia themselves must constantly tend the plant which grows on Pedro Orce's grave.

NOTES

[1] This is a metaphor which is used by Saramago himself within the text (see *Levantado do Chão* [Eighth Edition, Lisbon: Caminho, 1988], 223-24). All references to the text are taken from this edition. His ironic allusion to the Holy Trinity is also implicit in the speech of Sigisberto reported earlier in the text: 'este mundo é o único possível, tal como está, que só depois de morrer haverá paraíso, o padre Agamedes que explique isto melhor, e que só o trabalho dá dignidade e dinheiro . . . foi Deus que quis assim as coisas, o padre Agamedes que explique melhor . . . e se o padre não for suficiente, pede-se aí à guarda que dê um passeio pelas aldeias, só a mostrar-se, é um recado que eles entendem sem difficuldade' (72).

[2] Marie-Eve Letizia, 'O lugar da mulher dentro do espa o e o processo da sua conscientiza ão através da narrative *Levantado do Chão* de José Saramago', in *Taíra* (Grenoble: Centre de Recherche et d'Études Lusophones et Intertropicales, 1991), No. 3, 157-76.

[3] Interview with Carlos Cruz, *Carlos Cruz na Quarta-Feira*, RTP, 28 July 1993.

[4] References to *Memorial do Convento* are taken from the Nineteenth Edition (Lisbon: Caminho, 1989).

[5] *O Ano da Morte de Ricardo Reis* (Sixth Edition, Lisbon: Caminho, 1985), 127.

[6] The biblical tale of Belshazzar may be found in the Book of Daniel, chapter 5.

[7] References to *A Jangada de Pedra* are from the First Edition (Lisbon: Caminho, 1986).

[8] *O Evangelho Segundo Jesus Cristo* (Second Edition, Lisbon: Caminho, 1991), 185 and 251.

[9] *Viagem a Portugal* (Second Edition, Lisbon: Caminho, 1990), 7.

[10] See José Saramago, 'A Península Ibérica entre a Europa e a América Latina', in *Vértice*, 2nd series (March-April 1992), No. 47, 5-11.

[11] The story of Aaron's rod may be found in the Book of Numbers, chapter 17, verses 1-10.

[12] Interview with Carlos Cruz, *Carlos Cruz na Quarta-Feira*, RTP, 28 July 1993.

Giovanni Pontiero (essay date 1994)

SOURCE: "José Saramago and *O Ano da Morte de Ricardo Reis*: The Making of a Masterpiece," in *Bulletin of Hispanic Studies*, Vol. LXXI, No. 1, January, 1994, pp. 139-48.

[*Pontiero considers Saramago's novel a philosophical journey centering on Fernando Pessoa, Portuguese poet, and one of Pessoa's heteronyms, Ricardo Reis, both of whom are characters in Saramago's book.*]

As the title suggests, this fourth novel by José Saramago is dominated by the presence of Ricardo Reis, one of the heteronyms of the poet Fernando Pessoa (1888-1935), Portugal's most famous poet since Camoens. Pessoa insisted that his three main heteronyms (Álvaro de Campos, Alberto Caeiro and Ricardo Reis) were not mere pseudonyms but evidence of the multiple personalities we all possess and contrasting facets of our innumerable selves. Saramago ingeniously probes the relationship between Pessoa and Reis further, by allowing the heteronym to outlive his creator by nine months, while summoning Pessoa from his tomb to renew friendship with Reis, who has just returned to Portugal after sixteen years of exile in Brazil.

Reis' return to Portugal can be seen as a quest, a pilgrimage to his creator's grave, a return to his spiritual roots, spurred on by the need to renew an unfinished dialogue about life and art, reality and illusion. Both Pessoa and Reis are haunted by unresolved enigmas and the poet confides: ' . . . morri antes de ter percebido se é o poeta que se finge de homem ou o homem que se finge de poeta'.[1]

The Lisbon Reis encounters on his return is a sombre and silent city, its topography a labyrinth of reminiscences. A constant drizzle and darkness emphasize the all-pervading sense of alienation and the author suggests that what Reis needs is

> um cãozito de cego, uma bengalita, uma luz adiante, que este mundo e esta Lisboa são uma névoa escura onde se perde o sul e o norte, o leste e o oeste, onde o único caminho aberto é para baixo . . .
>
> (91)

The Lisbon depicted by Saramago is unmistakably that of the mid-1930s. The reader has the impression of scanning photographs of the period, the city's monuments and statues reminding us of Portugal's former glory, once a great sea-faring nation and mighty empire, but now much diminished. In the company of Reis, we discover the city's landmarks, a city of slopes and lookouts dominating the waters of the Tagus. Posters, advertisements and a wealth of visual detail provide a vivid picture of the city's commerce, the trading companies and products of the day, the time-honoured traditions and local customs, the numerous churches, convents, theatres, cinemas and music halls. A city of bustle and sharp contrasts, a nation much given to parades and processions, feast-days and carnival.

But once installed in the Hotel Bragança, a glass house at once confining and transparent, 'lugar neutro, sem compromisso, de trânsito e vida suspensa' (22), Reis gradually becomes aware of a clandestine Lisbon, of the anxieties and fears lurking in the background. The political events that were to change the face of Europe, notably the civil war in Spain and the upsurge of Fascism in Italy and Germany, also began to affect Portugal. A tiny country with reduced resources, Portugal could hope for little in the power game being played by stronger nations. The repressive régime introduced by Salazar's 'New State' aped the Fascist régimes of Italy and Germany with disastrous results. Salazar, Portugal's self-styled sage, protector and gentle potentate, courted the approval of these dubious allies, while leading his country into crippling isolation. The spirit of patriotism he invoked was to absolve all excesses and justify the most glaring contradictions.

Reis' pessimistic view of the political arena of the day and his contempt for political expediency provide Saramago with an irresistible opportunity to voice his own firm belief that deception is the very essence of politics:

> Lutam as nações umas com as otras, por interesses que não são de Jack nem de Pierre nem de Hans nem de Manolo nem de Giuseppe, tudo nomes de homem para simplificar, mas que os mesmos e outros homens tomam ingenuamente como seus, os interesses, ou virão a sê-lo à custa de pesado pagamento quando chegar a hora de liquidar a conta.
>
> (149

The voice we are listening to here is that of a committed communist who knows that powerful neighbours can either offer help or extermination. As a political force, Portugal comes across as a nation that has lost its nerve and initiative; servile and ineffectual, timid even on her home territory, she is patronized by the rest of Europe and is insultingly typecast as the 'loyal ally'.

Saramago frequently refers to the tiny voice of Portugal, and this sense of inferiority conditions the Portuguese people both at home and abroad. The author reminds us that no one can claim to be truly Portuguese unless he speaks another language better than his own, a nation of emigrants prepared to settle wherever they can find something to eat and earn some money. Patient, hard-working and submissive, the Portuguese have mastered the art of self-effacement: 'este povo ainda tem na memória inconsciente os costumes do deserto, continua a acreditar que o que defende do frio defende do calor, por isto se cobre todo, como se se escondesse' (310). Brainwashed by the politicians and clergy, the people are encouraged to confuse things human and divine and to believe that 'Portugal é Cristo e Cristo é Portugal' (281).

Seen through the eyes of an atheist who is not insensitive to the persuasive influence of religion, the Holy Shrine of Fatima is yet further proof of human gullibility. The faith and resignation of the pilgrims returning empty-handed fills Reis with quiet rage and frustration. In search of a miracle, these pilgrims advance from every cardinal and collateral point until they converge at the shrine: 'Fátima . . . uma enorme estrela . . . esta preciosa jóia de catolicidade resplandece por muitos lumes . . . sofrimento . . . fé . . . caridade . . . a indústria de bentinhos e similares . . . quinquilharia . . . comes e bebes . . . perdidos e achados' (317). A dispirited Reis retreats from the pilgrimage convinced that once we start believing in miracles we have lost all hope. Stoic resignation is preferable by far and will bring fewer disappointments: 'Não tentarás o Senhor teu Deus nem a Senhora Sua Mãe e, se bem pensasses, não deverias pedir, mas aceitar, isto mandaria a humildade, só Deus é que sabe o que nos convém' (318).

Reis is equally scornful of that other major instrument of manipulation, the Press, which misleads its readers while satisfying their curiosity. Perusing the newspapers of the day, Reis uncovers yet another labyrinth of information at once significant and trivial, true and false, selected and edited for maximum effect and couched in words which conceal as much as they reveal, the language pitched at the level of the masses they hope to brainwash. Salazar transformed the Press into a powerful instrument of propaganda and self-aggrandizement. We are reminded that the ideals and achievements of the New State were constantly being extolled in the newspapers. Thanks to Salazar, Divine Providence was pouring endless blessings on Portugal while the rest of the world faced doom and destruction, a farcical travesty not unlike the special edition printed daily for the senile John D. Rockefeller which reported nothing but prosperity, the end of unemployment, the death of communism in Russia, and the virtues of the American way of life, while suppressing every item of bad news.

Returning from the relaxed, not to say lax, atmosphere of Brazil, it is perhaps inevitable that Reis should be struck by the persistent rigidity of the social hierarchy in his native Portugal. He has his own ironic theory about social harmony:

> a paz social é uma questão de tacto, de finura, de psicologia, para tudo dizer numa palavra só, à vez três vezes, se ela ou elas coincidem rigorosamente com o pensamento é problema a cujo deslindamento já tínhamos renunciado.
>
> (217)

Beholding the spectacle of the world from his own privileged position, he is painfully aware of its ironies, injustices and inequalities. The lower orders, that backward clan, disconcert and exasperate him with their endless capacity for suffering and humiliation (whether it be sincere or false). Reis comments that if Lydia were not a maid at the Hotel Bragança, there is every possibility that she would make an excellent tightrope walker, juggler or musician, for she has talent enough for any of these professions. And this reflection squares with Saramago's firm conviction that even the most deprived members of society are exceptional human beings who only need the right conditions in order to show their true worth. Class distinctions are further explored when we meet the two women in Reis' life: the warm-hearted, uncomplaining Lydia who submits to the advances of hotel guests because 'a vida é triste', and the coy, elusive Marcenda who has the right social credentials but whose chances of a normal existence have been dashed by the embarrassing

disfigurement of a withered arm. The presence of Lydia and Marcenda satisfies two quite separate strands in Reis' nature: a man in search of his creature comforts and sexual gratification on the one hand, the poet in search of the ideal muse on the other, because even poets, after all, are not exempt from the demands both of the flesh and the spirit. Reis' warring emotions on both counts tell us everything we need to know about accepted attitudes between men and women in a society fettered by religious beliefs and social prejudices. And our protagonist speaks with two voices: pursuing his muse one minute as he works at a poem and engaging in a little erotic combat the next to steady his nerves and calm his thoughts. Uneasy relationships between men and women are probed in all Saramago's books and with disarming honesty. He confides that there are moments in life when we think we are experiencing passion and it is merely an outburst of gratitude. His limited experience of women has taught him the difference between love and companionship, the latter seemingly preferable because less painful and demanding.

So much for the personal dimension as Reis renews contact with his past and intellectual formation, but what of the universal dimension surrounding the charismatic figure of Fernando Pessoa—poet, philosopher and a pervasive presence even as a ghost?

Saramago's portrait of Pessoa is accurate in every detail: a fastidious and somewhat enigmatic human being, a keen observer of life and hypersensitive by nature. As an intellectual, Pessoa was impressive. A man with wide interests, a voracious reader and attuned to new philosophical ideas and literary trends then current in Europe. Avant-garde journals published in Lisbon provided Pessoa with a platform for his theories about art and life. In his poetry and essays, there is a lingering sense of disquiet: 'Não conheço quem fui no que hoje sou'.[2] In dialogue, Reis, his heteronym, alternately identifies with Pessoa or questions his creator's conclusions on every imaginable issue from political allegiances to the essence of true love. And to complicate matters, the voice of Saramago himself can be heard intermittently, adding his own note of agreement or dissent. The dialogues between Pessoa and Reis are wary and tense, they confess to never having really understood each other as they recapitulate and reiterate their convictions, qualify and revise certain opinions they once held. In both men there is a contagious pessimism and weariness, Pessoa the more resigned, Reis the more irritable and sceptical, 'a mais duvidosa das pessoas' (361); both are keenly aware of their inner solitude, of a profound silence (the half-brother of solitude). Like Pessoa before him, Reis feels overwhelmed by the enormity of the world, by too much talk, too much literature, and he declares himself exhausted after hours of listening to

> os pulmões portugueses tuberculosos, cansado também de ter palmilhado a cidade, no espaço limitado por onde incessantemente circula, como a mula que vai puxando a nora, de olhos vendados, e, apesar disso ou por causa disso, sentindo por momentos a vertigem do tempo, o

oscilar ameaçador das arquitecturas, a viscosa pasta do
chão, as pedras moles.

(267)

Here we find the same dark musings as in Pessoa's *Livro
do Desassossego,* but offset by the simple need to believe
that there are some good things in life such as love, for
example, or that happiness which unhappy people are continually talking about. Yet for the self-questioning Pessoa
and Reis, happiness and love might well prove to be impossible, given their difficulty in knowing themselves. And
this is where Lydia shows her inner strength. She possesses neither Reis' intellect nor powers of introspection, but
when it comes to knowing herself—she does not appear to
have the slightest doubt. Their relationship reveals the abyss
between what Pessoa defines as 'vida teórica' and 'vida
prática'.[3] The words she utters are simple and to the point,
yet somehow more meaningful than the fastidious discussions of Pessoa and Reis: 'singular rapariga esta Lídia, diz
as coisas mais simples e parece que as diz como se apenas
mostrasse a pele doutras palavras profundas que não pode
ou não quer pronunciar' (305).

The existential problem posed by Pessoa, Reis and Saramago, is that every human being is individual while
resembling every other human being. We are all unique,
yet innumerable, and this multiple personality exacer-
bates the problem of self-identity and our fragmentation. To complicate matters, the gods, too, are innumerable, but hopefully superfluous: 'quem não tem Deus
procura deuses, quem deuses abandonou a Deus inventa,
um dia nos livraremos deste e daqueles' (73). This fragmentation means that we can feel many, often contradictory, things at the same time. And this in turn can so
easily lead us into misunderstanding and misinterpreta-
tion; human error and its dire consequences being one
of Saramago's constant preoccupations.

Another obsessive preoccupation is the thought of encroaching death. Man is compared with an elephant that
senses its approaching end. A constant theme in his poetry and prose while alive, death is perceived somewhat
differently by the Pessoa who returns from the grave.
The poet's confidences to Reis give as much cause for
disquiet as reassurance. Looking back on life, Pessoa can
best describe it as a lingering convalescence:

> afinal a vida não é muito mais que estar deitado, convale-
> scendo duma enfermidade antiga, incurável e recidivante,
> com intervalos a que chamamos saúde, algum nome
> lhes havíamos de dar, vista a diferença que há entre os
> dois estados.

(171)

This uneasy pact between life and death extends to that
between memory and oblivion, and Pessoa warns Reis
that the wall separating the living from one another is no
less opaque than the wall that separates the living from
the dead. The poet's message would appear to be that,
when the laughter and the tears have subsided, we are left
with shadows, a sense of futility, a shaming recognition
of our own ineptitude when it comes to accepting funda-

mental truths, and when Reis accuses Pessoa of trivial
philosophizing, he warns him that everything loses its
significance once seen from his side of death.

Convinced that the works of mankind are ever incomplete, Pessoa can attest to lost opportunities, to missing
out on that one word that needed to be said, that one
gesture that needed to be made before time ran out. Once
dead, Pessoa becomes aware that being and existing are
not the same thing, and that in the final analysis none of
us is truly alive or dead, nor is anyone the wiser as to
whether 'this passing shadow we cast on the ground is
life because it resembles life'.

Pessoa's lifelong concern with the inevitability of fate is
echoed throughout Saramago's novel. We are constantly
being reminded that no man escapes his ironic destiny—
'o destino, além de obreiro, também sabe de ironias'
(258)—or can hope to win his battle against time: 'Não
há resposta para o tempo, estamos nele e assistimos nada
mais' (323). As Ricardo Reis lies in bed, he imagines
that he can see the palm of God's hand overhead and is
reading there the lines of life, of a life that narrows, is
interrupted and revived, becomes more and more tenuous, a besieged heart solitary behind those walls. In Saramago's firmament the gods are wise and indifferent,
and above them is fate, the supreme order to which even
gods are subject. Once he touches on the divinities, Saramago becomes cynical, rebellious, and subversive. Because the gods of Ricardo Reis are silent, unfeeling entities prepared to dupe and abandon us:

> para quem o mal e o bem são menos que palavras, por
> as não dizerem eles nunca, e como as diriam, se mesmo
> entre o bem e o mal não sabem distinguir, indo como
> nós vamos no rio das coisas, só deles distintos porque
> lhe chamamos deuses e às vezes acreditamos.

(60)

The challenge confronting mankind is to change fate without the assistance of god or gods, to change it for better
or worse, and to prevent fate from being fate.

In Saramago, critics worldwide have recognized a master
of irony, a writer with an unsparing eye for human foibles
and paradoxical situations. And when pressed on this point
he once explained: 'I de-dramatise life through irony'.[4] In
O Ano da Morte de Ricardo Reis, the registers of parody and satire are as unpredictable as they are varied.
Saramago can be biting yet compassionate, discerning yet
deeply moving. His most bitter remarks are directed at
the powerful and affluent who live in dread of some dangerous subversion of social class and ranking, a thing
greatly to be feared. New Year resolutions, he insists,
are only for the common people: the others, uncommon
and superior, have their own good reasons for being and
doing quite the opposite whenever it suits or profits them.
Mindful of the time-honoured rivalry between Spain and
Portugal, Reis mentally compares the subdued mutter-
ings and whispers of the Portuguese with the high-pitched
voices of wealthy Spanish refugees speaking the sonorous language of Cervantes and flaunting their triumph in

misfortune: his disgruntled thoughts echoing time-honoured grievances: 'os espanhóis são assim, querem logo tomar conta de tudo, é preciso estar sempre de olho neles' (393). The English fare no better. Perfidious Albion, we are reminded, has lived up to her reputation and given nearly every other nation just cause for complaint, and when Reis sees cricket being played on the deck of the ocean liner *The Highland Brigade,* he is even more convinced that for the British Empire nothing is impossible. The author can be engagingly witty when he suggests that the only real justification for statues is to provide perches for pigeons or suggests that Bovril might be the answer to the country's poverty, as he watches leaflets advertising the beverage's nutritious value dropping from the clouds on to the pilgrims at Fatima. The humour becomes rumbustious, not to say risqué, when Reis finally kisses the highly-strung Marcenda and can feel the blood rushing to his temples and his libido aroused, and there is a hint of playful irreverence when he retells the story of Adam and Eve and settles for an earthier vision of Paradise and its delights:

> Onde se reunirem homem e mulher, Deus estará entre eles, por estas novas palavras aprenderemos que o paraíso, afinal, não era onde nos tinham dito, é aqui, ali aonde Deus terá de ir, de cada vez, se quiser reconhecer-lhe o gosto.
>
> (224)

At times the humorist is reined in by the radical sceptic: 'Um homem, se estudou, aprende a duvidar, muito mais sendo os deuses tão inconstantes, certos apenas, eles por ciência, nós por experiência, de que tudo acaba, e o sempre antes do resto' (218). Life is looked at obliquely and with a questioning eye. But note that even the aloof and indifferent Reis is often stirred by unexpected emotions to the extent of finding himself quaking because a simple cloud has passed.

Like all important novels, **O Ano da Morte de Ricardo Reis** is also a book about reading and writing. Note the titles of the two books mentioned several times within the narrative: *The God of the Labyrinth* and *Conspiracy,* both titles embodying key themes throughout the novel. Drawing a clear distinction between the essential books and those which satisfy our inclinations, the author likes to think of his own books as a conversation with his reader. He frequently addresses the reader directly in mid-narrative, taking care to adopt a tone of voice which is challenging rather than confessional. This desire to be an 'oral narrator' has influenced his technique with its disregard for conventional punctuation. As he himself has stressed: 'the words written by me are intended as much to be read as to be heard . . . the oral narrator speaks as if he were composing music and uses the same elements as the musician: sounds and pauses, high or low, some short, others long'.[5] As readers, we are invited to ponder and tease out the contradictions he exposes, to probe the nuances of the words and moments of silence. To complicate matters, *thinking itself* intervenes as if it were a protagonist, and like the Argentinian writer, Jorge Luis Borges, the author believes there is no more elaborate

pleasure than that of thought. He makes frequent use of Borgesian images: the labyrinth, the chessboard, the compass, the river of time and the mirror, but the wealth of associations attributed to the last of these images shows just how skilfully he adapts these borrowings:

> talvez no espelho se tenha falado uma língua diferente, talvez outras palavras se tenham dito naquele cristalino lugar, então outros foram os sentidos expressos, parecendo que, como sombra, os gestos se repetiam, outro foi o discurso, perdido na inacessível dimensão, perdido também, afinal o que deste lado se disse, apenas conservados na lembrança alguns fragmentos, não iguais, não complementares, não capazes de reconstituir o discurso inteiro, o deste lado, insista-se, por isso os sentimentos de ontem não se repetem nos sentimentos de hoje, ficaram pelo caminho, irrecuperáveis, pedaços de espelho partido, a memória.
>
> (175-76)

Like Borges he specializes in tactical subtleties, dialectical cunning and rhetorical digressions. Saramago exploits philosophical preambles and frequent digressions to show just how deeply the human mind can burrow: 'a sensibilidade das pessoas tem recônditos tão profundos que, se por eles nos aventurarmos com ânimo de tudo examinar, há grande perigo de não sairmos de lá tão cedo' (122). As a writer he is motivated by the desire to establish patterns of symmetry amidst the chaos, to discover unexpected links between men and symbols; sometimes all too transparent, for example, a new automobile named The Dictator, or Marcenda's withered arm seen as a symbol of collective mutilation; at other times startlingly unreal, for instance, the image of St Francis of Assisi's stigmata linking him with the cross of Christ, and the crosses on the armbands of bank employees at a political rally.

In linguistic matters, Saramago is scrupulous, analysing, dissecting and contrasting words and their meaning; establishing different layers of meaning; investigating new formulations. He is particularly sensitive to words spoken from the heart as opposed to platitudes devoid of any human interest, and he leads us through an intricate mental process that derives from a succession of stimuli, sometimes unconscious, sometimes only pretending to be unconscious, which achieves new relationships of thought and expression. As with most of the important writers of our age, he cultivates that opacity of language whereby books are made out of words as much as out of characters and incidents. He neatly defines the tyranny of words:

> por que será que as palavras se servem tantas vezes de nós, vemo-las a aproximarem-se, a ameaçarem, e não somos capazes de afastá-las, de calá-las, e assim acabamos por dizer o que não queríamos, é como o abismo irresistível, vamos cair e avançamos.
>
> (214)

Yet much as he is worried by the inauthenticity of language and the danger of counterfeit emotions, he reassures us in the next breath that words are the best tools we can hope for in our attempt, ever frustrated, to express what we call thought. Language, for Saramago, owes much of its fascination to the inherent contradictions, and he warns us that unless we are prepared to use all words, however absurd, we will never say the essential words. The texture of his own prose owes much of its richness to multiple registers as he goes from description to philosophical speculation, from melancholy and despair to wry humour. By restricting punctuation to commas and full-stops, he creates his own verbal music and allows for a greater variety of inflections. The basic technique is that of counterpoint as he sets up a game of voices, each voice establishing its own truths, yet truths often saying different things.

Connecting the threads across time (a time at once linear and labyrinthine), finding certain threads without knots and certain knots without threads, Saramago shows us how the past and its ghosts can be more real and concrete than life in the present.

For Saramago, writing novels is a truly passionate way of living life and enlarging on the world. He does not subscribe to the idea of an absent, impartial narrator. In *O Ano da Morte de Ricardo Reis* our author is omniscient and omnipresent, and he shows an almost carnal relationship with his country and people while transcending all barriers of race and culture in his pursuit of a vision of totality. The novelist's art, as he understands and practises it, is not one of reflection or imitation but a skilful act of invention:

> O objecto da arte não é a imitação . . . a realidade não suporta o seu reflexo, rejeita-o, só uma outra realidade, qual seja, pode ser colocada no lugar daquela que se quis expressar, e, sendo diferentes entre si, mutuamente se mostram, explicam e enumeram a realidade como invenção que foi, a invenção como realidade que será.
>
> (109-10)

Or as Pessoa himself expressed it: 'Sobre a nudez forte da verdade o manto diáfano da fantasia' (62).

As in all of his major novels, the author's earthly journey leads him irresistibly back to the point of departure. The opening phrase—'Aqui o mar acaba e a terra principia' (11)—finds its completion in the closing sentence: 'Aqui, onde o mar se acabou e a terra espera' (415). Sea and earth, space and time, past and present merge in this kaleidoscopic vision of an awesome totality.

NOTES

[1] José Saramago, *O Ano da Morte de Ricardo Reis* (Sixth Edition, Lisbon: Caminho, 1985), 118. All quotations are taken from this edition.

[2] 'O Andaime', from the *Cancioneiro in Obra Poética* (Third Edition, Rio de Janeiro: José Aguilar Editora, 1969), 159.

[3] Fernando Pessoa, *Livro do Desassossego,* edited by Vicente Guedes and Bernardo Soares (Lisbon: Editorial Presença Lda., 1990), 228.

[4] Giovanni Pontiero: Interview with José Saramago, *PN Review,* XVI (1989), No. 4, 41.

[5] *Ibid.,* 39.

FURTHER READING

Daniel, Mary L. "Symbolism and Synchronicity: Jose Saramago's *Jangada de pedra.*" *Hispania,* Vol. 74, No. 3 (September 1991): 536-41.
Examines how diverse elements contribute to the unifying journey-symbolism in the novel.

Forrest, Gene Steven. "The Dialectics of History in Two Dramas of Jose Saramago." *Hispanofila,* 106 (September 1992): 59-68.
Illustrates the author's metaphoric use of history to further his own vision of society.

Howe, Irving. "Fueling the Passarola." *New York Times Book Review,* Vol. 102 (13 July 1997): 11.
Explains the construction and content of *Baltasar and Blimunda.*

Kaufman, Helena. "Evangelical Truths: José Saramago on the Life of Christ." *Revista Hispanica Moderna,* Vol. XLVII, No. 2 (December 1994): 449-58.
Assesses Saramago's version of Jesus's life, in which the author develops some non-traditional insights and interpretations.

Kerrigan, Michael. "The I of Saramago." *Times Literary Supplement,* No. 4942 (19 December 1997): 20.
Review of *Blindness.*

Preto-Rodas, Richard A. A review of *Cadernos de Lancarote: Diario-III. World Literature Today,* Vol. 71, No. 1 (Winter 1977): 133.
Describes Saramago's approach to the events in his life during 1995, published as Vol. 3 of his diaries.

Pontiero, Giovanni. "The Apotheosis of *Blimunda*: An Opera by Azio Corghi Based on Saramago's *Memorial do convento.*" *Bulletin of Hispanic Studies,* Special Homage Volume (1992). *Hispanic Studies in Honour of Geoffrey Ribbans,* Ann L. Mackenzie and Dorothy S. Severin, eds., pp. 335-43. Liverpool: Liverpool University Press, 1992.
Discusses how Saramago's novel was adapted for musical theater.

———. "Jose Saramago: An Introduction." *Bulletin of Hispanic Studies,* Vol. LXXI, No. 1 (January 1994): 115-17.
Brief summary of Saramago's career and themes.

———. A review of *Ensaio sobre a ceguieira. World Literature Today,* Vol. 70, No. 2 (Spring 1996): 385-86.
Asserts that the series of characters who experience blindness in the novel actually become ethically, rather than literally, blinded.

Additional coverage of Saramago's life and career is contained in the following sources published by the Gale Group: *Contemporary Authors*, Vol. 153; *Contemporary Literature Criticism*, Vol. 119.

Severo Sarduy
1937–1993

Cuban novelist, poet, and essayist.

INTRODUCTION

Sarduy is best known for experimental and linguistically complex literary works that explore Cuban culture and the ways in which language creates and transforms reality. His most famous work, the novel *Cobra* (1972), for which he received the Prix Médicis étranger, eschews linear narrative logic for a loosely structured series of images and dialogue scenes in which events are repeated with differing outcomes and the characters change form and gender. As one critic, Julia A. Kushigian observes: "[T]he strength of Sarduy's work lies . . . in his ability to duplicate the world through the chaotic, creative process mixing times, histories, cultures, and genders in an effort to stimulate readers through the brilliance and complexity of his prose."

Sarduy was born in Camagüey, Cuba, where he attended Instituto de Segunda Ensenanza. In 1956 he entered medical school in Havana, where he began writing poetry and advertisements for radio and television. The following year he published a short story entitled "El seguro." During the Cuban revolution Sarduy worked as an art critic for *Lunes de Revolución*; in the fall of 1959, Fidel Castro's new government awarded him a scholarship to study art criticism at the L'Ecole du Louvre in Paris. Sarduy became aligned with two highly influential French literary groups: one was associated with the literary journal *Mundo Nuevo*, and the other—which included Philippe Sollers, Julia Kristeva, Lucien Goldman, and Tzvetan Todorov—was associated with the radical structuralist and Maoist journal *Tel quel*; he also studied structuralist methodology under Roland Barthes at the Icole Pratique des Hautes Itudes of the Sorbonne. Sarduy's first novel, *Gestos*, was published in 1963 and was followed by numerous other works, including novels and collections of poems and essays. Sarduy died in Paris in 1993 from AIDS-related complications.

Gestos examines life in Cuba just before the Communist revolution of 1956-1959 and attempts to determine what it means to be Cuban. The novel is comprised of impressionistic vignettes, dialogue scenes, and monologues that depict the daily activities of an unnamed mulatto laundress and singer. *De donde son los cantantes* (1967; *From Cuba with a Song*), considered by many critics to be Sarduy's most experimental novel, includes three narrative sections: the first concerns a tortured romance between a Spanish general and a nightclub singer; the second depicts the career of a singer named Dolores Rondon, who was the unnamed main character from *Gestos*; the third section deals with the introduction of Spanish-European culture to Cuba. Sarduy's next novel, *Cobra*, tells the story of the title character, the star of a burlesque house run by a woman named La Seflora with whom Cobra—whose gender is at times difficult to ascertain—is romantically involved. The fantastical plot of this novel—one that includes such disparate characters as Tibetan monks, a motorcycle gang, and a Tangierian sex-change doctor named Dr. Ktazob who is reminiscent of Dr. Benway from William S. Burroughs's *Naked Lunch*—begins when Cobra and La Seflora are reduced to dwarf size by a drug both were taking to make Cobra's feet smaller. *Cobra* proceeds mainly as dialogue and is accompanied by Sarduy's comments on art and the creative process. *Maitreya* (1978; *Maitreya*), a novel many critics consider to be about the theme of exile, begins at the time of the Chinese invasion of Tibet when a Buddhist monk, the Master, dies after predicting his eventual reincarnation as the Instructor. The other monks find a young boy being cared for by two Chinese women, the Leng sisters, and declare him the reincarnation of the Master and the next Lama. Not wishing an ascetic life for the boy, the Leng sisters flee to Ceylon and then to Cuba during the revolution. The final section of the book concerns the death of Cuban author José Lezama Lima. Evincing a more traditional narrative structure than some of his previous novels, *Colibrí* (1984) centers on a house near a jungle where a woman named La Regenta provides wealthy male clients the spectacle of handsome young men wrestling. Colibrí, a young blond man who has just arrived, defeats an obese Japanese wrestler, El Japoneson, and becomes the hero of the club. After discovering that La Regenta is passionately in love with him, Colibrí flees into the jungle and meets up with El Japoneson. The two become friends and lovers. Once captured, Colibrí is returned to La Regenta, only to escape and be caught again. Upon his return the second time, however, Colibrí is treated like a god and orders La Regenta's house burnt to the ground and rebuilt. Colibrí then takes charge as the new "dictator" of the club. *Cocuyo* (1990) is an ironic *bildungsroman* set in pre-Castro Cuba that some critics have found reminiscent of Voltaire's *Candide*. Cocuyo, whose name means "firebeetle," is torn from his comfortable bourgeois life by a violent storm; he is injured and winds up in a hospital staffed by unreliable and untrustworthy doctors. He eventually flees to a girls' school where he takes a job running errands. Cocuyo's journey towards maturity leads to an awakening of his sexuality, specifically his love for a woman named Ada.

Most critics praise Sarduy's experimental approach to novel writing, aligning him with the avant-garde writers of the South American literary "Boom," post-Boom, and with European postmodern and post-structuralist authors. Sarduy's work is recognized for its distinctive blend of themes, including an abiding interest in Cuban identity and culture, as well as a fascination with Oriental and Western philosophies. Sarduy's work also deals with themes of sexuality and personal identity, offering often outrageous depictions of transvestism, transsexuality, homosexuality, and sadomasochism in an attempt to explore and critique the notion of a unified ego, or singular personality. While critics generally agree that Sarduy's work offers unique and original insights and experiences, most point out that his books are difficult—sometimes nearly inaccessible—because, in addition to the oblique, allusive nature of his writing and his frequent avoidance of linear narrative logic, Sarduy—by his own admission—often included in his works references to his personal life that could have been meaningful only to himself or to particularly close friends. Michael Wood concluded of *Cobra*: "There is a dizzy freedom in such writing. And while Sarduy has horrible slithers into cuteness and into sniggerings of camp, and while he is far more interested in blood and semen and leather jackets than I am ever going to be, . . .*Cobra* remains a remarkable book, a nervous, flighty homage to the life of language."

PRINCIPAL WORKS

Gestos [*Gestures*] (novel) 1963

De donde son los cantantes [*From Cuba with a Song*] (novel) 1967

Escrito sobre un cuerpo: Ensayos de critica [*Written on a Body*] (essays) 1969

Flamenco (poetry) 1969

Mood Indigo [with H. M. Erhardt] (poetry) 1970

Merveilles de la nature (poetry) 1971

Cobra (novel) 1972

Overdose (poetry) 1972

Barroco (essays) 1974

*Big Bang: Para situar en órbita cinco máquinas / Pour situer en orbite cinq machines de Ramon Alejandro [with Ramon Alejandro] (poetry) 1974

Maitreya [*Maitreya*] (novel) 1978

Para la voz [*For Voice*] (dramas) 1978

Daiquirí (poetry) 1980

La simulación (essays and lectures) 1982

Colibrí (novel) 1984

Un testigo fugaz y disfrazado (poetry) 1985

El Cristo de la rue Jacob [*Christ on the Rue Jacob*] (novel) 1987

Nueva inestabilidad (essays) 1987

Cocuyo (novella) 1990

Pájaros de la playa (novel) 1993

Epitafios, imitación, aforismos (poetry and prose) 1994

* This volume is in both French and Spanish.

CRITICISM

Severo Sarduy with Roberto González Echevarría (interview date 1972)

SOURCE: "Interview: Severo Sarduy," in *Diacritics*, Vol. 2, No. 2, Summer, 1972, pp. 41-5.

[*González Echevarría is a Cuban-born American educator and critic who specializes in Hispanic literature. In the following interview, Sarduy discusses the concept of "the baroque" and its significance in his work.*]

Severo Sarduy is a young Cuban writer (b. 1936) established in Paris, where he is director of the Latin American collection of Editions du Seuil. He began his literary career as a poet in pre-revolutionary Cuba. After the Revolution, in 1959-60, he was part of the team of writers who published *Lunes de Revolución*, an active literary weekly directed by the novelist Guillermo Cabrera Infante. At the end of 1960, a grant from the government sent Sarduy to Paris to study art history at the Ecole du Louvre. He has been in Paris since, where, after completing his studies, he joined two influential literary groups: the one formed around *Mundo Nuevo*, a monthly literary journal directed by Emir Rodríguez Monegal and the *Tel Quel* group. He had published two novels, *Gestos* (1963) and *De donde son los cantantes* (1967), and one book of critical essays, *Escrito sobre un cuerpo* (1969). These last two books, as well as his third novel *Cobra* (to appear this spring in Spanish; fragments have already appeared in *Tel Quel* translated by Philippe Sollers), show the influence of the structuralist *Tel Quel* group, which will be evident also in his answers in the following interview. Aside from his work as a novelist and playwright, Sarduy has served as intellectual bridge between the French literary theoreticians and the Latin American intellectual community.

[GONZÁLEZ ECHEVARRÍA]: *Severo, I know that you're preparing a lengthy essay on the Spanish-American baroque for a UNESCO book edited by the Peruvian critic, Julio Ortega. In addition, your interest in the works of Góngora and Lezama Lima qualify you as an expert in the baroque of the seventeenth century as well as in that of the contemporary period. I'd like you to speak first of Góngora, and then proceed to the baroque of Lezama Lima and of course, that of your own works.*

[SARDUY]: Góngora was born in 1561 and died in 1627. If I remember correctly, he wrote the first *Soledad* in 1612, the year in which he also wrote *Polifemo*. I am not the least bit interested in making a kind of literary and historical parallel with what happened in that period. I mean, as an example, all the biographers of Góngora point out that in 1604 peace was made in London, and the second part of the *Guzmán de Alfarache* was published. Or they can say that in 1609 the *moriscos* were expelled and there appeared, as well, Quevedo's translation of Anacreon, and Quevedo's polemic with Góngora was begun. What the biographers point out is a visible parallel, a visible synchrony with what happened in that moment. I am more interested in establishing a kind of table—and I would give the word "table" the meaning which it has in French when one speaks of a *table de correspondances*; that is, an interplay of different signs that correspond among themselves—establishing a table of the underlying elements that reverberate in the wording of the *Soledades*, and which are not marked by visible historical events. For example, we can keep in mind the following: What is the *episteme* which the baroque makes explicit and puts into practice? There is a factor which seems to me to be essential, which undoubtedly Eugenio d'Ors, the precursor of all that we can mention in this sense, foresaw: in this age which we have just situated, Kepler discovered that the rotation of the planets around the sun is not circular, as was believed and as Galileo continued to affirm for primarily esthetic reasons, but *elliptical*—I underline, obviously, the word "elliptical." At the same time, if I remember correctly, it was Harvey who discovered that the circulation of the blood traces a kind of ellipse around the heart. I should also add another thing to this *dossier*: the canonical structure of the Church was decentralized; in place of a central aisle leading the worshiper from the entrance to the high altar, it took the form of a building without specific entrances and exits, and whose plan was opened, just as the urbanism of the baroque city was opened. In other words, the baroque city was no longer a center around the cathedral, around the dome, but rather a decentralized organization—"polysemous" shall we say—with various comings and goings, with various interior sections. Thus we see here that there exists a kind of underlying battle—which interests me much more than those battles and those treaties that the biographers point out—between two forms characteristic of our western civilization: the circle and the ellipse. This struggle of circle and ellipse has various manifestations; it is fought in several fields. In painting, it is apparent for example, how in the works of Raphael, a circular structure continued to prevail. However, already in Pierre de Cortona, the central circle breaks apart and everything is organized into a kind of ellipse that defines the baroque, of which Cortona is perhaps the most characteristic Italian painter. Thus we see how in painting the circle and the ellipse confront each other. I believe that, forcing things a little, we could say that the figures in Guadalupe which carry on a dialogue in the paintings of Zurbarán can also be inscribed within a circle, while those of El Greco can not.

And how do you extend these ideas to literature?

The area to which I am most interested in extending these ideas is, obviously, literature. In Góngora, as in all of the baroque, the ellipse is the essential support, and the rhetorical ellipse here corresponds, metaphorically I think, to the geometric ellipse. This is not by chance. In the Gongorine ellipse, in the baroque ellipse, there are two centers: the suppressed term and the "suppressing" term. In an ellipse, there is always a term which is hidden, censured; and one which blossoms from the textural surface to serve as a *cachette* or a mask for the other. Instead of saying "Strait of Magellan," we would say, "the hinge, the narrow embracer of one ocean and another, etc." We know perfectly well that certain animal names are censured in Gongorine rhetoric, that one can not speak of hens, and so forth. We know that there is a series of pre-established *topoi,* so that one term may be censured and the other apparent one may cover it. In a Lacanian sense we can say that what Góngora shows is precisely what he hides from us. In other words, that which he shows, as in the metaphor that supports all of the Lacanian psychoanalysis, is that which never ceases to hide something. The Gongorine ellipse, in short then, functions as a table of events which are never historical, which can never be dated, but which constitute the epistemology underlying all the mechanisms of the baroque; which is to say, the struggle between Galileo and Kepler, between Raphael and Cortona, between Zurbarán and El Greco, between the "divine" Herrera and Góngora.

Let's move on to contemporary literature, or rather to the present baroque of Lezama Lima and Severo Sarduy.

We're going to begin exactly as we did with regard to the Spanish baroque of the seventeenth century—with cosmology. Which is to say, what does contemporary cosmology teach us? The latest theories are supported by data obtained not through instruments of observation but through radio, using high frequency waves. These waves have allowed us to construct a cosmological theory which is almost sure, to the extent that one can speak of cosmology beyond hypotheses. The universe is presently in expansion—this theory is called, precisely, the theory of the expanding universe. This expansion, which has verified that celestial bodies constantly distance themselves from each other, proves that at a certain moment—and to which undoubtedly corresponds the notice which heads the second part of *Enana Blanca* in **Cobra**—there was an explosion of a quasar, and this explosion gave origin to the universe such as we know it, which brings us to the following: the center of the universe is empty; it is a polyvalent and movable center. This theory of the empty center, this topology of the empty center, is going to reverberate in literature exactly as the theory of the ellipse resounded at a certain moment in the structure of the Gongorine metaphor. To wit: I believe that the textuality consistent with this theory is precisely one which stipulates an empty center. In other words, the censured word is going to form here that empty center; it will not exist any more, but its pulverizations at various levels will be legible in the textual surface, in that which Julia Kristeva calls the "phenotext," as opposed to the "genotext." The genotext is movable, plural, empty; the phenotext—that is, the visible, legible surface of the text—will, by means of a radial reading, make room for this word, this paragram which has been censured, eliminated. Here I will allow myself to give an example of radial reading found in **Cobra**, by means of the censured or suppressed paragram "morphine" at which one arrives through a series of signs that participate on different levels; on a phonetic level, when instead of "morphine" allusion is made to "Morpheus," to "morphologically," to "white morpheus" which is a cattle disease, etc. On the level of meaning, reference is made to a series of images of whiteness such as "snow," and an another level, to "horse," which, in slang, is another way of saying "morphine," etc. Thus one can read on various levels these signs which lead to a center which is no longer there, which is already missing.

I would like you to clarify a little more the difference between paragram and radial reading.

Radial reading is the process which can lead us, in this case, to a negative and absent paragram. In other words, the basic model, that which generates the visible text, the phenotext, is no longer there; it is missing. We could say, in a very Heideggerian sense certainly, that it shines by its absence.

But then, should the reader of that paragraph in **Cobra** *to which you were alluding—should he be able to recover the genotext?*

No, no, his reading would be innocent.

Then if the reading of such text were not innocent, it would not be considered a "good reading"?

I think it would be as if the seventeenth century reader had to recognize the zodiacal allusions Góngora makes in the first *Soledad* in order to know that he was speaking about the month of April. I think that the reader of the age generally read very naïvely. *Cobra* is full of such traps, some of which are for my friends, some for you as you know, some for Roland [Barthes], some for François [Wahl], and others strictly for me which no one knows. In other words, there is a series of formal secret mechanisms. Let me use a canonical example of this devotion: the sculptures of the Parthenon, situated at a great height on the metope of the pediment, and not visible except frontally or from below, are also minutely sculptured from behind. The craftsman who created them dedicated this work to the gods. That work, although not to be contemplated by men, had to be perfect. These "secrets of construction" were dedicated to God. In this sense, in the humble as well as minute composition of *Cobra*, there are many "secrets of construction"; the manuscript which in Benares I offered to the Ganges for example, was the object of great care.

Then an innocent, naïve reading is for those who have said that you alone understand **De donde son los cantantes***.*

In other words, the reading, with all of the mechanics to which we refer, is not accessible to everyone. I think it's evident that there are degrees of perception in all readings. That which interests me is to see how the whole *episteme* of his age is reflected in the practice of writing of each author. I repeat that I am not the least bit interested in lists of contemporary occurrences which point out to the author, for example, that there was a reform of customs and a high sense of authority in the year 1623, when Góngora received a pension of 400 *ducados!*

This brings us to a theme to which you have alluded in several of your works: the expulsion of the author, or the negation of a unique, individual emissive center.

Well, perhaps this stems in part from an observation by Philippe Sollers with regard to the absence of the author. Through a series of motives of an ideological nature, in Sollers the interesting thing is precisely the censure of that type of emissive center of the text which is the au-

thor, and which is, specifically, the Romantic author. Romanticism supposes—and this conception has been handed down to our age through a series of persistent prejudices—that there is a single, omnipotent emitter of the text, and that the text is an expressive entity which stems from a center and which is decoded by another center: the reader. Even in Sartre, the idea of language as practical-inert stems from this conception, since the author would be someone who uses that practical-inert entity to express something that is his own psychology, etc.

This is what you parody in **De donde son los cantantes***, when you appear in the novel . . .*

As author . . .

Yes, and later in **Cobra***, when you appear and threaten a character with exclusion from the chapter which you are writing.*

In other words, that which is being formulated there exactly is that there is no author. And why is there no author? Because if we carry our ideology to its ultimate consequences, we will know that there are no proprietors of language . . . Plagiarism, as Lautréamont proposed, is not only admissible, but advisable besides. One must totally suppress the idea of a central emitter of the voice.

But getting back to the expulsion of the author, how is it effected, how can we nullify him?

This idea of eliminating the author, of expelling him, can be realized by means of two practices. One of these practices is very obvious: the ultra-baroque. In other words, when we arrive, for example, at the temple of Kajuraho, that enormous Indian pyramid of copulating figures; or when we arrive at the temple of Konarak or Mahabzli-Puram or to Kanchi Puram, or to any of the great places of Indian architecture (also in this context: the window of Tomar, of Alcobaça, and of Batalha; as well as certain South American colonial architecture—the works of the Indian Condori, or the works of the authors of the Sacrarium of Mexico, the works of the Aleijandihno in Minas Gerais . . .) All of these works have no author . . . the baroque proliferation is so extreme that this type of bubbling up of the signifiers expels all personal ideology, all psychology. There is no author because the *horror vacui* eliminates any central emitter. In this sense I believe that all the works which I have just mentioned have no author. I believe that here that which is manifest is a grammar in proliferation; an exacerbated code which devours everything. The chapels "by" Churriguera in the cathedral at Burgos have no author. Gongorine literature, the literature of the extreme baroque, expels this omnipotent entity of which we were speaking.

The second possibility is that which has already been practiced in the United States by the sculptors of the school of "minimal art." For example, Bob Morris, Donald Judd, John McCracken, Larry Bell, Sol Lewitt, etc. And perhaps preceding these sculptors, the painter Barnett Newman. What do these sculptures of minimal art—or, as has been said, of primary structures—teach us? In the case of Barnett Newman, monochrome panels. In the case of the others, simple cubes, cylinders—in other words, pure geometric forms. These painters and sculptors, by reducing themselves to primary structures, that is, to the structures which engender all other possible forms in space, and by radically eliminating all expression, eliminate the author as well.

Thus it is the opposite of what you mentioned before about the ultra-baroque.

Yes, the opposite of what I had said. In this sense, I think that a painting of Barnett Newman also has no author. Showing a blue monochrome panel is precisely bringing us to that point of non-reducibility of expression.

Is this what you have tried to do in **La playa***?*

La playa, my dramatic piece whose subtitle is precisely *Primary Structures,* claims to do nothing other than show primary grammatical structures. There is practically no plot, and no development, since it is a fixed theater, and as it was represented in Kassel, there are no entrances or exits of characters, nor any movement. It is like a staged photograph. The sentences—*et pour cause*—are extremely simple, and they do not allow one to "see" or rather to hear more than the essential articulations of the composition of the sentence. The mechanics of this play consist of showing the support which from a subject leads to a predicate and to a direct object. As in the cube of Larry Bell, that which one sees is the essential support of all possible bodies in space. That is the second practice of the expulsion of the author; the first by hypergraphy, the second by the reduction of the support to the primary structure.

You say that there is no plot in **La playa***; however, you told me that . . .*

Of course, there is a kind of plot, shall we say, *grosso modo*, which can explain to a certain extent the acceptance of the play in Germany. It deals, putting between quotation marks the work "deals," with the story of a German gigolo in Cannes. The gigolo, as hero of the play, has business in the south of France with whatever people he meets, which gives rise to a whole series of possibilities of combination, and of sexual combination [. . .] but anyway, this is relatively marginal.

Why also the subtitle "Sequences"?

It is called "Sequences" simply because it stems in a sense from a play by Luciano Berio called *Sequences.*

But "sequence" indicates "progression," doesn't it?

It really refers to the strongest etymological meaning of the word "sequence," as the *Littré* defines it, and as was subject of an essay by François Wahl which you will probably read when the play comes out in print. Sequence is precisely the combining of various cards of the same suit in the deck.

Getting back to the baroque, I know you have on other occasions expressed some ideas about the morality of the baroque, especially in relation to eroticism, which is one of the preferred themes of your work—of creative work as well as of your critical work. What is the morality of the baroque, and to what extent is it manifested in the proliferation of signifiers of which you spoke earlier?

A morality of squandering, of waste. We should start off with the idea of baroque as waste and over-abundance of signifiers, as totally saturated information. The baroque is precisely the squandering of signifiers, or "media," and from there, I believe arises the censure of a moral order of which the baroque has been victim in civilizations as puritanical as the French. In France there has never been a perfect expression of the baroque. Remember the censure, and carrying things to their extreme, the expulsion in France of Bernini, whose project for the façade of the Louvre was rejected. I would say—exaggerating a bit—that neither in French architecture nor in painting is there a perfect baroque as there is in Italy or in Spain or in Germany.

And with regard to eroticism?

Eroticism, like the baroque, is a squandering, because eroticism is a game which carries with it no "information." Eroticism is not in function with reproduction, but with excess, with play. The erotic man is the *homo ludens*, not the man who reproduces. Eroticism then responds to a baroque phenomenon of waste, of loss.

Then Don Juan would be the typical case, wouldn't he?

Of course, Don Juan is the typical case, although Ives Bonnefoy, in his recent book *Roma 1630*, which won this year's prize for criticism and which is precisely about the baroque, says that Don Juan is not a baroque character since he doesn't fulfill to satiety a total adherence to the object, that he assumes the category of absolute in the baroque expenditure; a *hic et nunc* which for him is the condition of the baroque and which—and I continue to paraphrase Bonnefoy—Bernini exemplifies in the dais of San Marcos.

I haven't read Bonnefoy's book, but from what you tell me, I doubt that I could agree with him about Don Juan.

Anyway, that which I find interesting to note is that eroticism has been censored for the same reason that the baroque was censored. In other words because they are not functional, because they do not carry with them a mass of information, of utility. Genetic information is the penetration of the spermatazoid into the egg. Eroticism opposes this carrying of information. The baroque sentence does not lead us to a pure and simple meaning, but rather, through a series of ellipses, of zig-zags, of dé-tours, carries with it only a floating signifier—empty and polyvalent.

And how can we apply these observations to the case of present-day Cuba?

That which is happening in Cuba could be called a type of psychoanalysis of the Hispanic. The catharsis which is there being effected is that of all the repressed censures during the centuries beginning with the Inquisition.

But then, how can the work of Lezama Lima be explained within that context?

Lezama is precisely the reverse of the Torquemadesque coin, since he attacks the censure on two of its levels, on two levels of waste: on the level of the erotic—and I cite obviously the Farraluque episode in *Paradiso*—and on that of the baroque. In this sense, he has dealt a blow to the censure on an exterior level—thematic—but also on a profound level—structural, syntactic, in the immense metaphorical squandering of *Paradiso*.

Yes, and in the case of Carpentier?

It would be very difficult to speak of Carpentier. I wish to revise to a certain extent my thesis on Carpentier. I don't believe Carpentier is baroque in the sense which I have just given to this word.

I don't agree with you on that.

I believe that he deals with a type of very learned and proliferous organization, but one which doesn't imply semantic waste. I don't think there is this squandering of information in Carpentier. But, I have to work much more with this author. It certainly interests me to contradict his ideology of the baroque. For Carpentier—and he mentions it explicitly in the interview we read today at home—the baroque is a kind of metaphor of nature. He considers, as did d'Ors in *Lo barroco*, that the baroque mechanism is a natural metaphor. D'Ors says that there is nothing more baroque than a Portuguese park at noon; he speaks of the natural, Adamic state of the baroque; he formulates a paradisiacal state of genesis, a natural primogenial state. And Carpentier says that the Amazon River, the uncontrollable vegetal proliferation of America inevitably had to lead us to the baroque. I don't think that the thesis of the justification of the baroque by natural analogy is as convincing as that of its justification by textual metaphor.

I agree, but, as Emir Rodríguez Monegal has pointed out, there is a great difference between Carpentier as theorist and Carpenter as novelist.

Of course, of course [. . .]

I would say that in his novels, Carpentier is baroque almost in spite of—or perhaps in opposition to—that

which he himself has stated in his book of essays, Tientos y diferencias.

Well, in that case, yes, but I am using as a point of departure his explicit ideology, that which he has stated: his conception of the baroque is totally "d'Orsian." In this case I am putting into practice the basic structuralist opposition between *nature* and *culture.* I believe that the baroque is nothing other than a metonymy of cultural order, not a metaphor of natural disorder. It interests me more that the base be intertextual. Why? Because the intertextual base permits the conveying of an idea which seems to me essential in the baroque: the idea of "grafting."

Yes, but you know that in Los Pasos Perdidos, *Carpentier grafts from colonial texts and at times, as I told you this morning, from little-known ethnographic texts as well.*

Yes, I know. I believe that precisely in this case I agree to the extent that the baroque can be interpreted as a cultural metaphor. I cite the façades of colonial architecture to which I alluded, where we see that the elements of the Icaic art, pre-Cortés in general, have been grafted onto an architectural structure of Hispanic origin. In literature, of course, the quotation, plagiarism, reference, and reminiscence would correspond to this type of grafting. But I am still of the idea that the baroque is a phenomenon of intertextuality precisely because the intertextuality allows me to bring into function another element—to my judgment an essential one: the element of parody, very visible in Lezama and scarcely visible at all, excuse me, in Carpentier.

I agree.

I believe there can be no baroque without parody.

Without doubt, parody is the missing element in Carpentier.

There is no baroque without parody; parody is a distancing, grafting, and as we have already seen—and you alluded today to Calderón's *Life is a Dream*—the baroque stems from an image which contradicts itself, which hollows itself out. The baroque is the blind spot of the king.

Eugene R. Skinner (review date 1974)

SOURCE: A review of *Cobra*, in *Hispania*, Vol. 57, No. 3, September, 1974, pp. 606-07.

[*In the following favorable review, Skinner discusses the structure of* Cobra.]

Sarduy has participated in several influential literary journals: *Lunes de revolución* in Cuba and after his move to Paris in 1960, *Mundo nuevo* and *Tel quel*. His previous novels, **Gestos** (1963) and **De donde son los cantantes** (1967) have earned him recognition in Europe and in

Latin America as an important figure in contemporary narrative. To an original sensitivity for the baroque style of his Cuban mentor Lezama Lima, Sarduy has amalgamated the linguistic concerns of the *Tel quel* group. The result is a unique fiction, rich in surface texture and detail, that eschews traditional narrative content in order to focus upon the process of communication. Since language is both producer and product of culture, this emphasis leads to an objectification of the very supports of culture.

Cobra definitely represents Sarduy's most ambitious endeavor in this direction. Whereas *De donde son los cantantes* reveals the tripartite underpinning of Cuban culture (Chinese, African, Spanish), his latest novel achieves a global scope, comprising a dialog between contemporary Oriental and Occidental cultures. In 1970, Sarduy indicated to Jean Michel Fossey that his novel in progress would present two European interpretations of India. Both versions arise from a reductive process that falsifies otherness, in this case Indian culture. The first view is exemplified by the "Drugstore," where otherness is reduced to picturesque detail. For example, a poster intending to portray the goddess Parvati reveals only a superficial retouching of a Madonna by Murillo. The second view, that of the "Bookstore," decodifies the texts of Indian religion and translates them into the vocabulary of Christian mysticism. Both perspectives originate from a concept of the medium, visual or linguistic representation, as an inert practical instrument for the communication of information. This produces on the level of culture, an ethnocentrism that falsifies otherness, self, and is inconsistent with contemporary European epistemology.

For Sarduy, as expressed in an interview with Roberto González Echevarría in 1972, the contemporary period is characterized by the topology of the empty center and its analog in the physical world: the theory of the expanding universe. The textuality appropriate to this theory would consist of "pulverizations" moving away from a "center" that no longer exists. The latter can only be recovered through a "radical" reading of the "pulverizations" back toward the empty center. *Cobra* definitely requires such a reading.

The novel consists of two parts. "Cobra I" introduces the protagonist, a transvestite in La Señora's Lyric Puppet Theater, who is obsessed with the perfection of his body. La Señora willingly sacrifices everything in order that the next spectacle, *La Férie orientale*, please the public. They both travel to Tangier, where Dr. Ktazob effects the final transformation of Cobra's body. "Cobra II" narrates the protagonist's initiation, death, and funeral in Amsterdam. A gang of four youths, that traffics both in drugs and Oriental mysticism, conducts the rituals. This part concludes with a pilgrimage to an Oriental temple for the celebration of the vernal solstice. These basic narrative units, "Cobra I" and "Cobra II," parody the two European views of India: "Drugstore" and "Bookstore," respectively.

However, a third view, although not present as a narrative unit, is suggested by the novel. The structure of the nar-

Severo Sarduy

rative seems to lack a hierarchical organization: episodes are narrated and then negated in order to be re-narrated, scenes and characters from this work and from other works appear and disappear, commenting upon this text and being commented upon by it. These techniques tend to recreate the experience of a continual process of emanation and dissolution of forms, of composition and decomposition of the text. This thrid perspective, hopefully the result of a "radical" reading, reveals simultaneously the Indian reality of my and the text's matrix of the empty center.

Ronald Schwartz (essay date 1980)

SOURCE: "Sarduy: Cuban 'Camp,'" *Nomads, Exiles & Emigres: The Rebirth of the Latin American Narrative, 1960-80*, pp. 92-99. Metuchen: The Scarecrow Press, Inc., 1980.

[*Here, Schwartz reviews several of Sarduy's books, focusing primarily on his most popular title,* Cobra, *as a playful but senseless work.*]

If Manuel Puig is the Argentine exponent of camp, Severo Sarduy's fiction is the compleat embodiment of a camp manifesto that never takes anything seriously. It "takes the entire cosmos as its subject, adheres to mutilations and swift changes and deals with the disintegration and rebirth of the world."[1] Sarduy's campiness is the embodiment of everything that is playful, humorous, and wildly imaginative. Some critics consider his works to be the most experimental and challenging of all Latin American fiction today. Unlike Puig, Sarduy does not provide his readers with straightforward storytelling, remarkable insights, or identifiable protagonists. However, like Puig in his *Kiss of the Spiderwoman*, Sarduy does glorify the best aspects of camp, create and explode images and words in an attempt to portray "the ultimate mutability of human landscapes,"[2] a hallucinatory universe through his own interpretation of surface reality. Sarduy insists, as did his tutors and fellow celebrants Lezama Lima and Cabrera Infante, that language—metamorphized, transmuted, truncated, or syncretized, with its own inner logic, its metaphors as celebrations of themselves,—that language is *everything*.

Severo Sarduy was born on February 25, 1937, in Camagüey, Cuba. Very little is known about his youth and adolescence. When asked to write his own chronology, he commented: "I have no sense of time, I don't understand the sequence of events nor do they seem to correspond to precise moments for me. I don't believe in the idea of continuity."[3] This should give the reader some notion of the timeless character of Sarduy's fictions. At any event, in 1956 he was sent to Havana to begin studies at the university's medical school. He had published some early poems in *Ciclón*, "a dissident branch of *Orígines*, edited by José Rodríguez Feo and livened up by Virgilio Piñera, "4 and had always wanted to continue his "vocation" as a writer. As the Castro revolution gained momentum and Fidel made his official entry into Havana in 1959, Sarduy dropped his medical studies and wrote some poetry, which appeared in *Diario Libre* and *Lunes de Revolución*.

With a government grant in 1960 Sarduy went to Europe to study art history. He also took trips to Caracas, New York, and Tokyo in pursuit of his studies. Between 1960 and 1964 he lived mostly in Madrid and Paris, where he gave courses in the Louvre's School of Art and in the Sorbonne's School for Advanced Studies, and journeyed throughout Europe. It was Franz Kline's action paintings, "his fascination for the black bars . . . over white canvasses while dancing"[5] that inspired his first novel, *Gestures* (1963), a book of action writing.

Gestures dealt with a mulatto woman's activities as theatrical performer and as a partisan activist for the Castro revolution. Critics felt that the fragmented, parodic style was very reminiscent of the French *nouveau roman* as well as Kline's "new" action painting. In 1969 Sarduy began publishing many articles in French; he became associated with the *Tel Quel* group of experimental writers, although his themes were always Cuban. When he wrote in Spanish, like Cabrera Infante he preferred the "Cuban" method of expressing his themes. A quick review of his articles will demonstrate Sarduy's prolific and diverse contributions to a variety of magazines, including the prestigious *Tel Quel*, *Mundo Nuevo*, *Sur*, *La Quinzaine Litteraire*, *Art Press*, and *Plu-*

ral, as well as his critical participation in books about art, his prologues, prefaces, epilogues, and introductions to art catalogs.

In 1967 literary critic Emir Rodríguez Monegal rescued Sarduy's second novel, *From Cuba with a Song*, after its first rejection in manuscript. A more experimental work than *Gestures*, *Cuba* presents Sarduy's analysis of Cuban culture, using the Chinese, African, and Spanish contributions to demonstrate the racial intermingling that defines the Cuban nation and personality. Transvestites appear and disappear in the course of the narrative, imposing a unity over the diverse sections. Sarduy's tale is one of drugs, hallucinations, and eroticism, portrayed in poetic language that is moving and baroque. He described his narrative technique as "a collage that moves inward, made up of poetry, epitaphs, dialogues, activating the reader as the three aspects of Cuban culture become interrelated, deepening the significance of the book."[6]

Returning briefly to the essay, Sarduy composes *Written on a Body* in 1969, discussing once again his fascination with literature and transvestism, transgression, and eroticism. Monegal writes: "An erotic writer who has discovered the pleasures of the text, Sarduy is today not only the most experimental of Latin American writers but also the one who has completely erased the boundaries between prose and poetry."[7] In 1971 Sarduy wrote a radio script entitled *The Beach*, which was presented in Stuttgart, Germany, as well as two moderately successful books of poems, *Flamenco* and *Mood Indigo*. Other plays conceived in Sarduy's "theatre of immobility" concept and presented in Stuttgart were *Departure* and *The Fall*. It was not until 1972 that he became known internationally for his famous third novel *Cobra*, which was first published in France. *Cobra* won the Medicis Prize for Literature in 1972. It also led him to write another essay, *Baroque* (1974), which tries to link the roots of baroque art to the scientific discoveries of Newton, Galileo, and Kepler. In *Cobra*, Sarduy began to show fascination for the "rhetorical" figure of the ellipse. To quote Emir Rodríguez Monegal once again: "What [Sarduy] has found is not the certainty of a God, placed solidly in the center of the universe, as in Lezama, but the certainty of the void created by an elliptical system with one empty center."[8]

In 1973 Severo Sarduy made a tour of the East, visiting Singapore and Jakarta. He worked for French National Television in Paris in 1974 and wrote a weekly television and radio program *Science in France*. In the same year another book of poetry, *Big-Bang*, appeared, published while Sarduy was working on his fourth novel. Also in 1974 he returned to the Far East, visiting Turkey, Iran, and other places. Presently living in Paris, Sarduy in 1977 finished *Maitreya*, a kind of anti-*Cobra*, which was brought out in Spain the following year. Probably his most experimental work to date, *Maitreya* has as its theme mysticism, the role of the Buddha, and the double. The book capitalizes upon the parodies of language the author had attempted in his earlier novels and provides the reader with the word plays, palimpsets, erotic prose, and baroque stylistics for which Sarduy has come to be known.[9] *Cobra* is a short but complex work that defies complete analysis. So much has been written about it, pro and con, especially about its phantasmagorical, phenomenological, and linguistic aspects, that it is difficult to write a single, simple opinion about Sarduy's life and art. Let us turn to *Cobra* itself, its plot and its style, and then try to appraise it in light of the current resurgence of the Latin American narrative.

Cobra is organized into two sections. In Part One the protagonist Cobra is a transvestite, the star of a theater troupe somewhere in Europe or the chief prostitute in the Great Lyrical Theatre of Dolls, a brothel. Cobra may be female in the first part and male in the second, depending upon the use of the pronouns "he" and "she." *She* was created in Part One from a wax doll by Madame and resides in the brothel with other dolls named Dior, Cadillac, and Sontag who are jealous when she becomes Queen of the Lyrical Theatre. The "doll," however, becomes humanized, and Cobra tells Madame: "Why did you bring me into the world if it wasn't absolutely divine?" She demands a sex change. One evening s(he) discovers a White Dwarf named Pup, her self-image. Cobra moves in a world of theatricals, among Madame (who *perhaps* created her), the stud Estuchio, and Pup, who encourages her (his) transformation or conversion by a mysterious Dr. Ktazob. The doctor is finally found in a North African slum, *probably* in an abortion clinic somewhere in Tangiers, where he ritualistically "kills" and then revives Cobra in her (his) new form, *probably* as a male.

In Part Two we are *probably* in Paris at Le Drugstore, where Cobra takes up with a motorcycle gang and is summarily tortured, raped, and killed in a kinky religious ceremony by Tundra, Scorpio, Totem, and Tiger as they move on to Amsterdam. All the motorcyclists are in search of their own identity; a Guru in Amsterdam sets them on a path to India, where they attend some complex, cosmic funeral ceremony, and Cobra is united with Nirvana or the elusive Hindu God Shiva or some such diety.

> May the lotus flower
> be, by the Diamond joined.
>
> (p. 176)

The lotus symbolizes regeneration and is joined to the diamond or mystical center of Cobra's universe.[10]

Sarduy admits to finding the inspiration for his novel in a real event. Apparently, Cobra was a transvestite in a Parisian cabaret called Carousel who was actually killed in an air crash on Mt. Fujiyama as his (her) troupe was returning to Paris. Sarduy then met one of Cobra's lovers, who told the author about his (her) passion for physical perfection and achieving the absolute.[11] Enough said about Sarduy's "inspiration."

The novel's style is strange, alien to anything this writer has ever encountered by a Latin American novelist. In an amusing footnote, Sarduy himself says:

> Moronic reader: if even with these clues, thick as posts, you have not understood that we're dealing with a metamorphosis of the painter of the preceding chapter . . . [then] abandon this novel and devote yourself to screwing or to reading the novels of the Boom, which are much easier.
>
> (p. 42)

Sarduy's style is precious, pretentious, neo-baroque, gay, self-mocking, campy, and heavy. Like Puig, he delights in cinematic references and footnotes, and takes camp and trashiness for his themes. The following paragraph, a description of Cobra after a "performance," gives one an idea of Sarduy's style.

> The itch gnawed at her—"pernicious leprosy"; as soon as the canned applause would explode she'd run into the wings—she had sunk to those therapeutic depths—to splash in a bowl of ice. She would put on the imperial cothurnuses again and return to the stage, fresh as a cucumber. To these thermic surprises the invaders responded with great maneuvers: from her nails a vascular violet burst out which smacked of frozen orchid, of an asthmatic bishop's cloak: beneath a crumbling refectory he eats a pineapple.

> That Lezamesque purple was followed by cracks in her ankles, hives, and then abscesses rising from between her toes, dark green sores on her soles.
>
> (p. 19)

Notice Sarduy's homage to Lezama Lima, whose disciple he once was, and his attention to surfaces, use of spectacular adjectival constructions, and violent colors. Sarduy's portrayal of events in *Cobra*, writes Suzanne Jill Levine, "suggests that history is fiction, life is theater, a place is a textual painting."[12] *Cobra*'s theme is that life is pure theater, and as in a theater, the only true realities lie on the surfaces of its text, which is "a playful series of transmutations,"[13] a protean exercise for author and reader alike.

Within the novel Sarduy seems to present his own manifesto for writing, especially in Part One: "Writing is the art of ellipsis, the art of digression, the art of recreating reality, the art of restoring history, the art of disorganizing an order and organizing a disorder, the art of patchwork [*bricolage*]." These pronouncements are repeated throughout the novel, reaffirming to us (and perhaps to Sarduy) his own intentions.

It is easy to lose the continuity of *Cobra*'s plot, since much of the novel is clouded by esoterica, a constant return to the "teddy-boy" leather-jacket, motorcycle-gang philosophy of the 1950s (which may appear somewhat decadent and recherché in the 1970s), and a host of anagrams, puns, and surreal images (like flowers sprouting from motorbikes). Readers are grateful for Sarduy's occasional footnotes, especially the one that defines the multiple meanings of "Cobra": a poisonous snake in India; a motorcycle gang near St. Germain des Près; a group

of artists centered in Copenhagen, Brussels, and Amsterdam; the singer who died in a plane crash over Mt. Fujiyama; and the receipt of wages, from the Spanish verb *co-
brar.* Footnotes such as these help readers decode ***Cobra***'s reality, as they move through a narcotic-hazed theatrical world of whores, motorcycle freaks, pretentious
Indian mystics, and erratic symbols. According to Levine:

> In *Cobra*, ultimate reality is Sarduy's language focused
> on the significant value of each word skillfully mani-
> pulating signs and figures . . . , giving the surface and
> iconography of *Cobra* a worth both cultural and social.
> The text not only signifies in the traditional sense, but
> also helps to decode a reality without presuming to
> exhaust its meanings.[14]

I have deliberately avoided dealing with various critical
interpretations of ***Cobra***: Roland Barthes's utopic praise
of the book in his *Pleasures of the Text,* Claude Lévi-
Strauss's notion of "writing as *bricolage*" (patchwork),
Rodríguez Monegal's effort to prove that ***Cobra*** is a text
of continual metamorphosis, Sarduy's reading of Octavio
Paz's images of India in his text or the references to
Jacques Derrida or Lacan's hidden presence or Julia
Kristeva's reading of Bakhtine on Sarduy's notion of
parody and Lezama Lima's interpretation of the baroque
and his influence on Sarduy as manifested in ***Cobra***.

Cobra is a Fellini-esque, theatrical, and cinematic spectacular, heavily influenced by the French *nouveau roman,* or anti-novel. Although it expresses its own theories of literature, it is very difficult to determine if it is
an "entertainment" or a serious work in light of its own
heavy baroqueness, its grammatical and syntactical connotations, its meaningless, incomprehensible passages.
Cobra is a manipulated work, totally fabricated as the
language Sarduy uses. "His sentences surprise; the rhythms
confound and startle us, and exhaust us, with a frightened
beauty. . . ."[15] Sarduy is the master of wordscapes that
dip, shake, and explode.

Cobra has been considered a dazzling performance, tantalizing, kaleidoscopic, Brechtian, elliptical, in constant
flux. "Sarduy's novels," writes Rodríguez Monegal, "are
constructed with the rigor and fantasy of poems. They
are devoted not to the construction of narrative (like
those of Vargas Llosa) but to the 'deconstruction' of
language."[16] ***Cobra*** is ironic, parodic, macabre, bizarre,
strange, mercurial, inscrutable, enigmatic, a travesty, an
orgy, a nightmare, provocative, vertiginous, delirious,
carnivalesque, trashy, controversial, camp. It has been
compared to William Burroughs's American cult classic novel *Naked Lunch*—probably because it is also a
"naked" book demanding a "naked" response. This writer agrees with Robert M. Adams, who writes: "***Cobra*** is
a glossy, evasive book, from which this reader emerged
chiefly with a deep sense of astral chill."[17] There are
scenes of sadism told with stylistic baroque elegance,
shrill "chills of intergalactic space, which the baroque
stylistics only deepen."[18] S. J. Levine writes: "Cobra,
the snake, the actress, the verb, the symbol of a pictorial school is the novel . . . an infinite play (within its

finite nature) of transformations and repetitions branch-
ing from the vocable "cobra" as it winds its way along
its slippery, rootless route."[19] "***Cobra***," writes reviewer
Jerome Charnyn, "is crafty, slippery and poisonous."[20]

Although Sarduy has borrowed much from the experimental *nouveau roman* and remains faithful to his own
tropical setting of Cuba's myths, colors, movements, and
violence, he remains a hermetic stylist and a writer whose
works are simply not to everybody's taste. Like Manuel
Puig, he is omniscient, detached, almost alienated from
his own fiction, but with his intrusive footnotes, he lets
us admire his tour de force. However, unlike Puig's his
plots are distorted and dictated by phonetic associations
or by the internal logic of language itself. Because of
Sarduy's "astral" coldness, there exists for this reader a
void that baroque stylistics and linguistic dalliance cannot fulfill no matter how original, fantastic, creative, or
playful.

NOTES

[1] Jerome Charnyn, "Review of *Cobra*," *New York Times* (May 9, 1975),
p. 3.

[2] *Idem.*

[3] Severy Sarduy, "Chronology," *Review '72* No. 6 (1972), p. 24.

[4] *Idem.*

[5] *Ibid.,* p. 26.

[6] John Brushwood, *The Spanish American Novel* (Austin: University of
Texas Press, 1976), p. 300.

[7] Emir Rodríguez Monegal, *The Borzoi Anthology of Latin American
Literature*, Vol. II (New York: Knopf, 1977), p. 951.

[8] *Idem.*

[9] Much of the biographical information in the preceding paragraphs is
drawn from Severo Sarduy's own "Chronicle," *Review '72* No. 6 (1972),
pp. 24-27.

[10] It is in the lotus image that *Cobra* becomes recognizable as a continuation of Part One of *From Cuba with a Song*, metamorphosed into her
(his) new fictional presence.

[11] Jean-Michel Fossey, "From Boom to Big-Bang," *Review '74* No. 13
(1974), p. 12.

[12] Suzanne Jill Levine, "Preface," in S. Sarduy's *Cobra* (New York: Dutton, 1975), p. x.

[13] *Ibid.,* p. xi.

[14] Suzanne Jill Levine, "Translated Selection from *Cobra*," *Review '72*
No. 6 (1972), p. 37, footnote.

[15] Charnyn, p. 3.

[16] Monegal, p. 951.

[17] Robert M. Adams, "Shrill Chill," *Review '74* No. 13 (1974), p. 24.

[18] *Ibid.*, p. 25.

[19] Levine, "Preface," p. x.

[20] Charnyn, p. 3.

Sharon Ghertman   (essay date 1980)

SOURCE: "Language as Protagonist in Sarduy's *De Donde Son Los Cantantes*: A Linguistic Approach to Narrative Structure, *The Analysis of Literary Texts: Current Trends in Methodology*, Randolph D. Pope, ed., pp. 145-52. Ypsilanti: Bilingual Press, 1980.

[*In this essay, Ghertman concentrates on Sarduy's use of syntax and meaning* De donde son los cantantes.]

In his discussion with Rodríguez Monegal,[1] Severo Sarduy comments that language is the intermediary between the author and reality in his second novel, **De donde son los cantantes**. Sarduy, however, understands language as a binary opposition when he notes, "Sería más bien en la oposición binaria compacto / difuso utilizada por Jakobson, donde veríamos el paragramma de lectura más adecuado."[2] It is my contention that Sarduy uses this theory of language as a structure of continuum versus discontinuum, of expansion and contraction, as a narrative device through the transformation of oppositional syntactic relationship into characters, nominalized as the protagonists Auxilio and Socorro.

This synonymic relation Auxilio-Socorro is a starting point for the novel in "Curriculum cubense," its introduction. Auxilio represents the contextual, continuous function of language, which in terms of the narrative means that she attracts other people into her sphere, acquires a paradigmatic arrangement, and allows for expansion. Socorro then moves in the opposite direction, toward a structural zero, to be filled in the final chapter, "La entrada del Cristo en la Habana." She represents the contrastual, discontinuous function of language, as she stops the action, changes its course, or diverts it into another area. Sarduy, aware of this process, defines text as: "Texto que se repite, que se cita sin límites, que se plagia a sí mismo; tapiz que se desteje para hilar otros signos."[3] In the transformations throughout the novel, Auxilio and Socorro at times appear on the same syntactic level, at times on opposing syntactic levels, relating to each other as paradigm and syntagma, or vertical diachrony and horizontal synchrony.[4] In "Curriculum cubense," both the convergent and divergent relationships are operative. The subtitle in itself comprises a binary opposition essential to language structure: *curriculum* the noun indicates a continuum or series, while *cubense* the adjective delimits and controls its extension. This pattern is a base from which more complex relations derive, a process called

"la lectura radial del texto,"[5] commencing with the title **De donde son los cantantes. Donde** stands for a displaced antecedent; it is a kind of void,[6] to be replaced with the titular structure composed of a place name and a referent to person: "Junto al río de Cenizas de Rosa," *Cenizas de Rosa* being a substitute for the illusive *Flor de Loto,* the Shanghai Opera singer "La Dolores Rondón," marked by the absence of place, a means of contracting the pattern. The last chapter restores the original arrangement, "La entrada de Cristo en la Habana." Thus the title of the novel becomes a syntactic chain setting forth a dominant organizational pattern for the remaining titles, each realization leading toward new sets of internal relationships. Let us now examine the syntactic patterns in "Curriculum cubense" and view the ways in which they influence the narrative direction of the text.

I distinguish two opposing levels of discourse. The first is the contextual system of continuation, realized as a nominal series plus a displaced antecedent or pronoun in association with *ser* or with its omission as an ellypsis. The second level is the contrastual system of discontinuation, realized as a series of negations, imperative verbs, exclamations, and insults, providing an internal means of textual closure.[7] Changes in the pattern and shifting from one level to another are frequent occurrences, furnishing a dynamic for the text as well as a model for deciphering it.

The first paragraph of the novel is a highly contextual system, a description of Auxilio and the writing process itself, replete with impersonal objects and chance associations. All signs of continuum are present, including an affirmation *sí*: "Plumas, sí, deliciosas plumas de azufre, río de plumas arrastrando cabezas de mármol, plumas en la cabeza, sombrero de plumas, colibríes y frambuesas." Omission of the verb is characteristic of this level of syntactic arrangement in which Sarduy reverses any preconceived notion about nominal forms being discontinuous and static.[8] This nominal system points to analogies between dissimilar objects by forcing them into similar syntactic forms. The first expansion of *plumas, deliciosas* plus a noun modifier *de azufre,* unites the animal with the mineral. In the next set of nouns, *plumas* modifies *río* in connection with a present participle, *arrastrando,* and its object *cabezas de mármol.* However, *plumas en la cabeza* marks a return to the first combination only to produce *sombrero de plumas.* The remaining noun couple, *colibríes y frambuesas,* concludes the segment as equivalents to *plumas,* for *frambuesas* and *azufre* are used for their ability to perform an imagistic, adjectival function rather than a logical one. The text does not proceed in a linear fashion but in a radial one, emanating from *plumas* as a base. The noun used as adjective becomes a recognizable underpinning for this lectura radial, as the nominal group moves the text foward by relating *plumas* to different semantic components while preserving the same syntax.

The formula *río de* plus noun has other reverberations in the novel as a sign of continuum. The title of Chapter 1, "Junto al río de Cenizas de Rosa," is one example. Also,

Socorro's first appearance without Auxilio is marked by this equivalence and the omission of the verb *ser*:

> ¿Pero cómo no equivocarse? Eran miles. Miles de piececillos. Manitas carcomidas. Aquel chirrido. Platos de lata y cucharas. Salían verdosillos y arremetían contra las ollas. Sirena y aparecían. Chirrido, y desaparecían. Al mismo tiempo. Salía una mujer a cada uno de los vidrios. Y en cada uno sacudía un mantel negro. La fachada desaparecía detrás de una cortina de migas de pan. Río de plumas.

(p. 13)[9]

The *migas de pan* become a *río de plumas*, an aquatic metaphor of continuum that is transformed once more into hyperbole with: "Las migas de pan han blanqueado la copa de los árboles, el césped negro. ¡Es como nieve!" (p. 14). Further, in the last chapter, the snow scene is composed in a similar nominal sequence, with the dialogue of Auxilio and Socorro reminding the reader of the repetitive system of continuation: "Cortinas de migas de pan—Auxilio—¿Quién en lo alto sacude sus manteles?—Socorro" (p. 146). The aquatic image, however, finds its final expression in a destructive context as it shifts the noun *nieve* to a verb phrase counterpart, *llovió*: "Ya iban alcanzando los portales cuando desde los helicópteros, llovió la balacera" (p 149). Thus we have an interrelating system of nominal forms that explain or contradict one another, and in this manner provide a recognizable pattern for the text.

Textual re-elaboration emerges in the first paragraph of the novel, as the second part, beginning with *desde él*, explains the first part, *Plumas sí*:

> desde él caen hasta el suelo los cabellos anaranjados de Auxilio, lisos, de nylon enlazados con cintas rosadas y campanitas, desde él a los lados de la cara, de las caderas, de las botas de piel de cebra, hasta el asfalto la cascada albina. Y Auxilio rayada, pájaro indio detrás de la lluvia.

The vehicle of connections is created by the series of prepositional phrases from *caen hasta el suelo* to *hasta el asfalto la cascada*. Yet the sequence begins with the pronoun *él* referring to *sombrero*. Nominal analogues appear in rapid succession: *cabellos anaranjados* reworks *plumas de azufre*; enlazados con cintas rosadas y campanitas refers to *arrastrando cabezas de mármol*, with the equivalence *cabezas—campanitas*. The paragraph closes with an ellipsis, comparable to *colibríes y frambuesas*: "Y Auxilio rayada; pájaro indio detrás de la lluvia." This final equation, *Auxilio* and *pájaro*, completes and interprets the relationships between parts one and two of this segment. The noun *plumas*, a synecdoche for *pájaro*, *colibríes*, and Auxilio herself, begins the radial sequence, expanding with noun modification and then contracting with the ellipsis. The combination *pájaro indio detrás de la lluvia* is a re-elaboration of *río de plumas*, a controlling contextual image of the entire work, becoming the "imagen deshilachada y móvil" of Chapter 1 (p. 27). Thus the transformational possibilities of language, through the integration of dissimilar semantic components into similar syntactic structures, becomes a formal basis for the peregrinations of Auxilio and Socorro in their various nominal equivalents.

Now let us examine the second structural pattern in Sarduy's use of language. According to the structural theory of binary oppositions, the system of continuum must be accompanied by a system of discontinuum. If we read Sarduy metalingually, a term used by Jakobson for signs pointing to the internal structure of language,[10] we find: "Bueno querido, no todo puede ser coherente en la vida. Un poco de desorden en el orden, ¿no?" (p. 28). It is Auxilio, however, who introduces the system of discontinuum or contrast after the first paragraph of "Curriculum cubense" with a negative verb that effectively causes a break in the pattern at a point at which one would expect a continuation of it: "¡No puedo más!—chilla y abre un hueco en las migas de pan." Even the gestural symbol of breaking bread indicates discontinuity of the nominal descriptive system. It is Socorro's function to negate what has gone on before with the following verbal series:

> —¡Revienta!—es Socorro la que habla—Sí, revienta, aguanta, muérete, quéjate al estado, quéjate a los dioses, *drop dead*, cáete abierta en dos como una naranja, ahógate en cerveza, en frankfurter chucrute, jódete. Conviértete en polvo, en ceniza. Eso querías.

(p. 11)

It is not the pattern of seriation that explains this conflicting relationship between Socorro and Auxilio but the polarity between nominal description and verbal dynamics. In response to this verbal attack, Auxilio retorts with the formulaic equation of the continuous system: "—Seré ceniza, mas tendré sentido. Polvo seré, mas polvo enamorado." As a contrastual device, Sarduy integrates non-hispanic terms like, *drop dead*, or Socorro's response to Auxilio's Quevedian equation: "—Tu me casses les cothurnes! (en français dans le texte)," again a verbal negation.[11] This entire first segment of the novel is composed by alternating the two syntactic levels with Auxilio and Socorro on opposing levels. Yet when Auxilio begins her harangue on Socorro, the nominal series of apostrophic insults, "—Crápula. Granuja. Rana," progressively builds up to the series of verb clauses, integrating Socorro's system into her own: "Que te trague el Ser. Que te aspire. Que se te rompa el aire acondicionado. Que a tu alrededor se abra un hueco" (p. 12). After this convergence of the two systems, the narrative takes a new turn, leading to the separation of Auxilio and Socorro.

The next sequential arrangement I will examine appears in "Self-Service." Auxilio and Socorro appear on the same organizational level, joined in a convergence with a series of nominal substitutional names that unite the pair: *Deidades amarillas, pájaros flavios, Gamos, Las Floridas, Las Siempre-presentes.* "Self-Service" fluctuates between two oppositional levels, as Auxilio retains her function as a structure of continuum, characterized by the overturned plate of potatoes: "Papa por papa, papa por papa las recoge" (p. 15). Auxilio, however, reintroduces the contrastual system, emphasizing contraction and change, closing the text in upon itself: "—¡Quiero desaparecer!—Ya no es ardilla sino topo: se hace una esfera, esconde la cabeza" (p. 16). It is with the *tableau vivant* that the structural convergence point becomes operative in the text. Socorro and Auxilio reunite in a nominal chain in a triangular arrangement with the outside world. The convergence point is a kind of structural knot or stopping place:

> Ya están las dos sentadas, compuestas, ante una ventana de celuloide. Ni una mancha, ni un solo cabello desplazado, ni una gota de salsa de tomate en las mejillas. Fijas: las cabezas, separadas por unos centímetros, coinciden con el cruce de las diagonales del paisaje—domos azules perforados de ventanas, un campo de aviación de donde se levantan mosquitos y bimotores—, las manos pálidas sobre el pecho. Ni siquiera se mueven, pero es unútil, todo el mundo las mira. Se saben acusadas.
>
> (p. 16)

Here we have an example of what Sarduy calls "la geometrización del espacio"[12] with the synonymic pair integrated into a geometric environment, as indicated by the verb *coinciden* and the noun phrase *con el cruce de las diagonales del paisaje*. Sarduy juxtaposes a metaphoric equivalent for the pair as a means of re-elaborating this relationship. The visual effect of the two heads coincides with a diagonal crossing in the landscape seen through a window. Thus we have *cabezas* as equal to *domos azules perforados de ventanas,* whereas *un cruce de las diagonales* equates to *un campo de aviación*. As this diagonal crossing is seen through a window, two levels emerge: *bimotores* lift off the diagonal air strip outside, while *mosquitos* remain inside. The convergence point illustrates the way in which similar linguistic relationships, here the contextual system of nominal equivalents, change function to produce stasis in the text. The solution to this absence of movement is once again seriation, as Auxilio presents the fifty photographs of her in varying poses. Her statement "Tengo una idea" (p. 16) serves as a pronominal form, replacing *idea* with a multiple sequence of photos. Finally, the segment closes with a dialogue composed on the contrastual, negative level of Socorro: "Espera. Olvidaba la hoz" (p. 18). The nominal image *la hoz* becomes integrated into the horizontal function of contrastual finality, as Socorro reiterates this syntactic pattern of negativity through imperative verbs.

The third realization of the oppositional pattern, Auxilio versus Socorro, appears in the last segment of "Curriculum cubense." Nominal seriation expands into a more complex set of relations: the subordinate clause plus a pronoun. In "Una nueva versión de los hechos: parca y general," Auxilio attracts the General into her sphere.

> Que ella lo enredó con sus guedejas de champán, que él la pinchó con el broche abierto de una de sus medallas, que la confitura de cereza cayó sobre el kaki carmelita del uniforme, que él la cortó con un galón, que se enredaron ambos, que se callaron por cortesía, que se insultaron, que los espárragos a la crema quedaron entre

las condecoraciones, que el pírrico invocó a la patrona de los artilleros, la invencible Changó, que ella respondió apelando a la reina del río y del cielo, su antídoto y detente: no se sabe ya nada.

> (p. 19)

This passage, composed of ten clauses plus a contrastual negation, *no se sabe ya nada*, re-elaborates the section on the self-service. Even the title, "Una nueva versión de los hechos," indicates its re-elaborative function. Subordinate clauses introduced by *que* constitute a system of substitutions of the pronoun by a noun. The first pronoun *ella* is replaces by *confitura de cereza* in the third clause and *espárragos* in the eighth, both referents to the spilt food in the self-service. *Ella* recurs in the tenth clause, closing the sequence of continuum through a circular arrangement. *El* appears in the second and fourth clauses, replaced once with *el pírrico* (clause 9). In the fifth, sixth, and seventh clauses a convergence appears, marked by reflexive pronouns. This fusion is reinforced by the nominal series:

> Allí están los dos—serpientes emplumadas—*cheek to cheek*, pegados uno a otro, pegadas a las bandejas. Hermanos siameses forcejeando. Murciélago de la Bacardí, mancha de tinta, animal doble, ostra abierta, cuerpo con su reflejo; eso son Auxilio y el General.
>
> (p. 19)

This third realization of patterned syntax in Sarduy serves the function of integrating new material into the text. The structure of continuum characteristically transforms and expands using the same basic syntactic arrangement, while introducing a new character, the General, into the framework of the narrative. At this point, however, Socorro demonstrates her role as a discontinuous component in her metalingual comment: "Yo lo que quiero es que acaben de sacar a Auxilio de este enredo." The authorial first person remarks, on the contextual level: "Hija mía, ¿No ves que si el general se quita sus quincallas sería como el pájaro pinto de Lacan?" Yet if Auxilio escapes the continuous *enredo,* the novel will end. Socorro objects to the affirmation, "Ya volverá a su casa, modosa, presumida, casta" (p. 20), with a criticism of structures of continuum: "Oigan esto. Tres adjetivos de un golpe. En mi tiempo no era así. A dónde va la joven literatura. . . ." The text provides its own dynamic structures, while, as Sarduy states, "es tapiz que se desteje para hilar otros signos."[13] These contrastual structures called "characters" in the narrative are aspects of the same linguistic phenomenon: "Cuatro seres distintos y que son uno solo." Language itself is the model for the narrative organization of *De donde son los cantantes* because of its capacity to transform and expand and yet remain a unified whole.

In conclusion, the present essay is an attempt to view the synonymity of Socorro and Auxilio as an ordering device in the text. The syntactic arrangements for these characters give a formal basis for what Sarduy calls *la lectura radial*. I have examined those syntactic systems in "Curriculum cubense" that are responsible for textual cohesion, recurring at crucial points in the narrative development. The work establishes its own internal ground rules but then changes the function of the pattern from continuous to discontinuous. The search for this underlying model in linguistic patterning is both the technique and the objective of the author in his quest for *cubanidad.*

The search for identity is in itself an underlying theme in **De donde son los contantes**; even the title reflects a preoccupation with origins. Yet perhaps what is significant for the discipline of literary criticism is that Sarduy uses linguistic theory, the binary structures of opposition, as a creative mechanism for the narrative. In "Curriculum cubense" he lays the groundwork for the syntactic relationships that contract and expand in the novel to shape its course and direction. His innovative use of Auxilio and Socorro is the *Siempre-presentes* in the entire work. Auxilio is first a contextual system of continuum, while Socorro is her counterpart as a contrastual system of discontinuum. Thus the hypothesis that the text is a network of interconnections, demanding a "radial reading" rather than a linear one, becomes poetic practice, poetic in the Greek sense here, with the dual protagonists Auxilio and Socorro:

> Las dos mujeres ilustrarían aquí dos vertientes de la hispanidad—en el tapiz, la Fe y la Práctica—, opuestos que imantan los continuos virajes del texto: si el comienzo evoca cierta fastuosidad, Zurbarán, pronto aparecen las *vanidades*, Valdés Leal; si Socorro quijotiza, Auxilio es un refranero sanchesco.

>   (p. 152)

Further, this relation between Auxilio and Socorro is not only thematic but syntactic, as the nominal system introduced by Auxilio is contrasted and severed by the verbal system of Socorro. These opposing functions, however, are not fixed values in the text but are subject to change, providing a dynamic for the work. When Socorro enters the *Domus dei,* "la casa de Dios" in "Curriculum cubense," her first separation from Auxilio is characterized by her integration into the contextual system of nominal expansion. Thus the process by which linguistic signs, here syntactic relationships, change their function becomes a narrative device that influences the development of literary structure. In the last chapter, Auxilio assumes a horizontal, discontinual function, analogous to her search for the material object, the potatoes in the "Self-Service," while Socorro in representing faith moves vertically in a continuous function, reversing her role in "Curriculum cubense." Sarduy is indeed aware of the ever-changing linguistic sign, "Cada frase tuya, que parecía banal y gratuita, cobra un gran sentido, se integra a una maquinaria precisa" (p. 78). Each new contextual combination then changes the interpretation of the statement and refers to the underlying binary model of language, integrating the surface complexity of the text with narrative devices. Thus it is not enough to document isolated linguistic forms in a text in order to determine their literary function, for it is essential to understand not only what the signs are but what they become.

NOTES

[1] Severo Sarduy, "Las estructuras de la narración," *Mundo Nuevo,* 2 (agosto 1966), p. 17: "El arte me sirvió de intermediario con la realidad, como en la segunda novela, el lenguaje ha sido el intermediario."

[2] Severo Sarduy, *Escrito sobre un cuerpo* (Buenos Aires: Editorial Sudamericana, 1969), p. 49.

[3] *Ibid.,* p. 66.

[4] Sarduy, p. 83: "Auxilio (agitando sus cabellos anaranjados, de llamas, aspas incandescentes, vinílicas)—Querida, he descubierto que Lezama es uno de los más grandes escritores.—Socorro (pálida, cejijunta, de mármol)—¿De La Habana?—Auxilio (toda diacrónica ella)—¡No hija, de la HISTORIA!" Here we have another use of linguistic terms as metaphor.

[5] Phillipe Sollers, "La boca obra," in *Severo Sarduy* (Madrid: Editorial Fundamentos, 1976), p. 116.

[6] Roberto Gonzáles Echevarría, "Memorias de apariencias y ensayo sobre *Cobra,*" in *Severo Sarduy,* ibid., p. 72.

[7] Cervantes understood this combination of negation and nominal series; *Don Quijote de la Mancha,* ed. Martín de Riquer (Barcelona: Editorial Juventud, 1968), p. 227: "Y fue esta negación añadir llama a llama y deseo a deseo." For the term closure, see Barbara Herrnstein Smith, *Poetic Closure: A Study of How Poems End* (Chicago: University of Chicago Press, 1970).

[8] Rulon Wells, "Nominal and Verbal Style," in *Style in Language,* ed. T. Sebeok (Cambridge, Mass.: M. I. T. Press, 1968), p. 217: "Nouns are static, less vivid than verbs."

[9] The number in parenthesis refers to the page of Sarduy's *De donde son los cantantes* (México: Joaquín Mortiz, 1970). All quotations are from this edition.

[10] Roman Jakobson, "Linguistics and Poetics," in *Style in Language, op. cit.,* p. 356: "A distinction has been made in modern logic between two levels of language, 'object language' speaking of objects and 'metalanguage' speaking of language."

[11] Ferdinand de Saussure, *Cours de linguistique générale* (Paris: Payot, 1969), p. 168: "La langue est pour ainsi dire une algèbre qui n'aurait que des termes complexes. Parmi les oppositions qu'elle comprend, il y en a qui sont plus significatives que d'autres; mais unité et fait de grammaire ne sont que des noms différents pour désigner des aspects divers d'un même fait général: le jue des oppositions linguistiques." Also Severo Sarduy, *Escrito sobre un cuerpo, op cit.,* p. 52: " . . . el lenguaje aparecerá como el espacio de la *acción de cifrar,* como una superficie de transformaciones ilimitadas. El travestismo, las metamorfosis continuas de personajes, la referencia a otras culturas, la mezcla de idiomas, la división del libro en registros (o voces) serían, exaltando el cuerpo—danza, gestos, todos los significados somáticos—, las características de esa escritura."

[12] Severo Sarduy, *Barroco* (Buenos Aires: Editorial Sudamericana, 1975), p. 32.

[13] Sarduy, *Escrito sobre un cuerpo, op. cit.,* p. 66.

Julio Ortega   (essay date 1984)

SOURCE: *"From Cuba With a Song,"* in *Poetics of Change: The New Spanish-American Narrative*, University of Texas Press, 1984, pp. 173-79.

[*In the following essay, Ortega examines how the structure and literary style of* From Cuba With a Song *contribute to an examination of the heritage and history of Cuba.*]

From Cuba with a Song, by the young Cuban writer Severo Sarduy, is a novel that carries radicalism of form to a new level in the Latin-American novel. It is a novel, an antinovel, and a scrapbook of a possible novel. It strikes the reader first as a jumble of innovations, but it actually possesses a self-induced program within its obstinate will to transgress. This program takes the form of the draining of the traditional novel in new variations of the reshaping of cultural forms.

The book consists of an introduction followed by three segments, each dealing with one of the three racial components of Cuban culture:

(a) "Curriculum cubense," a sort of prologue, poses the idea of the text as iconographic writing. Through this writing, Sarduy will attempt to make visible the different and conjugated components of the Cuban world.

(b) The first segment, "By the River of Rose Ashes," is a mirrored recreation of the Chinese world of Havana. Its detailed descriptions, enumerations, and transformations are not intended as a snapshot of this world but as its possible metaphor: the masks are switched in this feverish transgression of its own design, in the play of its verbal fireworks. The humor found here is a form of criticism, of self-questioning. This text is, therefore, a brilliant pastiche sustained by the code of its baroque gratuitousness and is valid in its own right. The glossed world of this novel is drained—by the act of glossing itself—of signification and even of materiality, because the baroque line of this work is light and airy and the sensation it distills is an insinuation, a trace of desire, rather than the full sensation of desire itself.

(c) The second segment, "Dolores Rondón," is a pastiche of the Black component of a "Cubanness" brilliantly reduced by Sarduy to a myth of sensible forms. Whereas the Chinese spectacle implied a world of objects, a happy confusion of changing characters and masks, the Black spectacle implies a theatrical oralness. The tragic game of a feminine character sarcastically followed through the popular legends about her is developed here in another literary game. Through a popular theatrical performance we witness the lost cause of this Cuban mulattress who has been elevated to a national symbol. Sarduy once again constructs a rhetorical parable, a baroque, oratorical pastiche, intended as another mask of reality within language.

(d) The third segment, "The Entry of Christ in Havana," is the most accomplished part of the text. It too is a verbal parable, but its object is the Hispanic component of this "curriculum cubense," which we now realize has critical implications and a dynamics of festive interrogation. The hallucinating creation of a language as a totally imaginary adventure, a process whose very nature implies a radical criticism of the tradition of this genre and of representation, reaches it expressive culmination in this text through gratuitousness. Its most beautiful creative energy emerges from the play of free verbal invention.

This ethnic and cultural anthropology turns out to be a proposal for an antianthropology, so to speak. The conjugation of "cultural" and "ethnic" elements is presented here starting from a different perception: the pictorial and theatrical possibilities of language. The three glossed components are seen as pure spectacle; thus their essences are disclosed through appearances, through faces represented as masks. Hence the Chinese is only a repertoire of objects; the Black is a full-bodied voice; and the Hispanic is a rotting wooden statue (of Christ), a parable of signification. Pastiche and inversion, the novel's secret Sadian or satirical festivity provide the touchstones for an ironic criticism of the three cultural components and the key to the possible reshaping of popular creativeness in a textural fullness. This popular imagery is reduced to a few sensuous signs, and the novel thus becomes a radical rejection of the meanings of culture in the name of the liberation of the senses provided by art.

Appearance is inevitably also a cultural form in Sarduy's literary game. It is a form emptied of meaning but infused with another proposition, the baroque in this case. The baroque aspect of Sarduy's work is not, however, the allegoric and sensorial baroque encountered in Lezama Lima or the solar baroque of Octavio Paz; it is, instead, a hyperbole of pure form, a spiral of metaphorical accumulations, a double mask, perhaps because the pastiche implies a total suppression of density and at the same time a pure presence of language. Deprived of a signifying connection with all referents, Sarduy's baroque requires a formal relationship with them based on its own medium: the word, the phrase, the text. Therefore, this baroque is almost a parody of itself, because Sarduy longs for the idea of the baroque as a kind of verbal absolute. The text is thus produced as a recodification by the image and as a recovery of the world through the senses. Repeatedly proposed as an erotic activity, Sarduy's writing is also the nervous or tense desire for a fulfilling eroticism, which is found here as suggestion, as a beckoning. Thus, even if the lack of density does not imply an aleatory eroticism (as in Lezama Lima), the origin of writing does. For Sarduy, narration amounts to liberating meaning through the senses, to posing a parody of the world through empathy.

This reduction of reality to the image produces various rhythms and scenes in the novel, from the image constructed and then displaced ("By the River of Rose Ashes") to the spectacular and sonorous image ("Dolores Rondón"), and to the image playing with the irony of symbols ("The Entry of Christ in Havana"). A warm and festive current runs through the novel in these sequences.

This festive energy suggests the continuous displacement of the text's own findings, because the reader himself loses, in the barrage of images, the course of its reference; the text thus continues to unfold in a constant imagistic beginning.

Sarduy has found a way to reconcile the surrealist method of figurative exploration by the image (especially in the delirious final text) with the *nouveau roman*'s method of detachment and objectivity.

Through this dual method, his writing evinces a pictorial base that is immediately transformed into a theatrical space and then converted into a dream. Hence this novel is nothing other than the dream of an innocent apocalypse.

Guillermo Sucre has written as follows:

> Sarduy's novel is a metaphor, and this metaphor is nourished, above all, by art. Sarduy looks through art at what is real. Art is his mediator and it is knowledge, but not in the sacred way it was for Proust, Joyce, or Thomas Mann, for all of whom art was still an absolute. Although Sarduy superposes art on all his perceptions, he does it in a playfully ironic way.

> [Guillermo Sucre, *Imagen*, No. 20]

This accurate comment also points to the place of this novel within the Latin-American narrative. The baroque aspect of Sarduy's work is rooted in a transgression of culture in the name of art as a sensuous resumption of reality through words.

But this novel also engages in an obstinate effort to destroy the pathos of the everyday world and attempts, instead, to rescue the world through the possible formal purity, in the full simplicity of its sensible evidence. "The Entry of Christ in Havana," in particular, suggests a critical zeal in its progressive hollowing out of the great myth (myth of Meaning? of Humanism?). This amused rage is the patient and final reconstruction of reality, its reformulation in the synthesis of dreaming and verbal actions. Through its changing images and the playfulness of its forms, the radical criticism of this operation also suggests a parody of traditional works, but this parody finally becomes a fervent reconstruction of the pure spectacle of sensible forms, of language as an infinite metaphor of tradition.

The verbal action or the verbal liberation have the same motivation, the reshaping of the world in the pleasure of the word, the desire for a conjugated perception arousing the desire to live reality anew as though it were a language of feelings. The freedom of the word is also the freedom of desire in the fleeting perception that conjugates them through the magic of writing. But the lucidity of this dream in *From Cuba with a Song* carries with it the inevitable ambiguity that goes with creative criticism: when it is critiqued poetry is destroyed and empties its references in the neatness of sensoriality. In this case poetry perhaps sees itself as a mask, as gratuitous appearance and,

therefore, as ironic criticism of its own poetic game. Perhaps more critical than poetic in nature, this novel consumes itself as its own excessive example. Thus, its creative resolutions lie in the radical position gained by its own textual drama, because this novel is also on the cutting edge, on the edge of culture. But Sarduy's imagistic fervor and verbal passion will undoubtedly reveal to us that *culture* itself is just another form of the more radical art he is proposing.

Critic Emir Rodríguez Monegal has given us a key to the creative work of Severo Sarduy in an interesting interview with him (*Revista de Occidente,* No. 93). Referring to *Cobra,* the title of his best-known novel, Sarduy establishes various possibilities of association with it that are based on reference and allusion and imply an interplay between a given structural system and a peculiar mechanism of writing.

From Cuba with a Song (1967) also shares in this multiple interplay. The title in Spanish (*De donde son los cantantes*) is a line from a popular Cuban song, in which it is heard as a question, but in the novel it appears as an answer. In the song the singers are from Havana, but the novel tells us they are from Cuba. This phrase is thus an epithet. In addition to establishing an association with the song and Cuba, the title establishes an association, through popular culture, with the reader. The title is thus the first phrase of the book: its metaphor and its incitement.

In effect, the association is established through allusions, and this is the point at which writing formulates its design. As in *Three Trapped Tigers,* in *From Cuba with a Song* allusion operates actively and permanently, although in Cabrera Infante's novel it tends to the direct, obvious pastiche, to the play on words as proliferating material. In *Three Trapped Tigers* the allusions serve the novel; they are one of its levels but are not necessarily the basis of its structuring, which is to be found instead in the unfolding of a parody that alludes to itself. On the other hand, in Sarduy's novel the three-part structure itself is referential: the *curriculum cubense* implies the Chinese component, the Black element, and the Hispanic factor (names that are places, races, cultures). Hence the three levels of the novel allude, in the manner of a gloss or masquerade, to these "anthropological" components, which are stripped of their traditional meaning.

Sarduy realizes that the only way to speak separately of these three components is to approach them from a detached point of view and through the effusiveness of play and sensorial empathy. Thus the system that creates the novel (three "full" worlds that are emptied exultantly) permits the release of a writing that always alludes to a potentially "infinite," presupposed objective correlate.

The allusion can refer to literature but, above all, it begins by referring to the visible and formal characteristics of those three festive worlds. Consequently, this writing achieves the brilliance of a formal play that is ironic in its perspective and sensorial in its choices. These detached points of view and the approximations in the structure of the narrative allow the work to be self-sufficient, to require only the spectrum of its artifice, of its illusional game: sleight of hand, magic word, and final switch. We can say, then, that this novel is critical in its antitraditional formulation and "poetic" in its ritualization of the fantastic paraphernalia adopted by the three texts-worlds-glosses.

Therefore, the reductive activities of the novel (the sharp humor of its parodies and its "draining" of the meaningful levels) are countered by an accumulating and masquerading activity (the novel chooses to carnivalize the signs of a festive and spectacular reality).

Notwithstanding its lack of density, which is precisely what makes it a mirage or a chorus of echoes, *From Cuba with a Song* contains several books: first, those that are part of the basic structure, whose common space is the exalting parody constructed by empathy, by identification; second, the substratum of the three "full worlds" that are simultaneously present and absent and imply the area in which the author cuts, selects, and reassembles; third, the writing that constructs with masks, that is, on the "surface" levels of a purely verbal deduction; and, finally, the other book, the one with critical implications, because this play of unrestricted, gratuitous appearance—this pageant of appearance—implies the irrepressible and systematic criticism of literature and of the traditional need that explains by "meaning" while overlooking the "meaninglessness" of the "artificial" forms, which are no more and no less artificial or gratuitous than desire and its labyrinth.

In *La Maison de Rendez-Vous*, a novel by Robbe-Grillet, the sensuous nuance of the Chinese scene is also produced starting from a repertoire of objects relevant to a Western outlook: a dancing woman in a clinging silk dress, for example. The erotic suggestion emerges, in this case, from a very clear notion of femininity: full presence, pure object. In the Chinese chapter of Sarduy's novel, on the other hand, the sensuous suggestion emerges from an expectation, a proximity, a light touch—from the postponement, therefore, of the act itself—and from the successive incitements that permit the disguising and imagistic proliferation of what in the end is not a woman but an empty mask. Robbe-Grillet prefers to design the unhurried sensuality of a repeated and formalized scene duplicated in the sumptuous tradition of typical objects. Sarduy opts for a bric-a-brac, delirious, and multiform China stripped of its tradition and reduced to a game, to a buoyant spectacle.

In so doing Sarduy places himself within a characteristically Spanish-American tradition. His critique of literature operates by expansion. He selects a formal and imagistic repertoire that goes beyond verism and the need to correlate words with the "reality" that supposedly underlies them. Lezama Lima had already brought images of snow

close to his tropical landscape, but Sarduy goes one step further: he makes it snow in Havana. This mechanism has come to us from the baroque. The first Spanish-American baroque poets pretended to see European flowers among our own. This act is more audacious than comparing an Araucanian girl with some mythological goddess, or the environs of Mexico City with some classical longing.

The greatest audacity is not, however, the inducement of an imaginary reality; it is the attitude toward language, because the use of words becomes as decisive as the knowledge of the world: language seeks to be the final transparency. This use of language reveals, above all, a nominal faith: the poet need only say the names of the world to believe that the world is inexhaustible. Names, therefore, are the images, the birth of metaphors and figuration. The mechanics of Spanish-American Modernism are not much different: a nominative repertoire becomes a fantastic paraphernalia; the world is transformed into a series of prestigious images.

Like Lezama, Sarduy has developed a variation within this tradition. Lezama's dense baroque, full of symbolic implications, is followed by the light baroque constructed on pure figuration that characterizes this novel. But the exultation itself of its artifice discloses its critical slant. In the end, in its draining of the meaningful levels, Sarduy's writing acts significantly based on the irony of a questioning, demythifying criticism.

The component aspects of "Cubanness" expose in this novel the other side of their full appearance: their empty appearance. The Chinese factor exists only as a carnivalesque masquerade; the Black factor exists as a chorus of voices (a mulattress reviews her "career" from the vantage point of her death, of her legend); and the Hispanic factor is seen from the perspective of the traditional and meaningful symbol par excellence, a statue of Christ on the cross, gradually and spectacularly destroyed during a religious procession. Along with the festiveness of the characterizing images and the masquerading, we find again a reduction of the mirages. Thus, the celebration of "Cubanness" is also the discovery of its significant "nonexistence," in other words, of the sole *presence of its forms*, which language consecrates through a reuniting eroticism.

FURTHER READING

Filer, Malva E. "Salvador Elizondo and Severo Sarduy: Two Borgesian Writers." *Borges and His Successors*, Edna Aizenberg, ed., pp. 214-26. Columbia: University of Missouri Press, 1990.

　　Offers a comparison between Sarduy and Elizondo as writers who follow the fantastic tradition of time overlap and theological themes of Borges's traditional narrative.

Additional coverage of Sarduy's life and career is contained in the following sources published by the Gale Group: *Contemporary Authors*, Vols. 89-92, 142; *Contemporary Literature Criticism*, Vols. 6, 97; *Dictionary of Literary Biography*, Vol. 113; *Hispanic Writers*.

Domingo Faustino Sarmiento
1811–1888

Argentine essayist, historian, philosopher, politician, and educator.

INTRODUCTION

Domingo Faustino Sarmiento was a nineteenth-century Argentine politician, educator, and non-fiction writer, who by some estimates published the most important Latin American essay of the nineteenth-century, *Civilización y barbarie: La vida de Juan Facundo Quiroga* (1845; *Life in the Argentine Republic in the Days of the Tyrants or Civilization and Barbarism*, 1961). Sarmiento served as President of the Republic of Argentina, governor and senator of his native province, and Ambassador to the U.S. He also served as Minister of Education, earning comparisons to the American educator Horace Mann for his energetic promotion of public education, founding schools wherever he landed and staffing them with teachers from the normal schools which he also founded. Sarmiento was also a prolific writer in the areas of philosophy, history, biography, and political theory. His books, articles, education manuals, and correspondence fill fifty-two volumes, all marked by a prose remarkable for its fluidity, expressive richness, and intuitiveness. Yet, despite his accomplishments and renown, Sarmiento was, and is, controversial for his belief in natural determinism, a theory whereby nature dictates behavior and personality.

Born in 1811 in the isolated western province of San Juan, Argentina, Sarmiento was the only son and fifth child in a family of six children. His father, a soldier who fought Spanish loyalists in Chile, was restless and impractical, and often away from home. He nonetheless encouraged his son's education. Sarmiento's mother was ambitious and diligent, maintaining a well-run home and garden, and making all the family's clothes. Domingo was taught by his father and uncle to read at the age of four. Early on, Domingo excelled at school and his teachers awarded him the honorary title of the school's First Citizen. The largest influence on his education, however, was another uncle and priest, José de Oro, who trained his nephew in Spanish grammar, Latin, the Bible, and oratory. Sarmiento grew up in a rustic frontier environment during a period of tumultuous political change: the governorship of San Juan province changed five times in one year (1819-20), and the rural chieftains, known as *caudillos,* vied almost continuously for power for the next forty years. One of them was the eponymous *gaucho* villain of Sarmiento's *Civilización y barbarie: La vida de Juan Facundo Quiroga*. In the desire to eradicate *gaucho* culture, Sarmiento joined the Asociación de Mayo, a group intent on spreading a new nationalism and identity. Central to this outlook were notions of historical idealism, common sense, and national culture. For Sarmiento, the *gaucho* was an impediment to this level of progress. Sarmiento was a "Unitarist" (opposed to "Federalist") in wanting to unite all of Argentina under a central government, independent from Spain and the U.S., and anti-*caudillo*. Sarmiento became a lieutenant in the Unitarist forces, but was captured in battle by Facundo Quiroga and held under house arrest. Exiled to Chile for five years, Sarmiento taught reading by a new syllabic method in a small school in the Andes. He read all sixty volumes of Sir Walter Scott, studied English, and worked at an array of jobs including running a store and working in a silver mine. In 1836, he became ill with typhoid fever and was allowed by the new governor of San Juan to return home, presumably to die in the care of his family. But Sarmiento recovered and resumed his literary pursuits. In 1839, Sarmiento founded the Colegio de Santa Rosa de América in San Juan, a school for girls. That year, he, with assistance from a colleague, began publishing a weekly newspaper, *El Zonda*. But the Federalist governor opposed the paper's Unitarist slant and raised the tax on newsprint, driving the paper out of business. In and out of exile for the next several years, Sarmiento wrote his three most readable works: *Civilización y barbarie: La vida de Juan Facundo Quiroga* (1845), *Viajes por Europa, África y América* (1849; *Travels in Europe, Africa, and America*), and *Recuerdos de provincia* (1850; *Memoirs of Provincial Life*). Sarmiento's exile consisted of traveling throughout the U. S., Europe, and North Africa, inspecting educational systems, favoring the elementary schools founded by Horace Mann in the United States. Returning to Chile in 1848, Sarmiento married, but then left his wife in 1862, the same year he was elected governor of San Juan. His subsequent duties included serving as ambassador to the United States and, from 1868-74, President of the Republic of Argentina. Sarmiento died in Asunción, Paraguay in 1888.

Sarmiento's first and most famous work, *Civilización y barbarie: La vida de Juan Facundo Quiroga*, is a polemic attacking the *gaucho* cause and their leader, Quiroga. The first part of the book begins with a topographical analysis of Argentina and its effect on its people and governance, present and future. Sarmiento writes that the *gaucho* way of life, earned through the use of horse and cattle throughout the vast grasslands, inhibits the progression of modern civilization. He felt that the *gaucho* knows nothing but the domination of animals which maintains him as a selfish-individualist habituated to violence. Sarmiento sympathized with the Spanish-descended *gaucho* as a romantic figure, but felt that the barbarian—especially Quiroga—must be civilized or eradicated. *Viajes por Europa, África y América*, a travel narrative, is a richly descriptive account of his travels while in exile. Here Sarmiento criticizes the Mediterranean countries, finding Spain barbaric and primitive, Italy impoverished and money-grubbing, and France disorganized and dirty. Germany and Switzerland, on the other hand, were deemed worthy of emulation, and Sarmiento offers methods of attracting immigrants from these countries to settle in Argentina. Most honored among countries was the U.S., offered up as a model for Sarmiento's utopian vision for Argentina. *Recuerdos de provincia* is a set of memoirs of Sarmiento's childhood. His autobiography, *Recuerdos*, was written partly to clear Sarmiento's name from the slurs against him perpetrated by the Federalists, especially Juan Manuel Rosas, the dictator opposed to a government based in Buenos Aires. Today, Sarmiento's popularity has waned due to his outdated stance on national and racial issues.

In 1883 Sarmiento published his last major work, the unfinished *Conflictos y armonías de las razas* (Conflict and Harmony in the Races), an essay meant to continue the themes of *Civilización y barbarie*. As Sarmiento's career began with racial theories, so it ends. Here Sarmiento asserts that "primitive" people share the same size cranium, lending itself to a slower thought process and a heightened sense of emotion. He again maintained that the U.S. was superior to South America because it had not indulged in miscegenation and that Chileans took too much foolish pride in their Indian heritage. Although incredibly conservative in his ideals, Sarmiento's vision carried with it a basic fundamental of democratic ideology, based on societal progress and innovation, and directly opposed to tenets of tyranny.

PRINCIPAL WORKS

Mi defensa (essays) 1843
Civilización y barbarie: La vida de Juan Facundo Quiroga I físico, costumbres, y ábitos de la República Arjentina (history) 1845
Viajes por Europa, África y América, 1845–1847. 2 vols. (history) 1849
Arjirópolis o la capital de los estados confederados del Río de la Plata (testimony) 1850
Recuerdos de provincia (history and autobiography) 1850
Vida de Abrán Lincoln (history) 1865
Conflictos y armonías de las razas en América. 2 vols. (history) 1883
La vida de Dominguito: In memoriam del valiente I deplorado capitán Domingo Fidel Sarmiento, muerto en Curupaití a los veinte años de edad (essays) 1886
Obras. 52 vols. (collected works) 1885-1903

CRITICISM

Cathryn A. Ducey (essay date 1979)

SOURCE: "Travel Narratives of D. F. Sarmiento: A Seminal Frontier Thesis," in *America: Exploration and Travel,*

edited by Steven E. Kagle, Bowling Green State University Popular Press, 1979, pp. 50-66.

[In this essay, the critic analyzes Sarmiento's work in terms of his definition and use of the frontier in his writings.]

Until the relatively recent (1970) publication of Michael Rockland's translations of Domingo Faustino Sarmiento's *Travels*, interest in the Argentinaian theorist and statesman has been practically nonexistent. Although some writers mention him as an advocate of public and progressive education in South America, and some economic and political studies deal with him as a liberal Latin-American President, Sarmiento's interest in the frontier development in Argentina are largely ignored. His *El Facundo* is read by some undergraduate and graduate students, with an emphasis upon the attacks, political and personal, on Rosas and other of the "barbarous" dictators.[1] Neglected, overlooked aspects of *Facundo* must be examined, along with his *Travels*, as presaging the frontier thesis of Frederick Jackson Turner, for Sarmiento theorized, generalized and applied concepts of the frontier based upon travels and observation.

Faustino Valentin Sarmiento was born February 15, 1811, in the Argentinian frontier town of San Juan de la Frontera. Located between the Andes and the Pampas, it had a population in 1811 of about 3,000. His family was poor, as were most of the inhabitants of San Juan. Early in life the young man took the name of his patron saint and became known as Domingo Faustino Sarmiento. He attended the first established school in the frontier province of San Juan; in 1825 he left school to become apprenticed to a French engineer; he next accepted the offer of his priest-uncle, Jose de Oro, to travel far outside the province and to study; in 1827 Sarmiento returned home to San Juan and began work as a shopkeeper in his aunt's store.

Somehow copies of Benjamin Franklin's *Autobiography* and of some works by Thomas Paine came into his hands. These books led him to decide that a "rationally ordered and understandable universe should exist."[2] Yet he saw no evidence of it on the Argentine frontier. Instead he saw only poverty, ignorance and a chaotic political situation. *Caudillo* (strongman) leaders like Manuel Rosas and Juan Facundo Quiroga were unconcerned about organized programs to combat poverty, illiteracy and uncertain political conditions.

As civil dissension became widespread, Argentinians were forced to choose between bending to the will and whip of the caudillos or following revolutionaries in the hopes of bringing reform to the government of Argentina. Sarmiento fought the caudillos and was forced into exile during the years 1828 to 1832.

While in self-imposed exile in Chile he began writing for newspapers, expressing his bitter disgust for the Federalists who were raping his country and undertaking what was to become a life-long role: teacher and advocate of public education.

He learned English, became caught up with the fever of the Chilean silver rush, became a mine worker and then a foreman. Such work must not have been fully satisfying, even if physically tiring, for he also gave English lessons, wrote assiduously, and began to develop his first full reform work—a program to colonize the Colorado River Valley.

From 1832 to 1839, while political equilibrium in Argentina was shakily maintained, Sarmiento zealously applied himself to personal development and to reforming some of the conditions in San Juan. The soldier-miner-fledgling teacher phases of his life were over. While earning a sketchy living as a journalist, he also founded a literary society and edited reform newspapers. Sarmiento set out to become a European in education, a North American in politics and a South American in loyalty.

Sarmiento began his best known work, ***Civilization and Barbarism: the Life of Juan Facundo Quiroga*** (popularly known in South America as ***El Facundo*** and in the United States as ***Life in the Argentine Republic***), during the 1840s. This pseudobiography was a vehicle for his attack on caudillo government and an analysis of the social and political causes of Argentina's problems. Primarily for this work Sarmiento is considered the major reformer of South America and the "Father of Spanish-American sociology."[3]

With the exception of particular passages dealing solely with the tyrant Juan Facundo Quiroga most of Sarmiento's ***El Facundo*** presages in tone, style and content both Mark Twain's *Roughing It* and Turner's thesis. Sarmiento granted that he was not writing an unbiassed history of Argentina; he intended, rather, a study of "national antecedents, the features of the soil, in the popular customs and traditions."[4]

It is difficult to tell that it is Sarmiento writing of Argentina rather than Turner of the United States in the following passage from the end of ***El Facundo***:

> . . . Our future destiny is foretold in our numerous rivers, the boundless pasturage of our plains, our immense forests, and a climate favorable to the production of the whole world. If we lack an intelligent population, let the people of Europe once feel that there is permanent peace and freedom in our country, and multitudes of emigrants would find their way to a land where success is sure.[5]

A strong faith in Argentina's future is clear throughout ***El Facundo***. The primary concerns trace the geographical and political conditions which transformed Argentina and describe individuals, both specific and archetypal, who influenced change.

Of the fourteen provinces in Argentina all except San Juan and Mendoza were pastoral; the city-dwellers of Buenos Aires were Europeanized and civilized, while the plains-frontier people recognized only the brutishness in life:

> supremacy of the strongest, the absolute and irresponsible authority of rulers, the administration of justice without formalities or discussion.

Rule by force, whether by the leaders of cattle trains and caravans or by local gauchos (cowboys), is accepted and respected, as it was in the American West. Emigrants to the plains, enduring long journeys by caravan, learned to

> acquire the habit of living far from society, of struggling, single-handed with nature, of disregarding privation, and of depending for protection against the dangers ever imminent upon no other resources than personal strength and skill.

Although Sarmiento continues to emphasize the self-sufficiency of the pampas pioneer/frontiersman, he finds the frontier traits only half-admirable. He contends, unlike Turner, that the lack of a stable, unified government, the isolation of "self-concentrated feudal" families, the roving nature of the gaucho, the lack of public schools and lack of tolerance for religious differences, and the "dearth of all amenities of life induces all the externals leading to barbarism."

The continual struggle of "isolated man with untamed nature," the constant "defying and subduing of nature," develops the "consciousness of individual consequence and superior prowess," but for Sarmiento it does not foster those principles of concern for the common good and progress which he believed so necessary for the development of a republic.

Life and customs on the pastoral pampas contrasted sharply with life in the commercial, water-based cities:

> distinct, rival and incompatible forms of society, two differing kinds of civilization existed in the Argentine Republic: one being Spanish, European, and cultivated, the other barbarous, American, and almost wholly of native growth. The revolution which occurred in the cities acted only as the cause, the impulse, which set these two distinct forms of national existence face to face, and gave occasion for a contest between them, to be ended, after lasting many years, by the absorption of one into the other.

Sarmiento saw the struggle between Hispanic European civilization and native barbarism as a struggle between "mind and matter" quite different from anything else in the world.

Sarmiento's thesis is that the way of life on the pampas, the individualism, independence and anti-European traits of the gaucho, and the isolation from centers of culture, led directly to a confrontation of values culminating in the revolution.

It is important to note that the same traits which Turner cites as leading to democracy on the American frontier, as supportive to the principles of liberty and responsibility, are pointed to by Sarmiento as leading to precisely opposite goals and conditions. Just as these traits strengthened the North American Union they fractured Argentina.

Embarking on a fateful trip to the United States in 1847, arranged as a public relations gesture by his government, Sarmiento began a series of letters which later were published as his *Viajes*, translated as *Travels in the United States in 1847*.[6] Always perceptive and inquisitive, Sarmiento's discussions of and observations on American life in mid-century anticipate the personalistic reportorial genre of Mark Twain's *Roughing It* and *Life on the Mississippi*. Rambling, sympathetic, humorous, often disconnected, descriptions are recorded with the intention of suggesting some insights to the American character.

On his initial trip he visited twenty-one states and was impressed by the technology, the industrial growth of cities, and by the order resulting from a federal republic based upon allegiance to ideals.

> On the other side of the Alleghenies, the New World begins.... In the west, Yankee genius has more room to move about and expand to try new things that would seem impossible in the older states. In the West they try things which are superhuman, inconceivable, seemingly absurd.[7]

In his *Travels* the various stages in frontier development which he describes in *Facundo* are re-established and a model of the frontier is expanded. On the American frontier, he says, the first pioneer is the "Indian Hater" who persecutes the native inhabitants of the lands so that they will desert them. Then come the Squatters, "who are misanthropes looking for solitude in which to dwell, danger for excitement, and the work of felling trees. . . ." The real pioneers come next, "opening the forests, sowing the earth, and spreading themselves over a great area." Once they are established, the "capitalist impresarios" follow, nearly on their heels, along with immigrant laborers and fortune-hunting youth. Finally are established the proprietary class, the cities, and the commercial routes.[8]

Sarmiento suggests that the availability of free and open land partially contributes to the prospering western development of the United States. But he asks, ". . . then why in South America, where it is just as easy if not easier to take up new land, are population and wealth not increasing?"[9] There, with a greater amount of virgin land than in the United States "have the backwardness, poverty and . . . ignorance" continued unabated. The reason why the mere existence of free land cannot be accepted as the major impetus for prosperity is clear:

> The American is a man with a home or the certainty of having one, a man beyond the clutch of hunger or desperation, a man with hopes for the future as bright as the imagination can invent, a man with political sentiments and needs. He is, in short, master of himself with a spirit elevated by education and a sense of his own dignity.[10]

These are attributes the Hispano-American lacks, and until they can be developed through education the free land of

the Pampas will remain uncultivated, the masses of people will remain in poverty, and the nation of Argentina will not prosper. ". . . Being a new country does not mean anything if action is wanting."[11]

Americans, in contrast, are "free men and not disciplined prisoners whose lives are administered," and they are energetic and active.[12]

The North American frontier land belongs to the Union and is sold for a dollar an acre to any man; while in Argentina, says Sarmiento, the system of land distribution is different. There land concessions are granted first to the conquistadors

> . . . who established earldoms for themselves, while soldiers, fathers of the sharecropper, that worker without land who multiplies without increasing the number of his buildings, sheltered themselves in the shade of their improvised roofs. The passion to occupy lands in the name of the king drove men to dominion over entire districts, which put great distances between landowners so that after three centuries the intervening land still has not been cleared. The city, for this reason, has been suppressed in the vast design, and the few villages which have been created since the conquest have been *decreed* by presidents."[13]

On the other hand, the American takes possession of his lands "in the name of the kings of the world: Work and Good Will."[14]

Sarmiento's view of the American seeking to tame the wilderness is admittedly romantic. He sees the Yankee as "a born proprietor," dreaming of conquering the forests. The western wilderness is tamed by "American Alexanders, who wander through the wilds looking for points that a profound study of the future indicates will be centers of commerce. The Yankee, an inventor of cities, professes a speculative science which leads him by deduction to the divination of a site where a future city must flourish."[15] Unhampered by the stigmas of ignorance or poverty and unimpeded by governmental regulations he accepts the land as his. His is a free "colonizing spirit," untrammelled by outside forces. Thus do

> Americans cross six hundred leagues of wilderness for an ideal. . . . They sacrifice themselves for the future of the nation. . . . These people carry with them, like a political conscience, certain constitutive principles of association. Political science becomes moral sentiment, perfecting the man, the people, even the mob. The municipality is converted into a phenomenon dependent upon spontaneous association. There is liberty of conscience and of thought. There is trial by jury.[16]

How different are the Americans from the Argentinians of any class, who are unable to conceive of voluntary association for the common good, unable to consider a political system based upon the principle of liberty, unable to forget the strictures of both religion and class. For they, their revolution not withstanding, assume that government exists because of the necessity to regulate the actions of individuals according to a predetermined code. And, says Sarmiento, without a system of universal education, the Argentine Republic will not be able to provide man with the means to develop fully his moral and political conscience.

In his *Travels* Sarmiento is concerned with actions and attitudes and customs of people throughout the United States, although his recurring emphasis is upon the westward movement and progress. Various customs are a source of both interest and amusement. Lack of attention paid to leisurely eating is somewhat disconcerting to the fastidious Sarmiento: "The American has two minutes set aside for lunch, five for dinner, ten for a smoke or to chew tobacco. . . . The Yankee *pur sang* eats all his food, desserts, and fruit from the same plate, one at a time or all together."[17]

Lack of respect for privacy is rife in America: "In the reading rooms [of large hotels] four or five parasites support themselves heavily on your shoulders to read the same tiny bit of print you are reading. . . . If you are tranquilly smoking your cigar, a passerby will take it out of your mouth in order to light his own."[18] If certain niceties of manners are not observed as they are in Europe or in South America it is perhaps because the trappings of civilization are unimportant in a burgeoning, apparently classless society. More to the point, for Sarmiento, is the acceptance by the American of man by man, whatever he may be lacking in the social graces.

Tolerance for men, and for their vagaries and differences, impresses the Argentinian visitor. As a Hispano-Catholic, reared with the rigid authority of the Spanish church ubiquitous in his country, Sarmiento is amazed by the American acceptance of the number and variety of religious sects. Although some of the frenetic, enthusiastic, or faith healing sects are both strange and unusual, he is impressed by the tolerance among the people he meets of and for religious differences.

Related to the tolerance of religious attitudes and practices is the American development and support of philanthropic and improvement organizations, an interest unheard of among South Americans. That individuals would give away capital to help their fellow man, that others would crusade against drunkenness, that anyone would freely donate money to establish institutions for the sick, the insane, or for the education of orphans—these are aspects of the uniquely North American way of life which so intrigues Sarmiento, and of which he approves. Groups and individuals seeking the improvement of society, with nothing to gain personally, he believes are a reflection and product of the American's overwhelming interest in mass education.[19]

Even if he sees much of the country and the lives of its inhabitants through the proverbial rose-colored classes, even if he can believe that all the mill girls in Lowell are "educated . . . conscientious and devoted to their work."[20] one comes to understand that such seemingly naive conclusions and his almost child-like acceptance of anything

American are understandable. He reaches conclusions because he almost desperately wants to believe that somewhere in the world an ideal state for all men could exist.

Such was his dream for his homeland. If the North American model could be imposed upon, or accepted by, Argentina then there was reason to hope and dream that his country could one day be as settled, as prosperous, its lands as cultivated, its people as free as in the United States.

The United States progressed rapidly because Old World values were cast off, because Americans continually searched for ways of improving the land and society. Thus, Sarmiento reflects bitterly about South America. In his own country he deplores what the Spaniards had not done in three centuries compared to what had been acomplished in less time in the United States.

Sarmiento remains optimistic that there will be a change, for he believes that in the expansion and "mixing and juxtaposition" of peoples that someday all America will be "homogenous." He firmly accepts the idea of the "melting pot," although slavery was a jarring note.

Sarmiento sees slaves as unassimilated and suppressed, describing slavery in the United States as "the deep ulcer and the incurable fistula which threatens to corrupt the robust body of the Union!"[21] He believes that the Founding Fathers made a "fatal error" in allowing the injustice of man's subjugation to man to exist in a country founded on diametrically opposed principles. He astutely remarks that had slavery been abolished with the Declaration of Independence or the Constitution at a time when the number of slaves was relatively few that it would have been a much more acceptable act then than in the nineteenth century. He suggests that a "racial war within a century" will take place, for he sees the division between slave and free states and the increasing numbers of Negroes as portents for a dire future.[22] He is concerned that slavery is a blight upon a fruitful democratic nation.

In spite of such weaknesses in the North American system, by and large Sarmiento sees only good. As a thoroughly curious traveller he remarks upon the many freedoms that Americans have. Among these is the freedom to travel at will. "Since everyone travels, there is no impossible or unprofitable enterprise in the field of transportation. . . . The great number of travellers makes for cheap rates, and cheap rates in turn tempt those who have no precise object in mind to go somewhere."[23] Even in 1847 Sarmiento was aware that the peripatetic American was unique in the world.

As he moves about the country, Sarmiento observes that in this dynamic society "the hotels will be more important than any other kind of public construction." Not only do the hotels which accommodate the increasing number of travellers impress him with public and private appointments, but so also do other buildings, such as banks and municipal edifices. The eclectic attitude of the American architects suggests: "If the Americans have not, then, created a new kind of architecture, they have at least developed national applications, forms, and a character influenced by their political and social institutions."[24]

The "melting pot," adaptability, and ingenuity in architecture, manners, and customs contrast with differences in his own country. In the Argentinian population centers public and private architecture was solely Spanish-inspired, modified only by availability of materials. Country adobe huts were crude, built from available materials. Hispanic class and national attitudes were reflected in architecture. In the United States, however, the buildings reflect pride in monuments, a penchant for echoing styles of past, republican, ages, and general experimental uses of forms and materials.

As population moved restlessly the need for railroads and varieties of internal communication and transport systems developed. The westward movement and attendant growth of industrial cities Sarmiento attributes, partially, to "the infallible Yankee instinct for sensing places which will produce wealth. . . ."[25]

Sarmiento judged the adaptability of the new westerners to be important, but recognized that even as emigrants from the East Coast and immigrants from Europe and the Orient adapted to new conditions so also

> the land soon puts its stamp upon them. . . . So the fragments of old societies are coming together in the flood of immigrants, mixing and forming the newest, the youngest, and the most daring republic on the face of the earth.[26]

The words foreshadow Turner's assertion that the land makes an impression on the people who set out, initially, to conquer it; "Americanization" takes place.

Portents for success on the frontier include, says Sarmiento, not only the adaptability of the new westerners and their inherent native ingenuity, but also the development of towns. Sarmiento describes "the village, which is the center of political life, just as the family is the center of domestic life . . . the essence of the United States is to be found in its small towns. This cannot be said of any other country."[27]

Even in the poorest of villages, he notes, North Americans repect and use manufactured items (locks, kitchen utensils, plows, axes) rather than local, crudely crafted items. Amenities lacking in South American villages (signposts, hotels, newspapers, banks, churches, post office, streets) are omnipresent in even the newest of American villages. What he sees as a basic difference between life in semi-isolated areas on the two continents is "widespread distribution of civilized ways in the towns as well as in the cities and among men of all classes."[28]

Sarmiento is quick to accept, however, that the signs of "civilized ways" do diminish the further west one moves.

> "Westward, where civilization diminishes," he writes, "and in the FAR WEST, where it is almost non-existent

because of the sparseness of the population, things are, of course, different. Comfort is reduced to what is strictly necessary. . . . But even in these remote plantations there is an appearance of perfect equality among the population in their dress, in their manners, and even in their intelligence. The merchant, the doctor, the SHERIFF, the farmer—all look the same. . . . Americans do not wear jackets or ponchos, but have a dress common to all and a universal roughness of manner which gives an impression of equality in education."[29]

How different are these views, of dress and attitudes, from appearances on the Argentinian frontier! There class differences in clothing and manner are readily apparent. The peon would be recognized by poncho and hand woven garments, the cleric by black robes, and if perchance a wealthy merchant or doctor travelled through a farm region the European cut in jackets, trousers and imported linens would be signs of wealth.

Beyond the superficial similitude in clothing and roughness of manner what Sarmiento finds most characteristic of Americans

> Is their ability to appropriate for their own use, generalize, popularize, conserve, and perfect all the practices, tools, methods, and aids which the most advanced civilization has put in the hands of men. In this the United States is unique on earth. There are no unconquerable habits that retard for centuries the adoption of an obvious improvement, and, on the other hand, there is a predisposition to try anything. . . . You would have to wait a century for something like this to happen in Spain, or in France, or in our own part of America.[30]

In his continuation of a seminal "frontier thesis" Sarmiento says that civilization is comprised of "moral and physical perfection or the abilities which a civilized man develops in order to subject nature to his desires."[31] Such perfection and abilities exist on only one frontier in the world and only among the men who forge their way through that frontier. Only the American is able to adapt to conditions easily, accept man as man, believe in his own ability to conquer nature, to use technology, to rely on his own native gifts of intuition and intelligence not only to survive in the wilderness, but to succeed. The ability and the willingness to try new things, new ways, new lands, is intrinsic to the American: ". . . If you want to know if a machine, an invention, or a social doctrine is useful and can be applied or developed in the near future, you must test it on the touchstone of Yankee knowhow."[32] The pragmatic and utilitarian and ingenious American "far from barbarizing, as we have, the elements which European civilization handed him when he came as a settler, has worked to perfect them and even improve upon them."[33]

With the attributes Sarmiento describes he finds it understandable that American inventions, products, and business forms rapidly displace those of Europe. But America's greatest potential for development lies in the citizen's "possession of the land which will be the nursery of his new family,"[34] in the small free-hold system.

Again and again Sarmiento recalls the points first made in **El Facundo**: that an inevitable confrontation occurs when civilization and barbarism meet and that the outcome decides the future of a nation. At the beginning of **El Facundo** he writes:

> If any form of national literature should appear in these new American societies, it must result from the description of the mighty scenes of nature, and still more from the illustration of the struggle between European civilization and native barbarism, between mind and matter—a struggle of imposing magnitude in South America. . . . [35]

In North America only Cooper, Sarmiento suggests, was able to capture the sense of the struggle:

> by removing the scene of the events he described from the settled portion of the country to the border land between civilized life and that of the savage, the theatre of war for the possession of the soil waged against each other, by the native tribes and the saxon race.[36]

As he pursues these points as journalist and statesman he repeatedly affirms his frontier thesis.

Although the cultural historian Henry Nash Smith asserts Turner's

> most important debt to his intellectual tradition is the idea of savagery and civilization that he uses to define his central factor. His frontier is explicitly 'the meeting point between savagery and civilization.'[37]

Clearly Sarmiento's location of the scene of man's struggle as "the border land between civilized life and that of the savage" and his emphasis upon the battle between "European civilization and native barbarism," nearly fifty years before Turner, is equally, if not more, important to the intellectual tradition.

What makes Sarmiento unique is the background from which he writes. He was neither a semi-trained political theorist as was a de Tocqueville, nor was he a transplanted—but seemingly thoroughly adapted "American" as a de Crevecoeur. Nor was he a native-born, self-made, thoroughly new-world, North American as was Franklin. Although he could assess and accept the vagaries of American frontier life, he was not the native satirist, or the "adaptable" American that was a Mark Twain. Nor, indeed, was he a Ph.D. trained historian, a product of the West, of the East, of universities, of the Germanic "school" of analysis as Turner was. He was not the interesting romantic novelist, as Cooper was, nor an intellectual like Emerson, nor a politician-statesman like T. R. Roosevelt. He was none of these and yet all of them.

Sarmiento is examined, although rarely at length, by historians who concern themselves with developments in Latin and South American history and political theory. He, Echeverria and Mitre and Rivadavia, as Argentine political theorists and presidents, belong in histories and analyses of South American development. But only Sarmiento can be considered as an instigator of changes in Argentina based upon analyses of a North American model. For it is he alone who could look at his own country and decide that he needed to assess analogues before he could set forth possible changes. He alone looked to a North American model as a total possibility for a means to develop a free and prosperous Argentina.

Beyond and above all else, it is the traveller-statesman D. F. V. Sarmiento of Argentina who formulates a thesis concerning the American Frontier as coherent and complete—if not more complete—as that of Frederick Jackson Turner of the United States.

Many contemporary historians have dismissed Turner's thesis for its generalizations, its roots in a romantic view of the American West, and its over-emphasis upon individualism. Others have questioned his lack of emphasis upon economic changes and his over-emphasis of the frontier as a decisive factor in shaping American life and thought. Few argue, however, about his definition of the frontier as a meeting point between civilization and savagery as being uniquely American. And historians credit Turner with being the first commentator to approach the concept of the American frontier from an analytic viewpoint. It seems almost futile to dismiss his "Frontier Thesis" as unimportant in analyses of American culture. If nothing else, he precipitated arguments about the nature of American development, and thus prompted other historians to delve into reasons for what shaped "the American Character."

Turner wrote, primarily, in the late nineteenth century, and he is especially important for: 1) precipitating historiographical inquiry based on New World, not Old World, models, and, 2) attempting a definition of New World development unlike any previously recognized by the North American academic world. He wrote within a context; he was a westerner, a man brought up on the frontier past—its realities and myths. His was an "insider's" interpretation.

Turner was nurtured on generalizations about the American frontier. It was the "safety-valve," a place where Huck Finns could "light out," to, if necessary, to build a new life. Frontier life produced archetypal political characters in Daniel Boone and Andrew Jackson. Controversy over slavery was promoted because of the Territories. Travellers continually commented about the New American produced on the frontier. Many of the frontier aspects celebrated by Turner existed in a Tidewater Virginia or a Puritan Massachusetts; de Tocqueville and de Crevecoeur described many of the same concepts of the American Character as "foreigners" observing life in the New World. Turner wrote out of his understandings and experience about frontier attributes psychologically accepted by most nineteenth century Americans. He solidified concepts, myths and psychological viewpoints.

In contrast, D. F. Sarmiento's interpretation of the frontier arises from a different set of experiences and background. He is the "outsider," a Hispanic-American, self-educated, relatively uninformed about North America. His knowledge was very limited when he finished **Facundo** in 1845. Yet from that limited knowledge he expresses in **Facundo** and later in the **Viajes** some startling insights: 1) a redefinition of the frontier as a meeting place between barbarism and civilization; 2) a celebration of individuality as it develops away from the cities; and, 3) an elaboration of the several phases of frontier social development.

Sarmiento, like Turner, sees the frontier as a step in the development of a nation and a national character. From a totally different psychological, social and educational background he arrives at similar definitions. His travels in the United States solidified his impressions and interpretations, but did not create them.

NOTES

[1] *El Facundo* is best known in the English translation by Mary Peabody Mann, *Life in the Argentine Republic in the Days of the Tyrants; or, Civilization and Barbarism.* (New York: 1960). All quotations from *El Facundo* will be referenced hereinafter as *Life in the Argentine Republic.* . . .

[2] Allison Williams Bunkley, *The Life of Sarmiento* (Princeton: 1952), p. 63.

[3] Bunkley, pp. 179-80.

[4] *Life in the Argentine Republic*, p. 4.

[5] *Life in the Argentine Republic*, p. 247. Unless otherwise noted all successive quotations from Sarmiento are from this source.

[6] Michael Aaron Rockland, Sarmiento's *"Travels in the United States."* (Princeton: 1970).

[7] Quoted by Rockland, pp. 64-5, from "Hacia el Oeste."

[8] Rockland, p. 190.

[9] Rockland, p. 153.

[10] Rockland, p. 153.

[11] Rockland, p. 155.

[12] Rockland, p. 158.

[13] Rockland, p. 165.

[14] Rockland, p. 165.

[15] Rockland, p. 166.

[16] Rockland, p. 171.

[17] Rockland, pp. 147-8.

[18] Rockland, p. 148.

[19] Rockland, p. 244, and elsewhere in text.

[20] Rockland, p. 246.

[21] Rockland, p. 304.

[22] Rockland, p. 305.

[23] Rockland, pp. 133-4.

[24] Rockland, p. 145.

[25] Rockland, p. 123.

[26] Rockland, p. 124.

[27] Rockland, pp. 126-7.

[28] Rockland, p. 131.

[29] Rockland, pp. 131-2.

[30] Rockland, pp. 132-3.

[31] Rockland, p. 133.

[32] Rockland, p. 144.

[33] Rockland, pp. 162-3.

[34] Quoted in Edmundo Correas, *Sarmiento and the United States* (Gainesville: 1961), p. 19.

[35] *Life in the Argentine Republic*, p. 25.

[36] *Life in the Argentine Republic*, p. 25.

[37] Smith, p. 293.

William H. Katra (essay date 1986)

SOURCE: "Reading *Facundo* as Historical Novel," in *The Historical Novel in Latin America: A Symposium*, edited by Daniel Balderston, Ediciones Hispamérica and Roger Thayer Stone Center for Latin American Studies, Tulane University, 1986, pp. 31-46.

[*In the following essay, Katra provides a favorable critical assessment of* Facundo *on the basis of its historical meaning and significance.*]

Although Domingo Faustino Sarmiento's **Facundo** (1845) is known primarily as an essay, with its marvelous socio-scientific and historical treatment of Argentina's tortured national reality during the times of the civil wars and the Rosas dictatorship,[1] its second section, that treats the life of *caudillo* Juan Facundo Quiroga, merits the attention of literary critics and cultural historians on account of the author's fictionalized treatment of historical material. The analysis of **Facundo** as historical novel has given rise to three general types of readings. Here, I will treat only indirectly the *aesthetic* reading, since the existing criticism is almost unanimous in its evaluation of Sarmiento's undeniable genius in vitalizing the stuff of history through his narration and in appealing to the subliminal dimension of the reader's artistic senstivity. Instead, I begin with a consideration of the *ontological* reading, about which there exists no small amount of confusion and controversy, that assesses how or to what degree his novelistic rendering contributes to our understanding of the historical events or personages treated. Then, I discuss the third, *ontogenetic* reading, that considers **Facundo** in its function of *creating* historical meaning, that is to say, its prophetic and perverse power of imposing an interpretation over Argentina's historical past.

The first issue to be dealt with is the manner by which Sarmiento approriated historical material for his narrative treatment. Juan Facundo Quiroga, the most esteemed and influential of the caudillos from the interior, had been brutally assassinated in 1835, a whole decade before Sarmiento wrote his memorable book. The legend of Facundo was still very much alive: his exploits in the war for independence, his unrivaled prestige in the provinces of the interior, and the mysterious circumstances surrounding his death, were all topics not only for historians and political leaders, but also for rural bards whose songs entertained country gatherings everywhere. Sarmiento, whose youthful years in the Andean province of San Juan coincided largely with the period of Facundo's predominance in the neighboring province of La Rioja and then throughout the interior, was entirely familiar with the historical circumstances surrounding the latter's activities. In addition, Sarmiento drew upon the impressions gained from at least a few personal encounters with the caudillo and his followers that are described at some length in **Recuerdos de provincia** (1850). But his treatment in **Facundo** is most appropriately characterized as a mythical and novelistic rendering of historical material.[2] This romantic biography was conceived and hastily written more out of the imperatives of political expediency than from commitment to historiographical objectivity. Therefore, the work's contribution as history can only be evaluated by taking into account its insertion into the ideological field of the period.

Sarmiento's heated opposition to the league of Federalist caudillos controlling the country that was nominally headed by Buenos Aires tyrant, Juan Manuel de Rosas, and his passionate advocacy of a liberal or pre-positivist transformation of his homeland, became principal determinants in choosing the image of Facundo Quiroga that he recorded for posterity in the pages of his famous work. In the latter years of his residency in San Juan, and then during the half-decade spent in Chilean exile before the publication of **Facundo**, his attraction to European ideas on progress and civility grew at a pace that paralleled his hatred for the uncultured, brutal caudillos. The latter, he believed, were primarily responsible for his region's and the entire country's recent fall from peace, security, and progress. These issues were foremost in his mind when

he wrote the pages that outwardly treated events that already belonged to the past. His debatable thesis was that Quiroga, the most prestigious and powerful caudillo of the interior, represented virtually the same "barbaric" and antiprogressive values, but in an even more primitive form, as Rosas, his caudillo successor in Buenos Aires. In addition to its creative historical distortions, this was a decidedly partisan view. Instead of recording the generally positive image that rural people of the Mediterranean provinces almost unanimously held of Juan Facundo Quiroga,[3] Sarmiento appropriated and then exaggerated the negative image that prevailed among the commercial and cultural elites in both the provinces and the port city.[4] Whether or not one accepts the conclusions of David Peña, with regard to the personality and importance of Juan Facundo Quiroga, his opinion about the historical value of Sarmiento's treatment of the same is beyond dispute; according to Peña, what stands out about **Facundo** is "su falsa contextura, su perniciosa influencia como obra de historia . . . [a pesar de que es] libro de infinita belleza literaria y amparado por un nombre glorioso, ya inmortal."[5]

Although impartial readers, both then and now, have recognized the strong ideological flavor in Sarmiento's literary portrait of Facundo Quiroga, the existing evidence points to the likelihood that the writer himself was sincerely convinced, at least to some degree, of the historical merits of the work.[6] **Facundo**, he wrote in the letter-prologue to the 1851 edition, was his attempt, albeit preliminary, to analyze the South American reality of his time "con intachable imparcialidad en la justipreciación de los hechos . . ." (7:16-17).[7] He would utilize the social theories then in vogue in order to "penetrar en el interior de nuestra vida política," exactly as Tocqueville had done with the North American reality (7:6). But this supposed objectivity must again—be understood in relation to the ideas then embraced by the group of young Europeanized intellectuals in Sarmiento's midst.

Indeed, the historical content of the work bears the unmistakable influence of several liberal and (pre-)positivist thinkers whose ideas were enthusiastically embraced by Sarmiento, V. F. López, J. V. Lastarria, and other young Argentine and Chilean intellectuals who resided in Santiago, Chile, in the early 1840s.[8] The historical progress of societies, as they perceived it, was unilinear and impersonal, and proceeded in accordance with the development of science and technology. This view was simultaneously teleological and political: on the one hand, the young liberals in Santiago believed that Providential will, speaking through scientific principles, defined the direction for society's advancement that no person or interest could impede; on the other hand, they believed that the social leader who understood the supposedly universal *science* of history and society could take appropriate action in order to hasten or guide that process. Herein lay their strong ethnocentrism (their pro-North European and "bourgeois" biases) in interpreting the history of their own people up until then, and in projecting the path for future development.

In the writings of José Victorino Lastarria, one finds a rationalization for their "filosofia de la historia", as it was called at the time. The young liberals believed, and were appropriately criticized by as judicious a thinker as Andrés Bello on this account,[9] that a fidelity to the facts of a particular situation was of relatively minor importance provided the historian gave proper emphasis to the "necessary" and "inevitable" spread of progressive ideas that were associated with liberalism.[10] This meant that once the grand principles of progress were understood, then one need not pay undue attention to the particularities of a given situation. Concretely, this meant that as long as one assessed a society in relation to its historical past according to the criteria of *liberty* and *progress*, then inconsistencies with regard to details would hardly matter.[11]

More explicitly stated, Sarmiento's historiographic writing practice had the objective of promoting the ascendancy of the class, unnamed in his writings but identified today on the basis of function and value orientation as the bourgeoisie, that advocated a social transformation based on the principles of liberalism. To Sarmiento's way of thinking, this transformation necessitated the prior assimilation of the inhabitants of the interior to the newly dominant norms of the port city, even if that meant the elimination of Indians or gauchos as a people.

Thus, Sarmiento's "philosophical" objectives clearly assumed a political dimension in his historiographical endeavor. Indeed, his political and propagandistic motivations in writing *Facundo* are well known. The work, originally a libel, was intended to be an ideological cannon blast at the foundations of Rosism. This was an entirely justified practice, in his eyes. Rosism, with its followers among the caudillos of the interior, was considered to be the incarnation of retrograde ideological and organization tendencies: the feudal Spanish colonial past, a cattle-based rural economy, anti-democratic political practices, official actions against education, commerce, and, in general, against institutions promoting the cultivation of reason. Therefore, Sarmiento did not lack philosophical and ideological reasons for opposing the Rosas regime. Indeed, he believed that his "conspiracy" in any way or form was justified by the noble end it furthered. And this, in essence, legitimized his ideological rendering of historical material. He admitted as much in the December 22, 1845 letter to General Paz. His *Facundo* was "Obra improvisada, llena de necesidad de inexactitudes, a designio a veces, no tiene otra importancia que la de ser uno de tantos medios tocados para ayudar a destruir un gobierno absurdo, i preparar el camino a otro nuevo."[12] Undoubtedly, the section of the work treating the life and death of Juan Facundo Quiroga is replete with "inexactitudes" and creative distortions.[13]

Whether his motives were more appropriately historical, "philosophical" or political, Sarmiento's intentions in writing his work were clearly related to his objective of discrediting one "text" in the eyes of his countrymen and replacing it with another: he would supplant the largely lived "text" of history that was remembered by the impoverished population of the interior provinces who looked upon Facundo Quiroga as the highest and most representative example of their society and primitive civilization, with his own largely "fictionalized" account that emphasized the "barbarian" nature of that caudillo's character and acts. How should the contemporary reader react to this instance of textual violence? The uninformed reader, or one granting priority to aesthetic qualities, might not grant due consideration to the ontological merits of the respective texts. However, other readers with a sensitivity to the historical importance of such a work would realize the weighty social and political implications that its contents would have had in the moment of writing. They would recognize its intended role, one shared with many other nineteenth and early twentieth century Latin American historical texts, of constructing and disseminating a desirable image of nationality, or *patria*.[14] Historically, the cultural enterprise accompanied, and at times achieved the status of participant in, the fierce conflicts between rival groups, each of which struggled to institutionalize society according to its own vision of the future or its own sometimes narrow interests. In all but exceptional cases, these disputes between competing interests and rival cultural interpretations continue to this day in unresolved form: different groups still violently dispute others' claims to the national "patrimony" (the land and its resources) and its "paternal" offspring (the goods produced on that land).

As such, one's interest in the historical aspects of certain Latin American narratives is rarely innocent, for such inquiries inevitably touch upon issues of paramount social and political significance. This was clearly recognized by some of Sarmiento's contemporaries. Liberal cohort Valentin Alsina presented Sarmiento with a long list of factual errors and misleading distortions which he observed in *Facundo*, most of which were due to Sarmiento's practice of "systematizing" his observations according to a priori categories: Sarmiento was "propenso a los *sistemas*." These criticisms—that Sarmiento apparently solicited—were made in the hopes that the work be rewritten in such a way as to arrive better "al descubrimiento de la verdad . . ., el recto examen, . . . a la veraz exposición de ella."[15] Apparently, this negative assessment of *Facundo*'s historical merits was also shared by the foremost liberal leaders of Sarmiento's generation who hailed from Buenos Aires.[16] Although not persuaded by the logic of Sarmiento's arguments, Alsina nevertheless recognized the common interests uniting him to the young writer-militant that a text such as *Facundo* promoted.

There were other contemporaries, however, who severely criticized the work because they recognized how its distorted treatment promoted all too well the extratextual interests that they stalwartly opposed. Juan Bautista Alberdi, who collaborated with Sarmiento and others before 1852 in the generational struggle against the Rosas dictatorship, became after that year a trusted adviser and minister in the Urquiza-led Confederation. As such, Sarmiento and Alberdi became ideological spokesmen for the two forces that disputed each other's hegemonic claims over the entire country.[17] The details of this agonizing national conflict and the dramatic dispute between these two men are too complex to treat here. It is sufficient to mention here Alberdi's clear recognition of the port-city bias in the writings of Sarmiento.[18] Sarmiento's slander of Facundo, Alberdi stated, followed from the former's inflexible interpretation of European "civilization" and the excessive importance granted to Buenos Aires in the country's assimilation of that goal. In *Las cartas quillotanas* he called Sarmiento "el gaucho de la prensa" for the latter's tyrannical practice of the pen that differed only in form from what Alberdi held to be the lawless and anarchistic costumes of Argentina's rural population. (In the last half of this opinion he and Sarmiento were of one mind.) Mitre's and Sarmiento's writings, Alberdi stated, were examples of "la historia forjada por la vanidad, una especie de mitología política con base histórica."[19] He observed that an objective treatment of the nation's recent past hardly existed, given the strong political passions of the time: Buenos Aires's xenophobic leaders, who controlled most of the country's publishing facilities, worked to exclude the dissemination of an image of national culture and history that would place their province in an unfavorable light or would "wound the vanity" of its people.

Sarmiento's *Facundo* has survived into the twentieth century as *libro de fundación* not because of any "realist" quality to the treatment of historical events and personages, but rather on account of its expressive power in aesthetically transforming lived experience into the stuff of narrative. Indeed, it seems surprising that this highly partisan, novelized treatment of the La Riojan caudillo has been so widely acclaimed that rival interpretations have been largely obscured. One could argue that this has occurred because of the particularly persuasive power of that literary power. Another explanation would highlight the work's role in predicting the path of development that Argentina would follow during Sarmiento's lifetime. That is to say, he foresaw the inevitability of the gaucho's disappearance, the displacement of caudillo leadership in the interior provinces, and the eventual ascension of liberalism—in its "dependent" variant[20]—to the status of official doctrine of his country's ruling circles. In this light, it can be argued that whereas *Facundo* was deficient in objectively depicting the historical past, it was entirely successful in capturing—in its "deep" reading of—the history of the country's future.[21] According to this ontogenetic reading, Sarmiento's "realism" was in relation to the future that he prophetically foresaw for his country, and not in relation to his interpretation of past events; it was in relation to the ideals and expectations of his "civilized" or bourgeois reader, and not in relation to the values of his "barbaric" countrymen in the interior.

Our familiarity with the ontogenetic function of discourse comes mainly from the deliberations of Nietzsche and Foucault, both of whom claimed that knowledge was irremediably tied up the exercise of power.[22] Clearly, the ontogenetic reading resembles the Kantian or Heideggerian "aesthetic" reading, and might also be compared to the Barthian conception of the reader's function with a "texte scriptible," in that it proposes an alternative and what is held to be superior interpretation to lived reality with regard to "truth." The main problem here is that there exists no lexical bridge linking the "truth" in language to the "truth" of lived experience. The danger of the writer striving for an ontogenetic text "is to risk becoming trapped in an implausible and highly artificial form of historical idealism."[23] Taking this into account, my use of the term, ontogenetic, is only in relation to the intentions of a writer, or the retrospective interpretation of a reader, when the textual counter-reality is presumed or projected to be linked to non-discursive, non-linguistic, non-artistic, non-interpretative action in transforming lived reality in accordance with that textual image. In "Tema del traidor y del héroe" Jorge Luis Borges provides a clear literary example of how a falsified reading of lived events can become endowed in time with ontogenetic historical truth. György Lukács's theories vis-à-vis Marxist revolutionary praxis, and the latter Foucault's anarchistic-revolutionary writing praxis are other examples. Sarmiento's *Facundo* vis-à-vis dependent-liberalism is the paradigmatic example for nineteenth century Latin American writing.

One finds in Sarmiento, and specifically with regard to *Facundo*, an early example of a writing praxis that had the intention of contributing to the alteration of history. Foucault has penetratingly observed, "One 'fictions' history on the basis of a political reality that makes it true, one 'fictions' a politics not yet in existence on the basis of an historical truth."[24] Understood as such, Sarmiento did not aim to portray the past "as it actually was." The function of his writing was hardly to depict an objective, epistemological truth. Instead, he was aware of the myth-making function that his powerful prose could inspire. Knowledge, for him, was therefore understood as a perspective that aimed at causing a particular impact on his readers. He foresaw the "performative" function of his writing as "effective history". it would contribute to breaking up the present order by projecting a new interpretation that could claim social legitimacy.

The ontogenetic reading, which takes into account the socio-historical context into which the work was dialectically inserted, and thus the public to which it was addressed, therefore explains to some degree why *Facundo* has come to acquire its unrivaled status in the corpus of the country's literature and cultural discourse. Briefly stated, Sarmiento's *Facundo*, with its mystified treatment of the country's historical past, has enjoyed considerable esteem because, among other reasons, it has offered a literary and ideological justification for the imposition, then profundization, of Buenos Aires's dependent-liberal regime over the rest of the country. In fact, the growth in this work's prestige chronologically paralleled, by and large, the spread of Buenos Aires's predominance over the rest of the country. That is to say, the "truth" of Sarmiento's ontogenetic reading in *Facundo* is due to its uncanny prediction of the path chosen for the nation's future consolidation. One could argue that the work, when considered as a historical act in itself, participated in that self-fulfilling prophecy. In Borges's story, "Tema del traidor y del héroe," the "heroic" reading displaced the "treacherous" interpretation for remarkably similar reasons: the guns of the idealistic Irish revolutionaries, just like the Remington automatics employed by Sarmiento's "national" troops, vanquished the opposition and thus helped to establish the social and political circumstances conducive to the cultural operation of "violently forgetting" the rival interpretation of origins.

One can only speculate what the status of **Facundo** would be today had the Confederation won out over Buenos Aires in the early 1860s, that is to say, had the historical basis for the ontogenetic reading of the work been overturned. As it was, however, Buenos Aires put asunder the project of the Confederation, and the dependent-liberal creed embraced by the port-city's leadership progressively became incarnated in governmental programs and social institutions throughout the country. This meant that dissident voices such as Alberdi's were effectively exiled or silenced, and the literary rebellion of one such as José Hernández became assimilated to Buenos Aires's preponderant cultural production. Therefore, as long as the "New Argentina" that had been shaped and molded largely according to the dependent-liberal project enjoyed prosperity, the prestige of Sarmiento—and the work—was not seriously challenged. Up through the first decades of the present century, Sarmiento was universally considered to be precursor, and even "hero," of this success story in modernization.

For this and related reasons, **Facundo** is Latin America's paradigmatic example of the historical novel, according to the criteria set forth by Marxist literary theorist and historian, György Lukács. There is a striking similarity between the agendas of both Sarmiento and Lukács with regard to the ontogenetic function of such writing, and, implicitly, their respective agendas for social transformation. Lukács, like Sarmiento, depicted a "social mission" for literature: for both, it was an instrument to be used by the ascendant bourgeoisie in its "struggle to liquidate the political, ideological and artistic heritage" of a historical period in decline.[25] Lukács, like Sarmiento, embraced a teleological vision of historical development that tended to justify the means employed by "enlightened" leaders in transforming utopian projections of a "*new* democracy" into social fact. Both believed themselves to be the ideologues and protagonists of the "pitiless" march of progress; both would record a "divided and contradictory, dialectical" type of mourning on account of the "necessary destruction" of the already spent institutions of the past.[26] Both predicted the advent of a new society, new culture, and new form of literature that would relegate to insignificance any past attainments of a struggling humanity. And lastly, both harbored ethnocentric (elitist, culturalist, Eurocentric, positivist) values that inevitably influenced the nature of their utopian project and the means they envisioned for its realization.[27]

Given the striking similarity between the respective writing and revolutionary projects of "pre-bourgeois" Sarmiento and Stalinist-Marxist Lukács, it is not surprising that over the last century and a half the great majority of scholars and critics embracing either an "orthodox liberal" or "liberal Marxist" orientation have been Sarmientine apologists.[28] First, there are those of the liberal left: Héctor Félix Bravo, Carlos Octavio Bunge, American critic Allison Williams Bunkley, Juan Pablo Echagüe, Martín García Merou, José H. Guerrero, José Ingenieros, Alberto Palcos, Félix Weinberg and José María Zuviría. Second, there are the liberal Marxists: Aníbal Ponce, Peruvian José Carlos Mariátegui, French critic Noël Salomon, and recently, Alejandro Losada. All of these writers and critics have exalted Sarmiento for his promotion of Europeanized and elitist "civilization" against local "barbarism." All have interpreted his writing and social missions in the light of Argentina's supposedly successful struggle against retrograde influences and on behalf of progress.

Unfortunately, this largely uncritical approval of Sarmiento's "civilizing" mission has led orthodox liberals and liberal Marxists to ignore significant aspects of Sarmiento's advocacies and orientations. While they have emphasized the generosity implicitly promised in his Enlightenment-inspired beliefs on progress, they have ignored the "strict control" and (in more trying moments) the annihilation he prescribed for gauchos, Indians and other social "barbarians." While they have called attention to his promotion of a society based on mutual respect, mass participation, and democratic rights, they have passed over the authoritarian or elitist aspects of his advocacies, and the repressive and even violent means he engineered for achieving them. They have not come to grips with the seismic contradictions in Sarmiento's missions, that social harmony would arise upon the ashes of destruction and that freedom would emerge out of a previous but necessary intolerance.[29]

What is more, the thesis of orthodox liberals and liberal Marxists with regard to Argentina's supposedly exemplary development in the second half of the nineteenth century and the first decades of the twentieth has come under new fire recently. Political historians and economists (Ferrer and Halperín Donghi, in particular) have documented how national leaders during Sarmiento's lifetime guided the country on a path of development that has resulted in accentuated social inequality and structural dependency (financial penetration and technological dependence, an economy emphasizing cattle exports for manufactured imports, and opposition to local industrialization and financial control), factors that perhaps outweigh in importance, at least for the citizens of the present, the phenomenal economic growth and rise of living standards during the same period. Political scientists and historians (Scobie, Ferns, Burns, Mellid, Paso, M. Peña, and Viñas) have provided evidence of the enormous social and human costs that acompanied Argentina's insertion into the British-led world economy after 1852, which have to be considered along with the positive evidence of Argentina's modernization and impressive cultural attainments. The same historians have documented how the supposed "liberal" reform of Argentina institutions during that period occurred in compliance with, and not in opposition to— as was formerly argued—the cattle-exporting oligarchy's continued social and economic hegemony. This new documentation must lead to a fresh evaluation of Argentina's supposed nineteenth-century "bourgeois revolution," as exalted with differing terminology by both orthodox liberals and Marxists, because it points out that the national commercial bourgeoisie allied to foreign capital interests neither attempted nor succeeded in supplanting the then (and still) hegemonic cattle latifundia class, with its origins in the feudal practices and institutions of the Spanish colonial period. Lastly, these historians have resurrected the almost "forgotten" disillusionment of Sarmiento in the last years of his life, when he realized that the old provincial aristocracy of Buenos Aires in alliance with foreign commercial interests, and not a new capitalist class of small agricultural producers and industrialists, were the sometimes ruthless beneficiaries of the new society that had emerged largely as a result of his generation's dedication and energy.

All of this means that critics and readers will have to continue in the task of reassessing the historical value of a work like *Facundo*. They would do well to take into account the warning of Wellek and Warren, that studies done on a literary work with presumed value as social document "makes sense only if we know the artistic method of the novelist studied, and can say—not merely in general terms, but concretely—in what relation the picture stands to the social reality. Is it realistic by intention?"[30] Although readers for over a century and a half have recognized *Facundo*'s unsurpassed aesthetic quality—its expressive language and the evocative power of its imagery—the work's historical material is decidely *not* realistic by intention. On the contrary, its strong sociopolitical bias and mystified treatment constitute significant deficiencies with regard to an ontological impact.[31]

But *Facundo* has enjoyed remarkable success with regard to the ontogenetic function of imposing an interpretation over the national historical and cultural scene. Foucault could not have imagined the darker side of his message, that for many readers Sarmiento's prose exemplifies. This is because the violence of the latter writer's discourse—its distortions, intentional omissions and politicized rendering of historical reality—anticipated the sometimes vengeful program for national transformation directed by Sarmiento and his generation in the post-Rosas era. Ezequiel Martínez Estrada tersely articulated the negative legacy for the twentieth century that must be taken into account along side of Sarmiento's positive contributions to Latin American culture and society. Sarmiento's writing project, according to Martínez Estrada, has succeeded in relegating significant fragments of the nation's social reality to the subconscious: "Los fantasmas desalojaron a los hombres, la utopía devoró la verdad."[32] Inevitably, both perspectives must now color any present or future assessment of this important work with regard to its status as historical novel.

NOTES

[1] I discuss the role of "essayistic discourse" in *Facundo* in "Discourse Production and Sarmiento's Essayistic Style," in *Simposio: el ensayo hispano. Actas*, eds. Isaac Jack Lévy and Juan Loveluck (Columbia: University of South Carolina Press, 1984), 147-56.

[2] This is the studied opinion of Armando Zárate, *Facundo Quiroga, Barranca Yaco: juicios y testimonios* (Buenos Aires: Plus Ultra, 1985), who, on many pages, uses the information supplied by Sarmiento as a standard against which other accounts are evaluated.

[3] For an alternative, and sometimes equally tendentious, perspective of Juan Facundo Quiroga to that offered by Sarmiento, see Rodolfo Ortega Peña and Eduardo Luis Dehalde, *Facundo y la montonera: historia de la resistencia nacional a la penetración británica* (Buenos Aires: Plus Ultra, 1968); Pedro de Paoli's two works, *Facundo: vida del brigadier general don Juan Facundo Quiroga, víctima suprema de la impostura* (Buenos Aires: Ciordia & Caggiano) and *Sarmiento: su gravitación en le desarrollo nacional* (Buenos Aires: Theoría, 1964); and José María Rosa, *Rivadavia y el imperialismo financiero* (Buenos Aires: 1964).

[4] Noteworthy among the historians and commentators who generally coincided with Sarmiento in the presentation of a damning perspective of Juan Facundo Quiroga are: Unitarian General Tomás de Iriarte, *Memorias* (Buenos Aires: Sociedad Impresora Americana, 1947); liberal writer Eduardo Gutiérrez, *Juan Manuel de Rosas* (Buenos Aires: La Patria Argentina, 1882); and historian Ramón J. Cárcano, *Juan Facundo Quiroga* (Buenos Aires: Losada, 1960).

[5] David Peña, *Juan Facundo Quiroga*, 5th ed. (Buenos Aires: Americana, 1953;—originally published in 1906), 9. See also: David Peña and Jorge Mitre, *Facundo: polémica histórica* (Buenos Aires: 1907). Studies that provide a fairly balanced account of the life and deeds of Juan Facundo Quiroga are: Enrique M. Barba, ed. and "Estudio preliminar," *Correspondencia entre Rosas, Quiroga y López* (Buenos Aires: Hachette, 1958); Leonard Paso, *Los caudillos y la organización nacional* (Buenos Aires: 1965); Ricardo Piccirilli, *Rivadavia y su tiempo* (Buenos Aires: 1943); and Antonio Zinny, *Historia de los gobernadores*. Vol. IV: *Mendoza, San Juan, La Rioja, Catamarca* (Buenos Aires: 1921).

[6] In subsequent years Sarmiento was hardly consistent in how he characterized this work. In *Recuerdos de provincia*, *Facundo* was classified among the "biographies" he had written, which suggests his attempt to imbue it with historiographical significance and to downplay the predominantly political and artistic motivations at play in its composition. Decades later, in a letter to his nephew, Belín Sarmiento, he more appropriately called the work "una especie de poema, panfleta, historia."

[7] All quotes are from Domingo F. Sarmiento, *Obras Completas*, Buenos Aires: Luz del Día, 1948-1956.

[8] See my discussion of this issue in *Domingo F. Sarmiento: Public Writer (Between 1839 and 1852)* (Tempe: Center for Latin American Studies, Arizona State University, 1985), 183-85.

[9] Andrés Bello, who participated in the debates on historiography in Santiago, Chile during the period in question, called attention to how the historical writing of Lastarria sacrificed the pursuit of truth for objectives related to political expediency. He clearly perceived one of the shortcomings of the "philosophical" treatment of historical issues, that is mistakenly viewed the Latin American countries in the same historical framework as the more developed societies of France and England, but without taking into account the vast differences separating the two experiences with regard to the developments of economic, social and cultural institutions. See Bernardo Subercaseaux S., *Cultura y sociedad liberal en el siglo XIX: Lastarria: ideología y literatura* (Santiago: Editorial Aconcagua, 1981), 68.

[10] J. V. Lastarria, *Recuerdos literarios: datos para la historia literaria de la América española, del progreso intelectual en Chile* (Santiago: Librería de M. Servat, 1885).

[11] Subercaseaux, 73-78.

[12] Quoted from Domingo Faustino Sarmiento, *Facundo*, prol. Alberto Palcos (Buenos Aires: Ediciones Culturales Argentinas, 1961), 450.

[13] In *Sarmiento: Public Writer*, 146-49, I analyze how Sarmiento utilized contemporaneous sociological and historical theories, primarily the *Volksgeist* orientation learned from Herder via Michelet and Guizot, in the fictionalized, politicized treatment of his protagonist.

[14] This is the insight of Doris Sommer, in "Not Just Any Narrative: How Romance Can Love Us to Death," included in the present volume.

[15] "Notas de Valentín Alsina al libro 'Civilización y barbarie,'" in *Facundo*, ed. Palcos, 350.

[16] Paoli, in *Sarmiento*, 87, calls attention to the young Buenos Aires liberals' opinion that Sarmiento's work was little more than a politically inspired tirade against Rosas. Carlos Tejedor, in a long review of *Facundo*, called it a "libelo político," Vicente Fidel López, in similar fashion, called it "una historia beduina."

[17] Historian David Peña explicitly links the historical roles of both Quiroga and Urquiza: "Ahí yace la figura extraña que refleja toda la primitiva sociedad argentina y, en materia política, el precursor de Urquiza. Si no muere el año 35, a los 47 de edad, Quiroga habría llegado a fundar la organización de la República (V.F. López)." Quoted from Zárate, *Facundo Quiroga*, 85.

[18] Alberdi's criticisms were also extended to the historiographic project of Mitre and other porteño writers. According to Alberdi, "Mitre gasta su tiempo en escribir disertaciones de historia para probar que las provincias del Norte no hicieron nada por su libertad." (July, 1864, as quoted in Juan Bautista Alberdi, *Las cartas rosistas de Alberdi*, comentarios de Adolfo Saldías [Buenos Aires: Politeia, 1970], 119).

[19] José Acevedo, *Obras históricas. José Artigas: Jefe de los Orientales y Protector de los Pueblos Libres. Su obra cívica. Alegato histórico*, 2nd edition (Montevideo: Casa A. Barreiro y Ramos, 1933), 99-100.

[20] I discuss "dependent" liberalism in relation to Sarmiento's generation in *Sarmiento: Public Writer*, 199-201.

[21] In this respect I am in agreement with José Luis Romero, "*Facundo* o la historia profunda," in *Là experiencia argentina y otros ensayos*, Luis Alberto Romero, comp. (Buenos Aires: Belgrano, 1980), 220-23.

[22] Allen Megill, *Prophets of Extremity: Nietzsche, Heidegger, Foucault, Derrida* (Berkeley, Los Angeles and London: University of California Press, 1985), 150, 168, uses the term "ontogenetic," but unfortunately provides neither a clear definition nor a precise textual genealogy of its use.

[23] Megill, 63.

[24] Michel Foucault, "The History of Sexuality," as quoted by Megill, 234.

[25] All the quoted phrases in this paragraph are from Gyorgy Lukács, *The Historical Novel* (1938), are reproduced in Berel Lang and Forrest Wil-

liams, eds. *Marxism and Art: Writings in Aesthetics and Criticism* (New York: David McKay Company, 1972), 372.

[26] Lukács, *Historical Novel*, 384-85.

[27] I document all these issues with regard to the beliefs and writing practice of *Sarmiento: Public Writer*. Several of the following paragraphs draw from material presented in the Foreword and the Epilogue of this work. George Yúdice, in "Testimonials and Hegemony," presented at the Symposium on the Historical Novel in Latin America, Tulane University, November 14-16, 1985, intelligently argues that this characterization of the revolutionary project for both Sarmiento and Lukács must be understood in the proper historical perspective: Sarmiento, radically progressive for his period, struggled on behalf of a *bourgeois* revolution for a decrepit and underdeveloped society; Lukács, academically anachronistic, projected a revolutionary project for his own time that borrowed heavily upon readings of or about nineteenth century European society. Yúdice optimistically argues that the revolutionary project such as that lived in Nicaragua and projected for other areas of Central America already shows definite signs of going beyond the elitist and Eurocentric parameters of previous struggles due to its "popular" character.

[28] David Viñas, in *Rebeliones populares argentinas*. Vol. I: *De los montoneros a los anarquistas* (Buenos Aires: Carlos Pérez, 1971), makes this association. Tulio Halperín Donghi, *Jornadas de historia y economía argentinas en los siglos XVIII y XIX* (Buenos Aires—Rosario: Instituto de Investigaciones Históricas, Facultad de Filosofía de Rosario, e IDES, 1964), 21, states: "Tenemos entonces una historiografía marxista, que es en el fondo historiografía liberal con lenguaje y vocabulario cambiado. . . ."

[29] In the "Epilogue" to *Sarmiento: Public Writer* I briefly document these assertions.

[30] Rene Wellek and Austin Warren, *Theory of Literature,* 3rd edition (San Diego, New York and London: Harcourt, Brace, Jovanovich, 1977), 104.

[31] While the above paragraphs demonstrate the deficiencies of *Facundo* with regard to the ontological function of faithfully rendering the data of lived historical experience into a coherent narrative, this does not mean that the work is entirely without value in relation to its function of teaching the reader about history or human society. This is so, paradoxically, because its aesthetic merits inevitably and unerringly affect its ontological status. Regardless of Sarmiento's intentions, the work succeeds in looking beyond the historical anecdote for the profound truth of human acts. Sarmiento, in the words of Armando Zárate, "Busca, como un supersticioso, en los hechos humanos, valores imaginarios que una escritura de combate exalta y define. Pero en el fondo, Facundo es un símbolo espectral y como tal, un mito cuyo gesto sólo puede definirse según la energía de la ficción, en su realidad entera, en su *folktale*. He aquí el movimiento primitivo de una densidad constitutiva, congruentemente literaria." ("El *Facundo*: un héroe como su mito," *Revista Iberoamericana*, 44: 104-105 [1978], 475).

[32] Ezequiel Martínez Estrada, *Radiografía de la pampa*, 6th ed. (Buenos Aires: Losada, 1968), 341.

Diana Sorensen Goodrich   (essay date 1991)

SOURCE: "The Wars of Persuasion: Years of *Facundo*'s Reception," in *Revista Hispánica Moderna*, Vol. XLIV, December 1991, pp. 177-90.

[*Here, Goodrich provides a thorough analysis of both Latin America's initial response to Sarmiento's* Facundo *and the social conditions that caused it.*]

In **Mi defensa** Sarmiento proclaims he has learned to read very well:

> En mí no ha tenido otro origen mi afición a instruirme que el haber aprendido a leer muy bien.[1]

One of the tricks his orphaned texts play upon him is that they call into questions the very possibility of reading well. This is epitomized by his first major work, **Facundo**: though unquestionably an honored member of the Latin American canon, it has been read in such divergent ways that it problematizes the possibility of interpretive validity. Indeed, one can think of few classics which have produced so many conflicting readings as **Facundo** has, or which have in the history of their reception brought to the forefront the complexities and the distortions that may arise in interpretive understanding. Moreover, the deferral of meaning—an inevitable condition of our dealings with language—is extended when reading becomes tangled in politically charged conflicts of interpretation. As one studies the readings of Sarmiento's **Facundo** one is struck by the paradoxically quality of its status: classics tend to elicit a fairly homogeneous reception, but **Facundo** has kindled wars of persuasion intended to defend or attack it, to legitimize it or to debunk it altogether. Its readings can in fact be seen as the subject of a long-standing and very fertile communicative interaction characterized by conflicting validity claims rooted in ideological struggles.

We are all well aware that a text's meanings are not fixed once and for all; what I will explore here is how its meanings are in part determined by the situation of the interpreters: how contextual constraints shape the process of reception. **Facundo** has given life to a national literary circuit, it is a founding text, as it marks a beginning for a series of cultural phenomena centered on the book as an artefact of central importance. In order to examine these questions I will focus on a particular moment in the very eventful life of Sarmiento's first major book: the time of its initial publication, seen as a rich cultural event. Since the study of the canonization of **Facundo** is closely linked with the process of elaboration of Argentine cultural myths, I will trace the impact on the actual coming on stage of the text itself, the avatars of its publication, its moving from pamphlet to book, the very immediate dialogue that it established with its readers, the way in which a text seeks out an audience as it comes on the scene, and, in doing so, is actually struggling for influence and hegemony. We tend to view a canonized book through the hindsight of later versions, or maybe through the vast repository of the complete works, and this may entail losing any sense of the earlier versions as different but equally vital speech acts in the world. Because the complete works, or even the anotated editions tend to reify writing as a series of complete final products, they erase any sense of their mode of production and reception, and of their interaction with contexts which were particularly powerful at the time of their publication. By looking at **Facundo**'s

occasion and original readership, seeking the impact it had on its contemporaries and during its first few years of life, I will consider its emergence as a phenomenon inscribed in the tension between legitimation and contestation. I will attempt to see it, as Foucault says, as "discourse in its sudden irruption; in that punctuality in which it appears, and in that temporal dispersion that enables it to be repeated, known, forgotten, transformed, utterly erased and hidden, far from all view, in the dust of books." Rather than treating it as "the distant presence of the origin" I will see it "as and when it occurs."[2] Releasing it from the inertia of the book, and restoring some of its lost vitality, I will examine the circulation of meanings produced as a result of its beginning. We can thus observe the material and discursive conditions of the existence of **Facundo** as it appeared in serial form in *El Progreso*, the interplay of relations it brought into being as it was read and interpreted, and some of the implications of its transformation from pamphlet to book. My work is affiliated with the enterprise of cultural studies, as it presupposes that communicative exchanges are the root of the dynamic interactions of meanings and power relations.

Of course, any attempt to recapture the initial situation of a text's reception is itself caught up in the movement of history. Gadamer has written eloquently about the problems of the fusion of horizons, and I think it is as interesting to bring to the forefront what can be reconstructed as it is to note the gaps which the past makes it impossible for us to fill. Attempting to reach back to the multiple factors which came into play in the production and reception of **Facundo** around the decade of its publication, brings home to us in a powerful way the degree to which the past is beyond reach. In part, of course, this is due to the dynamics of my historically situated, present subjectivity, so well defined in Walter Benjamin's penetrating dictum: "History is the subject of a structure whose site is not homogeneous, empty time, but time filled by the presence of the now." My "now" evidently conditions my understanding of the past as well as the direction in which I will seek significant informations. Again, Benjamin comes to mind: ". . . every image of the past that is not recognized by the present as one of its own concerns threatens to disappear irretrievably."[3]

The image of the past which I will try to bring into existence has of course a purely textual status: it emerges from newspapers and letters, two discursive forms which sustained the communication among the intellectuals of this time. These textual materials constitute a fabric tightly woven of writing, inscription and action. The relationship has a powerful double fit which has to do with the community of Argentine exiles living in Chile during Rosas' era: while they were constantly in touch with each other, inscribing their doing in astonishingly numerous letters and newspaper articles, they were also keenly aware of the extent to which writing was transmuted into action. To peruse the letters and journalistic pieces written by Sarmiento and his acquaintances at this time is to become aware of the degree to which **Facundo** is manipulated as a power-gaining tool. With no other one of his works was Sarmiento as concerned to have it reach those readers who might respond favourably to him as its author. He was convinced that as his readership expanded so did his prestige and that this would bring him closer to public office. There are many eloquent proofs of this in Sarmiento's correspondence. There is a letter written on April 8 1851 to Modestino Pizarro from his quinta in Yungay, in which Sarmiento deals with the arrangements to be made as soon as Rosas is overthrown:

> En ese congreso, si tiene lugar, habría un asiento vacío si no estoy yo. Hecháranme [*sic*] de menos los pueblos, será incompleta y vacilante su marcha. Mi presencia daría a todos confianza, y sólo a Rosas miedo; porque a mí se ligan ideas ya formuladas y de todos conocidas. Hay más, y esto es lo peor, ese congreso será subyugado por Urquiza y creo que sólo mi presencia puede conservarle la majestad de la representación nacional.[4]

Sarmiento's legitimation as a potential member of Congress derives from his writings, from the fact that his readers have become acquainted with his thinking. The pragmatic connection between book and action is such that on the occasion of *Facundo*'s second edition, Sarmiento's choice of words to describe it is revealing: "*Civilización y barbarie* quedará empastada en la entrante semana, rica edición corregida, aumentada, afiladas las uñas . . ."[5] The metaphor is suggestive of the belligerent qualities that he attributes to his book, and of his conviction that it would have far-reaching repercussions in the world. When he wrote to Paz and Benavidez hoping to win their support, he saw to it that they received copies of *Facundo*, as though the relationship between author and book were metonymical. In the letter to Paz, written in Montevideo on December 22, 1845, *Facundo* is seen in the same pugnacious light: "Con el propósito de agitar todas las preocupaciones del interior escribí el *Facundo*, del que hice pasar a cordillera cerrada un cajón."[6] Sarmiento was not alone in attributing such efficacy to his writings. An eloquent letter written by Juan Andrés Ferrera from La Paz, Bolivia, encouraging him to continue his discrediting enterprise against Rosas assures him of his success in the following terms:

> *Aldao y Facundo* serán bien pronto dos poderes invisibles que arrastrarán hacia el cadalso al infame Rosas.[7]

Another early reader, Wenceslao Paunero, illustrates to what extent the early reception of *Facundo* privileged its pragmatic dimension:

> Ninguno de los escritores argentinos ha comprendido y explicado los diversos elementos de nuestra sociedad como Ud. Felicítese pues amigo de que su trabajo es hermoso y fecundo en resultados.[8]

This relationship between writing, action and power was one of Sarmiento's obsessions. His enemy Alberdi knew exactly how to nettle him in this regard, and he found subtle ways to berate his performance as a mere "escritor de la prensa periódica." Urquiza also mooted Sarmiento's

insistent claims to having waged an effective battle against Rosas with his pen, and he did so in very blunt terms through his secretary, Ángel Elías, shortly before Caseros, on January 2, 1852:

> El señor general ha leído la carta que ayer le ha escrito usted, y me encarga le diga respecto de los prodigios que dice usted que hace la imprenta asustando al enemigo, "que hace muchos años que las prensas chillan en Chile y en otras partes, y que hasta ahora don Juan Manuel de Rosas no se ha asustado; que antes al contrario cada día estaba más fuerte".[9]

Sarmiento's offended answer is dated the very next day, and what he responds to is the charge against the effectiveness of the written word:

> Es muy natural creer que yo me exagere a mis propios ojos la influencia de la prensa, es decir, de la palabra . . . Pero la prensa de Chile he sido yo durante muchos años, y en estos últimos no se ha ocupado de otra cosa que de predisponer la opinión pública en favor del señor general y de la digna empresa que iba a acometer. [. . .] Las armas que combaten a Rosas son invencibles; pero también es cierto que la opinión lo ha abandonado, y alguna parte, por pequeña que sea, debe concedérsele a los que han tenido el coraje de combatir su poder diez años . . . [10]

This compelling alliance between discourse and power, not limited specifically to the actual overthrow of Rosas but taken in more general terms, has had a bearing on the relationship between the reception of *Facundo* and the shaping of an Argentine cultural tradition, for, as Habermas might put it, the contents of a cultural tradition are the communicable meanings toward which social action is oriented. The questions which the countless readers of this book have addressed over the last almost one hundred and fifty years have touched upon the ways in which discursive practices regulate social and political relations. For indeed, as Foucault has so eloquently argued, power circulates, it functions in the form of a chain, and the production and circulation of discourse embodied in the letters and journalistic pieces connected with *Facundo* are defined by the ever-changing choreography of power which was being played out before and after the battle of Caseros.

We see also how the production of power, prestige and community are interconnected in the moment when this book made its appearance. The network of discursive practices I am discussing helped mold the concept of nationality which the cast of characters of the pre and post Caseros era helped define. The connection between exile and community is strong: the "proscriptos" (to borrow a term from Ricardo Rojas) became what in Benedict Anderson's suggestive terms can be called an "imagined community" which needed to fight its own sense of dispersion by turning to the binding force of writing.[11] If, as Victor Turner claims, the journey is a social process, we can see the journey into exile—a pilgrimage away from the fatherland—as a meaning-creating experience.[12] Only the power of writing could grant a sense of community and of nationhood to the men who were plotting the demise of Rosas from Chile, Montevideo, Perú, and Bolivia. Anderson attributes great importance to the newspaper in the formation of the cultural artifact of nationness. The perusal of such newspapers as *El Mercurio,* or *El Progreso,* in which Sarmiento played a pivotal role, gives us a sense of the cohesive way in which they created an assemblage of fellow readers. Of course, these fellow readers were not limited to Argentine exiles, for they included the Chilean reading public, but the Argentine hegemonic intellectuals like Sarmiento, Vicente Fidel López, Alberdi, Juan María Gutiérrez, Carlos Tejedor, and Félix Frías, established a remarkable network of communication among themselves and with their counterparts in Montevideo (Esteban Echeverría, Florencio Varela, Bartolomé Mitre, Valentín Alsina) by writing and reading letters and newspapers in a truly feverish manner. The emergence of Facundo in *El Progreso* must be seen within this field: it is part of a rich, sometimes dissonant conversation among them all, and as such, it seems to me, it was received. In what follows, then, I shall explore a field of questions designed to determine the conditions of existence of these discursive formations: the situations that provoked **Facundo** together with the consequences it gave rise to. In other words, as Arthur Danto has said about historical reconstruction, I will locate this discursive event in some stories, always bearing in mind his caveat that "Completely to describe an event is to locate it in all the right stories, and this we cannot do."[13] These "stories" will touch upon the contextual factors which might have conditioned the reception of the text, the forms of appropriation which were deployed, questions of distribution, circulation, readership, as well as the intricate counterpoint between consent and dissent, legitimation and contestation which **Facundo**'s appearance brought into play.

The first "story" deals with the author and his reading public. As Foucault has put it, "The author's name indicates the status of discourse within a society and a culture."[14] What did the name "Sarmiento" mean to the audience of the eighteen-forties? How was their reading of the "feuilleton" as it appeared in *El Progreso* between May 2 and June 21 1845 framed by the political and cultural discourses which were circulating at the time? Even though it was published in book-form as early as July 1845, it seems obvious that **Facundo** was a vital element of the journalistic field in which Sarmiento played so prominent a role and which Benedict Anderson considers crucial in the development of a sense of community.[15] When Sarmiento wrote to Urquiza, "La prensa de Chile he sido yo" he was committing only mild exaggeration. When he arrived in Chile, the only existing newspaper was *El Mercurio* of Valparaíso, founded in 1827, and shortly after the publication of an article of his commemorating the battle of Chacabuco, Sarmiento was offered the editorship of the paper. His centrality was soon sustained by an intricate mesh of controversy and power contests which pertained to both Argentines and Chileans, as well as to the founding discourses of culture and politics. In the Chilean environment, his writing was drawn into the struggle between the Conservative

and the Liberal parties ("pelucones" and "pipiolos"), which was played out in the founding of newspapers, in the recruitment of prestigious editors and in the daily battling of articles. Sarmiento's decision to support the conservative party was reached after a careful examination of the role of the Argentine exiles in the Chilean political arena (as he explained later in **Recuerdos de provincia**), and after considerable effort on the part of Las Heras and Montt to recruit his services for newspapers that were being founded to promote their respective causes. Shortly after he left *El Mercurio,* in 1842, Sarmiento established the first newspaper of Santiago, *El Progreso,* under the auspices of Manuel Montt. Clearly, this was the founding moment of journalistic discourse in Chile. Lastarria and his "pipiolo" associates founded *El Miliciano,* and, later on, *El Siglo.* It is significant that when *El Progreso* began the serialized publication of **Facundo** Sarmiento was involved in heated debates not only, as it well known, with Rosas's emissary, Baldomero García, but also with the "pipiolo" newspapers, most especially with *El Siglo.* These debates, in part focused on the Chilean presidential elections of 1846, framed the early readings of the text with controversy. Sarmiento describes one of the peaks of the disputation in a colourful letter to his friend Pepe Posse on January 29th 1845:

> Los de *El Siglo* se abandonaron a todo el furor que es costumbre entre todos estos canallas, cuando les aprieto los callos. Dijéronme "caballo cuyano", cobarde y qué sé yo. Instigado por López, me dirigí a la imprenta de *El Siglo,* requerí al ofensor, no me daban una explicación, escupíle la cara, y él entre si se le pasaba el susto, si hacía algo por lavarse la afrenta, trató de agarrarme, alcanzó a los cabellos, me desasí de él y lo eché en hora mala. Yo me aguardaba algo serio, algo de caballeros; media hora después empero estaba lleno Santiago, "bailaban de gusto! de qué sé yo qué cuentos, inventados a placer, me habían molido a patadas, sacándome los ojos, quince días después la república entera estaba llena, de que me habían destripado, etc., brindaban en Aconcagua, predicaban los curas, etc . . . [16]

The press did not merely report; its writing was the arena where the power struggle was staged. A letter addressed to Sarmiento by Santiago Cueto in 1845 conveys the sense of immediate pragmatic efficacy attained by print:

> Usted es nuestro salvador y no dudo que empleará todo su talento para dar por tierra contra los Lastarrias, infames calumniadores . . . El artículo de mañana, así como todos los que sigan en toda esta semana han de ser tales que apure usted todo su talento; que muevan al pueblo de Santiago: que lo hagan tomar horror a ese partido infernal: que nos den el triunfo, por el miedo que tengan esos imbéciles.[17]

The readers of *El Progreso, El Siglo* and the *Diario de Santiago,* which replaced *El Siglo* as of July 5, 1845, formed an interpretive community whose competence was marked by heated debate. Here is one example of the reception of **Facundo** by Pedro Godoy, a "pipiolo" who wrote in *El Siglo* and in the *Diario de Santiago*:

El autor de *Facundo* se forjó un plan, quiso llamarlo biografia de un hombre célebre en los anales de la revolución argentina, pretendió describir una de las épocas más sangrientas de esa revolución, intentó llamar la atención del público sobre su obra, y sin los conocimientos necesarios, sin ideas fijas sobre política ni sobre los acontecimientos que en parte, quizá haya presenciado, [. . .] y no contando, en suma, más que con su atrevimiento natural, sacó a la luz el tejido de absurdos que ahora examinamos.[18]

Sometimes the tone of the reviews was blatantly insulting, and the struggle became such that a press jury was summoned on behalf of Sarmiento, but Godoy was absolved.

In the cultural field Sarmiento's name became associated with controversies which had to do with the construction of a truly American cultural discourse, and which implied a break with the established tradition. As is well known, Sarmiento was deeply involved in the 1842 polemic with Bello and the strongholds of classicism, and it was played out in the daily newspapers (in this particular case *El Semanario*—the first weekly publication with literary pretensions to appear in Chile—and *El Mercurio*), which became display texts for the community of readers to participate in and consume. As in the controversy with *El Siglo,* it is remarkable to note how aggressive the writing is. Here is a brief sample, from Sarmiento's pen:

> . . . los redactores de *El Semanario* quieren habérselas con nosotros, y se las habrán, poque el que ataca al can ataca al sabadán, y el público no se mete en esas niñerías; gusta que se rompan lo cuernos los escritores, y sacar él solo la utilidad oyendo el pro y el contra de las cuestiones que se ventilan. Conque déjense de público los señores de *El Semanario,* que nosotros también tenemos nuestro publiquito diminuto, pero joven, ilustrado y amigo de su tiempo y de las cosas que no huelen a tocino rancio como el clasicismo.[19]

Sarmiento's hegemonic standing in the discourse of cultural formation and in the foundation of institutions at this time is eloquently revealed by the fact that on October 17 1843 he presented the first paper to be produced by the newly founded University of Chile. His ***Memoria sobre ortografía americana*** provoked heated debates, and it is interesting to examine the newspapers of the time and observe the degree of spelling instability which the ***Memoria*** triggered: while some ignored Sarmiento's suggestions, several of them adopted them and did away with the h, v and z, with the silent u in such combinations as "gue", "gui", "que" and "qui". It is of course relevant that Sarmiento's suggestion coincides with the foundation of the nation's institutions and the production of a national discourse, since clearly the new spelling model was ultimately designed to inscribe in the realm of writing a difference between Spain and the emerging nations.

Another relevant factor in the context of production and reception of *Facundo* was, as I anticipated, the visit to Chile of Rosas's emissary, Baldomero García in April 1845 —a month before the first "entrega" of the "feuilleton".

This event generated a rich array of journalistic articles ranging from discussions focussed on the trip's purpose to animated commendation of the heroic attibutes of an otherwise obscure Argentine exile, a certain Bedoya who had to face prosecution as the result of having torn a label reading "imueran los salvajes, asquerosos, inmundos unitarios!" from one of García's servants. García's presence galvanized some of the conflicts which pertained to both the inner workings of the Chilean political struggles and the agency of the Argentine exiles. As a result, tensions mounted to a point which, according to a piece written by Sarmiento on May 1 in *El Progreso,* announcing the forthcoming publication of the "Vida de Quiroga," made it imperative to bring out a text designed to halt "un mal que puede ser trascendental para nosotros." *Facundo* stands in the midst of this tangled web not merely because Sarmiento, as has been said, wanted to discredit García and, certainly, Rosas, but because he needed to address his enemies at *El Siglo.* In order to undermine the authority of the "pelucón" newspaper *(El Progreso)* they had adduced that Sarmiento was being silenced in his attacks of García by no other than Montt (his supporter, and, in fact the one the "pipiolos" wanted to bring disrepute to) in order to avoid problems between the governments of Chile and Argentina. Sarmiento's fiery response, entitled ""Por qué nos ataca *El Siglo*?" appeared in *El Progreso* on the very same day he announced the serialized publication of *Facundo;* the central thrust of his argument was that the issue at stake was freedom of speech:

> Pero entonces destrúyase la libertad de imprenta, como lo pide *El Siglo,* e impártase órdenes del ministerio, como lo aconseja y aprueba *El Siglo,* que sólo esta vez halla digna e ilustrada la conducta del ministro Montt.[20]

Thus, the questions of communicative understanding and misunderstanding were bound up with oppositional practices and situational constraints. In the "Anuncio" of May 1, Sarmiento sums it up in the following terms:

> Intereses mezquinos y de circunstancias, rencillas de periodistas, y propósitos de partido, tienden a sublevar pasiones y celos que con el designio manifiesto de comprometer a un individuo ante la opinión pública no van a nada menos que a levantar en Chile ecos al bárbaro sistema de Rosas.[21]

It was necessary to occupy a different discursive site in the struggle with a work of vaster scope, one which would grant authority by placing the debates within a broader framework and by bringing to bear on them the conceptual apparatus of the thinkers who, as he put in the *Ortografía americana,* "dirigen el pensamiento de hoy."[22]

As was stated at the beginning, the way we read *Facundo* now tends to reify writing in the form of the completed book. Here is a unity which we must question as artificial: it is always salutary to suspend, as Foucault says, "the material individualization of the book, which occupies a determined space, which has an economic value, and which itself indicates, by a number of signs, the limits of its beginning and its end." The frontiers of **Facundo** are fascinating because they have undergone numerous reconfigurations, always betraying their placement within a complex field of discourse, again, as Foucault put it, "caught up in a system of references . . . , as a node within a network."[23] As a serialized publication the text was read in a fragmentary way, and it was also framed by the other pieces which occupied the space of the newspapers - both within *El Progreso* and the other papers with which it established a dialogue. It is important to retain a sense of the material mode of existence of this text, its status as a publication and the forms of reception it might have invited. A piece Sarmiento wrote for *El Progreso* on August 30, 1845, suggestively entitled **"Nuestro pecado de los folletines"** conveys both the condemnation the "folletín" inspired in the reading public (derived, of course, from the "cosas pecaminosas" which it contained) and its communicative success, facetiously yet proudly presented as a disease ("la lepra del folletín ha ganado ya todos los diarios") which *El Mercurio* introduced during the early years of Sarmiento's stewardship. While this section favoured the consumption of romantic and truculent literature (Sue and Dumas might epitomize the preference here, but Balzac was not excluded), it did not rule out non fictional accounts of general interest: *El Mercurio,* for instance, was publishing the "Estractos del viaje al viejo mundo por el peruano D. Juan Bustamante" in August 1845, only a month after *El Progreso* had brought out **Facundo**. Here was a space slightly removed from the actual news coverage, but which shared its borders and its readers and which allowed concepts to gain currency and power. As Sarmiento observed in **Viajes**, "Un buen folletín puede decidir de los destinos del mundo dando una nueva dirección a los espíritus."[24] Evidently, it was the desirable medium for shaping opinion at a time of crisis, and Sarmiento saw to it that its readers encountered in the pages of *El Progreso* journalistic pieces which would orient interpretation in a supportive way. Thus, in May and June of 1845, the readers of the "folletín" "Vida de Quiroga" were presented with pieces which reinforced its central thesis, such as "Interés de Chile en la cuestión del Plata" (8·5·45), "El sistema de Rosas" (28·5·45), "La causa de Bedoya" (2, 3 and 6·6·45), or "Lo que a Rosas debe la América del Sur" (13·6·45). But the serialized "folletín," with its fragmentary reception, is especially prone to the dialectics of both legitimation and contestation: a reader who then turned to *El Siglo,* or later the *Diario de Santiago* would encounter all the possibilities of reading **Facundo** against the grain. Here is one brief example taken from *El Siglo,* on May 20: "El **Facundo** es una obra la más fecunda en desatinos, en plagios y en mentiras." Another, from *La Gaceta de Comercio* of Valparaíso: "Santo Dios despierten al señor Sarmiento, sacudanló [sic] para que se mire en su estatura y conozca que sólo llama la atención por la magnitud de su insolencia." *El Siglo*, on June 14: "lo único que logrará [Sarmiento] será que los Santiaguinos levantemos la voz para decir a los Provincianos que cuando lean Montt y Sarmiento again [sic] de cuenta que leen Bolívar y el Sargento Pino . . . , Montt y una Chancleta vieja."[25] Aggravating things was Montt's investiture to the Interior Ministry; by June 11 *El Siglo* announced "guerra

a muerte al redactor del *Progreso.*" In August the *Diario de Santiago* publishes a parody of **Facundo** with some aggressive distortions: the subject of the biography is now Sarmiento himself, renamed "Pantaleón del Carrascal" to allude to a poor quarter of the city of San Juan, and events in Sarmiento's life are incorporated in a derisive manner. This is no harmless scoff: Pantaleón-Sarmiento is even made to murder two federal soldiers. Evidently, what Hans Robert Jauss calls the "horizon of expectations" of the readers was deeply stamped by conflict, and the text was set in an interplay of relations existing within its textual boundaries but also outside of them. It is not surprising that by September 1845, when Sarmiento left *El Progreso* in the midst of such heated controversy, Félix Frías should make the following confidential remark at the end of a letter to Juan María Gutiérrez: "Sarmiento deja *El Progreso*. Se irá probablemente a Europa si pronto no podemos todos regresar a nuestro país. Está ya honrosamente inutilizado para la prensa."[26]

When in July 1845 the text changed its status from "folletín" to book the struggles did not subside, but there is a shift in the schemata of text use. We witness now the dynamics of circulation and distribution, the seeking out of a broader audience and the anxiety to exert influence beyond the sphere of the political debates which were being enacted in the Chilean newspapers. The little book is now received as a unit, removed from its previous fragmented journalistic frame. The text itself underwent the first of several future modifications, for there is good reason to believe that the folletin had ended after "Barranca Yaco!!!," with the murder of Quiroga. As a book, it entered a different system of distribution than the one it had had in the journalistic medium, and the numerous letters written by and addressed to Sarmiento about this attest to the difficulties inherent in promoting book circulation at this time. Sarmiento's plight was obviously aggravated by exile, and by the government's hostility in the territory he wished to penetrate. Whatever the effect of the difficulties to be faced, it is remarkable to observe how much Sarmiento wanted to be read, to have his book reach an audience which went even beyond the continental confines. Of the letters he wrote to Gutiérrez, very insistently making this kind of request, there is one that stands out as epitomizing the reach of his anxiety for readership: "Pero volvamos a su misión de derramar la Odisea por toda la redondez del orbe. "¿A que no a escrito una palabra a sus amigos de Francia, al National, la Democracia Pacífica, Revista de Paris y de Ambos Mundos, etc., etc.? Vamos, ágalo."[27] About fifty copies were furtively introduced to Buenos Aires, others given as presents to the patriots in Chile, or sent to powerful figures such as Paz, Varela, Echeverría or Rivera Indarte. In spite of such efforts, it was evidently very hard to have the book reach its readers. Juan María Gutiérrez, commissioned with what seems to me a major portion of the burden of the distribution of the book, and who at one point assured Sarmiento he would do what was necessary "para que el señor don Facundo se pasee por esas capitales," has difficulty obtaining the books in Valparaíso: "Quiero advertirle que de los ejemplares de **Facundo**, ni encuadernados ni a la rústica, hay uno solo en mi poder."[28] His friend Aberastain, who had helped Sarmiento gather information on Facundo Quiroga in March writes on August 5, 1845 from Copiapó: "Recibí su carta y no los cuarenta ejemplares del *Facundo*; pienso que éstos hayan llegado y estén demorados en el puerto a donde he encargado ya a Ríos establecido allí que me los mande en la primera oportunidad."[29] Wenceslao Paunero, writing from La Paz, has obviously been waiting long for his copy: "Nada sé de su *Facundo* hasta ésta; "¡Por qué demonio de vía lo ha dirigido usted!"[30] The vicissitudes of transportation made distribution tentative: a shipment of books to France, for example, never made it beyond Cape Horn, and Sarmiento had to give away his very last copy to the Revue des Deux Mondes when he presented it for review. Small wonder, then, that writing to Gutiérrez on his way to Europe, in January 1846, Sarmiento should express his discouragement: ""Qué libro tan desgraciado fue éste; todo, hasta la impresión, salió como si Rosas ubiese sido el que ponía la mano en él."[31]

Thus, *Facundo* sets in motion a process of circulation and distribution; it also engenders the discourse of literary criticism. A rich dialogue about it is established among the hegemonic intellectuals in Chile and Montevideo. In attempting to trace it, one is again struck by the situational nature of reading and interpretation, and by the problems of historically reconstructing the contextual constraints which are in place in a particular reading. From among the early readers of *Facundo* I have selected one who addresses both issues in an intriguing way: Juan María Gutiérrez. A man with a clear sense of the need to promote the emergence of a "Poética americana" (to quote the title of an anthology he was compiling), Gutiérrez was the one Sarmiento turned to for a favorable review. The pragmatic and textual circumstances surrounding this review heighten our awareness of the inferential or speculative grounds on which historical understanding takes place, of the extent to which one tentatively considers filling gaps, and then does so with varying degrees of success. The result is a suggestive mix of adequately and inadequately explained events, and an inevitable coming to terms with the slippage between text and reading. Sarmiento sent to him the very first copy on July 24 with the following letter:

> Remito a usted el primer ejemplar del *Facundo* que ve la luz pública. Ha salido como una cosa infamemente tratada.

> "Quiere usted encargarse de analizarlo, por *El Mercurio*, y decir que es un librote estupendo, magnífico, celebérrimo?[32]

On July 27th *El Mercurio* brings out an unsigned review which is full of praise and admiration, and which gives the book credit for having brilliantly understood the underlying causes of the political turmoil in Argentina; for having been written with the conceptual brilliance of a philosopher and with the beauty of an artist. Palcos attributes this review to Demetrio Rodríguez Peña, on the grounds that he was the editor of the paper, and he calls it "la más franca y abiertamente favorable."[33] Verdevoye, for his part,

considers Palcos's attribution in the light of the letters exchanged between Sarmiento and Gutiérrez and suggests that the author might be Gutiérrez.[34] Antonio Pagés Larraya does not waver: he ascribes it to Gutiérrez without further consideration, and so have other critics.[35] Complicating matters is a letter written by Sarmiento to Gutiérrez on August 8 which expresses considerable dissatisfaction with the review written by him.

> Escribió usted su salutación editorial en *El Mercurio* y se la agradezco. Si no fuera periodista yo hubiera creído que la chanza era pesada; pero como soy del métier, comprendí que hacía usted con el *Facundo* lo que yo he hecho tantas veces con otras cosas peores. No vaya usted a tener la falta de gusto de entrar en explicaciones sobre este punto.[36]

Now, the piece published by *El Mercurio* on July 27 (only three days after the letter with which Sarmiento sent the first copy) could hardly have inspired the comments I have just read, because it is enthusiastic in every respect. Moreover, on August 22, while writing again to Gutiérrez about the book, Sarmiento alludes to *Facundo* as "mi Odisea, como se ha complacido en llamarla usted"[37] and there is no allusion to Homer's work in the review of July 27, nor are there any letters in which Gutiérrez suggests the comparison. At this point one is acutely conscious of the precarious contact established with the past. If it is eminently textual, it is also subject to the gaps which this textuality is fraught with: either Sarmiento's reading of the review which appeared on July 27 totally misconstrued its stance, or else somewhere in *El Mercurio* between the 24th of July (when Sarmiento sent the book to Gutiérrez) and the 8th of August (when he wrote to him in clear displeasure about the review) there is another review which is less favourable. Obviously, one must go back to the historical record in search for a text which might help construct a plausible explanation. Here again we are confronted with the inaccessibility of the past: all the Microfilm copies of *El Mercurio* available in the U.S. (at Sterling Library, the Library of Congress and Bancroft Library at Berkeley) have one big hiatus which extends between the 30th of June and the 18th of August. Until I get an answer to my inquiries in the Biblioteca Nacional de Chile, I am left with this inadequately explained gap in the reconstruction of *Facundo*'s reception which has an eloquence of its own. Was there another review or did Sarmiento misread the one of the 27th? Aside from the cautionary effect it has on the researcher, the situation I have been describing is part and parcel of the early readings of this text.[38]

Interestingly, the striking interpretive instability which characterizes *Facundo* does not derive exclusively from the conflicts among readers, but also from discrepancies which can be detected in the same reader, and which seem to stem from the different circumstances within which his acts of reading take place. Hence, interpretations can differ depending on whether they are framed by the private space of a letter or the public one of a newspaper. Gutiérrez himself, whatever his actual review may have been, voices strong reservations about *Facundo* contained in a letter written to Alberdi on August 6, 1845. He assures

Alberdi that "todo hombre sensato verá en él una carica-tura," and adds:

> Es este libro como las pinturas que de nuestra sociedad hacen a veces los viajeros por decir cosas raras: el Matadero, la mulata en intimidad con la niña, el cigarro en boca de la señora mayor. [. . .] La República Argentina no es charca de sangre: la civilización nuestra no es el progreso de las escuelas primarias de San Juan.[39]

Likewise, Echeverría, who wrote a very positive apprecia-tion of the book in the "Ojeada retrospectiva" which is part of the *Dogma socialista* ("los apuntes biográficos de Fr. Aldao y la vida de Juan Facundo Quiroga son en concepto nuestro lo más completo y original que haya salido de la pluma de los jóvenes proscriptos argenti-nos"),[40] expressed a different, angry reaction in a letter to Alberdi of June 12, 1850: "'¿Qué cosa ha escrito él que no sean cuentos y novelas según su propia confesión? "¿Dónde está en sus obras la fuerza de raciocinio y las concepciones profundas? Yo no veo en ellas más que lucubraciones fantásticas, descripciones y raudal de chá-chara infecunda."[41] Within the community of exiles, *Fa-cundo* was judged in very mixed ways; even an admiring reader like Alsina deauthorized the book by writing his painstaking fifty one notes in 1846, intending to, as he put it, "no [. . .] dejar pasar errores, [. . .] acerca de los hechos como acerca de los juicios."[42] Alsina's corrections deserve a separate study; for my purposes here suffice it to say that Sarmiento alluded to them in the edition of 1851 in a way which reveals the destabilizing effect they had on his own validity claims.

The "stories" I have entertained so far beg the question of how *Facundo* came to occupy a central position in the accepted Latin American canon. It is a story that this exploration of beginnings cannot complete, for it would take us into the early years of the twentieth century and the production of national identity myths which is asso-ciated with the "Centenario" celebrations. Nevertheless, the book's appearance, as it maps out a multi-dimension-al space in which a variety of writings blend and clash, prefigures the conflicts which characterize the history of its reception. In the last analysis, it is a process in which reading is revealed in all its problematic—yet produc-tive—dimensions.

NOTES

[1] "Mi defensa," in *Sarmiento en el destierro*, ed. Armando Donoso (Buenos Aires: M. Gleizer, 1927) 160.

[2] Michel Foucault, *The Archaeology of Knowledge*, trans. A. M. Sheri-dan Smith (New York: Harper Colophon Books, 1976) 25.

[3] Walter Benjamin, *Illuminations* (Glasgow: Fontana/Collins, 1970) 263.

[4] *La correspondencia de Sarmiento*, ed. Carlos A. Segreti (Córdoba, R. A.: Poder Ejecutivo de la Provincia de Córdoba, 1988) 154-5. His idiosyn-cratic spelling has been respected.

[5] *La correspondencia de Sarmiento*, 154.

[6] *La correspondencia de Sarmiento*, 103.

[7] *La correspondencia de Sarmiento*, 78.

[8] *La correspondencia de Sarmiento*, 80.

[9] *La correspondencia de Sarmiento*, 183.

[10] *La correspondencia de Sarmiento*, 184.

[11] Benedict Anderson, *Imagined Communities. Reflections on the Origin and Spread of Nationalism* (London: Verso, 1983).

[12] See *Image and Pilgrimage in Christian Culture* (New York: Columbia University Press, 1978), and "Social Dramas and Stories about Them," *Critical Inquiry*, 7, 1 (Autumn 1980): 141-68.

[13] Arthur Danto, *Analytical Philosophy of History* (London and Cam-bridge: Cambridge University Press, 1968) 84.

[14] "What Is an Author?" in *Textual Strategies*, ed. Josue Harari (Ithaca, N. Y.: Cornell University Press, 1979) 147.

[15] For a thorough exploration of this aspect see Elizabeth Garrels, "El *Facundo* como folletín," *Revista Iberoamericana* 143 (abril-junio 1988): 419-47.

[16] *La correspondencia de Sarmiento*, 50.

[17] *La correspondencia de Sarmiento*, 49.

[18] In *Facundo*, ed. Alberto Palcos (Buenos Aires: Ediciones Culturales Argentinas, 1962) 24-5.

[19] *El Mercurio* 30 July 1842.

[20] Domingo F. Sarmiento, *Obras completas* (Buenos Aires: Editorial Luz del Día, 1948), vol. VI, 159-160.

[21] Sarmiento, *Obras . . .* , vol. VI, 160.

[22] This is a revealing passage in the *Ortografía*, for it lists the names of the "sabios" who underpin Sarmiento's cognitive authority, and most of them appear in the epigraphs of the *Facundo*: a legitimizing device, obviously. Disparaging the "nulidad de la Academia de la lengua castel-lana," he poses the following rhetorical questions: "'¿Son filósofos que puedan compararse con los filósofos de las naciones que nos transmiten las ideas de que vivimos? "¿Son historiadores como Guizot, Thierry, Niebuhr, Michelet y toda la grande escuela histórica de nuestra época? "¿Son sabios como Arago o Cuvier, literatos como Villemain, gramáticos como la nueva escuela francesa, poetas como Hugo, Chateaubriand, o Lamartine?" (*Obras completas*, vol. 6, 6).

[23] *The Archaeology . . .*, 23.

[24] *Viajes* (Buenos Aires: Editorial Belgrano, 1981) 116. Quoted by E. Garrels, "El *Facundo* como folletín," 428.

[25] *El Siglo*, June 14, 1845. Quoted in *Ilustración Argentina*, August 1, 1849.

[26] *Archivo de Juan María Gutiérrez* (Buenos Aires: Congreso de la Nación Argentina, 1979) 13.

[27] *Archivo Gutiérrez*, 9.

[28] *La correspondencia de Sarmiento*, 89.

[29] *La correspondencia de Sarmiento*, 83.

[30] *La correspondencia de Sarmiento*, 97.

[31] *Archivo Gutiérrez*, 48-9.

[32] *La correspondencia de Sarmiento*, 82.

[33] In his critical edition of *Facundo. Civilización y barbarie* (La Plata, R. A.: Universidad Nacional de La Plata, 1938) 320.

[34] In *Domingo Faustino Sarmiento. Éducateur et publiciste (entre 1839 et 1852)* (Paris: Institut des Hautes Études de L'Amérique Latine, 1963) 428.

[35] In "La recepción de un texto sarmientino," in *Boletín de la Academia Argentina de Letras* XLIX (1984), 241.

[36] *La correspondencia de Sarmiento*, 85.

[37] *La correspondencia de Sarmiento*, 86.

[38] There is, unquestionably, a provisional element in all this which might well beg the question of its inclusion here. However, it is highly revealing of the problems of historical reconstruction, and of the process itself more than of the finished product. The temporality of reading is fraught with problems of textual transmission. For an enlightened discussion of them, see Susan Noakes, *Timely Reading. Between Exegesis and Interpretation* (Ithaca and London: Cornell University Press, 1988).

[39] In *Atlántida* X (1913): 161.

[40] *Dogma socialista* (Buenos Aires: La Torre de Babel, 1958) 76.

[41] In *Escritos póstumos de J. B. Alberdi* (Buenos Aires: Imprenta Alberto Monkes, 1897) vol. XV, 790. Quoted in Pagés Larraya, "La recepción . . . ," 245. That Alberdi should be the addressee of these two letters by Gutiérrez and Echeverría is no mere coincidence: he was the ideal reader for objections of this sort as Sarmiento's most formidable conceptual enemy. For more on this, see Adolfo Prieto, "*Las ciento y una*. El escritor como mito político," *Revista Iberoamericana* 143 (abril-junio 1988): 477-489, and my "The Wiles of Disputation: Alberdi Reads *Facundo*," forthcoming in the proceedings of a symposium in honor of Domingo F. Sarmiento held at the University of California at Berkeley in October 1988.

[42] In *Facundo. Civilización y barbarie*, ed. Alberto Palcos, 1938, 426.

FURTHER READING

Allen, Esther. "The Paradoxes of Admiration: Sarmiento, Tocqueville, and the United States," in *Annals of Scholarship*, Vol. 11, Nos. 1 & 2 (1996): 61-81.

> Compares Sarmiento's written documentation of his visit to the United States (*Recuerdos de Provincia*) with French writer Alex de Tocqueville's written account of his overall negative impression of the States (*Democracy in America*).

Henríquez-Ureña, Pedro. "Romanticism and Anarchy: 1830-1860." In *Literary Currents in Hispanic America*, pp. 112-36. New York: Russel & Russel, Inc., 1963.

> Explores Sarmiento's life and his contribution to Latin American literature.

Torrés-Ríoseco, Arturo. "The Romantic Upheaval in Spanish America." In *The Epic of Latin American Literature*, pp. 44-85. New York: Oxford University Press, 1942.

> Praises Sarmiento as "the great apostle of romanticism" and discusses the romantic aspects of his writings.

Carlos de Sigüenza y Góngora
1645–1700

Mexican novelist, poet, cosmologist, and mathematician.

INTRODUCTION

One of the most learned and influential scholars and writers to emerge from seventeenth-century Latin America was Carlos de Sigüenza y Góngora. Though he wrote prolifically, much of his work is known only through the mention of other writers of the period. While his scientific writings mark Sigüenza y Góngora as one of Latin America's earliest proponents of inquiry and argument, his literary efforts are less radiant because of his lack of originality and his imitation of the baroque writers who preceeded him. His most memorable work is the short picaresque novel, *Infortunios de Alonso Ramírez* (1690; *The Misadventures of Alonso Ramírez*).

Sigüenza y Góngora was born in Mexico City on August 14, 1645, the eldest son of six children. His father, Carlos de Sigüenza, had been a tutor of Prince Baltasár Carlos in the royal household at Madrid, and his mother was a native of Seville and related to the famous Spanish poet Luis de Góngora from which the son acquired the latter part of his surname. The boy entered the Jesuit college at Tepotzolán as a novitiate when he was fifteen and excelled in philosophy, literature, and theology. He stayed seven years and in 1667, was expelled for "certain late-night escapades." Though he attempted several times to be readmitted into the Jesuit Order, he was unsuccessful until shortly before he died. His expulsion was a source of anguish for Sigüenza y Góngora, but he continued theological study at the Royal University of Mexico and developed an interest in mathematics. When he was twenty-seven he won the competition for Chair of Mathematics and Astrology at the same university. His two published *lunarios* (almanacs) were proof of his qualifications. It seems that Sigüenza y Góngora neglected his teaching, probably because of his growing fame, his dislike of bureaucracy, and his distaste for astrology, for which he was censored by the Inquisition. He was invited to the court of Louis XIV but couldn't go because his university forbade him. His work earned him the position of Royal Cosmographer of New Spain, a title given him by the king, though he said he scorned such titles "which sound like a great deal and are worth little." Sigüenza y Góngora's mathematical knowledge was more practical than theoretical and he applied it to the design of fortifications, canals, and other engineering projects. Astronomy was also a major interest and one which made his reputation, particularly in his *Manifesto filosófico contra los cometas* (1681; *Philosophical Manifesto Against Comets*) in which he refuted the notion that comets were tragic omens. When his work was questioned he responded with *El belerofonte matemático* (*The Mathematical Bellero-phon*) where he attempts to prove that comets are natural events, not divine signs, and that science is superior to astrology. His last and most famous work on the subject, *Libra astonómica y filosófica* (1690; *Treatise on Astronomy and Philosophy*), was the result of an attack by a Catholic priest in which Sigüenza y Góngora asserted the superiority of science in the Cartesian tradition over theology in the Christian tradition, particularly in deference to the analysis of natural phenomena. In 1693, Sigüenza y Góngora retired from the University of Mexico, apparently distressed at the deaths of several close friends and relatives, and his sufferings from a kidney stone. On August 22, 1700 he died in Mexico City and left a will requesting his body be autopsied to discover the location of the kidney stone. This knowledge, he hoped, could be used in future treatments of the painful ailment.

Sigüenza y Góngora's poetry went through various stages that reflect his status on various issues, both spiritual and political. An early work, *Primavera indiana* (1668; *Indian Spring*) is a poem in praise of the Virgin of Guadalupe and reflects his current affectation with the Catholic church. Another poem, *Glorias de Querétaro* (*Glories of Querétaro*) was published in 1680, the same year he was appointed Royal Cosmographer. This poem was also an encomium to the Virgin of Guadalupe, one in which the poet describes the dedication ceremonies of a church in the city of Querétaro erected in her honor. He also published the *Panegírico con que la muy noble e imperial ciudad de México aplaudió . . . al Marqués de la Laguna* (1680; *Panegyric with which the Very Noble and Imperial City of Mexico Applauded . . . the Marquis of the Laguna*), a poem of seventeen *ottava rima* stanzas recited by an allegorical figure on the occasion of the viceregal Marquis entering Mexico City. He also published a prose work integrating Mexico's Indian past with its Spanish colonial present, the *Teatro de virtudes políticas que constituten a un príncipe* (1680; *Theater of the Political Virtues that make a Prince*). Sigüenza y Góngora's most important literary work, *Infortunios de Alonso Ramírez*, is a narrative based on the struggles of a shipwrecked Puerto Rican who visited Sigüenza y Góngora in Mexico in 1690. The protagonist, Ramírez, tells of ocean adventures and shipwreck on the coast of Mexico. Ramírez is not the usual picaresque figure living by his wits at cost to others, but is, instead, honest and generous, hard-working and devoutly Catholic. The author's unique contribution to the picaresque is his extensive knowledge of geography, especially of Asia and America. He also employs a common characteristic of the picaresque—social criticism—and uses it to highlight the Mexicans' lack of charity, hypocrisy, and egregious ambitions. Another well-known work of Sigüenza y Góngora is *Alboroto y motín de los indios de Mexico del 8 de junio de 1692* (1932; *Riot and Revolt of the Indians of*

Mexico City, June 8, 1692), a long letter to his friend, Admiral Andrés de Pez. The letter concerns a riot caused by Indian suffering over a poor wheat harvest and the government's indifference. The revolt broke out in the marketplace and spread to the principal square of the capital. Small businesses were burned and the fire reached city hall. Sigüenza y Góngora witnessed the revolt and bravely helped save precious documents and paintings from the conflagration. In this letter, Sigüenza y Góngora's racism emerges, despite an interest in pre-Columbian indigenous cultures, as he represents the Indians as ungrateful complainers. In later letters, he recommends that Indians be kept far away from the center of the city and confined to certain areas. After this publication, Sigüenza y Góngora embarked for the northern littoral of the Gulf of Mexico toward Pensacola Bay to prepare accurate maps and reports of the terrain in order to establish a colony. His next publication, *Mercurio volante* (1693; *Flying Mercurio*) is an account of the peaceful reconquest of the Indians in the region known as New Mexico.

As a scientist, Sigüenza y Góngora contributed to Enlightenment thought, especially in his assertion that comets were natural phenomena and in his criticism of the astrology of his day. As a mapmaker, he provided accurate mappings of various rivers and bays. As a historian, he documented the re-conquering of New Mexico and the revolt of Indians in Mexico City. As a novelist, he wrote an important work, *Infortunios de Alonso Ramírez,* for the history of picaresque fiction. Few figures have made simultaneous impact on the worlds of both science and literature; Sigüenza y Góngora was able to do so.

PRINCIPAL WORKS

Primavera indiana, poema sacro-histórico, idea de María Santísima de Guadalupe (poetry) 1668

Glorias de Querétaro en la nueva congregación eclesiástica de María Santísima de Guadalupe (poetry) 1680

Panegírico con que la muy noble e imperial ciudad de México aplaudió . . . al Marqués de la Laguna (poetry) 1680

Teatro de virtudes políticas que constituten a un príncipe (history) 1680

Manifiesto filosófico contra los cometas, despojados del imperio que tenían sobre los tímidos (pamphlet) 1681

Triunfo parténico que en glorias de María Santísima, inmaculadamente concebida, celebró la Pontificia, Imperial y Regia Academia Mexicana (poetry and chronicle) 1683

Paraíso occidental, plantado y cultivado . . . en su magnífico Real Convento de Jesús María de México (history and biography) 1684

Infortunios de Alonso Ramírez (chronicle) 1690

Libra astronómica y filosófica (essay) 1690

Relación de lo sucedido a la Armada de Barlovento a

fines del año pasado y principios de este de 1691 (history) 1691

Trofeo de la justicia española en el castigo de la alevosía francesa (history) 1691

Mercurio volante, con la noticia de la recuperación de las provincias del Nuevo México (chronicle) 1693

Oriental planeta evangélico, epopeya sacro-panegírico al Apóstol grande de las Indias (poetry) 1700

Alboroto y motín de los indios de México del 8 de junio de 1692 (essays) 1932

Obras históricas (essays) 1944

Noticia cronológica de los reyes, emperadores, gobernadores, presidentes y virreyes de ésta nobilísima ciudad de México (essays) 1948

Informe sobre el Castillo de San Juan de Ulúa, 31 de diciembre de 1695 (essays) 1958

Libra astronómica y filosófica (essays) 1959

Documentos inéditos de don Carlos de Sigüenza y Góngora (essays) 1963

El belerofonte matemático [*The Mathematical Bellerophon*] (mathematics)

CRITICISM

Julie Greer Johnson (essay date 1981)

SOURCE: "Picaresque Elements in Carlos Sigüenza y Góngora's *Los Infortunios de Alonso Ramírez*," in *Hispania*, Vol. 64, No. 1, March, 1981, pp. 60-7.

[*In this essay, Johnson attributes the success and endurance of* Les Infortunios de Alonso Ramírez *to Sigüenza y Góngora's skillful fusion of history, adventure, and literary technique.*]

The intellectual pre-eminence of don Carlos Sigüenza y Góngora illuminates the entire spectrum of scholarship in Spanish colonial America and contrasts sharply with the oppression and obscurantism prevalent in seventeenth-century New Spain. As an antiquarian, poet, cosmographer, mathematician, and historian, this celebrated Mexican *savant* became known throughout the New World and Europe for his outstanding accomplishments as an invitation to join the dazzling court of Louis XIV of France attests. Although he declined this most auspicious request in order to become the Royal Cosmographer of Charles II, he decided to remain in the viceregal capital, and he, together with Sor Juana Inés de la Cruz, graced the cultural life of their native land for nearly half a century.[1]

While Sigüenza delved into many disciplines during his lifetime of study, his greatest and most enduring contribution to knowledge rests upon his remarkable ability as an historian. Firmly believing that the examination of history provided a sound basis for the future growth and development of mankind, this leading academician wrote many contemporary and pre-Columbian historical accounts on secular and religious themes. His most popular work, *Los infortunios de Alonso Ramírez*, owes much of its success to its literary qualities.[2]

Early in the year 1690, the Viceroy of New Spain, the Count of Galve, received at his court a Puerto Rican youth named Alonso Ramírez who had just returned from a voyage around the world. Amazed and shaken by the young man's account of his early life in the colonies and his heart-rending story of the mistreatment he endured at the hands of English pirates, the Viceroy sent him to Sigüenza, his official court chronicler who was in ill health at the time, with the hope that Alonso's awesome adventures might entertain his good friend. This distinguished member of the Viceroy's retinue expressed a personal interest in the young fellow and undertook to assist him to obtain money and a position with the Royal Fleet in the Gulf of Mexico.

On hearing the touching story of Alonso Ramírez, Sigüenza y Góngora quickly recognized the opportunity to capture effectively a moment in Spanish colonial history and he did so with the flare of a good writer. His account of an innocent boy who leaves home to make his own way in the world emulates one of the most popular forms of Spanish literature, the picaresque novel. In essence, this innovative prose fiction reflects the life and times of one who remains on the periphery of society but who displays a dauntless determination to survive and an instinctive drive to overcome his present circumstances and better his lot.[3]

Alonso's personal nature and his haphazard endeavors which were reminiscent of the life of the *pícaro,* especially that of Alemán's Guzmán de Alfarache, inspired Sigüenza to write **Los infortunios**.[4] Although the author's finished composition is basically an historical account, it is a striking example of the efficacious intertwining of history with literary technique prevalent in the picaresque genre.[5] The result of this delicate balance between historical documentation and creative form not only confirms Sigüenza's outstanding ability as an historian but distinguishes him as a gifted storyteller as well. The novelistic perspective which he employs enhances immeasurably the interest of this historical document and contributes substantially to its commendable stature as a literary work. Conclusive evidence linking Sigüenza's work to picaresque literature in general, and to Alemán's masterpiece in particular, may be found throughout his exciting account and may readily be seen in its main character, setting, structure, and style.

According to Sigüenza y Góngora's portrayal, Alonso Ramírez, like such Spanish literary models as Lazarillo, Pablos, and Guzmán,[6] is an anti-hero. He is a common boy vested with average abilities whose stalwart resolution to survive and courageous endurance to face the challenges of his daily life are unquestionably admirable and ultimately noteworthy. Sigüenza's young protagonist spends his uneventful childhood in the city of San Juan, Puerto Rico, a neglected stepping stone to more lucrative ports of call. Although Alonso seems to regard his parents with no particular affection, he does provide several significant details about his humble origins. His father, Lucas de Villanueva, is probably a native Andalusian, and his mother Ana Ramírez is a citizen of San Juan. In a respectful

tone touched perhaps with some bitterness, he mentions that his family had given him the only gift that poor people can give to their children which is "consejos para inclinar á la virtud" (Sigüenza, p. 9).

Although only a small portion of the narrative of the entire work is devoted to Alonso's early years, it is evident from several allusions to the abject poverty of the island and the gnawing hunger that plagued him continually that his adverse experiences and destitute surroundings made an indelible impression on such a tender child. It was probably a profound revulsion against this shocking ambience and his own inner feelings of inferiority that instilled in him a compulsive drive not only to subsist but to succeed in life as well.

In order to escape the ignominy of this privation, he leaves his parents and his island home to seek his fortune and enlists as a page on a sailing vessel bound for Cuba. He expresses some reservations about his destiny through the use of a pun, as this excerpt conveys:

> Valime de la ocasion, que me ofreció para esto vna Urqueta del Capitan *Iuan del Corcho* que salia de aquel Puerto para el de la *Habana* en que corriendo el año de 1675 y siendo menos de trece los de mi edad me recibieron por paje. No me pareció trabajosa la ocupacion considerandome en libertad, y sin la pension de cortar madera; pero confiesso, que tal vez presagiando lo por venir dudaba si podria prometerme algo que fuesse bueno, haviendome valido de vn corcho para principiar mi fortuna: Mas quien podrà negarme, que dudè bien advirtiendo consiguientes mis sucesos á aquel principio? (Sigüenza, p. 10)

As is all too often true, the abandonment of family and friends and a change of locality do not necessarily insure a modification in one's luck, and this would prove to be Alonso's unfortunate case. When he arrives in New Spain, he quickly discovers this sad truth since the bleak economic conditions prevalent in Puerto Rico exist throughout the Spanish Indies. His pathetic admission that "en la demora de seis meses que alli perdi experimentè mayor hambre que en Puerto-Rico" is a heart-breaking revelation for such a youth (Sigüenza, p. 11). With hopes of an easier, more plentiful existence cruelly dashed, his earlier positive outlook toward the prospects for employment and prosperity soon turns to pessimism and cynicism. As the son of a carpenter, Alonso had received some training in this trade, but he had no intention of engaging in such a laborious pursuit. Although his predilection for comfort and convenience would be paramount to his initial considerations of work, the lack of hiring and sheer hunger drove him aimlessly, almost hopelessly, from place to place.

After being in New Spain for a number of years, Alonso marries a young woman who dies in childbirth during their first year of marriage. Because of his roving nature and his defensive aloofness, Alonso only admits to feeling love in this particular instance. Otherwise it appears to be a rather remote emotion. At the end of a long series of degrading setbacks, he becomes exasperated with his deprived status and comes to a very crucial decision: "Desesperè entonces de poder ser algo, y hallándome en el Tribunal de mi propia conciencia no solo acusado, sino convencido de inutil, quise darme por pena de este delito, la que se da en Mexico à los que son delinquentes, que es embiarlos desterrados â las Philipinas" (Sigüenza, p. 15).

If his lack of productivity and growing indigence had caused despondency, his ill-fated seizure by English pirates soon after his arrival in the Orient only intensified it. However, it is through this experience that he learns to accept the burdensome responsibilities of manhood and to shun any semblance of resignation or defeat. While he abides the overbearance of his captors, he harbors much resentment toward them not only for their abominable conduct but for their slurs on his national origin as well. The following quotation is a defensive yet spirited reply to the privateers who recognize his capabilities and want him to join their ranks:

> Propusieronme entonces como ya otras vezes me la hauian dicho; el que jurase de acompañarlos siempre, y me darian armas. Agradeciles la merced, y haziendo reflexa â las obligaciones con que naci, les respondi con afectada humildad, el que mas me acomodaba â servirlos à ellos que â pelear con otros, por ser grande el temor que les tenia a las valas, tratandome de Español cobarde y gallina, y por esso indigno de estar en su compañia, que me honrara y valiera mucho, no me instaron mas. (Sigüenza, p. 38).

By the time Alonso is emancipated from the custody of these foreign agents and reaches *terra firma*, he is a self-confident adult who has won the respect of his fellowmen. He is cognizant of the quirks of fortune and is resolved to conduct his life in a prudent manner. The narrative closes on an exceedingly optimistic note as his prospects for a better life are clearly in the offing.

Just as the appearance of the *pícaro* in sixteenth- and seventeenth- century Spanish literature reflects the declining and decadent social and economic conditions of the country, so *Los infortunios de Alonso Ramírez* betrays a similar plight in the Spanish Indies. With skill and understanding, Sigüenza undertakes to portray accurately the turbulent years of a great empire which compose the colorful and lively backdrop for his protagonist's tale of woe. Although he focuses mainly upon the seamy side of life, a dominant feature of works written in the picaresque vein, by revealing some of the ugly aspects of existence in the colonies, he uses this particular perspective to dispel existing myths concerning Spain's wealth and power. It is by probing extensively the fascinating historical setting that Sigënza scrutinizes several aspects of social, economic, and political importance and exposes the discrepancy between appearances and reality.

Beginning in the sixteenth century and continuing through the next, the strains of Spain's imperialistic policies had become too great a burden for her to bear, and unquestionably reverberations of disastrous mismanagement were felt in outlying areas of the realm. In a final effort to bolster her own sagging economy, Spain undertook to enforce strict compliance with mercantilistic principles, thus dooming the colonies to an even worse fate than the mother country. Contrary to widely circulated rumors in Spain, the territories in the New World had ceased to offer aspiring young adventurers a chance to make their fortunes. A glorious era in Spanish history was coming to an inevitable close. Although Sigüenza gives little detailed information concerning the colonial economy, poverty looms everywhere in his narrative, and starvation constantly threatens the young Ramírez. In the colonies as well as in Spain, recurrent economic crises together with an inherent dislike of manual labor made vagabondage an ever present fact of life. Transients of all types roamed about Spain and her possessions ultimately signaling the further weakening of the Spanish empire.[7]

With the advent of the seventeenth century, Spain had to face a new and more challenging threat to her dominions in the New World. Latecomer nations, such as England, France, and the Netherlands sought to establish themselves there at the expense of the Spaniards. Despite financial reverses and political setbacks, Spain still fancied herself as the supreme power in the New World and eminent ruler of the seas as well. Alonso confirms the fact that the oceans were teeming with foreign vessels and that outlawing privateers were encroaching upon Spanish territory, looting and burning the belongings of the inhabitants, and seizing Spanish subjects. Spanish prestige was at increasingly low ebb, and colonists found themselves ill equipped to ward off enterprising and ruthless buccaneers.[8] After Alonso was abducted from his defenseless supply launch, he was appalled to see how well armed the English were and to hear them deride and jeer at his countrymen.

While revealing surprising weaknesses in the Spanish imperial structure, Sigüenza also unmasks the bold and repugnant nature of Spain's rivals. Because of the infamous Black Legend maliciously propagated by Spain's enemies, European public opinion had branded her as the cruelest, most unprincipled nation in the world.[9] This false impression, as well, is shattered by Sigüenza who continually narrates the heinous crimes of Spain's adversaries. One episode in which he recounts a cannibalistic celebration among Alonso's captors is an especially good example of this (Sigüenza, p. 29), and scenes of murder, torture, robbery, and destruction of property which dominate the narration of the protagonist's captivity add elements of fear and suspense to his story.

But Sigüenza's descriptions are not always grim and disturbing. On several occasions he depicts familiar American landmarks which stand like proud remnants of a once powerful empire and represent the diminishing vestiges of an opulent society. In his compendium of Alonso's childhood, he refers to the impressive, old fortifications around the port of San Juan, and he exalts the grandeur of the city of Mexico. Sigüenza has also captured the spirit of an era in which sea travel was critical to a nation's survival and scientific developments in this area were exceedingly vital. Because many of Alonso's experiences take place at sea, the narrative contains navigational information and cartographic references.

Los infortunios de Alonso Ramírez, like the classic representatives of the picaresque genre, *Lazarillo de Tormes, Guzmán de Alfarache*, and *El Buscón*, is a loosely constructed account presented in autobiographical form. After an introductory statement of purpose,[10] the protagonist embarks upon a chronological narrative of the events of his childhood, adolescence, and manhood. The unity of these separate entities is provided by the presence of the protagonist himself, and the composition of the work is deliberately left open, ostensibly to continue the main character's adventures at some future date.

While the structure of Sigüenza's account bears a certain resemblance to the Spanish picaresque works produced during the Golden Age, its numerous parallels with one in particular, *Guzmán de Alfarache*, are quite striking. These points of comparison may be found not only in some of the specific details of the lives of the two protagonists but in the duplication of select episodes as well.

Both Guzmán and Alonso preface a recapitulation of their respective adventures by divulging their family backgrounds and by alluding to the unpropitious circumstances of their departures from home. Poverty is a crucial factor in their decisions, and the two boys strike out on their own determined not only to survive but to encounter a better life as well. The following excerpt taken from a recounting of Alonso's childhood reveals the penury suffered by his parents and his unsuccessful apprenticeship with his father:

> Entre los que esta [pobreza] havia tomado muy â su cargo fueron mis Padres, y assi era fuerza que huviera sido porque no lo merecian sus procederes: pero ya es pension de las Indias el que assi sea. . . . Era mi Padre Carpintero de ribera, y impusome (en quanto permitia la edad) al proprio exercicio, pero reconociedo no ser continua la fabrica, y temiendome no vivir siempre, por esta causa, con las incomodidades, que aunque muchacho me hazian fuerza, determinè hurtarle el cuerpo á mi misma Patria para buscar en las agenas mas cõveniencia. (Sigüenza, p. 9)

Guzmán endures similar conditions in his native Seville as he sees family possessions dwindle away to buy the bare necessities of life: "Como quedé niño de poco entendimiento, no sentí su falta [la del padre]; aunque ya tenía de doce años adelante. Y no embargante que venimos en pobreza, la casa estaba con alhajas, de que tuvimos que vender para comer algunos días" (Alemán, I, i, 2, pp. 96-97). In the preceding quotation Guzmán mentions that he was twelve years old when his family fell upon hard times. Curiously enough, he and Alonso are exactly that same age when they go forth to seek their fortunes.

Just as Alonso's conclusion to leave Puerto Rico is marked by practicality, so a similar verdict is evoked by Guzmán's logical reasoning:

> El mejor medio que hallé fué probar la mano para salir de miseria, dejando mi madre y tierra. Hícelo así; y para no ser conocido no me quise valer del apellido de mi padre; púseme el Guzmán de mi madre, y Alfarache de

la heredad adonde tuve mi principio. Con esto salí a ver mundo, peregrinando por él, encomendándome a Dios y buenas gentes en quien hice confianza. (Alemán, I, i, 2, p. 101)

Because of his father's moral turpitude, Guzmán sought to detach himself from such disgrace by using his mother's maiden name. Alonso, likewise, is known by his mother's surname, although his reason for this change is never given.

The early upbringing and environment of these two juveniles bore a profound stigma for them, and as a result they sought to be rid of their all too familiar surroundings and escape to another country. Alonso naïvely contemplates the opportunities that await him in New Spain, and Guzmán seeks to elude parental opprobrium by traveling to Italy. The two undertake sea voyages, and both become the servants of captains to secure their passage.

As a means of obtaining a suitable position with celerity, Alonso and Guzmán contact relatives in their newly adopted countries. Although Alonso calls on his maternal relations, and Guzmán visits those on his father's side, both have extremely negative experiences. In the following passage Alonso learns that needy relatives are denied by the more affluent ones:

> El motivo que tube para salir de Mexico à la Ciudad de *Huaxaca* fue la noticia de que assistia en ella con el titulo, y exercicio honroso de Regidor D. Luis Ramirez en quien por parentesco, que con mi Madre tiene, afiancè, ya que no ascesos desproporcionados á los funda-mentos tales quales en que estrivaran; por lo menos alguna mano para subir vn poco: pero consegui despues de vn viage de ocheta leguas el que negandome con muy malas palabras el parentesco, tuviesse necessidad de valerme de los estraños por no poder sufrir despegos sensibilissimos por no esperados. . . . (Sigüenza, p. 12)[11]

Guzmán as well encounters a reception from his kinsmen analogous to that of Alonso and as the succeeding excerpt attests, he is reviled openly by them:

> Luego, pues, que dejé a mi amo el capitán, con todos mis harrapos y remiendos, hecho un espantajo de higuera, quise hacerme de los godos, emparentando con la nobleza de aquella ciudad, publicándome por quién era; y preguntando por la de mi padre, causó en ellos tanto enfado, que me aborrecieron de muerte. (Alemán, I, iii, 1, pp. 168-69)

In their quest for economic self-sufficiency, both youths travel widely and enter into the service of numerous masters. For seven years after leaving Puerto Rico and before departing for the Orient, Alonso's wanderings take him throughout the Viceroyalty of New Spain. During his meandering from Puebla de los Angeles to Mexico City and down to Guatemala, he is retained by at least six employers and at various times works as a carpenter, a page, a muleteer, a traveling salesman, an apprentice to an architect, and an aid to a gentleman named Cristóbal Medina.[12]

Throughout the travels of these two young protagonists, hunger is an important motivating force in their lives. In fact, as they journey from place to place, their immediate necessities seem to eclipse any recognition of the beauty of their environs. However, on one occasion, in each case, the overwhelming magnificence of a major cultural center, one in the New World, the other in Europe, receives their unending praise. On entering Mexico City, Alonso is awed and elated to find that the widely circulating rumors of its greatness are not unfounded, and Guzmán experiences the same sensations during his stay in Florence and expresses almost identical impressions of that great city.

After being out in the world for some time, both Alonso and Guzmán decide to marry. While the nature of their conjugal relationships is entirely different, their marriages are terminated abruptly by the death of their spouses after only a brief period of matrimony.

As both individuals find themselves down on their luck, Alonso reviews his situation carefully and sentences himself to be banished to the Philippines. Guzmán, on the other hand, accused and convicted of committing a crime, receives a very real sentence and is condemned to the galleys for life. While Alonso's self-imposed exile does not mean immediate confinement, it does eventually lead to his seizure by English corsairs. During the time that both Alonso and Guzmán, now men, spend as prisoners, they are both held captive on sailing vessels. Throughout their respective voyages, each protagonist experiences physical restraints of one sort or another, is betrayed by friends, and becomes involved in mutinies. As a result of their knowledge of these conspiracies on shipboard, both Alonso and Guzmán divulge the names of the participants as well as their plans to the proper authorities. This affirmation of loyalty, together with their previously established associations with certain officers in charge, earns them their freedom.

With the announcement of a pardon for Guzmán, Part II of Alemán's work comes to a close; however, for Alonso, set adrift in the Caribbean Sea, the series of tribulations is not yet over. From this point until his arrival back in the capital, he goes on to relate additional encounters and ordeals which are surprisingly reminiscent of earlier occurrences in the *Guzmán*. Here, however, the correlation is merely suggestive rather than explicit.

As is characteristic of human nature, it is a time of crisis that elicits a reaffirmation of faith, and both protagonists ascribe their very survival on several occasions to divine protection. The news of the release of Alonso and his companions is hailed by them with thankfulness and jubilation. Alonso, himself, attributes his personal salvation to his undying devotion to the Patron Saint of Mexico, as a small memento of hers was a source of great consolation to him. After surviving a devastating storm on his way home from Italy, Guzmán makes a solemn pledge to the Holy Matriarch of Seville whose timely intervention, he believes, delivered him from the throes of destruction.

While both instances represent isolated religious acts, respect and reverence for the divine is a constant factor in both *Los infortunios* and the *Guzmán*. The two protagonists are portrayed attending masses, both claim to have witnessed miracles, and both implore God or the Virgin to aid them with considerable frequency.

The storm previously referred to was quite a terrifying experience for Guzmán because by this time the guilt of having led a sinful life was weighing heavily upon his conscience. The following excerpt from his narration discloses a sober judgment on the part of the youthful main character: "venimos con bonanza hasta España, que no poco la tuve deseada, sin ferros, artillería, remos, postizas ni arrombadas. Porque todo fué a la mar y quedé yo vivo: que fuera más justo perecer en ella" (Alemán, II, ii, 9, p. 169).

Although this storm occurs before Guzmán's imprisonment, his American counterpart is caught in a raging tempest after his liberation from the English. In a desperate effort to save his fellow passengers, he risks his life by diving into the turbulent waters but manages to reach the shore safely. From the following quote it is clear that he feels a certain loathing for his miserable life: "Cónsiderando el peligro en la dilacion, haziendo fervorosos actos de contricion, y queriedo merecerle á Dios su misericordia sacrificandole mi vida por la de aquellos Pobres, ciñendome vn cabo delgado, para que lo fuesen largando me arrojé al agua" (Sigüenza, p. 58).

With the passage of the storm, Alonso and his crew reach the shores of the Yucatan Peninsula and begin their trek inland. After many trials and the loss of several of his comrades, they arrive at the town of Tejozuco where they are aided by the parish priest. Alonso tells of the beneficence of this man of the cloth and recounts his indebtedness to him. His account is suggestive of Guzmán's fortuitous encounter with a kind, charitable churchman while visiting the city of Rome. Because of the prelate's magnanimity, the young *pícaro* becomes a mischievous, overindulged servant in his household.

Before Alonso and the other survivors were freed from the brutal abuse of the English, their jailors had loaded their small craft with certain items that they had pillaged in the Orient. These commodities, of far greater worth in New Spain, aroused the greed of several parties. One example of their covetousness concerns the desires of a corrupt local *alcalde* to confiscate the unfortunate group's property, which in reality represented small recompense for their extreme hardships. On a number of occasions Guzmán, as well, confronted this same problem of the venality of certain officials. It was probably a matter of some concern to Alemán, as his criticism of these avaricious public servants is frequent and lengthy.[13]

Undoubtedly the most humorous episode of *Los infortunios*, which incidentally follows this same basic theme, involves the efforts of a purported friend of Alonso to deprive him of his slave, Pedro, by disclosing some alarming rumors. But, Alonso, now a man of experience, quickly prevents his feigned acquaintance's attempt to bilk him.

While Guzmán's expertise at executing clever tricks is well documented, he himself is subjected many times to chicanery of one type or another. However, as these incidents occur early in his life, he is deceived by such knavery.[14] Although similarities between these two works are numerous, Sigüenza's manner of presentation of these common elements is quite different.

Unlike the works of the picaresque genre previously mentioned, *Los infortunios de Alonso Ramírez* is the documentary record of historical fact. Its content, therefore, by its very nature, requires the clear, concise exposition that Sigüenza has accorded it to maintain the accuracy of his report. However, his intimate view of his protagonist's life and his informal manner of expression reflect the youthful vantage point from which he narrates his brief account and exude a human warmth designed to appeal to the sensitivity of his readers as well as to entertain them. Although the Baroque influence is visible in several passages, the general precision and clarity of Sigüenza's narration, together with the inclusion of scientific data, portend the writings characteristic of the Enlightenment in Spanish America.

Sigüenza's enthralling adventure story of an errant Puerto Rican youth serves as excellent testimony to his well-deserved reputation for being one of the best prose writers of the colonial period and provides a vital link between Spanish literary tradition and early Spanish American literature. While the extent of Sigüenza's knowledge of the entire gamut of picaresque writings remains undetermined, it is evident that he was well acquainted with *Guzmán de Alfarache* and that it influenced him to some degree in his literary rendering of the events of Alonso's life as well as the formulation of his personality. Sigüenza's clever adaptation of certain picaresque elements for his historical presentation proves the effectiveness of such a combination and serves as a forerunner of Spanish America's first novel and totally picaresque work, *El Periquillo Sarniento* by José Joaquín Fernández de Lizardi, published over a century after Sigüenza's pioneering creation.[15]

NOTES

[1] Irving A. Leonard, *Don Carlos Sigüenza y Góngora, a Mexican Savant of the Seventeenth Century* (Berkeley: University of California Press, 1929), p. 2.

[2] Carlos de Sigüenza y Góngora, *Infortvnios qve Alonso Ramírez natural de la Civdad de S. Juan de Pverto Rico padeció assi en poder de Ingleses Piratas que lo apresaron en las Islas Philipinas como navegando por si solo, y sin derrota, hasta varar en la Costa de Iucatan: Consiguiendo por este medio dar vuelta al Mundo* (México: Los herederos de la viuda de Bernardo Calderón, 1690), p. 84. The pagination is mine beginning with the title page.

[3] As decrees dating back to the time of Ferdinand and Isabella attest, works of pure fiction were officially banned from the Spanish territories shortly after the discovery of America to protect the impressionable Indians at a crucial point in their assimilation into the Spanish empire; however, books containing imaginative prose were clearly in evidence

in the colonies. The first conclusive proof that we have of the arrival of a picaresque novel to the New World is provided by a number of ship manifests preserved from the early part of the seventeenth century. In the year 1600 for example few of these listings pertaining to cargoes of books excluded these exceedingly popular works. Although records of consignments of books bound for the Spanish Indies are incomplete, extant documents corroborate the introduction, in quantity, of the first part of Alemán's masterpiece in the year 1600 and the arrival of Mateo Luján de Sayavedra's spurious continuation of the *Guzmán* as well as the true sequel in subsequent years. Even the appearance of the *Quijote,* a popular work in its own right among colonial readers, did not diminish the continual flow of picaresque literature to New Spain and Peru or detract from its apparent heyday there. Irving A. Leonard, "*Guzmán de Alfarache* in the Lima Book Trade, 1613," *Hispanic Review,* XI (1943), pp. 210-20.

[4] Mateo Alemán, *Guzmán de Alfarache,* introduction by Samuel Gili y Gaya, 5 volumes, (Madrid: Espasa-Calpe, S.A., 1962, 1955, 1961, 1953, 1956).

[5] Other important historical accounts of the colonial period which contain novelistic elements are: *Historia verdadera de la conquista de la Nueva España* by Bernal Díaz del Castillo, *Comentarios reales de los Incas* by the Inca, Garcilaso de la Vega, and *Cautiverio feliz* by Francisco Núñez de Pineda y Bascuñán.

[6] *Lazarillo de Tormes,* introduction by Joseph Virgil Ricapito, (Madrid: Cátedra, 1976); Francisco Quevedo y Villegas, *La vida del Buscón llamado don Pablos,* edición crítica por Fernando Lázaro Carreter, (Salamanca: Universidad de Salamanca, 1965).

[7] John Lynch, *Spain under the Hapsburgs,* Volume I, *Empire and Absolutism 1516-1598* (New York: Oxford University Press, 1964), pp. 345-48; 346, Volume II, *Spain and America 1598-1700* (Oxford: Basil Blackwell, 1969), pp. 194-95. Alonso refers to the fact that it was customary for delinquents to be shipped to the Philippines (Sigüenza, p. 15). The existence of groups of idle individuals is noted in both the *Guzmán* (I, iii, 3-6) and *El Buscón* (pp. 232-36).

[8] C. H. Haring, *The Buccaneers in the West Indies in the XVII Century* (London: Methuen and Co. Ltd., 1910), pp. 232-72. It is evident from an expedition which Sigüenza undertook to Pensacola Bay in 1693 that he was concerned about the vulnerability of Spanish territories to French incursions. Leonard, *Don Carlos Sigüenza y Góngora,* pp. 139, 146.

[9] The Black Legend grew out of exaggerated reports of atrocities committed by the Spaniards during the Conquest and was highly publicized by Bartolomé de Las Casas during his humanitarian campaign for the protection of the Indians.

[10] *Los infortunios de Alonso Ramírez* shares with other picaresque works the principal aim of offering entertainment to the reading public. However, the alleged didactic purpose delineated by Lazarillo, Pablos, and Guzmán is notably absent from Alonso's sensitive recollection as he hopes to solicit the sympathy of his reader, thus mitigating to some degree the grievous memories of his journey.

[11] The appearance of Alonso's notable relation in *Los infortunios* may also have personal significance. Sigüenza was a relative of the famous Spanish poet Luis de Góngora y Argote (1561-1627). His admiration for this illustrious writer is seen in his struggling at-

tempts to imitate Góngora's florid poetic style. Leonard, *Don Carlos Sigüenza y Góngora*, p. 4.

[12] Alonso mentions that he becomes a muleteer but does not disclose the name of his master. It would seem reasonable, however, to assume that there was one, as he could not have afforded his own team of mules. Alonso also serves Captain Bel, although involuntarily, when he is taken captive by the English. Considering his employment on these two occasions as well as those just cited, Alonso served a total of eight masters, precisely the number reported by Guzmán and Lazarillo.

[13] Two examples of such abuse in the *Guzmán* are: I, i, 3 in which corrupt officials are compared to voracious whales that swallow up everything and I, ii, 9 in which Guzmán explains the saying "en Malagón, en cada casa un ladrón y en la del alcalde, hijo y padre." In *Lazarillo* the pardoner and the *alguacil* team up to deceive the people, but Lazarillo does not fall prey to the carefully conceived sham (*Lazarillo,* Tratado V). Pablos is bled by prison officials who extort an exorbitant amount of money from him to gain his freedom (Quevedo, pp. 183-93).

[14] Shortly after Guzmán leaves home, he eats several disgusting meals at local inns (I, i, 3 and I, i, 5). Later he is tricked by women (I, ii, 8; II, i, 5; and II, iii, 1) and has his belongings stolen (II, iii, 1). Alemán scorns the use of lying (II, i, 1) and calls rumors the "hija natural del odio y de la envidia" (I, i, 8, p. 181). Pablos endures the pranks of fellow students at Alcalá (pp. 64-68) and loses his money on a couple of occasions to crooks (pp. 124-26; 220).

[15] José Joaquín Fernández de Lizardi, *El Periquillo Sarniento* (México: Editorial Porrúa, S.A., 1959). This work, which marks the official beginning of the novel in Spanish America, was first published in 1816.

J. S. Cummins (essay date 1984)

SOURCE: "*Infortunios de Alonso Ramírez*: 'A Just History of Fact'?," in *Bulletin of Hispanic Studies*, Vol. LXI, No. 3, July, 1984, pp. 295-303.

[*Here, Cummins provides detailed evidence to support his claim that Siguenza y Gongora's* Infortunios que Alonso Ramírez *is an accurate historical narrative.*]

The 1680s was one of the most eventful decades in the entire history of Spain's remotest colony, the Philippines. Those years witnessed an earthquake, an alarming comet, epidemics of smallpox and influenza (which killed millions throughout Asia), floods and famine, a rising in the Chinese quarter in Manila (the Parian), martyrdoms in the Jesuits' mission in the Marianas, the murder by pirates of friars working in the provinces, and the blockading (1686) of the annual Manila Galleon bound for Acapulco (the lifeline of the colony);[1] the *San Telmo,* another year's Galleon, arriving from Mexico, had to be escorted into Cavite by a hastily converted ship of war. And, if this was not enough, throughout the decade there raged a violent controversy between the civic authorities and the Archbishop, Felipe Pardo, O.P. Though high hopes had been

entertained of the abilities of the new Governor, Gabriel de Curuzeláegui (1684-89), who was described as 'impartial', and who did much to cool tempers, the crown officers in general failed to please anyone. The Jesuit Father Antonio Jaramillo, for instance, writing in 1682 to the Duchess of Aveiro, the celebrated 'Mother of the Missions', exclaimed that 'si para qualquiera es la Puerta del cielo angosta, para los que en Manila tienen los goviernos es un postigo mui estrecho por donde no caven animos tan vistidos de paciones como yndican en lo exterior los subcesos'.[2]

If the colony had its joint trials, some of the unfortunate members of it suffered special torments of their own. One of these, Alonso Ramírez, is of some interest to readers of Spanish-American colonial literature. In 1675, as a boy of twelve, Ramírez left his native Puerto Rico, mistakenly believing he had no future there at his late father's trade of ship's carpenter.[3] He found work in Havana but dissatisfied and impatient, soon moved to New Spain. There too he was unlucky, for a bid to ingratiate himself with an alleged relative was rejected; an attempt to better himself through a judicious marriage also failed, and, widowed within the year, he decided (1682) to emigrate again—this time to Manila, Mexico's East Asian 'colony' where he became a successful seaman.[4] After five years of this life he was captured by English pirates who held him prisoner for two years.[5] On his eventual release and return to Mexico City (1690) the Viceroy (the Conde de Galve) sent him to visit the eminent scholar Carlos de Sigüenza y Góngora who recorded Ramírez's 'peregrinación lastimosa'. The result of this collaboration was the ***Infortunios que Alonso Ramírez padeció*** (Mexico City 1690), a work which has been much discussed. A recital of adventures and mishaps, it is variously regarded as the first Spanish-American novel, even as a colonial picaresque novel; as a biography with novelesque overtones typical of that fusion of fact and fiction known as faction; or even as a first step towards periodical literature in the New World, since it related events too recent for it to be regarded as a chronicle. What is clear is that the framework of the narrative is factual, but that Sigüenza added details and interjections of his own.

The pirates who captured Ramírez cannot yet be identified with certainty although he names some of them, such as Captains Bell and Donkin. Unfortunately, he does not name the ship on which he was made to serve. The pirates themselves left no known account of their adventures and misdeeds, and so it fell to Sigüenza to record their story, as seen through Ramírez's eyes. Curiously enough, Ramírez very nearly fell into the hands of the celebrated Englishman, William Dampier. Dampier (1652-1715), explorer, buccaneer, seaman-scientist, writer, infinitely superior to the rough crew amongst whom he lived, was undoubtedly the most intelligent of the many buccaneers harassing the Spaniards in the South Sea between 1680 and 1720.

What happened was that some companions of Dampier, under Captain Read on board the *Cygnet,* had seized two Spanish rice ships in Manila Bay in roughly the place where Ramírez was taken, and at about the same time. He, knowing that there were two friendly vessels carrying rice somewhere in the Bay and, unaware that they had just been captured, mistook the two ships of his captors for fellow Spaniards. Off his guard therefore, he continued calmly on his way ('proseguí con mis bordos sin recelo alguno, porque no había de que tenerlo') and so fell into hostile hands. Clearly, since Dampier was prowling those same waters at that same time, Ramírez might well have been captured by him instead of by the nonentities Bell and Donkin. Had that happened, Ramírez would be known to us, not through Sigüenza's *Infortunios*, but through that classic of English travel literature (one of Daniel Defoe's source books for *Robinson Crusoe*), Dampier's *New Voyage around the World* (London 1697), arguably the greatest seafaring narrative in the language. But the choice of Sigüenza as recorder, reporter, editor and ghost-writer of Ramírez's misadventures was as obvious as it was suitable, for he was one of the two leading savants of the day, the male counterpart of the extraordinary blue-stocking nun Sor Juana Inés de la Cruz.

Carlos de Sigüenza y Góngora, born in Mexico (1645), was a realtive of Luis de Góngora. His mother, Dionisia Suárez de Figueroa y Góngora, came from Seville; his father from Madrid.[6] The boy Carlos, being of a studious temperament, had the ambition to become a Jesuit and in pursuit of his vocation he spent six years in the College of Puebla de los Ángeles. But in 1667 there occurred an incident—we shall never know what it was—which led to his expulsion, against his will, from the Jesuit Society.[7] He thereupon transferred to the University of Mexico, where his uncommon aptitude for mathematics was quickly recognized. In 1672 he won first the chair of Mathematics and then the title of Royal Cosmographer. Since these posts brought little financial reward ('títulos son éstos que suenan mucho y valen muy poco') he also acted as chaplain to the Hospital Real del Amor de Dios. The Viceroy respected him highly and the Archbishop, Francisco Aguiar y Seijas, made him his almoner. His versatility and the catalogue of his qualifications tax credulity: he was a theologian and philosopher, a mathematician, cartographer and geographer, a university accountant, a military and civil engineer, official examiner of gunners, an astronomer, archaeologist, antiquarian, philologist and historian. His poetry is mediocre though some of it has been Englished by Samuel Beckett. Apart from his scientific writings, and some historical essays, the *Infortunios* is the most popular of Sigüenza's works nowadays. In his own day, however, he gained an international reputation and allegedly received an invitation from Louis XIV to go to the French court. Amongst his many correspondents abroad were the Jesuit polymath Athanasius Kircher in Rome; Newton's collaborator and first Astronomer Royal of England, John Flamsteed in London; the Jesuit Pieter van Hamme in China;[8] the learned if bizarre Cistercian bishop ('mi grande amigo') Juan Caramuel Lobkowitz in Milan, and the Italian traveller Giovanni Francesco Gemelli Careri who met him in Mexico and who acknowledges his help in his *Giro intorno al Mondo* (1699).[9]

In short, as an encyclopaedic scholar he may be compared with his contemporaries Pedro de Peralta Barnuevo (1663-

1743) in Peru and the Puritan savant Cotton Mather (1663-1728) in New England. But in reality there was no one amongst his contemporaries in Spain or in either of the Americas to approach him in intellectual stature and international reputation.

The society in which Sigüenza lived, and to which Ramírez aspired, had developed rapidly after the Conquest and the colony was soon proud of itself and its achievements, as is shown by the Renaissance-style Latin dialogues of the humanist Francisco Cervantes de Salazar who, in his *Academia mexicana* (1554), conducts a Spanish visitor around the city and, with a quotation from Luis Vives, shows off the university where he himself teaches. And Mexicans had even greater reason for pride when, in 1565, the friar-cosmographer, fray Andrés de Urdaneta, discovered the return sea-route between Mexico and the Philippines. 'Westward the course of Empire' had indeed moved: New Spain was now at the centre of the world, lying between east and west, between Atlantic and Pacific, Europe and Asia, at the heart of the trade routes of the world's economy. In 1604 a poet in Mexico celebrated this:

> Mexico al mundo por igual divide
>
> . . . . .
>
> En ti se junta España con la China
> Italia con Japón, y finalmente
> un mundo entero en trato y disciplina.
> En ti de los tesoros del poniente
> se goza lo mejor; en ti la nata
> de cuanto entre su luz cría el oriente . . .

For Spaniards the seventeenth century was a period of industrial, commercial and financial debility; of faltering government and of repeated military defeats. But this was not true of Mexico and it is a mistake to regard this as a dead century, a monotonous round of routine and regular ceremonial affirmations of one's loyalty to the Crown and of one's own status in local society. For Mexico City had come of age: it was now a metropolitan centre of cultural and intellectual life.[10] González de Eslava, in the sixteenth of his *Coloquios* (1610), had said, rather irritably, that Mexico had 'más poetas que estiércol'. More sedately, but enthusiastically, the poet-cleric Bernardo de Balbuena described the glories of Mexico in his *Grandeza Mexicana* (1604). Literarily speaking, this long poem opens the century:

> Aquí hallarás más hombres eminentes
> en toda ciencia y todas facultades
> que arenas lleva el Gange en sus corrientes;
> Monstruos en perfección de habilidades,
> y en letras humanas y divinas
> eternos rastreadores de verdades . . .

The Renaissance in Europe might have remained little more significant than an antiquarian return to the Classics if it had not coincided with the age of discovery: the discovery of the sea and of exotic space, such as America. Out of the New World there came one of the fundamental tenets of the modern age: that saying of Cortés' chaplain,

López de Gómara, 'Experience gives the lie to philosophy'. And true to this, Sigüenza (together with Sor Juana Inés de la Cruz) stand out as harbingers of the new spirit of enquiry in the New World, demanding the right to think for themselves. In the controversy over the significance of the great comet of 1681 (the comet of Bayle's *Reflections*) it was the creole Sigüenza who rebuked a Jesuit mathematician from Europe, Father Eusebio Kino, in terms which would have been unthinkable two generations earlier: 'advierto que ni su reverencia, ni otro algún matemático, aunque sea el mismo Ptolemeo, puede asentar dogmas en estas ciencias, porque en ellas no sirve de cosa alguna la autoridad sino las pruebas y demostración'.[11]

Nevertheless, there were problems. This was the heyday of the buccaneers, those bands of French, English, Dutch, German and other smugglers, whose contraband activities (at first mainly in the Caribbean) the Spaniards sought to eliminate. Consequently, the buccaneers carried on a private war against Spain, even in periods of official peace.[12] The highlight of their operations came in 1671 with the pillage and destruction of Panama City by Henry Morgan.[13] After the Stuart Restoration the English tolerated the buccaneers in the Caribbean as an aid to preventing Spain from recapturing Jamaica. The Spaniards countered by setting up coastal defences, even though these sometimes cost more than the specie and merchandise being lost; in fact it was the decreasing importance of silver in Spanish America (as against land and cattle) which caused piracy in the area to dwindle. The Treaty of Ryswick (1697) formally recognized English and French settlements and commercial agents, so that buccaneer mercenaries were no longer needed or patronized by European states, and the day of the Caribbean pirate was over. But the buccaneers who had been so active and had flourished in the area, now spread into the Pacific and Indian Oceans where they raided, for instance, Spanish and Portuguese vessels, Chinese trading junks and ships of the Mogul emperors. The northern European nations entered the Iberian sphere of influence in Asia by means of powerful trading companies (the equivalents of the modern multinational). Of these the most formidable was the Dutch East India Company (1602) which eventually seized the monopoly of the Spice Islands' trade of immensely valuable cargoes of cloves, cinnamon, and nutmegs. The English East India Company (1600), a similar but smaller organization, traded with India, and a French Company (1664), enabled the French (1683) to secure Pondicherry and to trade at Canton. The main route across the Pacific (the 'Spanish Lake') was established by the annual Galleon from Acapulco to Manila, while in the Indian Ocean (where Ramírez's captors mainly operated), the English, Dutch, French and Portuguese followed routes from the Cape of Good Hope to Nagasaki. To this crowded canvas came the privateers—seaborne conquistadors, they might be defined as pirates with royal permission. They provided a cheap method of raising naval forces, since governments used them in wartime to harass and seize enemy shipping, and so at various times English, French and Dutch privateers operated against each others' merchantmen. In wartime, pirates such as Ramírez's captors called themselves privateers and became respectable for the duration of hostilities.

Soon after the Conquest Spaniards became aware of the hazards facing them in the Atlantic and in the Pacific. Their first shipment of Aztec loot was intercepted by French corsairs and ended up in Paris; fifteen years later so too did some of the first Peruvian booty. In defence the Spaniards established a convoy system for crossing the Atlantic: the Mexican fleet left Vera Cruz for Spain each June; in May the outward-bound fleet left Spain for Mexico, and in August the galleons set sail for South American ports. These measures proved successful, though inevitably losses continued.

The day of the pirate might be drawing to a close, but books about them now multiplied and for generations appealed to the romantically-minded, reaching a climax in Stevenson's *Treasure Island* (1883). Sigüenza's contribution to the vogue is divided into seven chapters, the first of which relates Ramírez's life up to his decision to 'exile' himself to the Philippines. This move ended the picaresque period in his story: the wandering in search of food and fortune; the rapid changing of employers with little or no sense of loyalty; the marriage partially designed to bring security; and, on one occasion (reminiscent of the pícaro-squire episode in the *Lazarillo*) the realization that he had adopted a master who was himself in dire need. Chapter Two describes the sea route to Manila. Though the ***Infortunios*** does not linger over the point, the *Santa Rosa,* on which Ramírez sailed, stopped over in accordance with policy and practice in the Marianas, considered an extension of the Philippines.[14] A Jesuit mission had recently been established there, and this was of considerable emotional significance to the Society, since the Fathers felt it brought them once more nearer to their beloved Japan mission, closed to them after 1640 by decree of the Shogun.[15] Unfortunately, however, others also saw the Marianas as a link with the Philippines, and so Guam was frequently visited by pirates who tried to appear respectable for the occasion. Some called only to take on fresh supplies, and for hungry buccaneers Guam was the 'Place of Plenty'. An equally strong reason for these unsolicited visits was to glean information about Spanish shipping movements and to sound out the possibility of an attack on Manila itself. The new Governor there, Curuzeláegui (a former admiral), was soon reporting to Madrid that all the surrounding seas were infested with pirates. For instance, in 1686—the year before Ramírez's capture—as the *Santo Niño* was preparing to return to Acapulco, it was reported that no fewer than eleven hostile ships were ranging round the islands in search of her. That same year Dampier (pretending to be Spanish) called at Guam hoping to capture that year's Galleon, but in the end he had to abandon his 'Golden Projects'. A Jesuit from the island who visited Dampier's ship was held hostage for some days but was graciously treated; indeed Dampier and Captain Swan confided their troubles to him and, when they released him, presented him with a telescope, clock and astrolabe.[16]

Ramírez, on his journey past Guam, was spared such alarms and reached Manila safely, where he became a sailor and travelled widely in South East Asia, visiting such places as Macao, Malacca, Madras and Batavia. But the years of comparative prosperity ended abruptly when he was captured by Bell and Donkin. The horror of that event is emphasized by the precision with which he had it recorded for him: 'Eran entonces las seis de la tarde del dia martes cuatro de marzo de mil seiscientos y ochenta y siete'. Those words, which close Chapter Two, read like an entry in a seaman's journal.

Chapter Three relates Ramírez's life as a prisoner. The pirates sailed out of Manila Bay with their booty, travelling restlessly across the Indian Ocean from Bengal to Australia, murdering, raping, robbing, burning, looting and capturing smaller craft; amongst others they took two richly laden ambassadorial vessels, one of which was bearing precious stones and other presents from Goa to Bangkok, and the other was carrying a mission from the Siamese king to the Governor of Manila. A third prize had on board a large cargo of silk from Macao bound for Europe. Eventually, after some two years of this, the pirates reached Madagascar where they decided to return home to England; after some debate as to whether they should kill their prisoners or not, it was decided to let them loose in a small vessel leaving them to fend for themselves.

Chapter Four, the axis of the work, pauses for a retrospective view of the story, enabling Ramírez to outline the trials he and other prisoners had suffered. This belated criticism of the corsairs and catalogue of their atrocities might suggest a subconscious fear inhibiting him in his dictation to Sigüenza until he was safely beyond their reach, not only in reality but even within the confines of the narrative itself.

The remaining three chapters of the book relate his further misadventures: he and his companions passed Trinidad, and reached Yucatán where, their vessel wrecked, Ramírez, in the manner of *Robinson Crusoe*, had to swim back from the beach to rescue the provisions and equipment aboard the sinking hulk. After further adventures Ramírez met the Viceroy in Mexico City, who, filled with compassion for him, not only sent him to Sigüenza but assisted him materially.[17] In 1690, with the publication of his biography, Alonso Ramírez vanishes, and his name is not further recorded.[18] If he ever returned to Manila he left no mark there; and there is no mention of him in the hospitable pages of Blair and Robertson's fifty-five volumes of Philippine history. But one can easily imagine him in his later years, proudly showing off his copy of the *Infortunios* (whether or not he could read it himself), reminiscing over his days as a sailor in Asia, and boasting like many another old sea-dog of his circumnavigation of the globe, involuntary though it was, which began on that terrible day in Manila Bay, precisely at 'six o'clock in the afternoon . . .'

Reference to Dampier and *Robinson Crusoe* raises another point. It would of course be absurd to seek any similarities between Defoe's 'just History of Fact' (which in reality is the first great English novel) and Sigüenza's 'first Spanish-American novel' (which in reality is a straight biographical narrative), except to note that neither author

had travelled, but that, for the nonce, each was playing a similar role.[19] Sigüenza was (what Defoe pretended to be) the reporter and editor of an informant's story, transmitting it to the press for the public interest. Sigüenza's was authentic, but Defoe's posture was that commonly adopted stratagem of passing off fiction as fact, because the Puritan code of those middle-class readers for whom he wrote linked 'invention' with lying and with the immorality of much Restoration literature.

But, on the other hand, there are instructive differences between each author and each work. If nothing else, the immense popularity of Defoe's work places it in a different category. The whole of English literature is full of references to it. For instance, Wilkie Collins' old butler in the *Moonstone* regarded it as the solution to his personal problems, something on a par with the Bible; George Borrow in *Lavengro* describes his intense emotion on first reading it; Coleridge thought 'You become a man while you read' *Robinson Crusoe*; earlier, Pope and Johnson had praised it. (Later, Karl Marx found lessons in it: lessons it was indeed meant to provide, though not the ones Marx found.) Defoe chose to defend his book, as has been said, by protesting that it was 'the Story of a private Man's Adventures in the World . . . and worth making Publick . . . The Editor believes the thing to be a just History of Fact; neither is there any Appearance of Fiction in it . . . and as such, he thinks without farther Compliment to the World, he does them a great Service in the Publication'. Later he added to this: 'All the Endeavours of envious People to reproach it with being a Romance, to search it for Errors in Geography, Inconsistency in the Relation, and Contradictions in the Fact, have proved abortive, and as impotent as malicious'. There is a moral and religious purpose in *Robinson Crusoe*, and Defoe complains that those who 'pretend that the Author has supply'd the Story out of his Invention, take from it the Improvement, which alone recommends that Invention to wise and good Men'.

Sigüenza, too, had a purpose in writing but it was different from Defoe's.[20] What seems to be his personal contribution to the *Infortunios* is the addition of geographical, navigational and cosmographical information reflecting his own interests. But he was not simply indulging his hobby: he was acting from a desire to educate, and to stimulate general concern as he sounded a warning of Spanish vulnerability both in the colonial territories and on the seas. When in his third chapter he, the expert on military matters, shows the reader the state of the defences of Manila, he was (marginally at least) within a seventeenth-century Spanish tradition: the 'preocupación de España'. It is revealing to find one or two Hispanic critics dismissing the navigational aspects of the book as tedious while by contrast, and significantly, information of precisely this sort was welcomed by British readers of books such as Dampier's. On the other hand, it must be admitted that in a narrative as short as the *Infortunios* there is no place for the minute technicalities relating to the Pacific route which open Chapter Two; such pages would be better in a seaman's manual. It is the sort of writing which in England drove Jonathan Swift to bitter parody: it is not the kind of mistake that Defoe would make.

Samuel Johnson thought that nothing written by man was ever wished longer by its readers, excepting only *Don Quixote*, *Robinson Crusoe* and *Pilgrim's Progress*. One might add Sigüenza's *Infortunios* to these, though for a different reason. Sigüenza seems almost to be following Defoe's later advice: 'There are so many travellers who have written a history of their voyages . . . that it would be very little diversion to anybody to give a long account of the places we went to, and the people who inhabit them; these things I leave to others, and refer the reader to those journals and travels . . . of which many are published and more promised every day'. Yet no such excuse could be made by Sigüenza in respect of Mexico. There is, then, a marked imbalance in the book, the first half being skimpy when compared to the second. Chapter Two, with its brief, almost bald, catalogue ('Estuve in Madrastapatan . . . Estuve en Malaca . . . Estuve en Batavia . . . Estuve tambien en Macan . . .') cries out for much more detail:[21] the detail that any novelist would be bound to give his reader. But Sigüenza was sick when he interviewed Ramírez and may have been still sick, or at best convalescent, when he wrote the first half of the book. In other circumstances he might have given a longer account or quizzed Ramírez more closely for further details. There may also have been reason to hurry the writing: it is noticeable that the work was ready for publication within a few weeks of Ramírez's return to Mexico City.[22]

The religious element in the *Infortunios* is formal and insignificant. The invocations to Our Lady of Guadalupe probably reflect Sigüenza's own particular devotion, which is also evident in other works by him. The stress on religious succour rings true, but the miraculous downpour of rain upon the men dying of thirst is a hagiographical cliché, and there is nowhere in the narrative the spirit of Defoe's *Serious Reflections*, so typical of the English age of self-scrutiny and moral earnestness.

It is not certain whether Defoe ever met Alexander Selkirk, (one of the two models for *Robinson Crusoe*) but he had excellent secondary sources to inspire him and to furnish background information. Mainly, there was Selkirk's story as told in the *Voyage* of Woodes Rogers, one of the most competent captains of the day. Also invaluable would be the *New Voyage* by Dampier who had been Rogers' pilot when they rescued Selkirk from Juan Fernandez Island; and Dampier also recounted the tale of Will, the Mosquito Indian who was the second source for Crusoe. Sigüenza had both primary and secondary sources. To fill out Ramírez's own story ('as told to . . .') he had available to him both Antonio de Morga's *Sucesos de las islas filipinas* (Mexico City 1609) and the Dominican Diego Aduarte's *Historia de la orden de predicadores en Philipinas* (Manila 1640).[23] Also useful would be Luis de Morales' Jesuit account of the Marianas published in Mexico, 1689; and A. O. Esquemeling's *Buccaneers of America* (Amsterdam 1678; Spanish edition 1681).

Evidence that the *Infortunios* tells a true story and is accurate in many details (especially the dating of episodes) can be found in contemporary English, Spanish, French and Dutch accounts. Many of those named in the text are persons of whom there is historical record: e.g., Antonio Nieto and Leandro Coello, admiral and pilot respectively of the (correctly named) Manila Galleon for the year 1682; and in the latter part of the story many of the clerics and officials (not to mention the Bishop and Viceroy) whom Ramírez claims to have met are verifiable. Again some of the incidents which took place in Asia and are referred to by him could only have come from an informant who had recently been there, since they would still be unknown in Mexico. The account of the Portuguese soldiers in Siam who were said to have had their hands cut off (though it is astray in minor detail) can be confirmed by contemporary French and Dutch records; the capture of the two rice ships in Manila Bay on the day Ramírez was taken, in the same place, can be confirmed. Ramírez's reference to English scheming in Borneo during his time there can be corroborated in contemporary English accounts. Though no evidence has been found in the archives of Goa or Macao to bear out the account of the embassies from Siam which were captured by the pirates the account is plausible, since there were frequent missions to and from that country during those years; sometimes there seem to have been almost as many embassies as pirates in those waters.[24] It must be admitted that some of the speeches attributed to the pirates sound apocryphal (e.g., that allegedly made by Captain Donkin at the opening of Chapter Four was surely embroidered by the rapporteur). On the other hand, and disconcertingly, there is no reference to Ramírez's captors in the copious contemporary literature, e.g. either in the East India Company records, letters, and recorded gossip, or in the pirate histories of the period, such as Charles Johnson's.[25] Yet depredations such as Ramírez relates, and the rumbustious passage of the two ships around the Indian Ocean, should have left some wake.

Recent research in the India Office suggested a Captain *Duncan* Mackintosh—a respectable seaman who 'turned rogue' in 1687—as Ramírez's 'Donkin', but a disparity in dating destroys the hypothesis. No doubt further research there will one day establish the identity of Donkin, Bell and the rest, and so establish that the *Infortunios* is indeed a 'just History of Fact'.

NOTES

[1] See W. L. Schurz, *The Manila Galleon* (New York: Dutton, 1959), an invaluable study for an understanding of the Galleon's significance and history.

[2] C. R. Boxer, 'Three Unpublished Jesuit Letters on the Philippine and Mariana Missions, 1681-89', *Philippine Studies*, X (1962), 434-42.

[3] Even as he was leaving home, a royal decree (signed in Madrid in 1670) was working its way through the bureaucracy: all unemployed youths in Puerto Rico were required to become apprentice ship's carpenters to meet future urgent naval demands. See Richard Konetz-

ke, *Colección de documentos para la historia de la formación social de Hispanoamérica, 1493-1810* (Madrid: CSIC, 1958), II (ii), 558-59.

4 His wife was a niece of archdeacon Juan de Poblete, brother of Miguel Millán de Poblete, archbishop of Manila, 1653-67; possibly this connection played some part in the decision to try his fortune in the Philippines.

5 Though in his first sentence Ramírez speaks of his 'tribulaciones de muerte por *muchos* años' (my italics).

6 Carlos de Sigüenza 'de 18 anos, cabello negro, natural de Madrid', went to Mexico in the suite of the Viceroy, the Marqués de Villena in 1640; see Dorothy Schons, *Notes from Spanish Archives* (Austin, Texas: Edwards Brothers, 1946), 19.

7 This is discussed by E. J. Burrus, 'Sigüenza y Góngora's Efforts for Readmission into the Jesuit Order', *HAHR*, XXXIII (1955), 387-91; there is a more satisfactory discussion in Jaime Delgado, ed., [Sigüenza's] *Piedad heroyca de Fernando Cortés* (Madrid: Porrua, 1960), xi-xxvi.

8 In early life Van Hamme had worked among the Tarahumara Indians: he knew Sigüenza personally; he always retained his interest in Mexico as is shown by his later letters from Peking: see P. Visschers, *Onuitgegeven* [Jesuit] *Brieven* (Arnhem: Josué Witz, 1857), 55, 171, 175, 176.

9 Gemelli praised the 'courtesy, industry, learning and unique antiquarian studies [of Sigüenza who] presented me with extraordinary rarities'.

10 For this see Richard Boyer, 'Mexico in the Seventeenth Century: Transition of a Colonial Society', *HAHR*, LVII (1977), 454-78.

11 *Libra astronomica* (Mexico City: Calderón, 1690), sect. 252.

12 Some were said to have been stimulated by hyped-up versions of Las Casas's *Brevissima* (such as that sponsored by Cromwell), so, nursing their selective consciences, these took to the seas to punish the Spaniards and dry the *Tears of the Indians*. Not all were English: the Frenchman Montbars, inflamed by his reading, saw himself as an instrument of divine justice, dedicated his sword 'Exterminator' to the God of Vengeance, and set sail on his divine commission: 'to execute vengeance upon the Heathen'. But the trials of the pacific were not all one-sided and some English merchantmen learnt to go in fear of the Spanish 'picaroons' [<pícaro-picarón] or privateers.

13 Pirate attacks sometimes brought apparent benefits: when Arica was in danger in 1682 there was a call-up which in Potosí embraced beggars and the unemployed: 'fue gran bien para esta Villa porque comenzaban a mover con la ociosidad algunos alborotos' (L. Hanke and G. Mendoza, eds., *Historia de . . . Potosí por Bartolomé Arzáns de Orsúa* (Providence: Brown U. P., 1965), II, 306.

14 Ramírez left Acapulco on Good Friday, 28 March 1682, and arrived in Manila on 23 July; he does not give the dates himself but they can be found in the notes of a Mexican diarist (A. de Robles, *Diario* (*1665-1703*), II [Mexico City 1946], 16) and a letter by a Manila Jesuit (Father Gerard Bouwens to the Duchess of Aveiro in Magg's Catalogue No.

442. *Bibliotheca Americana et Philippina*, Part III [London: Maggs, 1923], 155). For the Marianas see Domingo Abella, *An Introduction to the Study of Philippines-Marianas Relations* (Manila: IAHA, 1962), 1-50.

15 For the Jesuit mission see W. Barrett, *Mission in the Marianas* (Minneapolis: University of Minnesota Press, 1975) and the review by F. Zubillaga, 'América e Islas Marianas', *Archivum Historicum Societatis Jesu*, XLVI (1977), 254.

16 Possibly the priest was well treated because Dampier thought he was only a Friar; in fact he was a local Jesuit. Dampier's account of the affair (*A New Voyage round the World* [London: Knapton, 1697], X) is fascinatingly corroborated by Father Bouwens' reports to Carlos II and to the 'Mother of the Missions' which show the Jesuit had a sharp eye for weighing up men, ships and armaments. His reports, unknown until 1923, bear out Dampier, once allowance has been made for OS and NS dating. See Maggs' Catalogue 442, pp. 217, 219. Dampier gave the Governor powder, shot and arms, and in return received ample food supplies. The Governor also begged for their 'delicate large English Dog and had it given him very freely by the Captain, though much against the grain of his Men, who had a great value for that Dog'.

17 The Viceroy was known for his compassion: his *residencia* reports that he was accustomed to 'oir generalmente a todos en suma benignidad, atención y agasajo, sin dejar de consolar el más miserable e infirmo'; he was 'el alivio de los pobres' (L. Hanke, *Guía de fuentes virreinales* [Cologne: Böhlau Verlag, 1977], I, 174, 176). The Archbishop, Aguiar y Seijas, may also have been interested in Ramírez's story since his nephew, the Dominican friar José Seijas, had just previously been murdered in the Philippines by pirates.

18 Though we know where he went since the Viceroy arranged for him to join the fleet which sailed to victory against the French on 19 July 1690. Sigüenza recommended him to one of the captains, his friend Juan Enríquez Barroto, 'excelente Mathemático y a cuyos desvelos deberá la Náutica Americana grandes progresos'. Sigüenza wrote two enthusiastic accounts of this victory in which occurs the name of don Alonso Ramírez, captain of musketeers, who covered himself with glory in the storming of Guarico, and was awarded two sonnets. But Sigüenza was not a novelist: this gallant hero is not the pícaro-pirate of the *Infortunios* but another of the same name.

19 Defoe had at least crossed the Channel; as for Sigüenza 'aunque no he salido a peregrinar otras tierras (harto me pesa), por lo en extremo mucho que he leido, paréceme puedo hacer concepto de lo que son y de lo que en ellas se hace'.

20 It may be assumed Ramírez himself had many hidden reasons for wanting to see his story published; but his main declared aim was defined in the opening words of the narrative where he claimed that he was seeking only to ease his psychological wounds by eliciting compassion; the censor Ayerra noted this point.

21 Dampier, like Esquemeling and Basil Ringrose (as Percy G. Adams has pointed out), often paused in narrating an adventure to describe a town, an island, or occasionally a plant or animal. Dampier's description of Mindanao, for example, is a model.

[22] Possibly Sigüenza was more involved with his great work, the *Libra astronomica*, which appeared at the same time; it is worth noting that although Ramírez did not reach the city until early May 1690, the *Infortunios* had already passed the ecclesiastical censor by 26 June.

[23] Later, in 1694, Sigüenza bought himself a copy of the Morga (now in the Lilly Library, Bloomington); he already had a copy of Aduarte (now the property of Professor C. R. Boxer) which could have given him much material had he chosen to use it. Aduarte has a vivid description of one Manila Galleon voyage on which the ship's provisions were destroyed early on, and for the rest of the journey passengers and crew had to live on beans for three months; this diet seems to have had a deplorable effect on the crew who fell into two gangs and fought amongst themselves continually, 'como si fueran moros y cristianos' (Aduarte, Book I, ch. 8).

[24] For instance, there was a Siamese embassy to England in 1687 (*Records of Relations between Siam and Foreign Countries,* IV [Bangkok: National Library, 1920], 207); to England and Venice (*Records of Fort St. George: Diary for 1687* [Madras: Government Office, 1916], 158); to Manila in 1686 (J. S. Cummins 'A Spanish Sidelight on "Siamese" White', *Journal of Southeast Asian History,* V (1964), 129-32, and cf Dampier's *New Voyage,* ch. XVII); to Manila, 1683 (Casimiro Díaz, *Conquistas de las islas Filipinas,* segunda parte, [1718] [Manila, 1890], ch. XIII); in 1688 Dampier (*Voyage,* ch. 18) encountered 'a small Frigot from Siam, with an Ambassador from the King of Siam to the Queen of Achin. The Ambassador was a Frenchman'. But the most celebrated of all these embassies was that of Siam to France which made its mark in French literature when Fénelon preached to the ambassadors in Paris, 6 January 1685.

[25] Daniel Defoe published five hundred works, less than a dozen of which carried his name on the title page: the *General History of the Pyrates by Charles Johnson* (1724) was not identified as Defoe's until 1932: see the edition by Michael Schonhorn, (London: Dent, 1972) xxii-xxiii.

FURTHER READING

Cummins, James S. "The Phillipines Glimpsed in the First Latin American 'Novel'," in *Philippine Studies,* Vol. 26 (First and Second Quarter 1978): 91-101.

> Explores Alonso Ramírez's motivation for traveling to the Philippines, his subsequent return to Mexico, and Sigüenza y Góngora's transcription of Ramírez's experiences.

Henríquez-Ureña, Pedro. "The Flowering of the Colonial World: 1600-1800." In *Literary Currents in Hispanic America,* pp. 58-93. New York: Russel & Russel, Inc., 1963.

> Provides a comprehensive review of the European presence in Latin America, the fusion of those cultures, and the influence it had on Hispanic American writers and their works.

Leonard, Irving Albert. "Introduction." In *The Mercurio Volante of Don Carlos de Sigüenza Y Góngora,* pp. 13-47. New York: Arno Press, 1967.

> Offers a positive review of *Mercurio Volante* and an overview of Mexico's history at the time it was written.

Morris, Robert J. A review of *Infortunios de Alonso Ramírez,* in *Hispania,* Vol. 74, No. 3 (September 1991): 680.

> Provides a favorable review of Estelle Irizarry's edition of *Infortunios de Alonso Ramírez.*

Soons, Alan. "Alonso Ramírez in an Enchanted and a Disenchanted World," in *Bulletin of Hispanic Studies,* Vol. LIII, No. 3 (July 1976): 201-05.

> Discusses how Alonso Ramírez's optimistic attitude complemented and contrasted with his life and his voyages.

Additional coverage of Sigüenza y Góngora's life and career is contained in the following sources published by the Gale Group: *Literary Criticism from 1400-1800,* Vol. 8.

Piri Thomas
1928-

(Born Juan Pedro Tomás; also known as John Peter Thomas) American autobiographer, dramatist, short story writer, and poet.

INTRODUCTION

Considered the progenitor of the Nuyorican (New York Puerto Rican) literary movement, Piri Thomas has earned critical and popular acclaim for his straightforward writing style and accurately graphic depictions of prison, racism, and street life in America. Thomas chronicled the difficulties of growing up as a dark-skinned Puerto Rican in Depression-era New York in a series of three autobiographies, the first of which, *Down These Mean Streets* (1967), is the most famous. The other two memoirs, *Savior, Savior Hold My Hand* (1976) and *Seven Long Times* (1974), detail Thomas's release from prison, social rehabilitation, and decision to become a writer. Thomas is a founding member of the world-renowned Nuyorican Poets Café in New York City's East Village. A long-time children's advocate, he is also the author of *Stories from El Barrio* (1978), a book for young adults.

Born in Spanish Harlem, New York, Thomas was the oldest of six children. Thomas has noted that he first experienced the debilitating effects of racism within his own family, as he was the only *negrito* (dark-skinned person) in a house where light skin was highly valued. His father, a Cuban immigrant who often could not find work because of his race, was an embittered man who frequently vented rage on his family. Thomas's mother was a devoutly religious Puerto Rican who taught her children to believe in God and themselves, despite the squalor that surrounded them. Her untimely death at age 36 in 1945 sent Thomas into a severe depression and a downward spiral of gang involvement and drug use that culminated in a prison sentence at age 21 for shooting a police officer. Thomas served seven years of hard labor at Sing Sing Prison. Despite the physical and emotional degradation of incarceration, Thomas obtained his GED (high school diploma equivalency degree) while in prison and experienced a sequence of spiritual epiphanies that, upon his release in 1956, prompted him to dedicate his life to writing.

In his autobiographies, Thomas juxtaposed the ideal of the American Dream with the harsh living conditions in *el barrio*, and so expressed the discontent, alienation, and loneliness of many Hispanic Americans. As a child, Thomas's dark skin exposed him to the cruel, invasive effects of racism, which prevails as a theme in his works. *Down These Mean Streets*, for example, reveals that one of Thomas's most debilitating childhood fears is his father's contempt for him because of his skin color. Thomas's attempts to mask this fear and to assert his manhood by running with gangs and using drugs only increased his feelings of worthlessness. Thomas's freedom from the demons of his past came only after he was jailed and made a conscious effort to love himself. *Savior, Savior Hold My Hand* and *Seven Long Times* continue Thomas's themes of alienation, racism and self-acceptance. Thomas has also earned acclaim for *Stories from El Barrio*, a collection of stories for young adults that humorously detail the life in an Hispanic neighborhood.

Most critics have cited *Down These Mean Streets* as Thomas's most important and impressive work. Critics and the general reading public alike have praised the book's insightful treatment of growing up amid poverty and violence, and for exposing the challenge of Hispanic Americans to find their place in a society that despises them. Upon the 1967 publication of *Down These Mean Streets*, *New York Times Book Review* critic Daniel Stern praised the book for having "an undeniable power that . . . comes from the fact that it is a report from the guts and heart of a submerged population group . . . ." In his book *Hispanic Nation*, Geoffrey Fox calls *Down These Mean Streets* the "first important Puerto Rican memoir written in English." Reaction to *Savior, Savior Hold My Hand* and *Seven Long Times* has been less enthusiastic. Writing for *Library Journal*, Robert P. Haro cited *Savior, Savior Hold My Hand* as having "stylistic flaws and weaknesses," and critic William Kennedy panned *Seven Long Times*, calling it "a dull echo" of *Down These Mean Streets*. Despite the varied responses to his later writings, Thomas has earned lasting admiration for *Down These Mean Streets*, both for its own merit and the Nuyorican writing movement that it helped create.

PRINCIPAL WORKS

Down These Mean Streets (memoir) 1967
Savior, Savior Hold My Hand (memoir) 1972
Seven Long Times (memoir) 1974
Stories From El Barrio (short stories) 1978
The World of Piri Thomas (videorecording) 1980

CRITICISM

Nelson Aldrich (essay date 1967)

SOURCE: "Inside the Skin," in *Book Week—World Journal Tribune,* May 21, 1967, pp. 4, 17.

[In the following essay, Aldrich praises the grim honesty of Down These Mean Streets.*]*

The truthfulness of **Down These Mean Streets** goes beyond autobiographical integrity to illuminate not only that dubious concept, "the culture of poverty," but more importantly, the culture of Americans.

The book is punctuated with violence, and with fitful sex and the anesthetics of heroin as well. They end by engulfing the youth that Thomas writes about, but not his book. For these things are not perceived by him as "problems" or as a social outrage, but as elements of a *rite de passage* that he recalls now with an easy, even a proud, familiarity. Besides, his life was far more complicated and rich than sensational. . . . The really serious aspects of life were not drugs, but the unremitting and *unavoidable* struggle for status; not police brutality, but the terrible possibility that his father did not love him; not American racism, but the devastating thought that, being a dark-skinned Puerto Rican, he must *choose* what he would only appear to be.

As history, the important thing about Thomas's book may be that it presents a life differing little from that of hundreds of thousands of boys who grew up and continue to grow up under similar conditions. It is definitely *unimportant* to history that Thomas is now a "constructive member of society." But **Down These Mean Streets** is not a Puerto Rican sequel to Claude Brown's *Manchild in the Promised Land*, for it demands to be read as literature, not as raw data for social research. Thomas knows himself; his recollection of his youth is completely honest, and his writing—though occasionally flawed by self-conscious barbaric yawps—is wonderfully powerful. His achievement is to have so thoroughly taken the measure of his individuality that he adds significantly to our sense of the richness and shame of being an American.

Daniel Stern   (essay date 1967)

SOURCE: "One Who Got Away," in *The New York Times Book Review*, May 21, 1967, pp. 1, 44.

[Here, Stern cites Down These Mean Streets *as a testament to the often ignored discrimination that plagues Hispanic Americans.]*

[The literary qualities of **Down These Mean Streets**] are primitive. Yet it has an undeniable power that I think comes from the fact that it is a report from the guts and heart of a submerged population group, itself submerged in the guts and hearts of our cities. It claims our attention and emotional response because of the honesty and pain of a life led in outlaw, fringe status, where the dream is always to escape.

There is, in reports such as this, a certain lack of suspense. The reader knows from the start that the survivor who wrote the book is one of those who got away. There remains the question of how the escape was worked. And

there is the fascination of being told of it in a special language created in conflict. . . .

What I, for one, did not know until I read Piri Thomas's tough, lyrical autobiography was the pervasiveness of the Hispanic cultural and social legacy, particularly that phenomenon known as *machismo,* which can be roughly translated as a kind of insistent maleness.

In Piri Thomas's gutter world, *machismo* is even more roughly translated as "heart." It can lead a boy to a sense of his own worth--or to drugs and jail. **Down These Mean Streets** is the story of Piri Thomas and his "heart." But, more important, it is the odyssey of one member of a submerged population group whose claim on our attention is immediate and overdue.

Piri Thomas addresses us secondarily as a writer, but first as a messenger (not a man with a message; that is quite a different thing.)

Like the messenger in the Book of Job, he tells us: *I, only, am escaped alive to tell thee.* Sentimental, rough-hewn, and unliterary as his tale may be, behind it stands a submerged population group that has had few voices. As a black Puerto Rican he speaks for the *negritos* of this world, as well as for those captive Americans of Spanish descent and tradition, the Puerto Ricans of Spanish Harlem.

From the inferno of the sidewalks Thomas has written another stanza in the passionate poem of color and color hatred being written today all over the world. James Baldwin tells us he was brought up to believe white was good and black was bad. Piri Thomas had to prove for himself that this was not true. In speaking for the black as well as for the poor and alien, he speaks for all who are buried alive in a society that troubles itself only minimally with its inarticulate miserable, its humiliated, its defeated and self-defeating.

His is a cautionary voice informed with honesty, warmth and intelligence. It is up to us to listen.

Warren Sloat   (essay date 1967)

SOURCE: "Exploration of Color," in *Saturday Review*, August 5, 1967, p. 33.

[In the following essay, Sloat praises the vernacular and narrative integrity of Down These Mean Streets.*]*

"Pops," Piri Thomas writes at the onset of his autobiography, "how come me and you is always on the outs? Is it something we don't know nothing about? I wonder if it's something I done, or something I am."

The affront Piri Thomas committed that put him on the outs with his father and most of America was to get born with a dark skin—a Puerto Rican who is, according to one of America's millions of color experts, "black enuff to be a nigger." Even in his own family his fairer-skinned brothers are taken aback. Though he passes in a Southern whore house (by speaking Spanish), he is unwanted when he answers classified ads.

Drugs, violence, the street code, the sights and sounds of the Harlem *Barrio* play subsidiary and reinforcing roles to this exploration of color in white America. "If You Ain't Got Heart, You Ain't Got Nada," one chapter is entitled. From the time he is a small boy, when his family moves to an Italian neighborhood, Piri has to show heart—has to fight bullies to stay alive. With World War II and Depression's end, the Thomases move on to Long Island. His brothers appear to be making it in the white world, but Piri, unable to take the cruelty of a gym dance and other slights, returns to Harlem, where, living alone, he pushes pot and engages in petty theft.

Determined to accept himself as a Negro, Thomas goes to the Deep South with a black friend. He comes back shaken. Hating all whites—except Trina, his Puerto Rican love—he descends by notches into the hell of heroin addiction until he is strung out with a $15-a-day habit. Piri turns to stickups, and in an attempted nightclub hold-up he and a cop exchange fire. "I finally shot some Mr. Charlies," thinks Thomas, who is himself wounded. "I shot 'em in my mind often enough."

To preserve a chance at parole, after serving six years of a sentence for attempted armed robbery and felonious assault, he stays out of a prison riot and even walks away from a fight. There are times, he has learned, when one must punk out on the street code. Although he gives up the Black Muslim faith, which he has adopted for a time, he remembers what Muhammad, his teacher, has told him: "No matter a man's color or race, he has a need of dignity and he'll go anywhere, become anything, or do anything to get it—anything."

Down These Mean Streets is a powerful thrust at self-definition without apology or euphemism. Its language is swinging, masculine, gritty. Often awkward, the writing more often has a feline grace. Because the author bears down so mightly on his own search for identity, he dominates his book; Trina, friends, and family remain partially in shadow. Nevertheless, Thomas has a gift for pulling in minor characters for a telling scene that adds dimension to his theme: the stilted speech of a light-skinned Negro he meets in the South who claims to be mostly white and recites a litany of forebears; the mincing foolishness of a group of faggots trying to be what they are not.

Thomas reports nothing of his later rehabilitation work with junkies in Harlem and Puerto Rico--which was the subject of the prizewinning film *Petey and Johnny*--leaving off his narrative shortly after his release from prison at the age of twenty-eight. There is no grand resolution of problems, no big closing message. "I was a kid yesterday and my whole world was yesterday," he says in his new freedom. "I ain't got nothing but today and a whole lot of tomorrows."

Elmer Bendiner (essay date 1967)

SOURCE: "Machismo," in *The Nation*, Vol. 205, No. 9, 1967, pp. 283-84.

[*In this essay, Bendiner favorably reviews* Down These Mean Streets, *but criticizes Thomas's forbearance with the white society that almost destroyed him.*]

Piri Thomas in his autobiography, ***Down These Mean Streets***, describes the passionate, painful search to validate his manhood for which, with dead-pan cool, he had to fight, steal, submit to buggery, open his veins to any drug, take any dare, any risk. He has done it all in Harlem's mean streets and gone on from *machismo* to manhood, acquiring during the journey an understanding of man.

This is not a confirmation ritual imposed by what the sociologists call the "barrio subculture." This is a trial by ordeal that American society devises when it challenges a boy to feel like a man while he's up to his neck in the muck that is thrown at him.

Piri Thomas emerged from his ordeal like a phoenix out of the fire. . . . More important, perhaps, he has given us this document of how a boy grows up in hell.

His account is all the more effective because he has not written of his childhood as hell untempered by love. He writes fondly—almost sentimentally—of the barrio and its people as if there were no villains, Negro or white, but only victims. . . .

When he is not talking about the fight for manhood he is developing the second theme of man's development, what Whitman called, "the dear love of comrades." Comradeship to a boy does not depend on a cause or a banner. It is blind to human faults and deaf to reason.

There is one danger in Piri Thomas' book though not primarily of his making. Middle-class Americans may smile contentedly when they finish its horrors and say: "You see, I knew it could be done. There is some good in them after all, and if they only try like Piri Thomas, they can all make it."

To guard against that crushing smugness it would have been good if Piri had a bit more anger and a bit less of the Puerto Rican's Christ-like tolerance that bids them murmur sympathetically at the hostile world—"*Ay Bendito.*"

Robert P. Haro (essay date 1972)

SOURCE: "Book Reviews: 'Savior, Savior Hold My Hand'," in *Library Journal*, Vol. 97, No. 14, August, 1972, p. 2579.

[*Below, Haro favorably reviews* Savior, Savior Hold My Hand.]

Get this book as soon as possible. That's the best advice this reviewer can give. *Savior, Savior Hold My Hand* will be called urban ethnic history, social psychology, sociology, etc.; but it is, in fact, an excellent literary account of Puerto Rican life in America.

As a sequel to Thomas' successful *Down These Mean Streets*, this work continues the story of a dark Puerto Rican's struggle to avoid the disasters of drugs, prostitution, crime, gang wars, etc. . . .

Oh, to be sure, the book has stylistic flaws and weaknesses, but nothing that detracts from its impact. It is a potpourri of urban English slang, underworld terminology, and Puerto Rican Spanish à la New York. To assist the reader with this vocabulary, a glossary is included. This book is excellent. . . .

George Anderson (essay date 1972)

SOURCE: "Book Reviews: 'Savior, Savior, Hold My Hand'," in *America*, Vol. 127, No. 19, December 9, 1972, pp. 500, 502.

[*In the following essay, Anderson finds* Savior, Savior Hold My Hand *interesting, but not as accomplished as* Down These Mean Streets.]

For those familiar with *Down These Mean Streets*, reading Piri Thomas' new book, *Savior, Savior, Hold My Hand* is an interesting but disappointing experience. . . . [While] the former is strong and vital, the latter never really comes together as a living unified work.

Theoretically it is the sequel which should be the more powerful. It recounts the struggle in the early 1960's of a young Puerto Rican, embittered by poverty, drug addiction, prison and racism, to establish in his life some degree of unity and meaningfulness. . . .

Accompanying his religious conversion is an awakening social consciousness which . . . leads him to accept a position as counsellor in a street club begun by another ex-con and convert to Christianity, John Clause.

From this point on, the story revolves mainly around Thomas' activities as an organizer among teen-aged blacks, Puerto Ricans and Italians, and the growing tension and ultimate break with Clause. An important sub-theme is institutional racism.

By the end of the book, disillusioned with churches in general and with the hypocritical Clause, Thomas has rejected organized Christianity altogether. Instead, he sees salvation as lying in the unity of the poor against their oppressors. . . .

Despite such potentially powerful material, *Savior, Savior* never comes to life as an autobiography. It lacks the perceptiveness, the richness of detail, humor and rhythm of language found everywhere in *Down These Mean*

Streets. There is a thinness of texture and little cumulative effect. The characters in the first book--especially Thomas' mother and father--stand out with a vividness which brings them as close as the next room. But the figures in *Savior, Savior, Hold My Hand* remain largely one-dimensional and shadowy. To know Piri Thomas for the brave and imaginative man of integrity that he is, one would have to go to the earlier part of his autobiography rather than to this later and inferior work.

William Kennedy (essay date 1974)

SOURCE: "Meaner Streets," in *The New Republic*, Vol. 171, Nos. 6 & 7, August 10 & 17, 1974, pp. 26-7.

[*In the following essay, Kennedy unfavorably reviews* Seven Long Times.]

[*Down These Mean Streets*] was a document about a special condition, a special place, a special man. It was dense with the specificity of his world, of his head, of the forces that played on them both, and it was told in a quasi-poetic argot that suited the material, added to the density. . . .

Thomas has now, in the age of Attica, resurrected the essence of [a 70-page segment of *Down These Mean Streets*], retitled it *Seven Long Times* and told the story all over again. . . .

Now it is a dull echo. A second pot of tea made from the same teabag; but he doesn't seem to see that. He writes the new book as if the first one never existed. Worse, he relies on sentiment instead of specific thought, on generalizations instead of the fine detail that he lavished on the first work. . . .

Thomas does have some good moments: the Comstock riot of August 1955, for instance. He treated it in the first book and spoke of his own unwillingness to join the futile riot, a decision that probably saved him from nine more years. He avoids that personal issue in the second telling, but focuses sharply on the riot's aftermath, the ritual punishment of the rioters. . . .

The new book is more of a polemic than the first, an argument for meaningful rehabilitation of prisoners. . . . [Thomas] illuminates the racial divisions within the prison life, the blacks denied privileged jobs, the whites granted easier paroles. . . .

He is also good on the necessity for aggressive behavior, for any passive con will surely be raped and pillaged in every way. . . .

But for all the good touches, there are long stretches of banality, renderings of the overfamiliar and no really individualized style, structure or vision. His guards are uniformly evil (in the earlier book he found some good in at least one guard), and his vision of himself is as a total victim of society. The environment has failed him, and there is no real awareness in him that personal failures also account for the behavior that leads a man to prison.

I don't mean to patronize Thomas. He did seven years and he knows what the life is better than I'll ever know. But with this new book he doesn't get it down. *Seven Long Times* lacks specificity of life and of minds and stands as a timely but shallow use of leftover experience.

Larry Garvin (essay date 1975)

SOURCE: "The New World of Piri Thomas," in *The Crisis*, Vol. 82, No. 6, June-July, 1975, pp. 196-203.

[*In the following essay, Garvin discusses the similarities and differences among* Down These Mean Streets, Savior, Savior Hold My Hand, *and* Seven Long Times.]

Down These Mean Streets for me . . . is an account of the victory of innocent values over a dehumanizing environment.

This innocence comes from Piri's complete immersion in life, and his absolute commitment to telling the full story without selective omission. Piri's innocence survives the baptism of the street because he arms it with a survival tool: chameleon-like self-assertion. Thus the self-conscious voice of the prologue—"I am My Majesty Piri Thomas"—carries innocence to safety through the mean streets of brutalization.

Chronologically, *Savior* picks up where *Down These Mean Streets* ends. But a shifting of tone and a changing of style are evident, if not fully developed.

There is a tentativeness to *Savior*, reflecting the changes going on in the author's life itself. While much of the anger and self-assertiveness of *Down These Mean Streets* is retained, the writing as a whole is more controlled, the style more crafted.

Piri calls *Streets* his stylistic "kindergarten," and *Savior* his "grammar school." *Savior, Savior, Hold My Hand* doesn't always work as well as *Streets*. It moves uncertainly in a new direction. The chronological frame worked well in *Streets* because of the constant speed and intensity of delivery; but, it breaks down considerably in *Savior*, which sometimes lacks a consistency of style. The chapters often read like a quest for subject matter; Piri picking his way through the middle years of his life, looking for a viable hook on which to hang his creative expression.

He finds a hanger in the story of John Clause and the East Harlem youth gangs. But, by the time this story unfolds, the book is half finished. The early anecdotes are reminiscent of *Down These Mean Streets*, and deal with the first months after release from prison, the search for work, religion, and fair housing for his family. As such, the main theme of this book is racism. If the telling fal-

ters stylistically, it is because Piri bites off too much, not for lack of experienced insight. . . .

The story of John Clause is the real meat of this book. And if this work has a flaw, it is simply that it did not take that story and develop it into a more devastating blow against institutionalized Christian (*sic*) racism.

The telling of this story and its stylistic execution mark a shift in style for Piri. We no longer have the gut experience flung at us for what it's worth. Piri begins to place it within his own developing framework. If the result is tentative and seemingly incomplete at times, it is nevertheless compelling; if it doesn't stand on its own (though by and large, I think it does), it sits well as a transitional work between *Down These Mean Streets* and *Seven Long Times*. For in *Savior*, Piri has taken one step back from his experience; and that one step has provided a developing objectivity which comes to its fruition in *Seven Long Times*.

[*Seven Long Times*] is the logical end to years of self-analysis through creative expression; and, as such, adds a political framework which the first books lack. But the new Piri Thomas has a large spiritual direction as well, and this spirituality suggestively manifests itself in the title of this work.

The mystical number "seven" appears frequently in Piri's life. Thus, it is perhaps no accident that the seven years in prison are described in seven chapters of *Down These Mean Streets* and become part of the title in *Seven Long Times*. But there the similarities end. Whereas *Streets* presents the raw experience as subject matter within a context of multiple social abuses, *Times* places the experience under careful scrutiny, picking it apart into its components. In the end, the examination complete, Piri provides human alternatives for the future. *Times* presents a new stance; it is the voice of a man who sees himself rising above the stormy seas of inhumanity to gaze freely about.

Piri calls it his "high school" book. *Times* uses the subtle objectivity of time and style as much as *Down These Mean Streets* uses the primal scream of gut experience. In *Streets* the voice is deep inside of life; in *Times* the voice comes up from the depths, steps back, and speaks:

> What's the good of living in a present that's got no future, no nuttin' unless I make something. I fell into this life without no say and I'll be a . . . if I live without having nuttin' to say.

Piri brings much more than his prison experiences to this book; for, this man has bridged the rapids between the problem and the solution.

Not only does Piri Thomas represent a human being directly out of the experience, but a student of the subject, digging deep into the roots of oppresion, to find reasonable alternatives to the world we now live in. It is these very insights which give *Seven Long Times* its importance as a documentary of America's penal mentality, which gives the prison system its ostensible *raison d'etre*. . . .

Times is a psychologically penetrating account of how this tortuous system operates. Piri picks apart the details of prison experience and holds them up to the light of truth. . . .

[The] miracle of Piri Thomas is more than his survival; it is his great skill and insight in relating the truth of his victories and the truth of an oppressive system which made those victories absolutely necessary. And in *Times*, Piri brings these talents to a literary climax.

Seven Long Times is more than an account of prison life; it is a call to unity amongst all people, unity being the only force able to combat the inhumanity of the penal system and the society which requires medieval-style prisons in order to perpetuate itself.

With the publication of these three books, Piri Thomas has established himself as a writer deserving to be heard. But like many other Third World artists, Piri's publications have not meant economic success, and only sometimes sustenance. . . . [The] bumps Piri has received in life have not diminished significantly with publicaton: the "brand" society affixes to the "ex-anything" is permanent. Piri's struggle for survival as a creative artist is necessarily as intense as his struggle to survive the cruelties of his childhood.

Denise M. Wilms (essay date 1978)

SOURCE: "Children's Books: 'Stories from El Barrio'," in *Booklist*, Vol. 75, No. 7, December 1, 1978, pp. 620-21.

[*In the following excerpt, Wilms criticizes the restrictive narrative style of* Stories from El Barrio, *but praises the book's honesty.*]

Stylistically, these storied reminiscences [in *Stories from El Barrio*] suffer from restraints imposed by a writer not totally at home with a juvenile audience. They also lack the breadth of vision of, say, [Nicholasa Mohr's *El Bronx Remembered*]. . . . But there's a pervasive, gut-level honesty that breaks through that thin veneer of stiffness; personalities emerge intact, and pace is fluid. The stories, whether humorous, touching, or tragic, strongly voice their settings; their concerns . . . sharply present the barrio's multifaceted character. Street language is restrained and unexploitive. This is warm-serious-funny blend, authentic and stronger for it.

Sonia Nieto (essay 1981)

SOURCE: A review of *Stories from El Barrio*, in *Interracial Books for Children Bulletin*, Vol. 12, No. 6, 1981, pp. 18-19.

[*In the following review, Nieto praises the life experiences depicted in* Stories from El Barrio.]

Youngsters now have the opportunity to enjoy the story-telling skills of Piri Thomas just as older adolescents and adults have in the past. Matching his previous work in every way, these eight stories present an authentic look into Barrio life, from the stench of uncovered garbage in July to the sudden and violent death of gang members.

Anyone who has grown up in the ghetto can recognize and relive the joy and the pain of these experiences. The Barrio of the title is not limited here to Spanish Harlem; it encompasses the Loisaida (Lower East Side), as well as Brooklyn and the Bronx, representing the many places where Puerto Ricans live in New York.

The stories also represent a variety of experiences. We have, for example, in **"The Three Mosquiteers,"** the humiliating experiences of three youngsters who can hustle in Harlem but who are completely helpless as Boy Scouts in the swamps of New Jersey. In **"Amigo Brothers,"** which takes place on the Lower East Side, the author uses two "panitas" (close friends) to tell us about the invincibility of friendship in the ghetto. There is the fanciful and adventuresome **"Mighty Miguel,"** in which good triumphs over evil through the creative imaginings of a young boy left alone for an evening in his brownstone. There is also the stark realism of **"The Blue Wings and The Puerto Rican Knights,"** which begins as upbeat, cool and funny and ends with quick and surprising death, the death of children struggling to survive in a brutal environment.

Growing up Puerto Rican, the pride and the shame of it, is amply documented here. The searing pain of straightening nappy hair, in both a physical and an emotional sense, is vividly described in **"The Konk"** ("If you want white man's hair, there's a price you gotta pay," says the barber). Above all, the humanity of Thomas' characters jumps out at us. In spite of the oppression of El Barrio, the people enjoy one another, struggle through adversity, make mistakes and love their kids, whether embracing, forgiving or beating them. Throughout there is a sense of warmth and affection, of family ties and friendship as one's real strength in this life.

Humor is likewise present in every story, from the hilarious **"Three Mosquiteers"** to the poignant **"La Peseta"** (who among us does not remember stealing a quarter from our parents' bureau to have some illicit though fleeting pleasure at the candy store?).

Stories from El Barrio is anti-racist as well as anti-individualistic (friends are always hanging out together, fighting, teasing, helping and loving one another through a myriad of experiences), a welcome relief from stories extolling the virtues of "rugged individualism." Unfortunately, but perhaps inevitably, the majority of the characters in these stories are men, since they draw upon the youthful experiences and remembrances of a young man growing up in El Barrio. The women included are not necessarily presented in a sexist way, although one of the few mentioned is of course beautiful and dainty. On the other hand, there are the Honey Debutantes, a gang of girls that fights alongside the boys till the end. All in all, the accounts tend to be non-sexist. There is, however, an offensively stereotypic lisping and limp-wristed Devil in **"Mighty Miguel,"** and teachers and parents should be aware that some of the stories are realistically sprinkled with curses, both in English and Spanish.

Racing through all eight stories, I remembered my own childhood, at times laughing knowingly, at times profoundly saddened by these familiar vignettes of ghetto life. The humor which shines through the perplexities and twists of life will hopefully instill in both Puerto Rican and non-Puerto Rican youngsters who read the book a healthy respect for the people who populate the streets of all urban ghettos.

Piri Thomas   (essay date 1983)

SOURCE: "A Neorican in Puerto Rico: Or Coming Home," in *Images and Identities: The Puerto Rican in Two World Contexts*, edited by Asela Rodríguez de Laguna, Transaction Books, 1987, pp. 153-56.

[*In the following essay, which was originally presented at a conference at Rutgers University in April 1983, Thomas discusses his feelings about assimilation, racial pride, and growing up Puerto Rican in the United States.*]

I was born on September 30, 1928 in Harlem Hospital. My mother, Dolores Montañez, was born in Bayamón, Puerto Rico. My father, Juan Tomás, was born in Oriente, Cuba. My name at birth was supposed to be Juan Pedro Tomás Montañez. However, when I grew up and looked at my birth certificate I discovered that it said John Thomas. And, whoever heard of a *puertorriqueño* named John Thomas? I wondered at the time about the reasons behind this: Was it a planned program on the part of the hospital authorities for assimilation? Or had they convinced my parents that to have a name like John Thomas would give me a better chance in the United States of America?

I believe every child regardless of color, race, sex, or geographic location is born with a sense of either identifying with or being identified with others. When I was a child I would sit in a little corner because at that time the young ones were not to be seen or heard. I have always disagreed with this idea. How else can you learn if you cannot ask? I would listen to imaginal projections of Puerto Rico from my parents. My mother, Aunt Angelita, Aunt Otilia, neighbors, and friends would talk about the fantastic island in the Caribbean, using terms such as "Island of Enchantment" and "Borinquen," talking about its beaches, palm trees, and mountains. It never snowed there. I would look out the window while they were talking and as I looked at the gray streets below I wondered—why do we live here? I would ask the question: Hey, what are we doing here, Ma? and what I would get in return was a

little funny look. Of course, the situation was, and is, like it has been for every other immigrant that has come to this so-called Promised Land—it is always an economic problem. Believe me, those who have money in Puerto Rico only come here temporarily. They take a look and then they go back. It is only the poor who come here with a dream of someday going back to Puerto Rico, although they never quite make it in this sense.

When I was a child, like many others I wanted to "identify." I lived in three worlds: The world of the home; the world of the school; and the world of the street. At home, of course, it was very beautiful in many ways because Mami was a very spiritual woman.

I want all of you to know that I have written *Down These Mean Streets*. I could have written about Puerto Ricans living in penthouses, but Puerto Ricans were not living in penthouses on Fifth Avenue. If they were anywhere near the penthouses they were working as doormen.

Children are born with dignity and perceptiveness, and understanding, and they sense when they are loved or not loved. I am a human being who has not allowed the child-like qualities in me to be slaughtered by anyone. If you lose your childlike qualities, and this has nothing to do with childishness, you then lose that beautiful identity, your own personal dignity. That is what identity is all about, your sense of dignity.

I remember wanting to "identify" in school. I would dress in a white shirt, blue trousers, and a red tie. Doesn't that remind you of a walking flag? I did not mind at all. I would put my hand over my heart and pledge allegiance to the flag of the United States because it did say "with liberty and justice for all." I would sing just as loud the national anthem. I was a child and I wanted to belong.

Out in the streets, it was different. Racists could not make up their minds whether to call me a "nigger" or a "spik." I would say, "Hey you so-and-so, I am a human being, man. I'm beautiful, can't you see?" Like many children I was born very beautiful and natural, into a most unnatural atmosphere. I do not feel any shame or guilt for the things I wrote in *Down These Mean Streets* and my other book. I have learned within myself that I was not born a criminal from my mother's womb. I was born a very beautiful child in a very unnatural, criminal society, a society filled with racism, exploitation, and a complete lack of caring for human dignity.

It was not until I reached the age of thirty-two that I had a few revealing experiences. At times I thought that my youth would kill me, but one thing I had in my heart all the time was to see Puerto Rico. To visit Puerto Rico would be like a homecoming. In New York I felt that most of the time I would only be identifying with a fire hydrant. I could jump high over it but the funny thing was that many times I did not make it. I say this with humor because if I were to say it in the way it should be said, with the rage of emotion at the outrages and all the things that our people as a people have had to endure, my goodness!

I arrived in Puerto Rico in 1960, and once I got off the plane and felt the breeze I was dumbfounded. I got out of the tourist area and once I got past the Dorado Beach Club and the Hilton, I began to see that Puerto Rico was as beautiful as its people. I found out that in Puerto Rico there were green ghettos; there were grey ones here too, but I found beauty and dignity. Our country is beautiful because there is love and affection.

> **In my young fifty-four years, I want to continuously be able to identify with that which is positive. I have found out that we will never have unity unless we can have a unity that is born of truth, without hypocrisy, without envy. We are not to deal with greed, that exploits men, women, and children of all colors. I have learned to identify with the feeling of being universal. Wherever my feet are, that is my turf. I am an earth being, part of the earth and the universe. This way I can reach out more and I do not feel confined by being defined and thereby diminished. I am proud to be the mixture that I am, and I am proud to be part of a family. The worst thing in the world for any child is not to belong or to be completely kept from belonging. I have learned that in order for us as humans—and I speak to you, the young ones of all ages—to know where we are going, we also have to know from where we come. That is part of our dignity. My enemy is not color, sex, or geographic location. My enemy is the enemy of all children: indifference to human need.**

In Puerto Rico I discovered that my Spanish was atrocious. I spoke Spanish badly, but regardless of this fact I decided to go ahead because I was a Rican. Whenever I made a mistake someone would correct me without making me feel ashamed. One day I was talking and a little girl approached me and said, "Excuse me," and I said, "Don't mention it." She suddenly turned to me and asked: "Excuse me, are you from the North?" I said, "Hum." She added: "Are you from New York?" And when I asked her how she knew, she replied that it was because of the way I spoke Spanish. When she noticed my sadness, she asked for my forgiveness since she had not meant any offense. I only added that I wanted her to know that although I had been born in New York, my soul was Puerto Rican. And that I was proud of speaking the Spanish that I had learned from my mother.

I remember being in Puerto Rico in 1960 and working on a drug addiction program with Dr. Ramírez. I was exposed to a radio station where we could bring in parents for information. I remember my pride every Sunday morning when I got to that radio station. I sat in front of the microphone and said: "Buenos días, pueblo puertorriqueño. Este es Piri Thomas y con zapatos o sin zapatos, hablándoles en español" (Good morning Puerto Rico. This is Piri Thomas, with or without shoes, talking to you in Spanish). I was so proud to be in my country! I was born hung up in the middle, with no place to go. If you asked me now whether I have been accepted in Puerto Rico wholeheartedly, my goodness gracious! There is no way that I as a Puerto Rican here can be the same as a Puerto Rican from there. But one thing for sure is that we can certainly share, because being bilingual is not a crime, it is a knowledge, a way of flow, a means whereby we can defend each other to the best of our abilities and to the best of our souls.

In my young fifty-four years, I want to continuously be able to identify with that which is positive. I have found out that we will never have unity unless we can have a unity that is born of truth, without hypocrisy, without envy. We are not to deal with greed, that exploits men, women, and children of all colors. I have learned to identify with the feeling of being universal. Wherever my feet are, that is my turf. I am an earth being, part of the earth and the universe. This way I can reach out more and I do not feel confined by being defined and thereby diminished. I am proud to be the mixture that I am, and I am proud to be part of a family. The worst thing in the world for any child is not to belong or to be completely kept from belonging. I have learned that in order for us as humans—and I speak to you, the young ones of all ages—to know where we are going, we also have to know from where we come. That is part of our dignity. My enemy is not color, sex, or geographic location. My enemy is the enemy of all children: indifference to human need. I have learned to be very careful with words and feelings. I have learned to say what I mean and mean what I say because it is very important how your behavior can modify children's minds in the name of love. The children, young people, all of you were born highly perceptive, psychic if you will. When somebody says to me that we are a minority I take it as an offense. I get very angry because to me the word *minority* is just another synonym for "nigger" or "spik." *Minority* means less than and whoever heard of a child being born "less than"? I speak as a majority of one, similar to everyone but with different fingerprints.

If you ask me what I have learned about "identifying," it is that identification comes from within oneself. If you know what is inside of you, then you can relate to others. Relations begin at home, men-women relations, feelings. I come from a long line of machos and machismo and most big-mouthed macho mistakes. It is from good women that I have been able to learn. I had to first go in and check out the women spirit that is in me, that spirit that comes from my mother and will always last in my soul.

Geoffrey Fox   (essay date 1996)

SOURCE: "Jumping the Puddle," in *Hispanic Nation*, edited by Geoffrey Fox, Birch Lane Press, 1996, pp. 200-01.

[*In the following excerpt, Fox favorably reviews* Down These Mean Streets *and provides a brief summary of Puerto Rican life in New York.*]

The first important Puerto Rican memoir written in English was Piri Thomas's story of growing up among violence, decay, and drugs in Spanish Harlem in the late forties and fifties, ***Down These Mean Streets*** (1967). This was the precursor of the literary movement that in the mid-1970s would take the name "Nuyorican" (for New York Puerto Rican).[27]

Earlier generations of Puerto Rican writers in New York, such as the radical journalists Bernardo Vega and Jesón or the poet Julia de Burgos, remembered life on the island (Puerto Rico, not Manhattan) and were most comfortable writing in Spanish.[28] They had a clear idea of who they were and no reason to question their membership in one of the great cultural and intellectual traditions of the world, the one that had begun in Spain and been enriched by its mingling with other cultures in the Spanish-speaking New World. And this may be why they felt no urgent need to write exhaustively about their own childhoods. Childhood had been the least problematic period of their lives.

But the New York-born children of the poor and mostly poorly educated Puerto Ricans who "jumped the puddle"— *brincaron el charco*—in DC-7s to La Guardia Airport in the 1940s or who had arrived earlier packed onto steamers, like the famous *Marine Tiger*, lost their connection to that proud Spanish tradition. In a climate and concrete canyons that were nothing like the place their parents remembered, surrounded by people who had no comprehension of and little sympathy for their culture, these children knew Puerto Rico only as a chimera glimpsed in photographs and the stories of their elders.

Piri Thomas's was the first of this generation to write of being made to feel ashamed of speaking Spanish and of looking neither quite white nor quite black. That he could not only survive the mean streets but write a book about it—and in proper English, which must have astonished his early teachers—was a major triumph. He wrote of his confusion about whether he was "black" or "white" because he "came out" dark like his father and his siblings were lighter, like his mother—a confusion that was entirely the product of encounters with the racial values outside his household, because within his Puerto Rican family such distinctions had not carried any special privileges. His meditations on such experiences, a process of discovery and healing for himself, helped other New York Latinos find a vocabulary to talk about their own experiences and thus heal themselves.

NOTES

[27] Piri Thomas, *Mean Streets.*

[28] Bernardo Vega, *Memoirs of Bernardo Vega: A contribution to the history of the Puerto Rican community in New York*, trans. Juan Flores,

ed. César Andreu Iglesias (New York: Monthly Review Press, 1984); Julia de Burgos, *Canción de la verdad sencilla* (San Juan, P.R.: Imprenta Baldrich, 1939); Jesús Colón, *A Puerto Rican in New York, and Other Sketches* (New York: Mainstream Publishers, 1961). Colón wrote for radical Spanish-language papers for many years before beginning an English-language column for the *Daily Worker* in 1955.

Piri Thomas with Ilan Stevens (interview date 1996)

SOURCE: "Race and Mercy: A Conversation with Piri Thomas," in *Massachusetts Review*, Vol. 37, No. 3, Autumn, 1996, pp. 344-54.

[*In the following interview, Thomas discusses the impact that heritage, racism, and spirituality have had on his writing.*]

Piri Thomas was one of the leading voices of the 60's movement that forced the issues of race and discrimination into the minds of mainstream readers and publishers. After spending time in prison, Thomas found new clarity by reflecting on his plight as a dark-skinned, Spanish-speaking Caribbean in the United States. His first work, ***Down These Mean Streets***, is one of the best known works about growing up Puerto Rican in New York. Originally published in 1967, it is now considered a classic and has never been out of print. In a powerful and penetrating look at U.S. society, Thomas chronicles his adolescence and early adult years by focusing on the problems faced by a working-class Puerto Rican who is trying to find his place in the racist society which rejects him.

Thomas was born in 1928 and grew up in the streets of El Barrio. While fluent in Spanish, he became a bona fide English-speaking writer because, as he puts it, "this land is my land." He lives in Berkeley, California, with his wife and daughters, and remains active as a writer and public speaker, addressing issues of racial tension and ways to bring people back together. Some of his other books include ***Savior, Savior, Hold My Hand*** (1972), ***Seven Long Times*** (1974), and ***Stories from El Barrio*** (1974). This interview took place in mid-1995.

[ILAN STAVANS]: *I would like to start with the topic of language. Would you reflect on your relationship between Spanish and English? What does the Spanish language mean to you and what does the English language mean to you? How close or far away are you from each of them? What do you feel for each of them?*

[PIRI THOMAS]: I remember with all my heart and soul the first words that I learned from Mami and Papi were all in Spanish but as I grew up I knew that I was not speaking Spanish from Galicia or Barcelona in Spain. I was speaking the Spanish that is spoken in Puerto Rico, which I call Puerto Rican Spanish, because we kept our nuances and feelings and energies and words that came from Africa like *chévere*, which means great. We are a mixture of all those who conquered us over the centuries, taking our women with or without permission. We are a culmination of all that energy, but our spirit is as free as it was born to be. We are a conglomeration of manifestations.

And so Spanish is the language in which you expressed your first words.

Sí, I began to go through the same process that everyone has undergone under the system, beginning with the Native Americans: the assimilation process. I remember in my own childhood in the thirties being in this school and I could not understand what the teacher was saying so much because they spoke very fast sometimes and I could not catch the words. I'd lean over to my friend saying "José, mira, what did the teacher say?" He would tell me and I would continue to do my homework. And so that teacher came roaring upon me and said "listen, stop talking in that language," and I said "well, I am speaking my mother's language. My mother's from Puerto Rico, I was born in this country," and she says "well you stop talking that, you have to learn English, you are in America now. After all, how else do you expect to become President of the United States if you do not learn to speak English correctly." I thought in my young heart, "my God this teacher has more faith than I have in my someday becoming President of the United States if I learn my English well enough." And the tremendous assimilation happened to me. As a child, I first had to think in Spanish to speak in English. Then, I had to think in English to speak in Spanish, because I had forgotten the language. I had forgotten the lessons that were taught in my home where my mother taught me how to read, beginning with readings from the Bible. So I've made a determined effort to regain my inheritance back to where I came from, to learn where I had come from in order to know where I was going, to be able to then recognize my true reality, the true reality of what we are in the scheme of things. I learned that we are human beings, but that there were those who believed that there were only two kinds of people on this earth: those who ruled and those who were ruled.

But while we can reclaim our past through the Spanish language, we must acknowledge that Spanish is also the language used by the conquistadores *in the Americas.*

I'm with you totally. In fact, I said it's ironic, that we who are from all the pueblos, Chile, Nicaragua, Peru, Ecuador, Cuba, Santo Domingo, Puerto Rico, all the islands, Central and South America, Mexico, are bound, blended, and held together by the language of the conqueror, whose fever for gold destroyed us physically, mentally, spiritually, and morally. They stripped away the indigenous knowledge and the religious beliefs of those they found and forced everybody into their mold which was slavery.

When you talk about regaining one's own past, one's own background and heritage, you seem to imply that the way to do it is through language. I recently talked to a couple of Puerto Rican writers who are close friends and they were complaining that because they write in English in this country and are mainland Puer-

to Ricans, their work is almost totally ignored in the island because of the language issues. How about you? What is your situation? Is your work known in Puerto Rico?

Well let me tell you, my brother, with all sincerity I agree. I went into San Germán, I believe, where I met beautiful people. When I walked into the lobby, the walls were covered with photographs, beautiful photographs, of all the Puerto Rican brothers and sisters, writers, poets, and all the feelings, all the energies, Palés Matos, Lola. I looked to the walls for a picture of all of us from the Barrio and did not find one. So I asked the brother, "Why don't we have pictures of the poets and writers, brothers and sisters from El Barrio? Aren't we all puertorriqueños?" And he told me "Well, because you don't write in Spanish." I told him "and what about these writers who wrote in French? These ones write in French, this one could speak German" and he just looked. I added "you have to remember one of our national poets Antonio Corretjer, who said that no matter if we're born on the moon we are still puertorriqueños to our soul." And "nadie, nobody," I told him, "can take away my heritage, because I, Juan Pedro Tomás, was born from a Puerto Rican womb, boricua. Although I was born in el norte my soul is Puerto Rican." But things are so mixed up for Puerto Ricans. The only reason why I knew of Puerto Rico is because I sat in the corner and listened to the grown-ups speaking about places like Fajardo, Bayamón, and San Juan, among other places on the island. My beautiful child-energy absorbed all that information by osmosis. I finally went to Puerto Rico when I got out of prison at the age of thirty-two. My God, as that wall of green humidity enveloped me, it was like I was entering into my mother's arms. However, soon I began to see the reality of U.S. colonialism in Puerto Rico—a so-called Commonwealth, that really means common for the pueblo and wealth for the latter-day carpetbaggers who enjoy a favorable tax status with the U.S. government.

Let's focus on religion.

I am a spiritual man. We all have a spirit—good, bad, or indifferent. I come from a family of different denominations. My father was a deathbed Catholic. He was only going to see a priest when he was ready to kick the bucket, but he was a very good man, he did not drink, he did not smoke, he was a good athlete. He believed in doing unto others as you would like to be done to yourself. My lovely mother was a Seventh-Day Adventist, she cooked on Friday before the sun went down and did not cook again until Saturday when the sun went down. We went to church on the Sabbath, we were the closest thing to the children of Israel in that sense of being. And my aunt, Angelita, my mother's sister, she was Pentecostal and I loved that church the best because you could express yourself there, with loud Alleluias and Glorias a Díos. In the others, you had to stay very quiet. In the Catholic church they spoke in Latin and I could not understand. But in the Pentecostal church, I could express myself. I began to think about God and what God was. I could not see him but they told me I could feel him, but that changed as the years went on and I made my inner journey, especially when I went to prison where you have plenty of time. I was determined that I was going to educate my mind. I was not going to eradicate it. I made inner journeys within myself, so as to judge for myself on who I was in my sense of being. I wrote it into my poetry, "To me God is a smile on the face of a child that is not being wasted." "To me God is spelled G-O-O-D, good." Every child has their own gift of energy that can make direct contact with the power force within them as well as contact with others. Everything in life has had some kind of influence on me, in one way or another. In prison, I spent time reading books on the religions of Islam, Buddhism, Confucianism. I was looking for answers in my six-by-eight-by-nine prison cell.

When did literature become an answer to you, a tool for salvation? Was it in prison, as you suggest at the end of **Down These Mean Streets***? Or was it before?*

Long before prison. My mother had saved some money from the sewing machine, because she used to work in the sweat shops but she also used to bring home work from the job and work until two or three o'clock in the morning, because there was no work for my father. My father came running home one day happy, because he had hit the bolita, where you play los números—get three numbers and you win. And with that money and what my mother had saved we moved to a foreign country called Babylon, Long Island. I went to school out there, which became a battleground for me. I was the only little coffee grain for miles around in a sea of white milk. However, I had an English teacher, whose name was Mrs. Wright. She was very kind to me, this beautiful white teacher, and I loved her energy flows. One day she asked the class to write a composition about anything we wished. And I wrote a composition on how much I loved her beautiful brunette hair and her hazel eyes and how I loved the way she smelled when she came over to look at my work. However, I did not particularly care for her pronouns and adjectives and verbs because I did not know what the hell she was talking about. Then, days later, the papers came back and she asked me to turn mine over. I'd written two and a half pages; on the half-page that was left, it said in red pencil—I remember it to this day—"Son, your punctuation is lousy. Your grammar is non-existent. However, if you wish to be a writer someday, you will be. P.S. We both love my wife," signed her husband. Someone had recognized that I had a gift, an ability to express, to share feelings through words. I believe all children are born poets and that every poet is the child and what the children need is a world that will guide them towards creativity and not towards greed.

Was there ever any writer while you were at that time in Babylon or later on while you were in jail that influenced you, not in terms of the friendship that you had with her or with him, but whose book you thought was something to emulate?

I loved to read as a kid. The reason I loved to read was because I was introduced by a very caring teacher to a very caring librarian on 110th Street in my Barrio. She allowed me to take out two books and I would go to the fire escape and turn my blanket into a hammock and I'd just sit back reading. I'd read whatever I found. I loved adventure stories, I loved science fiction or traveling to other universes. I loved the energies of Jack London and the white wolf and fang, everything, the feelings. Actually, I didn't have a whole lot of time to read until I went to prison, where I found out that I could create a world in my mind that would take me away from all that if I really tuned myself to books and my imagination. One night, a brother whose nickname was Young Blood knocked on my prison cell. He knocked very low and I said "Aha" and he said "Tommy, Tommy, they wrote a book with my name on it, Young Blood, you know, and, man, I want you to read it. It's by a brother man, a black brother." At that time, we were calling each other black. And he handed me the book through the bars and it was called *Youngblood* by John Oliver Killens. He was an attorney who was also a very fine writer, a beautiful black human being. I read the book; it had been read by so many people that the pages were like onion skin. When I finished reading it, Young Blood asked, "what'd you think of it, Tommy?" and I said "Man, it was really dynamite, you live it, the whole feeling." And I added "Young Blood, you want to know something?" and he said "yeah" and I said, "I could write too." And he smiled at me and he said "yeah I know you can, Tommy" and that's when I began to write what would one day be known as **Down These Mean Streets**. At that time, it was entitled *Home Sweet Harlem*.

Race is an issue ubiquitous in your work. In fact, very few Latino writers today are brave enough to discuss it in such plain, uninhibited ways as you do.

Children have a spirit of discernment and the ability to perceive and to sense and to feel and they can look at a person and see the look of contempt or the outrage or the disgust on people's faces. It is very easy for children to read people like people read books. I was one of those children. So when you ask of racism and bigotry, yes, I began at the first stage of life in the barrio. As I grew older it grew harder. I remember the first time I went to the South with my friend Billy. I sat in the front of the bus and when the bus got to the Mason Dixon line, our driver got off and a new driver got on. Immediately, he said "all the colored to the back" and all the coloreds got up and went back and I just sat there. And he said "I want all of you colored people to go to the back" and I said "look I am puertorriqueño" and he looked at me and said "I don't care what kind of nigger you are" and he put his hand into his side pocket. Using the better part of my discretion and with a great nudging on my arm from Billy, because he knew we would be killed, I grudgingly but with dignity went to the back of the bus and sat for the rest of the ride staring at the back of his head determined that I would never forget this incident. And they'd call me "nigger!" and if it wasn't nigger they'd call me "spik." Racism was a horror to bear because most times it wasn't quite said. It was worse because they dug into your psyche with one little look of contempt or their nose would flare as you passed them as if they had smelled dirt. So I came to my mother enraged and feeling this, saying "mira mami, they called me this." So my mother said "listen to this, my son, I want you to learn this and remember it for the rest of your life. I want you to know that there is no one in this world better than you, only maybe better off, with money and so forth, and maybe only better off. You have your sense of beautiful dignity. Nobody can take that away. Only you can give it away or sell it, ¿entiendes?" My mother said, "they don't have to kill you with hatred my son, envy will suffice." Wisdom from my mother.

I've heard you say that literature is useful to fight racism. But how effective can it be? Writers are also depressive types. Whenever they realize that words are simply words—ephemeral, transient—they fall into an impossible abyss of fatalism.

Words are important because they awaken consciousness and thus can inspire action. So you have to be careful how you use words because they can be bullets or butterflies. Children become what they learn or don't learn. Children become what they are taught or not taught. For thousands of years we have heard propaganda about white supremacy and "might makes right." Because if you conquer people by might, strip away their education, their beliefs, their culture, and their land, then in two or three generations their children will be in the dark ages again. We had very bright minds when we first went into their schools, because children are not born stupid. The world has no right to judge intelligence by the color of one's skin. Different colors were meant to be very beautiful just like flowers come in different and beautiful colors. Birds are different colors. And this is the struggle that we have had to wage, to allow all the colors to express their humanity through literature and the other arts to learn from each other, as a people, for we are not only geographic locations, colors, sexes, or preferences. We are earthlings who share a common bond—our humanity.

When **Down These Mean Streets** *came out, there was an immediate uproar in terms of the sexual explicitness and there were even some legal problems. When you were writing the subsequent books,* **Savior, Savior,** *and* **Seven Long Times**, *and* **Stories From El Barrio**, *did the experience of the censorship with* **Down These Mean Streets** *affect you in any conscious or unconscious way when you were writing? Were you trying, in a sense, to be more defiant and explicit or less defiant and explicit?*

I didn't have too much time to think about all that. I was so elated with my gift of being able to write even though the first book had almost killed me because it was such an outpouring--I almost suffered an emotional burnout. I could not stand the agony anymore. So when I wrote *Savior, Savior, Hold my Hand*, I wrote it more gentle.

And when I wrote *Seven Long Times*, I was looking at it twenty-five years later, very objectively, like a scientist. But *Down These Mean Streets*, that was an explosion from my very soul and I will utilize part of that power in my upcoming book, *A Matter of Dignity*. I will have to go back to that time to relive it. Then, as my clarity of mind begins to rise, you will see that instead of rage without reason, there is now reason.

DOWN THESE MEAN STREETS INAUGURATED A NEW AWARENESS.

Everywhere I go, people congratulate me. Over the years I've received hundreds if not thousands of letters. People have said to me, "Bro, I had never read a book in my life but this was put in my hand and it opened my soul to reading. I never finished a book in my life, hey, bro, wow!" I was writing the rage out of me but at the same time, I was writing for all of us who were living in that hell. I was not born a criminal from my mother's womb, none of us who had been into the so-called criminal activity had been born criminals from our mother's womb. We were all born very beautiful children, just like any other little babies, into a very criminal society of racism and bigotry and horror to the nth degree, not to leave out promises that very rarely, if ever, came to be. Many people do not understand that to write that book I almost blew my mind. Because I had to force myself to go back in time and feel all the feelings again which included all the agony and the pain. That book was supposed to be something to be swept under the rug and forgotten but I went and opened Pandora's Box, and out came not only the demons, but also the truths. That's why I could not leave a chapter unfinished; I would work on it three or four days straight, reliving all the emotions from that time. But once I discovered that the truth brought relief from the pain, it was wonderful. I then added humor and when you have humor you can laugh, and when you can laugh, the demons go away.

And finally, let me go back to what that teacher told you when you were little, about becoming President of the United States. Did you ever consider running for public office?

I'd probably be assassinated on the first day. I don't have political ambitions. I decided to devote my whole life and energy to passing on the fruits of the learning tree—wisdoms, common sense. So I've stayed with the children. It gives me great satisfaction to be doing something very beautiful that no one can take away from me—sharing with the children the message that each one of us is very beautiful, that we are not sub-species, not sub-humans, not niggers nor spiks nor minorities. We are all human beings—born of earth and the universe. Colors were meant to be simple decorations and not declarations of war.

Additional coverage of Thomas's life and career is contained in the following sources published by the Gale Group: *Contemporary Authors*, Vols. 73-76; *Contemporary Literature Criticism*, Vol. 17; *Hispanic Writers*.

Sabine Ulibarrí
1919–

Chicano short story writer, poet, and essayist.

INTRODUCTION

As a poet, short story writer, and essayist, Sabine Ulibarrí is one of the most well-known Chicano writers in the United States. Ulibarrí's books of poetry and criticism were first published in Mexico and Spain because, while most of his works appear in bilingual editions, he has always written in Spanish which he, himself, translates into English. The bilingual appearance of his work has garnered Ulibarrí a diverse audience; his stories are reprinted in more than three dozen regional and national anthologies, many of which are textbooks used in elementary, high school, and university literature and culture courses. In addition to his scholarly works, textbooks, and essays, Ulibarrí has published two books of poetry and two collections of short stories, and edited another collection of prose and poetry written by his students. Most recently he published *Mayhem Was Our Business: Memorias de un veterano* (1996), a memoir of Ulibarrí's experiences as an airforce gunner in World War II. An educational and civic leader, and a prominent spokesman for Hispanic literature and culture, he was honored with a Governor's Award in 1987 in recognition of his contributions to education and literature.

Sabine R. Ulibarrí was born in Santa Fe, New Mexico, in 1919, but was raised in Tierra Amarilla in northern New Mexico. Educated in public schools, Ulibarrí began to teach when he was just nineteen. His first teaching position was in the Rio Arriba County Schools, where he taught for two years. He then transferred to the El Rito Normal School from 1940-42. From 1942-45, Ulibarrí fought in WWII in the air force and flew thirty-five combat missions over Europe for which he received the Distinguished Flying Cross and the Air Medal on four seperate occasions. After the war, he returned to study at the University of New Mexico under the G.I. Bill and graduated with degrees in Spanish and English. He later received an assistantship to teach Spanish, earning his M.A. after writing his thesis on the novelist Benito Pérez Galdós. After teaching at UNM for a period, he took a leave of absence to pursue a doctorate in Spanish at the University of California. He received his Ph.D. in 1958, and returned to full-time teaching in New Mexico. In 1962, his dissertation on the Spanish poet Juan Ramón Jiménez was published in Spain. Two years later, his first book of short stories, *Tierra Amarilla: Cuentos de Nuevo Mexico* (1964: *Tierra Amarilla: Stories of New Mexico*), was published in Ecuador. Ulibarrí also wrote poems collected in the volumes, *Al cielo se sube a pie* (1966; *One Gets to Heaven on Foot*) and *Amor y Ecua-dor* (1966; *Love and Ecuador*), both published in Spain. Ulbarrí had lived in Ecuador to coordinate educational programs for UNM and while there, became enamored of its people, culture, and natural beauty. For his work, he was given the Distinguished Citizen Award and Honorary Citizen Award from the city of Quito, the capital of Ecuador. After founding the Andean Center at UNM-Quito in 1968, Ulibarrí was elected president of the American Association of Teachers of Spanish and Portugese and was Executive Council Member from 1970-75. Beginning in 1973, he chaired the Department of Modern and Classical Languages at UNM for ten years, and then retired from UNM with a New Mexico Regents Meritorious Service Medal. During this period, Ulibarrí published a second collection of short stories, *Mi abuela fumaba puros y otros cuentos de Tierra Amarilla* (1977; *My Grandmother Smoked Cigars, and other Tales of Tierra Amarilla*). He has continued writing and teaching into the 1990s, most recently publishing his memoirs as a soldier in WWII.

Ulbarrí's first works were collections of poetry, *Al cielo se sube a pie*, published in Mexico, and *Amor y Ecuador*. Both are similar in content, language, and poetic expression. The language of *Al cielo* has been described as "deliberate and precise" in its exploration of love, women, Tierra Amarilla, uprootedness, solitude, and the frequently devastating effects of progress, among other things. The poetry of love dominates in Ulibarrí's poetry, its absence or transitory nature and his problems with finding the ideal woman. Like Eve, woman in these poems is the joy and bane of male existence. *Amor y Ecuador* is divided into sections on love and the poet's experience in Ecuador. In the first part, Ulibarrí shares the experience of his stay in Ecuador. Generally, Ecuador rejuvenated him, and the book recreates his joyful and exciting experience with subtle inflections of anger at the exploitation of the common people in the country. In the poem "Indosincrasia" the conflict is especially apparent. While the eyes of the Indian reveal a reservoir of strength and dignity, they also reveal the depths to which they have been frustrated since being conquered in the fifteenth and sixteenth centuries by Spanish conquistadors. Still the poem ends on a note of hope, as the poet himself has overcome the prejudice and ill treatment directed toward Hispanics in America. He calls on the Ecuadoreans to "Raise your eyes and speak, and leap from the trench." Love is an ongoing theme in this second collection, although the fruits of his quest are often marred by an illusory love. Ulibarrí's short fiction, written in the style of the *costumbrismo*, is a personal exploration of humanity, expressed in quirky characteristics and the animated oration of local legends. Together, the people of his stories comprise a community of Hispanics whose lives intertwine and weave through time and location.

Perhaps the most interesting story is "Sábelo," narrated by a nine-year old who tells of Don José Viejo, a sharp-tongued old man. After getting beyond his fear of the man, the child develops a friendship with him. Ulibarrí's essays describe a different facet of his community. For example, in "Cultural Heritage of the Southwest," he defends the necessity for bilingual education to school-age children in order to ease the learning gap and encourage native culture and history. He claims that this would develop a greater sense of cultural and social assimilation, encourage further education, and increase opportunities. Ulibarrí's most recent work is his memoir of World War II, in which he tells of his experiences as a ball-turret gunner. Initially resistant to enlisting and determined to sit out the war while obtaining his law degree, Ulibarrí's growing sense of shame and duty compelled him to join the U.S. Army Air Force. The experience changed his life. As a combat flier he was one of the elite, but a grueling combat tour brought him face to face with hysteria-induced exultation, fear, and the seductive power of violence and destruction. His calm assessment of the horrors of war is, however, tempered by stories of generosity and friendship.

Not only recognized and admired as a writer, administrator, and teacher, Ulibarrí is also a man whose well-articulated thoughts on today's crucial issues are still highly respected by the Chicano community and progressive educators across the United States. Although politics was not the main arena of Ulibarrí's efforts, he deserves recognition for his early stands on bilingual and bicultural education. His literary explorations of the interior terrain of the marginalized Hispanic community has brought him to the forefront of Spanish American literature.

PRINCIPAL WORKS

Spanish for the First Grade (instruction) 1957

El mundo poetico de Juan Ramon; estudio estilistico de la lengua poetica y de los simbolos (criticism) 1962

Fun Learning Elementary Spanish, 2 Vol. (instruction) 1965

Tierra Amarilla: Cuentos de Nuevo Mexico [Tierra Amarilla: Stories of New Mexico] (short stories) 1964

Al cielo se sube a pie (poetry) 1966

Amor y Ecuador (poetry) 1966

La fragua sin fuego/No Fire for the Forge (short stories and poems) 1971

El alma de la raza (poetry) 1971

Mi abuela fumaba puros y otros cuentos de Tierra Amarilla/My Grandma Smoked Cigars and Other Stories of Tierra Amarilla (short stories) 1977

Primeros encuentros/First Encounters (short stories) 1982

El gobernador Glu Glu (short stories) 1988

El condor, and Other Stories (short stories) 1989

Kissing Cousins: 1000 Words Common to Spanish and English (instruction) 1991

Flow of the River: Corre el Rio (short stories) 1992

Sueños/Dreams (poetry) 1994

Sabine R. Ulibarrí: Critical Essays (criticism) 1995

Mayhem Was Our Business/Memorias de un veterano (essays) 1996

CRITICISM

Donaldo W. Urioste (essay date 1986)

SOURCE: "Costumbrismo in Sabine R. Ulibarrí's *Tierra Amarilla: Cuentos de Nuevo Mexico*," *Missions in Conflict: Essays on U.S.-Mexican Relations and Chicano Culture*, Germany: Gunter Narr Verlag Tübingen, 1986, pp. 169-78.

[*In the following excerpt, Urioste highlights Ulibarrí's short stories as exemplary of the costumbrismo tradition in their exploration of the emotional growth and rites of passage of youth in America.*]

Among the oldest literary traditions in the Chicano Southwest is the short story. As with poetry and drama, this genre was initially introduced into the region in the form of folktales by the Spanish colonists of the sixteenth century, and was passed on orally from one generation to another. The vast majority of these folktales are of Old World origin and still represent the lore and cultural heritage that Hispanic settlers brought with them, when they first settled the area.[1] Moreover, during the colonial period the American Southwest also experienced great influxes of Mexican immigration which brought with them folk narratives originated in Mexico. Introduced by these settlers was lore dealing with such subjects and motifs as *la llorona, la malinche, las ánimas, la muerte, la Virgen de Guadalupe* and the lives and miracles of other Mexican saints. As with the earlier Spanish folktales, the Mexican *cuentos* were interwoven with local culture and geography to forge a new literary reality.

Following in the molds established by these traditions of folk literature, much of the early fiction written by Chicanos also drew heavily from elements of a folk existence.[2] With its multifaceted history of story and lore, rich in so many ways so as to function as a muse for literary inspiration, the Southwest first produced writers whose fiction was deeply rooted in the traditions, beliefs and customs of its people. Folklore, in this sense, forms an integral part of the writings of Nina Otero, Jovita Gonzales, Fray Angélico Chávez, Josefina Escajeda, and Arthur L. Campa,[3] and to this day continues to be a major source of inspiration for many writers of fiction and poetry.[4] However, whereas the primary intention of the earlier writers was generally limited to recapturing, recording and romantically depicting memories, forms, and images of a bygone time, the objective of the contemporary writers is more literary and social. That is, the latter group is not only inspired by the urge to recapture and salvage forms and meanings from the past, but also by the desire to create works of art and to record and critically reflect upon the present.

Among the short story writers notable for this trait is the New Mexican, Sabine Reyes Ulibarrí. To date, Ulibarrí stands out as one of the most versatile and prolific of Chicano writers. In addition to his highly acclaimed *Tierra Amarilla: cuentos de Nuevo México* (1964), he also has to his credit two other collections of short fiction, two books of poetry and a major work of literary criticism.[5] As the title of *Tierra Amarilla: cuentos de Nuevo México* suggests, these tales, as well as those in the other two collections, focus on the life and people of Tierra Amarilla, the northern New Mexican village of Ulbarrí's birth and childhood. They are, in essence, memories of a bygone day in which the author-narrator nostalgically recalls particular events, mysteries, and inhabitants of his native *pueblo*. Like the traditional *cuadros de costumbres* of Spanish and Spanish American letters, Ulibarrí skillfully and poetically describes that provincial milieu's most intimate life patterns: its customs, traditions, manners, beliefs, language, types, dress, etc. Notwithstanding this marked concern for the culturally quaint and picturesque, however, Ulibarrí's skillful use of language, irony, caricature, and humor add an ever present vitality to the stories.

Tierra Amarilla: cuentos de Nuevo México consists of five short stories and a novelette. Varying in theme and structure, all narrations are in the first person and with the exception of **"El hombre sin nombre,"** the novelette, all reflect recollections of childhood experiences and/or acquaintances. In this presentation we will limit our comments to three of the stories: **"Mi caballo mago," "Juan P.,"** and **"La fragua sin fuego."**

"Mi caballo mago," the first selection of the work, is a poetic rendition of a child's *rite de passage* into manhood. In a lyrical style and fairy tale-like quality reminiscent of Juan Ramón Jiménez' *Platero y yo*, an adult narrator recalls the circumstances leading to his capturing, as a youth, of a legendary white stallion that roamed the wilderness around Tierra Amarilla, an event that symbolically takes him to the threshold of manhood. The story begins with a metaphorical description of the white steed, establishing it as a symbol of masculine virility and the dream horse of all the local ranchmen:

> Era blanco. Blanco como el olvido. Era libre. Libre como la alegría. Era la ilusión, la libertad y la emoción. Poblaba y dominaba las serranías y las llanuras de las cercanías. Era un caballo blanco que llenó mi juventud de fantasía y poesía. Alrededor de las fogatas del campo y en las resolanas del pueblo los vaqueros de esas tierras hablaban de él con entusiasmo y admiración. Y la mirada se volvía turbia y borrosa de ensueño. La animada charla se apagaba. Todos atentos a la visión evocada. Mito del reino animal. Poema del mundo viril.[6]

The poetic imagery created by Ulibarrí's compact, telegraphic-like style evokes the impression that the stallion is indeed an illusion, a phantom horse that has eluded all attempts of capture and has left its pursuers, its would-be masters with only words of awe and admiration with which to describe their encounter.

As the story unfolds, the image of the stallion becomes more majestic and legendary. Through a series of metaphors and similes, he becomes lord of the animal kingdom, comparable to an Oriental monarch, proudly parading his harem throughout his bucolic kingdom. The more the horse is seen and avoids the lasso, the more he becomes the talk of the village *vaqueros*. In fact, such is his evasive presence that he has become more legend than reality, a distinction giving him the notoriety of "el caballo brujo" (p. 5). To capture and possess such a wonder horse would certainly raise one's stature within the community, gracing the captor with such qualities as valor, masculine strength, and sex appeal.

Like the village *vaqueros*, our narrator-protagonist is also entranced with the possibility, the illusion of possessing the phantom horse, and thereby entering the realm of manhood. Though he has never seen the animal, the tales of its feats have filled his young mind with ambition and imagination:

> Escuchaba embobado a mi padre y a sus vaqueros hablar del caballo fantasma que al atraparlo se volvía espuma y aire y nada. Participaba de la obsesión de todos, ambición de lotería, de algún día ponerle yo mi lazo, de hacerlo mío, y lucirlo los domingos por la tarde cuando las muchachas salen a paseo por la calle.
>
> (p. 5)

The boy's first sight of the stallion is one of everlasting durability. One summer evening, as he is lethargically herding cattle in the forest, he accidentally comes upon the animal. Like in a still-life picture, everything around seems to fall silent and come to a complete standstill, as he spots the horse in a nearby opening:

> ¡Allí está! ¡El caballo mago! Al extremo del abra, en un promontorio, rodeado de verde. Hecho estatua, hecho estampa. Línea y forma y mancha blanca en fondo verde. Orgullo, fama y arte en carne animal. Cuadro de belleza encendida y libertad varonil.
>
> (p. 7)

And just as quickly as this beautiful still-life image is formulated in the child's mind, it is shattered by the stallion who, also aware of the boy's presence, defiantly challenges his intrusion and escapes into the forest.

Subsequent to this brief encounter, the child becomes even more obsessed with the possibility of capturing the wonder horse. He dreams of the steed day and night, and is constantly investigating its whereabouts. Then on one wintery Sunday afternoon he again comes across the phantom steed. As with the first experience, this one is equally dramatic and poetic. This time however, our protagonist is determined to pursue and capture the animal, and he follows it for hours through the snow-covered hillside. Little by little the malnutritioned beast gives way to exhaustion and the boy apprehends and captures it, a feat no other individual, boy or man alike, had been able to accomplish. As the narrator recalls the dramatic incident, he utilizes the present tense to make the experience more immediate and vivid:

> Me siento seguro. Desato el cabestro. Abro el lazo. Las riendas tirantes. Cada nervio, cada músculo alerta y el alma en la boca. Espuelas tensas en ijares temblorosos. Arranca el caballo. Remolineo el cabestro y lanzo el lazo obediente.
>
> Vértigo de furia y rabia. Remolinos de luz y abanicos de transparente nieve. Cabestro que silba y quema en la teja de la silla. Guantes violentos que humean.
>
> Ojos ardientes en sus pozos. Boca seca. Frente caliente. Y el mundo se sacude y se estremece. Y se acaba la larga zanja blanca en un ancho charco blanco.
>
> Sosiego jadeante y denso. El caballo mago es mío.
>
> (p. 11)

Having captured the stallion, the boy's rite of passage into manhood is completed. He has, in essence, successfully met his initiatory trial of strength—his test of manhood—and is ready to be received by his father as a man. Sensing this coming-of-age, he triumphantly parades the steed through the village, leading it homeward where his father proudly acknowledges his feat with a handshake "un poco más fuerte que de ordinario"—and a very gratifying "'Esos son hombres'" (p. 15).

The child's victory over the wonder horse leaves him with mixed emotions. He is indeed overcome with joy that he has succeeded in capturing the majestic steed, that local symbol of masculinity and virility, and thereby entered into the world of manhood. Nevertheless, at the same time he is deeply saddened by the fact that in depriving the once indomitable stallion of its freedom to roam the wilderness, he has also deprived future generations of children and *vaqueros* of a dream or an ideal to pursue. Consequently, the following morning, when he discovers that *el Mago* has escaped from the pasture, his eyes fill with "lágrimas infantiles." The tears, however, are not out of sadness, but out of happiness. As the protagonist himself informs us:

> Lloraba de alegría. Estaba celebrando, por mucho que me dolía, la fuga y la libertad del Mago, la transcendencia de ese espíritu indomable. Ahora seguirá siendo el ideal, la ilusión y la emoción.
>
> (p. 17)

In other words, he is overjoyed that the phantom stallion was once again free to roam the wilderness and thus continue being "el brujo" and "el mago," or as so appropriately stated by Erlinda Gonzales Berry, "to fill the fantasies of both child and man with the transcending power of idealism and illusion."[7] In this light, **"Mi caballo mago"** stands out not only as a story in which the young protagonist comes of age physically and sexually, but also intellectually, for his final understanding and appreciation of the values of hope, freedom and the ideal certainly bear resemblance to those of a mature and sagacious humanist.

In **"Juan P."** and **"La fragua sin fuego,"** Ullibarrí takes a much more critical view of his native Tierra Amarilla and its inhabitants. Like in the previous story, both of these narrations are rendered from the perspective of an adult narrator recalling images of his childhood past in Tierra Amarilla; the focus here being on local personalities. However, whereas the outlook of the previous story is nostalgically happy and warm, the underlying tone of these two stories is melancholic and somewhat adverse.

"Juan P." is the tragic story of Juan Perrodo, the town drunk, and his spinster sisters who, once very promising and charming members of the community, were compelled into living a life of humiliation and seclusion due to the thoughtlessness and cruelty of their neighbors. In keeping with the *costumbrista* mode, the story begins with a detailed discussion of the origins of the rounded hummocks beside each of the village homes on which firewood was stacked during the winter months. These mounds, formed from the splinters, chips, and sawdust of cutting wood, not only provided the stacked firewood with the proper ventilation in times of rain and/or snow, but were also a means of determining the age and social status of the family living in the household: the higher and wider the heap, the older and more influential the family on the property. Moreover, the formation of these mounds entailed hard work in the chopping and sawing of the wood, and thereby provided a worthwhile activity to develop the young males into robust and strong men.

After introducing this age-old custom of Tierra Amarilla, the narrator informs us that, though unwillingly, as a young boy he, too, was involved in the molding of his family's wood pile. Annoyed by his son's preference for books and poetry, and obsessed with the idea of making a man out of the boy, the narrator's father set up a schedule of household chores that would assure his virile development. Of course, among the many tasks the boy had to perform was the cutting of the family firewood. On one occasion, while carrying out this duty, he is approached by Juan P. riding on a magnificent sorrel horse, the envy of all the local *vaqueros*, and the rider's only remaining symbol of his once prominent position in the community—a life that had been, a life that might have been. As the rider passes in his usual drunken state, he is singing a self-composed ballad:

> A mí me llaman Juan P.
> Soy el borracho del pueblo.
> Tengo dos hermanas escondidas:
> Son las perrodas del pueblo.
>
> (p. 41)

Though he senses something humiliating in the words of Juan P., until this time the child had been totally ignorant as to the tragic plight of Juan and his sisters. Since in Hispanic cultures it is a customary practice to give nicknames based on the physical and/or character handicaps of an individual, he assumed that the "P" of Juan's epithet was an abbreviated form of *pedo*, a term referring to the man's reputation as a drunk, and that the name of the sisters, *las perrodas*, was merely an extension of their brother's nickname. Now, upon noting the tragic words and tone of Juan's song, the child wants to learn more about the origin of the insulting epithet, of Juan's drunkenness and of the seclusion of the sisters; and at his insistence he is given an account of the situation by Brígido, one of his father's hired hands.

From Brígido's account (presented in the form of a *racconto*), we learn that Juan and his sisters came from one of the oldest and most prominent families in Tierra Amarilla, and that the people of the village were responsible for their tragic demise. This "riches to ruin" transition is explained to have begun, ironically, when Juan and the sisters, along with the entire community, were respectfully praying at the wake of a deceased neighbor. During one of the occasional pauses in the rosary, when all is absolutely silent in the church, one of the sisters shattered the silence with a burst of human explosion—"uno de esos ruidos que . . . Aun en privado, cuando nos ocurren, nos dejan un poco rebajados, un poco envilecidos" (p. 47). Of course, such an untimely outburst caught the immediate attention of all the villagers present, but it was not until later that they react. In the days following the incident, as gossip of the shocking incident spreads throughout the community, Juan and his sisters—until then, highly respected neighbors—begin to be known by their new and humiliating nickname: *Los Perrodos*.

In response to the humiliating gossip and the insulting epithet, the trio withdraws, in shame, into the solitude of their home and seclude themselves from the rest of the community, emerging from the household only on occasions: the women to attend mass, and Juan to patronize the local saloon. As Juan takes to drinking more and more, he neglects the homestead and crops, until finally the place appears to be totally deserted:

> Se secaron los rosales, antes tan cuidadosamente atendidos. Los campos, trigales y alfalfares, se veían cada día más tristes, más abandonados. . . . La tristeza, la soledad y el abandono invadieron la heredad y tomaron posesión de ella

> (pp. 47-49).

And as time takes its toll he peddles off the family possessions until all that remains are the house in which the sisters live in seclusion, and the beautiful sorrel horse on which Juan scornfully and dejectedly parades through the community singing his tragic ballad:

> A mí me llaman Juan P.
> Soy el borracho del pueblo.
> Tengo dos hermanas escondidas:
> Son las perrodas del pueblo.

By the time Brígido concludes the tragic story of Juan P. and his two spinster sisters, the young protagonist is overcome with indignation and anger directed toward that community that had senselessly and unjustly condemned those three human beings to an existence of shame and despair. And as he continues his initial chore of cutting the firewood he hacks furiously and vengefully, imagining each log to be the face of one of the ugly villagers who had poisoned the honorable family with their filthy gossip. In recalling his desire for vengeance the narrator informs us:

> Partí leña como loco. El montón, el promontorio de mi casa creció aquella tarde con la inmundicia de la mente y la lengua de los hombres. Y si ustedes pasan hoy por Tierra Amarilla fíjense en el montón de mi casa. Si escarban poco hallarán allí ojos y lenguas y sesos humanos. Son los de los que bautizaron a "los Perrodos".

> (p. 51)

As such, like the story previously discussed, Ulibarrí concludes **"Juan P."** with a profoundly humane and compassionate note. And as is typical of most narratives in the *costumbrista* mode, also evident in this story is its nostalgic depiction of the customs and traditions of a bygone day. However, what differs in **"Juan P."** is its critical perspective. While the other narrative alludes to village customs and/or traditions in a positive, somewhat romantic light, this story is critical and even disapproving of them; especially when they can lead to the senseless harm and demise of another human being, as they did in the case of Juan P. and his two beautiful sisters.

A similar note of criticism is found in **"La fragua sin fuego,"** a sketch in which Ulibarrí passionately censures narrow-minded social rejections. Like in **"Juan P.",** the focus of this story is on one of the many personalities who played an important role in the narrator's strides toward maturity while still a child growing up in Tierra Amarilla. Here he recalls Edumenio, the village blacksmith. Edumenio, who lives alone in a small white house at the village's edge, is portrayed as a quiet, hardworking, Atlas of a man, also living at the margins of the town's social structure. Nevertheless, he is quite taken in by the village children (our narrator included), who would spend many an afternoon in his blacksmith shop curiously observing him at work and joyfully playing with scrap metals and the tools of his trade. Moreover, because he treated the children as adults, their attraction toward him is enhanced. Our narrator recalls:

> Era muy bueno. Nos componía los juguetes rotos. Nos hacía trompos con unas puntas como espadas. Hacía maravillas con hoja de lata. Nos daba aros, tejas, y mil piezas de desperdicio que a los niños les gustan tanto. Nos dejaba hacer. . . . Otra cosa. Nunca nos trató con esa condescendencia que tienen los mayores para los niños. Nos hablaba de hombre a hombre. Cuando podíamos ayudarle en algo, traerle una herramienta, animar el brasero con el fuelle, ir a comprarle unos cigarros, eso nos llenaba de importancia.

> (p. 71)

A true companion to the children he was indeed. However, as the story unfolds, we also learn that he was a lonely man nonetheless, and, in order to fulfill his needs for adult companionship, he would occasionally close down his shop and go into the city where, as we are informed, "se ponía una borrachera imperial y se entregaba por completo al mal andar" (p. 75). On one such occasion Edumenio returned to the village accompanied by a beautiful young woman who immediately catches the attention of the community and our child narrator. In a poetic fashion reminiscent of Eduardo Barrios' child protagonist in *El niño que enloqueció de amor*,[8] he describes his infatuation for her:

> Se llamaba Henriqueta. Desde que la vi la primera vez quedé convencido que era la criatura más hermosa que Dios había puesto en la tierra.... Yo la miraba con ojos de becerro en cara de cordero, y la seguía como un perro. Era un amor que no pide nada y lo da todo: la inteligencia, la voluntad y la fuerza.... Amor limpio, puro, nuevo; sin manos, ni palabras, ni labios. Mudo y secreto, no va ni viene, ni siquiera está—sólo es.

> (pp. 75-77)

Undoubtedly, with the companionship of his newly acquired spouse things were due to change for Edumenio in the community; and change they did. The once unloquacious, introspective blacksmith became a talkative, jovial individual; backslapping and joking with all who came near him. No longer alone, he was indeed a happy man. The happiness, however, was short-lived. Soon after their arrival to the community, rumors began to spread that Henriqueta, who wore makeup, flashy jewelry, tight dresses and short skirts—that is, who dressed and carried herself in city fashion—was a loose woman. And when Edumenio began making courtesy calls, wishing to introduce his bride to all the good families of the community, they are coldly and snobbishly rejected. As a result of the snobbery Henriqueta eventually abandons the community and Edumenio, humiliated and emotionally distraught, soon follows suit; thus leaving forevermore, *la fragua sin fuego*.

Having witnessed this haughtiness even in his own home, our nine-year-old protagonist witness is overcome with indignation and anger, and later in life, as he narrates his account, he candidly directs himself to the victims of his village's social snobbery and fervently apologizes for its shameful behavior:

> Ya no tengo nueve años. Ya soy hombre. Pero recuerdo y lloro. Y me avergüenzo de la condición humana que les negó, a ti, Edumenio, a ti, Henriqueta, el don de la felicidad que Dios les dio. Dios manda y el hombre dispone.

> Edumenio, en dondequiera que estés, espero que tengas otra fragua, y que sigas haciéndole la guerra al hierro indócil. Espero que hayas encontrado a tu Henriqueta. Espero que tengas una casita blanca y limpia con macetas de geranios y claveles en el jardín. Henriqueta . . . espero que hayas conseguido la honradez que buscabas. Espero que en otro sitio, entre otras gentes más

generosas, tú y Edumenio hayan fraguado una vida llena de dulzura, de amor propio y de dignidad que los dos se merecen.

> (pp. 81-83)

Consequently, in a manner similar to that found in **"Juan P.,"** Ulibarrí closes **"La fragua sin fuego"** with a note of profound human compassion, and what had begun as a simple nostalgic sketch about one of the many villagers who once resided in Tierra Amarilla, ends up being a condemnation of this village's—and that of all small isolated communities'—narrow-minded social codes and suspicious nature.

That Sabine Reyes Ulibarrí's stories are *costumbrista*, there is no denying for, as we have seen, they do indeed focus on a facet of New Mexican life that is rapidly disappearing or is already bygone, and nostalgically depict regional customs, manners, language, types, and all the quaint local-colorist motifs that characterize this genre. But simple and local as these tales manifest themselves, they transcend the superficially picturesque and quaint intent of *costumbrismo* to present larger, more universal lessons about life and human conduct, be it man's eternal search for the ideal, the pursuit and/or negation of freedom, happiness and justice; or even more simply, the manifestation of innocent curiosity. Key to this subtle transition is the author's skillful manipulation of the adult/child points of view. By combining these two perspectives, Ulibarrí is able, not only to nostalgically recall images of a bygone day, but to restore a state of innocence and compassion lost collectively in the process of individual and/or social maturation. While the adult narrator functions primarily as the agent of recalling that golden age, the child protagonist-witness, innocent and uncorrupted by social constraints, focuses on and denounces the foibles and sometimes unwarranted behavior of the adults in his village; and thereby imbues these short sketches with a note of human compassion seldom found in the pages of traditional *costumbrista* literature.

NOTES

[1] As in Spain and other Mediterranean countries, many of these tales deal with such motifs as kings, castles, princesses, courtships, magic enchantments, animal lore, and the picaresque. Some tales are adapted to local customs while others introduce regional characteristics and types such as *brujerías* and indigenous themes; hence making the stories seem more realistic and dramatic to the reader. It is from this oral tradition that Chicanos have inherited the likes of "Los tres principes," "La niña perseguida," "El príncipe encantado," "La princesa encantada," "Juan el oso," "Juan el tonto," "Juan sin miedo," "Pedro Ordimales," "Los dos compadres," and "El tonto y la princesa." For these and additional folktales of Old World origin, see Juan B. Rael, *Cuentos españoles de Colorado y de Nuevo México* (Stanford: Stanford University Press, 1957); José M. Espinoza, *Spanish Folktales from New Mexico* (New York: American Folklore Society, 1937); and Aurora Lucero White, *Literary Folklore of the Hispanic Southwest* (San Antonio: The Naylor Company, 1953).

[2] Phillip D. Ortego, ed., *We Are Chicanos: An Anthology of Mexican American Literature* (New York: Washington Square Press, 1975), p. 272.

[3] See for example, Otero, "Count La Cerda's Treasure," Gonzales, "Don Tomás," Fray Angélico Cháves, "Hunchback Madonna," Escajeda, "Tales from San Elizario," and Campa, "The Cell of Heavenly Justice," all of which have been reprinted in Philip D. Ortego, ed., *We Are Chicanos: An Anthology of Mexican American Literature.*

[4] See for example, Sabine R. Ulibarrí, *Tierra Amarilla: Cuentos de Nuevo México* (Albuquerque: University of New Mexico Press, 1974); Alurista, *Floricanto en Aztlán* (Los Angeles: UCLA Press, 1971); Rudolfo Anaya, *Bless Me, Ultima* (Berkeley: Quinto Sol, 1972); Rolando Hinojosa, *Estampas de Valle y otras obras* (Berkeley: Quinto Sol, 1973); and Orlando Romero, *Nambé-Year One* (Berkeley: Tonatiuh International, 1976), all of which develop around or expound upon folk beliefs and lore of the Chicano Southwest.

[5] *Mi abuela fumaba puros y otros cuentos de Tierra Amarilla* (Berkeley: Quinto Sol, 1977), *Primeros encuentros* (Ypsilanti, Michigan: Editorial Bilingue, 1982), *Al cielo se sube a pie* (Madrid: Ediciones Alfaguara, 1966), *Amor y Ecuador* (Madrid: Ediciones Jose Porrua Turranzas, 1966), and *El mundo poético de Juan Ramón Jiménez* (Madrid: Artes y Grafical Clavileno, 1962).

[6] Sabine R. Ulibarrí, *Tierra Amarilla: Stories of New Mexico/ Cuentos de Nuevo México,* trans. Thelma C. Nason (Albuquerque: The University of New Mexico Press, 1974), p. 3. Quotations cited in this paper are from the Spanish text, and all subsequent references to this work will appear with page numbers in parentheses in the body of the text.

[7] Erlinda Gonzales Berry, "Chicano Literature in Spanish: Roots and Content," Diss. The University of New Mexico 1978, p. 53.

[8] Eduardo Barrios, *El niño que enloqueció de amor,* 1915.

Sabine Ulibarrí

Charles Tatum   (essay date 1989)

SOURCE: "Sabine Ulibarrí: Another Look at a Literary Master," *Paso por Aquí: Critical Essays on the New Mexican Literary Tradition, 1542-1988*, Erlinda Gonzales-Berry, ed., Albuquerque: University of New Mexico Press, 1989, pp. 231-41.

[*Here, Tatum presents an overview of Ulibarrí's poetry and fiction, focusing on recurring themes of love and the author's portrayal of character.*]

Poet, essayist, and prose writer, Sabine Ulibarrí holds an important place in contemporary Chicano literature. In addition to scholarly works, textbooks and thought-provoking essays, Sabine Ulibarrí has published two books of poetry, five collections of short stories, and he has edited another collection of his students' prose and poetry. All of his creative literature was originally written in Spanish although his short stories have also appeared in bilingual editions. When compared to other Chicano writers, his literary output is significant, particularly if one takes into account that he is one of a handful of contemporary Chicano writers who is completely comfortable with written literary Spanish. This fluency with written expression is a reflection of the writer's upbringing in a completely Spanish-speaking environment where Hispanics constituted the majority culture. In addition, literary Spanish was an important part of his childhood for his father would often read Spanish literature to his family. Ulibarrí's academic training and his rigorous study of the Spanish literary masters have undoubtedly reinforced his earlier language background and contributed significantly to his mastery of the language seen in his own creative works.

His two books of poetry, *Al cielo se sube a pie* and *Amor y Eduador*, were both published in 1966 and are similar in content, language, and poetic expression although the first is perhaps broader in its subject matter. In *Al cielo se sube a pie*, using a language the Spanish poet Angel González describes as "pausado y preciso," (deliberate and precise) Ulibarrí includes poetry that deals with love, the woman, his native Tierra Amarilla, uprootedness, solitude, the tragic consequences of progress, life as a transitory state, and several other themes. His poetry is filled with color, finely rendered images, and language carefully selected and appropriate to the content. Dominant in this collection is poetry dealing with various aspects of love: the elusiveness of authentic love; the transitory nature of passion; deceit and disillusionment in the love relationship. In general, the woman/lover is idealized and exists in a more real state in his imagination than in true life. This concept seems to be in keeping with his vision of the illusory nature of love, especially physical love. The poet/male depicts himself, as, on one hand, privileged by her attention, favor, and affection yet, on the other, victimized by her distance and abandonment of him. A related love theme is his belief in the easy conquest of woman. Her willing submission is doomed not to last; only love after sacrifice and intentional effort on the part of both parties will endure. His view of woman in her role as a lover in this collection of poetry is best characterized as distrustful. She is beautiful—as he aptly describes in his series of *pie* poems—but mindless, affectionate and undependable. Her world is a limited one and her view of herself and others is shortsighted. In her relationship to the male she is the source of much of his pain and agony.

Another dominant theme in *Al cielo se sube a pie* is the poet's sense of uprootedness in an alien world in which a premium is placed on success and achievement. In the poem, **"Fuego fatuo,"** he laments having left his native rural Northern New Mexico, having paid the price of loneliness and a feeling of abandonment for less authentic and ultimately less tangible rewards. The poet describes himself as the only member of his family who has left the mountain in pursuit of an elusive star, and while he has tasted success he is still searching for the "cima errante" (wandering summit). Although he is resigned to his self-chosen fate, the poet is saddened when he lets himself remember what he has sacrificed. In **"Patria de retorno"**, (**"Native Land of My Return"**) he recognizes the impossibility of returning to the comfort and security of his childhood home. Although he may be welcomed back by friends and family, nonetheless, he is still a "forastero en mi casa ancestral" (stranger in my ancestral home).

The poet is thus destined to wander the earth on a constant search, waiting for death, filled with hunger for permanence, plagued and saddened by his loss of roots and family. Poetry is his consolation, his vehicle to give expression to life's pain. Artistic expression provides a kind of salve for the poet's wounds and at the same time allows him to eternalize his pain.

As the title indicates, *Amor y Ecuador* has two major themes: poetry focusing on the poet's impressions and memories of Ecuador and poetry devoted to love. In the first section of the book on Ecuador, Ulibarrí shares with us the meaningfulness of his visit to the South American country in 1963. Always the keen and thoughtful observer, he records his visit in a way that allows us to share with him its personal significance. From the first poem, he draws us into the experience of passing time in the Andean country that is geographically so different from his native New Mexico yet has so much in common with it. They share a common heritage and the poet sees Albuquerque and Quito as two poles of the same Hispanic world. Ecuador in general and Quito in particular represent a positive element for the poet, something he has been out of touch with back home. He arrives in the Ecuadorian capital filled with hope and anticipation. He descends from his plane to find himself still in a world of clouds and sky and mystery. In one poem Quito is described as God's work and in another, the first line of each of a six-stanza poem devoted to Ecuador, he repeats: "Aquí todo me humaniza" (Here everything humanizes me).

The expected wonder and awe of Ecuador's rich Spanish-Indian history and its geographical splendor constitute only one aspect of his Ecuadorian poetry. In addition to this sensorial and cognitive awareness of geography and history, the poet is in touch with something deeply human that touches a sensitive chord in him. Perhaps he is at home here as he has not been since leaving his beloved mountainous Tierra Amarilla. The poet lets himself be touched by the people he passes on the streets and by the warmth and welcoming from Ecuadorian friends. He feels rejuvenated, joyful, excited and yet, profoundly saddened and angered by the misery and exploitation that surrounds him. In a poem titled **"Indosincrasia"** the poet reveals these conflicting feelings. The Indian is a reserve of dignity and strength, and at the same time the poet recognizes in his eyes the long history of frustrated hopes and suffering. The poet identifies with this experience and asks his brother, the inhabitant of the high and lonely Andes, to look into his New Mexican eyes where he will see reflected the same suffering of centuries. The poem ends on a note of solidarity and hope; together they can overcome their shared tragic history.

The poetry of the second part of *Amor y Ecuador* seems to have taken on a decidedly more melancholy tone than the love poems of *Al cielo se sube a pie*—this poetry has a bittersweet quality arising from the poet's belief that he cannot have what he wants; love, to him, is elusive, momentary, and even frightening. His own love overpowers him and he warns the beloved to flee lest she be destroyed by it. Images of abandonment, disillusionment after love making, and bitter memories of unrequited love abound. In one poem, he visits the birthplace of a past lover and is filled with the sadness of her absence. For the first time, we see references to sin and guilt associated with the poet's relationships with lovers. Tragically, the poet sees himself as destined to carry with him for life the burden of his guilt; he has altogether given up hope in salvation.

Ulibarrí's prose can best be characterized as a kind of intrahistory, a chronicling and recording of the values, sentiments, relationships, and texture of the daily lives of his friends and family, the Hispanic inhabitants of his beloved Tierra Amarilla. The writer himself has commented that with his short stories he has tried to document the history of the Hispanics of northern New Mexico, the history not yet recorded by the scholars who have written otherwise excellent studies of the region. Ulibarrí believes that these historians do not understand at a deep level the Hispanic heritage that predates by hundreds of years the arrival of the Anglo soldier and businessman in the mid-nineteenth century. He recognizes that the Hispanic world that he knew as a child is fast disappearing under the attack of the aggressive Anglo culture. His stories, then, constitute an attempt to document the *historia sentimental*, the essence of that culture before it completely disappears. In addition to this missionary zeal, his stories are just as importantly his attempt, as a personal objective, to regain his childhood experiences. As reflected in much of the poetry discussed earlier, he feels as though he has been uprooted from his culture and his family and in documenting his memories of a childhood and adolescence in Tierra Amarilla he is trying to resurrect for himself a repository of humanizing experiences. In answering the questions about his people—how they were (are); what it meant to live in an environment where Spanish was the dominant language; the significance of living daily the values and traditions of America's oldest non-Indian culture—he ultimately answers the questions about himself: Who am I? Where do I come from? What have I lost? How much of it can I regain?

Ulibarrí's short stories are more personal than documentary or social history. One looks in vain for explicitly social themes although they may be buried under a rich surface of local color, language, and family and community ties. He explains that he is different from many Chicano writers in that he was raised in a majority Hispanic culture and does not have an ax to grind in creating the world of Tierra Amarilla. This is not to say, however, that he is not socially committed—this side of him is clearly evident in his essays and in his comments made before groups such as the 1967 Cabinet hearings in El Paso.

Most of his short narrations are about individual personalities: relatives and acquaintances, those he knew well and those around whom local legends had developed; those he loved and those he feared as a child. All seem to have affected him strongly and together they make up a whole community of Hispanos from Tierra Amarilla. It is apt to compare both of his collections of short stories to Spanish and Spanish American *costumbrismo*, the literary genre that is characterized by sketches of different regional customs, language, rituals, types, and values. Local color, legends, and personalities are the stuff of his stories as he methodically sets out to recreate this world for us. His stories are not sterile reproductions but rendered so that his poetic sensibility shows through and enhances the sense of excitement and mystery he associates with those memories.

The first story of the volume *Tierra Amarilla* is an excellent example of how the author brings to bear his poetic sense upon his childhood memories. **"Mi caballo blanco"** reminds the reader of another poet, Juan Ramón Jiménez, who immortalized a little grey donkey in his memorable prose poem *Platero y yo*. Ulibarrí describes the magical qualities of a legendary horse that filled his childhood with poetry and fantasy. The young adolescent narrator tells us of the wonder with which he had heard of the marvelous feats, some real, some fictitious, of this unusual animal who roamed the high plateaus with his harem of mares. The horse symbolizes for the adolescent a world of masculine strength and sexuality, a world he is about to enter himself. He dreams of capturing this magnificent creature and parading him around the town plaza observed by lovely and awe-struck young women. He does capture the horse and goes to sleep believing that because of his feat he has finally entered the world of adulthood, yet the child in him remains; the inner excitement and laughter he feels betrays the exterior calm that for him is the proper demeanor for a real man. And when the horse escapes, not only does his fantasy world come tumbling down, but he recognizes that he's still very much a child at heart. He gratefully accepts his father's comforting words and decides that the glorious animal is better left an illusion in its freedom than being forced to enter the real world—the adult world—in captivity. Ulibarrí thus sensitively and skillfully reconstructs a pivotal moment in an adolescent's life—perhaps his own—where the battle between childhood and adulthood is fiercely waged.

The next three narrations of *Tierra Amarilla* are humorous accounts of personalities and the many stories, legends, and half-truths that developed in the community of which they were a part. The first is about Father Benito, a chubby angelic Franciscan friar who was assigned to the local parish. Although well-intentioned and loved by the parishioners he is described as somewhat naive. In addition, he was handicapped by knowing little Spanish. It was his ignorance of the language that was the source of much humor and mischief at his expense. Ulibarrí recounts that Sunday Mass was veritable torture for the parish-ioners who, anticipating that their dear Padre Benito was going to make a huge blunder during his sermon—he inevitably did when he gave it in his stumbling Spanish—would spend the entire mass desperately trying to keep from rolling in the aisles with laughter.

The third story of the volume is told from the perspective of a fifteen-year-old narrator who recalls how the local town drunk, Juan P., and his two spinster sisters got their name Perrodas. It seems one day many years before, the two sisters were attending a very solemn rosary for a dear friend who had passed away when one of them let pass a substantial amount of air. She fainted. The author speculates that this occurred either from embarrassment or because of the sheer amount of energy needed to contain the air. Only the dead person was not shaken by the explosion. The scandalous event was never fully discussed publicly but soon after it happened Juan and his sisters began to be called Perroda, a play on *pedorra* meaning flatulent. A more serious side of this story is the apparent delight with which the community labeled the family, thus destroying their reputation, turning Juan into a drunk, and dooming his two sisters to spinsterhood. The adolescent narrator is cognizant of this somewhat vicious side of his beloved community. The story also contains another serious subtheme having to do with the narrator's conflict with his father who wanted him to abandon his books and his poetry to cultivate more virile and more worthwhile—in his father's view—pursuits. The narrator keenly feels this disapproval and goes to great lengths to please him by performing such manly activities as chopping wood.

"Sabélo" is a good illustration of how legends were created in Northern New Mexican communities. Once again, the story is presented by a young narrator—nine years old in this case—who filters reality through his child's imagination to give birth to another character endowed with fantastic powers. The story focuses on Don José Viejo, a sharp-tongued old man who was as ancient as hunger itself. After overcoming his fear of the old man, the young narrator develops a warm friendship with him and an almost religious respect. Don José is gifted with an innate talent for story telling, especially fantastic ones with himself as the central figure; for example, how he killed a huge bear after being badly scratched on the back. But the story that really captures the young boy's imagination has to do with Don José's ability to remove honey from a beehive without receiving so much as one sting. According to Don José, he is not bothered by the bees because, in fact, he is a bee or at least indirectly descended from bees. After swearing his young friend to secrecy, the old man tells him how this came about. His father was kind of a pied piper for bees who rescued them from captivity and liberated them in the forest. His mother was a queen bee who one day kissed her savior on the lips; he magically turned into a bee; they had a child—Don José—who was raised in the hive and then, inexplicably, took on a human form. Further, the scratches on his back are really bumblebee stripes and not wounds received at the hand of the fierce bear. The impressionable child concludes: "Yo me quedé temblando. Yo sabía que don José Viejo no mentía." ("I was left trembling. I knew that Don José Viego wasn't lying").

The last story of **Tierra Amarilla** differs in length, form and content from the author's other fiction. Dealing with a number of philosophical themes such as life as a dream, the father-son relationship, the development of the individual personality, the story, which is divided into six short chapters, seems to focus on the struggle of the narrator, an author of thirty years, to free himself from his dead father's image and domination to become an autonomous individual. Alejandro the narrator has returned to his birthplace, a small Hispanic town, to celebrate the completion of his biography of his father. Shortly into the visit he begins to notice that his friends and especially the family members are behaving strangely towards him, but it is not until he sees a reflection of his father's face in a raised wine glass that he is able to explain their behavior. Finally, random remarks made earlier about his resemblance to his father fall into place; somehow he has assumed his father's personality to the extent that others mistakenly are reacting as though he were him. In addition, an inner voice from his subconscious suddenly speaks to him—Alejandro believes he is hearing his own father, especially when the voice tells him, "Desde tu edad más tierna, yo te absorbí, y viví en ti" ("From your most tender years, I absorbed you and I lived in you"). Here the confusion between the two personalities is heightened. Are these voices real? Are they the result of the narrator's insecurity about his own identity? Is life a dream? Is he his father's dream? Is he not autonomous? What importance do his own life experiences have in defining and shaping his per-

sonality? All of these questions rush over Alejandro leaving him in a confused and vulnerable state. During the remainder of the story the narrator tries to answer these questions, all the while harrassed by what he believes to be his father's voice, which repeats that he wants to eternalize himself through his son. Alejandro falls into a troubled sleep and wakes up suffering from amnesia. He does not remember who he is or who the woman is who tenderly nurses and shows him affection. Although he does partially recover his memory, he remains at the end precariously balanced on the edge of confusion, not fully knowing who he is and not fully trusting that the woman who shows such love for him is really his wife.

With **Mi abuela fumaba puros y otros cuentos de Tierra Amarilla**, Ulibarrí adds to his published work about his native northern New Mexico ten more sensitively rendered tales. In this attractive bilingual edition, beautifully illustrated by artist Dennis Martínez, Ulibarrí presents a tapestry of childhood memories of life among the hardy and proud Hispanos of Tierra Amarilla. His stories are a series of carefully drawn sketches of individuals—family, friends, acquaintances—who play an important role in a young boy's strides towards adulthood: the matriarchal grandmother, viewed with a combination of tenderness and fear; Uncle Cirilo of whose size and mighty voice the child lives in awe; the legendary Negro Aguilar whose feats as an indomitable *vaquero* and skilled horse-tamer are reputed in the furthest reaches of the county; the astute Elacio Sandoval, the biology teacher who talks himself out of marrying the woman he does not love; Roberto, who one day goes to town to buy more nails and does not return for four years.

With obvious enthusiasm, Ulibarrí shares with us the wide range of the young boy's feelings and experiences: his terror upon finding himself face-to-face with *la llorona* herself; the profound sadness upon learning of his father's sudden death; the proud response to his much admired childhood heroes when they deign to talk to him. The author draws on local legends and popular superstition and combines them with vivid details from his childhood to create a rich mixture of fact and fiction. His stories are tinged with hues of longing for a past that although he cannot relive, he has brought to life with deft and broad strokes of his pen. The book thus forms a composite of the memories of a writer sensitive to the child in him, who looks back nostalgically to a time of closeness and warmth among people who treated him with understanding and love.

As Rudolfo Anaya points out in his introduction to this attractive volume, what emerges in all of the stories is a strong sense of daily life and tradition among the Hispanos of Northern New Mexico as well as the bonds of their loving and sharing. Another important element is humor which, while present in his earlier stories, here is more ribald.

The title story is a sensitively created and tender description of the author's grandmother, a kind of silent matriarch who sustained the family for many decades through difficult periods and tragic events. In the narrator's memory her relationship to her husband, although somewhat tumultuous, was characterized by an underlying feeling of mutual respect and fear, "somewhere between tenderness and toughness." The narrator affectionately recalls that after his grandfather died, the grandmother would absent herself to her bedroom after the evening chores were done to smoke a cigar, symbol to the child of his grandfather's power over his family and ranch business and also of his grandmother's longing for her husband. As so many of the characters of his stories, the grandmother seems to represent for the author a graphic and vital connection with his past: his Hispano community, his family, his language, and his cultural roots.

The second story, **"Brujerías o tonterías"** (**"Sorcery or Foolishness"**) is a summary of local legends and characters (endowed with mysterious powers) who were prominent in Tierra Amarilla during the narrator's childhood: la Matilde de Ensenada who was reportedly a witch and go-between—*Trotaconventos*—between lovers; *el sanador* (the healer) another character whose knowledge of the supernatural properties of medicines and animals miraculously saves his uncle from certain death; and finally *la llorona* herself with whom the narrator has a terrifying encounter only to discover later that he had actually run into Atenencia, a mentally retarded woman who would relentlessly pursue her unfaithful husband and scare local inhabitants in the bargain.

The focus of the third story is the narrator's uncle by marriage, Cirilo, sheriff of Río Arriba County. He is described as big, fat, strong, and fearsome, especially from the point of view of the child who felt dwarfed in his presence. Not only did he capture and sometimes have to manhandle criminals, but he also kept the peace at the schoolhouse. On one occasion after the teacher could take no more harrassment from the young devils of students, Cirilo was called in. In a memorable scene, he quells the riot with merely his presence.

The next story is similar in that it also deals with another scandalously loved adventurer, who, most notably, wore no pants when he rode horseback and was punching cows. Other local characters central to other stories are: Elacio the astute biology teacher, who upon finding himself under pressure by her brothers to marry Erlinda Benavídez, arranges for his friend Jimmy Ortega to fall in love with her; Felix and Sally who found the restaurant La Casa KK—known locally as Casa CaCa—, prosper, and then split up; Mano Fashico, Don Cacahuate, Doña Cebolla, Pedro Urdemales, Bertoldo, all imaginary childhood friends from New Mexican folklore who in the words of the author "me endulzaron y enriquecieron la vida entonces y que ahora recuerdo con todo cariño" (They sweetened and enriched my life back then and I now remember them very tenderly).

In the final story of the collection, Ulibarrí describes the brotherhood of Penitentes, the secret religious organization of devout males of the community to whom, only in later years, he attributes their due and recognizes their importance in holding together the Hispano culture of northern New Mexico. It was they who filled the administrative religious and cultural vacuum of early New Mexico to give continuity and cohesiveness to the Hispano population. Ulibarrí cautions the reader not to believe all the exaggerated versions of the Penitentes' secret rituals—although in the story he does refer indirectly to some of their more extreme religious practices such as the ones that occurred during Lent.

As the title of Ulibarrí's third collection of short stories indicates, **Primeros encuentros, First Encounters** focuses on the author's early experiences with Anglos and Anglo culture. While at least one of the selections—**"Don Nicomedes"**—deals with dominant culture racism in northern New Mexico, most present a sympathetic view of the complex process of cultural melding. As in the two previous collections of short stories, the author draws heavily on his memories of growing up Hispano in Tierra Amarilla. Tinged with sadness due to the loss of childhood innocence, his young protagonists struggle to come to grips with their emergence into adulthood. Leaving the haven of the family, they venture forth to find their way in a different, but not necessarily hostile, environment.

"Un oso y un amor" (**"A Bear and a Love"**) typifies this process. The narrator remembers tenderly the joyful and carefree times he spent as a teenager playing with his friends in the woods, his developing friendship with Shirley Cantel, an attractive Anglo girl, and then their separation as their paths divided as young adults.

Ulibarrí portrays Anglos not as flat sociological entities but as multi-dimensional characters with feelings as diverse as those of his Hispano characters. Because he remembers the two groups intermingling freely in Tierra Amarilla, their interrelationships—as in the above study—are portrayed as natural and without racial conflict. This is seen throughout the collection. In **"El forastero gentil,"** for example, an Anglo cowboy—a Texan—is welcomed by a Hispano ranch family. Knowing little about his past, but sensing that he has suffered some deep disillusionment, Don Prudencio, the father, offers him his home and his family's companionship. The author deftly contrasts the stranger's rough exterior to his gentle response to the children. The Texan and the Hispanos develop a deep mutual respect.

This same respect is a characteristic found in other stories such as **"La güera," "Adolfo Miller," "Don Nicomedes," "Don Tomás Vernes,"** and **"Mónico."** Anglos, like Hispanos, are depicted as both good and bad, energetic and lazy, brutal and gentle. Although somewhat idealized, life in Tierra Amarilla is always interesting and varied as characters from the two cultures learn more about each other.

Pupurupú, Ulibarrí's latest collection of short stories, shows two clear tendencies: a return to the nostalgic, memory-laden stories of **Tierra Amarilla** and **Mi abuela fumaba puros** and an incursion into fantasy. **Pupurupú**

also contains stories that cannot neatly be classified as either predominantly nostalgic or fantastic, such as "**El juez, mi rehén,**" and "**Palomas negras.**"

Stories similar to these in Ulibarrí's first two collections need only be listed here, for they are of lesser interest than those that represent the author's experimentation with fantasy. They are: "**Adios carnero,**" and "**La niña que murió de amor.**"

Readers who have come to expect the simply told tales of growing up in and around Tierra Amarilla will be pleasantly surprised to find that Ulibarrí is equally comfortable exploring other literary veins. These stories are rich in tonality and psychological insight.

In "**El gobernador Glu Glu,**" the author creates a mythical land ruled by a buffoonish character, Antonio Zonto Glu Glu, who has risen to his position of power thanks to one remarkable trait: he can not utter a single word against women without biting his tongue and saying "Glu glu." These absurd syllables are somehow irresistible to women who come to adore this nondescript little man. Coached by his wife, Antonio launches his political career as a defender of women's rights, finally winning the gubernatorial election. Soon after, he dies a fulfilled and happy man. The author gently parodies the foibles of politicians and their tendency to seize upon current issues, using them for their own political gain.

"**Monte Niko**" is the finest example in *Pupurupú* of Ulibarrí's fantastic stories. He imbues the story's ambiance with qualities not found elsewhere in his writing. A fictitious people, the Nikoni, live harmoniously in the valley of Nikon blessed by nature and isolated from others' strife. They worship Talaniko, the god of love and peace, who has rewarded their loyalty and devotion by granting them fertile fields, spiritual tranquility, and leisure time to devote to the pursuit of art and philosophy. Niko, a young man of extraordinary sensitivity and intelligence, is chosen king to lead them. He defeats Peri Yodo, a terrible beast who is the incarnation of evil, gives his people commandments to live by, and dies soon after.

"**El conejo pionero**" and "**Mamá guantes**" are other stories in Ulibarrí's most recent collection that reflect the same mode as "**Monte Niko.**" The first is a playful treatment of a man's friendship with a rabbit, the second is a somber consideration of interpersonal relationships.

As we have seen from the virtuosity and variety of his writings, Sabine Ulibarrí is a salient figure on the Chicano literary scene. In terms of New Mexico, he has spent a lifetime putting into words the essence of Hispano life as he lived and remembers it in Tierra Amarilla.

Juan D. Bruce-Novoa   (review date 1990)

SOURCE: "Magical Regionalism," *The American Book Review,* Vol. 11, No. 6, January-February 1990, p. 14.

[*Bruce-Novoa is a distinguished Hispanic poet and critic. In this review of* El Cóndor and Other Stories, *he maintains that Ulibarrí's short stories are too realistic to uphold the "literary creations" necessary to support the genre.*]

Ulibarrí, a native New Mexican, is no novice. When Chicano political activism was surfacing in the mid 1960s, but before any major piece of literature associated with it had been published, two books of Ulibarrí's poetry appeared, *Al cielo se sube a pie* and *Amor y Ecuador,* in Madrid in 1966. Thus, some classify him as a precursor, one of a few established writers—including José Antonio Villarreal, John Rechy, and Fray Angélico Chávez—formed before the political activism of the sixties and never associated with the activities or the ideological stance of younger Chicanos. If his poetry supported the image of aloof author in its standard Spanish, personal instead of communal topics, and somewhat international flavor, his short fiction displayed his knowledge of and concern for the communal existence of Chicanos—he would probably call them Hispanos—in his native New Mexico. *Tierra Amarilla: Stories of New Mexico/Tierra Amarilla: Cuentos de Nuevo Mexico* (1971), *Mi abuela fumaba puros y otros cuentos de Tierra Amarilla/My Grandmother Smoked Cigars and Other Stories of Tierra Amarilla* (1977), *Primeros encuentros/First Encounters* (1982) all feature regional and ethnic specificity that belie charges of cultural alienation. In those stories Ulibarrí spoke of and for the Hispano people of his region, often assuming the tone and spirit of the community "cuentero" or teller of folktales.

The new stories are a peculiar mixture of Ulibarrí's personal antecedents—a peculiar and somewhat uneasy mixture. Here, the author has selected non-ethnic topics—for example, a Russian opera singer's reincarnation for ideal love, or a German scientists' creation of a beneficent vegetable Frankenstein, or a Greek goddess-turned-statue, and others. The stories could happen anywhere, but Ulibarrí places them in New Mexico, a detail both superfluous and distracting. The New Mexican setting adds nothing to their development. Even in the story of the Greek statue, where the magical revival of the goddess through the blood of her ardent rescuer recalls the romantic bent of traditional New Mexican folktales, the story's interior logic does not incorporate the local as a necessary ingredient. The same is true of several of the stories. The result is the impression that the author tries too hard to place his region into universal literature, but only achieves it at the simplest level, loudly proclaiming that interesting things can happen in New Mexico too, believe it or not. But to achieve his goal, the author must include information and plot twists that, since they are not necessary to the story, otherwise would be eliminated. The rule of the short story is to eliminate anything not directly related to the development. When Ulibarrí takes time and space to explain the here irrelevant fact of location, he breaks that rule.

His desire to place exotic characters in New Mexico forces this strategy on him. We can ask why it matters to Ulibarrí that a Russian opera singer decide to live in

Albuquerque and that her son seek love in Paris? Why must a Greek statue end up in a New Mexican museum? Why must two students study at Harvard, when that detail adds nothing to the plot? Not that these things could not happen in real life—they do and are believable—but short stories are not life, rather literary creations with generic demands. Superfluous material flaws the works. The explanation is that Ulibarrí still functions more as an oral-tradition storyteller than a literary short-story writer, despite obvious literary pretensions. One strategy of the oral-tradition performer is to relate the tale to the audience, often by placing it in their geographic or genealogic spaces. This is legitimate on Ulibarrí's part, but the stories come off as forced, too blatantly manipulated. The most disturbing flaw in the book arises, then, from the uneasy marriage of two similar, yet distinct modes of narration.

When the plot and the setting blend naturally, as in **"El cacique Cruzto,"** the story raises no such distractions. Mythical elements and strange coincidences are fully acceptable, here and in the other stories—readers are so used to what is loosely termed magical realism that Ulibarrí's fantastic plots will surprise no one at this point. When well blended, anything can go into the content; when awkwardly done, content matters little—the story rings false.

Many will consider magical realism the collection's defining mark. Ulibarrí continually mixes fantastic and realistic elements, blurring the boundary between them, a technique characteristic of this type of writing. However, once in a while Ulibarrí underestimates the reader's familiarity with the technique and explains too much. When Damian Karanova reads a letter from his deceased mother in which she speaks of people and events she could not have known, Ulibarrí adds:

> Damian remained pensive, strangely serene, thinking about the new perspectives now opening for him. What he had just read seemed perfectly logical, normal and natural to him. He did not wonder, for example, how his mother could have known twenty-five years before that there was going to be a famous singer by the name Amina Karavelha now and that she was going to give a performance on August 15th of this year. The coincidence in the names did not surprise him either.

A satire of magical realism would permit such a self-relative intervention, but nowhere does the author indicate that we are to read this as satire. The tactics of magical realism are seriously employed; no debunking is apparent, so explanation is uncalled-for and, thus, another distracting flaw.

In fact, **"Amena Karanova"** symbolizes the problems with the entire volume. Amena Karanova arrives in New Mexico by accident, decides to stay, chooses a New Mexican spouse to sire her child, and then dies, leaving the child to realize her failed dreams in a manner and in spaces that relegate the New Mexican elements to the periphery. Even the New Mexican father is a simple tool of the exotic beauty. She constructs a strange altar for her rituals, just as she builds a new room for her son to grow up in. And when the son reaches maturity, he is sent off to Europe to find a fit spouse. New Mexico is a mere setting; the New Mexican father is no more than a drone for the foreign Queen. That strangeness and estrangement permeate the text.

In the title story the contradictions of the good intentions of communal linkage and the misguided privileging of the foreign and exotic over the local come to a head. This utopian revindication of Native Americans by a non-Indian professor from the University of New Mexico could have been set in that state. Native Americans there share the necessary ingredients: an ancient tradition, the memory of independence and relative grandeur, and a condition of economic and cultural repression. Why then must Ulibarrí return to a topic of his earlier poetry, Ecuador, to find a setting? Why indulge the exoticist nostalgia for an Inca empire in South America? If readers are expected to accept the unrealistically simplistic details of a benevolent terrorism and the magical transformation of the New Mexican professor into a reincarnation of an Inca Emperor, could they not be asked to apply their imagination to a U.S. setting? Despite the apparently revolutionary plot, what is ultimately revealed here is the contradictory message of traditional U.S. mainstream imperialistic arrogance and paternalistic liberalism, both in the guise of a Latino superhero.

In **"El Condor"** the Ecuadorian underclasses, both mestizo and Native American, are pictured as unable to achieve their own liberation. Only a sensitive U.S. liberal, who has come to Ecuador for reasons far from political, can realize the extent of the oppression and create a revolution. It is he who will catalyze the native population by destroying the oppressor class, forcing a higher social consciousness among liberals, and eventually rediscovering and revitalizing native traditions. In the end, the U.S. savior becomes so steeped in the local myths and ethos that he becomes the new manifestation of a lost utopia. His physical features themselves metamorphose.

> At the same time that the color and the texture of the hair was changing, other, more radical, changes were taking place. Again the alteration was so slow that no one noticed it for a long time. Subtle deformations in the features and in the bone structure of the skull of the man who had been Dr. Garibay were taking place. The result was that the face of the old professor became the face of the posters that Ottozamìn had one day sketched [to invent the icon of the Inca hero El Condor]. He was rejuvenated entirely. He now had an athletic and heroic look. Sofía went through similar changes. She took on the appearance of an Inca princess, like the ones etched in ancient gold jewelry or painted on the ceramics of olden times. She started calling her lover 'Altor,' which in Quechua means 'king'. He called her 'Altora.'

This is all too familiar to students of Hollywood film, because it repeats one of the standard stereotypical plots about Latin America. Since *Aztec Treasure* (1914), Hollywood has filmed and refilmed avatars of **"El Condor"** set all over Latin America. Liberal good intentions aside, the result is usually the same: the establishment of an enlightened dictatorship by foreigners who somehow reincarnate the paternalistic dominance of ancient elitism—the Incas invoked here, after all, subjugated many tribes to create their empire. El Condor, having achieved absolute power in Ecuador, moves to a mountain palace, where he holds populist court. "Every day at six in the evening Altor came out on the balcony. The plaza was always full of Indians. He spoke to them of love, brotherhood, democracy, compassion, honesty, self-respect. He spoke to them as if they were children, his children." Latin Americans as children in need of redemption, even after they have been liberated—this is an elitist and colonialistic concept, one that all conquerors of the area have indulged in even as they presented themselves as Christian saviors and champions of democracy.

Perhaps it is too much to ask Chicanos to act outside the mainstream traditions of their country, the United States. One is what he is, and literature, no matter how much one manipulates it for personal ends, betrays underlying truths. Certainly Ulibarrí takes this venture seriously—the story contains intercalated elements from his earlier life—and we must read and criticize it with equal seriousness, and not overlook the fundamental contradictions.

Sabine Ulibarrí has produced an interesting, if not altogether successful, synthesis of New Mexican oral tradition and mainstream magical realism. Perhaps we could call it magical regionalism.

Additional coverage of Ulibarrí's life and career is contained in the following sources published by the Gale Group: *Contemporary Authors*, Vol. 131; *Contemporary Literature Criticism*, Vol. 83; *Dictionary of Literary Biography*, Vol. 82; *DISCovering Multicultural America*; *Hispanic Writers*.

Rodolfo Usigli
1905–1979

Mexican playwright, poet, essayist, and critic.

INTRODUCTION

As with most artists and intellectuals who lived at the time of the Mexican Revolution, Rodolfo Usigli was inspired with reformist energy which he applied to overhauling Mexican theater. Called the "apostle of Mexican drama" for his dedication to defining and establishing a distinct Mexican theater, Usigli rescued the Mexican dramatic arts from its imitation of Spanish theater. To prepare himself for the task, Usigli read, studied, and even attempted to imitate plays from the ancient Greeks, Spain's Golden Age, and the realist/naturalist forebears of Ibsen, Shaw, and Strindberg. In addition, Usigli formed his own repertory company, wrote newspaper reviews, histories of Mexican drama, and a manual of dramatic theory and composition. He translated plays for radio and theater and helped establish Mexico's first school of drama where he taught dramaturgy to the upcoming generation of playwrights. Most important, he wrote some of Mexico's most representative and best-known plays, especially *El gesticulador* (1947; *The Imposter*), widely considered the play that ushered in modern Mexican drama. The play was a box-office sensation when it premiered in 1947 but was also the object of attack, especially by unions and government, both of which thought it too critical. After two weeks the play was banned from the stage. This censorship combined with the present opinion of Usigli's mastery exhibited in *El gesticulador* finds relevence in one of Usigli's most famous lines: "A people without drama is a people without truth."

Born on November 17, 1905, in Mexico City, Rodolfo Usigli was a child of parents newly-immigrated to Mexico. His father, an Italian, died when Rodolfo was very young. His mother was Austro-Hungarian and raised her four children by herself with wages from shopkeeping and cleaning. Though the family was considered poor, Rodolfo was blessed with a mother who spoke Polish, German, and French to her children, and who instilled in them high aspirations in artistic and intellectual matters. Although he was legally blind until age three, permanently troubled by both ear and eye defects, and forced to work at an early age, Usigli cultivated an interest in puppets and theater, read voraciously, and learned English and French. But the disciplined boy never finished secondary school, though he did attend adult education classes offered to workers and the poor in the evening. At home, Usigli read six plays a day, tried to imitate them, and set down his evaluations which local papers were "glad to publish" as reviews. And so by age twenty, Usigli was already a respected theater critic. Still, his lack of offi-

cial schooling kept him mostly outside the circle of the playwrights of his time. Usigli's first play, *El apóstol* (1931; *The Apostle*), was a failure largely because Act II's earthquake could not be staged. Other early plays also found problems, some believing Usigli's cantankerous reputation hampered his efforts. But whatever unsuccesses these plays suffered, Usigli secured a position on the faculty at the National University of Mexico and an administrative job in the Ministry of Education where he created a radio program that broadcast drama classics from around the world. In 1935, along with Xavier Villaurrutia, Usigli received a scholarship to study drama at Yale. When he returned, he taught again at the university, worked as an administrator for the Institute of Fine Arts, and wrote some of his major plays, including, *El gesticulador*. Although Usigli had written sixteen plays; a literary diary; a poetry collection; a variety of reviews, prologues, and essays on Mexican drama; and fine translations of T. S. Eliot's poetry, his theater would not allow him the necessary break into Mexico's modern theatrical establishment. Much of Usigli's drama was focused on the emerging Mexican middle-class, which deviated from the formal experimentation and universal, cosmopolitan themes explored by his contemporaries. He decided to join the diplomatic service so he could leave the country. His first assignment in France afforded him a two-year stay, during which time he traveled to England. There he met the playwright who most influenced him, George Bernard Shaw. Shaw wrote to Usigli: "If you ever need an Irish certificate of vocation as a dramatic poet I will sign it. . . . Mexico can starve you; but it cannot deny your genius." Usigli also took time to interview T. S. Eliot and Jean Cocteau, collecting these and other visits, interviews, and memories in *Conversaciones y encuentros* (1974; *Conversations and Encounters*). When he returned, *El gesticulador* was produced and became a hit. Two other plays also became successful *El niño y la niebla* (1951; *The Child and the Mist*) and *Jano es una muchacha* (1952; *Janus is a Girl*). After a few years of inconsistent success, Usigli was forced to leave Mexico on what was called "diplomatic exile," and fled to Lebanon and then Norway until 1972. While in exile he wrote his Corona Trilogy, consisting of *Corona de sombra* (1947; *Crown of Shadows*), *Corona de fuego* (1961; *Crown of Fire*), *Corona de luz* (1969; *Crown of Light*), the first of these being one of Usigli's most renowned plays. But his exile hurt his career and by the time he returned to Mexico, a new generation of playwrights emerged and his plays seemed outdated. Still far from unknown, Usigli won Mexico's highest prize for literature in 1972. By the time he died in 1979, however, he was reportedly lonely and bitter, his last two plays critical of youth and reform.

Usigli thought that each country should develop its own theater representative of it own themes and concerns.

For this reason, plays should criticize the society in which their countrymen live and help inspire them to national greatness. But through these national preoccupations, Usigli also sought something universal since he believed that theater's essential material was human passion and ideas. He also focused the spotlight on the emerging middle class with its colloquialisms, mannerisms, and petty responsibilities and concerns. His dramatic themes are the relationship between the individual and the state, the function of art and artist in public affairs, the role of women in male-dominated society, and the changing values and resultant conflicts between age groups. Usigli's version of realist theater has been called "a poetry of selective realism" because it mixes a good deal of imagination and interpretation with history, traditional myth, and observation of persons and situations. Unlike the majority of the artists of his day who worked on grand historical themes of oppressor and oppressed against a national landscape, Usigli's drama is smaller, issue-oriented, and closer to the heart of the average Mexican citizen; his goal was to change society rather than merely instill it with pride or anger through portrayals of moments of glorious history. Usigli's dramatic career is often divided into three periods: social and political satires, psycho-realist dramas, and historical dramas. His most respected plays are *El niño y la niebla*, *El gesticulador*, and the Corona Trilogy. *El niño y la niebla* involves a neurotic wife attempting to get rid of her husband to be with her lover. To do so she tries to condition her somnambulist son to kill his father, her husband. But the overwrought boy shoots himself instead, leaving the woman in an even worse predicament. Usigli's greatest play, *El gesticulador*, is the story of a university history professor who takes on the identity of a legendary Mexican general with the same name and birthplace in order to give himself prestige. A U.S. historian writes up his "discovery" of this general who had been missing in action. Thrust into publicity and politics, the "general" becomes the leader of a revolutionary party through the ignorance and self-interest of local politicians. Though the imposter tries to rise to the occasion, he is killed before he can realize his ideas, preferring death to being found out. Usigli dedicated the tragedy to his "hypocritical fellow countrymen." Usigli's Corona Trilogy was his most ambitious project, an interpretation of three pivotal events in Mexican independence. The earliest drama and a contender for Usigli's best play, *Corona de sombra*, deals with the brief reign of Emperor Maximillian and France's bid to turn Mexico into a French monarchy. Usigli shows Maximillian as a latent democrat who secretly identifies with the liberal cause of a people's government, almost willingly sacrificing his life to save Mexico from European designs. Though *Corona de sombra* is the first play produced in the trilogy, it represents the last of the events leading to what Usigli saw as the three main events of Mexican sovereignty. The first historical event chronicles the clash between Spaniards and Aztecs as depicted in *Corona de fuego*. Usigli saw this as Mexico's phase of "material sovereignty." The second event, the establishment of Catholicism in Mexico, is represented in *Corona de luz*. This is said to represent Mexico's "spiritual sovereignty." Finally *Corona de sombra*, with its drama of European takeover, ushered in Mexico's last phase of independence, its "political sovereignty."

An accomplished essayist, poet, and novelist, Usigli was first and foremost a man of the theater. His efforts in defining and refining Mexican theater came largely through his portrayal of Mexican history, society, and people, especially the emerging middle-class. No other post-revolutionary dramatist was able to project so authentic and comprehensive an artistic vision of modern Mexico. Largely due to Usigli's consistent, creative and scholarly efforts, Mexico has one of the best theaters in the Spanish-speaking world.

PRINCIPAL WORKS

El apóstol: Comedia (drama) 1931

México en el teatro (history and criticism) 1932

Caminos del teatro en México (history and criticism) 1933

Estado de secreto: Comedia (drama) 1936

Medio tono: Comedia [*The Great Middle Class in Poet Lore*] (drama) 1937

Conversación desesperada (poems) 1938

La mujer no hace milagros: Comedia de malas maneras (drama) 1939

Sueño de día (drama) 1939

La crítica de "La mujer no hace milagros": Comedieta (drama) 1940

Itinerario del autor dramático, y otros ensayos (drama criticism) 1940

Vacaciones: Comedieta (drama) 1940

La familia cena en casa: Comedia   (drama) 1942

Ensayo de un crimen (novel) 1944

Otra primavera (drama) 1945

Corona de sombra: Pieza antihistórica (drama) 1947

El gesticulador: Pieza para demagogos (drama) 1947

La última puerta: Farsa impolítica (drama) 1948

Los fugitivos (drama) 1950

Noche de estío: Comedia (drama) 1950

El niño y la niebla (drama) 1951

Aguas estancadas (drama) 1952

Jano es una muchacha (drama) 1952

La función de despedida: Comedia (drama) 1953

Un día de éstos. . .: Farsa impolítica (drama) 1954

Vacaciones II: Comedieta (drama) 1956

Mientras amemos: Estudio en intensidad dramática (drama) 1956

La exposición: Comedia divertimiento (drama) 1959

Homenaje a Alfredo Gómez de la Vega [with Mauricio Magdaleno] (drama) 1959

Antonio Ruiz et l'art dangereux de la peinture (nonfiction) 1960

Corona de fuego: Primer esquema para una tragedia antihistórica americana (drama) 1961

Tres comedietas [includes *Un navío cargado de...: Comedia marítima*, *El testamento y el viudo: Comedia involuntaria*, and *El encuentro: Comedieta*] (drama) 1966

Juan Ruiz de Alarcón en el tiempo, Secretaria de Educacion Publica (history) 1967

Carta de amor: Monólogo heterodoxo (drama) 1968

Corona de luz: Comedia antihistórica [*Crown of Light* in *Two Plays*: *Crown of Light* and *One of These Days...*] (drama) 1969

El gran circo del mundo (drama) 1969

Los viejos: Duólogo imprevisto (drama) 1971

Buenos días, señor Presidente! Moralidad en dos actos y un interludio según "La vida es sueño" (drama) 1972

Obliteración (fiction) 1973

Conversaciones y encuentros: Bernard Shaw, Lenormand, Jean Cocteau, Clifford Odets, André Breton, Elmer Rice, Paul Muni, B. Traven, T. S. Eliot (interviews) 1974

Imagen y prisma de México; Presencia de Juárez en el teatro universal: Una paradoja (history) 1976

Teatro completo (collected works) 1963-1979

Corona de sombra, Corona de fuego, Corona de luz (collected plays) 1982

El gesticulador y otras obras de teatro (collected plays) 1983

El gesticulador [and] La mujer no hace milagros (collected plays) 1985

CRITICISM

R. Vance Savage (essay date 1971)

SOURCE: "Rodolfo Usigli's Idea of Mexican Theatre," in *Latin American Theatre Review*, Vol. 4, No. 2, Spring, 1971, pp. 13-20.

[*Savage outlines Usigli's components of ideal theater, including definite purpose, appropriate subject and treatment, and the author's belief in the necessity of examining one's own society for authentic elements of tragedy.*]

Rodolfo Usigli has gained fame as one of the most prominent playwrights of the twentieth-century Mexican theatre and "one of Latin America's greatest dramatists."[1] In spite of this fame, as Solomon H. Tilles has recently pointed-ed out, there have been very few attempts to examine critically the many prologues, epilogues and other essays in which Usigli presents his dramatic theory.[2] This apparent neglect is not surprising, since some of Usigli's critical writings remain unpublished, and others appeared in Mexican newspapers or magazines now difficult to locate.[3] Even in the available works his ideas must often be extracted from long, rambling dissertations on many aspects of Mexican life or from vituperative replies to comments by critics of his plays. These critical works deserve careful study, nevertheless, for in them Usigli presents his idea of the appropriate form and content for Mexican theatre; that is, the type of plays he believes Mexican dramatists must write if that country is ever to have a national theatre. Clarification of this idea is important, not just for the opportunity it provides to evaluate Usigli as a critic, but for a better understanding of his plays and, ultimately, his position in the Mexican theatre.

Throughout Usigli's writings runs his belief in the special role of the theatre in any society. The theatre, more than any other art form, according to Usigli, reflects the society that produces it: "Entre todas las formas de arte que sirven para identificar a una raza, el teatro es, a ciencia cierta, a más concluyente. . . . Flor compacta de una raza definida, el teatro es el verdadero perfil de los países."[4] If the theatre is the "profile" of a country, Usigli believes it is because the dramatist possesses special insights into his society. As Usigli states hyperbolically, "más que el profeta y más allá que el santo . . . es el único ser que cumple con su destino y que se busca, viviseccionándose."[5] Although other artists may have the same insights, they are not in the same position to interpret their findings for the average man. Unlike the novelist, poet or philosopher, who influence more select groups, the dramatist "se ve en la obligación de conducir multitudes impreparadas y no seleccionadas sobre las cuales debe regir él como gran unidad" (**"Primeros apuntes,"** p. 191). His responsibility, then, is a serious one, for he is potentially the leader of the masses and must decide what is beneficial for them.

This concept of the theatre is essentially social. The theatre serves to "abrir los ojos y para airear la conciencia del mundo."[6] The dramatist's role is one of public service, and the theatre he creates should serve as the conscience of society. Usigli admits that in formulating these ideas he was influenced chiefly by Shaw. He calls *Heartbreak House* the "punto de partida de mi conciencia del teatro."[7] His comments on the purpose of the theatre are similar to those of Shaw, who, according to Barrett H. Clark, "both in theory and in practice . . . maintained that it is the function of the drama to teach and serve a practical and immediate purpose for the community and society."[8]

The idea of a theatre that reflects Mexican society distinguishes Usigli from the dramatists of most of the experimental groups in Mexico during the 1920s to 1940s. The authors of *Ulises* and *Orientación*, for example, emphasized the importance of the universality of the theatre. Usigli emphasizes the uniqueness of the theatre of each country: "El teatro de un país es siempre y sólo de ese país, y no importa mucho que sus obras se universalicen o no."[9] As a result, Usigli's disillusionment with the experimental groups is stated often in his essays in the 1940s and 1950s. He accuses the experimentalists of making the mistake of considering the theatre an *afición* instead of a profession,[10] of making the Mexican theatre an imitation of foreign works,[11] and of writing for other writers instead of for the public.[12] He concludes that imitating what he calls the "semidioses europeos," who were writing for select audiences in countries with long literary traditions, has been of little help in determining the proper form and content for a Mexican theatre. He insists that Mexican authors must treat the realities of Mexico if they are to write "Mexican" drama (**"Ensayo,"** p. 290).

Usigli believes that one way Mexican dramatists may help themselves to choose subjects that reflect Mexican society is to study the classical Greek theatre. In his long article on tragedy, **"Primer ensayo hacia una tragedia**

mexicana,"[13] Usigli attributes part of the success of the Greek dramatists to the fact that they were able to relate past traditions to present reality: "Importa como escribe Sófocles la tragedia, o como la escribe Esquilo, porque cada uno representa la reunión del pasado supervivo con el presente en acción de vivir. . . . La tradición—influencia religiosa, política e histórica—y el público contemporáneo—entidad social—exigen de modo general que el dramaturgo trate un tema histórico o mitológico nativo, conocido de los espectadores." (p. 107). According to Usigli, Mexican dramatists should emulate the Greeks and look to their religious, political and historical traditions for subject matter that will be meaningful to the contemporary Mexican public.

One of the traditions that may be a source of valid dramatic material is the field of Mexican politics. In **"Anatomía del teatro"** Usigli supports this belief by citing *Le malade imaginaire,* Act III, Scene 3, where Molière's spokesman, Beraldo, defends bringing to the stage the different professions of men.[14] Usigli concludes that whereas most societies have other "professions" for dramatic themes, in Mexico there is only one: "La profesión del político es en la vida, como en el teatro . . . la única profesión nacional" (**"Anatomía,"** p. 290).

In the unpublished prologue to *Noche de estío,*[15] Usigli makes the same point by comparing Mexico to Spanish society during the Golden Age. Spanish dramatists of the time took their material from the court, from tradition, or from the professions. Although Mexico does not have a nobility to attract the dramatist's attention, it does have equally valid dramatic material: "Tenemos la política con todos sus repliegues, mezquindades, sombras pasajeras, grandezas, cómicas situaciones, ambiciones criminales y grotescas, la política, que, en realidad, ha substituido con ventaja a la nobleza por cuanto son ventajosos los señores políticos." (p. 143).

Usigli points out that the writers of the satirical *revistas* have proved that political themes are valid subject matter for Mexican theatre (**"Noche de estío,"** p. 143). It seems to him absurd to leave this material in the hands of such mediocre writers. Skilled writers of serious drama can use the same material and produce a much more meaningful theatre. In **"Anatomía del teatro"** he clarifies this point: "No hablo simplemente de un teatro político, en el que abundarían los temas satíricos y heroicos de la vida política, desde la espera en la antesala hasta la muerte por la sangre. El teatro es miedo a vivir si no contiene aquello que es universal para una raza o para un país o para un continente o para el mundo." (p. 10). Usigli emphasizes that he does not mean that politics constitute the only valid subject for a national theatre. A Mexican theatre must, however, have its roots in Mexican society, and since the national occupation is politics, "un teatro mexicano sin raíz política sería probablemente más difícil que hacer una revolución, o una dictadura, sin generales" (**"Ensayo,"** p. 276).

One of the aspects of Greek drama that Usigli considers most worthy of emulation is tragedy. He is especially concerned with recapturing the sense of tragedy, an element he considers lost in drama since classical antiquity. He believes that by examining the great classical tragedies, Mexican writers may extract that which is meaningful for Mexican drama.

This concern for the tragic genre is evident throughout Usigli's critical writings. As early as 1931 he was thinking of the possibility of Mexican tragedy: "Tenemos sin poder aprovecharlos correctamente, todos los elementos de la alta tragedia; todos los venenos que se embaten entre sí, un ideal para la revolución, un ideal para la paz y un ingenio robusto contra esos y otros ideales" (**"Primeros apuntes,"** p. 197). Two years later Usigli began to think of Mexican politics as a source for tragic themes. He was tempted to try to write tragedies in his earliest political plays, but decided on comedies in the style of Molière, Romains and Shaw (**"Noche de estío,"** p. 2). He believed that Aristotle's concept of the type of man who should be the object of imitation would include Mexican politicians, as well as other types who were in positions of power in Mexico (**"Noche de estío,"** p. 142). In 1937 Usigli put his idea into practice when he wrote *El gesticulador,* the work which he claims to be the first serious attempt at tragedy in the Mexican theatre.[16] Seven years later he wrote his second tragedy, *Corona de sombra,* considered by many to be his best play.

Usigli's continued interest in tragedy is best demonstrated by an essay written in 1950, "Primer ensayo hacia una tragedia mexicana." In this work he discusses tragedy in terms of Nietzsche's theory of the serene Apollonian elements and the chaotic Dionysian ones, which, in great drama, are blended artistically. After the period of the Greeks, the Apollonian aspects of tragedy seem to be replaced by the Dionysian drunkenness: "El espectador y el autor por parejo han conspirado durante siglos para extinguir en ellos y en sus descendientes, junto con otras virtudes externas, lo que Nietzsche llamaba el placer o el deleite de lo trágico. Uno y otro lo han reemplazado, subvenido o adulterado por el deleite o el placer de lo morboso, lo mismo en el aspecto sexual que en el aspecto sentimental." (p. 104). As one example of the failure of tragedians after the Greeks, Usigli cites Shakespeare, who comes close to capturing the sentiment and character of tragedy, but distorts the form. Usigli compares his plays to a painting by Picasso, with a leg protruding from the armpit or an eye shining from the stomach. (p. 105). In this distortion Shakespeare somehow misses what Usigli calls the sense of tragedy, a term he defines only as "la medida del hombre." (p. 112).

The failure of modern dramatists to capture the sense of tragedy seems to Usigli to be best illustrated by the works of Eugene O'Neill. O'Neill also emphasizes the Dionysian aspects and neglects the Apollonian serenity: "O'Neill posee el sentimiento pero no la proporción de lo trágico, ni su sentido más profundo. Su obra suscita el terror o el horror, pero no la piedad." (p. 111). In *Mourning Becomes Electra* O'Neill makes another mistake typical of many modern dramatists; instead of searching out the tragic elements in his own society, he attempts to borrow themes from the Greeks. The result is that "la transposición del tema lo hace caerse de falso." (p. 111).

Modern dramatists, concludes Usigli, have failed to capture the spirit of tragedy. Because of their obsession with the grotesque elements, they have failed to achieve the harmonious combination of the grotesque and the serene of the Greek classical theatre. Also, they have neglected to search out the tragic elements in their own society, and instead have made poor copies of classical tragedy. In order to avoid these errors, Usigli insists that Mexican authors study Mexican society. Then, by using Greek tragedy as a model, they may adapt contemporary content to a modern form, which will enable them to recapture some of the spirit of tragedy which was present in Greek drama.

Usigli supports his theory by providing a concrete example of appropriate material from Mexican history. He sees in Cuauhtémoc, the last of the Aztec emperors, the potential for revival of the tragic genre in Mexico: "Es particularmente este héroe—Cuauhtémoc—, es particularmente esta mezcla de una profecía antigua con una realidad moderna . . . lo que me mueve a pensar que en México, de todo el Continente, es donde existe la posibilidad de recrear la tragedia como género." (p. 125). Ten years later Usigli put his theory into practice by writing a tragedy in verse, complete with choruses, about the Aztec chief. *Corona de fuego*, like *El gesticulador* and *Corona de sombra*, demonstrates Usigli's desire to add grandeur to the Mexican theatre by creating a Mexican tragedy.

There is one other significant element in Usigli's ideal Mexican theatre. Having outlined the purpose of the theatre, appropriate subject matter and the need to search for tragic elements in Mexican society, there remains the question of an appropriate style that will enable Mexican dramatists to express their ideas. Moreover, if a national theatre is to have the support of the Mexican public, what is the form that will appeal to that public?

Usigli observes that the example which has existed for some twenty-five years in the *revista* has been ignored by Mexican dramatists. The *revista* gives the Mexican a realistic portrayal of the elements of Mexican society which are familiar to all Mexicans. In this sense, a national theatre should emulate the *revista*: "Hay que hacer algo por este mexicano que espía incómodamente su propia vida en los demás por el ojo de una cerradura. Hay que acercarle un sillón confortable, invitarlo a sentarse, apagar la luz en torno a él y encenderla sobre su imagen reflejada en otro."[17]

Because he finds that the realistic technique imposes certain limitations, Usigli personally prefers a more poetic theatre: "El teatro realista es deleznable, si no malo, por cuanto depende de un sistema de circunstancias externas, de movimiento dirigidos hacia un objeto inmediato, de acciones sujetas al denominador común de una fecha y a relaciones habitualmente objetivas, de familia y de clase."[18] Furthermore, the realistic theatre tends to become bogged down in trivial, ephemeral themes: "No es sólo la filtración de impurezas y de vulgaridad en los personajes; la banal-

idad y la repetición. . . . Es—la vida privada de sus seres, el aislamiento de sus escenarios, la intimidad, a menudo desnuda en su aspecto sexual; el módico egoísmo de sus sentimientos; la falta de alcance de sus catástrofes; lo dómestico de la vida; lo intrascendente de sus pasiones, la pequeñez de su radio de acción" (**"Noche de estío,"** p. 139). The appearance of Pirandello indicates to Usigli a protest against the limitations of realistic drama. He hopes that Pirandello, and other playwrights like Lorca, Cocteau and Giraudoux, will cause the return of poetry to the theatre (**"Noche de estío,"** p. 139). Usigli insists, however, that "mientras México no posea su propio teatro realista, las obras poéticas serán accidentes individuales, fechas para las historias de la literatura; pero no constituirán un teatro poético propio" (**"Discurso,"** p. 334). He believes, therefore, that social realism is the style to be preferred, although he envisions a gradual transition to a more poetic drama as public taste becomes more refined.

In formulating his idea of a Mexican theatre, Usigli is essentially an eclectic. He selects concepts from other writers, past and present, which he feels apply to Mexican drama. He derives his theory of the purpose of the theatre from Shaw; he looks to the classical Greeks, the Spanish Golden Age, diverse writers such as Molière, and to Mexican traditions to find meaningful subject matter; and he borrows Nietzsche's terminology to explain how modern dramatists can capture the spirit of tragedy in modern society. His originality lies in the selection and application of these ideas to the Mexican theatre.

Although Usigli's theoretical ideas are taken principally from writers of the past, they also demonstrate his involvement with contemporary trends in Mexico and other countries. The insistence on Mexican subject matter represents a rejection of the experimentalists' "universal" works On the other hand, his advocacy of political themes shows his agreement with the ideas of the authors of the *Teatro de Ahora* (1932) and with the prevalent trend on the stages of the United States. As Bamber Gascoigne points out, the "1930s stand out from the whole history of the theatre as *the* decade of political theatre."[19] Since Usigli spent 1935 studying drama at Yale, it is safe to assume that he was cognizant of this trend.

Usigli's desire for a tragic and poetic theatre also reflects contemporary dramatic thought. During the period he was formulating and recording his theoretical ideas, leading American and European playwrights, such as O'Neill, Lorca and Eliot, were experimenting with forms of modern tragedy, and many dramatists were attempting to achieve poetic effects in their plays. Authors such as Lorca and Eliot were experimenting with varied rhymes and rhythms. Other dramatists, such as O'Casey, were achieving poetic effect through rhythmic prose. Usigli knew modern drama well; it is understandable that he should share his contemporaries' enthusiasm for tragic and poetic drama.

Usigli's essays show his special concern for the role of the public. He envisions the theatre as a means of educating the public, but he also insists on subject matter that will be received well by a Mexican audience. He provides specific examples for some of the proper subjects for Mexican plays, such as the world of politics, and indicates how dramatists may look for other valid dramatic material in their society. The most confusing part of these critical ideas is the discussion of tragedy. Usigli's definition of the tragic sense as simply "la medida del hombre" is, at best, hazy. His adoption of Nietzsche's theory, which, as Nietzsche recognizes, is itself mystic and vague, does not help to clarify his meaning.[20] Also, Usigli's judgments of all tragedians since the Greeks seem excessively harsh. Although his disappointment with O'Neill's *Mourning Becomes Electra* (1931) is generally shared by other critics,[21] O'Neill's earlier work, *Desire Under the Elms* (1924), is considered by some to be one of the most successful attempts at modern tragedy.[22] Usigli's criticism of Shakespeare's freedom of form also seems unjustified, since Usigli himself recommends that dramatists should search out modern material, which may require modern form.

Usigli's idea of a Mexican theatre may be summarized as one modeled on the European realistic tradition, but treating meaningful national themes. Although this idea does not constitute a complete dramatic theory which describes a theatre that would be uniquely Mexican in form and content, it does offer flexible guidelines for plays of some significance and grandeur that, hopefully, will attract the Mexican public to the theatre. Once they have their audience, Mexican dramatists can move toward the poetic theatre that Usigli believes will be "la más grande hazaña del espíritu nativo" (**"Discurso,"** p. 334).

NOTES

[1] Willis Knapp Jones, *Behind Spanish American Footlights* (Austin: University of Texas Press, 1966), p. 502.

[2] "Rodolfo Usigli's Concept of Dramatic Art," *Latin American Theatre Review,* 3/2 (Spring 1970), pp. 31-38. There is one detailed study of Usigli's dramatic theory: D. L. Rosenberg, in "The Dramatic Theory of Rodolfo Usigli: The Poetry of Selective Realism," unpublished Ph.D. dissertation, State University of Iowa, 1962, evaluates Usigli's basic theoretical ideas, emphasizing his approach to realism. Although Rosenberg does not relate Usigli's theory to the Mexican theatre, his organization of Usigli's major ideas is useful. Also see my study, "The 'Mexican' Theater of Rodolfo Usigli: Theory and Practice," unpublished Ph.D. dissertation, University of Oregon, 1969.

[3] Ten of Usigli's prologues, epilogues or other essays (one of which—the prologue to *Un día de estos . . .* —numbers 151 pages) remain unpublished. In 1964 Fondo de Cultura Económica had the complete collection of manuscripts of Usigli's essays but decided not to publish them.

[4] "Primeros apuntes sobre el teatro," *México en el teatro* (Mexico: Imprenta Mundial, 1932), p. 197. This is a collection of five articles originally published in *El Universal Ilustrado* (Mexico), Sept. 10 and 24, Oct. 1 and 22, Nov. 5, 1931.

[5] "Poeta en libertad," *Cuadernos Americanos,* XLIX (Jan.-Feb., 1950), p. 297.

[6] "Un día de estos," unpublished prologue, 1953, p. 5.

[7] "Dos conversaciones con George Bernard Shaw y algunas cartas," *Cuadernos Americanos,* Part II, XXXI (Jan.-Feb., 1947), p. 238.

[8] *European Theories of the Drama* (New York: Crown Publishers, 1918), p. 471.

[9] "El teatro en lucha," *Hoy* (Mexico City), No. 335 (July 24, 1943), p. 61.

[10] "Addenda después del estreno," *Jano es una muchacha* (Mexico: Imprenta Nuevo Mundo, 1952), pp. 188-189.

[11] "El gran teatro del nuevo mundo," unpublished prologue to *Los fugitivos,* 1950, p. 24.

[12] "Ensayo sobre la actualidad de la poesía dramática," in *El gesticulador* (Mexico: Editorial Stylo, 1947), p. 290. Subsequent references appear in the text as "Ensayo."

[13] "Primer ensayo hacia una tragedia mexicana," *Cuadernos Americanos,* LII (July-August, 1950). Subsequent references appear as "Primer ensayo."

[14] "Anatomía del teatro," *El Nacional* (Mexico City), April 20, 1947, p. 10. Subsequent references appear in the text as "Anatomía."

[15] "Prólogo a *Noche de estío,*" unpublished, 1935. Subsequent references appear in the text as "Noche de estío."

[16] See "Doce notas," in *El gesticulador* (Mexico: Editorial Stylo, 1947), p. 241.

[17] "Anatomía del teatro," April 13, 1947, p. 6.

[18] "Discurso por un teatro realista," *América,* 1937, pp. 316-317. Subsequent references appear in the text as "Discurso."

[19] Bamber Gascoigne, *Twentieth Century Drama* (New York: Barnes and Noble, Inc., 1962), p. 26.

[20] See Otto Manthey-Zorn, *Dionysus: The Tragedy of Nietzsche* (Amherst: Amherst College Press, 1956), p. 28.

[21] Gascoigne, p. 115, is of the opinion that O'Neill only succeeded in belittling his archetypes.

[22] See Gascoigne, p. 91; Herbert J. Muller, *The Spirit of Tragedy* (New York: Alfred A. Knopf, 1956), p. 315.

John W. Kronik   (essay date 1977)

SOURCE: "Usigli's *El gesticulador* and the Fiction of Truth," in *Latin American Theatre Review*, Vol. 11, No. 1, pp. 5-16.

[*Kronik discusses* El gesticulador *in the context of the relationship between creator (the playwright) and his creation (the characters).*]

Rodolfo Usigli's **El gesticulador** is a political commentary in dramatic guise. It is by that token an accusing statement on contemporary Mexican reality, and as such it conforms to Usigli's frequently stated convictions about the needs of the Mexican stage. The critics have regularly interpreted the play in the light of its social immediacy, a typical view being that Usigli composes "teatro en una forma [. . .] concreta de análisis realista de la sociedad mexicana."[1] Some, like Octavio Paz, read *El gesticulador* as an expression of the Mexican character (a judgment with which Usigli would concur); and one critic argues, not unconvincingly and following Usigli's own self-analyses, that his theatre is an examination of man's intrinsic qualities, not only of his social relationships.[2] All these assessments are valid, but whatever the magnitude of its contribution to the operative discussions of modern Mexico, *El gesticulador* is not so shallow a play as to limit itself to such ideological engagement. In fact, as a directly political drama, the piece can be considered defective or unconvincing for its series of contrivances. But contrivance is precisely the stuff of this play, which moves in that richer terrain where the circumstantial subject matter is transcended in its very enactment. That circumstantial involvement is never abandoned, and *El gesticulador* is anything but the autistic exercise that Usigli was given to condemning so roundly. Yet, regardless of Usigli's personal proclamations in favor of a theatre of ideas and against his experimentally oriented contemporaries of the vanguard, his "pieza para demagogos" is one of those plays which all the while that it molds the theatrical medium into a vehicle of socio-political commentary also turns inward onto itself to unmask and probe the medium that it is. If the theatrical artifact that Usigli wields with *El gesticulador* is a mirror, the image reflected back to us is double: the Mexican scene and the play itself. Not only are fiction (in the sense of artistic invention) and language here vehicles for the expression of social and psychological concepts, but conversely, the historical reality of the play is a metaphor for the nature of fiction and the nature of language.

Usigli's volume of writings on the theatre and his prologues and epilogues to his plays give testimony to his concern for the state of the dramatic art in Mexico and also record his ponderings about the theatre as an instrument of esthetic expression.[3] It is not my contention that Usigli wrote *El gesticulador* as a paean to the birth of a play, but it is surprising that critics have not responded to the structural evidence in the work that reveals it as self-reflexive. *El gesticulador* is a play within a play. Furthermore, since plays are inventions and the subject of this play is invention, *El gesticulador*'s interior duplication contains the echo of its own making. What D. L. Shaw, in his useful and perceptive explication of Usigli's play,[4] sees as a radical alteration in all its aspects by the end of Act II, is actually the fictional elaboration of the play within the play. Only at the exclusive level of the outer play can we speak, as Shaw does, of a thematic, interpersonal, and psychological evolution. What Shaw takes to be a transformation in the play's initial components are, more accurately, the new components of the second or interior play, the one for whose creation and existence the protagonist of the outer play, César Rubio the professor, is responsible. That is, where Shaw's perfectly acceptable interpretation functions at the level of a single play with a single character named César Rubio, another and perhaps more productive understanding of *El gesticulador* enlists Usigli and César Rubio in their own

game and extracts from the text two plays, each with a character named César Rubio. To trace the interior recreation of César Rubio and subsequently to align the esthetic implications of his dual existence with the play's major thematic element will be our task in this essay.

That task is the more readily accomplished if, in view of the above discussion, we are willing to label *El gesticulador* as metatheatre. We shall then feel less constrained than Shaw to situate Usigli's play in the tradition of the classic tragedy, in the strict context of which it is likely a failure, and shall see it evolving more according to the Shakespearean and Calderonian vision of drama. *El gesticulador* is a metaplay first in the simple sense that it is self-reflexive. It is also a metaplay insofar as it fits into Abel's category of "theatre pieces about life seen as already theatricalized."[5] Can there be any doubt that the action of *El gesticulador* adheres to Abel's dictum that "in the metaplay life *must* be a dream and the *world* must be a stage"? That this indivisibility of life and theatre, reality and dream was on Usigli's mind at this time is corroborated by the fact that he prefaces an essay written in 1939, the year after *El gesticulador*, with the speech from *As You Like It* (II, vii) in which Jaques pronounces the famous lines, "All the world's a stage, and all the men and women merely players"; and then picking up the Shakespeare citation, Usigli reaffirms: "Así la anatomía del teatro se asemeja a la humana."[6] (The nebulous dividing line between lived and invented reality is a preoccupation in several of Usigli's plays.) The lengthy epilogue to *El gesticulador* had already drawn the connection between this philosophical stand, what Calderón called "el gran teatro del mundo," and the play's implication that offended so many viewers, namely that all Mexicans are gesticulators: "una escuela de teatro resultaba verdaderamente superflua en un lugar donde el teatro se vivía, donde todos eran políticos, es decir, actores consumados que actuaban cotidianamente en una farsa interminable."[7] A gesturer, an impostor, a hypocrite is an actor; conversely, imposture is an actor's lifeblood.

The characters within the play are themselves conscious of the existential and political metaphor that derives from this philosophical blurring. Miguel, soon after the play opens, by momentarily evoking the family's past as a lie, an unsuccessful comedy designed to camouflage their economic plight, presages the nature of the future action as a lie. Unlike Miguel, his father accepts the theatrical temper of existence. He sees as the only alternative to living one lie the living of another lie. The individual simply chooses to enact one or the other, so that in politics, the play makes clear, it is not a matter of authentic individuals versus role players. All are role players, and one can only hope that those who imitate goodness can conquer the impostors of evil. The two political gesturers in this play, Rubio and Navarro, are not of the same pith. César justifies his self-theatricalization both to his wife, Elena, and to his rival, Navarro, on the basis that humbug reigns in Mexico:

> Todo el mundo aquí vive de apariencias, de gestos.
> (II, 754)[8]

Puede que yo no sea el gran César Rubio. Pero, ¿quién eres tú? ¿Quién es cada uno en México? Dondequiera encuentras impostores, impersonadores, simuladores; asesinos disfrazados de héroes, burgueses disfrazados de líderes; ladrones disfrazados de diputados, ministros disfrazados de sabios, caciques disfrazados de demócratas, charlatanes disfrazados de licenciados, demagogos disfrazados de hombres. [. . .] Todos son unos gesticuladores hipócritas. [. . .] Todos usan ideas que no son suyas; todos son como las botellas que se usan en el teatro: con etiqueta de coñac, y rellenas de limonada.

(III, 782)

The interior fiction that César weaves in response to his personal dilemma and, secondarily, to his perception of the national scene has all the trappings of a play, including script, special rhetoric, costume, and actor's remuneration. For César and for his spectators, both those acting inside the play and those sitting outside it, that interior play, the enactment of dream-creation, constitutes the ultimate eradication of the frontiers between stage and street. Already by the time the spectator hears the recitation in Act II of Bolton's account that ends with "La verdad es siempre más extraña que la ficción," that irony has in turn been subjected to irony by the fact that the truth which is stranger than fiction is itself a fiction. "We are such stuff as dreams are made on" is one echo; "toda la vida es sueño, y los sueños sueños son" is another.[9] As man lives out his play, *El gesticulador* dramatizes man living out his play. There is no vehicle more ideal than a metaplay for the portrayal of a social order that lives by the lie. And as we shall see, in his ventilation of the theatre's artificial fabric, Usigli causes the mediating artifice to subvert the statement it appears to be making.

The raw material of *El gesticulador* is history—truth so rendered by time. Both the playwright and his principal character manipulate history in the interests of their respective fictions. That complex game circumscribes the relationship between creator and creation—that is, first between Usigli and César Rubio and then between Professor César Rubio and General César Rubio. Usigli recognizes that the theatre is not history, but anti-history, and is accepted on faith rather than on the basis of certifiable evidence. The poet (that is, creative artist) and the historian do not have the same mission, which is why the *Corona* trilogy bears the designation of "piezas antihistóricas." In *El gesticulador*, the poet Usigli, inspired by history, has invented a historian who is, figuratively, a poet and who avails himself of history in order to fulfill himself as a poet. In other words, César Rubio is a historian who, in order to take his own place in history, turns poet and transcends the factual limitations of history; yet to do so, he is dependent on his detailed knowledge of historical happenings, as the scenes with the visiting delegation and with Navarro prove. Usigli and César Rubio thus appear to be creatures of the same ilk. Neither is slave to the historical scenario that serves him as inspiration. Usigli's belief that the theatre is the imaginative reconstruction of the past finds literal duplication in the actions of César Rubio. When Rubio interprets a historical fact that is an invention of Usigli's derived from the latter's interpretation of Mexico's past, the two

have initiated a parallel process vis-à-vis history. We, sitting outside the play, know Usigli to be the fabricator of all these machinations; César Rubio, not so privileged, is responsible for the intricacies of his own involvements.

That responsibility devolves upon César Rubio as his creator casts the illusion of sharing his prerogatives as playwright in order to return to the realm of fiction, a fiction that he had made to appear historical. Initially, in the outer play—Usigli's exclusively—there is a fictional character named César Rubio, a university professor of history, protagonist of this drama. There is another fictional character, also the creation of Usigli, who by Usigli's designed coincidence likewise bears the name of César Rubio and was a famous general killed in the revolution. He is the fiction made to appear historical. (The pairing of Ambrose Bierce and César Rubio as Bolton's two research interests seems to legitimize the fiction historically.) From the perspective of the inner play, since Professor César Rubio has no Pirandellian insight into his fictionality, the general is a historical reality, and the drama is the professor's assumption of the fictional role of being the historical personage (the general). In that inner play, César Rubio is playwright and actor in one stroke. The creation of the general is accomplished in two phases, both of which are in the hands of the professor. The first is realized narratively when César tells Bolton the story of the general. The second is César's dramatization of the general in the body of the professor. How the general functions as a catalyst in the psychic development of the professor we shall remark on in a moment; for now it is significant that, thanks to the professor, the general has acquired dimensions far greater than those of his original pseudo-historic status, and even his mythic complexion has been reconfirmed. *El gesticulador* is in these terms the drama of Professor César Rubio's dramatization of General César Rubio. The tripartite division of the play reflects the course of this creative scheme:

Act I—Introduction (past): César Rubio, professor and historian: the personal dilemma is exposed, along with its possible resolution through fiction.

Act II—Transition (present): César Rubio, creator: the act of artistic invention is dramatized.

Act III—Resolution (future): César Rubio, general and politician: the fiction is realized; fiction and history together are transcended in the process of mythification.

As political drama, *El gesticulador* reaches its culminating point with the death of César Rubio. The interpretation of it as metatheatre, however, suggests a structural shift, with the climax of the outer play coming near the end of the first act when César allows Bolton to believe that he is the revolutionary general. That moment also constitutes the inception of the play within the play. César's acceptance of the deputation's political charge after lengthy discussion and probing in Act II is then the climax of the inner play. That leaves the final act as the occasion for the coalescence of identities.

To be fully accurate, the dynamics of that synthesis are manifested already in Act II, and the reaffirmation of identity is effected in the month that elapses before the action of the final act. Even the denial of the fiction is a step in the trajectory of its generation. When César says to the politicians, "Nunca pensé en resucitar el pasado, señores" (II, 760), reviving the past is exactly what he is doing. There is a further dramatic irony that underlines for the audience the dual level of the game in process when Treviño's question to César, "¿Por qué habla usted de sí mismo como si se tratara de otro?" receives the answer "Porque quizás así es" (II, 763). And as the interrogation draws to a close, two stage directions, of the sort that theatricalize the theatre, tell more than César's dialogue: "Involuntariamente en papel, viviendo ya el mito de César Rubio"; "Desamparado, arrastrado al fin por la farsa" (II, 765, 767).

Whether the professor's metamorphosis into the general is real or fictitious is a problem only for the spectator initiated into the two-tiered game of invention. César in the last act demonstrates both through his external demeanor and in his transmuted character that he has fully conformed to the role he had created for himself. If the professor in the outer play is unconscious of his fictionality in regard to Usigli, it is not so likely that the professor in the inner play forgets that as general he is role-playing; but the fiction has taken him over: that much is demonstrable. The César Rubio of Act III is an utterly new man, as distinct in personality, if not in identity, from the earlier César Rubio as that César Rubio is from Rodolfo Usigli. And like the playwright, César Rubio the historian disappears once the drama of the politician is under way. He can be present only in that portion of the play that is the staging of artistic creation. As the creation takes shape, its creator is expunged from the script, and when the act is consummated, only its effluence is visible. That visible entity in the end is the fruit of César's lie. He can say in full candor to Navarro in their confrontation: "Empecé mintiendo, pero me he vuelto verdadero" (III, 783). Those words reflect a conviction so strong that he repeats them to Elena: "Es que ya no hay mentira: fue necesaria al principio, para que de ella saliera la verdad. Pero ya me he vuelto verdadero, cierto" (III, 787). When Miguel, eavesdropping, hears César pronounce the words "No soy César Rubio" (III, 783), he believes he has heard the truth and, flushed with anguish, loses his faith in his father. But the irony is that his father *is* César Rubio—on two counts, no less: he is, as he has always been, César Rubio the professor; on top of that, he has *become,* and therefore is, César Rubio the general, psychically and in the eyes of the people. Ironically, too, he merits greater respect in his acquired condition than in his previous state. The ultimate irony is that the disappearance of the historian constitutes César Rubio's realization of himself as a historian. Unlike Bolton, César is a professor of history who does not write. He complains to Julia (I, 734) that, despite all his knowledge, he has been unable to create anything, even a book. Later he is to accomplish that more profoundly than he could have dreamed, far more perfectly than the productive but duped Bolton, for César's creation is flesh and book, subject

(myth, being) and object (word, play) all at once. César's conversion into the general is his composition of a text, his evocation of history for others to read. He thus fulfills himself at the same time as a man, as a creative artist, and as a historian.

Of course, César does not accomplish this pursuit without assistance. Man's eagerness to believe in fictions is César's closest collaborator. His principal abettor is Oliver Bolton, for César's lie was Bolton's truth before César ever invented his lie. To the extent that César Rubio, floundering about, was a character in search of an author, in Bolton he finds his opportunity for self-definition. The creative act depends on coincidence—a suggestion, an observation, an illumination—for its inception. The outside stimulus catalyzes the inner need. Bolton makes his appearance, not intent on historical truth, but on "una verdad que corresponda al carácter de César Rubio, a la lógica de las cosas" (I, 745). César improvises, tests out his invention on this knowledgeable listener one step at a time, and the incipient idea matures into a full-fledged fiction and subsequently into (apparent) fact. The path is from inspiration to (ambiguous) text. In the second act the five politicians take up the task where Bolton had left it and become César's unwitting prompters in the composition of his script. Elena, by failing to disclose the masquerade when she had the opportunity to do so on both occasions, is guilty of complicity in the creative act. Julia, who thrives on heroes, gleefully embraces her father's new identity and will have no truck with her doubting brother. Navarro also contributes to César's fictionalization and, setting up another fiction to accomplish the feat, assures the character's immortalization. Everyone helps César Rubio to compose the text that he becomes.

In Act III there are two César Rubios present on stage: the man in his double identity and the image on the election poster. The device accentuates the duality, particularly when César asks if the portrait resembles him. Guzmán's emphatic assent and his report of an old man's statement, "César no cambia" (III, 776), nurture the dramatic irony while confirming the imposition of the face depicted on the poster, that of the general, the fiction. The two entities have acquired the same face. In the end, as the creator has become his creation and the self has turned into the other, the other's past reinvented to be present transforms the self's illusions into reality. The simulacrum is on paper, not in the body of the living César Rubio. When César says, "el muerto no es César Rubio, sino yo, el que era yo . . ." (III, 787), we realize that both Rubios will have died twice: the professor when he became the general and when the politician is assassinated, the general first in his condition as historical fiction and then in his fictive reincarnation. By the time of the assassination, the two fictions—the one that usurped its creator's role and the one whose historicity was usurped—have fused in the process of mythification.

The continuing presence of César Rubio on stage, even after his death, in the form of his likeness on the placard symbolizes his mythification. The mythic dimension of

El gesticulador is of special importance in linking the play's metatheatrical structure with its thematic implications. It is the vehicle that extracts from César Rubio's interior recreation a commentary on the superiority of fiction, the ambiguity of language and art, and the relativity of truth.

Myth, to start with, is an amalgam of truth and lie: history recast as fiction or fiction become historical. *El gesticulador* is myth because history so revived as to be present and ever-present is myth. But if lie is a fundamental ingredient of myth, in Usigli's play myth is lie in a more problematic and disquieting fashion. If we follow the general's trajectory, we see that he has passed from history (or historical fiction) to myth before the action of the play opens. He is then, in the course of *El gesticulador*'s dramatic present, historically reborn only to be mythified once again and permanently. However, we descry a difference between the original and the ultimate mythic states: the one that precedes the action of the drama and is recast by it rings true, while the one that is newly contrived and legated to infinity stands on the hollow foundation of dishonesty. After all, it is the work of a trickster clever enough to appreciate the disparity between the mythic potential of a hag-ridden professor with a flypaper memory and a heroic revolutionary who suffered a mysterious fate. The myth appears further debased through the participation of Bolton, who in his innocence is more mythmaker than historian, and Navarro, whose mythmaking is clearly a function of his political demagoguery.

We are making a mistake, however, if we isolate the general from the professor, as the play does not, for the process of mythification is cumulative and *El gesticulador* is in any event the professor's, not the general's, drama. We commit a further error if we stop at the imprecations that *El gesticulador* hurls at the morality of its historical circumstance. The collectivization of a lie is demagoguery in a political context; in another it is mythification. The very failure of the revolution that César Rubio's fate dramatizes leaves him larger than life through the growth that he has experienced. If the existing myth of the general serves as the enabling agent for the professor's fictitious dispossessal of the general, then the weak professor's psychic accomplishment is as much to be wondered at as the deeds of a soldier in battle. The professor's maneuver of becoming another, which is the action of this play, automatically grants him the other's mythic stature, but that stature has been earned in the becoming. The sullying contribution of Navarro's mythmaking cannot be erased from the text; yet it does not diminish César Rubio's rights to mythic rank: it diminishes only itself.[10]

The elevation of César Rubio the man into a myth whose stature, on the one hand, he deserves but of whose falseness, on the other hand, the spectator is quite aware represents a tension that inheres to fiction insofar as fiction also demands faith in a falsehood. Rather than resolving that tension, the action of *El gesticulador* traces its elaboration through the blatant exposure of the inner play's

César Rubio as a fiction. Mythopoeia and the invention of fictions are thus equalized in the irresolvable tensions of their constituent qualities.

D. L. Shaw says: "while the man dies his imposture lives on." Precisely so: Cervantes, Unamuno, Pirandello, and history itself have demonstrated that the creation outlives its creator, that the fiction is not burdened with the finiteness of man. César confirms that idea from his perspective when, with an ironic smile, he assures Bolton that the general is more alive than the two of them. If one wonders how César Rubio can compose a script for himself that includes his own death, the answer is that as a man playing the role of another, he knows—and he proves so in his clash with Navarro—that his death is part of his performance. His death in the third act is the natural follow-up to the second-act suppression of the professor as he evolved into another. That process of subsumption, it would appear, engenders more lasting forms: fiction, myth, immortality. The murder and the permanent sequestration of the truth are, ironically, the guarantors of these happy states. Realizing—as Bolton does not—that the truth that is stranger than fiction *is* fiction, we find ourselves seduced by the notion that fiction is superior to truth.

Such a view of the privileged status of fiction is viable only if we relinquish our insistence on absolutes, as Miguel refuses to, and behold ambiguity as the inherent characteristic of language that allows such a posture. A play's self-examination as theatre must ultimately turn upon its agent of linguistic communication, the word. *El gesticulador*'s plot and structure are dependent on the same sign's reference to two initially distinct entities: "César Rubio."[11] That alone is an admission into Usigli's word game. A further embroilment at this level centers on the mythic connotations of "César": a literal or an ironic reading of the sign bestows contradictory personalities on its bearer and classifies the word as variably revealing or deceptive. Similarly, in the play's opening conversation among the family members, many of Julia's comments are made in a sarcastic tone. With bitter playfulness she inverts the surface meaning of her words and their intended thrust, thereby exposing the untruthfulness of the linguistic sign. By contrast, when Miguel says: "Ahora ya hemos empezado a hablar" (I, 730), the suggestion is that only through language can the truth be enunciated; the absence of discourse is the absence of truth.[12] César agrees that it is best to let language manifest itself: "No quiero que volvamos a estar [. . .] rodeados de pausas." Finally, the arbitrator in this situation, Elena, issues a double plea. First, she says that César owes his children no explanations: that is, silence is preferable to speech. Secondly, she admonishes him not to take the children's words at face value ("Ni debes tomar así lo que ellos digan" [I, 730]), which means that their words must be apprehended in context, interpreted. One concludes that language is untrustworthy and mystifying. That sentence, itself fraught with a multiplicity of meanings, which César addresses to his son, reverberates everywhere: "No conoces el precio de las palabras" (I, 731). Articulated or not, words can hide the truth, just as the furniture and dishes borrowed for the party on Elena's saint's day concealed the truth of the family's poverty. But, ever deceptive, the signs are reversed when the situation changes, and the contradiction between appearance and reality is perpetuated. In its period of poverty, the family professed economic comfort; now, when the family's fortunes are on the rise, "se advierte cierta ostentación de pobreza, una insistencia de César Rubio en presumir de modestia" (III, 773). At that same juncture in the play, language is shown to have a subversive potential even if it is not actively manipulated (at least, the manipulator here is not Rubio but Usigli): Estrella includes in his reading of the President's telegram the word "punto" after each sentence. The ideograph converted into word acts as a subverting agent that renders a serious document ludicrous.[13]

At the same time as language is truth's only hope, the ambiguity of language confers upon truth its relativity. Language is with equal ease the mediator of hypocrisy or truth, fiction or history. Exactly at the point where César Rubio's fictionality is consummated, the words that he pronounces in apparent affirmation of his identity ring out as a declaration of the subterfuge of language: "He dicho ya que soy César Rubio" (II, 760). Truth and lie are one here. The speaker is, indeed, César Rubio. But does the linguistic label, a convention, establish identity? Or does identity—truth—lie in the nature of the object independently of its signifier? If so, can we ever fathom the nature of anything through language? Is language then not a misleading instrument whose essence invites error and misuse? If the code is imperfect, the talented and the unscrupulous decoder operate in the same terrain. César Rubio evidently is a master of the word: "Sabe escuchar, callar, decir lo estrictamente preciso [. . .] Al señor Presidente lo conquistó a las cuatro palabras" (III, 773). He constructs his fictional self entirely through understatement, ellipsis, and insinuation. The ambiguity—multiplicity and duplicity—of language accomplishes the rest for him as his listeners cooperate. Meaning is attributed *to* the word; it does not emanate *from* it. The word thus fixes on an object the identity that others perceive in it (that is, fictionalize). Estrella's use of the title "mi general," first hesitatingly, then with assurance, suffices to make a general of César Rubio. The object comes into being upon conferral of a sign.[14]

Within *El gesticulador*, only Elena, in fear of the consequences, and Miguel, out of idealistic conviction, resist the apparent inversion of truth and lie. In addition to her timid effort to deflect her husband from his course, Elena tries to convince Julia to forget a young man in Mexico City, pointing out that he does not love her. Julia's hurt reaction triggers an oracular response that Elena utters as a reproach but that accurately describes the motives of Julia and the others about her: "La verdad es la que te hace daño, hija" (II, 750). Here the word is truth, and the truth impedes the soothing elaboration of a fiction. Her friend is forgotten later on as Julia, always in need of a *Lebenslüge*, becomes enraptured by the myth of César Rubio in which she is participating. At that point she protests to Elena like a latter-day Segismundo: "No hay mentira, mamá. Todo el pasado fue un sueño, y esto es

real" (III, 793). Miguel, unlike his sister, rejects the relativity of a positive present if it does not quench his thirst for totally unadulterated historical veracity. "Nada es más grande que la verdad," he shouts (III, 790), and the play ends with his plea, "¡La verdad!" He cannot accept his fate of having been born into a world of façades as bogus as the sets in a theatre and clamors to strip away the deceit that hides the truth. He is too naive to have captured the facts of life—and language and play; too fixed in his convictions to acknowledge the destructive powers of truth, to say nothing of its inaccessibility; and too one-dimensional in his fictional constitution to recognize that whatever César Rubio accomplishes internally and whatever Usigli accomplishes with *El gesticulador* has been accomplished by fiction. Usigli's own plays are eloquent statements of his belief in the expression of truth; but as a practicing dramatist, he chooses illusion as his vehicle. In his epilogue to *El gesticulador* and in his pronouncements elsewhere, he unwaveringly condemns the lie that the Mexican lives in every phase of his personal and national existence. Yet, in the play, the positions that emerge are not so clear-cut. César's lie has a positive moral dimension, while Miguel's passion for truth is touched by quixotism and inflexibility. The inventor of fictions garners the prize of immortality in myth; the seeker of truth is condemned to personal anxiety over the unbreachable mystery of the absolute. Certainly, *El gesticulador* paints all the evils of hypocrisy and cheating, but it also invests lying (fiction) with moral exemplariness. If on an ethical plane that lesson seems astonishing, cynically pragmatic, even Machiavellian, to the adherents of fiction and of the sustaining power of illusion, that formula comes as no surprise. As every critic knows, fiction is a religion that demands faith, yet does not crumble under rational scrutiny.

With language beyond the grasp of absolutes and meaning such an uncertain commodity, it becomes apparent why Usigli should opt for a play in the first place, and in particular one in which the fictive process is dramatized, in order to declare that the search for truth is best served by the recognition of its relativity. In a country where the university is mute, saddled with strikes and repression— "nadie enseñaba ni nadie aprendía ya" (I, 731)—the theatre must take over as the propagator of truth, as Usigli does with his play and César Rubio with his. "Un pueblo sin teatro es un pueblo sin verdad" is the motto for the epilogue, which is a way of saying that the absence of fiction equals the absence of truth. That the theatre is fiction, dependent on the brittle medium of language and on interpretation, does not hamper it in its function because fiction and truth occupy the same space. Julia accurately locates that space when she angrily says to her brother: "La verdad está dentro, no fuera de uno" (III, 791). César, himself, proclaims the pluralistic character of truth, at least implicitly, when in answering Elena's overtures that he abandon his illusions, he shifts his phrasing: "¡Mis sueños! Siempre he querido *la* realidad: es lo que tú no puedes entender. *Una* realidad . . ." (II, 753; my italics).[15] Miguel's final cry for *the* truth is accompanied by an action that suffuses his hope with the deepest irony: "el rollo de carteles [. . .] se abre como un abanico en una múltiple imagen de César Rubio" (III, 798). Those unfurling multiple images are the multiple images that the play has constructed: the multiple images of César Rubio, of language, of art, of truth. In many vanguard works, self-reflexivity is a voluntary divestiture of their illusionist status. *El gesticulador*'s self-referentiality as dramatic creation is, rather, a confrontation with reality and a proclamation in support of truthful expression. Miguel, however, is not its spokesman, for Usigli's play recognizes itself as an imposture that condemns posturing. Usigli alerts his spectator to the horrifying duplicity that marks politics and human relationships; but he has understood that in the inscrutable and privileged realms of language and of art this same duplicity harbors all the secrets of their delight.

NOTES

[1] Carlos Solórzano, *Teatro latinoamericano en el siglo XX* (Mexico: Pormaca, 1964), p. 132. I do not intend to enmesh myself here in the discussions of reality and realism, fanned by Usigli's own essays and taken up eagerly by his readers; for example, Vera F. de Beck, "La fuerza motriz, en la obra dramática de Rodolfo Usigli," *Revista Iberoamericana*, 18 (1953), 369-83.

[2] Solomon Tilles, "Rodolfo Usigli's Concept of Dramatic Art," *Latin American Theatre Review*, 3/2 (1970), 33.

[3] Eunice J. Gates has drawn attention to these in "Usigli As Seen in His Prefaces and Epilogues," *Hispania*, 37 (1954), 432-39; Tilles examines them further, as does R. Vance Savage, "Rodolfo Usigli's Idea of a Mexican Theatre," *Latin American Theatre Review*, 4/2 (1971), 13-20. An openly preceptive essay on how to fashion a play is Usigli's *Itinerario del autor dramático* (Mexico: La Casa de España, 1940).

[4] "Dramatic Technique in Usigli's *El gesticulador*," *Theatre Research International*, 1 (1976), 125-33.

[5] Lionel Abel, *Metatheatre* (New York: Hill and Wang, 1963), p. 60.

[6] *Anatomía del teatro* (Mexico: Ecuador 0°0'0", 1967), pp. 15, 26.

[7] "Epílogo sobre la hipocresía del mexicano," in *El gesticulador* (Mexico: Letras de México, 1944), p. 190.

[8] All textual references to *El gesticulador*, by act and page number, are to Rodolfo Usigli, *Teatro completo*, I (Mexico: Fondo de Cultura Económica, 1963), 727-802.

[9] Of the two historians in the play, Rubio is clearly the more sage. Bolton, who proclaims that "La historia no es una novela," falls into the trap of propelling a myth as history. César, for his part, says: "Sin embargo, la historia no es más que un sueño. Los que la hicieron soñaron con cosas que no se realizaron; los que la estudian sueñan con cosas pasadas; los que la enseñan *(con una sonrisa)* sueñan que poseen la verdad y que la entregan" (I, 746).

[10] Through a series of telltale strokes the spectators are readied for the mythic fettle of the character they see on stage from the outset. Not the least of these is the name that associates him with the Roman emperor, both the historical figure and the Shakespearean character, the story of

whose triumphs and betrayal has persisted as myth. The play twice makes specific reference to Caesar in open parallelism (II, 756; III, 786). At the same time, the first description of César blurs time-bound history and timeless myth in his very person: "su figura recuerda vagamente la de Emiliano Zapata y, en general, la de los hombres y las modas de 1910, aunque vista impersonalmente y sin moda" (I, 728). In short, Elena is confused when she defines César's flaw as his refusal to be himself, for César was created to be a role player. His name as a sign of Roman and Mexican history-become-myth, his identity as a character in a play, his socio-political circumstance, and the idea that the world is a stage all bear out his mythic and fictive ethos.

[11] Navarro, with Usigli guiding a careful choice of words, spells out the nature of the farce ("Te viene grande la figura de César Rubio, hombre. No sé cómo has tenido el descaro . . . el valor de meterte en esta farsa") and the role that the word plays in it ("Te llamas César y te apellidas Rubio, pero eso es todo lo que tienes del general. [. . .] Se acuerdan de tu cara, y cuando quieren nombrarte no tienen más remedio que decir César Rubio") (III, 781).

[12] Later, when the Bolton account is made public, Miguel is once more the first to implore that truth and fiction be sorted out, and he again sees the solution resting with the word: "¿Y por qué el silencio? No es más que una palabra . . ." (II, 757). But if César were to give his word, would Miguel then have solved the enigma? One need only take note of the political delegation's dependency on César's word.

[13] The element of political satire through language in *El gesticulador* should not escape the spectator. From the moment the politicians enter the scene in Act II, the dialogue takes on rhetorical overtones. With the coinage of the word "rubista" (III, 774), this dimension of the play reaches its apex. An individual who is a sham is the basis for a new word that consequently is informed of a meaning of whose emptiness all who use it are unaware. Their perception has led them to confer meaning on a sign; but in reality its referent and the meaning accorded it stand in contradiction to each other. Also, the following definition, in César's words, deserves some thought: "La política es una especie de filología de la vida que lo concatena todo" (III, 775).

[14] In the "Epílogo" Usigli attacks the practice that "los universitarios fracasados have of acquiring titles through political means: "el título es un escudo, una apariencia o máscara, una mentira individual en que el hombre se enconcha para esconder su incapacidad para hacer frente de otro modo a la vida. Y esta mentira se colectiviza con rapidez y despersonaliza a su propietario convirtiéndolo para siempre, de modo abstracto, en *el* doctor, *el* licenciado, etc." (p. 191). The first sentence applies in part to Professor César Rubio; the second then fits César Rubio become "*el* general." But the critical attitude with which Usigli makes this statement cannot be brashly connected to César because the moral context of his fictional existence is equivocal. Outside the play, the social reality to which the remark pertains makes it wholly condemnatory; but in the framework of his fictionality, César's behavior is as moral as it is immoral. "Es inútil añadir que *El gesticulador* no es precisamente César Rubio, sino que tiene una semejanza impresionante con México" (p. 204).

[15] I recognize that those who believe in the possibility of apprehending an absolute truth or a single legitimate textual meaning will reject such a relativist view, which they regard as crassly subjective. E. D. Hirsch, for example, in *The Aims of Interpretation* (Chicago: Univ. of Chicago Press, 1976), calls this relativistic fallacy "cognitive atheism" (p. 36). This objection, of course, constitutes a denial of all perspectivist theories. On the other hand, Abel, in his summary of *Metatheatre* (p. 113), gives his classification those traits that Usigli has attempted to articulate in *El gesticulador*: "Tragedy gives by far the stronger sense of the reality of

the world. Metatheatre gives by far the stronger sense that the world is a projection of human consciousness. / Tragedy glorifies the structure of the world, which it supposedly reflects in its own form. Metatheatre glorifies the unwillingness of the imagination to regard any image of the world as ultimate. [. . .] Metatheatre assumes there is no world except that created by human striving, human imagination."

Dennis Perri (essay date 1981)

SOURCE: "The Artistic Unity of *Corona de sombra*," in *Latin American Theatre Review*, Vol. 15, No. 1, pp. 13-19.

[*Perri outlines ways in which Usigli's use of journeys leads to a level of ultimate clarity in interpreting the characters in* Corona de Sombra.]

Corona de sombra has been the object of diverse critical interest since its controversial premiere in 1947. Attention has often centered on Usigli's adaptation and interpretation of Mexican history or the psychological characterization of the insane Carlota.[1] For other critics, *Corona de sombra* has served to illustrate the application of Usigli's theories of dramatic art.[2] Still others have elected to examine the play in relation to the *Corona* trilogy and its vision of Mexican reality.[3] In the main, discussion of the drama's formal elements has been limited to cursory praise for the innovative use of the split stage and lighting and to brief commentary of the symbolic value of the crown, light, and shadows. Peter Beardsell, however, has devoted his energies to a closer analysis of the play in which he relates Usigli's artistic manipulation of Carlota's insanity to its thematic function.[4] This essay intends to explore further the artistic dynamics of the play and in particular to demonstrate how structure, irony, imagery, and staging interact to communicate the drama's reinterpretation of the *Segundo imperio*.

The structure of *Corona de sombra* reflects the play's progressive movement toward the clarity of understanding. To give dramatic form to this process, Usigli relies on the pattern of the journey; on both a literal and figurative level the journey functions prominently in the ordering of the dramatic action. For example, the dramatic action is set in motion by Erasmo's trip to Belgium to discover the truth: "Busco la verdad, para decirla al mundo entero. Busco la verdad sobre Carlota."[5] Once initiated, the action unfolds in a series of flashbacks to the ill-fated reign of Maximilian and Carlota. Two historical journeys stand out in these scenes and signal the beginning and the end of the Empire: the voyage from Austria to Mexico and the trip from Mexico to Paris and Rome. Figuratively the flashbacks can be said to constitute a journey through the memory of the mad Carlota only to end in the restoration of her sanity. Before his death Maximilian compares his life to a sea voyage: "He viajado por todos los mares . . . sé que el mar se parece demasiado a la vida, y que su única misión es conducir al hombre a la tierra, tal como la misión de la vida es llevar al hombre a la muerte" (p. 102). The play, of course, serves to chronicle significant moments in this voyage. Simply

stated, whether conceived in temporal, spatial, or metaphorical terms, the journey governs the general organization of the drama and is well-suited to its central action: the gradual advance toward awareness.

The journeys of the characters reveal as well an interdependence which links the historical and psychological dimensions of the drama. Dissatisfied with traditional interpretations of the *Segundo imperio*, the historian Erasmo must travel with Carlota through her memory: "Quizás en lo que diga habrá algo, algo que me ayude en mi trabajo" (p. 35). Due to the historian's stimulus, Carlota, in turn, initiates a process through which she ultimately recovers her sanity: "Siento como si de pronto pudiera yo comprender todas las cosas" (p. 95). Ironically, Carlota's original trips to Mexico and then to Europe led to her loss of reason, but now when retold to Erasmo these trips result in the restoration of her reason. Carlota's return to the past occasions the reenactment of Maximilian's tragic journey whose end ultimately proves to complete that of Carlota and Erasmo. Awaiting his execution Maximilian sees clearly his role in the history of the Mexican nation: "Muero con la conciencia tranquila, porque no fue la simple ambición de poder la que me trajo aquí, ni pesa sobre mí la sombra de un solo crimen deliberado. En mis peores momentos respeté e hice respetar la integridad de México" (pp. 105-6). The historian has discovered the object of his journey: "Ahora lo veo claramente . . . México consumó su independencia en 1867 gracias a él" (p. 107). Maximilian protected Mexico from the real threat to its sovereignty, namely, Napoleon. Carlota has likewise completed her journey: "Siento en mí una paz profunda, la luz que me faltaba" (p. 107).

The journey not only gives form to the drama's action, but it is also visible in scenic construction. Numerous scenes occur during situations of arrivals and departures: Act I, scene ii, eve of the departure for Mexico; scene iii, arrival in Mexico; Act II, scene ii, eve of Carlota's departure for Europe; scene iii, arrival in Paris; scene iv, arrival in Rome. Departures and arrivals normally suggest moments of anticipation and apprehension. The atmosphere of heightened tension generates a sense of imminent action. Situations of departure and arrival, moreover, provide a logical setting for the characters to explain past motivations, to anticipate future actions, and to initiate action toward their goals. This interrelationship between past and present, cause and effect, is what Erasmo and Carlota must comprehend in order to arrive at their respective destinations.

Finally, the speeches of the characters reinforce the motif of a journey through the repeated references to sea, ship, and trips. For instance, Maximilian can be heard to remark: "He pensado que podríamos emprender viajes, ahora que hay nuevas rutas, nuevos medios de transporte" (p. 27); "Tú tienes que preparar tu viaje" (p. 65); "He viajado por todos los mares" (p. 102); "el mar se parece demasiado a la vida" (p. 102); "Cuando pienso en la cabalgata loca que han sido estos tres años del imperio . . ." (p. 103). The mention of boats and trips pervades the speeches of Carlota: "Ese viaje tan largo . . ." (p. 20); "Debo quitarme este horrible traje de viaje" (p. 20); "por eso he callado durante todo el viaje" (p. 23); "Lo descubrí al hacer el viaje de regreso" (p. 23); "Ese barco tan largo" (p. 24); "un camino tan largo" (p. 24); "Largo. Un viaje largo" (p. 66); "Ese viaje interminable puso a prueba mis nervios" (p. 69); "Pero no podía yo llegar al otro extremo del barco" (p. 76); "¿Cómo podría llegar al otro extremo del barco?" (p. 77); "Este barco tan largo" (p. 81).

In sum, structure, dramatic situation, and language all converge around the concept of the journey, a journey whose end is not a spatial point, but a state of understanding.

Irony complements the formal function of the journey by reminding the audience of the overall pattern even within individual scenes. Or in William Empson's words: "irony . . . offers an intelligible way of reminding the audience of the rest of the play when reading or seeing a single part of it."[6] One example of irony in *Corona de sombra* will illustrate its dramatic function and reinforcement of the pattern of journey. In Act II Carlota icily recommends that Juárez be murdered: "Lo destruiremos, te lo juro. . . . Mandaremos a alguien que acabe con él . . . ¿Qué es un asesinato político para salvar un imperio?" (p. 54). Her solution is ironic since it is Juárez who will have Maximilian executed and also since her obsessive thirst for power will drive her insane. As a result the irony increases the dramatic tension of her speech and reminds the audience that Carlota's journey leads toward punishment and grief. Yet the desire for Juárez's blood is ironic in another sense for it is expressed after the audience has heard Carlota remark to Erasmo (believing him to be Juárez): "Y me pareció desde entonces que os odiaba. Pero os veo aquí, frente a mí, y sé que no es verdad. Yo no os odio . . . Pero vos me inspiráis confianza" (p. 25). Thus, there is the suggestion that her journey will also bring about insight. The irony of this moment (the call for assassination) encourages the audience to evaluate Carlota's actions and attitudes as parts of a continuum or journey which on one level points to suffering and on another to a possibly clearer understanding of reality.

Imagery effectively punctuates relevant stages in the characters' unfolding journeys. To be specific, the changing images of the forest, sun, and crown underscore the movement of the characters toward their destination. The first mention of the Chapultepec forest describes it as a mysterious, fascinating haven for two lovers. "El bosque me tiene fascinado. Chapultepec, lugar de chapulines. . . . Escapemos del imperio . . . Como dos prometidos o como dos amantes. Vayamos a caminar por el bosque azteca cogidos de la mano" (p. 40). At the outset of their reign, this retreat from the duties of imperial rule symbolizes their illusory dreams for Mexico. Even the couple's conflicting attitudes toward Juárez cannot interfere:

CARLOTA—¿Para qué? Has roto el encanto. Yo pienso en ti y tú piensas en Juárez.

MAXIMILIANO—No podemos separarnos así, amor

mío. Vamos, te lo ruego. *(Le besa la mano; luego la rodea por la cintura con un brazo Ella apoya su cabeza en el hombro de él . . . Salen.)*

(p. 41)

During Act Two the cloud of politics and violence casts a shadow over the forest and impedes access to it:

MAXIMILIANO—Pero me siento inerte, perdido en un bosque de voces que me dan vértigo.

(p. 62)

MAXIMILIANO—Una cita en el bosque mientras el imperio arde.

CARLOTA—Eso es, Max: Una cita en el bosque, dentro de muy poco tiempo. Ahora hay que luchar, eso es todo—y hay que desconfiar—hay que matar.

(pp. 54-55)

Later, the forest appears as a sign of Carlota's delusions as she unrealistically anticipates a fruitful embassy to Paris and Rome: "volvemos a estar tan cerca como al principio, mi amor. . . . Nos veremos en el bosque, Max, pero a mi regreso. Sólo entonces podremos volver a ser nosotros mismos" (pp. 64-65). These are Carlota's last words to Maximilian and with an ironic twist they are prophetic. It is not a triumphant return from Europe, but an anguished return from 61 years of insanity which occasions the couple's reunion in the forest. Furthermore, they will not meet in the dream-like forest of Chapultepec, but in the final haven, death. Nevertheless, a peaceful resignation marks Carlota's entry into this forest:

(Carlota mira al frente. Sonríe. Se reclina en el respaldo del sillón con un gran suspiro de alivio.)

CARLOTA—En el bosque, Max. Ya estamos en el bosque.

(p. 108)

Maximilian has already foreseen this last reunion: "Hasta muy pronto Carla. Hasta muy pronto en el bosque" (p. 105). The forest has come to signify the definitive destination of life's journey, but it is a death which holds meaning and consolation for both Maximilian and Carlota.

Once Carlota faces the truth that her dreams have been destroyed and have caused destruction, she will reach the final stages of her journey. It is the evolving image of the sun which lends a lyric intensity to the progress of her journey. The sun can shed light and it can dazzle and blind. Both these traits and others are applied to Carlota's journey. Initially it is the sun which conveys the illusions of her youth: "deseé que el príncipe que me desposara se pareciera al sol como tú" (p. 31). For a brief moment, her personal fantasies and reality seem to converge in harmony as she contemplates her future in the land of the sun: "creen en el sol de la sangre y del rango . . . Es el país del sol y tú te pareces al sol. . . . ¿Tú crees que pueden odiar el sol en parte alguna?" (pp. 31, 32).

The image of the sun only compounds the irony since it is not the light of truth that Carlota observes, but the bedazzling brilliance of personal fortune. Foolishly she believes that the splendor of a European monarchy can outshine the Aztec sun of Mexico's origins.

Subsequent references to the sun produce ever increasing negative overtones. Once in Mexico, Carlota employs the image of the sun to accentuate the jealousy she feels, "Todas te miraban y te deseaban como el sol" (p. 39). This image foreshadows the obstacles Carlota will face in her selfish efforts to enjoy the sun of absolute power. In the stormy encounter with Napoleon, the frivolous Empress Eugenia declares: "La Emperatriz de México será el sol de nuestro baile" (p. 68). In the future Carlota had planned for herself, this image would have represented the attainment of her loftiest aspirations: power, respect, beauty. Instead the image strikes a bitterly ironic chord. On the verge of mental collapse and wildly clawing to save a crumbling empire, she must listen to platitudes from a woman she despises.

Pius XI emphasizes the temporal dimension of the solar image to affirm the finite nature of man, "El hombre es una sombra por la que pasan brevemente la sangre y el sol de la vida" (pp. 76-77). The sun signals the passing of time and fittingly appears at the point in which the sun of Carlota's obsessive ambition sets, to be replaced by 61 years of shadows. As will be discussed below, the sun of clarity will finally shine on Carlota in the form of theatrical lighting rather than linguistic imagery.

The recurrent image of the crown best reflects the effect on Carlota of the journey toward knowledge. The young Carlota considers the Mexican opportunity to be an adventure and a dream transformed into reality. Her state of euphoria prompts the usually idealistic Maximilian to warn her pragmatically: "Pero no será una corona de juego" (p. 31). Previous statements by the Empress prove that she quickly learns the seriousness of the game and totally dedicates herself to the political struggle. At this point, Pius XI underscores Carlota's misguided faith in a temporal crown: "Dios da su corona a los buenos y es una corona más bella que la corona imperial . . . las coronas son de humo" (pp. 76-77). Unable to deal with the ephemeral nature of power and the actual loss of her crown, Carlota loses her mind. Deprived of her worldly crown and undeserving of a heavenly one, she must wear one of suffering and punishment, "su corona es de espinas y de sombra" (p. 82). Carlota herself recognizes the punishment in Act Three and her use of the crown image underlines the torture of its weight: "¿Y no bastan acaso sesenta años de vivir en la noche, en la muerte, con esta corona de pesadilla en la frente, para merecer el perdón?" (p. 99). The image of the crown at last reflects Carlota's insight, and to some degree her salvation, once she realizes that her suffering has served a purpose: "Lo que quiero deciros es que Maximiliano volvería a morir por México, y que yo volvería a llevar esta corona de sombra sobre mi frente durante sesenta años para oír otra vez vuestras palabras. Para repetírselas al Emperador" (p. 108). In sum, the image of the crown has mirrored Carlota's development from being a blind, self-centered woman to an individual who has reached a deeper understanding of self and the events she helped shape.

Not only the linguistic images but the theatrical devices as well reinforce the pattern of the journey. The divided stage and the action which shifts from side to side visually represent the drama's movement through time and space. Thus, the abstract concept of a journey becomes actualized through the staging. At the outset of the play the glass wall between the two portions of the stage serves to separate, while at the play's end this "division de cristales," becomes a symbol of insight as it offers the final proof that Carlota has indeed been insane for 61 years: "Carlota se acerca lentamente y trata de mirarse en los cristales; vuelve la vista a todas partes, toma un candelabro, y se acerca nuevamente a la vidriera, donde mira atentamente su reflejo" (p. 95).

The verbal imagery concerning the sun has already been traced, but it is sunlight (stagelight) which frames the action of the entire play. Before the appearance of the characters the audience observes the set bathed in light: "Es de mañana y la luz del sol penetra tumultuosamente por el balcón y la terraza" (p. 11). The majority of the play takes place during night scenes or with the sunlight blocked by curtains. At the completion of the characters' journeys, the audience again sees full sunlight: "Entonces, sin una palabra, sopla una por una las bujías, se dirige al fondo y descorre las cortinas. La luz del sol penetra en una prodigiosa cascada, hasta iluminar la figura inmóvil de Carlota" (p. 109).

The everpresent candelabra in *Corona de sombra* acts as a symbol of sight and blindness which accentuates the paradoxical nature of the journey through the memories of the mad Carlota. Carlota's compulsion to substitute artificial for natural light graphically displays the depths of her madness, and nowhere is this madness more striking than in Act III, scene iii: "Se reconcentraba mirando al vacío. La luz de las doce bujías forma un círculo fantástico en torno a su rostro" (p. 95). The candelabra also announces the shift from one side to another of the divided stage. In these cases the candelabra figuratively illuminates the flashback scenes which in turn contribute to the characters' final awareness. Likewise it is the candlelight which assists Carlota to see that she has aged. It is the candelabra, then, that links the two dimensions of the journey through Carlota's memory. On the one hand the events as they occurred resulted in her loss of reason; on the other hand the recalling of them leads to sanity as Carlota and Erasmo form a more lucid perception of historical events and their significance.

In conclusion, *Corona de sombra* is a unified work which dramatizes the reassessment of the *Segundo imperio*.[8] Usigli creates a play in which structure, irony, imagery, and staging combine to involve the audience in this reinterpretation of history. As we have seen, the interaction of these formal elements encourages the audience to consider the divergent and sometimes paradoxical forces which determine events and their significance. The death of Rodolfo Usigli is cause for a serious reexamination of the richness of his theatre. *Corona de sombra* is certainly a notable example of Usigli's dramatic art.

NOTES

[1] For a more detailed discussion of such topics see: John B. Nomland, *Teatro mexicano contemporáneo: 1900-1950*, Tr. Paloma Gorostiza de Zozaya and Luis Reyes de la Maza (México: Instituto Nacional de Bellas Artes, Departamento de Literatura, 1965); Alyce de Kuehne, *Teatro mexicano contemporáneo; 1940-1962* (Mexico: Imprenta Benjamín Franklin, 1962); Francisco Monterde, "Juárez, Maximiliano y Carlota en las obras de los dramaturgos mexicanos," *Cuadernos Americanos*, CXXXVI (September-October, 1964), 231-240; Gordon Ragle, "Rodolfo Usigli and his Mexican Scene," *Hispania*, XLVI (1963), 307-311.

[2] Consult: Solomon H. Tilles, "Rodolfo Usigli's Concept of Dramatic Art," *Latin American Theatre Review*, 3/2 (Spring, 1970), 31-38; Vera F. Beck, "La fuerza motriz en la obra dramática de Rodolfo Usigli," *Revista Iberoamericana*, XVIII (September, 1953), 369-383; Eunice J. Gates, "Usigli as Seen in His Prefaces and Epilogues," *Hispania*, XXXVII (December, 1954), 432-439.

[3] See: Roberto R. Rodríguez, "La función de la imaginación en las *Coronas* de Rodolfo Usigli," *Latin American Theatre Review*, 10/2 (Spring, 1977), 37-44 and the introduction to Rodolfo Usigli, *Two Plays: Crown of Light, One of these Days*, trans. Thomas Bledsoe, ed. J. Cary Davis, introduction Willis Knapp Jones (Carbondale: Southern Illinois University Press, 1966), xix-xxi.

[4] Peter R. Beardsell, "Insanity and Poetic Justice in Usigli's *Corona de sombra*," *Latin American Theatre Review*, 10/1 (Fall 1976), 5-14.

[5] Rodolfo Usigli, *Corona de sombra*, ed Rex Edward Ballinger (New York: Appleton-Century-Crofts, Inc., 1961), 22. All further quotation from the play will be taken from this edition. Future citations will include page references and will be incorporated into the text.

[6] Bert O. States, *Irony and Drama: A Poetics* (Ithaca: Cornell University Press, 1971), p. 28.

[7] Beardsell, "Insanity and Poetic Justice . . . ," has also noted this interpretation of the "corona de espinas," when he states that it might, "suggest not only mockery and suffering but also the notion of sacrifice. It is possible to see Carlota, therefore, as a sacrificial victim, who wears her crown on behalf of Mexico, as Christ wore his on behalf of man" (p. 10).

[8] I cannot agree with Alyce de Kuehne's judgment of the drama's unity, as she claims *Corona de sombra* to be "una pieza de indiscutibles méritos, cuya falta de unidad se achaca a una caprichosa estructura cinematográfica." *Teatro mexicano contemporáneo: 1940-1962*, p. 65.

FURTHER READING

Beardsell, Peter R. "Insanity and Poetic Justice in Usigli's *Corona de sombra*." *Latin American Theatre Review*, Vol. 10, No. 1 (1976): 5-14.

Compares the historical Carlota of Mexico with his character in *Corona de sombra*.

———. "Usigli's Political Drama in Perspective." *Bulletin of Hispanic Studies*, Vol. LXVI, No. 3 (July, 1989): 251-61.

Focuses on Usigli's lesser-known political plays.

Finch, Mark S. "Rodolfo Usigli's *Corona de sombra, Corona de fuego, Corona de luz*: The Mythopoesis of Antihistory." *Romance Notes*, Vol. XXII, No. 2 (Winter 1981): 151-54.

Explains Usigli's ideas about life-as-drama and the artist as its interpreter.

Gates, Unice J. "Usigli as Seen in His Prefaces and Epilogues." *Hispania*, Vol. XXXVII, No. 4 (December 1954): 432-39.

Notes how Usigli's personal experiences were incorporated into his work.

Labinger, Andrea G. "Age, Alienation and the Artist in Usigli's *Los viejos*." *Latin American Theatre Review*, Vol. 14, No. 2 (Spring 1981): 41-7.

Considers the implications of generational conflict and estrangement.

Natella, Arthur A., Jr. "Christological Symbolism in Rodolfo Usigli's *El gesticulador*." *Discurso Literario*, Vol. 5, No. 2 (Spring 1988): 455-61.

Compares the recorded life of Christ to that of his protagonist in *El gesticulador*.

Nigro, Kirsten. "Light and Darkness in Usigli's *Corona de sombra*." *Chasqui*, Vol. XVII, No. 2 (November 1988): 27-34.

Outlines Usigli's antihistorical treatment of the Carlota and Maximilian story in the Mexico of 1866.

Scott, Wilder P. "Rodolfo Usigli and Contemporary Dramatic Theory." *Romance Notes*, Vol. XI, No. 3 (Spring 1970): 526-30.

Looks at Usigli's philosophy of drama and his influence on Mexican theater.

———. "French Literature and the Theater of Rodolfo Usigli." *Romance Notes*, Vol. XVI, No. 1 (Autumn 1974): 228-31.

Discusses the influence of French literature on Usigli's work.

———. "The Genesis and Development of a Female Character in Two Plays of Rodolfo Usigli." *South Atlantic Bulletin*, Vol. XXXIX, No. 4 (November 1974): 31-7.

Supports the opinion that Usigli used the same character in more than one work.

Tilles, Solomon T. "Rodolfo Usigli's Concept of Dramatic Art." *Latin American Theatre Review*, Vo. 3, No. 2 (Spring 1970): 31-8.

Contends that Usigli's works differ from the realists' in their focus on myth formation rather than social observation.

Additional coverage of Usigli's life and career is contained in the following sources published by the Gale Group: *Contemporary Authors*, Vol. 131; *Hispanic Writers*.

Luisa Valenzuela
1938–

Argentine-born novelist and short story writer.

INTRODUCTION

Within the United States, Argentine-born Luisa Valenzuela is one of the best-known and most-respected contemporary writers from Latin America, having had most of her novels, novellas, and short stories translated into English. In Argentina, Valenzuela wrote for various magazines, the newspapers *La Nación* and *El Mundo*, and for radio programs. She took part in the International Writers Program at the University of Iowa in 1969, and in 1972 received a grant from Argentina's National Arts Foundation to research North American literature. She has taught at Columbia University and New York University and won fellowships from the Institute for the Humanities and from the Guggenheim Foundation, and was named Distinguished Writer in Residence at NYU. Valenzuela's prose has been called "critical and revolutionary," and she is often classified among some of the greatest writers of the twentieth-century, including Carlos Fuentes, Julio Cortázar, and Gabriel Garcia Márquez. Valenzuela is a relentless and incisive critic of bourgeois conventions, political repression, and literary practice, i.e., the importance and use of language. Valenzuela's focus is on the need for change which she achieves through the use of cycles, defying conventions of traditional writing and showcasing narratives that predate history.

Luisa Valenzuela was born in Buenos Aires on November 26, 1938, and attended a girls' school. She began writing early on under the guidance of her mother, the well-known writer Luisa Mercedes Levinson. This assistance and her exposure to translated writings gave her a solid foundation that marked the beginning of her career. Valenzuela attended the Colegio Nacional Vincente López in Buenos Aires, earning her B.A. At twenty, Valenzuela moved to Paris after she married a French sailor. On trips to the forested park, the Bois de Bologna, Valenzuela became familiar with its prostitutes, providing her with the subject of her first novel, *Hay que sonreír* (1966; *Clara: Thirteen Short Stories and a Novel*, 1976) written when she was twenty-one. Prostitutes also make an appearances throughout Valenzuela's works, such as *Como en la guerra* (1977; *He Who Searches*). Valenzuela left Paris in 1961 and eventually became editor of the Sunday supplement of *La Nación* from 1964-69. During this time, Valenzuela developed an interest in the ancient beliefs and rituals of South American Indians, like the Afro-Brazilian Macumba, the Guaraní of Paraguay and Argentina, and Chile's Mapuche Indians. The result of her studies and ensuing travels is the magical overtones of her urbanized portraits of life depicted in *Los heréticos* (1967). In 1969,

Valenzuela came to the U.S. on a Fulbright scholarship to participate in the International Writer's Workshop at the University of Iowa. Here, she began her novel *El gato eficaz* (1972; *Cat-O-Nine-Deaths*), which she finished back in Argentina. From 1970-73, she freelanced for various newspapers in the U. S., Mexico, Europe, and, later, in Buenos Aires.

When she returned to her native city in 1974, Juan Perón had just died and his wife, Eva, assumed control. Eva Perón's even more repressive regime became the subject of Valenzuela's collection of short stories *Aquí pasan cosas raras* (1976; *Strange Things Happen Here*, 1979). In 1976, the military took over the Argentine government, and *Como en la guerra* had its first page, depicting torture, officially expurgated (the portion was included in the English translation). During these years in Buenos Aires, Valenzuela helped hide political outlaws. Throughout most of the eighties, Valenzuela lived in New York City, teaching at various institutions, and occasionally taking extended trips to Buenos Aires and Tepoztlán, Mexico. In 1981, she began one of her most talked-about pieces, *Cola de lagartija* (1983; *The Lizard's Tail*), a novel about José Lopéz Rega, Juan Perón's astrologer who became Minister of Social Welfare but was in de facto control of the government from 1974-76, during the administration of Eva Perón. As in *The Lizard's Tail*, Rega was known as "the sorcerer," partially because he wrote a book on witchcraft. Valenzuela's most recent novel, published in 1990, is *Bedside Manners*.

Perhaps the hallmark of Valenzuela's writing is her effort to break the stranglehold of censorship: "I believe that things must be said. That what must be avoided are the barriers of self-censorship, or worse than self-censorship, the barriers of that internal censorship which prevents you from saying that which deep down you really want to say without realizing it." The result of this desire is a form of writing that plays with language, shifts narrators, and alters perceptions and views, all rendered with a sense of humor. Not only does she attempt to free herself from the constraints of censorship through means of razor-sharp critique, but her scope broadens to fight for free expression for other people, as well. She targets society's institutions, customs, and taboos—culture, religion, politics, and mores—all of which allow poverty, hunger, and humiliation. Valenzuela's first novel, *Hay que sonreír*, recounts the efforts of a young prostitute to "use her head." Men attempt to save the girl in one way or another, although usually through exploiting and silencing her. At the end the girl ends up in a circus act as "The Aztec Flower" in which her body is hidden and only her objectified head shows. Her head is eventually cut off, presenting an indictment on a society and its ineffectual treatment of the struggle of its people to survive. Valenzuela's second novel, *El gato eficaz*, breaks from the traditional novel by shifting viewpoints and narrators. It serves to illuminate binaries like life/death, black/white, masculine/feminine by clouding the distinction between boundaries and seeking pluralistic notions of identity in order to transcend a fixed ideal. Valenzuela's short story collection, *Aquí pasan cosas raras*, is seasoned with a barbed humor aimed at the increasingly oppressive political situation in Argentina during Eva Perón's administration. This work focuses on the violence, fear, and brutality displayed by the government during so much of this period. Valenzuela's most acclaimed work is *Cola de lagartija*, a fictionalized account of the life and doings of "the sorcerer," the powerful López Rega. Endowed with three testicles, the thinly-disguised character names his third testicle "sister Estrella," indicating its feminine identity. Rega's plan for assuming power is achieved by reproducing himself through uniting the semen from his two male testicles with the hormonally-produced sister Estrella. Perched on a white pyramid, the sorcerer begins to conceive a son without the aid of a woman, his bid for self-sufficiency and omnipotence. Valenzuela said in a 1986 interview that "the separation between what we usually call reality and fiction is more tenuous than we can imagine. And there are people or historic moments that serve as pivots, bridges, or shifters. José López Rega, and the whole period of Perónism in which he was a major figure, is situated in that difficult limit that almost mediates with hell, above all with the infernos of Argentine superstition that we refuse to recognize." At the end of *The Lizard's Tail*, the sorcerer explodes—so swollen is he with his own offspring—and his blood runs down the pyramid to signal an era of peace through human sacrifice, which one observer, a character named Luisa Valenzuela, believes will be followed by another tyranny. Valenzuela's most recent novel, *Bedside Manners*, revolves around a bedridden woman who is completely ignorant of the political and military repression that surrounds her. The protagonist returns from New York to her native land "in search of refuge" from the spiritually destructive world and takes up residence in a country club to recuperate. There, she finds her bed becomes "a boat adrift on troubled waters." Though the country club is supposed to shelter her from the outside world, the violent and materialistic landscape of her country penetrates her room relentlessly. Defense mechanisms become literal as well as figurative, and the woman ends up taking part in the military offensive, Operation Identity, paralleling her own monumental struggle to recover her ability to think and to remember.

Through the use of fantasy, language, and irony, Luisa Valenzuela seeks freedom from any and all confines of predetermined literary and social structures. It's a struggle that finds free expression in her novels and short stories. Valenzuela's work is consistently praised for its unique characterization, viewpoint, and solutions to prevalent social issues. As one critic notes: "Luisa Valenzuela's narrative is a deep preoccupation with the use of power, the abuse of power, and the structures of domination which permeate the most basic aspects of our existence. . . One of the merits of Valenzuela's narrative is that she is able to create a fictional world which weaves together all these structures of domination to create a pattern that reflects the complex dynamics of an existence based on oppression."

PRINCIPAL WORKS

Hay que sonreir [*Clara: Thirteen Short Stories and a Novel*] (novel) 1966
Los hereticos (short stories) 1967
El gato eficaz (novel) 1972
Aquí pasan cosas raras [*Strange Things Happen Here: Twenty-Six Short Stories and a Novel*] 1976
Como en la guerra [*He Who Searches*] (novel) 1977
Libro que no muerde (short stories) 1980'
Cambio de armas [*Other Weapons*] (short stories) 1982
Cola de largartija [*The Lizard's Tail*] (novel) 1983
Donde viven las aguilas [*Up among the Eagles*] (short stories) 1983
Open Door (short stories) 1989
Novela negra con argentinos [*Black Novel (With Argentines)*] (novel) 1990
Realidad nacional desde la cama [*Bedside Manners*] (novel) 1990
The Censors: A Bilingual Selection of Stories (short stories) 1992
Simetrias [*Simetries*] (short stories) 1993
Hay que sonreir [film adaptation]

CRITICISM

Mary K. Addis (essay date 1990)

SOURCE: "Fictions of Motherhood: Three Short Stories by Luisa Valenzuela." *Romance Languages Annual*, Vol. I (1990): 353-60.

[*Addis uses Valenzuela's stories as an example of a true feminine voice in writing.*]

Both Luisa Valenzuela's narrative practice and her theorizing in several recent essays share with the linguistically radical French feminists a concern with the problems raised by women's relationship to language. Like Kristeva, Irigaray and Cixous, Valenzuela maintains that woman's experience, specifically woman's "desire," is what has been systematically repressed in the signifying practices of Western culture and that consequently, to quote Elaine Marks, "there has been only one voice, a male voice which women writers of the past obligatorily imitated" (**"Women"** 836). A felt need to resist and challenge these signifying practices, therefore, led the French feminists to search for a uniquely "feminine" mode of discourse outside or beyond the dominant discursive order. For Irigaray and Cixous, this would be an *écriture féminine,* a narrative or language of female desire (*jouissance*) whose power would derive from the female body and the mother's voice and that would therefore be radically disruptive and capable of seeing through and taking apart the structures and conventions of the phallocentric Symbolic order.[1]

Valenzuela also affirms the existence of a feminine writing, what she calls "un lenguaje hémbrico" (**"Brujas"** 91), and she too claims that it exists on the side of what has been repressed, "por el lado de las brujas," she writes in one essay (**"Brujas"** 88). As for the French feminists, this is a language that comes from the female body, for "language is sex" and "the word . . . is body . . . And we will be conscious of our bodies when it comes to the body of our writing" (**"Word"**). Moreover, this is a language that is disruptive in the French feminist sense because, as Valenzuela writes in **"La mala palabra,"** "puede eventualmente decir lo que no debe ser dicho, revelar el oscuro deseo, desencadenar las diferencias amenazadoras que subvierten el cómodo esquema del discurso falocéntrico, el muy paternalista." For Valenzuela, writing from the body, revealing the desire that has been repressed, both disrupts patriarchal constructs and frees women's expression. She sees it, therefore, as a transgressive and liberating act.[2]

The earliest examples of a transgression of patriarchal constructs through the narration of female desire in Valenzuela's fiction can be found in her first collection of short stories, **Los heréticos**, published in 1967. The narrative project of a number of the stories is the dismantling or subverting through irony of clearly masculinist codings of the world, especially codings or constructs of female identity and sexuality derived from religion, though other targets also emerge. I have chosen to discuss here three stories which focus on mother-son relationships at the moment of the Oedipal crisis and which in effect revise and rewrite the dominant psychoanalytic narrative of psycho-social development elaborated by Freud and Lacan by allowing the mother rather than the father to play the determining role. The scene of each of the stories is the resolution of the Oedipal complex, or, to use the Lacanian model, the scene of the young boy's passage from the realm of the Imaginary, the realm of the mother, into the realm of the Symbolic, the realm of the father and the father's law.

That it is the mother who motivates the child's passage from the Imaginary to the Symbolic is highly significant. Feminists in both the United States and France have repeatedly pointed out that psychoanalytic theory assigns a secondary role to the mother in the Oedipal drama (Wenzel). The primary role belongs to the father. It is his responsibility to break up the dyadic unity between mother and child in order that the child may make his way into the male world of the dominant order. From this perspective, according to Adrienne Rich, the mother-son relationship is understood to be "by nature regressive, circular, unproductive." "Culture," she writes, "depends on the father-son relationship." André Bleikasten reminds us of "the crucial function which psychoanalysis assigns to the father in the dialectic of desire and law that, under nor-

mal circumstances, leads to the achievement of selfhood." And Susan Suleiman complains that in psychoanalytic theory the mother functions as little more than an object of service. Her desire is supposed to be shaped solely by the child's interests and needs, and her own subjectivity is never examined.

In her review of the first published anthology of psychoanalytic feminist criticism, *The (M)other Tongue*, Jane Gallop singles out the Suleiman essay to which I have referred, "Writing and Motherhood," for being the only essay in the collection that effects a feminist reading of psychoanalytic theory. Gallop argues, in fact, that Suleiman's study "goes beyond the boundaries of the new field [psychoanalytic feminist criticism] into a critique of its very possibility." Unlike the authors of other essays in the collection, who all too easily fall prey to "the myth of the selfless mother," Suleiman notes with clarity one of the principle "blind spots" of psychoanalysis: its inability to see "the mother as an other subjectivity" (Gallop). What is missing in psychoanalytic accounts of development is, precisely, "the mother as other," the mother as a separate individual whose needs and desires do not always coincide with those of the child. The editors of *The (M)other Tongue* note this absence, if only in passing, in the introduction to the volume:

> Psychoanalysis, whether it posits in the beginning maternal presence or absence, has yet to develop a story of the mother as other than the object of the infant's desire or the matrix from which he or she develops an infant's subjectivity. The mother herself as speaking subject, as author, is missing from these dramas.

This gap in the narrative of psychoanalysis is what prompts Suleiman to call for feminists to pay more attention to "fictions of motherhood" written from the mother's rather than the child's or the psychoanalyst's perspective. Citing Julia Kristeva, Suleiman writes that as yet we know very little about the mother's "inner discourse." We have only the discourses constructed about her, discourses that have created and perpetuated the ideal of maternal altruism, the myth of the selfless mother.[3]

Clearly, it is against the ideal of the selfless mother that Valenzuela writes. In the three stories I have selected, the mother is represented as a subject in her own right, and what she wants and desires is central. Of particular interest is the fact that these are stories about the process of *her* move toward individuation and liberation, dramas necessarily played out against the dominant Symbolic order and its myths of motherhood and, in two of the stories, against the male child himself. Thus in **"Hijo de Kermaria"** and **"La profesora,"** it is the mother who, by affirming her separate identity and desire for sexual pleasure, forces the young male out of a narcissistic identification with her and into the world of the father, the world which for Lacan is synonymous with the order of culture and language. As we shall see, the moment of separation or rupture is experienced by the youth as a kind of momentary blindness or loss of sight, suggesting an inability to acknowledge difference.

The third story, **"Los menestreles,"** is quite different. Here it is the mother's linguistic creativity, closely linked to her procreativity and sexual desire, that is capable of creating an alternative Symbolic or language that will survive her own death and live on as the creative language of her son. In this case, the passage from the Imaginary to the Symbolic need never be negotiated since the two realms are one and the same. This evocation of the mother's linguistic power is not without its problems, however, since we shall see how the mother's success will depend, precisely, on *her* repression of difference. The story is marked by internal contradiction because, though sexual desire empowers the mother linguistically, the desire itself cannot be put into language.

It might be useful at this point to define briefly Lacan's terms and developmental scheme. Naomi Schor has defined them succinctly. The Imaginary, she writes, "is that psychic register which is synonymous with the exclusive, dual infant-mother relationship, what Freud called the pre-Oedipus." Schor is careful to emphasize the reason for Lacan's choice of the word "Imaginary." The choice reflects, according to Schor, "his emphasis on the image in the pre-Oedipus, on the manner in which the human subject's ego is constituted through a series of images: the image of the other as self (mother) or of the self as other (mirror image)." The Imaginary depends, therefore, on vision (Silverman; Moi). Toril Moi writes that the Imaginary "corresponds to the pre-Oedipal period when the child believes itself to be a part of the mother, and perceives no separation between itself and the world. In the Imaginary, there is no difference and no absence, only identity and presence. . . . The child, when looking at itself in the mirror—or at itself on the mother's arm, or simply at another child—only perceives another human being with whom it merges and identifies." Consequently, in the Imaginary or "mirror stage" there are only dual relationships (Moi). It is only at the moment of the Oedipal crisis—when the father intervenes to break up the dual mother-child relationship—that the child can see itself as separate and can enter the world of the dominant or Symbolic order. Lacan's Symbolic, then, according to Schor, "is presided over by the father and the cultural order he represents: the subject enters the Symbolic order at the very moment when [he] is inscribed in the kinship system and is, as it were, reinscribed when [he] acquires language and, through the mediation of the father, takes [his] place in society. Whereas the Imaginary implies identity as well as identification, the Symbolic relies on difference, sexual . . . as well as linguistic."

Since Valenzuela's stories challenge this narrative of development, especially its privileging of the paternal role, my analysis cannot simply subject the selected texts to the authority of psychoanalytic theory. Shoshana Felman has suggested a shift in emphasis. Felman notes that, traditionally, the relationship to literature to psychoanalysis has been one of subordination: literature, "a body of language," is subjected to the authority of psychoanalysis, "a body of knowledge." This is a relationship of slave to master in the Hegelian sense: "literature's function, like that of the slave, is to *serve* precisely the *desire* of

psychoanalytic theory—its desire for recognition; exercising its authority and *power* over the literary field, holding a discourse of masterly competence, psychoanalysis, in literature, thus seeks above all its own *satisfaction.*" If, however, as the French feminists affirm, female desire can disrupt patriarchal thought and authority, and there is little doubt at this point about the patriarchal bias of psychoanalysis, we must reconceptualize the relationship between the two fields in practicing any form of psychoanalytic feminist criticism. We must disrupt, in other words, psychoanalysis's position of mastery. Felman suggests we think of the relationship as one of mutual implication, a relationship between equals. Since there are no "*natural* boundaries between literature and psychoanalysis, which clearly define and distinguish them," since both are bodies of language *and* bodies of knowledge, it is important "to explore, bring to light and articulate the various (indirect) ways in which the two domains do indeed *implicate each other*, each one finding itself enlightened, informed, but also affected, displaced, by the other."

Valenzuela's stories and psychoanalysis "implicate each other" regarding their respective constructions of the figure of the mother. Psychoanalysis's theorizing about the good mother "who has no interests of her own" and whose sexuality is supposed to be "suppressed and diverted" by the "central emotional expression of motherliness" is challenged and displaced in Valenzuela's three short narratives, as we shall see, by the figure of a mother who seeks self-realization and who knows and follows her own desire. In the short story **"Hijo de Kermaria,"** for example, the mother's desire and the child's needs are in conflict. This story is set in a small, isolated village in Brittany, and the village chapel, which houses the statue of the Virgin of Kermaria with Child, is the center of community life, the source of its Symbolic order. The object of subversion in this story is the Christian discourse of ideal motherhood, the myth of the Virgin Mother. Suleiman has noted some of the affinities between the Christian construction of the ideal mother and the construction of the mother in psychoanalytic theory: both require, for example, the mother's selfless devotion to her son. "In both cases," Suleiman writes, "the mother is elevated precisely to the extent that she prostrates herself before her son." The difference between the psychoanalytic and the Christian construction, according to Suleiman, is that psychoanalysis takes the "moral obligation" of religion and turns it into a "psychological law."

The main characters of **"Hijo de Kermaria"** are an eleven-year old boy named Joseph, his young, widowed mother, and the mother's aging and blind father-in-law, Joseph's grandfather. The grandfather's stories about the different painted figures and statues of the chapel constitute the Symbolic order into which Joseph will soon be initiated. At the beginning of the narrative, we see, for example, how the grandfather's stories about the painted figures have already suggested to Joseph different games he can play with his friends. Specifically, the boys play a game of identification with the different painted figures that portray the dance of death on the walls of the church: "la ronda de gentiles y de muertos que estaba pintada desde hacía setecientos años en la capilla de Kermaria." That identification with death is preferred over identification with one of the Gentiles is made clear when Joseph breaks the rules of the game and identifies with death out of turn. One of the other boys protests: "¡Pajarón! Sabes muy bien que no puede haber dos muertes seguidas. Puedes ser el pobre, o el carnicero, o lo que se te antoje. Pero no, claro, justo se te ocurre ser la muerte cuando no te toca el turno." Joseph is indignant since he invented the game after his grandfather taught him the meaning of the painting.

The grandfather uses the feminine personal pronoun "ella" ("ella te hace bailar y bailar") to refer to the figure of death, and when, on the same page, he uses the feminine direct object pronoun "la" to refer to something being washed in the church, the reader is momentarily confused about the referent. Logically, it would refer again to the figure of death ("la muerte"), but it turns out to be a reference to the statue of the Virgin Mother, to whom the grandfather feels an erotic attachment, much to the dismay of the old women dressed in black who try to keep him out of the church. The grandfather blames the old women for his blindness and for denying him access to the Virgin's body:

> Son ellas las que hicieron conjuros para que me quedara ciego, porque yo era el único hombre que iba a la capilla a verlas arrodilladas, rezando las oraciones al revés frente a la imagen de la Virgen con el Niño, ese Niño que no quiere saber nada del gran pecho redondo que le ofrece la Virgen María y que pone cara de asco. Y ellas allí, rezando para que toda la leche en todos los pechos de madre se vuelva agria, para que todos los hijos se vuelvan lechuzas, o lobizones, de noche.

While the old women wish to deny the life-giving force of the mother's physical relationship with the infant, a wish to desex the mother, the grandfather maintains the illusion of an erotic possession of the Virgin's body in imagining his identity to be that of God the Father ("esas viejas de demonio . . . ni siquiera me dejan tocarla . . . como si Ella no estuviese allí en su casa y yo con Ella en la casa de todos." Both the old women and the grandfather, and shortly Joseph as well, are caught up in a Symbolic order that either denies female sexuality or appropriates it for the male's own satisfaction and self-aggrandizement.

In either case, female sexuality in the dominant order comes to be associated with death.[4] Joseph's choice of the Virgin's love as a way to resolve his own Oedipal jealousies will likewise, as we shall see, be a choice of death over life. The conflicting imperatives of the Imaginary and the Symbolic that define the Oedipal crisis for Lacan soon become apparent as Joseph begins to suspect that his mother wishes to remarry. He is already uncomfortably aware that she is unlike the other widows of the village, who are old and who always dress in black. And his fear of what the future holds stops him from following his mother on those afternoons when she secretly slips out of the house to meet her lover. His grandfather's stories, which carry the weight and prestige of the Symbolic, are powerful enough to keep Joseph at home: "nada lo retenía tanto en su lugar como las palabras del viejo y prefirió quedarse allí en vez de correr a descubrir lo que lo atormentaba."

The moment of painful separation that comes with or is motivated by the intuition of his mother's sexual difference and desire occurs during the time of the annual pilgrimage to the chapel made by women from the coast. During the time of the pilgrimage, the young boys of Kermaria feel they have been dispossessed of their chapel: "el grupo de chicos salvajes que vivía pendiente de la capilla no podía compartir la alegría y se sentía desposeído por esa gente. . . ." Moreover, their own mothers stay away: "sus madres, las mujeres de los labradores, se mantenían apartadas y no entraban a la capilla cuando entraban las otras. . . ." The story suggests that the women from the coast, the wives of fishermen, belong to a different, less repressive cultural order. They are associated with "un mito lejano, la antigüedad de la raza" and with water and the sea. Toril Moi has written that in the work of Hélène Cixous as well as in many ancient mythologies "water is the feminine element *par excellence.*" Similarly, Valenzuela uses "oceanic" water imagery to suggest female sexuality in her description of the women from the coast as they enter the chapel: "las otras, las mujeres de los pescadores . . . se balanceaban como las olas y parecían acunar a un hijo." When Joseph begins to try to win back his mother from her lover, who is also a fisherman, she asks him repeatedly what he knows about the sea: "¿Qué sabes tú del mar?—y a veces lo sacudía hasta hacerlo llorar." Joseph's response—"Joseph apenas atinaba a lamerse las lágrimas repitiéndose que esa era la única agua salada que existía en el mundo"—expresses his refusal to acknowledge that anyone other than he can be the object of his mother's love.

Significantly, only Joseph's mother enters the chapel with the strangers, and when he sees her enter, he becomes alarmed. As a prank to scare off the old widows, the boys of Kermaria have put small fish into the fonts of holy water. When Joseph's mother sees the fish, however, she is not surprised. As if the fish were a symbol in their own right, Joseph's mother clasps one in her hands and quietly leaves to meet her lover. Joseph tries to run after her, but is blinded by the sun: "en el umbral del atrio un sol repentino le hirió las pupilas y . . . tuvo que detenerse, cegado." When he regains his sight, his mother is only a shadowy white form disappearing into the wooded countryside. Joseph experiences a momentary blindness a second time when his mother finally joins the man she plans to marry. Blindness in this story, as in the next one I will discuss, seems to represent the distortions, delusions or blindness of the Symbolic order itself, its repression of the feminine and of sexual difference. For Kristeva, what is most severely repressed in the Symbolic order is "la mère qui jouit" or "the mother who knows sexual pleasure" (Marks and De Courtivon). This is precisely that aspect of his mother's life that Joseph cannot accept.

Joseph's mother had tried to teach him about love. "Para amar," she explained, "hay que ser maduro y sabio y lleno de piedad." But Joseph, still caught in the realm of Imaginary, narcissistic identifications, responds: "Cuando yo ame, mis hijos tendrán la cara del Niño de cera que está frente al altar." The reader intuits in Joseph's words some of the ways that, according to Naomi Schor, the Symbolic can intrude and structure the Imaginary dyad. For Joseph, the image of the Virgin and Child (a construct of the Symbolic order) reflects or mirrors his relationship with his mother; his own children, he imagines, will simply reproduce the image. Joseph's identification with the Christ Child expresses, to quote Jim Swan, a "desire for an origin of identity with one who is the same, an origin free of the disturbance of difference."

Hence Joseph sees his mother's decision to remarry as a betrayal: "si su madre había querido buscarse un nuevo marido . . . lo había traicionado vilmente al no elegir uno de los apóstoles del atrio o a una de las figuras del fresco que eran sus verdaderos amigos." Her choice, Pierre, a fisherman from the coast, betrays in turn her own needs and desires. Joseph's mother takes him with her on her trip to the coast to meet Pierre, but when Joseph sees his rival, he separates himself from his mother and flees, choosing the love of the desexed Virgin, the myth of the Symbolic, over the love of his own mother rather than confront and accept the fact of his mother's difference. He reconciles himself by reasoning that "el cariño que él necesitaba no era su madre quien podía dárselo, sino esa otra mujer que había en su pueblo, tan cálida, tan generosa, la capilla de Kermaria."

Joseph's choice is made, significantly enough, in the ossuary of a church and is, as I have already indicated, a choice of death over life. Joseph is even aware of this: "Pensó que después de todo no estaba tan mal que su madre se fuera con un hombre que estaba bien vivo y que no pertenecía a ese maldito mundo de los muertos." In **"Hijo de Kermaria,"** Valenzuela associates the Symbolic, and its repression of female desire, with death, thereby effectively reversing the more conventional masculinist association of death with the female body (Kahn Hartsock). The motif of death frames the story. It is present in the beginning details and in the closing imagery. It defines, tragically, Joseph's resolution of his Oedipal jealousies, his successful entry, in other words, into the world of the father and the father's law. The mother escapes this order by affirming her desire and by defying the authority of her "father-in-law," whom she in fact expels from the family home shortly before leaving for the coast.

The mother who follows her own desire is also the subject of the short story **"La profesora."** Here the rupture of an Imaginary identification is treated much more humorously. This narrative tells the story of a young male university graduate who, after receiving his degree in history, returns to visit his high school history teacher. He brings with him a highly idealized and clearly narcissistically-grounded image of a woman with no sexual or indeed human qualities whatsoever. He remembers her as always having been "tan majestuosamente fuera de su alcance," with "una austeridad que la dejaba fuera del tiempo," and he enters the gate to her house "en pos de un rodete, unos tacos bajos y un sombrío traje sastre." He comes hoping to find

in her presence confirmation that he has become what she wanted him to become, a mirror image of her own purity and a mirror image of the great heroes of the past whose stories she had taught him in class. The mirroring process will, however, shortly be disrupted. He arrives still believing she holds him in special regard and that when, in the past, she related the stories of the great heroes, she had imagined them having his face, his mouth and his eyes ("Mientras dictaba clase les ponía tu boca, tus ojos, que me miraban absortos y que seguían cada unos de mis gestos, como adorándome)." He believes, in other words, that she, not the dominant cultural order, has made him the person he now is, and he grossly overestimates his own importance in her life, as he is soon to discover.

Upon entering the garden of her house, the reality principle sets in and cognitive confusion begins. He discovers not the teacher but her seven children and finds he has unwittingly set foot in a realm about which he knows nothing, "el mundo mistificado de los niños." Rather than the little angels he had imagined her children must be, he finds them monstrous: "Le pareció que tenían máscaras de sangre porque la mermelada de frutilla les chorreaba por el mentón y pensó que se querían matar porque se estaban bombardeando con panes, sin saber que esa era la habitual diversión a la hora del té que siempre se estiraba en risas que él tomó por aullidos." The very materiality of the children, their disorder, their bodies, belie the corporality or the sexuality of the mother who, when she finally does appear, can no longer be seen as the former teacher but now, rather, as simply "un cuerpo de mujer."

His inability to confront difference, his need, like Joseph's, to split motherhood from sexuality, the same bipolar logic in the construction of female identity within the prevailing Symbolic order, will shortly cause him, as it did Joseph, to flee. After the seven impersonations (mirror images) of the mother given by the children, the real ("verdadera") Señora de Ortiz comes out of the house "y él la vio más grotesca que todos los disfraces de los chicos porque se había soltado el rodete y el pelo muy corto le daba una expresión adolescente que nada tenía que ver con su recuerdo." Communication is impossible because she does not say the words he wants to hear, nor does she give him the recognition he had expected.

Like Joseph's mother in **"Hijo de Kermaria,"** this mother gives up her role in a cultural order that denies her her selfhood. She gives up her teaching position in order to be with her children. Though Mendizábal, the former student, is deaf to her words, she explains her decision: "le confieso que me hartan los buenos alumnos, la cátedra, todas esas historias. . . . Ya va a ver lo arduo que es vivir entre héroes sin cara que se estereotipan y son siempre los mismos . . . Ahora soy tan feliz desde que me liberé de todo eso. Si hasta parezco mucho más joven ¿verdad, chicos? Tengo ganas de reír, de divertirme." In this mother's words, we see a positive valorizing of an Imaginary unstructured by the Symbolic. The mother seeks and finds pleasure in her close relationship with her children. Mendizábal's vision of the teacher-mother, on the other hand, is culturally mediated, and so evidence of her desire disrupts his fantasies.

Total rupture of the narcissistic identification occurs with the loss of his glasses, which accidentally fall to the ground when the teacher touches his shoulder. He is sunk, comically, into total blindness, accompanied by a sense of total helplessness, vulnerability and a fear of seduction which he equates, paradoxically, with both death and life. Panic, nevertheless, sends him groping his way to the gate and once on the other side, the children return his glasses. With the restoration of his vision, which signals a recovery of his sense of self and his definitive entry into the dominant order, he decides his imagination has simply played a trick on him. But when he looks back into the yard, once again from the perspective of the dominant cultural order, he sees an image of the teacher struggling in vain to pick herself up off the ground: "Un mal sueño, sí, de no haber sido porque entre las cabezas de los chicos y más allá de sus risas creyó ver la silueta de la profesora que trataba en vano de incorporarse." The pit is not far from the pedestal! Once securely outside the mother's garden ("dejó atrás el jardín endemoniado") and once the mirroring image has been destroyed, the youth achieves a position of mastery vis-à-vis the mother, never again to fall prey to the lure of the mother-child bond. His adult sense of self, his manhood, depends on repressing, this time definitively, the original attachment to one who is other, a woman.

In **"Hijo de Kermaria"** and **"La profesora,"** there is a sense of inevitability in the process that leads to the break-up of the dyadic unity between mother and son, though it is the mother's own difference, and her affirmation of this difference, that effects the break. The mother does not play a secondary role nor is her subjectivity ignored in Valenzuela's fictions about the Oedipal crisis. The third story I have chosen, however, is much more radical in its implications. **"Los Menestreles"** is a utopian evocation of the creative linguistic powers of women, and there is a much more explicit link in this narrative between language and desire, textuality and sexuality. In **"Los Menestreles,"** female sexuality is itself capable of generating an alternative Symbolic or language. The mother's son will not be forced to repress difference nor the original identification with the mother in order to achieve adulthood. The consequences for the mother, however, are less fortunate.

Like **"Hijo de Kermaria,"** **"Los Menestreles"** is set in the French countryside. The story portrays an especially close, symbiotic relationship between the peasant woman, Jeanne, and her son, Ariel. The story begins with the presentation of Ariel's inner discourse or child's subjectivity and desire, his need to hear his mother's voice, and his feelings about his name and his fathers' (plural) name. Ariel asks his mother repeatedly to tell him the name of his fathers, not because he has forgotten their name but because he derives pleasure from hearing his mother pronounce it: Ariel "no quería que le anduviera con vueltas, no le importaba saber cómo se llamaban, lo que quería era oírlo en boca de su madre porque cuando ella pronunciaba el nombre

se le escapaba ese campanilleo en la voz que a veces era triste pero que otras veces resonaba con un profundo placer." Jeanne would always reply "Se llamaban los Menestreles," and Ariel would realize that "Ariel rimaba con menestrel, Arieles y Menestreles." The mother's voice provides the basis of identity and identification in this story, not vision. The importance of the mother's voice in this narrative recalls Hélène Cixous's assertion that femininity in writing is to be discerned in the privileging of the voice: *"Writing and voice . . . are woven together,"* she writes in *La Jeune Née* (qtd. in Moi). Similarly, Marta Traba has speculated that women's writing is closer than men's to the oral tradition; it is closer to speech than to the printed word.

Ariel's feelings about his name are, nevertheless, ambivalent, at least at the beginning of the story, when he is only nine years old. He both loves and hates his name: "Ariel adoraba su nombre y lo odiaba al mismo tiempo." At night in bed, or alone in the fields, or in the presence of his mother, he likes the sound of his name and the sound of his mother's voice when she pronounces it. But his is not a common name, and at school it causes him shame. At school, he is afraid to pronounce it, and the older boys make fun of his shame: "Cómo te llamas, ricurita?" As we shall see, the name Ariel, derived from "menestrel," is a matronymic, not a patronymic, and so identifies him with his mother and not with his absent father, Georges Le Gouarnec, as the dominant order requires. Ariel's ambivalence suggests, surely, an opposition between the realm of the mother, the womb-like locus of the home, and the realm of the dominant cultural order, which the school represents.

The source of Ariel's ambivalence is revealed in his mother's inner discourse, which in the short story alternates with Ariel's and with intercalated dialogue between mother and son. The mother's inner discourse is the story of the "menestreles," a story, we realize by the end of the narrative, that is purely the product of Jeanne's sexual fantasy. It is a story, nevertheless, that provides the narrative of Ariel's own origin and identity. It is Jeanne's story about the arrival one day of nine workmen, "los menestreles," while her husband, Georges, is away at war. The "menestreles" sing songs and tell marvellous stories and are fleeing the war because, as one was to have said: "El gobierno quiere darnos rifles y nosotros sólo queremos blandir nuestras mandolinas. Al ruido de las balas, preferimos el de nuestras voces cuando cantan." Fleeing a world of hate and destruction, the workmen stay nine days and nine nights and, according to the logic of Jeanne's fantasy, each night she takes one to her bed. Her language and body tell her that nine is the sum of her happiness, the nine fathers of her son, one for each month of her pregnancy.

Though Jeanne omits certain details, the story of the "menestreles" is the story she tells Ariel about his own origin and identity, notwithstanding the fact that his biological father is the still absent Georges Le Gouarnec. From this imagined story or fantasy comes, furthermore, the language she teaches her son. She teaches him language by telling him every year on his birthday the stories she claims the "menestreles" once told her: "Un solo día del año la madre lo sienta sobre sus rodillas y le cuenta los cuentos que le gustaría escuchar a ella." This practice continues year after year until Ariel's thirteenth birthday, when Georges finally returns and Ariel realizes it is time for him to leave and assume the identity and language his mother has given him: "Se dio cuenta de que había llegado el momento de ser como ellos [los menestreles] y de seguir su propio camino ya que su cama que había sido la de ellos crujía bajo otro peso plebeyo, pegajoso." Ariel thus identifies with the fathers imagined for him by his mother and not with his biological father, whom he rejects. After Ariel leaves, Jeanne continues to tell him stories in letters she writes with great difficulty, but when she receives his first letter she realizes that he has acquired the language she had taught him: "Ariel ya había ascendido de categoría: ya era capaz de crear historias como los menestreles."

Although Ariel does not demonstrate his acquisition of language, the mother's alternative Symbolic, until after his physical separation from his mother, this was, nonetheless, a language he learned at his mother's knee, a "mother tongue" of great power.[5] Here it is the mother who facilitates the son's passage to adulthood, and it is a passage almost void of conflicting imperatives, though not void, we might notice, of repression. Rereading the story, we observe that Jeanne's success in creating the son's Symbolic requires the verbal repression, precisely, of *jouissance*: "Hay cosas que no se le pueden contar a un chico de ocho años"; "Lo que no puede contar son sus noches verdaderas con los Menestreles, sus noches que se convierten en palabras que le queman la boca." The experience of sexual pleasure itself, in other words, cannot be verbalized.

Hence the internal contradiction. The female body and its experience of sexual pleasure are the source of the power of Jeanne's language, yet that source is something which cannot be revealed, something which language cannot accomodate. This would seem to confirm the French feminists' assertions about the power of language and its repression of the feminine, and yet at the same time deny the possibility of an *écriture féminine*. The Lacanian Symbolic does make itself felt in this story.[6] For this reason, we need to read **"Los Menestreles,"** following Toril Moi's reading of Cixous, as "a utopian solution to the problem of desire." According to Moi, the utopian project is always marked by conflict and contradiction because "the utopian vision takes off from a negative analysis of its own society," or cultural order, with all the gaps, inconsistencies, and, we might add, repressions that define that order. The contradiction in **"Los Menestreles"**— Jeanne's creation of a Symbolic that derives its power from her sexual difference and yet must repress that difference in order to survive—must be understood, again following Toril Moi, as "structured by the conflict between an *already* contradictory patriarchal ideology[7] and the utopian thought that struggles to free itself from the patriarchal stranglehold" emphasis added). In other words,

since Valenzuela too resides within the patriarchal order, any attempt to escape its repressive effects requires both a confrontation with and an acknowledgment of the power of the repressive effects of the Symbolic order that gave rise to the utopia in the first place.

NOTES

[1] For a critical discussion of *l'écriture féminine*, see Toril Moi (Part II: "French Feminist Theory" 89-173) and Ann Rosalind Jones. For another application of French feminist theory to Hispanic texts by women, see Elizabeth J. Ordóñez.

[2] The connections between French feminist theory and Valenzuela's theoretical essays on writing by women merit further study.

[3] Suleiman is especially interested in the conjunction of writing and motherhood as expressed in the work of mothers who write. Since Valenzuela had a child in 1958, it seems safe to assume that at least some of the stories of *Los heréticas* (1967) were written by a mother. For a short biographical sketch of Valenzuela, see Garfield 143.

[4] Valenzuela makes the same point in her essay "Mis brujas favoritas" (89).

[5] This "mother tongue" in effect displaces the language he learned at school. His first songs and stories, learned at school, fail to please the mother. See *Los heréticos* 51.

[6] Georges's arrival can be read as a second intervention of the paternal or Lacanian Symbolic insofar as Jeanne has awaited Ariel's thirteenth birthday to tell him about what she had previously repressed: "Ariel ya cumplía los trece y por fin [Jeanne] podía vaciar en él su propio corazón, hablarle de su gran amor por ellos y saciar esa vieja sed que tenía de compartirlo con alguien" (55). Georges's arrival on the day of Ariel's birthday silences this desire. Jeanne must once again repress pleasure: "se encontró con que debía enquistar nuevamente su corazón" (58). The paternal signifier (Ariel's patronymic "Le Gouarnec") also appears on the last letter he receives: "En el sobre decía Ariel Le Gouarnec, no simplemente Ariel, y él supo que se trataba de una mala noticia" (58). This letter is sent by the village priest to inform Ariel that his mother is dying. Jeanne dies when she can no longer remember the name of the other fathers. Ariel does remember, however, and he leaves his biological father definitively in order to travel to the south in search of the "menestreles," thus complying with his mother's dying wish. The matronymic or maternal signifier, therefore, finally prevails.

[7] The primary contradiction with which this paper has been concerned is, to quote Jim Swan, the male "desire for sameness against the fact that at the origin of a man's identity is inevitably one who is different, other, a woman" (161).

WORKS CITED

Bleikasten, André. "Fathers in Faulkner." *The Fictional Father: Lacanian Readings of the Text.* Ed. Robert Con Davis. Amherst: U of Massachusetts P, 1981. 115-46.

Felman, Shoshana. "To Open the Question." *Yale French Studies* 55-56 (1977): 5-10.

Gallop, Jane. "Reading the Mother Tongue: Psychoanalytic Feminist Criticism." *The Trial(s) of Psychoanalysis.* Ed. Francoise Meltzer. Chicago: U of Chicago P, 1987. 125-40.

Garfield, Evelyn Picon. *Women's Voices from Latin America: Interviews with Six Contemporary Authors.* Detroit: Wayne State UP, 1985.

Garner, Shirley Nelson, et al., eds. *The (M)other Tongue: Essays in Feminist Psychoanalytic Interpretation.* Ithaca: Cornell UP, 1985.

Hartsock, Nancy C. M. *Money, Sex, and Power: Toward a Feminist Historical Materialism.* 1983. Boston: Northeastern UP, 1985.

Jones, Ann Rosalind. "Writing the Body: Toward an Understanding of *L'Ecriture féminine.*" *Feminist Studies* 7 (1981): 247-63.

Kahn, Coppélia. "The Hand That Rocks the Cradle: Recent Gender Theories and Their Implications." Garner et al. 72-88.

Marks, Elaine and Isabelle de Courtivron, eds. *New French Feminisms.* New York: Shoken Books, 1981.

Marks, Elaine. "Women and Literature in France." *Signs* 3 (1978): 832-42.

Moi, Toril. *Sexual/Textual Politics: Feminist Literary Theory.* New York: Metheun, 1985.

Ordóñez, Elizabeth J. "Inscribing Difference: 'L'Ecriture Féminine' and New Narrative by Women." *Anales de Literatura Española Contemporánea* 12 (1987): 45-58.

Rich, Adrienne. *Of Woman Born: Motherhood as Experience and Institution.* New York: Norton, 1976.

Schor, Naomi. "*Eugenie Grandet:* Mirrors and Melancholia." Garner et al. 217-37.

Silverman, Kaja. *The Subject of Semiotics.* New York: Oxford UP, 1983.

Suleiman, Susan Rubin. "Writing and Motherhood." Garner et al. 352-77.

Swan, Jim. "Difference and Silence: John Milton and the Question of Gender." Garner et al. 142-68.

Traba, Marta. "Hipótesis sobre una escritura diferente." *La sartén por el mango.* Eds. Patricia Elena González and Eliana Ortega. Río Piedras, Puerto Rico: Ediciones Huracán, 1985. 21-26.

Valenzuela, Luisa. *Los heréticos.* Buenos Aires: Paidós, 1967.

———. "La mala palabra." *Revista Iberoamericana.* 51 (1985): 489-91

———. "Mis brujas favoritas." *Theory and Practice of Feminist Literary Criticism.* Eds. Gabriele Mora and Karen S. Van Hooft. Ypsilanti: Bilingual Press, 1982. 88-95.

———. "The Word, That Milk Cow." *Contemporary Women Authors of Latin America.* Eds. Doris Meyer and Margarite Fernández Olmos. Brooklyn: Brooklyn College Press, 1983. 96-97.

Wenzel, Hélène Vivienne. "Introduction to Luce Irigaray's 'And the One Doesn't Stir Without the Other'." *Signs* 7 (1981): 56-59.

Juanamaría Cordones-Cook   (essay date 1995)

SOURCE: "*Novela negra con argentinos:* The Desire to Know." *World Literature Today,* Vol. 69, No. 4 (Autumn 1995): 745-50.

[*Cordones-Cook assesses the novel in terms of the "Dirty War" and its representation of the dichotomous nature of Argentinians, at once civilized and barbaric.*]

Without attempting resolutions, conclusions, or definitions of any kind, Luisa Valenzuela, in her writing, gives expression to a radical poetics and sexual/textual ethos. Her kaleidoscopic and protean texts constitute a celebration of the imagination and of Eros, of energy and of change. Guided by the desire to know and reveal the failures of esthetic, linguistic, social, and political categories, Valenzuela practices an esthetics of irreverence and transgression that corresponds to an absolutely radical ideology. She brings to bear a consciousness that is scarcely rational, a sensibility which, in the name of the pleasure principle, rebels against the reality principle, the castrater of expression and human liberty. In this way much of her writing can be read as an inquiry that, beginning with being, calls upon and exposes nonbeing, the repressed subjective and cultural unconscious.

With a profound lucidity marked by the violent political events of the "Dirty War,"[1] Valenzuela explores that unconscious in one of her latest novels, *Novela negra con argentinos* (1990).[2] In her previous novelistic work she had shown a gradual awakening of sociopolitical consciousness determined by the Argentine context.[3] Through *El gato eficaz* (1972), a text that breaks with all conventions and traditions, Valenzuela creates an open, seamless narrative space that inscribes an anarchic sign: it unfolds in seductive and Dionysian dynamics with subversive ideological implications. She continues with ever-increasing political awareness in *Como en la guerra* (1977), removing the patriarchal military government's mask of civilization and respect. Thus does she reveal the hidden face of opprobrium and violence in the Argentine political reality. *Cambio de armas* (1982) somberly exposes confrontational aspects in each of the narratives denouncing the Dirty War. *Cola de lagartija* (1983), a heterogeneous, mutable, and irreverent discourse in a bitter grimace of black humor, strips the political and military hierarchies of their fictitious solemnities.

Novela negra con argentinos follows this trajectory as a phase of reflection and understanding of the Argentine paradox that has intrigued the author for some time.[4] The novel treats the oxymoronic nature of the contemporary Argentine citizen, presumably civilized and respectable, who unexpectedly turns into a cruel assassin and reveals thereby the hidden face of barbarity thought not to exist or to be viable in a society of such high culture.

The text opens with an obscure incident in the early dawn hours of New York City. Agustín Palant, an Argentine writer, steps silently from an apartment with a revolver in his pocket, leaving behind a murdered—or at least he presumes her to be murdered—stage actress, Edwina Irving. She is a stranger whom Agustín has approached on this one and only occasion after her theatrical performance of a culinary scene in a rundown warehouse that serves as stage. Agustín accompanies Edwina to her apartment, and when she is about to surrender in his arms, after a tender recognition, he pulls the pistol from his pocket and without any explanation, simply "just because," he fires a shot into her temple. Immediately after this apparently gratuitous death, Agustín leaves the scene of the crime. Following two nights of anguished, paranoid ruminations, desolate, depressed, and so confused that he comes to doubt whether he even committed the crime, he goes to his lover, Roberta Aguilar, also a writer and an Argentine. Horrified, he recounts the story of his crime. Now face to face with this infamous act of murder, he feels alienated and asks himself: why did he kill? The inexplicable gratuitousness of the crime intrigues Roberta as well, who embarks with Agustín through mysterious conduits on an adventurous investigation in a search for possible answers to the enigma.

This study will explore the desire for signification that motivates Roberta and Agustín, which underlies the development of the entire narration and illuminates some of the strategies for access to the unconscious, the other scene, from the perspective of the psychoanalytic ideas of Jacques Lacan.[5]

Novela negra records with a provocative rhythm the story of an appetite for signification which, in its metonymic displacements and metaphoric projections, is interwoven with a creative obsession. The text constitutes what Peter Brooks, in *Reading for the Plot*, calls a narrative of desire and a desire for narrative (48). It represents the dynamics of a desire—in this case epistemological—which motivates the story and at the same time reveals the nature of narration as desire, the need to recount as a creative human drive.[6] Full of enigmas, this desire operates in contiguous planes in constant slippage. The discourse disseminates itself in libidinous linguistic play, effecting successive mutations that launch the subject in pursuit of an always elusive object—*la manque à être*—toward an infinite, unreachable abyss.

The text seduces the reader and absorbs him or her in a textual/sexual dynamics which Peter Brooks calls forepleasure or tropes of pleasure. In a thrust of that desire through which and toward which the narration is displaced, Valenzuela guides the reader through intricate meanderings filled with detours, delays, and ambiguities. The yearning for possession and dispossession, continuity and discontinuity, which dissolves already-constituted forms, traps the reader in fascination and horror from the first page to the last, in a search for an answer to the enigma of the crime's motive. The ambiguities that surround the act of the crime itself are never completely elucidated, for there is no empirical evidence of the deed. Perhaps the perpetration of the crime is inconsequential. At any rate, the fact is that it does not matter whether the murder occurred at the level of concrete facts or whether it belongs to the realm of hallucinations or desires. What

really matters is that it be inscribed in a place symbolic of the history of that subject, impunity and guilt being one and the same (208 English; 220 Spanish). Roberta attempts to recover that lost link in the chain of Agustín's internal story in order to arrive at a profound perception of a "real" experience that language is neither able nor allowed to express directly.

Roberta understands that, from a psychoanalytic perspective, the subject, upon acceding to the Symbolic order,[7] undergoes separation and castration, which carries with it an acceptance of the prohibition imposed by the Law of the Name-of-the-Father. The individual acquires the word, only to find the failure of linguistic representation that distances the subject from the Real. Aware of the barriers imposed by language, Roberta seeks to free herself from the word, which has lost its power to signify and which smears everything it tries to represent. With this objective, Roberta chooses to exercise an imagination expressed through her body, thus to return to her own primordial generative stage.

Since unconscious desire, according to Lacan, is inscribed on the body, Roberta with her body is able to record in the text an inexhaustible female imagery with its dynamic stream of phantasmagoric images. Roberta lets herself be carried away, which allows her body to write its history with inaudible words. Without the intermediary of the Symbolic order, Roberta can overcome internal barriers, and the immense resources of the unconscious will be able to bloom in their explosive potentiality. Uninhibited, Roberta opens a provocative communication, bringing to the surface anxieties, fears, and topics which had been excluded, prohibited, and silenced. Unfolding an expansive, creative feminine economy, Roberta frees her internal demons in order to recover her original strength. Her body, incited by the pleasure principle and by the vital drives toward union, constitutes a space traversed by Eros which pushes to establish even greater unities.

Like flowing energy, Roberta pours out her body in uncontrolled mutations that slip away always in search of something else. She manages to articulate a dialectical interplay between the constant diachrony mobilized by desire and the object of a desire impossible to grasp, which essentially tends toward the absolute unity of the self. Roberta asks questions about the nature of love and searches for totality in an open demand: "I want love. . . . I want there to be love, I want to feel love and I want to be able to express it. In all directions" (94 English; 95-96 Spanish). As for Agustín, who is moved by the death drive, he cannot satisfy that demand. Roberta chooses to exercise other processes of the imagination that will allow her to fill her emptiness and fulfill her desire for access to the lost scene.

In the course of her search and incursions, Roberta comes to a secondhand clothing shop, and with the help of Bill, a handsome green-eyed black man, she transfigures herself with masks, costumes, and transvestism. She cuts and colors her hair. She dresses as a man, as a swaggering "macho" from the forties. Starting with an impoverished and rudimentary reality, she improvises a theater. Writing with the body, she stages and acts out with Bill confirmatory erotic fantasies, in a series of spontaneous, dramatic, and spectacular transactions. In order to learn what one feels, Roberta even attempts to gain access to another scene that does not belong to her, that of Agustín. She adopts a theatricality filled with inversions and lethal mirrorings, which re-presents the crime, with Bill in the role of victim and she in that of Agustín (62-63 English; 61-62 Spanish).

As a strategy for access to Agustín's other scene, the theatrical act[8] is repeatedly inscribed in the text with the body performing aggressive, erotic, and ritualistic ceremonies. Lacan has pointed out a specific relationship between man and his body which is manifested in certain aggressive social practices, rituals that deny respect for the natural forms of the human body. In *Novela negra* these aggressive practices are realized through the ceremonial formalism of erotic and sadomasochistic rituals in the "homemade inferno" of Ava Taurel.[9] In that den of torture, with chambers equipped with all the paraphernalia for ritual, chimeras, erotic obsessions, savagery, and violence, black fantasies are performed. Darkest desires are unleashed, allowing pain to invade the realm of sexual arousal in order to provoke perverse pleasures. Through gestures, movements, and stagings, the dynamics of a sign system beyond language articulate with great intensity a deeply theatrical experience in the vein of Antonin Artaud. His appearance in the novel as an implicit and explicit intertext is very apropos, because the strategies of the Theater of Cruelty are used as a vehicle for access to the hidden face of reality. This dramatic genre exposes the audience to dangerous experiences in order to generate catharsis, purification, and transfiguration. Thus Roberta, searching for the human soul behind pain and pushing the limits to arrive at the hidden face of the mirror,[10] repeatedly visits Ava Taurel's den of sadomasochistic pleasures. Faced with that theater of cruelty, Roberta asks whether Agustín's story is not theater and his crime a stage montage.

Consistent with her desire to discover the mysterious motive for Agustín's crime as well as the secret memory of oblivion, Roberta searches different paths for an opening that will give her an entrance to Agustín's story. He cooperates, and in the course of this search the two attend a party in Lara's loft, a space that evokes, in a distorted and contemporary fashion, the great Gothic palaces. They ascend in a black cage, a freight elevator which, like Charon's boat, transports them in body and word to another territory. Once there, they find Lara, a primeval witch, in a kitchen stirring a big pot as she prepares a potion of strange herbs. Lara corporeally reinscribes the scene prior to Agustín's crime, when Edwina was making a soup, perhaps as an initiation rite both commemorative and preparatory to an internal voyage.

Inserted within a set of Chinese boxes which transports them initially to a theatrical stage in the loft, an imitation of those sets of the sixties, Roberta and Agustín witness distorted—not to mention disturbing and magical—spectacles. Inhabited by strange beings, a grotesque and chaotic decor of Haitian engravings, musical instruments, masks, and sculptures constructed with toilets, human organs, cardboard dolls, and other "treasures" gathered from the urban rubble and trash, this space forms a perverse scenography of clowns and monsters with bloody, ravenous jaws, joined in macabre rituals in a fantastic, fabulous bestiary. On a passage through bizarre scenes and lavish choreographic montages, they witness rites and magical exorcisms and undergo dramatic mutations. All this prepares them to communicate through experiences of recognition in other settings and allows them to cross the fourth wall to another scene.

Guided by a literary critic, Roberta and Agustín ascend again in the freight elevator, this time reaching the top floor. There lives Edouard, an aged dance teacher on his deathbed, and Antoine, his favorite pupil, who has managed to offer the decrepit old man the theatrical and voyeuristic pleasure of witnessing his erotic encounters with boys from the streets behind a translucent wall or one-way mirror. In Edouard's room, Roberta and Agustín arrive at "the depths of the mother cave," through which they can have access to the secret spectacle of another mask of fantasy, the face of human imagination whence the terrifying occult emerges (176 English; 186 Spanish). Facing this scene, Agustín, uneasy, anxious, and on the verge of sinking, seeks to flee. He asks himself, "Is this the movie I'm supposed to get back into? Is this the scene I must become a part of in order to reestablish an order that can never be reestablished in me?" (166 English; 176 Spanish).

Via meanderings through labyrinths and mirrors, with no unified idea of self, Agustín moves in the order of dual relationships of the Imaginary. He is ever in search of, in others and in their gaze, a whole image to give him the identity he lacks. Thus, from Edouard's bedroom, Agustín traverses other walls and curtains, until at last he leaves the darkness and enters another brightly lit scenario where he meets Héctor Bravo, a Uruguayan Tupamaro physician.

On this other stage, Agustín enters into a transitive fascination with the specular other that is Héctor Bravo. He seizes the word, searching for transparency in the opacity of language, and he achieves catharsis. For the first time he tells his story without fear of wounding any susceptibility, without fear of the dangers of confession, but without achieving any precision or certainty about the act of the crime.

It is not surprising that in this process Héctor Bravo, from the position to which Agustín implicitly assigns him, that of a subject supposed to know, should proceed by considering psychoanalytic speculations that revolve around the dialectic of the Imaginary order. Perhaps Edwina caused Agustín to confront the distant frustration of an unbearable past, and by firing the shot he believed he was achieving needed distance from that past. Or it may be that by killing Edwina, Agustín was eliminating his other, that the murder was a rejection of specular images of the mother he did not love. He probably sought to destroy his own feminine image, because of his incapacity to satisfy feminine demands, or he killed the image of all women, whom he fears because they force him to face unbearable frustrations (208 English; 220 Spanish).

If all these alternatives contemplated by Héctor Bravo are considered at a basic level, it will become clear that they suggestively aim at Roberta, who has temporarily filled the space of alterity in the mirror as Agustín's other. Metaphorically, Roberta embodies the phallic mother by virtue of possessing in Agustín's Imaginary the qualities which the Symbolic order attributes to the phallus,[11] namely initiative, activity, and power. Roberta represents a powerful specular image of the ideal of a unified gestalt to which Agustín aspires and which, in fact, he lacks. She is the subject that can give him everything, the object of his desire who at the same time desires him as an object. Face to face with Roberta, who in addition reminds him of a past that he wants to block out, Agustín feels threatened; he perceives his own weakness and vulnerability, all of which produces an ambivalent eroto-aggressive attitude, characteristic of certain manifestations of the mirror stage. Moreover, Agustín quivers with fear of women at the threat of castration which underlies the paranoid fantasy of the *vagina dentata*, to which he himself alludes during a ritual bath in aromatic and healing herbs given by Ro-berta. In fact, Roberta undergoes a process of identification with Edwina to the point of dreaming that she herself dies in a similar fashion.

Héctor Bravo's scheme of psychoanalytic arguments sheds light on the enigma of the crime's motives but does not elucidate them completely. The reader must investigate more deeply the text's other face in order to rescue other elusive diluted codes that might lead to the reconstruction of the repressed past of that subject's story.

It is remarkable that Agustín does not allow the unbearable experience of the horrors of the Dirty War to come into consciousness: " . . . an entire country left behind, an era and a horror not labeled as such (screams in the house next door and desaparecidos). No. Unbearable memories of other victims who . . . would be mentioned no further" (76-77 English; 77 Spanish). In accordance with certain dictatorial military interests, those recollections should be erased from collective memory, never again to resurface, thus imposing an amnesia that blocks reflection and analysis and maintains the equilibrium of that militarist Symbolic order.

As for politically aware Roberta, she certainly remembers that time filled with threats of torture for political reasons, bodies tossed from helicopters with their entrails spilling out, floating in the River Plate. In the exploratory games she initiates with Agustín in her apartment during a period of total isolation, Roberta evokes in a story the famous "Calera de Córdoba," a cement factory where political prisoners went to work as slaves and contracted insidious lung diseases.[12]

Nevertheless, though Agustín has exiled those unbearable memories from his consciousness to a preconscious or

unconscious level, such experiences have marked him indelibly. Like implacable phantoms, they return to him, transmuted into action to re-present events of a distant repressed past, in the re-acting of a gesture which he does not entirely recall making in the first place. The internal force that moved him to pull the trigger is revealed as an effect of a drive[13] that originated in the unconscious, the locus of otherness which has been repressed by the Law of the Name-of-the-Father. It is a death drive revealed as a desire to repeat behaviors and which, combined with aggressivity, is directed outward to destroy the object, his other.

According to Lacan, aggressivity in experience activates an intended aggression that stems from the formative stages of the individual in images of physical disintegration, dislocation, castration, mutilation, and dismembering—all destructive images, phantasmagorias which obsessively torment humanity and are present in dreams and psychosis. Aggressivity is linked to certain unconscious representations created through early relationships in the social environment, the imagos[14] of the premirror stage that appear as variations of the first matrices of the fragmented body.[15] The imago implies a specular fascination with the image which is revealed through drives in real or phantasmatic behaviors. The night of the supposed crime, Agustín, confronting Edwina, perceives her as the image of his likeness, his other. Edwina involuntarily evokes in him a threat of fragmentation and corporal dislocation, and offers a target for a death urge which will materialize an eroto-aggressive tension in the empirical plane of a concrete action, or in the imaginative plane of a fantasy.

During the investigative process, Agustin's early imagos have filtered with great difficulty through the fissures of his consciousness. He recalls his guilt-ridden incapacity to act when, in his apartment building in Buenos Aires, his neighbors begged for help, only to be dragged off wearing hoods, never to be seen again. These imagos also appear as a shifting series of phantasmagoria in nightmares filled with images of sadistic torture. Agustín, dressed as a woman, is seen in birth position staked and tied with cords and chains, on the point of being dismembered until only his sex organ remains, which is then burned by a powerful and frightening woman, a primeval witch who first appears as a strange figure of Roberta, later to become Edwina. Meanwhile, Edwina returns to Agustín in a photograph which he chews up and swallows, desperate in his desire for empowerment and identification by introjection into his other, or she returns to him in totally fragmented images.

The images of the fragmented body that come so obsessively to Agustín represent the imagos of his early experiences in Argentina. They are the imago of the terrifying Law of the Name-of-the-Father of the Dirty War, which he had attempted to block from his memory and which turned into an intrapsychic element. By shooting Edwina, Agustin has played out an imaginary script and has staged an eclipsed memory which, like a ghost from the past, struggles to return tangentially in a death drive. Agustín projects all his hostility onto the image of Edwina. Affected by the imagos intertwined in a play of negative transferences[16] that bring the past onto the present, Agustín displaces his ancient imagos, the representations that fix the experiences of brutality acquired by previous introjections excluded from his consciousness, onto Edwina.

Through displacement and condensation, the constitution and deformation suffered by the subject at the roots of its own history is manifested in Agustín, as he observes the castrating Law of the Name-of-the-Father represented by the dictates of corruption and violence of the regime in the Dirty War. Agustín's crime appears as a metaphor for an Argentine political and metaphysical disease, a symptom of the contradictions and aberrant incongruencies of that regime, and also a product of those political and social circumstances. Within this context, Agustín embodies a propitiatory victim of the social system reflecting a notion of collective responsibility: "The dead you kill are offspring of someone else's crimes" (220 English; 231-32 Spanish).

Seeking to understand the monstrousness of the contemporary Argentine citizen, seemingly civilized and respectable, Luisa Valenzuela in ***Novela negra con argentinos*** delivers her reflections on the Dirty War in a discourse overflowing with digressions, questionings, and metonymic displacements of the desire for signification. Valenzuela offers, through multiple, dispersive, and emancipatory strategies, access to Non-Being, to the other scene, the other of the cultural ethos, a shelter for repressed memories and collective messages; at the same time, like her protagonist Roberta, she refuses to eclipse the memory of the process of atrocities against wronged humanity in that somber and shameful chapter of Argentine history.

NOTES

[1] The Dirty War constitutes a black period of Argentine history. Preceded by a climate of terrorism from both the Right and the Left, the Argentine head of state carried out a coup on 23 May 1976, marking the beginning of the Dirty War. During this period, in the name of national security and patriotic Western Christian values, behind a façade of decorum and respect, every norm of integrity, every moral, social, and political propriety, all civil rights, were systematically violated. Thousands and thousands of people disappeared after being cruelly tortured and murdered, producing a climate of terror in the entire populace. Argentina ended this period of horror with the inauguration of Raúl Alfonsín as president of the republic, in December 1983.

[2] *Novela negra con argentinos*, second-place winner of the Plaza y Janés prize, was printed the same year in Spain by Plaza y Janés and in the United States by Ediciones del Norte. The translation by Toby Talbot, entitled *Black Novel (with Argentines)*, was published in New York by Simon & Schuster in 1992. The quotes included in this essay originate in the Ediciones del Norte text and also cite the Simon & Schuster translation.

[3] For a closer look at this trajectory in the novelistic work of Valenzuela before the publication of *Novela negra*, see Juanamaría Cordones-Cook, *Poética de transgresión en la novelística de Luisa Valenzuela*.

[4] See the commentaries by Luisa Valenzuela in her interview with Evelyn Picon Garfield on this subject, "Interview with Luisa Valenzuela."

[5] On the subject of Lacan's concepts, I have consulted *Ecrits: A Selection*, by Jacques Lacan, and *Jacques Lacan: A Philosophy of Psychoanalysis*, by Ellie Regland-Sullivan.

[6] Peter Brooks explains: "Narratives both tell of desire—typically present some story of desire—and arouse and make use of desire as a dynamic of signification. Desire is . . . a force including sexual desire but larger and more polymorphous" (37).

[7] These psychoanalytic concepts come from the theory of Lacan. He posits a system which functions through the discourse of the family. The self in its development passes, in the so-called Imaginary order—a field of fantasies and conscious and unconscious images—through an initial phase of plenitude with its mother, from whom it is rudely separated by the imposition of paternal authority, the Law of the Name-of-the-Father, by which it is left distanced from the Real. In this way a castrating lack is produced, a primordial void, which is associated and contemporary with the acquisition of language and the access to the culture of the society, to the Symbolic order.

[8] For a discussion of the dramatic and theatrical qualities in *Novela negra*, see the interview "Luisa Valenzuela habla sobre *Novela negra con argentinos y Realidad nacional desde la cama*," by Juanamaría Cordones-Cook.

[9] In a conversation at Columbia University in October 1992, Valenzuela affirmed that Ava Taurel was a curious character taken from real life. She had met her personally in New York, grown rich as the owner of a den of sadomasochistic pleasures. In fact, Ava Taurel had formulated theories on the psychology of such pleasures.

[10] According to Rosemary Jackson, the literary fantasies of Sade and those after him imply a search for the Imaginary, though paradoxically the horror and violence that such fantasies need to employ suggest the possibility of a return to that Imaginary.

[11] When referring to the phallus, the biological object or penis is not intended; rather, I mean the Law of the Name-of-the-Father, which Lacan represents through the phallus, as a symbol of lost plenitude, a privileged abstract signifier that marks a difference and an absence.

[12] Valenzuela commented that she took this idea of the cement factory from *La nave de los locos*, by Cristina Peri Rossi (October 1992 interview with Cordones-Cook).

[13] The term *drive* is used in the sense of an internal force whose end is to suppress a state of tension which impels the subject to perform certain acts likely to produce an energetic discharge of arousal (Laplanche and Pontalis).

[14] I refer to the unconscious representation given as an imaginary outline through which the subject confronts its other and which can be objectified in behaviors or images, and even in fantasies (Laplanche and Portalis).

[15] I use the notion of the fragmented body in the Lacanian sense, just as it is manifested in dreams upon encountering an aggressive disintegration (4-5).

[16] Lacan, referring to this concept, affirms: "[It] represents in the patient the imaginary transference onto our person of one of the more or less archaic *imagos*, which by an effect of symbolic subduction, degrades, diverts, or inhibits the cycle of such behavior, which, by an accident of repression, has excluded from the control of the ego this or that function or corporal segment, and which by an action of identification, has given its form to this or that agency of the personality" (14).

Gwendolyn Díaz (essay date 1995)

SOURCE: "Politics of the Body in Luisa Valenzuela's 'Cambio de armas' and 'Simetrías.'" *World Literature Today*, Vol. 69, No. 4 (Autumn 1995): 751-56.

[*Díaz uses Valenzuela's stories to demonstrate relationships among physical, verbal, and influential elements which allow one faction to hold sway over another.*]

At the heart of Luisa Valenzuela's narrative is a deep preoccupation with the use of power, the abuse of power, and the structures of domination which permeate the most basic aspects of our existence. These structures of domination are based on the struggle implied in the idea of politics. What is meant here by politics is the competition between diverse interest groups for power, leadership, and the allocation of value. These structures of domination surface in the politics of the body, the politics of sexuality, the politics of language, and the politics of the state, particularly the authoritarian state. The narrative of Luisa Valenzuela skillfully portrays the interdependence between each of these levels of political exchange and underscores the serious problems embedded in structures of domination and their repercussion from one level of our existence into others.

Valenzuela's two stories **"Cambio de armas"** (1982) and **"Simetrías"** (1993) explore the relationship between body, language, and power, as well as the coercive structures that privilege one gender, social order, or political view over another. Both of the stories, which deal with the plight of female torture victims, take place in Argentina during the period of military dictatorship called the "Dirty War" (1976-83), a period that was euphemistically referred to by the government as the "Proceso de reorganización nacional" (Process of National Reorganization). At this time all civil rights were suspended, and the military dictatorship had free rein to seize anyone suspected of being a subversive. This period of extreme military repression began with the coup of General Jorge Videla, whose main target was the urban guerrillas and leftist organizations responsible for terrorism. However, of the estimated six thousand to twenty thousand *desaparecidos* or "disappeared" victims, relatively few were actually terrorists. (Lewis, 449).

In these two stories the author not only analyzes the repression, subjugation, and violence exerted by the totalitarian regime on its victims, but also shows that this same repression is embedded in the culture through its perceptions of body and gender differences, as well as evident in the language which structures the social order. There-

fore, parallel to the study of the literature, this analysis reviews an evolution of the concept of dominance and subjugation that underlies human relations and is reflected in fiction. In doing so, it briefly focuses on common denominators in the views of G. W. F. Hegel, Jacques Lacan, and Michel Foucault, who offer valuable insight into the psychological, social, and political variables that structure society according to a system of power relationships. Hegel shapes his view of human relations in terms of the master-and-slave dichotomy explained in his *Phenomenology of the Mind* (217-27). The master/slave dialectic suggests that a subject is only conscious of itself when it has before it another consciousness. At this time it comes outside itself and finds itself in the other being. What it wants is the recognition of the other. The two subjects then must prove themselves in what Hegel calls a struggle for life and death in which they risk their life to obtain freedom in the form of the truth of their own being. The outcome of this struggle results in a subject that exists for itself, the master, and a subject that is dependent on the other, the slave.

Lacan, who studied Hegel, views the master/slave dialectic as a rationale for the way in which subjects constitute their gender identity. His reading of the dialectic places the emphasis on desire not so much for recognition, but desire for that which is lacking, which he calls the "object a" or missing object ("Desire," 15-16). What is crucial in Lacan's account of the formation of sexuality is that woman is construed as the one who is lacking. The most obvious lack is that of the male organ (as pointed out by Freud). Lacan explains that what the organ represents is the abstract concept of phallus, which he defines as language, authority, and power. Hence, he suggests, society is structured around a valorization of male discourse as represented in the association between possessing the phallus, possessing the word, and possessing the authority. Hegel's master/slave dialectic and Lacan's theory of the formation of sexuality vis-à-vis the phallus reflect a patriarchal view of society based on dominance and subordination. Woman is viewed as the other of man and as such is perceived (by man) as mystery, lack, and loss. In Hegelian terms, the man is positioned as the master who sees in the other a means of defining himself and his superior value. The woman, on the other hand, is positioned as the slave whose identity is dependent on that of the master and his desires. Lacan's sexual metaphor for the distribution of power within society has been taken to task by feminists such as Irigaray and Kristeva, who have critiqued his thought as implicated in the phallocentric system it describes. Others, such as Rose and Mitchell, have seen Lacan's theories not as a reflection of male supremacy, but as an exposition of the arbitrary nature of both male and female sexual identity.[2]

Whereas Lacan puts emphasis on the power of language to mold and affect our psyche and social relations, Michel Foucault focuses more literally on the body itself, developing a historical account of how the human body has been molded, manipulated, and conceptualized as the site in which power and knowledge exert their control. Lacan's metaphorical reading of the power relations implied in sexual difference takes on a physical and carnal emphasis in Foucault's *History of Sexuality*: "Sexual relations—always conceived in terms of the model act of penetration, assuming a polarity that opposed activity and passivity—were seen as being of the same type as the relationship between a superior and a subordinate, an individual who dominates and one who is dominated, one who commands and one who complies, one who vanquishes and one who is vanquished" (215). Since sexual relations were seen as social rivalries, the active role was valorized over the passive one because of its capacity of dominating, penetrating, and asserting itself.

One of the merits of Valenzuela's narrative is that she is able to create a fictional world which weaves together all these structures of domination to create a pattern that reflects the complex dynamics of an existence based on oppression. In her story **"Cambio de armas"** it becomes evident that authoritarian regimes are a reflection of the sexual and social organization of the culture. The story is constructed as a series of episodes each headed by a title that puts emphasis on a significant object or issue. The fragmented nature of the structure reflects the fragmented nature of the psyche of the protagonist, who has lost her memory and perceives reality only as she experiences it in the present. To her the past is a gap, a deep dark well of forgetfulness which she has repressed in her unconscious. What she has repressed is the fact that she has been apprehended by the colonel she had attempted to kill and that he has become her torturer as well as the abusive lover who uses her as a sexual slave. In the process she has lost her identity, and the colonel, who is called Héctor and later Roque, is reconstructing her identity in terms of what he wants her to be. He has called her Laura and has placed a photograph in the apartment where she is imprisoned, in which she appears in a wedding dress with an absent expression while he stands next to her looking triumphant. Her lack of identity is mirrored in the fact that the man who is supposed to be her husband could be any man to her; she calls him by many different names, not knowing for sure who he really is. This signals the fact that this specific colonel is important not as an individual but as a type, a dominating force, implied in the name with which he signs the wedding photo, Roque (hard like a rock).

The section called "The Mirrors" is a key to understanding the dynamics of the relationship between the torturer and his victim. He and the woman are in bed in a room where the walls and ceiling are covered with mirrors. Her reflection in the mirrors comes back to her "inverted and distant" (114); that is to say, she does not recognize herself as the sexual slave he has made of her. The scene is reminiscent of Lacan's mirror stage, in which the subject constitutes her image of herself as a whole being (*Ecrits*, 4). By seeing herself inverted, the protagonist understands subconsciously that her true self is not the one which she is experiencing in that bed. However, the colonel has chosen precisely the bed as the place to build her identity according to his view. When she closes her eyes, he orders her to open them and commands her to look at what he is about to do. He touches her body as if drawing

her piece by piece, first a leg, then a knee, then a thigh. This action, rather than erotic, implies Roque's perception of her as an object, as a series of body parts defined by him.

The episode brings to mind Hegel's view of the master, who sees the slave as merely another consciousness through which he can validate his superiority. In Lacanian words, man defines woman in terms of his own desire. When the woman once again closes her eyes, the colonel yells at her, calling her a "whore" and ordering her to open her eyes (115). It becomes evident that what he wants is for her to accept his definition of her, to see herself through his eyes, as a mere sex object, a whore. The woman seems to recall another order, her head being kicked in, her arm twisted, a voice commanding her to speak up, to sing, to give the names. This brief flashback is a confused memory of the period in which she was tortured and ordered to confess the names of her accomplices. When she yells "No," her scream is so loud that it "seems to shatter the mirror on the ceiling, that multiplies and maims and destroys his image, almost like a bullet shot" (115). This image recalls her own attempt to kill this colonel and challenge the military regime. In a similar fashion the image shows her desire to confront this man who has humiliated her. The "No" she emits underscores the fact that she has neither confessed the names of her accomplices nor accepted his perception of her as a sex object. Here, as throughout the story, the parallels between structures of domination in the realm of sexuality and those in the realms of language and of politics become intertwined.

In the episode called "The Colleagues" the woman is visited in her apartment by two military colleagues of the colonel. They question her as to her memories, and she realizes she is being interrogated. She is asked about her place of origin, which is Tucumán (a province where guerrilla activity was prominent), about her recollection of a particular bombing, about her health and her back problems (she has a severe scar on her back). Realizing that she has no memories, she feels completely empty, void of identity, and wants to vomit. The colonel stares at her, pleased with his work (119). The scene is a grotesque example of the concept of woman as lack. As in Hegel, the master triumphs over the slave, sublates his identity, and projects his own onto the slave. We encounter also the Lacanian idea of woman as lack and void. In *Encore* Lacan develops the theory that "the woman" does not exist, for the essence of woman cannot be defined except by her lack (69). Again, the cultural image of woman unfolds into the political realm, where the colonel attempts to fill this void which is woman with his own perception of her denigrated status and sexual servility. Nevertheless, the falsity of this assumption is reflected in the falsity of the environment of the apartment. In the apartment that serves as her prison everything is fictitious: a window that does not open, keys that do not work, a wedding photograph she does not recognize, the presence of One and Two (the bodyguards of the colonel), the medications she is forced to take—all this belies the false nature of this construed reality and underscores the falsity of social constructs of gender.

The section titled "The Peephole" reflects how the subject is created through the gaze of others. The colonel possesses the woman in the living room after having opened the peephole in the door to allow his colleagues to watch. He exposes her for all to see in a humiliating and violent act that places her in the position of sexual slave and himself in that of master. What is significant about this scene is that here the colonel flaunts himself in front of the public eye of the peephole. He faces the peephole (and the myriad onlookers it connotes) to "point toward it with his proud erection" (125). By so doing, he is asking to be recognized by the public as a sexual power, a dominant master with the force of a beast. He construes his identity in terms of his dominance and her subjugation. He needs the gaze of others, whose recognition will authenticate the presumed nature of his selfhood.

Hegel's thoughts on the subject's search for recognition of himself in the other and Lacan's views of the gaze of others as constituting the subject's identity (*The Four*, 74-77) come together in this denigrating episode, where both characters have been lowered to the status of animals, one by force and the other by choice. She feels like "an ambushed animal," and he roars and paces the room in a state of excitement. The twisted nature of this scene is reflected in the animal imagery used to describe the situation. She is referred to as a "bitch" while he "bellows" and "roars" like a "caged animal displaying the strength of his dissatisfaction" (126-27). This debasing ritual brings to mind Lacan's analysis of the dynamics of sexual politics: "For the soul to come into being, she, the woman, is differentiated from it . . . called woman and defamed" (*Encore*, 69). Man, hence, equates himself with the soul and denigrates woman, his other, by relegating her to the merely carnal (*Encore*, 69).

In **"Cambio de armas"** the issue of torture is rationalized in terms of a sick patient who needs treatment. The protagonist is referred to as a sick person recovering from an illness and taking medication for both physical and mental ailments. Foucault shows that the illness metaphor has traditionally been used as a way of justifying torture. It is metaphorized as a way of "treating" a criminal viewed as "sick," a "patient" in need of a "cure" (because the act of defiance is considered abnormal or unnatural; *Discipline*, 22). The metaphor of the sick body was also used by the Argentine military, whose authoritarian discourse described the political situation in terms of a nation whose body was "sick" and in need of radical "surgery" to extirpate the diseased parts. The metaphor was used as a rationale in order to justify the extreme measures to which they resorted in the process of "curing" the "infirm" body. The violence to bodies and identities was explained as a necessary means of healing the nation.[3]

In the denouement the colonel learns that he must leave the country, and he wants to tell his victim who he is and who she is so that his victory and revenge will be fulfilled. He tells her that he has broken her as one breaks a horse, that he has taken her apart piece by piece and put her back together again, rebuilding her to suit his whim (134).

He shows her the weapon which was taken from her and tells her that he has weapons too, referring to the sexual torture. Once more we see the idea of woman as a tabula rasa to be molded by the male signifier. The association between the phallus and the weapon indicates the superimposition of sexual domination and political authoritarianism. The story comes to a stop when the woman picks up the revolver and aims at the man's back. The lack of a final resolution (does she or doesn't she shoot?) is a question mark that leads the reader to think further about the structure of dominance. If she shoots him, then she too would be resorting to violence and aggression. If she does not, then she falls into the role of passive victim lacking in power and will. The question mark with which the story ends is an incitement to the reader to reconsider the structures that underlie the politics of relationships.

"Simetrías," the title story in Valenzuela's most recent collection of short fiction (1993), deals even more poignantly with the issue of torture during the "Dirty War." In a recent interview she says that this story is the book's pièce de résistance and that she weaves into it many incidents of female torture which were later revealed as having occurred during the repression. She adds that **"Simetrías"** serves as the other side of the coin, the symmetrical counterpart to **"Cambio de armas."**[4] **"Simetrías"** shares several parallels with the previous story. The protagonist is a female torture victim whose torturer has taken a fancy to her, set her aside for himself, and begun to focus obsessively on her. Also, the character of Héctor Bravo, who has surfaced before in Valenzuela's work (as a doctor and torturer in *Novela negra con argentinos*) and is referred to in **"Cambio de armas"** (where the torturer's name is Héctor before he changes it to Roque), serves in **"Simetrías"** as the narrator. Both stories develop the idea that sexual aggression is mirrored in political aggression, that torture is an extreme and perverted form of domination, and that the memory of the horror must be preserved in order to avoid its recurrence. Other parallels are the development of animal imagery to illustrate bestial tendencies and the recurrence of the military as perpetrator of sadistic acts.

"Simetrías" is structured as a series of monologues that alternate between the torturer and his victim and are strung together by means of the viewpoint of the narrator, Héctor Bravo, who relates the similarities between incidents that took place in 1947 and those taking place in 1977. The narrative set in 1947 (at the time of Perón's first presidency) focuses on a relationship between a woman who goes to the Buenos Aires zoo and an orangutan caged in that same zoo. Little by little, the woman and the orangutan become fascinated with each other. The orangutan takes on human characteristics and is said to have fallen in love with the woman, who in turn loses her composure and becomes animal-like. The woman's husband is a colonel who realizes he has been cuckolded by an animal and takes out his revolver to shoot the beast. Thirty years later, in 1977, during the height of the military repression in Argentina, another colonel tortures his female prisoner (a captured subversive) on the metal table of the dark, dank quarters of a hidden detention center, close to the Buenos Aires zoo. He has become obsessed with this particular woman and takes sadistic pleasure in torturing her by day and escorting her out on the town at night. An elaborate complex of associations is developed among these four figures: the female prisoner, the orangutan, the torturer, and the woman in the zoo. The torturer's obsession with the prisoner is mirrored in the obsession between the woman in the zoo and the caged orangutan.

The story reveals the sick relationship that forms between the torturer and his victim, while allowing the reader to witness the thoughts of both as exposed in the monologues. The discourse of the torturers reflects their belief in the fact that they possess the right to break these women in order to punish them for having dared to subvert the authority of the state: "Gloriosamente es como nosotros las matamos, por la gloria y el honor de la patria" (Gloriously is how we kill them, for the glory and honor of our fatherland [177]). Andrés Avellaneda's book on authoritarianism and culture presents a well-developed analysis of the discourse of the authoritarian regime in the specific case of Argentina in the years 1960-83. He explains that the discourse centered on establishing the government as the legitimate savior of the nation and its people, and to do so it developed a manipulative discourse that focused on upholding morals, sexual customs, religion, and national security (19-22). The female subversives were seen as particularly offensive because they dared to subvert not only the political order but also the sexual order; hence the sexual emphasis on female torture: "Las mujeres que están en nuestro poder . . . han perdido sus nombres . . . y saben dejarse atravesar porque nos hemos encargado de ablandarlas" (The women in our power have lost their names . . . they know how to let themselves be penetrated because we have taken charge of softening them [174]). The concept of "penetration" is later associated with that of the "word," which is seen as penetrating like a "bullet" (174). The phallus as signifier inscribes in the woman the structure of domination implicit in the patriarchal symbolic order and reflected in the association between the word, the phallus, and the bullet.

The tortured women have had their names and their senses stripped away from them. They are described as not being able to see (a reference to the blindfolds put on them when they were being tortured), as having an absent look in their eyes, as being mute or as having nothing but a "fine thread of a voice" left (175). These broken women are seen as empty receptacles for the inscribing power of the torturers: "Les metemos cosas mucho más tremendas que las nuestras porque esas cosas son también una prolongación de nosotros mismos y porque ellas son nuestras. Las mujeres" (We stick things in them that are many times more tremendous than ours because those things are also an extension of our very own selves and because they are ours. The women [176]). After stripping the women of their identity, the torturers literally "fill" them with new meaning, the meaning of terror and violence embedded in the structure they attempted to subvert. Foucault's comments on torture as a mechanism of inscribing the pa-

rameters of power show that, historically, the torture victim had to have his punishment "inscribed" on his body so that it would be "legible to all," making the guilty person the "herald of his own condemnation" (*Discipline*, 42). The victim walked through the streets in a procession wearing a placard that stated his or her crime as a way of "publishing" that crime (43). The linguistic metaphor illustrates the association between the body and a page on which the ruler publishes his own order. This underscores Lacan's perception that the phallic order structures society as well as Hegel's perception that human relations are based on dominance and subjugation. It also gives insight into the sexual nature of torture, in that the woman's act of subversion is considered a threat not only to the political structure but to the patriarchal organization of society as well.

In Valenzuela's story the crime of the victims is published through the grotesque charade of taking them out to dinner at night. The monologues of the women relate that the torturers dress them up in beautiful clothes, being careful to hide their scars, and take them out to eat. However, they can hardly taste the food because their dresses press so painfully on their thorax, and the torturers soon reinstitute them into the horror and make them vomit what they have eaten (173). Later one learns that these women have been taken out to show that the torturers have a power that is even more absolute and incontestable than the power of humiliation and punishment (179). That greater power is the power to break the human spirit and make a public display of it.

However, the torturers do not always succeed. In this story, as in **"Cambio de armas,"** they have failed to extract a confession from their victims. As Foucault points out, one of the aims of torture is to force a confession from the criminal in order to make him acknowledge the established order as "true" as well as provide knowledge of accomplices (35-40). The issue of confession is a crucial one in both stories, because the female victims have refused to confess anything at all to the torturers. The fact that the prisoners neither confess nor give up the names of any accomplices denotes, in a sense, their triumph and the failure of the torturers to extract any useful admissions or information.

The animal imagery alluded to in **"Cambio de armas"** is developed more fully in **"Simetrías."** Here the author develops a contrast between the human who is more savage than the beast and the beast that is more humane than the human. Héctor Bravo is obsessed with two occurrences: one is the sadistic relationship between the colonel and his prisoner; the other is the sexual attraction he witnesses earlier between the woman in the zoo and the orangutan. Bravo superimposes these two occurrences and often confuses them. During one of the woman's visits with the orangutan, they stare at each other through the bars of the cage and the once simple and comical animal is no longer the same; he looks at her with the eyes of a human in love (178). She, on the other hand, has become tattered and alienated, with the air of someone who lives in the jungle (181).

The second focal point of Bravo's obsession is the relationship between the colonel and his captive. The colonel, whose actions toward his victim are extremely savage, becomes so fascinated with her that he thinks he has fallen in love with her. He is no longer torturing her for the sake of the nation but realizes in her a sadistic passion that he construes as love. In a sense, his feelings for her seem to have softened him. When his superiors realize this, they send him away to Europe so that they can kill the woman. Conversely, his prisoner is described in terms of an animal. The colonel has ordered an expensive necklace for her, a tight choker that looks a bit like a dog collar, and a snakeskin belt he fancies as a leash with which he could walk her all over the world (183). The association between the caged orangutan and the captive woman reaches its peak in a grotesque scene in which the victim is being tortured with an electric cattle prod; in the same sentence her spasms are compared to the jerky movements of the orangutan who expresses his attraction for the woman in the zoo (181). The orangutan couple act as a parody of the other couple, reflecting the perverted nature of each relationship.

In the final lines of the story the two time periods appear to have become one and the same in the mind of Héctor Bravo. The bullet that kills the orangutan and the one that kills the torture victim also seem to be one and the same (187). The story ends by relating that when the two lovers return to the site of their desire, the woman to the zoo and the colonel from Europe, they find their respective cages empty and are stricken by terror and hate (187). Of the other two, the prisoner and the orangutan, we learn that they both die as a result of being loved too much.

Two hypotheses come to mind regarding the symmetries implied in this tale. First, in the symmetry reflected in the juxtaposition of the two couples we see that the zoo woman's desire for the orangutan has humanized the beast and that the beast's desire for her has animalized her. Similarly, the bestial colonel seems to acquire something akin to what he construes as the human ability to love, while the prisoner (who never does acknowledge him) is given animal characteristics attributed to her by the colonel. Each lover has become caged into the relationship. Each is trapped in his or her own desire for the other. These two examples suggest the Lucanian notion that the subject is trapped by the structure of its desire. They also show that people are the victims of their own passions as well as of the passions of others.

The second symmetry is that of the historical times. In 1947 Juan Perón had been president for a year. During that time, the police-state instruments which had been developed earlier (control of political activity by the police, almost unlimited power to search and detain, the use of torture) were all institutionalized (Weisman, 89). In 1977 the repressive mechanisms of the government ballooned into what became a war against its own citizens; hence the name "Dirty War." History came full circle, repeating the violence and oppression embedded in the system. As suggested in a passage that equates the screams of the torture victims with those of archaic wounded animals in the depths of Paleolithic caverns (182), the story shows that violence and domination have existed for ages and that they continue to surface in a world which exists under the illusion of being civilized.

Valenzuela does not offer any facile solutions to the recurring incidents of the abuse of power. What she does is effectively expose the acts of terror and the mechanisms of dominance and subjugation that permeate our sexual relationships and overlap into our sociolinguistic and political structures. The reader is challenged to give thought to these dilemmas and to take consciousness of the paradigms that mold our world and structure our psyche. Neither Hegel's master-and-slave dichotomy, nor Lacan's phallic order, nor Foucault's politics of the body reflects constructive paradigms. The challenge to all of us is not only to denounce these systems, as Valenzuela does, but also to actively deconstruct them in order to reconstruct a more humane way of relating to one another.

NOTES

[1] This quote by Hebe Bonafini, a *madre de la Plaza de Maya*, is from the *New York Times* article by Calvin Sims, "Argentine Tells of Dumping 'Dirty War' Captives into Sea," 13 March 1995, p. A1.

[2] *Feminine Sexuality: Jacques Lacan and the Ecole Freudienne*, eds. Juliet Mitchell and Jacqueline Rose, New York, Norton, 1982.

[3] Guillermo O'Donnell, "Tensions in the Bureaucratic-Authoritarian State and the Question of Democracy," *The New Authoritarianism in Latin America*, ed. David Collier, Princeton (N.J.), Princeton University Press, 1979.

[4] Gwendolyn Díaz, interview with Luisa Valenzuela, Emory University, Atlanta, November 1994.

FURTHER READING

Ainsa, Fernando. "Journey to Luisa Valenzuela's Land of Fear." *World Literature Today*, Vol. 69, No. 4 (Autumn 1995): 683-90.

> Discusses the nature of fear, individual and collective, in Valenzuela's writing.

Christoph, Nancy. "Bodily Matters: The Female Grotesque in Luisa Valenzuela's *Cola de lagartija*." *Revista Hispanica Moderna*, Vol. XLVIII, No. 2 (December 1995): 365-80.

> Points out the author's use of the female grotesque to challenge pervasive male control in society.

Cox, Victoria. "Political and Social Alienation in Valenzuela's *Novela negra con argentinos*." *Letras Femeninas*, Vol. XXIII, Nos. 1-2 (1997): 71-7.

> Examines Valenzuela's treatment of exile and estrangement.

Craig, Linda. "Women and Language: Luisa Valenzuela's *El gato eficaz*." *Feminist Readings on Spanish and Latin-American Literature*, L. P. Conde and S. M. Hart, eds., pp. 151-60. Lewiston, N.Y.: The Edwin Mellen Press, 1991.

Assesses the accepted role of women in society as indicated through language.

Dash, Robert C. "An Interview with Luisa Valenzuela." *Chasqui*, Vol. XXI, No. 1 (May 1992): 101-05.

Focuses on feminism, writing, politics, and society.

Kerr, Lucille. "Novels and 'Noir' in New York." *World Literature Today*, Vol. 69, No. 4 (Autumn 1995): 733-39.

Considers the mystery elements in *Novela negra con argentinos*.

Lagos, Maria Ines. "Displaced Subjects: Valenzuela and the Metropolis." *World Literature Today*, Vol. 69, No. 4 (Autumn, 1995): 726-32.

Concentrates on "decenteredness" and its repercussions.

Magnarelli, Sharon. "The Spectacle of Reality in Luisa Valenzuela's *Realidad nacional vista desde la cama*." *Letra Femeninas*, Vol. XIX, Nos. 1-2 (1993): 65-73.

Analyzes the "bi-directional" nature of the text.

———. "*Simetrias*: 'Mirror, Mirror, on the Wall . . .'" *World Literature Today*, Vol. 69, No. 4 (Autumn 1995): 717-25.

Likens stories in *Simetrias* to fairy tales: political and didactic.

———. "The New Novel / A New Novel: Spider's Webs and Detectives in Luisa Valenzuela's *Black Novel (with Argentines*.)" *Studies in Twentieth Century Literature*, Vol. 19, No. 1 (Winter 1995): 43-60.

Indicates that in this novel, captivity permits the exploration of human nature.

Martinez, Victoria. "In Search of the Word: Performance in Luisa Valenzuela's *Novela negra con argentinos*." *Chasqui*, Vol. XXIII, No. 2 (November 1994): 54-65.

Takes a theatrical approach to *Novela negra*.

Martinez, Z. Nelly. "Dangerous Messianisms: The World According to Valenzuela." *World Literature Today*, Vol. 69, No. 4 (Autumn 1995): 697-701.

Relates language to the repression and authoritarianism characteristic of paternalistic society.

Marting, Diane E. "Gender and Metaphoricity in Luisa Valenzuela's 'I'm Your Horse in the Night'." *World Literature Today*, Vol. 69, Vol. 4 (Autumn 1995): 702-08.

Weighs the implications and challenges of interpreting Valenzuela's multi-layered narratives.

Metzger, Mary Janell. "'Oedipal with a Vengeance': Narrative, Desire, and Violence in Luisa Valenzuela's 'Fourth Version'." *Tulsa Studies in Women's Literature*, Vol. 14, No. 2 (Fall 1995): 295-307.

Notes the elements of multiplicity in "Fourth Version."

Morello-Frosch, Marta. "The Subversion of Ritual in Luisa Valenzuela's *Other Weapons*." *World Literature Today*, Vol. 69, No. 4 (Autumn 1995): 691-96.

Outlines ways in which Valenzuela restructures ritual, thereby modifying its social context.

Mouat, Ricardo Gutierrez. "Luisa Valenzuela's Literal Writing." *World Literature Today*, Vol. 69, No. 4 (Autumn 1995): 709-16.

Surveys Valenzuela's uses of literal and figurative language.

Perricone, Catherine R. "Valenzuela's *Novela negra con argentinos*: a Metafictional Game." *Romance Notes*, Vol. XXXVI, No. 3 (Spring 1996): 237-42.

Demonstrates Valenzuela's use of metafiction in her search for "the key to literary creativity."

Additional coverage of Valenzuela's life and career is contained in the following sources published by the Gale Group: *Contemporary Authors*, **Vol. 101;** *Contemporary Authors New Revision Series*, **Vols. 32, 65;** *Contemporary Literature Criticism*, **Vols. 31, 104;** *Dictionary of Literary Biography*, **Vol. 113;** *DISCovering Multicultural America*; *Hispanic Writers*; *Short Story Criticism*, **Vol. 14.**

Lope de Vega
1562-1635

(Full name Lope Félix de Vega y Carpio) Spanish playwright, poet, novelist, short story writer, and critic.

INTRODUCTION

Acclaimed by Miguel Cervantes as a "prodigy of nature," Lope de Vega is acknowledged as one of the greatest Spanish dramatists and poets, as well as probably the most prolific writer the world has ever seen. Singlehandedly, he gave precise form to the *comedia* (full-length secular play), thus initiating the flowering of Spanish Golden Age drama which lasted from the 1580s to the 1680s. Lope elaborated upon the technical devices of medieval drama to produce an effective dramatic form known for its swiftly paced action, graceful plotting, witty dialogue, and emotive lyricism. His *comedias* reflect the history and concerns of Spanish society and focus on such themes as patriotism, love, honor, and religion. By his own estimation, Lope wrote over fifteen hundred dramatic works in addition to prose fiction and a large body of lyric poetry. His oeuvre is characterized by a high level of quality that made the phrase "It is by Lope" a byword denoting excellence.

The son of a craftsman in Madrid who wrote poetry and was passionately religious, Lope was an intellectually precocious boy who was said to have translated Latin poetry at the age of five and to have written his first play, *El verdante amante*, at twelve. During the years 1574-76 he studied at the Jesuit Theatine college in Madrid; subsequently, he worked in the household of the Bishop of Avila, where he is thought to have composed his early plays, and at the same time studied literature at the University of Alcalá de Hernares. In 1583 he began his career, spanning nearly fifty years, as a professional dramatist. That same year he conducted an adulterous affair with Elena Osorio, the heroine of his dramatic novel *La Dorotea* (1632) and the model for the character Filis in his pastoral ballads. At this time, Lope also served on a naval expedition to quell rebellion in the Azores. Upon his return to Madrid, he achieved notoriety as a brawler and philanderer. While continuing his affair with Elena, Lope succeeded in having several of his plays staged by her father, an influential impresario. After composing venomous diatribes against Elena's family, who deplored Lope's amorous advances, the dramatist was arrested in 1588 and banished to Valencia for eight years. Within several months he illegally returned to Madrid and eloped with the seventeen-year-old Isabel de Urbina, who appears as Belisa in much of his poetry. Shortly after their marriage, Lope joined the Spanish Armada, later recording the experience of defeat at the hands of the English in his epic poem on Sir Francis Drake, *La Dragontea* (1598).

In 1589 Lope returned to exile in Valencia with his wife. He quickly achieved eminence among dramatists there and became secretary to the Duke of Alba in the following year. At this time, Lope embarked on a period of vigorous poetic production that lasted until the deaths of his wife and two daughters in the years 1594-96. He returned to Madrid where he initiated two affairs and married the daughter of a wealthy butcher. Following the death of his second wife in 1613, Lope underwent a period of religious upheaval and entered the priesthood, vowing to lead a life of celibacy. However, he continued to have affairs with married women, one of whom, Marta de Nevares, bore him a daughter in 1617. During these years, Lope's fame as a dramatist was at its height both in Spain and abroad. In 1627 Pope Urban VIII awarded him an honorary doctorate in theology and the cross of the Order of St. John of Jerusalem. Despite such recognition, Lope's popularity was slightly eclipsed by the new generation of playwrights, especially Pedro Calderón de la Barca. Moreover, his personal life was beset by such concerns as Marta's gradual blindness, insanity, and death, and by the elopement of their daughter. After a period of declining health, which nevertheless did not impede his creative vigor, he died in 1635 and was publicly mourned by nobles and commoners alike.

Spanish drama of the late sixteenth century had evolved from a variety of influences, including medieval religious theater—a popular theatrical tradition employing stock characters—and pastoral pieces modelled on Latin and Italian literature, which were performed in aristocratic households. Eventually, full-length plays were written that were divided into several acts, composed in a variety of metrical forms, and patterned after Roman drama as perceived by writers of the Italian Renaissance. In his poetic treatise *Arte nuevo de hacer comedias en este tiempo* (1609; *The New Art of Writing Plays*) Lope expounded his dramaturgical method, stating that his *comedias* are based on an assimilation and refinement of classical rules and the Spanish popular tradition. He further asserted that the action of the *comedia* should be confined to three acts encompassing exposition, complication, and denouement respectively. Lope also explored in detail which of the Spanish and Italian meters are most appropriate for specific dramatic purposes. In opposition to the highly stylized and allusive poetic style of Luis de Góngora, Lope de Vega eschewed baroque conceits and effects, and developed an expressive metaphorical method of exposition aimed at capturing the richness of everyday life.

Some 450 of Lope's plays have survived. In addition to the *comedias*, they include *autos sacramentales* (single-act allegories for the Feast of Corpus Christi) and nativity plays. Scholars typically group the *comedias* under several genre headings, including religious plays, pastoral dramas, plays depicting mythological subjects, historical dramas, cloak-and-sword plays, and novelesque plays. Lope's religious plays treat Old and New Testament themes as well as the lives of the saints and traditional pious legends. The pastoral plays reflect the Italian Renaissance fashion of bucolic literature and focus on the attainment of love in an idyllic setting. Frequently derived from Ovid's *Metamorphoses*, the mythological plays are atypical of Lope's *comedias* in that they are closely modelled after classical versification and Renaissance aesthetic principles. The historical plays number some of Lope's most highly regarded works, including *Peribáñez y el comendador de Ocaña* (1605-12) and *Fuenteovejuna* (1612-14). They are often taken from historical narratives or contemporary events and interweave subplots concerning love with primary actions expressing the ideals of honor and nationalism. The cloak-and-sword plays are among Lope's most popular works and present elaborate plots of intrigue and adventure driven by jealousy and revenge. The novelesque plays are derived from Italian *novelle* and medieval European and Byzantine tales portraying the ideals of Platonic love and Christian chivalry. *Castelvines y Monteses* (1606-12), for example, is based on a novel by Matteo Bandello which also served as the basis for Shakespeare's *Romeo and Juliet*. Unlike his Elizabethan contemporary, however, Lope provided the story with a happy ending.

Considered one of Lope's most perfect works, *El castigo sin venganza* (1631; *Justice without Revenge*) is another novelesque play derived from Bandello. The plot concerns a philandering duke who arranges the deaths of his newly married wife and his illegitimate son upon discovery of their affair. In this *comedia*, Lope provides one of his most ironic and searching explorations of the themes of private vengeance and public justice. Critics have praised Lope's deft handling of the complex action of this play as well as his sensitive treatment of the moral implications of honor, revenge, and adulterous love.

The two historical plays *Peribáñez* and *Fuenteovejuna* have received particular attention from twentieth-century critics and audiences. *Peribáñez* is set in the reign of King Henry III, early in the fifteenth century, and concerns the wealthy and clever peasant, Peribáñez, who is forced to kill the lord of the town of Ocaña in order to safeguard his wife's honor. At the play's end, the king ennobles Peribáñez, declaring his killing of an aristocrat justified. Praised for its well-wrought plot and graceful poetic language, *Peribáñez* is also noted for the acute depiction of the contrasting worlds of the aristocracy and the peasantry. Similarly, *Fuenteovejuna* is set in the fifteenth century and focuses on the collective vengeance exacted by the rural community of Fuenteovejuna on their malevolent and rapacious overlord. In keeping with the aesthetic precepts expressed in his *The New Art of Writing Plays*, Lope uses seven verse forms in this play to produce exceptionally striking and luxurious poetry that serves to portray individual characters as well as a variety of viewpoints on the nature of good government.

Many scholars and critics regard Lope de Vega as one of the finest lyric poets in Western culture. They have noted that whereas Renaissance poets tended to explore the themes of Platonism and courtly love in a distant and abstract manner, Lope's secular poetry resonates with the experiences of his turbulent life and presents the women he loved as fully-realized beings. Stating that "poetry must cost great trouble to the poet, but little to the reader," Lope sought to create a tasteful balance of ideas, syntax, feeling, and movement. His *Rimas Sacras* (1614) reveal him to have been an equally fine religious poet. The collection contains a cycle of twenty-eight ballads which relate, often in excruciating detail, the Passion and Death of Christ.

Lope's few prose works reveal the same autobiographical element present in his secular poetry. His novellas, for example, are typically engaging bucolic tales in the vein of Menippean satire which have been described as love letters written solely for the entertainment of his mistress Marta de Nevares. More serious is the late work *La Dorotea*, which Lope called "action in prose." In this novel, presented in dialogue form in five acts, Lope recreates his early affair with Elena Osorio and produces what Leo Spitzer has called a masterpiece of "the literarizing of life."

In the twentieth century Lope de Vega's plays have frequently been translated and staged in Europe and North America, and have influenced such dramatists as Federico García Lorca, Albert Camus, and Thornton Wilder. While scholars and critics have universally acknowledged Lope's pioneering significance in the history of Spanish drama, his stature has occasionally been the subject of debate. Gerald Brenan, for example, has faulted Lope as a dramatist, arguing that his plays fail to achieve depth in their portrayal of human nature and that "there is no play or group of plays that one can point to in which he has condensed his gifts." Others, such as Bruce W. Wardropper, have regarded Lope as "above all a great poet—one who wrote, among the several kinds of poetry, dramatic poetry." Most critics, however, would concur with Ezra Pound that Lope de Vega's vast achievement defies systematic assessment: "Lope is like ten brilliant minds inhabiting one body. An attempt to enclose him in any formula is like trying to make one pair of boots to fit a centipede."

PRINCIPAL WORKS

Los hechos de Garcilaso de la Vega y el moro Tarfe (drama) 1579-83
Los locos de Valencia (drama) 1590-95
El caballero de milagro (drama) 1593-98
La Hermosura de Angelica, con otras diversas rimas, etc. [*La Dragontea*], 3 vols. (poetry) 1602
Peribáñez y el comendador de Ocaña [*Peribáñez*] (drama) 1605-12
Castelvines y Monteses (drama) 1606-12

Arte nuevo de hacer comedias en este tiempo [*The New Art of Writing Plays*] (criticism) 1609

Fuenteovejuna [*Fuente Ovejuna*] (drama) 1612-14

La dama boba [*The Idiot Lady*] (drama) 1613

El perro del hortelano [*The Dog in the Manger*] (drama) 1613

Rimas Sacras (poetry) 1614

El mejor alcalde, el rey [*The King the Greatest Alcalde*] (drama) 1620-23

El caballero de Olmedo [*The Knight from Olmedo*] (drama) 1622

La Estrella de Sevilla [*The Star of Seville*] (drama) c.1623

Novelas a la señora Marcia Leonarda (novellas) 1624

El castigo sin venganza [*Justice without Revenge*] (drama) 1631

La Dorotea (novel) 1632

La mayor virtud de un rey (drama) 1634

Obras de Lope de Vega, 15 vols. (drama, poetry, prose) 1890-1913

CRITICISM

George Henry Lewes (essay date 1846)

SOURCE: "Lope de Vega," in *Great Short Biographies of the World: A Collection of Short Biographies, Literary Portraits, and Memoirs Chosen from the Literatures of the Ancient and Modern World*, Barrett H. Clark, ed. Robert M. McBride & Company, 1928, pp. 572-601.

[*Lewes was one of the most versatile men of letters in the Victorian era. A prominent English journalist, he co-founded, with Leigh Hunt of* The Leader, *a radical political journal which he also edited from 1851 to 1854. He served as the first editor of the* Fortnightly Review *from 1865 to 1866, a journal which he also helped to establish. Critics often cite Lewes's influence on the novelist George Eliot, to whom he was companion and mentor, as his principal contribution to English letters, but they also credit him with critical acumen in his literary commentary, most notably in his dramatic criticism. In the following excerpt from his pioneering study* The Spanish Drama: Lope de Vega and Calderón (1846), *Lewes provides a favorable assessment of Lope's career, maintaining that he "not only far outstripped his rivals in the excellence of his comedies, but also in their fertility."*]

From the circumstances of his position [Lope de Vega] was forced to write in accordance with the public taste; and fortunate for him, and for his art, were the circumstances which forced this. I mean fortunate, inasmuch as they gave birth to a genuine national drama instead of a feeble imitation of antiquity. For it is only pedants who can consider him as the corrupter of the Spanish stage. On the other hand it may be supposed that had his genius been greater or his necessities less, he might have founded a national drama of a still higher character. Let us turn our eyes towards Molière. In his time the farces and improvised plays which delighted the crowd were even still less artistic than the plays which delighted the Spanish public when Lope de Vega appeared. Yet Molière created French comedy. He had to clear the stage of its masks and improvised buffooneries, and to substitute *character* and wit. On the first representation of *Les Précieuses Ridicules*, an old man in the pit, charmed with this novelty, cried out to Molière, who was playing Mascarille: "Bravo, Molière! take courage! that is true comedy!" At this cry, which he foresaw would be the real expression of the public sentiment, Molière felt his heart expand, and he let fall this pregnant remark: "I have now only to study mankind." He did so; and a series of immortal works attest his earnestness and power.

Lope de Vega was not a Molière. But he did that which lay in his power. He could not give a new direction to comedy; but in following the route chalked out for him by predecessors he founded a national drama, and became the idol of the public. In truth those who had written before him had produced but miserable works in comparison with those which he so rapidly threw off. Even the great Cervantes was thrown into the shade. His works, which have been lost, were greatly superior to those of his contemporaries; but they sank into insignificance beside the works of the young Lope; and he retired from all contest with this "prodigy of nature and phœnix of intelligence," as he called him. He yielded the throne to Lope, as in later times Scott yielded the throne to the impetuous Byron, who remained

Sole Napoleon of the realms of rhyme.

Cervantes retired to lay up stores, and meditate the composition of the greatest romance ever written—the First Part of *Don Quixote*.

It is curious, with our present knowledge and estimate of the two men, to think of Cervantes as inferior to Lope de Vega; not simply inferior in popularity, but also in dramatic talent. A lurking doubt must present itself as to whether, if the plays were extant, we should not find in them evidences of a far higher genius than was ever manifested by the Spanish phœnix. But this is hasty surmise. If we had not the poems of Shakspere to contradict the opinion, we should assuredly imagine that the poems of the author of the *Midsummer Night's Dream* surpassed anything in Spenser or Milton; but with the poems before us we cannot entertain the notion. So would it be with the comedies of Cervantes, were they extant. We may admit, as incontestable, that Cervantes was a man of greater genius than Lope de Vega; but it by no means follows that he had greater theatrical talent; it by no means follows that his faculties were so early matured as to have enabled him to surpass his rival at that period. Many a genius has been slow of growth. Oaks that flourish for a thousand years do not spring up into beauty like a reed. The excellence of Lope de Vega was not, like that of Cervantes, one demanding time for maturity, one demanding abundant materials difficult of mastery. To write plays of intrigue, such as his, he needed only a knowledge of manners and the elementary passions, with a quick perception of the requisites of the stage. With such food, a fanciful and ingenious intellect, stimulated by inexhaustible animal spirits, could produce masterpieces of this kind at an early age. To write *Don Quixote* other preparations were necessary. It required a profound and varied knowledge of mankind, founded on a minute and patient observation of moral complexities, and a clear insight into the sway exercised over our passions by our interests, and over our interests by our passions. In a word, Cervantes needed a rich psychological experience; not such knowledge as is written down in books, but such as is in action in the heads and hearts of men. Beyond this, he needed a complete and artistic mastery of his knowledge, so that he might reproduce it in the most harmonious form. A boy of twenty, with the requisite ability, could have written the best play by Lope de Vega; the same boy could not even have *understood Don Quixote* in all that constitutes its surpassing excellence. It was not until his fiftieth year, after a life wherein meditation and action held equal sway, that Cervantes commenced his immortal work. It was in his twelfth year that Lope wrote his first comedy; it was in his twenty-sixth that he was pronounced the Spanish phœnix.

There is no inconsistency then in supposing Cervantes inferior to the young Lope, and forced to yield him place. He was slowly growing while Lope was in full vigour. Nor would he have ever equalled Lope in theatrical excellence: his genius lay elsewhere. I assume this on the ground of his inferiority to Lope de Vega in those plays which he wrote after Lope had given him a model; the plays I mean published by Blas Nazarre. Hear what Cervantes himself says of them:

> Some years since I returned to the ancient occupation of my leisure hours, and imagining that the age had not passed away in which I used to hear the sound of praise, I again began to write comedies. The birds, however, had flown from their nest. I could find no manager to ask for my plays, though they knew that I had written them. I threw them, therefore, into the corner of a trunk, and condemned them to eternal obscurity. A bookseller then told me that he would have bought them from me had he not been told by a celebrated author that much dependence might be placed upon my prose, but none upon my poetry. To say the truth, this information mortified me much. I said to myself: "Certainly I am either changed, or the world, contrary to its custom, has become much wiser, for in past times I used to meet with praise." I read my comedies anew, together with some interludes which I had placed with them. I found that they were not so bad but that they might pass from what this author called darkness into what others may perhaps term noonday. I was angry, and sold them to the bookseller, who has now printed them. They have paid me tolerably, and I have pocketed my money with pleasure, and without troubling myself about the opinions of the actors. I was willing to make them as excellent as I could; and if, dear reader, thou findest anything good in them, I pray thee, when thou meetest any other calumniator, to tell him to amend his manners and not to judge so severely, since, after all, the plays contain not any incongruities or striking faults.

Now the plays thus spoken of, and which are said to contain no striking faults—no incongruities—are so bad, that the paradoxical and stupid admirer of Cervantes, Blas Nazarre, conceives them to have been written with the same purpose of exposing the irregularities and absurdities of the dramatists, as *Don Quixote* of exposing the follies of the romance writers: "Cervantes compusó sus comedias con la misma idea que el *Quijote*, haciéndolas de intento desarragladas y llenas de desatinos, á fin de purgar del mal gusto y mala moral el teatro." But this is preposterous. The satire in *Don Quixote* is transparent; in the comedies no one but Nazarre could suspect it. Besides, Cervantes tell us himself that he wrote the plays for representation, and thinks them worthy of it. Had he meant them as satires he would have taken pains to forewarn the public; the more so as they had been denied performance. In our days, when a tragedy is refused at every theatre, the author publishes it with a declaration that it is "meant for the closet."

I cannot bring these two great names together without endeavouring to settle the ill-conducted dispute respecting the opinion entertained of these men by each other. Some biographers and critics declare them to have been unjust towards each other. Others declare them to have been magnanimously courteous. Both sides have texts to quote; but both are wrong. The truth is that although occasional jealousies may have been excited, and harsh words have escaped during moments of irritation, these two men were fully aware of each other's greatness.

"Wherever Cervantes has mentioned the poet," says Lord Holland,

> in his printed works, he has spoken of his genius not only with respect, but admiration. It is true that he implies that his better judgment occasionally yielded to the temptation of immediate profit, and that he sometimes sacrificed his permanent fame to fleeting popularity with the comedians and the public. But in saying this, he says little more than Lope himself has repeatedly acknowledged; and throughout his works he speaks of him in a manner which, if Lope had possessed discernment enough to have perceived the real superiority of Cervantes, would have afforded him as much pleasure as the slight mixture of censure seems to have given him concern. The admirers, or rather the adorers of Lope, who had christened him the Phœnix of Spain, were very anxious to crush the reputation of Cervantes. With this view they excited rivals on whom they lavished extravagant praises; they at one time decried novels and romances, and at another extolled all those who wrote them, except the one who was most deserving of their praise. If the sonnet published by Pellicer in the Life prefixed to *Don Quixote* be genuine, Cervantes was at length provoked to attack more directly the formidable reputation of their idol. In this sonnet, which contains a sort of play upon words, by the omission of the last syllable of each, that cannot be translated, the works of Lope were somewhat severely handled; a sonnet compiled in four languages from various authors is ridiculed; the expediency of a sponge is suggested; and he is above all advised not to pursue his Jerusalem Conquistada, a work upon which he was then employed. Lope, who parodied the sonnet of Cervantes, rejected his advice, and published that

epic poem, in which his failure is generally acknowledged even by his most fervent admirers.

Lope retaliated; nor can we wonder at it. But only excessive irritation could have made him speak of *Don Quixote* as waste paper fit for enveloping spices, saffron dye, etc.

> Por el mundo va
> vendiendo especias, y azafran romi,
> y al fin en muladares parara.

This was, however, only a spurt of temper. When in his *Laurel de Apolo* he comes to chronicle his serious opinion of Cervantes, he speaks magnificently of him, and touchingly alluding to the arm Cervantes lost at Lepanto, says:

> ——————que una mano herida
> pudo dar a su dueño eterna vida.

"That single hand has given to its master eternal life." And Cervantes, on a similar occasion (in the *Viage de Parnaso*), says of his rival:

> Distinguished bard, whom no one of our time
> Could pass or equal in his prose or rhyme.

I need quote no more.

Lope de Vega not only far outstripped his rivals in the excellence of his comedies, but also in their fertility. No writer ever approached him in rapidity. There has been much exaggeration on this point; and one would think that biographers had pledged themselves to make the marvellous incredible, so resolutely do they exaggerate. Lord Holland, who suspected the truth of some of the Spanish estimates, was not altogether free from an excess of credulity. "Twenty-one million three hundred thousand of his lines," says he,

> are said to be actually printed; and no less than eighteen hundred plays of his composition to have been acted on the stage. He nevertheless asserts in one of his last poems, that

> *The printed part, though far too large, is less Than that which yet unprinted waits the press.*

It is true that the Castilian language is copious; that the verses are often extremely short, and that the laws of metre and of rhyme are by no means severe. Yet were we to give credit to such accounts, allowing him to begin his compositions at the age of thirteen, we must believe that upon an average he wrote more than nine hundred lines a day; a fertility of imagination, and a celerity of pen, which, when we consider the occupations of his life as a soldier, a secretary, a master of a family, and a priest; his acquirements in Latin, Italian, and Portuguese; and his reputation for erudition; become not only improbable, but absolutely, and, one may almost say, physically impossible.

As the credibility, however, of miracles must depend upon the weight of evidence, it will not be foreign to the purpose to examine the testimonies we possess of this extraordinary facility and exuberance of composition. There does not now exist the fourth part of the works which he and his admirers mention; yet enough remains to render him one of the most voluminous authors that ever put pen to paper. Such was his facility, that he informs us in his **Eclogue to Claudio**, that more than a hundred times he composed a play and produced it on the stage in twenty-four hours. Montalvan declares that he latterly wrote in metre with as much rapidity as in prose, and in confirmation of it relates the following story:

> "His pen was unable to keep pace with his mind, as he invented even more than his hand was capable of transcribing. He wrote a comedy in two days, which it would not be very easy for the most expeditious amanuensis to copy out in the time. At Toledo he wrote fifteen acts in fifteen days, which make five comedies. These he read at a private house, where Maestro Joseph de Valdebieso was present and was witness of the whole; but because this is variously related, I will mention what I myself know from my own knowledge. Roque de Figueroa, the writer for the theatre at Madrid, was at such a loss for comedies that the doors of the theatre de la Cruz were shut; but as it was in the Carnival, he was so anxious upon the subject that Lope and myself agreed to compose a joint comedy as fast as possible. It was the **Tercera Orden de San Francisco**, and is the very one in which Arias acted the part of the saint more naturally than was ever witnessed on the stage. The first act fell to Lope's lot, and the second to mine; we dispatched these in two days, and the third was to be divided into eight leaves each. As it was bad weather, I remained in his house that night; and knowing that I could not equal him in the execution, I had a fancy to beat him in the dispatch of the business: for this purpose I got up at two o'clock, and at eleven had completed my share of the work. I immediately went out to look for him, and found him very deeply occupied with an orange-tree that had been frost-bitten in the night. Upon my asking him how he had gone on with his task, he answered, 'I set about it at five; but I finished the act an hour ago; took a bit of ham for breakfast; wrote an epistle of fifty triplets; and have watered the whole of the garden: which has not a little fatigued me.' Then taking out the papers, he read me the eight leaves and the triplets; a circumstance that would have astonished me, had I not known the fertility of his genius, and the dominion he had over the rhymes of our language."

As to the number of his plays, all contemporary authors concur in representing it as prodigious. "At last appeared," says Cervantes in his prologue, "that prodigy of nature, the great Lope, and established his monarchy on the stage. He conquered and reduced under his jurisdiction every actor and author in the kingdom. He filled the world with plays written with purity, and the plot conducted with skill, in number so many that they exceed eighteen hundred sheets of paper; and what is the most wonderful of all that can be said upon the subject, every one of them have I seen acted, or heard of their being so from those that had seen them; and though there have been many who have attempted the same career, all their works together would not equal in quantity what this single man has composed." Montalvan asserts that he wrote eighteen hundred plays, and four hundred *autos sacramentales;* and asserts, that if the works of his literary idol were placed in one scale, and those of all ancient and modern poets in the other, the weight of the former would decide the comparison in point of quantity, and be a fair emblem of the superiority in point of merit of Lope's verses over those of all other poets together. What Lope himself says upon this subject will be most satisfactorily related in his own words, though the passages are far from poetical. Having given a list in his prologue to the *Pelegrino*, written in 1604, of three hundred and forty-three plays, in his *Art de hacer Comedias*, published five years afterwards, he says:

> None than myself more barbarous or more wrong,
> Who, hurried by the vulgar taste along,
> Dare give my precepts in despite of rule,
> Whence France and Italy pronounce me fool.
> But what am I to do? Who now of plays,
> With one complete within these seven days,
> Four hundred eighty-three in all have writ,
> And all, save six, against the rules of wit.

"In the *Eclogue to Claudio*, one of his last works, are the following curious though prosaic passages:

> Should I the titles now relate
>   Of plays my endless labour bore,
> Well might you doubt the list so great,
>   Such reams of paper scribbled o'er;
> Plots, imitations, scenes, and all the rest,
> To verse reduc'd, in flowers of rhetoric drest.
>
> The number of my fables told
>   Would seem the greatest of them all;
> For, strange, of dramas you behold
>   Full fifteen hundred mine I call;
> And full a hundred times,—within a day
> Passed from my muse upon the stage a play.

And again:

> The public, Avarice oft deceived,
>   And fix'd on others' works my name;
> Vile works! which Ignorance mine believed,
>   Or Malice call'd, to wound my fame:
> That crime I can't forgive, but much incline
> To pardon some who fix'd their names on mine.
> Then spare, indulgent Claudio, spare
>   The list of all my barbarous plays;
> For this with truth I can declare,
>   And though 'tis truth it is not praise,
> The printed part, though far too large, is less
> Than that which yet unprinted waits the press.

Though these passages seem to confirm the assertions of his biographers and contemporaries, yet the complaint contained in the last, which is yet more strongly urged in his prologue to the *Pelegrino,* proves the light authority upon which his name was given to dramatic composi-

tions, and consequently may suggest a probable mode of explaining the exaggeration which must have taken place with regard to their number. That there must be some exaggeration all will be disposed to admit. It is but just however to observe, that though Lope is the most wonderful, he is not the only Spanish author the number of whose verses approaches to a miracle. La Cueva mentions one who had written one thousand plays in four acts; some millions of Latin lines were composed by Mariner; and many hundred dramatic compositions are still extant of Calderón , as well as of authors of inferior merit. It was not uncommon even for the nobility of Philip the Fourth's time to converse for some minutes in extempore poetry; and in carelessness of metre, as well as in commonplace images, the verses of that time often remind us of the *improvisatori* of Italy.

Bouterwek is still more credulous. He says Lope required no more than four-and-twenty hours to write a versified drama of three acts in redondillas, interspersed with sonnets, tercets, and octaves. This is an amplification of what Lope de Vega has said of himself in the couplet quoted by Lord Holland, which I have before noticed. But I would here suggest that if the couplet is to be understood to say Lope actually wrote a play in the course of four-and-twenty hours, this can only be credible on the supposition of the play being an interlude of *one* act, not a comedy of *three*. Be this as it may, Bouterwek has not the shadow of an authority for saying, "Lope sometimes wrote a play in the short space of three or four hours;" this is a gratuitous bit of biographical exaggeration. Nor can I discover the source from which he learned that Lope wrote "upwards of two thousand comedies." The real number is not easily ascertained; but I concur with Schach and Damas Hinard in estimating them at about fifteen hundred, exclusive of *autos sacramentales* and interludes; in all eighteen hundred dramatic works. This calculation is founded upon Lope's own indications. It would be tedious to enumerate them here; let the single passage from his *Eclogue to Claudio* suffice.

> Pero si ahora el numero infinito
> De las fabulas comicas intento . . .
> Mil y quinientas fabulas admira . . .

"But if I now come to enumerate the infinite quantity of comic fables, you will be amazed to learn that I have composed fifteen hundred." This was written only five years before his death; and Montalvan assures us that for many years he had relinquished the theatre; so that fifteen hundred seems the highest number that can be accepted.

But fifteen hundred! and add thereto three hundred autos, and interludes, five epic poems, an *Arcadia*, an *Art of Comedy*, thirty-six romances supplied to the Romancero, the *Laurel de Apolo*, the *Gatomaquia*, a vast number of sonnets, epistles, and epitaphs, and some prose novels! It really takes one's breath away to hear of such achievements. If only as a prodigy of fecundity, this man ranks among the wonders of the world. Fifteen hundred plays, and all successful! They brought money to the treasury, competence to him, and delight to all Spain. Lope was no prodigious "unactable unacted" boasting of a barren rapidity. His fertility was owing to his mastery over the materials furnished by an ardent imagination; the rapidity of which some moderns boast is the mere torrent of words unobstructed by ideas. Lope's plays were acted, are acted still, and may still be read with pleasure. He was the idol of his nation. The nobility vied with each other in their expressions of admiration and friendship. The very Pope sent him the Cross of Malta and the degree of Doctor of Theology, accompanying them by a flattering epistle. His career as a dramatist was a bright track of glory. Whenever he appeared in the streets he was surrounded by crowds eager to catch a glimpse of the Phœnix. The boys ran shouting after him; and those whom old age prevented from keeping pace with the rest, stood and gazed on him in wonder as he passed.

In truth Lope had charmed, intoxicated the whole nation. He was the incarnation of the national genius in its Oriental prodigality. He threw gleams of sunny mirth into the dark countenances of the holy Inquisitors. He even charmed the sombre spirit of Philip the Second. He taught the hidalgos a refinement in the ingenuity of intrigue; and roused the joyous boisterous mirth of the common people. Those only who know the exuberance of the southern temperament—its vehemence of admiration or contempt—can understand the furor excited by Lope de Vega. I have seen an Italian singer obliged to obey the call, and appear before the curtain fifteen times at the conclusion of an opera in which she had enchanted the audience; and then the excited admirers, intoxicated with their own enthusiasm, rushed out of the theatre, took the horses from her carriage, and, like exulting slaves, drew the enchantress to her home. These men were ready to fight a duel with anyone who dared to question the singer's supremacy. So in Spain, the frantic admirers of Lope declared that Spongia, who had written a severe critique upon his works, deserved nothing short of *death;* and it is probable the critic would have met this fate had he not prudently retired to a foreign land. Pilgrimages from all parts of Spain were made to see this phoenix. Even the Italians left the land of Dante and Ariosto to pay homage to the great Lope de Vega. The Cardinal Barberini followed him with something little short of veneration. A fame so loud and spread so wide, no one has yet possessed. His name was an epithet of excellence: a Lope melon, a Lope cigar, a Lope horse, were perfect specimens. There must have been something great in the man who was thus throned on the imaginations of his countrymen. There have since been absurd popularities; but they have been fleeting, and the noisy shouts died away in faint echoes, till they became inaudible. Lope de Vega has survived two centuries of change, and still is acted, still is read.

Amidst this noisy popularity Lope was not so happy as in those early days of struggle, when hope threw a spring-like verdure over the future, and when the present was irradiated by the sunny smiles of wife and child. The priceless treasures—Love and Hope—had been snatched from him. Glory could not compensate him for their loss.

He was as active as ever; rather more so; fulfilled his religious duties, and solaced his leisure hours with the cultivation of his garden. This garden (*huerticillo*), if garden it could be called, having only a few feet of space, contained about a dozen plants, a vine, two trees, and a fountain rustically constructed out of a broken vase of earthenware. To vulgar eyes it was a strip of ground; to the poet's more imaginative mind it was a fairyland—

> donde vivo retirad
> Sí no virtuosa vida, nunco ociosa.

The space was small, but what was that to one who could make it large by peopling it with the creations of his fancy? it was humble, but he covered its poverty by the magnificence of his imagination.

Nor was his house altogether deserted. Towards 1620 one sees the graceful form of a young maiden gliding about the poet, like a guardian angel. Who was this Marcela? One knows not what to answer. Montalvan speaks of her with provoking reserve, which stimulates conjecture without satisfying it; he calls her a near relation. Lope, in his dedication to her of *El remedio en la desdicha*, calls her his daughter: whence the natural conclusion is that she was an illegitimate child. He loved her tenderly, and was proud of her beauty and talents. But he was soon to lose her also. She entered a convent; obeying the voice which spoke within her, she took the veil and left him who had loved her "more like a lover than a father" (*mas galan que padre*), to lament her loss. This he has done, in the epistle just quoted, where he describes the ceremony of her taking the veil.

The following year his second, now only, son, Lope, left him, to join the Marquis de Santa Cruz, son of the valiant captain under whom Lope himself had served during the campaign in Portugal. Soon afterwards his daughter Feliciana was engaged to be married to a young cavalier, Don Luis Usategui. But the bridegroom, though noble, was poor, and demanded a dowry. Lope, with the usual improvidence of poets, had spent easily the money he so easily earned, and was in no condition to bestow on his child a dowry. After due reflection he addressed the following to the king:—"Lope says, Sire, that he served your grandfather with his sword. He did nothing remarkable then, and has since done less; but he showed his zeal and his courage. He served your father with his pen. If it has not carried your father's name and praises from one end of the world to the other, it is the fault of his want of talent, not a deficiency of zeal. Lope has a daughter, and he is old. The Muses have made him honoured, but not rich. Assist me: I am endeavouring to get my child a husband. Spare me, O great Philip, a slight portion of your riches, and may you have more gold and diamonds than I have rhymes!"—The king's answer was a generous dowry.

The drama did not exclusively occupy his fruitful muse; but the drama was after all the scene of his great triumphs. As a poet he aspired no less to the approbation of the critics than to the applause of the crowd. His epics are, however, indifferent performances. Lord Holland says,

The *Hermosura de Angelica* is perhaps the best of his heroic poems, though during his life the *Corona Tragica*, his poem on Mary Queen of Scots, attracted more notice and secured him more praise. When however we consider the quarter in which these encomiums originated, we may suspect that they were bestowed on the orthodoxy rather than on the poetry of the work. When Lope published it, the passions which religious dissension had excited throughout Europe had not subsided. The indiscriminate abuse of one sect was still sufficient to procure any work a favourable reception with the other; and the *Corona Tragica*, the subject of which was fortunately chosen for such a purpose, was not deficient in that recommendation. Queen Elizabeth is a bloody Jezebel, a second Athaliah, an obdurate sphinx, and the incestuous progeny of a harpy. He tells us also in the preface, that any author who censures his king and natural master is a perfidious traitor, unworthy and incapable of all honours, civil or military. In the second book he proves himself fully exempt from such a reproach by selecting for the topics of his praise the actions of the Spanish monarch, which seem the least to admit of apology or excuse. He finds nothing in the wisdom or activity of Charles V so praiseworthy as his treachery to the Protestants. Philip II, whom he does everything but blame for not murdering Queen Elizabeth during her sister's reign, is most admired for sacrificing the interest of his crown, the peace and prosperity of his dominions, at the shrine of orthodoxy:

> How much the second Philip did it cost
>   Freedom *unjust* from Flanders to withhold!
> Rather than yield the world he would have lost,
>   His faith so steady and his heart so bold:
> The third, with *just* decree, to Afric's coast
>   Banish'd the remnants of that pest of old,
> The Moors; and nobly ventured to contemn
> Treasures which flowed from barbarous hordes like them.

The praise of the fourth Philip is founded on an anecdote with which I am unacquainted, viz., of his adoration of the sacrament in the presence of English heretics. There is no supernatural agency in this poem; but it has not sufficient merit in other respects to allow us to draw from its failure any argument in favour of such machinery. The speech of Mary when her sentence is announced is the only passage I found in it rising at all above mediocrity:

> Thanks for your news, illustrious lords, she cried;
>   I greet the doom that must my griefs decide:
> Sad though it be, though sense must shrink from pain,
> Yet the immortal soul the trial shall sustain.
>
> But had the fatal sentence reached my ears
>   In France, in Scotland, with my husband crown'd,
> Not age itself could have allayed my fears,
>   And my poor heart had shudder'd at the sound.
> But now immur'd for twenty tedious years,
>   Where naught my listening ears can catch around
> But fearful noise of danger and alarms,
> The frequent threat of death, and constant din of arms.

> Ah! what have I in dying to bemoan?
>   What punishment in death can they devise
> For her who living only lives to groan,
>   And see continual death before her eyes?
> Comfort's in death, where 't is in life unknown;
>   Who death expects feels more than he who dies:—
> Though too much valour may our fortune try,
> To live in fear of death is many times to die.
>
> Where have I e'er reposed in silent night,
>   But Death's stern image stalk'd around my bed?
> What morning e'er arose on me with light,
>   But on my health some sad disaster bred?
> Did fortune ever aid my war or flight,
>   Or grant a refuge for my hapless head?
> Still at my life some fearful phantom aim'd,
>   My draughts with poison drugg'd, my towers with treachery flamed.
>
> And now with fearful certainty I know
>   Is come the hour that my sad being ends,
> Where life must perish with a single blow;
>   Then mark her death whom steadfast faith attends
> My cheeks unchang'd, my inward calm shall show,
>   While free from foes, serene, my generous friends,
> I meet my death—or rather I should say,
> Meet my eternal life, my everlasting day.

The last line of the second stanza, quoted above, reminds one of a similar sentiment in Shakespere:

> Cowards die many times before their deaths,
> The valiant never taste of death but once.
>   *Julius Cæsar*, act. 2, sc. 2.

I have never read these ambitious efforts; but I have read, and with considerable amusement, his Burlesque Epic called *The Battle of the Cats—Gatomaquia*: in which the heroic deeds of Marramaquiz (that Achilles of *Toms*), and the charms of Zapaquilda (that Helen of *Pussies*), are narrated with immense gusto. Such burlesques are easy to write, but not easy to write well. Lope has hit the mock heroic tone to perfection. I have also read his *New Art of Writing Comedies*, which is interesting as regards the state of the drama, but has no intrinsic merit. His *Rimas Humanas* deserve more attention than has been accorded to them, both for their intrinsic merit and their biographical allusions. Many of them are worthless; many simply ingenious; but there are some fine touches of feeling and some gorgeous imagery, with a constant facility and mastery of versification. Among the playthings of his pen may be cited the following sonnet, compiled from Ariosto, Camoens, Petrarch, Tasso, Horace, Serafina, Boscan, and Garcilasso:

> Le donne, i cavalier, le arme, gli amori, (*Ariosto*)
> en dolces jogos en placer continuo, (*Camoens*)
> fuggo per piu non esser pellegrino, (*Petrarca*)
> ma su nel cielo infra i beati chori. (*Tasso*)
> Dulce et decorum est pro patria mori, (*Horace*)
> sforzame amor, fortuna, el mio destino (*Serafina*)

ni es mucho en tanto mal ser adivino, (*Boscan*)
seguendo l' ire e i giovenil furori. (*Ariosto*)
Satis beatus unicis Sabinis, (*Horace*)
parlo in rime aspre, e di dolceza ignude, (*Petrarca*)
deste passado ben, que nunca foro, (*Camoens*)
No hay bien que en mal no se convierta y mude,
(*Garcilasso*)
nec prata canis albicant pruinis (*Horace*)
la vita jugge, e non se arresta un hora. (*Petrarca*)

This sonnet is interesting as displaying the affinity between the Latin and the southern languages, and as showing also the differences.

Lope grew old, but he did not outlive his fame; nor did he lose that readiness and presence of mind which made him witty in ludicrous circumstances, and dignified in serious. One day a cavalier insulted him; and on Lope's expostulating, replied "If you are dissatisfied, Sir, let us hence," touching his sword. "Yes," replied the old soldier, now a priest, "let us hence, and to the altar; *I* to say a mass, *you to serve me!*" Is there not something very grand, and at the same time dramatic, in this? (pp. 587-600)

Brander Matthews   (essay date 1902)

SOURCE: "The Drama in Spain," in *The International Quarterly*, Vol. VI, September-December, 1902, pp. 241-59.

[*An American critic, playwright, and novelist, Matthews wrote extensively on world drama and served for twenty-five years at Columbia as professor of dramatic literature, the first to hold such a position in an American university. Matthews was also a founding member and president of the National Institute of Arts and Letters. In the following excerpt, he describes the origins of Spanish drama, assesses Lope de Vega's significance, and provides an analysis of* The Star of Seville.]

Lope molded the Spanish drama to suit his own gifts; he stamped it forever with the impress of his own personality; and even if we must admit that Calderón , who came after, also rose higher, and that the younger poet surpassed the elder in the lyrical elevation of several of his plays, none the less must we remember always that the greatest dramas of Calderón are examples of a class of which Lope had set the first model. If we acknowledge, as we may, that even Calderón trod only where Lope had first broken the path, we must record that all the other dramatists of Spain were also followers in his footsteps. From out the numerous mass of Lope de Vega's works, it would be possible to select a satisfactory specimen of every species of the drama as it has existed in Spain. What Lope was, so was the Spanish drama. He came first, and he was the most original of all, the most fertile, the most indefatigable, the most various, the most multifarious.

His influence on the stage of Spain was far more potent and more durable than that of Sophocles on the theater of Greece or of Shakspere on the drama of England. It was

Lope who earliest discovered how to hold the interest of a modern audience by the easy intricacy of his story and by the surprising variety of the successive situations, each artfully prepared for by its predecessor. If Schlegel found an ingenious felicity of plot-making to be so characteristic of the Spanish drama that he was led to suspect a Spanish origin for any play in which he observed this quality, it was to the practice and to the precept of Lope de Vega that his fellow-dramatists owed their possession of this merit. One of these fellow-dramatists it was who summed up the good points of the Spanish drama in lines which have been thus Englished by G. H. Lewes:—

Invention, interest, sprightly turns in plays,
Say what they will, are Spain's peculiar praise;
Hers are the plots which strict attention seize,
Full of intrigue and yet disclosed with ease:
Hence scenes and acts her fertile stage affords
Unknown, unrivaled on the foreign boards.

It was the lack of a metropolis which had helped to deprive the Italians of a drama worthy of their intellectual supremacy in the early Renascence; and it was the choice of Madrid as the capital which made possible the sudden outflowering of the Spanish dramatic literature. The many little bands of strolling players . . . containing performers of both sexes, looked longingly toward the court; and two of them were in time allowed to settle in the royal city, bringing with them their elementary repertory of songs and dances, of simple interludes and of lumbering chronicle-plays. The theater assigned to each of these companies was as primitive as the entertainment they proffered, for it was no more than the courtyard of a house. At the farther end of this courtyard was the shallow platform, which served as a stage, and which was shielded by a sloping roof. Near to the stage were a few benches, and then came the space where the main body of the rude public stood throughout the performance, unprotected from the weather. Behind them rose several tiers of seats, stretching back almost to the house, and affording accommodation for the women, who were kept apart from the men. Then the rooms of the house itself served as private boxes; and in time these came to be so highly valued that the right to one passed as an heirloom. A few privileged spectators were allowed seats on the sides of the stage. There was neither curtain nor scenery.

The performance took place by daylight in the early afternoon, so there was no need of artificial illumination. It began with the appearance of the musicians upon the stage itself, where they played on the guitar and sang popular ballads until an acceptable audience had gathered or until the boisterous impatience of those who had arrived compelled the actors to commence. Then the musicians withdrew; and a chief performer, often the manager himself, appeared to speak a prolog, amusing in itself and abounding in compliments to the audience. When at last he left the stage free, the actors who were to open the play came out and the first act was performed. Simple as was the medieval stage with its neutral ground backed by the stations, which became mansions in France and pageants in England, the Spanish stage was simpler still, since the stations were abolished and there remained only the neutral ground—the bare platform. Neither authors nor spectators ever bothered themselves about the place where the characters were at any moment supposed to be. The actors then engaged in carrying on the story were standing in sight of the audience; and this was the sole essential, the background being merely accidental. If by chance it became necessary for the audience to know just where the action was about to take place, then this information was furnished by the dialog itself, without any change of the stage-setting, the platform remaining bare of all scenery. Thus the dramatist was at liberty to select such incidents of his fable as he saw fit, not having to consider the difficulty of making the successive places visible in the eyes of the spectators.

When the first act was ended the actors left the stage; the musicians came forward again; and there followed a song-and-dance or even a little ballad-farce to fill the interval between the acts of the chief play. Then the second act was presented in its turn; and after it there came another song-and-dance or another comical interlude. The third act of the play was always the last, for the Spanish dramatists early accepted a division into three parts. When the chief play was finally concluded, it was at once followed by a farce, and often also by one of the national dances; and then at last the entertainment came to an end, and the noisy and turbulent spectators withdrew, having applauded boisterously if they thought they had had their money's worth, and having with equal freedom made vocal their dissatisfaction if they did not happen to think so.

These were the apparently unfavorable conditions under which were represented the works of the dramatic poets of Spain at the moment when the drama flourished most exuberantly; and no one who knows the circumstances of the contemporary theater in England under Elizabeth can fail to perceive the striking similarity. The dramatic poets of England, like the dramatic poets of Spain, saw their plays produced by daylight, on an unadorned platform, set up in what was no more than the courtyard of an inn, open to the sky. The English plays, like the Spanish, were acted without scenery, before a noisy throng of groundlings who stood in the pit; and in England also there were what were called "jigs" by the clown between acts. The English plays, like the Spanish, were devised to please the public as a whole and not to delight only a special class. Such differences as there are between the Spanish drama and the English are due not to the conditions of the performance, but directly to the characteristics of the two peoples; and Shakspere is not more representative of the Elizabethan Englishman than is Calderón of the contemporary Spaniard.

In Spain, as in England, the people had given proof that they possessed the first requisite of a truly national drama,—a steadfast determination, steeled for instant action. The Spanish kingdom was then seemingly at the very climax of its might; and having compacted the monarchy and driven out the Moors, having overrun half Europe and taken all America as their own, the Spaniards had the

pride of a chosen people. They thrilled with a consciousness of a lofty destiny, while at the same time they accepted with enthusiasm feudal and chivalrous ideals of fidelity and loyalty and honor. Men of very varied individuality, they were united in their devotion to the church, in which they had an unquestioning faith, and to the king, who ruled by divine right and could do no wrong. Lope de Vega, for example, had been in his youth a soldier on the Invincible Armada; and later he became a familiar of the Holy Inquisition. It is true that the religious fervor of the Spaniards was often only empty superstition; and that it was in no wise incompatible with a strangely contorted ethical code which approved of vengeance as a duty and justified murder to remove a stain from honor.

The Spanish language is a rich and sonorous tongue, as characteristic of the race that speaks it as is English or French; and in the hands of the dramatic poets Spanish lends itself readily to the display of an eloquence which only too often sinks into facile grandiloquence. One of the most marked peculiarities of these plays is a rhetorical redundancy which often rises into a lyrical copiousness, but which not infrequently also condenses itself into a sententious apothegm. The personages taking part are as likely to reveal a vehement luxuriance of phrase as they are to disclose a perverse subtlety of intellect. Formal and pompous their speech is on occasion; and at other times it is easy and natural, refreshing in its humorous lightness, sparkling with unpremeditated wit, and bristling with pungent proverbs. As we read these plays we are constantly reminded that Seneca and Lucan and Marcus Aurelius were all of them Spaniards.

These characteristics of the language itself, and of the people that spoke the language, are familiar to all who know *Don Quixote*; and they are made visible in the plays of every Spanish dramatist, especially in those of Lope de Vega, because there is scarcely any kind of drama which he was not the first to attempt. He has left us farces as slight in texture as those of Lope de Rueda; mysteries more artfully put together than those of the medieval scribes; chronicle-plays not unlike those of his immediate predecessors, but with a heightened dramatic interest; dramatized ballads and romances far more skilfully wrought than any seen on the stage before he took it for his own. He gave a lyric grace to the briefer religious plays, which were called sacramental-acts; and he himself invented the play of plot and intrigue and mystery which is known as the comedy-of-cloak-and-sword. He showed the same fertility of ingenuity in devising comedies of incident and of character. He solidly constructed somber tragedies of honor and revenge. He seems to have written hundreds of plays of every kind and description; and scores of them are still preserved in print. They vary greatly in merit; many of them are mere improvisations; but very few of them fail to display his dexterity, his perfect understanding of the theater, his mastery of stagecraft.

The art of the playwright is a finer art today, no doubt; it is at once firmer and more delicate than was possible in the Spain which was just emerging from the middle ages; but the dramatists of every modern language are greatly indebted to the models set by Lope de Vega,—and none the less because the most of these later writers are unconscious of their obligation. Nowhere has modern dramaturgic craftsmanship been carried to a higher pitch of perfection than in France; and it must never be forgotten that the *Cid*, the first of French tragedies, and the *Liar*, the first of French comedies, were both of them borrowed by Corneille from Spanish plays written by contemporary disciples of Lope de Vega's.

. . . The dramatists of every modern language are greatly indebted to the models set by Lope de Vega,—and none the less because the most of these later writers are unconscious of their obligation . . . From out the immense mass of Lope de Vega's dramatic works it is not easy to make choice of any single play as truly typical. The selection is indeed difficult when we have before us pieces of so many different classes, from the sacramental-acts and from mere dramatized anecdotes to comedies sometimes perfervidly lyrical and sometimes frankly prosaic, from chronicle-plays loosely epic in their structure to true tragedies with an ever-increasing tensity of emotion. . . . He seems to have written hundreds of plays of every kind and description; and scores of them are still preserved in print. They vary greatly in merit; many of them are mere improvisations; but very few of them fail to display his dexterity, his perfect understanding of the theater, his mastery of stagecraft.

From out the immense mass of Lope de Vega's dramatic works it is not easy to make choice of any single play as truly typical. The selection is indeed difficult when we have before us pieces of so many different classes, from the sacramental-acts and from mere dramatized anecdotes to comedies sometimes perfervidly lyrical and sometimes frankly prosaic, from chronicle-plays loosely epic in their structure to true tragedies with an ever-increasing tensity of emotion. But one of his most famous plays is the *Star of Seville*, and perhaps this will serve as well as any to suggest his method of handling a story on the stage.

The first act begins with the King of Castile and his evil counselor, Arias, coming upon the stage with two of the Alcaldes of Seville, who compliment the monarch on his arrival. After they withdraw, the King asks eagerly about a beautiful girl he had remarked as he entered the city. Arias tells him that she is Estrella, known as the Star of Seville because of her loveliness, and that she is a sister of Bustos Tabera. The King confesses his sudden passion, and sends Arias to fetch Bustos to him, hoping through the brother to get at the sister. Then two Officers enter in turn, each asking the King for a vacant governorship; but he dismisses them without deciding. Arias returns with Bustos, a man of blunt honesty, who is surprised when the King proffers the governorship to him. He conceals his suspicions when the King flatters him, asks about his family, and finally promises to provide a proper husband for his sister. After the men have left the stage Estrella enters, so that the spectators are supposed now to be witnesses of a scene in her home. Accompanying her is Don Sancho, to whom she is betrothed and with whom she exchanges protestations of love. Bustos appears and tells his friend of the King's intention of finding a fit husband for his sister; whereupon Don Sancho reproaches him for not having informed the monarch that their marriage had been agreed upon. When they depart, the King and Arias enter, and the dialog makes it clear that they are now to be imagined as standing at the door of Estrella's dwelling. The King has come to visit the brother in hope of getting speech with the sister: but Bustos, when he appears, finds excuses for not asking the King to enter the house. So the monarch takes the brother off with him, leaving Arias behind to corrupt the sister. When the stage is again left empty, Estrella enters with her maid-servant; and therefore the audience perceives that they are within the house as before. Arias presents himself to tell Estrella of the King's passion for her; but her sole answer is to turn her back on him and walk out of the room. Thereupon Arias promptly bribes the servant to admit the King that night. After they depart, there is a scene at the palace; Arias comes in to report, and the delighted monarch bids him see that the servant is well rewarded. Then the King and his evil counselor leave the stage empty and bring to an end the first act,—an act of swift and spirited exposition, taking the spectator at once into the heart of the situation and exciting the interest of expectancy.

The second act opens with the admission of the King into Estrella's house, and with the unexpected return of Bustos, who confronts the intruder in the dark and demands his name. The King has to declare himself; but the sturdy fellow pretends not to believe this, asserting that the monarch, being the fountain of honor, would never have come there to bring dishonor. The King is thus forced to cross swords with the subject, but he escapes unhurt as soon as the servants bring lights. Bustos hangs the treacherous maid-servant, and bids his sister prepare for her immediate wedding with Don Sancho. In the later scenes the King, resolved on a private vengeance for a private affront, decides to have Bustos made away with by some devoted soldier; and at the suggestion of Arias he sends for Don Sancho. The monarch explains that he needs to have a guilty man slain, and gives Don Sancho a written warrant for the deed; but the loyal subject prefers to rely on the royal word, and destroys the authorization, agreeing to slay the man whose name is written in the sealed paper given to him by the King. Don Sancho, left alone, receives a letter from Estrella, telling him that her brother desires them to be married that very day. The soldier is doubly overjoyed, for this is now his wedding morn, and the King has just confided to him a dangerous task. Then he opens the paper to find that the name of the man he is to kill is Bustos Tabera. Horror-stricken, he debates his duty, only to decide at last that he must obey the King's command, kill his best friend and thereby give up his bride. At this moment Estrella's brother enters, and, to his astonishment, Don Sancho forces a quarrel on him. They draw; Bustos is slain; and Don Sancho is led away to prison. Next the spectators are shown Estrella's happiness as she is decking herself for the bridal. But all too soon come the Alcaldes, bearing the body of Bustos, and telling her that the murderer of her brother is the bridegroom she is awaiting. And here ends the second act, wrought to a high pitch of intensity, with sudden alternations of hope and despair.

What happens in the third act may be more briefly indicated. Estrella comes to the King and claims vengeance on the murderer of her brother,—the man whom she herself loves. The monarch (whose passion has now faded as quickly as it had blazed up) gives her the key of Don Sancho's cell, and with it the power of disposing of the murderer as she pleases. Thickly veiled, she goes to the prison, leads her lover forth, and bids him go free. But when he discovers who it is has released him, he rejects his freedom at the hands of the sister of his victim. He returns to his cell, and as he refuses to give any motive for the murder, the civil authorities condemn him to death—altho the King tries to influence the sentence of the Alcaldes, and even thinks he has succeeded, only to be taken aback by their official independence. So the monarch has at last to declare that he himself gave Don Sancho the fatal order. With the fanatical loyalty of the time, one of the Alcaldes remarks that no doubt his Majesty had a good reason for this command. But none the less does the blood of Bustos separate the two lovers, and they bid each other farewell forever, to the astonishment and admiration of the sovran. The comic servant of Don Sancho has the last word, addressed straight to the audience: "You have heard the tragedy Lope has written for you, and never can you forget the Star of Seville."

Here we have a painting of the passions by means of the primary colors only and with the boldest contrasts. Here we have a rapid succession of surprising situations, following each other so closely that we have scarce time to grasp their full meaning. But whatever defects the drama may disclose when dissected critically in the library, there can be no doubt that it would always be interesting in the theater itself, before Spanish spectators in absolute sympathy with the high-strung magnanimity of the hero and the heroine. It is like a dramatized ballad; and not a little lyrical hyperbole lingers in the dialog, side by side with the homeliest directness of speech. This admixture of the top-lofty and of the matter-of-fact is most characteristic of the Spanish drama, which made no formal distinction between tragedy and comedy,—following the medieval practice rather than the doctrine of the Renascence. A play with a tragic climax might have comic incidents and comic characters, just as a play of humorous intention was likely to contain at least one duel with a possibly fatal termination.

In almost every piece we find the *gracioso*, as the Spaniards call the conventional comic servant of the hero, whose task it is to supply fun at intervals and to relax by a laugh the tension of the overwrought situations. Like the modern melodramatists, the Spanish playwrights understood the value of "comic relief," as it is termed today. The gracioso has a part of varying importance; sometimes he is a mere clown always trying to be funny and yet having but little to do with the plot; sometimes he is a clever fellow, quick-witted and sharp-tongued and therefore a chief factor in the intrigue; sometimes he serves as a chorus to voice a common-sense opinion as to the superfine heroics of his master,—and this he does at the end of the **Star of Seville**, for instance; and sometimes, with the assistance of a female partner, he provides in the underplot a parody of the main story of the play. The relation of Sancho Panza to Don Quixote is that of the gracioso to the hero; and indeed there is no better example of the gracioso anywhere than Sancho,—except that the hasty playwrights never gave the gracioso the vital individuality which the genius of the novelist bestowed on Don Quixote's squire. The gracioso is plain-spoken at times, but he is never so foul-mouthed as are not a few of the comic personages in the Elizabethan plays. Indeed, the Spanish drama is distinctly more decent, both in word and in deed, than the English drama which was contemporary with it.

In Lope's hands the gracioso was more easily witty than in Calderón's, just as Lope's lighter pieces were more gracefully humorous than were those of his great follower. Lope was naturally gay and seemed to improvise laughter-provoking intrigues, whereas Calderón laboriously constructed his humorous situations, with skilful certainty, no doubt, but with little spontaneity. The fun of Calderón's *House with Two Doors* is indisputable, but it is rather mechanical when contrasted with Lope's playful comedy, the title of which in English would be the **Dog in the Manger**. Here Lope revealed a delicacy of perception into feminine psychology; his heroine is a true woman, whereas his hero is a pitiful creature, finding a father by fraud; and in the author's bringing about the marriage which ends the play, we have another instance of the careless cynicism and of the moral obtuseness which accompanied the religious enthusiasm of the Spaniards. (pp. 249-56)

Hugo Albert Rennert   (essay date 1904)

SOURCE: *The Life of Lope de Vega (1562-1635)*, reprinted by Benjamin Blom, Inc., 1968, 587 p.

[*Rennert was a German-born American scholar best known for his works about the Golden age of Spanish drama,* The Spanish Stage in the Time of Lope de Vega *(1909) and* The Life of Lope de Vega *(1904). In the following excerpt, taken from the latter work, Rennert offers an assessment of Lope's stature, charts the course of his reputation in the centuries following his death, and compares him with Calderón de la Barca.]*

The principal source of his revenue—his comedias—[Lope de Vega] esteemed the least of all his literary productions. These, as he frequently said, he wrote for bread. "Necessity and I, going into the business of making verses, brought the comedias into fashion," he says. Like many another poet he was a poor critic of his own works, and under-valued what he did best. Petrarch, who was proud of his Latin epic *Africa*, lives almost wholly by his sonnets. And, as regards one other Spaniard, the foremost of them all,—Cervantes—there is nothing to show that he ever realized the supreme greatness of his *Don Quixote*; while, on the other hand, we know that he always pointed with pride to his very mediocre comedias, which any third-rate *ingenio* might have written, and, almost at his last gasp, spoke with affectionate regard of his dull and soporific pastoral romance, the *Galatea*. In like manner Lope de Vega rated his own epics and lyrics far above his comedias, while to the latter he owes his immense and enduring fame. His comedias are not all good; in the very nature of things it is impossible that they should be, and his most ardent devotee, I imagine, would not maintain that they were so. More than a score could be mentioned, however, that have not been, and probably never will be, surpassed. These vary from sublime tragedy to the brightest effects of humour, and all are authentic masterpieces in their various kinds. With the theatrical managers waiting at his door for these '*versos mercantiles*,' Lope wrote far too much; he also wrote too rapidly and too carelessly. But in all the countless number of his plays, judging from the many I have read, I will make bold to assert that there is not one which is wholly bad,—not one without repeated bursts of lofty poetry which only a splendid genius could have written. It is chiefly to his comedias, as I have said, that Lope owes his enduring fame,—and I say enduring fame, because I believe that now, more than ever, his fame shows unquestionable signs of a revival which is destined to be permanent. After the comparative obscurity of over two centuries, after the passing of the Calderón cult inaugurated in Germany in the early decades of the century just past, the world has once more turned back to him who was the idol of the Spanish nation at the beginning of the seventeenth century, and Lope de Vega has regained his kingdom. Nor is this renascence limited to Spain alone. Grillparzer re-established the repute of Lope throughout the continent of Europe, and in England there has been a corresponding revival which has been whimsically, or forgetfully, ascribed to Ormsby. In the interest of historical truth it should be placed on record that the credit for this revolution of opinion in England is due, in the first instance, to *The Athenæum*, a journal which rendered inestimable service to the cause by encouraging that great authority, John Rutter Chorley, to propagate sound doctrine in its columns [see Nos. 1360 and 1361, November 19 and November 26, 1853]. Towards the close of the nineteenth century the trium-

phal march of Lope has been unchecked, continuous, and universal. To withstand the great array of accomplished scholars ranged under Lope's conquering banner requires more self-assurance than could possibly be found in any modest student. The rehabilitation is now complete, and it would be difficult indeed to overpraise the part taken in the final stages of the victorious campaign by the eminent critic, Sr. Menéndez y Pelayo, in whom the Spanish Academy has found for its reprint of Lope de Vega's complete works an editor fully equipped with all the learning, penetration, and enthusiasm requisite for the fulfilment of his stupendous task.

It cannot be denied, even by the most zealous *Lopista*, that for a short time previous to his death the position of the "great Monarch of the Spanish theatre," had been rudely shaken by some of his own disciples and imitators who chanced to gain the applause of the play-going public. Tirso de Molina, Alarcon, and—in still greater degree—Calderón had won recognition. Lope saw himself, towards the close of his career, gradually pushed more and more aside. He knew it only too well and complains of it wistfully in a letter to his patron. He suffered the fate of all who court the fickle favour of the populace. He had lived too long and had outstayed his welcome; he survived to see others, who owed nearly everything to his magic pen, supplant him in the good graces of the common crowd—of that *vulgo* which he perhaps despised, but which he had always striven so assiduously to please. For, though Lope's popularity was immense,—greater in his own country than that of any other Spaniard of his age,—it was more superficial than the popularity of his follower Calderón. And yet Lope was, in more respects than one, a much greater poet than Calderón. In grandeur of theological conception and metaphysical subtlety, Calderón, the poet of Catholicism *par excellence*, is superior to any dramatic poet of his age. Yet Lope far surpasses Calderón in fertility of invention, in breadth of grasp and in simplicity and clearness of expression, for the *culteranismo* that so often mars the verse of Calderón, is rare in Lope. Moreover—and the point is capital—Lope is infinitely the superior in depicting character, as well as in vivacity and persuasiveness of dialogue, which he handles with an easy grace and dexterity unequalled by any other Spanish dramatist. Again, Calderón is distinctly inferior to Lope in his feminine types. In the former we miss the delicacy and charm—the noble tenderness, the gracious sincerity, the irresistible appeal—of Lope's enchanting heroines. The perennial freshness, the pulsation of emotion that vitalizes the theatre of Lope, is wanting in the cold, conventional, artificial world of his successor, in which the personages are frequently exaggerated to such a degree that they cease to be human. Here is the secret of Lope's greatness—his simplicity and truth to nature. In this quality he stands quite alone, and is not even approached by any of his fellow writers for the stage. Where Lope gives us individual men and women, his follower gives us mere types. Calderón, especially after his earlier period, accentuated and exaggerated what he found in Lope, and in his *comedias de capa y espada* (dramas of intrigue or of manners), which are the most characteristic part of his theatre, this tendency has degenerated into a mannerism that is often almost wooden. It is hard to believe that such characters as he presents really existed or could exist; we rebel against his detestable conception of honour which vindicates the most cold-blooded murder. The whole fabric which he has reared seems factitious and unreal. It would appear as though Spain had changed with the death of Lope; and indeed the audiences to which Calderón appealed were entirely different from those of Lope de Vega. The master wrote for the embodied Spanish nation; the disciple for the few—for the king and the courtiers. The unshackled freedom of social commerce, the everyday life of the people which Lope rendered with such vigour and such consummate mastery, gave place to the frigid atmosphere, the stilted manners of the Court. Lope meant his comedias, as he distinctly says, not to be read, but to be acted. He composed with a confident, breathless speed, often scattering his jewels with a spendthrift's prodigality; the musical verses tripped from his pen without effort and, to all seeming, spontaneously. In Calderón's dramas, on the other hand, we discern the conscious effort of the frugal craftsman with no abundant resources in reserve. Lope was the poet of the people: Calderón was the poet of the palace.

But for some time the countless creations of Lope's inexhaustible fancy had begun to lose their savour even with the general public—with the jaded *vulgo* ever clamouring for something new. His plays were no longer received with the rapturous enthusiasm of earlier years; some were even hissed, as we learn from his letters. The old attraction was waning. The glamour of Lope's name had begun to fade. The world about him had changed. The heroic days of Spain which he had delineated with convincing force in his comedias, had passed, and with them the taste for such productions. Spain had been declining, slowly but surely. With the accession of Philip IV., the decadence had begun to manifest itself most unmistakably. The argosies from the Indies were all mortgaged months and years before they reached the mouth of the Guadalquivir. A brave show was made to keep up the tradition of ancient splendour, but all was an empty pretence. And this sinister condition of things reacted on the national theatre. The emphatic, affected, monotonous comedia of Calderón and his school came into vogue. Once more, the people "called him noble that was now their hate, him vile that was their garland." Nature was thought vulgar by the superfine, and the mob aped its betters. The poignant simplicity, the engaging truth, the sunny humour of Lope de Vega, which had enthralled the whole Spanish race for half a century, ceased to move and to delight. The constant spell of fifty years was broken: the great enchanter's magic lost its power. But Lope had not degenerated with the times. Ever a fighter, he could not tamely acquiesce in his dethronement from the vast and glorious empire which his unaided genius had won, and which he had held by an unquestioned right of conquest. He must have known it was a forlorn hope to accept battle against a whole generation far younger than himself; but it was not in him to refuse a challenge, and, if he was to fall, he would perish sword in hand. Almost to the end he proved that his arm was not shortened nor his heart grown cold. One of his last comedias—if not his last—*Las Bizarrias*

de Belisa, written the year before his death, at the age of seventy-two, is in his best manner, blithe and radiant with immortal youth. Old and feeble in body, Lope displayed to the last a wit, an urbanity, an invention which defied the years. Still he could not but recognize that the sceptre was departing from him. In his closing hours of bitterness and trial he lacked the invincible buoyancy of his contemporary Cervantes. He had hitherto met the shocks of fortune with unabated valour,

> And ever with a frolic welcome took
> The thunder and the sunshine.

Now, during the last twelvemonth, the burden of domestic grief was, as he said, more than he could bear. Suffering from frequent attacks of melancholy, and bowed down by a mighty sorrow, he felt that his sun was setting. Yet it continued to flash forth fitfully with undiminished splendour. At last it sank on that August evening when Lope's soul was required of him, and the great light went out which had illumined the remotest corners of Spanish soil. But his works remain as an imperishable monument to one who, with all his faults, was among the greatest of mankind. (pp. 393-98)

Ezra Pound (essay date 1910)

SOURCE: "The Quality of Lope de Vega," in *The Spirit of Romance*, New Directions, 1929, pp. 179-213.

[*An American poet and critic, Pound is regarded as one of the most innovative and influential figures in twentieth-century Anglo-American poetry. He was instrumental in obtaining editorial and financial assistance for T. S. Eliot, James Joyce, and William Carlos Williams, among other writers. His* Cantos, *published throughout his life, are among the most ambitious poetic cycles of the century, and his series of satirical poems* Hugh Selwyn Mauberly (1920) *is ranked with Eliot's* The Waste Land (1922) *as one of the most incisive attacks upon the decadence of modern culture. In the following excerpt originally published in London in 1910, he examines Lope's dramatic and poetic styles as displayed in several plays, including* The Star of Seville *and* Castelvines y Monteses.]

The art of literature and the art of the theatre are neither identical nor concentric. A part of the art of poetry is included in the complete art of the drama. Words are the means of the art of poetry; men and women moving and speaking are the means of drama. A play, to be a good play, must come over the footlights.

A composition, so delicate that actual presentation of it must in its very nature spoil the illusion, is not drama. In a play, ordinary words can draw power from the actor; the words of poetry must depend upon themselves. A good play may, or may not, be literature or poetry. In a study of poetry, one is concerned only with such plays as happen to contain poetry; in a study of literature, one is concerned only with such plays as may be enjoyably read. The aims of poetry and drama differ essentially in this: poetry presents itself to the individual, drama presents itself to a collection of individuals. Poetry also presents itself to any number of individuals, but it can make its appeal in private, seriatim. Drama must appeal to a number of individuals simultaneously. This requires no essential difference in their subject-matters, but it may require a very great difference in the manner of presentation.

It cannot be understood too clearly that the first requirement of a play is that it hold the audience. If it does not succeed in this it may be a work of genius, or it may be, or contain a number of excellent things, but it is *not* a good play. Some of the means whereby a play holds its audience vary from age to age; the greater part of them do not. The æsthetic author may complain that these means are mere trickery, but they are in reality the necessary limitations of the dramatic form. They are, for the most part, devices for arousing expectation, for maintaining suspense, or devices of surprise. They are, it is true, mechanical or ingenious, but so is the technique of verse itself.

Rhyme, for instance, is in a way mechanical, and it also arouses expectation—an expectation of the ear for repetition of sound. In the delayed rhyming of Daniel, we have a maintaining of suspense. In every very beautiful or unusual arrangement of words we have "dénouement"—surprise.

The so-called tricks of the stage are its rhymes and its syntax. They are, perhaps, more easily analysed than the subtler technique of lyric poetry, but they cannot be neglected. After these restrictions, or conventions, or laws of the drama have been mastered, the author can add his beauty and his literary excellence. But without these, his excellences are as far from being drama, as a set of disconnected, or wrongly connected wheels and valves, is from being an engine. All great plays consist of this perfected mechanism, plus poetry, or philosophy, or some further excellence which is of enduring interest.

Because it is very difficult to write good poetry, and because the dramatist has so many other means at his command, he usually relapses into inferior poetry or neglects it altogether. When the paraphernalia of the stage were less complicated, this neglect was less easy.

The sources of English drama have been traced by Chambers in his *History of the Mediæval Stage,* to the satisfaction of nearly everyone. In Spain the sources and prime influences of the drama were: the church ceremonies, the elaborate services for Christmas and Easter, which result in the divers sorts of religious plays, saints' plays, and the like; the dialogue forms of the troubadour poetry, developing in "loas," and "entremes" or skits; and later, the effect of the travelling Italian company of a certain Ganasa, who brought the "Comedia del Arte" into Spain.

In this "Comedia del Arte" one finds the art of drama, the art of the stage; a complete art, as yet unalloyed by any admixture of the literary art. The comedians chose their subject; and each man for himself, given some rough plan, worked out his own salvation—to wit, the speeches of the character he represented. That is to say, you had a company of actor-authors, making plays as they spoke them. Hamlet's "O reform it altogether, and let those that play your clowns speak no more than is set down for them," shows that the effects of this custom lasted in England until Shakespear's time, at least in connection with "character" parts.

According to Lope de Vega, "comedies" in Spain are no older than Rueda. If one is to quibble over origins, one must name Gomez Manrique (1412-91) as author of liturgical drama of the simplest sort. He was not the originator, merely the first author whose name we know; and Juan del Encina (1468-1534) for "eclogas" or "skits."

Calisto and Melibea (the "Celestina") was published in 1499; and is probably by Fernando de Rojas. It is a novel in dialogue of twenty-two acts, unstageable.

The Portuguese, Gil Vincente, lived from 1470-1540; it is not known that his works were ever played in Spain. But Lope de Rueda (circa 1558), gold-beater, actor-manager, and playwright, began the theatre.

Whatever may be said to the credit of these originators, there is no interest except for the special student in any Spanish plays earlier than those of Lope de Vega, and Lope certainly found his stage in a much more rudimentary condition than Shakespear found the stage of England. Whatever be the intrinsic merit of Lope's work, this much is certain: he gave Spain her dramatic literature, and from Spain Europe derived her modern theatre. In his admirable essay on Lope, Fitz-Maurice Kelly says: "Schiller and Goethe combined, failed to create a national theatre at Weimar; no one but Lope could have succeeded in creating a national theatre at Madrid."

Shakespear is a consummation; nothing that is based on Shakespear excels him. Lope is a huge inception; Calderón and Tirso de Molina, Alarcon, De Castro, have made their enduring reputations solely by finishing what Lope had neglected to bring to perfection. They may excel him in careful workmanship, never in dramatic energy. When I say that Lope's plays are the first which are of general interest, I mean that he is the first who, having mastered the machinery of the drama, added to his plays those excellences which give to his works some enduring interest.

Lope was born 1562, led a varied, interesting life, which is best told by H. A. Rennert in his *Life of Lope de Vega.* He wrote a multitude of miscellaneous works, and from fifteen hundred to two thousand plays, of which about four hundred remain to us. Some of the plays are still as fresh and as actable as on the day they were written. Considering the haste of their composition, it is not remarkable that many others possess merely antiquarian interest. Montalban testifies to Lope's having written fifteen acts in fifteen consecutive days, and many of the plays were probably composed within twenty-four hours.

Lope is bound to the Middle Ages much more closely than are the Elizabethans by reason of his religious plays, a form of art practically uninfluenced by the Renaissance, and already out of fashion in London. Such plays were greatly in demand in Lope's time, and for long after, in Madrid. They attain their highest development at the hands of Calderón. Lope's religious plays scarcely belong to world literature, and it is not on their account that one seeks to resurrect the damaged shade of their author.

From my scant knowledge of the English religious plays, I should say that they are more vigorous than those written in Spanish; this does not mean that Lope's "obras santos" are without interest, and *El Serafin Humano*, his dramatization of the *Fioretti* of St. Francis is certainly entertaining.

In the opening scenes of the play we find Francisco, an over-generous young man, engaged in a flirtation with certain ladies of no great dignity. These ladies remark among themselves: "Ah, this is a new cock-sparrow; this will be easy." The ladies' "escudero," or serving-man, proceeds to "work" Francisco for inordinate tips. The lower action runs its course. Francisco gives his clothes to a beggar, and sees a vision; here the piety of the play begins. Francisco takes the cross; a "voice" tells him to give up the crusade, that he must fight a better battle where he is; and in this atmosphere of voices and visions the play proceeds, ending in Brother Gil's vision of the "holy tree."

If Lope's cycle of historical plays do not match Shakespear's cycle of the English kings, it is quite certain that they can be compared to nothing else. From the opening cry in *Amistad Pagada*,

> Al arma, al arma capitanes fuertes,
> Al arma capitanes valerosos,

through the sequence of the plays overflowing the five volumes of Pelayo's huge edition, the spirit of Spain and the spirit of the "romanceros" is set loose upon the boards. It is of "bellicosa Espana," more invincible than "Libia fiera," and of Leon, "already conquered, its walls razed to the ground, coming furious from the mountains."

There is about the cycle no effect of pageantry or of parade; it is a stream of swift-moving men, intent on action. The scope of the cycle may be judged from the following titles: *King Vamba*, *The Last Goth*, *The Deeds of Bernardo del Carpio's Youth*, *Feman Gonzalez*, *El Nuevo mondo descubierto por Cristobal Colon*. This last is, I believe, the finest literary presentation of Columbus known to exist. It is noble and human, and there is admirable drawing in the scene where Columbus is mocked by the King of Portugal. The further main action runs as follows: Bartolomeo brings the news of England's refusal to finance the venture. "Imagination" appears, after the manner of the Greek *deus ex machina*; and there is a play within the play, a little "morality" of Providence, Idolatry, and Christian religion. Columbus finally gets an

audience with King Ferdinand. Fragments of the dialogue are as follows:

> *Colon*:
>   The conquest of Granada brought to happy
>   end,
>   Now is the time to gain the world. . . .
>   The crux?
>   Lord, money, the money is the all,
>   The master and the north and the ship's track,
>   The way, the intellect, the toil, the power,
>   Is the foundation and the friend most sure.

> *The King*:
>   War with Granada has cost me
>   A sum, which you, perchance, may know.

But the money is finally provided.

Act II opens with the mutiny on shipboard. The eloquence of the strike leaders is of the sort one may hear at Marble Arch on any summer evening.

> *First Mutineers*:
>   Arrogant capitan
>   Of a band deceived,
>   Who in your cause
>   Are nearer unto death
>   Than to the land you seek,
>   Whereto, through thousand thousands
>   Of leagues and of oppressions,
>   You drag them o'er
>   A thousand deaths to feed
>   The fishes of such distant seas.
>   Where's this new world?
>   O maker of humbugs,
>   O double of Prometheus,
>   What of these dry presages,
>   Is not this all high sea?
>   What of your unseen land,
>   Your phantom conquest?
>   I ask no argosies.
>   Let go your boughs of gold
>   And give us barley beards
>   So they be dry.

The other mutineers continue with ridicule and sarcasm. Frey Buyl saves Columbus, and land is sighted. The third act is of the triumphant return.

Los novios de Hornachuelos (an incident in the reign of Henry III) contains one of the tensest scenes of all romantic drama; the greater part of this play is delightful comedy: Thus, from Act I, Scene 1:

> *Mendo* (servant):
>   Do you not fear the king?

> *Lope Melindez*:
>   The power of the king is not thus great.
>   My whim serves me for law.
>   There's no king else for me.

Lope Melindez and none other
Is king in Estremadura.
If Henry gain to rule,
Castile is wide.

Mendo:
You speak notable madness.
Doth not the whole wide world
Tremble for that sick man Henry
Whose valour is past belief.

Melindez threatens his squire, and Mendo replies:

Those who must please on all occasions must be
chameleons.
Must clothe themselves and seem their master's
colors.

From which lines we learn that the king is an invalid, that Lope Melindez, "the wolf" of Estremadura, is a braggart and rebel, and that his squire is a philosopher in fustian.

Continuing, we find that Melindez has in him "such might of love that he is affrighted of it"; that there is a gentlewoman called for her beauty the Star, "Estrella" de Estremadura, who is "the cipher of all human beauty." (It is always diverting to notice the manner in which Shakespear and Lope habitually boil down the similes of love into epigrammatic metaphor).

Next a servant announces: "The King-at-Arms of the King," with a letter. Melindez receives him, and says he will reply at leisure. The King-at-Arms replies that the King demands an immediate answer.

Melindez:
Ah! punctual fellows,
The Kings-at-Arms!

King-at-Arms:
Henry
Doth thee no small honor
When for Ambassador
He sendeth such an one as I.
We Kings-at-Arms
Move on no lesser service
Than to bear challenges
To Emperors or Kings.

Melindez:
The King defies me, then!

The King-at-Arms replies that the King challenges only equals. The letter is a summons for Melindez to present himself at Court with four servants and no more.

Melindez:
Oh, Mendo
I'm for throwing
This King-at-Arms from a
Balcony, into the castle moat.
He becomes too loquacious.

Melindez refuses to obey the summons, makes a long speech to the effect that from his castle, which beholds the sun's birth, he sees no land which hath other lord than himself, and that he has arms for four thousand. After having disburdened himself, he becomes polite, but the King-at-Arms will neither rest nor eat.

Melindez:
Heaven go with you.

King-at-Arms:
The King will take satisfaction.

Melindez:
Sword to sword, let's see
Who's vassal and who's King!

(*The King-at-Arms leaves.*)

Melindez:
I'm for Hornachuelos.

Scene 2 is at Hornachuelos. Estrella enters, and her character is in part shown by her attire. ("Enter Estrella, with javelin, sword, dagger, and plumed sombrero.")

This charming gentlewoman is marrying off a couple of her vassals tenant who have not the slightest desire to be so united. The manner of their unwillingness may be here gathered: ("They take hands without turning round, and Mariana gives Berueco a kick which makes him roll.")

Then Mariana:

I'll give you such a blow
As will make you spit
Teeth for two days.

The act ends with a speech of Estrella's:

Lope Melindez, if love is a flame,
Then am I snow frozen in the Alps.

In the beginning of the second act the King sees Estrella, and she falls in love with him. The King-at-Arms has delivered Melindez' answer to the King, who rides to Melindez' castle. Then comes the great scene, the duel between two kinds of strength; it is Lope's thesis for the rights of will and personality.

Servant:
Three horses with riders
Who would speak with you;
One has entered!

Melindez:
Great freedom, by God!

(*King Henry III enters alone.*)

Henry:
Which of the two

Calls himself Melindez,
I have wished to know him.

Melindez:
I call myself Melindez.

Henry:
I have a certain business
Of which I come to speak with you,
Because I love you.
It is of importance
That we be alone.

Melindez:
Leave us.

(The servants go out.)

Henry:
Fasten the door.

Melindez:
How fastidious we are!

(presumably after locking it)
It is locked.

Henry:
Take this chair, to please me.

Melindez:
I sit.

Henry:
Then listen.

Melindez:
I already listen,
And with wonder.

Henry:
El enfermo rey Enrique
[**The sickly King Henry**]

The speech is too long to quote in full. It summarizes the King's reign, begun at the age of fourteen, fraught with all difficulty. It tells of a kingdom set to rights and order drawn from civic chaos, the purport being: such has been my life, such have been its trials; who are you, Melindez, to stand against me, who to jeopardize the welfare of the kingdom by making it necessary for me to leave it in the hands of subordinates? The speech ends:

Henry:
. . . Lope Melindez, I am
*(The King here rises from his chair and
grasps his sword. Lope removes his hat.)*
Enrique, alone we are.
Draw your sword! for I would
Know between you and me,
Being in your house,
The two of us in this locked room,

Who in Castile deserves
To be king, and who
Wolf-vassal of Estremadura.
Show yourself now to me
Haughty and valorous,
Since you boast so much
In my absence. Come!
For my heart is sound
Though my body be sickly,
And my heart spurts the Spanish blood
Of the descendants of Pelayo!

Melindez:
My Lord, no more,
Your face without knowing you gives terror.
Mad have I been.
Blind I went.
Pardon! Señor
If I can please you with tears and surrender.
You have my arms crossed.
My steel at your feet,
And my lips also.
*(He casts his sword at the King's feet and kisses the
ground. Henry sets his foot upon Melindez's head.)*

Henry:
Lope Melindez, thus are humbled the gallant
necks of haughty vassals.
*(The King trembles with the chill of the quar-
tian ague. He walks.)*
Chance has brought on
The Quartian, have you
a bed near.

Melindez:
In the room below
The floor you tread,
But it's small sphere
For such a sovran king.

Henry:
Open
And tell my servants
To come undress me,
For by my trusted valor
I would pass the night
In your house.

Melindez:
Not in vain
Do the Castillians tremble at you,
O Enrique, terror of the world.

In the third act we return to comedy. The King refuses to marry Estrella, saying among other things that he is an invalid. Estrella and Melindez are ordered to marry each other, and the low-life troubles of Berueco and Mariana are travestied in the higher action. Berueco and Mariana have come to blows; Estrella and Melindez shoot across the stage playing the same game with swords, Melindez thinking the King has tricked him and Estrella, naturally resenting the insult. The King unravels the entanglement by divorcing the peasants and promising Estrella another husband.

Another delightful play of this historico-romantic sort is **Las Almenas de Toro**. It has an additional interest for us in that Ruy Diaz appears in it, the time treated being slightly earlier than that shown in the **Poema del Cid**.

The play in brief outline is as follows:

King Ferdinand had divided his kingdom at his death, leaving the cities Toro and Zamora to his daughters, Urraca and Elvira. The new King, Sancho, is not content. At the opening of the play we find the King, the Cid, and the Conde Ancures before the gates of Toro, which Elvira has closed through fear of her brother. The Cid advises the King to retire and return unarmed. He advises the King to let the sisters keep their cities. The King rejects this counsel, and the Cid is sent forward as ambassador.

Elvira comes forth upon the city wall, and replies with delightful irony to the King's proposition that she become a nun.

> *Elvira*:
>   Tell him, my Cid,
>   That I have turned Toro into a cloister
>   (Suffice it to see that the gate is well locked.)
>   It is unfitting that a cloister
>   Be opened to a secular person.

The King sees his sister on the battlements, and, without knowing who she is, falls in love with her.

> *The King*:
>   On the battlements of Toro
>   There passed a damozel, or
>   To speak more truly
>   'Twas the sun's self passed us,
>   Fair the form and light the passing.

> For her whom I saw on the wall that subtlety
> wherewith astronomy painteth aloft her divers
> sights upon the azure mantle of the sky, hath
> made me such that I believe many imagined
> things should be true.

The Cid tells him that it is his sister.

> *The King*:
>   An ill flame be kindled in her!

Pastoral action is brought into the play as relief, "contra el arte," as Lope says in his preface.

King Sancho attacks Toro and is repulsed. At the beginning of the second act Bellido Dolfos begins to plot. Then, under cover of night (a purely imaginary night) two soldiers with guitars come out onto the battlements. Lope is constantly opposed to new-fangled scenery and constantly scenic in imagination. Here the soldiers sing while the siege is in progress.

Dolfos, with a thousand men, approaches and pretends to be Diego Ordonez with relief from Zamora. The ruse succeeds, the town is taken, and Elvira flees.

Dolfos, who had been promised the King's sister in marriage if he took the town, is jealous, and says that the King, or Ancures, or the Cid, has hidden Elvira to cheat him and prevent her marrying below her station. In the meantime the pastoral action runs its course. The Duque de Borgoña, travelling incognito, meets with Elvira, who has disguised herself in country clothing. The people, despite the improbability of the minor entanglement, are convincingly drawn.

Bellido Dolfos finally murders King Sancho. Toro declares for his brother Alfonso, *"el de Leon,"* with whom we are familiar in the **Poema**, but Elvira returns, and the town receives her in triumph.

La Estrella de Sevilla is usually listed as a play of the Cloak and Sword. It is also a problem play of advanced disposition. The question set is this: Can a woman marry the man she loves if he have killed her brother, who was his friend? The King is unjustly angered with Bustos Tabera, the brother, and secretly orders Sancho Ortiz to slay him. Ortiz is bound in duty and honor to obey his King. Lope decides that the marriage is impossible. The handling of royalty in this play is most interesting. The King, Sancho el bravo, is a man subject to the passions, but the incentive to connect evil desire with action comes always from the courtier Arias; thus the evil proceeds, not from the King, but through him.

In reading a play of Lope's it is always worth while to notice which character precipitates the action. Sometimes the entire movement is projected by the gracioso. In this play Ortiz' serving-man is used solely for comic relief, and with a fine precision. His rôle is very short; he appears only about eight times, and each time at the exact moment when the tragic strain begins to oppress the audience. Almost imperceptibly he fades out of the play. Lope is past-master of "relief," and here it serves to keep the audience sensitive to the tragic, unjaded.

When Ortiz is arrested for murder, he refuses to divulge the cause, and the King is forced to confess that the death is by his order.

Estrella pardons Ortiz, but will not marry him. The dignity of this conclusion is sufficient refutation of those who say that Lope wrote nothing but melodrama, and to please the groundlings.

Three of Lope's surviving plays accord us opportunity for direct comparison with the works of his English contemporaries.

The first is **Castelvines y Monteses**, based on Bandello's novel of **Romeo and Julietta**, and the second, **La Nueva Ira de Dios y Gran Tamorlan de Persia**.

The construction of this play is perhaps more skilful than that of Marlowe's *Tamburlaine*. One misses, I think, the sense of Marlowe's unbridled personality moving behind the words: yet there is a tense vigor of phrase in this play of Lope's, and more lines than one in which Marlowe himself might have poured his turbulence of spirit:

Thus Tamorlan:

> Call me the crooked iron,
> Lame am I and mighty!

And again:

> El mundo mi viene estrecho,
> The world grows narrow for me.

And:

> I've to make me a city
> Of gold and silver, and my house of the bodies
>   of kings,
> Be they rocks of valor.

In the first act we find Bayaceto, the Grand Turk, in love with Aurelia, daughter of the Greek Emperor.

Lope naturally shows us **El Gran Turco** carrying on his courtship *in propria persona*; strolling in the Emperor's garden in the cool of the day he is taken captive. This imparts a characteristic briskness to the opening scenes of the play. Bayaceto proclaims himself, and is accepted by the Emperor. The betrothal takes place with ceremony.

Tamorlan is increasing in power. Lelia Eleazara, a Turkish lady in love with Bayaceto, curses him at his betrothal. Bayaceto boasts to Aurelia that to please her, he will go out to conquer the world. The passage presumably corresponds to Marlowe's "To entertain devine Zenocrite" and falls below it. News of Tamorlan is brought, and the act closes.

ACT II

(*Sound drums, and in form of squadrons there go forth by one door half the company clad in skins, Tamorlan behind them; and by the other door the other half, clad as Moors, Bayaceto behind them.*)

Tamorlan:
> I am the Tamorlan,
> I am the celestial wrath,
> I am the burning ray,
> Cause of death and dismay
> To whomso looketh upon me
> In mine anger. . . . .
> Son of myself and of my deeds.

Bayaceto is defeated in battle and taken prisoner.

Scene 2. Presumably in the palace of the Emperor.

Aurelia (*in soliloquy*):
> Presages sad, how now
> Do ye ill-treat me.
> Meseems ye announce
> Mine end with bale and grief
> Unto my new-sprung life;
> Grant comfort,
> Unless my death be fated
> For this day.
> So long the fray!

Aliatar brings news of the battle, with this fine description:

> One sea, fair April
> Mirroring the sky
> With plumes and pennons
> And resplendent arms.

Then, Aurelia, on hearing the outcome,

> No time's for weeping. On!
> Reform our host.
> Call the aged from the farms
> On to Belaquia.
> Homes, lives, and goods
> To bloody smoke be turned,
> Till one flame lap the vale
> That saw the birth
> Of this vile Tamorlan, . . .

Then Elizara comes out, dressed as a madman, and Ozman. Elizara wishes to free Bayaceto by going to Tamorlan disguised as a buffoon.

The next scene shows Tamorlan mocking Bayaceto, in a cage. Elizara enters; then enter the ambassadors from twenty-nine kings, wishing to ransom Bayaceto: they are refused.

Act III. Tamorlan is overthrown and dies. Elizara becomes a Christian nun.

The play here follows the usual lines of the plays of Spanish and Moorish contest, or the **Chançon de Roland**, for that matter. This sort of conquest play is, of course, no longer suitable for the stage.

Lope's work differs from Shakespear's in that it faces in two directions: thus, **Tamorlan** is a last exhalation of the spirit which produced the **"Cantares de Gesta."** The saints' plays are a transference to the stage of a literary form which had been long popular. The Spanish historical plays are far more vital than either of these, but their roots are in the older ballades and romances. (The term "romance" is applied in Spanish to a particular form of short narrative poem.) The plays of Lope, which are prophetic of the future stage, are those of the "cloak and sword." The best of which are as fresh and playable today as they were in 1600. It is on this pattern that Beaumarchais has written his *Barber of Seville*, and Shaw his *Arms and the Man*. It is true that Shaw has introduced chocolate creams, and electric bells in Bulgaria, and certain other minor details, but the stock situations and the sprightly spirit of impertinence date at least from Lope. The most diverting proof of this is **El Desprecio Agradecido**, which might have been written—bar certain vagaries of chronos—by Shaw in collaboration with Joachim du Bellay. The action begins with characteristic swiftness.

Personas

DON BERNARDO (from Seville)
SANCHO, his servant
LISARDA, Florela's sister
FLORELA, Lisarda's sister
INES, their maid
LUCINDO, their brother
DON ALEXANDRO, their father
MENDO, servant of this family
OCTAVIO, betrothed to Lisarda

Acto Primo

(*Come forth Bernardo and Sancho, with drawn swords and bucklers.*)

Bernardo:
What a rotten jump!
Sancho:
The walls were high.
Bernardo:
I should have thought you would have leapt the better, since you were the more afraid.
Sancho:
Who isn't afraid of the law, and we just leaving a man dead?
Bernardo:
Carelessness, I admit. Let who lives, live keenly. It's a fine house we've come into.
Sancho:
I'm flayed entirely. The wall's cost me blood.
Bernardo:
In the darkness I can see no more than that this is a garden.
Sancho:
And what are we going to do about it?
Bernardo:
To get out, Sancho, is what I should wish to do.
Sancho:
If they hear us, they'll take us for thieves.
Bernardo:
Zeal comes to men in straitened circumstance.
Sancho:
It's the Devil ever made us leave Seville!
Bernardo:
The parlor, shall we go in?
Sancho:
Yes.
Bernardo:
Women speak.
Sancho:
Notice that they say they are going to bed.
Bernardo:
But what shall we do?

Sancho:
We shall see what they are, from behind this hanging.

Twenty-eight lines have carried us thus far.

The shifting of the embarrassment indicated in the next to the last line is as keen as it is characteristic.

(*Come forth Lisarda, Florela, Ines, and ladies.*)

Lisarda:
Put the light on this table, let me see that tray. Take off these roses, I don't want them to wither.
Florela:
How dull Octavio was!
Lisarda:
There is nothing that bores one so much as a relative ready to be a husband and not a lover.
Florela:
Take this chain, Ines . . .

And so on until

(*Sancho's buckler falls.*)

Lisarda:
Good Lord! what's that?
Florela:
What fell?
Ines:
Don't be afraid.
Lisarda:
Lock the door, Ines.
Ines:
Which one?
Lisarda:
That which opens into the garden.
Ines:
It is open.
Lisarda:
Good care you take (of us)!
Ines:
We used to lock it later than this.
Lisarda:
Apologize, and get to work. Take this light, look quickly. What fell?
Ines:
What is this?
Lisarda:
How?
Ines:
This buckler here!
Lisarda:
My brother's guard would be like it.
Ines:
Yes! And since when have the curtains worn shoes?
Lisarda:
Jesus mil veces! Thieves!

Bernardo comes out, and with eloquent apologies casts himself on their mercy. Lope does justice to the delicate situation. Finally Lisarda says, "Ines, lock them both in this room, and bring me the key"; and then follows a charming bit of impertinence:

> *Bernardo*:
> Ines, I shall not sleep.
> *Ines*:
> Can you do with this light and a book?
> *Bernardo*:
> Depends on the book.
> *Ines*:
> Part 26 of Lope.
> *Bernardo*:
> Ah! spurious works printed with his name on 'em.

The further entanglement of the comedy is delightful. I have in part explained the characters in the list of *dramatis personœ*.

Bernardo has come from Seville with a letter for Octavio, whose cousin, Bernardo's brother, is about to marry. Octavio hears voices in Lisarda's house on the night of Bernardo's adventure, and is filled with jealousy. When Bernardo, on leaving, delivers his letter and narrates his strange adventures, speaking of the lovely lady and his departure, he says, in Lope's inimitable Spanish:

> Sali, no se si diga enamorado,
> Pero olvidado del amor pasado.

> I came out, I do not know that one would say,
> in love, But forgetful of past love.

Or,

> Not enamored, but forgetful of past enamorment.

The cadence and rhyme of the Spanish gives it a certain suavity which I cannot reproduce.

Nothing gives less idea of a play than an outline of its plot: the feelings of Octavio during Bernardo's narration can be readily guessed at, and Lope well displays them.

Both sisters fall in love with Bernardo, and the scene between them reminds one of a similar encounter in Wilde's *Importance of Being Earnest*.

The fact that women were at this time, contrary to the English custom, permitted on the Spanish stage; and Lope's greater familiarity with the sex, which he married frequently and with varying degrees of formality, accounts for a fuller development of the feminine rôles than one finds in the contemporary English plays. Lope is no mere wit and juggler. Lisarda's speech, when her love for Bernardo seems wholly thwarted by circumstance, brings into the play that poetry which is never far from the pen of "the Phœnix of Spain."

The following translation is appalling in its crudity. Lisarda is walking in the garden where Bernardo had entered the night before:

> Flowers of this garden
> Where entered Don Bernardo
> On whom I look, a sunflower,
> On the sun that is my doom;
> Rose, carnation, jasmine,
> That with a life securer
> Take joy in your swift beauty,
> Tho' ye make in one same day
> Your green sepulchres
> Of the cradles you were born in;
> Yet would I speak with you,
> Since my joy found beginning
> And ending in one day,
> Whence took it birth and death,
> And I await like ending.
> A flower I was as ye,
> I was born as ye are born,
> And if ye know not rightly
> That ye hold your life but lightly,
> Learn, O flowers, of me.
> The light of your colors,
> And the pomp of all your leaves,
> The blue, the white, the ruddy,
> Paint loves and jealousies.
> For this, O flowers, ye pass.
> Counsel I give and example.
> For yesterday I was, what today I am not,
> And if today I am not what I was but yesterday
> Now may ye learn from me,
> What things do pass away
> With the passing of one day.
> As ye are, I was certain
> That my fair hope would flower.
> But love's blossoms alway
> Bring forth fruit uncertain.
> Aspic living, amor hidden—
> Nay, I learnt it not from you—
> This killed and said to me:
> Whoso look on me now and find me
> Changèd so, would not believe
> The marvel that I was but yesterday.
> Be ye with colors lovely
> As those that ye saw love in,
> With the perfumed exhalations
> That are comets of the flower.
> And O, ye easy splendors,
> That I stand invoking,
> If I be marvellous today,
> Consider what yesterday gave shadow
> To the sun, with what I was
> Who today am not my shadow even.

The play winds on through the comic labyrinths. The man whom Bernardo killed for following his former flame from Seville, turns out not to have been killed, but appears as Lucindo, Lisarda's brother. He and his father try to marry Bernardo to the wrong sister: the marriage of Lisarda to Octavio seems inevitable. Sancho and Mendo, in their love for Ines, parody the main action. The high-flown language of the times' gallantry is mixed with Sancho's cynical matter-of-fact humor. Lope's *graciosos* are often without a sense of humor; at such times their remarks are usually unconscious, are humorous because of their position in the play: the position of the *gracioso* in Lope's plays is that occupied by Sancho Panza in *Don Quixote*. The chauffeur in Shaw's *Man and Superman* retains some of the *gracioso*'s functions. It is part of Lope's mastery of theatrical technique that he seems to whisper privately to each member of his audience, "What fools the rest are! But *you* and *I* see the thing in its true colors." Thus, to the young romantic, he seems to say, "Behold this gallant, whose nobility and ideals are so misunderstood by his vulgar serving-man"; and to the *gracioso* in the audience he says, "This 'high falutin' romance, these lofty ideals, this code of honor! What nonsense it is!" It is flattery, of course, not the subtlest, but practical flattery, harnessed to Lope's theatrical purpose.

Despite their number, Lope's plays are not filled with wooden figures, or masks, or types, but with individuals. There is repetition, small wonder and small harm; even in Shakespear, Toby Belch and Falstaff are to some extent and much girth the same character.

Any comparison of Shakespear and Lope must be based in part on their distinctly individual treatment of the same theme—that is, Bandello's tale of Romeo and Juliette. The comparison is a fair one, for if *Romeo and Juliet* is not one of Shakespear's greatest plays, it is one-fiftieth part of his work, while Lope's *Castelvines y Monteses* is less than one-fifteen-hundredth part of his.

An English translation of Lope's play by F. W. Cosens appeared in 1869, for private distribution; this translation should be reprinted, though Cosens is, I think, wrong in attempting a Shakespearian diction in his rendering of Lope's Spanish. Lope's dramatic convention differs from Shakespear's in this: Shakespear's convention is that of ennobled diction. His speech is characteristic of his people, but is more impressive than ordinary speech. Works of art attract us by a resembling unlikeness. Lope's convention is that of rhymes and assonance—that is, his lines differ from ordinary speech in that they are more suave: when Lope becomes ornate, irony is not far distant. The nature of the Spanish language permits rhyme and assonance, without such strain or cramping as these devices would generate in English. His effort is to make speeches which can be more easily pronounced "trippingly on the tongue." Shakespear also aims at this, but it is a secondary aim, and it is concealed by his verse structure, although such words as:

> Nymph, in thy orisons
> Be all my sins
> remembered,

have about them something of the Spanish smoothness. But Lope would have written, I think,

> Nymph,
> In thine orisons
> Be all our sins
> remembered.

Lope is all for speed in dialogue; his lines are shorter: thus a translation which has his own blemishes (*i.e.* those of carelessness), is a truer representation of him than one that retards his action by a richer phrasing. Not that he lacks eloquence or noble diction on occasion, but his constant aim is swiftness.

This criticism must only be applied to certain plays. No formula of criticism even approximately applies to all of Lope's work. What he does today, he does not tomorrow.

Dante and Shakespear are like giants. Lope is like ten brilliant minds inhabiting one body. An attempt to enclose him in any formula is like trying to make one pair of boots to fit a centipede.

Lope's **Castelvines y Monteses**, then, lacks Shakespear's richness of diction. He tends towards actual reproduction of life, while Shakespear tends towards a powerful symbolic art. In this play each of the masters has created his own vivid detail. In the Spanish play there is a delightful and continued "double entente" in the garden scene, where Julia sits talking to Octavio, in phrases which convey their real meaning only to Roselo. Shakespear portrays this maidenly subtlety in Act III, Scene 5, in the dialogue between Juliet and her mother.

Although Lope's play ends in comedy, it has a tragic emphasis, no lighter than Shakespear's: thus Julia drinks the sleeping draught, and, as it is beginning to take effect, doubts whether it be not some fatal poison; so all the fear of death is brought in. Lope is past-master at creating that sort of "atmospheric pressure," which we are apt to associate specifically with Ibsen and Maeterlinck. He envelops his audience with his sense of "doom impending" and his "approach of terror," or in any temper of emotion which most fits his words and makes most sure his illusion.

After Julia has been buried, Roselo comes into the tomb, and the fear of his *criado* (servant), the trusty Marin, in the place of death brings the comic relief.

(In **Los Bandos de Verona**, a later play on this subject by Rojas, the *gracioso* is omitted, and the nurse fills this office in the dramatic machinery, somewhat as the nurse in Shakespear.)

Julia awakes; Marin touches her by accident.

> *Julia:*
> Man, are you living or dead?
> *Marin:*
> *Muerto soy!*—Dead am I!

The lovers escape to the country, and live disguised as peasants. Antonio (Julia's father) goes [on] a journey, discovers Roselo, and is about to have him killed, when the voice of his supposedly dead daughter arrests him. The escaped Julia, impersonating her own ghost, terrifies him into forgiveness, and the play ends in restoration and gaiety. There is no absolute stage necessity for the general slaughter at the end of Shakespear's play. If one demand tragedy, Lope creates as intense an air of tragedy in the poison scene above mentioned. A decision as to the relative merits of these two plays depends solely on individual taste; the greatness of Shakespear is, however, manifest if we shift our ground of comparison to ***Acertar Errando***. This play and *The Tempest* are traceable to a common source, presumably of rich beauty. When Furness wrote his introduction to *The Tempest,* no source used by Shakespear in this play had been discovered. ***Acetar Errando*** is a far more ordinary affair than the English play, but then Lope probably wrote his version in three days or less. In the Spanish play we find a rightful heiress, Aurora Infanta of Calabria, on an island, and early in the course of the play this speech:

> *Aurora:*
> Fabio, Oton, there's a little ship in the offing
> Perplexed and buffeted.
> Proudly the sea with sledgy blows
> Disturbs and drives it on.
> They wait your aid.
> Thus before my eyes
> Die those that clamor there within,
> A prey of the brackish whirl . . .
> The winds play at *pelota* (make them their
>   tennis),
> Ah, boldness little availing!
> Now touch they the stars, and now the sandy
>   floor.

As in the Romeo tale, both authors from their fecundity supply their own detail, never hitting upon the same, but often upon equally enchanting methods of presentation.

Here, I think, we must presuppose much of the beauty to be that of the common source.

The beneficent Prospero is probably Shakespear's own creation, although in Lope's play we find mention of "the power of the stars," and of a "master of the island." I suspect an Italian, and ultimately Oriental, source for both the plays, but this is merest conjecture.

Both Ariel and the phantom music of Shakespear's play were perhaps suggested by Apuleius, but Lope's prince, in describing the tempest, personifies the winds, which had confused his mariners: with common names, to be sure, "Eolo," and "Austro," but it is personification nevertheless. In Lope's ***Tarquin*** we find a combination of our old friends Stephano and Trinculo: among other things, he, at landing, speaks thus familiarly: "Let me then bless the wine."

Caliban is Shakespear's; but Lope also mentions an unprepossessing creature, with one eye larger than the other.

Lope's further "enredo" or entanglement differs from that of the English play. He sets fewer characters on the boards, but there is parallel for Ferdinand's imprisonment, and for Sebastian's plot against Alonso (or Caliban's against Prospero—if one choose to regard it so).

In the end the Prince and Island Princess "ascertain by erring," after the manner of such adventure. A separate volume would be required for an adequate academic discussion of this play and the problems it involves.

One might continue giving synopses of Lope's plays almost *ad infinitum.* No formula of criticism is, as I have said, of any great use in trying to define him. He is not a man, he is a literature. A man of normal energy could spend a fairly active life in becoming moderately familiar with the 25 per cent of Lope's work which has survived him.

His ***Adonis y Venus*** does not seem particularly happy; it is perhaps typical of his dramatic treatment of classic themes. But if these imitations are without notable value, how gladly do we turn to those shorter poems, which are really Spanish. Thus:

> A mis soledades voy
> De mis soledades vengo
> Porque para andar conmigo
> Mi bastan mis pensamientos.

The true poet is most easily distinguished from the false, when he trusts himself to the simplest expression, and when he writes without adjectives.

> To my solitudes I go,
> From my solitudes return I,
> Sith for companions on the journey,
> Mine own thoughts (do well) suffice me.

These lines are at the beginning of some careless redondillas, representing the thoughts he takes with him journeying; among which this quatrain:

> Envy they paint with evil chere,
> But I confess that I possess it,
> For certain men who do not know
> The man that lives next door to them.

He is ever at these swift transitions. I think his thoughts outran even his pen's celerity, so that often he writes only their beginnings. It is this that gives him buoyancy, and inimitable freshness. For, notwithstanding the truth of Fitzmaurice Kelly's statement that in his non-dramatic work "Lope followed everyone who made a hit," there is about his plays nothing *fin de siècle,* but always an atmosphere of earliest morning. There is no kind of excellence (except that of sustained fineness) of which we dare say, "it was beyond him," since our refutation may be concealed anywhere in those surviving plays of his, which no living man has read.

Hood's delicacy in one corner of his mind, in another, the vigor of Marlowe. If haste or love of words has left some of his nature painting rhetorical, his

> A penas Leonora
> La blanca aurora
> Puso su pie de marfil

Sobre las flores de Abril,
Scarcely doth the white dawn press
Her ivory foot upon the April flowers,

is as descriptive of the pale dawn of Spain as is Shake-spear's "in russet mantle clad," of the more northern day's approaching.

As illustration of his suave, semi-ironical gallantry I quote this from a passage between "galan" and "gracioso."

> *Galan*:
>   Porque eso nombre mi dan?
> *Gracioso*:
>   No vienes desde Milan
>   Solo a ver un mujer?
> *Galan*:
>   No es una mujer mas que una ciudad
>   Siendo un mundo de pesar
>   Siendo un cielo de plazer?
> *Master*:
>   Why do they give me this name (*i.e.* fool)?
> *Man*:
>   Didn't you come all the way from Milan
>   Just to look at a woman?
> *Master*:
>   Isn't a woman more than a city,
>   Being a world of trouble
>   And a heaven of pleasure?

Between his vigor and his suavity, his wit and his tenderness, the intoxication grows within one. One may know him rather well and yet come upon him suddenly in some new phase; thus, if one knows only his irony, one comes upon the slumber song in the little book of devotions, *Los Pastores de Belen* (*The Bethlehem Shepherds*). One stanza is as follows, the Virgin singing it:

> Cold be the fierce winds
> Treacherous round him;
> Ye see that I have not
> Wherewith to guard him.
> O Angels, divine ones
> That pass us a-flying;
> Sith sleepeth my child here
> Still ye the branches.

If we at this late day are bewildered at his versatility, it is small wonder that the times which saw the man himself should have gone mad over him.

It is not in the least surprising that in 1647 there should have appeared a creed beginning "I believe in Lope de Vega the Almighty, the poet of heaven and earth"; the marvel is that the Inquisition should have been able to suppress it.

A Spaniard told me not long since that Lope prophesied the wireless telegraph. I have forgotten the exact passage which he used as substantiation, but I am quite ready to believe it.

At the end of this century Lope's works may be reasonably accessible. The best English sources of information concerning Lope are: H. A. Rennert's *Life of Lope de Vega*; Fitzmaurice Kelly's essay on Lope, in his *Chapters on Spanish Literature;* and the pages on Lope in his *History of Spanish Literature.* Synopses of a number of plays are given in A. F. Von Schack's *Geschichte des dramatischen Literatur und Kunst in Spanien.* There is a Spanish translation of this work by E. de Mier.

Anyone who can read Spanish would do well to apply himself to the plays themselves.

No prince of letters ever ruled such subjects as had Frey Lope Felix de Vega y Carpio. (pp. 179-210)

Salvador de Madariaga   (essay date 1920)

SOURCE: "English Sidelights on Spanish Literature," in *Shelley & Calderón and Other Essays on English and Spanish Poetry.* Constable and Company, 1920, pp. 50-83.

[*A versatile, accomplished man of letters, Madariaga is widely considered Spain's outstanding intellectual figure of the twentieth-century and was a prominent diplomat in pre-Revolutionary Spain. Trilingual, he wrote criticism, political treatises, histories, and biographies, as well as novels, poetry, and plays—all of which have been praised for their clarity and elegance of style—in Spanish, French, and English. In the following excerpt, he maintains that Lope's significance in the history of Spanish drama is analogous to that of Shakespeare in English drama.*]

Though the founder of the Spanish theatre, and by far its greatest figure, Lope de Vega had to wait until quite recently before posterity accorded him the fame which he deservedly enjoyed in his lifetime. Calderón, better known, preceded him into European renown. This fact explains why Calderón, believed to be the "central figure" of the Spanish theatre, should have been selected as the prototype with whom to compare Shakespeare. But in actual fact, the real Spanish equivalent to Shakespeare is Lope de Vega. Not only were they both the founders of their national theatres, but they were both of that spontaneous type of genius which most reminds us of the simplicity, fatality and almost awe-inspiring power of natural forces. Of nature, indeed, Shakespeare and Lope have the fecundity and the reckless extravagance and a calm disregard for mere polish, refinement and perfection. When they, as they often do, give us a rendering of apt and felicitous accuracy, we feel that we owe it, not to any painstaking effort of conscientious artistry but to that intuition which their genius gains in the all-pervading sympathy of their outlook. And like all fertile sources of creation, they both inspire in us a mysterious feeling of affection and gratitude, such as we feel for the sea or the earth or the life-giving sun.

Yet the parallel between Lope and Shakespeare cannot be carried much further without having to note down differences which curiously resemble the differences between Chaucer and Juan Ruiz. Lope's marvellous fecundity implied a facility of imagination, construction and execution as favourable to the quantity as harmful to the quality of his work. In the circumstances in which he wrote, his standard of quality is indeed incredibly high. His adventurous life did not leave him time enough to deepen and mature his philosophy of life, and of him, no less than of Juan Ruiz, it may be said that, compared to his English brother-spirit, he is inferior in that he failed to cultivate his mind in solitude. Little as we know of Shakespeare's life, he could hardly have grown some of the more complex flowers of his poetry without leisure and tranquillity. Thus it is that Shakespeare deepens into thought and erects a theatre of emotions in the very chambers of the human soul, while Lope spreads out into action and builds a theatre of situations in the open space of tangible reality. (pp. 76-8)

Additional coverage of Vega's life and career is contained in the following sources published by the Gale Group: *Literature Criticism from 1400 to 1800*, Vol. 23.

Helena María Viramontes
1954–

Chicana short story writer, novelist, and editor.

INTRODUCTION

Helena María Viramontes has published two single-authored books, *The Moth and Other Stories*, a collection of short stories, and *Under the Feet of Jesus*, a novel; and has co-edited two collections of non-fiction written by other Chicanas. At a time when the Hispanic population, and the Mexican-American population in particular, is increasing rapidly in the United States, Viramontes examines the challenges her people face in managing dual-cultural identities. Exploring the lives of characters who struggle to survive in a society which tends to be indifferent or hostile, Viramontes focuses on the hopes and dreams of citizens relegated to second-class status. In *The Moth and Other Stories* (1985), a collection of short stories and her first book, she depicts the humiliation and oppression that Chicana women endure in their everyday lives in Southern California. Viramontes's penchant for writing sometimes didactic prose was still evident in her first novel, *Under the Feet of Jesus*, published in 1995. The novel chronicles the life of Estrella, a young migrant worker who attempts to break free of the repressive dictates of family and church. Viramontes does not reserve her caustic critiques of patriarchy for the White American society which oppresses her people; she also investigates ways in which the Latino culture itself fosters gender oppression.

The fifth of eleven children, Viramontes was born in 1954 to working class parents in East Los Angeles, California, a predominantly Mexican-American part of the city. Viramontes learned about the politics of poverty first hand. Having met as farm laborers picking cotton, Viramontes's parents would take the family to pick grapes in the fields of Fresno, California. Though her family struggled to make ends meet, the Viramontes's always had a house full of guests: friends and family frequently came from Mexico to stay with them. Viramontes's mother was fond of saying, "If there's enough floor, there's enough bed." The constant stream of visitors, and the stories they told, helped shape Viramontes's own love of storytelling. This love blossomed during the 70s as Viramontes began reading African-American women writers such as Toni Morrison, Gwendolyn Brooks, and Alice Walker. This, she felt, opened avenues for her to write about her own culture. Her reading of Hispanic writers such as Gabriel Garcia Marquez, Julio Cortezar, and Jorge Luis Borges, inspired her to experiment with form. After graduating from Immaculate Heart College in 1975, Viramontes enrolled in the M.F.A. program at the University of California at Irvine, but she later dropped out because of clashes with the administration. In 1985 she published a collection of short stories, *The Moth and Other Stories*, which drew upon her own experience as a Chicana. In 1988 she and María Herrera-Sobek co-edited a collection of writing by and about Chicanas called *Chicana Creativity and Criticism: Charting New Frontiers in American Literature*. Viramontes then returned to the University of California at Irvine, graduating with an M.F.A. in 1993. Viramontes credits winning the Chicano Literature contest at Irvine with restoring her confidence as a writer, inspiring her to finish *Under the Feet of Jesus*. Viramontes studied with Irvine faculty members and writers Judith Grossman and Thomas Kenneally whom, along with Sandra Cisneros, are credited as influences on her writing. Married and a mother of two children, Viramontes is currently an associate professor of English and Creative Writing at Cornell University.

Though reviewers have criticized the overtly ideological nature of Viramontes's writing, they have also praised her commitment to exploring the lives of women, specifically poor Chicanas. In *The Moth and Other Stories*, Viramontes illustrates how cultural and societal values shape the lives of these women, often instilling in them a sense of inferiority and self-hatred. The wife of Tomas, a central character in "The Broken Web," for example, is given no name, to emphasize the character's own lack of self worth. Viramontes often presents events out of chronological order, and shifts point of view to underscore the complex nature of experience. In *Under the Feet of Jesus*, she continues with her theme of examining the relationship between a Chicana woman's material circumstances and her reaction to it. The novel, dedicated to farm labor activist César Chavez, is a *bildungsroman* narrated by Estrella, a young migrant worker sharing the story of her first love and the inevitable obstacles the couple face from their families and society. The characters in the novel are fashioned from Viramontes's personal life and experiences. The bleakness and poverty of the characters' lives are set against the stunning beauty of the California landscape, a juxtaposition which heightens the reader's sense of injustice. Viramontes's work is part of the growing body of Chicana literature being published in recent decades. Much of this literature has appeared in small press magazines such as *Xhisme Arte Magazine*, which she edited from 1978-81, and *Maize*, and many of the authors are being published by Arte Publico Press, the oldest and largest publisher of Hispanic literature in the United States. Viramontes's writing forms a vital part of the explosion of Latinas fostering the American literary scene. Her willingness to explore both the personal and the political lives of women marks her writing as fiction written with the purpose of expressing and celebrating a view previously unexplored in American fiction.

PRINCIPAL WORKS

The Moths and Other Stories (short stories) 1985
*"Miss Clairol" (short story) 1987
Chicana (W)Rites on Word and Film [editOR with María Herrera-Sobek] (anthology) 1988
†"'Nopalitos': The Making of Fiction" (essay) 1989
‡"Tears on My Pillow" (short story) 1992
Under the Feet of Jesus (novel) 1995
Chicana Creativity and Criticism: New Frontiers in American Literature [edited with María Herrera-Sobek] (anthology) 1996

* in *Chicana Creativity and Criticism: Charting New Frontiers in American Literature*, edited by Viramontes and María Herrera-Sobeck (Houston: Arte Público, 1987), pp. 101-105.

† in *Breaking Boundaries: Latina Writings and Critical Readings*, edited by Asunción Horno-Delgado, Eliana Ortega, Nina M. Scott, and Nancy Saporta Sternbach (Amherst: University of Massachusetts Press, 1989), pp. 33-38.

‡ in *New Chicana/Chicano Writing*, edited by Charles M. Tatum (Tucson: University of Arizona Press, 1992), pp. 110-115.

CRITICISM

Roberta Fernández (essay date 1989)

SOURCE: "'The Cariboo Café:' Helena María Viramontes Discourses with her Social and Cultural Contexts," in *Women's Studies: An Interdisciplinary Journal*, Vol. 17, 1989, pp. 71-85.

[*In this essay, critic Roberta Fernández offers an in-depth review of the varied themes, narratives, and socio-political Hispanic values in* "The Cariboo Café."]

The Moths and Other Stories is a collection of eight stories by Helena María Viramontes of which **"The Moths," "The Cariboo Cafe"** and **"Neighbors"** are the most powerful pieces.[1] All the stories deal with female characters of various ages struggling against the limitations imposed by religious values that support patriarchal dominance. Helena María Viramontes was born and grew up in East Los Angeles, the setting for her stories. Yet her best piece, **"The Cariboo Cafe,"** extends into the lives of women in Central America, specifically in El Salvador and is the most characteristic of her experimental style.

"The Cariboo Cafe" is an intricately narrated short story with three story lines, each narrated through a different perspective. The three stories converge inside the Cariboo Cafe, a geographical metaphor for the city of Los Angeles, port of entry for America's new immigrants. There Sonya and Macky, children of "illegal aliens," an Anglo-

American cook and "the woman" [my quotation marks] from El Salvador cross ill-fated paths. For Sonya, from whose perspective Viramontes opens the story, the Cariboo Cafe is "the zero, zero place." At the opening of the second section, the cook gives an explanation of Sonya's description of the cafe, noting that the sign has lost all its paint except for the two O's in Cariboo. It is "the double zero cafe. Story of my life."

Macky, the little boy, is given a personalized identity by each of the other three characters. For Sonya, he is the little brother, her charge, whose hand she holds tightly. For the cook he is "Short Orders" who reminds him of JoJo, the son he lost in VietNam. And for "the woman" he is Geraldo, the son who was "disappeared" in her country. Although both adults have suffered the loss of a child as a direct or indirect repercussion of ill-waged American foreign involvements, they will never be able to communicate this to each other, for in the Cariboo Cafe they are natural antagonists.

The story focuses on the continuation of various degrees of violence which displaced immigrants suffer in their new country. The opening lines emphasize this displacement:

> They arrived in the secrecy of night, as displaced people often do, stopping over for a week, a month, eventually staying a lifetime. The plan was simple. Mother would work too until they saved enough to move into a finer future where the toilet was one's own and the children needn't be frightened.

But in the opening sequence, Sonya, a latch-key child, is quite frightened, because she has broken one of the rules by which she survives. At her young age she has learned to live by three rules: 1) never talk to strangers; 2) avoid the police or "polie" who are La Migra in disguise; 3) keep your key with you at all times. Having lost her key she is forced to break rule number one, which eventually brings her and Macky into deadly contact with the dreaded police inside the Cariboo Cafe.

In her own narrative section, "the woman" takes us back to the point where the first section ended by implying that it was Geraldo, her little boy, whom she saw walking through the streets.

> I jumped the curb, dashed out into the street, but the street is becoming wider and wider. I've lost him once and can't lose him again and to hell with the screaching tires and the horns and the headlights barely touching my hips. I can't take my eyes off him because, you see, they are swift and cunning and can take your life with a snap of a finger. But God is a just man and His mistakes can be undone.

(p. 72)

The reference to God is in keeping with Viramontes's view that the god of established religion is a powerful man linked to the subjugation of women (and the poor). In these few lines she also insinuates the confused state of mind of "the woman" who seems to think she is still in her country where the police "are swift and cunning and can take your life with a snap of a finger" (p. 72). The author uses this confusion very effectively for ironic effect by balancing this scene with a second scene in which "the woman" discusses her anguish with her friend María about the loss of her five-year old Geraldo. She had last seen the boy when she sent him to the corner store for a mango only to have him picked up by the police who accused him of subversive actions against the government. "The woman" asks María.

> Don't these men have mothers, lovers, babies, sisters? Don't they see what they are doing? Later, María says, these men are babes farted out from the Devil's ass. We check to make sure no one has heard her say this.
>
> (p. 71)

At the end of the story Viramontes effectively ties the closing lines uttered by "the woman" back to this conversation which she had with her friend.

Because of the juxtaposition of the cook's story with "the woman's" story, the text makes many demands on the reader and requires several readings before the chronology can be ordered. Throughout, the cook is presented as a sympathetic character who gets caught in the series of events that take place in his cafe. On the night that Sonya and Macky are reported lost, "the woman" finds them in the street, then brings them to the cafe where the cook takes to the little boy right away. "I pinch his nose 'cause he's a real sweetheart like Jojo. You know, my boy" (p. 66). When "the woman" speaks Spanish, "Right off I know she's illegal which explains why she looks like a weirdo" (p. 66). After they leave, he sees a news bulletin on TV about two missing children. "I recognize the mugs right away. Short Order and his doggie sister" (p. 66). He's not quite sure whether or not he should call the police: "Cops ain't exactly my friends, and all I need is for bacon to be crawling all over my place" (p. 66). And he decides to go to sleep instead.

But the next morning he too is a victim of circumstances as the police come three times to his cafe. First they arrive in response to an overdose that his friend Paulie has in the cafe's bathroom. No sooner has he finished cleaning up the bathroom, than he sees "all these illegals running out of the factory to hide" (p. 67). They all run into his bathroom, and out of frustration with the incident with Paulie, "my stomach being all dizzy, and the cops all over the place, and the three illegals running in here, I was all confused, you know. . . . I guess that's why I pointed to the bathroom" when the police arrive (p. 68). Feeling guilty after the undocumented workers are taken away, he watches in frustration as "the woman" comes back with the two children.

Once again taken up with the boy, he begins to cry as he cooks over the hot stove. "For the first time since JoJo's death, he's crying. He becomes angry at the lady for returning" (p. 73). And when he finally notifies the police about the children, he does so out of a belief that "Children gotta be with their parents, family gotta be together" (p. 73). Viramontes's irony is at its best at the point

when the cook decides to call the police in order to keep the children together with their parents, for the author's main focus has been on the enforced separation of children from their parents as a result of police action and government repression.

This separation of mothers from their children is emphasized in the third section when a clear reference is made to La Llorona:

> The darkness becomes a serpent's tongue, swallowing us whole. It is the night of La Llorona. The women come up from the depths of sorrow to search for their children. I join them, frantic, desperate, and our eyes become scrutinizers, our bodies opiated with the scent of their smiles. Descending from door to door, the wind whips our faces. I hear the wailing of the women and know it to be my own. Geraldo is nowhere to be found.
>
> (pp. 68-69)

At this point the nameless woman's anonymity begins to take on a greater significance, for she becomes "every woman" who has suffered the political disappearance of a child. Viramontes's discourse with Third World feminism becomes evident when, in the scene which follows the reference to La Llorona, the woman addresses a boy-guard, only a few years older than Geraldo but already a caricature of *machismo* in his role as interrogator at the jail. "'We arrest spies. Criminals.' He says this with cigarette smoke spurting out of his nostrils like a nose bleed" (p. 69). As he continues intimidating her, the boy-guard spouts against the "contras." In his role as a representative of the government he tells her

> "Contras are tricksters. They exploit the ignorance of people like you.". . . He throws the stub on the floor, crushes it under his boot. "This," he says, screwing his boot into the ground, "is what the contras do to people like you."
>
> (p. 69)

The sequence is a striking example of the *machista-Marianista* relationship between the sexes in Latin America, where men, even when they are boys, possess institutional power over women.

Soon after her son's disappearance, the woman began to be ostracized from her society, "for to be associated with her is condemnation" (p. 70). She eventually made her way to Los Angeles, where her nephew Tavo helped her find work. Still, she had a hard time making adjustments: "The machines, their speed and dust, make me ill. But I can clean. I clean toilets, dump trash cans, sweep. Disinfect the sinks. I will gladly do whatever is necessary to repay Tavo" (p. 72). Yet, even in the close environment of home she felt displaced, for she knew that when Tavo's baby finally arrived his wife would "not let me hold it, for she thinks I am a bad omen. I know it" (p. 72).

Her strong maternal instincts together with her continuing anguish at losing her son to a possible violent end account for her confusion when she finds Sonya and Macky. She ignores the little girl and focuses her attention on the boy. At home she bathes him ritualistically. After the children go to sleep, "[f]or the first time in years, her mind is quiet of all noise and she had the desire to sleep" (p. 73). So dramatic is her change that the next day, the cook is surprised at how different she looked from the night before:

> so young. Her hair is combed slick back into one thick braid and her earrings hang like baskets of golden pears on her finely sculptured ears. He can't believe how different she looks. Almost beautiful.
>
> (p. 73)

But her happiness is short-lived, for as soon as the police arrive she thinks she is back in her country.

> She sees them opening the screen door, their guns taut and cold like steel erections. Something is wrong, and she looks to the cowering cook. She has been betrayed, and her heart is pounding like footsteps running, faster, louder, faster and she can't hear what they are saying to her.
>
> (p. 74)

All she knows is that she will not be separated from her son once again, and she must protect him from the violence that the police inflict on children who are "disappeared."

> she crushes Geraldo against her, so tight, as if she wants to conceal him in her body again, return him to her belly so that they will not castrate him and hang his small, blue penis on her door, not crush his face so that he is unrecognizable, not bury him among the heaps of bones, and ears and teeth and jaws, because no one but she cared to know that he cried.
>
> (p. 74)

Seconds before the woman is struck, Viramontes turns her into a symbol of La Llorona weeping for all the disappeared children of the world.

> She refuses to let go. For they will have to cut her arms off to take him, rip her mouth off to keep her from screaming for help . . . She begins screaming all over again, screaming so that the walls shake, screaming enough for all the women of murdered children, screaming, pleading for help from the people outside, and she pushes an open hand against an officer's nose, because no one will stop them and he pushes the gun barrel to her face.
>
> (p. 74)

In an astute use of her shifting points of view, Viramontes ends the story with the woman's voice. Even as she fades into unconsciousness she assumes a fighting mood. No longer the passive female whipped into place by social constraints greater than she, the woman reacts to the system(s) that have subjugated her. And she becomes the voice of all women fighting against injustice everywhere.

> To hell with you all, because you can no longer frighten me. I will fight you for my son until I have no hands left to hold a knife. I will fight you all because you're all farted out of the Devil's ass, and you'll not take us with you. I am laughing, howling at their stupidity.
>
> (p. 75)

II

In analyzing **"The Cariboo Cafe"** I shall follow the Bakhtinian principle of dialogism or the utterance in intertextual dimension, which allows for a multifaceted approach to a work. For Mikhail Bakhtin, all discourse was in dialogue with prior discourses on the same subject as well as with discourses yet to come, whose reactions it foresees and anticipates.[2] To study the intertextual dimensions of **"The Cariboo Cafe"**—the discourses with which the text is in dialogue—I will situate the text within three frameworks, viewing it as a) a postmodernist text; b) dependent upon the perspective of Third World feminist ideology; and c) culturally situated within the collective memory of Mexican political legends.

In so doing, I want to demonstrate how Helena María Viramontes, without leaving her own immediate locale, expands the thematic of her story beyond that of strictly ethnic concerns to include one of the most vital issues of our day, the presence of millions of immigrants from Latin America within the national territory that makes up the United States. By focusing her story on one of those immigrant women, she humanizes the faceless shadows in our midst and prods our conscience to the painful reality of women from the Third World who now live side by side with us. That Viramontes makes her point by updating "La Llorona," a figure from the political folk legends of the collective Mexican memory, is a stroke of literary genious and accounts for an artistically satisfying and a politically challenging Third World feminist text.

A) POSTMODERNISM: ENGAGING THE READER IN PROCESSES OF SIGNIFICATION

In an article entitled "The Context of the Concept," Charles Russell defines postmodernism through its contrast to modernism. For him

> what essentially defined modernism was its self-conscious formal experimentation . . . devoted to discovering the special validity of art and literature in a culture apparently indifferent to anything but a material and socially validating conception of art. . . . Modernist literature and art . . . consequently expressed its felt alienation both by consciously devaluing the referential dimension of the artwork—its subject matter—and by explicitly emphasizing its formal conventions—the idiosyncratic, personal style of the artist.[3]

Russell argues that what was revealed in modernism was essentially "the inability of individual action, private language, or artistic style to alter society and its institutions."[4]

Although Russell does not discuss feminist and ethnic

literatures, both fit the new socially concerned approach which for him characterizes postmodernism.

> Moving beyond the hermeticism and alienation of modernism, postmodern art engages the reader and audience in the *processes* of signification that shape the experience of art. . . . Instead of modernist transcendence of the social milieu, we are offered active participation in its being and potential transformation.[5]

It is this engagement in the potential transformation of the social milieu which links **"The Cariboo Cafe"** to postmodernism. Yet, in order to participate fully in the cultural continuity that is operative in the text of the story, the reader must have at least a minimal knowledge of the political situation of Central America and the contemporary reality of Los Angeles, where it is estimated that at least 300,000 Salvadorean refugees currently live. To assist in the reading of the text, the author must use the social discourse of the moment so that her readers can understand her intertextual message. Unfortunately, Viramontes fails to do this.

Although she has stated, in her public readings and in private conversation, that the woman in the story is from El Salvador, there is nothing in the text to place her there. In fact, through an unfortunate use of the world "contras" Viramontes seems to be alluding to Nicaragua as the woman's country of origin whose violence she was forced to flee. Although the author in actuality is referring to the insurgents of El Salvador, she fails to use the language of the general public's social discourse in reference to the turmoil in Central America. Clearly, Viramontes wishes to engage her readers in active participation in social transformation and must make clear to them just where it is that she positions herself in relationship to the political struggles in Central America.

B) Third World Feminism as Ideological Framework

Viramontes handles Third World feminist ideology more adroitly than issues of Central American politics. I take Third World feminism to mean feminist concerns beyond those of one's own ethnic group as well as an *actively* expressed desire to improve the conditions of women by improving the social circumstances of all people (especially those of people of color in the United States, Africa, Asia and Latin America). Because it perceives the interrelationship between race, class and gender, Third World feminism, then, has a broad scope and encompasses many goals.

To see how Viramontes is in discourse with Third World feminism in **"The Cariboo Cafe"** it is necessary to go beyond its text to its greater context or its metatext.

> (The metatext) is always the record of a dialogue of a particular kind; the complex correlation of the *text* (object of study and reflexion) and the *context* that frames it. . . . It is the encounter of two texts: the already given text and

the reacting text being created, and therefore, it is the encounter of two subjects, of two authors.[6]

Taking some liberties with this Bakhtinian principle I would like to juxtapose two voices in order to highlight the unspoken yet understood discourse to which the reader is reacting. On the one hand is the voice of the woman in the Viramontes text with its focus on the anguish and violence that the poor experience in "law and order" societies. This is the voice in the narrative whose misadventures the reader follows. To this voice I would like to juxtapose that of an Indian woman, closer in experience to the woman in **"The Cariboo Cafe"** than either we or the author can ever be. This particular voice was tape-recorded by Elizabeth Burgos-Debray, then was edited and adapted into a powerful book, *I. . . . Rigoberta Menchú, An Indian Woman in Guatemala.*[7]

Rigoberta Menchú is a Quiché Indian woman from the mountains of Guatemala, a country historically divided by differences of language, dress and custom. Determined to learn Spanish in order to take her message to the greater world, she joined the Peasant Unity Committee in 1979 and became one of the leaders in the struggle to liberate the Indian peasants from centuries of exploitation and injustice. As a result, her family was slowly eradicated. First, her brother was captured, tortured and burned to death in public; then her father was bombed inside the Spanish embassy which he and other campesinos had occupied. Finally, her mother suffered the most horrible of deaths. She was raped, tortured and mutilated, and then left to die slowly.

> On the third day of her torture, they cut off her ears. They cut her whole body bit by bit. They began with small tortures, small beatings and worked up to terrible tortures. The first tortures she'd received became infected. It was her turn to suffer the terrible pain her son had suffered too. . . . They didn't let my mother turn over, and her face was so disfigured, cut and infected: she could barely make any movement by herself. . . . My mother was covered in worms, because in the mountains there is a fly which goes straight into any wound, and if the wound isn't tended in two days, there are worms where the fly has been. Since all my mother's wounds were open, there were worms in all of them. She was still alive. My mother died in terrible agony. When my mother died, the soldiers stood over her and urinated in her mouth, even after she was dead.[8]

In a review of Menchú's narrative, Jean Franco connects this peculiarly modern horror

> to the effects of modernization which in Latin America was imposed by force and with extraordinary cruelty. . . . (I)t was first and foremost the army that was modernized, an army whose weapons were part of U.S. aid and whose methods of pacification included genocide. Torture and mutilation were intended to inspire fear as a method of control and to cause trauma in the population. But these methods are not peculiar to Guatemala. They have occurred everywhere when serious alternatives to capitalism have been pursued or in places where the population does not docilely accept modernization.[9]

Another critic, Ximena Bunster, notes that women like Rigoberta Menchú believe that

> a people's struggle should be fought simultaneously with the goal of liberating women and transforming the traditional *machista-Maríanist* relationship between the sexes. Class and gender inequalities have to be fought parallel to and as part of a common front; victory is only possible if women can participate successfully in the political leadership of their countries and fight in the rank and file as equals with men.[10]

Taking both Franco's and Bunster's comments into account, one can then point to Rigoberta Menchú as the personification of Third World feminism. Like many peasant (and urban) women of Latin America (and other parts of the Third World) she thinks that the liberation of women goes hand in hand with the liberation of all people in Latin America. Although it is not hard for many of us in this country to feel some form of solidarity with Rigoberta and her people, it is more difficult for us to comprehend the displacement that occurs when people are forced to flee a daily existence that becomes unbearable. Yet, thousands of those displaced people are among us, many living shadowy and desperate lives as "illegal immigrants."[11]

In "The Cariboo Cafe" Helena María Viramontes has individualized a few of these immigrants, dramatizing their situation by showing the continuation of violence that plagues them in their new country. In this way, she not only gives us the narrative as text but also engages us with its implied discourse. As a result of this dialogue, the context of the story acquires an even greater profundity than the text alone would have.

C) LA LLORONA AND THE DISCOURSE WITH THE POLITICAL COLLECTIVE MEMORY OF A PEOPLE

The double voice discourse of Chicana authors who are writing from the perspectives of women and minority is evident in the recent poetry of Lorna Dee Cervantes, Ana Castillo and Alma Villanueva. In prose fiction, *The House on Mango Street* by Sandra Cisneros and Viramontes's **The Moths and Other Stories** are the clearest examples of Chicanas questioning the traditional roles of women within their culture. This double voice discourse also is in dialogue with the historical and cultural models traditionally set before Mexican and Chicana women. Shirleen Soto has described three sixteenth century figures that have served as models of both ideal and negative womanhood within the Mexican and Chicano culture: the Virgen of Guadalupe, La Malinche and La Llorona.[12] It is to the latter two figures that I wish to draw attention, and in particular to La Llorona, for she is the dominant symbol behind the woman in **"The Cariboo Cafe."**

According to Soto, "La Llorona, descrita como un alma en pena, representa a la pecadora cuya conducta exige arrepentimiento, y cuya actitud dispuesta a tal arrepentimien-

to la hace un poco más tolerable que la Malinche." (The Weeping Woman, who appears in the guise of a sorrowful spirit, represents the sinner whose conduct demands repentance, and whose attitude towards that repentance makes her a figure more tolerable than La Malinche).[13] As a symbol of a repentant woman in mourning, La Llorona has undergone various transformations from her sixteenth century roots with their amalgamation of Aztec and Spanish folk legends. Historically, this Weeping Woman was an Aztec woman who was betrayed by her husband. Upon discovering his infidelity, she killed their children for revenge and was then condemned to wander forever in the night, weeping for her lost children. A victim of the oppressive Aztec laws governing women's rights, La Llorona was popularly converted into a symbol of a victimized woman forced to turn against her own children as her only means of defense. With regional variations throughout Mexico and in Mexican American communities the legend of La Llorona persists into the present. In all of its versions the legend fires the popular imagination with its wandering solitary figure lost in a world that refuses to accept her.

The political transformation of La Llorona occurs when she is merged with the figure of La Malinche, the progenitress of the Mexican mestizo race. Malinche was a Nahuatl-speaking princess sold into slavery by her mother so that the offspring of her second marriage could inherit what rightfully belonged to the first born.[14] When she was sixteen, Hernán Cortés made her his lover, his interpreter, and his adviser in Indian customs. Serving in the role of diplomat between the Nahuatl-speaking, the Mayan-speaking and the Spanish-speaking, Malinche's role in the conquest of Mexico has undergone varying interpretations in different periods of Mexican history, but it is only in modern Mexico that she has been completely maligned. In contemporary Mexico, the term "malinchista" is popularly used to refer to someone who is perceived as being disloyal to his or her people; hence, "malinchista" connotes a traitor. When this popular image of Malinche merges with the legend of La Llorona her weeping becomes a continuous lament for her supposed responsibility for the fall of the Aztec empire. Thus, the symbolic mother of the mestizo race is tainted with a Catholic sense of original sin.

The reinterpretation of La Llorona/Malinche has inspired the creative imagination of Chicana writers, who seem to be fascinated with the manner in which La Llorona and Malinche have become symbols of female marginality in Mexican and Chicano culture. The writers are not merely questioning misogynist views in their culture but are actively and creatively changing the symbology of the legends.

For example, a new feminist interpretation can be found in a dramatic work by Carmen Toscano called "La Llorona," in which a chorus of five women identify with the mournful lament of La Llorona.[15] One of the women states that "inside of herself, (La Llorona) carries the voices of many women," implying that the cry has now become a plea against patriarchy.

Another example of the reinterpretation of the legend with more of an ethnic than a feminist emphasis is that of Victoria Moreno's "La Llorona, Crying Lady of Creekbeds, 483 Years Old and Aging."[16] Through the use of a recurring refrain, "they took away her children," Moreno lashes out at feminist values that she perceives as a threat to the traditional Mexican esteem for the family. In this poem, La Llorona is transformed into a contemporary victim of a system that devalues the way of life of an entire people. The poem is thus representative of a period in Chicana ideology when the choice seemed to be either/or: between traditional ethnic values or loss of culture through "gabacha" feminism.

Helena María Viramontes gives an even more original interpretation to the literary potential of La Llorona in **"The Cariboo Cafe,"** where she extends the symbol in an entirely new way, linking it to the other discourses with which she is in dialogue. As we have already seen, in this story Viramontes connects the wailing attributes of La Llorona to the contemporary anguish of mothers in Latin America who suffer the political disappearance of a child: "I hear the wailing of the women and know it to be my own" (p. 69). In an attempt to involve the reader in an active participation in social transformation—one of the characteristics of the postmodernist text—Viramontes ends her story with the woman screaming, "pleading for help from the people outside" (p. 74). Thus, the woman/La Llorona undergoes a change from passive mourner to active accuser and we, the readers, must decide where we wish to position ourselves in relationship to the fight against injustice suffered by women (and the poor) in Third World nations as well as in our own backyard.

III

In a text as intricately structured as is **"The Cariboo Cafe,"** plot is the primary element that must be analyzed. But the ordering of the plot in itself would not do justice to many discourses with which the author is in dialogue. Hence, in this study I have tried to present its intertextual dimensions, that is, its discourse with contemporary postmodernist *engagement,* with Third World feminism, and with the political collective Mexican memory in its relationship to La Llorona.

The *processes* of signification characteristic of postmodernist literature, which request of the reader an active participation in the potential transformation of society, are focused around the second and third discourses I have presented: Third World feminist ideology and the political Mexican collective memory associated with La Llorona. I have gone outside of the text of **"The Cariboo Cafe"** to Rigoberta Menchú's story in order to present a firsthand account of the political situation from which the woman in the story emerges. Viramontes's clever handling of the woman's disorientation and confusion helps to make obvious the point of the story: the displaced of Latin America continue to live a persecuted life in the "zero, zero place" that is Los Angeles. The degree of persecution may be different, but it can be as deadly.

The shadowy presence that the woman assumed throughout her life is transformed in her last moments as she becomes incapsulated in a scream, a plead, a howl, a symbol of all mothers who have lost a child to the masculine violence that governs all dictatorships. She thus literally becomes the voice of Third World feminist ideology demanding a stop to the violence. The irony of the voice being heard precisely at the moment of the woman's death is transcended by her conversion into La Llorona, for in the collective memory La Llorona's voice will continue forever. Thus, Viramontes achieves a literary feat by transforming an ancient political legend into a contemporary political symbol of Third World feminism.

NOTES

[1] Helena María Viramontes, *The Moths and Other Stories* (Houston: Arte Público Press, 1985). Page references for this collection will be included within the text itself.

[2] Tzvetan Todorov, *Mikhail Bakhtin: The Dialogical Principle,* translated by Wlad Godzich (Minneapolis: University of Minnesota Press, 1984) p. x.

[3] Charles Russell, "The Context of the Concept," in *Romanticism, Modernism, Postmodernism* ed. by Harry R. Garvin (Cranbury, New Jersey: Associated University Presses, Inc., 1980) 183-184. In the same special issue, see Ihab Hassain, "The Question of Postmodernism," 117-126 and Julia Kristeva, "Postmodernism?" 136-141. See also Fredric Jameson, "Postmodernism, or The Cultural Logic of Late Capitalism," *New Left Review,* No. 146 (July-August, 1984) 53-92. A response to Jameson is found in Dan Latimer, "Jameson and Post-Modernism," *New Left Review,* No. 148 (Nov.-Dec., 1984) 117-128. See also Terry Eagleton, "Capitalism, Modernism and Postmodernism," *New Left Review,* No. 152 (July-August, 1985) 60-73.

[4] Ibid., 185.

[5] Ibid., 191-192.

[6] Mikhail Bakhtin, "The Problem of Text in Linguistics, Philology, and the Other Human Sciences: An Essay of Philosophical Analysis," in *Estetika slovesnogo tvorchestva* (Moscow: S. F. Bocharov, 1979). Quoted by Todorov in op. cit., p. 23.

[7] *I. . . . Rigoberta Menchú, an Indian Woman in Guatemala* edited and introduced by Elizabeth Burgos-Debray (New York: Schocken Books, 1984).

[8] Ibid., 198-199.

[9] Jean Franco, "Five Books on Guatemala," in *Fiction International* [Central American literary issue] 16/2 (Summer/Fall, 1986) 194.

[10] Ximena Bunster, "A Leader of Her People," *The Women's Review of Books* 3/1 (Oct., 1985) 12.

[11] The Immigration Reform and Control Act of November 1987 excludes most of the Salvadorean refugees from the amnesty program because most Salvadoreans have come to this country after 1982, the cut-off date for amnesty. For a moving account of Latin American immigrants in Los Angeles, see Stephanie Chávez and James Quinn, "Garages: Immigrant in, Cars Out," *The Los Angeles Times,* Sunday, May 24, 1987, part I/pages 1, 18-19.

[12] Shirlene Soto, "Tres modelos culturales: La Virgen de Guadalupe, la Malinche and la Llorona," *Fem* (Mexico City), Ano 10, n. 48 (Octubre-Noviembre, 1986) 13-16. An earlier, condensed version of this article appeared as "Three Historical Models of Chicana Feminism," *El Mirlo: A National Chicano Studies Newsletter,* UCLA 10/3 (Summer, 1983) 1, 7-8.

[13] Ibid., p. 13 [Translation Mine].

[14] For an excellent and detailed account of the shifting interpretation of Malinche in the Mexican psyche, see Rachel Phillips, "Marina/Malinche: Masks and Shadows," in *Women in Hispanic Literature: Icons and Fallen Idols* edited by Beth Miller (Berkeley, Los Angeles, London: University of California Press, 1983).

[15] Carmen Toscano, "La Llorona," in *The Third Woman: Minority Women Writers of the United States* edited by Dexter Fisher (Boston: Houghton Mifflin Company) 318.

[16] Victoria Moreno, "La Llorona, Crying Lady of the Creekbeds, 483 Years Old, and Aging," in Dexter Fisher, op. cit., 319-320.

Helena María Viramontes with Juanita Heredia and Silvia Pellarolo (essay date 1994)

SOURCE: "East of Downtown and Beyond: Interview with Helena María Viramontes," in *Mester,* Vol. XXIII, No. 2-3, Fall 1993-Spring 1994, pp. 165-80.

[*In this interview, Viramontes discusses the importance of free access to literature, her collaboration with accomplished Latino authors, and her hopes for the future of Latino writing.*]

A native of East Los Angeles, Helena María Viramontes has participated in many journals, literary contests, and community activities. She is best known for her internationally acclaimed *The Moths and Other Stories* published in 1985 by Arte Público Press. This collection of short stories brings to light the importance of the urban woman's voice, concerns, and perspectives within Chicano/Latino culture. Viramontes calls attention to the themes of sexuality in **"Growing"** and **"Birthday,"** changing cultural/sexual roles in **"The Broken Web,"** the relationships among women in **"The Moths,"** and the immigrant experience in **"Cariboo Café."**

In *Chicana Creativity and Criticism: Charting New Frontiers in American Literature* (1987), Viramontes and María Herrera-Sobek coedited a collection of critical articles, fiction, poetry, and essays on Chicana literature, a project that was inspired by a conference held at U.C. Irvine. The book proved to be very popular and re-cently sold out. The University of New Mexico Press will reissue the book in an expanded edition. In this collection, the short story **"Miss Clairol"** by Viramontes shows a new direction in the representation of the urban female factory worker in Chicano/Latino literature according to Herrera-Sobek. In **"Nopalitos"** (*Breaking Boundaries: Writings by Latinas* 1989), Viramontes cultivates the testimonial genre by giving us an autobiographical account of the importance of the oral tradition in her work.

Viramontes has been literary editor for *Xhismearte* and a coordinator for the Latino Writers Association. In 1990 she cofounded the nonprofit group, Latino Writers and Filmmakers, Inc. She has recently signed a contract for two novels and a book of short stories with New American Library Series/Dutton Publishers. She is presently working on a novel, *Under the Feet of Jesus*, to be published in 1995 with the support of the National Endowment for the Arts. Viramontes has also accepted a ladder-rank position as Assistant Professor of Creative Writing in the Department of English at Cornell University.

As one of the participants at the conference "Writing the Immigrant Experience" at the renovated public library in downtown Los Angeles, Viramontes reflected on the significance of the public library in her literary formation. Later on that afternoon, we met with Viramontes to discuss her role as a writer and a community activist.

Viramontes elaborated on the importance of her involvement with the public library. We asked her why this place means so much to her.

[VIRAMONTES] I'm a big advocate of public libraries because I grew up in a bookless home. I come from a family of eleven. It wasn't until my older brothers and sisters started going to school that there were books in the house. My father had bought us a set of *World Book Encyclopedias* that we were forbidden to touch because they hadn't been paid. Also my older sister had a *Bible* she guarded like her big jar of *Noxzema*. I was amazed by the pictures in this book and the temptation was too much for me to bear. For the longest time I thought that the encyclopedias contained all the information I needed to know in the world, and that the *Bible* had all the truth. What more could a hungry child want? That's all I really needed. It wasn't until very recently that I realized that this isn't altogether true. But that's where I developed my respect for the printed word. In any event, I was always really excited about books.

The library was my space. I would take two buses to come here to the Central Library. It was very much unlike the way it is now. You would walk into this huge domelike room and in it were rows and rows of catalogue card drawers and all those cards represented books ready to be accessed by the tip of my fingers. You're constantly moving, but you have to make contacts and connections. I like that thought because in many ways that's the way it was at the public library. I met all kinds of different people and worlds in this library.

[HEREDIA AND PELLROLO] *What do you remember about the library as a child?*

First of all, it was a place of warmth, great warmth. Someone always kept the heat just right. And nobody bothered you. And then to see the big huge boxes with catalogue cards in them and jot the numbers and go to the stacks and say *¡Ay! como tenían tantos libros* and then just pile them up. These many books [she extends her hands]. To go and sit down with them. There was always a homeless person or two or three or five or ten, either sleeping, reading or looking at odd things. I remember seeing some old lady reading page after page of old *T.V. Guides*, while another time, I saw some *viejito* reading a foreign book, but he was holding it backwards. I thought all this was so fascinating. It's always been my quiet, tripping out space, the library.

What did you read?

I liked reading about people's lives, biographies. I would read fiction and magazines but it was mostly biographies I remember. At that time I was very much struck by people's lives. I also read about California history. They had a California room where I would read sections of history books. More than anything else, I just enjoyed the freedom to be able to have access to these things, to pick a book on Harriet Tubman or Marilyn Monroe or whatever my heart desired. Nobody bothered me. It was incredible. That is basically what writers seek, you know: a little space. A little non-distractive time to be able to think or feel whatever you want.

What kinds of community services have you done with the public library?

Last year, for example, they started closing down public libraries. There was one public library in particular that I adopted. It was called *Friendly Stop Library* in the City of Orange. It's a barrio library. It's a trailer that pretty much served the small barrio there. I loved the work that they were doing. The librarian who worked there was a Chicano. One day I visited the library at about 3:30 in the afternoon. It was packed. All sorts of kids were there, reading, looking at magazines. I mean it was a place where the community came together, almost like a teen post, but the kids were reading or doing homework.

The librarian was able to disseminate the books that were relevant to the kids' cultures and concerns. It was a wonderful, wonderful place that belonged to them. Well sure enough they were going to close it up. I just couldn't believe this so I wrote this letter to all my friends. I said, "Listen, here *compas*. I mean we need to do something here. Don't you remember how important the libraries were to a lot of us because we just did not have enough books available to us?" And so on. I must have made about 75 copies of the letter and sent them out to all my friends who sent them out to their friends. Well, sure enough, the response was so big that the library was awarded another grant. All I did was write a letter and it worked. A lot of the writers, especially the Latino writ-

ers, responded. That was really, really very nice. It was wonderful to see that everybody took the time to write letters to say "Don't do this. This is really important. This is my own personal experience at the public library." Libraries have always been very close to my heart.

When you grow up in a family of eleven in a three bedroom house in East L.A. where do you study? I mean where can you go to study? *En la cocina.* Yeah, *bueno* after you wash the dishes. You know what I mean? The library also provided me with a place to exercise my imagination. I could sit for hours, read, sleep, and nobody bothered me. Plus I had access to the information that I wanted to have access to. It was really great.

When did you start to write?

I started writing seriously after college. Actually I did write a play in my drama class in high school. The play even had an underlying feminism that was subconscious. It dealt with the lives of five prostitutes. I mean what can I say? I was a high school student at the time. Ms. Duran, our Chicana drama teacher, said, "We are not going to censor here. You write whatever you want to write. And if you want to use curse words, you could use curse words." *¡Ay! Bueno.* You should have seen all the pieces that the students did. It was not so much the permission to use bad words, but the freedom to write unrestrictively. Mine was one that was selected to be read.

What were your college years like? Did you write then?

In 1971, I got accepted to this small, four-year, liberal arts college called Immaculate Heart College in Hollywood. People like Diane Keaton's sister for example and Mary Tyler Moore graduated from there. It was small, but very, very radical. The first year I attended, Tom Hayden came to teach there. What a controversy that was! *Las mujeres*, a lot of them called themselves nuns, had their own communities of sisters. It was my understanding that some of them were excommunicated from the Church for their radicalism. Nonetheless, they defined themselves, created their own communities of spirituality and although the school closed its doors, the community of women still offered a graduate course in feminist spirituality. Very interesting women.

As a student, I was hungry for the information they had to share. But going there I realized in many ways how the system had failed me in terms of not being prepared. There were five Chicanas and three Black women and we hung out like this, man. We were like this [a sign of unity]. In fact, Eloise Klein Healy, who was one of my teachers back then, came up to me after class once and asked: "God, we want to know what you guys are thinking about." We felt so intimidated, unprepared, and we always sat in the back really tight-lipped. But I have to hand it to Eloise; years later I thanked her. She was the first white woman who asked me what I thought. It was a terrifying experience coming into this white upper middle-class university because all of us came from very different backgrounds. It was an incredible experience.

How did your family react when you decided to continue your education?

I explained a little about my background in terms of the workload I had at the house. I remember getting up at five and helping my mother with the lunches, getting ready for school, going to school, coming home. She only let me take drama once a week the last year of high school. We weren't allowed to have after school activities. I had to come home, help with the dinner and then wash dishes. After eight or nine o'clock, I did my homework until about midnight. Then I'd go to sleep. I always remember saying a prayer, "Oh God, thank you for this day. Sleep is the best thing until five o'clock." I knew then that if I was going to go to a college or a university I would not be able to do it at the house because there was no space. That's when I realized, I needed to move into a dorm. At Immaculate Heart College, they gave me a room at the dorms. I was seventeen years old, and needed signed permission. My father, of course, said I would move out over his dead body. So I turned to my mother, who hardly went against my father. However, I used a different strategy. I asked her, "*Mamá*, do you want me to marry a doctor or lawyer?" How could a caring mother not respond affirmatively. "*¡Pues, sí!*" she said. Then I posed to her, "How can I meet these doctors and lawyers if I don't go to where they are studying?" All I had to do next is show my mother where to sign.

My roommate, this woman from Pacific Palisades, reminded me of Janis Joplin. She was a very rebellious wild person and that's why she fell in love with me because she said, "Come on over here. We're probably the same thing." So I ended up rooming with her. Two weeks later my parents come to check everything out. All my mother kept saying was "*¿Onde están las monjitas, onde están las monjitas?*" She was waiting for the nuns to come out and greet her. "*Pues allá están*, Mom, *es que están estudiando*," I said. God, it was crazy, crazy. Yeah, I remember those days. I always remember those days.

Why are those days significant?

It was hilarious because in many ways they were the most critical days of intellectualism that I had. When I talk to students especially, I tell them that this is an opportunity for them to get the information that they are going to need for the rest of their lives. When I was visiting Harvard and Yale, the first thing I did was check out the libraries. I'm thinking, hey, we need to have that too. This belongs to us too. We need to have access to this information.

Could you talk about your role as literary editor in **XhismeArte**, *the Latino literary and art magazine of Los Angeles? How did you contribute?*

Sure. I was involved from 1978 to 1981. Through informal literary workshops, about 25 writers met and shared their fiction works. I worked with the Pulitzer Prize winning journalist, Víctor Manuel Valle. We worked together submitting grants and receiving money to hold these literary workshops.

In 1981, I coordinated a special issue dedicated to *La Mujer* in an attempt to recognize and bring into perspective our creative force. I was the only woman on the editorial staff who brought forth particular gender issues. I can now say that this issue was a valuable and historical contribution to the Chicano/Latino literary tradition. The issue *La Mujer* was a publication designed for a special anthology, *Homenaje a la Ciudad de Los Angeles 1781-1981*. In this issue, we wanted to emphasize the other side of literary history that noticed *La Mujer* as an organizer as well as a worker in the fields and factories, a planner of revolutions, a generator of ideas, traditions, cultures, beliefs as well as propagator of her race. The onedimensional depiction of *La Mujer* in the arts and literature did not do justice to her. While the Anglo described her as dark and lustful with a sexual appetite, the Chicano/Latino painted her as strong, but sexless, or sensual but intellectually sterile. *La Mujer* knows better. Both Barbara Carrasco, who was the art editor, and myself agreed to collaborate on this issue that celebrated *La Mujer*.

A writer voices the lives and future of Chicanas/Latinas. In a society that represents inferiority by race and intelligence by sex, she must struggle endlessly to create forms and ideas against those negative images that portray her. We are powerful warriors because we can teach. In order to continue to develop our art, we must be connected to other women *artistas*. In a similar fashion, we must keep in touch with the men of our culture, educating them about the condition of *La Mujer* so that we can form a collective voice, a literary and artistic consciousness for the good of all. Some of the contributors of *La Mujer* issue, who were relatively unknown at the time, included Rosa Elvira Alvarez, Alma Villanueva, Lin Romero, Gina Valdés, and myself. The works we presented capture a reality often perceived as harsh and bitter, but honest. The art included wonderful work by Carrasco, Yreina Cervantes and Linda Vallejo.

How did the Latino Writers Association form?

This collectivity of writers grew out of the workshops we held for **Xhismearte** and speared by Valle. More than anything, its purpose was to provide critical and moral support so necessary for the development of *artistas*. It was a stimulating environment where an exchange of ideas, constructive criticism, and exploration of intellectual conversations took place. We had a grand vision. Víctor Manuel Valle, others and I met every Thursday religiously for about three years. At times it was frustrating because I was the only *mujer* in this community of writers. That is how we came up with the idea of *La Mujer* issue for **Xhismearte**.

Focusing more on your own development, who did you read?

When I was in college I was reading a lot of African-American writers like Ralph Ellison and Richard Wright. Anglo women writers like Doris Lessing and Virginia

Woolf. And, of course, the regulars of American literature. African-American women writers like Toni Morrison and Alice Walker came a little bit later. Angela Davis had an impact on me as well. I was very impressed by that kind of radical atmosphere of writing your roots and yourself and the urban city plight.

What also struck me at the time was the Latin American writers and their works: *One Hundred Years of Solitude, Pedro Páramo.* I had been reading a lot but this was so different than anything that I had ever read. It was so enjoyable. It was the type of reading that just drew me in. I just forgot about the hours. I was no longer reading but in the world of these writers, experiencing the sights and scents. Words no longer got in the way of the stories, you know what I mean? Oh! What a wonderful thing! I can't even describe it, to be in another world completely and not let anybody distract you from it until you are out of it. That's what I got from a lot of these Latin American writers. Now it's interesting that I probably would have started writing a lot sooner had I been exposed to Latin American women writers. But by and large I was exposed to the male writers because it was they who were being translated. I was very fascinated by their technique, by their storytelling, by the way they narrated, by their information. Yet I still didn't think of writing on my own.

What was the impact of reading Pedro Páramo?

Once I finished *Pedro Paramo,* that's when I wrote my first short story, **"Requiem for the Poor,"** which is about Chicanos and their parents, the cultural conflicts, and crossing the border from Tijuana. At the time, I took a creative writing course at Cal State L.A. where I wrote this short narrative. That's a little story in which I tried to do a Juan Rulfoesque kind of atmosphere. My professor said, "Submit it to the magazine." Sure, you know I'll submit it. And then I got a first place fiction award.

In *Pedro Páramo,* I admired the ghostlike consciousness he created and the blurry line between reality and phantoms. The form of the narrative and the art of telling a story amazed me most of all. As a reader, I enjoyed putting the pieces of the puzzle together. It was a mystery to me. There is a fine line between realism and magic. I am talking about the magic in curiosity and awareness of the reader's eye who learns to trust.

When was that?

This was in 1975 or 76. Still in his class, the professor asked us to write about something that felt personal to me. So I opened up my journal and I picked out a thing that happened to me. And in fact it was almost like a two or three day long monologue, which turned out to be **"Birthday."** In this story, I experimented with stream of consciousness. I combine the cosmic and the personal. As a writer, I tried to concern myself with how to tell a story as well as the subject matter of abortion and women's bodies. After I submitted this piece, my professor said to me, "You know you have such a unique vision. I have

never read anything like this before." I began thinking, well, let me try my hand at writing.

Speaking of the printed word, I find this rebellious spirit in many of your female characters. How does this relate to your writing process?

The rebellion in my soul is not apparent to me until I see it in my characters. You know it's interesting because when I was writing **Under the Feet of Jesus** I wrote to Sandra [Cisneros]: "You know, Sandra, I am a grateful woman for many things. But one thing I'm very thankful for are these characters. Though one thinks I gave them life, it is they who have given me life." That's the way I feel. Writing is so basic and so part of my own development as a human being that this is what I want to offer my readers too.

How did you come up with the idea to do **"The Moths"**, *one of your most famous stories which is published in numerous anthologies?*

The emotion comes from a very famous black and white *Life* magazine photo of a Japanese woman bathing her deformed child. I was overpowered by the love I saw between this mother and her child. While the child looks into space, the mother shows such love and compassion in bathing the child. I felt the strength of bonding, love and trust between the two. I wanted to capture this feeling in the relationship between the grandmother and her grandchild in **The Moths**. I chose the grandmother figure instead of the mother figure because she has more time to take care of the spirituality of the children. The mother figure is too close a generation to relate to her rebellious daughter. This story is a tribute to grandparents and the role they play in our lives. I also show that these people have real lives with complexities. There are no easy solutions.

This composite of characters in difficult situations is apparent in most of your works. In **"The Broken Web,"** *how did you develop these intense characters?*

I was always fascinated by women's stories. The idea for **"The Broken Web"** was given to me by this woman I knew. I went to the court and investigated her court records. It was an incredible story. Her experience reminded me of the movie, *Dance with a Stranger.* It's an interesting movie because it deals with this woman who works at a bar. She is also very confident about her sexuality. She is a single parent and she is doing well. But then she just falls in love with the wrong guy. They become obsessed with each other. They terrorize each other but then they can't live without each other. They are always drawn back to each other for one reason or another. In our lives, at least in the women that I've talked to, there's always been that occasion at one point in somebody's life, where you have this relationship in which you become obsessed with this person, including myself. Getting back to the story, she ended up killing the guy by shooting him so that she could be released emotionally. But the fascinating part is that she wrote a letter. She was the first woman in England to be hung, by the way. That's why they wrote a movie about it. But the fascinating part of the letter was that she wrote to his mother to say she loved him, but he just couldn't keep his pants on. He always kept wanting relationships with other women. Very interesting movie.

I see the parallel in **"The Broken Web,"** though I didn't see this woman until years and years later. This woman's husband terrorized her by doing horrible things to her and her children. That's when she just got the rifle not more than ten feet away and pulled the trigger once, twice and then reloaded. Did it again. Then she was tried. She was tried first for homicide but then the story began to unravel the torment. She got secondary manslaughter. She had written a *testimonio* in her *pocho* English of how much she loved her husband, but why she had to do what she did. I was so fascinated by that. I thought, "Oh, shoot! I want to write this in her voice. *Y no lo podía hacer.* I could not do it. Maybe I still will. Because it was so fascinating to have that kind of voice.

Why did you choose the daughter's voice?

Well the daughter is the one who told me about her mother. After I interviewed her mother I got the court transcripts. Because in a way, I felt a certain amount of responsibility to tell about this past nobody knew about. But when the daughter confessed it to me, she had to be very discrete. Then I asked her, "Do you think your Mom would talk to me about this so I could write something on it?" And she said, "Yeah, I think so. Let's talk to her." So I talked to that person. I got the court case first and then I returned to talk to that woman. But even then it was a very delicate balance that I had to take because I was really transgressing a lot of intimate information. But these women were very good about this mixed report. They even told me about some of the things that this man did. Even then the daughter instead of the mother would tell me about some of the things that she could not talk about.

Was it difficult to find a publisher for **The Moths and Other Stories** *at this time considering there were not many established Chicana/Latina writers?*

Why do you think we had such magazines as *Xhisme Arte,* and *Con Safos?* We just took publications into our own hands. Remember we had a group of Latino writers here in the association. We had people like Luis Rodríguez, *Always Running,* Luis. Luis was able to develop a panel of Latino writers to participate in an American Writers Congress which was held in New York. That was the first major conference with a Latino panel in years by American writers. Luis asked me to participate in the panel with Nick Kanellos whom I was just beginning to know through some of the books by Arte Público.

At the panel, I met Nick Kanellos for the first time. He was screaming and yelling. It's funny because when I share this story with everybody, they all say they have stories of Nick Kanellos. He was very upset because there were not many Latino writers invited, just a handful, a speck such as Rudolfo Anaya, myself, and a few others.

In any event, as we sat together, I leaned over and said "I have all these stories that I've written over the years. Maybe I can put them in a collection." He said, "Yeah, yeah, go ahead. Mail them to me." That was back in 1981. It didn't get published until 1985. It took a long time. At that time it took about two or three years to get a book out. I got the book on the very same day I brought my son Francisco home from the hospital. *Y me habló* Nick's public relation agent to set up a reading. I said that I couldn't because I had just come home from the hospital. "Are you okay?" she asked. "Yeah, I just had a baby." Shortly afterwards Denise's [Chávez] book *The Last of the Menu Girls* came. Denise and I actually did our tour together around Texas. That's how Denise and I got hooked up together.

While they [Cisneros and Chávez] continued to write, my writing still went up and down, sporadic in many ways. I have always written but I've just done it in short terms. Shortly before the book *The Moths* was published, **"The Cariboo Cafe"** was not even going to be included. I put it in as a last minute entry because another story, a love story about these two Chicano teachers at Garfield High School, was a weak link in the book.

"Cariboo Café" *is another significant landmark in expressing the concerns of the Latino immigrant experience. How did this idea come about?*

I was living in Vancouver at the time and I had just had Pilar. I became very obsessively involved with the politics of Central America. The *New York Times* did not provide sufficient information concerning Central America. I read a lot more through the Canadian papers. I was thinking, "My God, don't people in the U.S. know what's going on?" I kept a journal, mostly notes. On a personal level, my motherly instinct to protect my child became inherently stronger as well as my rage. For **"The Cariboo Cafe"** I did background reading. One day I started with this voice, a man's voice and the way he sees these particular people. The story is divided into three sections. I wrote the second section first, the third section second, and then the first section last. Not only was I developing the voice of the man, but I was also creating the story. I wanted readers to become part of the story, to stand there and witness what was going on. I managed to bring the readers in; they are the bystanders at the end of the story looking into the *café* in silence. At the same time, I wanted them to experience the pain of this woman in losing a child senselessly, a fact that was happening left and right in Central America.

That story took me a long time to do, because the story line was very difficult and very painful. At times, I cried as I was writing it. Other times, I even had nightmares about it. I remember one night when I woke up screaming because I saw this man take my child and run away. I was running. I was touching her fingertips. She was reaching out to me. I was running faster. It scared the hell out of me. I got up screaming. I did not know the power of the story or what I was doing but I felt that I needed to do something. I needed to do something fast to recognize the suffering of these women who were very much silenced because people were not covering this type of material in their articles.

I finished the piece in San Francisco. In fact, I had written the piece when Pilar would sleep and then I would get up and work for an hour and then suddenly she would wake up. The pattern would repeat itself. I remember the time I finished it. It was three o'clock in the morning. I was supposed to take a plane at seven o'clock that same morning to go to Long Beach because they had invited me to this Women Writers Conference. I wanted to finish the piece because I had not done anything new in a long time. While Pilar was sitting in my backpack, I was typing away. She eventually fell asleep at about four thirty. I put her back to bed, packed my stuff, and then I was off. I didn't have time to consider the impact that the story had on me until I got to the place where I was supposed to read it.

This was in 1984. There were two hundred women and then we each divided into groups. I did not know at the time that Tillie Olsen was in my audience. As I began reading the story, I literally fell apart. I began sobbing and sobbing because the pain was so close to my heart. It was an incredible experience. I kept crying and couldn't stop. When I finished the story, I felt like such a fool until I looked up. Everyone in the room was crying. People had tears rolling down their eyes. I just could not believe it.

I did not know who Tillie Olsen was physically, but I knew and admired her as a writer. She came up to me, took my hand and said "I'm so glad you're writing this. Nobody has ever written this kind of work. This is so special." So I said, "Thank you, thank you. What's your name?" She said, "Tillie Olsen." Later on that day, in her keynote speech she said, "I have just been to an incredible reading of a story. I think this is what we have to be writing about, the important aspects of life that we have to put down on paper." I decided to send this story to Nick telling him to pull out the other story and put this one in. So that's how **"The Cariboo Cafe"** got into this book. I'm glad that it did because it's a good story. It's also one that I could never read out publicly. I tried other times but I decided that I better not do it.

In **"Nopalitos,"** *you experiment with another genre, the testimonio. It's really moving. What motivated this change?*

Let me tell you. During those crazy times, when I was not actually writing, I was keeping journals. I was reading, basically keeping a time of silence. Those years that passed were really hard for me. When somebody contacted me and asked, "Why don't you write a *testimonio*?" I could not even come up with the time to do it. I was sorry that they wanted me to do it.

During that time I got a call from the Chicano Literary Prize, which I had won a few years back at Irvine. They asked me if I had wanted to be the keynote speaker along with Tomás Rivera. "Are you talking to me?" I asked. "Aren't you Helena María Viramontes?" they asked. I was vacuuming at the time. It was hilarious. I immediately put some thoughts together because I did not have that much time to prepare. I would write sentences on post-its, to put here and to put there. Then I just typed it up in four hours. It's good that I did that because that was the basis of **"Nopalitos."**

This incident is interesting because I did the presentation on Wednesday with Tomás Rivera. By Sunday, he died of a heart attack. It was incredible. The spirits have a way of pointing me out to people and being where I should be. It was so strange that I should be there with him and that we should talk and a few days later he's gone. It was very sad because we were making a date to meet in a couple of weeks.

From taking those notes that I did for **"Nopalitos,"** María [Herrera-Sobek] said that they were very good. But I was pissed off that I did not have enough time to sit down and write.

One day Nancy Sternbach called me to say that she really wanted me to do the *testimonio* for this anthology. I said OK that I would sit down that afternoon, type it up, and work from my notes. While my husband watched the kids, it took me about four hours to put everything together and send it out. The next day I regretted it completely. I said, "Oh! How could I have possibly sent her this! Oh! This is terribly written! What can I say? What can I do?" A couple of days later she calls me back. She says, "Helena, we loved it. We loved it." That was the product of just a few hours work, but it wasn't really. The thoughts and ideas had already been there. There were minimal changes done. I like it a lot. It gives tribute to my mother, that's what it does and the importance of growing up hearing stories.

Are you working more on **"Miss Clairol"**? *I loved that story. The sympathy you have for that character, Arlene.*

The series of Paris Rats? I would like to continue. I really respect Arlene. It is interesting because I received a lot of flack especially from the outer circles. "*Ay!* Look at the way you are portraying a Chicana! Look, she's stealing lipstick in front of her kids!" I asked "Don't you understand? *No tiene dinero.* Geez. Don't you understand that she is a young woman *también que trabaja* like you would not believe. Yeah, she wants to go out. Yeah, she wants to have a good time. A life!" Anyway, yeah, I have to get back to the series. There's a couple of stories that need to be reworked and there is a couple that need to be written.

Have you tried experimenting with other genres, theater for example?

I see myself writing film. I am very interested in developing a script that I did at the Sundance Institute. It deals

Helen María Viramontes

with a *mexicana* who is known as the first convicted felon in Orange County. *Pobre mujer.* I feel that I have to vindicate her. Her name was Modesta Avila. The only existing picture we have of her is the photo that was taken at San Quentin. This woman owned a little patch of land in 1884, *algo así.* The railroads were invading very fast, Huntington being one of the big railroad magnates. They wanted to draw a straight line, a boundary through California. They wanted to cross her land. At first, she said, "No!" But then she changed her mind and said, "OK, but give me some money." They said, "No!" She ended up going to the courts complaining that they were building on her land and not giving her any kind of compensation. The courts did not pay any attention to her. The story has it (which captured my imagination) that she hung a laundry line across the railroad tracks though the court records say otherwise. She had *calzones* telling them "Fuckers! I'm going to dry my laundry." The courts got so pissed off that they arrested her. They tried her and then she was acquitted. Because she was acquitted, she was tried again until they found her guilty of obstruction of the railroad. She was given three years in San Quentin. She was pregnant at the time. Of course, she died up there. Who knows what happened to her child? I was able to get her picture from a wonderful woman who did some research on her. I blew it up and she's staring at me everyday. Waiting with such mournful eyes.

So I wrote this piece for the Sundance Institute that I plan to develop and make it into a real great story. It really needs to be told. I am told that some of her family still live. The descendants of the Avila don't talk about her. They say that she is not part of the family or that she is another string of Avila or whatever because she is a convicted criminal. *Pobrecita*, you should see her. She is so *triste.* It was really the railroad magnates who just wanted to get their way. Then it was Orange County that had developed its own county away from Los Angeles and wanted to show that they were good, law abiding citizens. The people in town treated her terribly. They said that she was famous with the "Santa Ana boys all over town," this kind of b.s. Yeah, of course. Basically they were representing her like a lying slut. This woman had a lot of guts, a lot of spunk. So I see myself doing this in film, but there are so many stories that I could develop.

How did you become involved with the Sundance Institute?

As you may know, Gabo [Gabriel García Márquez] is a supporter of the Havana Film School. Robert Redford, an admirer of Gabo, was successful in getting him a visa to stay in the USA for this workshop he was putting together in 1989. Gabo agreed to come as long as he could work with five U.S. Latino writers. This was also part of the Latin American exchange program he had set up. That was the first stipulation. So then a big national pool of Latino writers submitted their best works. I did not think I would be nominated because I was not really a film, but a fiction writer and I also knew I was competing against major people. When I was finally accepted, I had to decline the offer at first. They gave me the business about my lacking a "proper" Spanish. Well, I gave them a history about the Chicano Movement and the condition of the working-class Latinos in the U.S. At the time, I was also living in Nuevo México with my kids and I could not just get up and go to the Sundance Institute in Utah. Gabo was so accommodating that it was hilarious. He said that I could bring my kids along and that I could speak in English if I wanted. So now I had no more excuses.

It was an incredible experience. Every day from 9 AM to 1 PM, Gabo instructed us to come in with a storyline that we discussed, pulling and challenging our imagination. Again I was in that literary environment where we exchanged ideas and I became familiar with the literary traditions and concerns of other Latino writers, Cubans, Nuyoricans. I also learned that Gabo was a very loving and sweet man. On the last day, he said that he was so sentimental that he did not know how to say good-bye and he left us with tears in his eyes and a wave of his hand. I was very moved.

What project are you working on now?

This novel, for example, is very small. But I leave it open for the characters who are so incredibly rich, so incredibly powerful that it calls for other stories. It is called **Under the Feet of Jesus**. It has taken me a little bit over a year to work on a consistent basis. That is why I'm a bit tired. I still have some expansion. In this work, I wanted to give a tribute to the *Mujer*. I wanted to make her fucking tough. And it works! I've received very, very wonderful responses. An editor at Dutton, a woman from New York told me, "I read this and I read it again. It gave me the sense of being a classic." I was in awe. I would not go that far, but if you want to consider it a classic that's OK with me. I told her that when I write I really have to take care of my characters. These are characters that some people have complete stereotypes about or are completely invisible. They have a right to come unto themselves. They have a right to exist, to show people that they love, to show people that they are strong, to show people that they are responsible, to show that they are responsible for the salad on the plates, for instance. Think about it. This woman, this young little Chicanita, comes out so strong. She is incredible. Her name is Estrella. So I feel really good about it.

By the way, how did you meet Sandra Cisneros?

Let me tell you. It was destined that Sandra and I should meet and become really good friends. A friend of mine in East L. A. said, "I just picked up this book *The House on Mango Street*. You got to read it, Helena. I thought of you. You got to read it." So then he sends it to me. I read it in one sitting. And I just think, "God, this is fabulous!" And then I am going to read it a second sitting, when another Chicana friend comes along and I said, "Listen, you got to read this book!" So then she takes it along, right. We start talking, we were already talking about "look how interesting she got the folk tales and she turned them into this and really made them real to us . . ." And that's when my friend says, "Well, let me borrow it because I need to use it for my class."

That very day I go home. I go to my mother's house in East L. A. It's late afternoon. As I am walking in, I see that my mother's mailbox door is open, so I get the mail for her. All of a sudden, there's a letter to Helena María Viramontes. The ribbon was all messed up so half of my name came but on the top it had Cisneros, S. Cisneros on it with an address, San Antonio, The Guadalupe Cultural Center. I looked and I said, "I wonder if this is Sandra Cisneros, the person who wrote *The House on Mango Street*." So then I open it and it was Sandra. She said, "I picked up *Cuentos: Stories by Latinas* edited by Cherríe Moraga. I read your two stories. I think they're wonderful. I want to invite you down to The Guadalupe Cultural Center." So I called her and I said, "You know it's quite ironic. I just finished your book." I did not get the sense at the time of the real importance of the book, which is incredible. It has already sold tons of copies. It's used in fourth grade classes right now all the way up to adult literacy programs and graduate level courses in literature, cultural, women, and sociology courses because it is so textured. It is so leveled in many, many ways that there is something for everybody. It will be a timeless piece. Pilar at that time was about seven months old. When we went down to San Antonio, Sandra and I hit it off real fast, *hablando, hablando, hablando*. In fact, she gave me a draft of "One Holy Night" [a story in *Woman Hollering Creek*]. After I read it I knew that she was such an incredible writer.

From then on each time that she would be around California, whether I was living up in San Francisco or back in Irvine, she would call me to make sure that we could meet and spend time together. It was always so nice. She would come over to the house in San Francisco and pull me out. "Come with me! So and so invited me over to go have some *pupusas* at this restaurant. Come with me, Helena." And it was funny because I was pregnant in San Francisco with my second son. Then she came to visit me. She had won the Before Columbus Book Award for *The House on Mango Street*. I always remember. I am in the kitchen about to vomit and she would say, "Hey, listen I met so and so at Stanford. He's going to take me to a jazz club. Come with me. Come on. Come on." And I'm like, "Yeah Sandra, right."

For a number of years, Sandra always kept me connected to writers and the aspect of writing. She would always call me. She would always write to me. Even in the long stretch of time when I was just going crazy with the kids, the evaluation of my life and trying to get it all together, she always reminded me that my writing was important. It should be a big priority for me to address. For a time, I actually felt myself in a black hole, and if it wasn't for Sandra who kept me afloat, literally, I would have died in my own frustration. She is one, if not the biggest, supporter of Chicana writers.

In 1989, I took a course called "Chicana Writers" with Professor Norma Alarcón at U. C. Berkeley. I was amazed because it was the first time I read any fiction by Chicana writers and that's how I was introduced to **The Moths and Other Stories**. *Do you consider yourself part of a Chicana literary movement?*

Yes, yes I do. I would also include Sandra Cisneros, Cherríe Moraga, Lorna Dee Cervantes and many others still. What this literary body has in common is that we all come from a specific social situation, a working-class background. We have a social consciousness of the sixties, the Chicano Movement, the Black Movement and the impact that those radical days had on us. We are connected with a concrete historical past.

In what direction do you see Chicana/Latina writers going?

We are doing some very, very wonderful work. We are providing a source of new breath in literature. We are giving life to people who have never been in literature before. That was one of the things that the editor had told me. She said, "I had never seen characters just like this. Never." Look at the voice of *The House on Mango Street*. Look at the Don Quijote kind of novel that Ana Castillo wrote. You know what I mean? We are not just writing stories. It is like we are redefining what literature is to us in many ways. One of the reasons I think we writers have to write essays is that we need to translate our own work. Give it the historical context by which the product was produced. It's all so very new. There is still discussion whether *The House on Mango Street* is a novel, a collection of vignettes, or short stories. There is still that type of problematics with the texts we have created. We have the women creating the works and right behind them you have the literary critics, by and large Chicanas, who are trying to contextualize it. I think the critics complement the writers. They give a bigger understanding to show people the importance of this work. It is not only stories. This is something more, a lot more to the movement.

In terms of historical and literary importance, there is a great need for this. That's where I see it. I think we are doing very exciting work. Now the bigger publishing houses are beginning to open up to us but that means little. We still need the control of our own presses to guarantee that our work will be published, popular or not, profitable or not. And time. We will have more time, space and compensation to work on the stories that keep us alive and well.

Cecelia Lawless (essay date 1996)

SOURCE: "Helena María Viramontes' Homing Devices in *Under the Feet of Jesus*," in *Homemaking: Women Writers and the Politics and Poetics of Home*, Garland Publishing, Inc., 1996, pp. 361-82.

[*Here, critic Cecelia Lawless analyzes the subject and symbolism of home in Viramontes's story "Under the Feet of Jesus."*]

Under the Feet of Jesus begins with a question: "Had they been heading for the barn all along?" (1). This interrogation introduces the idea of a journey and its potential destination, which is a fundamental and often-forgotten aspect of the idea of home. *Under the Feet of Jesus* explores the barn as home site, and as a barn-dweller for some years, I appreciate the home-like qualities of this living space. In the warp of boards and slant of roof, a history of communion between architectural structure and function exists. Although an integral part of the indigenous architecture of the United States, the barn is a structure no longer in much demand and often abandoned to time and the weather. As a home site, then, the barn evokes irony.[1] Even this one in *Under the Feet of Jesus* is a dangerous place that is no longer solid on the ground. Thus this symbol for home represents a fragile and perhaps outdated home at best.

In this essay I will map the topographical meanings of silence and the barn, and the spaces in between where I read the shadows of a house-building project in this story of a migrant family. The idea of home in *Under the Feet of Jesus* is not compatible with a traditional home icon complete with white picket fence pictured in the American dream nor an invincible home with the stability of four walls and a roof; rather, this home is a linguistic gesture of refuge for all those marginalized and disenfranchised by a socio-political system intent on silencing dissonant voices. The mythic home of the American dream functions as a useful rhetorical device for both those on the political Left and Right. However, for many, in particular for people of color, owning a house remains merely a dream. With the lack of a home-site and the supposed stability which that place implies, come a lack of voice in the community, in nation-building, and history-making. Estrella's family in *Under the Feet of Jesus* is emblematic of a Chicano migratory family, nomadic in their wanderings from job to job, whose voices do not participate in the continuing process of redefinition of national identity. But even though they do not own a house, they do begin to explore the possibilities for home-building within different sedimentary layers of language.[2]

In *Under the Feet of Jesus* characters do not speak to one another. Although words might overlap in the speakers' presence, no contact between people is made with them. Words follow their own path chiselled from stone, bone, and blood where meaning must be culled from surrounding gestures. Yet it is from the words uttered by the migrant workers in the novel that a home must be constructed, since there is no other material at hand: "It was always a question of work, and work depended on the harvest, the car running, their health, the conditions of the road, how long the money held out, and the weather, which meant they could depend on nothing" (2). Material options for this family are not dependable, and instead they must rely on another level of communicative signs: "The silence and the barn and the clouds meant many things" (2). The barn here becomes marked by its position between two ambiguous phenomena, silence and clouds. Thus framed, linguistic instability threatens to convert the barn into a space "in between."

A home transcends geometric space; a tar paper shack in Mexico or the various pieces of paraphernalia of an American street person can all represent a home, even if not so considered by conventional standards. In his socio-poetic study, Mexican architect Victor Manuel Ortiz capitalizes the word "house" [casa] to give it prominence and in some way establish a link between "casa" and "hogar" in Spanish, where the force of linguistic distinction remains less strong than in the English "house" and "home:" "La CASA ha sido siempre algo más que un techo: el marco físico ha operado como un abanico de posibilidades entre las cuales se hacen elecciones a través de tabúes, costumbres y caminos tradicionales de una cultura" [The house / home has always been more than a mere roof: the physical framework has functioned like a fan of possibilities among which one makes choices through traditional and cultural taboos, customs, and directions] (29). Through capitalization, Ortiz builds in his writing an actual structure for his concept since his form reflects the content of his work: he houses the word "house" at the same time that he analyses and explains it. I would further suggest that when we base our analysis in socio-linguistic, geographic, and architectural studies we can separate out layers of meaning between house and home.

The cover of Ortiz's book displays a naive, child-like drawing of a house. This image of a box with windows, doors, and a chimney crosses cultural boundaries. A house can be a two-dimensional construct. In contrast, a home is a socio-physical construct as well as a cultural icon. A home implies a dynamic tension, a continual dialectic of giving and taking, coming and going, falling away and building up. Thus, for my purposes, the word "house" will refer to structure only, whereas "home" will include the habitable, human implications of the house. This distinction directly relates to the differences already established in sociological studies between space—mathematically oriented—and place—historically oriented. As Yi-Fu Tuan has pointed out in one of his influential geographic studies, "space is a mathematical construct whereas place contains personal, human roots" (98). In other words, space and house are synchronic terms while place and home have diachronic implications.

When viewed through both its structural and existential implications, house/home also represents an institution of power, a defined private space, a middle-class domestic ideal, and hence the term is often manipulated by politicians and nationalists. Home and house have overlapped to such an extent that they have become emptied of meaning; for example, real estate agents no longer sell houses, they sell homes. Thus, these two words form an important linguistic strategy for the framing of social and private lives. But for Estrella in *Under the Feet of Jesus*, and her mother Petra, and many other working-class Chicana women, the house/home conceals as much terror as it projects supposed safety. In the house that the Chicana woman must convert into home, there is pressure to produce and care for children, to work inside and outside the house for economic reasons, and still to remain attractive for one's man. But as Rebolledo suggests, "[Chicanas] . . . have grown up and survived along the edges, along the borders of so many languages, worlds, cultures and social systems that we constantly fix and focus on the spaces in between" (136). If the idea of home, traditionally a central locus point, can be re-conceived as a space in between, rather than merely on the margin, then the home takes on a more powerful and dynamic luster because it becomes less a static space than a place in process. In fact, I would suggest that part of the project of *Under the Feet of Jesus* is to subvert and undermine the claim of the "safe house" so as to make us question the cultural significance of the place that in one way or another we all inhabit. The site of language as home may seem a paltry solace in the midst of the actual poverty of this family, but there is power in language.

Under the Feet of Jesus destabilizes the motifs of the house/home, the journey, and the girl-growing-into-woman, subverting its traditional American counterpart.[3] Such a textual interrogation of language opens the way for readers to review and renew their own participation in the production of discourse on political, racial, and feminist levels by revising cliches and casually held concepts such as "house," "home," "place," "space," "woman," and "culture."

Words are like tools used for building places to inhabit with others. Estrella, the growing thirteen-year-old girl in *Under the Feet of Jesus*, learns this from a man who is not her father, Perfecto Flores. Everyone calls him Perfecto because his work is always "perfecto": he has earned and now lives the word that identifies him. From Perfecto, Estrella connects objects with their function and thus the curves and tails of the worker's tools begin to make sense to her even as the chalky lines on school blackboards become more coherent:

> Tools to build, bury, tear down, rearrange and repair, a box of reasons his hands took pride in. She lifted the pry bar in her hand, felt the coolness of iron and power of function, weighed the significance it awarded her, and soon she came to understand how essential it was to know these things. That was when she began to read.

(22)

Reading and telling a story become related here to the act of building. Perfecto's tools are tangible; they lie heavily in Estrella's hands. She can wield these objects and they give her power. In knowing the names of these tools, she increases her independence because she explores simultaneously the use and utterance of language. This knowledge leads her to the place so simply expressed in the phrase, "That was when she began to read." This passage connecting tools to words, Perfecto to Estrella, reading to building, is of fundamental importance in understanding the unfolding story which demands sensitive tools for the interpretation of a home-site.

As Heidegger has shown through his etymological studies in "Building, Dwelling, Thinking," building *is* dwelling, and the idea of being harks back to dwelling as well. What interests me in Heidegger's work is his formulation of home and its connection to language: "Language is the house of Being" (86).[4] If we take this statement literally, we realize that we dwell in language, and in alienating ourselves from language we lose our potential to dwell, to make a home. In learning to build with tools, Perfecto perfects his sense of dwelling, just as Estrella, in seeing words as building tools, will also learn how to dwell with more thoughtfulness. This idea of dwelling, of "homing" oneself, is a touchstone for a family whose emotional and physical life consists of constant movement.

Estrella is the eldest child of Petra, a migrant worker whose maternal feelings extend beyond her own family, as she explains when she takes in the sick Alejo, another young migrant worker: "If we don't take care of each other, who would take care of us? We have to look out for our own" (81). Petra expresses her philosophy of life here, which includes a strong sense of solidarity and community, even amongst transient working people such as Alejo, who is from far away Texas.[5] Petra is a woman constantly on the move from field to field in search of work and food. She has two little boys and twin girls as well as Estrella, and now lives with Perfecto Flores, thirty-seven years her senior. Her husband, the father of her children, left her in search of something he could never articulate, and now Perfecto is also on the edge of leaving, compelled by his yearning for home, for "his real home, not the bungalow. The desire became as urgent as the money he brought in for Petra's family. . . . What would happen if he forgot his way home?" (67). A strong woman who combats varicose veins with large amounts of garlic, Petra has no home to call her own except for her children. At the same time, Estrella the girl-woman explores her potential for making homes through the tentative rapport she builds with Alejo, who will ultimately leave for the hospital because of an illness he has developed from breathing in the poison spray used for fumigation. Each character in the novel finds him/herself on a threshold or in-between space of leave-taking from the promise (or threat) of a traditional home. *Under the Feet of Jesus* relates the implied journeys of these characters, although it refrains from disclosing a final destination.

This migrant family on the border between Mexico and the United States is also on the border between home and homelessness. In the present moment Estrella, Perfecto, and Petra work the fields accompanied by the four younger children. They appear to do this for some months with no thought of school or other less strenuous work options. Perfecto does contemplate tearing down a barn near their desolate bungalow so he can sell the wood for cash, but Estrella refuses to help him because of her strange attachment to the building. The past mostly consists of derelict urban dwellings reminiscent of another Chicana's depiction of transient childhood in *The House on Mango Street*:

> We didn't always live on Mango Street. Before that we lived on Loomis on the third floor, and before that we lived on Keeler. Before Keeler it was Pauline, and before that I can't remember. But what I remember most is moving a lot. Each time it seemed there'd be one more of us.
>
> (3)

Although these two novels are very different, they both emphasize the effect of constant displacement on young children and how that displacement can motivate a desire for expression through language and story-telling.

Under the Feet of Jesus interrogates the unique quality of the traditional house / home that supposedly represents safety for the woman in flight. For as well as telling the story of a family who migrates from field to field, from job to job, *Under the Feet of Jesus* also tells the tale of flight from places. Migration is the working-class Chicana's journey through "space," and the various bungalows, shacks, or urban hovels represent the waiting stations or houses not yet homes. The act of flight reflects these women's despair regarding their sense of ideological, ontological "place." If migration is a movement towards some ideal—the house become home—then flight is a movement away from the fear of the house that has never become home. Thus, on the physical and existential levels, these women constantly combat the fear of homelessness that is so directly linked to the problematics of their cultural female identity.

Both Petra and her daughter Estrella are in different stages of flight. Petra, like many working-class Chicanas, finds

herself in the unenviable position of representing the stoic, strong, resourceful Mother.[6] In fact, she is tired, overburdened with economic problems, concerned for her five children, and abandoned by her husband. At one point we do see her in flight from a powerful scene of her children's hunger and her current despair. By inflicting pain on herself—she bites through her thumb—and then running out the door, she mentally and physically leaves the responsibilities of home behind her, but she does return. In this case, the four walls of the house / home have become a nightmarish, unsafe prison for her and her children. Because of such experiences, Petra has learned to shape the shelter of home from the people, the family that surrounds her rather than to seek stability from buildings. Estrella's flight, on the other hand, is not so self-conscious. In this chronicle of her growing from girl to woman, Estrella feels the pull of something beyond the circuit of migration in which she lives. The pull is both away from home and towards a reconceptualization of home, tenuously defined by Alejo, Maxine, Perfecto, and her mother, what an insider observer might call her community. It occurs to Estrella that picking vegetables might not be her life forever (101); words lay a path towards another option. Through Petra we already know that Estrella won a prize for a written essay, and once she has overcome her suspicion of Alejo's questions, his words begin to take on meaning for her, sink into her like the bones in the tar pits that he describes. Estrella is learning that words have substance and weight, like Perfecto's tools, and that with an understanding of language comes the fearlessness and the responsibility to use them.

From these reflections arise certain vital questions for Petra and Estrella: How does the house/home reflect and express their daily life? Do they learn to tell a story the same way that they learn to inhabit a house? Can reconstructed words such as "house" and "home" create a rhetorical foundation for effective social change? And, ultimately, can language act as home?

How do we get from one place to another? We can run, stroll, march, or dance, thus expressing different ways of taking possession of the environment. We can also read. In our lives we move through rooms as we move through stories to reveal and penetrate private realms. As an architectonic object, the text, and implicitly the act of narration, allows a reader or listener a place to inhabit. Many writers have intuited the importance of spatial sequence by playing with the linearity of the stories we read. For example, Cortázar's famous novel *Hopscotch* (1967) tells us explicitly that we can read the chapters in varying order. Ana Castillo's more recent *The Mixquiahuala Letters* (1986) and Sandra Cisneros's *The House on Mango Street* (1984) are two Chicana examples providing freedom of narrative movement. *Under the Feet of Jesus* also is a carefully patterned maneuvering towards an understanding of the Chicana growing into her domestic space, wherever and however that might be conceived. Viramontes' play with borders, with the inside and the outside so fundamental to the traditional notion of home, allows for a re-orienting of space that is not a dichotomy but "the space in between."

Aside from offering story-telling as a model for building a home in the transitory space in between, *Under the Feet of Jesus* demands the participation of the reader. This text does not work on only one narrative plane. Often *Under the Feet of Jesus* reads as a disconnected series of short story vignettes that the reader must in some way assemble. Perfecto likewise assembles his tools in his red tool chest to form a pattern that will help him with the work at hand. Through his knowledge of tools he can semiotically read the value of the walls, the supports, the fixtures and appliances of buildings so as to enter into the language of barter rather than monetary exchange. Instead of paying his bill at the local store, he fixes its run-down freezer. To pay for Alejo's clinic visit, he assesses the various decrepit aspects of the building and offers to fix them. Estrella watches, listens, and learns from Perfecto's "fix-it" lessons and begins to use words as tools to "fix" situations. In learning how to use words forcefully, Estrella also becomes a better reader of others' words. Thus, the give-and-take established in Perfecto's bartering with his tools is also enacted in Estrella's speaking and listening throughout the novel. The same situation of exchange is demanded of the reader of *Under the Feet of Jesus*, where we must use our tools of interpretation to understand the many implications of this story.

A linear time line does not exist in *Under the Feet of Jesus*. The narrative demands an active role from the reader, who must make an effort not to become lost amongst the different time locations framed by blank spaces. Often too, the blocks of text or individual paragraphs will swing back and forth between two characters to express simultaneity. Thus, scenes appearing on the same page, but in different textual places, render time both spatial and parallel. For example, in the beginning of Part II from pages 42-44, the narrative alternates between Estrella in the hot fields picking grapes, her thoughts and tired actions, and Alejo's movements and musings in this same field. We learn here of their different pasts and their reactions to the land. Estrella almost appears defeated by her circumstances: "Her tracks led to where she stood now. Morning, noon or night, four or fourteen or forty it was all the same. She stepped forward, her body never knowing how tired it was until she moved once again. Don't cry" (43). Alejo, in contrast, appears less concentrated on the task at hand, but more grounded in the significance of the land:

> He loved stones and the history of stones because he believed himself to be a solid mass of boulder thrusted out of the earth and not some particle lost in infinite and cosmic space. With a simple touch of a hand and a hungry wonder of his connection to it all, he not only became a part of the earth's history, but would exist as the boulders did, for eternity.
>
> (42)

Both characters think of the same themes here—their paths on earth, the act of touching, the sense of hunger—but their views are radically different. Spatially, however, they are in the same place: "Alejo had been working right next to Estrella all along. How could he not have known?" (45). The reader knows this information before Alejo

due to the preceding paragraph in which all the different workers are gathered together narratively in a semblance of community, despite their different thoughts and activities, by the evocative call of the train: "The lone train broke the sun and silence with its growing thunderous roar and the train reminded the *piscadores* of destinations, of arrivals and departures, of home and not of home" (45).[7] Time and space converge through the narrative play.

Just after the synchrony of Estrella and Alejo working together in the fields, Estrella decides to walk to her family's bungalow rather than take the truck with Alejo and the rest of the workers. It is almost as if she rejects the physical synchrony of working with Alejo for the mental asymmetry that they also experienced. She opts for independent flight and a potential journey evoked by the railroad tracks she walks. Earlier, the call of home had resonated for the workers from these same tracks, and the reader wonders where these tracks will lead and what division line they mark. As she walks, Estrella encounters a baseball diamond where running boys play the All-American game. She too runs, but her game is a matter of survival due to her tenuous status in American society. She can only observe here; she is not "at home." And then car lights blind her and she realizes that she does not known where home is. The game and its goal: "Destination: home plate" (49), become superimposed on the game of finding illegals and the fear it produces even for people like Estrella who are legal.

While focusing on the nature of home and the relation of Chicanos to home, *Under the Feet of Jesus* also gives the sense of *unheimlich* or "unhomelike" a precise form. As described by Freud, the *unheimlich* is a dis-ease bordering on fear of home. *Under the Feet of Jesus* articulates the *unheimlich's* marginality, whether spatial or temporal, and it recalls an Otherness that lies at the core of the bourgeois world, thus questioning the nature of established, accepted order. Implicitly, questions arise during the reading of this text, such as: why do migrant workers have to live like this? what are their options? what are the "white leaflets with black eagles on them" (72)? Why is there such fear of "la migra" (immigration) if the United States documents for Petra's children are "under the feet of Jesus" in her altar? How can they claim the States as home if they are in fear of its immigration officers? And so on. In this way, the novel functions as historical memory, a site that documents Chicana life in a migrant American context. The needed tools of interpretation for this text then include a focus on the movement and dislocation of boundaries, both spatial and social; the life-like qualities of the house/home; and the woman's role in the midst of these turbulent problems.

Sometimes words as well as people appear in flight in the novel, particularly when the characters try to speak to one another; like wayward winds their words do not catch onto anything. If Estrella represents a star, as her name indicates, then can she and her words act as a guiding star for others or as a falling star soon lost in darkness? Although Alejo and Estrella have some meaningful conversations, the following represents the apparent lack of connection between the addresser and the addressee:

—My papa was the one who named me that. . . .

—What does he call you now?

—My papa's gone.

—Dead?

—Things just happen.

(55)

Estrella is suspicious of too many words, too many questions. Alejo asks her a seemingly ordinary question about how many brothers she has and she responds,

—That's kinda a funny question.

—You don't like questions?

—Not really. Only asking maybe.

—What's your full name?

—Talk louder.

—Last name. What's your last name?

—What's it to you? she snapped back.

(56)

In this exchange Alejo is trying to "place" Estrella, and everything conspires against him: Estrella's discomfort with even ordinary conversation, the rumble and noise of the truck taking them to work, and his own nervousness caused by the lack of privacy of the truck filled with a listening and mocking audience.

Between Perfecto and Estrella the lines of conversation do not cross one another either; for example,

—I'm not your papa. But you're getting me old with your. . . .

—Where did you put the lantern?

—Stay away from the barn, hear me?

—You're right. You're not my papa.

—That should do it.

(22)

Such lack of conversation accentuates the homelessness of these characters while pointing towards other forms of home-building, perhaps not always considered by white, anglo, middle-class wage earners. The apparent lack of exchange between characters has been supplanted by a language of gesture that often speaks more strongly than English, Spanish, or the many instances of Spanglish used

in this text. Examples of this gestural language abound in the novel, for example: Alejo hardly speaks when he first meets Estrella's family, but he gives them a sack of peaches with no explanation, and Petra quietly returns the sack to him filled with pinto beans (38); in the nurse's office Estrella does not know what to do, or what to say and she holds out her hands, palms up, empty, for all to see (124); the exchanges between Petra's children and Perfecto are nonexistent but the twins love to hold on to his big hands, one on each side (87). All these examples and more speak volumes in a culture where one is judged by one's actions. When one is constantly on the edge of survival, on the border, literal and metaphorical, of becoming invisible to mainstream American society, then the impact and weight of words must shift.

Language as gesture becomes a product of fear and exhaustion and despair. People in this text are so very tired—everyone from Perfecto in his old age. "This was not a time for words . . . He wanted to rest, to lay down and never get up" (137), to Petra and her many burdens—who holds her eldest as if she "was trying to hide her back in her body" (146), and the young Estrella who feels "as if her body had been beaten into a pulp of ligaments and cartilage" (145). Too seldom in the theoretical world of the American academy are these mundane details taken into account in our analyses of textual, potentially innovative linguistic maneuvers.

This silencing of one kind of language and activating another kind is particularly crucial to the understanding of Estrella's growth as a woman when, towards the end of the novel, she appears to abandon language in favor of the use of force. In fact, at this point in her life, she couples language with the only tools (Perfecto's very real tools) she as yet knows how to manipulate. Under her instigation, the family has taken the sick Alejo to a run-down clinic where an insensitive nurse wants to take all their money for a cursory and graceless examination of the young man. Estrella uses her knowledge of the different functions of language—lies, bartering, pleading—but the nurse insists on charging them. Estrella takes up one of Perfecto's tools, a crowbar, and smashes it down on the nurse's desk to make her understand their terrible need. To the nurse such an act might appear like armed robbery:

> Estrella slammed the crowbar down on the desk, shattering the school pictures of the nurse's children, sending the pencils flying to the floor; breaking the porcelain cat with a nurse's cap into pieces. The nurse dropped her purse and shielded her face. Estrella waited.

(129)

In fact, this is Estrella's effort to fix the situation. She does not want to hurt anything or anyone, she just realizes that her words coupled with this action will rectify the situation she has concluded is unjust:

> She remembered the tar pits. Energy, money, the fossilized bones of energy matter. How bones made oil and oil made gasoline. The oil was made from their bones, and it was their bones that kept the nurse's car from not

halting on some highway, kept her on her way to Daisy-field to pick up her boys at six. It was their bones that kept the air conditioning in the cars humming, that kept them moving on the long dotted line of the map. Their bones. Why couldn't the nurse see that? Estrella had figured it out: the nurse owed them as much as they owed her.

(127)

For this nurse, and much of mainstream American society, Estrella and her family represent mere means to an end: they exist as part of a larger labor force, not as individuals with needs and desires. Estrella must have the money back because they need it for gas to get to the hospital. We can see here how Estrella has learned her reading lesson well from Perfecto and Alejo and her mother. For example, it is fitting that Estrella uses Perfecto's crowbar with her own words to pry apart the nurse's prejudices. And in Estrella's position as voiceless and invisible Other, which she is slowly beginning to understand, she must use her knowledge of tools to achieve what she wants and needs.

Estrella's development from girl to woman in **Under the Feet of Jesus** parallels her growing understanding and use of the tools Perfecto, Alejo, and Petra have imparted to her. I have already explained to some extent here Perfecto's tools and the legacy that he leaves with Estrella, but he is a complex character with his own ambivalence concerning home, as he lives a "travesty of laws" (71). Although Petra sees him as part of her family, when Perfecto dreams of home he dreams of his dead wife and their children with whom he has lost contact. Petra believes in him because he has lived his words to her, "trust me" (96) and to Estrella (131), but since they have arrived at the camps. "The desire to return home was now a tumor lodged under the muscle of Perfecto's heart and getting larger with every passing day" (70). This longing leads him to consider tearing down the barn, in some ways a home-site for Estrella: "With or without Estrella's help, he committed himself to tearing the barn down. The money was essential to get home before home became so distant, he wouldn't be able to remember his way back" (71). But Estrella in the end bargains with Perfecto: she will become his tool, and help to tear down the barn, if he will help her to take Alejo to the clinic. And from Perfecto and his knowledge of active tools, Estrella also learns the grace of language. When she thanks him for his help she lays a path for him to follow through her words and her tone which act like the bones in Alejo's tar pit stories. These markers possibly will help him, ultimately, to realize and accept her family as home.[8]

> He had given this country his all, and in this land that used his bones for kindling, in this land that never once in the thirty years he lived and worked, never once said thank you, this woman who could be his grand-daughter, had said the words with such honest gratitude, he was struck by how deeply these words touched him.
>
> (131-132)

Alejo has a different but related tool that he uses to communicate with and verbally seduce Estrella. In his

awkward adolescent fumbling with language to gain Estrella's attention, he tells her stories. These stories are about tar pits and bones and the oil that comes from these historical sites. And these musings resonate throughout the text in powerful ways to explain the situation of this migrant family, particularly the motif of bones that acts as a metaphor for home in the text, the ultimate home for all people, the bones that we inhabit and that we leave behind after death. The story of the tar pits explains Alejo's interests to Estrella and also "homes" her onto his ontological site as person: the story acts as an explanatory analogy of her own family's and others' sense of homelessness, of not belonging in the capital-based market of the United States. Only one of his stories tells of a person, a young girl whose bones were found in a field as if homeless and displaced: "They found her in a few bones. No details of her life were left behind, no piece of cloth, no ring, no doll. A few bits of bone displayed somewhere under a glass and nothing else" (112). This feeling of being lost and "boneless" is how Alejo feels when he breathes in the fumigation fumes: "No fingerprint or history, bone. No lava stone. No story or family, bone" (66). Through Alejo's words, Viramontes clarifies the significant relationship between bone, earth, stone, family story, and finally, home.

With her mother, Estrella learns the language of domesticity, where empty Quaker Oats boxes can be converted into musical drums to appease little children, and the everyday gesture of rolling early-morning tortillas becomes just another appendage of one's body. Rarely do Estrella and Petra speak to one another, but they do exchange glances and embraces. Petra instills in Estrella a respect for the power of home remedies such as garlic for varicose veins and a circle drawn in dirt round a shack to keep away scorpions. Estrella also learns from Petra the strategies of mothering which she constantly uses with the other children in the family. The mother teaches her daughter a home-based language, tools to construct her own home. On first arriving at their bungalow, for example, Petra inspects the cooking grill outside and evaluates the smell of former meals. In this way, the traditionally contained kitchen moves outside, and the art of cooking is established by sensual smells rather than by four walls. Through her language and her gestures Petra enforces the idea of an extended—nontraditional—family and hope for community.

Poet and playwright Cherríe Moraga explains the situation of many Chicana women that applies to Petra as well:

> So we fight back, we think, with our families—with our women pregnant and our men, the indisputable heads. We believe the more severely we protect the sex roles within the family, the stronger we will be as a unit in opposition to the anglo threat. And yet, our refusal to examine *all* the roots of lovelessness in our families is our weakest link and softest spot.
>
> (181)

In **Under the Feet of Jesus** the woman acts as participant—not passive object—in the restructuring or redefining of a language laden with "house-bound" ideology. She moves inside and outside the walls of the house to expand domestic intimacy into the public world: she makes the inside become outside. Viramontes gives us an alternative to the borders so glorified in texts such as Bachelard's topophilia studies of the house/home, or an early article by Rivera praising "la casa, el barrio and la lucha as constant elements in the ritual of Chicano literature" (441); *Under the Feet of Jesus* presents an alternative view. It explores "the dialectic of inside and outside, that is, here and there, integration and alienation, comfort and anxiety" that the traditional house / home offers (Olivares 161), and then it questions these dichotomies. Conventional Mexican American texts, especially those written in the sixties and seventies by male writers, implicitly support the idea of the contented woman as the domestic angel, while Viramontes' text explicitly undermines any unthinking acceptance of such ideology. The inside is not necessarily good and safe for the female. Instead the Chicana must explore new layers of language to furnish a home-site, almost as if, using Alejo's motif of bones and stones, she must dig deep into geological layers of language to unearth the bones with which to reconstruct a different home to inhabit.

Unlike the traditional anglo-European view of home, the reader sees here the different cultural approaches that Chicanas from Mexico and Southern California have employed in their reconstruction of a sense of home. The tension between male and female goals in this novel reflects the impasse between individual insight and the unchanging social codes faced by the Chicana heroine. Clearly these clashes are seen in the case of Petra's husband abandoning her, and then Perfecto's more ambiguous leave-taking. And Alejo's courtship of Estrella, though conventional, leads not to her merely mothering him in his sickness but to her letting go of him for his own good and that of her family.

Estrella and her family can barely visualize the kind of home that comes readily to mind for most middle-class white Americans. Estrella and her family are migrant workers—piscadores. The whole premise behind the twentieth century's political rhetoric about a stable and secure home is completely undermined by this family's constant movement, displacement, and potential eviction from both home and country. At one point the little boy comments to Petra, "Maybe we can stay in one place" (130). Even a small child can feel the instinctual appeal of constancy, of not always working, not moving. Hence this story, like so many untold stories, articulates different ways of conceptualizing the home-site. Mohanty and Martin write: "Far too often . . . both male leftists and feminists have responded to the appeal of a rhetoric of home and family by merely reproducing the most conventional articulations of those terms in their own writings" (191). *Under the Feet of Jesus* does not reproduce homey nostalgia, nor do its characters long for the anglo version of home. And in this recognition comes a need for, and an acceptance of making space and place available within the diverse layers of the States for various kinds of home. The family in *Under the Feet of Jesus* appears isolated, regardless of whether they are legal or not, for many reasons: economic, racial, linguistic, to name a few. In rejecting a conventional idea of home, they need the practical means to envision another kind of home. In any case, their idea is not a cozy embroidery-stitched picture of "home, sweet, home;" instead, home should be viewed as a vital, thriving reality lived through language, people, and habitable structures. As the sociologist Muntañola explains, "La noción de lugar para vivir es un constante y triple encuentro entre el medio externo, nosotros mismo y los demás, y cada lugar construido es una síntesis y un resultado de este triple encuentro" [The notion of a place to live is a constant and triple encounter between the outside world, ourselves, and others, and every constructed place is a synthesis and a result of this triple encounter] (55). A home cannot be conceived as a private, protected, and individualistic place. Without the interaction with others, and the varieties of religion, race, sexuality, political views that they bring with them, the concept of home as expounded in this paper could not exist.

Future constructions of home sites depend not only on architecture, but in socio-political possibilities for home-building as well. My goal in this study has been to suggest that the act of narration can be a form of "home" where self-identity emerges. Disintegrating language and actual homelessness have become current arenas of debate for many societies. For example, the newly passed proposition 187 in California denies social services to illegal immigrants and in effect denies them a home site in physical and political reality. According to the *San Francisco Chronicle*, the state of California is host to almost half of the nation's undocumented population (11). The proposition has sowed fear and bitterness among many voters. It brings out the xenophobia and racism that often lie just under the surface of the American social fabric. I note that amongst various Other groups who are denied a home-site for racial and/or legal reasons, the "master's tools" are denied them,[9] and an opportunity to found a site of solidarity is missed.

With the passage of proposition 187, people on both sides of the issue lose the potential for home-building. As Martin and Mohanty put it in their example of a women's community:

> The relationship between the loss of community and the loss of self is crucial. To the extent that identity is collapsed with home and community and based on homogeneity and comfort, on skin, blood, and heart, the giving up of home will necessarily mean the giving up of self and vice versa.
>
> (209)

Skin, blood, and heart can also stand in for the bones so often evoked in *Under the Feet of Jesus*. These specific, body-structuring details are vital parts of a home community, but laws like proposition 187 forget these human elements in the legal analysis of immigration problems. Identity is related to place, so that when people are denied a place to live, their identity is undermined. The fear that provokes such propositions also acts as a threat to the anglo community because it highlights the presence of the Other instead of incorporating Others in the sedimentary levels of language and society.

Within these layers of sedimentation a Chicana/o discourse is in process. As Rebolledo writes, "I think we would all agree that Chicana criticism and theory are still in a state of flux, looking for a theoretical, critical framework that is our own" (350). In *Under the Feet of Jesus* language in flux and a shifting home are represented by the space in between—the barn. The barn acts almost as another character in the text as well as being a potential home-site for Estrella. Even if not made originally for human habitation, a barn instills a sense of quiet and respect from most people. In its simple and vernacular architectural style, a barn connects the present with the past. Perhaps it is this sense of being grounded that attracts Estrella to the barn from the beginning. It seems to be a structure that will not move, that shelters, that marks time. At the same time, through its holes and cracks it lets through air and light. Estrella personifies the barn when she imagines tearing it down with Perfecto, "pulling the resistant long rusted nails out of the woodsheet walls. The nails would screech and the wood would moan and she would pull the veins out" (63). And this image of destruction, an almost human portrayal of blood and bones, leads her to reflect on a much larger picture: "Is that what happens? Estrella thought, people just use you until you're all used up, then rip you into pieces when they're finished with you?" (63).

In *Under the Feet of Jesus* the barn represents many things: a mysterious place, a refuge, money, a base for flight into other realms, and the home that Estrella has never had. At the end of the novel, after leaving Alejo behind at the hospital, perhaps forever, after her mother verges on collapse as her figure of Christ breaks in two, after Perfecto poises himself in indecisive flight, Estrella goes to the barn in the dark to climb to the roof and feel the power of open skies, stars, and strength in its structure. Grounded, "[l]ike the chiming bells of the great cathedrals, she believed her heart powerful enough to summon *home* all those who strayed" (151, my emphasis). The question arises whether Estrella has the power to be a beacon of home or will fall into disrepair like her barn. In my reading, Estrella finds herself in a discursive exile, on the edge of a threshold, where language becomes the tool to implement an odyssey of self-exploration. Homeless, even within her domestic spheres, this woman will become, I contend, a builder engaged in establishing strong foundations for future homes. I have tried to interweave the ideas of language as home, and the learning of a new language to build a new home, in this essay. An early scene in the novel, between Alejo and Estrella, illustrates this intersection:

> Yeah, and Estrella pointed to the bottle because she wanted to tell him how good she felt but didn't know how to build the house of words she could invite him in. That was real good, she said, and they looked at one another and waited. Build rooms as big as barns. . . .

Wide-open windows where she could put candlelights and people from across the way would point at the glow and not feel so alone in the night.

(59)

Estrella then takes the empty bottle and shows Alejo how to make music, a different kind of language that they can share and that will house them. By exploring different languages and opening up different silences, Estrella—Star—will be true to her name and thus guide as beacon those around her who need a different kind of home. Such languages of difference act as homing devices in Viramontes' *Under the Feet of Jesus*.

NOTES

[1] The fate of the barns parallels the fate of families like Estrella's: both are abandoned by mainstream society after they have been "used up"; both belong to a world in which labor is not depersonalized through mechanization.

[2] I borrow the metaphor "sedimentary layers of language" from Bakhtin's concept of heteroglossia, which he defines as the plurality of voices or discourses and their potentially creative interconnections and overlappings.

[3] *The Grapes of Wrath* is a classic American counterpart to *Under the Feet of Jesus*. Although Viramontes's novel also deals with migrant workers, it focuses more on an interior voyage than does Steinbeck's lengthier novel.

[4] Philosophers and architects such as Heidegger, Bachelard, Le Corbusier, and Norberg-Schulz demonstrate uniformly positive reactions to and interpretations of the idea of home, usually within rather strict terminology. It is only recently in North and South America that the influence of sociological and feminist studies have broadened and deepened the critique of the home site.

[5] The following passage from the novel illustrates the geographic and historical distance of Texas in the minds of the field workers: "-De donde eres? —Del Rio Grande Valle. —Es un estado de México? -Texas ya es parte de los Estados Unidos. —Ay . . ." (53).

[6] Traditionally, the options for Chicanas have included two extremes of the madre santa/wife and the feminist/whore. These essentializing poles have been mitigated by recent theoretical and literary work of such writers as Gloria Anzaldúa, Norma Alarcón, Tey Diana Rebolledo, Cherríe Moraga, Sandra Cisneros, and Helena María Viramontes.

[7] *Piscadores*—fruit or vegetable pickers—is a linguistic marker of a Chicano word entering into the English narrative. A different investigation than mine here would trace the socio-linguistic implications of code-switching in the novel and their effect in producing another level of home through language.

[8] I use "realize" in the Spanish sense of the word *realizar,* to actualize something in the performative sense.

9. See Audre Lorde's insightful essay, "The Master's Tools Will Never Dismantle the Master's House."

WORKS CITED

Alarcón, Norma. "Making Familia From Scratch: Split Subjectivities in the Work of Helena María Viramontes and Cherríe Moraga." In Herrera-Sobek, 147-159.

Alarcón, Norma, ed. *Chicana Critical Issues.* Berkeley: Third Woman Press, 1993.

Anzaldúa, Gloria, ed. *Making Face, Making Soul: Haciendo Caras. Creative and Critical Perspectives by Women of Color.* San Francisco: Aunt Lute, 1990.

Arthur, Eric, and Dudley Witney. *The Barn: A Vanishing Landmark in North America.* Toronto: McClelland and Stewart Ltd., 1972.

Bachelard, Gaston. *The Poetics of Space.* 1958. Trans. María Jolas. Boston: Beacon Press, 1969.

Castillo, Debra A. *Talking Back: Toward a Latin American Feminist Criticism.* Ithaca: Cornell UP, 1992.

Editorial, "The Resonances of Proposition 187 for California," *San Francisco Chronicle,* Sunday, October 23, 1994, sec. TW, 11.

Heidegger, Martin. *Poetry, Language, Thought.* Trans. Albert Hofstadter, New York: Harper Colophon Books, 1971.

Herrera-Sobek, María, and Helena María Viramontes, eds. *Chicana Creativity and Criticism: Charting New Frontiers in American Literature.* Houston: Arte Público Press, 1988.

de Lauretis, Teresa, ed. *Feminist Studies/Critical Studies.* Bloomington: Indiana UP, 1986.

Lorde, Audre. *Sister Outsider.* Trumansburg: The Crossing Press, 1984.

Martin, Biddy, and Chandra Talpade Mohanty. "Feminist Politics: What's Home Got to Do with It?" In de Lauretis, 191-121.

Moraga, Cherríe. "From a Long Line of Vendidas: Chicanas and Feminism." In de Lauretis, 173-190.

Muntañola, Josep. *La arquitectura como lugar.* Barcelona: Editorial Gustavo Gili, 1974.

Norburg-Schulz, Christian. *Genius Loci: Towards a Phenomenology of Architecture.* 1979. London: Academy Editions, 1980.

Olivares, Julián. "Sandra Cisneros' 'The House on Mango Street' and the Poetics of Space," In Herrera-Sobek, 160-169.

Ortiz, Victor Manuel. *La casa, una aproximación.* Mexico: Universidad Autonoma Metropolitana de Xochimilco, 1984.

Rebolledo, Tey Diana, and Eliana S. Rivero, eds. *Infinite Divisions: An Anthology of Chicana Literature.* Tucson: U of Arizona P, 1993.

Rivera, Tomás. "Chicano Literature: Fiesta of the Living." *Books Abroad* 49.3 (1975):439-452.

Tuan, Yi-Fu. *Space and Place: The Perspective of Experience.* Minneapolis: U of Minnesota P, 1977.

Viramontes, Helena María. *Under the Feet of Jesus.* New York: Dutton, 1995.

FURTHER READING

Alarcón, Norma. "Making *Familia* From Scratch: Split Subjectivities in the Work of Helena María Viramontes and Cherríe Moraga." *Chicana Creativity and Criticism: Charting New Frontiers in American Literature,* edited by María Herrera-Sobek and Helena María Viramontes, pp. 147-59, Houston: Arte Publico Press, 1988.

> Analyzes and compares Viramontes' deconstruction of female stereotypes with the feminist writing style of Cherríe Moraga.

Pavletich, JoAnn and Margot Gayle Backus. "With His Pistol in *Her* Hand: Rearticulation the Corrido Narrative in Helena María Viramontes' 'Neighbors'." *Cultural Critique,* Vol. 27 (September / December 1981): 127-52.

> Reviews the reversal of traditional sex roles in Viramontes's story "Neighbors."

Saldivar-Hull, Sonia. "Political Identities in Contemporary Chicana Literature Helena María Viramontes's Visions of the U.S. Third World." *'Writing' Nationa and 'Writing' Region in America,* edited by Theo D'haen and Hans Bertens, pp. 156-65, Amsterdam: Vu University Press, 1996.

> Reviews Viramontes's writings as narratives that transcend literary constrictions and seek to modify sexist Latin American traditions.

Stockton, Sharon. "Rereading the Maternal Body: Viramontes' *The Moths* and the Construction of the New Chicana." *The Americas Review,* Vol. 22, Nos. 1-2 (Spring-Summer 1994): 212-29.

> Analyzes Viramontes's incorporation and reconstruction of the Latina virgin/whore stereotype in her short story collection *The Moths.*

Viramontes, Helena María. "'Nopalitos': The Making of Fiction." *Breaking Boundaries: Latina Writing and Critical Readings,* edited by Asunción Horno-Delgado et al., pp. 33-8, Amherst: University of Massachusetts Press, 1989.

> Discusses the beginnings of her love for writing, her feelings as a Chicana, her literary influences, and her conviction that writing can influence destiny.

Additional coverage of Viramontes's life and career is contained in the following sources published by the Gale Group: *Contemporary Authors*, **Vol. 159;** *Dictionary of Literary Biography*, **Vol. 122.**

HISPANIC LITERATURE

CRITICISM

SUPPLEMENT

Indexes

How to Use This Index

The main references

Calvino, Italo
    1923–1985 .... CLC 5, 8, 11, 22, 33, 39,
                           73; SSC 3

list all author entries in the following Gale Literary Criticism series:

BLC(S) = Black Literature Criticism (Supplement)
CLC = Contemporary Literary Criticism
CLR = Children's Literature Review
CMLC = Classical and Medieval Literature Criticism
DA = DISCovering Authors
DAB = DISCovering Authors: British
DAC = DISCovering Authors: Canadian
DAM = DISCovering Authors: Modules
        DRAM: Dramatists Module; MST: Most-Studied Authors Module;
        MULT: Multicultural Authors Module; NOV: Novelists Module;
        POET: Poets Module; POP: Popular Fiction and Genre Authors Module
DC = Drama Criticism
HLC(S) = Hispanic Literature Criticism Supplement
LC = Literature Criticism from 1400 to 1800
NCLC = Nineteenth-Century Literature Criticism
PC = Poetry Criticism
SSC = Short Story Criticism
TCLC = Twentieth-Century Literary Criticism
WLC = World Literature Criticism, 1500 to the Present

The cross-references

See also CANR 23; CA 85-88;
   obituary CA116

list all author entries in the following Gale biographical and literary sources:

AAYA = Authors & Artists for Young Adults
AITN = Authors in the News
BEST = Bestsellers
BW = Black Writers
CA = Contemporary Authors
CAAS = Contemporary Authors Autobiography Series
CABS = Contemporary Authors Bibliographical Series
CANR = Contemporary Authors New Revision Series
CAP = Contemporary Authors Permanent Series
CDALB = Concise Dictionary of American Literary Biography
CDBLB = Concise Dictionary of British Literary Biography
DLB = Dictionary of Literary Biography
DLBD = Dictionary of Literary Biography Documentary Series
DLBY = Dictionary of Literary Biography Yearbook
HW = Hispanic Writers
JRDA = Junior DISCovering Authors
MAICYA = Major Authors and Illustrators for Children and Young Adults
MTCW = Major 20th-Century Writers
NNAL = Native North American Literature
SAAS = Something about the Author Autobiography Series
SATA = Something about the Author
YABC = Yesterday's Authors of Books for Children

Hispanic Literature Criticism: Supplement
Cumulative Author Index

Author Index

Hispanic Literary Criticism: Supplement
Cumulative Nationality Index

HLCS Cumulative Title Index

Title Index

Title Index

Title Index